W9-CDV-829

# Artificial Intelligence

## A Modern Approach

*Second Edition*

**PRENTICE HALL SERIES**
**IN ARTIFICIAL INTELLIGENCE**
*Stuart Russell and Peter Norvig, Editors*

| | |
|---|---|
| FORSYTH & PONCE | *Computer Vision: A Modern Approach* |
| GRAHAM | ANSI *Common Lisp* |
| JURAFSKY & MARTIN | *Speech and Language Processing* |
| NEAPOLITAN | *Learning Bayesian Networks* |
| RUSSELL & NORVIG | *Artificial Intelligence: A Modern Approach* |

# Artificial Intelligence

## A Modern Approach

## *Second Edition*

Stuart J. Russell and Peter Norvig

*Contributing writers:*
John F. Canny
Douglas D. Edwards
Jitendra M. Malik
Sebastian Thrun

*Pearson Education, Inc., Upper Saddle River, New Jersey 07458*

*Library of Congress Cataloging-in-Publication Data*

CIP Data on file.

Vice President and Editorial Director, ECS: Marcia J. Horton
Publisher: Alan R. Apt
Associate Editor: Toni Dianne Holm
Editorial Assistant: Patrick Lindner
Vice President and Director of Production and Manufacturing, ESM: David W. Riccardi
Executive Managing Editor: Vince O'Brien
Assistant Managing Editor: Camille Trentacoste
Production Editor: Irwin Zucker
Manufacturing Manager: Trudy Pisciotti
Manufacturing Buyer: Lisa McDowell
Director, Creative Services: Paul Belfanti
Creative Director: Carole Anson
Art Editor: Greg Dulles
Art Director: Heather Scott
Assistant to Art Director: Geoffrey Cassar
Cover Designers: Stuart Russell and Peter Norvig
Cover Image Creation: Stuart Russell and Peter Norvig; Tamara Newnam and Patrice Van Acker
Interior Designer: Stuart Russell and Peter Norvig
Marketing Manager: Pamela Shaffer
Marketing Assistant: Barrie Reinhold

Pearson Education, Inc.,
Upper Saddle River, New Jersey 07458



Printed in the United States of America

10 9 8 7

ISBN 0-13-790395-2

Pearson Education Ltd., *London*
Pearson Education Australia Pty. Ltd., *Sydney*
Pearson Education Singapore, Pte. Ltd.
Pearson Education North Asia Ltd., *Hong Kong*
Pearson Education Canada, Inc., *Toronto*
Pearson Educación de Mexico, S.A. de C.V.
Pearson Education—Japan, *Tokyo*
Pearson Education Malaysia, Pte. Ltd.
Pearson Education, Inc., *Upper Saddle River, New Jersey*

*For Loy, Gordon, and Lucy* — S.J.R.

*For Kris, Isabella, and Juliet* — P.N.

# Preface

**Artificial Intelligence** (AI) is a big field, and this is a big book. We have tried to explore the full breadth of the field, which encompasses logic, probability, and continuous mathematics; perception, reasoning, learning, and action; and everything from microelectronic devices to robotic planetary explorers. The book is also big because we go into some depth in presenting results, although we strive to cover only the most central ideas in the main part of each chapter. Pointers are given to further results in the bibliographical notes at the end of each chapter.

The subtitle of this book is "A Modern Approach." The intended meaning of this rather empty phrase is that we have tried to synthesize what is now known into a common framework, rather than trying to explain each subfield of AI in its own historical context. We apologize to those whose subfields are, as a result, less recognizable than they might otherwise have been.

The main unifying theme is the idea of an **intelligent agent**. We define AI as the study of agents that receive percepts from the environment and perform actions. Each such agent implements a function that maps percept sequences to actions, and we cover different ways to represent these functions, such as production systems, reactive agents, real-time conditional planners, neural networks, and decision-theoretic systems. We explain the role of learning as extending the reach of the designer into unknown environments, and we show how that role constrains agent design, favoring explicit knowledge representation and reasoning. We treat robotics and vision not as independently defined problems, but as occurring in the service of achieving goals. We stress the importance of the task environment in determining the appropriate agent design.

Our primary aim is to convey the *ideas* that have emerged over the past fifty years of AI research and the past two millenia of related work. We have tried to avoid excessive formality in the presentation of these ideas while retaining precision. Wherever appropriate, we have included pseudocode algorithms to make the ideas concrete; our pseudocode is described briefly in Appendix B. Implementations in several programming languages are available on the book's Web site, **aima.cs.berkeley.edu**.

This book is primarily intended for use in an undergraduate course or course sequence. It can also be used in a graduate-level course (perhaps with the addition of some of the primary sources suggested in the bibliographical notes). Because of its comprehensive coverage and large number of detailed algorithms, it is useful as a primary reference volume for AI graduate students and professionals wishing to branch out beyond their own subfield. The only prerequisite is familiarity with basic concepts of computer science (algorithms, data structures, complexity) at a sophomore level. Freshman calculus is useful for understanding neural networks and statistical learning in detail. Some of the required mathematical background is supplied in Appendix A.

## Overview of the book

The book is divided into eight parts. Part I, **Artificial Intelligence**, offers a view of the AI enterprise based around the idea of intelligent agents—systems that can decide what to do and then do it. Part II, **Problem Solving**, concentrates on methods for deciding what to do when one needs to think ahead several steps—for example in navigating across a country or playing chess. Part III, **Knowledge and Reasoning**, discusses ways to represent knowledge about the world—how it works, what it is currently like, and what one's actions might do—and how to reason logically with that knowledge. Part IV, **Planning**, then discusses how to use these reasoning methods to decide what to do, particularly by constructing *plans*. Part V, **Uncertain Knowledge and Reasoning**, is analogous to Parts III and IV, but it concentrates on reasoning and decision making in the presence of *uncertainty* about the world, as might be faced, for example, by a system for medical diagnosis and treatment.

Together, Parts II–V describe that part of the intelligent agent responsible for reaching decisions. Part VI, **Learning**, describes methods for generating the knowledge required by these decision-making components. Part VII, **Communicating, Perceiving, and Acting**, describes ways in which an intelligent agent can perceive its environment so as to know what is going on, whether by vision, touch, hearing, or understanding language, and ways in which it can turn its plans into real actions, either as robot motion or as natural language utterances. Finally, Part VIII, **Conclusions**, analyzes the past and future of AI and the philosophical and ethical implications of artificial intelligence.

## Changes from the first edition

Much has changed in AI since the publication of the first edition in 1995, and much has changed in this book. Every chapter has been significantly rewritten to reflect the latest work in the field, to reinterpret old work in a way that is more cohesive with new findings, and to improve the pedagogical flow of ideas. Followers of AI should be encouraged that current techniques are much more practical than those of 1995; for example the planning algorithms in the first edition could generate plans of only dozens of steps, while the algorithms in this edition scale up to tens of thousands of steps. Similar orders-of-magnitude improvements are seen in probabilistic inference, language processing, and other subfields. The following are the most notable changes in the book:

- In Part I, we acknowledge the historical contributions of control theory, game theory, economics, and neuroscience. This helps set the tone for a more integrated coverage of these ideas in subsequent chapters.
- In Part II, online search algorithms are covered and a new chapter on constraint satisfaction has been added. The latter provides a natural connection to the material on logic.
- In Part III, propositional logic, which was presented as a stepping-stone to first-order logic in the first edition, is now presented as a useful representation language in its own right, with fast inference algorithms and circuit-based agent designs. The chapters on first-order logic have been reorganized to present the material more clearly and we have added the Internet shopping domain as an example.
- In Part IV, we include newer planning methods such as GRAPHPLAN and satisfiability-based planning, and we increase coverage of scheduling, conditional planning, hierarchical planning, and multiagent planning.
- In Part V, we have augmented the material on Bayesian networks with new algorithms, such as variable elimination and Markov Chain Monte Carlo, and we have created a new chapter on uncertain temporal reasoning, covering hidden Markov models, Kalman filters, and dynamic Bayesian networks. The coverage of Markov decision processes is deepened, and we add sections on game theory and mechanism design.
- In Part VI, we tie together work in statistical, symbolic, and neural learning and add sections on boosting algorithms, the EM algorithm, instance-based learning, and kernel methods (support vector machines).
- In Part VII, coverage of language processing adds sections on discourse processing and grammar induction, as well as a chapter on probabilistic language models, with applications to information retrieval and machine translation. The coverage of robotics stresses the integration of uncertain sensor data, and the chapter on vision has updated material on object recognition.
- In Part VIII, we introduce a section on the ethical implications of AI.

## Using this book

The book has 27 chapters, each requiring about a week's worth of lectures, so working through the whole book requires a two-semester sequence. Alternatively, a course can be tailored to suit the interests of the instructor and student. Through its broad coverage, the book can be used to support such courses, whether they are short, introductory undergraduate courses or specialized graduate courses on advanced topics. Sample syllabi from the more than 600 universities and colleges that have adopted the first edition are shown on the Web at aima.cs.berkeley.edu, along with suggestions to help you find a sequence appropriate to your needs.

The book includes 385 exercises. Exercises requiring significant programming are marked with a keyboard icon. These exercises can best be solved by taking advantage of the code repository at aima.cs.berkeley.edu. Some of them are large enough to be considered term projects. A number of exercises require some investigation of the literature; these are marked with a book icon.

Throughout the book, important points are marked with a pointing icon. We have included an extensive index of around 10,000 items to make it easy to find things in the book. Wherever a **new term** is first defined, it is also marked in the margin.

NEW TERM

## Using the Web site

At the **aima.cs.berkeley.edu** Web site you will find:

- implementations of the algorithms in the book in several programming languages,
- a list of over 600 schools that have used the book, many with links to online course materials,
- an annotated list of over 800 links to sites around the web with useful AI content,
- a chapter by chapter list of supplementary material and links,
- instructions on how to join a discussion group for the book,
- instructions on how to contact the authors with questions or comments,
- instructions on how to report errors in the book, in the likely event that some exist, and
- copies of the figures in the book, along with slides and other material for instructors.

## Acknowledgments

Jitendra Malik wrote most of Chapter 24 (on vision). Most of Chapter 25 (on robotics) was written by Sebastian Thrun in this edition and by John Canny in the first edition. Doug Edwards researched the historical notes for the first edition. Tim Huang, Mark Paskin, and Cynthia Bruyns helped with formatting of the diagrams and algorithms. Alan Apt, Sondra Chavez, Toni Holm, Jake Warde, Irwin Zucker, and Camille Trentacoste at Prentice Hall tried their best to keep us on schedule and made many helpful suggestions on the book's design and content.

Stuart would like to thank his parents for their continued support and encouragement and his wife, Loy Sheflott, for her endless patience and boundless wisdom. He hopes that Gordon and Lucy will soon be reading this. RUGS (Russell's Unusual Group of Students) have been unusually helpful.

Peter would like to thank his parents (Torsten and Gerda) for getting him started, and his wife (Kris), children, and friends for encouraging and tolerating him through the long hours of writing and longer hours of rewriting.

We are indebted to the librarians at Berkeley, Stanford, MIT, and NASA, and to the developers of CiteSeer and Google, who have revolutionized the way we do research.

We can't thank all the people who have used the book and made suggestions, but we would like to acknowledge the especially helpful comments of Eyal Amir, Krzysztof Apt, Ellery Aziel, Jeff Van Baalen, Brian Baker, Don Barker, Tony Barrett, James Newton Bass, Don Beal, Howard Beck, Wolfgang Bibel, John Binder, Larry Bookman, David R. Boxall, Gerhard Brewka, Selmer Bringsjord, Carla Brodley, Chris Brown, Wilhelm Burger, Lauren Burka, Joao Cachopo, Murray Campbell, Norman Carver, Emmanuel Castro, Anil Chakravarthy, Dan Chisarick, Roberto Cipolla, David Cohen, James Coleman, Julie Ann Comparini, Gary Cottrell, Ernest Davis, Rina Dechter, Tom Dietterich, Chuck Dyer, Barbara Engelhardt, Doug Edwards, Kutluhan Erol, Oren Etzioni, Hana Filip, Douglas

Fisher, Jeffrey Forbes, Ken Ford, John Fosler, Alex Franz, Bob Futrelle, Marek Galecki, Stefan Gerberding, Stuart Gill, Sabine Glesner, Seth Golub, Gosta Grahne, Russ Greiner, Eric Grimson, Barbara Grosz, Larry Hall, Steve Hanks, Othar Hansson, Ernst Heinz, Jim Hendler, Christoph Herrmann, Vasant Honavar, Tim Huang, Seth Hutchinson, Joost Jacob, Magnus Johansson, Dan Jurafsky, Leslie Kaelbling, Keiji Kanazawa, Surekha Kasibhatla, Simon Kasif, Henry Kautz, Gernot Kerschbaumer, Richard Kirby, Kevin Knight, Sven Koenig, Daphne Koller, Rich Korf, James Kurien, John Lafferty, Gus Larsson, John Lazzaro, Jon LeBlanc, Jason Leatherman, Frank Lee, Edward Lim, Pierre Louveaux, Don Loveland, Sridhar Mahadevan, Jim Martin, Andy Mayer, David McGrane, Jay Mendelsohn, Brian Milch, Steve Minton, Vibhu Mittal, Leora Morgenstern, Stephen Muggleton, Kevin Murphy, Ron Musick, Sung Myaeng, Lee Naish, Pandu Nayak, Bernhard Nebel, Stuart Nelson, XuanLong Nguyen, Illah Nourbakhsh, Steve Omohundro, David Page, David Palmer, David Parkes, Ron Parr, Mark Paskin, Tony Passera, Michael Pazzani, Wim Pijls, Ira Pohl, Martha Pollack, David Poole, Bruce Porter, Malcolm Pradhan, Bill Pringle, Lorraine Prior, Greg Provan, William Rapaport, Philip Resnik, Francesca Rossi, Jonathan Schaeffer, Richard Scherl, Lars Schuster, Soheil Shams, Stuart Shapiro, Jude Shavlik, Satinder Singh, Daniel Sleator, David Smith, Bryan So, Robert Sproull, Lynn Stein, Larry Stephens, Andreas Stolcke, Paul Stradling, Devika Subramanian, Rich Sutton, Jonathan Tash, Austin Tate, Michael Thielscher, William Thompson, Sebastian Thrun, Eric Tiedemann, Mark Torrance, Randall Upham, Paul Utgoff, Peter van Beek, Hal Varian, Sunil Vemuri, Jim Waldo, Bonnie Webber, Dan Weld, Michael Wellman, Michael Dean White, Kamin Whitehouse, Brian Williams, David Wolfe, Bill Woods, Alden Wright, Richard Yen, Weixiong Zhang, Shlomo Zilberstein, and the anonymous reviewers provided by Prentice Hall.

## About the Cover

The cover image was designed by the authors and executed by Lisa Marie Sardegna and Maryann Simmons using SGI Inventor™ and Adobe Photoshop™. The cover depicts the following items from the history of AI:

1. Aristotle's planning algorithm from *De Motu Animalium* (c. 400 B.C.).
2. Ramon Lull's concept generator from *Ars Magna* (c. 1300 A.D.).
3. Charles Babbage's Difference Engine, a prototype for the first universal computer (1848).
4. Gottlob Frege's notation for first-order logic (1789).
5. Lewis Carroll's diagrams for logical reasoning (1886).
6. Sewall Wright's probabilistic network notation (1921).
7. Alan Turing (1912–1954).
8. Shakey the Robot (1969–1973).
9. A modern diagnostic expert system (1993).

# About the Authors

**Stuart Russell** was born in 1962 in Portsmouth, England. He received his B.A. with first-class honours in physics from Oxford University in 1982, and his Ph.D. in computer science from Stanford in 1986. He then joined the faculty of the University of California at Berkeley, where he is a professor of computer science, director of the Center for Intelligent Systems, and holder of the Smith–Zadeh Chair in Engineering. In 1990, he received the Presidential Young Investigator Award of the National Science Foundation, and in 1995 he was cowinner of the Computers and Thought Award. He was a 1996 Miller Professor of the University of California and was appointed to a Chancellor's Professorship in 2000. In 1998, he gave the Forsythe Memorial Lectures at Stanford University. He is a Fellow and former Executive Council member of the American Association for Artificial Intelligence. He has published over 100 papers on a wide range of topics in artificial intelligence. His other books include *The Use of Knowledge in Analogy and Induction* and (with Eric Wefald) *Do the Right Thing: Studies in Limited Rationality.*

**Peter Norvig** is director of Search Quality at Google, Inc. He is a Fellow and Executive Council member of the American Association for Artificial Intelligence. Previously, he was head of the Computational Sciences Division at NASA Ames Research Center, where he oversaw NASA's research and development in artificial intelligence and robotics. Before that he served as chief scientist at Junglee, where he helped develop one of the first Internet information extraction services, and as a senior scientist at Sun Microsystems Laboratories working on intelligent information retrieval. He received a B.S. in applied mathematics from Brown University and a Ph.D. in computer science from the University of California at Berkeley. He has been a professor at the University of Southern California and a research faculty member at Berkeley. He has over 50 publications in computer science including the books *Paradigms of AI Programming: Case Studies in Common Lisp*, *Verbmobil: A Translation System for Face-to-Face Dialog*, and *Intelligent Help Systems for UNIX.*

# Summary of Contents

# Contents

## I Artificial Intelligence

# IV Planning

# 1 INTRODUCTION

*In which we try to explain why we consider artificial intelligence to be a subject most worthy of study, and in which we try to decide what exactly it is, this being a good thing to decide before embarking.*

We call ourselves *Homo sapiens*—man the wise—because our mental capacities are so important to us. For thousands of years, we have tried to understand *how we think*; that is, how a mere handful of stuff can perceive, understand, predict, and manipulate a world far larger and more complicated than itself. The field of **artificial intelligence**, or AI, goes further still: it attempts not just to understand but also to *build* intelligent entities.

ARTIFICIAL INTELLIGENCE

AI is one of the newest sciences. Work started in earnest soon after World War II, and the name itself was coined in 1956. Along with molecular biology, AI is regularly cited as the "field I would most like to be in" by scientists in other disciplines. A student in physics might reasonably feel that all the good ideas have already been taken by Galileo, Newton, Einstein, and the rest. AI, on the other hand, still has openings for several full-time Einsteins.

AI currently encompasses a huge variety of subfields, ranging from general-purpose areas, such as learning and perception to such specific tasks as playing chess, proving mathematical theorems, writing poetry, and diagnosing diseases. AI systematizes and automates intellectual tasks and is therefore potentially relevant to any sphere of human intellectual activity. In this sense, it is truly a universal field.

## 1.1 WHAT IS AI?

We have claimed that AI is exciting, but we have not said what it *is*. Definitions of artificial intelligence according to eight textbooks are shown in Figure 1.1. These definitions vary along two main dimensions. Roughly, the ones on top are concerned with *thought processes* and *reasoning*, whereas the ones on the bottom address *behavior*. The definitions on the left measure success in terms of fidelity to *human* performance, whereas the ones on the right measure against an *ideal* concept of intelligence, which we will call **rationality**. A system is rational if it does the "right thing," given what it knows.

RATIONALITY

| Systems that think like humans | Systems that think rationally |
|---|---|
| "The exciting new effort to make computers think ... *machines with minds*, in the full and literal sense." (Haugeland, 1985)<br><br>"[The automation of] activities that we associate with human thinking, activities such as decision-making, problem solving, learning ..." (Bellman, 1978) | "The study of mental faculties through the use of computational models." (Charniak and McDermott, 1985)<br><br>"The study of the computations that make it possible to perceive, reason, and act." (Winston, 1992) |
| **Systems that act like humans** | **Systems that act rationally** |
| "The art of creating machines that perform functions that require intelligence when performed by people." (Kurzweil, 1990)<br><br>"The study of how to make computers do things at which, at the moment, people are better." (Rich and Knight, 1991) | "Computational Intelligence is the study of the design of intelligent agents." (Poole *et al.*, 1998)<br><br>"AI ...is concerned with intelligent behavior in artifacts." (Nilsson, 1998) |

**Figure 1.1** Some definitions of artificial intelligence, organized into four categories.

Historically, all four approaches to AI have been followed. As one might expect, a tension exists between approaches centered around humans and approaches centered around rationality.[1] A human-centered approach must be an empirical science, involving hypothesis and experimental confirmation. A rationalist approach involves a combination of mathematics and engineering. Each group has both disparaged and helped the other. Let us look at the four approaches in more detail.

### Acting humanly: The Turing Test approach

TURING TEST

The **Turing Test**, proposed by Alan Turing (1950), was designed to provide a satisfactory operational definition of intelligence. Rather than proposing a long and perhaps controversial list of qualifications required for intelligence, he suggested a test based on indistinguishability from undeniably intelligent entities—human beings. The computer passes the test if a human interrogator, after posing some written questions, cannot tell whether the written responses come from a person or not. Chapter 26 discusses the details of the test and whether a computer is really intelligent if it passes. For now, we note that programming a computer to pass the test provides plenty to work on. The computer would need to possess the following capabilities:

NATURAL LANGUAGE PROCESSING

◇ **natural language processing** to enable it to communicate successfully in English.

[1] We should point out that, by distinguishing between *human* and *rational* behavior, we are not suggesting that humans are necessarily "irrational" in the sense of "emotionally unstable" or "insane." One merely need note that we are not perfect: we are not all chess grandmasters, even those of us who know all the rules of chess; and, unfortunately, not everyone gets an A on the exam. Some systematic errors in human reasoning are cataloged by Kahneman *et al.* (1982).

KNOWLEDGE REPRESENTATION

◇ **knowledge representation** to store what it knows or hears;

AUTOMATED REASONING

◇ **automated reasoning** to use the stored information to answer questions and to draw new conclusions;

MACHINE LEARNING

◇ **machine learning** to adapt to new circumstances and to detect and extrapolate patterns.

TOTAL TURING TEST

Turing's test deliberately avoided direct physical interaction between the interrogator and the computer, because *physical* simulation of a person is unnecessary for intelligence. However, the so-called **total Turing Test** includes a video signal so that the interrogator can test the subject's perceptual abilities, as well as the opportunity for the interrogator to pass physical objects "through the hatch." To pass the total Turing Test, the computer will need

COMPUTER VISION

◇ **computer vision** to perceive objects, and

ROBOTICS

◇ **robotics** to manipulate objects and move about.

These six disciplines compose most of AI, and Turing deserves credit for designing a test that remains relevant 50 years later. Yet AI researchers have devoted little effort to passing the Turing test, believing that it is more important to study the underlying principles of intelligence than to duplicate an exemplar. The quest for "artificial flight" succeeded when the Wright brothers and others stopped imitating birds and learned about aerodynamics. Aeronautical engineering texts do not define the goal of their field as making "machines that fly so exactly like pigeons that they can fool even other pigeons."

### Thinking humanly: The cognitive modeling approach

COGNITIVE SCIENCE

If we are going to say that a given program thinks like a human, we must have some way of determining how humans think. We need to get *inside* the actual workings of human minds. There are two ways to do this: through introspection—trying to catch our own thoughts as they go by—and through psychological experiments. Once we have a sufficiently precise theory of the mind, it becomes possible to express the theory as a computer program. If the program's input/output and timing behaviors match corresponding human behaviors, that is evidence that some of the program's mechanisms could also be operating in humans. For example, Allen Newell and Herbert Simon, who developed GPS, the "General Problem Solver" (Newell and Simon, 1961), were not content to have their program solve problems correctly. They were more concerned with comparing the trace of its reasoning steps to traces of human subjects solving the same problems. The interdisciplinary field of **cognitive science** brings together computer models from AI and experimental techniques from psychology to try to construct precise and testable theories of the workings of the human mind.

Cognitive science is a fascinating field, worthy of an encyclopedia in itself (Wilson and Keil, 1999). We will not attempt to describe what is known of human cognition in this book. We will occasionally comment on similarities or differences between AI techniques and human cognition. Real cognitive science, however, is necessarily based on experimental investigation of actual humans or animals, and we assume that the reader has access only to a computer for experimentation.

In the early days of AI there was often confusion between the approaches: an author would argue that an algorithm performs well on a task and that it is *therefore* a good model of human performance, or vice versa. Modern authors separate the two kinds of claims; this distinction has allowed both AI and cognitive science to develop more rapidly. The two fields continue to fertilize each other, especially in the areas of vision and natural language. Vision in particular has recently made advances via an integrated approach that considers neurophysiological evidence and computational models.

### Thinking rationally: The "laws of thought" approach

SYLLOGISMS

LOGIC

The Greek philosopher Aristotle was one of the first to attempt to codify "right thinking," that is, irrefutable reasoning processes. His **syllogisms** provided patterns for argument structures that always yielded correct conclusions when given correct premises—for example, "Socrates is a man; all men are mortal; therefore, Socrates is mortal." These laws of thought were supposed to govern the operation of the mind; their study initiated the field called **logic**.

LOGICIST

Logicians in the 19th century developed a precise notation for statements about all kinds of things in the world and about the relations among them. (Contrast this with ordinary arithmetic notation, which provides mainly for equality and inequality statements about numbers.) By 1965, programs existed that could, in principle, solve *any* solvable problem described in logical notation.[2] The so-called **logicist** tradition within artificial intelligence hopes to build on such programs to create intelligent systems.

There are two main obstacles to this approach. First, it is not easy to take informal knowledge and state it in the formal terms required by logical notation, particularly when the knowledge is less than 100% certain. Second, there is a big difference between being able to solve a problem "in principle" and doing so in practice. Even problems with just a few dozen facts can exhaust the computational resources of any computer unless it has some guidance as to which reasoning steps to try first. Although both of these obstacles apply to *any* attempt to build computational reasoning systems, they appeared first in the logicist tradition.

### Acting rationally: The rational agent approach

AGENT

RATIONAL AGENT

An **agent** is just something that acts (*agent* comes from the Latin *agere*, to do). But computer agents are expected to have other attributes that distinguish them from mere "programs," such as operating under autonomous control, perceiving their environment, persisting over a prolonged time period, adapting to change, and being capable of taking on another's goals. A **rational agent** is one that acts so as to achieve the best outcome or, when there is uncertainty, the best expected outcome.

In the "laws of thought" approach to AI, the emphasis was on correct inferences. Making correct inferences is sometimes *part* of being a rational agent, because one way to act rationally is to reason logically to the conclusion that a given action will achieve one's goals and then to act on that conclusion. On the other hand, correct inference is not *all* of rationality, because there are often situations where there is no provably correct thing to do, yet something must still be done. There are also ways of acting rationally that cannot be said to involve inference. For example, recoiling from a hot stove is a reflex action that is usually more successful than a slower action taken after careful deliberation.

---

[2] If there is no solution, the program might never stop looking for one.

All the skills needed for the Turing Test are there to allow rational actions. Thus, we need the ability to represent knowledge and reason with it because this enables us to reach good decisions in a wide variety of situations. We need to be able to generate comprehensible sentences in natural language because saying those sentences helps us get by in a complex society. We need learning not just for erudition, but because having a better idea of how the world works enables us to generate more effective strategies for dealing with it. We need visual perception not just because seeing is fun, but to get a better idea of what an action might achieve—for example, being able to see a tasty morsel helps one to move toward it.

For these reasons, the study of AI as rational-agent design has at least two advantages. First, it is more general than the "laws of thought" approach, because correct inference is just one of several possible mechanisms for achieving rationality. Second, it is more amenable to scientific development than are approaches based on human behavior or human thought because the standard of rationality is clearly defined and completely general. Human behavior, on the other hand, is well-adapted for one specific environment and is the product, in part, of a complicated and largely unknown evolutionary process that still is far from producing perfection. *This book will therefore concentrate on general principles of rational agents and on components for constructing them.* We will see that despite the apparent simplicity with which the problem can be stated, an enormous variety of issues come up when we try to solve it. Chapter 2 outlines some of these issues in more detail.

One important point to keep in mind: We will see before too long that achieving perfect rationality—always doing the right thing—is not feasible in complicated environments. The computational demands are just too high. For most of the book, however, we will adopt the working hypothesis that perfect rationality is a good starting point for analysis. It simplifies the problem and provides the appropriate setting for most of the foundational material in the field. Chapters 6 and 17 deal explicitly with the issue of **limited rationality**—acting appropriately when there is not enough time to do all the computations one might like.

## 1.2 THE FOUNDATIONS OF ARTIFICIAL INTELLIGENCE

In this section, we provide a brief history of the disciplines that contributed ideas, viewpoints, and techniques to AI. Like any history, this one is forced to concentrate on a small number of people, events, and ideas and to ignore others that also were important. We organize the history around a series of questions. We certainly would not wish to give the impression that these questions are the only ones the disciplines address or that the disciplines have all been working toward AI as their ultimate fruition.

### Philosophy (428 B.C.–present)

- Can formal rules be used to draw valid conclusions?
- How does the mental mind arise from a physical brain?
- Where does knowledge come from?
- How does knowledge lead to action?

Aristotle (384-322 B.C.) was the first to formulate a precise set of laws governing the rational part of the mind. He developed an informal system of syllogisms for proper reasoning, which in principle allowed one to generate conclusions mechanically, given initial premises. Much later, Ramon Lull (d. 1315) had the idea that useful reasoning could actually be carried out by a mechanical artifact. His "concept wheels" are on the cover of this book. Thomas Hobbes (1588–1679) proposed that reasoning was like numerical computation, that "we add and subtract in our silent thoughts." The automation of computation itself was already well under way; around 1500, Leonardo da Vinci (1452–1519) designed but did not build a mechanical calculator; recent reconstructions have shown the design to be functional. The first known calculating machine was constructed around 1623 by the German scientist Wilhelm Schickard (1592–1635), although the Pascaline, built in 1642 by Blaise Pascal (1623–1662), is more famous. Pascal wrote that "the arithmetical machine produces effects which appear nearer to thought than all the actions of animals." Gottfried Wilhelm Leibniz (1646–1716) built a mechanical device intended to carry out operations on concepts rather than numbers, but its scope was rather limited.

Now that we have the idea of a set of rules that can describe the formal, rational part of the mind, the next step is to consider the mind as a physical system. René Descartes (1596–1650) gave the first clear discussion of the distinction between mind and matter and of the problems that arise. One problem with a purely physical conception of the mind is that it seems to leave little room for free will: if the mind is governed entirely by physical laws, then it has no more free will than a rock "deciding" to fall toward the center of the earth. Although a strong advocate of the power of reasoning, Descartes was also a proponent of **dualism**. He held that there is a part of the human mind (or soul or spirit) that is outside of nature, exempt from physical laws. Animals, on the other hand, did not possess this dual quality; they could be treated as machines. An alternative to dualism is **materialism**, which holds that the brain's operation according to the laws of physics *constitutes* the mind. Free will is simply the way that the perception of available choices appears to the choice process.

DUALISM

MATERIALISM

Given a physical mind that manipulates knowledge, the next problem is to establish the source of knowledge. The **empiricism** movement, starting with Francis Bacon's (1561–1626) *Novum Organum*,[3] is characterized by a dictum of John Locke (1632–1704): "Nothing is in the understanding, which was not first in the senses." David Hume's (1711–1776) *A Treatise of Human Nature* (Hume, 1739) proposed what is now known as the principle of **induction**: that general rules are acquired by exposure to repeated associations between their elements. Building on the work of Ludwig Wittgenstein (1889–1951) and Bertrand Russell (1872–1970), the famous Vienna Circle, led by Rudolf Carnap (1891–1970), developed the doctrine of **logical positivism**. This doctrine holds that all knowledge can be characterized by logical theories connected, ultimately, to **observation sentences** that correspond to sensory inputs.[4] The **confirmation theory** of Carnap and Carl Hempel (1905–1997) attempted to understand how knowledge can be acquired from experience. Carnap's book *The Logical Structure of*

EMPIRICISM

INDUCTION

LOGICAL POSITIVISM

OBSERVATION SENTENCES

CONFIRMATION THEORY

[3] An update of Aristotle's *Organon*, or instrument of thought.

[4] In this picture, all meaningful statements can be verified or falsified either by analyzing the meaning of the words or by carrying out experiments. Because this rules out most of metaphysics, as was the intention, logical positivism was unpopular in some circles.

*the World* (1928) defined an explicit computational procedure for extracting knowledge from elementary experiences. It was probably the first theory of mind as a computational process.

The final element in the philosophical picture of the mind is the connection between knowledge and action. This question is vital to AI, because intelligence requires action as well as reasoning. Moreover, only by understanding how actions are justified can we understand how to build an agent whose actions are justifiable (or rational). Aristotle argued that actions are justified by a logical connection between goals and knowledge of the action's outcome (the last part of this extract also appears on the front cover of this book):

> But how does it happen that thinking is sometimes accompanied by action and sometimes not, sometimes by motion, and sometimes not? It looks as if almost the same thing happens as in the case of reasoning and making inferences about unchanging objects. But in that case the end is a speculative proposition ... whereas here the conclusion which results from the two premises is an action. ... I need covering; a cloak is a covering. I need a cloak. What I need, I have to make; I need a cloak. I have to make a cloak. And the conclusion, the "I have to make a cloak," is an action. (Nussbaum, 1978, p. 40)

In the *Nicomachean Ethics* (Book III. 3, 1112b), Aristotle further elaborates on this topic, suggesting an algorithm:

> We deliberate not about ends, but about means. For a doctor does not deliberate whether he shall heal, nor an orator whether he shall persuade, ... They assume the end and consider how and by what means it is attained, and if it seems easily and best produced thereby; while if it is achieved by one means only they consider *how* it will be achieved by this and by what means *this* will be achieved, till they come to the first cause, ... and what is last in the order of analysis seems to be first in the order of becoming. And if we come on an impossibility, we give up the search, e.g. if we need money and this cannot be got; but if a thing appears possible we try to do it.

Aristotle's algorithm was implemented 2300 years later by Newell and Simon in their GPS program. We would now call it a regression planning system. (See Chapter 11.)

Goal-based analysis is useful, but does not say what to do when several actions will achieve the goal, or when no action will achieve it completely. Antoine Arnauld (1612–1694) correctly described a quantitative formula for deciding what action to take in cases like this (see Chapter 16). John Stuart Mill's (1806–1873) book *Utilitarianism* (Mill, 1863) promoted the idea of rational decision criteria in all spheres of human activity. The more formal theory of decisions is discussed in the following section.

### Mathematics (c. 800–present)

- What are the formal rules to draw valid conclusions?
- What can be computed?
- How do we reason with uncertain information?

Philosophers staked out most of the important ideas of AI, but the leap to a formal science required a level of mathematical formalization in three fundamental areas: logic, computation, and probability.

The idea of formal logic can be traced back to the philosophers of ancient Greece (see Chapter 7), but its mathematical development really began with the work of George Boole

(1815–1864), who worked out the details of propositional, or Boolean, logic (Boole, 1847). In 1879, Gottlob Frege (1848–1925) extended Boole's logic to include objects and relations, creating the first-order logic that is used today as the most basic knowledge representation system.[5] Alfred Tarski (1902–1983) introduced a theory of reference that shows how to relate the objects in a logic to objects in the real world. The next step was to determine the limits of what could be done with logic and computation.

ALGORITHM

The first nontrivial **algorithm** is thought to be Euclid's algorithm for computing greatest common denominators. The study of algorithms as objects in themselves goes back to al-Khowarazmi, a Persian mathematician of the 9th century, whose writings also introduced Arabic numerals and algebra to Europe. Boole and others discussed algorithms for logical deduction, and, by the late 19th century, efforts were under way to formalize general mathematical reasoning as logical deduction. In 1900, David Hilbert (1862–1943) presented a list of 23 problems that he correctly predicted would occupy mathematicians for the bulk of the century. The final problem asks whether there is an algorithm for deciding the truth of any logical proposition involving the natural numbers—the famous *Entscheidungsproblem*, or decision problem. Essentially, Hilbert was asking whether there were fundamental limits to the power of effective proof procedures. In 1930, Kurt Gödel (1906–1978) showed that there exists an effective procedure to prove any true statement in the first-order logic of Frege and Russell, but that first-order logic could not capture the principle of mathematical induction needed to characterize the natural numbers. In 1931, he showed that real limits do exist.

INCOMPLETENESS THEOREM

His **incompleteness theorem** showed that in any language expressive enough to describe the properties of the natural numbers, there are true statements that are undecidable in the sense that their truth cannot be established by any algorithm.

This fundamental result can also be interpreted as showing that there are some functions on the integers that cannot be represented by an algorithm—that is, they cannot be computed. This motivated Alan Turing (1912–1954) to try to characterize exactly which functions *are* capable of being computed. This notion is actually slightly problematic, because the notion of a computation or effective procedure really cannot be given a formal definition. However, the Church–Turing thesis, which states that the Turing machine (Turing, 1936) is capable of computing any computable function, is generally accepted as providing a sufficient definition. Turing also showed that there were some functions that no Turing machine can compute. For example, no machine can tell *in general* whether a given program will return an answer on a given input or run forever.

INTRACTABILITY

Although undecidability and noncomputability are important to an understanding of computation, the notion of **intractability** has had a much greater impact. Roughly speaking, a problem is called intractable if the time required to solve instances of the problem grows exponentially with the size of the instances. The distinction between polynomial and exponential growth in complexity was first emphasized in the mid-1960s (Cobham, 1964; Edmonds, 1965). It is important because exponential growth means that even moderately large instances cannot be solved in any reasonable time. Therefore, one should strive to divide

[5] Frege's proposed notation for first-order logic never became popular, for reasons that are apparent immediately from the example on the front cover.

the overall problem of generating intelligent behavior into tractable subproblems rather than intractable ones.

NP-COMPLETENESS

How can one recognize an intractable problem? The theory of **NP-completeness**, pioneered by Steven Cook (1971) and Richard Karp (1972), provides a method. Cook and Karp showed the existence of large classes of canonical combinatorial search and reasoning problems that are NP-complete. Any problem class to which the class of NP-complete problems can be reduced is likely to be intractable. (Although it has not been proved that NP-complete problems are necessarily intractable, most theoreticians believe it.) These results contrast with the optimism with which the popular press greeted the first computers—"Electronic Super-Brains" that were "Faster than Einstein!" Despite the increasing speed of computers, careful use of resources will characterize intelligent systems. Put crudely, the world is an *extremely* large problem instance! In recent years, AI has helped explain why some instances of NP-complete problems are hard, yet others are easy (Cheeseman *et al.*, 1991).

PROBABILITY

Besides logic and computation, the third great contribution of mathematics to AI is the theory of **probability**. The Italian Gerolamo Cardano (1501–1576) first framed the idea of probability, describing it in terms of the possible outcomes of gambling events. Probability quickly became an invaluable part of all the quantitative sciences, helping to deal with uncertain measurements and incomplete theories. Pierre Fermat (1601–1665), Blaise Pascal (1623–1662), James Bernoulli (1654–1705), Pierre Laplace (1749–1827), and others advanced the theory and introduced new statistical methods. Thomas Bayes (1702–1761) proposed a rule for updating probabilities in the light of new evidence. Bayes' rule and the resulting field called Bayesian analysis form the basis of most modern approaches to uncertain reasoning in AI systems.

### Economics (1776–present)

- How should we make decisions so as to maximize payoff?
- How should we do this when others may not go along?
- How should we do this when the payoff may be far in the future?

The science of economics got its start in 1776, when Scottish philosopher Adam Smith (1723–1790) published *An Inquiry into the Nature and Causes of the Wealth of Nations*. While the ancient Greeks and others had made contributions to economic thought, Smith was the first to treat it as a science, using the idea that economies can be thought of as consisting of individual agents maximizing their own economic well-being. Most people think of economics as being about money, but economists will say that they are really studying how people make choices that lead to preferred outcomes. The mathematical treatment of "preferred outcomes" or **utility** was first formalized by Léon Walras (pronounced "Valrasse") (1834-1910) and was improved by Frank Ramsey (1931) and later by John von Neumann and Oskar Morgenstern in their book *The Theory of Games and Economic Behavior* (1944).

DECISION THEORY

**Decision theory**, which combines probability theory with utility theory, provides a formal and complete framework for decisions (economic or otherwise) made under uncertainty—that is, in cases where probabilistic descriptions appropriately capture the decision-maker's environment. This is suitable for "large" economies where each agent need pay no attention to the actions of other agents as individuals. For "small" economies, the situation is much more like a **game**: the actions of one player can significantly affect the utility of another (either positively or negatively). Von Neumann and Morgenstern's development of **game theory** (see also Luce and Raiffa, 1957) included the surprising result that, for some games, a rational agent should act in a random fashion, or at least in a way that appears random to the adversaries.

GAME THEORY

For the most part, economists did not address the third question listed above, namely, how to make rational decisions when payoffs from actions are not immediate but instead result from several actions taken *in sequence*. This topic was pursued in the field of **operations research**, which emerged in World War II from efforts in Britain to optimize radar installations, and later found civilian applications in complex management decisions. The work of Richard Bellman (1957) formalized a class of sequential decision problems called **Markov decision processes**, which we study in Chapters 17 and 21.

OPERATIONS RESEARCH

Work in economics and operations research has contributed much to our notion of rational agents, yet for many years AI research developed along entirely separate paths. One reason was the apparent **complexity** of making rational decisions. Herbert Simon (1916–2001), the pioneering AI researcher, won the Nobel prize in economics in 1978 for his early work showing that models based on **satisficing**–making decisions that are "good enough," rather than laboriously calculating an optimal decision–gave a better description of actual human behavior (Simon, 1947). In the 1990s, there has been a resurgence of interest in decision-theoretic techniques for agent systems (Wellman, 1995).

SATISFICING

### Neuroscience (1861–present)

- How do brains process information?

NEUROSCIENCE

**Neuroscience** is the study of the nervous system, particularly the brain. The exact way in which the brain enables thought is one of the great mysteries of science. It has been appreciated for thousands of years that the brain is somehow involved in thought, because of the evidence that strong blows to the head can lead to mental incapacitation. It has also long been known that human brains are somehow different; in about 335 B.C. Aristotle wrote, "Of all the animals, man has the largest brain in proportion to his size." [6] Still, it was not until the middle of the 18th century that the brain was widely recognized as the seat of consciousness. Before then, candidate locations included the heart, the spleen, and the pineal gland.

Paul Broca's (1824–1880) study of aphasia (speech deficit) in brain-damaged patients in 1861 reinvigorated the field and persuaded the medical establishment of the existence of localized areas of the brain responsible for specific cognitive functions. In particular, he showed that speech production was localized to a portion of the left hemisphere now called Broca's area.[7] By that time, it was known that the brain consisted of nerve cells or **neurons**, but it was not until 1873 that Camillo Golgi (1843–1926) developed a staining technique allowing the observation of individual neurons in the brain (see Figure 1.2). This technique

NEURONS

[6] Since then, it has been discovered that some species of dolphins and whales have relatively larger brains. The large size of human brains is now thought to be enabled in part by recent improvements in its cooling system.

[7] Many cite Alexander Hood (1824) as a possible prior source.

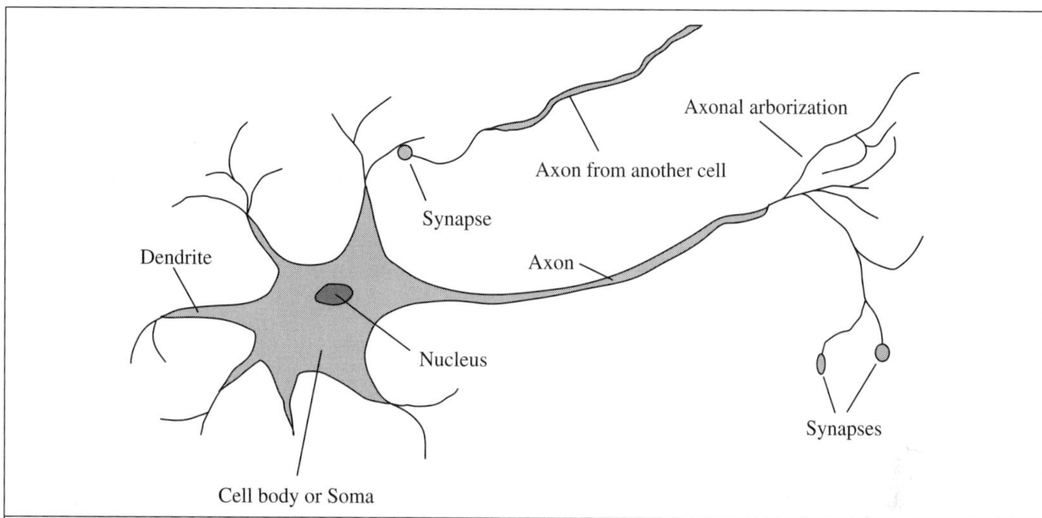


**Figure 1.2** The parts of a nerve cell or neuron. Each neuron consists of a cell body, or soma, that contains a cell nucleus. Branching out from the cell body are a number of fibers called dendrites and a single long fiber called the axon. The axon stretches out for a long distance, much longer than the scale in this diagram indicates. Typically they are 1 cm long (100 times the diameter of the cell body), but can reach up to 1 meter. A neuron makes connections with 10 to 100,000 other neurons at junctions called synapses. Signals are propagated from neuron to neuron by a complicated electrochemical reaction. The signals control brain activity in the short term, and also enable long-term changes in the position and connectivity of neurons. These mechanisms are thought to form the basis for learning in the brain. Most information processing goes on in the cerebral cortex, the outer layer of the brain. The basic organizational unit appears to be a column of tissue about 0.5 mm in diameter, extending the full depth of the cortex, which is about 4 mm in humans. A column contains about 20,000 neurons.

was used by Santiago Ramon y Cajal (1852–1934) in his pioneering studies of the brain's neuronal structures.[8]

We now have some data on the mapping between areas of the brain and the parts of the body that they control or from which they receive sensory input. Such mappings are able to change radically over the course of a few weeks, and some animals seem to have multiple maps. Moreover, we do not fully understand how other areas can take over functions when one area is damaged. There is almost no theory on how an individual memory is stored.

The measurement of intact brain activity began in 1929 with the invention by Hans Berger of the electroencephalograph (EEG). The recent development of functional magnetic resonance imaging (fMRI) (Ogawa *et al.*, 1990) is giving neuroscientists unprecedentedly detailed images of brain activity, enabling measurements that correspond in interesting ways to ongoing cognitive processes. These are augmented by advances in single-cell recording of

[8] Golgi persisted in his belief that the brain's functions were carried out primarily in a continuous medium in which neurons were embedded, whereas Cajal propounded the "neuronal doctrine." The two shared the Nobel prize in 1906 but gave rather antagonistic acceptance speeches.

| | Computer | Human Brain |
|---|---|---|
| Computational units | 1 CPU, $10^8$ gates | $10^{11}$ neurons |
| Storage units | $10^{10}$ bits RAM | $10^{11}$ neurons |
| | $10^{11}$ bits disk | $10^{14}$ synapses |
| Cycle time | $10^{-9}$ sec | $10^{-3}$ sec |
| Bandwidth | $10^{10}$ bits/sec | $10^{14}$ bits/sec |
| Memory updates/sec | $10^9$ | $10^{14}$ |

**Figure 1.3** A crude comparison of the raw computational resources available to computers (*circa* 2003) and brains. The computer's numbers have all increased by at least a factor of 10 since the first edition of this book, and are expected to do so again this decade. The brain's numbers have not changed in the last 10,000 years.

neuron activity. Despite these advances, we are still a long way from understanding how any of these cognitive processes actually work.

The truly amazing conclusion is that *a collection of simple cells can lead to thought, action, and consciousness* or, in other words, that *brains cause minds* (Searle, 1992). The only real alternative theory is mysticism: that there is some mystical realm in which minds operate that is beyond physical science.

Brains and digital computers perform quite different tasks and have different properties. Figure 1.3 shows that there are 1000 times more neurons in the typical human brain than there are gates in the CPU of a typical high-end computer. Moore's Law[9] predicts that the CPU's gate count will equal the brain's neuron count around 2020. Of course, little can be inferred from such predictions; moreover, the difference in storage capacity is minor compared to the difference in switching speed and in parallelism. Computer chips can execute an instruction in a nanosecond, whereas neurons are millions of times slower. Brains more than make up for this, however, because all the neurons and synapses are active simultaneously, whereas

most current computers have only one or at most a few CPUs. Thus, *even though a computer is a million times faster in raw switching speed, the brain ends up being 100,000 times faster at what it does.*

### Psychology (1879–present)

- How do humans and animals think and act?

The origins of scientific psychology are usually traced to the work of the German physicist Hermann von Helmholtz (1821–1894) and his student Wilhelm Wundt (1832–1920). Helmholtz applied the scientific method to the study of human vision, and his *Handbook of Physiological Optics* is even now described as "the single most important treatise on the physics and physiology of human vision" (Nalwa, 1993, p.15). In 1879, Wundt opened the first laboratory of experimental psychology at the University of Leipzig. Wundt insisted on carefully controlled experiments in which his workers would perform a perceptual or associa-

[9] Moore's Law says that the number of transistors per square inch doubles every 1 to 1.5 years. Human brain capacity doubles roughly every 2 to 4 million years.

tive task while introspecting on their thought processes. The careful controls went a long way toward making psychology a science, but the subjective nature of the data made it unlikely that an experimenter would ever disconfirm his or her own theories. Biologists studying animal behavior, on the other hand, lacked introspective data and developed an objective methodology, as described by H. S. Jennings (1906) in his influential work *Behavior of the Lower Organisms*. Applying this viewpoint to humans, the **behaviorism** movement, led by John Watson (1878–1958), rejected *any* theory involving mental processes on the grounds that introspection could not provide reliable evidence. Behaviorists insisted on studying only objective measures of the percepts (or *stimulus*) given to an animal and its resulting actions (or *response*). Mental constructs such as knowledge, beliefs, goals, and reasoning steps were dismissed as unscientific "folk psychology." Behaviorism discovered a lot about rats and pigeons, but had less success at understanding humans. Nevertheless, it exerted a strong hold on psychology (especially in the United States) from about 1920 to 1960.

BEHAVIORISM

The view of the brain as an information-processing device, which is a principal characteristic of **cognitive psychology**, can be traced back at least to the works of William James[10] (1842–1910). Helmholtz also insisted that perception involved a form of unconscious logical inference. The cognitive viewpoint was largely eclipsed by behaviorism in the United States, but at Cambridge's Applied Psychology Unit, directed by Frederic Bartlett (1886–1969), cognitive modeling was able to flourish. *The Nature of Explanation*, by Bartlett's student and successor Kenneth Craik (1943), forcefully reestablished the legitimacy of such "mental" terms as beliefs and goals, arguing that they are just as scientific as, say, using pressure and temperature to talk about gases, despite their being made of molecules that have neither. Craik specified the three key steps of a knowledge-based agent: (1) the stimulus must be translated into an internal representation, (2) the representation is manipulated by cognitive processes to derive new internal representations, and (3) these are in turn retranslated back into action. He clearly explained why this was a good design for an agent:

COGNITIVE PSYCHOLOGY

> If the organism carries a "small-scale model" of external reality and of its own possible actions within its head, it is able to try out various alternatives, conclude which is the best of them, react to future situations before they arise, utilize the knowledge of past events in dealing with the present and future, and in every way to react in a much fuller, safer, and more competent manner to the emergencies which face it. (Craik, 1943)

After Craik's death in a bicycle accident in 1945, his work was continued by Donald Broadbent, whose book *Perception and Communication* (1958) included some of the first information-processing models of psychological phenomena. Meanwhile, in the United States, the development of computer modeling led to the creation of the field of **cognitive science**. The field can be said to have started at a workshop in September 1956 at MIT. (We shall see that this is just two months after the conference at which AI itself was "born.") At the workshop, George Miller presented *The Magic Number Seven*, Noam Chomsky presented *Three Models of Language*, and Allen Newell and Herbert Simon presented *The Logic Theory Machine*. These three influential papers showed how computer models could be used to

COGNITIVE SCIENCE

[10] William James was the brother of novelist Henry James. It is said that Henry wrote fiction as if it were psychology and William wrote psychology as if it were fiction.

address the psychology of memory, language, and logical thinking, respectively. It is now a common view among psychologists that "a cognitive theory should be like a computer program" (Anderson, 1980), that is, it should describe a detailed information-processing mechanism whereby some cognitive function might be implemented.

### Computer engineering (1940–present)

- How can we build an efficient computer?

For artificial intelligence to succeed, we need two things: intelligence and an artifact. The computer has been the artifact of choice. The modern digital electronic computer was invented independently and almost simultaneously by scientists in three countries embattled in World War II. The first *operational* computer was the electromechanical Heath Robinson,[11] built in 1940 by Alan Turing's team for a single purpose: deciphering German messages. In 1943, the same group developed the Colossus, a powerful general-purpose machine based on vacuum tubes.[12] The first operational *programmable* computer was the Z-3, the invention of Konrad Zuse in Germany in 1941. Zuse also invented floating-point numbers and the first high-level programming language, Plankalkül. The first *electronic* computer, the ABC, was assembled by John Atanasoff and his student Clifford Berry between 1940 and 1942 at Iowa State University. Atanasoff's research received little support or recognition; it was the ENIAC, developed as part of a secret military project at the University of Pennsylvania by a team including John Mauchly and John Eckert, that proved to be the most influential forerunner of modern computers.

In the half-century since then, each generation of computer hardware has brought an increase in speed and capacity and a decrease in price. Performance doubles every 18 months or so, with a decade or two to go at this rate of increase. After that, we will need molecular engineering or some other new technology.

Of course, there were calculating devices before the electronic computer. The earliest automated machines, dating from the 17th century, were discussed on page 6. The first *programmable* machine was a loom devised in 1805 by Joseph Marie Jacquard (1752–1834) that used punched cards to store instructions for the pattern to be woven. In the mid-19th century, Charles Babbage (1792–1871) designed two machines, neither of which he completed. The "Difference Engine," which appears on the cover of this book, was intended to compute mathematical tables for engineering and scientific projects. It was finally built and shown to work in 1991 at the Science Museum in London (Swade, 1993). Babbage's "Analytical Engine" was far more ambitious: it included addressable memory, stored programs, and conditional jumps and was the first artifact capable of universal computation. Babbage's colleague Ada Lovelace, daughter of the poet Lord Byron, was perhaps the world's first programmer. (The programming language Ada is named after her.) She wrote programs for the unfinished Analytical Engine and even speculated that the machine could play chess or compose music.

---

[11] Heath Robinson was a cartoonist famous for his depictions of whimsical and absurdly complicated contraptions for everyday tasks such as buttering toast.

[12] In the postwar period, Turing wanted to use these computers for AI research—for example, one of the first chess programs (Turing *et al.*, 1953). His efforts were blocked by the British government.

AI also owes a debt to the software side of computer science, which has supplied the operating systems, programming languages, and tools needed to write modern programs (and papers about them). But this is one area where the debt has been repaid: work in AI has pioneered many ideas that have made their way back to mainstream computer science, including time sharing, interactive interpreters, personal computers with windows and mice, rapid development environments, the linked list data type, automatic storage management, and key concepts of symbolic, functional, dynamic, and object-oriented programming.

### Control theory and Cybernetics (1948–present)

- How can artifacts operate under their own control?

Ktesibios of Alexandria (c. 250 B.C.) built the first self-controlling machine: a water clock with a regulator that kept the flow of water running through it at a constant, predictable pace. This invention changed the definition of what an artifact could do. Previously, only living things could modify their behavior in response to changes in the environment. Other examples of self-regulating feedback control systems include the steam engine governor, created by James Watt (1736–1819), and the thermostat, invented by Cornelis Drebbel (1572–1633), who also invented the submarine. The mathematical theory of stable feedback systems was developed in the 19th century.

CONTROL THEORY

The central figure in the creation of what is now called **control theory** was Norbert Wiener (1894–1964). Wiener was a brilliant mathematician who worked with Bertrand Russell, among others, before developing an interest in biological and mechanical control systems and their connection to cognition. Like Craik (who also used control systems as psychological models), Wiener and his colleagues Arturo Rosenblueth and Julian Bigelow challenged the behaviorist orthodoxy (Rosenblueth *et al.*, 1943). They viewed purposive behavior as arising from a regulatory mechanism trying to minimize "error"—the difference between current state and goal state. In the late 1940s, Wiener, along with Warren McCulloch, Walter Pitts, and John von Neumann, organized a series of conferences that explored the new mathematical and computational models of cognition and influenced many other researchers in the behavioral sciences. Wiener's book *Cybernetics* (1948) became a bestseller and awoke the public to the possibility of artificially intelligent machines.

CYBERNETICS

OBJECTIVE FUNCTION

Modern control theory, especially the branch known as stochastic optimal control, has as its goal the design of systems that maximize an **objective function** over time. This roughly matches our view of AI: designing systems that behave optimally. Why, then, are AI and control theory two different fields, especially given the close connections among their founders? The answer lies in the close coupling between the mathematical techniques that were familiar to the participants and the corresponding sets of problems that were encompassed in each world view. Calculus and matrix algebra, the tools of control theory, lend themselves to systems that are describable by fixed sets of continuous variables; furthermore, exact analysis is typically feasible only for *linear* systems. AI was founded in part as a way to escape from the limitations of the mathematics of control theory in the 1950s. The tools of logical inference and computation allowed AI researchers to consider some problems such as language, vision, and planning, that fell completely outside the control theorist's purview.

### Linguistics (1957–present)

- How does language relate to thought?

In 1957, B. F. Skinner published *Verbal Behavior.* This was a comprehensive, detailed account of the behaviorist approach to language learning, written by the foremost expert in the field. But curiously, a review of the book became as well known as the book itself, and served to almost kill off interest in behaviorism. The author of the review was Noam Chomsky, who had just published a book on his own theory, *Syntactic Structures.* Chomsky showed how the behaviorist theory did not address the notion of creativity in language—it did not explain how a child could understand and make up sentences that he or she had never heard before. Chomsky's theory—based on syntactic models going back to the Indian linguist Panini (c. 350 B.C.)—could explain this, and unlike previous theories, it was formal enough that it could in principle be programmed.

Modern linguistics and AI, then, were "born" at about the same time, and grew up together, intersecting in a hybrid field called **computational linguistics** or **natural language processing**. The problem of understanding language soon turned out to be considerably more complex than it seemed in 1957. Understanding language requires an understanding of the subject matter and context, not just an understanding of the structure of sentences. This might seem obvious, but it was not widely appreciated until the 1960s. Much of the early work in **knowledge representation** (the study of how to put knowledge into a form that a computer can reason with) was tied to language and informed by research in linguistics, which was connected in turn to decades of work on the philosophical analysis of language.

COMPUTATIONAL LINGUISTICS

## 1.3 The History of Artificial Intelligence

With the background material behind us, we are ready to cover the development of AI itself.

### The gestation of artificial intelligence (1943–1955)

The first work that is now generally recognized as AI was done by Warren McCulloch and Walter Pitts (1943). They drew on three sources: knowledge of the basic physiology and function of neurons in the brain; a formal analysis of propositional logic due to Russell and Whitehead; and Turing's theory of computation. They proposed a model of artificial neurons in which each neuron is characterized as being "on" or "off," with a switch to "on" occurring in response to stimulation by a sufficient number of neighboring neurons. The state of a neuron was conceived of as "factually equivalent to a proposition which proposed its adequate stimulus." They showed, for example, that any computable function could be computed by some network of connected neurons, and that all the logical connectives (and, or, not, etc.) could be implemented by simple net structures. McCulloch and Pitts also suggested that suitably defined networks could learn. Donald Hebb (1949) demonstrated a simple updating rule for modifying the connection strengths between neurons. His rule, now called **Hebbian learning**, remains an influential model to this day.

Two undergraduate students at Harvard, Marvin Minsky and Dean Edmonds, built the first neural network computer in 1950. The SNARC, as it was called, used 3000 vacuum tubes and a surplus automatic pilot mechanism from a B-24 bomber to simulate a network of 40 neurons. Later, at Princeton, Minsky studied universal computation in neural networks. His Ph.D. committee was skeptical about whether this kind of work should be considered mathematics, but von Neumann reportedly said, "If it isn't now, it will be someday." Minsky was later to prove influential theorems showing the limitations of neural network research.

There were a number of early examples of work that can be characterized as AI, but it was Alan Turing who first articulated a complete vision of AI in his 1950 article "Computing Machinery and Intelligence." Therein, he introduced the Turing test, machine learning, genetic algorithms, and reinforcement learning.

### The birth of artificial intelligence (1956)

Princeton was home to another influential figure in AI, John McCarthy. After graduation, McCarthy moved to Dartmouth College, which was to become the official birthplace of the field. McCarthy convinced Minsky, Claude Shannon, and Nathaniel Rochester to help him bring together U.S. researchers interested in automata theory, neural nets, and the study of intelligence. They organized a two-month workshop at Dartmouth in the summer of 1956. There were 10 attendees in all, including Trenchard More from Princeton, Arthur Samuel from IBM, and Ray Solomonoff and Oliver Selfridge from MIT.

Two researchers from Carnegie Tech,[13] Allen Newell and Herbert Simon, rather stole the show. Although the others had ideas and in some cases programs for particular applications such as checkers, Newell and Simon already had a reasoning program, the Logic Theorist (LT), about which Simon claimed, "We have invented a computer program capable of thinking non-numerically, and thereby solved the venerable mind–body problem."[14] Soon after the workshop, the program was able to prove most of the theorems in Chapter 2 of Russell and Whitehead's *Principia Mathematica*. Russell was reportedly delighted when Simon showed him that the program had come up with a proof for one theorem that was shorter than the one in *Principia*. The editors of the *Journal of Symbolic Logic* were less impressed; they rejected a paper coauthored by Newell, Simon, and Logic Theorist.

The Dartmouth workshop did not lead to any new breakthroughs, but it did introduce all the major figures to each other. For the next 20 years, the field would be dominated by these people and their students and colleagues at MIT, CMU, Stanford, and IBM. Perhaps the longest-lasting thing to come out of the workshop was an agreement to adopt McCarthy's new name for the field: **artificial intelligence**. Perhaps "computational rationality" would have been better, but "AI" has stuck.

Looking at the proposal for the Dartmouth workshop (McCarthy *et al.*, 1955), we can see why it was necessary for AI to become a separate field. Why couldn't all the work done

---

[13] Now Carnegie Mellon University (CMU).

[14] Newell and Simon also invented a list-processing language, IPL, to write LT. They had no compiler, and translated it into machine code by hand. To avoid errors, they worked in parallel, calling out binary numbers to each other as they wrote each instruction to make sure they agreed.

in AI have taken place under the name of control theory, or operations research, or decision theory, which, after all, have objectives similar to those of AI? Or why isn't AI a branch of mathematics? The first answer is that AI from the start embraced the idea of duplicating human faculties like creativity, self-improvement, and language use. None of the other fields were addressing these issues. The second answer is methodology. AI is the only one of these fields that is clearly a branch of computer science (although operations research does share an emphasis on computer simulations), and AI is the only field to attempt to build machines that will function autonomously in complex, changing environments.

### Early enthusiasm, great expectations (1952–1969)

The early years of AI were full of successes—in a limited way. Given the primitive computers and programming tools of the time, and the fact that only a few years earlier computers were seen as things that could do arithmetic and no more, it was astonishing whenever a computer did anything remotely clever. The intellectual establishment, by and large, preferred to believe that "a machine can never do $X$." (See Chapter 26 for a long list of $X$'s gathered by Turing.) AI researchers naturally responded by demonstrating one $X$ after another. John McCarthy referred to this period as the "Look, Ma, no hands!" era.

Newell and Simon's early success was followed up with the General Problem Solver, or GPS. Unlike Logic Theorist, this program was designed from the start to imitate human problem-solving protocols. Within the limited class of puzzles it could handle, it turned out that the order in which the program considered subgoals and possible actions was similar to that in which humans approached the same problems. Thus, GPS was probably the first program to embody the "thinking humanly" approach. The success of GPS and subsequent programs as models of cognition led Newell and Simon (1976) to formulate the famous **physical symbol system** hypothesis, which states that "a physical symbol system has the necessary and sufficient means for general intelligent action." What they meant is that any system (human or machine) exhibiting intelligence must operate by manipulating data structures composed of symbols. We will see later that this hypothesis has been challenged from many directions.

PHYSICAL SYMBOL SYSTEM

At IBM, Nathaniel Rochester and his colleagues produced some of the first AI programs. Herbert Gelernter (1959) constructed the Geometry Theorem Prover, which was able to prove theorems that many students of mathematics would find quite tricky. Starting in 1952, Arthur Samuel wrote a series of programs for checkers (draughts) that eventually learned to play at a strong amateur level. Along the way, he disproved the idea that computers can do only what they are told to: his program quickly learned to play a better game than its creator. The program was demonstrated on television in February 1956, creating a very strong impression. Like Turing, Samuel had trouble finding computer time. Working at night, he used machines that were still on the testing floor at IBM's manufacturing plant. Chapter 6 covers game playing, and Chapter 21 describes and expands on the learning techniques used by Samuel.

John McCarthy moved from Dartmouth to MIT and there made three crucial contributions in one historic year: 1958. In MIT AI Lab Memo No. 1, McCarthy defined the high-level language **Lisp**, which was to become the dominant AI programming language. Lisp is the

LISP

second-oldest major high-level language in current use, one year younger than FORTRAN. With Lisp, McCarthy had the tool he needed, but access to scarce and expensive computing resources was also a serious problem. In response, he and others at MIT invented time sharing. Also in 1958, McCarthy published a paper entitled *Programs with Common Sense*, in which he described the Advice Taker, a hypothetical program that can be seen as the first complete AI system. Like the Logic Theorist and Geometry Theorem Prover, McCarthy's program was designed to use knowledge to search for solutions to problems. But unlike the others, it was to embody general knowledge of the world. For example, he showed how some simple axioms would enable the program to generate a plan to drive to the airport to catch a plane. The program was also designed so that it could accept new axioms in the normal course of operation, thereby allowing it to achieve competence in new areas *without being reprogrammed*. The Advice Taker thus embodied the central principles of knowledge representation and reasoning: that it is useful to have a formal, explicit representation of the world and of the way an agent's actions affect the world and to be able to manipulate these representations with deductive processes. It is remarkable how much of the 1958 paper remains relevant even today.

1958 also marked the year that Marvin Minsky moved to MIT. His initial collaboration with McCarthy did not last, however. McCarthy stressed representation and reasoning in formal logic, whereas Minsky was more interested in getting programs to work and eventually developed an anti-logical outlook. In 1963, McCarthy started the AI lab at Stanford. His plan to use logic to build the ultimate Advice Taker was advanced by J. A. Robinson's discovery of the resolution method (a complete theorem-proving algorithm for first-order logic; see Chapter 9). Work at Stanford emphasized general-purpose methods for logical reasoning. Applications of logic included Cordell Green's question-answering and planning systems (Green, 1969b) and the Shakey robotics project at the new Stanford Research Institute (SRI). The latter project, discussed further in Chapter 25, was the first to demonstrate the complete integration of logical reasoning and physical activity.

MICROWORLDS

Minsky supervised a series of students who chose limited problems that appeared to require intelligence to solve. These limited domains became known as **microworlds**. James Slagle's SAINT program (1963a) was able to solve closed-form calculus integration problems typical of first-year college courses. Tom Evans's ANALOGY program (1968) solved geometric analogy problems that appear in IQ tests, such as the one in Figure 1.4. Daniel Bobrow's STUDENT program (1967) solved algebra story problems, such as the following:

> If the number of customers Tom gets is twice the square of 20 percent of the number of advertisements he runs, and the number of advertisements he runs is 45, what is the number of customers Tom gets?

The most famous microworld was the blocks world, which consists of a set of solid blocks placed on a tabletop (or more often, a simulation of a tabletop), as shown in Figure 1.5. A typical task in this world is to rearrange the blocks in a certain way, using a robot hand that can pick up one block at a time. The blocks world was home to the vision project of David Huffman (1971), the vision and constraint-propagation work of David Waltz (1975), the learning theory of Patrick Winston (1970), the natural language understanding program

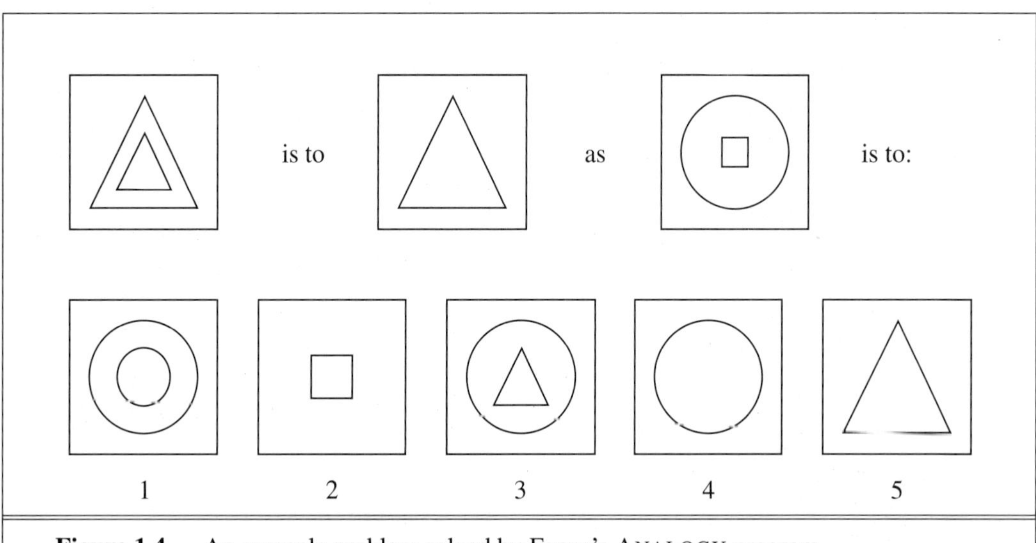


**Figure 1.4** An example problem solved by Evans's ANALOGY program.

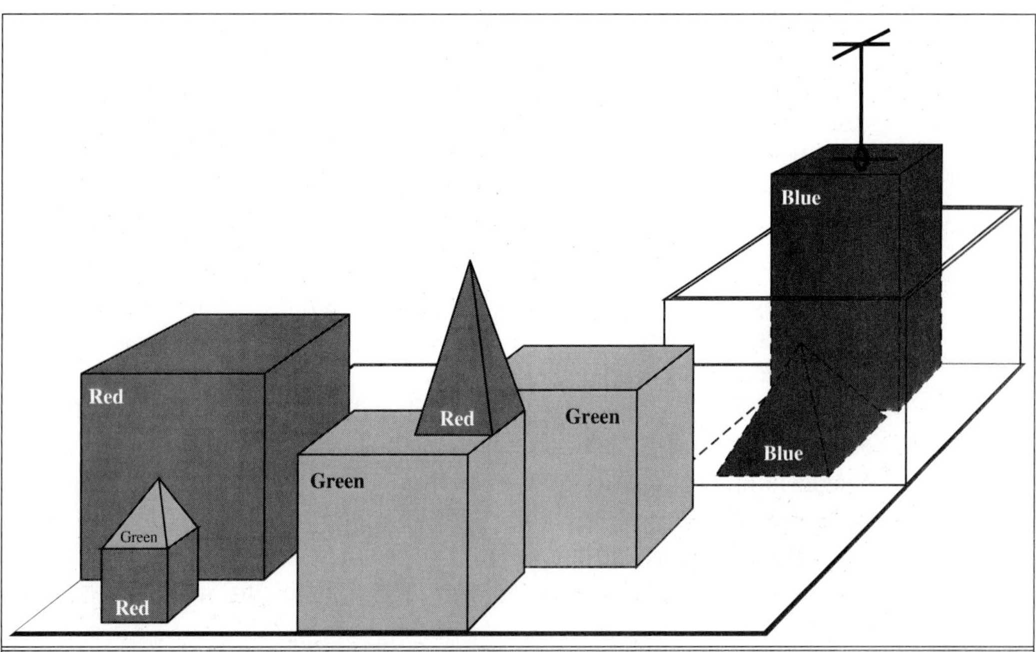


**Figure 1.5** A scene from the blocks world. SHRDLU (Winograd, 1972) has just completed the command, "Find a block which is taller than the one you are holding and put it in the box."

of Terry Winograd (1972), and the planner of Scott Fahlman (1974).

Early work building on the neural networks of McCulloch and Pitts also flourished. The work of Winograd and Cowan (1963) showed how a large number of elements could collectively represent an individual concept, with a corresponding increase in robustness and parallelism. Hebb's learning methods were enhanced by Bernie Widrow (Widrow and Hoff,

1960; Widrow, 1962), who called his networks **adalines**, and by Frank Rosenblatt (1962) with his **perceptrons**. Rosenblatt proved the **perceptron convergence theorem**, showing that his learning algorithm could adjust the connection strengths of a perceptron to match any input data, provided such a match existed. These topics are covered in Chapter 20.

### A dose of reality (1966–1973)

From the beginning, AI researchers were not shy about making predictions of their coming successes. The following statement by Herbert Simon in 1957 is often quoted:

> It is not my aim to surprise or shock you—but the simplest way I can summarize is to say that there are now in the world machines that think, that learn and that create. Moreover, their ability to do these things is going to increase rapidly until—in a visible future—the range of problems they can handle will be coextensive with the range to which the human mind has been applied.

Terms such as "visible future" can be interpreted in various ways, but Simon also made a more concrete prediction: that within 10 years a computer would be chess champion, and a significant mathematical theorem would be proved by machine. These predictions came true (or approximately true) within 40 years rather than 10. Simon's over-confidence was due to the promising performance of early AI systems on simple examples. In almost all cases, however, these early systems turned out to fail miserably when tried out on wider selections of problems and on more difficult problems.

The first kind of difficulty arose because most early programs contained little or no knowledge of their subject matter; they succeeded by means of simple syntactic manipulations. A typical story occurred in early machine translation efforts, which were generously funded by the U.S. National Research Council in an attempt to speed up the translation of Russian scientific papers in the wake of the Sputnik launch in 1957. It was thought initially that simple syntactic transformations based on the grammars of Russian and English, and word replacement using an electronic dictionary, would suffice to preserve the exact meanings of sentences. The fact is that translation requires general knowledge of the subject matter in order to resolve ambiguity and establish the content of the sentence. The famous re-translation of "the spirit is willing but the flesh is weak" as "the vodka is good but the meat is rotten" illustrates the difficulties encountered. In 1966, a report by an advisory committee found that "there has been no machine translation of general scientific text, and none is in immediate prospect." All U.S. government funding for academic translation projects was canceled. Today, machine translation is an imperfect but widely used tool for technical, commercial, government, and Internet documents.

The second kind of difficulty was the intractability of many of the problems that AI was attempting to solve. Most of the early AI programs solved problems by trying out different combinations of steps until the solution was found. This strategy worked initially because microworlds contained very few objects and hence very few possible actions and very short solution sequences. Before the theory of computational complexity was developed, it was widely thought that "scaling up" to larger problems was simply a matter of faster hardware and larger memories. The optimism that accompanied the development of resolution theorem

proving, for example, was soon dampened when researchers failed to prove theorems involving more than a few dozen facts. *The fact that a program can find a solution in principle does not mean that the program contains any of the mechanisms needed to find it in practice.*

MACHINE EVOLUTION

The illusion of unlimited computational power was not confined to problem-solving programs. Early experiments in **machine evolution** (now called **genetic algorithms**) (Friedberg, 1958; Friedberg *et al.*, 1959) were based on the undoubtedly correct belief that by making an appropriate series of small mutations to a machine code program, one can generate a program with good performance for any particular simple task. The idea, then, was to try random mutations with a selection process to preserve mutations that seemed useful. Despite thousands of hours of CPU time, almost no progress was demonstrated. Modern genetic algorithms use better representations and have shown more success.

Failure to come to grips with the "combinatorial explosion" was one of the main criticisms of AI contained in the Lighthill report (Lighthill, 1973), which formed the basis for the decision by the British government to end support for AI research in all but two universities. (Oral tradition paints a somewhat different and more colorful picture, with political ambitions and personal animosities whose description is beside the point.)

A third difficulty arose because of some fundamental limitations on the basic structures being used to generate intelligent behavior. For example, Minsky and Papert's book *Perceptrons* (1969) proved that, although perceptrons (a simple form of neural network) could be shown to learn anything they were capable of representing, they could represent very little. In particular, a two-input perceptron could not be trained to recognize when its two inputs were different. Although their results did not apply to more complex, multilayer networks, research funding for neural-net research soon dwindled to almost nothing. Ironically, the new back-propagation learning algorithms for multilayer networks that were to cause an enormous resurgence in neural-net research in the late 1980s were actually discovered first in 1969 (Bryson and Ho, 1969).

### Knowledge-based systems: The key to power? (1969–1979)

WEAK METHODS

The picture of problem solving that had arisen during the first decade of AI research was of a general-purpose search mechanism trying to string together elementary reasoning steps to find complete solutions. Such approaches have been called **weak methods**, because, although general, they do not scale up to large or difficult problem instances. The alternative to weak methods is to use more powerful, domain-specific knowledge that allows larger reasoning steps and can more easily handle typically occurring cases in narrow areas of expertise. One might say that to solve a hard problem, you have to almost know the answer already.

The DENDRAL program (Buchanan *et al.*, 1969) was an early example of this approach. It was developed at Stanford, where Ed Feigenbaum (a former student of Herbert Simon), Bruce Buchanan (a philosopher turned computer scientist), and Joshua Lederberg (a Nobel laureate geneticist) teamed up to solve the problem of inferring molecular structure from the information provided by a mass spectrometer. The input to the program consists of the elementary formula of the molecule (e.g., $C_6H_{13}NO_2$) and the mass spectrum giving the masses of the various fragments of the molecule generated when it is bombarded by an electron beam.

For example, the mass spectrum might contain a peak at $m = 15$, corresponding to the mass of a methyl ($CH_3$) fragment.

The naive version of the program generated all possible structures consistent with the formula, and then predicted what mass spectrum would be observed for each, comparing this with the actual spectrum. As one might expect, this is intractable for decent-sized molecules. The DENDRAL researchers consulted analytical chemists and found that they worked by looking for well-known patterns of peaks in the spectrum that suggested common substructures in the molecule. For example, the following rule is used to recognize a ketone (C=O) subgroup (which weighs 28):

> **if** there are two peaks at $x_1$ and $x_2$ such that
> (a) $x_1 + x_2 = M + 28$ ($M$ is the mass of the whole molecule);
> (b) $x_1 - 28$ is a high peak;
> (c) $x_2 - 28$ is a high peak;
> (d) At least one of $x_1$ and $x_2$ is high.
> **then** there is a ketone subgroup

Recognizing that the molecule contains a particular substructure reduces the number of possible candidates enormously. DENDRAL was powerful because

> All the relevant theoretical knowledge to solve these problems has been mapped over from its general form in the [spectrum prediction component] ("first principles") to efficient special forms ("cookbook recipes"). (Feigenbaum *et al.*, 1971)

The significance of DENDRAL was that it was the first successful *knowledge-intensive* system: its expertise derived from large numbers of special-purpose rules. Later systems also incorporated the main theme of McCarthy's Advice Taker approach—the clean separation of the knowledge (in the form of rules) from the reasoning component.

With this lesson in mind, Feigenbaum and others at Stanford began the Heuristic Programming Project (HPP), to investigate the extent to which the new methodology of **expert systems** could be applied to other areas of human expertise. The next major effort was in the area of medical diagnosis. Feigenbaum, Buchanan, and Dr. Edward Shortliffe developed MYCIN to diagnose blood infections. With about 450 rules, MYCIN was able to perform as well as some experts, and considerably better than junior doctors. It also contained two major differences from DENDRAL. First, unlike the DENDRAL rules, no general theoretical model existed from which the MYCIN rules could be deduced. They had to be acquired from extensive interviewing of experts, who in turn acquired them from textbooks, other experts, and direct experience of cases. Second, the rules had to reflect the uncertainty associated with medical knowledge. MYCIN incorporated a calculus of uncertainty called **certainty factors** (see Chapter 14), which seemed (at the time) to fit well with how doctors assessed the impact of evidence on the diagnosis.

EXPERT SYSTEMS

The importance of domain knowledge was also apparent in the area of understanding natural language. Although Winograd's SHRDLU system for understanding natural language had engendered a good deal of excitement, its dependence on syntactic analysis caused some of the same problems as occurred in the early machine translation work. It was able to overcome ambiguity and understand pronoun references, but this was mainly because it was designed specifically for one area—the blocks world. Several researchers, including Eugene Charniak, a fellow graduate student of Winograd's at MIT, suggested that robust language understanding would require general knowledge about the world and a general method for using that knowledge.

At Yale, the linguist-turned-AI-researcher Roger Schank emphasized this point, claiming, "There is no such thing as syntax," which upset a lot of linguists, but did serve to start a useful discussion. Schank and his students built a series of programs (Schank and Abelson, 1977; Wilensky, 1978; Schank and Riesbeck, 1981; Dyer, 1983) that all had the task of understanding natural language. The emphasis, however, was less on language *per se* and more on the problems of representing and reasoning with the knowledge required for language understanding. The problems included representing stereotypical situations (Cullingford, 1981), describing human memory organization (Rieger, 1976; Kolodner, 1983), and understanding plans and goals (Wilensky, 1983).

The widespread growth of applications to real-world problems caused a concurrent increase in the demands for workable knowledge representation schemes. A large number of different representation and reasoning languages were developed. Some were based on logic—for example, the Prolog language became popular in Europe, and the PLANNER family in the United States. Others, following Minsky's idea of **frames** (1975), adopted a more structured approach, assembling facts about particular object and event types and arranging the types into a large taxonomic hierarchy analogous to a biological taxonomy.

FRAMES

## AI becomes an industry (1980–present)

The first successful commercial expert system, R1, began operation at the Digital Equipment Corporation (McDermott, 1982). The program helped configure orders for new computer systems; by 1986, it was saving the company an estimated $40 million a year. By 1988, DEC's AI group had 40 expert systems deployed, with more on the way. Du Pont had 100 in use and 500 in development, saving an estimated $10 million a year. Nearly every major U.S. corporation had its own AI group and was either using or investigating expert systems.

In 1981, the Japanese announced the "Fifth Generation" project, a 10-year plan to build intelligent computers running Prolog. In response the United States formed the Microelectronics and Computer Technology Corporation (MCC) as a research consortium designed to assure national competitiveness. In both cases, AI was part of a broad effort, including chip design and human-interface research. However, the AI components of MCC and the Fifth Generation projects never met their ambitious goals. In Britain, the Alvey report reinstated the funding that was cut by the Lighthill report.[15]

Overall, the AI industry boomed from a few million dollars in 1980 to billions of dollars in 1988. Soon after that came a period called the "AI Winter," in which many companies suffered as they failed to deliver on extravagant promises.

[15] To save embarrassment, a new field called IKBS (Intelligent Knowledge-Based Systems) was invented because Artificial Intelligence had been officially canceled.

### The return of neural networks (1986–present)

Although computer science had largely abandoned the field of neural networks in the late 1970s, work continued in other fields. Physicists such as John Hopfield (1982) used techniques from statistical mechanics to analyze the storage and optimization properties of networks, treating collections of nodes like collections of atoms. Psychologists including David Rumelhart and Geoff Hinton continued the study of neural-net models of memory. As we discuss in Chapter 20, the real impetus came in the mid-1980s when at least four different groups reinvented the back-propagation learning algorithm first found in 1969 by Bryson and Ho. The algorithm was applied to many learning problems in computer science and psychology, and the widespread dissemination of the results in the collection *Parallel Distributed Processing* (Rumelhart and McClelland, 1986) caused great excitement.

CONNECTIONIST

These so-called **connectionist** models of intelligent systems were seen by some as direct competitors both to the symbolic models promoted by Newell and Simon and to the logicist approach of McCarthy and others (Smolensky, 1988). It might seem obvious that at some level humans manipulate symbols—in fact, Terrence Deacon's book *The Symbolic Species* (1997) suggests that this is the *defining characteristic* of humans, but the most ardent connectionists questioned whether symbol manipulation had any real explanatory role in detailed models of cognition. This question remains unanswered, but the current view is that connectionist and symbolic approaches are complementary, not competing.

### AI becomes a science (1987–present)

Recent years have seen a revolution in both the content and the methodology of work in artificial intelligence.[16] It is now more common to build on existing theories than to propose brand new ones, to base claims on rigorous theorems or hard experimental evidence rather than on intuition, and to show relevance to real-world applications rather than toy examples.

AI was founded in part as a rebellion against the limitations of existing fields like control theory and statistics, but now it is embracing those fields. As David McAllester (1998) put it,

> In the early period of AI it seemed plausible that new forms of symbolic computation, e.g., frames and semantic networks, made much of classical theory obsolete. This led to a form of isolationism in which AI became largely separated from the rest of computer science. This isolationism is currently being abandoned. There is a recognition that machine learning should not be isolated from information theory, that uncertain reasoning should not be isolated from stochastic modeling, that search should not be isolated from classical optimization and control, and that automated reasoning should not be isolated from formal methods and static analysis.

In terms of methodology, AI has finally come firmly under the scientific method. To be accepted, hypotheses must be subjected to rigorous empirical experiments, and the results must

[16] Some have characterized this change as a victory of the **neats**—those who think that AI theories should be grounded in mathematical rigor—over the **scruffies**—those who would rather try out lots of ideas, write some programs, and then assess what seems to be working. Both approaches are important. A shift toward neatness implies that the field has reached a level of stability and maturity. Whether that stability will be disrupted by a new scruffy idea is another question.

be analyzed statistically for their importance (Cohen, 1995). Through the use of the Internet and shared repositories of test data and code, it is now possible to replicate experiments.

The field of speech recognition illustrates the pattern. In the 1970s, a wide variety of different architectures and approaches were tried. Many of these were rather *ad hoc* and fragile, and were demonstrated on only a few specially selected examples. In recent years, approaches based on **hidden Markov models** (HMMs) have come to dominate the area. Two aspects of HMMs are relevant. First, they are based on a rigorous mathematical theory. This has allowed speech researchers to build on several decades of mathematical results developed in other fields. Second, they are generated by a process of training on a large corpus of real speech data. This ensures that the performance is robust, and in rigorous blind tests the HMMs have been improving their scores steadily. Speech technology and the related field of handwritten character recognition are already making the transition to widespread industrial and consumer applications.

Neural networks also fit this trend. Much of the work on neural nets in the 1980s was done in an attempt to scope out what could be done and to learn how neural nets differ from "traditional" techniques. Using improved methodology and theoretical frameworks, the field arrived at an understanding in which neural nets can now be compared with corresponding techniques from statistics, pattern recognition, and machine learning, and the most promising technique can be applied to each application. As a result of these developments, so-called

DATA MINING

**data mining** technology has spawned a vigorous new industry.

Judea Pearl's (1988) *Probabilistic Reasoning in Intelligent Systems* led to a new acceptance of probability and decision theory in AI, following a resurgence of interest epitomized by Peter Cheeseman's (1985) article "In Defense of Probability." The **Bayesian network** formalism was invented to allow efficient representation of, and rigorous reasoning with, uncertain knowledge. This approach largely overcomes many problems of the probabilistic reasoning systems of the 1960s and 1970s; it now dominates AI research on uncertain reasoning and expert systems. The approach allows for learning from experience, and it combines the best of classical AI and neural nets. Work by Judea Pearl (1982a) and by Eric Horvitz and David Heckerman (Horvitz and Heckerman, 1986; Horvitz *et al.*, 1986) promoted the idea of *normative* expert systems: ones that act rationally according to the laws of decision theory and do not try to imitate the thought steps of human experts. The Windows™ operating system includes several normative diagnostic expert systems for correcting problems. Chapters 13 to 16 cover this area.

Similar gentle revolutions have occurred in robotics, computer vision, and knowledge representation. A better understanding of the problems and their complexity properties, combined with increased mathematical sophistication, has led to workable research agendas and robust methods. In many cases, formalization and specialization have also led to fragmentation: topics such as vision and robotics are increasingly isolated from "mainstream" AI work. The unifying view of AI as rational agent design is one that can bring unity back to these disparate fields.

### The emergence of intelligent agents (1995–present)

Perhaps encouraged by the progress in solving the subproblems of AI, researchers have also started to look at the "whole agent" problem again. The work of Allen Newell, John Laird, and Paul Rosenbloom on SOAR (Newell, 1990; Laird *et al.*, 1987) is the best-known example of a complete agent architecture. The so-called situated movement aims to understand the workings of agents embedded in real environments with continuous sensory inputs. One of the most important environments for intelligent agents is the Internet. AI systems have become so common in web-based applications that the "-bot" suffix has entered everyday language. Moreover, AI technologies underlie many Internet tools, such as search engines, recommender systems, and Web site construction systems.

Besides the first edition of this text (Russell and Norvig, 1995), other recent texts have also adopted the agent perspective (Poole *et al.*, 1998; Nilsson, 1998). One consequence of trying to build complete agents is the realization that the previously isolated subfields of AI might need to be reorganized somewhat when their results are to be tied together. In particular, it is now widely appreciated that sensory systems (vision, sonar, speech recognition, etc.) cannot deliver perfectly reliable information about the environment. Hence, reasoning and planning systems must be able to handle uncertainty. A second major consequence of the agent perspective is that AI has been drawn into much closer contact with other fields, such as control theory and economics, that also deal with agents.

## 1.4 THE STATE OF THE ART

What can AI do today? A concise answer is difficult, because there are so many activities in so many subfields. Here we sample a few applications; others appear throughout the book.

**Autonomous planning and scheduling:** A hundred million miles from Earth, NASA's Remote Agent program became the first on-board autonomous planning program to control the scheduling of operations for a spacecraft (Jonsson *et al.*, 2000). Remote Agent generated plans from high-level goals specified from the ground, and it monitored the operation of the spacecraft as the plans were executed—detecting, diagnosing, and recovering from problems as they occurred.

**Game playing:** IBM's Deep Blue became the first computer program to defeat the world champion in a chess match when it bested Garry Kasparov by a score of 3.5 to 2.5 in an exhibition match (Goodman and Keene, 1997). Kasparov said that he felt a "new kind of intelligence" across the board from him. *Newsweek* magazine described the match as "The brain's last stand." The value of IBM's stock increased by $18 billion.

**Autonomous control:** The ALVINN computer vision system was trained to steer a car to keep it following a lane. It was placed in CMU's NAVLAB computer-controlled minivan and used to navigate across the United States—for 2850 miles it was in control of steering the vehicle 98% of the time. A human took over the other 2%, mostly at exit ramps. NAVLAB has video cameras that transmit road images to ALVINN, which then computes the best direction to steer, based on experience from previous training runs.

**Diagnosis:** Medical diagnosis programs based on probabilistic analysis have been able to perform at the level of an expert physician in several areas of medicine. Heckerman (1991) describes a case where a leading expert on lymph-node pathology scoffs at a program's diagnosis of an especially difficult case. The creators of the program suggest he ask the computer for an explanation of the diagnosis. The machine points out the major factors influencing its decision and explains the subtle interaction of several of the symptoms in this case. Eventually, the expert agrees with the program.

**Logistics Planning:** During the Persian Gulf crisis of 1991, U.S. forces deployed a Dynamic Analysis and Replanning Tool, DART (Cross and Walker, 1994), to do automated logistics planning and scheduling for transportation. This involved up to 50,000 vehicles, cargo, and people at a time, and had to account for starting points, destinations, routes, and conflict resolution among all parameters. The AI planning techniques allowed a plan to be generated in hours that would have taken weeks with older methods. The Defense Advanced Research Project Agency (DARPA) stated that this single application more than paid back DARPA's 30-year investment in AI.

**Robotics:** Many surgeons now use robot assistants in microsurgery. HipNav (DiGioia *et al.*, 1996) is a system that uses computer vision techniques to create a three-dimensional model of a patient's internal anatomy and then uses robotic control to guide the insertion of a hip replacement prosthesis.

**Language understanding and problem solving:** PROVERB (Littman *et al.*, 1999) is a computer program that solves crossword puzzles better than most humans, using constraints on possible word fillers, a large database of past puzzles, and a variety of information sources including dictionaries and online databases such as a list of movies and the actors that appear in them. For example, it determines that the clue "Nice Story" can be solved by "ETAGE" because its database includes the clue/solution pair "Story in France/ETAGE" and because it recognizes that the patterns "Nice *X*" and "*X* in France" often have the same solution. The program does not know that Nice is a city in France, but it can solve the puzzle.

These are just a few examples of artificial intelligence systems that exist today. Not magic or science fiction—but rather science, engineering, and mathematics, to which this book provides an introduction.

## 1.5 SUMMARY

This chapter defines AI and establishes the cultural background against which it has developed. Some of the important points are as follows:

- Different people think of AI differently. Two important questions to ask are: Are you concerned with thinking or behavior? Do you want to model humans or work from an ideal standard?
- In this book, we adopt the view that intelligence is concerned mainly with **rational action**. Ideally, an **intelligent agent** takes the best possible action in a situation. We will study the problem of building agents that are intelligent in this sense.

- Philosophers (going back to 400 B.C.) made AI conceivable by considering the ideas that the mind is in some ways like a machine, that it operates on knowledge encoded in some internal language, and that thought can be used to choose what actions to take.
- Mathematicians provided the tools to manipulate statements of logical certainty as well as uncertain, probabilistic statements. They also set the groundwork for understanding computation and reasoning about algorithms.
- Economists formalized the problem of making decisions that maximize the expected outcome to the decision-maker.
- Psychologists adopted the idea that humans and animals can be considered information-processing machines. Linguists showed that language use fits into this model.
- Computer engineers provided the artifacts that make AI applications possible. AI programs tend to be large, and they could not work without the great advances in speed and memory that the computer industry has provided.
- Control theory deals with designing devices that act optimally on the basis of feedback from the environment. Initially, the mathematical tools of control theory were quite different from AI, but the fields are coming closer together.
- The history of AI has had cycles of success, misplaced optimism, and resulting cutbacks in enthusiasm and funding. There have also been cycles of introducing new creative approaches and systematically refining the best ones.
- AI has advanced more rapidly in the past decade because of greater use of the scientific method in experimenting with and comparing approaches.
- Recent progress in understanding the theoretical basis for intelligence has gone hand in hand with improvements in the capabilities of real systems. The subfields of AI have become more integrated, and AI has found common ground with other disciplines.

## BIBLIOGRAPHICAL AND HISTORICAL NOTES

The methodological status of artificial intelligence is investigated in *The Sciences of the Artificial*, by Herb Simon (1981), which discusses research areas concerned with complex artifacts. It explains how AI can be viewed as both science and mathematics. Cohen (1995) gives an overview of experimental methodology within AI. Ford and Hayes (1995) give an opinionated view of the usefulness of the Turing Test.

*Artificial Intelligence: The Very Idea*, by John Haugeland (1985) gives a readable account of the philosophical and practical problems of AI. Cognitive science is well described by several recent texts (Johnson-Laird, 1988; Stillings *et al.*, 1995; Thagard, 1996) and by the *Encyclopedia of the Cognitive Sciences* (Wilson and Keil, 1999). Baker (1989) covers the syntactic part of modern linguistics, and Chierchia and McConnell-Ginet (1990) cover semantics. Jurafsky and Martin (2000) cover computational linguistics.

Early AI is described in Feigenbaum and Feldman's *Computers and Thought* (1963), Minsky's *Semantic Information Processing* (1968), and the *Machine Intelligence* series edited by Donald Michie. A large number of influential papers have been anthologized by Webber and Nilsson (1981) and by Luger (1995). Early papers on neural networks are collected in *Neurocomputing* (Anderson and Rosenfeld, 1988). The *Encyclopedia of AI* (Shapiro, 1992) contains survey articles on almost every topic in AI. These articles usually provide a good entry point into the research literature on each topic.

The most recent work appears in the proceedings of the major AI conferences: the biennial International Joint Conference on AI (IJCAI), the annual European Conference on AI (ECAI), and the National Conference on AI, more often known as AAAI, after its sponsoring organization. The major journals for general AI are *Artificial Intelligence*, *Computational Intelligence*, the *IEEE Transactions on Pattern Analysis and Machine Intelligence*, *IEEE Intelligent Systems*, and the electronic *Journal of Artificial Intelligence Research*. There are also many conferences and journals devoted to specific areas, which we cover in the appropriate chapters. The main professional societies for AI are the American Association for Artificial Intelligence (AAAI), the ACM Special Interest Group in Artificial Intelligence (SIGART), and the Society for Artificial Intelligence and Simulation of Behaviour (AISB). AAAI's *AI Magazine* contains many topical and tutorial articles, and its website, aaai.org, contains news and background information.

## EXERCISES

These exercises are intended to stimulate discussion, and some might be set as term projects. Alternatively, preliminary attempts can be made now, and these attempts can be reviewed after the completion of the book.

**1.1** Define in your own words: (a) intelligence, (b) artificial intelligence, (c) agent.

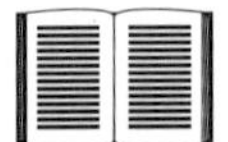

**1.2** Read Turing's original paper on AI (Turing, 1950). In the paper, he discusses several potential objections to his proposed enterprise and his test for intelligence. Which objections still carry some weight? Are his refutations valid? Can you think of new objections arising from developments since he wrote the paper? In the paper, he predicts that, by the year 2000, a computer will have a 30% chance of passing a five-minute Turing Test with an unskilled interrogator. What chance do you think a computer would have today? In another 50 years?

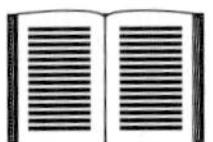

**1.3** Every year the Loebner prize is awarded to the program that comes closest to passing a version of the Turing test. Research and report on the latest winner of the Loebner prize. What techniques does it use? How does it advance the state of the art in AI?

**1.4** There are well-known classes of problems that are intractably difficult for computers, and other classes that are provably undecidable. Does this mean that AI is impossible?

**1.5** Suppose we extend Evans's ANALOGY program so that it can score 200 on a standard IQ test. Would we then have a program more intelligent than a human? Explain.

**1.6** How could introspection—reporting on one's inner thoughts—be inaccurate? Could I be wrong about what I'm thinking? Discuss.

**1.7** Examine the AI literature to discover whether the following tasks can currently be solved by computers:

**a**. Playing a decent game of table tennis (ping-pong).
**b**. Driving in the center of Cairo.
**c**. Buying a week's worth of groceries at the market.
**d**. Buying a week's worth of groceries on the web.
**e**. Playing a decent game of bridge at a competitive level.
**f**. Discovering and proving new mathematical theorems.
**g**. Writing an intentionally funny story.
**h**. Giving competent legal advice in a specialized area of law.
**i**. Translating spoken English into spoken Swedish in real time.
**j**. Performing a complex surgical operation.

For the currently infeasible tasks, try to find out what the difficulties are and predict when, if ever, they will be overcome.

**1.8** Some authors have claimed that perception and motor skills are the most important part of intelligence, and that "higher level" capacities are necessarily parasitic—simple add-ons to these underlying facilities. Certainly, most of evolution and a large part of the brain have been devoted to perception and motor skills, whereas AI has found tasks such as game playing and logical inference to be easier, in many ways, than perceiving and acting in the real world. Do you think that AI's traditional focus on higher-level cognitive abilities is misplaced?

**1.9** Why would evolution tend to result in systems that act rationally? What goals are such systems designed to achieve?

**1.10** Are reflex actions (such as moving your hand away from a hot stove) rational? Are they intelligent?

**1.11** "Surely computers cannot be intelligent—they can do only what their programmers tell them." Is the latter statement true, and does it imply the former?

**1.12** "Surely animals cannot be intelligent—they can do only what their genes tell them." Is the latter statement true, and does it imply the former?

**1.13** "Surely animals, humans, and computers cannot be intelligent—they can do only what their constituent atoms are told to do by the laws of physics." Is the latter statement true, and does it imply the former?

# 2 INTELLIGENT AGENTS

*In which we discuss the nature of agents, perfect or otherwise, the diversity of environments, and the resulting menagerie of agent types.*

Chapter 1 identified the concept of **rational agents** as central to our approach to artificial intelligence. In this chapter, we make this notion more concrete. We will see that the concept of rationality can be applied to a wide variety of agents operating in any imaginable environment. Our plan in this book is to use this concept to develop a small set of design principles for building successful agents—systems that can reasonably be called **intelligent**.

We will begin by examining agents, environments, and the coupling between them. The observation that some agents behave better than others leads naturally to the idea of a rational agent—one that behaves as well as possible. How well an agent can behave depends on the nature of the environment; some environments are more difficult than others. We give a crude categorization of environments and show how properties of an environment influence the design of suitable agents for that environment. We describe a number of basic "skeleton" agent designs, which will be fleshed out in the rest of the book.

## 2.1 AGENTS AND ENVIRONMENTS

ENVIRONMENT
SENSOR
ACTUATOR

An **agent** is anything that can be viewed as perceiving its **environment** through **sensors** and acting upon that environment through **actuators**. This simple idea is illustrated in Figure 2.1. A human agent has eyes, ears, and other organs for sensors and hands, legs, mouth, and other body parts for actuators. A robotic agent might have cameras and infrared range finders for sensors and various motors for actuators. A software agent receives keystrokes, file contents, and network packets as sensory inputs and acts on the environment by displaying on the screen, writing files, and sending network packets. We will make the general assumption that every agent can perceive its own actions (but not always the effects).

PERCEPT
PERCEPT SEQUENCE

We use the term **percept** to refer to the agent's perceptual inputs at any given instant. An agent's **percept sequence** is the complete history of everything the agent has ever perceived. In general, *an agent's choice of action at any given instant can depend on the entire percept sequence observed to date.* If we can specify the agent's choice of action for every possible

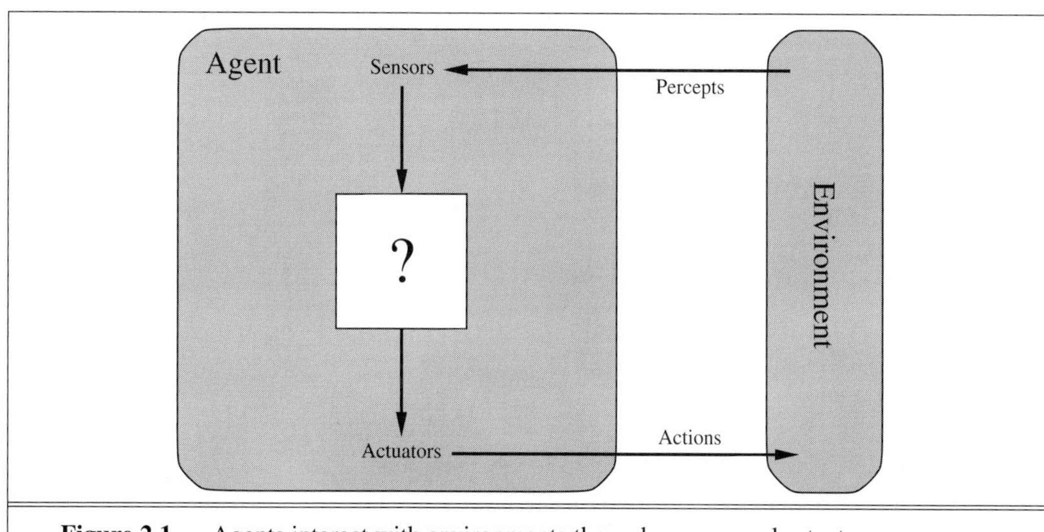


**Figure 2.1** Agents interact with environments through sensors and actuators.

percept sequence, then we have said more or less everything there is to say about the agent. Mathematically speaking, we say that an agent's behavior is described by the **agent function** that maps any given percept sequence to an action.

AGENT FUNCTION

We can imagine *tabulating* the agent function that describes any given agent; for most agents, this would be a very large table—infinite, in fact, unless we place a bound on the length of percept sequences we want to consider. Given an agent to experiment with, we can, in principle, construct this table by trying out all possible percept sequences and recording which actions the agent does in response.[1] The table is, of course, an *external* characterization of the agent. *Internally*, the agent function for an artificial agent will be implemented by an **agent program**. It is important to keep these two ideas distinct. The agent function is an abstract mathematical description; the agent program is a concrete implementation, running on the agent architecture.

AGENT PROGRAM

To illustrate these ideas, we will use a very simple example—the vacuum-cleaner world shown in Figure 2.2. This world is so simple that we can describe everything that happens; it's also a made-up world, so we can invent many variations. This particular world has just two locations: squares $A$ and $B$. The vacuum agent perceives which square it is in and whether there is dirt in the square. It can choose to move left, move right, suck up the dirt, or do nothing. One very simple agent function is the following: if the current square is dirty, then suck, otherwise move to the other square. A partial tabulation of this agent function is shown in Figure 2.3. A simple agent program for this agent function is given later in the chapter, in Figure 2.8.

Looking at Figure 2.3, we see that various vacuum-world agents can be defined simply by filling in the right-hand column in various ways. The obvious question, then, is this: *What*

[1] If the agent uses some randomization to choose its actions, then we would have to try each sequence many times to identify the probability of each action. One might imagine that acting randomly is rather silly, but we'll see later in this chapter that it can be very intelligent.

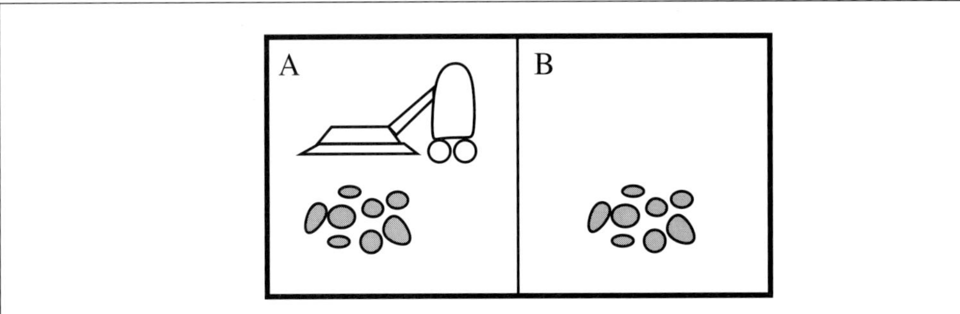


**Figure 2.2** A vacuum-cleaner world with just two locations.

| Percept sequence | Action |
|---|---|
| $[A, Clean]$ | *Right* |
| $[A, Dirty]$ | *Suck* |
| $[B, Clean]$ | *Left* |
| $[B, Dirty]$ | *Suck* |
| $[A, Clean], [A, Clean]$ | *Right* |
| $[A, Clean], [A, Dirty]$ | *Suck* |
| ⋮ | ⋮ |
| $[A, Clean], [A, Clean], [A, Clean]$ | *Right* |
| $[A, Clean], [A, Clean], [A, Dirty]$ | *Suck* |
| ⋮ | ⋮ |

**Figure 2.3** Partial tabulation of a simple agent function for the vacuum-cleaner world shown in Figure 2.2.

*is the right way to fill out the table?* In other words, what makes an agent good or bad, intelligent or stupid? We answer these questions in the next section.

Before closing this section, we will remark that the notion of an agent is meant to be a tool for analyzing systems, not an absolute characterization that divides the world into agents and non-agents. One could view a hand-held calculator as an agent that chooses the action of displaying "4" when given the percept sequence "2 + 2 =," but such an analysis would hardly aid our understanding of the calculator.

## 2.2 GOOD BEHAVIOR: THE CONCEPT OF RATIONALITY

RATIONAL AGENT

A **rational agent** is one that does the right thing—conceptually speaking, every entry in the table for the agent function is filled out correctly. Obviously, doing the right thing is better than doing the wrong thing, but what does it mean to do the right thing? As a first approximation, we will say that the right action is the one that will cause the agent to be most successful. Therefore, we will need some way to measure success. Together with the description of the environment and the sensors and actuators of the agent, this will provide a complete specification of the task facing the agent. Given this, we can define more precisely what it means to be rational.

### Performance measures

PERFORMANCE MEASURE

A **performance measure** embodies the criterion for success of an agent's behavior. When an agent is plunked down in an environment, it generates a sequence of actions according to the percepts it receives. This sequence of actions causes the environment to go through a sequence of states. If the sequence is desirable, then the agent has performed well. Obviously, there is not one fixed measure suitable for all agents. We could ask the agent for a subjective opinion of how happy it is with its own performance, but some agents would be unable to answer, and others would delude themselves.[2] Therefore, we will insist on an objective performance measure, typically one imposed by the designer who is constructing the agent.

Consider the vacuum-cleaner agent from the preceding section. We might propose to measure performance by the amount of dirt cleaned up in a single eight-hour shift. With a rational agent, of course, what you ask for is what you get. A rational agent can maximize this performance measure by cleaning up the dirt, then dumping it all on the floor, then cleaning it up again, and so on. A more suitable performance measure would reward the agent for having a clean floor. For example, one point could be awarded for each clean square at each time step (perhaps with a penalty for electricity consumed and noise generated). *As a general rule, it is better to design performance measures according to what one actually wants in the environment, rather than according to how one thinks the agent should behave.*

The selection of a performance measure is not always easy. For example, the notion of "clean floor" in the preceding paragraph is based on average cleanliness over time. Yet the same average cleanliness can be achieved by two different agents, one of which does a mediocre job all the time while the other cleans energetically but takes long breaks. Which is preferable might seem to be a fine point of janitorial science, but in fact it is a deep philosophical question with far-reaching implications. Which is better—a reckless life of highs and lows, or a safe but humdrum existence? Which is better—an economy where everyone lives in moderate poverty, or one in which some live in plenty while others are very poor? We will leave these questions as an exercise for the diligent reader.

### Rationality

What is rational at any given time depends on four things:

- The performance measure that defines the criterion of success.
- The agent's prior knowledge of the environment.
- The actions that the agent can perform.
- The agent's percept sequence to date.

[2] Human agents in particular are notorious for "sour grapes"—believing they did not really want something after not getting it, as in, "Oh well, never mind, I didn't want that stupid Nobel prize anyway."

DEFINITION OF A RATIONAL AGENT

This leads to a **definition of a rational agent**:

> *For each possible percept sequence, a rational agent should select an action that is expected to maximize its performance measure, given the evidence provided by the percept sequence and whatever built-in knowledge the agent has.*

Consider the simple vacuum-cleaner agent that cleans a square if it is dirty and moves to the other square if not; this is the agent function tabulated in Figure 2.3. Is this a rational agent? That depends! First, we need to say what the performance measure is, what is known about the environment, and what sensors and actuators the agent has. Let us assume the following:

- The performance measure awards one point for each clean square at each time step, over a "lifetime" of 1000 time steps.
- The "geography" of the environment is known *a priori* (Figure 2.2) but the dirt distribution and the initial location of the agent are not. Clean squares stay clean and sucking cleans the current square. The $Left$ and $Right$ actions move the agent left and right except when this would take the agent outside the environment, in which case the agent remains where it is.
- The only available actions are $Left$, $Right$, $Suck$, and $NoOp$ (do nothing).
- The agent correctly perceives its location and whether that location contains dirt.

We claim that *under these circumstances* the agent is indeed rational; its expected performance is at least as high as any other agent's. Exercise 2.4 asks you to prove this.

One can see easily that the same agent would be irrational under different circumstances. For example, once all the dirt is cleaned up it will oscillate needlessly back and forth; if the performance measure includes a penalty of one point for each movement left or right, the agent will fare poorly. A better agent for this case would do nothing once it is sure that all the squares are clean. If clean squares can become dirty again, the agent should occasionally check and re-clean them if needed. If the geography of the environment is unknown, the agent will need to explore it rather than stick to squares $A$ and $B$. Exercise 2.4 asks you to design agents for these cases.

### Omniscience, learning, and autonomy

OMNISCIENCE

We need to be careful to distinguish between rationality and **omniscience**. An omniscient agent knows the *actual* outcome of its actions and can act accordingly; but omniscience is impossible in reality. Consider the following example: I am walking along the Champs Elysées one day and I see an old friend across the street. There is no traffic nearby and I'm not otherwise engaged, so, being rational, I start to cross the street. Meanwhile, at 33,000 feet, a cargo door falls off a passing airliner,[3] and before I make it to the other side of the street I am flattened. Was I irrational to cross the street? It is unlikely that my obituary would read "Idiot attempts to cross street."

This example shows that rationality is not the same as perfection. Rationality maximizes *expected* performance, while perfection maximizes *actual* performance. Retreating from a requirement of perfection is not just a question of being fair to agents. The point is

[3] See N. Henderson, "New door latches urged for Boeing 747 jumbo jets," *Washington Post*, August 24, 1989.

that if we expect an agent to do what turns out to be the best action after the fact, it will be impossible to design an agent to fulfill this specification—unless we improve the performance of crystal balls or time machines.

Our definition of rationality does not require omniscience, then, because the rational choice depends only on the percept sequence *to date*. We must also ensure that we haven't inadvertently allowed the agent to engage in decidedly underintelligent activities. For example, if an agent does not look both ways before crossing a busy road, then its percept sequence will not tell it that there is a large truck approaching at high speed. Does our definition of rationality say that it's now OK to cross the road? Far from it! First, it would not be rational to cross the road given this uninformative percept sequence: the risk of accident from crossing without looking is too great. Second, a rational agent should choose the "looking" action before stepping into the street, because looking helps maximize the expected performance. Doing actions *in order to modify future percepts*—sometimes called **information gathering**—is an important part of rationality and is covered in depth in Chapter 16. A second example of information gathering is provided by the **exploration** that must be undertaken by a vacuum-cleaning agent in an initially unknown environment.

INFORMATION GATHERING

EXPLORATION

LEARNING

Our definition requires a rational agent not only to gather information, but also to **learn** as much as possible from what it perceives. The agent's initial configuration could reflect some prior knowledge of the environment, but as the agent gains experience this may be modified and augmented. There are extreme cases in which the environment is completely known *a priori*. In such cases, the agent need not perceive or learn; it simply acts correctly. Of course, such agents are very fragile. Consider the lowly dung beetle. After digging its nest and laying its eggs, it fetches a ball of dung from a nearby heap to plug the entrance. If the ball of dung is removed from its grasp *en route*, the beetle continues on and pantomimes plugging the nest with the nonexistent dung ball, never noticing that it is missing. Evolution has built an assumption into the beetle's behavior, and when it is violated, unsuccessful behavior results. Slightly more intelligent is the sphex wasp. The female sphex will dig a burrow, go out and sting a caterpillar and drag it to the burrow, enter the burrow again to check all is well, drag the caterpillar inside, and lay its eggs. The caterpillar serves as a food source when the eggs hatch. So far so good, but if an entomologist moves the caterpillar a few inches away while the sphex is doing the check, it will revert back to the "drag" step of its plan, and will continue the plan without modification, even after dozens of caterpillar-moving interventions. The sphex is unable to learn that its innate plan is failing, and thus will not change it.

Successful agents split the task of computing the agent function into three different periods: when the agent is being designed, some of the computation is done by its designers; when it is deliberating on its next action, the agent does more computation; and as it learns from experience, it does even more computation to decide how to modify its behavior.

AUTONOMY

To the extent that an agent relies on the prior knowledge of its designer rather than on its own percepts, we say that the agent lacks **autonomy**. A rational agent should be autonomous—it should learn what it can to compensate for partial or incorrect prior knowledge. For example, a vacuum-cleaning agent that learns to foresee where and when additional dirt will appear will do better than one that does not. As a practical matter, one seldom requires complete autonomy from the start: when the agent has had little or no experience, it would have to act randomly unless the designer gave some assistance. So, just as evolution provides animals with enough built-in reflexes so that they can survive long enough to learn for themselves, it would be reasonable to provide an artificial intelligent agent with some initial knowledge as well as an ability to learn. After sufficient experience of its environment, the behavior of a rational agent can become effectively *independent* of its prior knowledge. Hence, the incorporation of learning allows one to design a single rational agent that will succeed in a vast variety of environments.

## 2.3 The Nature of Environments

TASK ENVIRONMENTS

Now that we have a definition of rationality, we are almost ready to think about building rational agents. First, however, we must think about **task environments**, which are essentially the "problems" to which rational agents are the "solutions." We begin by showing how to specify a task environment, illustrating the process with a number of examples. We then show that task environments come in a variety of flavors. The flavor of the task environment directly affects the appropriate design for the agent program.

### Specifying the task environment

In our discussion of the rationality of the simple vacuum-cleaner agent, we had to specify the performance measure, the environment, and the agent's actuators and sensors. We will group all these together under the heading of the **task environment**. For the acronymically minded, we call this the **PEAS** (**P**erformance, **E**nvironment, **A**ctuators, **S**ensors) description. In designing an agent, the first step must always be to specify the task environment as fully as possible.

PEAS

The vacuum world was a simple example; let us consider a more complex problem: an automated taxi driver. We will use this example throughout the rest of the chapter. We should point out, before the reader becomes alarmed, that a fully automated taxi is currently somewhat beyond the capabilities of existing technology. (See page 27 for a description of an existing driving robot, or look at recent proceedings of the conferences on Intelligent Transportation Systems.) The full driving task is extremely *open-ended*. There is no limit to the novel combinations of circumstances that can arise—another reason we chose it as a focus for discussion. Figure 2.4 summarizes the PEAS description for the taxi's task environment. We discuss each element in more detail in the following paragraphs.

First, what is the **performance measure** to which we would like our automated driver to aspire? Desirable qualities include getting to the correct destination; minimizing fuel consumption and wear and tear; minimizing the trip time and/or cost; minimizing violations of traffic laws and disturbances to other drivers; maximizing safety and passenger comfort; maximizing profits. Obviously, some of these goals conflict, so there will be tradeoffs involved.

Next, what is the driving **environment** that the taxi will face? Any taxi driver must deal with a variety of roads, ranging from rural lanes and urban alleys to 12-lane freeways. The roads contain other traffic, pedestrians, stray animals, road works, police cars, puddles,

| Agent Type | Performance Measure | Environment | Actuators | Sensors |
|---|---|---|---|---|
| Taxi driver | Safe, fast, legal, comfortable trip, maximize profits | Roads, other traffic, pedestrians, customers | Steering, accelerator, brake, signal, horn, display | Cameras, sonar, speedometer, GPS, odometer, accelerometer, engine sensors, keyboard |

**Figure 2.4** PEAS description of the task environment for an automated taxi.

and potholes. The taxi must also interact with potential and actual passengers. There are also some optional choices. The taxi might need to operate in Southern California, where snow is seldom a problem, or in Alaska, where it seldom is not. It could always be driving on the right, or we might want it to be flexible enough to drive on the left when in Britain or Japan. Obviously, the more restricted the environment, the easier the design problem.

The **actuators** available to an automated taxi will be more or less the same as those available to a human driver: control over the engine through the accelerator and control over steering and braking. In addition, it will need output to a display screen or voice synthesizer to talk back to the passengers, and perhaps some way to communicate with other vehicles, politely or otherwise.

To achieve its goals in the driving environment, the taxi will need to know where it is, what else is on the road, and how fast it is going. Its basic **sensors** should therefore include one or more controllable TV cameras, the speedometer, and the odometer. To control the vehicle properly, especially on curves, it should have an accelerometer; it will also need to know the mechanical state of the vehicle, so it will need the usual array of engine and electrical system sensors. It might have instruments that are not available to the average human driver: a satellite global positioning system (GPS) to give it accurate position information with respect to an electronic map, and infrared or sonar sensors to detect distances to other cars and obstacles. Finally, it will need a keyboard or microphone for the passenger to request a destination.

In Figure 2.5, we have sketched the basic PEAS elements for a number of additional agent types. Further examples appear in Exercise 2.5. It may come as a surprise to some readers that we include in our list of agent types some programs that operate in the entirely artificial environment defined by keyboard input and character output on a screen. "Surely," one might say, "this is not a real environment, is it?" In fact, what matters is not the distinction between "real" and "artificial" environments, but the complexity of the relationship among the behavior of the agent, the percept sequence generated by the environment, and the performance measure. Some "real" environments are actually quite simple. For example, a robot designed to inspect parts as they come by on a conveyor belt can make use of a number of simplifying assumptions: that the lighting is always just so, that the only thing on the conveyer belt will be parts of a kind that it knows about, and that there are only two actions (accept or reject).

| Agent Type | Performance Measure | Environment | Actuators | Sensors |
|---|---|---|---|---|
| Medical diagnosis system | Healthy patient, minimize costs, lawsuits | Patient, hospital, staff | Display questions, tests, diagnoses, treatments, referrals | Keyboard entry of symptoms, findings, patient's answers |
| Satellite image analysis system | Correct image categorization | Downlink from orbiting satellite | Display categorization of scene | Color pixel arrays |
| Part-picking robot | Percentage of parts in correct bins | Conveyor belt with parts; bins | Jointed arm and hand | Camera, joint angle sensors |
| Refinery controller | Maximize purity, yield, safety | Refinery, operators | Valves, pumps, heaters, displays | Temperature, pressure, chemical sensors |
| Interactive English tutor | Maximize student's score on test | Set of students, testing agency | Display exercises, suggestions, corrections | Keyboard entry |

**Figure 2.5** Examples of agent types and their PEAS descriptions.

SOFTWARE AGENTS
SOFTBOTS

In contrast, some **software agents** (or software robots or **softbots**) exist in rich, unlimited domains. Imagine a softbot designed to fly a flight simulator for a large commercial airplane. The simulator is a very detailed, complex environment including other aircraft and ground operations, and the software agent must choose from a wide variety of actions in real time. Or imagine a softbot designed to scan Internet news sources and show the interesting items to its customers. To do well, it will need some natural language processing abilities, it will need to learn what each customer is interested in, and it will need to change its plans dynamically—for example, when the connection for one news source goes down or when a new one comes online. The Internet is an environment whose complexity rivals that of the physical world and whose inhabitants include many artificial agents.

### Properties of task environments

The range of task environments that might arise in AI is obviously vast. We can, however, identify a fairly small number of dimensions along which task environments can be categorized. These dimensions determine, to a large extent, the appropriate agent design and the applicability of each of the principal families of techniques for agent implementation. First, we list the dimensions, then we analyze several task environments to illustrate the ideas. The definitions here are informal; later chapters provide more precise statements and examples of each kind of environment.

FULLY OBSERVABLE

◇ **Fully observable** vs. **partially observable**.
If an agent's sensors give it access to the complete state of the environment at each point in time, then we say that the task environment is fully observable.[4] A task environment is effectively fully observable if the sensors detect all aspects that are *relevant* to the choice of action; relevance, in turn, depends on the performance measure. Fully observable environments are convenient because the agent need not maintain any internal state to keep track of the world. An environment might be partially observable because of noisy and inaccurate sensors or because parts of the state are simply missing from the sensor data—for example, a vacuum agent with only a local dirt sensor cannot tell whether there is dirt in other squares, and an automated taxi cannot see what other drivers are thinking.

DETERMINISTIC

STOCHASTIC

◇ **Deterministic** vs. **stochastic**.
If the next state of the environment is completely determined by the current state and the action executed by the agent, then we say the environment is deterministic; otherwise, it is stochastic. In principle, an agent need not worry about uncertainty in a fully observable, deterministic environment. If the environment is partially observable, however, then it could *appear* to be stochastic. This is particularly true if the environment is complex, making it hard to keep track of all the unobserved aspects. Thus, it is often better to think of an environment as deterministic or stochastic *from the point of view of the agent*. Taxi driving is clearly stochastic in this sense, because one can never predict the behavior of traffic exactly; moreover, one's tires blow out and one's engine seizes up without warning. The vacuum world as we described it is deterministic, but variations can include stochastic elements such as randomly appearing dirt and an unreliable suction mechanism (Exercise 2.12). If the environment is deterministic except for the actions of other agents, we say that the environment is **strategic**.

STRATEGIC

EPISODIC

SEQUENTIAL

◇ **Episodic** vs. **sequential**.[5]
In an episodic task environment, the agent's experience is divided into atomic episodes. Each episode consists of the agent perceiving and then performing a single action. Crucially, the next episode does not depend on the actions taken in previous episodes. In episodic environments, the choice of action in each episode depends only on the episode itself. Many classification tasks are episodic. For example, an agent that has to spot defective parts on an assembly line bases each decision on the current part, regardless of previous decisions; moreover, the current decision doesn't affect whether the next

[4] The first edition of this book used the terms **accessible** and **inaccessible** instead of **fully** and **partially observable**; **nondeterministic** instead of **stochastic**; and **nonepisodic** instead of **sequential**. The new terminology is more consistent with established usage.

[5] The word "sequential" is also used in computer science as the antonym of "parallel." The two meanings are largely unrelated.

part is defective. In sequential environments, on the other hand, the current decision could affect all future decisions. Chess and taxi driving are sequential: in both cases, short-term actions can have long-term consequences. Episodic environments are much simpler than sequential environments because the agent does not need to think ahead.

STATIC
DYNAMIC

◇ **Static** vs. **dynamic**.
If the environment can change while an agent is deliberating, then we say the environment is dynamic for that agent; otherwise, it is static. Static environments are easy to deal with because the agent need not keep looking at the world while it is deciding on an action, nor need it worry about the passage of time. Dynamic environments, on the other hand, are continuously asking the agent what it wants to do; if it hasn't decided yet, that counts as deciding to do nothing. If the environment itself does not change with the passage of time but the agent's performance score does, then we say the environment is **semidynamic**. Taxi driving is clearly dynamic: the other cars and the taxi itself keep moving while the driving algorithm dithers about what to do next. Chess, when played with a clock, is semidynamic. Crossword puzzles are static.

SEMIDYNAMIC

DISCRETE
CONTINUOUS

◇ **Discrete** vs. **continuous**.
The discrete/continuous distinction can be applied to the *state* of the environment, to the way *time* is handled, and to the *percepts* and *actions* of the agent. For example, a discrete-state environment such as a chess game has a finite number of distinct states. Chess also has a discrete set of percepts and actions. Taxi driving is a continuous-state and continuous-time problem: the speed and location of the taxi and of the other vehicles sweep through a range of continuous values and do so smoothly over time. Taxi-driving actions are also continuous (steering angles, etc.). Input from digital cameras is discrete, strictly speaking, but is typically treated as representing continuously varying intensities and locations.

SINGLE AGENT
MULTIAGENT

◇ **Single agent** vs. **multiagent**.
The distinction between single-agent and multiagent environments may seem simple enough. For example, an agent solving a crossword puzzle by itself is clearly in a single-agent environment, whereas an agent playing chess is in a two-agent environment. There are, however, some subtle issues. First, we have described how an entity *may* be viewed as an agent, but we have not explained which entities *must* be viewed as agents. Does an agent $A$ (the taxi driver for example) have to treat an object $B$ (another vehicle) as an agent, or can it be treated merely as a stochastically behaving object, analogous to waves at the beach or leaves blowing in the wind? The key distinction is whether $B$'s behavior is best described as maximizing a performance measure whose value depends on agent $A$'s behavior. For example, in chess, the opponent entity $B$ is trying to maximize its performance measure, which, by the rules of chess, minimizes agent $A$'s performance measure. Thus, chess is a **competitive** multiagent environment. In the taxi-driving environment, on the other hand, avoiding collisions maximizes the performance measure of all agents, so it is a partially **cooperative** multiagent environment. It is also partially competitive because, for example, only one car can occupy a parking space. The agent-design problems arising in multiagent environments are often

COMPETITIVE

COOPERATIVE

| Task Environment | Observable | Deterministic | Episodic | Static | Discrete | Agents |
|---|---|---|---|---|---|---|
| Crossword puzzle | Fully | Deterministic | Sequential | Static | Discrete | Single |
| Chess with a clock | Fully | Strategic | Sequential | Semi | Discrete | Multi |
| Poker | Partially | Stochastic | Sequential | Static | Discrete | Multi |
| Backgammon | Fully | Stochastic | Sequential | Static | Discrete | Multi |
| Taxi driving | Partially | Stochastic | Sequential | Dynamic | Continuous | Multi |
| Medical diagnosis | Partially | Stochastic | Sequential | Dynamic | Continuous | Single |
| Image-analysis | Fully | Deterministic | Episodic | Semi | Continuous | Single |
| Part-picking robot | Partially | Stochastic | Episodic | Dynamic | Continuous | Single |
| Refinery controller | Partially | Stochastic | Sequential | Dynamic | Continuous | Single |
| Interactive English tutor | Partially | Stochastic | Sequential | Dynamic | Discrete | Multi |

**Figure 2.6** Examples of task environments and their characteristics.

quite different from those in single-agent environments; for example, **communication** often emerges as a rational behavior in multiagent environments; in some partially observable competitive environments, **stochastic behavior** is rational because it avoids the pitfalls of predictability.

As one might expect, the hardest case is *partially observable*, *stochastic*, *sequential*, *dynamic*, *continuous*, and *multiagent*. It also turns out that most real situations are so complex that whether they are *really* deterministic is a moot point. For practical purposes, they must be treated as stochastic. Taxi driving is hard in all these senses.

Figure 2.6 lists the properties of a number of familiar environments. Note that the answers are not always cut and dried. For example, we have listed chess as fully observable; strictly speaking, this is false because certain rules about castling, *en passant* capture, and draws by repetition require remembering some facts about the game history that are not observable as part of the board state. These exceptions to observability are of course minor compared to those faced by the taxi driver, the English tutor, or the medical diagnosis system.

Some other answers in the table depend on how the task environment is defined. We have listed the medical-diagnosis task as single-agent because the disease process in a patient is not profitably modeled as an agent; but a medical-diagnosis system might also have to deal with recalcitrant patients and skeptical staff, so the environment could have a multiagent aspect. Furthermore, medical diagnosis is episodic if one conceives of the task as selecting a diagnosis given a list of symptoms; the problem is sequential if the task can include proposing a series of tests, evaluating progress over the course of treatment, and so on. Also, many environments are episodic at higher levels than the agent's individual actions. For example, a chess tournament consists of a sequence of games; each game is an episode, because (by and large) the contribution of the moves in one game to the agent's overall performance is not affected by the moves in its previous game. On the other hand, decision making within a single game is certainly sequential.

The code repository associated with this book (aima.cs.berkeley.edu) includes implementations of a number of environments, together with a general-purpose environment simulator that places one or more agents in a simulated environment, observes their behavior over time, and evaluates them according to a given performance measure. Such experiments are often carried out not for a single environment, but for many environments drawn from an **environment class**. For example, to evaluate a taxi driver in simulated traffic, we would want to run many simulations with different traffic, lighting, and weather conditions. If we designed the agent for a single scenario, we might be able to take advantage of specific properties of the particular case but might not identify a good design for driving in general. For this reason, the code repository also includes an **environment generator** for each environment class that selects particular environments (with certain likelihoods) in which to run the agent. For example, the vacuum environment generator initializes the dirt pattern and agent location randomly. We are then interested in the agent's average performance over the environment class. A rational agent for a given environment class maximizes this average performance. Exercises 2.7 to 2.12 take you through the process of developing an environment class and evaluating various agents therein.

ENVIRONMENT CLASS

ENVIRONMENT GENERATOR

## 2.4 The Structure of Agents

So far we have talked about agents by describing *behavior*—the action that is performed after any given sequence of percepts. Now, we will have to bite the bullet and talk about how the insides work. The job of AI is to design the **agent program** that implements the agent function mapping percepts to actions. We assume this program will run on some sort of computing device with physical sensors and actuators—we call this the **architecture**:

AGENT PROGRAM

ARCHITECTURE

$$agent = architecture + program\ .$$

Obviously, the program we choose has to be one that is appropriate for the architecture. If the program is going to recommend actions like *Walk*, the architecture had better have legs. The architecture might be just an ordinary PC, or it might be a robotic car with several onboard computers, cameras, and other sensors. In general, the architecture makes the percepts from the sensors available to the program, runs the program, and feeds the program's action choices to the actuators as they are generated. Most of this book is about designing agent programs, although Chapters 24 and 25 deal directly with the sensors and actuators.

### Agent programs

The agent programs that we will design in this book all have the same skeleton: they take the current percept as input from the sensors and return an action to the actuators.[6] Notice the difference between the agent program, which takes the current percept as input, and the agent function, which takes the entire percept history. The agent program takes just the current

[6] There are other choices for the agent program skeleton; for example, we could have the agent programs be **coroutines** that run asynchronously with the environment. Each such coroutine has an input and output port and consists of a loop that reads the input port for percepts and writes actions to the output port.

```
function TABLE-DRIVEN-AGENT(percept) returns an action
  static: percepts, a sequence, initially empty
          table, a table of actions, indexed by percept sequences, initially fully specified

  append percept to the end of percepts
  action ← LOOKUP(percepts, table)
  return action
```

**Figure 2.7** The TABLE-DRIVEN-AGENT program is invoked for each new percept and returns an action each time. It keeps track of the percept sequence using its own private data structure.

percept as input because nothing more is available from the environment; if the agent's actions depend on the entire percept sequence, the agent will have to remember the percepts.

We will describe the agent programs via the simple pseudocode language that is defined in Appendix B. (The online code repository contains implementations in real programming languages.) For example, Figure 2.7 shows a rather trivial agent program that keeps track of the percept sequence and then uses it to index into a table of actions to decide what to do. The table represents explicitly the agent function that the agent program embodies. To build a rational agent in this way, we as designers must construct a table that contains the appropriate action for every possible percept sequence.

It is instructive to consider why the table-driven approach to agent construction is doomed to failure. Let $\mathcal{P}$ be the set of possible percepts and let $T$ be the lifetime of the agent (the total number of percepts it will receive). The lookup table will contain $\sum_{t=1}^{T} |\mathcal{P}|^t$ entries. Consider the automated taxi: the visual input from a single camera comes in at the rate of roughly 27 megabytes per second (30 frames per second, $640 \times 480$ pixels with 24 bits of color information). This gives a lookup table with over $10^{250,000,000,000}$ entries for an hour's driving. Even the lookup table for chess—a tiny, well-behaved fragment of the real world—would have at least $10^{150}$ entries. The daunting size of these tables (the number of atoms in the observable universe is less than $10^{80}$) means that (a) no physical agent in this universe will have the space to store the table, (b) the designer would not have time to create the table, (c) no agent could ever learn all the right table entries from its experience, and (d) even if the environment is simple enough to yield a feasible table size, the designer still has no guidance about how to fill in the table entries.

Despite all this, TABLE-DRIVEN-AGENT *does* do what we want: it implements the desired agent function. The key challenge for AI is to find out how to write programs that, to the extent possible, produce rational behavior from a small amount of code rather than from a large number of table entries. We have many examples showing that this can be done successfully in other areas: for example, the huge tables of square roots used by engineers and schoolchildren prior to the 1970s have now been replaced by a five-line program for Newton's method running on electronic calculators. The question is, can AI do for general intelligent behavior what Newton did for square roots? We believe the answer is yes.

```
function REFLEX-VACUUM-AGENT([location,status]) returns an action
  if status = Dirty then return Suck
  else if location = A then return Right
  else if location = B then return Left
```

**Figure 2.8** The agent program for a simple reflex agent in the two-state vacuum environment. This program implements the agent function tabulated in Figure 2.3.

In the remainder of this section, we outline four basic kinds of agent program that embody the principles underlying almost all intelligent systems:

- Simple reflex agents;
- Model-based reflex agents;
- Goal-based agents; and
- Utility-based agents.

We then explain in general terms how to convert all these into *learning agents*.

### Simple reflex agents

SIMPLE REFLEX AGENT

The simplest kind of agent is the **simple reflex agent**. These agents select actions on the basis of the *current* percept, ignoring the rest of the percept history. For example, the vacuum agent whose agent function is tabulated in Figure 2.3 is a simple reflex agent, because its decision is based only on the current location and on whether that contains dirt. An agent program for this agent is shown in Figure 2.8.

Notice that the vacuum agent program is very small indeed compared to the corresponding table. The most obvious reduction comes from ignoring the percept history, which cuts down the number of possibilities from $4^T$ to just 4. A further, small reduction comes from the fact that, when the current square is dirty, the action does not depend on the location.

CONDITION–ACTION RULE

Imagine yourself as the driver of the automated taxi. If the car in front brakes, and its brake lights come on, then you should notice this and initiate braking. In other words, some processing is done on the visual input to establish the condition we call "The car in front is braking." Then, this triggers some established connection in the agent program to the action "initiate braking." We call such a connection a **condition–action rule**,[7] written as

**if** *car-in-front-is-braking* **then** *initiate-braking*.

Humans also have many such connections, some of which are learned responses (as for driving) and some of which are innate reflexes (such as blinking when something approaches the eye). In the course of the book, we will see several different ways in which such connections can be learned and implemented.

The program in Figure 2.8 is specific to one particular vacuum environment. A more general and flexible approach is first to build a general-purpose interpreter for condition–

[7] Also called **situation–action rules**, **productions**, or **if–then rules**.

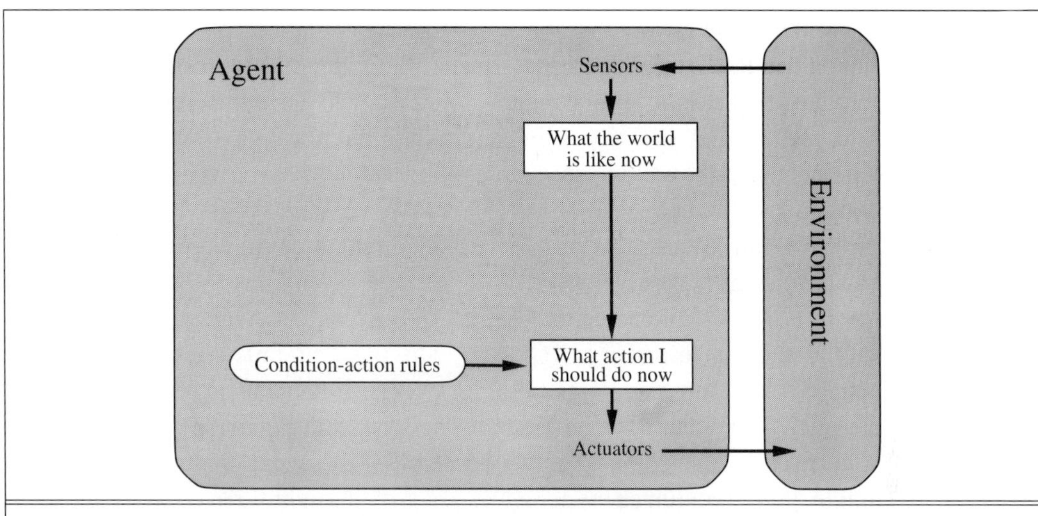


**Figure 2.9** Schematic diagram of a simple reflex agent.

**function** SIMPLE-REFLEX-AGENT($percept$) **returns** an action
  **static**: $rules$, a set of condition–action rules

  $state \leftarrow$ INTERPRET-INPUT($percept$)
  $rule \leftarrow$ RULE-MATCH($state$, $rules$)
  $action \leftarrow$ RULE-ACTION[$rule$]
  **return** $action$

**Figure 2.10** A simple reflex agent. It acts according to a rule whose condition matches the current state, as defined by the percept.

action rules and then to create rule sets for specific task environments. Figure 2.9 gives the structure of this general program in schematic form, showing how the condition–action rules allow the agent to make the connection from percept to action. (Do not worry if this seems trivial; it gets more interesting shortly.) We use rectangles to denote the current internal state of the agent's decision process and ovals to represent the background information used in the process. The agent program, which is also very simple, is shown in Figure 2.10. The INTERPRET-INPUT function generates an abstracted description of the current state from the percept, and the RULE-MATCH function returns the first rule in the set of rules that matches the given state description. Note that the description in terms of "rules" and "matching" is purely conceptual; actual implementations can be as simple as a collection of logic gates implementing a Boolean circuit.

Simple reflex agents have the admirable property of being simple, but they turn out to be of very limited intelligence. The agent in Figure 2.10 will work *only if the correct decision can be made on the basis of only the current percept—that is, only if the environment is fully observable.* Even a little bit of unobservability can cause serious trouble. For example, the braking rule given earlier assumes that the condition *car-in-front-is-braking* can be determined from the current percept—the current video image—if the car in front has a centrally mounted brake light. Unfortunately, older models have different configurations of taillights, brake lights, and turn-signal lights, and it is not always possible to tell from a single image whether the car is braking. A simple reflex agent driving behind such a car would either brake continuously and unnecessarily, or, worse, never brake at all.

We can see a similar problem arising in the vacuum world. Suppose that a simple reflex vacuum agent is deprived of its location sensor, and has only a dirt sensor. Such an agent has just two possible percepts: $[Dirty]$ and $[Clean]$. It can $Suck$ in response to $[Dirty]$; what should it do in response to $[Clean]$? Moving $Left$ fails (for ever) if it happens to start in square $A$, and moving $Right$ fails (for ever) if it happens to start in square $B$. Infinite loops are often unavoidable for simple reflex agents operating in partially observable environments.

RANDOMIZATION

Escape from infinite loops is possible if the agent can **randomize** its actions. For example, if the vacuum agent perceives $[Clean]$, it might flip a coin to choose between $Left$ and $Right$. It is easy to show that the agent will reach the other square in an average of two steps. Then, if that square is dirty, it will clean it and the cleaning task will be complete. Hence, a randomized simple reflex agent might outperform a deterministic simple reflex agent.

We mentioned in Section 2.3 that randomized behavior of the right kind can be rational in some multiagent environments. In single-agent environments, randomization is usually *not* rational. It is a useful trick that helps a simple reflex agent in some situations, but in most cases we can do much better with more sophisticated deterministic agents.

### Model-based reflex agents

The most effective way to handle partial observability is for the agent to *keep track of the part of the world it can't see now*. That is, the agent should maintain some sort of **internal state** that depends on the percept history and thereby reflects at least some of the unobserved aspects of the current state. For the braking problem, the internal state is not too extensive—just the previous frame from the camera, allowing the agent to detect when two red lights at the edge of the vehicle go on or off simultaneously. For other driving tasks such as changing lanes, the agent needs to keep track of where the other cars are if it can't see them all at once.

INTERNAL STATE

Updating this internal state information as time goes by requires two kinds of knowledge to be encoded in the agent program. First, we need some information about how the world evolves independently of the agent—for example, that an overtaking car generally will be closer behind than it was a moment ago. Second, we need some information about how the agent's own actions affect the world—for example, that when the agent turns the steering wheel clockwise, the car turns to the right or that after driving for five minutes northbound on the freeway one is usually about five miles north of where one was five minutes ago. This knowledge about "how the world works"—whether implemented in simple Boolean circuits or in complete scientific theories—is called a **model** of the world. An agent that uses such a model is called a **model-based agent**.

MODEL-BASED AGENT

Figure 2.11 gives the structure of the reflex agent with internal state, showing how the current percept is combined with the old internal state to generate the updated description

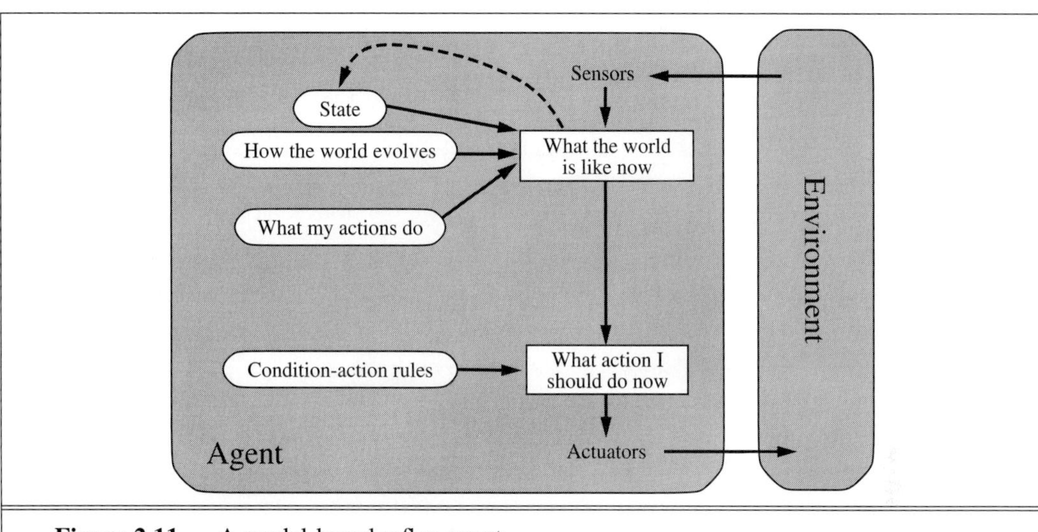


**Figure 2.11** A model-based reflex agent.

**function** REFLEX-AGENT-WITH-STATE(*percept*) **returns** an action
  **static**: *state*, a description of the current world state
    *rules*, a set of condition–action rules
    *action*, the most recent action, initially none

  *state* ← UPDATE-STATE(*state*, *action*, *percept*)
  *rule* ← RULE-MATCH(*state*, *rules*)
  *action* ← RULE-ACTION[*rule*]
  **return** *action*

**Figure 2.12** A model-based reflex agent. It keeps track of the current state of the world using an internal model. It then chooses an action in the same way as the reflex agent.

of the current state. The agent program is shown in Figure 2.12. The interesting part is the function UPDATE-STATE, which is responsible for creating the new internal state description. As well as interpreting the new percept in the light of existing knowledge about the state, it uses information about how the world evolves to keep track of the unseen parts of the world, and also must know about what the agent's actions do to the state of the world. Detailed examples appear in Chapters 10 and 17.

## Goal-based agents

Knowing about the current state of the environment is not always enough to decide what to do. For example, at a road junction, the taxi can turn left, turn right, or go straight on. The correct decision depends on where the taxi is trying to get to. In other words, as well as a current state description, the agent needs some sort of **goal** information that describes situations that are desirable—for example, being at the passenger's destination. The agent

GOAL

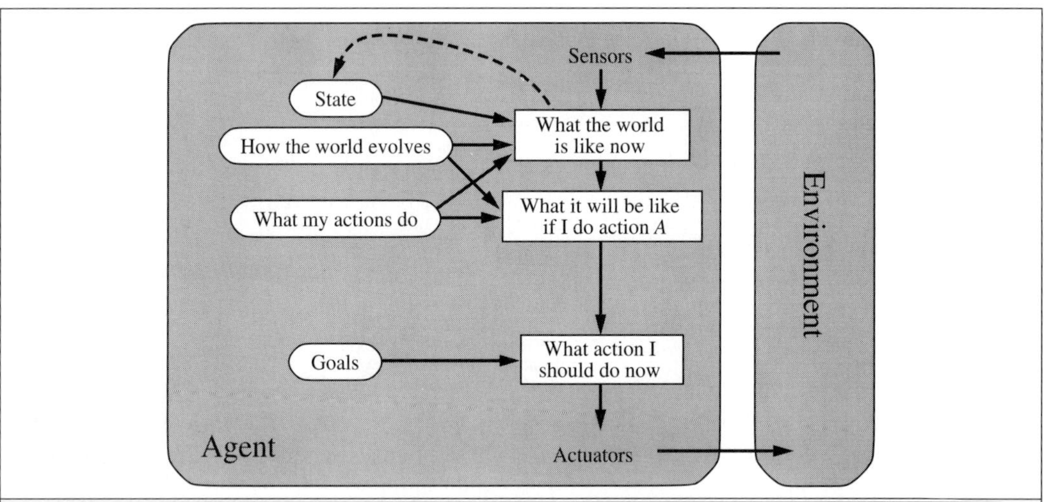


**Figure 2.13** A model-based, goal-based agent. It keeps track of the world state as well as a set of goals it is trying to achieve, and chooses an action that will (eventually) lead to the achievement of its goals.

program can combine this with information about the results of possible actions (the same information as was used to update internal state in the reflex agent) in order to choose actions that achieve the goal. Figure 2.13 shows the goal-based agent's structure.

Sometimes goal-based action selection is straightforward, when goal satisfaction results immediately from a single action. Sometimes it will be more tricky, when the agent has to consider long sequences of twists and turns to find a way to achieve the goal. **Search** (Chapters 3 to 6) and **planning** (Chapters 11 and 12) are the subfields of AI devoted to finding action sequences that achieve the agent's goals.

Notice that decision making of this kind is fundamentally different from the condition–action rules described earlier, in that it involves consideration of the future—both "What will happen if I do such-and-such?" and "Will that make me happy?" In the reflex agent designs, this information is not explicitly represented, because the built-in rules map directly from percepts to actions. The reflex agent brakes when it sees brake lights. A goal-based agent, in principle, could reason that if the car in front has its brake lights on, it will slow down. Given the way the world usually evolves, the only action that will achieve the goal of not hitting other cars is to brake.

Although the goal-based agent appears less efficient, it is more flexible because the knowledge that supports its decisions is represented explicitly and can be modified. If it starts to rain, the agent can update its knowledge of how effectively its brakes will operate; this will automatically cause all of the relevant behaviors to be altered to suit the new conditions. For the reflex agent, on the other hand, we would have to rewrite many condition–action rules. The goal-based agent's behavior can easily be changed to go to a different location. The reflex agent's rules for when to turn and when to go straight will work only for a single destination; they must all be replaced to go somewhere new.

## Utility-based agents

Goals alone are not really enough to generate high-quality behavior in most environments. For example, there are many action sequences that will get the taxi to its destination (thereby achieving the goal) but some are quicker, safer, more reliable, or cheaper than others. Goals just provide a crude binary distinction between "happy" and "unhappy" states, whereas a more general performance measure should allow a comparison of different world states according to exactly how happy they would make the agent if they could be achieved. Because "happy" does not sound very scientific, the customary terminology is to say that if one world state is preferred to another, then it has higher **utility** for the agent.[8]

UTILITY

UTILITY FUNCTION

A **utility function** maps a state (or a sequence of states) onto a real number, which describes the associated degree of happiness. A complete specification of the utility function allows rational decisions in two kinds of cases where goals are inadequate. First, when there are conflicting goals, only some of which can be achieved (for example, speed and safety), the utility function specifies the appropriate tradeoff. Second, when there are several goals that the agent can aim for, none of which can be achieved with certainty, utility provides a way in which the likelihood of success can be weighed up against the importance of the goals.

In Chapter 16, we will show that any rational agent must behave *as if* it possesses a utility function whose expected value it tries to maximize. An agent that possesses an *explicit* utility function therefore can make rational decisions, and it can do so via a general-purpose algorithm that does not depend on the specific utility function being maximized. In this way, the "global" definition of rationality—designating as rational those agent functions that have the highest performance—is turned into a "local" constraint on rational-agent designs that can be expressed in a simple program.

The utility-based agent structure appears in Figure 2.14. Utility-based agent programs appear in Part V, where we design decision making agents that must handle the uncertainty inherent in partially observable environments.

## Learning agents

We have described agent programs with various methods for selecting actions. We have not, so far, explained how the agent programs *come into being*. In his famous early paper, Turing (1950) considers the idea of actually programming his intelligent machines by hand. He estimates how much work this might take and concludes "Some more expeditious method seems desirable." The method he proposes is to build learning machines and then to teach them. In many areas of AI, this is now the preferred method for creating state-of-the-art systems. Learning has another advantage, as we noted earlier: it allows the agent to operate in initially unknown environments and to become more competent than its initial knowledge alone might allow. In this section, we briefly introduce the main ideas of learning agents. In almost every chapter of the book, we will comment on opportunities and methods for learning in particular kinds of agents. Part VI goes into much more depth on the various learning algorithms themselves.

---

[8] The word "utility" here refers to "the quality of being useful," not to the electric company or water works.

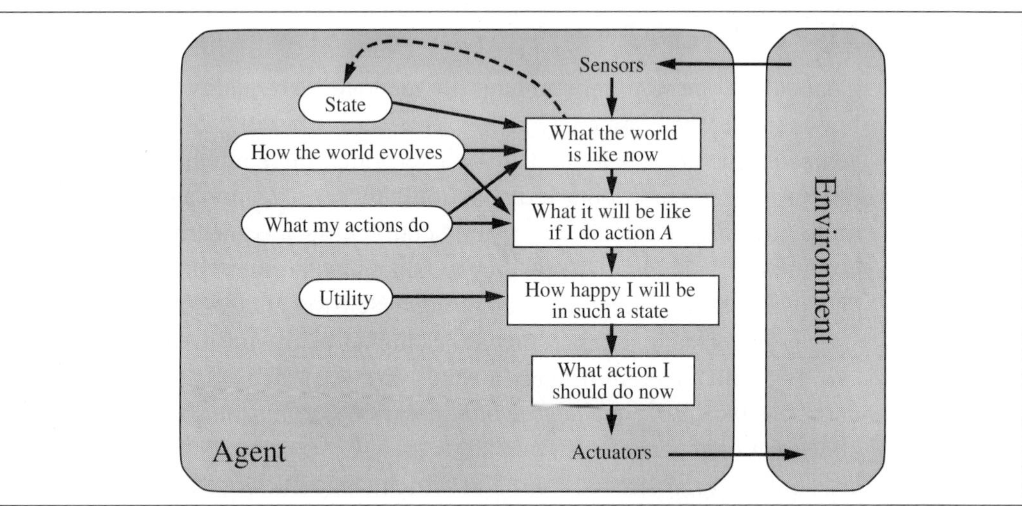


**Figure 2.14** A model-based, utility-based agent. It uses a model of the world, along with a utility function that measures its preferences among states of the world. Then it chooses the action that leads to the best expected utility, where expected utility is computed by averaging over all possible outcome states, weighted by the probability of the outcome.

A learning agent can be divided into four conceptual components, as shown in Figure 2.15. The most important distinction is between the **learning element**, which is responsible for making improvements, and the **performance element**, which is responsible for selecting external actions. The performance element is what we have previously considered to be the entire agent: it takes in percepts and decides on actions. The learning element uses feedback from the **critic** on how the agent is doing and determines how the performance element should be modified to do better in the future.

LEARNING ELEMENT

PERFORMANCE ELEMENT

CRITIC

The design of the learning element depends very much on the design of the performance element. When trying to design an agent that learns a certain capability, the first question is not "How am I going to get it to learn this?" but "What kind of performance element will my agent need to do this once it has learned how?" Given an agent design, learning mechanisms can be constructed to improve every part of the agent.

The critic tells the learning element how well the agent is doing with respect to a fixed performance standard. The critic is necessary because the percepts themselves provide no indication of the agent's success. For example, a chess program could receive a percept indicating that it has checkmated its opponent, but it needs a performance standard to know that this is a good thing; the percept itself does not say so. It is important that the performance standard be fixed. Conceptually, one should think of it as being outside the agent altogether, because the agent must not modify it to fit its own behavior.

PROBLEM GENERATOR

The last component of the learning agent is the **problem generator**. It is responsible for suggesting actions that will lead to new and informative experiences. The point is that if the performance element had its way, it would keep doing the actions that are best, given what it knows. But if the agent is willing to explore a little, and do some perhaps suboptimal actions in the short run, it might discover much better actions for the long run. The problem

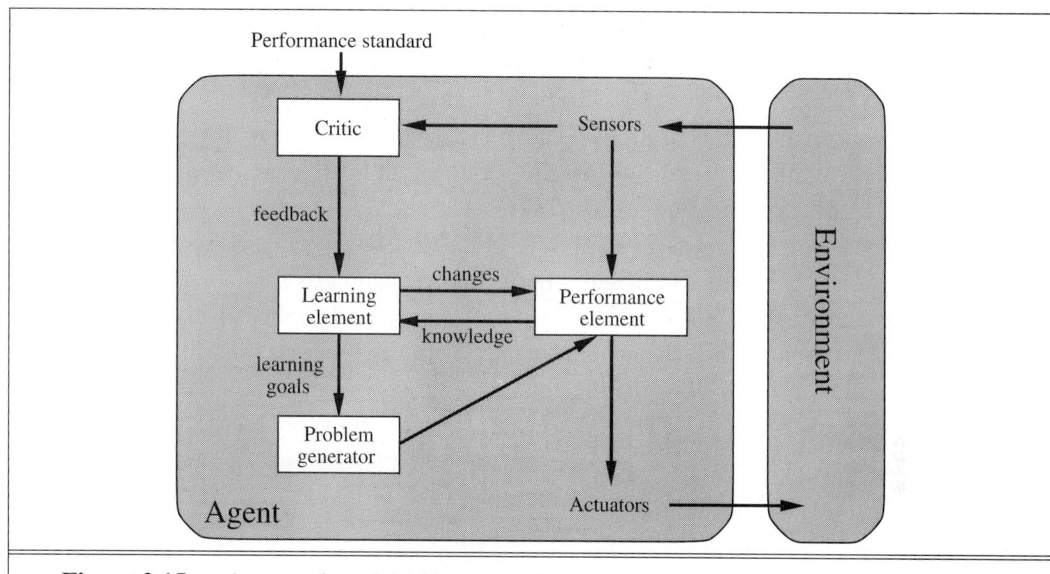


**Figure 2.15** A general model of learning agents.

generator's job is to suggest these exploratory actions. This is what scientists do when they carry out experiments. Galileo did not think that dropping rocks from the top of a tower in Pisa was valuable in itself. He was not trying to break the rocks, nor to modify the brains of unfortunate passers-by. His aim was to modify his own brain, by identifying a better theory of the motion of objects.

To make the overall design more concrete, let us return to the automated taxi example. The performance element consists of whatever collection of knowledge and procedures the taxi has for selecting its driving actions. The taxi goes out on the road and drives, using this performance element. The critic observes the world and passes information along to the learning element. For example, after the taxi makes a quick left turn across three lanes of traffic, the critic observes the shocking language used by other drivers. From this experience, the learning element is able to formulate a rule saying this was a bad action, and the performance element is modified by installing the new rule. The problem generator might identify certain areas of behavior in need of improvement and suggest experiments, such as trying out the brakes on different road surfaces under different conditions.

The learning element can make changes to any of the "knowledge" components shown in the agent diagrams (Figures 2.9, 2.11, 2.13, and 2.14). The simplest cases involve learning directly from the percept sequence. Observation of pairs of successive states of the environment can allow the agent to learn "How the world evolves," and observation of the results of its actions can allow the agent to learn "What my actions do." For example, if the taxi exerts a certain braking pressure when driving on a wet road, then it will soon find out how much deceleration is actually achieved. Clearly, these two learning tasks are more difficult if the environment is only partially observable.

The forms of learning in the preceding paragraph do not need to access the external performance standard—in a sense, the standard is the universal one of making predictions that agree with experiment. The situation is slightly more complex for a utility-based agent that wishes to learn utility information. For example, suppose the taxi-driving agent receives no tips from passengers who have been thoroughly shaken up during the trip. The external performance standard must inform the agent that the loss of tips is a negative contribution to its overall performance; then the agent might be able to learn that violent maneuvers do not contribute to its own utility. In a sense, the performance standard distinguishes part of the incoming percept as a **reward** (or **penalty**) that provides direct feedback on the quality of the agent's behavior. Hard-wired performance standards such as pain and hunger in animals can be understood in this way. This issue is discussed further in Chapter 21.

In summary, agents have a variety of components, and those components can be represented in many ways within the agent program, so there appears to be great variety among learning methods. There is, however, a single unifying theme. Learning in intelligent agents can be summarized as a process of modification of each component of the agent to bring the components into closer agreement with the available feedback information, thereby improving the overall performance of the agent.

## 2.5 SUMMARY

This chapter has been something of a whirlwind tour of AI, which we have conceived of as the science of agent design. The major points to recall are as follows:

- An **agent** is something that perceives and acts in an environment. The **agent function** for an agent specifies the action taken by the agent in response to any percept sequence.
- The **performance measure** evaluates the behavior of the agent in an environment. A **rational agent** acts so as to maximize the expected value of the performance measure, given the percept sequence it has seen so far.
- A **task environment** specification includes the performance measure, the external environment, the actuators, and the sensors. In designing an agent, the first step must always be to specify the task environment as fully as possible.
- Task environments vary along several significant dimensions. They can be fully or partially observable, deterministic or stochastic, episodic or sequential, static or dynamic, discrete or continuous, and single-agent or multiagent.
- The **agent program** implements the agent function. There exists a variety of basic agent-program designs, reflecting the kind of information made explicit and used in the decision process. The designs vary in efficiency, compactness, and flexibility. The appropriate design of the agent program depends on the nature of the environment.
- **Simple reflex agents** respond directly to percepts, whereas **model-based reflex agents** maintain internal state to track aspects of the world that are not evident in the current percept. **Goal-based agents** act to achieve their goals, and **utility-based agents** try to maximize their own expected "happiness."
- All agents can improve their performance through **learning**.

## Bibliographical and Historical Notes

The central role of action in intelligence—the notion of practical reasoning—goes back at least as far as Aristotle's *Nicomachean Ethics*. Practical reasoning was also the subject of McCarthy's (1958) influential paper "Programs with Common Sense." The fields of robotics and control theory are, by their very nature, concerned principally with the construction of physical agents. The concept of a **controller** in control theory is identical to that of an agent in AI. Perhaps surprisingly, AI has concentrated for most of its history on isolated components of agents—question-answering systems, theorem-provers, vision systems, and so on—rather than on whole agents. The discussion of agents in the text by Genesereth and Nilsson (1987) was an influential exception. The whole-agent view is now widely accepted in the field and is a central theme in recent texts (Poole *et al.*, 1998; Nilsson, 1998).

CONTROLLER

Chapter 1 traced the roots of the concept of rationality in philosophy and economics. In AI, the concept was of peripheral interest until the mid-1980s, when it began to suffuse many discussions about the proper technical foundations of the field. A paper by Jon Doyle (1983) predicted that rational agent design would come to be seen as the core mission of AI, while other popular topics would spin off to form new disciplines.

Careful attention to the properties of the environment and their consequences for rational agent design is most apparent in the control theory tradition—for example, classical control systems (Dorf and Bishop, 1999) handle fully observable, deterministic environments; stochastic optimal control (Kumar and Varaiya, 1986) handles partially observable, stochastic environments; and hybrid control (Henzinger and Sastry, 1998) deals with environments containing both discrete and continuous elements. The distinction between fully and partially observable environments is also central in the **dynamic programming** literature developed in the field of operations research (Puterman, 1994), which we will discuss in Chapter 17.

Reflex agents were the primary model for psychological behaviorists such as Skinner (1953), who attempted to reduce the psychology of organisms strictly to input/output or stimulus/response mappings. The advance from behaviorism to functionalism in psychology, which was at least partly driven by the application of the computer metaphor to agents (Putnam, 1960; Lewis, 1966), introduced the internal state of the agent into the picture. Most work in AI views the idea of pure reflex agents with state as too simple to provide much leverage, but work by Rosenschein (1985) and Brooks (1986) questioned this assumption (see Chapter 25). In recent years, a great deal of work has gone into finding efficient algorithms for keeping track of complex environments (Hamscher *et al.*, 1992). The Remote Agent program that controlled the Deep Space One spacecraft (described on page 27) is a particularly impressive example (Muscettola *et al.*, 1998; Jonsson *et al.*, 2000).

Goal-based agents are presupposed in everything from Aristotle's view of practical reasoning to McCarthy's early papers on logical AI. Shakey the Robot (Fikes and Nilsson, 1971; Nilsson, 1984) was the first robotic embodiment of a logical, goal-based agent. A full logical analysis of goal-based agents appeared in Genesereth and Nilsson (1987), and a goal-based programming methodology called agent-oriented programming was developed by Shoham (1993).

The goal-based view also dominates the cognitive psychology tradition in the area of problem solving, beginning with the enormously influential *Human Problem Solving* (Newell and Simon, 1972) and running through all of Newell's later work (Newell, 1990). Goals, further analyzed as *desires* (general) and *intentions* (currently pursued), are central to the theory of agents developed by Bratman (1987). This theory has been influential both in natural language understanding and multiagent systems.

Horvitz *et al.* (1988) specifically suggest the use of rationality conceived as the maximization of expected utility as a basis for AI. The text by Pearl (1988) was the first in AI to cover probability and utility theory in depth; its exposition of practical methods for reasoning and decision making under uncertainty was probably the single biggest factor in the rapid shift towards utility-based agents in the 1990s (see Part V).

The general design for learning agents portrayed in Figure 2.15 is classic in the machine learning literature (Buchanan *et al.*, 1978; Mitchell, 1997). Examples of the design, as embodied in programs, go back at least as far as Arthur Samuel's (1959, 1967) learning program for playing checkers. Learning agents are discussed in depth in Part VI.

Interest in agents and in agent design has risen rapidly in recent years, partly because of the growth of the Internet and the perceived need for automated and mobile **softbots** (Etzioni and Weld, 1994). Relevant papers are collected in *Readings in Agents* (Huhns and Singh, 1998) and *Foundations of Rational Agency* (Wooldridge and Rao, 1999). *Multiagent Systems* (Weiss, 1999) provides a solid foundation for many aspects of agent design. Conferences devoted to agents include the International Conference on Autonomous Agents, the International Workshop on Agent Theories, Architectures, and Languages, and the International Conference on Multiagent Systems. Finally, *Dung Beetle Ecology* (Hanski and Cambefort, 1991) provides a wealth of interesting information on the behavior of dung beetles.

## EXERCISES

**2.1** Define in your own words the following terms: agent, agent function, agent program, rationality, autonomy, reflex agent, model-based agent, goal-based agent, utility-based agent, learning agent.

**2.2** Both the performance measure and the utility function measure how well an agent is doing. Explain the difference between the two.

**2.3** This exercise explores the differences between agent functions and agent programs.

**a.** Can there be more than one agent program that implements a given agent function? Give an example, or show why one is not possible.

**b.** Are there agent functions that cannot be implemented by any agent program?

**c.** Given a fixed machine architecture, does each agent program implement exactly one agent function?

**d.** Given an architecture with $n$ bits of storage, how many different possible agent programs are there?

**2.4** Let us examine the rationality of various vacuum-cleaner agent functions.

**a.** Show that the simple vacuum-cleaner agent function described in Figure 2.3 is indeed rational under the assumptions listed on page 36.

**b.** Describe a rational agent function for the modified performance measure that deducts one point for each movement. Does the corresponding agent program require internal state?

**c.** Discuss possible agent designs for the cases in which clean squares can become dirty and the geography of the environment is unknown. Does it make sense for the agent to learn from its experience in these cases? If so, what should it learn?

**2.5** For each of the following agents, develop a PEAS description of the task environment:

**a.** Robot soccer player;

**b.** Internet book-shopping agent;

**c.** Autonomous Mars rover;

**d.** Mathematician's theorem-proving assistant.

**2.6** For each of the agent types listed in Exercise 2.5, characterize the environment according to the properties given in Section 2.3, and select a suitable agent design.

The following exercises all concern the implementation of environments and agents for the vacuum-cleaner world.

**2.7** Implement a performance-measuring environment simulator for the vacuum-cleaner world depicted in Figure 2.2 and specified on page 36. Your implementation should be modular, so that the sensors, actuators, and environment characteristics (size, shape, dirt placement, etc.) can be changed easily. (*Note:* for some choices of programming language and operating system there are already implementations in the online code repository.)

**2.8** Implement a simple reflex agent for the vacuum environment in Exercise 2.7. Run the environment simulator with this agent for all possible initial dirt configurations and agent locations. Record the agent's performance score for each configuration and its overall average score.

**2.9** Consider a modified version of the vacuum environment in Exercise 2.7, in which the agent is penalized one point for each movement.

**a.** Can a simple reflex agent be perfectly rational for this environment? Explain.

**b.** What about a reflex agent with state? Design such an agent.

**c.** How do your answers to **a** and **b** change if the agent's percepts give it the clean/dirty status of every square in the environment?

**2.10** Consider a modified version of the vacuum environment in Exercise 2.7, in which the geography of the environment—its extent, boundaries, and obstacles—is unknown, as is the initial dirt configuration. (The agent can go *Up* and *Down* as well as *Left* and *Right*.)

**a.** Can a simple reflex agent be perfectly rational for this environment? Explain.

**b.** Can a simple reflex agent with a *randomized* agent function outperform a simple reflex agent? Design such an agent and measure its performance on several environments.

**c.** Can you design an environment in which your randomized agent will perform very poorly? Show your results.

**d.** Can a reflex agent with state outperform a simple reflex agent? Design such an agent and measure its performance on several environments. Can you design a rational agent of this type?

**2.11** Repeat Exercise 2.10 for the case in which the location sensor is replaced with a "bump" sensor that detects the agent's attempts to move into an obstacle or to cross the boundaries of the environment. Supposc the bump sensor stops working; how should the agent behave?

**2.12** The vacuum environments in the preceding exercises have all been deterministic. Discuss possible agent programs for each of the following stochastic versions:

**a.** Murphy's law: twenty-five percent of the time, the *Suck* action fails to clean the floor if it is dirty and deposits dirt onto the floor if the floor is clean. How is your agent program affected if the dirt sensor gives the wrong answer 10% of the time?

**b.** Small children: At each time step, each clean square has a 10% chance of becoming dirty. Can you come up with a rational agent design for this case?

# 3 SOLVING PROBLEMS BY SEARCHING

*In which we see how an agent can find a sequence of actions that achieves its goals, when no single action will do.*

The simplest agents discussed in Chapter 2 were the reflex agents, which base their actions on a direct mapping from states to actions. Such agents cannot operate well in environments for which this mapping would be too large to store and would take too long to learn. Goal-based agents, on the other hand, can succeed by considering future actions and the desirability of their outcomes.

PROBLEM-SOLVING AGENT

This chapter describes one kind of goal-based agent called a **problem-solving agent**. Problem-solving agents decide what to do by finding sequences of actions that lead to desirable states. We start by defining precisely the elements that constitute a "problem" and its "solution," and give several examples to illustrate these definitions. We then describe several general-purpose search algorithms that can be used to solve these problems and compare the advantages of each algorithm. The algorithms are **uninformed**, in the sense that they are given no information about the problem other than its definition. Chapter 4 deals with **informed** search algorithms, ones that have some idea of where to look for solutions.

This chapter uses concepts from the analysis of algorithms. Readers unfamiliar with the concepts of asymptotic complexity (that is, $O()$ notation) and NP-completeness should consult Appendix A.

## 3.1 PROBLEM-SOLVING AGENTS

Intelligent agents are supposed to maximize their performance measure. As we mentioned in Chapter 2, achieving this is sometimes simplified if the agent can adopt a **goal** and aim at satisfying it. Let us first look at why and how an agent might do this.

Imagine an agent in the city of Arad, Romania, enjoying a touring holiday. The agent's performance measure contains many factors: it wants to improve its suntan, improve its Romanian, take in the sights, enjoy the nightlife (such as it is), avoid hangovers, and so on. The decision problem is a complex one involving many tradeoffs and careful reading of guidebooks. Now, suppose the agent has a nonrefundable ticket to fly out of Bucharest the following day. In that case, it makes sense for the agent to adopt the **goal** of getting to Bucharest. Courses of action that don't reach Bucharest on time can be rejected without further consideration and the agent's decision problem is greatly simplified. Goals help organize behavior by limiting the objectives that the agent is trying to achieve. **Goal formulation**, based on the current situation and the agent's performance measure, is the first step in problem solving.

GOAL FORMULATION

We will consider a goal to be a set of world states—exactly those states in which the goal is satisfied. The agent's task is to find out which sequence of actions will get it to a goal state. Before it can do this, it needs to decide what sorts of actions and states to consider. If it were to try to consider actions at the level of "move the left foot forward an inch" or "turn the steering wheel one degree left," the agent would probably never find its way out of the parking lot, let alone to Bucharest, because at that level of detail there is too much uncertainty in the world and there would be too many steps in a solution. **Problem formulation** is the process of deciding what actions and states to consider, given a goal. We will discuss this process in more detail later. For now, let us assume that the agent will consider actions at the level of driving from one major town to another. The states it will consider therefore correspond to being in a particular town.[1]

PROBLEM FORMULATION

Our agent has now adopted the goal of driving to Bucharest, and is considering where to go from Arad. There are three roads out of Arad, one toward Sibiu, one to Timisoara, and one to Zerind. None of these achieves the goal, so unless the agent is very familiar with the geography of Romania, it will not know which road to follow.[2] In other words, the agent will not know which of its possible actions is best, because it does not know enough about the state that results from taking each action. If the agent has no additional knowledge, then it is stuck. The best it can do is choose one of the actions at random.

But suppose the agent has a map of Romania, either on paper or in its memory. The point of a map is to provide the agent with information about the states it might get itself into, and the actions it can take. The agent can use this information to consider subsequent stages of a hypothetical journey via each of the three towns, trying to find a journey that eventually gets to Bucharest. Once it has found a path on the map from Arad to Bucharest, it can achieve its goal by carrying out the driving actions that correspond to the legs of the journey. In general, *an agent with several immediate options of unknown value can decide what to do by first examining different possible* sequences *of actions that lead to states of known value, and then choosing the best sequence.*

SEARCH
SOLUTION
EXECUTION

This process of looking for such a sequence is called **search**. A search algorithm takes a problem as input and returns a **solution** in the form of an action sequence. Once a solution is found, the actions it recommends can be carried out. This is called the **execution** phase. Thus, we have a simple "formulate, search, execute" design for the agent, as shown in Figure 3.1. After formulating a goal and a problem to solve, the agent calls a search procedure to solve it. It then uses the solution to guide its actions, doing whatever the solution recommends as

[1] Notice that each of these "states" actually corresponds to a large *set* of world states, because a real world state specifies every aspect of reality. It is important to keep in mind the distinction between states in problem solving and world states.

[2] We are assuming that most readers are in the same position and can easily imagine themselves to be as clueless as our agent. We apologize to Romanian readers who are unable to take advantage of this pedagogical device.

```
function SIMPLE-PROBLEM-SOLVING-AGENT(percept) returns an action
  inputs: percept, a percept
  static: seq, an action sequence, initially empty
          state, some description of the current world state
          goal, a goal, initially null
          problem, a problem formulation

  state ← UPDATE-STATE(state, percept)
  if seq is empty then do
     goal ← FORMULATE-GOAL(state)
     problem ← FORMULATE-PROBLEM(state, goal)
     seq ← SEARCH(problem)
  action ← FIRST(seq)
  seq ← REST(seq)
  return action
```

**Figure 3.1** A simple problem-solving agent. It first formulates a goal and a problem, searches for a sequence of actions that would solve the problem, and then executes the actions one at a time. When this is complete, it formulates another goal and starts over. Note that when it is executing the sequence it ignores its percepts: it assumes that the solution it has found will always work.

the next thing to do—typically, the first action of the sequence—and then removing that step from the sequence. Once the solution has been executed, the agent will formulate a new goal.

We first describe the process of problem formulation, and then devote the bulk of the chapter to various algorithms for the SEARCH function. We will not discuss the workings of the UPDATE-STATE and FORMULATE-GOAL functions further in this chapter.

Before plunging into the details, let us pause briefly to see where problem-solving agents fit into the discussion of agents and environments in Chapter 2. The agent design in Figure 3.1 assumes that the environment is **static**, because formulating and solving the problem is done without paying attention to any changes that might be occurring in the environment. The agent design also assumes that the initial state is known; knowing it is easiest if the environment is **observable**. The idea of enumerating "alternative courses of action" assumes that the environment can be viewed as **discrete**. Finally, and most importantly, the agent design assumes that the environment is **deterministic**. Solutions to problems are single sequences of actions, so they cannot handle any unexpected events; moreover, solutions are executed without paying attention to the percepts! An agent that carries out its plans with its eyes closed, so to speak, must be quite certain of what is going on. (Control theorists call this an **open-loop** system, because ignoring the percepts breaks the loop between agent and environment.) All these assumptions mean that we are dealing with the easiest kinds of environments, which is one reason this chapter comes early on in the book. Section 3.6 takes a brief look at what happens when we relax the assumptions of observability and determinism. Chapters 12 and 17 go into much greater depth.

OPEN-LOOP

### Well-defined problems and solutions

PROBLEM

A **problem** can be defined formally by four components:

INITIAL STATE

- The **initial state** that the agent starts in. For example, the initial state for our agent in Romania might be described as $In(Arad)$.

SUCCESSOR FUNCTION

- A description of the possible **actions** available to the agent. The most common formulation[3] uses a **successor function**. Given a particular state $x$, SUCCESSOR-FN($x$) returns a set of $\langle action, successor \rangle$ ordered pairs, where each action is one of the legal actions in state $x$ and each successor is a state that can be reached from $x$ by applying the action. For example, from the state $In(Arad)$, the successor function for the Romania problem would return

  $$\{\langle Go(Sibiu), In(Sibiu)\rangle, \ \langle Go(Timisoara), In(Timisoara)\rangle, \ \langle Go(Zerind), In(Zerind)\rangle\}$$

  STATE SPACE

  Together, the initial state and successor function implicitly define the **state space** of the problem—the set of all states reachable from the initial state. The state space forms a graph in which the nodes are states and the arcs between nodes are actions. (The map of Romania shown in Figure 3.2 can be interpreted as a state space graph if we view each road as standing for two driving actions, one in each direction.) A **path** in the state space is a sequence of states connected by a sequence of actions.

  PATH

GOAL TEST

- The **goal test**, which determines whether a given state is a goal state. Sometimes there is an explicit set of possible goal states, and the test simply checks whether the given state is one of them. The agent's goal in Romania is the singleton set $\{In(Bucharest)\}$. Sometimes the goal is specified by an abstract property rather than an explicitly enumerated set of states. For example, in chess, the goal is to reach a state called "checkmate," where the opponent's king is under attack and can't escape.

PATH COST

- A **path cost** function that assigns a numeric cost to each path. The problem-solving agent chooses a cost function that reflects its own performance measure. For the agent trying to get to Bucharest, time is of the essence, so the cost of a path might be its length in kilometers. In this chapter, we assume that the cost of a path can be described as the sum of the costs of the individual actions along the path. The **step cost** of taking action $a$ to go from state $x$ to state $y$ is denoted by $c(x, a, y)$. The step costs for Romania are shown in Figure 3.2 as route distances. We will assume that step costs are nonnegative.[4]

  STEP COST

The preceding elements define a problem and can be gathered together into a single data structure that is given as input to a problem-solving algorithm. A **solution** to a problem is a path from the initial state to a goal state. Solution quality is measured by the path cost function, and an **optimal solution** has the lowest path cost among all solutions.

OPTIMAL SOLUTION

### Formulating problems

In the preceding section we proposed a formulation of the problem of getting to Bucharest in terms of the initial state, successor function, goal test, and path cost. This formulation seems

[3] An alternative formulation uses a set of **operators** that can be applied to a state to generate successors.

[4] The implications of negative costs are explored in Exercise 3.17.

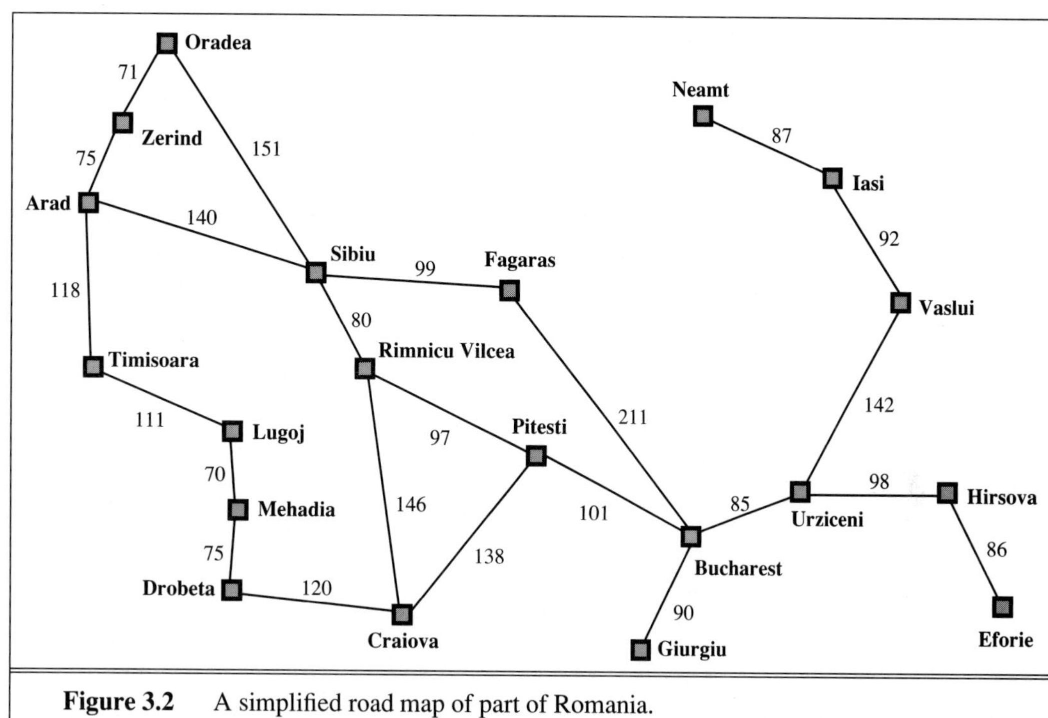


**Figure 3.2** A simplified road map of part of Romania.

reasonable, yet it omits a great many aspects of the real world. Compare the simple state description we have chosen, *In(Arad)*, to an actual cross-country trip, where the state of the world includes so many things: the traveling companions, what is on the radio, the scenery out of the window, whether there are any law enforcement officers nearby, how far it is to the next rest stop, the condition of the road, the weather, and so on. All these considerations are left out of our state descriptions because they are irrelevant to the problem of finding a route to Bucharest. The process of removing detail from a representation is called **abstraction**.

ABSTRACTION

In addition to abstracting the state description, we must abstract the actions themselves. A driving action has many effects. Besides changing the location of the vehicle and its occupants, it takes up time, consumes fuel, generates pollution, and changes the agent (as they say, travel is broadening). In our formulation, we take into account only the change in location. Also, there are many actions that we will omit altogether: turning on the radio, looking out of the window, slowing down for law enforcement officers, and so on. And of course, we don't specify actions at the level of "turn steering wheel to the left by three degrees."

Can we be more precise about defining the appropriate level of abstraction? Think of the abstract states and actions we have chosen as corresponding to large sets of detailed world states and detailed action sequences. Now consider a solution to the abstract problem: for example, the path from Arad to Sibiu to Rimnicu Vilcea to Pitesti to Bucharest. This abstract solution corresponds to a large number of more detailed paths. For example, we could drive with the radio on between Sibiu and Rimnicu Vilcea, and then switch it off for the rest of the trip. The abstraction is *valid* if we can expand any abstract solution into a solution in the more detailed world; a sufficient condition is that for every detailed state that is "in Arad," there is a detailed path to some state that is "in Sibiu," and so on. The abstraction is *useful* if carrying out each of the actions in the solution is easier than the original problem; in this case they are easy enough that they can be carried out without further search or planning by an average driving agent. The choice of a good abstraction thus involves removing as much detail as possible while retaining validity and ensuring that the abstract actions are easy to carry out. Were it not for the ability to construct useful abstractions, intelligent agents would be completely swamped by the real world.

## 3.2 EXAMPLE PROBLEMS

The problem-solving approach has been applied to a vast array of task environments. We list some of the best known here, distinguishing between *toy* and *real-world* problems. A **toy problem** is intended to illustrate or exercise various problem-solving methods. It can be given a concise, exact description. This means that it can be used easily by different researchers to compare the performance of algorithms. A **real-world problem** is one whose solutions people actually care about. They tend not to have a single agreed-upon description, but we will attempt to give the general flavor of their formulations.

TOY PROBLEM

REAL-WORLD PROBLEM

### Toy problems

The first example we will examine is the **vacuum world** first introduced in Chapter 2. (See Figure 2.2.) This can be formulated as a problem as follows:

- ◇ **States**: The agent is in one of two locations, each of which might or might not contain dirt. Thus there are $2 \times 2^2 = 8$ possible world states.
- ◇ **Initial state**: Any state can be designated as the initial state.
- ◇ **Successor function**: This generates the legal states that result from trying the three actions (*Left*, *Right*, and *Suck*). The complete state space is shown in Figure 3.3.
- ◇ **Goal test**: This checks whether all the squares are clean.
- ◇ **Path cost**: Each step costs 1, so the path cost is the number of steps in the path.

Compared with the real world, this toy problem has discrete locations, discrete dirt, reliable cleaning, and it never gets messed up once cleaned. (In Section 3.6, we will relax these assumptions.) One important thing to note is that the state is determined by both the agent location and the dirt locations. A larger environment with $n$ locations has $n\,2^n$ states.

8-PUZZLE

The **8-puzzle**, an instance of which is shown in Figure 3.4, consists of a $3\times3$ board with eight numbered tiles and a blank space. A tile adjacent to the blank space can slide into the space. The object is to reach a specified goal state, such as the one shown on the right of the figure. The standard formulation is as follows:

- ◇ **States**: A state description specifies the location of each of the eight tiles and the blank in one of the nine squares.
- ◇ **Initial state**: Any state can be designated as the initial state. Note that any given goal can be reached from exactly half of the possible initial states (Exercise 3.4).

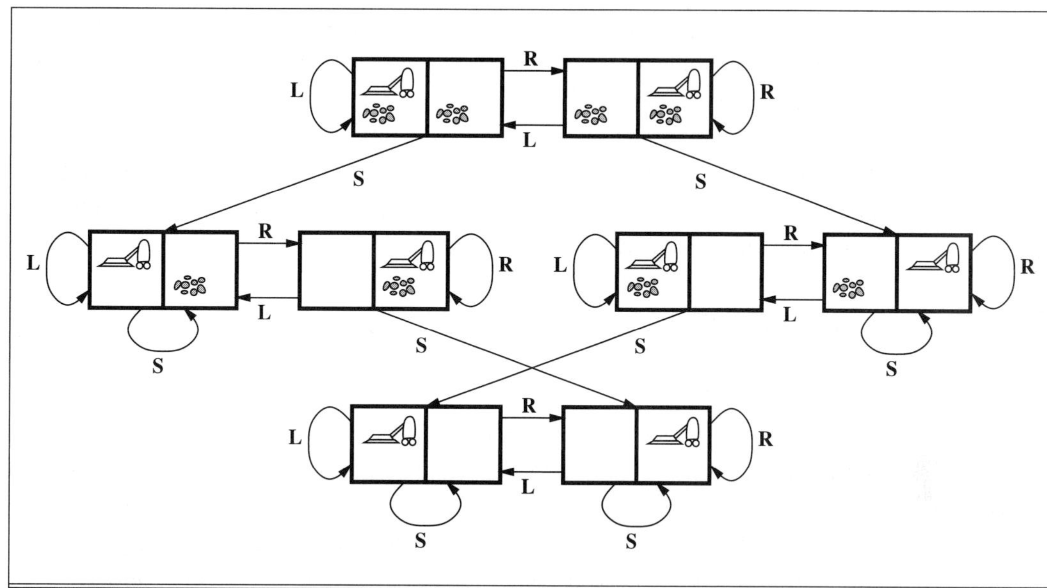


**Figure 3.3** The state space for the vacuum world. Arcs denote actions: L = *Left*, R = *Right*, S = *Suck*.

◇ **Successor function**: This generates the legal states that result from trying the four actions (blank moves *Left*, *Right*, *Up*, or *Down*).

◇ **Goal test**: This checks whether the state matches the goal configuration shown in Figure 3.4. (Other goal configurations are possible.)

◇ **Path cost**: Each step costs 1, so the path cost is the number of steps in the path.

What abstractions have we included here? The actions are abstracted to their beginning and final states, ignoring the intermediate locations where the block is sliding. We've abstracted away actions such as shaking the board when pieces get stuck, or extracting the pieces with a knife and putting them back again. We're left with a description of the rules of the puzzle, avoiding all the details of physical manipulations.

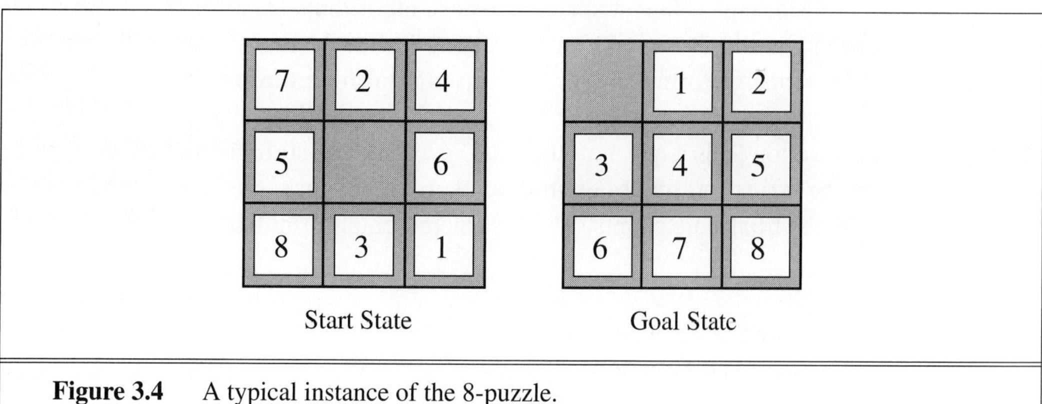


**Figure 3.4** A typical instance of the 8-puzzle.

SLIDING-BLOCK PUZZLES

The 8-puzzle belongs to the family of **sliding-block puzzles**, which are often used as test problems for new search algorithms in AI. This general class is known to be NP-complete, so one does not expect to find methods significantly better in the worst case than the search algorithms described in this chapter and the next. The 8-puzzle has $9!/2 = 181,440$ reachable states and is easily solved. The 15-puzzle (on a $4 \times 4$ board) has around 1.3 trillion states, and random instances can be solved optimally in a few milliseconds by the best search algorithms. The 24-puzzle (on a $5 \times 5$ board) has around $10^{25}$ states, and random instances are still quite difficult to solve optimally with current machines and algorithms.

8-QUEENS PROBLEM

The goal of the **8-queens problem** is to place eight queens on a chessboard such that no queen attacks any other. (A queen attacks any piece in the same row, column or diagonal.) Figure 3.5 shows an attempted solution that fails: the queen in the rightmost column is attacked by the queen at the top left.

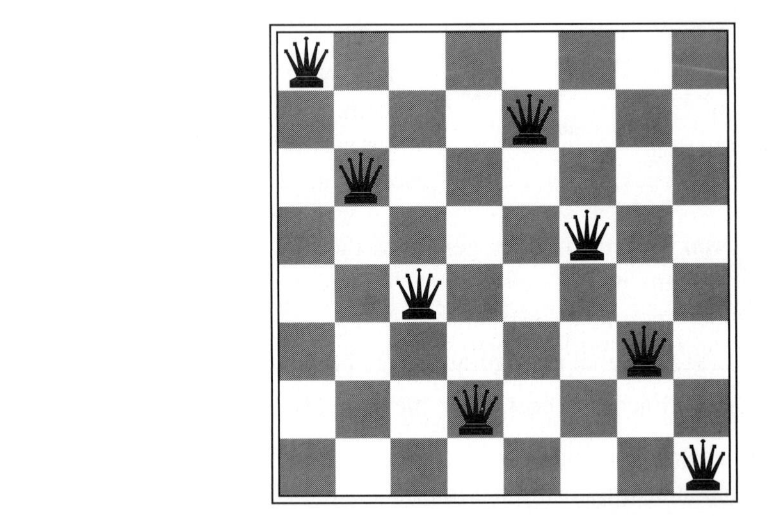

**Figure 3.5** Almost a solution to the 8-queens problem. (Solution is left as an exercise.)

INCREMENTAL FORMULATION

COMPLETE-STATE FORMULATION

Although efficient special-purpose algorithms exist for this problem and the whole $n$-queens family, it remains an interesting test problem for search algorithms. There are two main kinds of formulation. An **incremental formulation** involves operators that *augment* the state description, starting with an empty state; for the 8-queens problem, this means that each action adds a queen to the state. A **complete-state formulation** starts with all 8 queens on the board and moves them around. In either case, the path cost is of no interest because only the final state counts. The first incremental formulation one might try is the following:

- ◇ **States**: Any arrangement of 0 to 8 queens on the board is a state.
- ◇ **Initial state**: No queens on the board.
- ◇ **Successor function**: Add a queen to any empty square.
- ◇ **Goal test**: 8 queens are on the board, none attacked.

In this formulation, we have $64 \cdot 63 \cdots 57 \approx 1.8 \times 10^{14}$ possible sequences to investigate. A better formulation would prohibit placing a queen in any square that is already attacked:

◇ **States**: Arrangements of $n$ queens ($0 \leq n \leq 8$), one per column in the leftmost $n$ columns, with no queen attacking another are states.

◇ **Successor function**: Add a queen to any square in the leftmost empty column such that it is not attacked by any other queen.

This formulation reduces the 8-queens state space from $3 \times 10^{14}$ to just 2,057, and solutions are easy to find. On the other hand, for 100 queens the initial formulation has roughly $10^{400}$ states whereas the improved formulation has about $10^{52}$ states (Exercise 3.5). This is a huge reduction, but the improved state space is still too big for the algorithms in this chapter to handle. Chapter 4 describes the complete-state formulation and Chapter 5 gives a simple algorithm that makes even the million-queens problem easy to solve.

### Real-world problems

ROUTE-FINDING PROBLEM

We have already seen how the **route-finding problem** is defined in terms of specified locations and transitions along links between them. Route-finding algorithms are used in a variety of applications, such as routing in computer networks, military operations planning, and airline travel planning systems. These problems are typically complex to specify. Consider a simplified example of an airline travel problem specified as follows:

◇ **States**: Each is represented by a location (e.g., an airport) and the current time.

◇ **Initial state**: This is specified by the problem.

◇ **Successor function**: This returns the states resulting from taking any scheduled flight (perhaps further specified by seat class and location), leaving later than the current time plus the within-airport transit time, from the current airport to another.

◇ **Goal test**: Are we at the destination by some prespecified time?

◇ **Path cost**: This depends on monetary cost, waiting time, flight time, customs and immigration procedures, seat quality, time of day, type of airplane, frequent-flyer mileage awards, and so on.

Commercial travel advice systems use a problem formulation of this kind, with many additional complications to handle the byzantine fare structures that airlines impose. Any seasoned traveller knows, however, that not all air travel goes according to plan. A really good system should include contingency plans—such as backup reservations on alternate flights—to the extent that these are justified by the cost and likelihood of failure of the original plan.

TOURING PROBLEMS

**Touring problems** are closely related to route-finding problems, but with an important difference. Consider, for example, the problem, "Visit every city in Figure 3.2 at least once, starting and ending in Bucharest." As with route finding, the actions correspond to trips between adjacent cities. The state space, however, is quite different. Each state must include not just the current location but also the *set of cities the agent has visited.* So the initial state would be "In Bucharest; visited {Bucharest}," a typical intermediate state would be "In Vaslui; visited {Bucharest,Urziceni,Vaslui}," and the goal test would check whether the agent is in Bucharest and all 20 cities have been visited.

TRAVELING SALESPERSON PROBLEM

The **traveling salesperson problem** (TSP) is a touring problem in which each city must be visited exactly once. The aim is to find the *shortest* tour. The problem is known to be NP-hard, but an enormous amount of effort has been expended to improve the capabilities of TSP algorithms. In addition to planning trips for traveling salespersons, these algorithms have been used for tasks such as planning movements of automatic circuit-board drills and of stocking machines on shop floors.

VLSI LAYOUT

A **VLSI layout** problem requires positioning millions of components and connections on a chip to minimize area, minimize circuit delays, minimize stray capacitances, and maximize manufacturing yield. The layout problem comes after the logical design phase, and is usually split into two parts: **cell layout** and **channel routing**. In cell layout, the primitive components of the circuit are grouped into cells, each of which performs some recognized function. Each cell has a fixed footprint (size and shape) and requires a certain number of connections to each of the other cells. The aim is to place the cells on the chip so that they do not overlap and so that there is room for the connecting wires to be placed between the cells. Channel routing finds a specific route for each wire through the gaps between the cells. These search problems are extremely complex, but definitely worth solving. In Chapter 4, we will see some algorithms capable of solving them.

ROBOT NAVIGATION

**Robot navigation** is a generalization of the route-finding problem described earlier. Rather than a discrete set of routes, a robot can move in a continuous space with (in principle) an infinite set of possible actions and states. For a circular robot moving on a flat surface, the space is essentially two-dimensional. When the robot has arms and legs or wheels that must also be controlled, the search space becomes many-dimensional. Advanced techniques are required just to make the search space finite. We examine some of these methods in Chapter 25. In addition to the complexity of the problem, real robots must also deal with errors in their sensor readings and motor controls.

AUTOMATIC ASSEMBLY SEQUENCING

**Automatic assembly sequencing** of complex objects by a robot was first demonstrated by FREDDY (Michie, 1972). Progress since then has been slow but sure, to the point where the assembly of intricate objects such as electric motors is economically feasible. In assembly problems, the aim is to find an order in which to assemble the parts of some object. If the wrong order is chosen, there will be no way to add some part later in the sequence without undoing some of the work already done. Checking a step in the sequence for feasibility is a difficult geometrical search problem closely related to robot navigation. Thus, the generation of legal successors is the expensive part of assembly sequencing. Any practical algorithm must avoid exploring all but a tiny fraction of the state space. Another important assembly problem is **protein design**, in which the goal is to find a sequence of amino acids that will fold into a three-dimensional protein with the right properties to cure some disease.

PROTEIN DESIGN

INTERNET SEARCHING

In recent years there has been increased demand for software robots that perform **Internet searching**, looking for answers to questions, for related information, or for shopping deals. This is a good application for search techniques, because it is easy to conceptualize the Internet as a graph of nodes (pages) connected by links. A full description of Internet search is deferred until Chapter 10.

## 3.3 SEARCHING FOR SOLUTIONS

Having formulated some problems, we now need to solve them. This is done by a search through the state space. This chapter deals with search techniques that use an explicit **search tree** that is generated by the initial state and the successor function that together define the state space. In general, we may have a search *graph* rather than a search *tree*, when the same state can be reached from multiple paths. We defer consideration of this important complication until Section 3.5.

SEARCH TREE

Figure 3.6 shows some of the expansions in the search tree for finding a route from Arad to Bucharest. The root of the search tree is a **search node** corresponding to the initial state, *In(Arad)*. The first step is to test whether this is a goal state. Clearly it is not, but it is important to check so that we can solve trick problems like "starting in Arad, get to Arad." Because this is not a goal state, we need to consider some other states. This is done by **expanding** the current state; that is, applying the successor function to the current state, thereby **generating** a new set of states. In this case, we get three new states: *In(Sibiu)*, *In(Timisoara)*, and *In(Zerind)*. Now we must choose which of these three possibilities to consider further.

SEARCH NODE

EXPANDING

GENERATING

This is the essence of search—following up one option now and putting the others aside for later, in case the first choice does not lead to a solution. Suppose we choose Sibiu first. We check to see whether it is a goal state (it is not) and then expand it to get *In(Arad)*, *In(Fagaras)*, *In(Oradea)*, and *In(RimnicuVilcea)*. We can then choose any of these four, or go back and choose Timisoara or Zerind. We continue choosing, testing, and expanding until either a solution is found or there are no more states to be expanded. The choice of which state to expand is determined by the **search strategy**. The general tree-search algorithm is described informally in Figure 3.7.

SEARCH STRATEGY

It is important to distinguish between the state space and the search tree. For the route finding problem, there are only 20 states in the state space, one for each city. But there are an infinite number of paths in this state space, so the search tree has an infinite number of nodes. For example, the three paths Arad–Sibiu, Arad–Sibiu–Arad, Arad–Sibiu–Arad–Sibiu are the first three of an infinite sequence of paths. (Obviously, a good search algorithm avoids following such repeated paths; Section 3.5 shows how.)

There are many ways to represent nodes, but we will assume that a node is a data structure with five components:

- STATE: the state in the state space to which the node corresponds;
- PARENT-NODE: the node in the search tree that generated this node;
- ACTION: the action that was applied to the parent to generate the node;
- PATH-COST: the cost, traditionally denoted by $g(n)$, of the path from the initial state to the node, as indicated by the parent pointers; and
- DEPTH: the number of steps along the path from the initial state.

It is important to remember the distinction between nodes and states. A node is a bookkeeping data structure used to represent the search tree. A state corresponds to a configuration of the world. Thus, nodes are on particular paths, as defined by PARENT-NODE pointers, whereas states are not. Furthermore, two different nodes can contain the same world state, if that state is generated via two different search paths. The node data structure is depicted in Figure 3.8.

FRINGE

LEAF NODE

We also need to represent the collection of nodes that have been generated but not yet expanded—this collection is called the **fringe**. Each element of the fringe is a **leaf node**, that

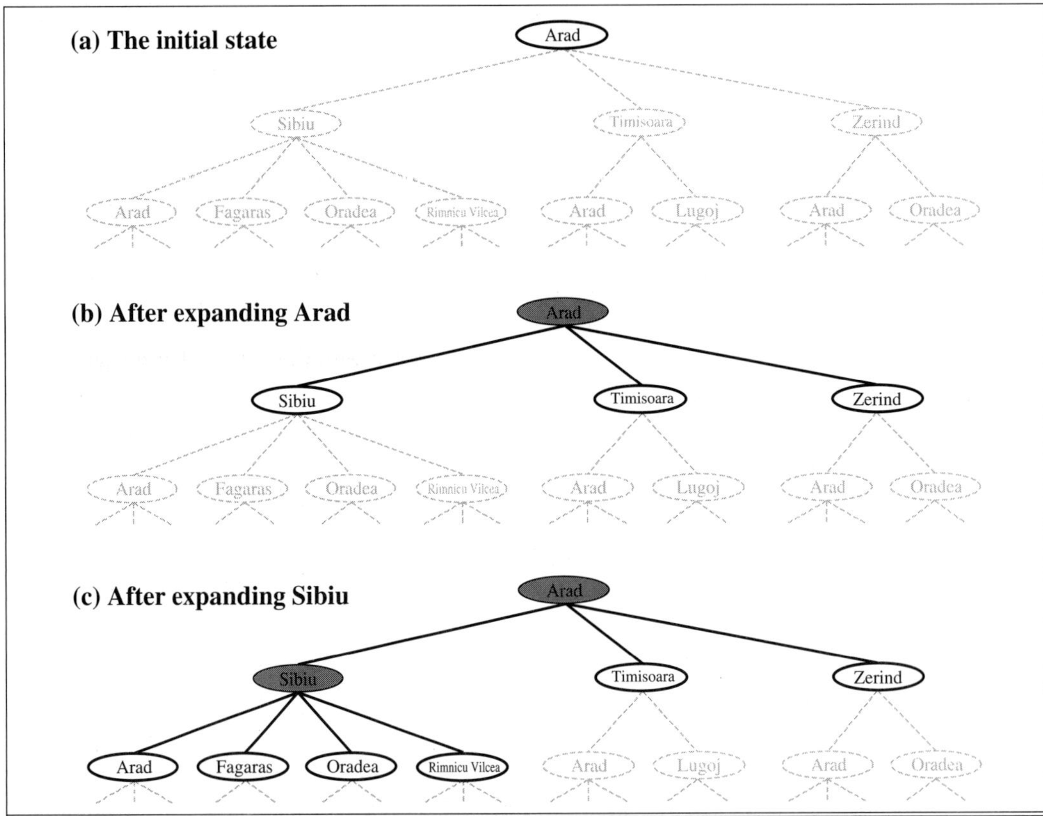


**Figure 3.6** Partial search trees for finding a route from Arad to Bucharest. Nodes that have been expanded are shaded; nodes that have been generated but not yet expanded are outlined in bold; nodes that have not yet been generated are shown in faint dashed lines.

**function** TREE-SEARCH(*problem*, *strategy*) **returns** a solution, or failure
  initialize the search tree using the initial state of *problem*
  **loop do**
    **if** there are no candidates for expansion **then return** failure
    choose a leaf node for expansion according to *strategy*
    **if** the node contains a goal state **then return** the corresponding solution
    **else** expand the node and add the resulting nodes to the search tree

**Figure 3.7** An informal description of the general tree-search algorithm.

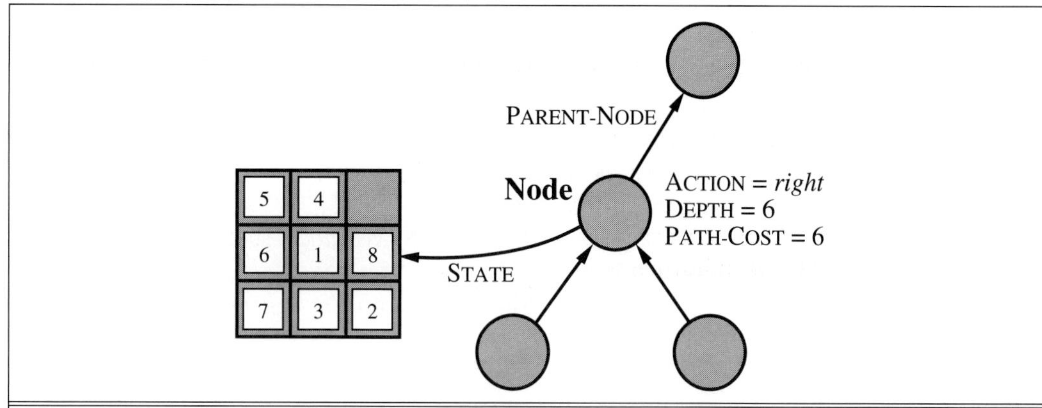


**Figure 3.8** Nodes are the data structures from which the search tree is constructed. Each has a parent, a state, and various bookkeeping fields. Arrows point from child to parent.

is, a node with no successors in the tree. In Figure 3.6, the fringe of each tree consists of those nodes with bold outlines. The simplest representation of the fringe would be a set of nodes. The search strategy then would be a function that selects the next node to be expanded from this set. Although this is conceptually straightforward, it could be computationally expensive, because the strategy function might have to look at every element of the set to choose the best one. Therefore, we will assume that the collection of nodes is implemented as a **queue**. The operations on a queue are as follows:

QUEUE

- MAKE-QUEUE(*element*, ...) creates a queue with the given element(s).
- EMPTY?(*queue*) returns true only if there are no more elements in the queue.
- FIRST(*queue*) returns the first element of the queue.
- REMOVE-FIRST(*queue*) returns FIRST(*queue*) and removes it from the queue.
- INSERT(*element*, *queue*) inserts an element into the queue and returns the resulting queue. (We will see that different types of queues insert elements in different orders.)
- INSERT-ALL(*elements*, *queue*) inserts a set of elements into the queue and returns the resulting queue.

With these definitions, we can write the more formal version of the general tree-search algorithm shown in Figure 3.9.

### Measuring problem-solving performance

The output of a problem-solving algorithm is either *failure* or a solution. (Some algorithms might get stuck in an infinite loop and never return an output.) We will evaluate an algorithm's performance in four ways:

COMPLETENESS

◇ **Completeness**: Is the algorithm guaranteed to find a solution when there is one?

OPTIMALITY

◇ **Optimality**: Does the strategy find the optimal solution, as defined on page 62?

TIME COMPLEXITY

◇ **Time complexity**: How long does it take to find a solution?

SPACE COMPLEXITY

◇ **Space complexity**: How much memory is needed to perform the search?

```
function TREE-SEARCH(problem, fringe) returns a solution, or failure

  fringe ← INSERT(MAKE-NODE(INITIAL-STATE[problem]), fringe)
  loop do
     if EMPTY?(fringe) then return failure
     node ← REMOVE-FIRST(fringe)
     if GOAL-TEST[problem] applied to STATE[node] succeeds
        then return SOLUTION(node)
     fringe ← INSERT-ALL(EXPAND(node, problem), fringe)
```

```
function EXPAND(node, problem) returns a set of nodes

  successors ← the empty set
  for each ⟨action, result⟩ in SUCCESSOR-FN[problem](STATE[node]) do
     s ← a new NODE
     STATE[s] ← result
     PARENT-NODE[s] ← node
     ACTION[s] ← action
     PATH-COST[s] ← PATH-COST[node] + STEP-COST(STATE[node], action, result)
     DEPTH[s] ← DEPTH[node] + 1
     add s to successors
  return successors
```

**Figure 3.9** The general tree-search algorithm. (Note that the *fringe* argument must be an empty queue, and the type of the queue will affect the order of the search.) The SOLUTION function returns the sequence of actions obtained by following parent pointers back to the root.

Time and space complexity are always considered with respect to some measure of the problem difficulty. In theoretical computer science, the typical measure is the size of the state space graph, because the graph is viewed as an explicit data structure that is input to the search program. (The map of Romania is an example of this.) In AI, where the graph is represented implicitly by the initial state and successor function and is frequently infinite, complexity is expressed in terms of three quantities: $b$, the **branching factor** or maximum number of successors of any node; $d$, the depth of the shallowest goal node; and $m$, the maximum length of any path in the state space.

BRANCHING FACTOR

Time is often measured in terms of the number of nodes generated[5] during the search, and space in terms of the maximum number of nodes stored in memory.

SEARCH COST

TOTAL COST

To assess the effectiveness of a search algorithm, we can consider just the **search cost**—which typically depends on the time complexity but can also include a term for memory usage—or we can use the **total cost**, which combines the search cost and the path cost of the solution found. For the problem of finding a route from Arad to Bucharest, the search cost

[5] Some texts measure time in terms of the number of node *expansions* instead. The two measures differ by at most a factor of $b$. It seems to us that the execution time of a node expansion increases with the number of nodes generated in that expansion.

is the amount of time taken by the search and the solution cost is the total length of the path in kilometers. Thus, to compute the total cost, we have to add kilometers and milliseconds. There is no "official exchange rate" between the two, but it might be reasonable in this case to convert kilometers into milliseconds by using an estimate of the car's average speed (because time is what the agent cares about). This enables the agent to find an optimal tradeoff point at which further computation to find a shorter path becomes counterproductive. The more general problem of tradeoffs between different goods will be taken up in Chapter 16.

## 3.4 Uninformed Search Strategies

UNINFORMED SEARCH

This section covers five search strategies that come under the heading of **uninformed search** (also called **blind search**). The term means that they have no additional information about states beyond that provided in the problem definition. All they can do is generate successors and distinguish a goal state from a nongoal state. Strategies that know whether one non-goal state is "more promising" than another are called **informed search** or **heuristic search** strategies; they will be covered in Chapter 4. All search strategies are distinguished by the *order* in which nodes are expanded.

INFORMED SEARCH

HEURISTIC SEARCH

### Breadth-first search

BREADTH-FIRST SEARCH

**Breadth-first search** is a simple strategy in which the root node is expanded first, then all the successors of the root node are expanded next, then *their* successors, and so on. In general, all the nodes are expanded at a given depth in the search tree before any nodes at the next level are expanded.

Breadth-first search can be implemented by calling TREE-SEARCH with an empty fringe that is a first-in-first-out (FIFO) queue, assuring that the nodes that are visited first will be expanded first. In other words, calling TREE-SEARCH(*problem*,FIFO-QUEUE()) results in a breadth-first search. The FIFO queue puts all newly generated successors at the end of the queue, which means that shallow nodes are expanded before deeper nodes. Figure 3.10 shows the progress of the search on a simple binary tree.

We will evaluate breadth-first search using the four criteria from the previous section. We can easily see that it is *complete*—if the shallowest goal node is at some finite depth $d$, breadth-first search will eventually find it after expanding all shallower nodes (provided the branching factor $b$ is finite). The *shallowest* goal node is not necessarily the *optimal* one; technically, breadth-first search is optimal if the path cost is a nondecreasing function of the depth of the node. (For example, when all actions have the same cost.)

So far, the news about breadth-first search has been good. To see why it is not always the strategy of choice, we have to consider the amount of time and memory it takes to complete a search. To do this, we consider a hypothetical state space where every state has $b$ successors. The root of the search tree generates $b$ nodes at the first level, each of which generates $b$ more nodes, for a total of $b^2$ at the second level. Each of *these* generates $b$ more nodes, yielding $b^3$ nodes at the third level, and so on. Now suppose that the solution is at depth $d$. In the worst case, we would expand all but the last node at level $d$ (since the goal itself is not expanded), generating $b^{d+1} - b$ nodes at level $d+1$. Then the total number of nodes generated is

$$b + b^2 + b^3 + \cdots + b^d + (b^{d+1} - b) = O(b^{d+1}) .$$

Every node that is generated must remain in memory, because it is either part of the fringe or is an ancestor of a fringe node. The space complexity is, therefore, the same as the time complexity (plus one node for the root).

Those who do complexity analysis are worried (or excited, if they like a challenge) by exponential complexity bounds such as $O(b^{d+1})$. Figure 3.11 shows why. It lists the time and memory required for a breadth-first search with branching factor $b = 10$, for various values of the solution depth $d$. The table assumes that 10,000 nodes can be generated per second and that a node requires 1000 bytes of storage. Many search problems fit roughly within these assumptions (give or take a factor of 100) when run on a modern personal computer.

There are two lessons to be learned from Figure 3.11. First, *the memory requirements are a bigger problem for breadth-first search than is the execution time.* 31 hours would not be too long to wait for the solution to an important problem of depth 8, but few computers have the terabyte of main memory it would take. Fortunately, there are other search strategies that require less memory.

The second lesson is that the time requirements are still a major factor. If your problem has a solution at depth 12, then (given our assumptions) it will take 35 years for breadth-first search (or indeed any uninformed search) to find it. In general, *exponential-complexity search problems cannot be solved by uninformed methods for any but the smallest instances.*

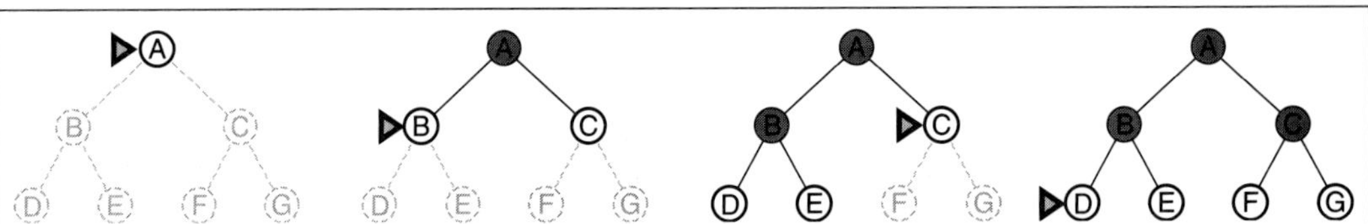


**Figure 3.10** Breadth-first search on a simple binary tree. At each stage, the node to be expanded next is indicated by a marker.

| Depth | Nodes | Time | Memory |
|---|---|---|---|
| 2 | 1100 | .11 seconds | 1 megabyte |
| 4 | 111,100 | 11 seconds | 106 megabytes |
| 6 | $10^7$ | 19 minutes | 10 gigabytes |
| 8 | $10^9$ | 31 hours | 1 terabytes |
| 10 | $10^{11}$ | 129 days | 101 terabytes |
| 12 | $10^{13}$ | 35 years | 10 petabytes |
| 14 | $10^{15}$ | 3,523 years | 1 exabyte |

**Figure 3.11** Time and memory requirements for breadth-first search. The numbers shown assume branching factor $b = 10$; 10,000 nodes/second; 1000 bytes/node.

### Uniform-cost search

UNIFORM-COST SEARCH

Breadth-first search is optimal when all step costs are equal, because it always expands the *shallowest* unexpanded node. By a simple extension, we can find an algorithm that is optimal with any step cost function. Instead of expanding the shallowest node, **uniform-cost search** expands the node $n$ with the *lowest path cost*. Note that if all step costs are equal, this is identical to breadth-first search.

Uniform-cost search does not care about the *number* of steps a path has, but only about their total cost. Therefore, it will get stuck in an infinite loop if it ever expands a node that has a zero-cost action leading back to the same state (for example, a $NoOp$ action). We can guarantee completeness provided the cost of every step is greater than or equal to some small positive constant $\epsilon$. This condition is also sufficient to ensure *optimality*. It means that the cost of a path always increases as we go along the path. From this property, it is easy to see that the algorithm expands nodes in order of increasing path cost. Therefore, the first goal node selected for expansion is the optimal solution. (Remember that TREE-SEARCH applies the goal test only to the nodes that are selected for expansion.) We recommend trying the algorithm out to find the shortest path to Bucharest.

Uniform-cost search is guided by path costs rather than depths, so its complexity cannot easily be characterized in terms of $b$ and $d$. Instead, let $C^*$ be the cost of the optimal solution, and assume that every action costs at least $\epsilon$. Then the algorithm's worst-case time and space complexity is $O(b^{1+\lfloor C^*/\epsilon \rfloor})$, which can be much greater than $b^d$. This is because uniform-cost search can, and often does, explore large trees of small steps before exploring paths involving large and perhaps useful steps. When all step costs are equal, of course, $b^{1+\lfloor C^*/\epsilon \rfloor}$ is just $b^d$.

### Depth-first search

DEPTH-FIRST SEARCH

**Depth-first search** always expands the *deepest* node in the current fringe of the search tree. The progress of the search is illustrated in Figure 3.12. The search proceeds immediately to the deepest level of the search tree, where the nodes have no successors. As those nodes are expanded, they are dropped from the fringe, so then the search "backs up" to the next shallowest node that still has unexplored successors.

This strategy can be implemented by TREE-SEARCH with a last-in-first-out (LIFO) queue, also known as a stack. As an alternative to the TREE-SEARCH implementation, it is common to implement depth-first search with a recursive function that calls itself on each of its children in turn. (A recursive depth-first algorithm incorporating a depth limit is shown in Figure 3.13.)

Depth-first search has very modest memory requirements. It needs to store only a single path from the root to a leaf node, along with the remaining unexpanded sibling nodes for each node on the path. Once a node has been expanded, it can be removed from memory as soon as all its descendants have been fully explored. (See Figure 3.12.) For a state space with branching factor $b$ and maximum depth $m$, depth-first search requires storage of only $bm + 1$ nodes. Using the same assumptions as Figure 3.11, and assuming that nodes at the same depth as the goal node have no successors, we find that depth-first search would require 118 kilobytes instead of 10 petabytes at depth $d = 12$, a factor of 10 billion times less space.

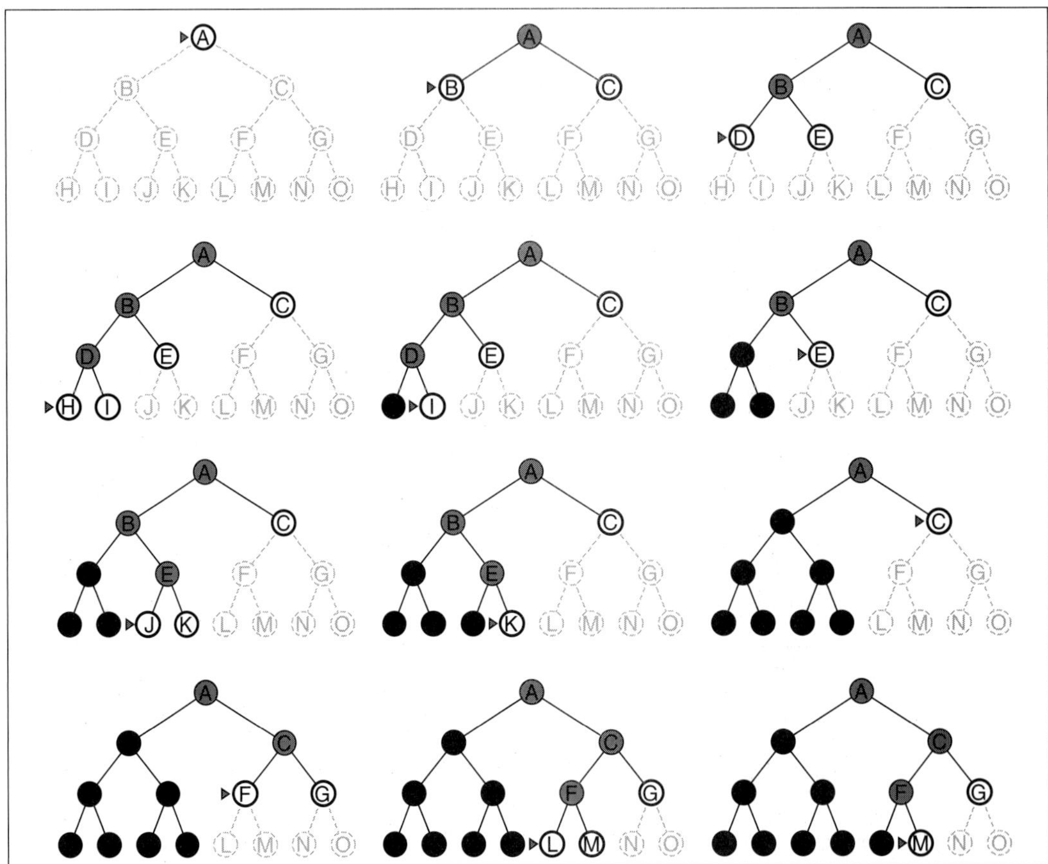


**Figure 3.12** Depth-first search on a binary tree. Nodes that have been expanded and have no descendants in the fringe can be removed from memory; these are shown in black. Nodes at depth 3 are assumed to have no successors and $M$ is the only goal node.

BACKTRACKING SEARCH

A variant of depth-first search called **backtracking search** uses still less memory. In backtracking, only one successor is generated at a time rather than all successors; each partially expanded node remembers which successor to generate next. In this way, only $O(m)$ memory is needed rather than $O(bm)$. Backtracking search facilitates yet another memory-saving (and time-saving) trick: the idea of generating a successor by *modifying* the current state description directly rather than copying it first. This reduces the memory requirements to just one state description and $O(m)$ actions. For this to work, we must be able to undo each modification when we go back to generate the next successor. For problems with large state descriptions, such as robotic assembly, these techniques are critical to success.

The drawback of depth-first search is that it can make a wrong choice and get stuck going down a very long (or even infinite) path when a different choice would lead to a solution near the root of the search tree. For example, in Figure 3.12, depth-first search will explore the entire left subtree even if node $C$ is a goal node. If node $J$ were also a goal node, then depth-first search would return it as a solution; hence, depth-first search is not optimal. If

```
function DEPTH-LIMITED-SEARCH(problem, limit) returns a solution, or failure/cutoff
   return RECURSIVE-DLS(MAKE-NODE(INITIAL-STATE[problem]), problem, limit)

function RECURSIVE-DLS(node, problem, limit) returns a solution, or failure/cutoff
   cutoff_occurred? ← false
   if GOAL-TEST[problem](STATE[node]) then return SOLUTION(node)
   else if DEPTH[node] = limit then return cutoff
   else for each successor in EXPAND(node, problem) do
       result ← RECURSIVE-DLS(successor, problem, limit)
       if result = cutoff then cutoff_occurred? ← true
       else if result ≠ failure then return result
   if cutoff_occurred? then return cutoff else return failure
```

**Figure 3.13** A recursive implementation of depth-limited search.

the left subtree were of unbounded depth but contained no solutions, depth-first search would never terminate; hence, it is not complete. In the worst case, depth-first search will generate all of the $O(b^m)$ nodes in the search tree, where $m$ is the maximum depth of any node. Note that $m$ can be much larger than $d$ (the depth of the shallowest solution), and is infinite if the tree is unbounded.

### Depth-limited search

DEPTH-LIMITED SEARCH

The problem of unbounded trees can be alleviated by supplying depth-first search with a predetermined depth limit $\ell$. That is, nodes at depth $\ell$ are treated as if they have no successors. This approach is called **depth-limited search**. The depth limit solves the infinite-path problem. Unfortunately, it also introduces an additional source of incompleteness if we choose $\ell < d$, that is, the shallowest goal is beyond the depth limit. (This is not unlikely when $d$ is unknown.) Depth-limited search will also be nonoptimal if we choose $\ell > d$. Its time complexity is $O(b^\ell)$ and its space complexity is $O(b\ell)$. Depth-first search can be viewed as a special case of depth-limited search with $\ell = \infty$.

Sometimes, depth limits can be based on knowledge of the problem. For example, on the map of Romania there are 20 cities. Therefore, we know that if there is a solution, it must be of length 19 at the longest, so $\ell = 19$ is a possible choice. But in fact if we studied the map carefully, we would discover that any city can be reached from any other city in at most 9 steps. This number, known as the **diameter** of the state space, gives us a better depth limit, which leads to a more efficient depth-limited search. For most problems, however, we will not know a good depth limit until we have solved the problem.

DIAMETER

Depth-limited search can be implemented as a simple modification to the general tree-search algorithm or to the recursive depth-first search algorithm. We show the pseudocode for recursive depth-limited search in Figure 3.13. Notice that depth-limited search can terminate with two kinds of failure: the standard *failure* value indicates no solution; the *cutoff* value indicates no solution within the depth limit.

### Iterative deepening depth-first search

ITERATIVE DEEPENING SEARCH

**Iterative deepening search** (or iterative deepening depth-first search) is a general strategy, often used in combination with depth-first search, that finds the best depth limit. It does this by gradually increasing the limit—first 0, then 1, then 2, and so on—until a goal is found. This will occur when the depth limit reaches $d$, the depth of the shallowest goal node. The algorithm is shown in Figure 3.14. Iterative deepening combines the benefits of depth-first and breadth-first search. Like depth-first search, its memory requirements are very modest: $O(bd)$ to be precise. Like breadth-first search, it is complete when the branching factor is finite and optimal when the path cost is a nondecreasing function of the depth of the node. Figure 3.15 shows four iterations of ITERATIVE-DEEPENING-SEARCH on a binary search tree, where the solution is found on the fourth iteration.

Iterative deepening search may seem wasteful, because states are generated multiple times. It turns out this is not very costly. The reason is that in a search tree with the same (or nearly the same) branching factor at each level, most of the nodes are in the bottom level, so it does not matter much that the upper levels are generated multiple times. In an iterative deepening search, the nodes on the bottom level (depth $d$) are generated once, those on the next to bottom level are generated twice, and so on, up to the children of the root, which are generated $d$ times. So the total number of nodes generated is

$$N(\text{IDS}) = (d)b + (d-1)b^2 + \cdots + (1)b^d\,,$$

which gives a time complexity of $O(b^d)$. We can compare this to the nodes generated by a breadth-first search:

$$N(\text{BFS}) = b + b^2 + \cdots + b^d + (b^{d+1} - b)\,.$$

Notice that breadth-first search generates some nodes at depth $d+1$, whereas iterative deepening does not. The result is that iterative deepening is actually *faster* than breadth-first search, despite the repeated generation of states. For example, if $b = 10$ and $d = 5$, the numbers are

$$\begin{aligned} N(\text{IDS}) &= 50 + 400 + 3{,}000 + 20{,}000 + 100{,}000 = 123{,}450 \\ N(\text{BFS}) &= 10 + 100 + 1{,}000 + 10{,}000 + 100{,}000 + 999{,}990 = 1{,}111{,}100\,. \end{aligned}$$

*In general, iterative deepening is the preferred uninformed search method when there is a large search space and the depth of the solution is not known.*

```
function ITERATIVE-DEEPENING-SEARCH(problem) returns a solution, or failure
   inputs: problem, a problem

   for depth ← 0 to ∞ do
      result ← DEPTH-LIMITED-SEARCH(problem, depth)
      if result ≠ cutoff then return result
```

**Figure 3.14** The iterative deepening search algorithm, which repeatedly applies depth-limited search with increasing limits. It terminates when a solution is found or if the depth-limited search returns *failure*, meaning that no solution exists.

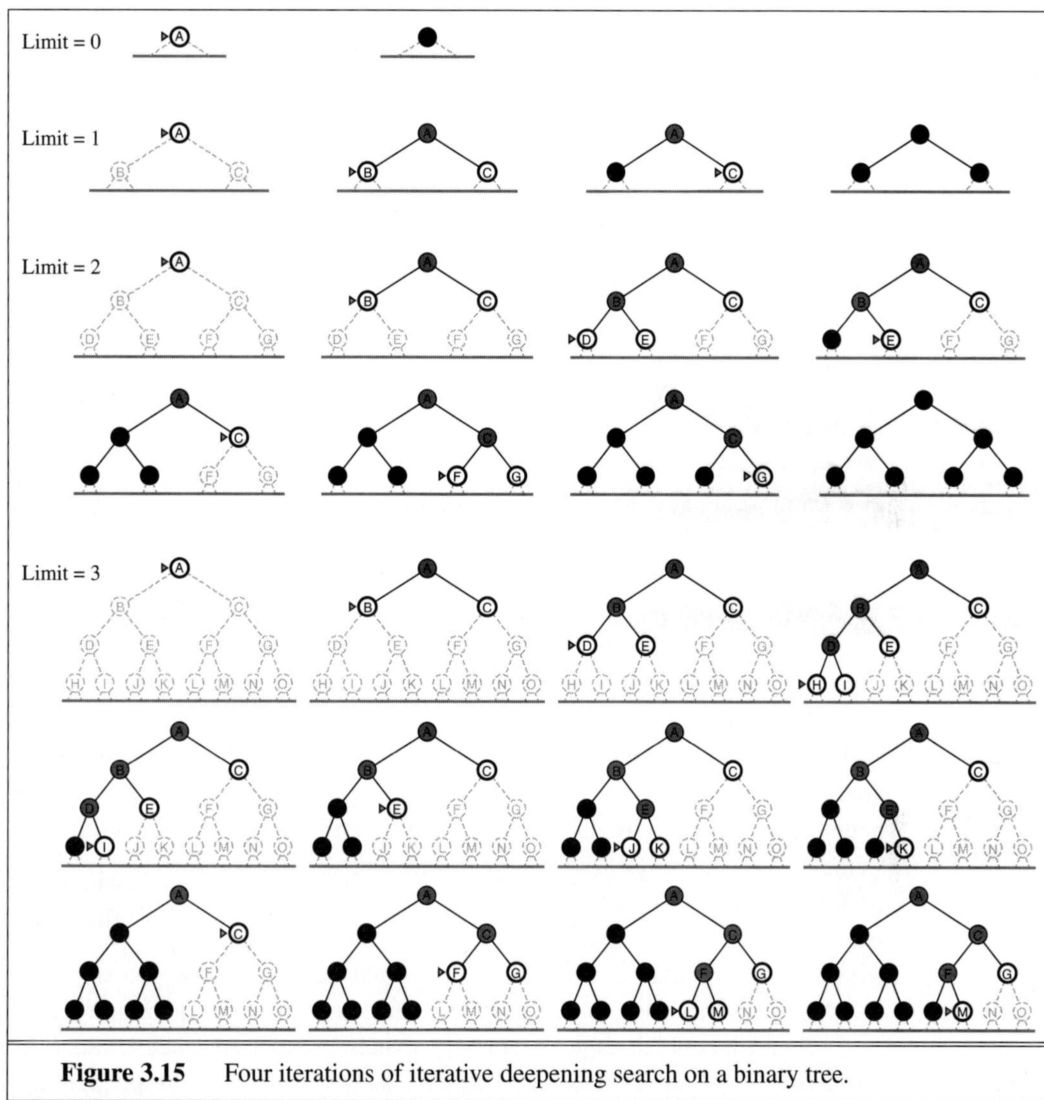


**Figure 3.15** Four iterations of iterative deepening search on a binary tree.

Iterative deepening search is analogous to breadth-first search in that it explores a complete layer of new nodes at each iteration before going on to the next layer. It would seem worthwhile to develop an iterative analog to uniform-cost search, inheriting the latter algorithm's optimality guarantees while avoiding its memory requirements. The idea is to use increasing path-cost limits instead of increasing depth limits. The resulting algorithm, called **iterative lengthening search**, is explored in Exercise 3.11. It turns out, unfortunately, that iterative lengthening incurs substantial overhead compared to uniform-cost search.

ITERATIVE LENGTHENING SEARCH

## Bidirectional search

The idea behind bidirectional search is to run two simultaneous searches—one forward from the initial state and the other backward from the goal, stopping when the two searches meet

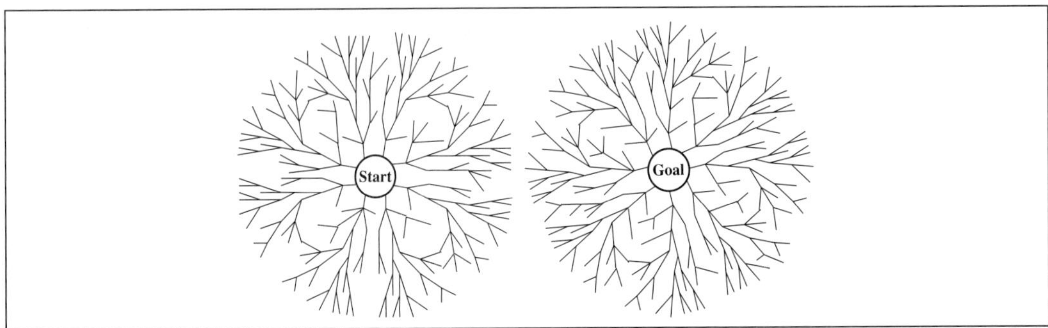


**Figure 3.16** A schematic view of a bidirectional search that is about to succeed, when a branch from the start node meets a branch from the goal node.

in the middle (Figure 3.16). The motivation is that $b^{d/2} + b^{d/2}$ is much less than $b^d$, or in the figure, the area of the two small circles is less than the area of one big circle centered on the start and reaching to the goal.

Bidirectional search is implemented by having one or both of the searches check each node before it is expanded to see if it is in the fringe of the other search tree; if so, a solution has been found. For example, if a problem has solution depth $d = 6$, and each direction runs breadth-first search one node at a time, then in the worst case the two searches meet when each has expanded all but one of the nodes at depth 3. For $b = 10$, this means a total of 22,200 node generations, compared with 11,111,100 for a standard breadth-first search. Checking a node for membership in the other search tree can be done in constant time with a hash table, so the time complexity of bidirectional search is $O(b^{d/2})$. At least one of the search trees must be kept in memory so that the membership check can be done, hence the space complexity is also $O(b^{d/2})$. This space requirement is the most significant weakness of bidirectional search. The algorithm is complete and optimal (for uniform step costs) if both searches are breadth-first; other combinations may sacrifice completeness, optimality, or both.

PREDECESSORS

The reduction in time complexity makes bidirectional search attractive, but how do we search backwards? This is not as easy as it sounds. Let the **predecessors** of a state $x$, $Pred(x)$, be all those states that have $x$ as a successor. Bidirectional search requires that $Pred(x)$ be efficiently computable. The easiest case is when all the actions in the state space are reversible, so that $Pred(x) = Succ(x)$. Other cases may require substantial ingenuity.

Consider the question of what we mean by "the goal" in searching "backward from the goal." For the 8-puzzle and for finding a route in Romania, there is just one goal state, so the backward search is very much like the forward search. If there are several *explicitly listed* goal states—for example, the two dirt-free goal states in Figure 3.3—then we can construct a new dummy goal state whose immediate predecessors are all the actual goal states. Alternatively, some redundant node generations can be avoided by viewing the set of goal states as a single state, each of whose predecessors is also a set of states—specifically, the set of states having a corresponding successor in the set of goal states. (See also Section 3.6.)

The most difficult case for bidirectional search is when the goal test gives only an implicit description of some possibly large set of goal states—for example, all the states satisfying the "checkmate" goal test in chess. A backward search would need to construct compact descriptions of "all states that lead to checkmate by move $m_1$" and so on; and those descriptions would have to be tested against the states generated by the forward search. There is no general way to do this efficiently.

### Comparing uninformed search strategies

Figure 3.17 compares search strategies in terms of the four evaluation criteria set forth in Section 3.4.

| Criterion | Breadth-First | Uniform-Cost | Depth-First | Depth-Limited | Iterative Deepening | Bidirectional (if applicable) |
|---|---|---|---|---|---|---|
| Complete? | Yes$^a$ | Yes$^{a,b}$ | No | No | Yes$^a$ | Yes$^{a,d}$ |
| Time | $O(b^{d+1})$ | $O(b^{1+\lfloor C^*/\epsilon \rfloor})$ | $O(b^m)$ | $O(b^\ell)$ | $O(b^d)$ | $O(b^{d/2})$ |
| Space | $O(b^{d+1})$ | $O(b^{1+\lfloor C^*/\epsilon \rfloor})$ | $O(bm)$ | $O(b\ell)$ | $O(bd)$ | $O(b^{d/2})$ |
| Optimal? | Yes$^c$ | Yes | No | No | Yes$^c$ | Yes$^{c,d}$ |

**Figure 3.17** Evaluation of search strategies. $b$ is the branching factor; $d$ is the depth of the shallowest solution; $m$ is the maximum depth of the search tree; $l$ is the depth limit. Superscript caveats are as follows: $^a$ complete if $b$ is finite; $^b$ complete if step costs $\geq \epsilon$ for positive $\epsilon$; $^c$ optimal if step costs are all identical; $^d$ if both directions use breadth-first search.

## 3.5 AVOIDING REPEATED STATES

Up to this point, we have all but ignored one of the most important complications to the search process: the possibility of wasting time by expanding states that have already been encountered and expanded before. For some problems, this possibility never comes up; the state space is a tree and there is only one path to each state. The efficient formulation of the 8-queens problem (where each new queen is placed in the leftmost empty column) is efficient in large part because of this—each state can be reached only through one path. If we formulate the 8-queens problem so that a queen can be placed in any column, then each state with $n$ queens can be reached by $n!$ different paths.

For some problems, repeated states are unavoidable. This includes all problems where the actions are reversible, such as route-finding problems and sliding-blocks puzzles. The search trees for these problems are infinite, but if we prune some of the repeated states, we can cut the search tree down to finite size, generating only the portion of the tree that spans the state-space graph. Considering just the search tree up to a fixed depth, it is easy to find cases where eliminating repeated states yields an exponential reduction in search cost. In the extreme case, a state space of size $d+1$ (Figure 3.18(a)) becomes a tree with $2^d$ leaves (Figure 3.18(b)). A more realistic example is the **rectangular grid** as illustrated in Figure 3.18(c). On a grid, each state has four successors, so the search tree including repeated

RECTANGULAR GRID

states has $4^d$ leaves; but there are only about $2d^2$ distinct states within $d$ steps of any given state. For $d = 20$, this means about a trillion nodes but only about 800 distinct states.

Repeated states, then, can cause a solvable problem to become unsolvable if the algorithm does not detect them. Detection usually means comparing the node about to be expanded to those that have been expanded already; if a match is found, then the algorithm has discovered two paths to the same state and can discard one of them.

For depth-first search, the only nodes in memory are those on the path from the root to the current node. Comparing those nodes to the current node allows the algorithm to detect looping paths that can be discarded immediately. This is fine for ensuring that finite state spaces do not become infinite search trees because of loops; unfortunately, it does not avoid the exponential proliferation of nonlooping paths in problems such as those in Figure 3.18. The only way to avoid these is to keep more nodes in memory. There is a fundamental tradeoff between space and time. *Algorithms that forget their history are doomed to repeat it.*

If an algorithm remembers every state that it has visited, then it can be viewed as exploring the state-space graph directly. We can modify the general TREE-SEARCH algorithm to include a data structure called the **closed list**, which stores every expanded node. (The fringe of unexpanded nodes is sometimes called the **open list**.) If the current node matches a node on the closed list, it is discarded instead of being expanded. The new algorithm is called GRAPH-SEARCH (Figure 3.19). On problems with many repeated states, GRAPH-SEARCH is much more efficient than TREE-SEARCH. Its worst-case time and space requirements are proportional to the size of the state space. This may be much smaller than $O(b^d)$.

CLOSED LIST

OPEN LIST

Optimality for graph search is a tricky issue. We said earlier that when a repeated state is detected, the algorithm has found two paths to the same state. The GRAPH-SEARCH algorithm in Figure 3.19 always discards the *newly discovered* path; obviously, if the newly discovered path is shorter than the original one, GRAPH-SEARCH could miss an optimal solution. Fortunately, we can show (Exercise 3.12) that this cannot happen when using either

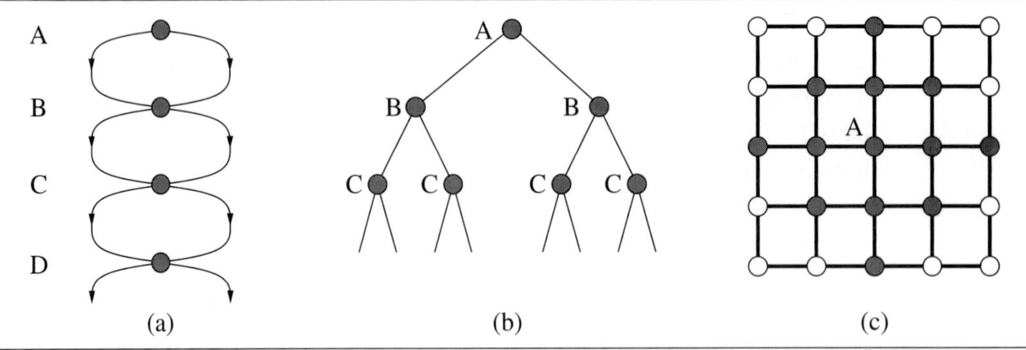


**Figure 3.18** State spaces that generate an exponentially larger search tree. (a) A state space in which there are two possible actions leading from A to B, two from B to C, and so on. The state space contains $d + 1$ states, where $d$ is the maximum depth. (b) The corresponding search tree, which has $2^d$ branches corresponding to the $2^d$ paths through the space. (c) A rectangular grid space. States within 2 steps of the initial state (A) are shown in gray.

```
function GRAPH-SEARCH(problem, fringe) returns a solution, or failure

  closed ← an empty set
  fringe ← INSERT(MAKE-NODE(INITIAL-STATE[problem]), fringe)
  loop do
     if EMPTY?(fringe) then return failure
     node ← REMOVE-FIRST(fringe)
     if GOAL-TEST[problem](STATE[node]) then return SOLUTION(node)
     if STATE[node] is not in closed then
        add STATE[node] to closed
        fringe ← INSERT-ALL(EXPAND(node, problem), fringe)
```

**Figure 3.19** The general graph-search algorithm. The set *closed* can be implemented with a hash table to allow efficient checking for repeated states. This algorithm assumes that the first path to a state $s$ is the cheapest (see text).

uniform-cost search or breadth-first search with constant step costs; hence, these two optimal tree-search strategies are also optimal graph-search strategies. Iterative deepening search, on the other hand, uses depth-first expansion and can easily follow a suboptimal path to a node before finding the optimal one. Hence, iterative deepening graph search needs to check whether a newly discovered path to a node is better than the original one, and if so, it might need to revise the depths and path costs of that node's descendants.

Note that the use of a closed list means that depth-first search and iterative deepening search no longer have linear space requirements. Because the GRAPH-SEARCH algorithm keeps every node in memory, some searches are infeasible because of memory limitations.

## 3.6 SEARCHING WITH PARTIAL INFORMATION

In Section 3.3 we assumed that the environment is fully observable and deterministic and that the agent knows what the effects of each action are. Therefore, the agent can calculate exactly which state results from any sequence of actions and always knows which state it is in. Its percepts provide no new information after each action. What happens when knowledge of the states or actions is incomplete? We find that different types of incompleteness lead to three distinct problem types:

1. **Sensorless problems** (also called **conformant problems**): If the agent has no sensors at all, then (as far as it knows) it could be in one of several possible initial states, and each action might therefore lead to one of several possible successor states.
2. **Contingency problems**: If the environment is partially observable or if actions are uncertain, then the agent's percepts provide *new* information after each action. Each possible percept defines a contingency that must be planned for. A problem is called **adversarial** if the uncertainty is caused by the actions of another agent.

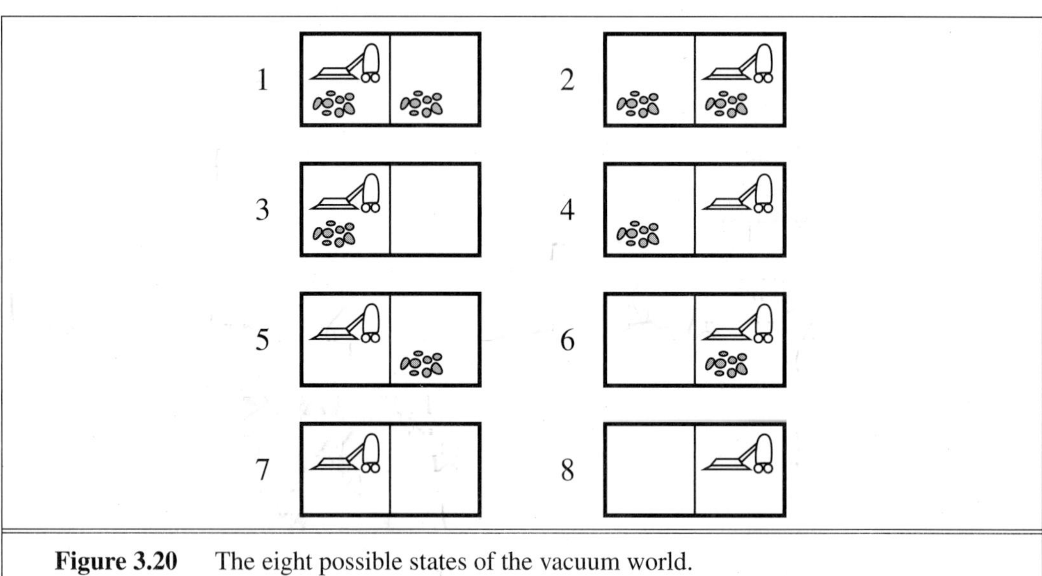


**Figure 3.20** The eight possible states of the vacuum world.

3. **Exploration problems**: When the states and actions of the environment are unknown, the agent must act to discover them. Exploration problems can be viewed as an extreme case of contingency problems.

As an example, we will use the vacuum world environment. Recall that the state space has eight states, as shown in Figure 3.20. There are three actions—*Left*, *Right*, and *Suck*—and the goal is to clean up all the dirt (states 7 and 8). If the environment is observable, deterministic, and completely known, then the problem is trivially solvable by any of the algorithms we have described. For example, if the initial state is 5, then the action sequence [*Right*,*Suck*] will reach a goal state, 8. The remainder of this section deals with the sensorless and contingency versions of the problem. Exploration problems are covered in Section 4.5, adversarial problems in Chapter 6.

## Sensorless problems

Suppose that the vacuum agent knows all the effects of its actions, but has no sensors. Then it knows only that its initial state is one of the set $\{1, 2, 3, 4, 5, 6, 7, 8\}$. One might suppose that the agent's predicament is hopeless, but in fact it can do quite well. Because it knows what its actions do, it can, for example, calculate that the action *Right* will cause it to be in one of the states $\{2, 4, 6, 8\}$, and the action sequence [*Right*,*Suck*] will always end up in one of the states $\{4, 8\}$. Finally, the sequence [*Right*,*Suck*,*Left*,*Suck*] is guaranteed to reach the goal state 7 no matter what the start state. We say that the agent can **coerce** the world into state 7, even when it doesn't know where it started. To summarize: when the world is not fully observable, the agent must reason about *sets* of states that it might get to, rather than single states. We call each such set of states a **belief state**, representing the agent's current belief about the possible physical states it might be in. (In a fully observable environment, each belief state contains one physical state.)

COERCION

BELIEF STATE

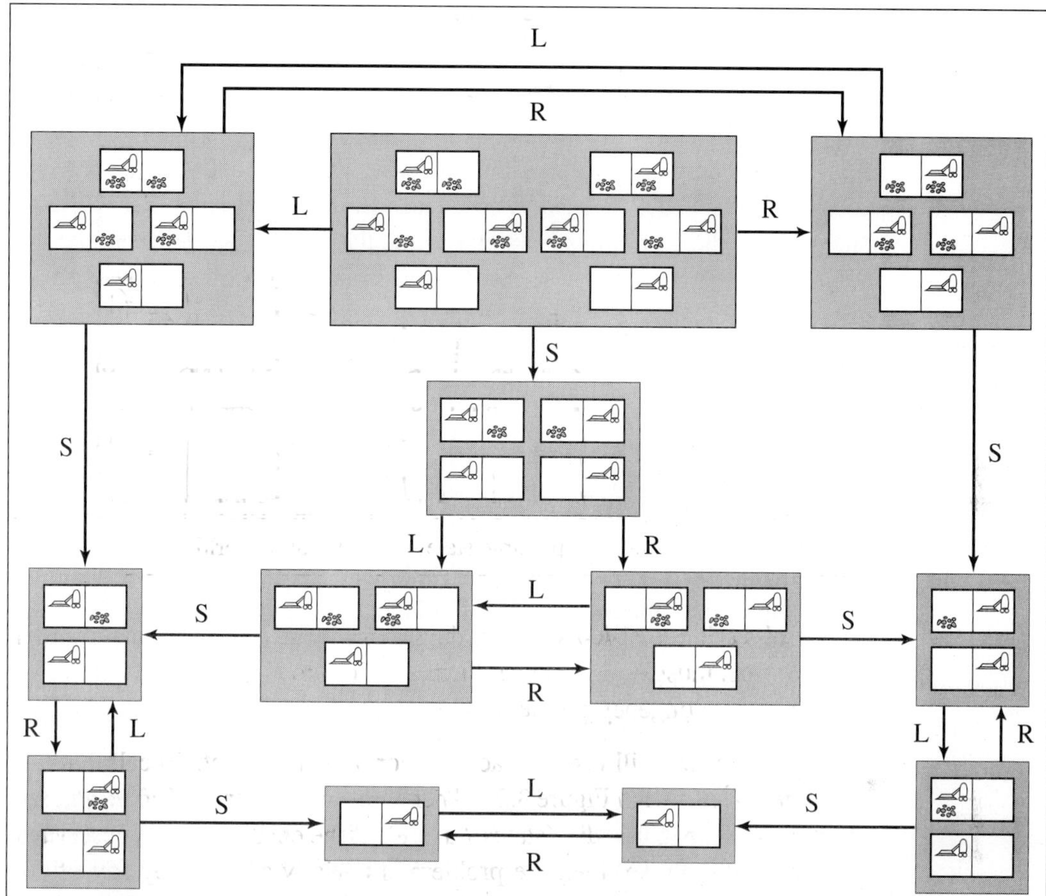


**Figure 3.21** The reachable portion of the belief state space for the deterministic, sensorless vacuum world. Each shaded box corresponds to a single belief state. At any given point, the agent is in a particular belief state but does not know which physical state it is in. The initial belief state (complete ignorance) is the top center box. Actions are represented by labeled arcs. Self-loops are omitted for clarity.

To solve sensorless problems, we search in the space of belief states rather than physical states. The initial state is a belief state, and each action maps from a belief state to another belief state. An action is applied to a belief state by unioning the results of applying the action to each physical state in the belief state. A path now connects several belief states, and a solution is now a path that leads to a belief state, *all of whose members* are goal states. Figure 3.21 shows the reachable belief-state space for the deterministic, sensorless vacuum world. There are only 12 reachable belief states, but the entire belief state space contains every possible set of physical states, i.e., $2^8 = 256$ belief states. In general, if the physical state space has $S$ states, the belief state space has $2^S$ belief states.

Our discussion of sensorless problems so far has assumed deterministic actions, but the analysis is essentially unchanged if the environment is nondeterministic—that is, if actions may have several possible outcomes. The reason is that, in the absence of sensors, the agent has no way to tell which outcome actually occurred, so the various possible outcomes are just additional physical states in the successor belief state. For example, suppose the environment obeys Murphy's Law: the so-called *Suck* action *sometimes* deposits dirt on the carpet *but only if there is no dirt there already*.[6] Then, if $Suck$ is applied in physical state 4 (see Figure 3.20), there are two possible outcomes: states 2 and 4. Applied to the initial belief state, $\{1, 2, 3, 4, 5, 6, 7, 8\}$, $Suck$ now leads to the belief state that is the union of the outcome sets for the eight physical states. Calculating this, we find that the new belief state is $\{1, 2, 3, 4, 5, 6, 7, 8\}$. So, for a sensorless agent in the Murphy's Law world, the $Suck$ action leaves the belief state unchanged! In fact, the problem is unsolvable. (See Exercise 3.18.) Intuitively, the reason is that the agent cannot tell whether the current square is dirty and hence cannot tell whether the $Suck$ action will clean it up or create more dirt.

### Contingency problems

CONTINGENCY PROBLEM

When the environment is such that the agent can obtain new information from its sensors after acting, the agent faces a **contingency problem**. The solution to a contingency problem often takes the form of a *tree*, where each branch may be selected depending on the percepts received up to that point in the tree. For example, suppose that the agent is in the Murphy's Law world and that it has a position sensor and a local dirt sensor, but no sensor capable of detecting dirt in other squares. Thus, the percept $[L, Dirty]$ means that the agent is in one of the states $\{1, 3\}$. The agent might formulate the action sequence [*Suck*, *Right*, *Suck*]. Sucking would change the state to one of $\{5, 7\}$, and moving right would then change the state to one of $\{6, 8\}$. Executing the final *Suck* action in state 6 takes us to state 8, a goal, but executing it in state 8 might take us back to state 6 (by Murphy's Law), in which case the plan fails.

By examining the belief-state space for this version of the problem, it can easily be determined that no fixed action sequence guarantees a solution to this problem. There is, however, a solution if we don't insist on a *fixed* action sequence:

$$[Suck, Right, \textbf{\textit{if}}\ [R,Dirty]\ \textbf{\textit{then}}\ Suck]\ .$$

This extends the space of solutions to include the possibility of selecting actions based on contingencies arising during execution. Many problems in the real, physical world are contingency problems, because exact prediction is impossible. For this reason, many people keep their eyes open while walking around or driving.

Contingency problems *sometimes* allow purely sequential solutions. For example, consider a *fully observable* Murphy's Law world. Contingencies arise if the agent performs a $Suck$ action in a clean square, because dirt might or might not be deposited in the square. As long as the agent never does this, no contingencies arise and there is a sequential solution from every initial state (Exercise 3.18).

The algorithms for contingency problems are more complex than the standard search algorithms in this chapter; they are covered in Chapter 12. Contingency problems also lend themselves to a somewhat different agent design, in which the agent can act *before* it has found a guaranteed plan. This is useful because rather than considering in advance every

[6] We assume that most readers face similar problems and can sympathize with our agent. We apologize to owners of modern, efficient home appliances who cannot take advantage of this pedagogical device.

possible contingency that *might* arise during execution, it is often better to start acting and see which contingencies *do* arise. The agent can then continue to solve the problem, taking into account the additional information. This type of **interleaving** of search and execution is also useful for exploration problems (see Section 4.5) and for game playing (see Chapter 6).

INTERLEAVING

## 3.7 SUMMARY

This chapter has introduced methods that an agent can use to select actions in environments that are deterministic, observable, static, and completely known. In such cases, the agent can construct sequences of actions that achieve its goals; this process is called **search**.

- Before an agent can start searching for solutions, it must formulate a **goal** and then use the goal to formulate a **problem**.
- A problem consists of four parts: the **initial state**, a set of **actions**, a **goal test** function, and a **path cost** function. The environment of the problem is represented by a **state space**. A **path** through the state space from the initial state to a goal state is a **solution**.
- A single, general TREE-SEARCH algorithm can be used to solve any problem; specific variants of the algorithm embody different strategies.
- Search algorithms are judged on the basis of **completeness**, **optimality**, **time complexity**, and **space complexity**. Complexity depends on $b$, the branching factor in the state space, and $d$, the depth of the shallowest solution.
- **Breadth-first search** selects the shallowest unexpanded node in the search tree for expansion. It is complete, optimal for unit step costs, and has time and space complexity of $O(b^{d+1})$. The space complexity makes it impractical in most cases. **Uniform-cost search** is similar to breadth-first search but expands the node with lowest path cost, $g(n)$. It is complete and optimal if the cost of each step exceeds some positive bound $\epsilon$.
- **Depth-first search** selects the deepest unexpanded node in the search tree for expansion. It is neither complete nor optimal, and has time complexity of $O(b^m)$ and space complexity of $O(bm)$, where $m$ is the maximum depth of any path in the state space.
- **Depth-limited search** imposes a fixed depth limit on a depth-first search.
- **Iterative deepening search** calls depth-limited search with increasing limits until a goal is found. It is complete, optimal for unit step costs, and has time complexity of $O(b^d)$ and space complexity of $O(bd)$.
- **Bidirectional search** can enormously reduce time complexity, but it is not always applicable and may require too much space.
- When the state space is a graph rather than a tree, it can pay off to check for repeated states in the search tree. The GRAPH-SEARCH algorithm eliminates all duplicate states.
- When the environment is partially observable, the agent can apply search algorithms in the space of **belief states**, or sets of possible states that the agent might be in. In some cases, a single solution sequence can be constructed; in other cases, the agent needs a **contingency plan** to handle unknown circumstances that may arise.

## Bibliographical and Historical Notes

Most of the state-space search problems analyzed in this chapter have a long history in the literature and are less trivial than they might seem. The missionaries and cannibals problem used in Exercise 3.9 was analyzed in detail by Amarel (1968). It had been considered earlier in AI by Simon and Newell (1961), and in operations research by Bellman and Dreyfus (1962). Studies such as these and Newell and Simon's work on the Logic Theorist (1957) and GPS (1961) led to the establishment of search algorithms as the primary weapons in the armory of 1960s AI researchers and to the establishment of problem solving as the canonical AI task. Unfortunately, very little work was done on the automation of the problem formulation step. A more recent treatment of problem representation and abstraction, including AI programs that themselves perform these tasks (in part), is in Knoblock (1990).

The 8-puzzle is a smaller cousin of the 15-puzzle, which was invented by the famous American game designer Sam Loyd (1959) in the 1870s. The 15-puzzle quickly achieved immense popularity in the United States, comparable to the more recent sensation caused by Rubik's Cube. It also quickly attracted the attention of mathematicians (Johnson and Story, 1879; Tait, 1880). The editors of the *American Journal of Mathematics* stated "The '15' puzzle for the last few weeks has been prominently before the American public, and may safely be said to have engaged the attention of nine out of ten persons of both sexes and all ages and conditions of the community. But this would not have weighed with the editors to induce them to insert articles upon such a subject in the *American Journal of Mathematics*, but for the fact that . . ." (there follows a summary of the mathematical interest of the 15-puzzle). An exhaustive analysis of the 8-puzzle was carried out with computer aid by Schofield (1967). Ratner and Warmuth (1986) showed that the general $n \times n$ version of the 15-puzzle belongs to the class of NP-complete problems.

The 8-queens problem was first published anonymously in the German chess magazine *Schach* in 1848; it was later attributed to one Max Bezzel. It was republished in 1850 and at that time drew the attention of the eminent mathematician Carl Friedrich Gauss, who attempted to enumerate all possible solutions, but found only 72. Nauck published all 92 solutions later in 1850. Netto (1901) generalized the problem to $n$ queens, and Abramson and Yung (1989) found an $O(n)$ algorithm.

Each of the real-world search problems listed in the chapter has been the subject of a good deal of research effort. Methods for selecting optimal airline flights remain proprietary for the most part, but Carl de Marcken (personal communication) has shown that airline ticket pricing and restrictions have become so convoluted that the problem of selecting an optimal flight is formally *undecidable*. The traveling-salesperson problem is a standard combinatorial problem in theoretical computer science (Lawler, 1985; Lawler *et al.*, 1992). Karp (1972) proved the TSP to be NP-hard, but effective heuristic approximation methods were developed (Lin and Kernighan, 1973). Arora (1998) devised a fully polynomial approximation scheme for Euclidean TSPs. VLSI layout methods are surveyed by Shahookar and Mazumder (1991), and many layout optimization papers appear in VLSI journals. Robotic navigation and assembly problems are discussed in Chapter 25.

Uninformed search algorithms for problem solving are a central topic of classical computer science (Horowitz and Sahni, 1978) and operations research (Dreyfus, 1969); Deo and Pang (1984) and Gallo and Pallottino (1988) give more recent surveys. Breadth-first search was formulated for solving mazes by Moore (1959). The method of **dynamic programming** (Bellman and Dreyfus, 1962), which systematically records solutions for all subproblems of increasing lengths, can be seen as a form of breadth-first search on graphs. The two-point shortest-path algorithm of Dijkstra (1959) is the origin of uniform-cost search.

A version of iterative deepening designed to make efficient use of the chess clock was first used by Slate and Atkin (1977) in the CHESS 4.5 game-playing program, but the application to shortest path graph search is due to Korf (1985a). Bidirectional search, which was introduced by Pohl (1969, 1971), can also be very effective in some cases.

Partially observable and nondeterministic environments have not been studied in great depth within the problem-solving approach. Some efficiency issues in belief-state search have been investigated by Genesereth and Nourbakhsh (1993). Koenig and Simmons (1998) studied robot navigation from an unknown initial position, and Erdmann and Mason (1988) studied the problem of robotic manipulation without sensors, using a continuous form of belief-state search. Contingency search has been studied within the planning subfield. (See Chapter 12.) For the most part, planning and acting with uncertain information have been handled using the tools of probability and decision theory (see Chapter 17).

The textbooks by Nilsson (1971, 1980) are good general sources of information about classical search algorithms. A comprehensive and more up-to-date survey can be found in Korf (1988). Papers about new search algorithms—which, remarkably, continue to be discovered—appear in journals such as *Artificial Intelligence*.

## EXERCISES

**3.1** Define in your own words the following terms: state, state space, search tree, search node, goal, action, successor function, and branching factor.

**3.2** Explain why problem formulation must follow goal formulation.

**3.3** Suppose that LEGAL-ACTIONS($s$) denotes the set of actions that are legal in state $s$, and RESULT($a, s$) denotes the state that results from performing a legal action $a$ in state $s$. Define SUCCESSOR-FN in terms of LEGAL-ACTIONS and RESULT, and *vice versa*.

**3.4** Show that the 8-puzzle states are divided into two disjoint sets, such that no state in one set can be transformed into a state in the other set by any number of moves. (*Hint:* See Berlekamp *et al.* (1982).) Devise a procedure that will tell you which class a given state is in, and explain why this is a good thing to have for generating random states.

**3.5** Consider the $n$-queens problem using the "efficient" incremental formulation given on page 67. Explain why the state space size is at least $\sqrt[3]{n!}$ and estimate the largest $n$ for which exhaustive exploration is feasible. (*Hint*: Derive a lower bound on the branching factor by considering the maximum number of squares that a queen can attack in any column.)

**3.6** Does a finite state space always lead to a finite search tree? How about a finite state space that is a tree? Can you be more precise about what types of state spaces always lead to finite search trees? (Adapted from Bender, 1996.)

**3.7** Give the initial state, goal test, successor function, and cost function for each of the following. Choose a formulation that is precise enough to be implemented.

**a.** You have to color a planar map using only four colors, in such a way that no two adjacent regions have the same color.

**b.** A 3-foot-tall monkey is in a room where some bananas are suspended from the 8-foot ceiling. He would like to get the bananas. The room contains two stackable, movable, climbable 3-foot-high crates.

**c.** You have a program that outputs the message "illegal input record" when fed a certain file of input records. You know that processing of each record is independent of the other records. You want to discover what record is illegal.

**d.** You have three jugs, measuring 12 gallons, 8 gallons, and 3 gallons, and a water faucet. You can fill the jugs up or empty them out from one to another or onto the ground. You need to measure out exactly one gallon.

**3.8** Consider a state space where the start state is number 1 and the successor function for state $n$ returns two states, numbers $2n$ and $2n + 1$.

**a.** Draw the portion of the state space for states 1 to 15.

**b.** Suppose the goal state is 11. List the order in which nodes will be visited for breadth-first search, depth-limited search with limit 3, and iterative deepening search.

**c.** Would bidirectional search be appropriate for this problem? If so, describe in detail how it would work.

**d.** What is the branching factor in each direction of the bidirectional search?

**e.** Does the answer to (c) suggest a reformulation of the problem that would allow you to solve the problem of getting from state 1 to a given goal state with almost no search?

**3.9** The **missionaries and cannibals** problem is usually stated as follows. Three missionaries and three cannibals are on one side of a river, along with a boat that can hold one or two people. Find a way to get everyone to the other side, without ever leaving a group of missionaries in one place outnumbered by the cannibals in that place. This problem is famous in AI because it was the subject of the first paper that approached problem formulation from an analytical viewpoint (Amarel, 1968).

**a.** Formulate the problem precisely, making only those distinctions necessary to ensure a valid solution. Draw a diagram of the complete state space.

**b.** Implement and solve the problem optimally using an appropriate search algorithm. Is it a good idea to check for repeated states?

**c.** Why do you think people have a hard time solving this puzzle, given that the state space is so simple?

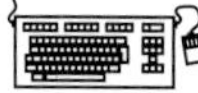

**3.10** Implement two versions of the successor function for the 8-puzzle: one that generates all the successors at once by copying and editing the 8-puzzle data structure, and one that generates one new successor each time it is called and works by modifying the parent state directly (and undoing the modifications as needed). Write versions of iterative deepening depth-first search that use these functions and compare their performance.

**3.11** On page 79, we mentioned **iterative lengthening search**, an iterative analog of uniform cost search. The idea is to use increasing limits on path cost. If a node is generated whose path cost exceeds the current limit, it is immediately discarded. For each new iteration, the limit is set to the lowest path cost of any node discarded in the previous iteration.

**a.** Show that this algorithm is optimal for general path costs.

**b.** Consider a uniform tree with branching factor $b$, solution depth $d$, and unit step costs. How many iterations will iterative lengthening require?

**c.** Now consider step costs drawn from the continuous range $[0, 1]$ with a minimum positive cost $\epsilon$. How many iterations are required in the worst case?

**d.** Implement the algorithm and apply it to instances of the 8-puzzle and traveling salesperson problems. Compare the algorithm's performance to that of uniform-cost search, and comment on your results.

**3.12** Prove that uniform-cost search and breadth-first search with constant step costs are optimal when used with the GRAPH-SEARCH algorithm. Show a state space with varying step costs in which GRAPH-SEARCH using iterative deepening finds a suboptimal solution.

**3.13** Describe a state space in which iterative deepening search performs much worse than depth-first search (for example, $O(n^2)$ vs. $O(n)$).

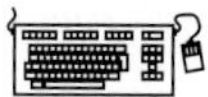

**3.14** Write a program that will take as input two Web page URLs and find a path of links from one to the other. What is an appropriate search strategy? Is bidirectional search a good idea? Could a search engine be used to implement a predecessor function?

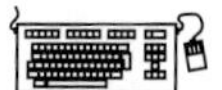

**3.15** Consider the problem of finding the shortest path between two points on a plane that has convex polygonal obstacles as shown in Figure 3.22. This is an idealization of the problem that a robot has to solve to navigate its way around a crowded environment.

**a.** Suppose the state space consists of all positions $(x, y)$ in the plane. How many states are there? How many paths are there to the goal?

**b.** Explain briefly why the shortest path from one polygon vertex to any other in the scene must consist of straight-line segments joining some of the vertices of the polygons. Define a good state space now. How large is this state space?

**c.** Define the necessary functions to implement the search problem, including a successor function that takes a vertex as input and returns the set of vertices that can be reached in a straight line from the given vertex. (Do not forget the neighbors on the same polygon.) Use the straight-line distance for the heuristic function.

**d.** Apply one or more of the algorithms in this chapter to solve a range of problems in the domain, and comment on their performance.

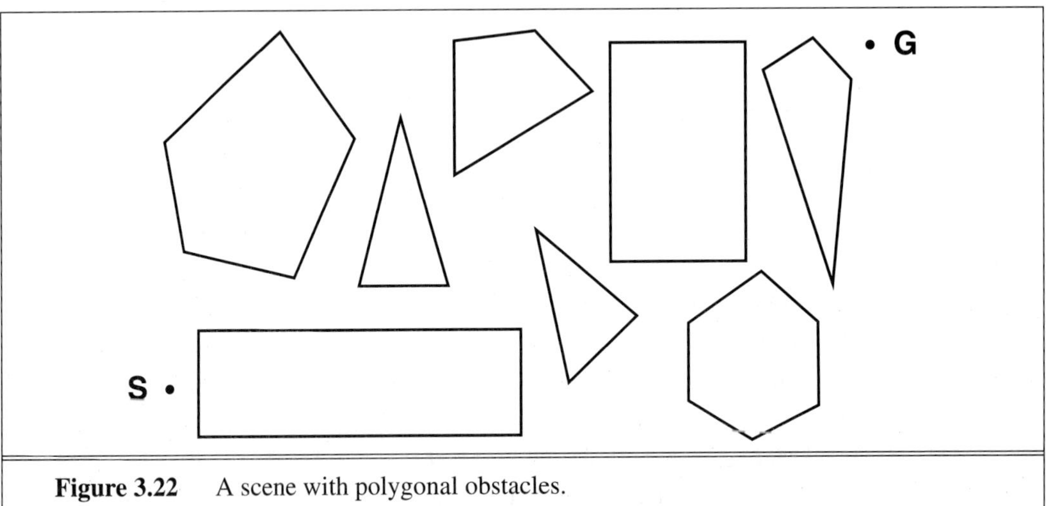


**Figure 3.22** A scene with polygonal obstacles.

**3.16** We can turn the navigation problem in Exercise 3.15 into an environment as follows:

- The percept will be a list of the positions, *relative to the agent*, of the visible vertices. The percept does *not* include the position of the robot! The robot must learn its own position from the map; for now, you can assume that each location has a different "view."
- Each action will be a vector describing a straight-line path to follow. If the path is unobstructed, the action succeeds; otherwise, the robot stops at the point where its path first intersects an obstacle. If the agent returns a zero motion vector and is at the goal (which is fixed and known), then the environment should teleport the agent to a *random location* (not inside an obstacle).
- The performance measure charges the agent 1 point for each unit of distance traversed and awards 1000 points each time the goal is reached.

**a.** Implement this environment and a problem-solving agent for it. The agent will need to formulate a new problem after each teleportation, which will involve discovering its current location.

**b.** Document your agent's performance (by having the agent generate suitable commentary as it moves around) and report its performance over 100 episodes.

**c.** Modify the environment so that 30% of the time the agent ends up at an unintended destination (chosen randomly from the other visible vertices if any, otherwise no move at all). This is a crude model of the motion errors of a real robot. Modify the agent so that when such an error is detected, it finds out where it is and then constructs a plan to get back to where it was and resume the old plan. Remember that sometimes getting back to where it was might also fail! Show an example of the agent successfully overcoming two successive motion errors and still reaching the goal.

**d.** Now try two different recovery schemes after an error: (1) Head for the closest vertex on the original route; and (2) replan a route to the goal from the new location. Compare the performance of the three recovery schemes. Would the inclusion of search costs affect the comparison?

**e.** Now suppose that there are locations from which the view is identical. (For example, suppose the world is a grid with square obstacles.) What kind of problem does the agent now face? What do solutions look like?

**3.17** On page 62, we said that we would not consider problems with negative path costs. In this exercise, we explore this in more depth.

**a.** Suppose that actions can have arbitrarily large negative costs; explain why this possibility would force any optimal algorithm to explore the entire state space.

**b.** Does it help if we insist that step costs must be greater than or equal to some negative constant $c$? Consider both trees and graphs.

**c.** Suppose that there is a set of operators that form a loop, so that executing the set in some order results in no net change to the state. If all of these operators have negative cost, what does this imply about the optimal behavior for an agent in such an environment?

**d.** One can easily imagine operators with high negative cost, even in domains such as route finding. For example, some stretches of road might have such beautiful scenery as to far outweigh the normal costs in terms of time and fuel. Explain, in precise terms, within the context of state-space search, why humans do not drive round scenic loops indefinitely, and explain how to define the state space and operators for route finding so that artificial agents can also avoid looping.

**e.** Can you think of a real domain in which step costs are such as to cause looping?

**3.18** Consider the sensorless, two-location vacuum world under Murphy's Law. Draw the belief state space reachable from the initial belief state $\{1, 2, 3, 4, 5, 6, 7, 8\}$, and explain why the problem is unsolvable. Show also that if the world is fully observable then there is a solution sequence for each possible initial state.

**3.19** Consider the vacuum-world problem defined in Figure 2.2.

**a.** Which of the algorithms defined in this chapter would be appropriate for this problem? Should the algorithm check for repeated states?

**b.** Apply your chosen algorithm to compute an optimal sequence of actions for a $3 \times 3$ world whose initial state has dirt in the three top squares and the agent in the center.

**c.** Construct a search agent for the vacuum world, and evaluate its performance in a set of $3 \times 3$ worlds with probability 0.2 of dirt in each square. Include the search cost as well as path cost in the performance measure, using a reasonable exchange rate.

**d.** Compare your best search agent with a simple randomized reflex agent that sucks if there is dirt and otherwise moves randomly.

**e.** Consider what would happen if the world were enlarged to $n \times n$. How does the performance of the search agent and of the reflex agent vary with $n$?

# 4 INFORMED SEARCH AND EXPLORATION

*In which we see how information about the state space can prevent algorithms from blundering about in the dark.*

Chapter 3 showed that uninformed search strategies can find solutions to problems by systematically generating new states and testing them against the goal. Unfortunately, these strategies are incredibly inefficient in most cases. This chapter shows how an informed search strategy—one that uses problem-specific knowledge—can find solutions more efficiently. Section 4.1 describes informed versions of the algorithms in Chapter 3, and Section 4.2 explains how the necessary problem-specific information can be obtained. Sections 4.3 and 4.4 cover algorithms that perform purely **local search** in the state space, evaluating and modifying one or more current states rather than systematically exploring paths from an initial state. These algorithms are suitable for problems in which the path cost is irrelevant and all that matters is the solution state itself. The family of local-search algorithms includes methods inspired by statistical physics (**simulated annealing**) and evolutionary biology (**genetic algorithms**). Finally, Section 4.5 investigates **online search**, in which the agent is faced with a state space that is completely unknown.

## 4.1 INFORMED (HEURISTIC) SEARCH STRATEGIES

INFORMED SEARCH

This section shows how an **informed search** strategy—one that uses problem-specific knowledge beyond the definition of the problem itself—can find solutions more efficiently than an uninformed strategy.

BEST-FIRST SEARCH

EVALUATION FUNCTION

The general approach we will consider is called **best-first search**. Best-first search is an instance of the general TREE-SEARCH or GRAPH-SEARCH algorithm in which a node is selected for expansion based on an **evaluation function**, $f(n)$. Traditionally, the node with the *lowest* evaluation is selected for expansion, because the evaluation measures distance to the goal. Best-first search can be implemented within our general search framework via a priority queue, a data structure that will maintain the fringe in ascending order of $f$-values.

The name "best-first search" is a venerable but inaccurate one. After all, if we could *really* expand the best node first, it would not be a search at all; it would be a straight march to the goal. All we can do is choose the node that *appears* to be best according to the evaluation function. If the evaluation function is exactly accurate, then this will indeed be the best node; in reality, the evaluation function will sometimes be off, and can lead the search astray. Nevertheless, we will stick with the name "best-first search," because "seemingly-best-first search" is a little awkward.

HEURISTIC FUNCTION

There is a whole family of BEST-FIRST-SEARCH algorithms with different evaluation functions.[1] A key component of these algorithms is a **heuristic function**,[2] denoted $h(n)$:

$$h(n) = \text{ estimated cost of the cheapest path from node } n \text{ to a goal node.}$$

For example, in Romania, one might estimate the cost of the cheapest path from Arad to Bucharest via the straight-line distance from Arad to Bucharest.

Heuristic functions are the most common form in which additional knowledge of the problem is imparted to the search algorithm. We will study heuristics in more depth in Section 4.2. For now, we will consider them to be arbitrary problem-specific functions, with one constraint: if $n$ is a goal node, then $h(n) = 0$. The remainder of this section covers two ways to use heuristic information to guide search.

### Greedy best-first search

GREEDY BEST-FIRST SEARCH

**Greedy best-first search**[3] tries to expand the node that is closest to the goal, on the grounds that this is likely to lead to a solution quickly. Thus, it evaluates nodes by using just the heuristic function: $f(n) = h(n)$.

STRAIGHT-LINE DISTANCE

Let us see how this works for route-finding problems in Romania, using the **straight-line distance** heuristic, which we will call $h_{SLD}$. If the goal is Bucharest, we will need to know the straight-line distances to Bucharest, which are shown in Figure 4.1. For example, $h_{SLD}(In(Arad)) = 366$. Notice that the values of $h_{SLD}$ cannot be computed from the problem description itself. Moreover, it takes a certain amount of experience to know that $h_{SLD}$ is correlated with actual road distances and is, therefore, a useful heuristic.

| | | | |
|---|---|---|---|
| **Arad** | 366 | **Mehadia** | 241 |
| **Bucharest** | 0 | **Neamt** | 234 |
| **Craiova** | 160 | **Oradea** | 380 |
| **Drobeta** | 242 | **Pitesti** | 100 |
| **Eforie** | 161 | **Rimnicu Vilcea** | 193 |
| **Fagaras** | 176 | **Sibiu** | 253 |
| **Giurgiu** | 77 | **Timisoara** | 329 |
| **Hirsova** | 151 | **Urziceni** | 80 |
| **Iasi** | 226 | **Vaslui** | 199 |
| **Lugoj** | 244 | **Zerind** | 374 |

**Figure 4.1** Values of $h_{SLD}$—straight-line distances to Bucharest.

[1] Exercise 4.3 asks you to show that this family includes several familiar uninformed algorithms.

[2] A heuristic function $h(n)$ takes a *node* as input, but it depends only on the *state* at that node.

[3] Our fi rst edition called this **greedy search**; other authors have called it **best-first search**. Our more general usage of the latter term follows Pearl (1984).

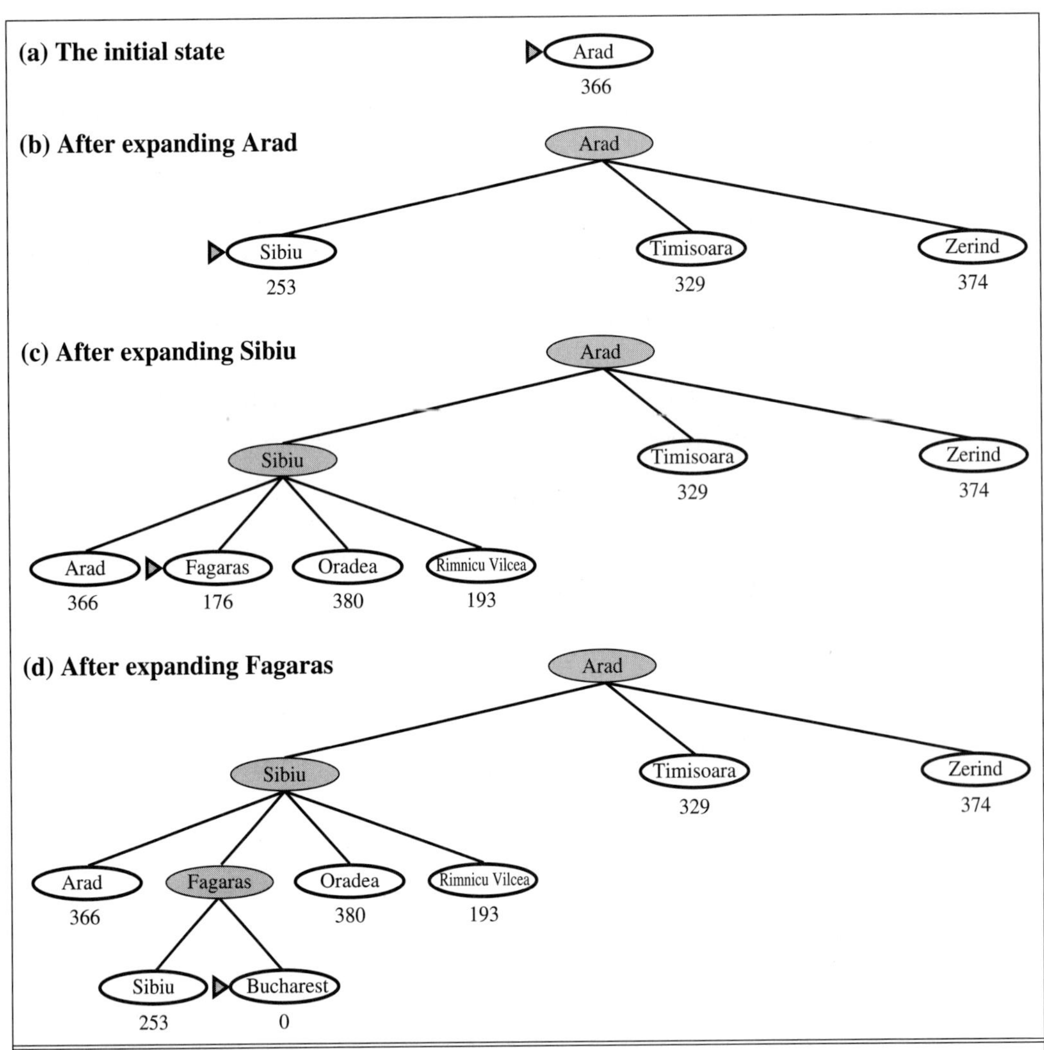


**Figure 4.2** Stages in a greedy best-first search for Bucharest using the straight-line distance heuristic $h_{SLD}$. Nodes are labeled with their $h$-values.

Figure 4.2 shows the progress of a greedy best-first search using $h_{SLD}$ to find a path from Arad to Bucharest. The first node to be expanded from Arad will be Sibiu, because it is closer to Bucharest than either Zerind or Timisoara. The next node to be expanded will be Fagaras, because it is closest. Fagaras in turn generates Bucharest, which is the goal. For this particular problem, greedy best-first search using $h_{SLD}$ finds a solution without ever expanding a node that is not on the solution path; hence, its search cost is minimal. It is not optimal, however: the path via Sibiu and Fagaras to Bucharest is 32 kilometers longer than the path through Rimnicu Vilcea and Pitesti. This shows why the algorithm is called "greedy"—at each step it tries to get as close to the goal as it can.

Minimizing $h(n)$ is susceptible to false starts. Consider the problem of getting from Iasi to Fagaras. The heuristic suggests that Neamt be expanded first, because it is closest to Fagaras, but it is a dead end. The solution is to go first to Vaslui—a step that is actually farther from the goal according to the heuristic—and then to continue to Urziceni, Bucharest, and Fagaras. In this case, then, the heuristic causes unnecessary nodes to be expanded. Furthermore, if we are not careful to detect repeated states, the solution will never be found—the search will oscillate between Neamt and Iasi.

Greedy best-first search resembles depth-first search in the way it prefers to follow a single path all the way to the goal, but will back up when it hits a dead end. It suffers from the same defects as depth-first search—it is not optimal, and it is incomplete (because it can start down an infinite path and never return to try other possibilities). The worst-case time and space complexity is $O(b^m)$, where $m$ is the maximum depth of the search space. With a good heuristic function, however, the complexity can be reduced substantially. The amount of the reduction depends on the particular problem and on the quality of the heuristic.

### A* search: Minimizing the total estimated solution cost

A* SEARCH

The most widely-known form of best-first search is called **A* search** (pronounced "A-star search"). It evaluates nodes by combining $g(n)$, the cost to reach the node, and $h(n)$, the cost to get from the node to the goal:

$$f(n) = g(n) + h(n) .$$

Since $g(n)$ gives the path cost from the start node to node $n$, and $h(n)$ is the estimated cost of the cheapest path from $n$ to the goal, we have

$$f(n) = \text{ estimated cost of the cheapest solution through } n .$$

Thus, if we are trying to find the cheapest solution, a reasonable thing to try first is the node with the lowest value of $g(n) + h(n)$. It turns out that this strategy is more than just reasonable: provided that the heuristic function $h(n)$ satisfies certain conditions, A* search is both complete and optimal.

The optimality of A* is straightforward to analyze if it is used with TREE-SEARCH.

ADMISSIBLE HEURISTIC

In this case, A* is optimal if $h(n)$ is an **admissible heuristic**—that is, provided that $h(n)$ *never overestimates* the cost to reach the goal. Admissible heuristics are by nature optimistic, because they think the cost of solving the problem is less than it actually is. Since $g(n)$ is the exact cost to reach $n$, we have as immediate consequence that $f(n)$ never overestimates the true cost of a solution through $n$.

An obvious example of an admissible heuristic is the straight-line distance $h_{SLD}$ that we used in getting to Bucharest. Straight-line distance is admissible because the shortest path between any two points is a straight line, so the straight line cannot be an overestimate. In Figure 4.3, we show the progress of an A* tree search for Bucharest. The values of $g$ are computed from the step costs in Figure 3.2, and the values of $h_{SLD}$ are given in Figure 4.1. Notice in particular that Bucharest first appears on the fringe at step (e), but it is not selected for expansion because its $f$-cost (450) is higher than that of Pitesti (417). Another way to say this is that there *might* be a solution through Pitesti whose cost is as low as 417, so the algorithm will not settle for a solution that costs 450. From this example, we can extract

a general proof that *A* using* TREE-SEARCH *is optimal if* $h(n)$ *is admissible.* Suppose a

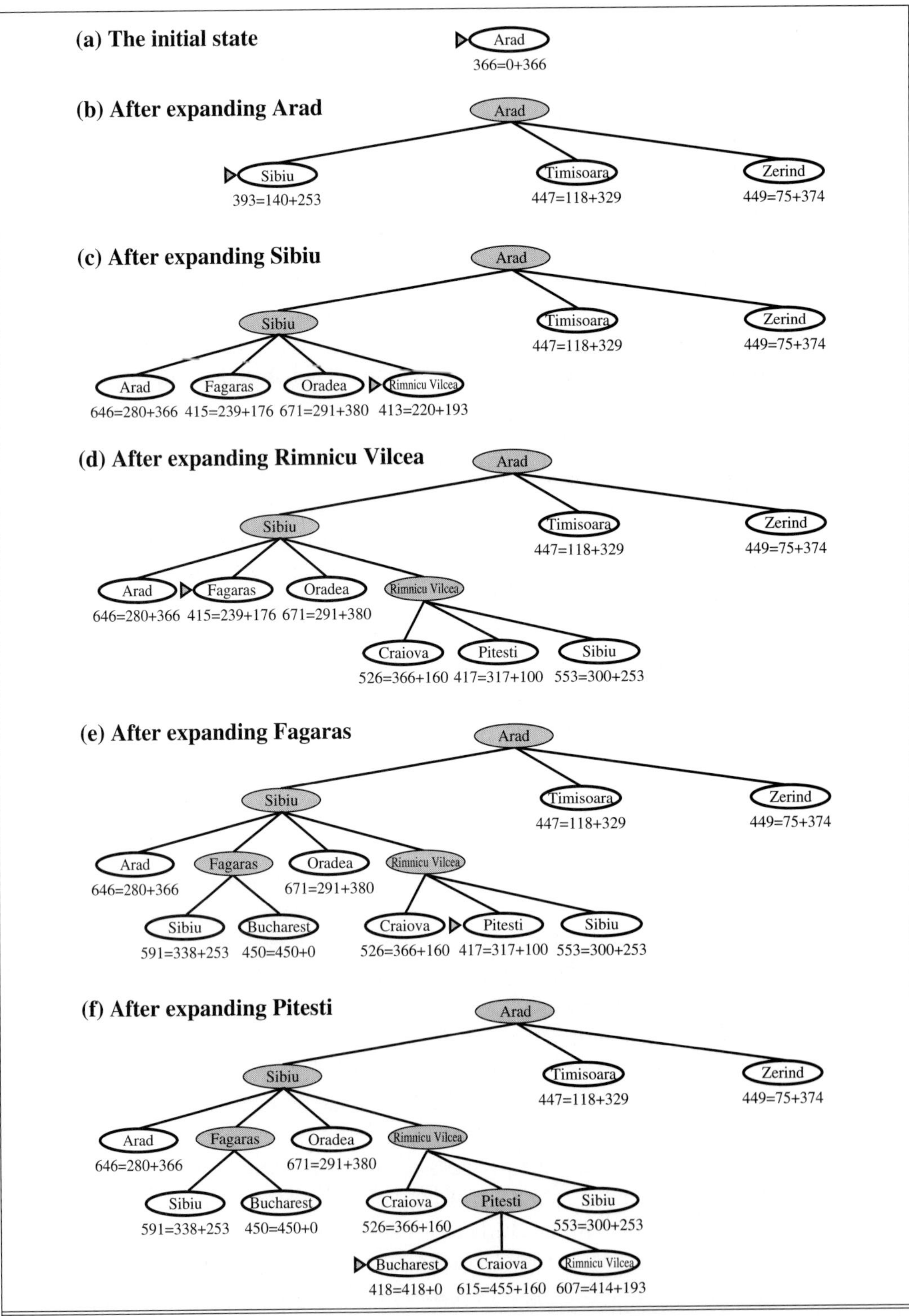


**Figure 4.3** Stages in an A* search for Bucharest. Nodes are labeled with $f = g + h$. The $h$ values are the straight-line distances to Bucharest taken from Figure 4.1.

suboptimal goal node $G_2$ appears on the fringe, and let the cost of the optimal solution be $C^*$. Then, because $G_2$ is suboptimal and because $h(G_2) = 0$ (true for any goal node), we know

$$f(G_2) = g(G_2) + h(G_2) = g(G_2) > C^* .$$

Now consider a fringe node $n$ that is on an optimal solution path—for example, Pitesti in the example of the preceding paragraph. (There must always be such a node if a solution exists.) If $h(n)$ does not overestimate the cost of completing the solution path, then we know that

$$f(n) = g(n) + h(n) \leq C^* .$$

Now we have shown that $f(n) \leq C^* < f(G_2)$, so $G_2$ will not be expanded and A* must return an optimal solution.

If we use the GRAPH-SEARCH algorithm of Figure 3.19 instead of TREE-SEARCH, then this proof breaks down. Suboptimal solutions can be returned because GRAPH-SEARCH can discard the optimal path to a repeated state if it is not the first one generated. (See Exercise 4.4.) There are two ways to fix this problem. The first solution is to extend GRAPH-SEARCH so that it discards the more expensive of any two paths found to the same node. (See the discussion in Section 3.5.) The extra bookkeeping is messy, but it does guarantee optimality. The second solution is to ensure that the optimal path to any repeated state is always the first one followed—as is the case with uniform-cost search. This property holds if we impose an extra requirement on $h(n)$, namely the requirement of **consistency** (also called **monotonicity**). A heuristic $h(n)$ is consistent if, for every node $n$ and every successor $n'$ of $n$ generated by any action $a$, the estimated cost of reaching the goal from $n$ is no greater than the step cost of getting to $n'$ plus the estimated cost of reaching the goal from $n'$:

CONSISTENCY

MONOTONICITY

$$h(n) \leq c(n, a, n') + h(n') .$$

TRIANGLE INEQUALITY

This is a form of the general **triangle inequality**, which stipulates that each side of a triangle cannot be longer than the sum of the other two sides. Here, the triangle is formed by $n$, $n'$, and the goal closest to $n$. It is fairly easy to show (Exercise 4.7) that every consistent heuristic is also admissible. The most important consequence of consistency is the following: *A* using* GRAPH-SEARCH *is optimal if* $h(n)$ *is consistent.*

Although consistency is a stricter requirement than admissibility, one has to work quite hard to concoct heuristics that are admissible but not consistent. All the admissible heuristics we discuss in this chapter are also consistent. Consider, for example, $h_{SLD}$. We know that the general triangle inequality is satisfied when each side is measured by the straight-line distance, and that the straight-line distance between $n$ and $n'$ is no greater than $c(n, a, n')$. Hence, $h_{SLD}$ is a consistent heuristic.

Another important consequence of consistency is the following: *If* $h(n)$ *is consistent, then the values of* $f(n)$ *along any path are nondecreasing.* The proof follows directly from the definition of consistency. Suppose $n'$ is a successor of $n$; then $g(n') = g(n) + c(n, a, n')$ for some $a$, and we have

$$f(n') = g(n') + h(n') = g(n) + c(n, a, n') + h(n') \geq g(n) + h(n) = f(n) .$$

It follows that the sequence of nodes expanded by A* using GRAPH-SEARCH is in nondecreasing order of $f(n)$. Hence, the first goal node selected for expansion must be an optimal solution, since all later nodes will be at least as expensive.

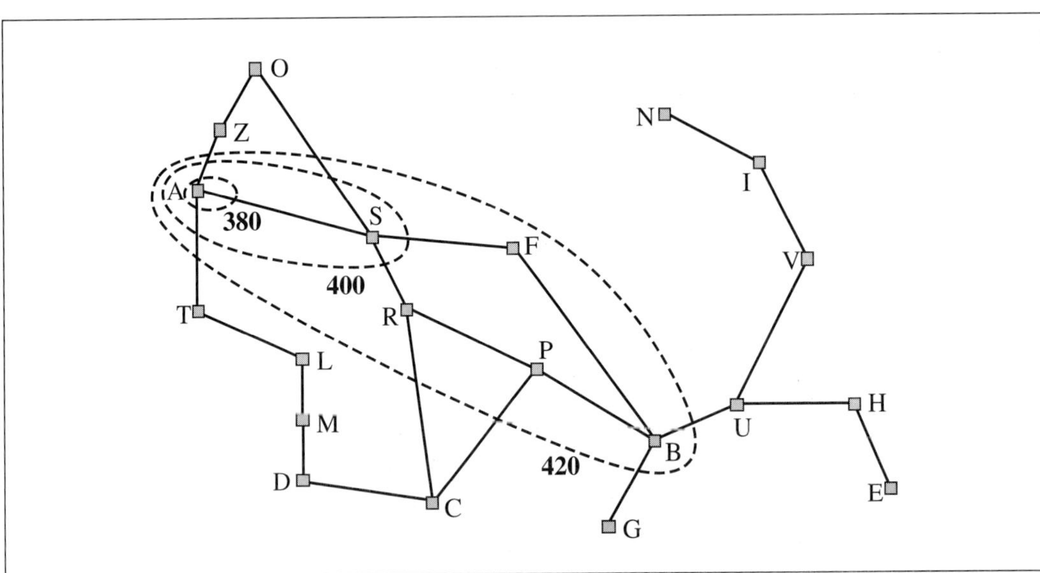


**Figure 4.4** Map of Romania showing contours at $f = 380$, $f = 400$ and $f = 420$, with Arad as the start state. Nodes inside a given contour have $f$-costs less than or equal to the contour value.

CONTOURS

The fact that $f$-costs are nondecreasing along any path also means that we can draw **contours** in the state space, just like the contours in a topographic map. Figure 4.4 shows an example. Inside the contour labeled 400, all nodes have $f(n)$ less than or equal to 400, and so on. Then, because A* expands the fringe node of lowest $f$-cost, we can see that an A* search fans out from the start node, adding nodes in concentric bands of increasing $f$-cost.

With uniform-cost search (A* search using $h(n) = 0$), the bands will be "circular" around the start state. With more accurate heuristics, the bands will stretch toward the goal state and become more narrowly focused around the optimal path. If $C^*$ is the cost of the optimal solution path, then we can say the following:

- A* expands all nodes with $f(n) < C^*$.
- A* might then expand some of the nodes right on the "goal contour" (where $f(n) = C*$) before selecting a goal node.

Intuitively, it is obvious that the first solution found must be an optimal one, because goal nodes in all subsequent contours will have higher $f$-cost, and thus higher $g$-cost (because all goal nodes have $h(n) = 0$). Intuitively, it is also obvious that A* search is complete. As we add bands of increasing $f$, we must eventually reach a band where $f$ is equal to the cost of the path to a goal state.[4]

Notice that A* expands no nodes with $f(n) > C^*$—for example, Timisoara is not expanded in Figure 4.3 even though it is a child of the root. We say that the subtree below Timisoara is **pruned**; because $h_{SLD}$ is admissible, the algorithm can safely ignore this subtree

PRUNING

[4] Completeness requires that there be only finitely many nodes with cost less than or equal to $C^*$, a condition that is true if all step costs exceed some finite $\epsilon$ and if $b$ is finite.

while still guaranteeing optimality. The concept of pruning—eliminating possibilities from consideration without having to examine them—is important for many areas of AI.

OPTIMALLY EFFICIENT

One final observation is that among optimal algorithms of this type—algorithms that extend search paths from the root—A* is **optimally efficient** for any given heuristic function. That is, no other optimal algorithm is guaranteed to expand fewer nodes than A* (except possibly through tie-breaking among nodes with $f(n) = C^*$). This is because any algorithm that *does not* expand all nodes with $f(n) < C^*$ runs the risk of missing the optimal solution.

That A* search is complete, optimal, and optimally efficient among all such algorithms is rather satisfying. Unfortunately, it does not mean that A* is the answer to all our searching needs. The catch is that, for most problems, the number of nodes within the goal contour search space is still exponential in the length of the solution. Although the proof of the result is beyond the scope of this book, it has been shown that exponential growth will occur unless the error in the heuristic function grows no faster than the logarithm of the actual path cost. In mathematical notation, the condition for subexponential growth is that

$$|h(n) - h^*(n)| \leq O(\log h^*(n)) ,$$

where $h^*(n)$ is the *true* cost of getting from $n$ to the goal. For almost all heuristics in practical use, the error is at least proportional to the path cost, and the resulting exponential growth eventually overtakes any computer. For this reason, it is often impractical to insist on finding an optimal solution. One can use variants of A* that find suboptimal solutions quickly, or one can sometimes design heuristics that are more accurate, but not strictly admissible. In any case, the use of a good heuristic still provides enormous savings compared to the use of an uninformed search. In Section 4.2, we will look at the question of designing good heuristics.

Computation time is not, however, A*'s main drawback. Because it keeps all generated nodes in memory (as do all GRAPH-SEARCH algorithms), A* usually runs out of space long before it runs out of time. For this reason, A* is not practical for many large-scale problems. Recently developed algorithms have overcome the space problem without sacrificing optimality or completeness, at a small cost in execution time. These are discussed next.

## Memory-bounded heuristic search

The simplest way to reduce memory requirements for A* is to adapt the idea of iterative deepening to the heuristic search context, resulting in the iterative-deepening A* (IDA*) algorithm. The main difference between IDA* and standard iterative deepening is that the cutoff used is the $f$-cost $(g + h)$ rather than the depth; at each iteration, the cutoff value is the smallest $f$-cost of any node that exceeded the cutoff on the previous iteration. IDA* is practical for many problems with unit step costs and avoids the substantial overhead associated with keeping a sorted queue of nodes. Unfortunately, it suffers from the same difficulties with real-valued costs as does the iterative version of uniform-cost search described in Exercise 3.11. This section briefly examines two more recent memory-bounded algorithms, called RBFS and MA*.

RECURSIVE BEST-FIRST SEARCH

**Recursive best-first search** (RBFS) is a simple recursive algorithm that attempts to mimic the operation of standard best-first search, but using only linear space. The algorithm is shown in Figure 4.5. Its structure is similar to that of a recursive depth-first search, but rather

```
function RECURSIVE-BEST-FIRST-SEARCH(problem) returns a solution, or failure
   RBFS(problem, MAKE-NODE(INITIAL-STATE[problem]), ∞)

function RBFS(problem, node, f_limit) returns a solution, or failure and a new f-cost limit
   if GOAL-TEST[problem](STATE[node]) then return node
   successors ← EXPAND(node, problem)
   if successors is empty then return failure, ∞
   for each s in successors do
      f[s] ← max(g(s) + h(s), f[node])
   repeat
      best ← the lowest f-value node in successors
      if f[best] > f_limit then return failure, f[best]
      alternative ← the second-lowest f-value among successors
      result, f[best] ← RBFS(problem, best, min(f_limit, alternative))
      if result ≠ failure then return result
```

**Figure 4.5** The algorithm for recursive best-first search.

than continuing indefinitely down the current path, it keeps track of the $f$-value of the best alternative path available from any ancestor of the current node. If the current node exceeds this limit, the recursion unwinds back to the alternative path. As the recursion unwinds, RBFS replaces the $f$-value of each node along the path with the best $f$-value of its children. In this way, RBFS remembers the $f$-value of the best leaf in the forgotten subtree and can therefore decide whether it's worth reexpanding the subtree at some later time. Figure 4.6 shows how RBFS reaches Bucharest.

RBFS is somewhat more efficient than IDA*, but still suffers from excessive node regeneration. In the example in Figure 4.6, RBFS first follows the path via Rimnicu Vilcea, then "changes its mind" and tries Fagaras, and then changes its mind back again. These mind changes occur because every time the current best path is extended, there is a good chance that its $f$-value will increase—$h$ is usually less optimistic for nodes closer to the goal. When this happens, particularly in large search spaces, the second-best path might become the best path, so the search has to backtrack to follow it. Each mind change corresponds to an iteration of IDA*, and could require many reexpansions of forgotten nodes to recreate the best path and extend it one more node.

Like A*, RBFS is an optimal algorithm if the heuristic function $h(n)$ is admissible. Its space complexity is linear in the depth of the deepest optimal solution, but its time complexity is rather difficult to characterize: it depends both on the accuracy of the heuristic function and on how often the best path changes as nodes are expanded. Both IDA* and RBFS are subject to the potentially exponential increase in complexity associated with searching on graphs (see Section 3.5), because they cannot check for repeated states other than those on the current path. Thus, they may explore the same state many times.

IDA* and RBFS suffer from using *too little* memory. Between iterations, IDA* retains only a single number: the current $f$-cost limit. RBFS retains more information in memory,

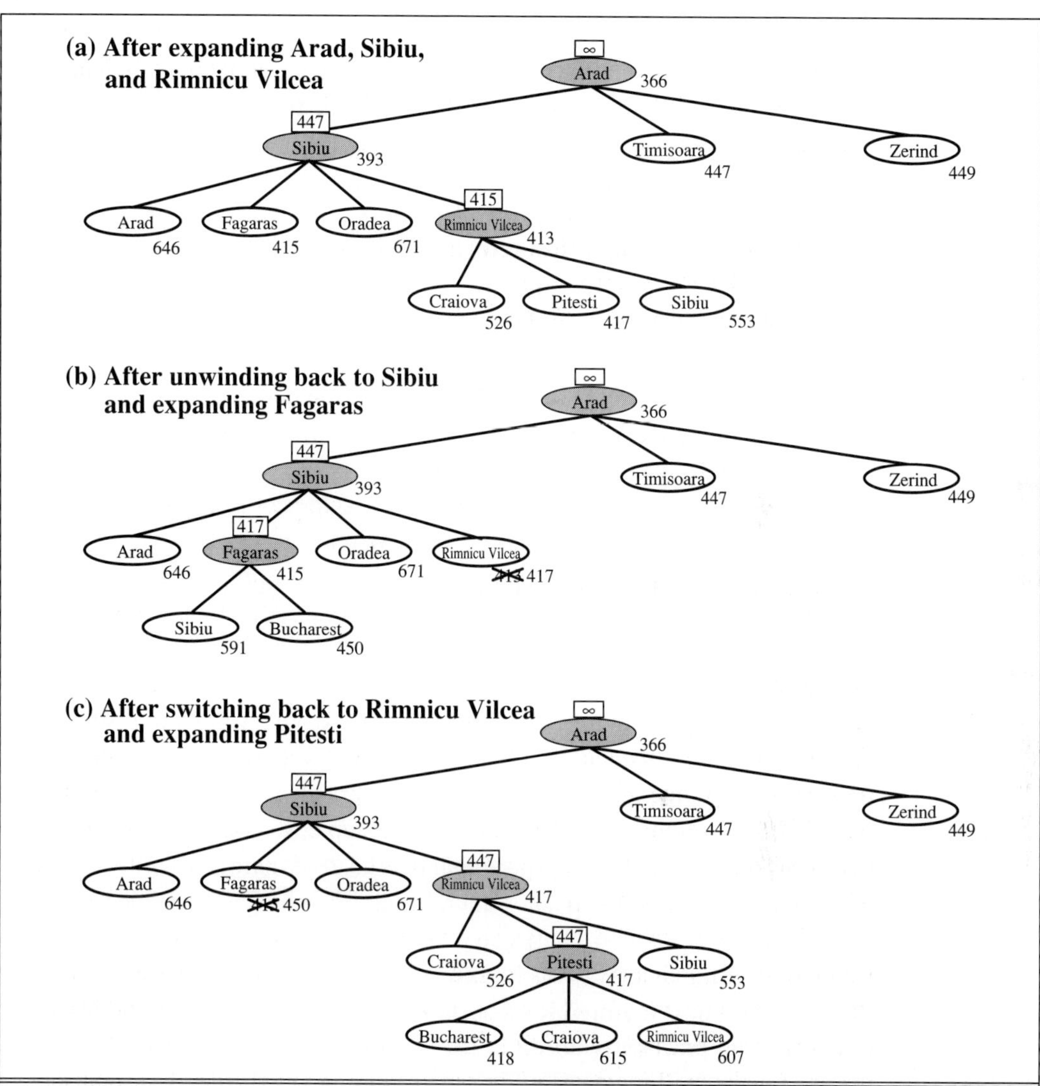


**Figure 4.6** Stages in an RBFS search for the shortest route to Bucharest. The $f$-limit value for each recursive call is shown on top of each current node. (a) The path via Rimnicu Vilcea is followed until the current best leaf (Pitesti) has a value that is worse than the best alternative path (Fagaras). (b) The recursion unwinds and the best leaf value of the forgotten subtree (417) is backed up to Rimnicu Vilcea; then Fagaras is expanded, revealing a best leaf value of 450. (c) The recursion unwinds and the best leaf value of the forgotten subtree (450) is backed up to Fagaras; then Rimnicu Vilcea is expanded. This time, because the best alternative path (through Timisoara) costs at least 447, the expansion continues to Bucharest.

but it uses only linear space: even if more memory were available, RBFS has no way to make use of it.

MA*
SMA*

It seems sensible, therefore, to use all available memory. Two algorithms that do this are **MA*** (memory-bounded A*) and **SMA*** (simplified MA*). We will describe SMA*, which is—well—simpler. SMA* proceeds just like A*, expanding the best leaf until memory is full. At this point, it cannot add a new node to the search tree without dropping an old one. SMA* always drops the *worst* leaf node—the one with the highest $f$-value. Like RBFS, SMA* then backs up the value of the forgotten node to its parent. In this way, the ancestor of a forgotten subtree knows the quality of the best path in that subtree. With this information, SMA* regenerates the subtree only when *all other paths* have been shown to look worse than the path it has forgotten. Another way of saying this is that, if all the descendants of a node $n$ are forgotten, then we will not know which way to go from $n$, but we will still have an idea of how worthwhile it is to go anywhere from $n$.

The complete algorithm is too complicated to reproduce here,[5] but there is one subtlety worth mentioning. We said that SMA* expands the best leaf and deletes the worst leaf. What if *all* the leaf nodes have the same $f$-value? Then the algorithm might select the same node for deletion and expansion. SMA* solves this problem by expanding the *newest* best leaf and deleting the *oldest* worst leaf. These can be the same node only if there is only one leaf; in that case, the current search tree must be a single path from root to leaf that fills all of memory. If the leaf is not a goal node, then *even if it is on an optimal solution path*, that solution is not reachable with the available memory. Therefore, the node can be discarded exactly as if it had no successors.

SMA* is complete if there is any reachable solution—that is, if $d$, the depth of the shallowest goal node, is less than the memory size (expressed in nodes). It is optimal if any optimal solution is reachable; otherwise it returns the best reachable solution. In practical terms, SMA* might well be the best general-purpose algorithm for finding optimal solutions, particularly when the state space is a graph, step costs are not uniform, and node generation is expensive compared to the additional overhead of maintaining the open and closed lists.

On very hard problems, however, it will often be the case that SMA* is forced to switch back and forth continually between a set of candidate solution paths, only a small subset of which can fit in memory. (This resembles the problem of **thrashing** in disk paging systems.) Then the extra time required for repeated regeneration of the same nodes means that problems that would be practically solvable by A*, given unlimited memory, become intractable for SMA*. That is to say, *memory limitations can make a problem intractable from the point of view of computation time.* Although there is no theory to explain the tradeoff between time and memory, it seems that this is an inescapable problem. The only way out is to drop the optimality requirement.

THRASHING

### Learning to search better

We have presented several fixed strategies—breadth-first, greedy best-first, and so on—that have been designed by computer scientists. Could an agent *learn* how to search better? The answer is yes, and the method rests on an important concept called the **metalevel state space**. Each state in a metalevel state space captures the internal (computational) state of a program that is searching in an **object-level state space** such as Romania. For example, the internal state of the A* algorithm consists of the current search tree. Each action in the metalevel state

METALEVEL STATE SPACE

OBJECT-LEVEL STATE SPACE

5 A rough sketch appeared in the first edition of this book.

space is a computation step that alters the internal state; for example, each computation step in A* expands a leaf node and adds its successors to the tree. Thus, Figure 4.3, which shows a sequence of larger and larger search trees, can be seen as depicting a path in the metalevel state space where each state on the path is an object-level search tree.

METALEVEL LEARNING

Now, the path in Figure 4.3 has five steps, including one step, the expansion of Fagaras, that is not especially helpful. For harder problems, there will be many such missteps, and a **metalevel learning** algorithm can learn from these experiences to avoid exploring unpromising subtrees. The techniques used for this kind of learning are described in Chapter 21. The goal of learning is to minimize the **total cost** of problem solving, trading off computational expense and path cost.

## 4.2 HEURISTIC FUNCTIONS

In this section, we will look at heuristics for the 8-puzzle, in order to shed light on the nature of heuristics in general.

The 8-puzzle was one of the earliest heuristic search problems. As mentioned in Section 3.2, the object of the puzzle is to slide the tiles horizontally or vertically into the empty space until the configuration matches the goal configuration (Figure 4.7).

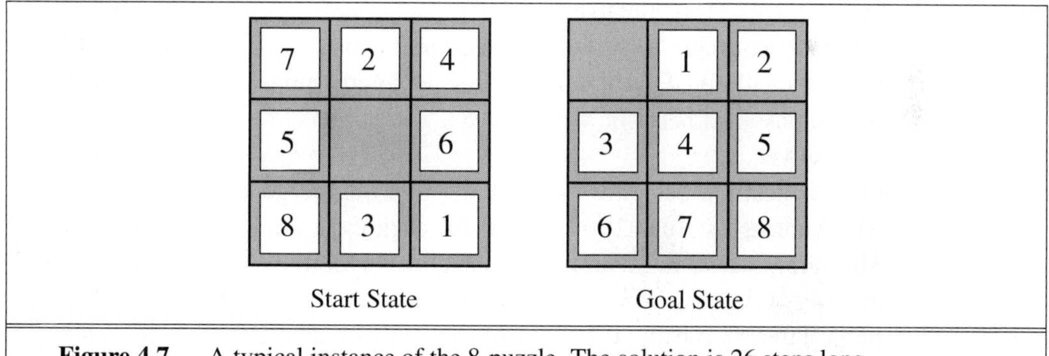


**Figure 4.7** A typical instance of the 8-puzzle. The solution is 26 steps long.

The average solution cost for a randomly generated 8-puzzle instance is about 22 steps. The branching factor is about 3. (When the empty tile is in the middle, there are four possible moves; when it is in a corner there are two; and when it is along an edge there are three.) This means that an exhaustive search to depth 22 would look at about $3^{22} \approx 3.1 \times 10^{10}$ states. By keeping track of repeated states, we could cut this down by a factor of about 170,000, because there are only $9!/2 = 181,440$ distinct states that are reachable. (See Exercise 3.4.) This is a manageable number, but the corresponding number for the 15-puzzle is roughly $10^{13}$, so the next order of business is to find a good heuristic function. If we want to find the shortest solutions by using A*, we need a heuristic function that never overestimates the number of steps to the goal. There is a long history of such heuristics for the 15-puzzle; here are two commonly-used candidates:

- $h_1$ = the number of misplaced tiles. For Figure 4.7, all of the eight tiles are out of position, so the start state would have $h_1 = 8$. $h_1$ is an admissible heuristic, because it is clear that any tile that is out of place must be moved at least once.
- $h_2$ = the sum of the distances of the tiles from their goal positions. Because tiles cannot move along diagonals, the distance we will count is the sum of the horizontal and vertical distances. This is sometimes called the **city block distance** or **Manhattan distance**. $h_2$ is also admissible, because all any move can do is move one tile one step closer to the goal. Tiles 1 to 8 in the start state give a Manhattan distance of

MANHATTAN DISTANCE

$$h_2 = 3 + 1 + 2 + 2 + 2 + 3 + 3 + 2 = 18 .$$

As we would hope, neither of these overestimates the true solution cost, which is 26.

### The effect of heuristic accuracy on performance

EFFECTIVE BRANCHING FACTOR

One way to characterize the quality of a heuristic is the **effective branching factor** $b^*$. If the total number of nodes generated by A* for a particular problem is $N$, and the solution depth is $d$, then $b^*$ is the branching factor that a uniform tree of depth $d$ would have to have in order to contain $N + 1$ nodes. Thus,

$$N + 1 = 1 + b^* + (b^*)^2 + \cdots + (b^*)^d .$$

For example, if A* finds a solution at depth 5 using 52 nodes, then the effective branching factor is 1.92. The effective branching factor can vary across problem instances, but usually it is fairly constant for sufficiently hard problems. Therefore, experimental measurements of $b^*$ on a small set of problems can provide a good guide to the heuristic's overall usefulness. A well-designed heuristic would have a value of $b^*$ close to 1, allowing fairly large problems to be solved.

To test the heuristic functions $h_1$ and $h_2$, we generated 1200 random problems with solution lengths from 2 to 24 (100 for each even number) and solved them with iterative deepening search and with A* tree search using both $h_1$ and $h_2$. Figure 4.8 gives the average number of nodes generated by each strategy and the effective branching factor. The results suggest that $h_2$ is better than $h_1$, and is far better than using iterative deepening search. On our solutions with length 14, A* with $h_2$ is 30,000 times more efficient than uninformed iterative deepening search.

DOMINATION

One might ask whether $h_2$ is *always* better than $h_1$. The answer is yes. It is easy to see from the definitions of the two heuristics that, for any node $n$, $h_2(n) \geq h_1(n)$. We thus say that $h_2$ **dominates** $h_1$. Domination translates directly into efficiency: A* using $h_2$ will never expand more nodes than A* using $h_1$ (except possibly for some nodes with $f(n) = C^*$). The argument is simple. Recall the observation on page 100 that every node with $f(n) < C^*$ will surely be expanded. This is the same as saying that every node with $h(n) < C^* - g(n)$ will surely be expanded. But because $h_2$ is at least as big as $h_1$ for all nodes, every node that is surely expanded by A* search with $h_2$ will also surely be expanded with $h_1$, and $h_1$ might also cause other nodes to be expanded as well. Hence, it is always better to use a heuristic function with higher values, provided it does not overestimate and that the computation time for the heuristic is not too large.

| | Search Cost | | | Effective Branching Factor | | |
|---|---|---|---|---|---|---|
| $d$ | IDS | A*($h_1$) | A*($h_2$) | IDS | A*($h_1$) | A*($h_2$) |
| 2 | 10 | 6 | 6 | 2.45 | 1.79 | 1.79 |
| 4 | 112 | 13 | 12 | 2.87 | 1.48 | 1.45 |
| 6 | 680 | 20 | 18 | 2.73 | 1.34 | 1.30 |
| 8 | 6384 | 39 | 25 | 2.80 | 1.33 | 1.24 |
| 10 | 47127 | 93 | 39 | 2.79 | 1.38 | 1.22 |
| 12 | 3644035 | 227 | 73 | 2.78 | 1.42 | 1.24 |
| 14 | – | 539 | 113 | – | 1.44 | 1.23 |
| 16 | – | 1301 | 211 | – | 1.45 | 1.25 |
| 18 | – | 3056 | 363 | – | 1.46 | 1.26 |
| 20 | – | 7276 | 676 | – | 1.47 | 1.27 |
| 22 | – | 18094 | 1219 | – | 1.48 | 1.28 |
| 24 | – | 39135 | 1641 | – | 1.48 | 1.26 |

**Figure 4.8** Comparison of the search costs and effective branching factors for the ITERATIVE-DEEPENING-SEARCH and A* algorithms with $h_1$, $h_2$. Data are averaged over 100 instances of the 8-puzzle, for various solution lengths.

### Inventing admissible heuristic functions

We have seen that both $h_1$ (misplaced tiles) and $h_2$ (Manhattan distance) are fairly good heuristics for the 8-puzzle and that $h_2$ is better. How might one have come up with $h_2$? Is it possible for a computer to invent such a heuristic mechanically?

$h_1$ and $h_2$ are estimates of the remaining path length for the 8-puzzle, but they are also perfectly accurate path lengths for *simplified* versions of the puzzle. If the rules of the puzzle were changed so that a tile could move anywhere, instead of just to the adjacent empty square, then $h_1$ would give the exact number of steps in the shortest solution. Similarly, if a tile could move one square in any direction, even onto an occupied square, then $h_2$ would give the exact number of steps in the shortest solution. A problem with fewer restrictions on the actions is called a **relaxed problem**. *The cost of an optimal solution to a relaxed problem is an admissible heuristic for the original problem.* The heuristic is admissible because the optimal solution in the original problem is, by definition, also a solution in the relaxed problem and therefore must be at least as expensive as the optimal solution in the relaxed problem. Because the derived heuristic is an exact cost for the relaxed problem, it must obey the triangle inequality and is therefore **consistent** (see page 99).

RELAXED PROBLEM

If a problem definition is written down in a formal language, it is possible to construct relaxed problems automatically.[6] For example, if the 8-puzzle actions are described as

A tile can move from square A to square B if
A is horizontally or vertically adjacent to B **and** B is blank,

[6] In Chapters 8 and 11, we will describe formal languages suitable for this task; with formal descriptions that can be manipulated, the construction of relaxed problems can be automated. For now, we will use English.

we can generate three relaxed problems by removing one or both of the conditions:

(a) A tile can move from square A to square B if A is adjacent to B.
(b) A tile can move from square A to square B if B is blank.
(c) A tile can move from square A to square B.

From (a), we can derive $h_2$ (Manhattan distance). The reasoning is that $h_2$ would be the proper score if we moved each tile in turn to its destination. The heuristic derived from (b) is discussed in Exercise 4.9. From (c), we can derive $h_1$ (misplaced tiles), because it would be the proper score if tiles could move to their intended destination in one step. Notice that it is crucial that the relaxed problems generated by this technique can be solved essentially *without search*, because the relaxed rules allow the problem to be decomposed into eight independent subproblems. If the relaxed problem is hard to solve, then the values of the corresponding heuristic will be expensive to obtain.[7]

A program called ABSOLVER can generate heuristics automatically from problem definitions, using the "relaxed problem" method and various other techniques (Prieditis, 1993). ABSOLVER generated a new heuristic for the 8-puzzle better than any preexisting heuristic and found the first useful heuristic for the famous Rubik's cube puzzle.

One problem with generating new heuristic functions is that one often fails to get one "clearly best" heuristic. If a collection of admissible heuristics $h_1 \ldots h_m$ is available for a problem, and none of them dominates any of the others, which should we choose? As it turns out, we need not make a choice. We can have the best of all worlds, by defining

$$h(n) = \max\{h_1(n), \ldots, h_m(n)\} .$$

This composite heuristic uses whichever function is most accurate on the node in question. Because the component heuristics are admissible, $h$ is admissible; it is also easy to prove that $h$ is consistent. Furthermore, $h$ dominates all of its component heuristics.

SUBPROBLEM

Admissible heuristics can also be derived from the solution cost of a **subproblem** of a given problem. For example, Figure 4.9 shows a subproblem of the 8-puzzle instance in Figure 4.7. The subproblem involves getting tiles 1, 2, 3, 4 into their correct positions. Clearly, the cost of the optimal solution of this subproblem is a lower bound on the cost of the complete problem. It turns out to be substantially more accurate than Manhattan distance in some cases.

PATTERN DATABASES

The idea behind **pattern databases** is to store these exact solution costs for every possible subproblem instance—in our example, every possible configuration of the four tiles and the blank. (Notice that the locations of the other four tiles are irrelevant for the purposes of solving the subproblem, but moves of those tiles do count towards the cost.) Then, we compute an admissible heuristic $h_{DB}$ for each complete state encountered during a search simply by looking up the corresponding subproblem configuration in the database. The database itself is constructed by searching backwards from the goal state and recording the cost of each new pattern encountered; the expense of this search is amortized over many subsequent problem instances.

---

[7] Note that a perfect heuristic can be obtained simply by allowing $h$ to run a full breadth-first search "on the sly." Thus, there is a tradeoff between accuracy and computation time for heuristic functions.

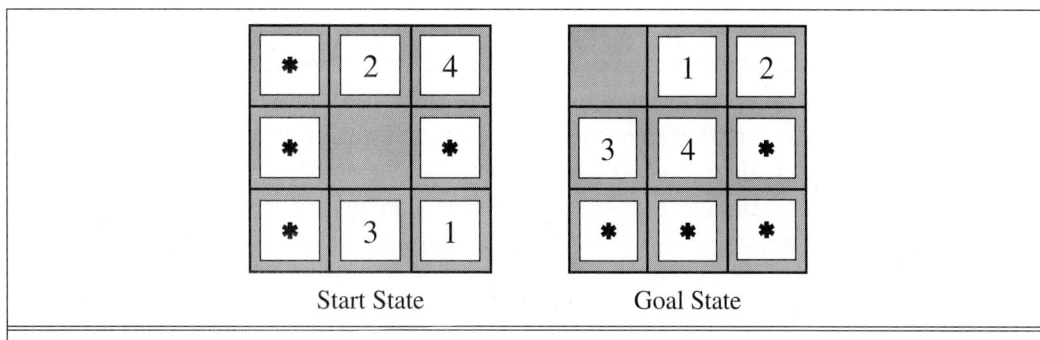


**Figure 4.9** A subproblem of the 8-puzzle instance given in Figure 4.7. The task is to get tiles 1, 2, 3, and 4 into their correct positions, without worrying about what happens to the other tiles.

The choice of 1-2-3-4 is fairly arbitrary; we could also construct databases for 5-6-7-8, and for 2-4-6-8, and so on. Each database yields an admissible heuristic, and these heuristics can be combined, as explained earlier, by taking the maximum value. A combined heuristic of this kind is much more accurate than the Manhattan distance; the number of nodes generated when solving random 15-puzzles can be reduced by a factor of 1000.

One might wonder whether the heuristics obtained from the 1-2-3-4 database and the 5-6-7-8 could be *added*, since the two subproblems seem not to overlap. Would this still give an admissible heuristic? The answer is no, because the solutions of the 1-2-3-4 subproblem and the 5-6-7-8 subproblem for a given state will almost certainly share some moves—it is unlikely that 1-2-3-4 can be moved into place without touching 5-6-7-8, and *vice versa*. But what if we don't count those moves? That is, we record not the total cost of solving the 1-2-3-4 subproblem, but just the number of moves involving 1-2-3-4. Then it is easy to see that the sum of the two costs is still a lower bound on the cost of solving the entire problem. This is the idea behind **disjoint pattern databases**. Using such databases, it is possible to solve random 15-puzzles in a few milliseconds—the number of nodes generated is reduced by a factor of 10,000 compared with using Manhattan distance. For 24-puzzles, a speedup of roughly a million can be obtained.

DISJOINT PATTERN DATABASES

Disjoint pattern databases work for sliding-tile puzzles because the problem can be divided up in such a way that each move affects only one subproblem—because only one tile is moved at a time. For a problem such as Rubik's cube, this kind of subdivision cannot be done because each move affects 8 or 9 of the 26 cubies. Currently, it is not clear how to define disjoint databases for such problems.

### Learning heuristics from experience

A heuristic function $h(n)$ is supposed to estimate the cost of a solution beginning from the state at node $n$. How could an agent construct such a function? One solution was given in the preceding section—namely, to devise relaxed problems for which an optimal solution can be found easily. Another solution is to learn from experience. "Experience" here means solving lots of 8-puzzles, for instance. Each optimal solution to an 8-puzzle problem provides examples from which $h(n)$ can be learned. Each example consists of a state from the solution path and the actual cost of the solution from that point. From these examples, an **inductive learning** algorithm can be used to construct a function $h(n)$ that can (with luck) predict solution costs for other states that arise during search. Techniques for doing just this using neural nets, decision trees, and other methods are demonstrated in Chapter 18. (The reinforcement learning methods described in Chapter 21 are also applicable.)

FEATURES

Inductive learning methods work best when supplied with **features** of a state that are relevant to its evaluation, rather than with just the raw state description. For example, the feature "number of misplaced tiles" might be helpful in predicting the actual distance of a state from the goal. Let's call this feature $x_1(n)$. We could take 100 randomly generated 8-puzzle configurations and gather statistics on their actual solution costs. We might find that when $x_1(n)$ is 5, the average solution cost is around 14, and so on. Given these data, the value of $x_1$ can be used to predict $h(n)$. Of course, we can use several features. A second feature $x_2(n)$ might be "number of pairs of adjacent tiles that are also adjacent in the goal state." How should $x_1(n)$ and $x_2(n)$ be combined to predict $h(n)$? A common approach is to use a linear combination:

$$h(n) = c_1 x_1(n) + c_2 x_2(n) .$$

The constants $c_1$ and $c_2$ are adjusted to give the best fit to the actual data on solution costs. Presumably, $c_1$ should be positive and $c_2$ should be negative.

## 4.3 Local Search Algorithms and Optimization Problems

The search algorithms that we have seen so far are designed to explore search spaces systematically. This systematicity is achieved by keeping one or more paths in memory and by recording which alternatives have been explored at each point along the path and which have not. When a goal is found, the *path* to that goal also constitutes a *solution* to the problem.

In many problems, however, the path to the goal is irrelevant. For example, in the 8-queens problem (see page 66), what matters is the final configuration of queens, not the order in which they are added. This class of problems includes many important applications such as integrated-circuit design, factory-floor layout, job-shop scheduling, automatic programming, telecommunications network optimization, vehicle routing, and portfolio management.

LOCAL SEARCH

CURRENT STATE

If the path to the goal does not matter, we might consider a different class of algorithms, ones that do not worry about paths at all. **Local search** algorithms operate using a single **current state** (rather than multiple paths) and generally move only to neighbors of that state. Typically, the paths followed by the search are not retained. Although local search algorithms are not systematic, they have two key advantages: (1) they use very little memory—usually a constant amount; and (2) they can often find reasonable solutions in large or infinite (continuous) state spaces for which systematic algorithms are unsuitable.

OPTIMIZATION PROBLEMS

OBJECTIVE FUNCTION

In addition to finding goals, local search algorithms are useful for solving pure **optimization problems**, in which the aim is to find the best state according to an **objective function**. Many optimization problems do not fit the "standard" search model introduced in

Chapter 3. For example, nature provides an objective function—reproductive fitness—that Darwinian evolution could be seen as attempting to optimize, but there is no "goal test" and no "path cost" for this problem.

STATE SPACE LANDSCAPE

GLOBAL MINIMUM

GLOBAL MAXIMUM

To understand local search, we will find it very useful to consider the **state space landscape** (as in Figure 4.10). A landscape has both "location" (defined by the state) and "elevation" (defined by the value of the heuristic cost function or objective function). If elevation corresponds to cost, then the aim is to find the lowest valley—a **global minimum**; if elevation corresponds to an objective function, then the aim is to find the highest peak—a **global maximum**. (You can convert from one to the other just by inserting a minus sign.) Local search algorithms explore this landscape. A **complete** local search algorithm always finds a goal if one exists; an **optimal** algorithm always finds a global minimum/maximum.

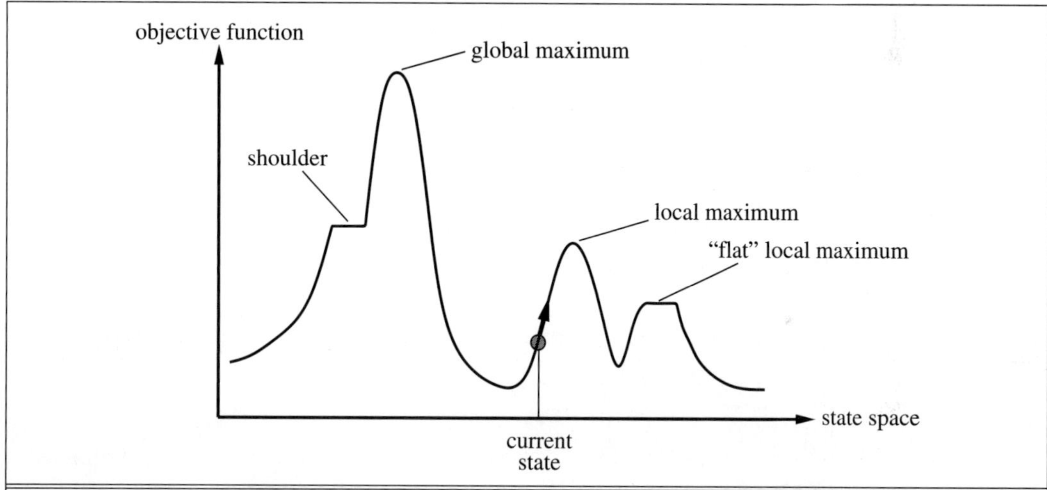


**Figure 4.10** A one-dimensional state space landscape in which elevation corresponds to the objective function. The aim is to find the global maximum. Hill-climbing search modifies the current state to try to improve it, as shown by the arrow. The various topographic features are defined in the text.

## Hill-climbing search

HILL-CLIMBING

The **hill-climbing** search algorithm is shown in Figure 4.11. It is simply a loop that continually moves in the direction of increasing value—that is, uphill. It terminates when it reaches a "peak" where no neighbor has a higher value. The algorithm does not maintain a search tree, so the current node data structure need only record the state and its objective function value. Hill-climbing does not look ahead beyond the immediate neighbors of the current state. This resembles trying to find the top of Mount Everest in a thick fog while suffering from amnesia.

To illustrate hill-climbing, we will use the **8-queens problem** introduced on page 66. Local-search algorithms typically use a **complete-state formulation**, where each state has 8 queens on the board, one per column. The successor function returns all possible states generated by moving a single queen to another square in the same column (so each state has

```
function HILL-CLIMBING(problem) returns a state that is a local maximum
   inputs: problem, a problem
   local variables: current, a node
                    neighbor, a node

   current ← MAKE-NODE(INITIAL-STATE[problem])
   loop do
      neighbor ← a highest-valued successor of current
      if VALUE[neighbor] ≤ VALUE[current] then return STATE[current]
      current ← neighbor
```

**Figure 4.11** The hill-climbing search algorithm (**steepest ascent** version), which is the most basic local search technique. At each step the current node is replaced by the best neighbor; in this version, that means the neighbor with the highest VALUE, but if a heuristic cost estimate $h$ is used, we would find the neighbor with the lowest $h$.

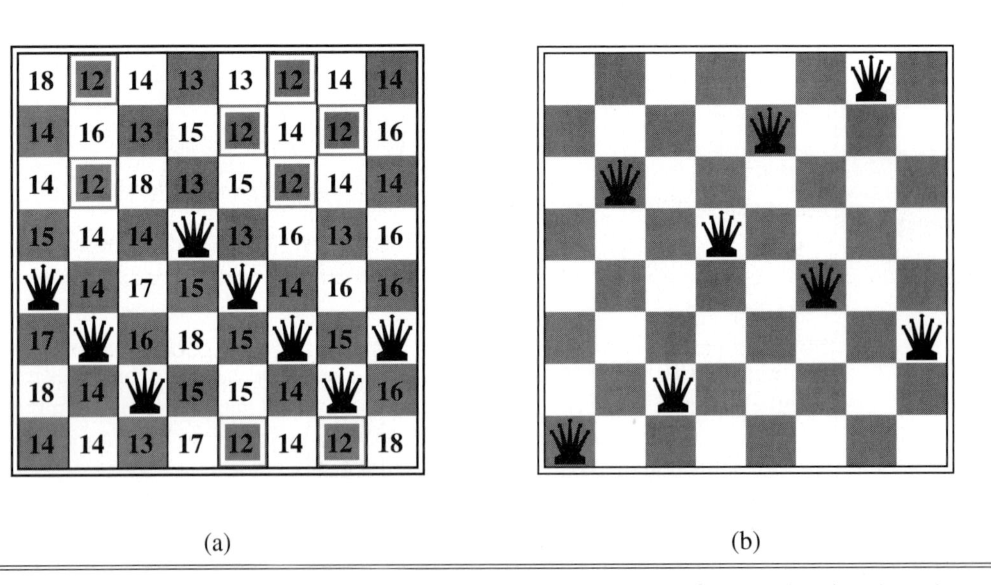


**Figure 4.12** (a) An 8-queens state with heuristic cost estimate $h = 17$, showing the value of $h$ for each possible successor obtained by moving a queen within its column. The best moves are marked. (b) A local minimum in the 8-queens state space; the state has $h = 1$ but every successor has a higher cost.

$8 \times 7 = 56$ successors). The heuristic cost function $h$ is the number of pairs of queens that are attacking each other, either directly or indirectly. The global minimum of this function is zero, which occurs only at perfect solutions. Figure 4.12(a) shows a state with $h = 17$. The figure also shows the values of all its successors, with the best successors having $h = 12$. Hill-climbing algorithms typically choose randomly among the set of best successors, if there is more than one.

GREEDY LOCAL SEARCH

Hill climbing is sometimes called **greedy local search** because it grabs a good neighbor state without thinking ahead about where to go next. Although greed is considered one of the seven deadly sins, it turns out that greedy algorithms often perform quite well. Hill climbing often makes very rapid progress towards a solution, because it is usually quite easy to improve a bad state. For example, from the state in Figure 4.12(a), it takes just five steps to reach the state in Figure 4.12(b), which has $h = 1$ and is very nearly a solution. Unfortunately, hill climbing often gets stuck for the following reasons:

◇ **Local maxima**: a local maximum is a peak that is higher than each of its neighboring states, but lower than the global maximum. Hill-climbing algorithms that reach the vicinity of a local maximum will be drawn upwards towards the peak, but will then be stuck with nowhere else to go. Figure 4.10 illustrates the problem schematically. More concretely, the state in Figure 4.12(b) is in fact a local maximum (i.e., a local minimum for the cost $h$); every move of a single queen makes the situation worse.

◇ **Ridges**: a ridge is shown in Figure 4.13. Ridges result in a sequence of local maxima that is very difficult for greedy algorithms to navigate.

SHOULDER

◇ **Plateaux**: a plateau is an area of the state space landscape where the evaluation function is flat. It can be a flat local maximum, from which no uphill exit exists, or a **shoulder**, from which it is possible to make progress. (See Figure 4.10.) A hill-climbing search might be unable to find its way off the plateau.

In each case, the algorithm reaches a point at which no progress is being made. Starting from a randomly generated 8-queens state, steepest-ascent hill climbing gets stuck 86% of the time, solving only 14% of problem instances. It works quickly, taking just 4 steps on average when it succeeds and 3 when it gets stuck—not bad for a state space with $8^8 \approx 17$ million states.

SIDEWAYS MOVE

The algorithm in Figure 4.11 halts if it reaches a plateau where the best successor has the same value as the current state. Might it not be a good idea to keep going—to allow a **sideways move** in the hope that the plateau is really a shoulder, as shown in Figure 4.10? The answer is usually yes, but we must take care. If we always allow sideways moves when there are no uphill moves, an infinite loop will occur whenever the algorithm reaches a flat local maximum that is not a shoulder. One common solution is to put a limit on the number of consecutive sideways moves allowed. For example, we could allow up to, say, 100 consecutive sideways moves in the 8-queens problem. This raises the percentage of problem instances solved by hill-climbing from 14% to 94%. Success comes at a cost: the algorithm averages roughly 21 steps for each successful instance and 64 for each failure.

STOCHASTIC HILL CLIMBING

FIRST-CHOICE HILL CLIMBING

Many variants of hill-climbing have been invented. **Stochastic hill climbing** chooses at random from among the uphill moves; the probability of selection can vary with the steepness of the uphill move. This usually converges more slowly than steepest ascent, but in some state landscapes it finds better solutions. **First-choice hill climbing** implements stochastic hill climbing by generating successors randomly until one is generated that is better than the current state. This is a good strategy when a state has many (e.g., thousands) of successors. Exercise 4.16 asks you to investigate.

The hill-climbing algorithms described so far are incomplete—they often fail to find a goal when one exists because they can get stuck on local maxima. **Random-restart hill**

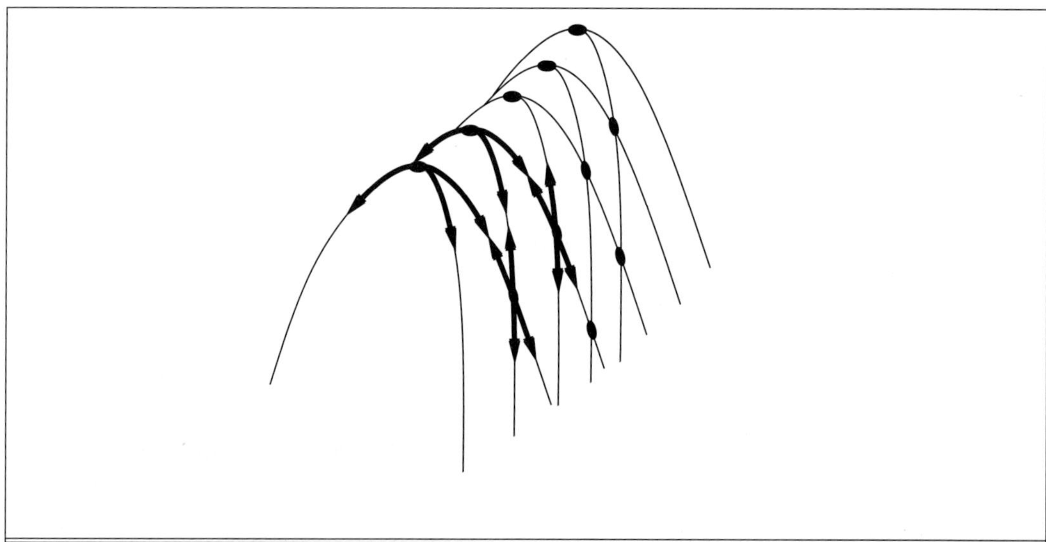

**Figure 4.13** Illustration of why ridges cause difficulties for hill-climbing. The grid of states (dark circles) is superimposed on a ridge rising from left to right, creating a sequence of local maxima that are not directly connected to each other. From each local maximum, all the available actions point downhill.

RANDOM-RESTART HILL CLIMBING

**climbing** adopts the well known adage, "If at first you don't succeed, try, try again." It conducts a series of hill-climbing searches from randomly generated initial states,[8] stopping when a goal is found. It is complete with probability approaching 1, for the trivial reason that it will eventually generate a goal state as the initial state. If each hill-climbing search has a probability $p$ of success, then the expected number of restarts required is $1/p$. For 8-queens instances with no sideways moves allowed, $p \approx 0.14$, so we need roughly 7 iterations to find a goal (6 failures and 1 success). The expected number of steps is the cost of one successful iteration plus $(1-p)/p$ times the cost of failure, or roughly 22 steps. When we allow sideways moves, $1/0.94 \approx 1.06$ iterations are needed on average and $(1 \times 21)+(0.06/0.94) \times 64 \approx 25$ steps. For 8-queens, then, random-restart hill climbing is very effective indeed. Even for three million queens, the approach can find solutions in under a minute.[9]

The success of hill climbing depends very much on the shape of the state-space landscape: if there are few local maxima and plateaux, random-restart hill climbing will find a good solution very quickly. On the other hand, many real problems have a landscape that looks more like a family of porcupines on a flat floor, with miniature porcupines living on the tip of each porcupine needle, *ad infinitum*. NP-hard problems typically have an exponential number of local maxima to get stuck on. Despite this, a reasonably good local maximum can often be found after a small number of restarts.

---

[8] Generating a *random* state from an implicitly specified state space can be a hard problem in itself.

[9] Luby *et al.* (1993) prove that it is best, in some cases, to restart a randomized search algorithm after a particular, fixed amount of time and that this can be *much* more efficient than letting each search continue indefinitely. Disallowing or limiting the number of sideways moves is an example of this.

### Simulated annealing search

A hill-climbing algorithm that *never* makes "downhill" moves towards states with lower value (or higher cost) is guaranteed to be incomplete, because it can get stuck on a local maximum. In contrast, a purely random walk—that is, moving to a successor chosen uniformly at random from the set of successors—is complete, but extremely inefficient. Therefore, it seems reasonable to try to combine hill climbing with a random walk in some way that yields both efficiency and completeness. **Simulated annealing** is such an algorithm. In metallurgy, **annealing** is the process used to temper or harden metals and glass by heating them to a high temperature and then gradually cooling them, thus allowing the material to coalesce into a low-energy crystalline state. To understand simulated annealing, let's switch our point of view from hill climbing to **gradient descent** (i.e., minimizing cost) and imagine the task of getting a ping-pong ball into the deepest crevice in a bumpy surface. If we just let the ball roll, it will come to rest at a local minimum. If we shake the surface, we can bounce the ball out of the local minimum. The trick is to shake just hard enough to bounce the ball out of local minima, but not hard enough to dislodge it from the global minimum. The simulated-annealing solution is to start by shaking hard (i.e., at a high temperature) and then gradually reduce the intensity of the shaking (i.e., lower the temperature).

SIMULATED ANNEALING

GRADIENT DESCENT

The innermost loop of the simulated-annealing algorithm (Figure 4.14) is quite similar to hill climbing. Instead of picking the *best* move, however, it picks a *random* move. If the move improves the situation, it is always accepted. Otherwise, the algorithm accepts the move with some probability less than 1. The probability decreases exponentially with the "badness" of the move—the amount $\Delta E$ by which the evaluation is worsened. The probability also decreases as the "temperature" $T$ goes down: "bad" moves are more likely to be allowed at the start when temperature is high, and they become more unlikely as $T$ decreases. One can prove that if the *schedule* lowers $T$ slowly enough, the algorithm will find a global optimum with probability approaching 1.

Simulated annealing was first used extensively to solve VLSI layout problems in the early 1980s. It has been applied widely to factory scheduling and other large-scale optimization tasks. In Exercise 4.16, you are asked to compare its performance to that of random-restart hill climbing on the $n$-queens puzzle.

### Local beam search

LOCAL BEAM SEARCH

Keeping just one node in memory might seem to be an extreme reaction to the problem of memory limitations. The **local beam search** algorithm[10] keeps track of $k$ states rather than just one. It begins with $k$ randomly generated states. At each step, all the successors of all $k$ states are generated. If any one is a goal, the algorithm halts. Otherwise, it selects the $k$ best successors from the complete list and repeats.

At first sight, a local beam search with $k$ states might seem to be nothing more than running $k$ random restarts in parallel instead of in sequence. In fact, the two algorithms are quite different. In a random-restart search, each search process runs independently of

[10] Local beam search is an adaptation of **beam search**, which is a path-based algorithm.

```
function SIMULATED-ANNEALING(problem, schedule) returns a solution state
  inputs: problem, a problem
          schedule, a mapping from time to "temperature"
  local variables: current, a node
                   next, a node
                   T, a "temperature" controlling the probability of downward steps

  current ← MAKE-NODE(INITIAL-STATE[problem])
  for t ← 1 to ∞ do
     T ← schedule[t]
     if T = 0 then return current
     next ← a randomly selected successor of current
     ΔE ← VALUE[next] – VALUE[current]
     if ΔE > 0 then current ← next
     else current ← next only with probability e^(ΔE/T)
```

**Figure 4.14** The simulated annealing search algorithm, a version of stochastic hill climbing where some downhill moves are allowed. Downhill moves are accepted readily early in the annealing schedule and then less often as time goes on. The *schedule* input determines the value of $T$ as a function of time.

the others. *In a local beam search, useful information is passed among the $k$ parallel search threads.* For example, if one state generates several good successors and the other $k-1$ states all generate bad successors, then the effect is that the first state says to the others, "Come over here, the grass is greener!" The algorithm quickly abandons unfruitful searches and moves its resources to where the most progress is being made.

In its simplest form, local beam search can suffer from a lack of diversity among the $k$ states—they can quickly become concentrated in a small region of the state space, making the search little more than an expensive version of hill climbing. A variant called **stochastic beam search**, analogous to stochastic hill climbing, helps to alleviate this problem. Instead of choosing the best $k$ from the the pool of candidate successors, stochastic beam search chooses $k$ successors at random, with the probability of choosing a given successor being an increasing function of its value. Stochastic beam search bears some resemblance to the process of natural selection, whereby the "successors" (offspring) of a "state" (organism) populate the next generation according to its "value" (fitness).

STOCHASTIC BEAM SEARCH

## Genetic algorithms

GENETIC ALGORITHM

A **genetic algorithm** (or GA) is a variant of stochastic beam search in which successor states are generated by combining *two* parent states, rather than by modifying a single state. The analogy to natural selection is the same as in stochastic beam search, except now we are dealing with sexual rather than asexual reproduction.

Like beam search, GAs begin with a set of $k$ randomly generated states, called the **population**. Each state, or **individual**, is represented as a string over a finite alphabet—most

POPULATION

INDIVIDUAL

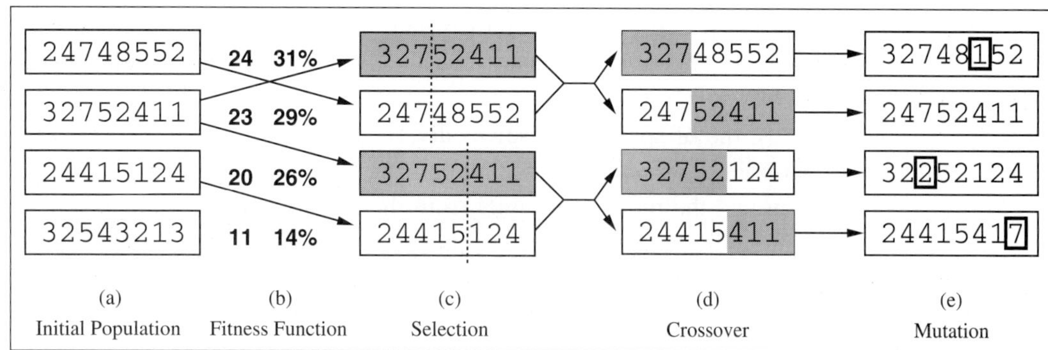


**Figure 4.15** The genetic algorithm. The initial population in (a) is ranked by the fitness function in (b), resulting in pairs for mating in (c). They produce offspring in (d), which are subject to mutation in (e).

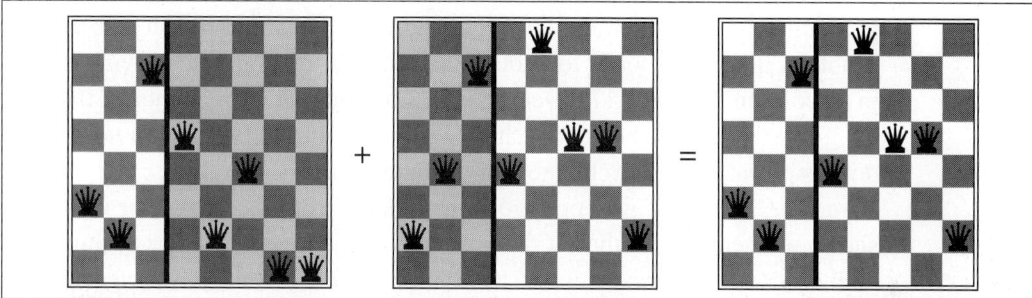


**Figure 4.16** The 8-queens states corresponding to the first two parents in Figure 4.15(c) and the first offspring in Figure 4.15(d). The shaded columns are lost in the crossover step and the unshaded columns are retained.

commonly, a string of 0s and 1s. For example, an 8-queens state must specify the positions of 8 queens, each in a column of 8 squares, and so requires $8 \times \log_2 8 = 24$ bits. Alternatively, the state could be represented as 8 digits, each in the range from 1 to 8. (We will see later that the two encodings behave differently.) Figure 4.15(a) shows a population of four 8-digit strings representing 8-queens states.

FITNESS FUNCTION

The production of the next generation of states is shown in Figure 4.15(b)–(e). In (b), each state is rated by the evaluation function or (in GA terminology) the **fitness function**. A fitness function should return higher values for better states, so, for the 8-queens problem we use the number of *nonattacking* pairs of queens, which has a value of 28 for a solution. The values of the four states are 24, 23, 20, and 11. In this particular variant of the genetic algorithm, the probability of being chosen for reproducing is directly proportional to the fitness score, and the percentages are shown next to the raw scores.

In (c), a random choice of two pairs is selected for reproduction, in accordance with the probabilities in (b). Notice that one individual is selected twice and one not at all.[11] For each

[11] There are many variants of this selection rule. The method of **culling**, in which all individuals below a given threshold are discarded, can be shown to converge faster than the random version (Baum *et al.*, 1995).

CROSSOVER

pair to be mated, a **crossover** point is randomly chosen from the positions in the string. In Figure 4.15 the crossover points are after the third digit in the first pair and after the fifth digit in the second pair.[12]

In (d), the offspring themselves are created by crossing over the parent strings at the crossover point. For example, the first child of the first pair gets the first three digits from the first parent and the remaining digits from the second parent, whereas the second child gets the first three digits from the second parent and the rest from the first parent. The 8-queens states involved in this reproduction step are shown in Figure 4.16. The example illustrates the fact that, when two parent states are quite different, the crossover operation can produce a state that is a long way from either parent state. It is often the case that the population is quite diverse early on in the process, so crossover (like simulated annealing) frequently takes large steps in the state space early in the search process and smaller steps later on when most individuals are quite similar.

MUTATION

Finally, in (e), each location is subject to random **mutation** with a small independent probability. One digit was mutated in the first, third, and fourth offspring. In the 8-queens problem, this corresponds to choosing a queen at random and moving it to a random square in its column. Figure 4.17 describes an algorithm that implements all these steps.

Like stochastic beam search, genetic algorithms combine an uphill tendency with random exploration and exchange of information among parallel search threads. The primary advantage, if any, of genetic algorithms comes from the crossover operation. Yet it can be shown mathematically that, if the positions of the genetic code is permuted initially in a random order, crossover conveys no advantage. Intuitively, the advantage comes from the ability of crossover to combine large blocks of letters that have evolved independently to perform useful functions, thus raising the level of granularity at which the search operates. For example, it could be that putting the first three queens in positions 2, 4, and 6 (where they do not attack each other) constitutes a useful block that can be combined with other blocks to construct a solution.

SCHEMA

The theory of genetic algorithms explains how this works using the idea of a **schema**, which is a substring in which some of the positions can be left unspecified. For example, the schema 246***** describes all 8-queens states in which the first three queens are in positions 2, 4, and 6 respectively. Strings that match the schema (such as 24613578) are called **instances** of the schema. It can be shown that, if the average fitness of the instances of a schema is above the mean, then the number of instances of the schema within the population will grow over time. Clearly, this effect is unlikely to be significant if adjacent bits are totally unrelated to each other, because then there will be few contiguous blocks that provide a consistent benefit. Genetic algorithms work best when schemas correspond to meaningful components of a solution. For example, if the string is a representation of an antenna, then the schemas may represent components of the antenna, such as reflectors and deflectors. A good component is likely to be good in a variety of different designs. This suggests that successful use of genetic algorithms requires careful engineering of the representation.

[12] It is here that the encoding matters. If a 24-bit encoding is used instead of 8 digits, then the crossover point has a 2/3 chance of being in the middle of a digit, which results in an essentially arbitrary mutation of that digit.

```
function GENETIC-ALGORITHM(population, FITNESS-FN) returns an individual
  inputs: population, a set of individuals
          FITNESS-FN, a function that measures the fitness of an individual

  repeat
     new_population ← empty set
     loop for i from 1 to SIZE(population) do
        x ← RANDOM-SELECTION(population, FITNESS-FN)
        y ← RANDOM-SELECTION(population, FITNESS-FN)
        child ← REPRODUCE(x, y)
        if (small random probability) then child ← MUTATE(child)
        add child to new_population
     population ← new_population
  until some individual is fit enough, or enough time has elapsed
  return the best individual in population, according to FITNESS-FN
```

```
function REPRODUCE(x, y) returns an individual
  inputs: x, y, parent individuals

  n ← LENGTH(x)
  c ← random number from 1 to n
  return APPEND(SUBSTRING(x, 1, c), SUBSTRING(y, c + 1, n))
```

**Figure 4.17** A genetic algorithm. The algorithm is the same as the one diagrammed in Figure 4.15, with one variation: in this more popular version, each mating of two parents produces only one offspring, not two.

In practice, genetic algorithms have had a widespread impact on optimization problems, such as circuit layout and job-shop scheduling. At present, it is not clear whether the appeal of genetic algorithms arises from their performance or from their æsthetically pleasing origins in the theory of evolution. Much work remains to be done to identify the conditions under which genetic algorithms perform well.

## 4.4 LOCAL SEARCH IN CONTINUOUS SPACES

In Chapter 2, we explained the distinction between discrete and continuous environments, pointing out that most real-world environments are continuous. Yet none of the algorithms we have described can handle continuous state spaces—the successor function would in most cases return infinitely many states! This section provides a *very brief* introduction to some local search techniques for finding optimal solutions in continuous spaces. The literature on this topic is vast; many of the basic techniques originated in the 17th century, after the development of calculus by Newton and Leibniz.[13] We will find uses for these techniques at

[13] A basic knowledge of multivariate calculus and vector arithmetic is useful when one is reading this section.

### EVOLUTION AND SEARCH

The theory of **evolution** was developed in Charles Darwin's *On the Origin of Species by Means of Natural Selection* (1859). The central idea is simple: variations (known as **mutations**) occur in reproduction and will be preserved in successive generations approximately in proportion to their effect on reproductive fitness.

Darwin's theory was developed with no knowledge of how the traits of organisms can be inherited and modified. The probabilistic laws governing these processes were first identified by Gregor Mendel (1866), a monk who experimented with sweet peas using what he called artificial fertilization. Much later, Watson and Crick (1953) identified the structure of the DNA molecule and its alphabet, AGTC (adenine, guanine, thymine, cytosine). In the standard model, variation occurs both by point mutations in the letter sequence and by "crossover" (in which the DNA of an offspring is generated by combining long sections of DNA from each parent).

The analogy to local search algorithms has already been described; the principal difference between stochastic beam search and evolution is the use of *sexual* reproduction, wherein successors are generated from *multiple* organisms rather than just one. The actual mechanisms of evolution are, however, far richer than most genetic algorithms allow. For example, mutations can involve reversals, duplications, and movement of large chunks of DNA; some viruses borrow DNA from one organism and insert it in another; and there are transposable genes that do nothing but copy themselves many thousands of times within the genome. There are even genes that poison cells from potential mates that do not carry the gene, thereby increasing their chances of replication. Most important is the fact that the *genes themselves encode the mechanisms* whereby the genome is reproduced and translated into an organism. In genetic algorithms, those mechanisms are a separate program that is not represented within the strings being manipulated.

Darwinian evolution might well seem to be an inefficient mechanism, having generated blindly some $10^{45}$ or so organisms without improving its search heuristics one iota. Fifty years before Darwin, however, the otherwise great French naturalist Jean Lamarck (1809) proposed a theory of evolution whereby traits *acquired by adaptation during an organism's lifetime* would be passed on to its offspring. Such a process would be effective, but does not seem to occur in nature. Much later, James Baldwin (1896) proposed a superficially similar theory: that behavior learned during an organism's lifetime could accelerate the rate of evolution. Unlike Lamarck's, Baldwin's theory is entirely consistent with Darwinian evolution, because it relies on selection pressures operating on individuals that have found local optima among the set of possible behaviors allowed by their genetic makeup. Modern computer simulations confirm that the "Baldwin effect" is real, provided that "ordinary" evolution can create organisms whose internal performance measure is somehow correlated with actual fitness.

several places in the book, including the chapters on learning, vision, and robotics. In short, anything that deals with the real world.

Let us begin with an example. Suppose we want to place three new airports anywhere in Romania, such that the sum of squared distances from each city on the map (Figure 3.2) to its nearest airport is minimized. Then the state space is defined by the coordinates of the airports: $(x_1, y_1)$, $(x_2, y_2)$, and $(x_3, y_3)$. This is a *six-dimensional* space; we also say that states are defined by six **variables**. (In general, states are defined by an $n$-dimensional vector of variables, $\mathbf{x}$.) Moving around in this space corresponds to moving one or more of the airports on the map. The objective function $f(x_1, y_1, x_2, y_2, x_3, y_3)$ is relatively easy to compute for any particular state once we compute the closest cities, but rather tricky to write down in general.

One way to avoid continuous problems is simply to **discretize** the neighborhood of each state. For example, we can move only one airport at a time in either the $x$ or $y$ direction by a fixed amount $\pm\delta$. With 6 variables, this gives 12 possible successors for each state. We can then apply any of the local search algorithms described previously. One can also apply stochastic hill climbing and simulated annealing directly, without discretizing the space. These algorithms choose successors randomly, which can be done by generating random vectors of length $\delta$.

GRADIENT

There are many methods that attempt to use the **gradient** of the landscape to find a maximum. The gradient of the objective function is a vector $\nabla f$ that gives the magnitude and direction of the steepest slope. For our problem, we have

$$\nabla f = \left( \frac{\partial f}{\partial x_1}, \frac{\partial f}{\partial y_1}, \frac{\partial f}{\partial x_2}, \frac{\partial f}{\partial y_2}, \frac{\partial f}{\partial x_3}, \frac{\partial f}{\partial y_3} \right) .$$

In some cases, we can find a maximum by solving the equation $\nabla f = 0$. (This could be done, for example, if we were placing just one airport; the solution is the arithmetic mean of all the cities' coordinates.) In many cases, however, this equation cannot be solved in closed form. For example, with three airports, the expression for the gradient depends on what cities are closest to each airport in the current state. This means we can compute the gradient *locally* but not *globally*. Even so, we can still perform steepest-ascent hill climbing by updating the current state via the formula

$$\mathbf{x} \leftarrow \mathbf{x} + \alpha \nabla f(\mathbf{x}) ,$$

where $\alpha$ is a small constant. In other cases, the objective function might not be available in a differentiable form at all—for example, the value of a particular set of airport locations may be determined by running some large-scale economic simulation package. In those cases, a so-called **empirical gradient** can be determined by evaluating the response to small increments and decrements in each coordinate. Empirical gradient search is the same as steepest-ascent hill climbing in a discretized version of the state space.

EMPIRICAL GRADIENT

Hidden beneath the phrase "$\alpha$ is a small constant" lies a huge variety of methods for adjusting $\alpha$. The basic problem is that, if $\alpha$ is too small, too many steps are needed; if $\alpha$ is too large, the search could overshoot the maximum. The technique of **line search** tries to overcome this dilemma by extending the current gradient direction—usually by repeatedly doubling $\alpha$—until $f$ starts to decrease again. The point at which this occurs becomes the new

LINE SEARCH

current state. There are several schools of thought about how the new direction should be chosen at this point.

NEWTON–RAPHSON

For many problems, the most effective algorithm is the venerable **Newton–Raphson** method (Newton, 1671; Raphson, 1690). This is a general technique for finding roots of functions—that is, solving equations of the form $g(x)=0$. It works by computing a new estimate for the root $x$ according to Newton's formula

$$x \leftarrow x - g(x)/g'(x) .$$

To find a maximum or minimum of $f$, we need to find $\mathbf{x}$ such that the *gradient* is zero (i.e., $\nabla f(\mathbf{x})=\mathbf{0}$). Thus $g(x)$ in Newton's formula becomes $\nabla f(\mathbf{x})$, and the update equation can be written in matrix–vector form as

$$\mathbf{x} \leftarrow \mathbf{x} - \mathbf{H}_f^{-1}(\mathbf{x})\nabla f(\mathbf{x}) ,$$

HESSIAN

where $\mathbf{H}_f(\mathbf{x})$ is the **Hessian** matrix of second derivatives, whose elements $H_{ij}$ are given by $\partial^2 f/\partial x_i \partial x_j$. Since the Hessian has $n^2$ entries, Newton–Raphson becomes expensive in high-dimensional spaces, and many approximations have been developed.

Local search methods suffer from local maxima, ridges, and plateaux in continuous state spaces just as much as in discrete spaces. Random restarts and simulated annealing can be used and are often helpful. High-dimensional continuous spaces are, however, big places in which it is easy to get lost.

CONSTRAINED OPTIMIZATION

A final topic with which a passing acquaintance is useful is **constrained optimization**. An optimization problem is constrained if solutions must satisfy some hard constraints on the values of each variable. For example, in our airport-siting problem, we might constrain sites to be inside Romania and on dry land (rather than in the middle of lakes). The difficulty of constrained optimization problems depends on the nature of the constraints and the objective function. The best-known category is that of **linear programming** problems, in which constraints must be linear inequalities forming a *convex* region and the objective function is also linear. Linear programming problems can be solved in time polynomial in the number of variables. Problems with different types of constraints and objective functions have also been studied—quadratic programming, second-order conic programming, and so on.

LINEAR PROGRAMMING

## 4.5 Online Search Agents and Unknown Environments

OFFLINE SEARCH

ONLINE SEARCH

So far we have concentrated on agents that use **offline search** algorithms. They compute a complete solution before setting foot in the real world (see Figure 3.1), and then execute the solution without recourse to their percepts. In contrast, an **online search**[14] agent operates by **interleaving** computation and action: first it takes an action, then it observes the environment and computes the next action. Online search is a good idea in dynamic or semidynamic domains—domains where there is a penalty for sitting around and computing too long. Online search is an even better idea for stochastic domains. In general, an offline search would

[14] The term "online" is commonly used in computer science to refer to algorithms that must process input data as they are received, rather than waiting for the entire input data set to become available.

have to come up with an exponentially large contingency plan that considers all possible happenings, while an online search need only consider what actually does happen. For example, a chess playing agent is well-advised to make its first move long before it has figured out the complete course of the game.

EXPLORATION PROBLEM

Online search is a *necessary* idea for an **exploration problem**, where the states and actions are unknown to the agent. An agent in this state of ignorance must use its actions as experiments to determine what to do next, and hence must interleave computation and action.

The canonical example of online search is a robot that is placed in a new building and must explore it to build a map that it can use for getting from $A$ to $B$. Methods for escaping from labyrinths—required knowledge for aspiring heroes of antiquity—are also examples of online search algorithms. Spatial exploration is not the only form of exploration, however. Consider a newborn baby: it has many possible actions, but knows the outcomes of none of them, and it has experienced only a few of the possible states that it can reach. The baby's gradual discovery of how the world works is, in part, an online search process.

### Online search problems

An online search problem can be solved only by an agent executing actions, rather than by a purely computational process. We will assume that the agent knows just the following:

- ACTIONS($s$), which returns a list of actions allowed in state $s$;
- The step-cost function $c(s, a, s')$—note that this cannot be used until the agent knows that $s'$ is the outcome; and
- GOAL-TEST($s$).

Note in particular that the agent *cannot* access the successors of a state except by actually trying all the actions in that state. For example, in the maze problem shown in Figure 4.18, the agent does not know that going *Up* from (1,1) leads to (1,2); nor, having done that, does it know that going *Down* will take it back to (1,1). This degree of ignorance can be reduced in some applications—for example, a robot explorer might know how its movement actions work and be ignorant only of the locations of obstacles.

We will assume that the agent can always recognize a state that it has visited before, and we will assume that the actions are deterministic. (These last two assumptions are relaxed in Chapter 17.) Finally, the agent might have access to an admissible heuristic function $h(s)$ that estimates the distance from the current state to a goal state. For example, in Figure 4.18, the agent might know the location of the goal and be able to use the Manhattan distance heuristic.

Typically, the agent's objective is to reach a goal state while minimizing cost. (Another possible objective is simply to explore the entire environment.) The cost is the total path cost of the path that the agent actually travels. It is common to compare this cost with the path cost of the path the agent would follow *if it knew the search space in advance*—that is, the actual shortest path (or shortest complete exploration). In the language of online algorithms, this is called the **competitive ratio**; we would like it to be as small as possible.

COMPETITIVE RATIO

Although this sounds like a reasonable request, it is easy to see that the best achievable competitive ratio is infinite in some cases. For example, if some actions are irreversible, the online search might accidentally reach a dead-end state from which no goal state is reachable.

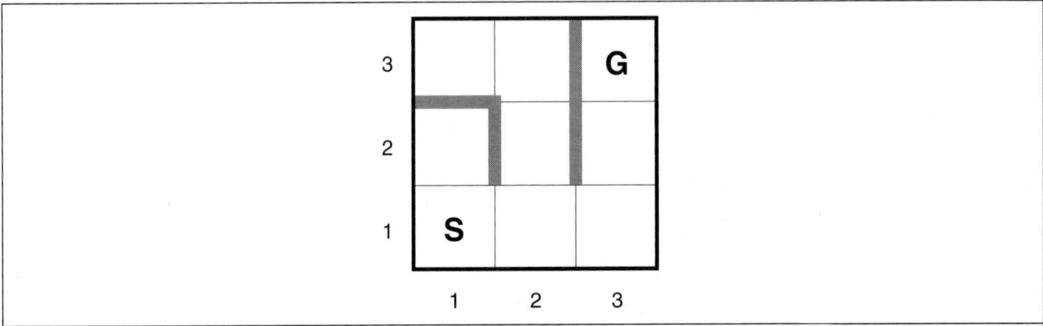


**Figure 4.18** A simple maze problem. The agent starts at $S$ and must reach $G$, but knows nothing of the environment.

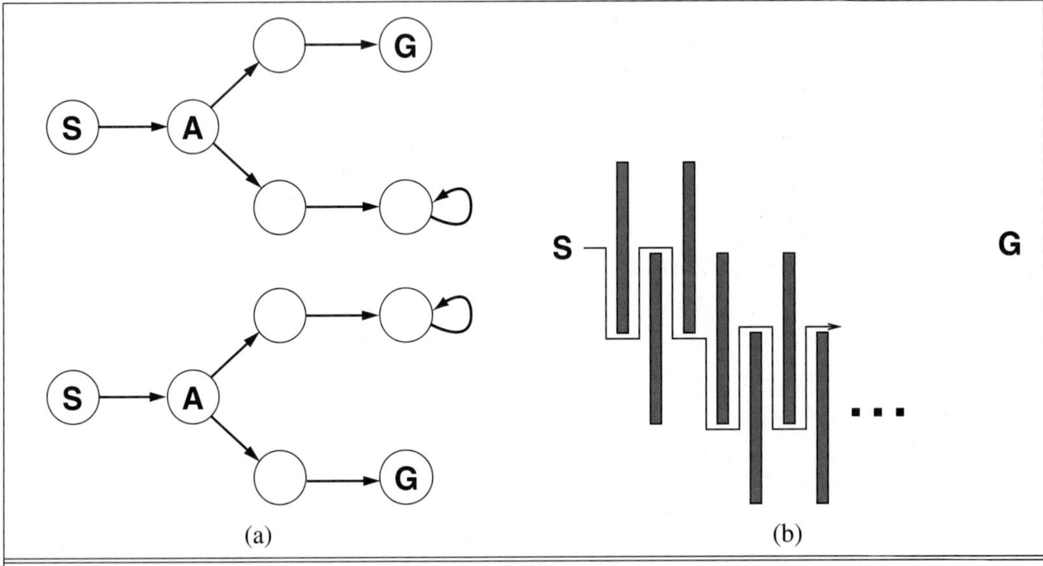


**Figure 4.19** (a) Two state spaces that might lead an online search agent into a dead end. Any given agent will fail in at least one of these spaces. (b) A two-dimensional environment that can cause an online search agent to follow an arbitrarily inefficient route to the goal. Whichever choice the agent makes, the adversary blocks that route with another long, thin wall, so that the path followed is much longer than the best possible path.

Perhaps you find the term "accidentally" unconvincing—after all, there might be an algorithm that happens not to take the dead-end path as it explores. Our claim, to be more precise, is that *no algorithm can avoid dead ends in all state spaces.* Consider the two dead-end state spaces in Figure 4.19(a). To an online search algorithm that has visited states $S$ and $A$, the two state spaces look *identical*, so it must make the same decision in both. Therefore, it will fail in one of them. This is an example of an **adversary argument**—we can imagine an adversary that constructs the state space while the agent explores it and can put the goals and dead ends wherever it likes.

ADVERSARY ARGUMENT

Dead ends are a real difficulty for robot exploration—staircases, ramps, cliffs, and all kinds of natural terrain present opportunities for irreversible actions. To make progress, we will simply assume that the state space is **safely explorable**—that is, some goal state is reachable from every reachable state. State spaces with reversible actions, such as mazes and 8-puzzles, can be viewed as undirected graphs and are clearly safely explorable.

SAFELY EXPLORABLE

Even in safely explorable environments, no bounded competitive ratio can be guaranteed if there are paths of unbounded cost. This is easy to show in environments with irreversible actions, but in fact it remains true for the reversible case as well, as Figure 4.19(b) shows. For this reason, it is common to describe the performance of online search algorithms in terms of the size of the entire state space rather than just the depth of the shallowest goal.

### Online search agents

After each action, an online agent receives a percept telling it what state it has reached; from this information, it can augment its map of the environment. The current map is used to decide where to go next. This interleaving of planning and action means that online search algorithms are quite different from the offline search algorithms we have seen previously. For example, offline algorithms such as A* have the ability to expand a node in one part of the space and then immediately expand a node in another part of the space, because node expansion involves simulated rather than real actions. An online algorithm, on the other hand, can expand only a node that it physically occupies. To avoid traveling all the way across the tree to expand the next node, it seems better to expand nodes in a *local* order. Depth-first search has exactly this property, because (except when backtracking) the next node expanded is a child of the previous node expanded.

An online depth-first search agent is shown in Figure 4.20. This agent stores its map in a table, $result[a, s]$, that records the state resulting from executing action $a$ in state $s$. Whenever an action from the current state has not been explored, the agent tries that action. The difficulty comes when the agent has tried all the actions in a state. In offline depth-first search, the state is simply dropped from the queue; in an online search, the agent has to backtrack physically. In depth-first search, this means going back to the state from which the agent entered the current state most recently. That is achieved by keeping a table that lists, for each state, the predecessor states to which the agent has not yet backtracked. If the agent has run out of states to which it can backtrack, then its search is complete.

We recommend that the reader trace through the progress of ONLINE-DFS-AGENT when applied to the maze given in Figure 4.18. It is fairly easy to see that the agent will, in the worst case, end up traversing every link in the state space exactly twice. For exploration, this is optimal; for finding a goal, on the other hand, the agent's competitive ratio could be arbitrarily bad if it goes off on a long excursion when there is a goal right next to the initial state. An online variant of iterative deepening solves this problem; for an environment that is a uniform tree, the competitive ratio of such an agent is a small constant.

Because of its method of backtracking, ONLINE-DFS-AGENT works only in state spaces where the actions are reversible. There are slightly more complex algorithms that work in general state spaces, but no such algorithm has a bounded competitive ratio.

```
function ONLINE-DFS-AGENT(s') returns an action
  inputs: s', a percept that identifies the current state
  static: result, a table, indexed by action and state, initially empty
          unexplored, a table that lists, for each visited state, the actions not yet tried
          unbacktracked, a table that lists, for each visited state, the backtracks not yet tried
          s, a, the previous state and action, initially null

  if GOAL-TEST(s') then return stop
  if s' is a new state then unexplored[s'] ← ACTIONS(s')
  if s is not null then do
      result[a, s] ← s'
      add s to the front of unbacktracked[s']
  if unexplored[s'] is empty then
      if unbacktracked[s'] is empty then return stop
      else a ← an action b such that result[b, s'] = POP(unbacktracked[s'])
  else a ← POP(unexplored[s'])
  s ← s'
  return a
```

**Figure 4.20** An online search agent that uses depth-first exploration. The agent is applicable only in bidirected search spaces.

### Online local search

Like depth-first search, **hill-climbing search** has the property of locality in its node expansions. In fact, because it keeps just one current state in memory, hill-climbing search is *already* an online search algorithm! Unfortunately, it is not very useful in its simplest form because it leaves the agent sitting at local maxima with nowhere to go. Moreover, random restarts cannot be used, because the agent cannot transport itself to a new state.

RANDOM WALK

Instead of random restarts, one might consider using a **random walk** to explore the environment. A random walk simply selects at random one of the available actions from the current state; preference can be given to actions that have not yet been tried. It is easy to prove that a random walk will *eventually* find a goal or complete its exploration, provided that the space is finite.[15] On the other hand, the process can be very slow. Figure 4.21 shows an environment in which a random walk will take exponentially many steps to find the goal, because, at each step, backward progress is twice as likely as forward progress. The example is contrived, of course, but there are many real-world state spaces whose topology causes these kinds of "traps" for random walks.

Augmenting hill climbing with *memory* rather than randomness turns out to be a more effective approach. The basic idea is to store a "current best estimate" $H(s)$ of the cost to reach the goal from each state that has been visited. $H(s)$ starts out being just the heuristic

[15] The infinite case is much more tricky. Random walks are complete on infinite one-dimensional and two dimensional grids, but not on three-dimensional grids! In the latter case, the probability that the walk ever returns to the starting point is only about 0.3405. (See Hughes, 1995, for a general introduction.)

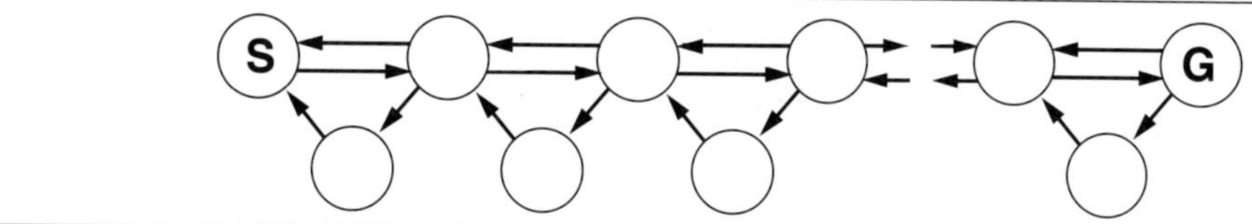


**Figure 4.21** An environment in which a random walk will take exponentially many steps to find the goal.

estimate $h(s)$ and is updated as the agent gains experience in the state space. Figure 4.22 shows a simple example in a one-dimensional state space. In (a), the agent seems to be stuck in a flat local minimum at the shaded state. Rather than staying where it is, the agent should follow what seems to be the best path to the goal based on the current cost estimates for its neighbors. The estimated cost to reach the goal through a neighbor $s'$ is the cost to get to $s'$ plus the estimated cost to get to a goal from there—that is, $c(s, a, s') + H(s')$. In the example, there are two actions with estimated costs $1 + 9$ and $1 + 2$, so it seems best to move right. Now, it is clear that the cost estimate of 2 for the shaded state was overly optimistic. Since the best move cost 1 and led to a state that is at least 2 steps from a goal, the shaded state must be at least 3 steps from a goal, so its $H$ should be updated accordingly, as shown in Figure 4.22(b). Continuing this process, the agent will move back and forth twice more, updating $H$ each time and "flattening out" the local minimum until it escapes to the right.

LRTA*

An agent implementing this scheme, which is called learning real-time A* (**LRTA***), is shown in Figure 4.23. Like ONLINE-DFS-AGENT, it builds a map of the environment using the *result* table. It updates the cost estimate for the state it has just left and then chooses the "apparently best" move according to its current cost estimates. One important detail is that actions that have not yet been tried in a state $s$ are always assumed to lead immediately to the goal with the least possible cost, namely $h(s)$. This **optimism under uncertainty** encourages the agent to explore new, possibly promising paths.

OPTIMISM UNDER UNCERTAINTY

An LRTA* agent is guaranteed to find a goal in any finite, safely explorable environment. Unlike A*, however, it is not complete for infinite state spaces—there are cases where it can be led infinitely astray. It can explore an environment of $n$ states in $O(n^2)$ steps in the worst case, but often does much better. The LRTA* agent is just one of a large family of online agents that can be defined by specifying the action selection rule and the update rule in different ways. We will discuss this family, which was developed originally for stochastic environments, in Chapter 21.

### Learning in online search

The initial ignorance of online search agents provides several opportunities for learning. First, the agents learn a "map" of the environment—more precisely, the outcome of each action in each state—simply by recording each of their experiences. (Notice that the assumption of deterministic environments means that one experience is enough for each action.) Second, the local search agents acquire more accurate estimates of the value of each state by using local updating rules, as in LRTA*. In Chapter 21 we will see that these updates eventually

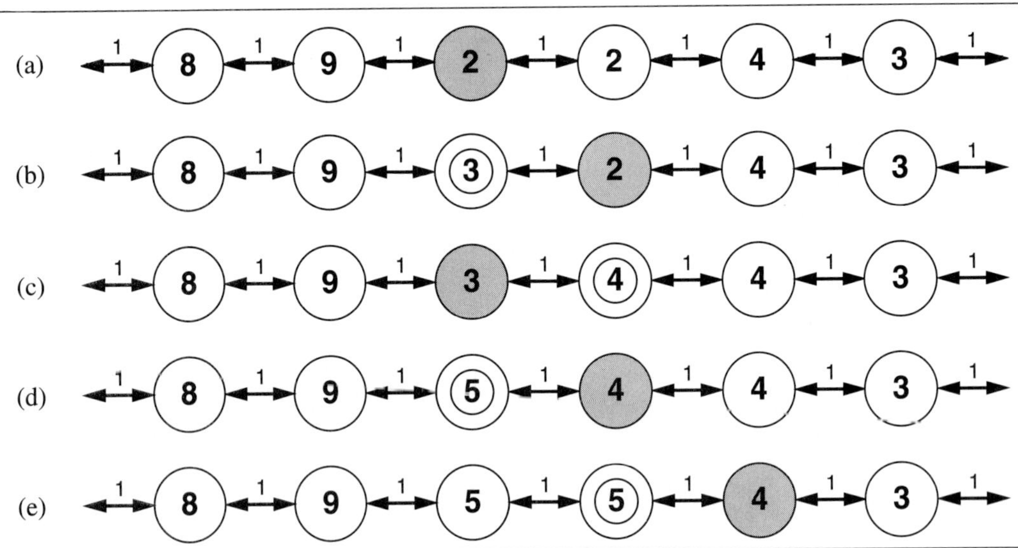


**Figure 4.22** Five iterations of LRTA* on a one-dimensional state space. Each state is labeled with $H(s)$, the current cost estimate to reach a goal, and each arc is labeled with its step cost. The shaded state marks the location of the agent, and the updated values at each iteration are circled.

```
function LRTA*-AGENT(s′) returns an action
   inputs: s′, a percept that identifies the current state
   static: result, a table, indexed by action and state, initially empty
           H, a table of cost estimates indexed by state, initially empty
           s, a, the previous state and action, initially null

   if GOAL-TEST(s′) then return stop
   if s′ is a new state (not in H) then H[s′] ← h(s′)
   unless s is null
      result[a, s] ← s′
      H[s] ←       min       LRTA*-COST(s, b, result[b, s], H)
              b∈ ACTIONS(s)
   a ← an action b in ACTIONS(s′) that minimizes LRTA*-COST(s′, b, result[b, s′], H)
   s ← s′
   return a

function LRTA*-COST(s, a, s′, H) returns a cost estimate
   if s′ is undefined then return h(s)
   else return c(s, a, s′) + H[s′]
```

**Figure 4.23** LRTA*-AGENT selects an action according to the values of neighboring states, which are updated as the agent moves about the state space.

converge to *exact* values for every state, provided that the agent explores the state space in the right way. Once exact values are known, optimal decisions can be taken simply by moving to the highest-valued successor—that is, pure hill climbing is then an optimal strategy.

If you followed our suggestion to trace the behavior of ONLINE-DFS-AGENT in the environment of Figure 4.18, you will have noticed that the agent is not very bright. For example, after it has seen that the $Up$ action goes from (1,1) to (1,2), the agent still has no idea that the $Down$ action goes back to (1,1), or that the $Up$ action also goes from (2,1) to (2,2), from (2,2) to (2,3), and so on. In general, we would like the agent to learn that $Up$ increases the $y$-coordinate unless there is a wall in the way, that $Down$ reduces it, and so on. For this to happen, we need two things. First, we need a formal and explicitly manipulable representation for these kinds of general rules; so far, we have hidden the information inside the black box called the successor function. Part III is devoted to this issue. Second, we need algorithms that can construct suitable general rules from the specific observations made by the agent. These are covered in Chapter 18.

## 4.6 SUMMARY

This chapter has examined the application of **heuristics** to reduce search costs. We have looked at a number of algorithms that use heuristics and found that optimality comes at a stiff price in terms of search cost, even with good heuristics.

- **Best-first search** is just GRAPH-SEARCH where the minimum-cost unexpanded nodes (according to some measure) are selected for expansion. Best-first algorithms typically use a **heuristic** function $h(n)$ that estimates the cost of a solution from $n$.
- **Greedy best-first search** expands nodes with minimal $h(n)$. It is not optimal, but is often efficient.
- **A* search** expands nodes with minimal $f(n) = g(n) + h(n)$. A* is complete and optimal, provided that we guarantee that $h(n)$ is admissible (for TREE-SEARCH) or consistent (for GRAPH-SEARCH). The space complexity of A* is still prohibitive.
- The performance of heuristic search algorithms depends on the quality of the heuristic function. Good heuristics can sometimes be constructed by relaxing the problem definition, by precomputing solution costs for subproblems in a pattern database, or by learning from experience with the problem class.
- **RBFS** and **SMA*** are robust, optimal search algorithms that use limited amounts of memory; given enough time, they can solve problems that A* cannot solve because it runs out of memory.
- *Local search* methods such as **hill climbing** operate on complete-state formulations, keeping only a small number of nodes in memory. Several stochastic algorithms have been developed, including **simulated annealing**, which returns optimal solutions when given an appropriate cooling schedule. Many local search methods can also be used to solve problems in continuous spaces.

- A **genetic algorithm** is a stochastic hill-climbing search in which a large population of states is maintained. New states are generated by **mutation** and by **crossover**, which combines pairs of states from the population.
- **Exploration problems** arise when the agent has no idea about the states and actions of its environment. For safely explorable environments, **online search** agents can build a map and find a goal if one exists. Updating heuristic estimates from experience provides an effective method to escape from local minima.

## BIBLIOGRAPHICAL AND HISTORICAL NOTES

The use of heuristic information in problem solving appears in an early paper by Simon and Newell (1958), but the phrase "heuristic search" and the use of heuristic functions that estimate the distance to the goal came somewhat later (Newell and Ernst, 1965; Lin, 1965). Doran and Michie (1966) conducted extensive experimental studies of heuristic search as applied to a number of problems, especially the 8-puzzle and the 15-puzzle. Although Doran and Michie carried out theoretical analyses of path length and "penetrance" (the ratio of path length to the total number of nodes examined so far) in heuristic search, they appear to have ignored the information provided by current path length. The A* algorithm, incorporating the current path length into heuristic search, was developed by Hart, Nilsson, and Raphael (1968), with some later corrections (Hart *et al.*, 1972). Dechter and Pearl (1985) demonstrated the optimal efficiency of A*.

The original A* paper introduced the consistency condition on heuristic functions. The monotone condition was introduced by Pohl (1977) as a simpler replacement, but Pearl (1984) showed that the two were equivalent. A number of algorithms predating A* used the equivalent of open and closed lists; these include breadth-first, depth-first, and uniform-cost search (Bellman, 1957; Dijkstra, 1959). Bellman's work in particular showed the importance of additive path costs in simplifying optimization algorithms.

Pohl (1970, 1977) pioneered the study of the relationship between the error in heuristic functions and the time complexity of A*. The proof that A* runs in linear time if the error in the heuristic function is bounded by a constant can be found in Pohl (1977) and in Gaschnig (1979). Pearl (1984) strengthened this result to allow a logarithmic growth in the error. The "effective branching factor" measure of the efficiency of heuristic search was proposed by Nilsson (1971).

There are many variations on the A* algorithm. Pohl (1973) proposed the use of *dynamic weighting*, which uses a weighted sum $f_w(n) = w_g g(n) + w_h h(n)$ of the current path length and the heuristic function as an evaluation function, rather than the simple sum $f(n) = g(n) + h(n)$ used in A*. The weights $w_g$ and $w_h$ are adjusted dynamically as the search progresses. Pohl's algorithm can be shown to be $\epsilon$-admissible—that is, guaranteed to find solutions within a factor $1 + \epsilon$ of the optimal solution—where $\epsilon$ is a parameter supplied to the algorithm. The same property is exhibited by the $A^*_\epsilon$ algorithm (Pearl, 1984), which can select any node from the fringe provided its $f$-cost is within a factor $1 + \epsilon$ of the lowest-$f$-cost fringe node. The selection can be done so as to minimize search cost.

$A^*$ and other state-space search algorithms are closely related to the *branch-and-bound* techniques that are widely used in operations research (Lawler and Wood, 1966). The relationships between state-space search and branch-and-bound have been investigated in depth (Kumar and Kanal, 1983; Nau *et al.*, 1984; Kumar *et al.*, 1988). Martelli and Montanari (1978) demonstrate a connection between dynamic programming (see Chapter 17) and certain types of state-space search. Kumar and Kanal (1988) attempt a "grand unification" of heuristic search, dynamic programming, and branch-and-bound techniques under the name of CDP—the "composite decision process."

Because computers in the late 1950s and early 1960s had at most a few thousand words of main memory, memory-bounded heuristic search was an early research topic. The Graph Traverser (Doran and Michie, 1966), one of the earliest search programs, commits to an operator after searching best first up to the memory limit. IDA* (Korf, 1985a, 1985b) was the first widely used optimal, memory-bounded, heuristic search algorithm, and a large number of variants have been developed. An analysis of the efficiency of IDA* and of its difficulties with real-valued heuristics appears in Patrick *et al.* (1992).

ITERATIVE EXPANSION

RBFS (Korf, 1991, 1993) is actually somewhat more complicated than the algorithm shown in Figure 4.5, which is closer to an independently developed algorithm called **iterative expansion**, or IE (Russell, 1992). RBFS uses a lower bound as well as the upper bound; the two algorithms behave identically with admissible heuristics, but RBFS expands nodes in best-first order even with an inadmissible heuristic. The idea of keeping track of the best alternative path appeared earlier in Bratko's (1986) elegant Prolog implementation of $A^*$ and in the DTA* algorithm (Russell and Wefald, 1991). The latter work also discusses metalevel state spaces and metalevel learning.

The MA* algorithm appeared in Chakrabarti *et al.* (1989). SMA*, or Simplified MA*, emerged from an attempt to implement MA* as a comparison algorithm for IE (Russell, 1992). Kaindl and Khorsand (1994) have applied SMA* to produce a bidirectional search algorithm that is substantially faster than previous algorithms. Korf and Zhang (2000) describe a divide-and-conquer approach, and Zhou and Hansen (2002) introduce memory-bounded $A^*$ graph search. Korf (1995) surveys memory-bounded search techniques.

The idea that admissible heuristics can be derived by problem relaxation appears in the seminal paper by Held and Karp (1970), who used the the minimum-spanning-tree heuristic to solve the TSP. (See Exercise 4.8.)

The automation of the relaxation process was implemented successfully by Prieditis (1993), building on earlier work with Mostow (Mostow and Prieditis, 1989). The use of pattern databases to derive admissible heuristics is due to Gasser (1995) and Culberson and Schaeffer (1998); disjoint pattern databases are described by Korf and Felner (2002). The probabilistic interpretation of heuristics was investigated in depth by Pearl (1984) and Hansson and Mayer (1989).

By far the most comprehensive source on heuristics and heuristic search algorithms is Pearl's (1984) *Heuristics* text. This book provides especially good coverage of the wide variety of offshoots and variations of $A^*$, including rigorous proofs of their formal properties. Kanal and Kumar (1988) present an anthology of important articles on heuristic search. New results on search algorithms appear regularly in the journal *Artificial Intelligence*.

Local-search techniques have a long history in mathematics and computer science. Indeed, the Newton–Raphson method (Newton, 1671; Raphson, 1690) can be seen as a very efficient local-search method for continuous spaces in which gradient information is available. Brent (1973) is a classic reference for optimization algorithms that do not require such information. Beam search, which we have presented as a local-search algorithm, originated as a bounded-width variant of dynamic programming for speech recognition in the HARPY system (Lowerre, 1976). A related algorithm is analyzed in depth by Pearl (1984, Ch. 5).

The topic of local search has been reinvigorated in recent years by surprisingly good results for large constraint satisfaction problems such as $n$-queens (Minton *et al.*, 1992) and logical reasoning (Selman *et al.*, 1992) and by the incorporation of randomness, multiple simultaneous searches, and other improvements. This renaissance of what Christos Papadimitriou has called "New Age" algorithms has also sparked increased interest among theoretical computer scientists (Koutsoupias and Papadimitriou, 1992; Aldous and Vazirani, 1994). In the field of operations research, a variant of hill climbing called **tabu search** has gained popularity (Glover, 1989; Glover and Laguna, 1997). Drawing on models of limited short-term memory in humans, this algorithm maintains a tabu list of $k$ previously visited states that cannot be revisited; as well as improving efficiency when searching graphs, this can allow the algorithm to escape from some local minima. Another useful improvement on hill climbing is the STAGE algorithm (Boyan and Moore, 1998). The idea is to use the local maxima found by random-restart hill climbing to get an idea of the overall shape of the landscape. The algorithm fits a smooth surface to the set of local maxima and then calculates the global maximum of that surface analytically. This becomes the new restart point. The algorithm has been shown to work in practice on hard problems. (Gomes *et al.*, 1998) showed that the run time distributions of systematic backtracking algorithms often have a **heavy-tailed distribution**, which means that the probability of a very long run time is more than would be predicted if the run times were normally distributed. This provides a theoretical justification for random restarts.

TABU SEARCH

HEAVY-TAILED DISTRIBUTION

Simulated annealing was first described by Kirkpatrick *et al.* (1983), who borrowed directly from the **Metropolis algorithm** (which is used to simulate complex systems in physics (Metropolis *et al.*, 1953) and was supposedly invented at a Los Alamos dinner party). Simulated annealing is now a field in itself, with hundreds of papers published every year.

Finding optimal solutions in continuous spaces is the subject matter of several fields, including **optimization theory**, **optimal control theory**, and the **calculus of variations**. Suitable (and practical) entry points are provided by Press *et al.* (2002) and Bishop (1995). **Linear programming** (LP) was one of the first applications of computers; the **simplex algorithm** (Wood and Dantzig, 1949; Dantzig, 1949) is still used despite worst-case exponential complexity. Karmarkar (1984) developed a practical polynomial-time algorithm for LP.

Work by Sewall Wright (1931) on the concept of a **fitness landscape** was an important precursor to the development of genetic algorithms. In the 1950s, several statisticians, including Box (1957) and Friedman (1959), used evolutionary techniques for optimization problems, but it wasn't until Rechenberg (1965, 1973) introduced **evolution strategies** to solve optimization problems for airfoils that the approach gained popularity. In the 1960s and 1970s, John Holland (1975) championed genetic algorithms, both as a useful tool and

EVOLUTION STRATEGIES

as a method to expand our understanding of adaptation, biological or otherwise (Holland, 1995). The **artificial life** movement (Langton, 1995) takes this idea one step further, viewing the products of genetic algorithms as *organisms* rather than solutions to problems. Work in this field by Hinton and Nowlan (1987) and Ackley and Littman (1991) has done much to clarify the implications of the Baldwin effect. For general background on evolution, we strongly recommend Smith and Szathmáry (1999).

ARTIFICIAL LIFE

Most comparisons of genetic algorithms to other approaches (especially stochastic hill-climbing) have found that the genetic algorithms are slower to converge (O'Reilly and Oppacher, 1994; Mitchell *et al.*, 1996; Juels and Wattenberg, 1996; Baluja, 1997). Such findings are not universally popular within the GA community, but recent attempts within that community to understand population-based search as an approximate form of Bayesian learning (see Chapter 20) might help to close the gap between the field and its critics (Pelikan *et al.*, 1999). The theory of **quadratic dynamical systems** may also explain the performance of GAs (Rabani *et al.*, 1998). See Lohn *et al.* (2001) for an example of GAs applied to antenna design, and Larrañaga *et al.* (1999) for an application to the traveling salesperson problem.

GENETIC PROGRAMMING

The field of **genetic programming** is closely related to genetic algorithms. The principal difference is that the representations that are mutated and combined are programs rather than bit strings. The programs are represented in the form of expression trees; the expressions can be in a standard language such as Lisp or can be specially designed to represent circuits, robot controllers, and so on. Crossover involves splicing together subtrees rather than substrings. This form of mutation guarantees that the offspring are well-formed expressions, which would not be the case if programs were manipulated as strings.

Recent interest in genetic programming was spurred by John Koza's work (Koza, 1992, 1994), but it goes back at least to early experiments with machine code by Friedberg (1958) and with finite-state automata by Fogel *et al.* (1966). As with genetic algorithms, there is debate about the effectiveness of the technique. Koza *et al.* (1999) describe a variety of experiments on the automated design of circuit devices using genetic programming.

The journals *Evolutionary Computation* and *IEEE Transactions on Evolutionary Computation* cover genetic algorithms and genetic programming; articles are also found in *Complex Systems*, *Adaptive Behavior*, and *Artificial Life*. The main conferences are the *International Conference on Genetic Algorithms* and the *Conference on Genetic Programming*, recently merged to form the *Genetic and Evolutionary Computation Conference*. The texts by Melanie Mitchell (1996) and David Fogel (2000) give good overviews of the field.

Algorithms for exploring unknown state spaces have been of interest for many centuries. Depth-first search in a maze can be implemented by keeping one's left hand on the wall; loops can be avoided by marking each junction. Depth-first search fails with irreversible actions; the more general problem of exploring of **Eulerian graphs** (i.e., graphs in which each node has equal numbers of incoming and outgoing edges) was solved by an algorithm due to Hierholzer (1873). The first thorough algorithmic study of the exploration problem for arbitrary graphs was carried out by Deng and Papadimitriou (1990), who developed a completely general algorithm, but showed that no bounded competitive ratio is possible for exploring a general graph. Papadimitriou and Yannakakis (1991) examined the question of finding paths to a goal in geometric path-planning environments (where all actions are reversible). They showed that

EULERIAN GRAPHS

a small competitive ratio is achievable with square obstacles, but with general rectangular obstacles no bounded ratio can be achieved. (See Figure 4.19.)

REAL-TIME SEARCH

The LRTA* algorithm was developed by Korf (1990) as part of an investigation into **real-time search** for environments in which the agent must act after searching for only a fixed amount of time (a much more common situation in two-player games). LRTA* is in fact a special case of reinforcement learning algorithms for stochastic environments (Barto *et al.*, 1995). Its policy of optimism under uncertainty—always head for the closest unvisited state—can result in an exploration pattern that is less efficient in the uninformed case than simple depth-first search (Koenig, 2000). Dasgupta *et al.* (1994) show that online iterative deepening search is optimally efficient for finding a goal in a uniform tree with no heuristic information. Several informed variants on the LRTA* theme have been developed with different methods for searching and updating within the known portion of the graph (Pemberton and Korf, 1992). As yet, there is no good understanding of how to find goals with optimal efficiency when using heuristic information.

PARALLEL SEARCH

The topic of **parallel search** algorithms was not covered in the chapter, partly because it requires a lengthy discussion of parallel computer architectures. Parallel search is becoming an important topic in both AI and theoretical computer science. A brief introduction to the AI literature can be found in Mahanti and Daniels (1993).

## EXERCISES

**4.1** Trace the operation of A* search applied to the problem of getting to Bucharest from Lugoj using the straight-line distance heuristic. That is, show the sequence of nodes that the algorithm will consider and the $f$, $g$, and $h$ score for each node.

**4.2** The **heuristic path algorithm** is a best-first search in which the objective function is $f(n) = (2 - w)g(n) + wh(n)$. For what values of $w$ is this algorithm guaranteed to be optimal? (You may assume that $h$ is admissible.) What kind of search does this perform when $w = 0$? When $w = 1$? When $w = 2$?

**4.3** Prove each of the following statements:

**a.** Breadth-first search is a special case of uniform-cost search.

**b.** Breadth-first search, depth-first search, and uniform-cost search are special cases of best-first search.

**c.** Uniform-cost search is a special case of A* search.

**4.4** Devise a state space in which A* using GRAPH-SEARCH returns a suboptimal solution with an $h(n)$ function that is admissible but inconsistent.

**4.5** We saw on page 96 that the straight-line distance heuristic leads greedy best-first search astray on the problem of going from Iasi to Fagaras. However, the heuristic is perfect on the opposite problem: going from Fagaras to Iasi. Are there problems for which the heuristic is misleading in both directions?

**4.6** Invent a heuristic function for the 8-puzzle that sometimes overestimates, and show how it can lead to a suboptimal solution on a particular problem. (You can use a computer to help if you want.) Prove that, if $h$ never overestimates by more than $c$, A* using $h$ returns a solution whose cost exceeds that of the optimal solution by no more than $c$.

**4.7** Prove that if a heuristic is consistent, it must be admissible. Construct an admissible heuristic that is not consistent.

**4.8** The traveling salesperson problem (TSP) can be solved via the minimum spanning tree (MST) heuristic, which is used to estimate the cost of completing a tour, given that a partial tour has already been constructed. The MST cost of a set of cities is the smallest sum of the link costs of any tree that connects all the cities.

**a.** Show how this heuristic can be derived from a relaxed version of the TSP.

**b.** Show that the MST heuristic dominates straight-line distance.

**c.** Write a problem generator for instances of the TSP where cities are represented by random points in the unit square.

**d.** Find an efficient algorithm in the literature for constructing the MST, and use it with an admissible search algorithm to solve instances of the TSP.

**4.9** On page 108, we defined the relaxation of the 8-puzzle in which a tile can move from square A to square B if B is blank. The exact solution of this problem defines **Gaschnig's heuristic** (Gaschnig, 1979). Explain why Gaschnig's heuristic is at least as accurate as $h_1$ (misplaced tiles), and show cases where it is more accurate than both $h_1$ and $h_2$ (Manhattan distance). Can you suggest a way to calculate Gaschnig's heuristic efficiently?

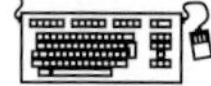

**4.10** We gave two simple heuristics for the 8-puzzle: Manhattan distance and misplaced tiles. Several heuristics in the literature purport to improve on this—see, for example, Nilsson (1971), Mostow and Prieditis (1989), and Hansson *et al.* (1992). Test these claims by implementing the heuristics and comparing the performance of the resulting algorithms.

**4.11** Give the name of the algorithm that results from each of the following special cases:

**a.** Local beam search with $k = 1$.

**b.** Local beam search with one initial state and no limit on the number of states retained.

**c.** Simulated annealing with $T = 0$ at all times (and omitting the termination test).

**d.** Genetic algorithm with population size $N = 1$.

**4.12** Sometimes there is no good evaluation function for a problem, but there is a good comparison method: a way to tell whether one node is better than another, without assigning numerical values to either. Show that this is enough to do a best-first search. Is there an analog of A*?

**4.13** Relate the time complexity of LRTA* to its space complexity.

**4.14** Suppose that an agent is in a $3 \times 3$ maze environment like the one shown in Figure 4.18. The agent knows that its initial location is (1,1), that the goal is at (3,3), and that the four actions *Up*, *Down*, *Left*, *Right* have their usual effects unless blocked by a wall. The agent does *not* know where the internal walls are. In any given state, the agent perceives the set of legal actions; it can also tell whether the state is one it has visited before or a new state.

**a.** Explain how this online search problem can be viewed as an offline search in belief state space, where the initial belief state includes all possible environment configurations. How large is the initial belief state? How large is the space of belief states?

**b.** How many distinct percepts are possible in the initial state?

**c.** Describe the first few branches of a contingency plan for this problem. How large (roughly) is the complete plan?

Notice that this contingency plan is a solution for *every possible environment* fitting the given description. Therefore, interleaving of search and execution is not strictly necessary even in unknown environments.

**4.15** In this exercise, we will explore the use of local search methods to solve TSPs of the type defined in Exercise 4.8.

**a.** Devise a hill-climbing approach to solve TSPs. Compare the results with optimal solutions obtained via the A* algorithm with the MST heuristic (Exercise 4.8).

**b.** Devise a genetic algorithm approach to the traveling salesperson problem. Compare results to the other approaches. You may want to consult Larrañaga *et al.* (1999) for some suggestions for representations.

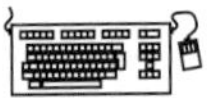

**4.16** Generate a large number of 8-puzzle and 8-queens instances and solve them (where possible) by hill climbing (steepest-ascent and first-choice variants), hill climbing with random restart, and simulated annealing. Measure the search cost and percentage of solved problems and graph these against the optimal solution cost. Comment on your results.

**4.17** In this exercise, we will examine hill climbing in the context of robot navigation, using the environment in Figure 3.22 as an example.

**a.** Repeat Exercise 3.16 using hill climbing. Does your agent ever get stuck in a local minimum? Is it *possible* for it to get stuck with convex obstacles?

**b.** Construct a nonconvex polygonal environment in which the agent gets stuck.

**c.** Modify the hill-climbing algorithm so that, instead of doing a depth-1 search to decide where to go next, it does a depth-$k$ search. It should find the best $k$-step path and do one step along it, and then repeat the process.

**d.** Is there some $k$ for which the new algorithm is guaranteed to escape from local minima?

**e.** Explain how LRTA* enables the agent to escape from local minima in this case.

**4.18** Compare the performance of A* and RBFS on a set of randomly generated problems in the 8-puzzle (with Manhattan distance) and TSP (with MST—see Exercise 4.8) domains. Discuss your results. What happens to the performance of RBFS when a small random number is added to the heuristic values in the 8-puzzle domain?

# 5 CONSTRAINT SATISFACTION PROBLEMS

*In which we see how treating states as more than just little black boxes leads to the invention of a range of powerful new search methods and a deeper understanding of problem structure and complexity.*

Chapters 3 and 4 explored the idea that problems can be solved by searching in a space of **states**. These states can be evaluated by domain-specific heuristics and tested to see whether they are goal states. From the point of view of the search algorithm, however, each state is a **black box** with no discernible internal structure. It is represented by an arbitrary data structure that can be accessed only by the *problem-specific* routines—the successor function, heuristic function, and goal test.

BLACK BOX

This chapter examines **constraint satisfaction problems**, whose states and goal test conform to a standard, structured, and very simple **representation** (Section 5.1). Search algorithms can be defined that take advantage of the structure of states and use *general-purpose* rather than *problem-specific* heuristics to enable the solution of large problems (Sections 5.2–5.3). Perhaps most importantly, the standard representation of the goal test reveals the structure of the problem itself (Section 5.4). This leads to methods for problem decomposition and to an understanding of the intimate connection between the structure of a problem and the difficulty of solving it.

REPRESENTATION

## 5.1 CONSTRAINT SATISFACTION PROBLEMS

CONSTRAINT SATISFACTION PROBLEM
VARIABLES
CONSTRAINTS
DOMAIN
VALUES
ASSIGNMENT
CONSISTENT
OBJECTIVE FUNCTION

Formally speaking, a **constraint satisfaction problem** (or CSP) is defined by a set of **variables**, $X_1, X_2, \ldots, X_n$, and a set of **constraints**, $C_1, C_2, \ldots, C_m$. Each variable $X_i$ has a nonempty **domain** $D_i$ of possible **values**. Each constraint $C_i$ involves some subset of the variables and specifies the allowable combinations of values for that subset. A state of the problem is defined by an **assignment** of values to some or all of the variables, $\{X_i = v_i, X_j = v_j, \ldots\}$. An assignment that does not violate any constraints is called a **consistent** or legal assignment. A complete assignment is one in which every variable is mentioned, and a **solution** to a CSP is a complete assignment that satisfies all the constraints. Some CSPs also require a solution that maximizes an **objective function**.

So what does all this mean? Suppose that, having tired of Romania, we are looking at a map of Australia showing each of its states and territories, as in Figure 5.1(a), and that we are given the task of coloring each region either red, green, or blue in such a way that no neighboring regions have the same color. To formulate this as a CSP, we define the variables to be the regions: $WA$, $NT$, $Q$, $NSW$, $V$, $SA$, and $T$. The domain of each variable is the set $\{red, green, blue\}$. The constraints require neighboring regions to have distinct colors; for example, the allowable combinations for $WA$ and $NT$ are the pairs

$$\{(red, green), (red, blue), (green, red), (green, blue), (blue, red), (blue, green)\} .$$

(The constraint can also be represented more succinctly as the inequality $WA \neq NT$, provided the constraint satisfaction algorithm has some way to evaluate such expressions.) There are many possible solutions, such as

$$\{ WA = red, NT = green, Q = red, NSW = green, V = red, SA = blue, T = red \}.$$

CONSTRAINT GRAPH

It is helpful to visualize a CSP as a **constraint graph**, as shown in Figure 5.1(b). The nodes of the graph correspond to variables of the problem and the arcs correspond to constraints.

Treating a problem as a CSP confers several important benefits. Because the representation of states in a CSP conforms to a *standard* pattern—that is, a set of variables with assigned values—the successor function and goal test can be written in a generic way that applies to all CSPs. Furthermore, we can develop effective, generic heuristics that require no additional, domain-specific expertise. Finally, the structure of the constraint graph can be used to simplify the solution process, in some cases giving an exponential reduction in complexity. The CSP representation is the first, and simplest, in a series of representation schemes that will be developed throughout the book.

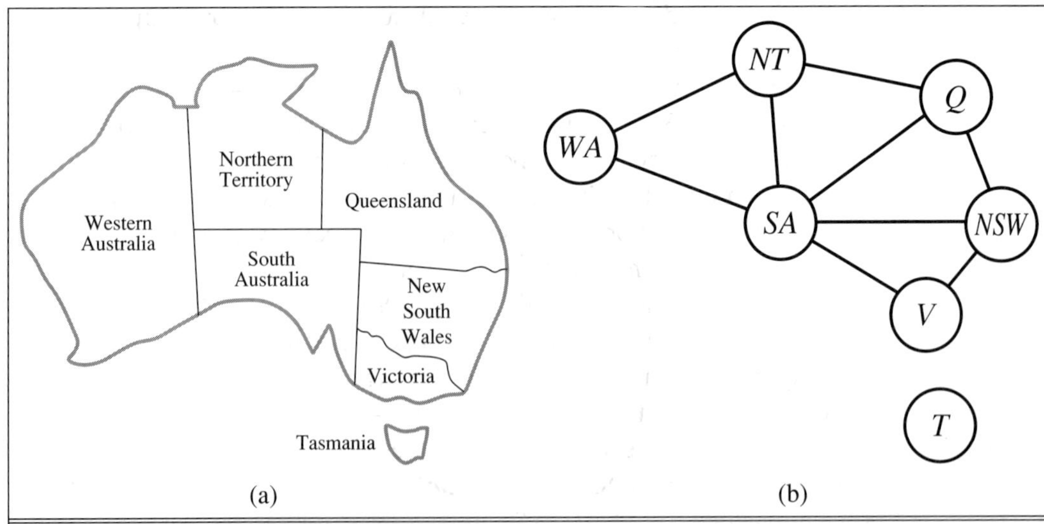


**Figure 5.1** (a) The principal states and territories of Australia. Coloring this map can be viewed as a constraint satisfaction problem. The goal is to assign colors to each region so that no neighboring regions have the same color. (b) The map-coloring problem represented as a constraint graph.

It is fairly easy to see that a CSP can be given an **incremental formulation** as a standard search problem as follows:

- ◊ **Initial state**: the empty assignment $\{\}$, in which all variables are unassigned.
- ◊ **Successor function**: a value can be assigned to any unassigned variable, provided that it does not conflict with previously assigned variables.
- ◊ **Goal test**: the current assignment is complete.
- ◊ **Path cost**: a constant cost (e.g., 1) for every step.

Every solution must be a complete assignment and therefore appears at depth $n$ if there are $n$ variables. Furthermore, the search tree extends only to depth $n$. For these reasons, depth-first search algorithms are popular for CSPs. (See Section 5.2.) It is also the case that *the path by which a solution is reached is irrelevant.* Hence, we can also use a **complete-state formulation**, in which every state is a complete assignment that might or might not satisfy the constraints. Local search methods work well for this formulation. (See Section 5.3.)

FINITE DOMAINS

The simplest kind of CSP involves variables that are **discrete** and have **finite domains**. Map-coloring problems are of this kind. The 8-queens problem described in Chapter 3 can also be viewed as a finite-domain CSP, where the variables $Q_1, \ldots, Q_8$ are the positions of each queen in columns $1, \ldots, 8$ and each variable has the domain $\{1, 2, 3, 4, 5, 6, 7, 8\}$. If the maximum domain size of any variable in a CSP is $d$, then the number of possible complete assignments is $O(d^n)$—that is, exponential in the number of variables. Finite-domain CSPs include **Boolean CSPs**, whose variables can be either *true* or *false*. Boolean CSPs include as special cases some NP-complete problems, such as 3SAT. (See Chapter 7.) In the worst case, therefore, we cannot expect to solve finite-domain CSPs in less than exponential time. In most practical applications, however, general-purpose CSP algorithms can solve problems *orders of magnitude* larger than those solvable via the general-purpose search algorithms that we saw in Chapter 3.

BOOLEAN CSPS

INFINITE DOMAINS

Discrete variables can also have **infinite domains**—for example, the set of integers or the set of strings. For example, when scheduling construction jobs onto a calendar, each job's start date is a variable and the possible values are integer numbers of days from the current date. With infinite domains, it is no longer possible to describe constraints by enumerating all allowed combinations of values. Instead, a **constraint language** must be used. For example, if $Job_1$, which takes five days, must precede $Job_3$, then we would need a constraint language of algebraic inequalities such as $StartJob_1 + 5 \leq StartJob_3$. It is also no longer possible to solve such constraints by enumerating all possible assignments, because there are infinitely many of them. Special solution algorithms (which we will not discuss here) exist for **linear constraints** on integer variables—that is, constraints, such as the one just given, in which each variable appears only in linear form. It can be shown that no algorithm exists for solving general **nonlinear constraints** on integer variables. In some cases, we can reduce integer constraint problems to finite-domain problems simply by bounding the values of all the variables. For example, in a scheduling problem, we can set an upper bound equal to the total length of all the jobs to be scheduled.

CONSTRAINT LANGUAGE

LINEAR CONSTRAINTS

NONLINEAR CONSTRAINTS

CONTINUOUS DOMAINS

Constraint satisfaction problems with **continuous domains** are very common in the real world and are widely studied in the field of operations research. For example, the scheduling of experiments on the Hubble Space Telescope requires very precise timing of observations; the start and finish of each observation and maneuver are continuous-valued variables that must obey a variety of astronomical, precedence, and power constraints. The best-known category of continuous-domain CSPs is that of **linear programming** problems, where constraints must be linear inequalities forming a *convex* region. Linear programming problems can be solved in time polynomial in the number of variables. Problems with different types of constraints and objective functions have also been studied—quadratic programming, second-order conic programming, and so on.

LINEAR PROGRAMMING

In addition to examining the types of variables that can appear in CSPs, it is useful to look at the types of constraints. The simplest type is the **unary constraint**, which restricts the value of a single variable. For example, it could be the case that South Australians actively dislike the color *green*. Every unary constraint can be eliminated simply by preprocessing the domain of the corresponding variable to remove any value that violates the constraint. A **binary constraint** relates two variables. For example, $SA \neq NSW$ is a binary constraint. A binary CSP is one with only binary constraints; it can be represented as a constraint graph, as in Figure 5.1(b).

UNARY CONSTRAINT

BINARY CONSTRAINT

Higher-order constraints involve three or more variables. A familiar example is provided by **cryptarithmetic** puzzles. (See Figure 5.2(a).) It is usual to insist that each letter in a cryptarithmetic puzzle represent a different digit. For the case in Figure 5.2(a)), this would be represented as the six-variable constraint $Alldiff(F, T, U, W, R, O)$. Alternatively, it can be represented by a collection of binary constraints such as $F \neq T$. The addition constraints on the four columns of the puzzle also involve several variables and can be written as

CRYPTARITHMETIC

$$O + O = R + 10 \cdot X_1$$
$$X_1 + W + W = U + 10 \cdot X_2$$
$$X_2 + T + T = O + 10 \cdot X_3$$
$$X_3 = F$$

where $X_1$, $X_2$, and $X_3$ are **auxiliary variables** representing the digit (0 or 1) carried over into the next column. Higher-order constraints can be represented in a **constraint hypergraph**, such as the one shown in Figure 5.2(b). The sharp-eyed reader will have noticed that the *Alldiff* constraint can be broken down into binary constraints—$F \neq T$, $F \neq U$, and so on. In fact, as Exercise 5.11 asks you to prove, every higher-order, finite-domain constraint can be reduced to a set of binary constraints if enough auxiliary variables are introduced. Because of this, we will deal only with binary constraints in this chapter.

AUXILIARY VARIABLES

CONSTRAINT HYPERGRAPH

The constraints we have described so far have all been **absolute** constraints, violation of which rules out a potential solution. Many real-world CSPs include **preference** constraints indicating which solutions are preferred. For example, in a university timetabling problem, Prof. X might prefer teaching in the morning whereas Prof. Y prefers teaching in the afternoon. A timetable that has Prof. X teaching at 2 p.m. would still be a solution (unless Prof. X happens to be the department chair), but would not be an optimal one. Preference constraints can often be encoded as costs on individual variable assignments—for example, assigning an afternoon slot for Prof. X costs 2 points against the overall objective function, whereas a morning slot costs 1. With this formulation, CSPs with preferences can be solved using opti-

PREFERENCE

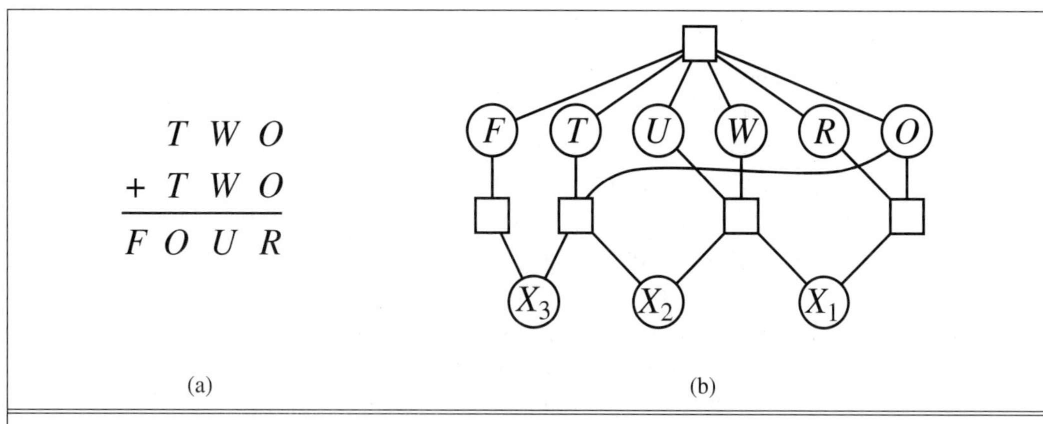


**Figure 5.2** (a) A cryptarithmetic problem. Each letter stands for a distinct digit; the aim is to find a substitution of digits for letters such that the resulting sum is arithmetically correct, with the added restriction that no leading zeroes are allowed. (b) The constraint hypergraph for the cryptarithmetic problem, showing the *Alldiff* constraint as well as the column addition constraints. Each constraint is a square box connected to the variables it constrains.

mization search methods, either path-based or local. We do not discuss such CSPs further in this chapter, but we provide some pointers in the bibliographical notes section.

## 5.2 BACKTRACKING SEARCH FOR CSPS

The preceding section gave a formulation of CSPs as search problems. Using this formulation, any of the search algorithms from Chapters 3 and 4 can solve CSPs. Suppose we apply breadth-first search to the generic CSP problem formulation given in the preceding section. We quickly notice something terrible: the branching factor at the top level is $nd$, because any of $d$ values can be assigned to any of $n$ variables. At the next level, the branching factor is $(n-1)d$, and so on for $n$ levels. We generate a tree with $n! \cdot d^n$ leaves, even though there are only $d^n$ possible complete assignments!

COMMUTATIVITY

Our seemingly reasonable but naïve problem formulation has ignored a crucial property common to all CSPs: **commutativity**. A problem is commutative if the order of application of any given set of actions has no effect on the outcome. This is the case for CSPs because, when assigning values to variables, we reach the same partial assignment, regardless of order. Therefore, *all CSP search algorithms generate successors by considering possible assignments for only a* single *variable at each node in the search tree.* For example, at the root node of a search tree for coloring the map of Australia, we might have a choice between $SA = red$, $SA = green$, and $SA = blue$, but we would never choose between $SA = red$ and $WA = blue$. With this restriction, the number of leaves is $d^n$, as we would hope.

BACKTRACKING SEARCH

The term **backtracking search** is used for a depth-first search that chooses values for one variable at a time and backtracks when a variable has no legal values left to assign. The algorithm is shown in Figure 5.3. Notice that it uses, in effect, the one-at-a-time method of

```
function BACKTRACKING-SEARCH(csp) returns a solution, or failure
  return RECURSIVE-BACKTRACKING({ }, csp)

function RECURSIVE-BACKTRACKING(assignment, csp) returns a solution, or failure
  if assignment is complete then return assignment
  var ← SELECT-UNASSIGNED-VARIABLE(VARIABLES[csp], assignment, csp)
  for each value in ORDER-DOMAIN-VALUES(var, assignment, csp) do
     if value is consistent with assignment according to CONSTRAINTS[csp] then
        add {var = value} to assignment
        result ← RECURSIVE-BACKTRACKING(assignment, csp)
        if result ≠ failure then return result
        remove {var = value} from assignment
  return failure
```

**Figure 5.3** A simple backtracking algorithm for constraint satisfaction problems. The algorithm is modeled on the recursive depth-first search of Chapter 3. The functions SELECT-UNASSIGNED-VARIABLE and ORDER-DOMAIN-VALUES can be used to implement the general-purpose heuristics discussed in the text.

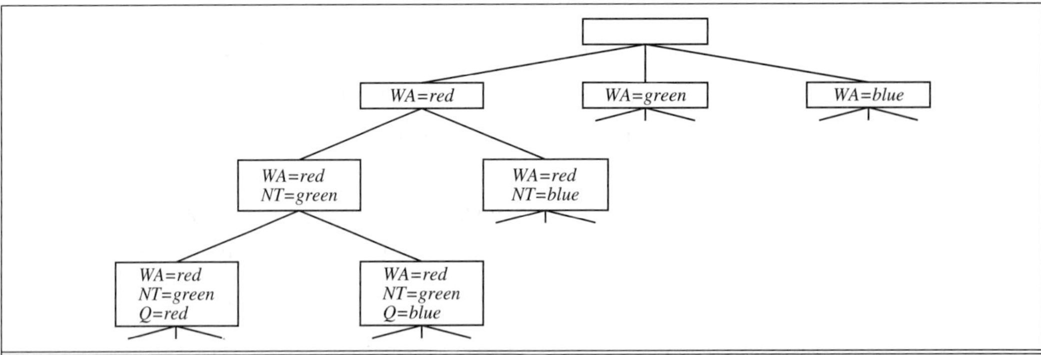


**Figure 5.4** Part of the search tree generated by simple backtracking for the map-coloring problem in Figure 5.1.

incremental successor generation described on page 76. Also, it extends the current assignment to generate a successor, rather than copying it. Because the representation of CSPs is standardized, there is no need to supply BACKTRACKING-SEARCH with a domain-specific initial state, successor function, or goal test. Part of the search tree for the Australia problem is shown in Figure 5.4, where we have assigned variables in the order $WA, NT, Q, \ldots$.

Plain backtracking is an uninformed algorithm in the terminology of Chapter 3, so we do not expect it to be very effective for large problems. The results for some sample problems are shown in the first column of Figure 5.5 and confirm our expectations.

In Chapter 4 we remedied the poor performance of uninformed search algorithms by supplying them with domain-specific heuristic functions derived from our knowledge of the problem. It turns out that we can solve CSPs efficiently without such domain-specific knowl-

| Problem | Backtracking | BT+MRV | Forward Checking | FC+MRV | Min-Conflicts |
|---|---|---|---|---|---|
| USA | (> 1,000K) | (> 1,000K) | 2K | 60 | 64 |
| $n$-Queens | (> 40,000K) | 13,500K | (> 40,000K) | 817K | 4K |
| Zebra | 3,859K | 1K | 35K | 0.5K | 2K |
| Random 1 | 415K | 3K | 26K | 2K | |
| Random 2 | 942K | 27K | 77K | 15K | |

**Figure 5.5** Comparison of various CSP algorithms on various problems. The algorithms from left to right, are simple backtracking, backtracking with the MRV heuristic, forward checking, forward checking with MRV, and minimum conflicts local search. Listed in each cell is the median number of consistency checks (over five runs) required to solve the problem; note that all entries except the two in the upper right are in thousands (K). Numbers in parentheses mean that no answer was found in the allotted number of checks. The first problem is finding a 4-coloring for the 50 states of the United States of America. The remaining problems are taken from Bacchus and van Run (1995), Table 1. The second problem counts the total number of checks required to solve all $n$-Queens problems for $n$ from 2 to 50. The third is the "Zebra Puzzle," as described in Exercise 5.13. The last two are artificial random problems. (Min-conflicts was not run on these.) The results suggest that forward checking with the MRV heuristic is better on all these problems than the other backtracking algorithms, but not always better than min-conflicts local search.

edge. Instead, we find general-purpose methods that address the following questions:

1. Which variable should be assigned next, and in what order should its values be tried?
2. What are the implications of the current variable assignments for the other unassigned variables?
3. When a path fails—that is, a state is reached in which a variable has no legal values—can the search avoid repeating this failure in subsequent paths?

The subsections that follow answer each of these questions in turn.

### Variable and value ordering

The backtracking algorithm contains the line

$var \leftarrow$ SELECT-UNASSIGNED-VARIABLE(VARIABLES[$csp$], $assignment$, $csp$).

By default, SELECT-UNASSIGNED-VARIABLE simply selects the next unassigned variable in the order given by the list VARIABLES[$csp$]. This static variable ordering seldom results in the most efficient search. For example, after the assignments for $WA = red$ and $NT = green$, there is only one possible value for $SA$, so it makes sense to assign $SA = blue$ next rather than assigning $Q$. In fact, after $SA$ is assigned, the choices for $Q$, $NSW$, and $V$ are all forced. This intuitive idea—choosing the variable with the fewest "legal" values—is called the **minimum remaining values** (MRV) heuristic. It also has been called the "most constrained variable" or "fail-first" heuristic, the latter because it picks a variable that is most likely to cause a failure soon, thereby pruning the search tree. If there is a variable $X$ with zero legal values remaining, the MRV heuristic will select $X$ and failure will be detected immediately—avoiding pointless searches through other variables which always will fail when $X$ is finally selected.

MINIMUM REMAINING VALUES

The second column of Figure 5.5, labeled BT+MRV, shows the performance of this heuristic. The performance is 3 to 3,000 times better than simple backtracking, depending on the problem. Note that our performance measure ignores the extra cost of computing the heuristic values; the next subsection describes a method that makes this cost manageable.

DEGREE HEURISTIC

The MRV heuristic doesn't help at all in choosing the first region to color in Australia, because initially every region has three legal colors. In this case, the **degree heuristic** comes in handy. It attempts to reduce the branching factor on future choices by selecting the variable that is involved in the largest number of constraints on other unassigned variables. In Figure 5.1, $SA$ is the variable with highest degree, 5; the other variables have degree 2 or 3, except for $T$, which has 0. In fact, once $SA$ is chosen, applying the degree heuristic solves the problem without any false steps—you can choose any consistent color at each choice point and still arrive at a solution with no backtracking. The minimum remaining values heuristic is usually a more powerful guide, but the degree heuristic can be useful as a tie-breaker.

LEAST-CONSTRAINING-VALUE

Once a variable has been selected, the algorithm must decide on the order in which to examine its values. For this, the **least-constraining-value** heuristic can be effective in some cases. It prefers the value that rules out the fewest choices for the neighboring variables in the constraint graph. For example, suppose that in Figure 5.1 we have generated the partial assignment with $WA = red$ and $NT = green$, and that our next choice is for $Q$. Blue would be a bad choice, because it eliminates the last legal value left for $Q$'s neighbor, $SA$. The least-constraining-value heuristic therefore prefers red to blue. In general, the heuristic is trying to leave the maximum flexibility for subsequent variable assignments. Of course, if we are trying to find all the solutions to a problem, not just the first one, then the ordering does not matter because we have to consider every value anyway. The same holds if there are no solutions to the problem.

## Propagating information through constraints

So far our search algorithm considers the constraints on a variable only at the time that the variable is chosen by SELECT-UNASSIGNED-VARIABLE. But by looking at some of the constraints earlier in the search, or even before the search has started, we can drastically reduce the search space.

### Forward checking

FORWARD CHECKING

One way to make better use of constraints during search is called **forward checking**. Whenever a variable $X$ is assigned, the forward checking process looks at each unassigned variable $Y$ that is connected to $X$ by a constraint and deletes from $Y$'s domain any value that is inconsistent with the value chosen for $X$. Figure 5.6 shows the progress of a map-coloring search with forward checking. There are two important points to notice about this example. First, notice that after assigning $WA = red$ and $Q = green$, the domains of $NT$ and $SA$ are reduced to a single value; we have eliminated branching on these variables altogether by propagating information from $WA$ and $Q$. The MRV heuristic, which is an obvious partner for forward checking, would automatically select $SA$ and $NT$ next. (Indeed, we can view forward checking as an efficient way to incrementally compute the information that the

| | *WA* | *NT* | *Q* | *NSW* | *V* | *SA* | *T* |
|---|---|---|---|---|---|---|---|
| Initial domains | R G B | R G B | R G B | R G B | R G B | R G B | R G B |
| After *WA*=*red* | Ⓡ | G B | R G B | R G B | R G B | G B | R G B |
| After *Q*=*green* | Ⓡ | B | Ⓖ | R B | R G B | B | R G B |
| After *V*=*blue* | Ⓡ | B | Ⓖ | R | Ⓑ | | R G B |

**Figure 5.6** The progress of a map-coloring search with forward checking. $WA = red$ is assigned first; then forward checking deletes $red$ from the domains of the neighboring variables $NT$ and $SA$. After $Q = green$, $green$ is deleted from the domains of $NT$, $SA$, and $NSW$. After $V = blue$, $blue$ is deleted from the domains of $NSW$ and $SA$, leaving $SA$ with no legal values.

MRV heuristic needs to do its job.) A second point to notice is that, after $V = blue$, the domain of $SA$ is empty. Hence, forward checking has detected that the partial assignment $\{WA = red, Q = green, V = blue\}$ is inconsistent with the constraints of the problem, and the algorithm will therefore backtrack immediately.

### Constraint propagation

Although forward checking detects many inconsistencies, it does not detect all of them. For example, consider the third row of Figure 5.6. It shows that when $WA$ is $red$ and $Q$ is $green$, both $NT$ and $SA$ are forced to be blue. But they are adjacent and so cannot have the same value. Forward checking does not detect this as an inconsistency, because it does not look far enough ahead. **Constraint propagation** is the general term for propagating the implications of a constraint on one variable onto other variables; in this case we need to propagate from $WA$ and $Q$ onto $NT$ and $SA$, (as was done by forward checking) and then onto the constraint between $NT$ and $SA$ to detect the inconsistency. And we want to do this fast: it is no good reducing the amount of search if we spend more time propagating constraints than we would have spent doing a simple search.

CONSTRAINT PROPAGATION

ARC CONSISTENCY

The idea of **arc consistency** provides a fast method of constraint propagation that is substantially stronger than forward checking. Here, "arc" refers to a *directed* arc in the constraint graph, such as the arc from $SA$ to $NSW$. Given the current domains of $SA$ and $NSW$, the arc is consistent if, for *every* value $x$ of $SA$, there is *some* value $y$ of $NSW$ that is consistent with $x$. In the third row of Figure 5.6, the current domains of $SA$ and $NSW$ are $\{blue\}$ and $\{red, blue\}$ respectively. For $SA = blue$, there is a consistent assignment for $NSW$, namely, $NSW = red$; therefore, the arc from $SA$ to $NSW$ is consistent. On the other hand, the reverse arc from $NSW$ to $SA$ is not consistent: for the assignment $NSW = blue$, there is no consistent assignment for $SA$. The arc can be made consistent by deleting the value $blue$ from the domain of $NSW$.

We can also apply arc consistency to the arc from $SA$ to $NT$ at the same stage in the search process. The third row of the table in Figure 5.6 shows that both variables have the domain $\{blue\}$. The result is that $blue$ must be deleted from the domain of $SA$, leaving the domain empty. Thus, applying arc consistency has resulted in early detection of an inconsis-

```
function AC-3(csp) returns the CSP, possibly with reduced domains
  inputs: csp, a binary CSP with variables {X1, X2, ..., Xn}
  local variables: queue, a queue of arcs, initially all the arcs in csp

  while queue is not empty do
    (Xi, Xj) ← REMOVE-FIRST(queue)
    if REMOVE-INCONSISTENT-VALUES(Xi, Xj) then
      for each Xk in NEIGHBORS[Xi] - {Xj} do
        add (Xk, Xi) to queue
```

```
function REMOVE-INCONSISTENT-VALUES(Xi, Xj) returns true iff we remove a value
  removed ← false
  for each x in DOMAIN[Xi] do
    if no value y in DOMAIN[Xj] allows (x,y) to satisfy the constraint between Xi and Xj
      then delete x from DOMAIN[Xi]; removed ← true
  return removed
```

**Figure 5.7** The arc consistency algorithm AC-3. After applying AC-3, either every arc is arc-consistent, or some variable has an empty domain, indicating that the CSP cannot be made arc-consistent (and thus the CSP cannot be solved). The name "AC-3" was used by the algorithm's inventor (Mackworth, 1977) because it's the third version developed in the paper.

tency that is not detected by pure forward checking.

Arc consistency checking can be applied either as a preprocessing step before the beginning of the search process, or as a propagation step (like forward checking) after every assignment during search. (The latter algorithm is sometimes called MAC, for *Maintaining Arc Consistency*.) In either case, the process must be applied *repeatedly* until no more inconsistencies remain. This is because, whenever a value is deleted from some variable's domain to remove an arc inconsistency, a new arc inconsistency could arise in arcs pointing to that variable. The full algorithm for arc consistency, AC-3, uses a queue to keep track of the arcs that need to be checked for inconsistency. (See Figure 5.7.) Each arc $(X_i, X_j)$ in turn is removed from the agenda and checked; if any values need to be deleted from the domain of $X_i$, then every arc $(X_k, X_i)$ pointing to $X_i$ must be reinserted on the queue for checking. The complexity of arc consistency checking can be analyzed as follows: a binary CSP has at most $O(n^2)$ arcs; each arc $(X_k, X_i)$ can be inserted on the agenda only $d$ times, because $X_i$ has at most $d$ values to delete; checking consistency of an arc can be done in $O(d^2)$ time; so the total worst-case time is $O(n^2d^3)$. Although this is substantially more expensive than forward checking, the extra cost is usually worthwhile.[1]

Because CSPs include 3SAT as a special case, we do not expect to find a polynomial-time algorithm that can decide whether a given CSP is consistent. Hence, we deduce that arc consistency does not reveal every possible inconsistency. For example, in Figure 5.1, the partial assignment $\{WA = red, NSW = red\}$ is inconsistent, but AC-3 will not find the incon-

[1] The AC-4 algorithm, due to Mohr and Henderson (1986), runs in $O(n^2d^2)$. See Exercise 5.10.

K-CONSISTENCY

sistency. Stronger forms of propagation can be defined using the notion called **$k$-consistency**. A CSP is $k$-consistent if, for any set of $k-1$ variables and for any consistent assignment to those variables, a consistent value can always be assigned to any $k$th variable. For example, 1-consistency means that each individual variable by itself is consistent; this is also called **node consistency**. 2-consistency is the same as arc consistency. 3-consistency means that any pair of adjacent variables can always be extended to a third neighboring variable; this is also called **path consistency**.

NODE CONSISTENCY

PATH CONSISTENCY

STRONGLY K-CONSISTENT

A graph is **strongly $k$-consistent** if it is $k$-consistent and is also $(k-1)$-consistent, $(k-2)$-consistent, ... all the way down to 1-consistent. Now suppose we have a CSP problem with $n$ nodes and make it strongly $n$-consistent (i.e., strongly $k$-consistent for $k=n$). We can then solve the problem with no backtracking. First, we choose a consistent value for $X_1$. We are then guaranteed to be able to choose a value for $X_2$ because the graph is 2-consistent, for $X_3$ because it is 3-consistent, and so on. For each variable $X_i$, we need only search through the $d$ values in the domain to find a value consistent with $X_1, \ldots, X_{i-1}$. We are guaranteed to find a solution in time $O(nd)$. Of course, there is no free lunch: any algorithm for establishing $n$-consistency must take time exponential in $n$ in the worst case.

There is a broad middle ground between $n$-consistency and arc consistency: running stronger consistency checks will take more time, but will have a greater effect in reducing the branching factor and detecting inconsistent partial assignments. It is possible to calculate the smallest value $k$ such that running $k$-consistency ensures that the problem can be solved without backtracking (see Section 5.4), but this is often impractical. In practice, determining the appropriate level of consistency checking is mostly an empirical science.

### Handling special constraints

Certain types of constraints occur frequently in real problems and can be handled using special-purpose algorithms that are more efficient than the general-purpose methods described so far. For example, the *Alldiff* constraint says that all the variables involved must have distinct values (as in the cryptarithmetic problem). One simple form of inconsistency detection for *Alldiff* constraints works as follows: if there are $m$ variables involved in the constraint, and if they have $n$ possible distinct values altogether, and $m > n$, then the constraint cannot be satisfied.

This leads to the following simple algorithm: First, remove any variable in the constraint that has a singleton domain, and delete that variable's value from the domains of the remaining variables. Repeat as long as there are singleton variables. If at any point an empty domain is produced or there are more variables than domain values left, then an inconsistency has been detected.

We can use this method to detect the inconsistency in the partial assignment $\{WA = red, NSW = red\}$ for Figure 5.1. Notice that the variables $SA$, $NT$, and $Q$ are effectively connected by an *Alldiff* constraint because each pair must be a different color. After applying AC-3 with the partial assignment, the domain of each variable is reduced to $\{green, blue\}$. That is, we have three variables and only two colors, so the *Alldiff* constraint is violated. Thus, a simple consistency procedure for a higher-order constraint is sometimes more effective than applying arc consistency to an equivalent set of binary constraints.

RESOURCE CONSTRAINT

Perhaps the most important higher-order constraint is the **resource constraint**, sometimes called the $atmost$ constraint. For example, let $PA_1, \ldots, PA_4$ denote the numbers of personnel assigned to each of four tasks. The constraint that no more than 10 personnel are assigned in total is written as $atmost(10, PA_1, PA_2, PA_3, PA_4)$. An inconsistency can be detected simply by checking the sum of the minimum values of the current domains; for example, if each variable has the domain $\{3, 4, 5, 6\}$, the $atmost$ constraint cannot be satisfied. We can also enforce consistency by deleting the maximum value of any domain if it is not consistent with the minimum values of the other domains. Thus, if each variable in our example has the domain $\{2, 3, 4, 5, 6\}$, the values 5 and 6 can be deleted from each domain.

For large resource-limited problems with integer values—such as logistical problems involving moving thousands of people in hundreds of vehicles—it is usually not possible to represent the domain of each variable as a large set of integers and gradually reduce that set by consistency checking methods. Instead, domains are represented by upper and lower bounds and are managed by bounds propagation. For example, let's suppose there are two flights, 271 and 272, for which the planes have capacities 165 and 385, respectively. The initial domains for the numbers of passengers on each flight are then

$$Flight271 \in [0, 165] \quad \text{and} \quad Flight272 \in [0, 385] .$$

Now suppose we have the additional constraint that the two flights together must carry 420 people: $Flight271 + Flight272 \in [420, 420]$. Propagating bounds constraints, we reduce the domains to

$$Flight271 \in [35, 165] \quad \text{and} \quad Flight272 \in [255, 385] .$$

We say that a CSP is bounds-consistent if for every variable $X$, and for both the lower bound and upper bound values of $X$, there exists some value of $Y$ that satisfies the constraint between $X$ and $Y$, for every variable $Y$. This kind of **bounds propagation** is widely used in practical constraint problems.

BOUNDS PROPAGATION

### Intelligent backtracking: looking backward

The BACKTRACKING-SEARCH algorithm in Figure 5.3 has a very simple policy for what to do when a branch of the search fails: back up to the preceding variable and try a different value for it. This is called **chronological backtracking**, because the *most recent* decision point is revisited. In this subsection, we will see that there are much better ways.

CHRONOLOGICAL BACKTRACKING

Consider what happens when we apply simple backtracking in Figure 5.1 with a fixed variable ordering $Q$, $NSW$, $V$, $T$, $SA$, $WA$, $NT$. Suppose we have generated the partial assignment $\{Q = red, NSW = green, V = blue, T = red\}$. When we try the next variable, $SA$, we see that every value violates a constraint. We back up to $T$ and try a new color for Tasmania! Obviously this is silly—recoloring Tasmania cannot resolve the problem with South Australia.

A more intelligent approach to backtracking is to go all the way back to one of the set of variables that *caused the failure*. This set is called the **conflict set**; here, the conflict set for $SA$ is $\{Q, NSW, V\}$. In general, the conflict set for variable $X$ is the set of previously assigned variables that are connected to $X$ by constraints. The **backjumping** method

CONFLICT SET

BACKJUMPING

backtracks to the *most recent* variable in the conflict set; in this case, backjumping would jump over Tasmania and try a new value for $V$. This is easily implemented by modifying BACKTRACKING-SEARCH so that it accumulates the conflict set while checking for a legal value to assign. If no legal value is found, it should return the most recent element of the conflict set along with the failure indicator.

The sharp-eyed reader will have noticed that forward checking can supply the conflict set with no extra work: whenever forward checking based on an assignment to $X$ deletes a value from $Y$'s domain, it should add $X$ to $Y$'s conflict set. Also, every time the last value is deleted from $Y$'s domain, the variables in the conflict set of $Y$ are added to the conflict set of $X$. Then, when we get to $Y$, we know immediately where to backtrack if needed.

The eagle-eyed reader will have noticed something odd: backjumping occurs when every value in a domain is in conflict with the current assignment; but forward checking detects this event and prevents the search from ever reaching such a node! In fact, it can be shown that *every branch pruned by backjumping is also pruned by forward checking.* Hence, simple backjumping is redundant in a forward-checking search or, indeed, in a search that uses stronger consistency checking, such as MAC.

Despite the observations of the preceding paragraph, the idea behind backjumping remains a good one: to backtrack based on the reasons for failure. Backjumping notices failure when a variable's domain becomes empty, but in many cases a branch is doomed long before this occurs. Consider again the partial assignment $\{WA = red, NSW = red\}$ (which, from our earlier discussion, is inconsistent). Suppose we try $T = red$ next and then assign $NT$, $Q$, $V$, $SA$. We know that no assignment can work for these last four variables, so eventually we run out of values to try at $NT$. Now, the question is, where to backtrack? Backjumping cannot work, because $NT$ *does* have values consistent with the preceding assigned variables—$NT$ doesn't have a complete conflict set of preceding variables that caused it to fail. We know, however, that the four variables $NT$, $Q$, $V$, and $SA$, *taken together*, failed because of a set of preceding variables, which must be those variables which directly conflict with the four. This leads to a deeper notion of the conflict set for a variable such as $NT$: it is that set of preceding variables that caused $NT$, *together with any subsequent variables*, to have no consistent solution. In this case, the set is $WA$ and $NSW$, so the algorithm should backtrack to $NSW$ and skip over Tasmania. A backjumping algorithm that uses conflict sets defined in this way is called **conflict-directed backjumping**.

CONFLICT-DIRECTED BACKJUMPING

We must now explain how these new conflict sets are computed. The method is in fact very simple. The "terminal" failure of a branch of the search always occurs because a variable's domain becomes empty; that variable has a standard conflict set. In our example, $SA$ fails, and its conflict set is (say) $\{WA, NT, Q\}$. We backjump to $Q$, and $Q$ *absorbs* the conflict set from $SA$ (minus $Q$ itself, of course) into its own direct conflict set, which is $\{NT, NSW\}$; the new conflict set is $\{WA, NT, NSW\}$. That is, there is no solution from $Q$ onwards, given the preceding assignment to $\{WA, NT, NSW\}$. Therefore, we backtrack to $NT$, the most recent of these. $NT$ absorbs $\{WA, NT, NSW\} - \{NT\}$ into its own direct conflict set $\{WA\}$, giving $\{WA, NSW\}$ (as stated in the previous paragraph). Now the algorithm backjumps to $NSW$, as we would hope. To summarize: let $X_j$ be the current variable, and let $conf(X_j)$ be its conflict set. If every possible value for $X_j$ fails, backjump to the most recent variable $X_i$ in $conf(X_j)$, and set

$$conf(X_i) \leftarrow conf(X_i) \cup conf(X_j) - \{X_i\} .$$

CONSTRAINT LEARNING

Conflict-directed backjumping takes us back to the right point in the search tree, but doesn't prevent us from making the same mistakes in another branch of the tree. **Constraint learning** actually modifies the CSP by adding a new constraint that is induced from these conflicts.

## 5.3 LOCAL SEARCH FOR CONSTRAINT SATISFACTION PROBLEMS

Local search algorithms (see Section 4.3) turn out to be very effective in solving many CSPs. They use a complete-state formulation: the initial state assigns a value to every variable, and the successor function usually works by changing the value of one variable at a time. For example, in the 8-queens problem, the initial state might be a random configuration of 8 queens in 8 columns, and the successor function picks one queen and considers moving it elsewhere in its column. Another possibility would be start with the 8 queens, one per column in a permutation of the 8 rows, and to generate a successor by having two queens swap rows.[2] We have actually already seen an example of local search for CSP solving: the application of hill climbing to the $n$-queens problem (page 112). The application of WALKSAT (page 223) to solve satisfiability problems, which are a special case of CSPs, is another.

MIN-CONFLICTS

In choosing a new value for a variable, the most obvious heuristic is to select the value that results in the minimum number of conflicts with other variables—the **min-conflicts** heuristic. The algorithm is shown in Figure 5.8 and its application to an 8-queens problem is diagrammed in Figure 5.9 and quantified in Figure 5.5.

Min-conflicts is surprisingly effective for many CSPs, particularly when given a reasonable initial state. Its performance is shown in the last column of Figure 5.5. Amazingly, on the $n$-queens problem, if you don't count the initial placement of queens, the runtime of min-conflicts is roughly *independent of problem size*. It solves even the *million*-queens problem in an average of 50 steps (after the initial assignment). This remarkable observation was the stimulus leading to a great deal of research in the 1990s on local search and the distinction between easy and hard problems, which we take up in Chapter 7. Roughly speaking, $n$-queens is easy for local search because solutions are densely distributed throughout the state space. Min-conflicts also works well for hard problems. For example, it has been used to schedule observations for the Hubble Space Telescope, reducing the time taken to schedule a week of observations from three weeks (!) to around 10 minutes.

Another advantage of local search is that it can be used in an online setting when the problem changes. This is particularly important in scheduling problems. A week's airline schedule may involve thousands of flights and tens of thousands of personnel assignments, but bad weather at one airport can render the schedule infeasible. We would like to repair the schedule with a minimum number of changes. This can be easily done with a local search algorithm starting from the current schedule. A backtracking search with the new set of

[2] Local search can easily be extended to CSPs with objective functions. In that case, all the techniques for hill climbing and simulated annealing can be applied to optimize the objective function.

```
function MIN-CONFLICTS(csp, max_steps) returns a solution or failure
  inputs: csp, a constraint satisfaction problem
          max_steps, the number of steps allowed before giving up

  current ← an initial complete assignment for csp
  for i = 1 to max_steps do
     if current is a solution for csp then return current
     var ← a randomly chosen, conflicted variable from VARIABLES[csp]
     value ← the value v for var that minimizes CONFLICTS(var, v, current, csp)
     set var = value in current
  return failure
```

**Figure 5.8** The MIN-CONFLICTS algorithm for solving CSPs by local search. The initial state may be chosen randomly or by a greedy assignment process that chooses a minimal-conflict value for each variable in turn. The CONFLICTS function counts the number of constraints violated by a particular value, given the rest of the current assignment.

**Figure 5.9** A two-step solution for an 8-queens problem using min-conflicts. At each stage, a queen is chosen for reassignment in its column. The number of conflicts (in this case, the number of attacking queens) is shown in each square. The algorithm moves the queen to the min-conflict square, breaking ties randomly.

constraints usually requires much more time and might find a solution with many changes from the current schedule.

## 5.4 THE STRUCTURE OF PROBLEMS

In this section, we examine ways in which the *structure* of the problem, as represented by the constraint graph, can be used to find solutions quickly. Most of the approaches here are very general and are applicable to other problems besides CSPs, for example probabilistic reasoning. After all, the only way we can possibly hope to deal with the real world is to decompose it into many subproblems. Looking again at Figure 5.1(b) with a view to identifying problem

INDEPENDENT SUBPROBLEMS

CONNECTED COMPONENTS

structure, one fact stands out: Tasmania is not connected to the mainland.[3] Intuitively, it is obvious that coloring Tasmania and coloring the mainland are **independent subproblems**—any solution for the mainland combined with any solution for Tasmania yields a solution for the whole map. Independence can be ascertained simply by looking for **connected components** of the constraint graph. Each component corresponds to a subproblem $CSP_i$. If assignment $S_i$ is a solution of $CSP_i$, then $\bigcup_i S_i$ is a solution of $\bigcup_i CSP_i$. Why is this important? Consider the following: suppose each $CSP_i$ has $c$ variables from the total of $n$ variables, where $c$ is a constant. Then there are $n/c$ subproblems, each of which takes at most $d^c$ work to solve. Hence, the total work is $O(d^c n/c)$, which is *linear* in $n$; without the decomposition, the total work is $O(d^n)$, which is exponential in $n$. Let's make this more concrete: dividing a Boolean CSP with $n = 80$ into four subproblems with $c = 20$ reduces the worst-case solution time from the lifetime of the universe down to less than a second.

Completely independent subproblems are delicious, then, but rare. In most cases, the subproblems of a CSP are connected. The simplest case is when the constraint graph forms a **tree**: any two variables are connected by at most one path. Figure 5.10(a) shows a schematic example.[4] We will show that *any tree-structured CSP can be solved in time linear in the number of variables.* The algorithm has the following steps:

1. Choose any variable as the root of the tree, and order the variables from the root to the leaves in such a way that every node's parent in the tree precedes it in the ordering. (See Figure 5.10(b).) Label the variables $X_1, \ldots, X_n$ in order. Now, every variable except the root has exactly one parent variable.
2. For $j$ from $n$ down to 2, apply arc consistency to the arc $(X_i, X_j)$, where $X_i$ is the parent of $X_j$, removing values from DOMAIN[$X_i$] as necessary.
3. For $j$ from 1 to $n$, assign any value for $X_j$ consistent with the value assigned for $X_i$, where $X_i$ is the parent of $X_j$.

There are two key points to note. First, after step 2 the CSP is directionally arc-consistent, so the assignment of values in step 3 requires no backtracking. (See the discussion of $k$-consistency on page 147.) Second, by applying the arc-consistency checks in reverse order in step 2, the algorithm ensures that any deleted values cannot endanger the consistency of arcs that have been processed already. The complete algorithm runs in time $O(nd^2)$.

Now that we have an efficient algorithm for trees, we can consider whether more general constraint graphs can be *reduced* to trees somehow. There are two primary ways to do this, one based on removing nodes and one based on collapsing nodes together.

The first approach involves assigning values to some variables so that the remaining variables form a tree. Consider the constraint graph for Australia, shown again in Figure 5.11(a). If we could delete South Australia, the graph would become a tree, as in (b). Fortunately, we can do this (in the graph, not the continent) by fixing a value for $SA$ and deleting from the domains of the other variables any values that are inconsistent with the value chosen for $SA$.

---

3 A careful cartographer or patriotic Tasmanian might object that Tasmania should not be colored the same as its nearest mainland neighbor, to avoid the impression that it *might* be part of that state.

4 Sadly, very few regions of the world, with the possible exception of Sulawesi, have tree-structured maps.

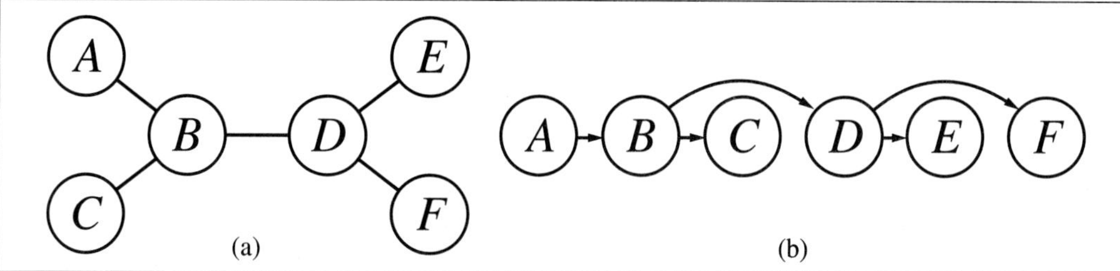


**Figure 5.10** (a) The constraint graph of a tree-structured CSP. (b) A linear ordering of the variables consistent with the tree with $A$ as the root.

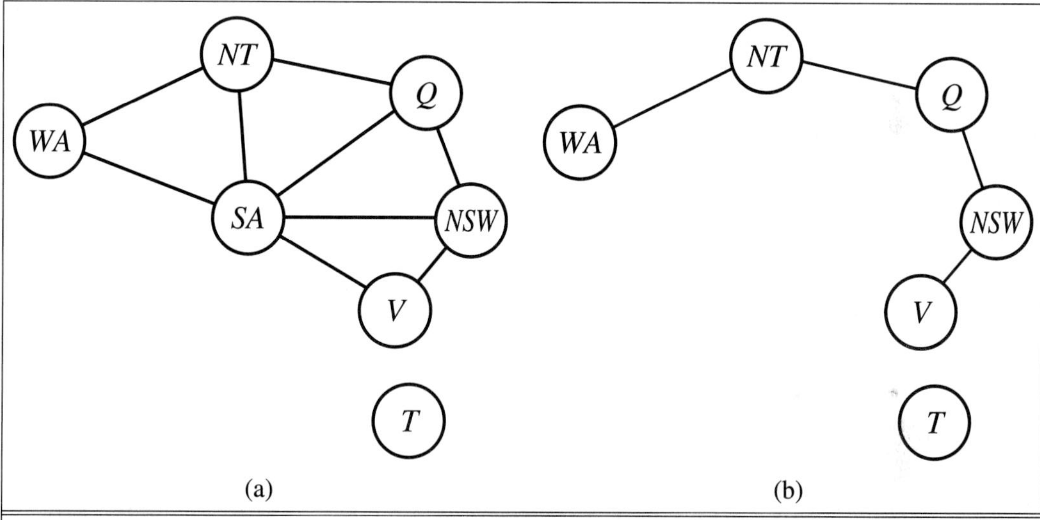


**Figure 5.11** (a) The original constraint graph from Figure 5.1. (b) The constraint graph after the removal of $SA$.

Now, any solution for the CSP after $SA$ and its constraints are removed will be consistent with the value chosen for $SA$. (This works for binary CSPs; the situation is more complicated with higher-order constraints.) Therefore, we can solve the remaining tree with the algorithm given above and thus solve the whole problem. Of course, in the general case (as opposed to map coloring) the value chosen for $SA$ could be the wrong one, so we would need to try each of them. The general algorithm is as follows:

CYCLE CUTSET

1. Choose a subset $S$ from VARIABLES[*csp*] such that the constraint graph becomes a tree after removal of $S$. $S$ is called a **cycle cutset**.
2. For each possible assignment to the variables in $S$ that satisfies all constraints on $S$,
   (a) remove from the domains of the remaining variables any values that are inconsistent with the assignment for $S$, and
   (b) If the remaining CSP has a solution, return it together with the assignment for $S$.

If the cycle cutset has size $c$, then the total runtime is $O(d^c \cdot (n - c)d^2)$. If the graph is "nearly a tree" then $c$ will be small and the savings over straight backtracking will be huge.

In the worst case, however, $c$ can be as large as $(n-2)$. Finding the *smallest* cycle cutset is NP-hard, but several efficient approximation algorithms are known for this task. The overall algorithmic approach is called **cutset conditioning**; we will see it again in Chapter 14, where it is used for reasoning about probabilities.

CUTSET CONDITIONING

TREE DECOMPOSITION

The second approach is based on constructing a **tree decomposition** of the constraint graph into a set of connected subproblems. Each subproblem is solved independently, and the resulting solutions are then combined. Like most divide-and-conquer algorithms, this works well if no subproblem is too large. Figure 5.12 shows a tree decomposition of the map-coloring problem into five subproblems. A tree decomposition must satisfy the following three requirements:

- Every variable in the original problem appears in at least one of the subproblems.
- If two variables are connected by a constraint in the original problem, they must appear together (along with the constraint) in at least one of the subproblems.
- If a variable appears in two subproblems in the tree, it must appear in every subproblem along the path connecting those subproblems.

The first two conditions ensure that all the variables and constraints are represented in the decomposition. The third condition seems rather technical, but simply reflects the constraint that any given variable must have the same value in every subproblem in which it appears; the links joining subproblems in the tree enforce this constraint. For example, $SA$ appears in all four of the connected subproblems in Figure 5.12. You can verify from Figure 5.11 that this decomposition makes sense.

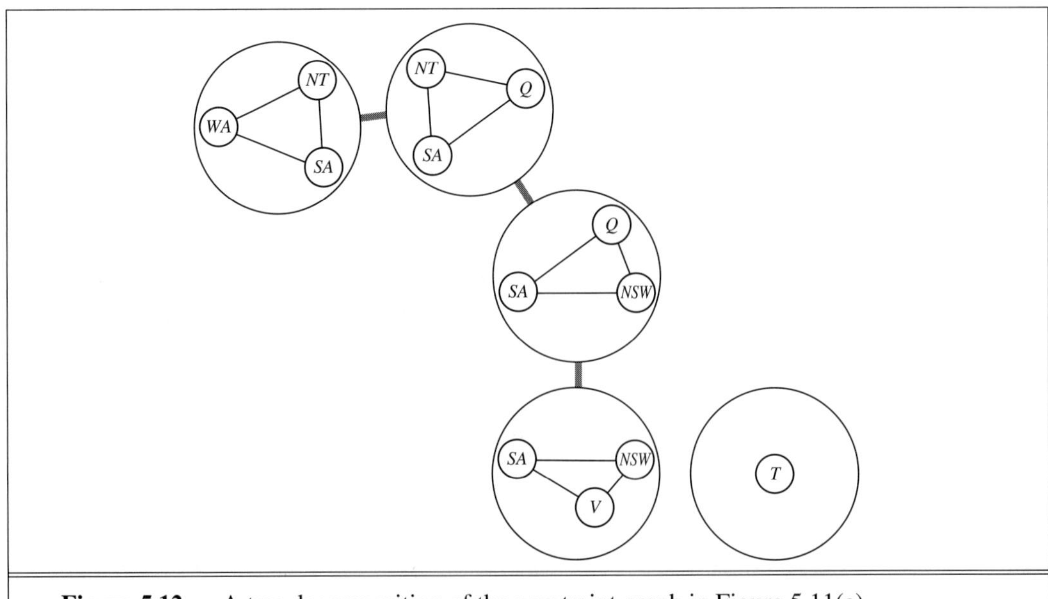


**Figure 5.12** A tree decomposition of the constraint graph in Figure 5.11(a).

We solve each subproblem independently; if any one has no solution, we know the entire problem has no solution. If we can solve all the subproblems, then we attempt to construct a global solution as follows. First, we view each subproblem as a "mega-variable" whose domain is the set of all solutions for the subproblem. For example, the leftmost subproblems in Figure 5.12 is a map-coloring problem with three variables and hence has six solutions—one is $\{WA = red, SA = blue, NT = green\}$. Then, we solve the constraints connecting the subproblems using the efficient algorithm for trees given earlier. The constraints between subproblems simply insist that the subproblem solutions agree on their shared variables. For example, given the solution $\{WA = red, SA = blue, NT = green\}$ for the first subproblem, the only consistent solution for the next subproblem is $\{SA = blue, NT = green, Q = red\}$.

A given constraint graph admits many tree decompositions; in choosing a decomposition, the aim is to make the subproblems as small as possible. The **tree width** of a tree decomposition of a graph is one less than the size of the largest subproblem; the tree width of the graph itself is defined to be the minimum tree width among all its tree decompositions. If a graph has tree width $w$, and we are given the corresponding tree decomposition, then the problem can be solved in $O(nd^{w+1})$ time. Hence, *CSPs with constraint graphs of bounded tree width are solvable in polynomial time.* Unfortunately, finding the decomposition with minimal tree width is NP-hard, but there are heuristic methods that work well in practice.

TREE WIDTH

## 5.5 SUMMARY

- **Constraint satisfaction problems** (or CSPs) consist of variables with constraints on them. Many important real-world problems can be described as CSPs. The structure of a CSP can be represented by its **constraint graph**.
- **Backtracking search**, a form of depth-first search, is commonly used for solving CSPs.
- The **minimum remaining values** and **degree** heuristics are domain-independent methods for deciding which variable to choose next in a backtracking search. The **least-constraining-value** heuristic helps in ordering the variable values.
- By propagating the consequences of the partial assignments that it constructs, the backtracking algorithm can reduce greatly the branching factor of the problem. **Forward checking** is the simplest method for doing this. **Arc consistency** enforcement is a more powerful technique, but can be more expensive to run.
- Backtracking occurs when no legal assignment can be found for a variable. **Conflict-directed backjumping** backtracks directly to the source of the problem.
- Local search using the **min-conflicts** heuristic has been applied to constraint satisfaction problems with great success.
- The complexity of solving a CSP is strongly related to the structure of its constraint graph. Tree-structured problems can be solved in linear time. **Cutset conditioning** can reduce a general CSP to a tree-structured one and is very efficient if a small cutset can be found. **Tree decomposition** techniques transform the CSP into a tree of subproblems and are efficient if the **tree width** of the constraint graph is small.

## BIBLIOGRAPHICAL AND HISTORICAL NOTES

The earliest work related to constraint satisfaction dealt largely with numerical constraints. Equational constraints with integer domains were studied by the Indian mathematician Brahmagupta in the seventh century; they are often called **Diophantine equations**, after the Greek mathematician Diophantus (c. 200–284), who actually considered the domain of positive rationals. Systematic methods for solving linear equations by variable elimination were studied by Gauss (1829); the solution of linear inequality constraints goes back to Fourier (1827).

DIOPHANTINE EQUATIONS

Finite-domain constraint satisfaction problems also have a long history. For example, **graph coloring** (of which map coloring is a special case) is an old problem in mathematics. According to Biggs *et al.* (1986), the four-color conjecture (that every planar graph can be colored with four or fewer colors) was first made by Francis Guthrie, a student of De Morgan, in 1852. It resisted solution—despite several published claims to the contrary—until a proof was devised, with the aid of a computer, by Appel and Haken (1977).

GRAPH COLORING

Specific classes of constraint satisfaction problems occur throughout the history of computer science. One of the most influential early examples was the SKETCHPAD system (Sutherland, 1963), which solved geometric constraints in diagrams and was the forerunner of modern drawing programs and CAD tools. The identification of CSPs as a *general* class is due to Ugo Montanari (1974). The reduction of higher-order CSPs to purely binary CSPs with auxiliary variables (see Exercise 5.11) is due originally to the 19th-century logician Charles Sanders Peirce. It was introduced into the CSP literature by Dechter (1990b) and was elaborated by Bacchus and van Beek (1998). CSPs with preferences among solutions are studied widely in the optimization literature; see Bistarelli *et al.* (1997) for a generalization of the CSP framework to allow for preferences. The bucket-elimination algorithm (Dechter, 1999) can also be applied to optimization problems.

Backtracking search for constraint satisfaction is due to Bitner and Reingold (1975), although they trace the basic algorithm back to the 19th century. Bitner and Reingold also introduced the MRV heuristic, which they called the *most-constrained-variable* heuristic. Brelaz (1979) used the degree heuristic as a tie-breaker after applying the MRV heuristic. The resulting algorithm, despite its simplicity, is still the best method for $k$-coloring arbitrary graphs. Haralick and Elliot (1980) proposed the *least-constraining-value heuristic.*

Constraint propagation methods were popularized by Waltz's (1975) success on polyhedral line-labeling problems for computer vision. Waltz showed that, in many problems, propagation completely eliminates the need for backtracking. Montanari (1974) introduced the notion of constraint networks and propagation by path consistency. Alan Mackworth (1977) proposed the AC-3 algorithm for enforcing arc consistency as well as the general idea of combining backtracking with some degree of consistency enforcement. AC-4, a more efficient arc consistency algorithm, was developed by Mohr and Henderson (1986). Soon after Mackworth's paper appeared, researchers began experimenting with the tradeoff between the cost of consistency enforcement and the benefits in terms of search reduction. Haralick and Elliot (1980) favored the minimal forward checking algorithm described by McGregor (1979), whereas Gaschnig (1979) suggested full arc consistency checking after each variable assignment—an algorithm later called MAC by Sabin and Freuder (1994). The latter paper provides somewhat convincing evidence that, on harder CSPs, full arc consistency checking pays off. Freuder (1978, 1982) investigated the notion of $k$-consistency and its relationship to the complexity of solving CSPs. Apt (1999) describes a generic algorithmic framework within which consistency propagation algorithms can be analyzed.

Special methods for handling higher-order constraints have been developed primarily within the context of **constraint logic programming**. Marriott and Stuckey (1998) provide excellent coverage of research in this area. The *Alldiff* constraint was studied by Regin (1994). Bounds constraints were incorporated into constraint logic programming by Van Hentenryck *et al.* (1998).

The basic backjumping method is due to John Gaschnig (1977, 1979). Kondrak and van Beek (1997) showed that this algorithm is essentially subsumed by forward checking. Conflict-directed backjumping was devised by Prosser (1993). The most general and powerful form of intelligent backtracking was actually developed very early on by Stallman and Sussman (1977). Their technique of **dependency-directed backtracking** led to the development of **truth maintenance systems** (Doyle, 1979), which we will discuss in Section 10.8. The connection between the two areas is analyzed by de Kleer (1989).

DEPENDENCY-DIRECTED BACKTRACKING

The work of Stallman and Sussman also introduced the idea of **constraint recording**, in which partial results obtained by search can be saved and reused later in the search. The idea was introduced formally into backtracking search by Dechter (1990a). **Backmarking** (Gaschnig, 1979) is a particularly simple method in which consistent and inconsistent pairwise assignments are saved and used to avoid rechecking constraints. Backmarking can be combined with conflict-directed backjumping; Kondrak and van Beek (1997) present a hybrid algorithm that provably subsumes either method taken separately. The method of **dynamic backtracking** (Ginsberg, 1993) retains successful partial assignments from later subsets of variables when backtracking over an earlier choice that does not invalidate the later success.

CONSTRAINT RECORDING

BACKMARKING

DYNAMIC BACKTRACKING

Local search in constraint satisfaction problems was popularized by the work of Kirkpatrick *et al.* (1983) on **simulated annealing** (see Chapter 4), which is widely used for scheduling problems. The *min-conflicts* heuristic was first proposed by Gu (1989) and was developed independently by Minton *et al.* (1992). Sosic and Gu (1994) showed how it could be applied to solve the 3,000,000 queens problem in less than a minute. The astounding success of local search using min-conflicts on the $n$-queens problem led to a reappraisal of the nature and prevalence of "easy" and "hard" problems. Peter Cheeseman *et al.* (1991) explored the difficulty of randomly generated CSPs and discovered that almost all such problems either are trivially easy or have no solutions. Only if the parameters of the problem generator are set in a certain narrow range, within which roughly half of the problems are solvable, do we find "hard" problem instances. We discuss this phenomenon further in Chapter 7.

Work relating the structure and complexity of CSPs originates with Freuder (1985), who showed that search on arc-consistent trees works without any backtracking. A similar result, with extensions to acyclic hypergraphs, was developed in the database community (Beeri *et al.*, 1983). Since those papers were published, there has been a great deal of progress in developing more general results relating the complexity of solving a CSP to the structure of its constraint graph. The notion of tree width was introduced by the graph theorists Robertson and Seymour (1986). Dechter and Pearl (1987, 1989), building on the work of Freuder, applied the same notion (which they called **induced width**) to constraint satisfaction problems and developed the tree decomposition approach sketched in Section 5.4. Drawing on this work and on results from database theory, Gottlob *et al.* (1999a, 1999b) developed a notion, **hypertree width**, that is based on the characterization of the CSP as a hypergraph. In addition to showing that any CSP with hypertree width $w$ can be solved in time $O(n^{w+1} \log n)$, they also showed that hypertree width subsumes all previously defined measures of "width" in the sense that there are cases where the hypertree width is bounded and the other measures are unbounded.

There are several good surveys of CSP techniques, including those by Kumar (1992), Dechter and Frost (1999), and Bartak (2001); and the encyclopedia articles by Dechter (1992) and Mackworth (1992). Pearson and Jeavons (1997) survey tractable classes of CSPs, covering both structural decomposition methods and methods that rely on properties of the domains or constraints themselves. Kondrak and van Beek (1997) give an analytical survey of backtracking search algorithms, and Bacchus and van Run (1995) give a more empirical survey. The texts by Tsang (1993) and by Marriott and Stuckey (1998) go into much more depth than has been possible in this chapter. Several interesting applications are described in the collection edited by Freuder and Mackworth (1994). Papers on constraint satisfaction appear regularly in *Artificial Intelligence* and in the specialist journal, *Constraints*. The primary conference venue is the International Conference on Principles and Practice of Constraint Programming, often called *CP*.

## EXERCISES

**5.1** Define in your own words the terms constraint satisfaction problem, constraint, backtracking search, arc consistency, backjumping and min-conflicts.

**5.2** How many solutions are there for the map-coloring problem in Figure 5.1?

**5.3** Explain why it is a good heuristic to choose the variable that is *most* constrained, but the value that is *least* constraining in a CSP search.

**5.4** Consider the problem of constructing (not solving) crossword puzzles:[5] fitting words into a rectangular grid. The grid, which is given as part of the problem, specifies which squares are blank and which are shaded. Assume that a list of words (i.e., a dictionary) is provided and that the task is to fill in the blank squares using any subset of the list. Formulate this problem precisely in two ways:

**a.** As a general search problem. Choose an appropriate search algorithm, and specify a heuristic function, if you think one is needed. Is it better to fill in blanks one letter at a time or one word at a time?

[5] Ginsberg *et al.* (1990) discuss several methods for constructing crossword puzzles. Littman *et al.* (1999) tackle the harder problem of solving them.

**b.** As a constraint satisfaction problem. Should the variables be words or letters?

Which formulation do you think will be better? Why?

**5.5** Give precise formulations for each of the following as constraint satisfaction problems:

FLOOR-PLANNING

**a.** Rectilinear **floor-planning**: find nonoverlapping places in a large rectangle for a number of smaller rectangles.

CLASS SCHEDULING

**b.** **Class scheduling**: There is a fixed number of professors and classrooms, a list of classes to be offered, and a list of possible time slots for classes. Each professor has a set of classes that he or she can teach.

**5.6** Solve the cryptarithmetic problem in Figure 5.2 by hand, using backtracking, forward checking, and the MRV and least-constraining-value heuristics.

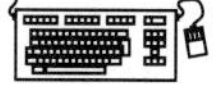

**5.7** Figure 5.5 tests out various algorithms on the $n$-queens problem. Try these same algorithms on map-coloring problems generated randomly as follows: scatter $n$ points on the unit square; selecting a point $X$ at random, connect $X$ by a straight line to the nearest point $Y$ such that $X$ is not already connected to $Y$ and the line crosses no other line; repeat the previous step until no more connections are possible. Construct the performance table for the largest $n$ you can manage, using both $d = 3$ and $d = 4$ colors. Comment on your results.

**5.8** Use the AC-3 algorithm to show that arc consistency is able to detect the inconsistency of the partial assignment $\{WA = red, V = blue\}$ for the problem shown in Figure 5.1.

**5.9** What is the worst-case complexity of running AC-3 on a tree-structured CSP?

**5.10** AC-3 puts back on the queue *every* arc $(X_k, X_i)$ whenever *any* value is deleted from the domain of $X_i$, even if each value of $X_k$ is consistent with several remaining values of $X_i$. Suppose that, for every arc $(X_k, X_i)$, we keep track of the number of remaining values of $X_i$ that are consistent with each value of $X_k$. Explain how to update these numbers efficiently and hence show that arc consistency can be enforced in total time $O(n^2d^2)$.

**5.11** Show how a single ternary constraint such as "$A + B = C$" can be turned into three binary constraints by using an auxiliary variable. You may assume finite domains. (*Hint:* consider a new variable that takes on values which are pairs of other values, and consider constraints such as "$X$ is the first element of the pair $Y$.") Next, show how constraints with more than three variables can be treated similarly. Finally, show how unary constraints can be eliminated by altering the domains of variables. This completes the demonstration that any CSP can be transformed into a CSP with only binary constraints.

**5.12** Suppose that a graph is known to have a cycle cutset of no more than $k$ nodes. Describe a simple algorithm for finding a minimal cycle cutset whose runtime is not much more than $O(n^k)$ for a CSP with $n$ variables. Search the literature for methods for finding approximately minimal cycle cutsets in time that is polynomial in the size of the cutset. Does the existence of such algorithms make the cycle cutset method practical?

**5.13** Consider the following logic puzzle: In five houses, each with a different color, live 5 persons of different nationalities, each of whom prefer a different brand of cigarette, a different drink, and a different pet. Given the following facts, the question to answer is "Where does the zebra live, and in which house do they drink water?"

The Englishman lives in the red house.
The Spaniard owns the dog.
The Norwegian lives in the first house on the left.
Kools are smoked in the yellow house.
The man who smokes Chesterfields lives in the house next to the man with the fox.
The Norwegian lives next to the blue house.
The Winston smoker owns snails.
The Lucky Strike smoker drinks orange juice.
The Ukrainian drinks tea.
The Japanese smokes Parliaments.
Kools are smoked in the house next to the house where the horse is kept.
Coffee is drunk in the green house.
The Green house is immediately to the right (your right) of the ivory house.
Milk is drunk in the middle house.

Discuss different representations of this problem as a CSP. Why would one prefer one representation over another?

# 6 ADVERSARIAL SEARCH

*In which we examine the problems that arise when we try to plan ahead in a world where other agents are planning against us.*

## 6.1 GAMES

Chapter 2 introduced **multiagent environments**, in which any given agent will need to consider the actions of other agents and how they affect its own welfare. The unpredictability of these other agents can introduce many possible **contingencies** into the agent's problem-solving process, as discussed in Chapter 3. The distinction between **cooperative** and **competitive** multiagent environments was also introduced in Chapter 2. Competitive environments, in which the agents' goals are in conflict, give rise to **adversarial search** problems—often known as **games**.

GAMES

Mathematical **game theory**, a branch of economics, views any multiagent environment as a game provided that the impact of each agent on the others is "significant," regardless of whether the agents are cooperative or competitive.[1] In AI, "games" are usually of a rather specialized kind—what game theorists call deterministic, turn-taking, two-player, **zero-sum games** of **perfect information**. In our terminology, this means deterministic, fully observable environments in which there are two agents whose actions must alternate and in which the utility values at the end of the game are always equal and opposite. For example, if one player wins a game of chess (+1), the other player necessarily loses (–1). It is this opposition between the agents' utility functions that makes the situation adversarial. We will consider multiplayer games, non-zero-sum games, and stochastic games briefly in this chapter, but will delay discussion of game theory proper until Chapter 17.

ZERO-SUM GAMES

PERFECT INFORMATION

Games have engaged the intellectual faculties of humans—sometimes to an alarming degree—for as long as civilization has existed. For AI researchers, the abstract nature of games makes them an appealing subject for study. The state of a game is easy to represent, and agents are usually restricted to a small number of actions whose outcomes are defined by

[1] Environments with very many agents are best viewed as **economies** rather than games.

precise rules. Physical games, such as croquet and ice hockey, have much more complicated descriptions, a much larger range of possible actions, and rather imprecise rules defining the legality of actions. With the exception of robot soccer, these physical games have not attracted much interest in the AI community.

Game playing was one of the first tasks undertaken in AI. By 1950, almost as soon as computers became programmable, chess had been tackled by Konrad Zuse (the inventor of the first programmable computer and the first programming language), by Claude Shannon (the inventor of information theory), by Norbert Wiener (the creator of modern control theory), and by Alan Turing. Since then, there has been steady progress in the standard of play, to the point that machines have surpassed humans in checkers and Othello, have defeated human champions (although not every time) in chess and backgammon, and are competitive in many other games. The main exception is Go, in which computers perform at the amateur level.

Games, unlike most of the toy problems studied in Chapter 3, are interesting *because* they are too hard to solve. For example, chess has an average branching factor of about 35, and games often go to 50 moves by each player, so the search tree has about $35^{100}$ or $10^{154}$ nodes (although the search graph has "only" about $10^{40}$ distinct nodes). Games, like the real world, therefore require the ability to make *some* decision even when calculating the *optimal* decision is infeasible. Games also penalize inefficiency severely. Whereas an implementation of A* search that is half as efficient will simply cost twice as much to run to completion, a chess program that is half as efficient in using its available time probably will be beaten into the ground, other things being equal. Game-playing research has therefore spawned a number of interesting ideas on how to make the best possible use of time.

We begin with a definition of the optimal move and an algorithm for finding it. We then look at techniques for choosing a good move when time is limited. **Pruning** allows us to ignore portions of the search tree that make no difference to the final choice, and heuristic **evaluation functions** allow us to approximate the true utility of a state without doing a complete search. Section 6.5 discusses games such as backgammon that include an element of chance; we also discuss bridge, which includes elements of **imperfect information** because not all cards are visible to each player. Finally, we look at how state-of-the-art game-playing programs fare against human opposition and at directions for future developments.

IMPERFECT INFORMATION

## 6.2 OPTIMAL DECISIONS IN GAMES

We will consider games with two players, whom we will call MAX and MIN for reasons that will soon become obvious. MAX moves first, and then they take turns moving until the game is over. At the end of the game, points are awarded to the winning player and penalties are given to the loser. A game can be formally defined as a kind of search problem with the following components:

- The **initial state**, which includes the board position and identifies the player to move.
- A **successor function**, which returns a list of (*move, state*) pairs, each indicating a legal move and the resulting state.

TERMINAL TEST

- A **terminal test**, which determines when the game is over. States where the game has ended are called **terminal states**.
- A **utility function** (also called an objective function or payoff function), which gives a numeric value for the terminal states. In chess, the outcome is a win, loss, or draw, with values $+1$, $-1$, or 0. Some games have a wider variety of possible outcomes; the payoffs in backgammon range from $+192$ to $-192$. This chapter deals mainly with zero-sum games, although we will briefly mention non-zero-sum games.

GAME TREE

The initial state and the legal moves for each side define the **game tree** for the game. Figure 6.1 shows part of the game tree for tic-tac-toe (noughts and crosses). From the initial state, MAX has nine possible moves. Play alternates between MAX's placing an X and MIN's placing an O until we reach leaf nodes corresponding to terminal states such that one player has three in a row or all the squares are filled. The number on each leaf node indicates the utility value of the terminal state from the point of view of MAX; high values are assumed to be good for MAX and bad for MIN (which is how the players get their names). It is MAX's job to use the search tree (particularly the utility of terminal states) to determine the best move.

## Optimal strategies

STRATEGY

In a normal search problem, the optimal solution would be a sequence of moves leading to a goal state—a terminal state that is a win. In a game, on the other hand, MIN has something to say about it. MAX therefore must find a contingent **strategy**, which specifies MAX's move in the initial state, then MAX's moves in the states resulting from every possible response by MIN, then MAX's moves in the states resulting from every possible response by MIN to *those* moves, and so on. Roughly speaking, an optimal strategy leads to outcomes at least as good as any other strategy when one is playing an infallible opponent. We will begin by showing how to find this optimal strategy, even though it should be infeasible for MAX to compute it for games more complex than tic-tac-toe.

PLY

Even a simple game like tic-tac-toe is too complex for us to draw the entire game tree, so we will switch to the trivial game in Figure 6.2. The possible moves for MAX at the root node are labeled $a_1$, $a_2$, and $a_3$. The possible replies to $a_1$ for MIN are $b_1$, $b_2$, $b_3$, and so on. This particular game ends after one move each by MAX and MIN. (In game parlance, we say that this tree is one move deep, consisting of two half-moves, each of which is called a **ply**.) The utilities of the terminal states in this game range from 2 to 14.

MINIMAX VALUE

Given a game tree, the optimal strategy can be determined by examining the **minimax value** of each node, which we write as MINIMAX-VALUE($n$). The minimax value of a node is the utility (for MAX) of being in the corresponding state, *assuming that both players play optimally* from there to the end of the game. Obviously, the minimax value of a terminal state is just its utility. Furthermore, given a choice, MAX will prefer to move to a state of maximum value, whereas MIN prefers a state of minimum value. So we have the following:

$$\text{MINIMAX-VALUE}(n) = \begin{cases} \text{UTILITY}(n) & \text{if } n \text{ is a terminal state} \\ \max_{s \in Successors(n)} \text{MINIMAX-VALUE}(s) & \text{if } n \text{ is a MAX node} \\ \min_{s \in Successors(n)} \text{MINIMAX-VALUE}(s) & \text{if } n \text{ is a MIN node.} \end{cases}$$

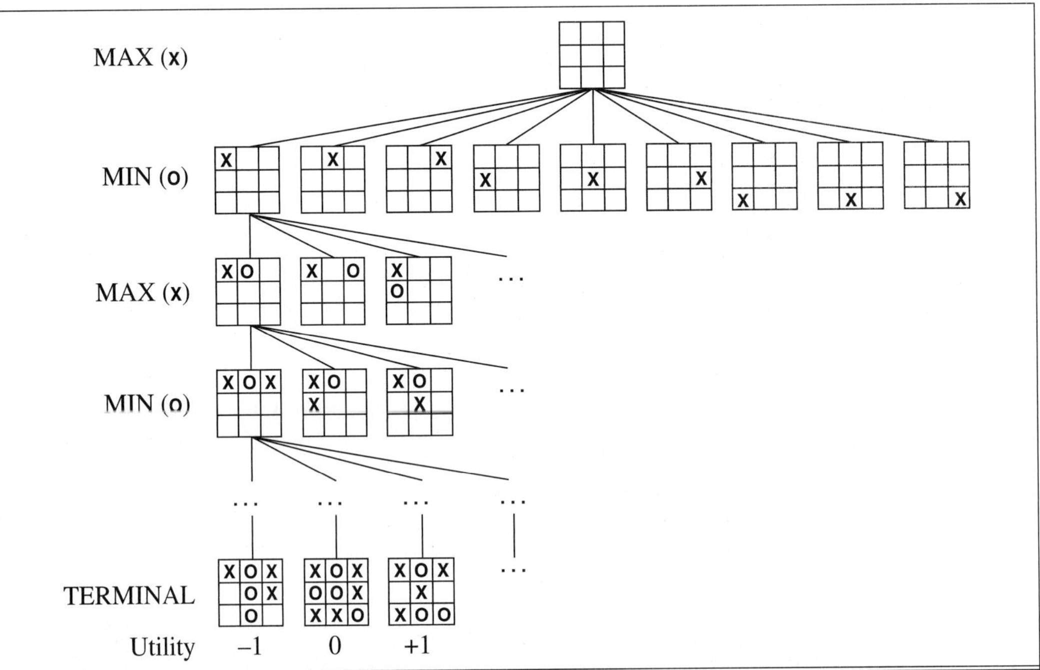


**Figure 6.1** A (partial) search tree for the game of tic-tac-toe. The top node is the initial state, and MAX moves first, placing an X in an empty square. We show part of the search tree, giving alternating moves by MIN (O) and MAX, until we eventually reach terminal states, which can be assigned utilities according to the rules of the game.

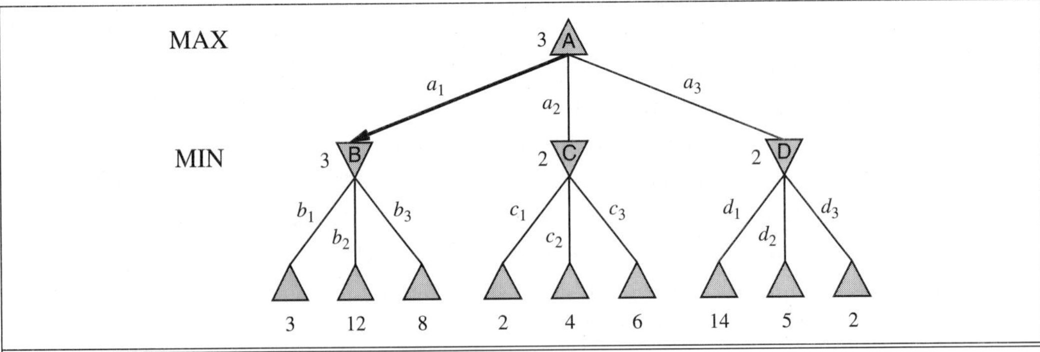


**Figure 6.2** A two-ply game tree. The △ nodes are "MAX nodes," in which it is MAX's turn to move, and the ▽ nodes are "MIN nodes." The terminal nodes show the utility values for MAX; the other nodes are labeled with their minimax values. MAX's best move at the root is $a_1$, because it leads to the successor with the highest minimax value, and MIN's best reply is $b_1$, because it leads to the successor with the lowest minimax value.

Let us apply these definitions to the game tree in Figure 6.2. The terminal nodes on the bottom level are already labeled with their utility values. The first MIN node, labeled $B$, has three successors with values 3, 12, and 8, so its minimax value is 3. Similarly, the other two MIN nodes have minimax value 2. The root node is a MAX node; its successors have minimax

MINIMAX DECISION

values 3, 2, and 2; so it has a minimax value of 3. We can also identify the **minimax decision** at the root: action $a_1$ is the optimal choice for MAX because it leads to the successor with the highest minimax value.

This definition of optimal play for MAX assumes that MIN also plays optimally—it maximizes the *worst-case* outcome for MAX. What if MIN does not play optimally? Then it is easy to show (Exercise 6.2) that MAX will do even better. There may be other strategies against suboptimal opponents that do better than the minimax strategy; but these strategies necessarily do worse against optimal opponents.

### The minimax algorithm

MINIMAX ALGORITHM

BACKED UP

The **minimax algorithm** (Figure 6.3) computes the minimax decision from the current state. It uses a simple recursive computation of the minimax values of each successor state, directly implementing the defining equations. The recursion proceeds all the way down to the leaves of the tree, and then the minimax values are **backed up** through the tree as the recursion unwinds. For example, in Figure 6.2, the algorithm first recurses down to the three bottom-left nodes, and uses the UTILITY function on them to discover that their values are 3, 12, and 8 respectively. Then it takes the minimum of these values, 3, and returns it as the backed-up value of node $B$. A similar process gives the backed up values of 2 for $C$ and 2 for $D$. Finally, we take the maximum of 3, 2, and 2 to get the backed-up value of 3 for the root node.

The minimax algorithm performs a complete depth-first exploration of the game tree. If the maximum depth of the tree is $m$, and there are $b$ legal moves at each point, then the time complexity of the minimax algorithm is $O(b^m)$. The space complexity is $O(bm)$ for an algorithm that generates all successors at once, or $O(m)$ for an algorithm that generates successors one at a time (see page 76). For real games, of course, the time cost is totally impractical, but this algorithm serves as the basis for the mathematical analysis of games and for more practical algorithms.

### Optimal decisions in multiplayer games

Many popular games allow more than two players. Let us examine how to extend the minimax idea to multiplayer games. This is straightforward from the technical viewpoint, but raises some interesting new conceptual issues.

First, we need to replace the single value for each node with a *vector* of values. For example, in a three-player game with players $A$, $B$, and $C$, a vector $\langle v_A, v_B, v_C\rangle$ is associated with each node. For terminal states, this vector gives the utility of the state from each player's viewpoint. (In two-player, zero-sum games, the two-element vector can be reduced to a single value because the values are always opposite.) The simplest way to implement this is to have the UTILITY function return a vector of utilities.

Now we have to consider nonterminal states. Consider the node marked $X$ in the game tree shown in Figure 6.4. In that state, player $C$ chooses what to do. The two choices lead to terminal states with utility vectors $\langle v_A = 1, v_B = 2, v_C = 6\rangle$ and $\langle v_A = 4, v_B = 2, v_C = 3\rangle$. Since 6 is bigger than 3, $C$ should choose the first move. This means that if state $X$ is reached, subsequent play will lead to a terminal state with utilities $\langle v_A = 1, v_B = 2, v_C = 6\rangle$. Hence,

```
function MINIMAX-DECISION(state) returns an action
  inputs: state, current state in game

  v ← MAX-VALUE(state)
  return the action in SUCCESSORS(state) with value v
```

```
function MAX-VALUE(state) returns a utility value
  if TERMINAL-TEST(state) then return UTILITY(state)
  v ← −∞
  for a, s in SUCCESSORS(state) do
    v ← MAX(v, MIN-VALUE(s))
  return v
```

```
function MIN-VALUE(state) returns a utility value
  if TERMINAL-TEST(state) then return UTILITY(state)
  v ← ∞
  for a, s in SUCCESSORS(state) do
    v ← MIN(v, MAX-VALUE(s))
  return v
```

**Figure 6.3** An algorithm for calculating minimax decisions. It returns the action corresponding to the best possible move, that is, the move that leads to the outcome with the best utility, under the assumption that the opponent plays to minimize utility. The functions MAX-VALUE and MIN-VALUE go through the whole game tree, all the way to the leaves, to determine the backed-up value of a state.

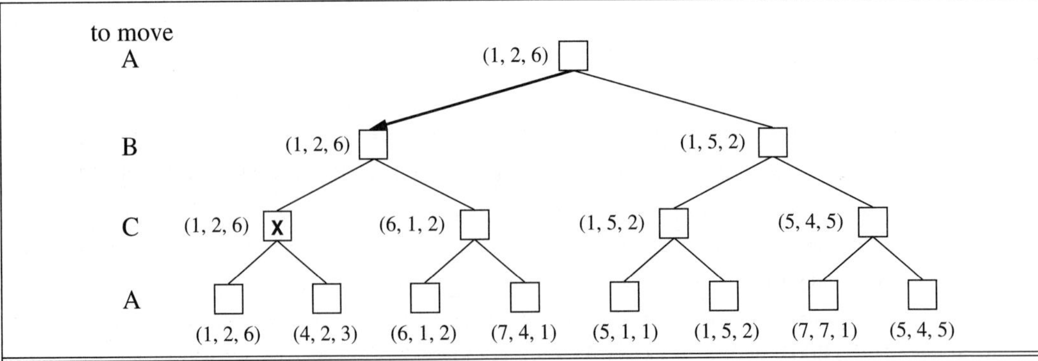


**Figure 6.4** The first three ply of a game tree with three players ($A$, $B$, $C$). Each node is labeled with values from the viewpoint of each player. The best move is marked at the root.

the backed-up value of $X$ is this vector. In general, the backed-up value of a node $n$ is the utility vector of whichever successor has the highest value for the player choosing at $n$.

ALLIANCES

Anyone who plays multiplayer games, such as Diplomacy$^{\text{TM}}$, quickly becomes aware that there is a lot more going on than in two-player games. Multiplayer games usually involve **alliances**, whether formal or informal, among the players. Alliances are made and broken as the game proceeds. How are we to understand such behavior? Are alliances a natural consequence of optimal strategies for each player in a multiplayer game? It turns out that they can be. For example suppose $A$ and $B$ are in weak positions and $C$ is in a stronger position. Then it is often optimal for both $A$ and $B$ to attack $C$ rather than each other, lest $C$ destroy each of them individually. In this way, collaboration emerges from purely selfish behavior. Of course, as soon as $C$ weakens under the joint onslaught, the alliance loses its value, and either $A$ or $B$ could violate the agreement. In some cases, explicit alliances merely make concrete what would have happened anyway. In other cases there is a social stigma to breaking an alliance, so players must balance the immediate advantage of breaking an alliance against the long-term disadvantage of being perceived as untrustworthy. See Section 17.6 for more on these complications.

If the game is not zero-sum, then collaboration can also occur with just two players. Suppose, for example, that there is a terminal state with utilities $\langle v_A = 1000, v_B = 1000\rangle$, and that 1000 is the highest possible utility for each player. Then the optimal strategy is for both players to do everything possible to reach this state—that is, the players will automatically cooperate to achieve a mutually desirable goal.

## 6.3 Alpha–Beta Pruning

The problem with minimax search is that the number of game states it has to examine is exponential in the number of moves. Unfortunately we can't eliminate the exponent, but we can effectively cut it in half. The trick is that it is possible to compute the correct minimax decision without looking at every node in the game tree. That is, we can borrow the idea of **pruning** from Chapter 4 in order to eliminate large parts of the tree from consideration.

ALPHA–BETA PRUNING

The particular technique we will examine is called **alpha–beta pruning**. When applied to a standard minimax tree, it returns the same move as minimax would, but prunes away branches that cannot possibly influence the final decision.

Consider again the two-ply game tree from Figure 6.2. Let's go through the calculation of the optimal decision once more, this time paying careful attention to what we know at each point in the process. The steps are explained in Figure 6.5. The outcome is that we can identify the minimax decision without ever evaluating two of the leaf nodes.

Another way to look at this is as a simplification of the formula for MINIMAX-VALUE. Let the two unevaluated successors of node $C$ in Figure 6.5 have values $x$ and $y$ and let $z$ be the minimum of $x$ and $y$. The value of the root node is given by

$$\begin{aligned}
\text{MINIMAX-VALUE}(\mathit{root}) &= \max(\min(3,12,8), \min(2,x,y), \min(14,5,2)) \\
&= \max(3, \min(2,x,y), 2) \\
&= \max(3, z, 2) \qquad \text{where } z \le 2 \\
&= 3.
\end{aligned}$$

In other words, the value of the root and hence the minimax decision are *independent* of the values of the pruned leaves $x$ and $y$.

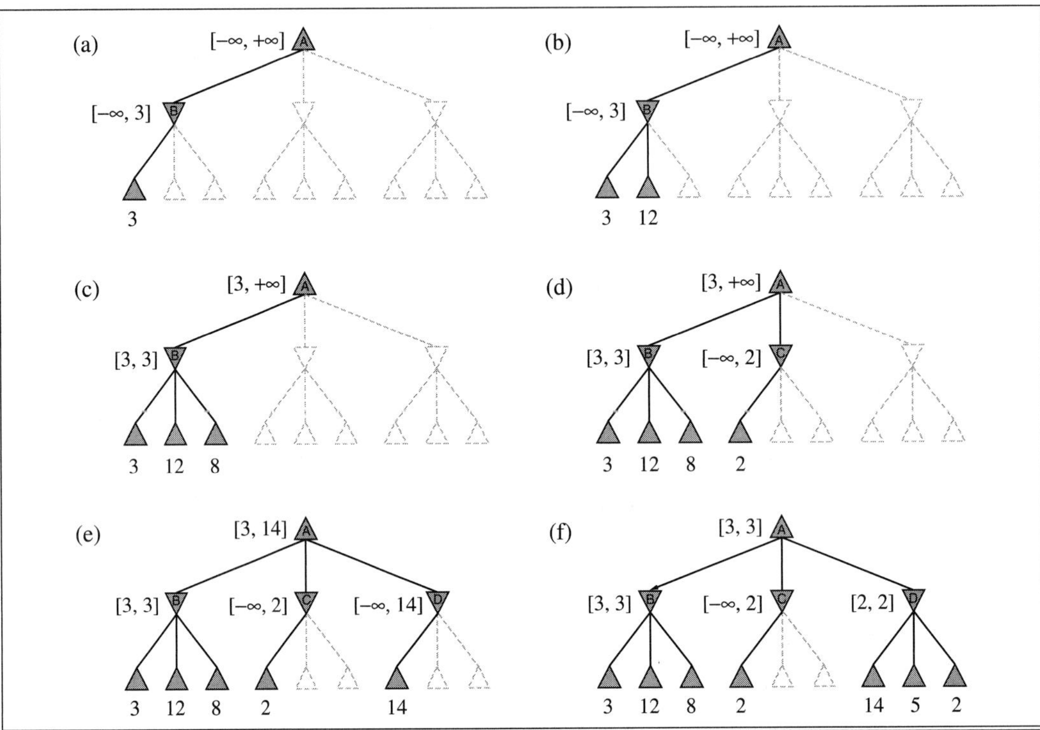


**Figure 6.5** Stages in the calculation of the optimal decision for the game tree in Figure 6.2. At each point, we show the range of possible values for each node. (a) The first leaf below $B$ has the value 3. Hence, $B$, which is a MIN node, has a value of *at most* 3. (b) The second leaf below $B$ has a value of 12; MIN would avoid this move, so the value of $B$ is still at most 3. (c) The third leaf below $B$ has a value of 8; we have seen all $B$'s successors, so the value of $B$ is exactly 3. Now, we can infer that the value of the root is *at least* 3, because MAX has a choice worth 3 at the root. (d) The first leaf below $C$ has the value 2. Hence, $C$, which is a MIN node, has a value of *at most* 2. But we know that $B$ is worth 3, so MAX would never choose $C$. Therefore, there is no point in looking at the other successors of $C$. This is an example of alpha–beta pruning. (e) The first leaf below $D$ has the value 14, so $D$ is worth *at most* 14. This is still higher than MAX's best alternative (i.e., 3), so we need to keep exploring $D$'s successors. Notice also that we now have bounds on all of the successors of the root, so the root's value is also at most 14. (f) The second successor of $D$ is worth 5, so again we need to keep exploring. The third successor is worth 2, so now $D$ is worth exactly 2. MAX's decision at the root is to move to $B$, giving a value of 3.

Alpha–beta pruning can be applied to trees of any depth, and it is often possible to prune entire subtrees rather than just leaves. The general principle is this: consider a node $n$ somewhere in the tree (see Figure 6.6), such that Player has a choice of moving to that node. If Player has a better choice $m$ either at the parent node of $n$ or at any choice point further up, then *$n$ will never be reached in actual play.* So once we have found out enough about $n$ (by examining some of its descendants) to reach this conclusion, we can prune it.

Remember that minimax search is depth-first, so at any one time we just have to consider the nodes along a single path in the tree. Alpha–beta pruning gets its name from the

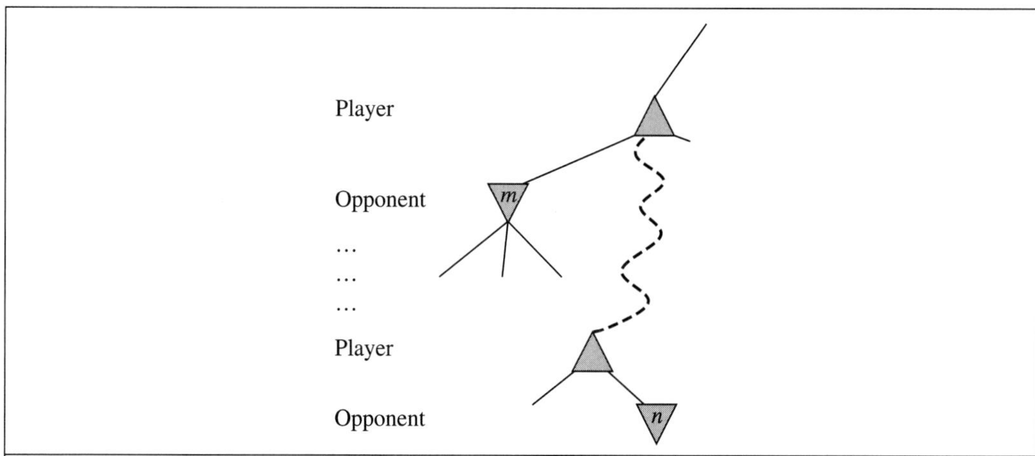


**Figure 6.6** Alpha–beta pruning: the general case. If $m$ is better than $n$ for Player, we will never get to $n$ in play.

following two parameters that describe bounds on the backed-up values that appear anywhere along the path:

$\alpha =$ the value of the best (i.e., highest-value) choice we have found so far at any choice point along the path for MAX.

$\beta =$ the value of the best (i.e., lowest-value) choice we have found so far at any choice point along the path for MIN.

Alpha–beta search updates the values of $\alpha$ and $\beta$ as it goes along and prunes the remaining branches at a node (i.e., terminates the recursive call) as soon as the value of the current node is known to be worse than the current $\alpha$ or $\beta$ value for MAX or MIN, respectively. The complete algorithm is given in Figure 6.7. We encourage the reader to trace its behavior when applied to the tree in Figure 6.5.

The effectiveness of alpha–beta pruning is highly dependent on the order in which the successors are examined. For example, in Figure 6.5(e) and (f), we could not prune any successors of $D$ at all because the worst successors (from the point of view of MIN) were generated first. If the third successor had been generated first, we would have been able to prune the other two. This suggests that it might be worthwhile to try to examine first the successors that are likely to be best.

If we assume that this can be done,[2] then it turns out that alpha–beta needs to examine only $O(b^{m/2})$ nodes to pick the best move, instead of $O(b^m)$ for minimax. This means that the effective branching factor becomes $\sqrt{b}$ instead of $b$—for chess, 6 instead of 35. Put another way, alpha–beta can look ahead roughly twice as far as minimax in the same amount of time. If successors are examined in random order rather than best-first, the total number of nodes examined will be roughly $O(b^{3m/4})$ for moderate $b$. For chess, a fairly simple ordering function (such as trying captures first, then threats, then forward moves, and then backward moves) gets you to within about a factor of 2 of the best-case $O(b^{m/2})$ result. Adding dynamic

[2] Obviously, it cannot be done perfectly; otherwise the ordering function could be used to play a perfect game!

```
function ALPHA-BETA-SEARCH(state) returns an action
  inputs: state, current state in game

  v ← MAX-VALUE(state, −∞, +∞)
  return the action in SUCCESSORS(state) with value v

function MAX-VALUE(state, α, β) returns a utility value
  inputs: state, current state in game
          α, the value of the best alternative for MAX along the path to state
          β, the value of the best alternative for MIN along the path to state

  if TERMINAL-TEST(state) then return UTILITY(state)
  v ← −∞
  for a, s in SUCCESSORS(state) do
    v ← MAX(v, MIN-VALUE(s, α, β))
    if v ≥ β then return v
    α ← MAX(α, v)
  return v

function MIN-VALUE(state, α, β) returns a utility value
  inputs: state, current state in game
          α, the value of the best alternative for MAX along the path to state
          β, the value of the best alternative for MIN along the path to state

  if TERMINAL-TEST(state) then return UTILITY(state)
  v ← +∞
  for a, s in SUCCESSORS(state) do
    v ← MIN(v, MAX-VALUE(s, α, β))
    if v ≤ α then return v
    β ← MIN(β, v)
  return v
```

**Figure 6.7** The alpha–beta search algorithm. Notice that these routines are the same as the MINIMAX routines in Figure 6.3, except for the two lines in each of MIN-VALUE and MAX-VALUE that maintain $\alpha$ and $\beta$ (and the bookkeeping to pass these parameters along).

move-ordering schemes, such as trying first the moves that were found to be best last time, brings us quite close to the theoretical limit.

TRANSPOSITIONS

In Chapter 3, we noted that repeated states in the search tree can cause an exponential increase in search cost. In games, repeated states occur frequently because of **transpositions**—different permutations of the move sequence that end up in the same position. For example, if White has one move $a_1$ that can be answered by Black with $b_1$ and an unrelated move $a_2$ on the other side of the board that can be answered by $b_2$, then the sequences $[a_1, b_1, a_2, b_2]$ and $[a_1, b_2, a_2, b_1]$ both end up in the same position (as do the permutations beginning with $a_2$). It is worthwhile to store the evaluation of this position in a hash table the first time it is encountered, so that we don't have to recompute it on subsequent occurrences.

TRANSPOSITION TABLE

The hash table of previously seen positions is traditionally called a **transposition table**; it is essentially identical to the *closed* list in GRAPH-SEARCH (page 83). Using a transposition table can have a dramatic effect, sometimes as much as doubling the reachable search depth in chess. On the other hand, if we are evaluating a million nodes per second, it is not practical to keep *all* of them in the transposition table. Various strategies have been used to choose the most valuable ones.

## 6.4 IMPERFECT, REAL-TIME DECISIONS

The minimax algorithm generates the entire game search space, whereas the alpha–beta algorithm allows us to prune large parts of it. However, alpha–beta still has to search all the way to terminal states for at least a portion of the search space. This depth is usually not practical, because moves must be made in a reasonable amount of time—typically a few minutes at most. Shannon's 1950 paper, *Programming a computer for playing chess*, proposed instead that programs should cut off the search earlier and apply a heuristic **evaluation function** to states in the search, effectively turning nonterminal nodes into terminal leaves. In other words, the suggestion is to alter minimax or alpha–beta in two ways: the utility function is replaced by a heuristic evaluation function EVAL, which gives an estimate of the position's utility, and the terminal test is replaced by a **cutoff test** that decides when to apply EVAL.

CUTOFF TEST

### Evaluation functions

An evaluation function returns an *estimate* of the expected utility of the game from a given position, just as the heuristic functions of Chapter 4 return an estimate of the distance to the goal. The idea of an estimator was not new when Shannon proposed it. For centuries, chess players (and aficionados of other games) have developed ways of judging the value of a position, because humans are even more limited in the amount of search they can do than are computer programs. It should be clear that the performance of a game-playing program is dependent on the quality of its evaluation function. An inaccurate evaluation function will guide an agent toward positions that turn out to be lost. How exactly do we design good evaluation functions?

First, the evaluation function should order the *terminal* states in the same way as the true utility function; otherwise, an agent using it might select suboptimal moves even if it can see ahead all the way to the end of the game. Second, the computation must not take too long! (The evaluation function could call MINIMAX-DECISION as a subroutine and calculate the exact value of the position, but that would defeat the whole purpose: to save time.) Third, for nonterminal states, the evaluation function should be strongly correlated with the actual chances of winning.

One might well wonder about the phrase "chances of winning." After all, chess is not a game of chance: we know the current state with certainty, and there are no dice involved. But if the search must be cut off at nonterminal states, then the algorithm will necessarily be *uncertain* about the final outcomes of those states. This type of uncertainty is induced by computational, rather than informational, limitations. Given the limited amount of computation that the evaluation function is allowed to do for a given state, the best it can do is make a guess about the final outcome.

Let us make this idea more concrete. Most evaluation functions work by calculating various **features** of the state—for example, the number of pawns possessed by each side in a game of chess. The features, taken together, define various *categories* or *equivalence classes* of states: the states in each category have the same values for all the features. Any given category, generally speaking, will contain some states that lead to wins, some that lead to draws, and some that lead to losses. The evaluation function cannot know which states are which, but it can return a single value that reflects the *proportion* of states with each outcome. For example, suppose our experience suggests that 72% of the states encountered in the category lead to a win (utility +1); 20% to a loss (–1), and 8% to a draw (0). Then a reasonable evaluation for states in the category is the weighted average or **expected value**: $(0.72 \times +1) + (0.20 \times -1) + (0.08 \times 0) = 0.52$. In principle, the expected value can be determined for each category, resulting in an evaluation function that works for any state. As with terminal states, the evaluation function need not return actual expected values, as long as the *ordering* of the states is the same.

FEATURES

EXPECTED VALUE

In practice, this kind of analysis requires too many categories and hence too much experience to estimate all the probabilities of winning. Instead, most evaluation functions compute separate numerical contributions from each feature and then *combine* them to find the total value. For example, introductory chess books give an approximate **material value** for each piece: each pawn is worth 1, a knight or bishop is worth 3, a rook 5, and the queen 9. Other features such as "good pawn structure" and "king safety" might be worth half a pawn, say. These feature values are then simply added up to obtain the evaluation of the position. A secure advantage equivalent to a pawn gives a substantial likelihood of winning, and a secure advantage equivalent to three pawns should give almost certain victory, as illustrated in Figure 6.8(a). Mathematically, this kind of evaluation function is called a **weighted linear function**, because it can be expressed as

MATERIAL VALUE

WEIGHTED LINEAR FUNCTION

$$\textsc{Eval}(s) = w_1 f_1(s) + w_2 f_2(s) + \cdots + w_n f_n(s) = \sum_{i=1}^{n} w_i f_i(s) \, ,$$

where each $w_i$ is a weight and each $f_i$ is a feature of the position. For chess, the $f_i$ could be the numbers of each kind of piece on the board, and the $w_i$ could be the values of the pieces (1 for pawn, 3 for bishop, etc.).

Adding up the values of features seems like a reasonable thing to do, but in fact it involves a very strong assumption: that the contribution of each feature is *independent* of the values of the other features. For example, assigning the value 3 to a bishop ignores the fact that bishops are more powerful in the endgame, when they have a lot of space to maneuver. For this reason, current programs for chess and other games also use *nonlinear* combinations of features. For example, a pair of bishops might be worth slightly more than twice the value of a single bishop, and a bishop is worth more in the endgame than at the beginning.

The astute reader will have noticed that the features and weights are *not* part of the rules of chess! They come from centuries of human chess-playing experience. Given the

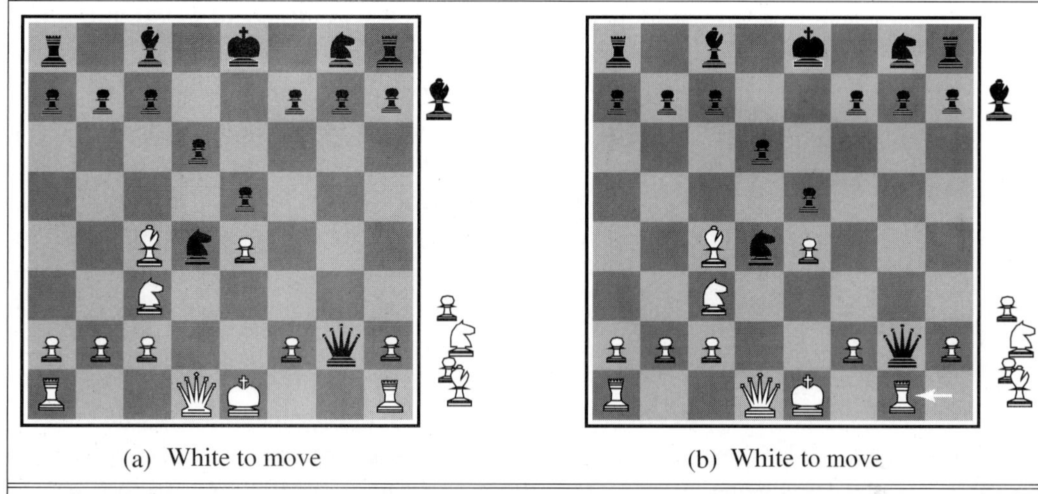


**Figure 6.8** Two slightly different chess positions. In (a), black has an advantage of a knight and two pawns and will win the game. In (b), black will lose after white captures the queen.

linear form of the evaluation, the features and weights result in the best approximation to the true ordering of states by value. In particular, experience suggests that a secure material advantage of more than one point will probably win the game, all other things being equal; a three-point advantage is sufficient for near-certain victory. In games where this kind of experience is not available, the weights of the evaluation function can be estimated by the machine learning techniques of Chapter 18. Reassuringly, applying these techniques to chess has confirmed that a bishop is indeed worth about three pawns.

## Cutting off search

The next step is to modify ALPHA-BETA-SEARCH so that it will call the heuristic EVAL function when it is appropriate to cut off the search. In terms of implementation, we replace the two lines in Figure 6.7 that mention TERMINAL-TEST with the following line:

**if** CUTOFF-TEST($state$, $depth$) **then return** EVAL($state$)

We also must arrange for some bookkeeping so that the current $depth$ is incremented on each recursive call. The most straightforward approach to controlling the amount of search is to set a fixed depth limit, so that CUTOFF-TEST($state$, $depth$) returns $true$ for all $depth$ greater than some fixed depth $d$. (It must also return $true$ for all terminal states, just as TERMINAL-TEST did.) The depth $d$ is chosen so that the amount of time used will not exceed what the rules of the game allow.

A more robust approach is to apply iterative deepening, as defined in Chapter 3. When time runs out, the program returns the move selected by the deepest completed search. However, these approaches can lead to errors due to the approximate nature of the evaluation function. Consider again the simple evaluation function for chess based on material advantage. Suppose the program searches to the depth limit, reaching the position in Figure 6.8(b), where Black is ahead by a knight and two pawns. It would report this as the heuristic value of the state, thereby declaring that the state will likely lead to a win by Black. But White's next move captures Black's queen with no compensation. Hence, the position is really won for White, but this can be seen only by looking ahead one more ply.

QUIESCENCE

Obviously, a more sophisticated cutoff test is needed. The evaluation function should be applied only to positions that are **quiescent**—that is, unlikely to exhibit wild swings in value in the near future. In chess, for example, positions in which favorable captures can be made are not quiescent for an evaluation function that just counts material. Nonquiescent positions can be expanded further until quiescent positions are reached. This extra search is called a **quiescence search**; sometimes it is restricted to consider only certain types of moves, such as capture moves, that will quickly resolve the uncertainties in the position.

QUIESCENCE SEARCH

HORIZON EFFECT

The **horizon effect** is more difficult to eliminate. It arises when the program is facing a move by the opponent that causes serious damage and is ultimately unavoidable. Consider the chess game in Figure 6.9. Black is ahead in material, but if White can advance its pawn from the seventh row to the eighth, the pawn will become a queen and create an easy win for White. Black can forestall this outcome for 14 ply by checking White with the rook, but inevitably the pawn will become a queen. The problem with fixed-depth search is that it believes that these stalling moves have avoided the queening move—we say that the stalling moves push the inevitable queening move "over the search horizon" to a place where it cannot be detected.

SINGULAR EXTENSIONS

As hardware improvements lead to deeper searches, one expects that the horizon effect will occur less frequently—very long delaying sequences are quite rare. The use of **singular extensions** has also been quite effective in avoiding the horizon effect without adding too much search cost. A singular extension is a move that is "clearly better" than all other moves in a given position. A singular-extension search can go beyond the normal depth limit without incurring much cost because its branching factor is 1. (Quiescence search can be thought of as a variant of singular extensions.) In Figure 6.9, a singular extension search will find the eventual queening move, provided that black's checking moves and white's king moves can be identified as "clearly better" than the alternatives.

FORWARD PRUNING

So far we have talked about cutting off search at a certain level and about doing alpha–beta pruning that provably has no effect on the result. It is also possible to do **forward pruning**, meaning that some moves at a given node are pruned immediately without further consideration. Clearly, most humans playing chess only consider a few moves from each position (at least consciously). Unfortunately, the approach is rather dangerous because there is no guarantee that the best move will not be pruned away. This can be disastrous if applied near the root, because every so often the program will miss some "obvious" moves. Forward pruning can be used safely in special situations—for example, when two moves are symmetric or otherwise equivalent, only one of them need be considered—or for nodes that are deep in the search tree.

Combining all the techniques described here results in a program that can play creditable chess (or other games). Let us assume we have implemented an evaluation function for chess, a reasonable cutoff test with a quiescence search, and a large transposition table. Let us also assume that, after months of tedious bit-bashing, we can generate and evaluate

Black to move

**Figure 6.9** The horizon effect. A series of checks by the black rook forces the inevitable queening move by white "over the horizon" and makes this position look like a win for black, when it is really a win for white.

around a million nodes per second on the latest PC, allowing us to search roughly 200 million nodes per move under standard time controls (three minutes per move). The branching factor for chess is about 35, on average, and $35^5$ is about 50 million, so if we used minimax search we could look ahead only about five plies. Though not incompetent, such a program can be fooled easily by an average human chess player, who can occasionally plan six or eight plies ahead. With alpha–beta search we get to about 10 ply, which results in an expert level of play. Section 6.7 describes additional pruning techniques that can extend the effective search depth to roughly 14 plies. To reach grandmaster status we would need an extensively tuned evaluation function and a large database of optimal opening and endgame moves. It wouldn't hurt to have a supercomputer to run the program on.

## 6.5 GAMES THAT INCLUDE AN ELEMENT OF CHANCE

In real life, there are many unpredictable external events that put us into unforeseen situations. Many games mirror this unpredictability by including a random element, such as the throwing of dice. In this way, they take us a step nearer reality, and it is worthwhile to see how this affects the decision-making process.

Backgammon is a typical game that combines luck and skill. Dice are rolled at the beginning of a player's turn to determine the legal moves. In the backgammon position of Figure 6.10, for example, white has rolled a 6–5, and has four possible moves.

Although White knows what his or her own legal moves are, White does not know what Black is going to roll and thus does not know what Black's legal moves will be. That means White cannot construct a standard game tree of the sort we saw in chess and tic-tac-toe. A

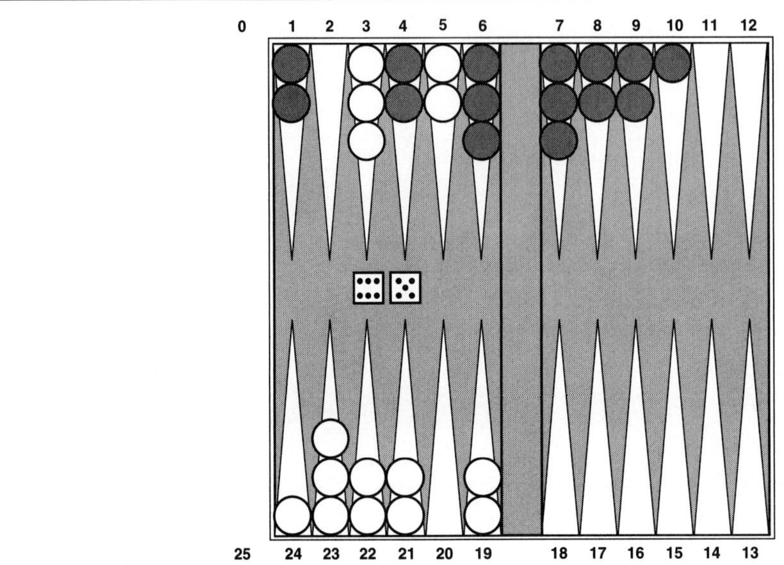


**Figure 6.10** A typical backgammon position. The goal of the game is to move all one's pieces off the board. White moves clockwise toward 25, and black moves counterclockwise toward 0. A piece can move to any position unless there are multiple opponent pieces there; if there is one opponent, it is captured and must start over. In the position shown, White has rolled 6–5 and must choose among four legal moves: (5–10,5–11), (5–11,19–24), (5–10,10–16), and (5–11,11–16).

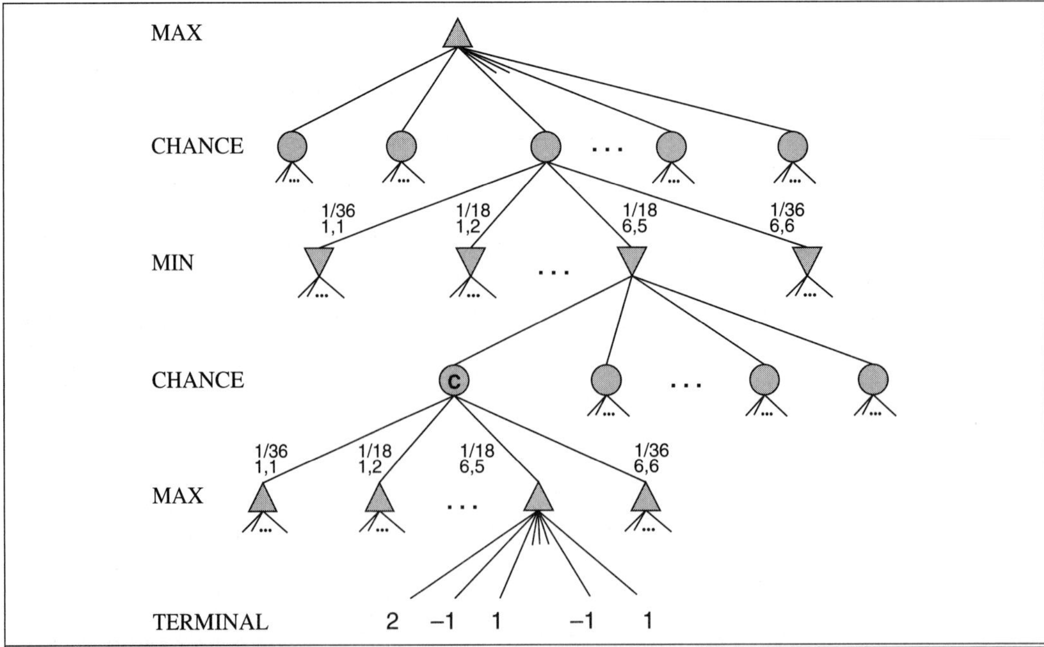


**Figure 6.11** Schematic game tree for a backgammon position.

CHANCE NODES

game tree in backgammon must include **chance nodes** in addition to MAX and MIN nodes. Chance nodes are shown as circles in Figure 6.11. The branches leading from each chance node denote the possible dice rolls, and each is labeled with the roll and the chance that it will occur. There are 36 ways to roll two dice, each equally likely; but because a 6–5 is the same as a 5–6, there are only 21 distinct rolls. The six doubles (1–1 through 6–6) have a 1/36 chance of coming up, the other 15 distinct rolls a 1/18 chance each.

EXPECTIMINIMAX VALUE

The next step is to understand how to make correct decisions. Obviously, we still want to pick the move that leads to the best position. However, the resulting positions do not have definite minimax values. Instead, we can only calculate the **expected value**, where the expectation is taken over all the possible dice rolls that could occur. This leads us to generalize the **minimax value** for deterministic games to an **expectiminimax value** for games with chance nodes. Terminal nodes and MAX and MIN nodes (for which the dice roll is known) work exactly the same way as before; chance nodes are evaluated by taking the weighted average of the values resulting from all possible dice rolls, that is,

$$
\text{EXPECTIMINIMAX}(n) =
\begin{cases}
\text{UTILITY}(n) & \text{if } n \text{ is a terminal state} \\
\max_{s \in Successors(n)} \text{EXPECTIMINIMAX}(s) & \text{if } n \text{ is a MAX node} \\
\min_{s \in Successors(n)} \text{EXPECTIMINIMAX}(s) & \text{if } n \text{ is a MIN node} \\
\sum_{s \in Successors(n)} P(s) \cdot \text{EXPECTIMINIMAX}(s) & \text{if } n \text{ is a chance node}
\end{cases}
$$

where the successor function for a chance node $n$ simply augments the state of $n$ with each possible dice roll to produce each successor $s$ and $P(s)$ is the probability that that dice roll occurs. These equations can be backed up recursively all the way to the root of the tree, just as in minimax. We leave the details of the algorithm as an exercise.

## Position evaluation in games with chance nodes

As with minimax, the obvious approximation to make with expectiminimax is to cut the search off at some point and apply an evaluation function to each leaf. One might think that evaluation functions for games such as backgammon should be just like evaluation functions for chess—they just need to give higher scores to better positions. But in fact, the presence of chance nodes means that one has to be more careful about what the evaluation values mean. Figure 6.12 shows what happens: with an evaluation function that assigns values [1, 2, 3, 4] to the leaves, move $A_1$ is best; with values [1, 20, 30, 400], move $A_2$ is best. Hence, the program behaves totally differently if we make a change in the scale of some evaluation values! It turns out that, to avoid this sensitivity, the evaluation function must be a *positive linear* transformation of the probability of winning from a position (or, more generally, of the expected utility of the position). This is an important and general property of situations in which uncertainty is involved, and we discuss it further in Chapter 16.

## Complexity of expectiminimax

If the program knew in advance all the dice rolls that would occur for the rest of the game, solving a game with dice would be just like solving a game without dice, which minimax

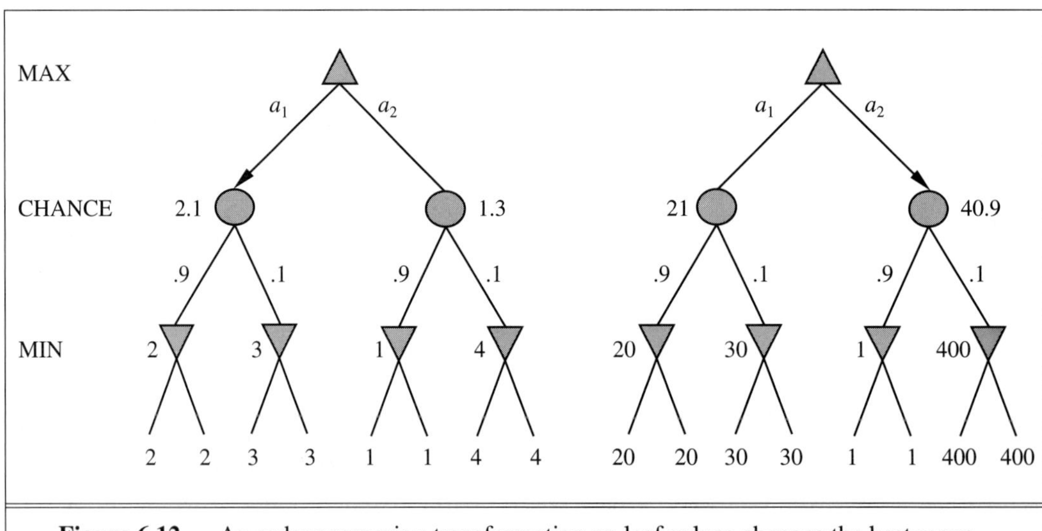


**Figure 6.12** An order-preserving transformation on leaf values changes the best move.

does in $O(b^m)$ time. Because expectiminimax is also considering all the possible dice-roll sequences, it will take $O(b^m n^m)$, where $n$ is the number of distinct rolls.

Even if the search depth is limited to some small depth $d$, the extra cost compared with that of minimax makes it unrealistic to consider looking ahead very far in most games of chance. In backgammon $n$ is 21 and $b$ is usually around 20, but in some situations can be as high as 4000 for dice rolls that are doubles. Three plies is probably all we could manage.

Another way to think about the problem is this: the advantage of alpha–beta is that it ignores future developments that just are not going to happen, given best play. Thus, it concentrates on likely occurrences. In games with dice, there are *no* likely sequences of moves, because for those moves to take place, the dice would first have to come out the right way to make them legal. This is a general problem whenever uncertainty enters the picture: the possibilities are multiplied enormously, and forming detailed plans of action becomes pointless, because the world probably will not play along.

No doubt it will have occurred to the reader that perhaps something like alpha–beta pruning could be applied to game trees with chance nodes. It turns out that it can. The analysis for MIN and MAX nodes is unchanged, but we can also prune chance nodes, using a bit of ingenuity. Consider the chance node $C$ in Figure 6.11 and what happens to its value as we examine and evaluate its children. Is it possible to find an upper bound on the value of $C$ before we have looked at all its children? (Recall that this is what alpha–beta needs to prune a node and its subtree.) At first sight, it might seem impossible, because the value of $C$ is the *average* of its children's values. Until we have looked at all the dice rolls, this average could be anything, because the unexamined children might have any value at all. But if we put bounds on the possible values of the utility function, then we can arrive at bounds for the average. For example, if we say that all utility values are between $+3$ and $-3$, then the value of leaf nodes is bounded, and in turn we *can* place an upper bound on the value of a chance node without looking at all its children.

### Card games

Card games are interesting for many reasons besides their connection with gambling. Among the huge variety of games, we will focus on those in which cards are dealt randomly at the beginning of the game, with each player receiving a hand of cards that is not visible to the other players. Such games include bridge, whist, hearts, and some forms of poker.

At first sight, it might seem that card games are just like dice games: the cards are dealt randomly and determine the moves available to each player, but all the dice are rolled at the beginning! We will pursue this observation further. It will turn out to be quite useful in practice. It is also quite wrong, for interesting reasons.

Imagine two players, MAX and MIN, playing some practice hands of four-card two handed bridge with all the cards showing. The hands are as follows, with MAX to play first:

MAX : ♡6 ♢6 ♣9 8    MIN : ♡4 ♠2 ♣10 5 .

Suppose that MAX leads the ♣9. MIN must now follow suit, playing either the ♣10 or the ♣5. MIN plays the ♣10 and wins the trick. MIN goes next and leads the ♠2. MAX has no spades (and so cannot win the trick) and therefore must throw away some card. The obvious choice is the ♢6 because the other two remaining cards are winners. Now, whichever card MIN leads for the next trick, MAX will win both remaining tricks and the game will be tied at two tricks each. It is easy to show, using a suitable variant of minimax (Exercise 6.12), that MAX's lead of the ♣9 is in fact an optimal choice.

Now let's modify MIN's hand, replacing the ♡4 with the ♢4:

MAX : ♡6 ♢6 ♣9 8    MIN : ♢4 ♠2 ♣10 5 .

The two cases are entirely symmetric: play will be identical, except that on the second trick MAX will throw away the ♡6. Again, the game will be tied at two tricks each and the lead of the ♣9 is an optimal choice.

So far, so good. Now let's hide one of MIN's cards: MAX knows that MIN has either the first hand (with the ♡4) or the second hand (with the ♢4), but has no idea which. MAX reasons as follows:

> The ♣9 is an optimal choice against MIN's first hand and against MIN's second hand, so it must be optimal now because I know that MIN has one of the two hands.

More generally, MAX is using what we might call "averaging over clairvoyancy." The idea is to evaluate a given course of action when there are unseen cards by first computing the minimax value of that action for each possible deal of the cards, and then computing the expected value over all deals using the probability of each deal.

If you think this is reasonable (or if you have no idea because you don't understand bridge), consider the following story:

> Day 1: Road *A* leads to a heap of gold pieces; Road *B* leads to a fork. Take the left fork and you'll find a mound of jewels, but take the right fork and you'll be run over by a bus.
> Day 2: Road *A* leads to a heap of gold pieces; Road *B* leads to a fork. Take the right fork and you'll find a mound of jewels, but take the left fork and you'll be run over by a bus.
> Day 3: Road *A* leads to a heap of gold pieces; Road *B* leads to a fork. Guess correctly and you'll find a mound of jewels, but guess incorrectly and you'll be run over by a bus.

Obviously, it's not unreasonable to take Road *B* on the first two days. No sane person, though, would take Road *B* on Day 3. Yet this is exactly what averaging over clairvoyancy suggests: Road *B* is optimal in the situations of Day 1 and Day 2; therefore it is optimal on Day 3, because one of the two previous situations must hold. Let us return to the card game: after MAX leads the ♣9, MIN wins with the ♣10. As before, MIN leads the ♠2, and now MAX is at the fork in the road without any instructions. If MAX throws away the ♡6 and MIN still has the ♡4, the ♡4 becomes a winner and MAX loses the game. Similarly, If MAX throws away the ♢6 and MIN still has the ♢4, MAX also loses. Therefore, playing the ♣9 first leads to a situation where MAX has a 50% chance of losing. (It would be much better to play the ♡6 and the ♢6 first, guaranteeing a tied game.)

The lesson to be drawn from all this is that when information is missing, one must consider *what information one will have* at each point in the game. The problem with MAX's algorithm is that it assumes that in each possible deal, play will proceed *as if all the cards are visible*. As our example shows, this leads MAX to act as if all *future* uncertainty will be resolved when the time comes. MAX's algorithm will also never decide to *gather* information (or *provide* information to a partner), because within each deal there's no need to do so; yet in games such as bridge, it is often a good idea to play a card that will help one discover things about one's opponent's cards or that will tell one's partner about one's own cards. These kinds of behaviors are generated automatically by an optimal algorithm for games of imperfect information. Such an algorithm searches not in the space of world states (hands of cards), but in the space of **belief states** (beliefs about who has which cards, with what probabilities). We will be able to explain the algorithm properly in Chapter 17, once we have developed the necessary probabilistic machinery. In that chapter, we will also expand on one final and very important point: in games of imperfect information, it's best to give away as little information to the opponent as possible, and often the best way to do this is to act *unpredictably*. This is why restaurant hygiene inspectors do random inspection visits.

## 6.6 STATE-OF-THE-ART GAME PROGRAMS

One might say that game playing is to AI as Grand Prix motor racing is to the car industry: state-of-the-art game programs are blindingly fast, incredibly well-tuned machines that incorporate very advanced engineering techniques, but they aren't much use for doing the shopping. Although some researchers believe that game playing is somewhat irrelevant to mainstream AI, it continues to generate both excitement and a steady stream of innovations that have been adopted by the wider community.

CHESS

**Chess**: In 1957, Herbert Simon predicted that within 10 years computers would beat the human world champion. Forty years later, the Deep Blue program defeated Garry Kasparov in a six-game exhibition match. Simon was wrong, but only by a factor of 4. Kasparov wrote:

> The decisive game of the match was Game 2, which left a scar in my memory . . . we saw something that went well beyond our wildest expectations of how well a computer would be able to foresee the long-term positional consequences of its decisions. The machine

> refused to move to a position that had a decisive short-term advantage—showing a very human sense of danger. (Kasparov, 1997)

Deep Blue was developed by Murray Campbell, Feng-Hsiung Hsu, and Joseph Hoane at IBM (see Campbell *et al.*, 2002), building on the Deep Thought design developed earlier by Campbell and Hsu at Carnegie Mellon. The winning machine was a parallel computer with 30 IBM RS/6000 processors running the "software search" and 480 custom VLSI chess processors that performed move generation (including move ordering), the "hardware search" for the last few levels of the tree, and the evaluation of leaf nodes. Deep Blue searched 126 million nodes per second on average, with a peak speed of 330 million nodes per second. It generated up to 30 billion positions per move, reaching depth 14 routinely. The heart of the machine is a standard iterative-deepening alpha–beta search with a transposition table, but the key to its success seems to have been its ability to generate extensions beyond the depth limit for sufficiently interesting lines of forcing/forced moves. In some cases the search reached a depth of 40 plies. The evaluation function had over 8000 features, many of them describing highly specific patterns of pieces. An "opening book" of about 4000 positions was used, as well as a database of 700,000 grandmaster games from which consensus recommendations could be extracted. The system also used a large endgame database of solved positions, containing all positions with five pieces and many with six pieces. This database has the effect of substantially extending the effective search depth, allowing Deep Blue to play perfectly in some cases even when it is many moves away from checkmate.

The success of Deep Blue reinforced the widely held belief that progress in computer game-playing has come primarily from ever-more-powerful hardware—a view encouraged by IBM. Deep Blue's creators, on the other hand, state that the search extensions and evaluation function were also critical (Campbell *et al.*, 2002). Moreover, we know that several recent algorithmic improvements have allowed programs running on standard PCs to win every World Computer-Chess Championship since 1992, often defeating massively parallel opponents that could search 1000 times more nodes. A variety of pruning heuristics are used to reduce the effective branching factor to less than 3 (compared with the actual branching factor of about 35). The most important of these is the **null move** heuristic, which generates a good lower bound on the value of a position, using a shallow search in which the opponent gets to move twice at the beginning. This lower bound often allows alpha–beta pruning without the expense of a full-depth search. Also important is **futility pruning**, which helps decide in advance which moves will cause a beta cutoff in the successor nodes.

NULL MOVE

FUTILITY PRUNING

The Deep Blue team declined a chance for a rematch with Kasparov. Instead, the most recent major competition in 2002 featured the program FRITZ against world champion Vladimir Kramnik. The eight game match ended in a draw. The conditions of the match were much more favorable to the human, and the hardware was an ordinary PC, not a supercomputer. Still, Kramnik commented that "It is now clear that the top program and the world champion are approximately equal."

CHECKERS

**Checkers**: Beginning in 1952, Arthur Samuel of IBM, working in his spare time, developed a checkers program that learned its own evaluation function by playing itself thousands of times. We describe this idea in more detail in Chapter 21. Samuel's program began as a novice, but after only a few days' self-play had improved itself beyond Samuel's own level (although he was not a strong player). In 1962 it defeated Robert Nealy, a champion at "blind checkers," through an error on his part. Many people felt that this meant computers were superior to people at checkers, but this was not the case. Still, when one considers that Samuel's computing equipment (an IBM 704) had 10,000 words of main memory, magnetic tape for long-term storage, and a .000001–GHz processor, the win remains a great accomplishment.

Few other people attempted to do better until Jonathan Schaeffer and colleagues developed Chinook, which runs on regular PCs and uses alpha–beta search. Chinook uses a precomputed database of all 444 billion positions with eight or fewer pieces on the board to make its endgame play flawless. Chinook came in second in the 1990 U.S. Open and earned the right to challenge for the world championship. It then ran up against a problem, in the form of Marion Tinsley. Dr. Tinsley had been world champion for over 40 years, losing only three games in all that time. In the first match against Chinook, Tinsley suffered his fourth and fifth losses, but won the match 20.5–18.5. The world championship match in August 1994 between Tinsley and Chinook ended prematurely when Tinsley had to withdraw for health reasons. Chinook became the official world champion.

Schaeffer believes that, with enough computing power, the database of endgames could be enlarged to the point where a forward search from the initial position would always reach solved positions, i.e., checkers would be completely solved. (Chinook has announced a win as early as move 5.) This kind of exhaustive analysis can be done by hand for $3 \times 3$ tic-tac-toe and has been done by computer for Qubic ($4 \times 4 \times 4$ tic-tac-toe), Go-Moku (five in a row), and Nine-Men's Morris (Gasser, 1998). Remarkable work by Ken Thompson and Lewis Stiller (1992) solved all five-piece and some six-piece chess endgames, making them available on the Internet. Stiller discovered one case where a forced mate existed but required 262 moves; this caused some consternation because the rules of chess require some "progress" to occur within 50 moves.

OTHELLO

**Othello**, also called Reversi, is probably more popular as a computer game than as a board game. It has a smaller search space than chess, usually 5 to 15 legal moves, but evaluation expertise had to be developed from scratch. In 1997, the Logistello program (Buro, 2002) defeated the human world champion, Takeshi Murakami , by six games to none. It is generally acknowledged that humans are no match for computers at Othello.

BACKGAMMON

**Backgammon**: Section 6.5 explained why the inclusion of uncertainty from dice rolls makes deep search an expensive luxury. Most work on backgammon has gone into improving the evaluation function. Gerry Tesauro (1992) combined Samuel's reinforcement learning method with neural network techniques (Chapter 20) to develop a remarkably accurate evaluator that is used with a search to depth 2 or 3. After playing more than a million training games against itself, Tesauro's program, TD-GAMMON, is reliably ranked among the top three players in the world. The program's opinions on the opening moves of the game have in some cases radically altered the received wisdom.

GO

**Go** is the most popular board game in Asia, requiring at least as much discipline from its professionals as chess. Because the board is $19 \times 19$, the branching factor starts at 361, which is too daunting for regular search methods. Up to 1997 there were no competent programs at all, but now programs often play respectable moves. Most of the best programs combine pattern recognition techniques (when the following pattern of pieces appears, this move should be considered) with limited search (decide whether these pieces can be captured, staying within the local area). The strongest programs at the time of writing are probably Chen Zhixing's Goemate and Michael Reiss' Go4++, each rated somewhere around 10 kyu (weak amateur). Go is an area that is likely to benefit from intensive investigation using more sophisticated reasoning methods. Success may come from finding ways to integrate several lines of local reasoning about each of the many, loosely connected "subgames" into which Go can be decomposed. Such techniques would be of enormous value for intelligent systems in general.

BRIDGE

**Bridge** is a game of imperfect information: a player's cards are hidden from the other players. Bridge is also a *multiplayer* game with four players instead of two, although the players are paired into two teams. As we saw in Section 6.5, optimal play in bridge can include elements of information-gathering, communication, bluffing, and careful weighing of probabilities. Many of these techniques are used in the Bridge Baron™ program (Smith *et al.*, 1998), which won the 1997 computer bridge championship. While it does not play optimally, Bridge Baron is one of the few successful game-playing systems to use complex, hierarchical plans (see Chapter 12) involving high-level ideas such as **finessing** and **squeezing** that are familiar to bridge players.

The GIB program (Ginsberg, 1999) won the 2000 championship quite decisively. GIB uses the "averaging over clairvoyancy" method, with two crucial modifications. First, rather than examining how well each choice works for every possible arrangement of the hidden cards—of which there can be up to 10 million—it examines a random sample of 100 arrangements. Second, GIB uses **explanation-based generalization** to compute and cache general rules for optimal play in various standard classes of situations. This enables it to solve each deal *exactly*. GIB's tactical accuracy makes up for its inability to reason about information. It finished 12th in a field of 35 in the par contest (involving just play of the hand) at the 1998 human world championship, far exceeding the expectations of many human experts.

## 6.7 DISCUSSION

Because calculating optimal decisions in games is intractable in most cases, all algorithms must make some assumptions and approximations. The standard approach, based on minimax, evaluation functions, and alpha–beta, is just one way to do this. Probably because it was proposed so early on, the standard approach had been developed intensively and dominates other methods in tournament play. Some in the field believe that this has caused game playing to become divorced from the mainstream of AI research, because the standard approach no longer provides much room for new insight into general questions of decision making. In this section, we look at the alternatives.

First, let us consider minimax. Minimax selects an optimal move in a given search tree *provided that the leaf node evaluations are exactly correct.* In reality, evaluations are

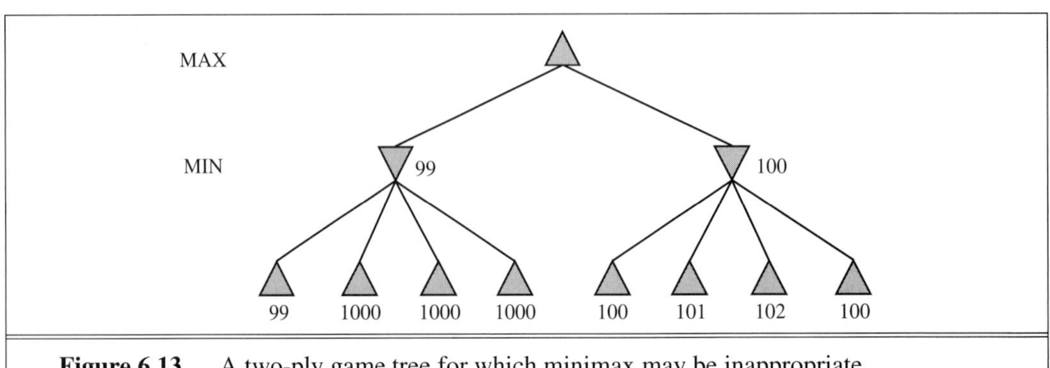


**Figure 6.13** A two-ply game tree for which minimax may be inappropriate.

usually crude estimates of the value of a position and can be considered to have large errors associated with them. Figure 6.13 shows a two-ply game tree for which minimax seems inappropriate. Minimax suggests taking the right-hand branch, whereas it is quite likely that the true value of the left-hand branch is higher. The minimax choice relies on the assumption that *all* of the nodes labeled with values 100, 101, 102, and 100 are *actually* better than the node labeled with value 99. However, the fact that the node labeled 99 has siblings labeled 1000 suggests that in fact it might have a higher true value. One way to deal with this problem is to have an evaluation that returns a *probability distribution* over possible values. Then one can calculate the probability distribution for the parent's value using standard statistical techniques. Unfortunately, the values of sibling nodes are usually highly correlated, so this can be an expensive calculation, requiring hard to obtain information.

Next, we consider the search algorithm that generates the tree. The aim of an algorithm designer is to specify a computation that runs quickly and yields a good move. The most obvious problem with the alpha–beta algorithm is that it is designed not just to select a good move, but also to calculate bounds on the values of all the legal moves. To see why this extra information is unnecessary, consider a position in which there is only one legal move. Alpha–beta search still will generate and evaluate a large, and totally useless, search tree. Of course, we can insert a test into the algorithm, but this merely hides the underlying problem: many of the calculations done by alpha–beta are largely irrelevant. Having only one legal move is not much different from having several legal moves, one of which is fine and the rest of which are obviously disastrous. In a "clear favorite" situation like this, it would be better to reach a quick decision after a small amount of search than to waste time that could be more productively used later on a more problematic position. This leads to the idea of the *utility of a node expansion*. A good search algorithm should select node expansions of high utility—that is, ones that are likely to lead to the discovery of a significantly better move. If there are no node expansions whose utility is higher than their cost (in terms of time), then the algorithm should stop searching and make a move. Notice that this works not only for clear-favorite situations, but also for the case of *symmetrical* moves, for which no amount of search will show that one move is better than another.

METAREASONING

This kind of reasoning about what computations to do is called **metareasoning** (reasoning about reasoning). It applies not just to game playing, but to any kind of reasoning at all. All computations are done in the service of trying to reach better decisions, all have costs, and all have some likelihood of resulting in a certain improvement in decision quality. Alpha–beta incorporates the simplest kind of metareasoning, namely, a theorem to the effect that certain branches of the tree can be ignored without loss. It is possible to do much better. In Chapter 16, we will see how these ideas can be made precise and implementable.

Finally, let us reexamine the nature of search itself. Algorithms for heuristic search and for game playing work by generating sequences of concrete states, starting from the initial state and then applying an evaluation function. Clearly, this is not how humans play games. In chess, one often has a particular goal in mind—for example, trapping the opponent's queen—and can use this goal to *selectively* generate plausible plans for achieving it. This kind of **goal-directed reasoning** or **planning** sometimes eliminates combinatorial search altogether. (See Part IV.) David Wilkins' (1980) PARADISE is the only program to have used goal-directed reasoning successfully in chess: it was capable of solving some chess problems requiring an 18-move combination. As yet there is no good understanding of how to *combine* the two kinds of algorithm into a robust and efficient system, although Bridge Baron might be a step in the right direction. A fully integrated system would be a significant achievement not just for game-playing research, but also for AI research in general, because it would be a good basis for a general intelligent agent.

## 6.8 SUMMARY

We have looked at a variety of games to understand what optimal play means and to understand how to play well in practice. The most important ideas are as follows:

- A game can be defined by the **initial state** (how the board is set up), the legal **actions** in each state, a **terminal test** (which says when the game is over), and a **utility function** that applies to terminal states.
- In two-player zero-sum games with **perfect information**, the **minimax** algorithm can select optimal moves using a depth-first enumeration of the game tree.
- The **alpha–beta** search algorithm computes the same optimal move as minimax, but achieves much greater efficiency by eliminating subtrees that are provably irrelevant.
- Usually, it is not feasible to consider the whole game tree (even with alpha–beta), so we need to cut the search off at some point and apply an **evaluation function** that gives an estimate of the utility of a state.
- Games of chance can be handled by an extension to the minimax algorithm that evaluates a **chance node** by taking the average utility of all its children nodes, weighted by the probability of each child.
- Optimal play in games of **imperfect information**, such as bridge, requires reasoning about the current and future **belief states** of each player. A simple approximation can be obtained by averaging the value of an action over each possible configuration of missing information.

- Programs can match or beat the best human players in checkers, Othello, and backgammon and are close behind in bridge. A program has beaten the world chess champion in one exhibition match. Programs remain at the amateur level in Go.

## BIBLIOGRAPHICAL AND HISTORICAL NOTES

The early history of mechanical game playing was marred by numerous frauds. The most notorious of these was Baron Wolfgang von Kempelen's (1734-1804) "The Turk," a supposed chess-playing automaton that defeated Napoleon before being exposed as a magician's trick cabinet housing a human chess expert (see Levitt, 2000). It played from 1769 to 1854. In 1846, Charles Babbage (who had been fascinated by the Turk) appears to have contributed the first serious discussion of the feasibility of computer chess and checkers (Morrison and Morrison, 1961). He also designed, but did not build, a special-purpose machine for playing tic-tac-toe. The first true game-playing machine was built around 1890 by the Spanish engineer Leonardo Torres y Quevedo. It specialized in the "KRK" (king and rook vs. king) chess endgame, guaranteeing a win with king and rook from any position.

The minimax algorithm is often traced to a paper published in 1912 by Ernst Zermelo, the developer of modern set theory. The paper unfortunately contained several errors and did not describe minimax correctly. A solid foundation for game theory was developed in the seminal work *Theory of Games and Economic Behavior* (von Neumann and Morgenstern, 1944), which included an analysis showing that some games *require* strategies that are randomized (or otherwise unpredictable). See Chapter 17 for more information.

Many influential figures of the early computer era were intrigued by the possibility of computer chess. Konrad Zuse (1945), the first person to design a programmable computer, developed fairly detailed ideas about how it might be done. Norbert Wiener's (1948) influential book *Cybernetics* discussed one possible design for a chess program, including the ideas of minimax search, depth cutoffs, and evaluation functions. Claude Shannon (1950) laid out the basic principles of modern game-playing programs in much more detail than Wiener. He introduced the idea of quiescence search and described some ideas for selective (nonexhaustive) game-tree search. Slater (1950) and the commentators on his article also explored the possibilities for computer chess play. In particular, I. J. Good (1950) developed the notion of quiescence independently of Shannon.

In 1951, Alan Turing wrote the first computer program capable of playing a full game of chess (see Turing *et al.*, 1953). But Turing's program never actually ran on a computer; it was tested by hand simulation against a very weak human player, who defeated it. Meanwhile D. G. Prinz (1952) had written, and actually run, a program that solved chess problems, although it did not play a full game. Alex Bernstein wrote the first program to play a full game of standard chess (Bernstein and Roberts, 1958; Bernstein *et al.*, 1958).[3]

John McCarthy conceived the idea of alpha–beta search in 1956, although he did not publish it. The NSS chess program (Newell *et al.*, 1958) used a simplified version of alpha–

[3] Newell *et al.* (1958) mention a Russian program, BESM, that may have predated Bernstein's program.

beta; it was the first chess program to do so. According to Nilsson (1971), Arthur Samuel's checkers program (Samuel, 1959, 1967) also used alpha–beta, although Samuel did not mention it in the published reports on the system. Papers describing alpha–beta were published in the early 1960s (Hart and Edwards, 1961; Brudno, 1963; Slagle, 1963b). An implementation of full alpha–beta is described by Slagle and Dixon (1969) in a program for playing the game of Kalah. Alpha–beta was also used by the "Kotok–McCarthy" chess program written by a student of John McCarthy (Kotok, 1962). Knuth and Moore (1975) provide a history of alpha–beta, along with a proof of its correctness and a time complexity analysis. Their analysis of alpha–beta with random successor ordering showed an asymptotic complexity of $O((b/\log b)^d)$, which seemed rather dismal because the effective branching factor $b/\log b$ is not much less than $b$ itself. They then realized that the asymptotic formula is accurate only for $b > 1000$ or so, whereas the often-quoted $O(b^{3d/4})$ applies to the range of branching factors encountered in actual games. Pearl (1982b) shows alpha–beta to be asymptotically optimal among all fixed-depth game-tree search algorithms.

The first computer chess match featured the Kotok-McCarthy program and the "ITEP" program written in the mid-1960s at Moscow's Institute of Theoretical and Experimental Physics (Adelson-Velsky *et al.*, 1970). This intercontinental match was played by telegraph. It ended with a 3–1 victory for the ITEP program in 1967. The first chess program to compete successfully with humans was MacHack 6 (Greenblatt *et al.*, 1967). Its rating of approximately 1400 was well above the novice level of 1000, but it fell far short of the rating of 2800 or more that would have been needed to fulfill Herb Simon's 1957 prediction that a computer program would be world chess champion within 10 years (Simon and Newell, 1958).

Beginning with the first ACM North American Computer-Chess Championship in 1970, competition among chess programs became serious. Programs in the early 1970s became extremely complicated, with various kinds of tricks for eliminating some branches of search, for generating plausible moves, and so on. In 1974, the first World Computer-Chess Championship was held in Stockholm and won by Kaissa (Adelson-Velsky *et al.*, 1975), another program from ITEP. Kaissa used the much more straightforward approach of exhaustive alpha–beta search combined with quiescence search. The dominance of this approach was confirmed by the convincing victory of CHESS 4.6 in the 1977 World Computer-Chess Championship. CHESS 4.6 examined up to 400,000 positions per move and had a rating of 1900.

A later version of Greenblatt's MacHack 6 was the first chess program to run on custom hardware designed specifically for chess (Moussouris *et al.*, 1979), but the first program to achieve notable success through the use of custom hardware was Belle (Condon and Thompson, 1982). Belle's move generation and position evaluation hardware enabled it to explore several million positions per move. Belle achieved a rating of 2250, becoming the first master-level program. The HITECH system, also a special-purpose computer, was designed by former World Correspondence Chess Champion Hans Berliner and his student Carl Ebeling at CMU to allow rapid calculation of evaluation functions (Ebeling, 1987; Berliner and Ebeling, 1989). Generating about 10 million positions per move, HITECH became North American computer champion in 1985 and was the first program to defeat a human grandmaster, in 1987. Deep Thought, which was also developed at CMU, went further in the direction of pure search speed (Hsu *et al.*, 1990). It achieved a rating of 2551 and was the forerunner of Deep Blue. The Fredkin Prize, established in 1980, offered $5000 to the first program to achieve a master rating, $10,000 to the first program to achieve a USCF (United States Chess Federation) rating of 2500 (near the grandmaster level), and $100,000 for the first program to defeat the human world champion. The $5000 prize was claimed by Belle in 1983, the $10,000 prize by Deep Thought in 1989, and the $100,000 prize by Deep Blue for its victory over Garry Kasparov in 1997. It is important to remember that Deep Blue's success was due to algorithmic improvements as well as hardware (Hsu, 1999; Campbell *et al.*, 2002). Techniques such as the null-move heuristic (Beal, 1990) have led to programs that are quite selective in their searches. The last three World Computer-Chess Championships in 1992, 1995, and 1999 were won by programs running on standard PCs. Probably the most complete description of a modern chess program is provided by Ernst Heinz (2000), whose DARKTHOUGHT program was the highest-ranked noncommercial PC program at the 1999 world championships.

Several attempts have been made to overcome the problems with the "standard approach" that were outlined in Section 6.7. The first selective search algorithm with some theoretical grounding was probably B* (Berliner, 1979), which attempts to maintain interval bounds on the possible value of a node in the game tree, rather than giving it a single point-valued estimate. Leaf nodes are selected for expansion in an attempt to refine the top-level bounds until one move is "clearly best." Palay (1985) extends the B* idea using probability distributions on values in place of intervals. David McAllester's (1988) conspiracy number search expands leaf nodes that, by changing their values, could cause the program to prefer a new move at the root. MGSS* (Russell and Wefald, 1989) uses the decision-theoretic techniques of Chapter 16 to estimate the value of expanding each leaf in terms of the expected improvement in decision quality at the root. It outplayed an alpha–beta algorithm at Othello despite searching an order of magnitude fewer nodes. The MGSS* approach is, in principle, applicable to the control of any form of deliberation.

Alpha–beta search is in many ways the two-player analog of depth-first branch-and-bound, which is dominated by A* in the single-agent case. The SSS* algorithm (Stockman, 1979) can be viewed as a two-player A* and never expands more nodes than alpha–beta to reach the same decision. The memory requirements and computational overhead of the queue make SSS* in its original form impractical, but a linear-space version has been developed from the RBFS algorithm (Korf and Chickering, 1996). Plaat *et al.* (1996) developed a new view of SSS* as a combination of alpha–beta and transposition tables, showing how to overcome the drawbacks of the original algorithm and developing a new variant called MTD(*f*) that has been adopted by a number of top programs.

D. F. Beal (1980) and Dana Nau (1980, 1983) studied the weaknesses of minimax applied to approximate evaluations. They showed that under certain independence assumptions about the distribution of leaf values in the tree, minimaxing can yield values at the root that are actually *less* reliable than the direct use of the evaluation function itself. Pearl's book *Heuristics* (1984) partially explains this apparent paradox and analyzes many game-playing algorithms. Baum and Smith (1997) propose a probability-based replacement for minimax, showing that it results in better choices in certain games. There is still little theory of the effects of cutting off search at different levels and applying evaluation functions.

The expectiminimax algorithm was proposed by Donald Michie (1966), although of course it follows directly from the principles of game-tree evaluation due to von Neumann and Morgenstern. Bruce Ballard (1983) extended alpha–beta pruning to cover trees with chance nodes. The first successful backgammon program was BKG (Berliner, 1977, 1980b); it used a complex, manually constructed evaluation function and searched only to depth 1. It was the first program to defeat a human world champion at a major classic game (Berliner, 1980a). Berliner readily acknowledged that this was a very short exhibition match (not a world championship match) and that BKG was very lucky with the dice. Work by Gerry Tesauro, first on NEUROGAMMON (Tesauro, 1989) and later on TD-GAMMON (Tesauro, 1995), showed that much better results could be obtained via reinforcement learning, which we will cover in Chapter 21.

Checkers, rather than chess, was the first of the classic games fully played by a computer. Christopher Strachey (1952) wrote the first working program for checkers. Schaeffer (1997) gives a highly readable, "warts and all" account of the development of his Chinook world champion checkers program.

The first Go-playing programs were developed somewhat later than those for checkers and chess (Lefkovitz, 1960; Remus, 1962) and have progressed more slowly. Ryder (1971) used a pure search-based approach with a variety of selective pruning methods to overcome the enormous branching factor. Zobrist (1970) used condition–action rules to suggest plausible moves when known patterns appeared. Reitman and Wilcox (1979) combined rules and search to good effect, and most modern programs have followed this hybrid approach. Müller (2002) summarizes the state of the art of computerized Go and provides a wealth of references. Anshelevich (2000) uses related techniques for the game of Hex. The *Computer Go Newsletter*, published by the Computer Go Association, describes current developments.

Papers on computer game playing appear in a variety of venues. The rather misleadingly named conference proceedings *Heuristic Programming in Artificial Intelligence* report on the Computer Olympiads, which include a wide variety of games. There are also several edited collections of important papers on game-playing research (Levy, 1988a, 1988b; Marsland and Schaeffer, 1990). The International Computer Chess Association (ICCA), founded in 1977, publishes the quarterly *ICGA Journal* (formerly the *ICCA Journal*). Important papers have been published in the serial anthology *Advances in Computer Chess*, starting with Clarke (1977). Volume 134 of the journal *Artificial Intelligence* (2002) contains descriptions of state-of-the-art programs for chess, Othello, Hex, shogi, Go, backgammon, poker, Scrabble.™and other games.

## EXERCISES

**6.1** This problem exercises the basic concepts of game playing, using tic-tac-toe (noughts and crosses) as an example. We define $X_n$ as the number of rows, columns, or diagonals with exactly $n$ $X$'s and no $O$'s. Similarly, $O_n$ is the number of rows, columns, or diagonals with just $n$ $O$'s. The utility function assigns $+1$ to any position with $X_3 = 1$ and $-1$ to any position with $O_3 = 1$. All other terminal positions have utility 0. For nonterminal positions, we use a linear evaluation function defined as $Eval(s) = 3X_2(s)+X_1(s)-(3O_2(s)+O_1(s))$.

**a.** Approximately how many possible games of tic-tac-toe are there?

**b.** Show the whole game tree starting from an empty board down to depth 2 (i.e., one $X$ and one $O$ on the board), taking symmetry into account.

**c.** Mark on your tree the evaluations of all the positions at depth 2.

**d.** Using the minimax algorithm, mark on your tree the backed-up values for the positions at depths 1 and 0, and use those values to choose the best starting move.

**e.** Circle the nodes at depth 2 that would *not* be evaluated if alpha–beta pruning were applied, assuming the nodes are generated *in the optimal order for alpha–beta pruning*.

**6.2** Prove the following assertion: for every game tree, the utility obtained by MAX using minimax decisions against a suboptimal MIN will be never be lower than the utility obtained playing against an optimal MIN. Can you come up with a game tree in which MAX can do still better using a *suboptimal* strategy against a suboptimal MIN?

**6.3** Consider the two-player game described in Figure 6.14.

**a.** Draw the complete game tree, using the following conventions:

- Write each state as $(s_A, s_B)$ where $s_A$ and $s_B$ denote the token locations.
- Put each terminal state in a square boxes and write its game value in a circle.
- Put *loop states* (states that already appear on the path to the root) in double square boxes. Since it is not clear how to assign values to loop states, annotate each with a "?" in a circle.

**b.** Now mark each node with its backed-up minimax value (also in a circle). Explain how you handled the "?" values and why.

**c.** Explain why the standard minimax algorithm would fail on this game tree and briefly sketch how you might fix it, drawing on your answer to (b). Does your modified algorithm give optimal decisions for all games with loops?

**d.** This 4-square game can be generalized to $n$ squares for any $n > 2$. Prove that $A$ wins if $n$ is even and loses if $n$ is odd.

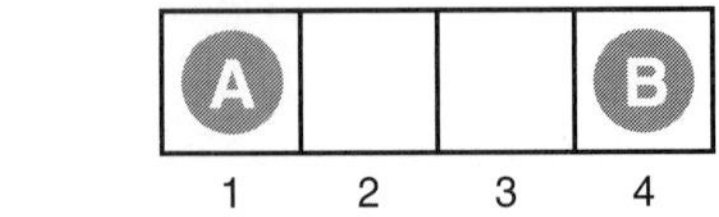


**Figure 6.14** The starting position of a simple game. Player $A$ moves first. The two players take turns moving, and each player must move his token to an open adjacent space *in either direction*. If the opponent occupies an adjacent space, then a player may jump over the opponent to the next open space if any. (For example, if $A$ is on 3 and $B$ is on 2, then $A$ may move back to 1.) The game ends when one player reaches the opposite end of the board. If player $A$ reaches space 4 first, then the value of the game to $A$ is $+1$; if player $B$ reaches space 1 first, then the value of the game to $A$ is $-1$.

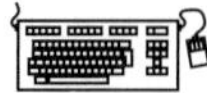

**6.4** Implement move generators and evaluation functions for one or more of the following games: Kalah, Othello, checkers, and chess. Construct a general alpha–beta game-playing agent that uses your implementation. Compare the effect of increasing search depth, improving move ordering, and improving the evaluation function. How close does your effective branching factor come to the ideal case of perfect move ordering?

**6.5** Develop a formal proof of correctness for alpha-beta pruning. To do this, consider the situation shown in Figure 6.15. The question is whether to prune node $n_j$, which is a max-node and a descendant of node $n_1$. The basic idea is to prune it if and only if the minimax value of $n_1$ can be shown to be independent of the value of $n_j$.

**a**. The value of $n_1$ is given by

$$n_1 = \min(n_2, n_{21}, \ldots, n_{2b_2}) .$$

Find a similar expression for $n_2$ and hence an expression for $n_1$ in terms of $n_j$.

**b**. Let $l_i$ be the minimum (or maximum) value of the nodes to the *left* of node $n_i$ at depth $i$, whose minimax value is already known. Similarly, let $r_i$ be the minimum (or maximum) value of the unexplored nodes to the right of $n_i$ at depth $i$. Rewrite your expression for $n_1$ in terms of the $l_i$ and $r_i$ values.

**c**. Now reformulate the expression to show that in order to affect $n_1$, $n_j$ must not exceed a certain bound derived from the $l_i$ values.

**d**. Repeat the process for the case where $n_j$ is a min-node.

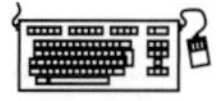

**6.6** Implement the expectiminimax algorithm and the *-alpha–beta algorithm, which is described by Ballard (1983), for pruning game trees with chance nodes. Try them on a game such as backgammon and measure the pruning effectiveness of *-alpha–beta.

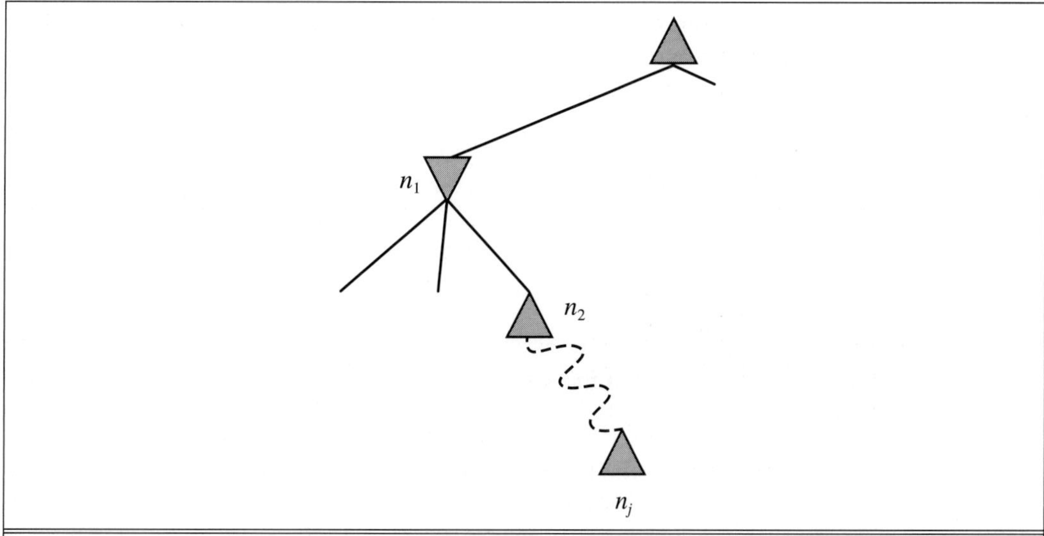


**Figure 6.15** Situation when considering whether to prune node $n_j$.

**6.7** Prove that with a positive linear transformation of leaf values (i.e., transforming a value $x$ to $ax + b$ where $a > 0$), the choice of move remains unchanged in a game tree, even when there are chance nodes.

**6.8** Consider the following procedure for choosing moves in games with chance nodes:

- Generate some die-roll sequences (say, 50) down to a suitable depth (say, 8).
- With known die rolls, the game tree becomes deterministic. For each die-roll sequence, solve the resulting deterministic game tree using alpha–beta.
- Use the results to estimate the value of each move and to choose the best.

Will this procedure work well? Why (not)?

**6.9** Describe and implement a *real-time, multiplayer* game-playing environment, where time is part of the environment state and players are given fixed time allocations.

**6.10** Describe or implement state descriptions, move generators, terminal tests, utility functions, and evaluation functions for one or more of the following games: Monopoly, Scrabble, bridge (assuming a given contract), and poker (choose your favorite variety).

**6.11** Consider carefully the interplay of chance events and partial information in each of the games in Exercise 6.10.

**a.** For which is the standard expectiminimax model appropriate? Implement the algorithm and run it in your game-playing agent, with appropriate modifications to the game-playing environment.

**b.** For which would the scheme described in Exercise 6.8 be appropriate?

**c.** Discuss how you might deal with the fact that in some of the games, the players do not have the same knowledge of the current state.

**6.12** The minimax algorithm assumes that players take turns moving, but in card games such as whist and bridge, the winner of the previous trick plays first on the next trick.

**a.** Modify the algorithm to work properly for these games. You may assume that a function WINNER($s$) is available that reports which player won the trick just completed (if any).

**b.** Draw the game tree for the first pair of hands shown on page 179.

**6.13** The Chinook checkers program makes extensive use of endgame databases, which provide exact values for every position with eight or fewer pieces. How might such databases be generated efficiently?

**6.14** Discuss how well the standard approach to game playing would apply to games such as tennis, pool, and croquet, which take place in a continuous physical state space.

**6.15** Describe how the minimax and alpha–beta algorithms change for two-player, **non-zero-sum games** in which each player has his or her own utility function. You may assume that each player knows the other's utility function. If there are no constraints on the two terminal utilities, is it possible for any node to be pruned by alpha–beta?

**6.16** Suppose you have a chess program that can evaluate 1 million nodes per second. Decide on a compact representation of a game state for storage in a transposition table. About how many entries can you fit in a 500MB in-memory table? Will that be enough for the three minutes of search allocated for one move? How many table lookups can you do in the time it would take to do one evaluation? Now suppose the transposition table is larger than can fit in memory. About how many evaluations could you do in the time it takes to do one disk seek with standard disk hardware?

# 7 LOGICAL AGENTS

*In which we design agents that can form representations of the world, use a process of inference to derive new representations about the world, and use these new representations to deduce what to do.*

This chapter introduces knowledge-based agents. The concepts that we discuss—the *representation* of knowledge and the *reasoning* processes that bring knowledge to life—are central to the entire field of artificial intelligence.

Humans, it seems, know things and do reasoning. Knowledge and reasoning are also important for artificial agents because they enable successful behaviors that would be very hard to achieve otherwise. We have seen that knowledge of action outcomes enables problem-solving agents to perform well in complex environments. A reflex agent could only find its way from Arad to Bucharest by dumb luck. The knowledge of problem-solving agents is, however, very specific and inflexible. A chess program can calculate the legal moves of its king, but does not know in any useful sense that no piece can be on two different squares at the same time. Knowledge-based agents can benefit from knowledge expressed in very general forms, combining and recombining information to suit myriad purposes. Often, this process can be quite far removed from the needs of the moment—as when a mathematician proves a theorem or an astronomer calculates the earth's life expectancy.

Knowledge and reasoning also play a crucial role in dealing with *partially observable* environments. A knowledge-based agent can combine general knowledge with current percepts to infer hidden aspects of the current state prior to selecting actions. For example, a physician diagnoses a patient—that is, infers a disease state that is not directly observable—prior to choosing a treatment. Some of the knowledge that the physician uses is in the form of rules learned from textbooks and teachers, and some is in the form of patterns of association that the physician may not be able to consciously describe. If it's inside the physician's head, it counts as knowledge.

Understanding natural language also requires inferring hidden state, namely, the intention of the speaker. When we hear, "John saw the diamond through the window and coveted it," we know "it" refers to the diamond and not the window—we reason, perhaps unconsciously, with our knowledge of relative value. Similarly, when we hear, "John threw the brick through the window and broke it," we know "it" refers to the window. Reasoning allows us to cope with the virtually infinite variety of utterances using a finite store of commonsense knowledge. Problem-solving agents have difficulty with this kind of ambiguity because their representation of contingency problems is inherently exponential.

Our final reason for studying knowledge-based agents is their flexibility. They are able to accept new tasks in the form of explicitly described goals, they can achieve competence quickly by being told or learning new knowledge about the environment, and they can adapt to changes in the environment by updating the relevant knowledge.

We begin in Section 7.1 with the overall agent design. Section 7.2 introduces a simple new environment, the wumpus world, and illustrates the operation of a knowledge-based agent without going into any technical detail. Then, in Section 7.3, we explain the general principles of **logic**. Logic will be the primary vehicle for representing knowledge throughout Part III of the book. The knowledge of logical agents is always *definite*—each proposition is either true or false in the world, although the agent may be agnostic about some propositions.

Logic has the pedagogical advantage of being a simple example of a representation for knowledge-based agents, but logic has some severe limitations. Clearly, a large portion of the reasoning carried out by humans and other agents in partially observable environments depends on handling knowledge that is *uncertain*. Logic cannot represent this uncertainty well, so in Part V we cover probability, which can. In Part VI and Part VII we cover many representations, including some based on continuous mathematics such as mixtures of Gaussians, neural networks, and other representations.

Section 7.4 of this chapter defines a simple logic called **propositional logic**. While much less expressive than **first-order logic** (Chapter 8), propositional logic serves to illustrate all the basic concepts of logic. There is also a well-developed technology for reasoning in propositional logic, which we describe in sections 7.5 and 7.6. Finally, Section 7.7 combines the concept of logical agents with the technology of propositional logic to build some simple agents for the wumpus world. Certain shortcomings in propositional logic are identified, motivating the development of more powerful logics in subsequent chapters.

## 7.1 KNOWLEDGE-BASED AGENTS

KNOWLEDGE BASE
SENTENCE
KNOWLEDGE REPRESENTATION LANGUAGE

The central component of a knowledge-based agent is its **knowledge base**, or KB. Informally, a knowledge base is a set of **sentences**. (Here "sentence" is used as a technical term. It is related but is not identical to the sentences of English and other natural languages.) Each sentence is expressed in a language called a **knowledge representation language** and represents some assertion about the world.

INFERENCE
LOGICAL AGENTS

There must be a way to add new sentences to the knowledge base and a way to query what is known. The standard names for these tasks are TELL and ASK, respectively. Both tasks may involve **inference**—that is, deriving new sentences from old. In **logical agents**, which are the main subject of study in this chapter, inference must obey the fundamental requirement that when one ASKs a question of the knowledge base, the answer should follow from what has been told (or rather, TELLed) to the knowledge base previously. Later in the

```
function KB-AGENT(percept) returns an action
   static: KB, a knowledge base
           t, a counter, initially 0, indicating time

   TELL(KB, MAKE-PERCEPT-SENTENCE(percept, t))
   action ← ASK(KB, MAKE-ACTION-QUERY(t))
   TELL(KB, MAKE-ACTION-SENTENCE(action, t))
   t ← t + 1
   return action
```

**Figure 7.1** A generic knowledge-based agent.

chapter, we will be more precise about the crucial word "follow." For now, take it to mean that the inference process should not just make things up as it goes along.

Figure 7.1 shows the outline of a knowledge-based agent program. Like all our agents, it takes a percept as input and returns an action. The agent maintains a knowledge base, $KB$, which may initially contain some **background knowledge**. Each time the agent program is called, it does three things. First, it TELLs the knowledge base what it perceives. Second, it ASKs the knowledge base what action it should perform. In the process of answering this query, extensive reasoning may be done about the current state of the world, about the outcomes of possible action sequences, and so on. Third, the agent records its choice with TELL and executes the action. The second TELL is necessary to let the knowledge base know that the hypothetical *action* has actually been executed.

BACKGROUND KNOWLEDGE

The details of the representation language are hidden inside three functions that implement the interface between the sensors and actuators and the core representation and reasoning system. MAKE-PERCEPT-SENTENCE constructs a sentence asserting that the agent perceived the given percept at the given time. MAKE-ACTION-QUERY constructs a sentence that asks what action should be done at the current time. Finally, MAKE-ACTION-SENTENCE constructs a sentence asserting that the chosen action was executed. The details of the inference mechanisms are hidden inside TELL and ASK. Later sections will reveal these details.

The agent in Figure 7.1 appears quite similar to the agents with internal state described in Chapter 2. Because of the definitions of TELL and ASK, however, the knowledge-based agent is not an arbitrary program for calculating actions. It is amenable to a description at the **knowledge level**, where we need specify only what the agent knows and what its goals are, in order to fix its behavior. For example, an automated taxi might have the goal of delivering a passenger to Marin County and might know that it is in San Francisco and that the Golden Gate Bridge is the only link between the two locations. Then we can expect it to cross the Golden Gate Bridge *because it knows that that will achieve its goal*. Notice that this analysis is independent of how the taxi works at the **implementation level**. It doesn't matter whether its geographical knowledge is implemented as linked lists or pixel maps, or whether it reasons by manipulating strings of symbols stored in registers or by propagating noisy signals in a network of neurons.

KNOWLEDGE LEVEL

IMPLEMENTATION LEVEL

As we mentioned in the introduction to the chapter, *one can build a knowledge-based agent simply by* TELL*ing it what it needs to know.* The agent's initial program, before it starts to receive percepts, is built by adding one by one the sentences that represent the designer's knowledge of the environment. Designing the representation language to make it easy to express this knowledge in the form of sentences simplifies the construction problem enormously. This is called the **declarative** approach to system building. In contrast, the **procedural** approach encodes desired behaviors directly as program code; minimizing the role of explicit representation and reasoning can result in a much more efficient system. We will see agents of both kinds in Section 7.7. In the 1970s and 1980s, advocates of the two approaches engaged in heated debates. We now understand that a successful agent must combine both declarative and procedural elements in its design.

DECLARATIVE

In addition to TELLing it what it needs to know, we can provide a knowledge-based agent with mechanisms that allow it to learn for itself. These mechanisms, which are discussed in Chapter 18, create general knowledge about the environment out of a series of percepts. This knowledge can be incorporated into the agent's knowledge base and used for decision making. In this way, the agent can be fully autonomous.

All these capabilities—representation, reasoning, and learning—rest on the centuries-long development of the theory and technology of logic. Before explaining that theory and technology, however, we will create a simple world with which to illustrate them.

## 7.2 THE WUMPUS WORLD

WUMPUS WORLD

The **wumpus world** is a cave consisting of rooms connected by passageways. Lurking somewhere in the cave is the wumpus, a beast that eats anyone who enters its room. The wumpus can be shot by an agent, but the agent has only one arrow. Some rooms contain bottomless pits that will trap anyone who wanders into these rooms (except for the wumpus, which is too big to fall in). The only mitigating feature of living in this environment is the possibility of finding a heap of gold. Although the wumpus world is rather tame by modern computer game standards, it makes an excellent testbed environment for intelligent agents. Michael Genesereth was the first to suggest this.

A sample wumpus world is shown in Figure 7.2. The precise definition of the task environment is given, as suggested in Chapter 2, by the PEAS description:

- ◊ **Performance measure**: +1000 for picking up the gold, –1000 for falling into a pit or being eaten by the wumpus, –1 for each action taken and –10 for using up the arrow.
- ◊ **Environment**: A $4 \times 4$ grid of rooms. The agent always starts in the square labeled [1,1], facing to the right. The locations of the gold and the wumpus are chosen randomly, with a uniform distribution, from the squares other than the start square. In addition, each square other than the start can be a pit, with probability 0.2.
- ◊ **Actuators**: The agent can move forward, turn left by $90°$, or turn right by $90°$. The agent dies a miserable death if it enters a square containing a pit or a live wumpus. (It is safe, albeit smelly, to enter a square with a dead wumpus.) Moving forward has no

effect if there is a wall in front of the agent. The action *Grab* can be used to pick up an object that is in the same square as the agent. The action *Shoot* can be used to fire an arrow in a straight line in the direction the agent is facing. The arrow continues until it either hits (and hence kills) the wumpus or hits a wall. The agent only has one arrow, so only the first *Shoot* action has any effect.

◇ **Sensors**: The agent has five sensors, each of which gives a single bit of information:

- In the square containing the wumpus and in the directly (not diagonally) adjacent squares the agent will perceive a stench.
- In the squares directly adjacent to a pit, the agent will perceive a breeze.
- In the square where the gold is, the agent will perceive a glitter.
- When an agent walks into a wall, it will perceive a bump.
- When the wumpus is killed, it emits a woeful scream that can be perceived anywhere in the cave.

The percepts will be given to the agent in the form of a list of five symbols; for example, if there is a stench and a breeze, but no glitter, bump, or scream, the agent will receive the percept $[Stench, Breeze, None, None, None]$.

Exercise 7.1 asks you to define the wumpus environment along the various dimensions given in Chapter 2. The principal difficulty for the agent is its initial ignorance of the configuration of the environment; overcoming this ignorance seems to require logical reasoning. In most instances of the wumpus world, it is possible for the agent to retrieve the gold safely. Occasionally, the agent must choose between going home empty-handed and risking death to find the gold. About 21% of the environments are utterly unfair, because the gold is in a pit or surrounded by pits.

Let us watch a knowledge-based wumpus agent exploring the environment shown in Figure 7.2. The agent's initial knowledge base contains the rules of the environment, as listed

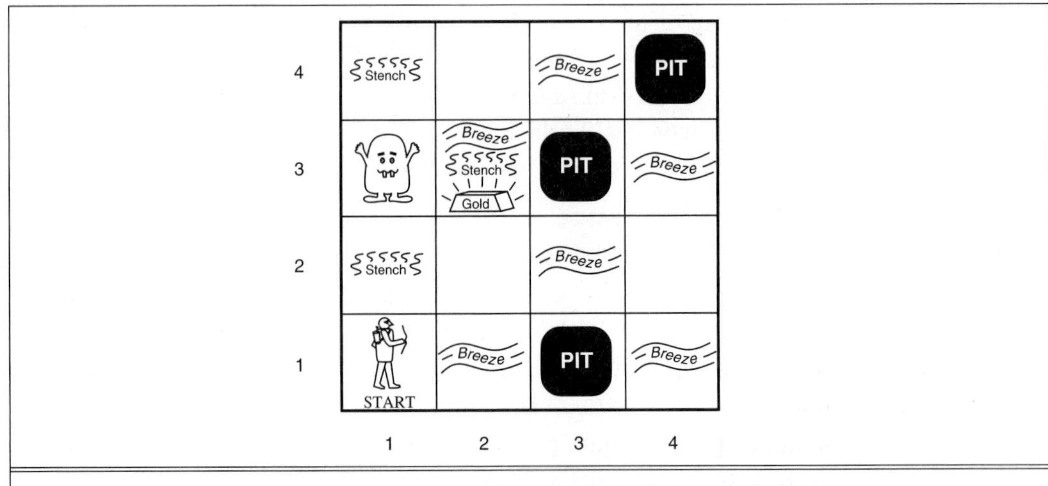


**Figure 7.2** A typical wumpus world. The agent is in the bottom left corner.

previously; in particular, it knows that it is in [1,1] and that [1,1] is a safe square. We will see how its knowledge evolves as new percepts arrive and actions are taken.

The first percept is $[None, None, None, None, None]$, from which the agent can conclude that its neighboring squares are safe. Figure 7.3(a) shows the agent's state of knowledge at this point. We list (some of) the sentences in the knowledge base using letters such as $B$ (breezy) and $OK$ (safe, neither pit nor wumpus) marked in the appropriate squares. Figure 7.2, on the other hand, depicts the world itself.

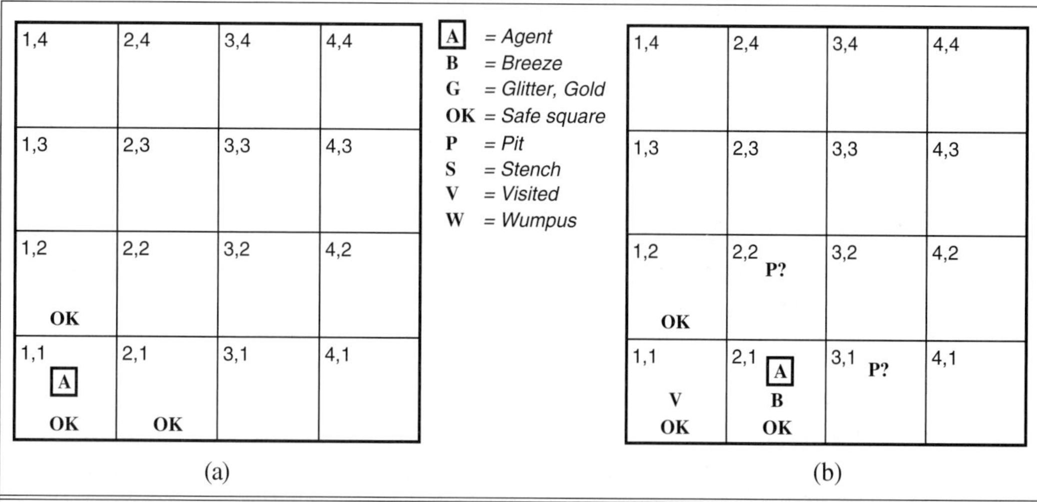


**Figure 7.3** The first step taken by the agent in the wumpus world. (a) The initial situation, after percept $[None, None, None, None, None]$. (b) After one move, with percept $[None, Breeze, None, None, None]$.

From the fact that there was no stench or breeze in [1,1], the agent can infer that [1,2] and [2,1] are free of dangers. They are marked with an $OK$ to indicate this. A cautious agent will move only into a square that it knows is $OK$. Let us suppose the agent decides to move forward to [2,1], giving the scene in Figure 7.3(b).

The agent detects a breeze in [2,1], so there must be a pit in a neighboring square. The pit cannot be in [1,1], by the rules of the game, so there must be a pit in [2,2] or [3,1] or both. The notation $P?$ in Figure 7.3(b) indicates a possible pit in those squares. At this point, there is only one known square that is $OK$ and has not been visited yet. So the prudent agent will turn around, go back to [1,1], and then proceed to [1,2].

The new percept in [1,2] is $[Stench, None, None, None, None]$, resulting in the state of knowledge shown in Figure 7.4(a). The stench in [1,2] means that there must be a wumpus nearby. But the wumpus cannot be in [1,1], by the rules of the game, and it cannot be in [2,2] (or the agent would have detected a stench when it was in [2,1]). Therefore, the agent can infer that the wumpus is in [1,3]. The notation $W!$ indicates this. Moreover, the lack of a $Breeze$ in [1,2] implies that there is no pit in [2,2]. Yet we already inferred that there must be a pit in either [2,2] or [3,1], so this means it must be in [3,1]. This is a fairly difficult inference, because it combines knowledge gained at different times in different places and

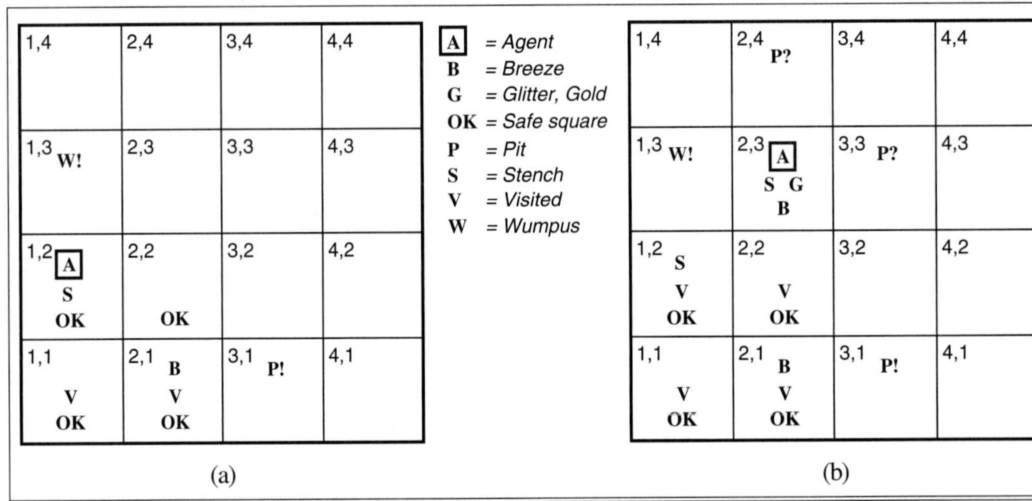


**Figure 7.4** Two later stages in the progress of the agent. (a) After the third move, with percept $[Stench, None, None, None, None]$. (b) After the fifth move, with percept $[Stench, Breeze, Glitter, None, None]$.

relies on the lack of a percept to make one crucial step. The inference is beyond the abilities of most animals, but it is typical of the kind of reasoning that a logical agent does.

The agent has now proved to itself that there is neither a pit nor a wumpus in [2,2], so it is $OK$ to move there. We will not show the agent's state of knowledge at [2,2]; we just assume that the agent turns and moves to [2,3], giving us Figure 7.4(b). In [2,3], the agent detects a glitter, so it should grab the gold and thereby end the game.

*In each case where the agent draws a conclusion from the available information, that conclusion is* guaranteed *to be correct if the available information is correct.* This is a fundamental property of logical reasoning. In the rest of this chapter, we describe how to build logical agents that can represent the necessary information and draw the conclusions that were described in the preceding paragraphs.

## 7.3 LOGIC

This section provides an overview of all the fundamental concepts of logical representation and reasoning. We postpone the technical details of any particular form of logic until the next section. We will instead use informal examples from the wumpus world and from the familiar realm of arithmetic. We adopt this rather unusual approach because the ideas of logic are far more general and beautiful than is commonly supposed.

SYNTAX

In Section 7.1, we said that knowledge bases consist of sentences. These sentences are expressed according to the **syntax** of the representation language, which specifies all the sentences that are well formed. The notion of syntax is clear enough in ordinary arithmetic: "$x + y = 4$" is a well-formed sentence, whereas "$x2y+ =$" is not. The syntax of logical languages (and of arithmetic, for that matter) is usually designed for writing papers and books. There are literally dozens of different syntaxes, some with lots of Greek letters and exotic mathematical symbols, and some with rather visually appealing diagrams with arrows and bubbles. In all cases, however, sentences in an agent's knowledge base are real physical configurations of (parts of) the agent. Reasoning will involve generating and manipulating those configurations.

SEMANTICS

A logic must also define the **semantics** of the language. Loosely speaking, semantics has to do with the "meaning" of sentences. In logic, the definition is more precise. The semantics of the language defines the **truth** of each sentence with respect to each **possible world**. For example, the usual semantics adopted for arithmetic specifies that the sentence "$x + y = 4$" is true in a world where $x$ is 2 and $y$ is 2, but false in a world where $x$ is 1 and $y$ is 1.[1] In standard logics, every sentence must be either true or false in each possible world—there is no "in between."[2]

TRUTH

POSSIBLE WORLD

MODEL

When we need to be precise, we will use the term **model** in place of "possible world." (We will also use the phrase "$m$ is a model of $\alpha$" to mean that sentence $\alpha$ is true in model $m$.) Whereas possible worlds might be thought of as (potentially) real environments that the agent might or might not be in, models are mathematical abstractions, each of which simply fixes the truth or falsehood of every relevant sentence. Informally, we may think of $x$ and $y$ as the number of men and women sitting at a table playing bridge, for example, and the sentence $x + y = 4$ is true when there are four in total; formally, the possible models are just all possible assignments of numbers to the variables $x$ and $y$. Each such assignment fixes the truth of any sentence of arithmetic whose variables are $x$ and $y$.

ENTAILMENT

Now that we have a notion of truth, we are ready to talk about logical reasoning. This involves the relation of logical **entailment** between sentences—the idea that a sentence *follows logically* from another sentence. In mathematical notation, we write as

$$\alpha \models \beta$$

to mean that the sentence $\alpha$ entails the sentence $\beta$. The formal definition of entailment is this: $\alpha \models \beta$ if and only if, in every model in which $\alpha$ is true, $\beta$ is also true. Another way to say this is that if $\alpha$ is true, then $\beta$ *must* also be true. Informally, the truth of $\beta$ is "contained" in the truth of $\alpha$. The relation of entailment is familiar from arithmetic; we are happy with the idea that the sentence $x + y = 4$ entails the sentence $4 = x + y$. Obviously, in any model where $x + y = 4$—such as the model in which $x$ is 2 and $y$ is 2—it is the case that $4 = x + y$. We will see shortly that a knowledge base can be considered a statement, and we often talk of a knowledge base entailing a sentence.

We can apply the same kind of analysis to the wumpus-world reasoning example given in the preceding section. Consider the situation in Figure 7.3(b): the agent has detected nothing in [1,1] and a breeze in [2,1]. These percepts, combined with the agent's knowledge of the rules of the wumpus world (the PEAS description on page 197), constitute the KB. The

---

[1] The reader will no doubt have noticed the similarity between the notion of truth of sentences and the notion of satisfaction of constraints in Chapter 5. This is no accident—constraint languages are indeed logics and constraint solving is a form of logical reasoning.

[2] **Fuzzy logic**, discussed in Chapter 14, allows for degrees of truth.

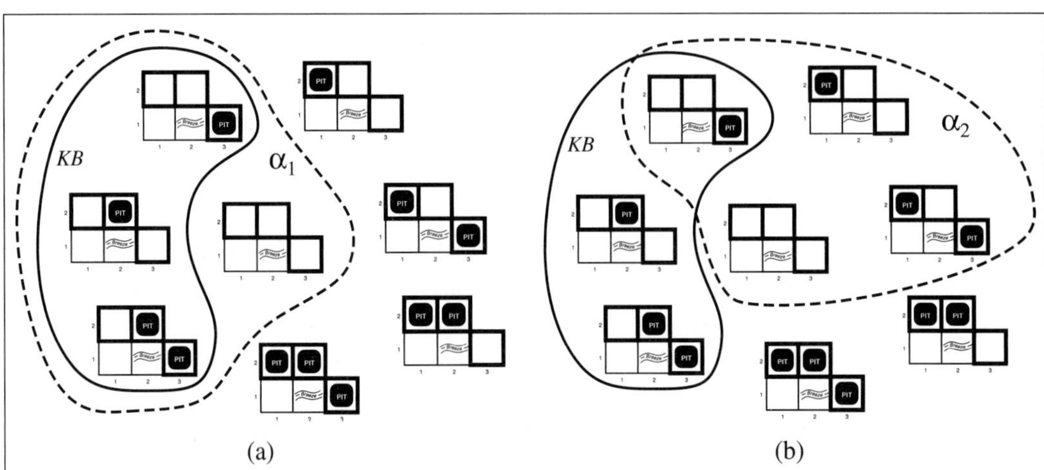


**Figure 7.5** Possible models for the presence of pits in squares [1,2], [2,2], and [3,1], given observations of nothing in [1,1] and a breeze in [2,1]. (a) Models of the knowledge base and $\alpha_1$ (no pit in [1,2]). (b) Models of the knowledge base and $\alpha_2$ (no pit in [2,2]).

agent is interested (among other things) in whether the adjacent squares [1,2], [2,2], and [3,1] contain pits. Each of the three squares might or might not contain a pit, so (for the purposes of this example) there are $2^3 = 8$ possible models. These are shown in Figure 7.5.[3]

The KB is false in models that contradict what the agent knows—for example, the KB is false in any model in which [1,2] contains a pit, because there is no breeze in [1,1]. There are in fact just three models in which the KB is true, and these are shown as a subset of the models in Figure 7.5. Now let us consider two possible conclusions:

$$\alpha_1 = \text{"There is no pit in [1,2]."}$$
$$\alpha_2 = \text{"There is no pit in [2,2]."}$$

We have marked the models of $\alpha_1$ and $\alpha_2$ in Figures 7.5(a) and 7.5(b) respectively. By inspection, we see the following:

in every model in which $KB$ is true, $\alpha_1$ is also true.

Hence, $KB \models \alpha_1$: there is no pit in [1,2]. We can also see that

in some models in which $KB$ is true, $\alpha_2$ is false.

Hence, $KB \not\models \alpha_2$: the agent *cannot* conclude that there is no pit in [2,2]. (Nor can it conclude that there *is* a pit in [2,2].)[4]

The preceding example not only illustrates entailment, but also shows how the definition of entailment can be applied to derive conclusions—that is, to carry out **logical inference**. The inference algorithm illustrated in Figure 7.5 is called **model checking**, because it enumerates all possible models to check that $\alpha$ is true in all models in which $KB$ is true.

LOGICAL INFERENCE

MODEL CHECKING

[3] Although the figure shows the models as partial wumpus worlds, they are really nothing more than assignments of *true* and *false* to the sentences "there is a pit in [1,2]" etc. Models, in the mathematical sense, do not need to have 'orrible 'airy wumpuses in them.

[4] The agent can calculate the *probability* that there is a pit in [2,2]; Chapter 13 shows how.

In understanding entailment and inference, it might help to think of the set of all consequences of $KB$ as a haystack and of $\alpha$ as a needle. Entailment is like the needle being in the haystack; inference is like finding it. This distinction is embodied in some formal notation: if an inference algorithm $i$ can derive $\alpha$ from $KB$, we write

$$KB \vdash_i \alpha ,$$

which is pronounced "$\alpha$ is derived from $KB$ by $i$" or "$i$ derives $\alpha$ from $KB$."

SOUND

TRUTH-PRESERVING

An inference algorithm that derives only entailed sentences is called **sound** or **truth-preserving**. Soundness is a highly desirable property. An unsound inference procedure essentially makes things up as it goes along—it announces the discovery of nonexistent needles. It is easy to see that model checking, when it is applicable,[5] is a sound procedure.

COMPLETENESS

The property of **completeness** is also desirable: an inference algorithm is complete if it can derive any sentence that is entailed. For real haystacks, which are finite in extent, it seems obvious that a systematic examination can always decide whether the needle is in the haystack. For many knowledge bases, however, the haystack of consequences is infinite, and completeness becomes an important issue.[6] Fortunately, there are complete inference procedures for logics that are sufficiently expressive to handle many knowledge bases.

We have described a reasoning process whose conclusions are guaranteed to be true in any world in which the premises are true; in particular, *if KB is true in the* real *world, then any sentence $\alpha$ derived from KB by a sound inference procedure is also true in the real world.* So, while an inference process operates on "syntax"—internal physical configurations such as bits in registers or patterns of electrical blips in brains—the process *corresponds* to the real-world relationship whereby some aspect of the real world is the case[7] by virtue of other aspects of the real world being the case. This correspondence between world and representation is illustrated in Figure 7.6.

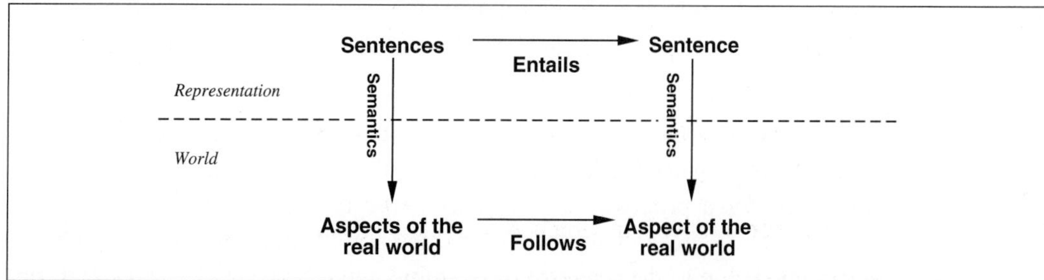


**Figure 7.6** Sentences are physical configurations of the agent, and reasoning is a process of constructing new physical configurations from old ones. Logical reasoning should ensure that the new configurations represent aspects of the world that actually follow from the aspects that the old configurations represent.

5 Model checking works if the space of models is finite—for example, in wumpus worlds of fixed size. For arithmetic, on the other hand, the space of models is infinite: even if we restrict ourselves to the integers, there are infinitely many pairs of values for $x$ and $y$ in the sentence $x + y = 4$.

6 Compare with the case of infinite search spaces in Chapter 3, where depth-first search is not complete.

7 As Wittgenstein (1922) put it in his famous *Tractatus*: "The world is everything that is the case."

GROUNDING

The final issue that must be addressed by an account of logical agents is that of **grounding**—the connection, if any, between logical reasoning processes and the real environment in which the agent exists. In particular, *how do we know that $KB$ is true in the real world?* (After all, $KB$ is just "syntax" inside the agent's head.) This is a philosophical question about which many, many books have been written. (See Chapter 26.) A simple answer is that the agent's sensors create the connection. For example, our wumpus-world agent has a smell sensor. The agent program creates a suitable sentence whenever there is a smell. Then, whenever that sentence is in the knowledge base, it is true in the real world. Thus, the meaning and truth of percept sentences are defined by the processes of sensing and sentence construction that produce them. What about the rest of the agent's knowledge, such as its belief that wumpuses cause smells in adjacent squares? This is not a direct representation of a single percept, but a general rule—derived, perhaps, from perceptual experience but not identical to a statement of that experience. General rules like this are produced by a sentence construction process called **learning**, which is the subject of Part VI. Learning is fallible. It could be the case that wumpuses cause smells *except on February 29 in leap years*, which is when they take their baths. Thus, $KB$ may not be true in the real world, but with good learning procedures there is reason for optimism.

## 7.4 Propositional Logic: A Very Simple Logic

PROPOSITIONAL LOGIC

We now present a very simple logic called **propositional logic**.[8] We cover the syntax of propositional logic and its semantics—the way in which the truth of sentences is determined. Then we look at **entailment**—the relation between a sentence and another sentence that follows from it—and see how this leads to a simple algorithm for logical inference. Everything takes place, of course, in the wumpus world.

### Syntax

ATOMIC SENTENCES

PROPOSITION SYMBOL

The **syntax** of propositional logic defines the allowable sentences. The **atomic sentences**—the indivisible syntactic elements—consist of a single **proposition symbol**. Each such symbol stands for a proposition that can be true or false. We will use uppercase names for symbols: $P$, $Q$, $R$, and so on. The names are arbitrary but are often chosen to have some mnemonic value to the reader. For example, we might use $W_{1,3}$ to stand for the proposition that the wumpus is in [1,3]. (Remember that symbols such as $W_{1,3}$ are *atomic*, i.e., $W$, 1, and 3 are not meaningful parts of the symbol.) There are two proposition symbols with fixed meanings: $True$ is the always-true proposition and $False$ is the always-false proposition.

COMPLEX SENTENCES

LOGICAL CONNECTIVES

**Complex sentences** are constructed from simpler sentences using **logical connectives**. There are five connectives in common use:

NEGATION

LITERAL

- $\neg$ (not). A sentence such as $\neg W_{1,3}$ is called the **negation** of $W_{1,3}$. A **literal** is either an atomic sentence (a **positive literal**) or a negated atomic sentence (a **negative literal**).

[8] Propositional logic is also called **Boolean logic**, after the logician George Boole (1815–1864).

CONJUNCTION

$\land$ (and). A sentence whose main connective is $\land$, such as $W_{1,3} \land P_{3,1}$, is called a **conjunction**; its parts are the **conjuncts**. (The $\land$ looks like an "A" for "And.")

DISJUNCTION

$\lor$ (or). A sentence using $\lor$, such as $(W_{1,3} \land P_{3,1}) \lor W_{2,2}$, is a **disjunction** of the **disjuncts** $(W_{1,3} \land P_{3,1})$ and $W_{2,2}$. (Historically, the $\lor$ comes from the Latin "vel," which means "or." For most people, it is easier to remember as an upside-down $\land$.)

IMPLICATION
PREMISE
CONCLUSION

$\Rightarrow$ (implies). A sentence such as $(W_{1,3} \land P_{3,1}) \Rightarrow \neg W_{2,2}$ is called an **implication** (or conditional). Its **premise** or **antecedent** is $(W_{1,3} \land P_{3,1})$, and its **conclusion** or **consequent** is $\neg W_{2,2}$. Implications are also known as **rules** or **if–then** statements. The implication symbol is sometimes written in other books as $\supset$ or $\rightarrow$.

BICONDITIONAL

$\Leftrightarrow$ (if and only if). The sentence $W_{1,3} \Leftrightarrow \neg W_{2,2}$ is a **biconditional**.

Figure 7.7 gives a formal grammar of propositional logic; see page 984 if you are not familiar with the BNF notation.

$$
\begin{array}{rcl}
\mathit{Sentence} & \rightarrow & \mathit{AtomicSentence} \mid \mathit{ComplexSentence} \\
\mathit{AtomicSentence} & \rightarrow & \mathbf{True} \mid \mathbf{False} \mid \mathit{Symbol} \\
\mathit{Symbol} & \rightarrow & \mathbf{P} \mid \mathbf{Q} \mid \mathbf{R} \mid \ldots \\
\mathit{ComplexSentence} & \rightarrow & \neg\, \mathit{Sentence} \\
 & \mid & (\ \mathit{Sentence} \land \mathit{Sentence}\ ) \\
 & \mid & (\ \mathit{Sentence} \lor \mathit{Sentence}\ ) \\
 & \mid & (\ \mathit{Sentence} \Rightarrow \mathit{Sentence}\ ) \\
 & \mid & (\ \mathit{Sentence} \Leftrightarrow \mathit{Sentence}\ )
\end{array}
$$

**Figure 7.7** A BNF (Backus–Naur Form) grammar of sentences in propositional logic.

Notice that the grammar is very strict about parentheses: every sentence constructed with binary connectives must be enclosed in parentheses. This ensures that the syntax is completely unambiguous. It also means that we have to write $((A \land B) \Rightarrow C)$ instead of $A \land B \Rightarrow C$, for example. To improve readability, we will often omit parentheses, relying instead on an order of precedence for the connectives. This is similar to the precedence used in arithmetic—for example, $ab + c$ is read as $((ab) + c)$ rather than $a(b + c)$ because multiplication has higher precedence than addition. The order of precedence in propositional logic is (from highest to lowest): $\neg$, $\land$, $\lor$, $\Rightarrow$, and $\Leftrightarrow$. Hence, the sentence

$$\neg P \lor Q \land R \Rightarrow S$$

is equivalent to the sentence

$$((\neg P) \lor (Q \land R)) \Rightarrow S\,.$$

Precedence does not resolve ambiguity in sentences such as $A \land B \land C$, which could be read as $((A \land B) \land C)$ or as $(A \land (B \land C))$. Because these two readings mean the same thing according to the semantics given in the next section, sentences such as $A \land B \land C$ are allowed. We also allow $A \lor B \lor C$ and $A \Leftrightarrow B \Leftrightarrow C$. Sentences such as $A \Rightarrow B \Rightarrow C$ are not allowed because the two readings have different meanings; we insist on parentheses in this case. Finally, we will sometimes use square brackets instead of parentheses when it makes the sentence clearer.

### Semantics

Having specified the syntax of propositional logic, we now specify its semantics. The semantics defines the rules for determining the truth of a sentence with respect to a particular model. In propositional logic, a model simply fixes the truth value—*true* or *false*—for every proposition symbol. For example, if the sentences in the knowledge base make use of the proposition symbols $P_{1,2}$, $P_{2,2}$, and $P_{3,1}$, then one possible model is

$$m_1 = \{P_{1,2} = false,\ P_{2,2} = false,\ P_{3,1} = true\}\ .$$

With three proposition symbols, there are $2^3 = 8$ possible models—exactly those depicted in Figure 7.5. Notice, however, that because we have pinned down the syntax, the models become purely mathematical objects with no necessary connection to wumpus worlds. $P_{1,2}$ is just a symbol; it might mean "there is a pit in [1,2]" or "I'm in Paris today and tomorrow."

The semantics for propositional logic must specify how to compute the truth value of *any* sentence, given a model. This is done recursively. All sentences are constructed from atomic sentences and the five connectives; therefore, we need to specify how to compute the truth of atomic sentences and how to compute the truth of sentences formed with each of the five connectives. Atomic sentences are easy:

- $True$ is true in every model and $False$ is false in every model.
- The truth value of every other proposition symbol must be specified directly in the model. For example, in the model $m_1$ given earlier, $P_{1,2}$ is false.

For complex sentences, we have rules such as

- For any sentence $s$ and any model $m$, the sentence $\neg s$ is true in $m$ if and only if $s$ is false in $m$.

TRUTH TABLE

Such rules reduce the truth of a complex sentence to the truth of simpler sentences. The rules for each connective can be summarized in a **truth table** that specifies the truth value of a complex sentence for each possible assignment of truth values to its components. Truth tables for the five logical connectives are given in Figure 7.8. Using these tables, the truth value of any sentence $s$ can be computed with respect to any model $m$ by a simple process of recursive evaluation. For example, the sentence $\neg P_{1,2} \land (P_{2,2} \lor P_{3,1})$, evaluated in $m_1$, gives $true \land (false \lor true) = true \land true = true$. Exercise 7.3 asks you to write the algorithm PL-TRUE?($s, m$), which computes the truth value of a propositional logic sentence $s$ in a model $m$.

Previously we said that a knowledge base consists of a set of sentences. We can now see that a logical knowledge base is a conjunction of those sentences. That is, if we start with an empty $KB$ and do TELL($KB, S_1$) ... TELL($KB, S_n$) then we have $KB = S_1 \land \ldots \land S_n$. This means that we can treat knowledge bases and sentences interchangeably.

The truth tables for "and," "or," and "not" are in close accord with our intuitions about the English words. The main point of possible confusion is that $P \lor Q$ is true when $P$ is true

| $P$ | $Q$ | $\neg P$ | $P \wedge Q$ | $P \vee Q$ | $P \Rightarrow Q$ | $P \Leftrightarrow Q$ |
|---|---|---|---|---|---|---|
| *false* | *false* | *true* | *false* | *false* | *true* | *true* |
| *false* | *true* | *true* | *false* | *true* | *true* | *false* |
| *true* | *false* | *false* | *false* | *true* | *false* | *false* |
| *true* | *true* | *false* | *true* | *true* | *true* | *true* |

**Figure 7.8** Truth tables for the five logical connectives. To use the table to compute, for example, the value of $P \vee Q$ when $P$ is true and $Q$ is false, first look on the left for the row where $P$ is *true* and $Q$ is *false* (the third row). Then look in that row under the $P \vee Q$ column to see the result: *true*. Another way to look at this is to think of each row as a model, and the entries under each column for that row as saying whether the corresponding sentence is true in that model.

or $Q$ is true *or both*. There is a different connective called "exclusive or" ("xor" for short) that yields false when both disjuncts are true.[9] There is no consensus on the symbol for exclusive or; two choices are $\dot{\vee}$ and $\oplus$.

The truth table for $\Rightarrow$ may seem puzzling at first, because it might not quite fit one's intuitive understanding of "$P$ implies $Q$" or "if $P$ then $Q$." For one thing, propositional logic does not require any relation of causation or relevance between $P$ and $Q$. The sentence "5 is odd implies Tokyo is the capital of Japan" is a true sentence of propositional logic (under the normal interpretation), even though it is a decidedly odd sentence of English. Another point of confusion is that any implication is true whenever its antecedent is false. For example, "5 is even implies Sam is smart" is true, regardless of whether Sam is smart. This seems bizarre, but it makes sense if you think of "$P \Rightarrow Q$" as saying, "If $P$ is true, then I am claiming that $Q$ is true. Otherwise I am making no claim." The only way for this sentence to be *false* is if $P$ is true but $Q$ is false.

The truth table for a biconditional, $P \Leftrightarrow Q$, shows that it is true whenever both $P \Rightarrow Q$ and $Q \Rightarrow P$ are true. In English, this is often written as "$P$ if and only if $Q$" or "$P$ iff $Q$." The rules of the wumpus world are best written using $\Leftrightarrow$. For example, a square is breezy *if* a neighboring square has a pit, and a square is breezy *only if* a neighboring square has a pit. So we need biconditionals such as

$$B_{1,1} \Leftrightarrow (P_{1,2} \vee P_{2,1}) ,$$

where $B_{1,1}$ means that there is a breeze in [1,1]. Notice that the one-way implication

$$B_{1,1} \Rightarrow (P_{1,2} \vee P_{2,1})$$

is true in the wumpus world, but incomplete. It does not rule out models in which $B_{1,1}$ is false and $P_{1,2}$ is true, which would violate the rules of the wumpus world. Another way of putting it is that the implication requires the presence of pits if there is a breeze, whereas the biconditional also requires the absence of pits if there is no breeze.

9 Latin has a separate word, *aut*, for exclusive or.

### A simple knowledge base

Now that we have defined the semantics for propositional logic, we can construct a knowledge base for the wumpus world. For simplicity, we will deal only with pits; the wumpus itself is left as an exercise. We will provide enough knowledge to carry out the inference that was done informally in Section 7.3.

First, we need to choose our vocabulary of proposition symbols. For each $i, j$:

- Let $P_{i,j}$ be true if there is a pit in $[i, j]$.
- Let $B_{i,j}$ be true if there is a breeze in $[i, j]$.

The knowledge base includes the following sentences, each one labeled for convenience:

- There is no pit in [1,1]:

$$R_1: \quad \neg P_{1,1} .$$

- A square is breezy if and only if there is a pit in a neighboring square. This has to be stated for each square; for now, we include just the relevant squares:

$$R_2: \quad B_{1,1} \quad \Leftrightarrow \quad (P_{1,2} \lor P_{2,1}) .$$
$$R_3: \quad B_{2,1} \quad \Leftrightarrow \quad (P_{1,1} \lor P_{2,2} \lor P_{3,1}) .$$

- The preceding sentences are true in all wumpus worlds. Now we include the breeze percepts for the first two squares visited in the specific world the agent is in, leading up to the situation in Figure 7.3(b).

$$R_4: \quad \neg B_{1,1} .$$
$$R_5: \quad B_{2,1} .$$

The knowledge base, then, consists of sentences $R_1$ through $R_5$. It can also be considered as a single sentence—the conjunction $R_1 \land R_2 \land R_3 \land R_4 \land R_5$—because it asserts that all the individual sentences are true.

### Inference

Recall that the aim of logical inference is to decide whether $KB \models \alpha$ for some sentence $\alpha$. For example, is $P_{2,2}$ entailed? Our first algorithm for inference will be a direct implementation of the definition of entailment: enumerate the models, and check that $\alpha$ is true in every model in which $KB$ is true. For propositional logic, models are assignments of *true* or *false* to every proposition symbol. Returning to our wumpus-world example, the relevant proposition symbols are $B_{1,1}$, $B_{2,1}$, $P_{1,1}$, $P_{1,2}$, $P_{2,1}$, $P_{2,2}$, and $P_{3,1}$. With seven symbols, there are $2^7 = 128$ possible models; in three of these, $KB$ is true (Figure 7.9). In those three models, $\neg P_{1,2}$ is true, hence there is no pit in [1,2]. On the other hand, $P_{2,2}$ is true in two of the three models and false in one, so we cannot yet tell whether there is a pit in [2,2].

Figure 7.9 reproduces in a more precise form the reasoning illustrated in Figure 7.5. A general algorithm for deciding entailment in propositional logic is shown in Figure 7.10. Like the BACKTRACKING-SEARCH algorithm on page 76, TT-ENTAILS? performs a recursive enumeration of a finite space of assignments to variables. The algorithm is **sound**, because it

| $B_{1,1}$ | $B_{2,1}$ | $P_{1,1}$ | $P_{1,2}$ | $P_{2,1}$ | $P_{2,2}$ | $P_{3,1}$ | $R_1$ | $R_2$ | $R_3$ | $R_4$ | $R_5$ | $KB$ |
|---|---|---|---|---|---|---|---|---|---|---|---|---|
| *false* | *false* | *false* | *false* | *false* | *false* | *false* | *true* | *true* | *true* | *true* | *false* | *false* |
| *false* | *false* | *false* | *false* | *false* | *false* | *true* | *true* | *true* | *false* | *true* | *false* | *false* |
| ⋮ | ⋮ | ⋮ | ⋮ | ⋮ | ⋮ | ⋮ | ⋮ | ⋮ | ⋮ | ⋮ | ⋮ | ⋮ |
| *false* | *true* | *false* | *false* | *false* | *false* | *false* | *true* | *true* | *false* | *true* | *true* | *false* |
| *false* | *true* | *false* | *false* | *false* | *false* | *true* | *true* | *true* | *true* | *true* | *true* | *true* |
| *false* | *true* | *false* | *false* | *false* | *true* | *false* | *true* | *true* | *true* | *true* | *true* | *true* |
| *false* | *true* | *false* | *false* | *false* | *true* | *true* | *true* | *true* | *true* | *true* | *true* | *true* |
| *false* | *true* | *false* | *false* | *true* | *false* | *false* | *true* | *false* | *false* | *true* | *true* | *false* |
| ⋮ | ⋮ | ⋮ | ⋮ | ⋮ | ⋮ | ⋮ | ⋮ | ⋮ | ⋮ | ⋮ | ⋮ | ⋮ |
| *true* | *true* | *true* | *true* | *true* | *true* | *true* | *false* | *true* | *true* | *false* | *true* | *false* |

**Figure 7.9** A truth table constructed for the knowledge base given in the text. *KB* is true if $R_1$ through $R_5$ are true, which occurs in just 3 of the 128 rows. In all 3 rows, $P_{1,2}$ is false, so there is no pit in [1,2]. On the other hand, there might (or might not) be a pit in [2,2].

```
function TT-ENTAILS?(KB, α) returns true or false
  inputs: KB, the knowledge base, a sentence in propositional logic
          α, the query, a sentence in propositional logic

  symbols ← a list of the proposition symbols in KB and α
  return TT-CHECK-ALL(KB, α, symbols, [ ])
```

```
function TT-CHECK-ALL(KB, α, symbols, model) returns true or false
  if EMPTY?(symbols) then
      if PL-TRUE?(KB, model) then return PL-TRUE?(α, model)
      else return true
  else do
      P ← FIRST(symbols); rest ← REST(symbols)
      return TT-CHECK-ALL(KB, α, rest, EXTEND(P, true, model)) and
               TT-CHECK-ALL(KB, α, rest, EXTEND(P, false, model))
```

**Figure 7.10** A truth-table enumeration algorithm for deciding propositional entailment. TT stands for truth table. PL-TRUE? returns true if a sentence holds within a model. The variable *model* represents a partial model—an assignment to only some of the variables. The function call EXTEND(*P, true, model*) returns a new partial model in which $P$ has the value *true*.

implements directly the definition of entailment, and **complete**, because it works for any $KB$ and $\alpha$ and always terminates—there are only finitely many models to examine.

Of course, "finitely many" is not always the same as "few." If $KB$ and $\alpha$ contain $n$ symbols in all, then there are $2^n$ models. Thus, the time complexity of the algorithm is $O(2^n)$. (The space complexity is only $O(n)$ because the enumeration is depth-first.) Later in this

$$
\begin{aligned}
(\alpha \wedge \beta) &\equiv (\beta \wedge \alpha) \quad \text{commutativity of } \wedge \\
(\alpha \vee \beta) &\equiv (\beta \vee \alpha) \quad \text{commutativity of } \vee \\
((\alpha \wedge \beta) \wedge \gamma) &\equiv (\alpha \wedge (\beta \wedge \gamma)) \quad \text{associativity of } \wedge \\
((\alpha \vee \beta) \vee \gamma) &\equiv (\alpha \vee (\beta \vee \gamma)) \quad \text{associativity of } \vee \\
\neg(\neg \alpha) &\equiv \alpha \quad \text{double-negation elimination} \\
(\alpha \Rightarrow \beta) &\equiv (\neg \beta \Rightarrow \neg \alpha) \quad \text{contraposition} \\
(\alpha \Rightarrow \beta) &\equiv (\neg \alpha \vee \beta) \quad \text{implication elimination} \\
(\alpha \Leftrightarrow \beta) &\equiv ((\alpha \Rightarrow \beta) \wedge (\beta \Rightarrow \alpha)) \quad \text{biconditional elimination} \\
\neg(\alpha \wedge \beta) &\equiv (\neg \alpha \vee \neg \beta) \quad \text{De Morgan} \\
\neg(\alpha \vee \beta) &\equiv (\neg \alpha \wedge \neg \beta) \quad \text{De Morgan} \\
(\alpha \wedge (\beta \vee \gamma)) &\equiv ((\alpha \wedge \beta) \vee (\alpha \wedge \gamma)) \quad \text{distributivity of } \wedge \text{ over } \vee \\
(\alpha \vee (\beta \wedge \gamma)) &\equiv ((\alpha \vee \beta) \wedge (\alpha \vee \gamma)) \quad \text{distributivity of } \vee \text{ over } \wedge
\end{aligned}
$$

**Figure 7.11** Standard logical equivalences. The symbols $\alpha$, $\beta$, and $\gamma$ stand for arbitrary sentences of propositional logic.

chapter, we will see algorithms that are much more efficient in practice. Unfortunately, *every known inference algorithm for propositional logic has a worst-case complexity that is exponential in the size of the input.* We do not expect to do better than this because propositional entailment is co-NP-complete. (See Appendix A.)

### Equivalence, validity, and satisfiability

Before we plunge into the details of logical inference algorithms, we will need some additional concepts related to entailment. Like entailment, these concepts apply to all forms of logic, but they are best illustrated for a particular logic, such as propositional logic.

LOGICAL EQUIVALENCE

The first concept is **logical equivalence**: two sentences $\alpha$ and $\beta$ are logically equivalent if they are true in the same set of models. We write this as $\alpha \equiv \beta$. For example, we can easily show (using truth tables) that $P \wedge Q$ and $Q \wedge P$ are logically equivalent; other equivalences are shown in Figure 7.11. They play much the same role in logic as arithmetic identities do in ordinary mathematics. An alternative definition of equivalence is as follows: for any two sentences $\alpha$ and $\beta$,

$$\alpha \equiv \beta \quad \text{if and only if} \quad \alpha \models \beta \text{ and } \beta \models \alpha\,.$$

(Recall that $\models$ means entailment.)

VALIDITY

The second concept we will need is **validity**. A sentence is valid if it is true in *all* models. For example, the sentence $P \vee \neg P$ is valid. Valid sentences are also known as

TAUTOLOGY

**tautologies**—they are *necessarily* true and hence vacuous. Because the sentence *True* is true in all models, every valid sentence is logically equivalent to *True*.

What good are valid sentences? From our definition of entailment, we can derive the

DEDUCTION THEOREM

**deduction theorem**, which was known to the ancient Greeks:

*For any sentences $\alpha$ and $\beta$, $\alpha \models \beta$ if and only if the sentence $(\alpha \Rightarrow \beta)$ is valid.*

(Exercise 7.4 asks for a proof.) We can think of the inference algorithm in Figure 7.10 as checking the validity of $(KB \Rightarrow \alpha)$. Conversely, every valid implication sentence describes a legitimate inference.

SATISFIABILITY

The final concept we will need is **satisfiability**. A sentence is satisfiable if it is true in *some* model. For example, the knowledge base given earlier, $(R_1 \land R_2 \land R_3 \land R_4 \land R_5)$, is satisfiable because there are three models in which it is true, as shown in Figure 7.9. If a sentence $\alpha$ is true in a model $m$, then we say that $m$ **satisfies** $\alpha$, or that $m$ **is a model of** $\alpha$. Satisfiability can be checked by enumerating the possible models until one is found that satisfies the sentence. Determining the satisfiability of sentences in propositional logic was the first problem proved to be NP-complete.

SATISFIES

Many problems in computer science are really satisfiability problems. For example, all the constraint satisfaction problems in Chapter 5 are essentially asking whether the constraints are satisfiable by some assignment. With appropriate transformations, search problems can also be solved by checking satisfiability. Validity and satisfiability are of course connected: $\alpha$ is valid iff $\neg\alpha$ is unsatisfiable; contrapositively, $\alpha$ is satisfiable iff $\neg\alpha$ is not valid. We also have the following useful result:

$\alpha \models \beta$ *if and only if the sentence* $(\alpha \land \neg\beta)$ *is unsatisfiable.*

REDUCTIO AD ABSURDUM

REFUTATION

Proving $\beta$ from $\alpha$ by checking the unsatisfiability of $(\alpha \land \neg\beta)$ corresponds exactly to the standard mathematical proof technique of *reductio ad absurdum* (literally, "reduction to an absurd thing"). It is also called proof by **refutation** or proof by **contradiction**. One assumes a sentence $\beta$ to be false and shows that this leads to a contradiction with known axioms $\alpha$. This contradiction is exactly what is meant by saying that the sentence $(\alpha \land \neg\beta)$ is unsatisfiable.

## 7.5 REASONING PATTERNS IN PROPOSITIONAL LOGIC

INFERENCE RULES

MODUS PONENS

This section covers standard patterns of inference that can be applied to derive chains of conclusions that lead to the desired goal. These patterns of inference are called **inference rules**. The best-known rule is called **Modus Ponens** and is written as follows:

$$\frac{\alpha \Rightarrow \beta, \quad \alpha}{\beta} .$$

The notation means that, whenever any sentences of the form $\alpha \Rightarrow \beta$ and $\alpha$ are given, then the sentence $\beta$ can be inferred. For example, if $(WumpusAhead \land WumpusAlive) \Rightarrow Shoot$ and $(WumpusAhead \land WumpusAlive)$ are given, then $Shoot$ can be inferred.

AND-ELIMINATION

Another useful inference rule is **And-Elimination**, which says that, from a conjunction, any of the conjuncts can be inferred:

$$\frac{\alpha \land \beta}{\alpha} .$$

For example, from $(WumpusAhead \land WumpusAlive)$, $WumpusAlive$ can be inferred.

By considering the possible truth values of $\alpha$ and $\beta$, one can show easily that Modus Ponens and And-Elimination are sound once and for all. These rules can then be used in any particular instances where they apply, generating sound inferences without the need for enumerating models.

All of the logical equivalences in Figure 7.11 can be used as inference rules. For example, the equivalence for biconditional elimination yields the two inference rules

$$\frac{\alpha \Leftrightarrow \beta}{(\alpha \Rightarrow \beta) \wedge (\beta \Rightarrow \alpha)} \quad \text{and} \quad \frac{(\alpha \Rightarrow \beta) \wedge (\beta \Rightarrow \alpha)}{\alpha \Leftrightarrow \beta} .$$

Not all inference rules work in both directions like this. For example, we cannot run Modus Ponens in the opposite direction to obtain $\alpha \Rightarrow \beta$ and $\alpha$ from $\beta$.

Let us see how these inference rules and equivalences can be used in the wumpus world. We start with the knowledge base containing $R_1$ through $R_5$, and show how to prove $\neg P_{1,2}$, that is, there is no pit in [1,2]. First, we apply biconditional elimination to $R_2$ to obtain

$$R_6 : \quad (B_{1,1} \Rightarrow (P_{1,2} \vee P_{2,1})) \wedge ((P_{1,2} \vee P_{2,1}) \Rightarrow B_{1,1}) .$$

Then we apply And-Elimination to $R_6$ to obtain

$$R_7 : \quad ((P_{1,2} \vee P_{2,1}) \Rightarrow B_{1,1}) .$$

Logical equivalence for contrapositives gives

$$R_8 : \quad (\neg B_{1,1} \Rightarrow \neg(P_{1,2} \vee P_{2,1})) .$$

Now we can apply Modus Ponens with $R_8$ and the percept $R_4$ (i.e., $\neg B_{1,1}$), to obtain

$$R_9 : \quad \neg(P_{1,2} \vee P_{2,1}) .$$

Finally, we apply De Morgan's rule, giving the conclusion

$$R_{10} : \quad \neg P_{1,2} \wedge \neg P_{2,1} .$$

That is, neither [1,2] nor [2,1] contains a pit.

PROOF

The preceding derivation—a sequence of applications of inference rules—is called a **proof**. Finding proofs is exactly like finding solutions to search problems. In fact, if the successor function is defined to generate all possible applications of inference rules, then all of the search algorithms in Chapters 3 and 4 can be applied to find proofs. Thus, searching for proofs is an alternative to enumerating models. The search can go forward from the initial knowledge base, applying inference rules to derive the goal sentence, or it can go backward from the goal sentence, trying to find a chain of inference rules leading from the initial knowledge base. Later in this section, we will see two families of algorithms that use these techniques.

The fact that inference in propositional logic is NP-complete suggests that, in the worst case, searching for proofs is going to be no more efficient than enumerating models. In many practical cases, however, *finding a proof can be highly efficient simply because it can ignore irrelevant propositions, no matter how many of them there are.* For example, the proof given earlier leading to $\neg P_{1,2} \wedge \neg P_{2,1}$ does not mention the propositions $B_{2,1}$, $P_{1,1}$, $P_{2,2}$, or $P_{3,1}$. They can be ignored because the goal proposition, $P_{1,2}$, appears only in sentence $R_4$; the other propositions in $R_4$ appear only in $R_4$ and $R_2$; so $R_1$, $R_3$, and $R_5$ have no bearing on the proof. The same would hold even if we added a million more sentences to the knowledge base; the simple truth-table algorithm, on the other hand, would be overwhelmed by the exponential explosion of models.

MONOTONICITY

This property of logical systems actually follows from a much more fundamental property called **monotonicity**. Monotonicity says that the set of entailed sentences can only *in-*

*crease* as information is added to the knowledge base.[10] For any sentences $\alpha$ and $\beta$,

$$\text{if} \quad KB \models \alpha \quad \text{then} \quad KB \land \beta \models \alpha .$$

For example, suppose the knowledge base contains the additional assertion $\beta$ stating that there are exactly eight pits in the world. This knowledge might help the agent draw *additional* conclusions, but it cannot invalidate any conclusion $\alpha$ already inferred—such as the conclusion that there is no pit in [1,2]. Monotonicity means that inference rules can be applied whenever suitable premises are found in the knowledge base—the conclusion of the rule must follow *regardless of what else is in the knowledge base.*

### Resolution

We have argued that the inference rules covered so far are *sound*, but we have not discussed the question of *completeness* for the inference algorithms that use them. Search algorithms such as iterative deepening search (page 78) are complete in the sense that they will find any reachable goal, but if the available inference rules are inadequate, then the goal is not reachable—no proof exists that uses only those inference rules. For example, if we removed the biconditional elimination rule, the proof in the preceding section would not go through. The current section introduces a single inference rule, **resolution**, that yields a complete inference algorithm when coupled with any complete search algorithm.

We begin by using a simple version of the resolution rule in the wumpus world. Let us consider the steps leading up to Figure 7.4(a): the agent returns from [2,1] to [1,1] and then goes to [1,2], where it perceives a stench, but no breeze. We add the following facts to the knowledge base:

$$R_{11}: \quad \neg B_{1,2} .$$
$$R_{12}: \quad B_{1,2} \Leftrightarrow (P_{1,1} \lor P_{2,2} \lor P_{1,3}) .$$

By the same process that led to $R_{10}$ earlier, we can now derive the absence of pits in [2,2] and [1,3] (remember that [1,1] is already known to be pitless):

$$R_{13}: \quad \neg P_{2,2} .$$
$$R_{14}: \quad \neg P_{1,3} .$$

We can also apply biconditional elimination to $R_3$, followed by modus ponens with $R_5$, to obtain the fact that there is a pit in [1,1], [2,2], or [3,1]:

$$R_{15}: \quad P_{1,1} \lor P_{2,2} \lor P_{3,1} .$$

Now comes the first application of the resolution rule: the literal $\neg P_{2,2}$ in $R_{13}$ *resolves with* the literal $P_{2,2}$ in $R_{15}$ to give

$$R_{16}: \quad P_{1,1} \lor P_{3,1} .$$

In English; if there's a pit in one of [1,1], [2,2], and [3,1], and it's not in [2,2], then it's in [1,1] or [3,1]. Similarly, the literal $\neg P_{1,1}$ in $R_1$ resolves with the literal $P_{1,1}$ in $R_{16}$ to give

$$R_{17}: \quad P_{3,1} .$$

[10] **Nonmonotonic** logics, which violate the monotonicity property, capture a common property of human reasoning: changing one's mind. They are discussed in Section 10.7.

In English: if there's a pit in [1,1] or [3,1], and it's not in [1,1], then it's in [3,1]. These last two inference steps are examples of the **unit resolution** inference rule,

UNIT RESOLUTION

$$\frac{\ell_1 \vee \cdots \vee \ell_k, \qquad m}{\ell_1 \vee \cdots \vee \ell_{i-1} \vee \ell_{i+1} \vee \cdots \vee \ell_k},$$

COMPLEMENTARY LITERALS

CLAUSE

where each $\ell$ is a literal and $\ell_i$ and $m$ are **complementary literals** (i.e., one is the negation of the other). Thus, the unit resolution rule takes a **clause**—a disjunction of literals—and a literal and produces a new clause. Note that a single literal can be viewed as a disjunction of one literal, also known as a **unit clause**.

UNIT CLAUSE

RESOLUTION

The unit resolution rule can be generalized to the full **resolution** rule,

$$\frac{\ell_1 \vee \cdots \vee \ell_k, \qquad m_1 \vee \cdots \vee m_n}{\ell_1 \vee \cdots \vee \ell_{i-1} \vee \ell_{i+1} \vee \cdots \vee \ell_k \vee m_1 \vee \cdots \vee m_{j-1} \vee m_{j+1} \vee \cdots \vee m_n},$$

where $\ell_i$ and $m_j$ are complementary literals. If we were dealing only with clauses of length two we could write this as

$$\frac{\ell_1 \vee \ell_2, \qquad \neg\ell_2 \vee \ell_3}{\ell_1 \vee \ell_3}.$$

That is, resolution takes two clauses and produces a new clause containing all the literals of the two original clauses *except* the two complementary literals. For example, we have

$$\frac{P_{1,1} \vee P_{3,1}, \qquad \neg P_{1,1} \vee \neg P_{2,2}}{P_{3,1} \vee \neg P_{2,2}}.$$

FACTORING

There is one more technical aspect of the resolution rule: the resulting clause should contain only one copy of each literal.[11] The removal of multiple copies of literals is called **factoring**. For example, if we resolve $(A \vee B)$ with $(A \vee \neg B)$, we obtain $(A \vee A)$, which is reduced to just $A$.

The *soundness* of the resolution rule can be seen easily by considering the literal $\ell_i$. If $\ell_i$ is true, then $m_j$ is false, and hence $m_1 \vee \cdots \vee m_{j-1} \vee m_{j+1} \vee \cdots \vee m_n$ must be true, because $m_1 \vee \cdots \vee m_n$ is given. If $\ell_i$ is false, then $\ell_1 \vee \cdots \vee \ell_{i-1} \vee \ell_{i+1} \vee \cdots \vee \ell_k$ must be true because $\ell_1 \vee \cdots \vee \ell_k$ is given. Now $\ell_i$ is either true or false, so one or other of these conclusions holds—exactly as the resolution rule states.

What is more surprising about the resolution rule is that it forms the basis for a family of *complete* inference procedures. *Any complete search algorithm, applying only the resolution rule, can derive any conclusion entailed by any knowledge base in propositional logic.* There is a caveat: resolution is complete in a specialized sense. Given that $A$ is true, we cannot use resolution to automatically generate the consequence $A \vee B$. However, we can use resolution to answer the question of whether $A \vee B$ is true. This is called **refutation completeness**, meaning that resolution can always be used to either confirm or refute a sentence, but it cannot be used to enumerate true sentences. The next two subsections explain how resolution accomplishes this.

REFUTATION COMPLETENESS

[11] If a clause is viewed as a *set* of literals, then this restriction is automatically respected. Using set notation for clauses makes the resolution rule much cleaner, at the cost of introducing additional notation.

### Conjunctive normal form

The resolution rule applies only to disjunctions of literals, so it would seem to be relevant only to knowledge bases and queries consisting of such disjunctions. How, then, can it lead to a complete inference procedure for all of propositional logic? The answer is that *every sentence of propositional logic is logically equivalent to a conjunction of disjunctions of literals.* A sentence expressed as a conjunction of disjunctions of literals is said to be in **conjunctive normal form** or **CNF**. We will also find it useful later to consider the restricted family of $k$-**CNF** sentences. A sentence in $k$-CNF has exactly $k$ literals per clause:

CONJUNCTIVE NORMAL FORM

K-CNF

$$(\ell_{1,1} \vee \ldots \vee \ell_{1,k}) \wedge \ldots \wedge (\ell_{n,1} \vee \ldots \vee \ell_{n,k}) .$$

It turns out that every sentence can be transformed into a 3-CNF sentence that has an equivalent set of models.

Rather than prove these assertions (see Exercise 7.10), we describe a simple conversion procedure. We illustrate the procedure by converting $R_2$, the sentence $B_{1,1} \Leftrightarrow (P_{1,2} \vee P_{2,1})$, into CNF. The steps are as follows:

1. Eliminate $\Leftrightarrow$, replacing $\alpha \Leftrightarrow \beta$ with $(\alpha \Rightarrow \beta) \wedge (\beta \Rightarrow \alpha)$.

   $$(B_{1,1} \Rightarrow (P_{1,2} \vee P_{2,1})) \wedge ((P_{1,2} \vee P_{2,1}) \Rightarrow B_{1,1}) .$$

2. Eliminate $\Rightarrow$, replacing $\alpha \Rightarrow \beta$ with $\neg\alpha \vee \beta$:

   $$(\neg B_{1,1} \vee P_{1,2} \vee P_{2,1}) \wedge (\neg(P_{1,2} \vee P_{2,1}) \vee B_{1,1}) .$$

3. CNF requires $\neg$ to appear only in literals, so we "move $\neg$ inwards" by repeated application of the following equivalences from Figure 7.11:

   $\neg(\neg\alpha) \equiv \alpha$ (double-negation elimination)
   $\neg(\alpha \wedge \beta) \equiv (\neg\alpha \vee \neg\beta)$ (De Morgan)
   $\neg(\alpha \vee \beta) \equiv (\neg\alpha \wedge \neg\beta)$ (De Morgan)

   In the example, we require just one application of the last rule:

   $$(\neg B_{1,1} \vee P_{1,2} \vee P_{2,1}) \wedge ((\neg P_{1,2} \wedge \neg P_{2,1}) \vee B_{1,1}) .$$

4. Now we have a sentence containing nested $\wedge$ and $\vee$ operators applied to literals. We apply the distributivity law from Figure 7.11, distributing $\vee$ over $\wedge$ wherever possible.

   $$(\neg B_{1,1} \vee P_{1,2} \vee P_{2,1}) \wedge (\neg P_{1,2} \vee B_{1,1}) \wedge (\neg P_{2,1} \vee B_{1,1}) .$$

The original sentence is now in CNF, as a conjunction of three clauses. It is much harder to read, but it can be used as input to a resolution procedure.

### A resolution algorithm

Inference procedures based on resolution work by using the principle of proof by contradiction discussed at the end of Section 7.4. That is, to show that $KB \models \alpha$, we show that $(KB \wedge \neg\alpha)$ is unsatisfiable. We do this by proving a contradiction.

A resolution algorithm is shown in Figure 7.12. First, $(KB \wedge \neg\alpha)$ is converted into CNF. Then, the resolution rule is applied to the resulting clauses. Each pair that contains complementary literals is resolved to produce a new clause, which is added to the set if it is not already present. The process continues until one of two things happens:

```
function PL-RESOLUTION(KB, α) returns true or false
  inputs: KB, the knowledge base, a sentence in propositional logic
          α, the query, a sentence in propositional logic

  clauses ← the set of clauses in the CNF representation of KB ∧ ¬α
  new ← { }
  loop do
     for each Ci, Cj in clauses do
        resolvents ← PL-RESOLVE(Ci, Cj)
        if resolvents contains the empty clause then return true
        new ← new ∪ resolvents
     if new ⊆ clauses then return false
     clauses ← clauses ∪ new
```

**Figure 7.12** A simple resolution algorithm for propositional logic. The function PL-RESOLVE returns the set of all possible clauses obtained by resolving its two inputs.

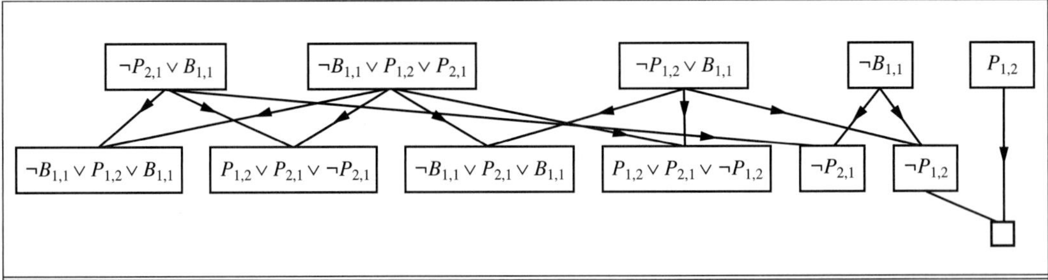


**Figure 7.13** Partial application of PL-RESOLUTION to a simple inference in the wumpus world. $\neg P_{1,2}$ is shown to follow from the first four clauses in the top row.

- there are no new clauses that can be added, in which case $KB$ does not entail $\alpha$; or,
- two clauses resolve to yield the *empty* clause, in which case $KB$ entails $\alpha$.

The empty clause—a disjunction of no disjuncts—is equivalent to *False* because a disjunction is true only if at least one of its disjuncts is true. Another way to see that an empty clause represents a contradiction is to observe that it arises only from resolving two complementary unit clauses such as $P$ and $\neg P$.

We can apply the resolution procedure to a very simple inference in the wumpus world. When the agent is in [1,1], there is no breeze, so there can be no pits in neighboring squares. The relevant knowledge base is

$$KB = R_2 \wedge R_4 = (B_{1,1} \Leftrightarrow (P_{1,2} \vee P_{2,1})) \wedge \neg B_{1,1}$$

and we wish to prove $\alpha$ which is, say, $\neg P_{1,2}$. When we convert $(KB \wedge \neg\alpha)$ into CNF, we obtain the clauses shown at the top of Figure 7.13. The second row of the figure shows all the clauses obtained by resolving pairs in the first row. Then, when $P_{1,2}$ is resolved with $\neg P_{1,2}$, we obtain the empty clause, shown as a small square. Inspection of Figure 7.13 reveals that many resolution steps are pointless. For example, the clause $B_{1,1} \lor \neg B_{1,1} \lor P_{1,2}$ is equivalent to $True \lor P_{1,2}$ which is equivalent to $True$. Deducing that $True$ is true is not very helpful. Therefore, any clause in which two complementary literals appear can be discarded.

### Completeness of resolution

RESOLUTION CLOSURE

To conclude our discussion of resolution, we now show why PL-RESOLUTION is complete. To do this, it will be useful to introduce the **resolution closure** $RC(S)$ of a set of clauses $S$, which is the set of all clauses derivable by repeated application of the resolution rule to clauses in $S$ or their derivatives. The resolution closure is what PL-RESOLUTION computes as the final value of the variable $clauses$. It is easy to see that $RC(S)$ must be finite, because there are only finitely many distinct clauses that can be constructed out of the symbols $P_1, \ldots, P_k$ that appear in $S$. (Notice that this would not be true without the factoring step that removes multiple copies of literals.) Hence, PL-RESOLUTION always terminates.

GROUND RESOLUTION THEOREM

The completeness theorem for resolution in propositional logic is called the **ground resolution theorem**:

> If a set of clauses is unsatisfiable, then the resolution closure of those clauses contains the empty clause.

We prove this theorem by demonstrating its contrapositive: if the closure $RC(S)$ does *not* contain the empty clause, then $S$ is satisfiable. In fact, we can construct a model for $S$ with suitable truth values for $P_1, \ldots, P_k$. The construction procedure is as follows:

For $i$ from 1 to $k$,

- If there is a clause in $RC(S)$ containing the literal $\neg P_i$ such that all its other literals are false under the assignment chosen for $P_1, \ldots, P_{i-1}$, then assign $false$ to $P_i$.
- Otherwise, assign $true$ to $P_i$.

It remains to show that this assignment to $P_1, \ldots, P_k$ is a model of $S$, provided that $RC(S)$ is closed under resolution and does not contain the empty clause. The proof of this is left as an exercise.

## Forward and backward chaining

HORN CLAUSES

The completeness of resolution makes it a very important inference method. In many practical situations, however, the full power of resolution is not needed. Real-world knowledge bases often contain only clauses of a restricted kind called **Horn clauses**. A Horn clause is a disjunction of literals of which *at most one is positive*. For example, the clause $(\neg L_{1,1} \lor \neg Breeze \lor B_{1,1})$, where $L_{1,1}$ means that the agent's location is [1,1], is a Horn clause, whereas $(\neg B_{1,1} \lor P_{1,2} \lor P_{2,1})$ is not.

The restriction to just one positive literal may seem somewhat arbitrary and uninteresting, but it is actually very important for three reasons:

1. Every Horn clause can be written as an implication whose premise is a conjunction of positive literals and whose conclusion is a single positive literal. (See Exercise 7.12.) For example, the Horn clause $(\neg L_{1,1} \lor \neg Breeze \lor B_{1,1})$ can be written as the implication

$(L_{1,1} \wedge Breeze) \Rightarrow B_{1,1}$. In the latter form, the sentence is much easier to read: it says that if the agent is in [1,1] and there is a breeze, then [1,1] is breezy. People find it easy to read and write sentences in this form for many domains of knowledge.

DEFINITE CLAUSES
HEAD
BODY
FACT

Horn clauses like this one with *exactly* one positive literal are called **definite clauses**. The positive literal is called the **head** and the negative literals form the **body** of the clause. A definite clause with no negative literals simply asserts a given proposition—sometimes called a **fact**. Definite clauses form the basis for **logic programming**, which is discussed in Chapter 9. A Horn clause with *no* positive literals can be written as an implication whose conclusion is the literal $False$. For example, the clause $(\neg W_{1,1} \vee \neg W_{1,2})$—the wumpus cannot be in both [1,1] and [1,2]—is equivalent to $W_{1,1} \wedge W_{1,2} \Rightarrow False$. Such sentences are called **integrity constraints** in the database world, where they are used to signal errors in the data. In the algorithms that follow, we assume for simplicity that the knowledge base contains only definite clauses and no integrity constraints. We say these knowledge bases are in Horn form.

INTEGRITY CONSTRAINTS

FORWARD CHAINING
BACKWARD CHAINING

2. Inference with Horn clauses can be done through the **forward chaining** and **backward chaining** algorithms, which we explain next. Both of these algorithms are very natural, in that the inference steps are obvious and easy to follow for humans.

3. Deciding entailment with Horn clauses can be done in time that is *linear* in the size of the knowledge base.

This last fact is a pleasant surprise. It means that logical inference is very cheap for many propositional knowledge bases that are encountered in practice.

The forward-chaining algorithm PL-FC-ENTAILS?$(KB, q)$ determines whether a single proposition symbol $q$—the query—is entailed by a knowledge base of Horn clauses. It begins from known facts (positive literals) in the knowledge base. If all the premises of an implication are known, then its conclusion is added to the set of known facts. For example, if $L_{1,1}$ and $Breeze$ are known and $(L_{1,1} \wedge Breeze) \Rightarrow B_{1,1}$ is in the knowledge base, then $B_{1,1}$ can be added. This process continues until the query $q$ is added or until no further inferences can be made. The detailed algorithm is shown in Figure 7.14; the main point to remember is that it runs in linear time.

The best way to understand the algorithm is through an example and a picture. Figure 7.15(a) shows a simple knowledge base of Horn clauses with $A$ and $B$ as known facts. Figure 7.15(b) shows the same knowledge base drawn as an **AND–OR graph**. In AND–OR graphs, multiple links joined by an arc indicate a conjunction—every link must be proved—while multiple links without an arc indicate a disjunction—any link can be proved. It is easy to see how forward chaining works in the graph. The known leaves (here, $A$ and $B$) are set, and inference propagates up the graph as far as possible. Wherever a conjunction appears, the propagation waits until all the conjuncts are known before proceeding. The reader is encouraged to work through the example in detail.

AND–OR GRAPH

It is easy to see that forward chaining is **sound**: every inference is essentially an application of Modus Ponens. Forward chaining is also **complete**: every entailed atomic sentence will be derived. The easiest way to see this is to consider the final state of the $inferred$ table (after the algorithm reaches a **fixed point** where no new inferences are possible). The table

FIXED POINT

```
function PL-FC-ENTAILS?(KB, q) returns true or false
  inputs: KB, the knowledge base, a set of propositional Horn clauses
          q, the query, a proposition symbol
  local variables: count, a table, indexed by clause, initially the number of premises
                   inferred, a table, indexed by symbol, each entry initially false
                   agenda, a list of symbols, initially the symbols known to be true in KB

  while agenda is not empty do
     p ← POP(agenda)
     if p = q then return true
     unless inferred[p] do
        inferred[p] ← true
        for each Horn clause c in whose premise p appears do
           decrement count[c]
           if count[c] = 0 then
              PUSH(HEAD[c], agenda)
  return false
```

**Figure 7.14** The forward-chaining algorithm for propositional logic. The *agenda* keeps track of symbols known to be true but not yet "processed." The *count* table keeps track of how many premises of each implication are as yet unknown. Whenever a new symbol $p$ from the agenda is processed, the count is reduced by one for each implication in whose premise $p$ appears. (These can be identified in constant time if $KB$ is indexed appropriately.) If a count reaches zero, all the premises of the implication are known so its conclusion can be added to the agenda. Finally, we need to keep track of which symbols have been processed; an inferred symbol need not be added to the agenda if it has been processed previously. This avoids redundant work; it also prevents infinite loops that could be caused by implications such as $P \Rightarrow Q$ and $Q \Rightarrow P$.

contains *true* for each symbol inferred during the process, and *false* for all other symbols. We can view the table as a logical model; moreover, *every definite clause in the original KB is true in this model.* To see this, assume the opposite, namely that some clause $a_1 \wedge \ldots \wedge a_k \Rightarrow b$ is false in the model. Then $a_1 \wedge \ldots \wedge a_k$ must be true in the model and $b$ must be false in the model. But this contradicts our assumption that the algorithm has reached a fi xed point! We can conclude, therefore, that the set of atomic sentences inferred at the fi xed point defi nes a model of the original KB. Furthermore, any atomic sentence $q$ that is entailed by the KB must be true in all its models and in this model in particular. Hence, every entailed sentence $q$ must be inferred by the algorithm.

DATA-DRIVEN

Forward chaining is an example of the general concept of **data-driven** reasoning—that is, reasoning in which the focus of attention starts with the known data. It can be used within an agent to derive conclusions from incoming percepts, often without a specifi c query in mind. For example, the wumpus agent might TELL its percepts to the knowledge base using an incremental forward-chaining algorithm in which new facts can be added to the agenda to initiate new inferences. In humans, a certain amount of data-driven reasoning occurs as new

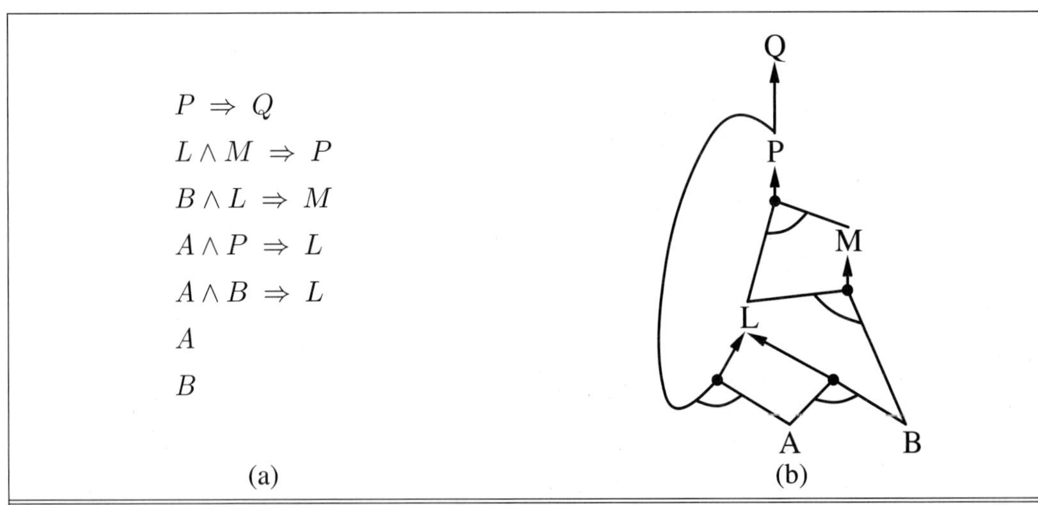


**Figure 7.15** (a) A simple knowledge base of Horn clauses. (b) The corresponding AND–OR graph.

information arrives. For example, if I am indoors and hear rain starting to fall, it might occur to me that the picnic will be canceled. Yet it will probably not occur to me that the seventeenth petal on the largest rose in my neighbor's garden will get wet; humans keep forward chaining under careful control, lest they be swamped with irrelevant consequences.

The backward-chaining algorithm, as its name suggests, works backwards from the query. If the query $q$ is known to be true, then no work is needed. Otherwise, the algorithm finds those implications in the knowledge base that conclude $q$. If all the premises of one of those implications can be proved true (by backward chaining), then $q$ is true. When applied to the query $Q$ in Figure 7.15, it works back down the graph until it reaches a set of known facts that forms the basis for a proof. The detailed algorithm is left as an exercise; as with forward chaining, an efficient implementation runs in linear time.

GOAL-DIRECTED REASONING

Backward chaining is a form of **goal-directed reasoning**. It is useful for answering specific questions such as "What shall I do now?" and "Where are my keys?" Often, the cost of backward chaining is *much less* than linear in the size of the knowledge base, because the process touches only relevant facts. In general, an agent should share the work between forward and backward reasoning, limiting forward reasoning to the generation of facts that are likely to be relevant to queries that will be solved by backward chaining.

## 7.6 EFFECTIVE PROPOSITIONAL INFERENCE

In this section, we describe two families of efficient algorithms for propositional inference based on model checking: one approach based on backtracking search, and one on hillclimbing search. These algorithms are part of the "technology" of propositional logic. This section can be skimmed on a first reading of the chapter.

The algorithms we describe are for checking satisfiability. We have already noted the connection between finding a satisfying model for a logical sentence and finding a solution for a constraint satisfaction problem, so it is perhaps not surprising that the two families of algorithms closely resemble the backtracking algorithms of Section 5.2 and the local-search algorithms of Section 5.3. They are, however, extremely important in their own right because so many combinatorial problems in computer science can be reduced to checking the satisfiability of a propositional sentence. Any improvement in satisfiability algorithms has huge consequences for our ability to handle complexity in general.

## A complete backtracking algorithm

DAVIS–PUTNAM ALGORITHM

The first algorithm we will consider is often called the **Davis–Putnam algorithm**, after the seminal paper by Martin Davis and Hilary Putnam (1960). The algorithm is in fact the version described by Davis, Logemann, and Loveland (1962), so we will call it DPLL after the initials of all four authors. DPLL takes as input a sentence in conjunctive normal form—a set of clauses. Like BACKTRACKING-SEARCH and TT-ENTAILS?, it is essentially a recursive, depth-first enumeration of possible models. It embodies three improvements over the simple scheme of TT-ENTAILS?:

- *Early termination*: The algorithm detects whether the sentence must be true or false, even with a partially completed model. A clause is true if *any* literal is true, even if the other literals do not yet have truth values; hence, the sentence as a whole could be judged true even before the model is complete. For example, the sentence $(A \lor B) \land (A \lor C)$ is true if $A$ is true, regardless of the values of $B$ and $C$. Similarly, a sentence is false if *any* clause is false, which occurs when each of its literals is false. Again, this can occur long before the model is complete. Early termination avoids examination of entire subtrees in the search space.

PURE SYMBOL

- *Pure symbol heuristic*: A **pure symbol** is a symbol that always appears with the same "sign" in all clauses. For example, in the three clauses $(A \lor \neg B)$, $(\neg B \lor \neg C)$, and $(C \lor A)$, the symbol $A$ is pure because only the positive literal appears, $B$ is pure because only the negative literal appears, and $C$ is impure. It is easy to see that if a sentence has a model, then it has a model with the pure symbols assigned so as to make their literals $true$, because doing so can never make a clause false. Note that, in determining the purity of a symbol, the algorithm can ignore clauses that are already known to be true in the model constructed so far. For example, if the model contains $B = false$, then the clause $(\neg B \lor \neg C)$ is already true, and $C$ becomes pure because it appears only in $(C \lor A)$.
- *Unit clause heuristic*: A **unit clause** was defined earlier as a clause with just one literal. In the context of DPLL, it also means clauses in which all literals but one are already assigned $false$ by the model. For example, if the model contains $B = false$, then $(B \lor \neg C)$ becomes a unit clause because it is equivalent to $(False \lor \neg C)$, or just $\neg C$. Obviously, for this clause to be true, $C$ must be set to $false$. The unit clause heuristic assigns all such symbols before branching on the remainder. One important consequence of the heuristic is that any attempt to prove (by refutation) a literal that is

```
function DPLL-SATISFIABLE?(s) returns true or false
  inputs: s, a sentence in propositional logic

  clauses ← the set of clauses in the CNF representation of s
  symbols ← a list of the proposition symbols in s
  return DPLL(clauses, symbols, [ ])
```

```
function DPLL(clauses, symbols, model) returns true or false

  if every clause in clauses is true in model then return true
  if some clause in clauses is false in model then return false
  P, value ← FIND-PURE-SYMBOL(symbols, clauses, model)
  if P is non-null then return DPLL(clauses, symbols – P, EXTEND(P, value, model))
  P, value ← FIND-UNIT-CLAUSE(clauses, model)
  if P is non-null then return DPLL(clauses, symbols – P, EXTEND(P, value, model))
  P ← FIRST(symbols); rest ← REST(symbols)
  return DPLL(clauses, rest, EXTEND(P, true, model)) or
         DPLL(clauses, rest, EXTEND(P, false, model))
```

**Figure 7.16** The DPLL algorithm for checking satisfiability of a sentence in propositional logic. FIND-PURE-SYMBOL and FIND-UNIT-CLAUSE are described in the text; each returns a symbol (or null) and the truth value to assign to that symbol. Like TT-ENTAILS?, it operates over partial models.

already in the knowledge base will succeed immediately (Exercise 7.16). Notice also that assigning one unit clause can create another unit clause—for example, when $C$ is set to *false*, $(C \lor A)$ becomes a unit clause, causing true to be assigned to $A$. This "cascade" of forced assignments is called **unit propagation**. It resembles the process of forward chaining with Horn clauses, and indeed, if the CNF expression contains only Horn clauses then DPLL essentially replicates forward chaining. (See Exercise 7.17.)

UNIT PROPAGATION

The DPLL algorithm is shown in Figure 7.16. We have given the essential skeleton of the algorithm, which describes the search process itself. We have not described the data structures that must be maintained in order to make each search step efficient, nor the tricks that can be added to improve performance: clause learning, variable selection heuristics, and randomized restarts. When these are included DPLL is one of the fastest satisfiability algorithms yet developed, despite its antiquity. The CHAFF implementation is used to solve hardware verification problems with a million variables.

## Local-search algorithms

We have seen several local-search algorithms so far in this book, including HILL-CLIMBING (page 112) and SIMULATED-ANNEALING (page 116). These algorithms can be applied directly to satisfiability problems, provided that we choose the right evaluation function. Because the goal is to find an assignment that satisfies every clause, an evaluation function that counts the number of unsatisfied clauses will do the job. In fact, this is exactly the measure

```
function WALKSAT(clauses, p, max_flips) returns a satisfying model or failure
  inputs: clauses, a set of clauses in propositional logic
          p, the probability of choosing to do a "random walk" move, typically around 0.5
          max_flips, number of flips allowed before giving up

  model ← a random assignment of true/false to the symbols in clauses
  for i = 1 to max_flips do
     if model satisfies clauses then return model
     clause ← a randomly selected clause from clauses that is false in model
     with probability p flip the value in model of a randomly selected symbol from clause
     else flip whichever symbol in clause maximizes the number of satisfied clauses
  return failure
```

**Figure 7.17** The WALKSAT algorithm for checking satisfiability by randomly flipping the values of variables. Many versions of the algorithm exist.

used by the MIN-CONFLICTS algorithm for CSPs (page 151). All these algorithms take steps in the space of complete assignments, flipping the truth value of one symbol at a time. The space usually contains many local minima, to escape from which various forms of randomness are required. In recent years, there has been a great deal of experimentation to find a good balance between greediness and randomness.

One of the simplest and most effective algorithms to emerge from all this work is called WALKSAT (Figure 7.17). On every iteration, the algorithm picks an unsatisfied clause and picks a symbol in the clause to flip. It chooses randomly between two ways to pick which symbol to flip: (1) a "min-conflicts" step that minimizes the number of unsatisfied clauses in the new state, and (2) a "random walk" step that picks the symbol randomly.

Does WALKSAT actually work? Clearly, if it returns a model, then the input sentence is indeed satisfiable. What if it returns *failure*? Unfortunately, in that case we cannot tell whether the sentence is unsatisfiable or we need to give the algorithm more time. We could try setting *max_flips* to infinity. In that case, it is easy to show that WALKSAT will eventually return a model (if one exists), provided that the probability $p > 0$. This is because there is always a sequence of flips leading to a satisfying assignment, and eventually the random walk steps will generate that sequence. Alas, if *max_flips* is infinity and the sentence is unsatisfiable, then the algorithm never terminates!

What this suggests is that local-search algorithms such as WALKSAT are most useful when we expect a solution to exist—for example, the problems discussed in Chapters 3 and 5 usually have solutions. On the other hand, local search cannot always detect *unsatisfiability*, which is required for deciding entailment. For example, an agent cannot *reliably* use local search to prove that a square is safe in the wumpus world. Instead, it can say, "I thought about it for an hour and couldn't come up with a possible world in which the square *isn't* safe." If the local-search algorithm is usually really fast at finding a model when one exists, the agent might be justified in assuming that failure to find a model indicates unsatisfiability. This isn't the same as a proof, of course, and the agent should think twice before staking its life on it.

### Hard satisfiability problems

We now look at how DPLL and WALKSAT perform in practice. We are particularly interested in *hard* problems, because *easy* problems can be solved by any old algorithm. In Chapter 5, we saw some surprising discoveries about certain kinds of problems. For example, the $n$-queens problem—thought to be quite tricky for backtracking search algorithms—turned out to be trivially easy for local-search methods, such as min-conflicts. This is because solutions are very densely distributed in the space of assignments, and any initial assignment is guaranteed to have a solution nearby. Thus, $n$-queens is easy because it is **underconstrained**.

UNDERCONSTRAINED

When we look at satisfiability problems in conjunctive normal form, an underconstrained problem is one with relatively *few* clauses constraining the variables. For example, here is a randomly generated[12] 3-CNF sentence with five symbols and five clauses:

$$(\neg D \vee \neg B \vee C) \wedge (B \vee \neg A \vee \neg C) \wedge (\neg C \vee \neg B \vee E)$$
$$\wedge (E \vee \neg D \vee B) \wedge (B \vee E \vee \neg C) .$$

16 of the 32 possible assignments are models of this sentence, so, on average, it would take just two random guesses to find a model.

So where are the hard problems? Presumably, if we *increase* the number of clauses, keeping the number of symbols fixed, we make the problem more constrained, and solutions become harder to find. Let $m$ be the number of clauses and $n$ be the number of symbols. Figure 7.18(a) shows the probability that a random 3-CNF sentence is satisfiable, as a function of the clause/symbol ratio, $m/n$, with $n$ fixed at 50. As we expect, for small $m/n$ the probability is close to 1, and at large $m/n$ the probability is close to 0. The probability drops fairly sharply around $m/n = 4.3$. CNF sentences near this **critical point** could be described as "nearly satisfiable" or "nearly unsatisfiable." Is this where the hard problems are?

CRITICAL POINT

Figure 7.18(b) shows the runtime for DPLL and WALKSAT around this point, where we have restricted attention to just the *satisfiable* problems. Three things are clear: First, problems near the critical point are *much* more difficult than other random problems. Second, even on the hardest problems, DPLL is quite effective—an average of a few thousand steps compared with $2^{50} \approx 10^{15}$ for truth-table enumeration. Third, WALKSAT is much faster than DPLL throughout the range.

Of course, these results are only for randomly generated problems. Real problems do not necessarily have the same structure—in terms of proportions of positive and negative literals, densities of connections among clauses, and so on—as random problems. Yet, in practice, WALKSAT and related algorithms are very good at solving real problems too—often as good as the best special-purpose algorithms for those tasks. Problems with thousands of symbols and millions of clauses are routinely handled by solvers such as CHAFF. These observations suggest that some combination of the min-conflicts heuristic and random-walk behavior provides a *general-purpose* capability for resolving most situations in which combinatorial reasoning is required.

---

[12] Each clause contains three randomly selected *distinct* symbols, each of which is negated with 50% probability.

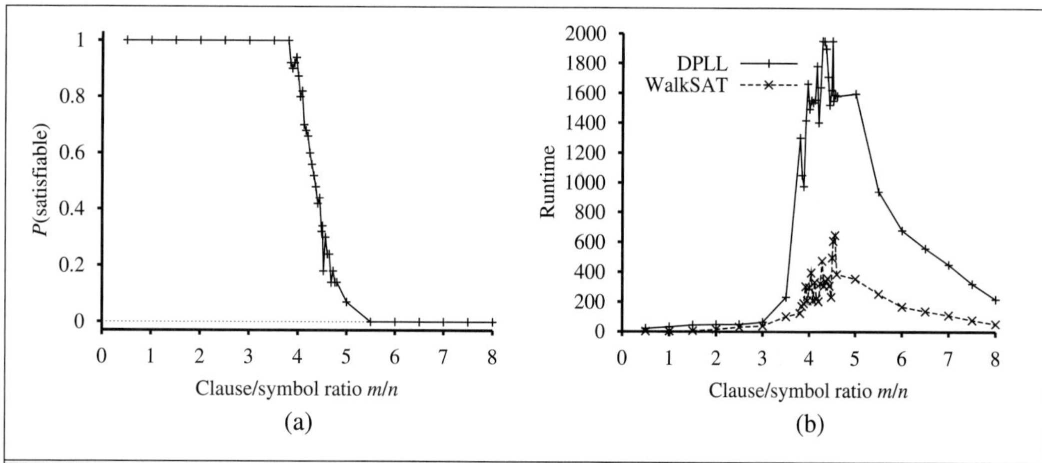


**Figure 7.18** (a) Graph showing the probability that a random 3-CNF sentence with $n = 50$ symbols is satisfiable, as a function of the clause/symbol ratio $m/n$. (b) Graph of the median runtime of DPLL and WALKSAT on 100 *satisfiable* random 3-CNF sentences with $n = 50$, for a narrow range of $m/n$ around the critical point.

## 7.7 AGENTS BASED ON PROPOSITIONAL LOGIC

In this section, we bring together what we have learned so far in order to construct agents that operate using propositional logic. We will look at two kinds of agents: those which use inference algorithms and a knowledge base, like the generic knowledge-based agent in Figure 7.1, and those which evaluate logical expressions directly in the form of circuits. We will demonstrate both kinds of agents in the wumpus world, and will find that both suffer from serious drawbacks.

### Finding pits and wumpuses using logical inference

Let us begin with an agent that reasons logically about the location of pits, wumpuses, and safe squares. It begins with a knowledge base that states the "physics" of the wumpus world. It knows that [1,1] does not contain a pit or a wumpus; that is, $\neg P_{1,1}$ and $\neg W_{1,1}$. For every square $[x, y]$, it knows a sentence stating how a breeze arises:

$$B_{x,y} \Leftrightarrow (P_{x,y+1} \lor P_{x,y-1} \lor P_{x+1,y} \lor P_{x-1,y}) . \tag{7.1}$$

For every square $[x, y]$, it knows a sentence stating how a stench arises:

$$S_{x,y} \Leftrightarrow (W_{x,y+1} \lor W_{x,y-1} \lor W_{x+1,y} \lor W_{x-1,y}) . \tag{7.2}$$

Finally, it knows that there is exactly one wumpus. This is expressed in two parts. First, we have to say that there is *at least one* wumpus:

$$W_{1,1} \lor W_{1,2} \lor \cdots \lor W_{4,3} \lor W_{4,4} .$$

Then, we have to say that there is *at most one* wumpus. One way to do this is to say that for any two squares, one of them must be wumpus-free. With $n$ squares, we get $n(n-1)/2$

```
function PL-WUMPUS-AGENT(percept) returns an action
   inputs: percept, a list, [stench,breeze,glitter]
   static: KB, a knowledge base, initially containing the "physics" of the wumpus world
           x, y, orientation, the agent's position (initially 1,1) and orientation (initially right)
           visited, an array indicating which squares have been visited, initially false
           action, the agent's most recent action, initially null
           plan, an action sequence, initially empty

   update x,y,orientation, visited based on action
   if stench then TELL(KB, S_x,y) else TELL(KB, ¬ S_x,y)
   if breeze then TELL(KB, B_x,y) else TELL(KB, ¬ B_x,y)
   if glitter then action ← grab
   else if plan is nonempty then action ← POP(plan)
   else if for some fringe square [i,j], ASK(KB, (¬ P_i,j ∧ ¬ W_i,j)) is true or
           for some fringe square [i,j], ASK(KB, (P_i,j ∨ W_i,j)) is false then do
      plan ← A*-GRAPH-SEARCH(ROUTE-PROBLEM([x,y], orientation, [i,j],visited))
      action ← POP(plan)
   else action ← a randomly chosen move
   return action
```

**Figure 7.19** A wumpus-world agent that uses propositional logic to identify pits, wumpuses, and safe squares. The subroutine ROUTE-PROBLEM constructs a search problem whose solution is a sequence of actions leading from $[x,y]$ to $[i,j]$ and passing through only previously visited squares.

sentences such as $\neg W_{1,1} \vee \neg W_{1,2}$. For a $4 \times 4$ world, then, we begin with a total of 155 sentences containing 64 distinct symbols.

The agent program, shown in Figure 7.19, TELLs its knowledge base about each new breeze and stench percept. (It also updates some ordinary program variables to keep track of where it is and where it has been—more on this later.) Then, the program chooses where to look next among the fringe squares—that is, the squares adjacent to those already visited. A fringe square $[i,j]$ is *provably safe* if the sentence $(\neg P_{i,j} \wedge \neg W_{i,j})$ is entailed by the knowledge base. The next best thing is a *possibly safe* square, for which the agent cannot prove that there *is* a pit or a wumpus—that is, for which $(P_{i,j} \vee W_{i,j})$ is *not* entailed.

The entailment computation in ASK can be implemented using any of the methods described earlier in the chapter. TT-ENTAILS? (Figure 7.10) is obviously impractical, since it would have to enumerate $2^{64}$ rows. DPLL (Figure 7.16) performs the required inferences in a few milliseconds, thanks mainly to the unit propagation heuristic. WALKSAT can also be used, with the usual caveats about incompleteness. In wumpus worlds, failures to find a model, given 10,000 flips, invariably correspond to unsatisfiability, so no errors are likely due to incompleteness.

PL-WUMPUS-AGENT works quite well in a small wumpus world. There is, however, something deeply unsatisfying about the agent's knowledge base. *KB* contains "physics" sentences of the form given in Equations (7.1) and (7.2) *for every single square*. The larger the environment, the larger the initial knowledge base needs to be. We would much prefer to have just two sentences that say how breezes and stenches arise in *all* squares. These are beyond the powers of propositional logic to express. In the next chapter, we will see a more expressive logical language in which such sentences are easy to express.

### Keeping track of location and orientation

The agent program in Figure 7.19 "cheats" because it keeps track of location *outside* the knowledge base, instead of using logical reasoning.[13] To do it "properly," we will need propositions for location. One's first inclination might be to use a symbol such as $L_{1,1}$ to mean that the agent is in [1,1]. Then the initial knowledge base might include sentences like

$$L_{1,1} \wedge \mathit{FacingRight} \wedge \mathit{Forward} \;\Rightarrow\; L_{2,1} \,.$$

Instantly, we see that this won't work. If the agent starts in [1,1] facing right and moves forward, the knowledge base will entail both $L_{1,1}$ (the original location) and $L_{2,1}$ (the new location). Yet these propositions cannot both be true! The problem is that the location propositions should refer to two different times. We need $L^1_{1,1}$ to mean that the agent is in [1,1] at time 1, $L^2_{2,1}$ to mean that the agent is in [2,1] at time 2, and so on. The orientation and action propositions also need to depend on time. Therefore, the correct sentence is

$$\begin{array}{l} L^1_{1,1} \wedge \mathit{FacingRight}^1 \wedge \mathit{Forward}^1 \;\Rightarrow\; L^2_{2,1} \\ \mathit{FacingRight}^1 \wedge \mathit{TurnLeft}^1 \;\Rightarrow\; \mathit{FacingUp}^2 \,, \end{array}$$

and so on. It turns out to be quite tricky to build a complete and correct knowledge base for keeping track of everything in the wumpus world; we will defer the full discussion until Chapter 10. The point we want to make here is that the initial knowledge base will contain sentences like the preceding two examples for every time $t$, as well as for every location. That is, for every time $t$ and location $[x, y]$, the knowledge base contains a sentence of the form

$$L^t_{x,y} \wedge \mathit{FacingRight}^t \wedge \mathit{Forward}^t \;\Rightarrow\; L^{t+1}_{x+1,y} \,. \qquad (7.3)$$

Even if we put an upper limit on the number of time steps allowed—100, perhaps—we end up with tens of thousands of sentences. The same problem arises if we add the sentences "as needed" for each new time step. This proliferation of clauses makes the knowledge base unreadable for a human, but fast propositional solvers can still handle the $4 \times 4$ Wumpus world with ease (they reach their limit at around $100 \times 100$). The circuit-based agents in the next subsection offer a partial solution to this clause proliferation problem, but the full solution will have to wait until we have developed first-order logic in Chapter 8.

### Circuit-based agents

CIRCUIT-BASED AGENT
SEQUENTIAL CIRCUIT
GATES
REGISTERS

A **circuit-based agent** is a particular kind of reflex agent with state, as defined in Chapter 2. The percepts are inputs to a **sequential circuit**—a network of **gates**, each of which implements a logical connective, and **registers**, each of which stores the truth value of a single proposition. The outputs of the circuit are registers corresponding to actions—for example,

[13] The observant reader will have noticed that this allowed us to finesse the connection between the raw percepts such as *Breeze* and the location-specific propositions such as $B_{1,1}$.

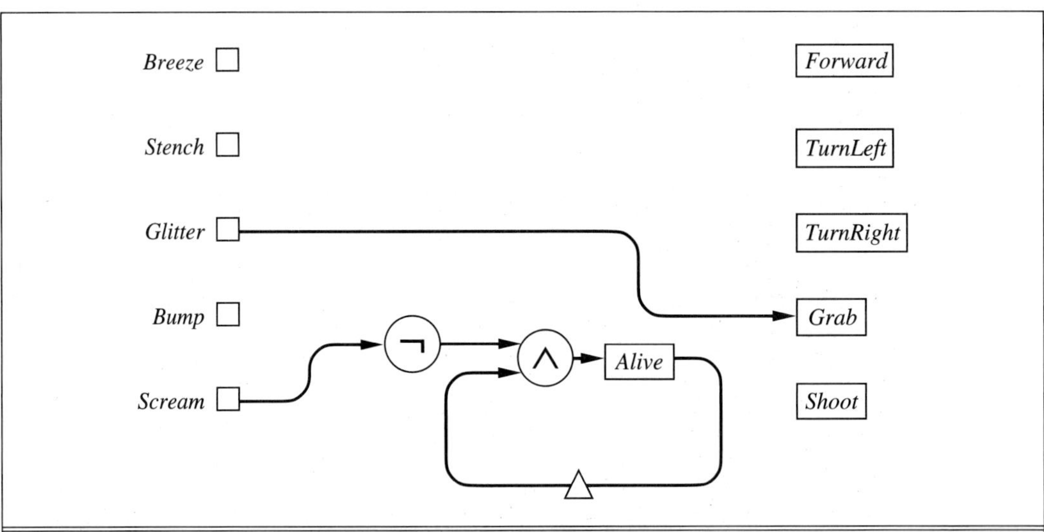


**Figure 7.20** Part of a circuit-based agent for the wumpus world, showing inputs, outputs, the circuit for grabbing the gold, and the circuit for determining whether the wumpus is alive. Registers are shown as rectangles and one-step delays are shown as small triangles.

the $Grab$ output is set to $true$ if the agent wants to grab something. If the $Glitter$ input is connected directly to the $Grab$ output, the agent will grab the goal whenever it sees it. (See Figure 7.20.)

DATAFLOW

Circuits are evaluated in a **dataflow** fashion: at each time step, the inputs are set and the signals propagate through the circuit. Whenever a gate has all its inputs, it produces an output. This process is closely related to the process of forward chaining in an AND–OR graph such as Figure 7.15(b).

We said in the preceding section that circuit-based agents handle time more satisfactorily than propositional inference-based agents. This is because the value stored in each register gives the truth value of the corresponding proposition symbol *at the current time* $t$, rather than having a different copy for each different time step. For example, we might have an $Alive$ register that should contain $true$ when the wumpus is alive and $false$ when it is dead. This register corresponds to the proposition symbol $Alive^t$, so on each time step it refers to a different proposition. The internal state of the agent—i.e., its memory—is maintained by connecting the output of a register back into the circuit through a **delay line**. This delivers the value of the register at the *previous* time step. Figure 7.20 shows an example. The value for $Alive$ is given by the conjunction of the negation of $Scream$ and the delayed value of $Alive$ itself. In terms of propositions, the circuit for $Alive$ implements the biconditional

DELAY LINE

$$Alive^t \Leftrightarrow \neg Scream^t \wedge Alive^{t-1} . \tag{7.4}$$

which says that the wumpus is alive at time $t$ *if and only if* there was no scream perceived at time $t$ (from a scream at $t-1$) *and* it was alive at $t-1$. We assume that the circuit is initialized with $Alive$ set to $true$. Therefore, $Alive$ will remain true until there is a scream, whereupon it will become false and stay false. This is exactly what we want.

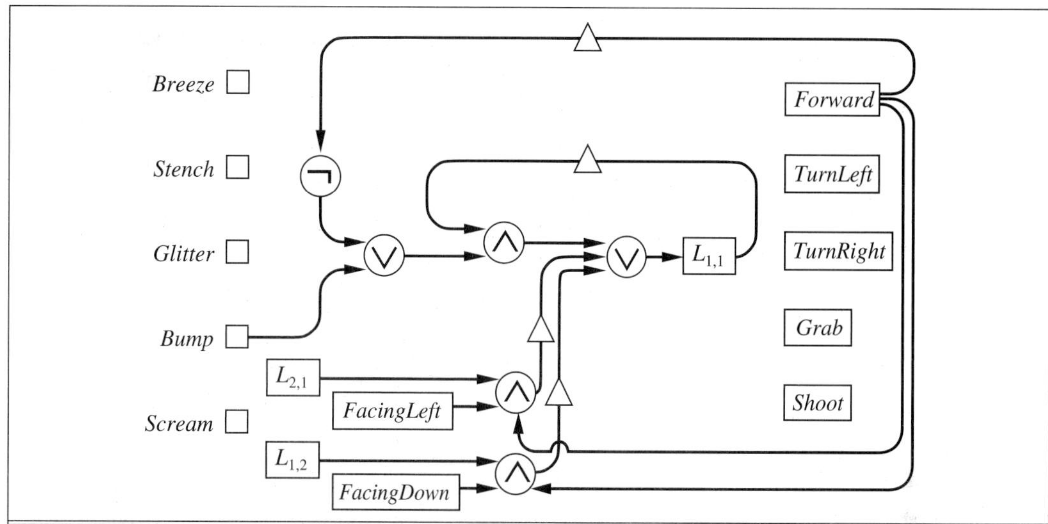


**Figure 7.21** The circuit for determining whether the agent is at [1,1]. Every location and orientation register has a similar circuit attached.

The agent's location can be handled in much the same way as the wumpus's health. We need an $L_{x,y}$ register for each $x$ and $y$; its value should be $true$ if the agent is at $[x, y]$. The circuit that sets the value of $L_{x,y}$ is, however, much more complicated than the circuit for $Alive$. For example, the agent is at [1,1] at time $t$ if (a) it was there at $t-1$ and either didn't move forward or tried but bumped into a wall; or (b) it was at [1,2] facing down and moved forward; or (c) it was at [2,1] facing left and moved forward:

$$\begin{aligned} L_{1,1}^{t} \quad \Leftrightarrow \quad & (L_{1,1}^{t-1} \wedge (\neg Forward^{t-1} \vee Bump^{t})) \\ \vee \; & (L_{1,2}^{t-1} \wedge (FacingDown^{t-1} \wedge Forward^{t-1})) \\ \vee \; & (L_{2,1}^{t-1} \wedge (FacingLeft^{t-1} \wedge Forward^{t-1}))\,. \end{aligned} \tag{7.5}$$

The circuit for $L_{1,1}$ is shown in Figure 7.21. Every location register has a similar circuit attached to it. Exercise 7.13(b) asks you to design a circuit for the orientation propositions.

The circuits in Figures 7.20 and 7.21 maintain the correct truth values for $Alive$ and $L_{x,y}$ for all time. These propositions are unusual, however, in that *their correct truth values can always be ascertained.* Consider instead the proposition $B_{4,4}$: square [4,4] is breezy. Although this proposition's truth value remains fixed, the agent cannot learn that truth value until it has visited [4,4] (or deduced that there is an adjacent pit). Propositional and first-order logic are designed to represent true, false, and unknown propositions automatically, but circuits are not: the register for $B_{4,4}$ must contain *some* value, either $true$ or $false$, even before the truth has been discovered. The value in the register might well be the wrong one, and this could lead the agent astray. In other words, we need to represent three possible states ($B_{4,4}$ is known true, known false, or unknown) and we only have one bit to do it with.

The solution to this problem is to use two bits instead of one. $B_{4,4}$ is represented by two registers that we will call $K(B_{4,4})$ and $K(\neg B_{4,4})$, where $K$ stands for "known.". (Remember that these are still just symbols with complicated names, even though they look like structured expressions!) When both $K(B_{4,4})$ and $K(\neg B_{4,4})$ are false, it means the truth value of $B_{4,4}$ is unknown. (If both are true, there's a bug in the knowledge base!) Now whenever we would use $B_{4,4}$ in some part of the circuit, we use $K(B_{4,4})$ instead ; and whenever we would use $\neg B_{4,4}$, we use $K(\neg B_{4,4})$. In general, we represent each potentially indeterminate proposition with two **knowledge propositions** that state whether the underlying proposition is known to be true and known to be false.

KNOWLEDGE PROPOSITION

We will see an example of how to use knowledge propositions shortly. First, we need to work out how to determine the truth values of the knowledge propositions themselves. Notice that, whereas $B_{4,4}$ has a fixed truth value, $K(B_{4,4})$ and $K(\neg B_{4,4})$ *do* change as the agent finds out more about the world. For example, $K(B_{4,4})$ starts out false and then becomes true as soon as $B_{4,4}$ can be determined to be true—that is, when the agent is in [4,4] and detects a breeze. It stays true thereafter. So we have

$$K(B_{4,4})^t \Leftrightarrow K(B_{4,4})^{t-1} \vee (L^t_{4,4} \wedge Breeze^t) . \tag{7.6}$$

A similar equation can be written for $K(\neg B_{4,4})^t$.

Now that the agent knows about breezy squares, it can deal with pits. The absence of a pit in a square can be ascertained if and only if one of the neighboring squares is known not to be breezy. For example, we have

$$K(\neg P_{4,4})^t \Leftrightarrow K(\neg B_{3,4})^t \vee K(\neg B_{4,3})^t . \tag{7.7}$$

Determining that there *is* a pit in a square is more difficult—there must be a breeze in an adjacent square that cannot be accounted for by another pit:

$$\begin{aligned} K(P_{4,4})^t \quad \Leftrightarrow \quad & (K(B_{3,4})^t \wedge K(\neg P_{2,4})^t \wedge K(\neg P_{3,3})^t) \\ \vee \quad & (K(B_{4,3})^t \wedge K(\neg P_{4,2})^t \wedge K(\neg P_{3,3})^t) . \end{aligned} \tag{7.8}$$

While the circuits for determining the presence or absence of pits are somewhat hairy, *they have only a constant number of gates for each square.* This property is essential if we are to build circuit-based agents that scale up in a reasonable way. It is really a property of the wumpus world itself; we say that an environment exhibits **locality** if the truth of each proposition of interest can be determined looking only at a constant number of other propositions. Locality is very sensitive to the precise "physics" of the environment. For example, the minesweeper domain (Exercise 7.11) is nonlocal because determining that a mine is in a given square can involve looking at squares arbitrarily far away. For nonlocal domains, circuit-based agents are not always practical.

ACYCLICITY

There is one issue around which we have tiptoed carefully: the question of **acyclicity**. A circuit is acyclic if every path that connects the output of a register back to its input has an intervening delay element. We require that all circuits be acyclic because cyclic circuits, as physical devices, do not work! They can go into unstable oscillations resulting in undefined values. As an example of a cyclic circuit, consider the following augmentation of Equation (7.6):

$$K(B_{4,4})^t \Leftrightarrow K(B_{4,4})^{t-1} \vee (L^t_{4,4} \wedge Breeze^t) \vee K(P_{3,4})^t \vee K(P_{4,3})^t . \tag{7.9}$$

The extra disjuncts, $K(P_{3,4})^t$ and $K(P_{4,3})^t$, allow the agent to determine breeziness from the known presence of adjacent pits, which seems entirely reasonable. Now, unfortunately, breeziness depends on adjacent pits, and pits depend on adjacent breeziness through equations such as Equation (7.8). Therefore, the complete circuit would contain cycles.

The difficulty is not that the augmented Equation (7.9) is *incorrect*. Rather, the problem is that the interlocking dependencies represented by these equations cannot be resolved by the simple mechanism of propagating truth values in the corresponding Boolean circuit. The acyclic version using Equation (7.6), which determines breeziness only from direct observation, is *incomplete* in the sense that at some points the circuit-based agent might know less than an inference-based agent using a complete inference procedure. For example, if there is a breeze in [1,1], the inference-based agent can conclude that there is also a breeze in [2,2], whereas the acyclic circuit-based agent using Equation (7.6) cannot. A complete circuit *can* be built—after all, sequential circuits can emulate any digital computer—but it would be significantly more complex.

## A comparison

The inference-based agent and the circuit-based agent represent the declarative and procedural extremes in agent design. They can be compared along several dimensions:

- *Conciseness*: The circuit-based agent, unlike the inference-based agent, need not have separate copies of its "knowledge" for every time step. Instead, it refers only to the current and previous time steps. Both agents need copies of the "physics" (expressed as sentences or circuits) for every square and therefore do not scale well to larger environments. In environments with many objects related in complex ways, the number of propositions will swamp any propositional agent. Such environments require the expressive power of first-order logic. (See Chapter 8.) Propositional agents of both kinds are also poorly suited for expressing or solving the problem of finding a path to a nearby safe square. (For this reason, PL-WUMPUS-AGENT falls back on a search algorithm.)
- *Computational efficiency*: In the *worst* case, inference can take time exponential in the number of symbols, whereas evaluating a circuit takes time linear in the size of the circuit (or linear in the *depth* of the circuit if realized as a physical device). In *practice*, however, we saw that DPLL completed the required inferences very quickly.[14]
- *Completeness*: We suggested earlier that the circuit-based agent might be incomplete because of the acyclicity restriction. The reasons for incompleteness are actually more fundamental. First, remember that a circuit executes in time linear in the circuit size. This means that, for some environments, a circuit that is complete (i.e., one that computes the truth value of every determinable proposition) must be exponentially larger than the inference-based agent's KB. Otherwise, we would have a way to solve the propositional entailment problem in less than exponential time, which is very unlikely. A second reason is the nature of the internal state of the agent. The inference-based agent remembers every percept and knows, either implicitly or explicitly, every sentence that follows from the percepts and initial KB. For example, given $B_{1,1}$, it knows the disjunction $P_{1,2} \lor P_{2,1}$, from which $B_{2,2}$ follows. The circuit-based agent, on the

[14] In fact, all the inferences done by a circuit can be done in linear time by DPLL! This is because evaluating a circuit, like forward chaining, can be emulated by DPLL using the unit propagation rule.

other hand, forgets all previous percepts and remembers just the individual propositions stored in registers. Thus, $P_{1,2}$ and $P_{2,1}$ remain *individually* unknown after the first percept, so no conclusion will be drawn about $B_{2,2}$.

- *Ease of construction*: This is a very important issue about which it is hard to be precise. Certainly, this author found it much easier to state the "physics" declaratively, whereas devising small, acyclic, not-too-incomplete circuits for direct detection of pits seemed quite difficult.

In sum, it seems there are *tradeoffs* among computational efficiency, conciseness, completeness, and ease of construction. When the connection between percepts and actions is simple—as in the connection between *Glitter* and *Grab*—a circuit seems optimal. For more complex connections, the declarative approach may be better. In a domain such as chess, for example, the declarative rules are concise and easily encoded (at least in first-order logic), but a circuit for computing moves directly from board states would be unimaginably vast.

We see different points on these tradeoffs in the animal kingdom. The lower animals with very simple nervous systems are probably circuit-based, whereas higher animals, including humans, seem to perform inference on explicit representations. This enables them to compute much more complex agent functions. Humans also have circuits to implement reflexes, and perhaps also **compile** declarative representations into circuits when certain inferences become routine. In this way, a **hybrid agent** design (see Chapter 2) can have the best of both worlds.

COMPILATION

## 7.8 Summary

We have introduced knowledge-based agents and have shown how to define a logic with which such agents can reason about the world. The main points are as follows:

- Intelligent agents need knowledge about the world in order to reach good decisions.
- Knowledge is contained in agents in the form of **sentences** in a **knowledge representation language** that are stored in a **knowledge base**.
- A knowledge-based agent is composed of a knowledge base and an inference mechanism. It operates by storing sentences about the world in its knowledge base, using the inference mechanism to infer new sentences, and using these sentences to decide what action to take.
- A representation language is defined by its **syntax**, which specifies the structure of sentences, and its **semantics**, which defines the **truth** of each sentence in each **possible world** or **model**.
- The relationship of **entailment** between sentences is crucial to our understanding of reasoning. A sentence $\alpha$ entails another sentence $\beta$ if $\beta$ is true in all worlds where $\alpha$ is true. Equivalent definitions include the **validity** of the sentence $\alpha \Rightarrow \beta$ and the **unsatisfiability** of the sentence $\alpha \land \neg\beta$.

- Inference is the process of deriving new sentences from old ones. **Sound** inference algorithms derive *only* sentences that are entailed; **complete** algorithms derive *all* sentences that are entailed.
- **Propositional logic** is a very simple language consisting of **proposition symbols** and **logical connectives**. It can handle propositions that are known true, known false, or completely unknown.
- The set of possible models, given a fixed propositional vocabulary, is finite, so entailment can be checked by enumerating models. Efficient **model-checking** inference algorithms for propositional logic include backtracking and local-search methods and can often solve large problems very quickly.
- **Inference rules** are patterns of sound inference that can be used to find proofs. The **resolution** rule yields a complete inference algorithm for knowledge bases that are expressed in **conjunctive normal form**. **Forward chaining** and **backward chaining** are very natural reasoning algorithms for knowledge bases in **Horn form**.
- Two kinds of agents can be built on the basis of propositional logic: **inference-based agents** use inference algorithms to keep track of the world and deduce hidden properties, whereas **circuit-based agents** represent propositions as bits in registers and update them using signal propagation in logical circuits.
- Propositional logic is reasonably effective for certain tasks within an agent, but does not scale to environments of unbounded size because it lacks the expressive power to deal concisely with time, space, and universal patterns of relationships among objects.

## BIBLIOGRAPHICAL AND HISTORICAL NOTES

John McCarthy's paper "Programs with Common Sense" (McCarthy, 1958, 1968) promulgated the notion of agents that use logical reasoning to mediate between percepts and actions. It also raised the flag of declarativism, pointing out that telling an agent what it needs to know is a very elegant way to build software. Allen Newell's (1982) article "The Knowledge Level" makes the case that rational agents can be described and analyzed at an abstract level defined by the knowledge they possess rather than the programs they run. The declarative and procedural approaches to AI are compared in Boden (1977). The debate was revived by, among others, Brooks (1991) and Nilsson (1991).

Logic itself had its origins in ancient Greek philosophy and mathematics. Various logical principles—principles connecting the syntactic structure of sentences with their truth and falsity, with their meaning, or with the validity of arguments in which they figure—are scattered in the works of Plato. The first known systematic study of logic was carried out by Aristotle, whose work was assembled by his students after his death in 322 B.C. as a treatise called the *Organon*. Aristotle's **syllogisms** were what we would now call inference rules. Although the syllogisms included elements of both propositional and first-order logic, the system as a whole was very weak by modern standards. It did not allow for patterns of inference that apply to sentences of arbitrary complexity, as in modern propositional logic.

SYLLOGISMS

The closely related Megarian and Stoic schools (originating in the fifth century B.C. and continuing for several centuries thereafter) introduced the systematic study of implication and other basic constructs still used in modern propositional logic. The use of truth tables for defining logical connectives is due to Philo of Megara. The Stoics took five basic inference rules as valid without proof, including the rule we now call Modus Ponens. They derived a number of other rules from these five, using among other principles the deduction theorem (page 210) and were much clearer about the notion of proof than Aristotle was. The Stoics claimed that their logic was complete in the sense of capturing all valid inferences, but what remains is too fragmentary to tell. A good account of the history of Megarian and Stoic logic, as far as it is known, is given by Benson Mates (1953).

The idea of reducing logical inference to a purely mechanical process applied to a formal language is due to Wilhelm Leibniz (1646–1716). Leibniz's own mathematical logic, however, was severely defective, and he is better remembered simply for introducing these ideas as goals to be attained than for his attempts at realizing them.

George Boole (1847) introduced the first comprehensive and workable system of formal logic in his book *The Mathematical Analysis of Logic*. Boole's logic was closely modeled on the ordinary algebra of real numbers and used substitution of logically equivalent expressions as its primary inference method. Although Boole's system still fell short of full propositional logic, it was close enough that other mathematicians could quickly fill in the gaps. Schröder (1877) described conjunctive normal form, while Horn form was introduced much later by Alfred Horn (1951). The first comprehensive exposition of modern propositional logic (and first-order logic) is found in Gottlob Frege's (1879) *Begriffschrift* ("Concept Writing" or "Conceptual Notation").

The first mechanical device to carry out logical inferences was constructed by the third Earl of Stanhope (1753–1816). The Stanhope Demonstrator could handle syllogisms and certain inferences in the theory of probability. William Stanley Jevons, one of those who improved upon and extended Boole's work, constructed his "logical piano" in 1869 to perform inferences in Boolean logic. An entertaining and instructive history of these and other early mechanical devices for reasoning is given by Martin Gardner (1968). The first published computer program for logical inference was the Logic Theorist of Newell, Shaw, and Simon (1957). This program was intended to model human thought processes. Martin Davis (1957) had actually designed a program that came up with a proof in 1954, but the Logic Theorist's results were published slightly earlier. Both Davis's 1954 program and the Logic Theorist were based on somewhat ad hoc methods that did not strongly influence later automated deduction.

Truth tables as a method of testing the validity or unsatisfiability of sentences in the language of propositional logic were introduced independently by Ludwig Wittgenstein (1922) and Emil Post (1921). In the 1930s, a great deal of progress was made on inference methods for first-order logic. In particular, Gödel (1930) showed that a complete procedure for inference in first-order logic could be obtained via a reduction to propositional logic, using Herbrand's theorem (Herbrand, 1930). We will take up this history again in Chapter 9; the important point here is that the development of efficient propositional algorithms in the 1960s was motivated largely by the interest of mathematicians in an effective theorem prover for first-order logic. The Davis–Putnam algorithm (Davis and Putnam, 1960) was the first effective algorithm for propositional resolution but was in most cases much less efficient than the DPLL backtracking algorithm introduced two years later (1962). The full resolution rule and a proof of its completeness appeared in a seminal paper by J. A. Robinson (1965), which also showed how to do first-order reasoning without resort to propositional techniques.

Stephen Cook (1971) showed that deciding satisfiability of a sentence in propositional logic is NP-complete. Since deciding entailment is equivalent to deciding unsatisfiability, it is co-NP-complete. Many subsets of propositional logic are known for which the satisfiability problem is polynomially solvable; Horn clauses are one such subset. The linear-time forward-chaining algorithm for Horn clauses is due to Dowling and Gallier (1984), who describe their algorithm as a dataflow process similar to the propagation of signals in a circuit. Satisfiability has become one of the canonical examples for NP reductions; for example Kaye (2000) showed that the Minesweeper game (see Exercise 7.11) is NP-complete.

Local search algorithms for satisfiability were tried by various authors throughout the 1980s; all of the algorithms were based on the idea of minimizing the number of unsatisfied clauses (Hansen and Jaumard, 1990). A particularly effective algorithm was developed by Gu (1989) and independently by Selman *et al.* (1992), who called it GSAT and showed that it was capable of solving a wide range of very hard problems very quickly. The WALKSAT algorithm described in the chapter is due to Selman *et al.* (1996).

The "phase transition" in satisfiability of random $k$-SAT problems was first observed by Simon and Dubois (1989). Empirical results due to Crawford and Auton (1993) suggest that it lies at a clause/variable ratio of around 4.24 for large random 3-SAT problems; this paper also describes a very efficient implementation of DPLL. Bayardo and Schrag (1997) describe another efficient DPLL implementation using techniques from constraint satisfaction, and Moskewicz *et al.* (2001) describe CHAFF, which solves million-variable hardware verification problems and was the winner of the SAT 2002 Competition. Li and Anbulagan (1997) discuss heuristics based on unit propagation that allow for fast solvers. Cheeseman *et al.* (1991) provide data on a number of related problems and conjecture that all NP hard problems have a phase transition. Kirkpatrick and Selman (1994) describe ways in which techniques from statistical physics might provide insight into the precise "shape" of the phase transition. Theoretical analysis of its *location* is still rather weak: all that can be proved is that it lies in the range [3.003,4.598] for random 3-SAT. Cook and Mitchell (1997) give an excellent survey of results on this and several other satisfiability-related topics.

Early theoretical investigations showed that DPLL has polynomial average-case complexity for certain natural distributions of problems. This potentially exciting fact became less exciting when Franco and Paull (1983) showed that the same problems could be solved in constant time simply by guessing random assignments. The random-generation method described in the chapter produces much harder problems. Motivated by the empirical success of local search on these problems, Koutsoupias and Papadimitriou (1992) showed that a simple hill-climbing algorithm can solve *almost all* satisfiability problem instances very quickly, suggesting that hard problems are rare. Moreover, Schöning (1999) exhibited a randomized variant of GSAT whose *worst-case* expected runtime on 3-SAT problems is $1.333^n$—still exponential, but substantially faster than previous worst-case bounds. Satisfiability algorithms are still a very active area of research; the collection of articles in Du *et al.* (1999) provides a good starting point.

Circuit-based agents can be traced back to the seminal paper of McCulloch and Pitts (1943), which initiated the field of neural networks. Contrary to popular supposition, the paper was concerned with the implementation of a Boolean circuit-based agent design in the brain. Circuit-based agents have received little attention in AI, however. The most notable exception is the work of Stan Rosenschein (Rosenschein, 1985; Kaelbling and Rosenschein, 1990), who developed ways to compile circuit-based agents from declarative descriptions of the task environment. The circuits for updating propositions stored in registers are closely related to the **successor-state axiom** developed for first-order logic by Reiter (1991). The work of Rod Brooks (1986, 1989) demonstrates the effectiveness of circuit-based designs for controlling robots—a topic we take up in Chapter 25. Brooks (1991) argues that circuit-based designs are *all* that is needed for AI—that representation and reasoning are cumbersome, expensive, and unnecessary. In our view, neither approach is sufficient by itself.

The wumpus world was invented by Gregory Yob (1975). Ironically, Yob developed it because he was bored with games played on a grid: the topology of his original wumpus world was a dodecahedron; we put it back in the boring old grid. Michael Genesereth was the first to suggest that the wumpus world be used as an agent testbed.

## EXERCISES

**7.1** Describe the wumpus world according to the properties of task environments listed in Chapter 2.

**7.2** Suppose the agent has progressed to the point shown in Figure 7.4(a), having perceived nothing in [1,1], a breeze in [2,1], and a stench in [1,2]. and is now concerned with the contents of [1,3], [2,2], and [3,1]. Each of these can contain a pit and at most one can contain a wumpus. Following the example of Figure 7.5, construct the set of possible worlds. (You should find 32 of them.) Mark the worlds in which the KB is true and those in which each of the following sentences is true:

$\alpha_2$ = "There is no pit in [2,2]."
$\alpha_3$ = "There is a wumpus in [1,3]."

Hence show that $KB \models \alpha_2$ and $KB \models \alpha_3$.

**7.3** Consider the problem of deciding whether a propositional logic sentence is true in a given model.

**a.** Write a recursive algorithm PL-TRUE?$(s, m)$ that returns *true* if and only if the sentence $s$ is true in the model $m$ (where $m$ assigns a truth value for every symbol in $s$). The algorithm should run in time linear in the size of the sentence. (Alternatively, use a version of this function from the online code repository.)

**b.** Give three examples of sentences that can be determined to be true or false in a *partial* model that does not specify a truth value for some of the symbols.

**c.** Show that the truth value (if any) of a sentence in a partial model cannot be determined efficiently in general.

**d.** Modify your PL-TRUE? algorithm so that it can sometimes judge truth from partial models, while retaining its recursive structure and linear runtime. Give three examples of sentences whose truth in a partial model is *not* detected by your algorithm.

**e.** Investigate whether the modified algorithm makes TT-ENTAILS? more efficient.

**7.4** Prove each of the following assertions:

**a.** $\alpha$ is valid if and only if $True \models \alpha$.

**b.** For any $\alpha$, $False \models \alpha$.

**c.** $\alpha \models \beta$ if and only if the sentence $(\alpha \Rightarrow \beta)$ is valid.

**d.** $\alpha \equiv \beta$ if and only if the sentence $(\alpha \Leftrightarrow \beta)$ is valid.

**e.** $\alpha \models \beta$ if and only if the sentence $(\alpha \land \neg\beta)$ is unsatisfiable.

**7.5** Consider a vocabulary with only four propositions, $A$, $B$, $C$, and $D$. How many models are there for the following sentences?

**a.** $(A \land B) \lor (B \land C)$

**b.** $A \lor B$

**c.** $A \Leftrightarrow B \Leftrightarrow C$

**7.6** We have defined four different binary logical connectives.

**a.** Are there any others that might be useful?

**b.** How many binary connectives can there be?

**c.** Why are some of them not very useful?

**7.7** Using a method of your choice, verify each of the equivalences in Figure 7.11.

**7.8** Decide whether each of the following sentences is valid, unsatisfiable, or neither. Verify your decisions using truth tables or the equivalence rules of Figure 7.11.

**a.** $Smoke \Rightarrow Smoke$

**b.** $Smoke \Rightarrow Fire$

**c.** $(Smoke \Rightarrow Fire) \Rightarrow (\neg Smoke \Rightarrow \neg Fire)$

**d.** $Smoke \lor Fire \lor \neg Fire$

**e.** $((Smoke \land Heat) \Rightarrow Fire) \Leftrightarrow ((Smoke \Rightarrow Fire) \lor (Heat \Rightarrow Fire))$

**f.** $(Smoke \Rightarrow Fire) \Rightarrow ((Smoke \land Heat) \Rightarrow Fire)$

**g.** $Big \lor Dumb \lor (Big \Rightarrow Dumb)$

**h.** $(Big \land Dumb) \lor \neg Dumb$

**7.9** (Adapted from Barwise and Etchemendy (1993).) Given the following, can you prove that the unicorn is mythical? How about magical? Horned?

> If the unicorn is mythical, then it is immortal, but if it is not mythical, then it is a mortal mammal. If the unicorn is either immortal or a mammal, then it is horned. The unicorn is magical if it is horned.

**7.10** Any propositional logic sentence is logically equivalent to the assertion that each possible world in which it would be false is not the case. From this observation, prove that any sentence can be written in CNF.

**7.11** Minesweeper, the well-known computer game, is closely related to the wumpus world. A minesweeper world is a rectangular grid of $N$ squares with $M$ invisible mines scattered among them. Any square may be probed by the agent; instant death follows if a mine is probed. Minesweeper indicates the presence of mines by revealing, in each probed square, the *number* of mines that are directly or diagonally adjacent. The goal is to have probed every unmined square.

**a.** Let $X_{i,j}$ be true iff square $[i, j]$ contains a mine. Write down the assertion that there are exactly two mines adjacent to [1,1] as a sentence involving some logical combination of $X_{i,j}$ propositions.

**b.** Generalize your assertion from (a) by explaining how to construct a CNF sentence asserting that $k$ of $n$ neighbors contain mines.

**c.** Explain precisely how an agent can use DPLL to prove that a given square does (or does not) contain a mine, ignoring the global constraint that there are exactly $M$ mines in all.

**d.** Suppose that the global constraint is constructed via your method from part (b). How does the number of clauses depend on $M$ and $N$? Suggest a way to modify DPLL so that the global constraint does not need to be represented explicitly.

**e.** Are any conclusions derived by the method in part (c) invalidated when the global constraint is taken into account?

**f.** Give examples of configurations of probe values that induce *long-range dependencies* such that the contents of a given unprobed square would give information about the contents of a far-distant square. [*Hint*: consider an $N \times 1$ board.]

**7.12** This exercise looks into the relationship between clauses and implication sentences.

**a.** Show that the clause $(\neg P_1 \lor \cdots \lor \neg P_m \lor Q)$ is logically equivalent to the implication sentence $(P_1 \land \cdots \land P_m) \Rightarrow Q$.

**b.** Show that every clause (regardless of the number of positive literals) can be written in the form $(P_1 \land \cdots \land P_m) \Rightarrow (Q_1 \lor \cdots \lor Q_n)$, where the $P$s and $Q$s are proposition symbols. A knowledge base consisting of such sentences is in **implicative normal form** or **Kowalski form**.

IMPLICATIVE NORMAL FORM

**c.** Write down the full resolution rule for sentences in implicative normal form.

**7.13** In this exercise, you will design more of the circuit-based wumpus agent.

**a**. Write an equation, similar to Equation (7.4), for the $Arrow$ proposition, which should be true when the agent still has an arrow. Draw the corresponding circuit.

**b**. Repeat part (a) for $FacingRight$, using Equation (7.5) as a model.

**c**. Create versions of Equations 7.7 and 7.8 for finding the wumpus, and draw the circuit.

**7.14** Discuss what is meant by *optimal* behavior in the wumpus world. Show that our definition of the PL-WUMPUS-AGENT is not optimal, and suggest ways to improve it.

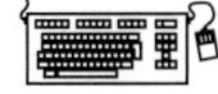

**7.15** Extend PL-WUMPUS-AGENT so that it keeps track of all relevant facts *within* the knowledge base.

**7.16** How long does it take to prove $KB \models \alpha$ using DPLL when $\alpha$ is a literal *already contained in* $KB$? Explain.

**7.17** Trace the behavior of DPLL on the knowledge base in Figure 7.15 when trying to prove $Q$, and compare this behavior with that of the forward chaining algorithm.

# 8 FIRST-ORDER LOGIC

*In which we notice that the world is blessed with many objects, some of which are related to other objects, and in which we endeavor to reason about them.*

In Chapter 7, we showed how a knowledge-based agent could represent the world in which it operates and deduce what actions to take. We used propositional logic as our representation language because it sufficed to illustrate the basic concepts of logic and knowledge-based agents. Unfortunately, propositional logic is too puny a language to represent knowledge of complex environments in a concise way. In this chapter, we examine **first-order logic**,[1] which is sufficiently expressive to represent a good deal of our commonsense knowledge. It also either subsumes or forms the foundation of many other representation languages and has been studied intensively for many decades. We begin in Section 8.1 with a discussion of representation languages in general; Section 8.2 covers the syntax and semantics of first-order logic; Sections 8.3 and 8.4 illustrate the use of first-order logic for simple representations.

FIRST-ORDER LOGIC

## 8.1 REPRESENTATION REVISITED

In this section, we will discuss the nature of representation languages. Our discussion will motivate the development of first-order logic, a much more expressive language than the propositional logic introduced in Chapter 7. We will look at propositional logic and at other kinds of languages to understand what works and what fails. Our discussion will be cursory, compressing centuries of thought, trial, and error into a few paragraphs.

Programming languages (such as C++ or Java or Lisp) are by far the largest class of formal languages in common use. Programs themselves represent, in a direct sense, only computational processes. Data structures within programs can represent facts; for example, a program could use a $4 \times 4$ array to represent the contents of the wumpus world. Thus, the programming language statement $World[2,2] \leftarrow Pit$ is a fairly natural way to assert that there is a pit in square [2,2]. (Such representations might be considered *ad hoc*; database systems were developed precisely to provide a more general, domain-independent way to

[1] Also called **first-order predicate calculus**, sometimes abbreviated as **FOL** or **FOPC**.

store and retrieve facts.) What programming languages lack is any general mechanism for deriving facts from other facts; each update to a data structure is done by a domain-specific procedure whose details are derived by the programmer from his or her own knowledge of the domain. This **procedural** approach can be contrasted with the **declarative** nature of propositional logic, in which knowledge and inference are separate, and inference is entirely domain-independent.

A second drawback of data structures in programs (and of databases, for that matter) is the lack of any easy way to say, for example, "There is a pit in [2,2] or [3,1]" or "If the wumpus is in [1,1] then he is not in [2,2]." Programs can store a single value for each variable, and some systems allow the value to be "unknown," but they lack the expressiveness required to handle partial information.

Propositional logic is a declarative language because its semantics is based on a truth relation between sentences and possible worlds. It also has sufficient expressive power to deal with partial information, using disjunction and negation. Propositional logic has a third property that is desirable in representation languages, namely **compositionality**. In a compositional language, the meaning of a sentence is a function of the meaning of its parts. For example, "$S_{1,4} \wedge S_{1,2}$" is related to the meanings of "$S_{1,4}$" and "$S_{1,2}$." It would be very strange if "$S_{1,4}$" meant that there is a stench in square [1,4] and "$S_{1,2}$" meant that there is a stench in square [1,2], but "$S_{1,4} \wedge S_{1,2}$" meant that France and Poland drew 1–1 in last week's ice hockey qualifying match. Clearly, noncompositionality makes life much more difficult for the reasoning system.

COMPOSITIONALITY

As we saw in Chapter 7, propositional logic lacks the expressive power to describe an environment with many objects *concisely*. For example, we were forced to write a separate rule about breezes and pits for each square, such as

$$B_{1,1} \Leftrightarrow (P_{1,2} \vee P_{2,1}) .$$

In English, on the other hand, it seems easy enough to say, once and for all, "Squares adjacent to pits are breezy." The syntax and semantics of English somehow make it possible to describe the environment concisely.

A moment's thought suggests that natural languages (such as English or Spanish) are very expressive indeed. We managed to write almost this whole book in natural language, with only occasional lapses into other languages (including logic, mathematics, and the language of diagrams). There is a long tradition in linguistics and the philosophy of language that views natural language as essentially a declarative knowledge representation language and attempts to pin down its formal semantics. Such a research program, if successful, would be of great value to artificial intelligence because it would allow a natural language (or some derivative) to be used within representation and reasoning systems.

The modern view of natural language is that it serves a somewhat different purpose, namely as a medium for **communication** rather than pure representation. When a speaker points and says, "Look!" the listener comes to know that, say, Superman has finally appeared over the rooftops. Yet we would not want to say that the sentence "Look!" encoded that fact. Rather, the meaning of the sentence depends both on the sentence itself and on the **context** in which the sentence was spoken. Clearly, one could not store a sentence such as "Look!" in a knowledge base and expect to recover its meaning without also storing a representation of the context—which raises the question of how the context itself can be represented. Natural languages are also noncompositional—the meaning of a sentence such as "Then she saw it" can depend on a context constructed by many preceding and succeeding sentences. Finally, natural languages suffer from **ambiguity**, which would cause difficulties for thinking. As Pinker (1995) puts it: "When people think about *spring*, surely they are not confused as to whether they are thinking about a season or something that goes *boing*—and if one word can correspond to two thoughts, thoughts can't be words."

Our approach will be to adopt the foundation of propositional logic—a declarative, compositional semantics that is context-independent and unambiguous—and build a more expressive logic on that foundation, borrowing representational ideas from natural language while avoiding its drawbacks. When we look at the syntax of natural language, the most obvious elements are nouns and noun phrases that refer to **objects** (squares, pits, wumpuses) and verbs and verb phrases that refer to **relations** among objects (is breezy, is adjacent to, shoots). Some of these relations are **functions**—relations in which there is only one "value" for a given "input." It is easy to start listing examples of objects, relations, and functions:

OBJECTS

RELATIONS

FUNCTIONS

- Objects: people, houses, numbers, theories, Ronald McDonald, colors, baseball games, wars, centuries ...
- Relations: these can be unary relations or **properties** such as red, round, bogus, prime, multistoried ..., or more general $n$-ary relations such as brother of, bigger than, inside, part of, has color, occurred after, owns, comes between, ...
- Functions: father of, best friend, third inning of, one more than, beginning of ...

PROPERTIES

Indeed, almost any assertion can be thought of as referring to objects and properties or relations. Some examples follow:

- "One plus two equals three"
  Objects: one, two, three, one plus two; Relation: equals; Function: plus. ("One plus two" is a name for the object that is obtained by applying the function "plus" to the objects "one" and "two." Three is another name for this object.)
- "Squares neighboring the wumpus are smelly."
  Objects: wumpus, squares; Property: smelly; Relation: neighboring.
- "Evil King John ruled England in 1200."
  Objects: John, England, 1200; Relation: ruled; Properties: evil, king.

The language of **first-order logic**, whose syntax and semantics we will define in the next section, is built around objects and relations. It has been so important to mathematics, philosophy, and artificial intelligence precisely because those fields—and indeed, much of everyday human existence—can be usefully thought of as dealing with objects and the relations among them. First-order logic can also express facts about *some* or *all* of the objects in the universe. This enables one to represent general laws or rules, such as the statement "Squares neighboring the wumpus are smelly."

The primary difference between propositional and first-order logic lies in the **ontological commitment** made by each language—that is, what it assumes about the nature of *reality*.

ONTOLOGICAL COMMITMENT

## THE LANGUAGE OF THOUGHT

Philosophers and psychologists have long pondered how it is that humans and other animals represent knowledge. It is clear that the evolution of natural language has played an important role in developing this ability in humans. On the other hand, much psychological evidence suggests that humans do not employ language directly in their internal representations. For example, which of the following two phrases formed the opening of Section 8.1?

> "In this section, we will discuss the nature of representation languages . . ."
>
> "This section covers the topic of knowledge representation languages . . ."

Wanner (1974) found that subjects made the right choice in such tests at chance level—about 50% of the time—but remembered the content of what they read with better than 90% accuracy. This suggests that people process the words to form some kind of nonverbal representation, which we call **memory**.

The exact mechanism by which language enables and shapes the representation of ideas in humans remains a fascinating question. The famous **Sapir–Whorf hypothesis** claims that the language we speak profoundly influences the way in which we think and make decisions, in particular by setting up the category structure by which we divide up the world into different sorts of objects. Whorf (1956) claimed that Eskimos have many words for snow and thus experience snow in a different way from speakers of other languages. Some linguists dispute the factual basis for this claim—Pullum (1991) argues that Inuit, Yupik, and other related languages seem to have about the same number of words for snow-related concepts as English—while others support it (Fortescue, 1984). It seems unarguably true that populations having greater familiarity with some aspects of the world develop much more detailed vocabularies—for example, field entomologists divide what most of us call *beetles* into hundreds of thousands of species and are personally familiar with many of these. (The evolutionary biologist J. B. S. Haldane once complained of "An inordinate fondness for beetles" on the part of the Creator.) Moreover, expert skiers have many terms for snow—powder, chowder, mashed potatoes, crud, corn, cement, crust, sugar, asphalt, corduroy, fluff, glop, and so on—that represent distinctions unfamiliar to the lay person. What is unclear is the direction of causality—do skiers become aware of the distinctions only by learning the words, or do the distinctions emerge from individual experience and become matched with the labels current in the community? This question is especially important in the study of child development. As yet, we have little understanding of the extent to which learning language and learning to think are intertwined. For example, does the knowledge of a name for a concept, such as *bachelor*, make it easier to construct and reason with more complex concepts that include that name, such as *eligible bachelor*?

For example, propositional logic assumes that there are facts that either hold or do not hold in the world. Each fact can be in one of two states: true or false.[2] First-order logic assumes more; namely, that the world consists of objects with certain relations among them that do or do not hold. Special-purpose logics make still further ontological commitments; for example, **temporal logic** assumes that facts hold at particular *times* and that those times (which may be points or intervals) are ordered. Thus, special-purpose logics give certain kinds of objects (and the axioms about them) "first-class" status within the logic, rather than simply defining them within the knowledge base. **Higher-order logic** views the relations and functions referred to by first-order logic as objects in themselves. This allows one to make assertions about *all* relations—for example, one could wish to define what it means for a relation to be transitive. Unlike most special-purpose logics, higher-order logic is strictly more expressive than first-order logic, in the sense that some sentences of higher-order logic cannot be expressed by any finite number of first-order logic sentences.

TEMPORAL LOGIC

HIGHER-ORDER LOGIC

EPISTEMOLOGICAL COMMITMENTS

A logic can also be characterized by its **epistemological commitments**—the possible states of knowledge that it allows with respect to each fact. In both propositional and first-order logic, a sentence represents a fact and the agent either believes the sentence to be true, believes it to be false, or has no opinion. These logics therefore have three possible states of knowledge regarding any sentence. Systems using **probability theory**, on the other hand, can have any *degree of belief*, ranging from 0 (total disbelief) to 1 (total belief).[3] For example, a probabilistic wumpus-world agent might believe that the wumpus is in [1,3] with probability 0.75. The ontological and epistemological commitments of five different logics are summarized in Figure 8.1.

| Language | Ontological Commitment (What exists in the world) | Epistemological Commitment (What an agent believes about facts) |
|---|---|---|
| Propositional logic | facts | true/false/unknown |
| First-order logic | facts, objects, relations | true/false/unknown |
| Temporal logic | facts, objects, relations, times | true/false/unknown |
| Probability theory | facts | degree of belief $\in [0, 1]$ |
| Fuzzy logic | facts with degree of truth $\in [0, 1]$ | known interval value |

**Figure 8.1** Formal languages and their ontological and epistemological commitments.

In the next section, we will launch into the details of first-order logic. Just as a student of physics requires some familiarity with mathematics, a student of AI must develop a talent for working with logical notation. On the other hand, it is also important *not* to get too concerned with the *specifics* of logical notation—after all, there are dozens of different versions. The main things to keep hold of are how the language facilitates concise representations and how its semantics leads to sound reasoning procedures.

[2] In contrast, facts in **fuzzy logic** have a **degree of truth** between 0 and 1. For example, the sentence "Vienna is a large city" might be true in our world only to degree 0.6.

[3] It is important not to confuse the degree of belief in probability theory with the degree of truth in fuzzy logic. Indeed, some fuzzy systems allow uncertainty (degree of belief) about degrees of truth.

## 8.2 SYNTAX AND SEMANTICS OF FIRST-ORDER LOGIC

We begin this section by specifying more precisely the way in which the possible worlds of first-order logic reflect the ontological commitment to objects and relations. Then we introduce the various elements of the language, explaining their semantics as we go along.

### Models for first-order logic

Recall from Chapter 7 that the models of a logical language are the formal structures that constitute the possible worlds under consideration. Models for propositional logic are just sets of truth values for the proposition symbols. Models for first-order logic are more interesting. First, they have objects in them! The **domain** of a model is the set of objects it contains; these objects are sometimes called **domain elements**. Figure 8.2 shows a model with five objects: Richard the Lionheart, King of England from 1189 to 1199; his younger brother, the evil King John, who ruled from 1199 to 1215; the left legs of Richard and John; and a crown.

DOMAIN

DOMAIN ELEMENTS

The objects in the model may be related in various ways. In the figure, Richard and John are brothers. Formally speaking, a relation is just the set of **tuples** of objects that are related. (A tuple is a collection of objects arranged in a fixed order and is written with angle brackets surrounding the objects.) Thus, the brotherhood relation in this model is the set

TUPLES

$$\{ \langle \text{Richard the Lionheart, King John} \rangle, \langle \text{King John, Richard the Lionheart} \rangle \} . \quad (8.1)$$

(Here we have named the objects in English, but you may, if you wish, mentally substitute the pictures for the names.) The crown is on King John's head, so the "on head" relation contains

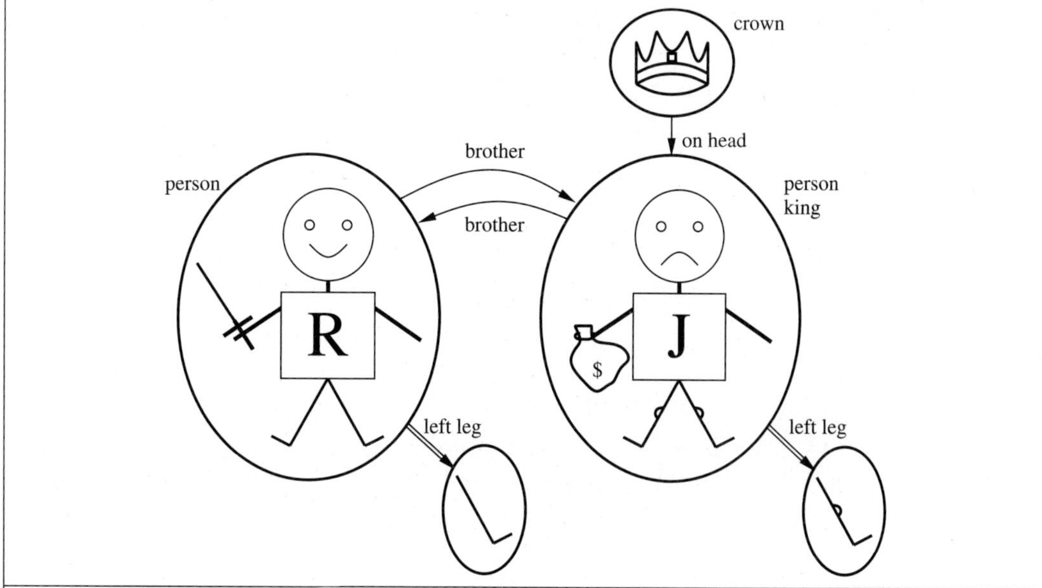


**Figure 8.2** A model containing five objects, two binary relations, three unary relations (indicated by labels on the objects), and one unary function, left-leg.

just one tuple, ⟨the crown, King John⟩. The "brother" and "on head" relations are binary relations—that is, they relate pairs of objects. The model also contains unary relations, or properties: the "person" property is true of both Richard and John; the "king" property is true only of John (presumably because Richard is dead at this point); and the "crown" property is true only of the crown.

Certain kinds of relationships are best considered as functions, in that a given object must be related to exactly one object in this way. For example, each person has one left leg, so the model has a unary "left leg" function that includes the following mappings:

$$\begin{aligned}&\langle \text{Richard the Lionheart} \rangle \rightarrow \text{Richard's left leg} \\ &\langle \text{King John} \rangle \rightarrow \text{John's left leg}\ .\end{aligned} \tag{8.2}$$

TOTAL FUNCTIONS

Strictly speaking, models in first-order logic require **total functions**, that is, there must be a value for every input tuple. Thus, the crown must have a left leg and so must each of the left legs. There is a technical solution to this awkward problem involving an additional "invisible" object that is the left leg of everything that has no left leg, including itself. Fortunately, as long as one makes no assertions about the left legs of things that have no left legs, these technicalities are of no import.

### Symbols and interpretations

We turn now to the syntax of the language. The impatient reader can obtain a complete description from the formal grammar of first-order logic in Figure 8.3.

CONSTANT SYMBOLS

PREDICATE SYMBOLS

FUNCTION SYMBOLS

The basic syntactic elements of first-order logic are the symbols that stand for objects, relations, and functions. The symbols, therefore, come in three kinds: **constant symbols**, which stand for objects; **predicate symbols**, which stand for relations; and **function symbols**, which stand for functions. We adopt the convention that these symbols will begin with uppercase letters. For example, we might use the constant symbols *Richard* and *John*; the predicate symbols *Brother*, *OnHead*, *Person*, *King*, and *Crown*; and the function symbol *LeftLeg*. As with proposition symbols, the choice of names is entirely up to the user. Each predicate and function symbol comes with an **arity** that fixes the number of arguments.

ARITY

INTERPRETATION

INTENDED INTERPRETATION

The semantics must relate sentences to models in order to determine truth. For this to happen, we need an **interpretation** that specifies exactly which objects, relations and functions are referred to by the constant, predicate, and function symbols. One possible interpretation for our example—which we will call the **intended interpretation**—is as follows:

- *Richard* refers to Richard the Lionheart and *John* refers to the evil King John.
- *Brother* refers to the brotherhood relation, that is, the set of tuples of objects given in Equation (8.1); *OnHead* refers to the "on head" relation that holds between the crown and King John; *Person*, *King*, and *Crown* refer to the sets of objects that are persons, kings, and crowns.
- *LeftLeg* refers to the "left leg" function, that is, the mapping given in Equation (8.2).

There are many other possible interpretations relating these symbols to this particular model. For example, one interpretation maps *Richard* to the crown and *John* to King John's left leg. There are five objects in the model, so there are 25 possible interpretations just for the

$$
\begin{aligned}
\textit{Sentence} &\rightarrow \textit{AtomicSentence} \\
&\quad\mid\ (\ \textit{Sentence Connective Sentence}\ ) \\
&\quad\mid\ \textit{Quantifier Variable}, \ldots\ \textit{Sentence} \\
&\quad\mid\ \neg\ \textit{Sentence} \\[1em]
\textit{AtomicSentence} &\rightarrow \textit{Predicate}(\textit{Term}, \ldots) \mid \textit{Term} = \textit{Term} \\[1em]
\textit{Term} &\rightarrow \textit{Function}(\textit{Term}, \ldots) \\
&\quad\mid\ \textit{Constant} \\
&\quad\mid\ \textit{Variable} \\[1em]
\textit{Connective} &\rightarrow\ \Rightarrow \mid\ \wedge \mid \vee \mid \Leftrightarrow \\
\textit{Quantifier} &\rightarrow \forall \mid \exists \\
\textit{Constant} &\rightarrow A \mid X_1 \mid \textit{John} \mid \cdots \\
\textit{Variable} &\rightarrow a \mid x \mid s \mid \cdots \\
\textit{Predicate} &\rightarrow \textit{Before} \mid \textit{HasColor} \mid \textit{Raining} \mid \cdots \\
\textit{Function} &\rightarrow \textit{Mother} \mid \textit{LeftLeg} \mid \cdots
\end{aligned}
$$

**Figure 8.3** The syntax of first-order logic with equality, specified in Backus–Naur form. (See page 984 if you are not familiar with this notation.) The syntax is strict about parentheses; the comments about parentheses and operator precedence on page 205 apply equally to first-order logic.

constant symbols *Richard* and *John*. Notice that not all the objects need have a name—for example, the intended interpretation does not name the crown or the legs. It is also possible for an object to have several names; there is an interpretation under which both *Richard* and *John* refer to the crown. If you find this possibility confusing, remember that, in propositional logic, it is perfectly possible to have a model in which *Cloudy* and *Sunny* are both true; it is the job of the knowledge base to rule out models that are inconsistent with our knowledge.

The truth of any sentence is determined by a model and an interpretation for the sentence's symbols. Therefore, entailment, validity, and so on are defined in terms of *all possible models* and *all possible interpretations*. It is important to note that the number of domain elements in each model may be unbounded—for example, the domain elements may be integers or real numbers. Hence, the number of possible models is unbounded, as is the number of interpretations. Checking entailment by the enumeration of all possible models, which works for propositional logic, is not an option for first-order logic. Even if the number of objects is restricted, the number of combinations can be very large. With the symbols in our example, there are roughly $10^{25}$ combinations for a domain with five objects. (See Exercise 8.5.)

### Terms

TERM

A **term** is a logical expression that refers to an object. Constant symbols are therefore terms, but it is not always convenient to have a distinct symbol to name every object. For example, in English we might use the expression "King John's left leg" rather than giving a name to his leg. This is what function symbols are for: instead of using a constant symbol, we use $LeftLeg(John)$. In the general case, a complex term is formed by a function symbol followed by a parenthesized list of terms as arguments to the function symbol. It is important to remember that a complex term is just a complicated kind of name. It is not a "subroutine call" that "returns a value." There is no $LeftLeg$ subroutine that takes a person as input and returns a leg. We can reason about left legs (e.g., stating the general rule that everyone has one and then deducing that John must have one) without ever providing a definition of $LeftLeg$. This is something that cannot be done with subroutines in programming languages.[4]

The formal semantics of terms is straightforward. Consider a term $f(t_1, \ldots, t_n)$. The function symbol $f$ refers to some function in the model (call it $F$); the argument terms refer to objects in the domain (call them $d_1, \ldots, d_n$); and the term as a whole refers to the object that is the value of the function $F$ applied to $d_1, \ldots, d_n$. For example, suppose the $LeftLeg$ function symbol refers to the function shown in Equation (8.2) and $John$ refers to King John, then $LeftLeg(John)$ refers to King John's left leg. In this way, the interpretation fixes the referent of every term.

### Atomic sentences

Now that we have both terms for referring to objects and predicate symbols for referring to relations, we can put them together to make **atomic sentences** that state facts. An atomic sentence is formed from a predicate symbol followed by a parenthesized list of terms:

$$Brother(Richard, John).$$

This states, under the intended interpretation given earlier, that Richard the Lionheart is the brother of King John.[5] Atomic sentences can have complex terms as arguments. Thus,

$$Married(Father(Richard), Mother(John))$$

states that Richard the Lionheart's father is married to King John's mother (again, under a suitable interpretation).

*An atomic sentence is* ***true*** *in a given model, under a given interpretation, if the relation referred to by the predicate symbol holds among the objects referred to by the arguments.*

---

4 **$\lambda$-expressions** provide a useful notation in which new function symbols are constructed "on the fly." For example, the function that squares its argument can be written as $(\lambda x\ x \times x)$ and can be applied to arguments just like any other function symbol. A $\lambda$-expression can also be defined and used as a predicate symbol. (See Chapter 22.) The `lambda` operator in Lisp plays exactly the same role. Notice that the use of $\lambda$ in this way does *not* increase the formal expressive power of first-order logic, because any sentence that includes a $\lambda$-expression can be rewritten by "plugging in" its arguments to yield an equivalent sentence.

5 We will usually follow the argument ordering convention that $P(x, y)$ is interpreted as "$x$ is a $P$ of $y$."

## Complex sentences

We can use **logical connectives** to construct more complex sentences, just as in propositional calculus. The semantics of sentences formed with logical connectives is identical to that in the propositional case. Here are four sentences that are true in the model of Figure 8.2 under our intended interpretation:

$$\neg Brother(LeftLeg(Richard), John)$$
$$Brother(Richard, John) \land Brother(John, Richard)$$
$$King(Richard) \lor King(John)$$
$$\neg King(Richard) \Rightarrow King(John) .$$

## Quantifiers

QUANTIFIERS

Once we have a logic that allows objects, it is only natural to want to express properties of entire collections of objects, instead of enumerating the objects by name. **Quantifiers** let us do this. First-order logic contains two standard quantifiers, called *universal* and *existential.*

### Universal quantification ($\forall$)

Recall the difficulty we had in Chapter 7 with the expression of general rules in propositional logic. Rules such as "Squares neighboring the wumpus are smelly" and "All kings are persons" are the bread and butter of first-order logic. We will deal with the first of these in Section 8.3. The second rule, "All kings are persons," is written in first-order logic as

$$\forall x \;\; King(x) \Rightarrow Person(x) .$$

VARIABLE

GROUND TERM

$\forall$ is usually pronounced "For all ...". (Remember that the upside-down A stands for "all.") Thus, the sentence says, "For all $x$, if $x$ is a king, then $x$ is a person." The symbol $x$ is called a **variable**. By convention, variables are lowercase letters. A variable is a term all by itself, and as such can also serve as the argument of a function—for example, $LeftLeg(x)$. A term with no variables is called a **ground term**.

EXTENDED INTERPRETATION

Intuitively, the sentence $\forall x \; P$, where $P$ is any logical expression, says that $P$ is true for every object $x$. More precisely, $\forall x \; P$ is true in a given model under a given interpretation if $P$ is true in all possible **extended interpretations** constructed from the given interpretation, where each extended interpretation specifies a domain element to which $x$ refers.

This sounds complicated, but it is really just a careful way of stating the intuitive meaning of universal quantification. Consider the model shown in Figure 8.2 and the intended interpretation that goes with it. We can extend the interpretation in five ways:

$x \rightarrow$ Richard the Lionheart,
$x \rightarrow$ King John,
$x \rightarrow$ Richard's left leg,
$x \rightarrow$ John's left leg,
$x \rightarrow$ the crown.

The universally quantified sentence $\forall x \;\; King(x) \Rightarrow Person(x)$ is true under the original interpretation if the sentence $King(x) \Rightarrow Person(x)$ is true in each of the five extended interpretations. That is, the universally quantified sentence is equivalent to asserting the following five sentences:

Richard the Lionheart is a king $\Rightarrow$ Richard the Lionheart is a person.
King John is a king $\Rightarrow$ King John is a person.
Richard's left leg is a king $\Rightarrow$ Richard's left leg is a person.
John's left leg is a king $\Rightarrow$ John's left leg is a person.
The crown is a king $\Rightarrow$ the crown is a person.

Let us look carefully at this set of assertions. Since, in our model, King John is the only king, the second sentence asserts that he is a person, as we would hope. But what about the other four sentences, which appear to make claims about legs and crowns? Is that part of the meaning of "All kings are persons"? In fact, the other four assertions are true in the model, but make no claim whatsoever about the personhood qualifications of legs, crowns, or indeed Richard. This is because none of these objects is a king. Looking at the truth table for $\Rightarrow$ (Figure 7.8), we see that the implication is true whenever its premise is false—*regardless* of the truth of the conclusion. Thus, by asserting the universally quantified sentence, which is equivalent to asserting a whole list of individual implications, we end up asserting the conclusion of the rule just for those objects for whom the premise is true and saying nothing at all about those individuals for whom the premise is false. Thus, the truth-table entries for $\Rightarrow$ turn out to be perfect for writing general rules with universal quantifiers.

A common mistake, made frequently even by diligent readers who have read this paragraph several times, is to use conjunction instead of implication. The sentence

$$\forall x \;\; King(x) \land Person(x)$$

would be equivalent to asserting

Richard the Lionheart is a king $\land$ Richard the Lionheart is a person,
King John is a king $\land$ King John is a person,
Richard's left leg is a king $\land$ Richard's left leg is a person,

and so on. Obviously, this does not capture what we want.

### Existential quantification ($\exists$)

Universal quantification makes statements about every object. Similarly, we can make a statement about *some* object in the universe without naming it, by using an existential quantifier. To say, for example, that King John has a crown on his head, we write

$$\exists x \;\; Crown(x) \land OnHead(x, John) \, .$$

$\exists x$ is pronounced "There exists an $x$ such that ..." or "For some $x$ ...".

Intuitively, the sentence $\exists x \; P$ says that $P$ is true for at least one object $x$. More precisely, $\exists x \; P$ is true in a given model under a given interpretation if $P$ is true in *at least one* extended interpretation that assigns $x$ to a domain element. For our example, this means that at least one of the following must be true:

Richard the Lionheart is a crown $\wedge$ Richard the Lionheart is on John's head;
King John is a crown $\wedge$ King John is on John's head;
Richard's left leg is a crown $\wedge$ Richard's left leg is on John's head;
John's left leg is a crown $\wedge$ John's left leg is on John's head;
The crown is a crown $\wedge$ the crown is on John's head.

The fifth assertion is true in the model, so the original existentially quantified sentence is true in the model. Notice that, by our definition, the sentence would also be true in a model in which King John was wearing two crowns. This is entirely consistent with the original sentence "King John has a crown on his head." [6]

Just as $\Rightarrow$ appears to be the natural connective to use with $\forall$, $\wedge$ is the natural connective to use with $\exists$. Using $\wedge$ as the main connective with $\forall$ led to an overly strong statement in the example in the previous section; using $\Rightarrow$ with $\exists$ usually leads to a very weak statement, indeed. Consider the following sentence:

$$\exists x \;\; \mathit{Crown}(x) \;\Rightarrow\; \mathit{OnHead}(x, \mathit{John}) \; .$$

On the surface, this might look like a reasonable rendition of our sentence. Applying the semantics, we see that the sentence says that at least one of the following assertions is true:

Richard the Lionheart is a crown $\Rightarrow$ Richard the Lionheart is on John's head;
King John is a crown $\Rightarrow$ King John is on John's head;
Richard's left leg is a crown $\Rightarrow$ Richard's left leg is on John's head;

and so on. Now an implication is true if both premise and conclusion are true, *or if its premise is false*. So if Richard the Lionheart is not a crown, then the first assertion is true and the existential is satisfied. So, an existentially quantified implication sentence is true in any model containing an object for which the premise of the implication is false; hence such sentences really do not say much at all.

### Nested quantifiers

We will often want to express more complex sentences using multiple quantifiers. The simplest case is where the quantifiers are of the same type. For example, "Brothers are siblings" can be written as

$$\forall x \;\; \forall y \;\; \mathit{Brother}(x, y) \;\Rightarrow\; \mathit{Sibling}(x, y) \; .$$

Consecutive quantifiers of the same type can be written as one quantifier with several variables. For example, to say that siblinghood is a symmetric relationship, we can write

$$\forall x, y \;\; \mathit{Sibling}(x, y) \;\Leftrightarrow\; \mathit{Sibling}(y, x) \; .$$

In other cases we will have mixtures. "Everybody loves somebody" means that for every person, there is someone that person loves:

$$\forall x \;\; \exists y \;\; \mathit{Loves}(x, y) \; .$$

[6] There is a variant of the existential quantifi er, usually written $\exists^1$ or $\exists!$, that means "There exists exactly one." The same meaning can be expressed using equality statements.

On the other hand, to say "There is someone who is loved by everyone," we write

$$\exists\, y\ \forall\, x\ \ Loves(x, y)\ .$$

The order of quantification is therefore very important. It becomes clearer if we insert parentheses. $\forall\, x\ (\exists\, y\ Loves(x, y))$ says that *everyone* has a particular property, namely, the property that they love someone. On the other hand, $\exists\, y\ (\forall\, x\ Loves(x, y))$ says that *someone* in the world has a particular property, namely the property of being loved by everybody.

Some confusion can arise when two quantifiers are used with the same variable name. Consider the sentence

$$\forall\, x\ \ [Crown(x) \lor (\exists\, x\ \ Brother(Richard, x))]\ .$$

Here the $x$ in $Brother(Richard, x)$ is *existentially* quantified. The rule is that the variable belongs to the innermost quantifier that mentions it; then it will not be subject to any other quantification.[7] Another way to think of it is this: $\exists\, x\ Brother(Richard, x)$ is a sentence about Richard (that he has a brother), not about $x$; so putting a $\forall\, x$ outside it has no effect. It could equally well have been written $\exists\, z\ Brother(Richard, z)$. Because this can be a source of confusion, we will always use different variables.

### Connections between $\forall$ and $\exists$

The two quantifiers are actually intimately connected with each other, through negation. Asserting that everyone dislikes parsnips is the same as asserting there does not exist someone who likes them, and vice versa:

$$\forall\, x\ \ \neg Likes(x, Parsnips) \quad \text{is equivalent to} \quad \neg\exists\, x\ \ Likes(x, Parsnips)\ .$$

We can go one step further: "Everyone likes ice cream" means that there is no one who does not like ice cream:

$$\forall\, x\ \ Likes(x, IceCream) \quad \text{is equivalent to} \quad \neg\exists\, x\ \ \neg Likes(x, IceCream)\ .$$

Because $\forall$ is really a conjunction over the universe of objects and $\exists$ is a disjunction, it should not be surprising that they obey De Morgan's rules. The De Morgan rules for quantified and unquantified sentences are as follows:

$$\begin{array}{llll}
\forall\, x\ \neg P \equiv \neg\exists\, x\ P & \qquad & \neg P \land \neg Q \equiv \neg(P \lor Q) \\
\neg\forall\, x\ P \equiv \exists\, x\ \neg P & & \neg(P \land Q) \equiv \neg P \lor \neg Q \\
\forall\, x\ P \equiv \neg\exists\, x\ \neg P & & P \land Q \equiv \neg(\neg P \lor \neg Q) \\
\exists\, x\ P \equiv \neg\forall\, x\ \neg P & & P \lor Q \equiv \neg(\neg P \land \neg Q)\ .
\end{array}$$

Thus, we do not really need both $\forall$ and $\exists$, just as we do not really need both $\land$ and $\lor$. Still, readability is more important than parsimony, so we will keep both of the quantifiers.

[7] It is the potential for interference between quantifi ers using the same variable name that motivates the slightly baroque mechanism of extended interpretations in the semantics of quantifi ed sentences. The more intuitively obvious approach of substituting objects for every occurrence of $x$ fails in our example because the $x$ in $Brother(Richard, x)$ would be "captured" by the substitution. Extended interpretations handle this correctly because the inner quantifi er's assignment for $x$ overrides the outer quantifi er's.

### Equality

EQUALITY SYMBOL

First-order logic includes one more way to make atomic sentences, other than using a predicate and terms as described earlier. We can use the **equality symbol** to make statements to the effect that two terms refer to the same object. For example,

$$Father(John) = Henry$$

says that the object referred to by $Father(John)$ and the object referred to by $Henry$ are the same. Because an interpretation fixes the referent of any term, determining the truth of an equality sentence is simply a matter of seeing that the referents of the two terms are the same object.

The equality symbol can be used to state facts about a given function, as we just did for the $Father$ symbol. It can also be used with negation to insist that two terms are not the same object. To say that Richard has at least two brothers, we would write

$$\exists x, y \;\; Brother(x, Richard) \land Brother(y, Richard) \land \neg(x = y) .$$

The sentence

$$\exists x, y \;\; Brother(x, Richard) \land Brother(y, Richard) ,$$

does not have the intended meaning. In particular, it is true in the model of Figure 8.2, where Richard has only one brother. To see this, consider the extended interpretation in which both $x$ and $y$ are assigned to King John. The addition of $\neg(x = y)$ rules out such models. The notation $x \neq y$ is sometimes used as an abbreviation for $\neg(x = y)$.

## 8.3 USING FIRST-ORDER LOGIC

Now that we have defined an expressive logical language, it is time to learn how to use it. The best way to do this is through examples. We have seen some simple sentences illustrating the various aspects of logical syntax; in this section, we will provide more systematic representations of some simple **domains**. In knowledge representation, a domain is just some part of the world about which we wish to express some knowledge.

DOMAINS

We will begin with a brief description of the TELL/ASK interface for first-order knowledge bases. Then we will look at the domains of family relationships, numbers, sets, and lists, and at the wumpus world. The next section contains a more substantial example (electronic circuits) and Chapter 10 covers everything in the universe.

### Assertions and queries in first-order logic

ASSERTIONS

Sentences are added to a knowledge base using TELL, exactly as in propositional logic. Such sentences are called **assertions**. For example, we can assert that John is a king and that kings are persons:

$$\text{TELL}(KB, King(John)) .$$
$$\text{TELL}(KB, \forall x \;\; King(x) \Rightarrow Person(x)) .$$

We can ask questions of the knowledge base using ASK. For example,

$$\text{ASK}(KB,\ King(John))$$

QUERIES
GOALS

returns $true$. Questions asked using ASK are called **queries** or **goals** (not to be confused with goals as used to describe an agent's desired states). Generally speaking, any query that is logically entailed by the knowledge base should be answered affirmatively. For example, given the two assertions in the preceding paragraph, the query

$$\text{ASK}(KB,\ Person(John))$$

should also return $true$. We can also ask quantified queries, such as

$$\text{ASK}(KB,\ \exists\, x\ \ Person(x))\ .$$

SUBSTITUTION
BINDING LIST

The answer to this query could be $true$, but this is neither helpful nor amusing. (It is rather like answering "Can you tell me the time?" with "Yes.") A query with existential variables is asking "Is there an $x$ such that ...," and we solve it by providing such an $x$. The standard form for an answer of this sort is a **substitution** or **binding list**, which is a set of variable/term pairs. In this particular case, given just the two assertions, the answer would be $\{x/John\}$. If there is more than one possible answer, a list of substitutions can be returned.

### The kinship domain

The first example we consider is the domain of family relationships, or kinship. This domain includes facts such as "Elizabeth is the mother of Charles" and "Charles is the father of William" and rules such as "One's grandmother is the mother of one's parent."

Clearly, the objects in our domain are people. We will have two unary predicates, $Male$ and $Female$. Kinship relations—parenthood, brotherhood, marriage, and so on—will be represented by binary predicates: $Parent$, $Sibling$, $Brother$, $Sister$, $Child$, $Daughter$, $Son$, $Spouse$, $Wife$, $Husband$, $Grandparent$, $Grandchild$, $Cousin$, $Aunt$, and $Uncle$. We will use functions for $Mother$ and $Father$, because every person has exactly one of each of these (at least according to nature's design).

We can go through each function and predicate, writing down what we know in terms of the other symbols. For example, one's mother is one's female parent:

$$\forall\, m, c\ \ Mother(c) = m\ \Leftrightarrow\ Female(m) \land Parent(m, c)\ .$$

One's husband is one's male spouse:

$$\forall\, w, h\ \ Husband(h, w)\ \Leftrightarrow\ Male(h) \land Spouse(h, w)\ .$$

Male and female are disjoint categories:

$$\forall\, x\ \ Male(x)\ \Leftrightarrow\ \neg Female(x)\ .$$

Parent and child are inverse relations:

$$\forall\, p, c\ \ Parent(p, c)\ \Leftrightarrow\ Child(c, p)\ .$$

A grandparent is a parent of one's parent:

$$\forall\, g, c\ \ Grandparent(g, c)\ \Leftrightarrow\ \exists\, p\ \ Parent(g, p) \land Parent(p, c)\ .$$

A sibling is another child of one's parents:

$$\forall x, y \;\; Sibling(x, y) \;\Leftrightarrow\; x \neq y \wedge \exists p \;\; Parent(p, x) \wedge Parent(p, y) \,.$$

We could go on for several more pages like this, and Exercise 8.11 asks you to do just that.

AXIOM

Each of these sentences can be viewed as an **axiom** of the kinship domain. Axioms are commonly associated with purely mathematical domains—we will see some axioms for numbers shortly—but they are needed in all domains. They provide the basic factual information from which useful conclusions can be derived. Our kinship axioms are also **definitions**; they have the form $\forall x, y \;\; P(x, y) \;\Leftrightarrow\; \ldots$. The axioms define the *Mother* function and the *Husband*, *Male*, *Parent*, *Grandparent*, and *Sibling* predicates in terms of other predicates. Our definitions "bottom out" at a basic set of predicates (*Child*, *Spouse*, and *Female*) in terms of which the others are ultimately defined. This is a very natural way in which to build up the representation of a domain, and it is analogous to the way in which software packages are built up by successive definitions of subroutines from primitive library functions. Notice that there is not necessarily a unique set of primitive predicates; we could equally well have used *Parent*, *Spouse*, and *Male*. In some domains, as we will see, there is no clearly identifiable basic set.

DEFINITION

THEOREM

Not all logical sentences about a domain are axioms. Some are **theorems**—that is, they are entailed by the axioms. For example, consider the assertion that siblinghood is symmetric:

$$\forall x, y \;\; Sibling(x, y) \;\Leftrightarrow\; Sibling(y, x) \,.$$

Is this an axiom or a theorem? In fact, it is a theorem that follows logically from the axiom that defines siblinghood. If we ASK the knowledge base this sentence, it should return *true*.

From a purely logical point of view, a knowledge base need contain only axioms and no theorems, because the theorems do not increase the set of conclusions that follow from the knowledge base. From a practical point of view, theorems are essential to reduce the computational cost of deriving new sentences. Without them, a reasoning system has to start from first principles every time, rather like a physicist having to rederive the rules of calculus for every new problem.

Not all axioms are definitions. Some provide more general information about certain predicates without constituting a definition. Indeed, some predicates have no complete definition because we do not know enough to characterize them fully. For example, there is no obvious way to complete the sentence:

$$\forall x \;\; Person(x) \;\Leftrightarrow\; \ldots$$

Fortunately, first-order logic allows us to make use of the *Person* predicate without completely defining it. Instead, we can write partial specifications of properties that every person has and properties that make something a person:

$$\forall x \;\; Person(x) \;\Rightarrow\; \ldots$$
$$\forall x \;\; \ldots \;\Rightarrow\; Person(x) \,.$$

Axioms can also be "just plain facts," such as $Male(Jim)$ and $Spouse(Jim, Laura)$. Such facts form the descriptions of specific problem instances, enabling specific questions to be answered. The answers to these questions will then be theorems that follow from the axioms. Often, one finds that the expected answers are not forthcoming—for example, from $Male(George)$ and $Spouse(George, Laura)$, one expects to be able to infer $Female(Laura)$; but this does not follow from the axioms given earlier. This is a sign that an axiom is missing. Exercise 8.8 asks you to supply it.

### Numbers, sets, and lists

NATURAL NUMBERS

PEANO AXIOMS

Numbers are perhaps the most vivid example of how a large theory can be built up from a tiny kernel of axioms. We will describe here the theory of **natural numbers** or nonnegative integers. We need a predicate $NatNum$ that will be true of natural numbers; we need one constant symbol, 0; and we need one function symbol, $S$ (successor). The **Peano axioms** define natural numbers and addition.[8] Natural numbers are defined recursively:

$$NatNum(0) .$$
$$\forall n \;\; NatNum(n) \Rightarrow NatNum(S(n)) .$$

That is, 0 is a natural number, and for every object $n$, if $n$ is a natural number then $S(n)$ is a natural number. So the natural numbers are 0, $S(0)$, $S(S(0))$, and so on. We also need axioms to constrain the successor function:

$$\forall n \;\; 0 \neq S(n) .$$
$$\forall m, n \;\; m \neq n \Rightarrow S(m) \neq S(n) .$$

Now we can define addition in terms of the successor function:

$$\forall m \;\; NatNum(m) \Rightarrow +(0, m) = m .$$
$$\forall m, n \;\; NatNum(m) \land NatNum(n) \Rightarrow +(S(m), n) = S(+(m, n)) .$$

INFIX

PREFIX

The first of these axioms says that adding 0 to any natural number $m$ gives $m$ itself. Notice the use of the binary function symbol "+" in the term $+(m, 0)$; in ordinary mathematics, the term would be written $m + 0$ using **infix** notation. (The notation we have used for first-order logic is called **prefix**.) To make our sentences about numbers easier to read, we will allow the use of infix notation. We can also write $S(n)$ as $n + 1$, so that the second axiom becomes

$$\forall m, n \;\; NatNum(m) \land NatNum(n) \Rightarrow (m + 1) + n = (m + n) + 1 .$$

This axiom reduces addition to repeated application of the successor function.

SYNTACTIC SUGAR

The use of infix notation is an example of **syntactic sugar**, that is, an extension to or abbreviation of the standard syntax that does not change the semantics. Any sentence that uses sugar can be "de-sugared" to produce an equivalent sentence in ordinary first-order logic.

Once we have addition, it is straightforward to define multiplication as repeated addition, exponentiation as repeated multiplication, integer division and remainders, prime numbers, and so on. Thus, the whole of number theory (including cryptography) can be built up from one constant, one function, one predicate and four axioms.

SETS

The domain of **sets** is also fundamental to mathematics as well as to commonsense reasoning. (In fact, it is possible to build number theory on top of set theory.) We want to be able to represent individual sets, including the empty set. We need a way to build up sets by

[8] The Peano axioms also include the principle of induction, which is a sentence of second-order logic rather than of first-order logic. The importance of this distinction is explained in Chapter 9.

adding an element to a set or taking the union or intersection of two sets. We will want to know whether an element is a member of a set and to be able to distinguish sets from objects that are not sets.

We will use the normal vocabulary of set theory as syntactic sugar. The empty set is a constant written as $\{\}$. There is one unary predicate, *Set*, which is true of sets. The binary predicates are $x \in s$ ($x$ is a member of set $s$) and $s_1 \subseteq s_2$ (set $s_1$ is a subset, not necessarily proper, of set $s_2$). The binary functions are $s_1 \cap s_2$ (the intersection of two sets), $s_1 \cup s_2$ (the union of two sets), and $\{x|s\}$ (the set resulting from adjoining element $x$ to set $s$). One possible set of axioms is as follows:

1. The only sets are the empty set and those made by adjoining something to a set:
$$\forall s \;\; Set(s) \Leftrightarrow (s = \{\}) \lor (\exists x, s_2 \;\; Set(s_2) \land s = \{x|s_2\}) \, .$$
2. The empty set has no elements adjoined into it. In other words, there is no way to decompose $\{\}$ into a smaller set and an element:
$$\neg \exists x, s \;\; \{x|s\} = \{\} \, .$$
3. Adjoining an element already in the set has no effect:
$$\forall x, s \;\; x \in s \Leftrightarrow s = \{x|s\} \, .$$
4. The only members of a set are the elements that were adjoined into it. We express this recursively, saying that $x$ is a member of $s$ if and only if $s$ is equal to some set $s_2$ adjoined with some element $y$, where either $y$ is the same as $x$ or $x$ is a member of $s_2$:
$$\forall x, s \;\; x \in s \Leftrightarrow [\exists y, s_2 \;\; (s = \{y|s_2\} \land (x = y \lor x \in s_2))] \, .$$
5. A set is a subset of another set if and only if all of the first set's members are members of the second set:
$$\forall s_1, s_2 \;\; s_1 \subseteq s_2 \Leftrightarrow (\forall x \;\; x \in s_1 \Rightarrow x \in s_2) \, .$$
6. Two sets are equal if and only if each is a subset of the other:
$$\forall s_1, s_2 \;\; (s_1 = s_2) \Leftrightarrow (s_1 \subseteq s_2 \land s_2 \subseteq s_1) \, .$$
7. An object is in the intersection of two sets if and only if it is a member of both sets:
$$\forall x, s_1, s_2 \;\; x \in (s_1 \cap s_2) \Leftrightarrow (x \in s_1 \land x \in s_2) \, .$$
8. An object is in the union of two sets if and only if it is a member of either set:
$$\forall x, s_1, s_2 \;\; x \in (s_1 \cup s_2) \Leftrightarrow (x \in s_1 \lor x \in s_2) \, .$$

LISTS

**Lists** are similar to sets. The differences are that lists are ordered and the same element can appear more than once in a list. We can use the vocabulary of Lisp for lists: *Nil* is the constant list with no elements; *Cons*, *Append*, *First*, and *Rest* are functions; and *Find* is the predicate that does for lists what *Member* does for sets. *List?* is a predicate that is true only of lists. As with sets, it is common to use syntactic sugar in logical sentences involving lists. The empty list is $[\,]$. The term $Cons(x, y)$, where $y$ is a nonempty list, is written $[x|y]$. The term $Cons(x, Nil)$, (i.e., the list containing the element $x$), is written as $[x]$. A list of several elements, such as $[A, B, C]$, corresponds to the nested term $Cons(A, Cons(B, Cons(C, Nil)))$. Exercise 8.14 asks you to write out the axioms for lists.

### The wumpus world

Some propositional logic axioms for the wumpus world were given in Chapter 7. The first-order axioms in this section are much more concise, capturing in a very natural way exactly what we want to say.

Recall that the wumpus agent receives a percept vector with five elements. The corresponding first-order sentence stored in the knowledge base must include both the percept and the time at which it occurred; otherwise the agent will get confused about when it saw what. We will use integers for time steps. A typical percept sentence would be

$$Percept([Stench, Breeze, Glitter, None, None], 5) .$$

Here, $Percept$ is a binary predicate and $Stench$ and so on are constants placed in a list. The actions in the wumpus world can be represented by logical terms:

$$Turn(Right),\;\; Turn(Left),\;\; Forward,\;\; Shoot,\;\; Grab,\;\; Release,\;\; Climb .$$

To determine which is best, the agent program constructs a query such as

$$\exists\, a \;\; BestAction(a, 5) .$$

ASK should solve this query and return a binding list such as $\{a/Grab\}$. The agent program can then return $Grab$ as the action to take, but first it must TELL its own knowledge base that it is performing a $Grab$.

The raw percept data implies certain facts about the current state. For example:

$$\forall\, t, s, g, m, c \;\; Percept([s, Breeze, g, m, c], t) \;\Rightarrow\; Breeze(t) ,$$
$$\forall\, t, s, b, m, c \;\; Percept([s, b, Glitter, m, c], t) \;\Rightarrow\; Glitter(t) ,$$

and so on. These rules exhibit a trivial form of the reasoning process called **perception**, which we study in depth in Chapter 24. Notice the quantification over time $t$. In propositional logic, we would need copies of each sentence for each time step.

Simple "reflex" behavior can also be implemented by quantified implication sentences. For example, we have

$$\forall\, t \;\; Glitter(t) \;\Rightarrow\; BestAction(Grab, t) .$$

Given the percept and rules from the preceding paragraphs, this would yield the desired conclusion $BestAction(Grab, 5)$—that is, $Grab$ is the right thing to do. Notice the correspondence between this rule and the direct percept–action connection in the circuit-based agent in Figure 7.20; the circuit connection *implicitly* quantifies over time.

SYNCHRONIC

DIACHRONIC

So far in this section, the sentences dealing with time have been **synchronic** ("same time") sentences, that is, they relate properties of a world state to other properties of the same world state. Sentences that allow reasoning "across time" are called **diachronic**; for example, the agent needs to know how to combine information about its previous location with information about the action just taken in order to determine its current location. We will defer discussion of diachronic sentences until Chapter 10; for now, just assume that the required inferences have been made for location and other time-dependent predicates.

We have represented the percepts and actions; now it is time to represent the environment itself. Let us begin with objects. Obvious candidates are squares, pits, and the wumpus.

We could name each square—$Square_{1,2}$ and so on—but then the fact that $Square_{1,2}$ and $Square_{1,3}$ are adjacent would have to be an "extra" fact, and we would need one such fact for each pair of squares. It is better to use a complex term in which the row and column appear as integers; for example, we can simply use the list term $[1, 2]$. Adjacency of any two squares can be defined as

$$\forall x, y, a, b \ \ Adjacent([x, y], [a, b]) \Leftrightarrow \\ [a, b] \in \{[x+1, y], [x-1, y], [x, y+1], [x, y-1]\} .$$

We could also name each pit, but this would be inappropriate for a different reason: there is no reason to distinguish among the pits.[9] It is much simpler to use a unary predicate *Pit* that is true of squares containing pits. Finally, since there is exactly one wumpus, a constant $Wumpus$ is just as good as a unary predicate (and perhaps more dignified from the wumpus's viewpoint). The wumpus lives in exactly one square, so it is a good idea to use a function such as $Home(Wumpus)$ to name that square. This completely avoids the cumbersome set of sentences required in propositional logic to say that exactly one square contains a wumpus. (It would be even worse for propositional logic with two wumpuses.)

The agent's location changes over time, so we will write $At(Agent, s, t)$ to mean that the agent is at square $s$ at time $t$. Given its current location, the agent can infer properties of the square from properties of its current percept. For example, if the agent is at a square and perceives a breeze, then that square is breezy:

$$\forall s, t \ \ At(Agent, s, t) \wedge Breeze(t) \Rightarrow Breezy(s) .$$

It is useful to know that a *square* is breezy because we know that the pits cannot move about. Notice that *Breezy* has no time argument.

Having discovered which places are breezy (or smelly) and, very importantly, *not* breezy (or *not* smelly), the agent can deduce where the pits are (and where the wumpus is). There are two kinds of synchronic rules that could allow such deductions:

DIAGNOSTIC RULES

◇ **Diagnostic rules**:
Diagnostic rules lead from observed effects to hidden causes. For finding pits, the obvious diagnostic rules say that if a square is breezy, some adjacent square must contain a pit, or

$$\forall s \ \ Breezy(s) \Rightarrow \exists r \ \ Adjacent(r, s) \wedge Pit(r) ,$$

and that if a square is not breezy, no adjacent square contains a pit: [10]

$$\forall s \ \ \neg Breezy(s) \Rightarrow \neg\exists r \ \ Adjacent(r, s) \wedge Pit(r) .$$

Combining these two, we obtain the biconditional sentence

$$\forall s \ \ Breezy(s) \Leftrightarrow \exists r \ \ Adjacent(r, s) \wedge Pit(r) . \tag{8.3}$$

---

[9] Similarly, most of us do not name each bird that flies overhead as it migrates to warmer regions in winter. An ornithologist wishing to study migration patterns, survival rates, and so on *does* name each bird, by means of a ring on its leg, because individual birds must be tracked.

[10] There is a natural human tendency to forget to write down negative information such as this. In conversation, this tendency is entirely normal—it would be strange to say "There are two cups on the table *and there are not three or more*," even though "There are two cups on the table" is, strictly speaking, still true when there are three. We will return to this topic in Chapter 10.

CAUSAL RULES

◇ **Causal rules**:
Causal rules reflect the assumed direction of causality in the world: some hidden property of the world causes certain percepts to be generated. For example, a pit causes all adjacent squares to be breezy:

$$\forall\, r\ \ Pit(r)\ \Rightarrow\ [\forall\, s\ \ Adjacent(r,s)\ \Rightarrow\ Breezy(s)]$$

and if all squares adjacent to a given square are pitless, the square will not be breezy:

$$\forall\, s\ \ [\forall\, r\ \ Adjacent(r,s)\ \Rightarrow\ \neg Pit(r)]\ \Rightarrow\ \neg Breezy(s)\ .$$

With some work, it is possible to show that these two sentences together are logically equivalent to the biconditional sentence in Equation (8.3). The biconditional itself can also be thought of as causal, because it states how the truth value of $Breezy$ is generated from the world state.

MODEL-BASED REASONING

Systems that reason with causal rules are called **model-based reasoning** systems, because the causal rules form a model of how the environment operates. The distinction between model-based and diagnostic reasoning is important in many areas of AI. Medical diagnosis in particular has been an active area of research, in which approaches based on direct associations between symptoms and diseases (a diagnostic approach) have gradually been replaced by approaches using an explicit model of the disease process and how it manifests itself in symptoms. The issues come up again in Chapter 13.

Whichever kind of representation the agent uses, *if the axioms correctly and completely describe the way the world works and the way that percepts are produced, then any complete logical inference procedure will infer the strongest possible description of the world state, given the available percepts.* Thus, the agent designer can concentrate on getting the knowledge right, without worrying too much about the processes of deduction. Furthermore, we have seen that first-order logic can represent the wumpus world no less concisely than the original English-language description given in Chapter 7.

## 8.4 KNOWLEDGE ENGINEERING IN FIRST-ORDER LOGIC

KNOWLEDGE ENGINEERING

The preceding section illustrated the use of first-order logic to represent knowledge in three simple domains. This section describes the general process of knowledge base construction—a process called **knowledge engineering**. A knowledge engineer is someone who investigates a particular domain, learns what concepts are important in that domain, and creates a formal representation of the objects and relations in the domain. We will illustrate the knowledge engineering process in an electronic circuit domain that should already be fairly familiar, so that we can concentrate on the representational issues involved. The approach we will take is suitable for developing *special-purpose* knowledge bases whose domain is carefully circumscribed and whose range of queries is known in advance. *General-purpose* knowledge bases, which are intended to support queries across the full range of human knowledge, are discussed in Chapter 10.

### The knowledge engineering process

Knowledge engineering projects vary widely in content, scope, and difficulty, but all such projects include the following steps:

1. *Identify the task.* The knowledge engineer must delineate the range of questions that the knowledge base will support and the kinds of facts that will be available for each specific problem instance. For example, does the wumpus knowledge base need to be able to choose actions or is it required to answer questions only about the contents of the environment? Will the sensor facts include the current location? The task will determine what knowledge must be represented in order to connect problem instances to answers. This step is analogous to the PEAS process for designing agents in Chapter 2.

2. *Assemble the relevant knowledge.* The knowledge engineer might already be an expert in the domain, or might need to work with real experts to extract what they know—a process called **knowledge acquisition**. At this stage, the knowledge is not represented formally. The idea is to understand the scope of the knowledge base, as determined by the task, and to understand how the domain actually works.

   KNOWLEDGE ACQUISITION

   For the wumpus world, which is defined by an artificial set of rules, the relevant knowledge is easy to identify. (Notice, however, that the definition of adjacency was not supplied explicitly in the wumpus-world rules.) For real domains, the issue of relevance can be quite difficult—for example, a system for simulating VLSI designs might or might not need to take into account stray capacitances and skin effects.

3. *Decide on a vocabulary of predicates, functions, and constants.* That is, translate the important domain-level concepts into logic-level names. This involves many questions of knowledge engineering *style*. Like programming style, this can have a significant impact on the eventual success of the project. For example, should pits be represented by objects or by a unary predicate on squares? Should the agent's orientation be a function or a predicate? Should the wumpus's location depend on time? Once the choices have been made, the result is a vocabulary that is known as the **ontology** of the domain. The word *ontology* means a particular theory of the nature of being or existence. The ontology determines what kinds of things exist, but does not determine their specific properties and interrelationships.

   ONTOLOGY

4. *Encode general knowledge about the domain.* The knowledge engineer writes down the axioms for all the vocabulary terms. This pins down (to the extent possible) the meaning of the terms, enabling the expert to check the content. Often, this step reveals misconceptions or gaps in the vocabulary that must be fixed by returning to step 3 and iterating through the process.

5. *Encode a description of the specific problem instance.* If the ontology is well thought out, this step will be easy. It will involve writing simple atomic sentences about instances of concepts that are already part of the ontology. For a logical agent, problem instances are supplied by the sensors, whereas a "disembodied" knowledge base is supplied with additional sentences in the same way that traditional programs are supplied with input data.

6. *Pose queries to the inference procedure and get answers.* This is where the reward is: we can let the inference procedure operate on the axioms and problem-specific facts to derive the facts we are interested in knowing.
7. *Debug the knowledge base.* Alas, the answers to queries will seldom be correct on the first try. More precisely, the answers will be correct *for the knowledge base as written*, assuming that the inference procedure is sound, but they will not be the ones that the user is expecting. For example, if an axiom is missing, some queries will not be answerable from the knowledge base. A considerable debugging process could ensue. Missing axioms or axioms that are too weak can be identified easily by noticing places where the chain of reasoning stops unexpectedly. For example, if the knowledge base includes one of the diagnostic axioms for pits,

   $$\forall s \; Breezy(s) \;\Rightarrow\; \exists r \;\; Adjacent(r, s) \wedge Pit(r) \; ,$$

   but not the other, then the agent will never be able to prove the *absence* of pits. Incorrect axioms can be identified because they are false statements about the world. For example, the sentence

   $$\forall x \;\; NumOfLegs(x, 4) \;\Rightarrow\; Mammal(x)$$

   is false for reptiles, amphibians, and, more important, tables. *The falsehood of this sentence can be determined independently of the rest of the knowledge base.* In contrast, a typical error in a program looks like this:

   ```
   offset = position + 1 .
   ```

   It is impossible to tell whether this statement is correct without looking at the rest of the program to see whether, for example, `offset` is used to refer to the current position, or to one beyond the current position, or whether the value of `position` is changed by another statement and so `offset` should also be changed again.

To understand this seven-step process better, we now apply it to an extended example—the domain of electronic circuits.

### The electronic circuits domain

We will develop an ontology and knowledge base that allow us to reason about digital circuits of the kind shown in Figure 8.4. We follow the seven-step process for knowledge engineering.

#### Identify the task

There are many reasoning tasks associated with digital circuits. At the highest level, one analyzes the circuit's functionality. For example, does the circuit in Figure 8.4 actually add properly? If all the inputs are high, what is the output of gate A2? Questions about the circuit's structure are also interesting. For example, what are all the gates connected to the first input terminal? Does the circuit contain feedback loops? These will be our tasks in this section. There are more detailed levels of analysis, including those related to timing delays, circuit area, power consumption, production cost, and so on. Each of these levels would require additional knowledge.

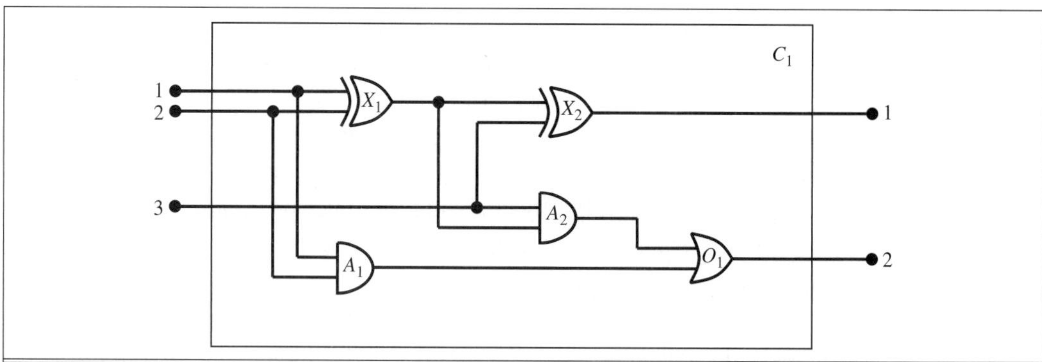


**Figure 8.4** A digital circuit C1, purporting to be a one-bit full adder. The first two inputs are the two bits to be added and the third input is a carry bit. The first output is the sum, and the second output is a carry bit for the next adder. The circuit contains two XOR gates, two AND gates and one OR gate.

### Assemble the relevant knowledge

What do we know about digital circuits? For our purposes, they are composed of wires and gates. Signals flow along wires to the input terminals of gates, and each gate produces a signal on the output terminal that flows along another wire. To determine what these signals will be, we need to know how the gates transform their input signals. There are four types of gates: AND, OR, and XOR gates have two input terminals, and NOT gates have one. All gates have one output terminal. Circuits, like gates, have input and output terminals.

To reason about functionality and connectivity, we do not need to talk about the wires themselves, the paths the wires take, or the junctions where two wires come together. All that matters is the connections between terminals—we can say that one output terminal is connected to another input terminal without having to mention the wire that actually connects them. There are many other factors of the domain that are irrelevant to our analysis, such as the size, shape, color, or cost of the various components.

If our purpose were something other than verifying designs at the gate level, the ontology would be different. For example, if we were interested in debugging faulty circuits, then it would probably be a good idea to include the wires in the ontology, because a faulty wire can corrupt the signal flowing along it. For resolving timing faults, we would need to include gate delays. If we were interested in designing a product that would be profitable, then the cost of the circuit and its speed relative to other products on the market would be important.

### Decide on a vocabulary

We now know that we want to talk about circuits, terminals, signals, and gates. The next step is to choose functions, predicates, and constants to represent them. We will start from individual gates and move up to circuits.

First, we need to be able to distinguish a gate from other gates. This is handled by naming gates with constants: $X_1, X_2$, and so on. Although each gate is connected into the circuit in its own individual way, its *behavior*—the way it transforms input signals into output signals—depends only on its *type*. We can use a function to refer to the type of the gate.[11] For example, we can write $Type(X_1) = XOR$. This introduces the constant $XOR$ for a particular type of gate; the other constants will be called $OR$, $AND$, and $NOT$. The $Type$ function is not the only way to encode the ontological distinction. We could have used a binary predicate, $Type(X_1, XOR)$, or several individual type predicates, such as $XOR(X_1)$. Either of these choices would work fine, but by choosing the function $Type$, we avoid the need for an axiom which says that each individual gate can have only one type. The semantics of functions already guarantees this.

Next we consider terminals. A gate or circuit can have one or more input terminals and one or more output terminals. We could simply name each one with a constant, just as we named gates. Thus, gate $X_1$ could have terminals named $X_1In_1$, $X_1In_2$, and $X_1Out_1$. The tendency to generate long compound names should be avoided, however. Calling something $X_1In_1$ does not make it the first input of $X_1$; we would still need to say this using an explicit assertion. It is probably better to name the gate using a function, just as we named King John's left leg $LeftLeg(John)$. Thus, let $In(1, X_1)$ denote the first input terminal for gate $X_1$. A similar function $Out$ is used for output terminals.

The connectivity between gates can be represented by the predicate $Connected$, which takes two terminals as arguments, as in $Connected(Out(1, X_1), In(1, X_2))$.

Finally, we need to know whether a signal is on or off. One possibility is to use a unary predicate, $On$, which is true when the signal at a terminal is on. This makes it a little difficult, however, to pose questions such as "What are all the possible values of the signals at the output terminals of circuit C1 ?" We will therefore introduce as objects two "signal values" 1 and 0, and a function $Signal$ that takes a terminal as argument and denotes the signal value for that terminal.

### Encode general knowledge of the domain

One sign that we have a good ontology is that there are very few general rules which need to be specified. A sign that we have a good vocabulary is that each rule can be stated clearly and concisely. With our example, we need only seven simple rules to describe everything we need to know about circuits:

1. If two terminals are connected, then they have the same signal:
   $\forall t_1, t_2 \;\; Connected(t_1, t_2) \Rightarrow Signal(t_1) = Signal(t_2)$
2. The signal at every terminal is either 1 or 0 (but not both):
   $\forall t \;\; Signal(t) = 1 \lor Signal(t) = 0$
   $1 \neq 0$
3. Connected is a commutative predicate:
   $\forall t_1, t_2 \;\; Connected(t_1, t_2) \Leftrightarrow Connected(t_2, t_1)$
4. An OR gate's output is 1 if and only if any of its inputs is 1:
   $\forall g \;\; Type(g) = OR \Rightarrow$
   $\quad Signal(Out(1, g)) = 1 \Leftrightarrow \exists n \;\; Signal(In(n, g)) = 1$

[11] Note that we have used names beginning with appropriate letters—$A_1$, $X_1$, and so on—purely to make the example easier to read. The knowledge base must still contain type information for the gates.

5. An AND gate's output is 0 if and only if any of its inputs is 0:
$$\forall g \;\; Type(g) = AND \Rightarrow$$
$$Signal(Out(1,g)) = 0 \Leftrightarrow \exists n \;\; Signal(In(n,g)) = 0$$
6. An XOR gate's output is 1 if and only if its inputs are different:
$$\forall g \;\; Type(g) = XOR \Rightarrow$$
$$Signal(Out(1,g)) = 1 \Leftrightarrow Signal(In(1,g)) \neq Signal(In(2,g))$$
7. A NOT gate's output is different from its input:
$$\forall g \;\; (Type(g) = NOT) \Rightarrow Signal(Out(1,g)) \neq Signal(In(1,g))$$

**Encode the specific problem instance**

The circuit shown in Figure 8.4 is encoded as circuit $C_1$ with the following description. First, we categorize the gates:

$$\begin{array}{ll} Type(X_1) = XOR & Type(X_2) = XOR \\ Type(A_1) = AND & Type(A_2) = AND \\ Type(O_1) = OR & \end{array}$$

Then, we show the connections between them:

$$\begin{array}{ll} Connected(Out(1,X_1), In(1,X_2)) & Connected(In(1,C_1), In(1,X_1)) \\ Connected(Out(1,X_1), In(2,A_2)) & Connected(In(1,C_1), In(1,A_1)) \\ Connected(Out(1,A_2), In(1,O_1)) & Connected(In(2,C_1), In(2,X_1)) \\ Connected(Out(1,A_1), In(2,O_1)) & Connected(In(2,C_1), In(2,A_1)) \\ Connected(Out(1,X_2), Out(1,C_1)) & Connected(In(3,C_1), In(2,X_2)) \\ Connected(Out(1,O_1), Out(2,C_1)) & Connected(In(3,C_1), In(1,A_2)) . \end{array}$$

**Pose queries to the inference procedure**

What combinations of inputs would cause the first output of $C_1$ (the sum bit) to be 0 and the second output of $C_1$ (the carry bit) to be 1?

$$\exists i_1, i_2, i_3 \;\; Signal(In(1,C_1)) = i_1 \wedge Signal(In(2,C_1)) = i_2 \wedge Signal(In(3,C_1)) = i_3$$
$$\wedge \; Signal(Out(1,C_1)) = 0 \wedge Signal(Out(2,C_1)) = 1 .$$

The answers are substitutions for the variables $i_1$, $i_2$, and $i_3$ such that the resulting sentence is entailed by the knowledge base. There are three such substitutions:

$$\{i_1/1,\, i_2/1,\, i_3/0\} \quad \{i_1/1,\, i_2/0,\, i_3/1\} \quad \{i_1/0,\, i_2/1,\, i_3/1\} .$$

What are the possible sets of values of all the terminals for the adder circuit?

$$\exists i_1, i_2, i_3, o_1, o_2 \;\; Signal(In(1,C_1)) = i_1 \wedge Signal(In(2,C_1)) = i_2$$
$$\wedge \; Signal(In(3,C_1)) = i_3 \wedge Signal(Out(1,C_1)) = o_1 \wedge Signal(Out(2,C_1)) = o_2 .$$

This final query will return a complete input–output table for the device, which can be used to check that it does in fact add its inputs correctly. This is a simple example of **circuit verification**. We can also use the definition of the circuit to build larger digital systems, for which the same kind of verification procedure can be carried out. (See Exercise 8.17.) Many domains are amenable to the same kind of structured knowledge-base development, in which more complex concepts are defined on top of simpler concepts.

### Debug the knowledge base

We can perturb the knowledge base in various ways to see what kinds of erroneous behaviors emerge. For example, suppose we omit the assertion that $1 \neq 0$.[12] Suddenly, the system will be unable to prove any outputs for the circuit, except for the input cases 000 and 110. We can pinpoint the problem by asking for the outputs of each gate. For example, we can ask

$$\exists\, i_1, i_2, o \;\; Signal(In(1, C_1)) = i_1 \wedge Signal(In(2, C_1)) = i_2 \wedge Signal(Out(1, X_1))$$

which reveals that no outputs are known at $X_1$ for the input cases 10 and 01. Then, we look at the axiom for XOR gates, as applied to $X_1$:

$$Signal(Out(1, X_1)) = 1 \;\Leftrightarrow\; Signal(In(1, X_1)) \neq Signal(In(2, X_1))\,.$$

If the inputs are known to be, say, 1 and 0, then this reduces to

$$Signal(Out(1, X_1)) = 1 \;\Leftrightarrow\; 1 \neq 0\,.$$

Now the problem is apparent: the system is unable to infer that $Signal(Out(1, X_1)) = 1$, so we need to tell it that $1 \neq 0$.

## 8.5 SUMMARY

This chapter has introduced **first-order logic**, a representation language that is far more powerful than propositional logic. The important points are as follows:

- Knowledge representation languages should be declarative, compositional, expressive, context-independent, and unambiguous.
- Logics differ in their **ontological commitments** and **epistemological commitments**. While propositional logic commits only to the existence of facts, first-order logic commits to the existence of objects and relations and thereby gains expressive power.
- A **possible world**, or **model**, for first-order logic is defined by a set of objects, the relations among them, and the functions that can be applied to them.
- **Constant symbols** name objects, **predicate symbols** name relations, and **function symbols** name functions. An **interpretation** specifies a mapping from symbols to the model. **Complex terms** apply function symbols to terms to name an object. Given an interpretation and a model, the truth of a sentence is determined.
- An **atomic sentence** consists of a predicate applied to one or more terms; it is true just when the relation named by the predicate holds between the objects named by the terms. **Complex sentences** use connectives just like propositional logic, and **quantified sentences** allow the expression of general rules.
- Developing a knowledge base in first-order logic requires a careful process of analyzing the domain, choosing a vocabulary, and encoding the axioms required to support the desired inferences.

[12] This kind of omission is quite common because humans typically assume that different names refer to different things. Logic programming systems, described in Chapter 9, also make this assumption.

## Bibliographical and Historical Notes

Although even Aristotle's logic deals with generalizations over objects, true first-order logic dates from the introduction of quantifiers in Gottlob Frege's (1879) *Begriffschrift* ("Concept Writing" or "Conceptual Notation"). Frege's ability to nest quantifiers was a big step forward, but he used an awkward notation. (An example appears on the front cover of this book.) The present notation for first-order logic is due substantially to Giuseppe Peano (1889), but the semantics is virtually identical to Frege's. Oddly enough, Peano's axioms were due in large measure to Grassmann (1861) and Dedekind (1888).

A major barrier to the development of first-order logic had been the concentration on one-place predicates to the exclusion of many-place relational predicates. This fixation on one-place predicates had been nearly universal in logical systems from Aristotle up to and including Boole. The first systematic treatment of relations was given by Augustus De Morgan (1864), who cited the following example to show the sorts of inferences that Aristotle's logic could not handle: "All horses are animals; therefore, the head of a horse is the head of an animal." This inference is inaccessible to Aristotle because any valid rule that can support this inference must first analyze the sentence using the two-place predicate "$x$ is the head of $y$." The logic of relations was studied in depth by Charles Sanders Peirce (1870), who also developed first-order logic independently of Frege, although slightly later (Peirce, 1883).

Leopold Löwenheim (1915) gave a systematic treatment of model theory for first-order logic in 1915. This paper also treated the equality symbol as an integral part of logic. Löwenheim's results were further extended by Thoralf Skolem (1920). Alfred Tarski (1935, 1956) gave an explicit definition of truth and model-theoretic satisfaction in first-order logic, using set theory.

McCarthy (1958) was primarily responsible for the introduction of first-order logic as a tool for building AI systems. The prospects for logic-based AI were advanced significantly by Robinson's (1965) development of resolution, a complete procedure for first-order inference described in Chapter 9. The logicist approach took root at Stanford. Cordell Green (1969a, 1969b) developed a first-order reasoning system, QA3, leading to the first attempts to build a logical robot at SRI (Fikes and Nilsson, 1971). First-order logic was applied by Zohar Manna and Richard Waldinger (1971) for reasoning about programs and later by Michael Genesereth (1984) for reasoning about circuits. In Europe, logic programming (a restricted form of first-order reasoning) was developed for linguistic analysis (Colmerauer *et al.*, 1973) and for general declarative systems (Kowalski, 1974). Computational logic was also well entrenched at Edinburgh through the LCF (Logic for Computable Functions) project (Gordon *et al.*, 1979). These developments are chronicled further in Chapters 9 and 10.

There are a number of good modern introductory texts on first-order logic. Quine (1982) is one of the most readable. Enderton (1972) gives a more mathematically oriented perspective. A highly formal treatment of first-order logic, along with many more advanced topics in logic, is provided by Bell and Machover (1977). Manna and Waldinger (1985) give a readable introduction to logic from a computer science perspective. Gallier (1986) provides an extremely rigorous mathematical exposition of first-order logic, along with a great deal of material on its use in automated reasoning. *Logical Foundations of Artificial Intelligence* (Genesereth and Nilsson, 1987) provides both a solid introduction to logic and the first systematic treatment of logical agents with percepts and actions.

## EXERCISES

**8.1** A logical knowledge base represents the world using a set of sentences with no explicit structure. An **analogical** representation, on the other hand, has physical structure that corresponds directly to the structure of the thing represented. Consider a road map of your country as an analogical representation of facts about the country. The two-dimensional structure of the map corresponds to the two-dimensional surface of the area.

**a.** Give five examples of *symbols* in the map language.

**b.** An *explicit* sentence is a sentence that the creator of the representation actually writes down. An *implicit* sentence is a sentence that results from explicit sentences because of properties of the analogical representation. Give three examples each of *implicit* and *explicit* sentences in the map language.

**c.** Give three examples of facts about the physical structure of your country that cannot be represented in the map language.

**d.** Give two examples of facts that are much easier to express in the map language than in first-order logic.

**e.** Give two other examples of useful analogical representations. What are the advantages and disadvantages of each of these languages?

**8.2** Consider a knowledge base containing just two sentences: $P(a)$ and $P(b)$. Does this knowledge base entail $\forall\, x\ P(x)$? Explain your answer in terms of models.

**8.3** Is the sentence $\exists\, x, y\ \ x = y$ valid? Explain.

**8.4** Write down a logical sentence such that every world in which it is true contains exactly one object.

**8.5** Consider a symbol vocabulary that contains $c$ constant symbols, $p_k$ predicate symbols of each arity $k$, and $f_k$ function symbols of each arity $k$, where $1 \leq k \leq A$. Let the domain size be fixed at $D$. For any given interpretation–model combination, each predicate or function symbol is mapped onto a relation or function, respectively, of the same arity. You may assume that the functions in the model allow some input tuples to have no value for the function (i.e., the value is the invisible object). Derive a formula for the number of possible interpretation–model combinations for a domain with $D$ elements. Don't worry about eliminating redundant combinations.

**8.6** Represent the following sentences in first-order logic, using a consistent vocabulary (which you must define):

**a.** Some students took French in spring 2001.

**b.** Every student who takes French passes it.

**c.** Only one student took Greek in spring 2001.

**d.** The best score in Greek is always higher than the best score in French.

**e.** Every person who buys a policy is smart.

**f.** No person buys an expensive policy.

**g.** There is an agent who sells policies only to people who are not insured.

**h.** There is a barber who shaves all men in town who do not shave themselves.

**i.** A person born in the UK, each of whose parents is a UK citizen or a UK resident, is a UK citizen by birth.

**j.** A person born outside the UK, one of whose parents is a UK citizen by birth, is a UK citizen by descent.

**k.** Politicians can fool some of the people all of the time, and they can fool all of the people some of the time, but they can't fool all of the people all of the time.

**8.7** Represent the sentence "All Germans speak the same languages" in predicate calculus. Use $\mathit{Speaks}(x, l)$, meaning that person $x$ speaks language $l$.

**8.8** What axiom is needed to infer the fact $\mathit{Female}(\mathit{Laura})$ given the facts $\mathit{Male}(\mathit{Jim})$ and $\mathit{Spouse}(\mathit{Jim}, \mathit{Laura})$?

**8.9** Write a general set of facts and axioms to represent the assertion "Wellington heard about Napoleon's death" and to correctly answer the question "Did Napoleon hear about Wellington's death?"

**8.10** Rewrite the propositional wumpus world facts from Section 7.5 into first-order logic. How much more compact is this version?

**8.11** Write axioms describing the predicates *GrandChild*, *GreatGrandparent*, *Brother*, *Sister*, *Daughter*, *Son*, *Aunt*, *Uncle*, *BrotherInLaw*, *SisterInLaw*, and *FirstCousin*. Find out the proper definition of $m$th cousin $n$ times removed, and write the definition in first-order logic.

Now write down the basic facts depicted in the family tree in Figure 8.5. Using a suitable logical reasoning system, TELL it all the sentences you have written down, and ASK it who are Elizabeth's grandchildren, Diana's brothers-in-law, and Zara's great-grandparents.

**8.12** Write down a sentence asserting that + is a commutative function. Does your sentence follow from the Peano axioms? If so, explain why; if not, give a model in which the axioms are true and your sentence is false.

**8.13** Explain what is wrong with the following proposed definition of the set membership predicate $\in$ :

$$\forall x, s \;\; x \in \{x|s\}$$
$$\forall x, s \;\; x \in s \Rightarrow \forall y \;\; x \in \{y|s\} .$$

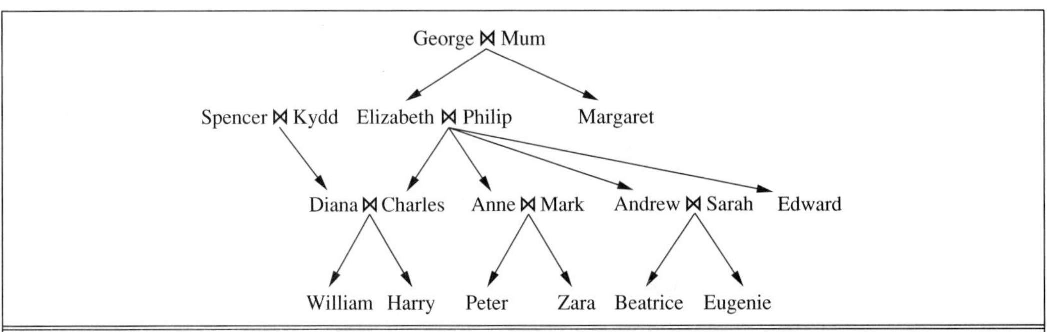


**Figure 8.5** A typical family tree. The symbol "⋈" connects spouses and arrows point to children.

**8.14** Using the set axioms as examples, write axioms for the list domain, including all the constants, functions, and predicates mentioned in the chapter.

**8.15** Explain what is wrong with the following proposed definition of adjacent squares in the wumpus world:

$$\forall x, y \;\; Adjacent([x, y], [x+1, y]) \land Adjacent([x, y], [x, y+1]) \, .$$

**8.16** Write out the axioms required for reasoning about the wumpus's location, using a constant symbol *Wumpus* and a binary predicate *In*(*Wumpus*, *Location*). Remember that there is only one wumpus.

**8.17** Extend the vocabulary from Section 8.4 to define addition for $n$-bit binary numbers. Then encode the description of the four-bit adder in Figure 8.6, and pose the queries needed to verify that it is in fact correct.

**8.18** The circuit representation in the chapter is more detailed than necessary if we care only about circuit functionality. A simpler formulation describes any $m$-input, $n$-output gate or circuit using a predicate with $m+n$ arguments, such that the predicate is true exactly when

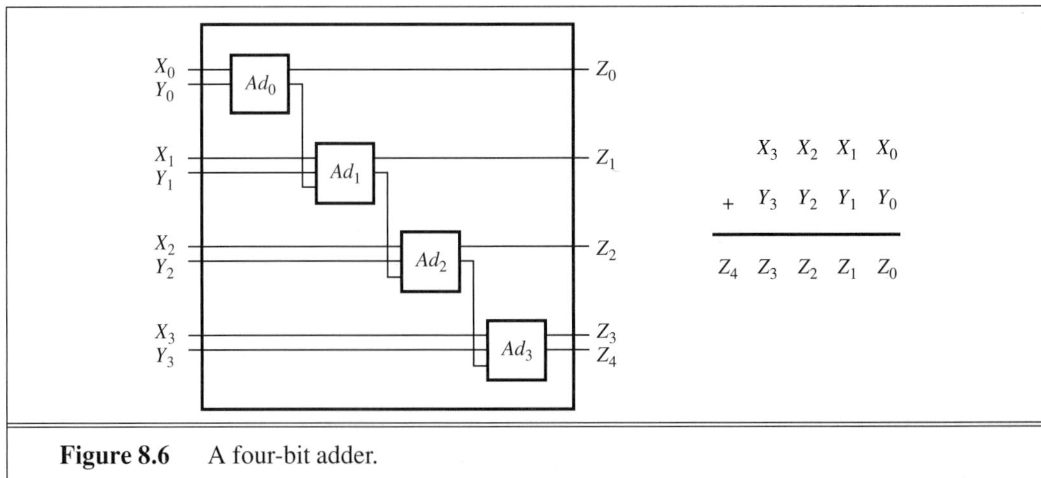


**Figure 8.6** A four-bit adder.

the inputs and outputs are consistent. For example, NOT-gates are described by the binary predicate $NOT(i, o)$, for which $NOT(0, 1)$ and $NOT(1, 0)$ are known. Compositions of gates are defined by conjunctions of gate predicates in which shared variables indicate direct connections. For example, a NAND circuit can be composed from $AND$s and $NOT$s:

$$\forall\, i_1, i_2, o_a, o \;\; NAND(i_1, i_2, o) \Leftarrow AND(i_1, i_2, o_a) \land NOT(o_a, o)\,.$$

Using this representation, define the one-bit adder in Figure 8.4 and the four-bit adder in Figure 8.6, and explain what queries you would use to verify the designs. What kinds of queries are *not* supported by this representation that *are* supported by the representation in Section 8.4?

**8.19** Obtain a passport application for your country, identify the rules determining eligibility for a passport, and translate them into first-order logic, following the steps outlined in Section 8.4.

# 9 INFERENCE IN FIRST-ORDER LOGIC

*In which we define effective procedures for answering questions posed in first-order logic.*

Chapter 7 defined the notion of **inference** and showed how sound and complete inference can be achieved for propositional logic. In this chapter, we extend those results to obtain algorithms that can answer any answerable question stated in first-order logic. This is significant, because more or less anything can be stated in first-order logic if you work hard enough at it.

Section 9.1 introduces inference rules for quantifiers and shows how to reduce first-order inference to propositional inference, albeit at great expense. Section 9.2 describes the idea of **unification**, showing how it can be used to construct inference rules that work directly with first-order sentences. We then discuss three major families of first-order inference algorithms: **forward chaining** and its applications to **deductive databases** and **production systems** are covered in Section 9.3; **backward chaining** and **logic programming** systems are developed in Section 9.4; and resolution-based **theorem-proving** systems are described in Section 9.5. In general, one tries to use the most efficient method that can accommodate the facts and axioms that need to be expressed. Reasoning with fully general first-order sentences using resolution is usually less efficient than reasoning with definite clauses using forward or backward chaining.

## 9.1 PROPOSITIONAL VS. FIRST-ORDER INFERENCE

This section and the next introduce the ideas underlying modern logical inference systems. We begin with some simple inference rules that can be applied to sentences with quantifiers to obtain sentences without quantifiers. These rules lead naturally to the idea that *first-order* inference can be done by converting the knowledge base to *propositional* logic and using *propositional* inference, which we already know how to do. The next section points out an obvious shortcut, leading to inference methods that manipulate first-order sentences directly.

### Inference rules for quantifiers

Let us begin with universal quantifiers. Suppose our knowledge base contains the standard folkloric axiom stating that all greedy kings are evil:

$$\forall x \;\; King(x) \land Greedy(x) \;\Rightarrow\; Evil(x) .$$

Then it seems quite permissible to infer any of the following sentences:

$$King(John) \land Greedy(John) \;\Rightarrow\; Evil(John) .$$
$$King(Richard) \land Greedy(Richard) \;\Rightarrow\; Evil(Richard) .$$
$$King(Father(John)) \land Greedy(Father(John)) \;\Rightarrow\; Evil(Father(John)) .$$
$$\vdots$$

UNIVERSAL INSTANTIATION

The rule of **Universal Instantiation** (UI for short) says that we can infer any sentence obtained by substituting a **ground term** (a term without variables) for the variable.[1] To write out the inference rule formally, we use the notion of **substitutions** introduced in Section 8.3. Let $\text{SUBST}(\theta, \alpha)$ denote the result of applying the substitution $\theta$ to the sentence $\alpha$. Then the rule is written

$$\frac{\forall v \;\; \alpha}{\text{SUBST}(\{v/g\}, \alpha)}$$

for any variable $v$ and ground term $g$. For example, the three sentences given earlier are obtained with the substitutions $\{x/John\}$, $\{x/Richard\}$, and $\{x/Father(John)\}$.

EXISTENTIAL INSTANTIATION

The corresponding **Existential Instantiation** rule for the existential quantifier is slightly more complicated. For any sentence $\alpha$, variable $v$, and constant symbol $k$ that does not appear elsewhere in the knowledge base,

$$\frac{\exists v \;\; \alpha}{\text{SUBST}(\{v/k\}, \alpha)} .$$

For example, from the sentence

$$\exists x \;\; Crown(x) \land OnHead(x, John)$$

we can infer the sentence

$$Crown(C_1) \land OnHead(C_1, John)$$

as long as $C_1$ does not appear elsewhere in the knowledge base. Basically, the existential sentence says there is some object satisfying a condition, and the instantiation process is just giving a name to that object. Naturally, that name must not already belong to another object. Mathematics provides a nice example: suppose we discover that there is a number that is a little bigger than 2.71828 and that satisfies the equation $d(x^y)/dy = x^y$ for $x$. We can give this number a name, such as $e$, but it would be a mistake to give it the name of an existing object, such as $\pi$. In logic, the new name is called a **Skolem constant**. Existential Instantiation is a special case of a more general process called **skolemization**, which we cover in Section 9.5.

SKOLEM CONSTANT

[1] Do not confuse these substitutions with the extended interpretations used to define the semantics of quantifiers. The substitution replaces a variable with a term (a piece of syntax) to produce a new sentence, whereas an interpretation maps a variable to an object in the domain.

As well as being more complicated than Universal Instantiation, Existential Instantiation plays a slightly different role in inference. Whereas Universal Instantiation can be applied many times to produce many different consequences, Existential Instantiation can be applied once, and then the existentially quantified sentence can be discarded. For example, once we have added the sentence $Kill(Murderer, Victim)$, we no longer need the sentence $\exists\, x\ Kill(x, Victim)$. Strictly speaking, the new knowledge base is not logically equivalent to the old, but it can be shown to be **inferentially equivalent** in the sense that it is satisfiable exactly when the original knowledge base is satisfiable.

INFERENTIAL EQUIVALENCE

### Reduction to propositional inference

Once we have rules for inferring nonquantified sentences from quantified sentences, it becomes possible to reduce first-order inference to propositional inference. In this section we will give the main ideas; the details are given in Section 9.5.

The first idea is that, just as an existentially quantified sentence can be replaced by one instantiation, a universally quantified sentence can be replaced by the set of *all possible* instantiations. For example, suppose our knowledge base contains just the sentences

$$\begin{array}{l} \forall\, x\ \ King(x) \land Greedy(x)\ \Rightarrow\ Evil(x) \\ King(John) \\ Greedy(John) \\ Brother(Richard, John)\ . \end{array} \tag{9.1}$$

Then we apply UI to the first sentence using all possible ground term substitutions from the vocabulary of the knowledge base—in this case, $\{x/John\}$ and $\{x/Richard\}$. We obtain

$$\begin{array}{l} King(John) \land Greedy(John)\ \Rightarrow\ Evil(John)\ , \\ King(Richard) \land Greedy(Richard)\ \Rightarrow\ Evil(Richard)\ , \end{array}$$

and we discard the universally quantified sentence. Now, the knowledge base is essentially propositional if we view the ground atomic sentences—$King(John)$, $Greedy(John)$, and so on—as proposition symbols. Therefore, we can apply any of the complete propositional algorithms in Chapter 7 to obtain conclusions such as $Evil(John)$.

PROPOSITIONALIZATION

This technique of **propositionalization** can be made completely general, as we show in Section 9.5; that is, every first-order knowledge base and query can be propositionalized in such a way that entailment is preserved. Thus, we have a complete decision procedure for entailment ... or perhaps not. There is a problem: When the knowledge base includes a function symbol, the set of possible ground term substitutions is infinite! For example, if the knowledge base mentions the $Father$ symbol, then infinitely many nested terms such as $Father(Father(Father(John)))$ can be constructed. Our propositional algorithms will have difficulty with an infinitely large set of sentences.

Fortunately, there is a famous theorem due to Jacques Herbrand (1930) to the effect that if a sentence is entailed by the original, first-order knowledge base, then there is a proof involving just a *finite* subset of the propositionalized knowledge base. Since any such subset has a maximum depth of nesting among its ground terms, we can find the subset by first generating all the instantiations with constant symbols ($Richard$ and $John$), then all terms of depth 1 ($Father(Richard)$ and $Father(John)$), then all terms of depth 2, and so on, until we are able to construct a propositional proof of the entailed sentence.

We have sketched an approach to first-order inference via propositionalization that is **complete**—that is, any entailed sentence can be proved. This is a major achievement, given that the space of possible models is infinite. On the other hand, we do not know until the proof is done that the sentence *is* entailed! What happens when the sentence is *not* entailed? Can we tell? Well, for first-order logic, it turns out that we cannot. Our proof procedure can go on and on, generating more and more deeply nested terms, but we will not know whether it is stuck in a hopeless loop or whether the proof is just about to pop out. This is very much like the halting problem for Turing machines. Alan Turing (1936) and Alonzo Church (1936) both proved, in rather different ways, the inevitability of this state of affairs. *The question of entailment for first-order logic is* ***semidecidable****—that is, algorithms exist that say yes to every entailed sentence, but no algorithm exists that also says no to every nonentailed sentence.*

## 9.2 UNIFICATION AND LIFTING

The preceding section described the understanding of first-order inference that existed up to the early 1960s. The sharp-eyed reader (and certainly the computational logicians of the early 1960s) will have noticed that the propositionalization approach is rather inefficient. For example, given the query $Evil(x)$ and the knowledge base in Equation (9.1), it seems perverse to generate sentences such as $King(Richard) \land Greedy(Richard) \Rightarrow Evil(Richard)$. Indeed, the inference of $Evil(John)$ from the sentences

$$\forall x \;\; King(x) \land Greedy(x) \;\Rightarrow\; Evil(x)$$
$$King(John)$$
$$Greedy(John)$$

seems completely obvious to a human being. We now show how to make it completely obvious to a computer.

### A first-order inference rule

The inference that John is evil works like this: find some $x$ such that $x$ is a king and $x$ is greedy, and then infer that this $x$ is evil. More generally, if there is some substitution $\theta$ that makes the premise of the implication identical to sentences already in the knowledge base, then we can assert the conclusion of the implication, after applying $\theta$. In this case, the substitution $\{x/John\}$ achieves that aim.

We can actually make the inference step do even more work. Suppose that instead of knowing $Greedy(John)$, we know that *everyone* is greedy:

$$\forall y \;\; Greedy(y) \,. \tag{9.2}$$

Then we would still like to be able to conclude that $Evil(John)$, because we know that John is a king (given) and John is greedy (because everyone is greedy). What we need for this to work is find a substitution both for the variables in the implication sentence and for the variables in the sentences to be matched. In this case, applying the substitution $\{x/John, y/John\}$ to the implication premises $King(x)$ and $Greedy(x)$ and the knowledge base sentences $King(John)$ and $Greedy(y)$ will make them identical. Thus, we can infer the conclusion of the implication.

GENERALIZED MODUS PONENS

This inference process can be captured as a single inference rule that we call **Generalized Modus Ponens**: For atomic sentences $p_i$, $p_i{}'$, and $q$, where there is a substitution $\theta$ such that $\text{SUBST}(\theta, p_i{}') = \text{SUBST}(\theta, p_i)$, for all $i$,

$$\frac{p_1{}',\ p_2{}',\ \ldots,\ p_n{}',\ (p_1 \wedge p_2 \wedge \ldots \wedge p_n \Rightarrow q)}{\text{SUBST}(\theta, q)}\ .$$

There are $n+1$ premises to this rule: the $n$ atomic sentences $p_i{}'$ and the one implication. The conclusion is the result of applying the substitution $\theta$ to the consequent $q$. For our example:

$p_1{}'$ is $King(John)$ $\qquad$ $p_1$ is $King(x)$
$p_2{}'$ is $Greedy(y)$ $\qquad$ $p_2$ is $Greedy(x)$
$\theta$ is $\{x/John, y/John\}$ $\qquad$ $q$ is $Evil(x)$
$\text{SUBST}(\theta, q)$ is $Evil(John)$ .

It is easy to show that Generalized Modus Ponens is a sound inference rule. First, we observe that, for any sentence $p$ (whose variables are assumed to be universally quantified) and for any substitution $\theta$,

$$p \models \text{SUBST}(\theta, p)\ .$$

This holds for the same reasons that the Universal Instantiation rule holds. It holds in particular for a $\theta$ that satisfies the conditions of the Generalized Modus Ponens rule. Thus, from $p_1{}', \ldots, p_n{}'$ we can infer

$$\text{SUBST}(\theta, p_1{}') \wedge \ldots \wedge \text{SUBST}(\theta, p_n{}')$$

and from the implication $p_1 \wedge \ldots \wedge p_n \Rightarrow q$ we can infer

$$\text{SUBST}(\theta, p_1) \wedge \ldots \wedge \text{SUBST}(\theta, p_n) \ \Rightarrow\ \text{SUBST}(\theta, q)\ .$$

Now, $\theta$ in Generalized Modus Ponens is defined so that $\text{SUBST}(\theta, p_i{}') = \text{SUBST}(\theta, p_i)$, for all $i$; therefore the first of these two sentences matches the premise of the second exactly. Hence, $\text{SUBST}(\theta, q)$ follows by Modus Ponens.

LIFTING

Generalized Modus Ponens is a **lifted** version of Modus Ponens—it raises Modus Ponens from propositional to first-order logic. We will see in the rest of the chapter that we can develop lifted versions of the forward chaining, backward chaining, and resolution algorithms introduced in Chapter 7. The key advantage of lifted inference rules over propositionalization is that they make only those substitutions which are required to allow particular inferences to proceed. One potentially confusing point is that in one sense Generalized Modus Ponens is less general than Modus Ponens (page 211): Modus Ponens allows any single $\alpha$ on the left-hand side of the implication, while Generalized Modus Ponens requires a special format for this sentence. It is generalized in the sense that it allows any number of $P_i'$.

### Unification

UNIFICATION

Lifted inference rules require finding substitutions that make different logical expressions look identical. This process is called **unification** and is a key component of all first-order

UNIFIER

inference algorithms. The UNIFY algorithm takes two sentences and returns a **unifier** for them if one exists:

$$\text{UNIFY}(p, q) = \theta \text{ where } \text{SUBST}(\theta, p) = \text{SUBST}(\theta, q) .$$

Let us look at some examples of how UNIFY should behave. Suppose we have a query $Knows(John, x)$: whom does John know? Some answers to this query can be found by finding all sentences in the knowledge base that unify with $Knows(John, x)$. Here are the results of unification with four different sentences that might be in the knowledge base.

$$\begin{aligned}
&\text{UNIFY}(Knows(John, x),\ Knows(John, Jane)) = \{x/Jane\}\\
&\text{UNIFY}(Knows(John, x),\ Knows(y, Bill)) = \{x/Bill, y/John\}\\
&\text{UNIFY}(Knows(John, x),\ Knows(y, Mother(y))) = \{y/John, x/Mother(John)\}\\
&\text{UNIFY}(Knows(John, x),\ Knows(x, Elizabeth)) = fail .
\end{aligned}$$

The last unification fails because $x$ cannot take on the values *John* and *Elizabeth* at the same time. Now, remember that $Knows(x, Elizabeth)$ means "Everyone knows Elizabeth," so we *should* be able to infer that John knows Elizabeth. The problem arises only because the two sentences happen to use the same variable name, $x$. The problem can be avoided by **standardizing apart** one of the two sentences being unified, which means renaming its variables to avoid name clashes. For example, we can rename $x$ in $Knows(x, Elizabeth)$ to $z_{17}$ (a new variable name) without changing its meaning. Now the unification will work:

STANDARDIZING APART

$$\text{UNIFY}(Knows(John, x),\ Knows(z_{17}, Elizabeth)) = \{x/Elizabeth, z_{17}/John\} .$$

Exercise 9.7 delves further into the need for standardizing apart.

There is one more complication: we said that UNIFY should return a substitution that makes the two arguments look the same. But there could be more than one such unifier. For example, $\text{UNIFY}(Knows(John, x), Knows(y, z))$ could return $\{y/John, x/z\}$ or $\{y/John, x/John, z/John\}$. The first unifier gives $Knows(John, z)$ as the result of unification, whereas the second gives $Knows(John, John)$. The second result could be obtained from the first by an additional substitution $\{z/John\}$; we say that the first unifier is *more general* than the second, because it places fewer restrictions on the values of the variables. It turns out that, for every unifiable pair of expressions, there is a single **most general unifier** (or MGU) that is unique up to renaming of variables. In this case it is $\{y/John, x/z\}$.

MOST GENERAL UNIFIER

An algorithm for computing most general unifiers is shown in Figure 9.1. The process is very simple: recursively explore the two expressions simultaneously "side by side," building up a unifier along the way, but failing if two corresponding points in the structures do not match. There is one expensive step: when matching a variable against a complex term, one must check whether the variable itself occurs inside the term; if it does, the match fails because no consistent unifier can be constructed. This so-called **occur check** makes the complexity of the entire algorithm quadratic in the size of the expressions being unified. Some systems, including all logic programming systems, simply omit the occur check and sometimes make unsound inferences as a result; other systems use more complex algorithms with linear-time complexity.

OCCUR CHECK

```
function UNIFY(x, y, θ) returns a substitution to make x and y identical
  inputs: x, a variable, constant, list, or compound
          y, a variable, constant, list, or compound
          θ, the substitution built up so far (optional, defaults to empty)

  if θ = failure then return failure
  else if x = y then return θ
  else if VARIABLE?(x) then return UNIFY-VAR(x, y, θ)
  else if VARIABLE?(y) then return UNIFY-VAR(y, x, θ)
  else if COMPOUND?(x) and COMPOUND?(y) then
     return UNIFY(ARGS[x], ARGS[y], UNIFY(OP[x], OP[y], θ))
  else if LIST?(x) and LIST?(y) then
     return UNIFY(REST[x], REST[y], UNIFY(FIRST[x], FIRST[y], θ))
  else return failure
```

```
function UNIFY-VAR(var, x, θ) returns a substitution
  inputs: var, a variable
          x, any expression
          θ, the substitution built up so far

  if {var/val} ∈ θ then return UNIFY(val, x, θ)
  else if {x/val} ∈ θ then return UNIFY(var, val, θ)
  else if OCCUR-CHECK?(var, x) then return failure
  else return add {var/x} to θ
```

**Figure 9.1** The unification algorithm. The algorithm works by comparing the structures of the inputs, element by element. The substitution $\theta$ that is the argument to UNIFY is built up along the way and is used to make sure that later comparisons are consistent with bindings that were established earlier. In a compound expression, such as $F(A, B)$, the function OP picks out the function symbol $F$ and the function ARGS picks out the argument list $(A, B)$.

### Storage and retrieval

Underlying the TELL and ASK functions used to inform and interrogate a knowledge base are the more primitive STORE and FETCH functions. STORE($s$) stores a sentence $s$ into the knowledge base and FETCH($q$) returns all unifiers such that the query $q$ unifies with some sentence in the knowledge base. The problem we used to illustrate unification—finding all facts that unify with $Knows(John, x)$—is an instance of FETCHing.

The simplest way to implement STORE and FETCH is to keep all the facts in the knowledge base in one long list; then, given a query $q$, call UNIFY$(q, s)$ for every sentence $s$ in the list. Such a process is inefficient, but it works, and it's all you need to understand the rest of the chapter. The remainder of this section outlines ways to make retrieval more efficient, and can be skipped on first reading.

We can make FETCH more efficient by ensuring that unifications are attempted only with sentences that have *some* chance of unifying. For example, there is no point in trying to unify $Knows(John, x)$ with $Brother(Richard, John)$. We can avoid such unifications by **indexing** the facts in the knowledge base. A simple scheme called **predicate indexing** puts all the $Knows$ facts in one bucket and all the $Brother$ facts in another. The buckets can be stored in a hash table[2] for efficient access.

INDEXING

PREDICATE INDEXING

Predicate indexing is useful when there are many predicate symbols but only a few clauses for each symbol. In some applications, however, there are many clauses for a given predicate symbol. For example, suppose that the tax authorities want to keep track of who employs whom, using a predicate $Employs(x, y)$. This would be a very large bucket with perhaps millions of employers and tens of millions of employees. Answering a query such as $Employs(x, Richard)$ with predicate indexing would require scanning the entire bucket.

For this particular query, it would help if facts were indexed both by predicate and by second argument, perhaps using a combined hash table key. Then we could simply construct the key from the query and retrieve exactly those facts that unify with the query. For other queries, such as $Employs(AIMA.org, y)$, we would need to have indexed the facts by combining the predicate with the first argument. Therefore, facts can be stored under multiple index keys, rendering them instantly accessible to various queries that they might unify with.

Given a sentence to be stored, it is possible to construct indices for *all possible* queries that unify with it. For the fact $Employs(AIMA.org, Richard)$, the queries are

| | |
|---|---|
| $Employs(AIMA.org, Richard)$ | Does AIMA.org employ Richard? |
| $Employs(x, Richard)$ | Who employs Richard? |
| $Employs(AIMA.org, y)$ | Whom does AIMA.org employ? |
| $Employs(x, y)$ | Who employs whom? |

SUBSUMPTION LATTICE

These queries form a **subsumption lattice**, as shown in Figure 9.2(a). The lattice has some interesting properties. For example, the child of any node in the lattice is obtained from its parent by a single substitution; and the "highest" common descendant of any two nodes is the result of applying their most general unifier. The portion of the lattice above any ground fact can be constructed systematically (Exercise 9.5). A sentence with repeated constants has a slightly different lattice, as shown in Figure 9.2(b). Function symbols and variables in the sentences to be stored introduce still more interesting lattice structures.

The scheme we have described works very well whenever the lattice contains a small number of nodes. For a predicate with $n$ arguments, the lattice contains $O(2^n)$ nodes. If function symbols are allowed, the number of nodes is also exponential in the size of the terms in the sentence to be stored. This can lead to a huge number of indices. At some point, the benefits of indexing are outweighed by the costs of storing and maintaining all the indices. We can respond by adopting a fixed policy, such as maintaining indices only on keys composed of a predicate plus each argument, or by using an adaptive policy that creates indices to meet the demands of the kinds of queries being asked. For most AI systems, the number of facts to be stored is small enough that efficient indexing is considered a solved problem. For industrial and commercial databases, the problem has received substantial technology development.

2 A hash table is a data structure for storing and retrieving information indexed by fixed *keys*. For practical purposes, a hash table can be considered to have constant storage and retrieval times, even when the table contains a very large number of items.

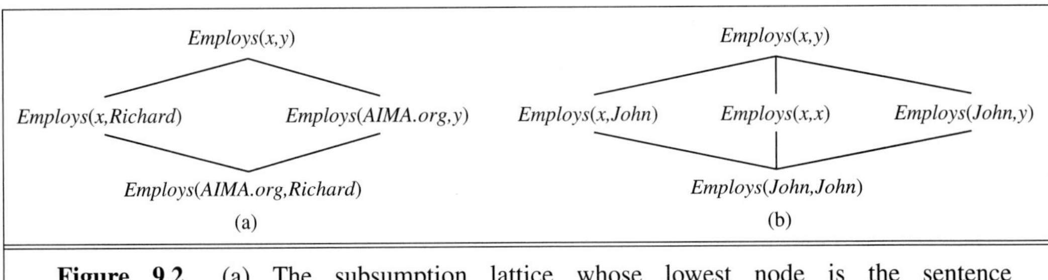


**Figure 9.2** (a) The subsumption lattice whose lowest node is the sentence $Employs(AIMA.org, Richard)$. (b) The subsumption lattice for the sentence $Employs(John, John)$.

## 9.3 FORWARD CHAINING

A forward-chaining algorithm for propositional definite clauses was given in Section 7.5. The idea is simple: start with the atomic sentences in the knowledge base and apply Modus Ponens in the forward direction, adding new atomic sentences, until no further inferences can be made. Here, we explain how the algorithm is applied to first-order definite clauses and how it can be implemented efficiently. Definite clauses such as $Situation \Rightarrow Response$ are especially useful for systems that make inferences in response to newly arrived information. Many systems can be defined this way, and reasoning with forward chaining can be much more efficient than resolution theorem proving. Therefore it is often worthwhile to try to build a knowledge base using only definite clauses so that the cost of resolution can be avoided.

### First-order definite clauses

First-order definite clauses closely resemble propositional definite clauses (page 217): they are disjunctions of literals of which *exactly one is positive*. A definite clause either is atomic or is an implication whose antecedent is a conjunction of positive literals and whose consequent is a single positive literal. The following are first-order definite clauses:

$$King(x) \land Greedy(x) \Rightarrow Evil(x) .$$
$$King(John) .$$
$$Greedy(y) .$$

Unlike propositional literals, first-order literals can include variables, in which case those variables are assumed to be universally quantified. (Typically, we omit universal quantifiers when writing definite clauses.) Definite clauses are a suitable normal form for use with Generalized Modus Ponens.

Not every knowledge base can be converted into a set of definite clauses, because of the single-positive-literal restriction, but many can. Consider the following problem:

> The law says that it is a crime for an American to sell weapons to hostile nations. The country Nono, an enemy of America, has some missiles, and all of its missiles were sold to it by Colonel West, who is American.

We will prove that West is a criminal. First, we will represent these facts as first-order definite clauses. The next section shows how the forward-chaining algorithm solves the problem.

"... it is a crime for an American to sell weapons to hostile nations":

$$American(x) \land Weapon(y) \land Sells(x, y, z) \land Hostile(z) \Rightarrow Criminal(x) . \tag{9.3}$$

"Nono ... has some missiles." The sentence $\exists\, x\ Owns(Nono, x) \land Missile(x)$ is transformed into two definite clauses by Existential Elimination, introducing a new constant $M_1$:

$$Owns(Nono, M_1) \tag{9.4}$$

$$Missile(M_1) \tag{9.5}$$

"All of its missiles were sold to it by Colonel West":

$$Missile(x) \land Owns(Nono, x) \Rightarrow Sells(West, x, Nono) . \tag{9.6}$$

We will also need to know that missiles are weapons:

$$Missile(x) \Rightarrow Weapon(x) \tag{9.7}$$

and we must know that an enemy of America counts as "hostile":

$$Enemy(x, America) \Rightarrow Hostile(x) . \tag{9.8}$$

"West, who is American ...":

$$American(West) . \tag{9.9}$$

"The country Nono, an enemy of America ...":

$$Enemy(Nono, America) . \tag{9.10}$$

DATALOG

This knowledge base contains no function symbols and is therefore an instance of the class of **Datalog** knowledge bases—that is, sets of first-order definite clauses with no function symbols. We will see that the absence of function symbols makes inference much easier.

### A simple forward-chaining algorithm

RENAMING

The first forward chaining algorithm we will consider is a very simple one, as shown in Figure 9.3. Starting from the known facts, it triggers all the rules whose premises are satisfied, adding their conclusions to the known facts. The process repeats until the query is answered (assuming that just one answer is required) or no new facts are added. Notice that a fact is not "new" if it is just a **renaming** of a known fact. One sentence is a renaming of another if they are identical except for the names of the variables. For example, $Likes(x, IceCream)$ and $Likes(y, IceCream)$ are renamings of each other because they differ only in the choice of $x$ or $y$; their meanings are identical: everyone likes ice cream.

We will use our crime problem to illustrate how FOL-FC-ASK works. The implication sentences are (9.3), (9.6), (9.7), and (9.8). Two iterations are required:

- On the first iteration, rule (9.3) has unsatisfied premises.
  Rule (9.6) is satisfied with $\{x/M_1\}$, and $Sells(West, M_1, Nono)$ is added.
  Rule (9.7) is satisfied with $\{x/M_1\}$, and $Weapon(M_1)$ is added.
  Rule (9.8) is satisfied with $\{x/Nono\}$, and $Hostile(Nono)$ is added.

```
function FOL-FC-ASK(KB, α) returns a substitution or false
  inputs: KB, the knowledge base, a set of first-order definite clauses
          α, the query, an atomic sentence
  local variables: new, the new sentences inferred on each iteration

  repeat until new is empty
     new ← { }
     for each sentence r in KB do
        (p1 ∧ ... ∧ pn ⇒ q) ← STANDARDIZE-APART(r)
        for each θ such that SUBST(θ, p1 ∧ ... ∧ pn) = SUBST(θ, p'1 ∧ ... ∧ p'n)
                     for some p'1, ..., p'n in KB
           q' ← SUBST(θ, q)
           if q' is not a renaming of some sentence already in KB or new then do
              add q' to new
              φ ← UNIFY(q', α)
              if φ is not fail then return φ
     add new to KB
  return false
```

**Figure 9.3** A conceptually straightforward, but very inefficient, forward-chaining algorithm. On each iteration, it adds to $KB$ all the atomic sentences that can be inferred in one step from the implication sentences and the atomic sentences already in $KB$.

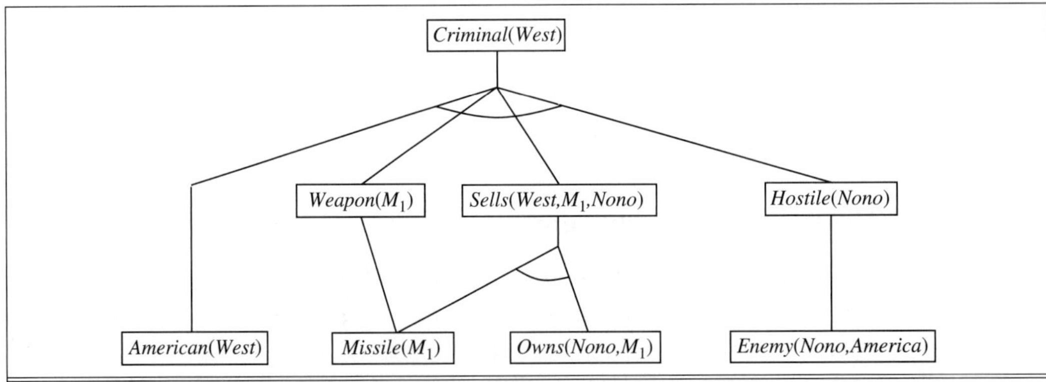


**Figure 9.4** The proof tree generated by forward chaining on the crime example. The initial facts appear at the bottom level, facts inferred on the first iteration in the middle level, and facts inferred on the second iteration at the top level.

- On the second iteration, rule (9.3) is satisfied with $\{x/West, y/M_1, z/Nono\}$, and $Criminal(West)$ is added.

Figure 9.4 shows the proof tree that is generated. Notice that no new inferences are possible at this point because every sentence that could be concluded by forward chaining is already contained explicitly in the KB. Such a knowledge base is called a **fixed point** of the inference process. Fixed points reached by forward chaining with first-order definite clauses are similar to those for propositional forward chaining (page 219); the principal difference is that a first-order fixed point can include universally quantified atomic sentences.

FOL-FC-ASK is easy to analyze. First, it is **sound**, because every inference is just an application of Generalized Modus Ponens, which is sound. Second, it is **complete** for definite clause knowledge bases; that is, it answers every query whose answers are entailed by any knowledge base of definite clauses. For Datalog knowledge bases, which contain no function symbols, the proof of completeness is fairly easy. We begin by counting the number of possible facts that can be added, which determines the maximum number of iterations. Let $k$ be the maximum **arity** (number of arguments) of any predicate, $p$ be the number of predicates, and $n$ be the number of constant symbols. Clearly, there can be no more than $pn^k$ distinct ground facts, so after this many iterations the algorithm must have reached a fixed point. Then we can make an argument very similar to the proof of completeness for propositional forward chaining. (See page 219.) The details of how to make the transition from propositional to first-order completeness are given for the resolution algorithm in Section 9.5.

For general definite clauses with function symbols, FOL-FC-ASK can generate infinitely many new facts, so we need to be more careful. For the case in which an answer to the query sentence $q$ is entailed, we must appeal to Herbrand's theorem to establish that the algorithm will find a proof. (See Section 9.5 for the resolution case.) If the query has no answer, the algorithm could fail to terminate in some cases. For example, if the knowledge base includes the Peano axioms

$$NatNum(0)$$
$$\forall n \;\; NatNum(n) \Rightarrow NatNum(S(n))$$

then forward chaining adds $NatNum(S(0))$, $NatNum(S(S(0)))$, $NatNum(S(S(S(0))))$, and so on. This problem is unavoidable in general. As with general first-order logic, entailment with definite clauses is semidecidable.

### Efficient forward chaining

The forward chaining algorithm in Figure 9.3 is designed for ease of understanding rather than for efficiency of operation. There are three possible sources of complexity. First, the "inner loop" of the algorithm involves finding all possible unifiers such that the premise of a rule unifies with a suitable set of facts in the knowledge base. This is often called **pattern matching** and can be very expensive. Second, the algorithm rechecks every rule on every iteration to see whether its premises are satisfied, even if very few additions are made to the knowledge base on each iteration. Finally, the algorithm might generate many facts that are irrelevant to the goal. We will address each of these sources in turn.

PATTERN MATCHING

#### Matching rules against known facts

The problem of matching the premise of a rule against the facts in the knowledge base might seem simple enough. For example, suppose we want to apply the rule

$$Missile(x) \Rightarrow Weapon(x) \; .$$

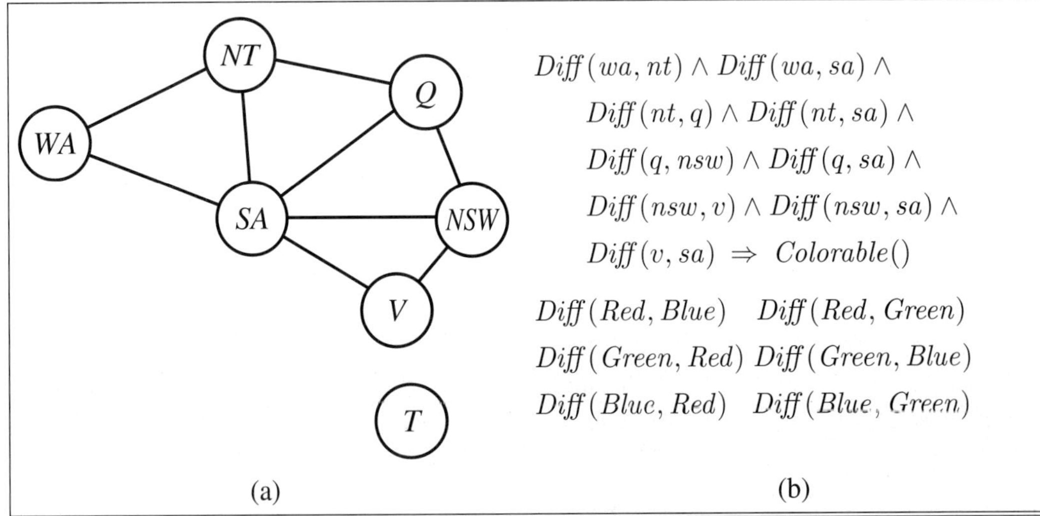


**Figure 9.5** (a) Constraint graph for coloring the map of Australia (from Figure5.1). (b) The map-coloring CSP expressed as a single definite clause. Note that the domains of the variables are defined implicitly by the constants given in the ground facts for $Diff$.

Then we need to find all the facts that unify with $Missile(x)$; in a suitably indexed knowledge base, this can be done in constant time per fact. Now consider a rule such as

$$Missile(x) \land Owns(Nono, x) \Rightarrow Sells(West, x, Nono) .$$

Again, we can find all the objects owned by Nono in constant time per object; then, for each object, we could check whether it is a missile. If the knowledge base contains many objects owned by Nono and very few missiles, however, it would be better to find all the missiles first and then check whether they are owned by Nono. This is the **conjunct ordering** problem: find an ordering to solve the conjuncts of the rule premise so that the total cost is minimized. It turns out that finding the optimal ordering is NP-hard, but good heuristics are available. For example, the **most constrained variable** heuristic used for CSPs in Chapter 5 would suggest ordering the conjuncts to look for missiles first if there are fewer missiles than objects that are owned by Nono.

The connection between pattern matching and constraint satisfaction is actually very close. We can view each conjunct as a constraint on the variables that it contains—for example, $Missile(x)$ is a unary constraint on $x$. Extending this idea, *we can express every finite-domain CSP as a single definite clause together with some associated ground facts.* Consider the map-coloring problem from Figure 5.1, shown again in Figure 9.5(a). An equivalent formulation as a single definite clause is given in Figure 9.5(b). Clearly, the conclusion $Colorable()$ can be inferred only if the CSP has a solution. Because CSPs in general include 3SAT problems as special cases, we can conclude that *matching a definite clause against a set of facts is NP-hard.*

It might seem rather depressing that forward chaining has an NP-hard matching problem in its inner loop. There are three ways to cheer ourselves up:

- We can remind ourselves that most rules in real-world knowledge bases are small and simple (like the rules in our crime example) rather than large and complex (like the CSP formulation in Figure 9.5). It is common in the database world to assume that both the sizes of rules and the arities of predicates are bounded by a constant and to worry only about **data complexity**—that is, the complexity of inference as a function of the number of ground facts in the database. It is easy to show that the data complexity of forward chaining is polynomial.

DATA COMPLEXITY

- We can consider subclasses of rules for which matching is efficient. Essentially every Datalog clause can be viewed as defining a CSP, so matching will be tractable just when the corresponding CSP is tractable. Chapter 5 describes several tractable families of CSPs. For example, if the constraint graph (the graph whose nodes are variables and whose links are constraints) forms a tree, then the CSP can be solved in linear time. Exactly the same result holds for rule matching. For instance, if we remove South Australia from the map in Figure 9.5, the resulting clause is

$$Diff(wa, nt) \land Diff(nt, q) \land Diff(q, nsw) \land Diff(nsw, v) \Rightarrow Colorable()$$

  which corresponds to the reduced CSP shown in Figure 5.11. Algorithms for solving tree-structured CSPs can be applied directly to the problem of rule matching.

- We can work hard to eliminate redundant rule matching attempts in the forward chaining algorithm, which is the subject of the next section.

### Incremental forward chaining

When we showed how forward chaining works on the crime example, we cheated; in particular, we omitted some of the rule matching done by the algorithm shown in Figure 9.3. For example, on the second iteration, the rule

$$Missile(x) \Rightarrow Weapon(x)$$

matches against $Missile(M_1)$ (again), and of course the conclusion $Weapon(M_1)$ is already known so nothing happens. Such redundant rule matching can be avoided if we make the following observation: *Every new fact inferred on iteration $t$ must be derived from at least one new fact inferred on iteration $t-1$.* This is true because any inference that does not require a new fact from iteration $t-1$ could have been done at iteration $t-1$ already.

This observation leads naturally to an incremental forward chaining algorithm where, at iteration $t$, we check a rule only if its premise includes a conjunct $p_i$ that unifies with a fact $p'_i$ newly inferred at iteration $t-1$. The rule matching step then fixes $p_i$ to match with $p'_i$, but allows the other conjuncts of the rule to match with facts from any previous iteration. This algorithm generates exactly the same facts at each iteration as the algorithm in Figure 9.3, but is much more efficient.

With suitable indexing, it is easy to identify all the rules that can be triggered by any given fact, and indeed many real systems operate in an "update" mode wherein forward chaining occurs in response to each new fact that is TELLed to the system. Inferences cascade through the set of rules until the fixed point is reached, and then the process begins again for the next new fact.

Typically, only a small fraction of the rules in the knowledge base are actually triggered by the addition of a given fact. This means that a great deal of redundant work is done in constructing partial matches repeatedly that have some unsatisfied premises. Our crime example is rather too small to show this effectively, but notice that a partial match is constructed on the first iteration between the rule

$$American(x) \land Weapon(y) \land Sells(x, y, z) \land Hostile(z) \Rightarrow Criminal(x)$$

and the fact $American(West)$. This partial match is then discarded and rebuilt on the second iteration (when the rule succeeds). It would be better to retain and gradually complete the partial matches as new facts arrive, rather than discarding them.

RETE

The **rete** algorithm[3] was the first to address this problem seriously. The algorithm preprocesses the set of rules in the knowledge base to construct a sort of dataflow network in which each node is a literal from a rule premise. Variable bindings flow through the network and are filtered out when they fail to match a literal. If two literals in a rule share a variable—for example, $Sells(x, y, z) \land Hostile(z)$ in the crime example—then the bindings from each literal are filtered through an equality node. A variable binding reaching a node for an $n$-ary literal such as $Sells(x, y, z)$ might have to wait for bindings for the other variables to be established before the process can continue. At any given point, the state of a rete network captures all the partial matches of the rules, avoiding a great deal of recomputation.

PRODUCTION SYSTEMS

Rete networks, and various improvements thereon, have been a key component of so-called **production systems**, which were among the earliest forward chaining systems in widespread use.[4] The XCON system (originally called R1, McDermott, 1982) was built using a production system architecture. XCON contained several thousand rules for designing configurations of computer components for customers of the Digital Equipment Corporation. It was one of the first clear commercial successes in the emerging field of expert systems. Many other similar systems have been built using the same underlying technology, which has been implemented in the general-purpose language OPS-5.

COGNITIVE ARCHITECTURES

Production systems are also popular in **cognitive architectures**—that is, models of human reasoning—such as ACT (Anderson, 1983) and SOAR (Laird *et al.*, 1987). In such systems, the "working memory" of the system models human short-term memory, and the productions are part of long-term memory. On each cycle of operation, productions are matched against the working memory of facts. A production whose conditions are satisfied can add or delete facts in working memory. In contrast to the typical situation in databases, production systems often have many rules and relatively few facts. With suitably optimized matching technology, some modern systems can operate in real time with over a million rules.

### Irrelevant facts

The final source of inefficiency in forward chaining appears to be intrinsic to the approach and also arises in the propositional context. (See Section 7.5.) Forward chaining makes all allowable inferences based on the known facts, *even if they are irrelevant to the goal at hand.* In our crime example, there were no rules capable of drawing irrelevant conclusions,

[3] Rete is Latin for net. The English pronunciation rhymes with treaty.

[4] The word **production** in **production systems** denotes a condition–action rule.

so the lack of directedness was not a problem. In other cases (e.g., if we have several rules describing the eating habits of Americans and the prices of missiles), FOL-FC-ASK will generate many irrelevant conclusions.

One way to avoid drawing irrelevant conclusions is to use backward chaining, as described in Section 9.4. Another solution is to restrict forward chaining to a selected subset of rules; this approach was discussed in the propositional context. A third approach has emerged in the deductive database community, where forward chaining is the standard tool. The idea is to rewrite the rule set, using information from the goal, so that only relevant variable bindings—those belonging to a so-called **magic set**—are considered during forward inference. For example, if the goal is $Criminal(West)$, the rule that concludes $Criminal(x)$ will be rewritten to include an extra conjunct that constrains the value of $x$:

MAGIC SET

$$Magic(x) \wedge American(x) \wedge Weapon(y) \wedge Sells(x, y, z) \wedge Hostile(z) \Rightarrow Criminal(x) .$$

The fact $Magic(West)$ is also added to the KB. In this way, even if the knowledge base contains facts about millions of Americans, only Colonel West will be considered during the forward inference process. The complete process for defining magic sets and rewriting the knowledge base is too complex to go into here, but the basic idea is to perform a sort of "generic" backward inference from the goal in order to work out which variable bindings need to be constrained. The magic sets approach can therefore be thought of as a kind of hybrid between forward inference and backward preprocessing.

## 9.4 BACKWARD CHAINING

The second major family of logical inference algorithms uses the **backward chaining** approach introduced in Section 7.5. These algorithms work backward from the goal, chaining through rules to find known facts that support the proof. We describe the basic algorithm, and then we describe how it is used in **logic programming**, which is the most widely used form of automated reasoning. We will also see that backward chaining has some disadvantages compared with forward chaining, and we look at ways to overcome them. Finally, we will look at the close connection between logic programming and constraint satisfaction problems.

### A backward chaining algorithm

Figure 9.6 shows a simple backward-chaining algorithm, FOL-BC-ASK. It is called with a list of goals containing a single element, the original query, and returns the set of all substitutions satisfying the query. The list of goals can be thought of as a "stack" waiting to be worked on; if *all* of them can be satisfied, then the current branch of the proof succeeds. The algorithm takes the first goal in the list and finds every clause in the knowledge base whose positive literal, or **head**, unifies with the goal. Each such clause creates a new recursive call in which the premise, or **body**, of the clause is added to the goal stack. Remember that facts are clauses with a head but no body, so when a goal unifies with a known fact, no new subgoals are added to the stack and the goal is solved. Figure 9.7 is the proof tree for deriving $Criminal(West)$ from sentences (9.3) through (9.10).

```
function FOL-BC-ASK(KB, goals, θ) returns a set of substitutions
  inputs: KB, a knowledge base
          goals, a list of conjuncts forming a query (θ already applied)
          θ, the current substitution, initially the empty substitution { }
  local variables: answers, a set of substitutions, initially empty

  if goals is empty then return {θ}
  q′ ← SUBST(θ, FIRST(goals))
  for each sentence r in KB where STANDARDIZE-APART(r) = (p1 ∧ ... ∧ pn ⇒ q)
        and θ′ ← UNIFY(q, q′) succeeds
     new_goals ← [p1, ..., pn|REST(goals)]
     answers ← FOL-BC-ASK(KB, new_goals, COMPOSE(θ′, θ)) ∪ answers
  return answers
```

**Figure 9.6** A simple backward-chaining algorithm.

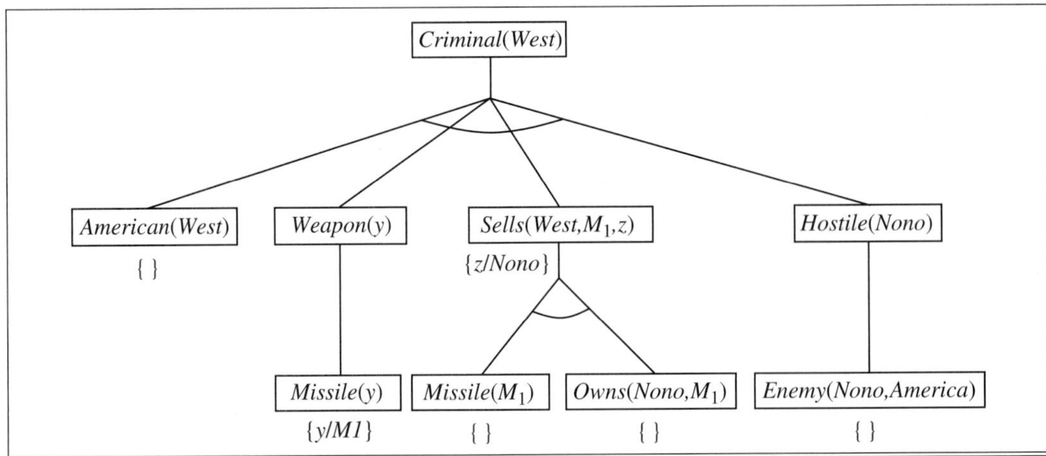


**Figure 9.7** Proof tree constructed by backward chaining to prove that West is a criminal. The tree should be read depth first, left to right. To prove $Criminal(West)$, we have to prove the four conjuncts below it. Some of these are in the knowledge base, and others require further backward chaining. Bindings for each successful unification are shown next to the corresponding subgoal. Note that once one subgoal in a conjunction succeeds, its substitution is applied to subsequent subgoals. Thus, by the time FOL-BC-ASK gets to the last conjunct, originally $Hostile(z)$, $z$ is already bound to $Nono$.

COMPOSITION

The algorithm uses **composition** of substitutions. COMPOSE$(\theta_1, \theta_2)$ is the substitution whose effect is identical to the effect of applying each substitution in turn. That is,

$$\text{SUBST}(\text{COMPOSE}(\theta_1, \theta_2), p) = \text{SUBST}(\theta_2, \text{SUBST}(\theta_1, p)) .$$

In the algorithm, the current variable bindings, which are stored in $\theta$, are composed with the bindings resulting from unifying the goal with the clause head, giving a new set of current bindings for the recursive call.

Backward chaining, as we have written it, is clearly a depth-first search algorithm. This means that its space requirements are linear in the size of the proof (neglecting, for now, the space required to accumulate the solutions). It also means that backward chaining (unlike forward chaining) suffers from problems with repeated states and incompleteness. We will discuss these problems and some potential solutions, but first we will see how backward chaining is used in logic programming systems.

### Logic programming

Logic programming is a technology that comes fairly close to embodying the declarative ideal described in Chapter 7: that systems should be constructed by expressing knowledge in a formal language and that problems should be solved by running inference processes on that knowledge. The ideal is summed up in Robert Kowalski's equation,

$$Algorithm = Logic + Control\ .$$

PROLOG

**Prolog** is by far the most widely used logic programming language. Its users number in the hundreds of thousands. It is used primarily as a rapid-prototyping language and for symbol-manipulation tasks such as writing compilers (Van Roy, 1990) and parsing natural language (Pereira and Warren, 1980). Many expert systems have been written in Prolog for legal, medical, financial, and other domains.

Prolog programs are sets of definite clauses written in a notation somewhat different from standard first-order logic. Prolog uses uppercase letters for variables and lowercase for constants. Clauses are written with the head preceding the body; ":-" is used for left-implication, commas separate literals in the body, and a period marks the end of a sentence:

```
criminal(X) :- american(X), weapon(Y), sells(X,Y,Z), hostile(Z).
```

Prolog includes "syntactic sugar" for list notation and arithmetic. As an example, here is a Prolog program for `append(X,Y,Z)`, which succeeds if list `Z` is the result of appending lists `X` and `Y`:

```
append([],Y,Y).
append([A|X],Y,[A|Z]) :- append(X,Y,Z).
```

In English, we can read these clauses as (1) appending an empty list with a list `Y` produces the same list `Y` and (2) `[A|Z]` is the result of appending `[A|X]` onto `Y`, provided that `Z` is the result of appending `X` onto `Y`. This definition of `append` appears fairly similar to the corresponding definition in Lisp, but is actually much more powerful. For example, we can ask the query `append(A,B,[1,2])`: what two lists can be appended to give `[1,2]`? We get back the solutions

```
A=[]     B=[1,2]
A=[1]    B=[2]
A=[1,2]  B=[]
```

The execution of Prolog programs is done via depth-first backward chaining, where clauses are tried in the order in which they are written in the knowledge base. Some aspects of Prolog fall outside standard logical inference:

- There is a set of built-in functions for arithmetic. Literals using these function symbols are "proved" by executing code rather than doing further inference. For example, the goal "`X is 4+3`" succeeds with `X` bound to 7. On the other hand, the goal "`5 is X+Y`" fails, because the built-in functions do not do arbitrary equation solving.[5]
- There are built-in predicates that have side effects when executed. These include input–output predicates and the `assert/retract` predicates for modifying the knowledge base. Such predicates have no counterpart in logic and can produce some confusing effects—for example, if facts are asserted in a branch of the proof tree that eventually fails.
- Prolog allows a form of negation called **negation as failure**. A negated goal `not P` is considered proved if the system fails to prove `P`. Thus, the sentence

  ```
  alive(X) :- not dead(X).
  ```

  can be read as "Everyone is alive if not provably dead."
- Prolog has an equality operator, =, but it lacks the full power of logical equality. An equality goal succeeds if the two terms are *unifiable* and fails otherwise. So `X+Y=2+3` succeeds with `X` bound to `2` and `Y` bound to `3`, but `morningstar=eveningstar` fails. (In classical logic, the latter equality might or might not be true.) No facts or rules about equality can be asserted.
- The **occur check** is omitted from Prolog's unification algorithm. This means that some unsound inferences can be made; these are seldom a problem except when using Prolog for mathematical theorem proving.

The decisions made in the design of Prolog represent a compromise between declarativeness and execution efficiency—inasmuch as efficiency was understood at the time Prolog was designed. We will return to this subject after looking at how Prolog is implemented.

### Efficient implementation of logic programs

The execution of a Prolog program can happen in two modes: interpreted and compiled. Interpretation essentially amounts to running the FOL-BC-ASK algorithm from Figure 9.6, with the program as the knowledge base. We say "essentially," because Prolog interpreters contain a variety of improvements designed to maximize speed. Here we consider only two.

First, instead of constructing the list of all possible answers for each subgoal before continuing to the next, Prolog interpreters generate one answer and a "promise" to generate the rest when the current answer has been fully explored. This promise is called a **choice point**. When the depth-first search completes its exploration of the possible solutions arising from the current answer and backs up to the choice point, the choice point is expanded to yield a new answer for the subgoal and a new choice point. This approach saves both time and space. It also provides a very simple interface for debugging because at all times there is only a single solution path under consideration.

CHOICE POINT

Second, our simple implementation of FOL-BC-ASK spends a good deal of time generating and composing substitutions. Prolog implements substitutions using logic variables

[5] Note that if the Peano axioms are provided, such goals can be solved by inference within a Prolog program.

**procedure** APPEND($ax, y, az, continuation$)

$trail \leftarrow$ GLOBAL-TRAIL-POINTER()
**if** $ax$ = [ ] and UNIFY($y, az$) **then** CALL($continuation$)
RESET-TRAIL($trail$)
$a \leftarrow$ NEW-VARIABLE(); $x \leftarrow$ NEW-VARIABLE(); $z \leftarrow$ NEW-VARIABLE()
**if** UNIFY($ax, [a \mid x]$) and UNIFY($az, [a \mid z]$) **then** APPEND($x, y, z, continuation$)

**Figure 9.8** Pseudocode representing the result of compiling the `Append` predicate. The function NEW-VARIABLE returns a new variable, distinct from all other variables so far used. The procedure CALL($continuation$) continues execution with the specified continuation.

that can remember their current binding. At any point in time, every variable in the program either is unbound or is bound to some value. Together, these variables and values implicitly define the substitution for the current branch of the proof. Extending the path can only add new variable bindings, because an attempt to add a different binding for an already bound variable results in a failure of unification. When a path in the search fails, Prolog will back up to a previous choice point, and then it might have to unbind some variables. This is done by keeping track of all the variables that have been bound in a stack called the **trail**. As each new variable is bound by UNIFY-VAR, the variable is pushed onto the trail. When a goal fails and it is time to back up to a previous choice point, each of the variables is unbound as it is removed from the trail.

TRAIL

Even the most efficient Prolog interpreters require several thousand machine instructions per inference step because of the cost of index lookup, unification, and building the recursive call stack. In effect, the interpreter always behaves as if it has never seen the program before; for example, it has to *find* clauses that match the goal. A compiled Prolog program, on the other hand, is an inference procedure for a specific set of clauses, so it *knows* what clauses match the goal. Prolog basically generates a miniature theorem prover for each different predicate, thereby eliminating much of the overhead of interpretation. It is also possible to **open-code** the unification routine for each different call, thereby avoiding explicit analysis of term structure. (For details of open-coded unification, see Warren *et al.* (1977).)

OPEN-CODE

The instruction sets of today's computers give a poor match with Prolog's semantics, so most Prolog compilers compile into an intermediate language rather than directly into machine language. The most popular intermediate language is the Warren Abstract Machine, or WAM, named after David H. D. Warren, one of the implementors of the first Prolog compiler. The WAM is an abstract instruction set that is suitable for Prolog and can be either interpreted or translated into machine language. Other compilers translate Prolog into a high-level language such as Lisp or C and then use that language's compiler to translate to machine language. For example, the definition of the `Append` predicate can be compiled into the code shown in Figure 9.8. There are several points worth mentioning:

- Rather than having to search the knowledge base for `Append` clauses, the clauses become a procedure and the inferences are carried out simply by calling the procedure.

- As described earlier, the current variable bindings are kept on a trail. The first step of the procedure saves the current state of the trail, so that it can be restored by RESET-TRAIL if the first clause fails. This will undo any bindings generated by the first call to UNIFY.

CONTINUATIONS

- The trickiest part is the use of **continuations** to implement choice points. You can think of a continuation as packaging up a procedure and a list of arguments that together define what should be done next whenever the current goal succeeds. It would not do just to return from a procedure like APPEND when the goal succeeds, because it could succeed in several ways, and each of them has to be explored. The continuation argument solves this problem because it can be called each time the goal succeeds. In the APPEND code, if the first argument is empty, then the APPEND predicate has succeeded. We then CALL the continuation, with the appropriate bindings on the trail, to do whatever should be done next. For example, if the call to APPEND were at the top level, the continuation would print the bindings of the variables.

Before Warren's work on the compilation of inference in Prolog, logic programming was too slow for general use. Compilers by Warren and others allowed Prolog code to achieve speeds that are competitive with C on a variety of standard benchmarks (Van Roy, 1990). Of course, the fact that one can write a planner or natural language parser in a few dozen lines of Prolog makes it somewhat more desirable than C for prototyping most small-scale AI research projects.

OR-PARALLELISM

AND-PARALLELISM

Parallelization can also provide substantial speedup. There are two principal sources of parallelism. The first, called **OR-parallelism**, comes from the possibility of a goal unifying with many different clauses in the knowledge base. Each gives rise to an independent branch in the search space that can lead to a potential solution, and all such branches can be solved in parallel. The second, called **AND-parallelism**, comes from the possibility of solving each conjunct in the body of an implication in parallel. AND-parallelism is more difficult to achieve, because solutions for the whole conjunction require consistent bindings for all the variables. Each conjunctive branch must communicate with the other branches to ensure a global solution.

### Redundant inference and infinite loops

We now turn to the Achilles heel of Prolog: the mismatch between depth-first search and search trees that include repeated states and infinite paths. Consider the following logic program that decides if a path exists between two points on a directed graph:

```
path(X,Z) :- link(X,Z).
path(X,Z) :- path(X,Y), link(Y,Z).
```

A simple three-node graph, described by the facts `link(a,b)` and `link(b,c)`, is shown in Figure 9.9(a). With this program, the query `path(a,c)` generates the proof tree shown in Figure 9.10(a). On the other hand, if we put the two clauses in the order

```
path(X,Z) :- path(X,Y), link(Y,Z).
path(X,Z) :- link(X,Z).
```

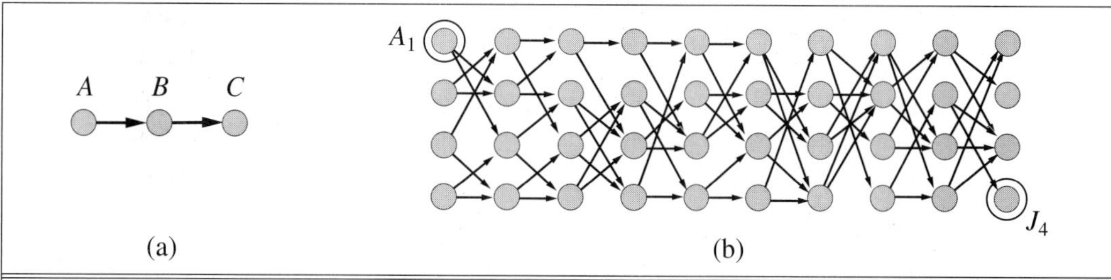


**Figure 9.9** (a) Finding a path from $A$ to $C$ can lead Prolog into an infinite loop. (b) A graph in which each node is connected to two random successors in the next layer. Finding a path from $A_1$ to $J_4$ requires 877 inferences.

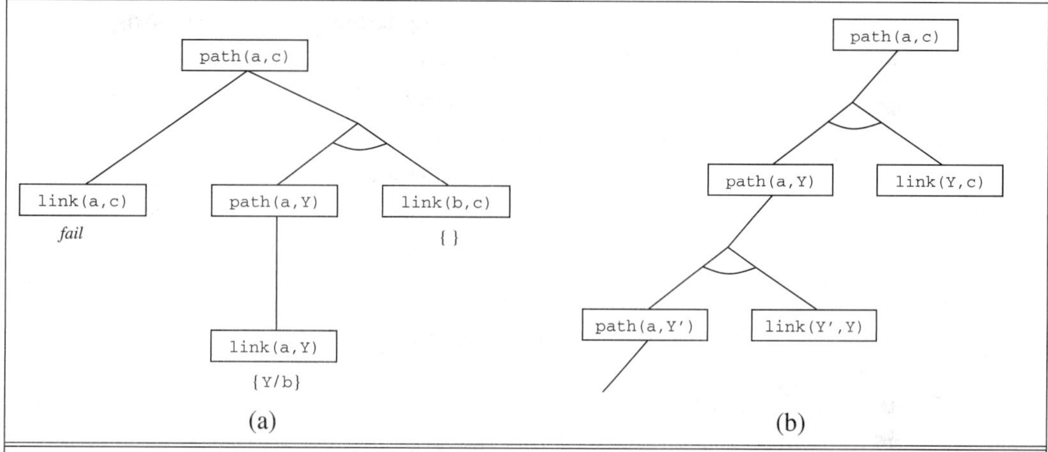


**Figure 9.10** (a) Proof that a path exists from $A$ to $C$. (b) Infinite proof tree generated when the clauses are in the "wrong" order.

then Prolog follows the infinite path shown in Figure 9.10(b). Prolog is therefore **incomplete** as a theorem prover for definite clauses—even for Datalog programs, as this example shows—because, for some knowledge bases, it fails to prove sentences that are entailed. Notice that forward chaining does not suffer from this problem: once `path(a,b)`, `path(b,c)`, and `path(a,c)` are inferred, forward chaining halts.

Depth-first backward chaining also has problems with redundant computations. For example, when finding a path from $A_1$ to $J_4$ in Figure 9.9(b), Prolog performs 877 inferences, most of which involve finding all possible paths to nodes from which the goal is unreachable. This is similar to the repeated-state problem discussed in Chapter 3. The total amount of inference can be exponential in the number of ground facts that are generated. If we apply forward chaining instead, at most $n^2$ `path(X,Y)` facts can be generated linking $n$ nodes. For the problem in Figure 9.9(b), only 62 inferences are needed.

DYNAMIC PROGRAMMING

Forward chaining on graph search problems is an example of **dynamic programming**, in which the solutions to subproblems are constructed incrementally from those of smaller subproblems and are cached to avoid recomputation. We can obtain a similar effect in a backward chaining system using **memoization**—that is, caching solutions to subgoals as they are found and then reusing those solutions when the subgoal recurs, rather than repeating the previous computation. This is the approach taken by **tabled logic programming** systems, which use efficient storage and retrieval mechanisms to perform memoization. Tabled logic programming combines the goal-directedness of backward chaining with the dynamic programming efficiency of forward chaining. It is also complete for Datalog programs, which means that the programmer need worry less about infinite loops.

TABLED LOGIC PROGRAMMING

### Constraint logic programming

In our discussion of forward chaining (Section 9.3), we showed how constraint satisfaction problems (CSPs) can be encoded as definite clauses. Standard Prolog solves such problems in exactly the same way as the backtracking algorithm given in Figure 5.3.

Because backtracking enumerates the domains of the variables, it works only for **finite domain** CSPs. In Prolog terms, there must be a finite number of solutions for any goal with unbound variables. (For example, the goal `diff(q,sa)`, which says that Queensland and South Australia must be different colors, has six solutions if three colors are allowed.) Infinite-domain CSPs—for example with integer or real-valued variables—require quite different algorithms, such as bounds propagation or linear programming.

The following clause succeeds if three numbers satisfy the triangle inequality:

```
triangle(X,Y,Z) :-
    X>=0, Y>=0, Z>=0, X+Y>=Z, Y+Z>=X, X+Z>=Y.
```

If we ask Prolog the query `triangle(3,4,5)`, this works fine. On the other hand, if we ask `triangle(3,4,Z)`, no solution will be found, because the subgoal `Z>=0` cannot be handled by Prolog. The difficulty is that variables in Prolog must be in one of two states: unbound or bound to a particular term.

CONSTRAINT LOGIC PROGRAMMING

Binding a variable to a particular term can be viewed as an extreme form of constraint, namely an equality constraint. **Constraint logic programming** (CLP) allows variables to be *constrained* rather than *bound*. A solution to a constraint logic program is the most specific set of constraints on the query variables that can be derived from the knowledge base. For example, the solution to the `triangle(3,4,Z)` query is the constraint `7 >= Z >= 1`. Standard logic programs are just a special case of CLP in which the solution constraints must be equality constraints—that is, bindings.

CLP systems incorporate various constraint-solving algorithms for the constraints allowed in the language. For example, a system that allows linear inequalities on real-valued variables might include a linear programming algorithm for solving those constraints. CLP systems also adopt a much more flexible approach to solving standard logic programming queries. For example, instead of depth-first, left-to-right backtracking, they might use any of the more efficient algorithms discussed in Chapter 5, including heuristic conjunct ordering, backjumping, cutset conditioning, and so on. CLP systems therefore combine elements of constraint satisfaction algorithms, logic programming, and deductive databases.

CLP systems can also take advantage of the variety of CSP search optimizations described in Chapter 5, such as variable and value ordering, forward checking, and intelligent backtracking. Several systems have been defined that allow the programmer more control over the search order for inference. For example, the MRS Language (Genesereth and Smith, 1981; Russell, 1985) allows the programmer to write **metarules** to determine which conjuncts are tried first. The user could write a rule saying that the goal with the fewest variables should be tried first or could write domain-specific rules for particular predicates.

METARULES

## 9.5 RESOLUTION

The last of our three families of logical systems is based on **resolution**. We saw in Chapter 7 that propositional resolution is a refutation complete inference procedure for propositional logic. In this section, we will see how to extend resolution to first-order logic.

The question of the existence of complete proof procedures is of direct concern to mathematicians. If a complete proof procedure can be found for mathematical statements, two things follow: first, all conjectures can be established mechanically; second, all of mathematics can be established as the logical consequence of a set of fundamental axioms. The question of completeness has therefore generated some of the most important mathematical work of the 20th century. In 1930, the German mathematician Kurt Gödel proved the first **completeness theorem** for first-order logic, showing that any entailed sentence has a finite proof. (No really *practical* proof procedure was found until J. A. Robinson published the resolution algorithm in 1965.) In 1931, Gödel proved an even more famous **incompleteness theorem**. The theorem states that a logical system that includes the principle of induction—without which very little of discrete mathematics can be constructed—is necessarily incomplete. Hence, there are sentences that are entailed, but have no finite proof within the system. The needle may be in the metaphorical haystack, but no procedure can guarantee that it will be found.

COMPLETENESS THEOREM

INCOMPLETENESS THEOREM

Despite Gödel's theorem, resolution-based theorem provers have been applied widely to derive mathematical theorems, including several for which no proof was known previously. Theorem provers have also been used to verify hardware designs and to generate logically correct programs, among other applications.

### Conjunctive normal form for first-order logic

As in the propositional case, first-order resolution requires that sentences be in **conjunctive normal form** (CNF)—that is, a conjunction of clauses, where each clause is a disjunction of literals.[6] Literals can contain variables, which are assumed to be universally quantified. For example, the sentence

$$\forall x \;\; American(x) \land Weapon(y) \land Sells(x, y, z) \land Hostile(z) \;\Rightarrow\; Criminal(x)$$

becomes, in CNF,

$$\neg American(x) \lor \neg Weapon(y) \lor \neg Sells(x, y, z) \lor \neg Hostile(z) \lor Criminal(x) \,.$$

[6] A clause can also be represented as an implication with a conjunction of atoms on the left and a disjunction of atoms on the right, as shown in Exercise 7.12. This form, sometimes called **Kowalski form** when written with a right-to-left implication symbol (Kowalski, 1979b), is often much easier to read.

*Every sentence of first-order logic can be converted into an inferentially equivalent CNF sentence.* In particular, the CNF sentence will be unsatisfiable just when the original sentence is unsatisfiable, so we have a basis for doing proofs by contradiction on the CNF sentences.

The procedure for conversion to CNF is very similar to the propositional case, which we saw on page 215. The principal difference arises from the need to eliminate existential quantifiers. We will illustrate the procedure by translating the sentence "Everyone who loves all animals is loved by someone," or

$$\forall x \ [\forall y \ \ Animal(y) \Rightarrow Loves(x,y)] \Rightarrow [\exists y \ \ Loves(y,x)] .$$

The steps are as follows:

◇ **Eliminate implications**:

$$\forall x \ [\neg \forall y \ \ \neg Animal(y) \lor Loves(x,y)] \lor [\exists y \ \ Loves(y,x)] .$$

◇ **Move ¬ inwards**: In addition to the usual rules for negated connectives, we need rules for negated quantifiers. Thus, we have

| | | |
|---|---|---|
| $\neg \forall x \ \ p$ | becomes | $\exists x \ \ \neg p$ |
| $\neg \exists x \ \ p$ | becomes | $\forall x \ \ \neg p$ . |

Our sentence goes through the following transformations:

$$\forall x \ [\exists y \ \ \neg(\neg Animal(y) \lor Loves(x,y))] \lor [\exists y \ \ Loves(y,x)] .$$
$$\forall x \ [\exists y \ \ \neg\neg Animal(y) \land \neg Loves(x,y)] \lor [\exists y \ \ Loves(y,x)] .$$
$$\forall x \ [\exists y \ \ Animal(y) \land \neg Loves(x,y)] \lor [\exists y \ \ Loves(y,x)] .$$

Notice how a universal quantifier ($\forall y$) in the premise of the implication has become an existential quantifier. The sentence now reads "Either there is some animal that $x$ doesn't love, or (if this is not the case) someone loves $x$." Clearly, the meaning of the original sentence has been preserved.

◇ **Standardize variables**: For sentences like $(\forall x \ \ P(x)) \lor (\exists x \ \ Q(x))$ which use the same variable name twice, change the name of one of the variables. This avoids confusion later when we drop the quantifiers. Thus, we have

$$\forall x \ [\exists y \ \ Animal(y) \land \neg Loves(x,y)] \lor [\exists z \ \ Loves(z,x)] .$$

SKOLEMIZATION

◇ **Skolemize**: **Skolemization** is the process of removing existential quantifiers by elimination. In the simple case, it is just like the Existential Instantiation rule of Section 9.1: translate $\exists x \ P(x)$ into $P(A)$, where $A$ is a new constant. If we apply this rule to our sample sentence, however, we obtain

$$\forall x \ [Animal(A) \land \neg Loves(x,A)] \lor Loves(B,x)$$

which has the wrong meaning entirely: it says that everyone either fails to love a particular animal $A$ or is loved by some particular entity $B$. In fact, our original sentence allows each person to fail to love a different animal or to be loved by a different person. Thus, we want the Skolem entities to depend on $x$:

$$\forall x \ [Animal(F(x)) \land \neg Loves(x,F(x))] \lor Loves(G(x),x) .$$

SKOLEM FUNCTION

Here $F$ and $G$ are **Skolem functions**. The general rule is that the arguments of the

Skolem function are all the universally quantified variables in whose scope the existential quantifier appears. As with Existential Instantiation, the Skolemized sentence is satisfiable exactly when the original sentence is satisfiable.

◇ **Drop universal quantifiers**: At this point, all remaining variables must be universally quantified. Moreover, the sentence is equivalent to one in which all the universal quantifiers have been moved to the left. We can therefore drop the universal quantifiers:

$$[Animal(F(x)) \land \neg Loves(x, F(x))] \lor Loves(G(x), x) .$$

◇ **Distribute $\lor$ over $\land$**:

$$[Animal(F(x)) \lor Loves(G(x), x)] \land [\neg Loves(x, F(x)) \lor Loves(G(x), x)] .$$

This step may also require flattening out nested conjunctions and disjunctions.

The sentence is now in CNF and consists of two clauses. It is quite unreadable. (It may help to explain that the Skolem function $F(x)$ refers to the animal potentially unloved by $x$, whereas $G(x)$ refers to someone who might love $x$.) Fortunately, humans seldom need look at CNF sentences—the translation process is easily automated.

### The resolution inference rule

The resolution rule for first-order clauses is simply a lifted version of the propositional resolution rule given on page 214. Two clauses, which are assumed to be standardized apart so that they share no variables, can be resolved if they contain complementary literals. Propositional literals are complementary if one is the negation of the other; first-order literals are complementary if one *unifies with* the negation of the other. Thus we have

$$\frac{\ell_1 \lor \cdots \lor \ell_k, \qquad m_1 \lor \cdots \lor m_n}{\textsc{Subst}(\theta, \ell_1 \lor \cdots \lor \ell_{i-1} \lor \ell_{i+1} \lor \cdots \lor \ell_k \lor m_1 \lor \cdots \lor m_{j-1} \lor m_{j+1} \lor \cdots \lor m_n)}$$

where $\textsc{Unify}(\ell_i, \neg m_j) = \theta$. For example, we can resolve the two clauses

$$[Animal(F(x)) \lor Loves(G(x), x)] \quad \text{and} \quad [\neg Loves(u, v) \lor \neg Kills(u, v)]$$

by eliminating the complementary literals $Loves(G(x), x)$ and $\neg Loves(u, v)$, with unifier $\theta = \{u/G(x), v/x\}$, to produce the **resolvent** clause

$$[Animal(F(x)) \lor \neg Kills(G(x), x)] .$$

BINARY RESOLUTION

The rule we have just given is the **binary resolution** rule, because it resolves exactly two literals. The binary resolution rule by itself does not yield a complete inference procedure. The full resolution rule resolves subsets of literals in each clause that are unifiable. An alternative approach is to extend **factoring**—the removal of redundant literals—to the first-order case. Propositional factoring reduces two literals to one if they are *identical*; first-order factoring reduces two literals to one if they are *unifiable*. The unifier must be applied to the entire clause. The combination of binary resolution and factoring is complete.

### Example proofs

Resolution proves that $KB \models \alpha$ by proving $KB \land \neg\alpha$ unsatisfiable, i.e., by deriving the empty clause. The algorithmic approach is identical to the propositional case, described in

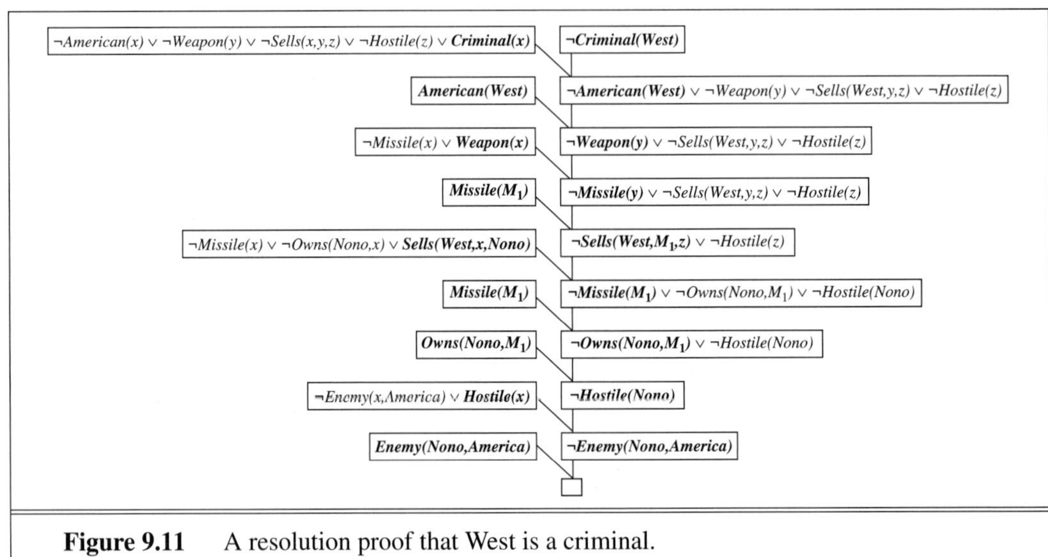


**Figure 9.11** A resolution proof that West is a criminal.

Figure 7.12, so we will not repeat it here. Instead, we will give two example proofs. The first is the crime example from Section 9.3. The sentences in CNF are

$$\neg American(x) \lor \neg Weapon(y) \lor \neg Sells(x,y,z) \lor \neg Hostile(z) \lor Criminal(x) .$$
$$\neg Missile(x) \lor \neg Owns(Nono,x) \lor Sells(West,x,Nono) .$$
$$\neg Enemy(x, America) \lor Hostile(x) .$$
$$\neg Missile(x) \lor Weapon(x) .$$
$$Owns(Nono, M_1) . \qquad Missile(M_1) .$$
$$American(West) . \qquad Enemy(Nono, America) .$$

We also include the negated goal $\neg Criminal(West)$. The resolution proof is shown in Figure 9.11. Notice the structure: single "spine" beginning with the goal clause, resolving against clauses from the knowledge base until the empty clause is generated. This is characteristic of resolution on Horn clause knowledge bases. In fact, the clauses along the main spine correspond *exactly* to the consecutive values of the $goals$ variable in the backward chaining algorithm of Figure 9.6. This is because we always chose to resolve with a clause whose positive literal unified with the leftmost literal of the "current" clause on the spine; this is exactly what happens in backward chaining. Thus, backward chaining is really just a special case of resolution with a particular control strategy to decide which resolution to perform next.

Our second example makes use of Skolemization and involves clauses that are not definite clauses. This results in a somewhat more complex proof structure. In English, the problem is as follows:

Everyone who loves all animals is loved by someone.
Anyone who kills an animal is loved by no one.
Jack loves all animals.
Either Jack or Curiosity killed the cat, who is named Tuna.
Did Curiosity kill the cat?

First, we express the original sentences, some background knowledge, and the negated goal G in first-order logic:

A. $\forall x\ [\forall y\ Animal(y) \Rightarrow Loves(x,y)] \Rightarrow [\exists y\ Loves(y,x)]$

B. $\forall x\ [\exists y\ Animal(y) \wedge Kills(x,y)] \Rightarrow [\forall z\ \neg Loves(z,x)]$

C. $\forall x\ Animal(x) \Rightarrow Loves(Jack,x)$

D. $Kills(Jack, Tuna) \vee Kills(Curiosity, Tuna)$

E. $Cat(Tuna)$

F. $\forall x\ Cat(x) \Rightarrow Animal(x)$

¬G. $\neg Kills(Curiosity, Tuna)$

Now we apply the conversion procedure to convert each sentence to CNF:

A1. $Animal(F(x)) \vee Loves(G(x), x)$

A2. $\neg Loves(x, F(x)) \vee Loves(G(x), x)$

B. $\neg Animal(y) \vee \neg Kills(x,y) \vee \neg Loves(z,x)$

C. $\neg Animal(x) \vee Loves(Jack, x)$

D. $Kills(Jack, Tuna) \vee Kills(Curiosity, Tuna)$

E. $Cat(Tuna)$

F. $\neg Cat(x) \vee Animal(x)$

¬G. $\neg Kills(Curiosity, Tuna)$

The resolution proof that Curiosity killed the cat is given in Figure 9.12. In English, the proof could be paraphrased as follows:

> Suppose Curiosity did not kill Tuna. We know that either Jack or Curiosity did; thus Jack must have. Now, Tuna is a cat and cats are animals, so Tuna is an animal. Because anyone who kills an animal is loved by no one, we know that no one loves Jack. On the other hand, Jack loves all animals, so someone loves him; so we have a contradiction. Therefore, Curiosity killed the cat.

The proof answers the question "Did Curiosity kill the cat?" but often we want to pose more general questions, such as "Who killed the cat?" Resolution can do this, but it takes a little

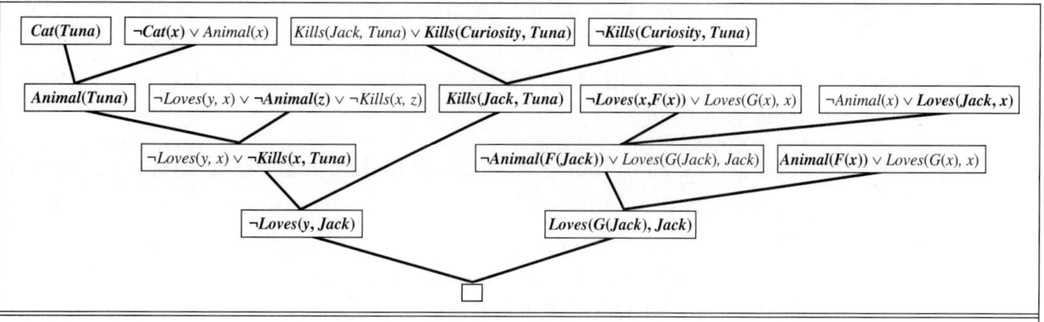


**Figure 9.12** A resolution proof that Curiosity killed the cat. Notice the use of factoring in the derivation of the clause $Loves(G(Jack), Jack)$.

more work to obtain the answer. The goal is $\exists w\ Kills(w, Tuna)$, which, when negated, becomes $\neg Kills(w, Tuna)$ in CNF. Repeating the proof in Figure 9.12 with the new negated goal, we obtain a similar proof tree, but with the substitution $\{w/Curiosity\}$ in one of the steps. So, in this case, finding out who killed the cat is just a matter of keeping track of the bindings for the query variables in the proof.

NONCONSTRUCTIVE PROOF

Unfortunately, resolution can produce **nonconstructive proofs** for existential goals. For example, $\neg Kills(w, Tuna)$ resolves with $Kills(Jack, Tuna) \vee Kills(Curiosity, Tuna)$ to give $Kills(Jack, Tuna)$, which resolves again with $\neg Kills(w, Tuna)$ to yield the empty clause. Notice that $w$ has two different bindings in this proof; resolution is telling us that, yes, someone killed Tuna—either Jack or Curiosity. This is no great surprise! One solution is to restrict the allowed resolution steps so that the query variables can be bound only once in a given proof; then we need to be able to backtrack over the possible bindings. Another solution is to add a special **answer literal** to the negated goal, which becomes $\neg Kills(w, Tuna) \vee Answer(w)$. Now, the resolution process generates an answer whenever a clause is generated containing just a *single* answer literal. For the proof in Figure 9.12, this is $Answer(Curiosity)$. The nonconstructive proof would generate the clause $Answer(Curiosity) \vee Answer(Jack)$, which does not constitute an answer.

ANSWER LITERAL

### Completeness of resolution

This section gives a completeness proof of resolution. It can be safely skipped by those who are willing to take it on faith.

REFUTATION COMPLETENESS

We will show that resolution is **refutation-complete**, which means that *if* a set of sentences is unsatisfiable, then resolution will always be able to derive a contradiction. Resolution cannot be used to generate all logical consequences of a set of sentences, but it can be used to establish that a given sentence is entailed by the set of sentences. Hence, it can be used to find all answers to a given question, using the negated-goal method that we described earlier in the Chapter.

We will take it as given that any sentence in first-order logic (without equality) can be rewritten as a set of clauses in CNF. This can be proved by induction on the form of the sentence, using atomic sentences as the base case (Davis and Putnam, 1960). Our goal therefore is to prove the following: *if $S$ is an unsatisfiable set of clauses, then the application of a finite number of resolution steps to $S$ will yield a contradiction.*

Our proof sketch follows the original proof due to Robinson, with some simplifications from Genesereth and Nilsson (1987). The basic structure of the proof is shown in Figure 9.13; it proceeds as follows:

1. First, we observe that if $S$ is unsatisfiable, then there exists a particular set of *ground instances* of the clauses of $S$ such that this set is also unsatisfiable (Herbrand's theorem).
2. We then appeal to the **ground resolution theorem** given in Chapter 7, which states that propositional resolution is complete for ground sentences.
3. We then use a **lifting lemma** to show that, for any propositional resolution proof using the set of ground sentences, there is a corresponding first-order resolution proof using the first-order sentences from which the ground sentences were obtained.

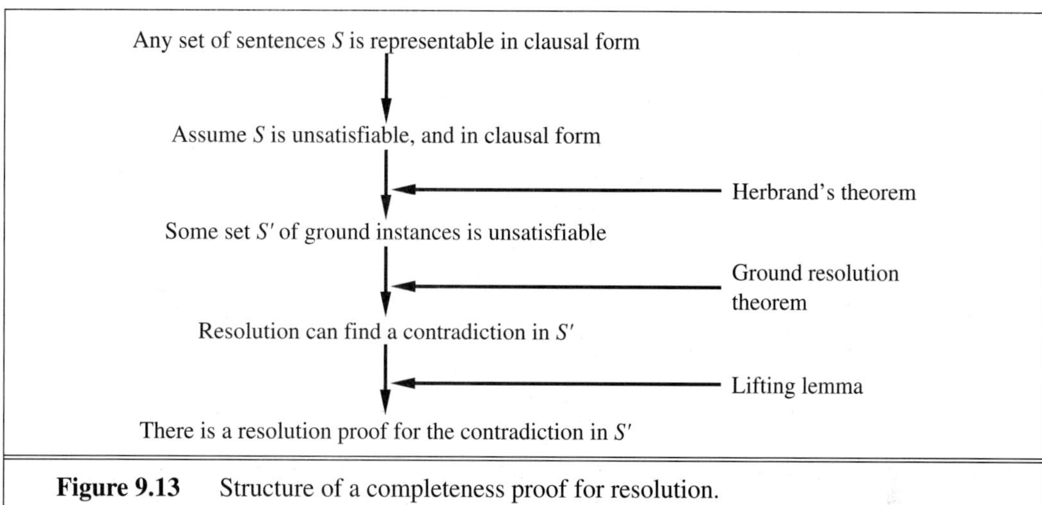


**Figure 9.13** Structure of a completeness proof for resolution.

To carry out the first step, we will need three new concepts:

HERBRAND UNIVERSE

◇ **Herbrand universe**: If $S$ is a set of clauses, then $H_S$, the Herbrand universe of $S$, is the set of all ground terms constructible from the following:

a. The function symbols in $S$, if any.
b. The constant symbols in $S$, if any; if none, then the constant symbol $A$.

For example, if $S$ contains just the clause $\neg P(x, F(x, A)) \vee \neg Q(x, A) \vee R(x, B)$, then $H_S$ is the following infinite set of ground terms:

$$\{A, B, F(A, A), F(A, B), F(B, A), F(B, B), F(A, F(A, A)), \ldots\} .$$

SATURATION

◇ **Saturation**: If $S$ is a set of clauses and $P$ is a set of ground terms, then $P(S)$, the saturation of $S$ with respect to $P$, is the set of all ground clauses obtained by applying all possible consistent substitutions of ground terms in $P$ with variables in $S$.

HERBRAND BASE

◇ **Herbrand base**: The saturation of a set $S$ of clauses with respect to its Herbrand universe is called the Herbrand base of $S$, written as $H_S(S)$. For example, if $S$ contains solely the clause just given, then $H_S(S)$ is the infinite set of clauses

$$\begin{aligned}&\{\neg P(A, F(A, A)) \vee \neg Q(A, A) \vee R(A, B),\\ &\neg P(B, F(B, A)) \vee \neg Q(B, A) \vee R(B, B),\\ &\neg P(F(A, A), F(F(A, A), A)) \vee \neg Q(F(A, A), A) \vee R(F(A, A), B),\\ &\neg P(F(A, B), F(F(A, B), A)) \vee \neg Q(F(A, B), A) \vee R(F(A, B), B), \ldots\}\end{aligned}$$

HERBRAND'S THEOREM

These definitions allow us to state a form of **Herbrand's theorem** (Herbrand, 1930):

> If a set $S$ of clauses is unsatisfiable, then there exists a finite subset of $H_S(S)$ that is also unsatisfiable.

Let $S'$ be this finite subset of ground sentences. Now, we can appeal to the ground resolution theorem (page 217) to show that the **resolution closure** $RC(S')$ contains the empty clause. That is, running propositional resolution to completion on $S'$ will derive a contradiction.

Now that we have established that there is always a resolution proof involving some finite subset of the Herbrand base of $S$, the next step is to show that there is a resolution

## GÖDEL'S INCOMPLETENESS THEOREM

By slightly extending the language of first-order logic to allow for the **mathematical induction schema** in arithmetic, Gödel was able to show, in his **incompleteness theorem**, that there are true arithmetic sentences that cannot be proved.

The proof of the incompleteness theorem is somewhat beyond the scope of this book, occupying, as it does, at least 30 pages, but we can give a hint here. We begin with the logical theory of numbers. In this theory, there is a single constant, 0, and a single function, $S$ (the successor function). In the intended model, $S(0)$ denotes 1, $S(S(0))$ denotes 2, and so on; the language therefore has names for all the natural numbers. The vocabulary also includes the function symbols $+$, $\times$, and $Expt$ (exponentiation) and the usual set of logical connectives and quantifiers. The first step is to notice that the set of sentences that we can write in this language can be enumerated. (Imagine defining an alphabetical order on the symbols and then arranging, in alphabetical order, each of the sets of sentences of length 1, 2, and so on.) We can then number each sentence $\alpha$ with a unique natural number $\#\alpha$ (the **Gödel number**). This is crucial: number theory contains a name for each of its own sentences. Similarly, we can number each possible proof $P$ with a Gödel number $G(P)$, because a proof is simply a finite sequence of sentences.

Now suppose we have a recursively enumerable set $A$ of sentences that are true statements about the natural numbers. Recalling that $A$ can be named by a given set of integers, we can imagine writing in our language a sentence $\alpha(j, A)$ of the following sort:

> $\forall i \;\; i$ is not the Gödel number of a proof of the sentence whose Gödel number is $j$, where the proof uses only premises in $A$.

Then let $\sigma$ be the sentence $\alpha(\#\sigma, A)$, that is, a sentence that states its own unprovability from $A$. (That this sentence always exists is true but not entirely obvious.)

Now we make the following ingenious argument: Suppose that $\sigma$ *is* provable from $A$; then $\sigma$ is false (because $\sigma$ says it cannot be proved). But then we have a false sentence that is provable from $A$, so $A$ cannot consist of only true sentences—a violation of our premise. Therefore $\sigma$ is *not* provable from $A$. But this is exactly what $\sigma$ itself claims; hence $\sigma$ is a true sentence.

So, we have shown (barring $29\frac{1}{2}$ pages) that for any set of true sentences of number theory, and in particular any set of basic axioms, there are other true sentences that *cannot* be proved from those axioms. This establishes, among other things, that we can never prove all the theorems of mathematics *within any given system of axioms*. Clearly, this was an important discovery for mathematics. Its significance for AI has been widely debated, beginning with speculations by Gödel himself. We take up the debate in Chapter 26.

proof using the clauses of $S$ itself, which are not necessarily ground clauses. We start by considering a single application of the resolution rule. Robinson's basic lemma implies the following fact:

> Let $C_1$ and $C_2$ be two clauses with no shared variables, and let $C'_1$ and $C'_2$ be ground instances of $C_1$ and $C_2$. If $C'$ is a resolvent of $C'_1$ and $C'_2$, then there exists a clause $C$ such that (1) $C$ is a resolvent of $C_1$ and $C_2$ and (2) $C'$ is a ground instance of $C$.

LIFTING LEMMA

This is called a **lifting lemma**, because it lifts a proof step from ground clauses up to general first-order clauses. In order to prove his basic lifting lemma, Robinson had to invent unification and derive all of the properties of most general unifiers. Rather than repeat the proof here, we simply illustrate the lemma:

$$\begin{aligned}
C_1 &= \neg P(x, F(x, A)) \vee \neg Q(x, A) \vee R(x, B)\\
C_2 &= \neg N(G(y), z) \vee P(H(y), z)\\
C'_1 &= \neg P(H(B), F(H(B), A)) \vee \neg Q(H(B), A) \vee R(H(B), B)\\
C'_2 &= \neg N(G(B), F(H(B), A)) \vee P(H(B), F(H(B), A))\\
C' &= \neg N(G(B), F(H(B), A)) \vee \neg Q(H(B), A) \vee R(H(B), B)\\
C &= \neg N(G(y), F(H(y), A)) \vee \neg Q(H(y), A) \vee R(H(y), B)\,.
\end{aligned}$$

We see that indeed $C'$ is a ground instance of $C$. In general, for $C'_1$ and $C'_2$ to have any resolvents, they must be constructed by first applying to $C_1$ and $C_2$ the most general unifier of a pair of complementary literals in $C_1$ and $C_2$. From the lifting lemma, it is easy to derive a similar statement about any sequence of applications of the resolution rule:

> For any clause $C'$ in the resolution closure of $S'$ there is a clause $C$ in the resolution closure of $S$, such that $C'$ is a ground instance of $C$ and the derivation of $C$ is the same length as the derivation of $C'$.

From this fact, it follows that if the empty clause appears in the resolution closure of $S'$, it must also appear in the resolution closure of $S$. This is because the empty clause cannot be a ground instance of any other clause. To recap: we have shown that if $S$ is unsatisfiable, then there is a finite derivation of the empty clause using the resolution rule.

The lifting of theorem proving from ground clauses to first-order clauses provides a vast increase in power. This increase comes from the fact that the first-order proof need instantiate variables only as far as necessary for the proof, whereas the ground-clause methods were required to examine a huge number of arbitrary instantiations.

### Dealing with equality

None of the inference methods described so far in this chapter handle equality. There are three distinct approaches that can be taken. The first approach is to axiomatize equality—to write down sentences about the equality relation in the knowledge base. We need to say that equality is reflexive, symmetric, and transitive, and we also have to say that we can substitute equals for equals in any predicate or function. So we need three basic axioms, and then one for each predicate and function:

$$\begin{array}{l} \forall x \;\; x = x \\ \forall x, y \;\; x = y \;\Rightarrow\; y = x \\ \forall x, y, z \;\; x = y \land y = z \;\Rightarrow\; x = z \\ \forall x, y \;\; x = y \;\Rightarrow\; (P_1(x) \;\Leftrightarrow\; P_1(y)) \\ \forall x, y \;\; x = y \;\Rightarrow\; (P_2(x) \;\Leftrightarrow\; P_2(y)) \\ \quad\vdots \\ \forall w, x, y, z \;\; w = y \land x = z \;\Rightarrow\; (F_1(w, x) = F_1(y, z)) \\ \forall w, x, y, z \;\; w = y \land x = z \;\Rightarrow\; (F_2(w, x) = F_2(y, z)) \\ \quad\vdots \end{array}$$

Given these sentences, a standard inference procedure such as resolution can perform tasks requiring equality reasoning, such as solving mathematical equations.

Another way to deal with equality is with an additional inference rule. The simplest rule, **demodulation**, takes a unit clause $x = y$ and substitutes $y$ for any term that unifies with $x$ in some other clause. More formally, we have

DEMODULATION

◇ **Demodulation**: For any terms $x$, $y$, and $z$, where $\text{UNIFY}(x, z) = \theta$ and $m_n[z]$ is a literal containing $z$:

$$\frac{x = y, \qquad m_1 \lor \cdots \lor m_n[z]}{m_1 \lor \cdots \lor m_n[\text{SUBST}(\theta, y)]} .$$

Demodulation is typically used for simplifying expressions using collections of assertions such as $x + 0 = x$, $x^1 = x$, and so on. The rule can also be extended to handle non-unit clauses in which an equality literal appears:

PARAMODULATION

◇ **Paramodulation**: For any terms $x$, $y$, and $z$, where $\text{UNIFY}(x, z) = \theta$,

$$\frac{\ell_1 \lor \cdots \lor \ell_k \lor x = y, \qquad m_1 \lor \cdots \lor m_n[z]}{\text{SUBST}(\theta, \ell_1 \lor \cdots \lor \ell_k \lor m_1 \lor \cdots \lor m_n[y])} .$$

Unlike demodulation, paramodulation yields a complete inference procedure for first-order logic with equality.

EQUATIONAL UNIFICATION

A third approach handles equality reasoning entirely within an extended unification algorithm. That is, terms are unifiable if they are *provably* equal under some substitution, where "provably" allows for some amount of equality reasoning. For example, the terms $1 + 2$ and $2 + 1$ normally are not unifiable, but a unification algorithm that knows that $x + y = y + x$ could unify them with the empty substitution. **Equational unification** of this kind can be done with efficient algorithms designed for the particular axioms used (commutativity, associativity, and so on), rather than through explicit inference with those axioms. Theorem provers using this technique are closely related to the constraint logic programming systems described in Section 9.4.

### Resolution strategies

We know that repeated applications of the resolution inference rule will eventually find a proof if one exists. In this subsection, we examine strategies that help find proofs *efficiently*.

### Unit preference

This strategy prefers to do resolutions where one of the sentences is a single literal (also known as a **unit clause**). The idea behind the strategy is that we are trying to produce an empty clause, so it might be a good idea to prefer inferences that produce shorter clauses. Resolving a unit sentence (such as $P$) with any other sentence (such as $\neg P \lor \neg Q \lor R$) always yields a clause (in this case, $\neg Q \lor R$) that is shorter than the other clause. When the unit preference strategy was first tried for propositional inference in 1964, it led to a dramatic speedup, making it feasible to prove theorems that could not be handled without the preference. Unit preference by itself does not, however, reduce the branching factor in medium-sized problems enough to make them solvable by resolution. It is, nonetheless, a useful heuristic that can be combined with other strategies.

UNIT RESOLUTION

**Unit resolution** is a restricted form of resolution in which every resolution step must involve a unit clause. Unit resolution is incomplete in general, but complete for Horn knowledge bases. Unit resolution proofs on Horn knowledge bases resemble forward chaining.

### Set of support

SET OF SUPPORT

Preferences that try certain resolutions first are helpful, but in general it is more effective to try to eliminate some potential resolutions altogether. The set-of-support strategy does just that. It starts by identifying a subset of the sentences called the **set of support**. Every resolution combines a sentence from the set of support with another sentence and adds the resolvent into the set of support. If the set of support is small relative to the whole knowledge base, the search space will be reduced dramatically.

We have to be careful with this approach, because a bad choice for the set of support will make the algorithm incomplete. However, if we choose the set of support $S$ so that the remainder of the sentences are jointly satisfiable, then set-of-support resolution will be complete. A common approach is to use the negated query as the set of support, on the assumption that the original knowledge base is consistent. (After all, if it is not consistent, then the fact that the query follows from it is vacuous.) The set-of-support strategy has the additional advantage of generating proof trees that are often easy for humans to understand, because they are goal-directed.

### Input resolution

INPUT RESOLUTION

In the **input resolution** strategy, every resolution combines one of the input sentences (from the KB or the query) with some other sentence. The proof in Figure 9.11 uses only input resolutions and has the characteristic shape of a single "spine" with single sentences combining onto the spine. Clearly, the space of proof trees of this shape is smaller than the space of all proof graphs. In Horn knowledge bases, Modus Ponens is a kind of input resolution strategy, because it combines an implication from the original KB with some other sentences. Thus, it is no surprise that input resolution is complete for knowledge bases that are in Horn form, but incomplete in the general case. The **linear resolution** strategy is a slight generalization that allows $P$ and $Q$ to be resolved together either if $P$ is in the original $KB$ or if $P$ is an ancestor of $Q$ in the proof tree. Linear resolution is complete.

LINEAR RESOLUTION

### Subsumption

SUBSUMPTION

The **subsumption** method eliminates all sentences that are subsumed by (i.e., more specific than) an existing sentence in the KB. For example, if $P(x)$ is in the KB, then there is no sense in adding $P(A)$ and even less sense in adding $P(A) \lor Q(B)$. Subsumption helps keep the KB small, and thus helps keep the search space small.

## Theorem provers

Theorem provers (also known as automated reasoners) differ from logic programming languages in two ways. First, most logic programming languages handle only Horn clauses, whereas theorem provers accept full first-order logic. Second, Prolog programs intertwine logic and control. The programmer's choice `A :- B, C` instead of `A :- C, B` affects the execution of the program. In most theorem provers, the syntactic form chosen for sentences does not affect the results. Theorem provers still need control information to operate efficiently, but that information is usually kept distinct from the knowledge base, rather than being part of the knowledge representation itself. Most of the research in theorem provers involves finding control strategies that are generally useful, as well as increasing the speed.

### Design of a theorem prover

In this section, we describe the theorem prover OTTER (Organized Techniques for Theorem-proving and Effective Research) (McCune, 1992), with particular attention to its control strategy. In preparing a problem for OTTER, the user must divide the knowledge into four parts:

- A set of clauses known as the **set of support** (or $sos$), which defines the important facts about the problem. Every resolution step resolves a member of the set of support against another axiom, so the search is focused on the set of support.
- A set of **usable axioms** that are outside the set of support. These provide background knowledge about the problem area. The boundary between what is part of the problem (and thus in $sos$) and what is background (and thus in the usable axioms) is up to the user's judgment.
- A set of equations known as **rewrites** or **demodulators**. Although demodulators are equations, they are always applied in the left to right direction. Thus, they define a canonical form into which all terms will be simplified. For example, the demodulator $x + 0 = x$ says that every term of the form $x + 0$ should be replaced by the term $x$.
- A set of parameters and clauses that defines the control strategy. In particular, the user specifies a heuristic function to control the search and a filtering function to eliminate some subgoals as uninteresting.

OTTER works by continually resolving an element of the set of support against one of the usable axioms. Unlike Prolog, it uses a form of best-first search. Its heuristic function measures the "weight" of each clause, where lighter clauses are preferred. The exact choice of heuristic is up to the user, but generally, the weight of a clause should be correlated with its size or difficulty. Unit clauses are treated as light; the search can thus be seen as a generalization of the unit preference strategy. At each step, OTTER moves the "lightest" clause in the set of support to the usable list and adds to the set of support some immediate consequences of resolving the lightest clause with elements of the usable list. OTTER halts when it has found a refutation or when there are no more clauses in the set of support. The algorithm is shown in more detail in Figure 9.14.

```
procedure OTTER(sos, usable)
  inputs: sos, a set of support—clauses defining the problem (a global variable)
          usable, background knowledge potentially relevant to the problem

  repeat
     clause ← the lightest member of sos
     move clause from sos to usable
     PROCESS(INFER(clause, usable), sos)
  until sos = [] or a refutation has been found
----------------------------------------------------------------
function INFER(clause, usable) returns clauses

  resolve clause with each member of usable
  return the resulting clauses after applying FILTER
----------------------------------------------------------------
procedure PROCESS(clauses, sos)

  for each clause in clauses do
     clause ← SIMPLIFY(clause)
     merge identical literals
     discard clause if it is a tautology
     sos ← [clause | sos]
     if clause has no literals then a refutation has been found
     if clause has one literal then look for unit refutation
```

**Figure 9.14** Sketch of the OTTER theorem prover. Heuristic control is applied in the selection of the "lightest" clause and in the FILTER function that eliminates uninteresting clauses from consideration.

### Extending Prolog

An alternative way to build a theorem prover is to start with a Prolog compiler and extend it to get a sound and complete reasoner for full first-order logic. This was the approach taken in the Prolog Technology Theorem Prover, or PTTP (Stickel, 1988). PTTP includes five significant changes to Prolog to restore completeness and expressiveness:

- The occurs check is put back into the unification routine to make it sound.
- The depth-first search is replaced by an iterative deepening search. This makes the search strategy complete and takes only a constant factor more time.
- Negated literals (such as $\neg P(x)$) are allowed. In the implementation, there are two separate routines, one trying to prove $P$ and one trying to prove $\neg P$.

- A clause with $n$ atoms is stored as $n$ different rules. For example, $A \Leftarrow B \wedge C$ would also be stored as $\neg B \Leftarrow C \wedge \neg A$ and as $\neg C \Leftarrow B \wedge \neg A$. This technique, known as **locking**, means that the current goal need be unified with only the head of each clause, yet it still allows for proper handling of negation.

LOCKING

- Inference is made complete (even for non-Horn clauses) by the addition of the linear input resolution rule: If the current goal unifies with the negation of one of the goals on the stack, then that goal can be considered solved. This is a way of reasoning by contradiction. Suppose the original goal is $P$ and this is reduced by a series of inferences to the goal $\neg P$. This establishes that $\neg P \Rightarrow P$, which is logically equivalent to $P$.

Despite these changes, PTTP retains the features that make Prolog fast. Unifications are still done by modifying variables directly, with unbinding done by unwinding the trail during backtracking. The search strategy is still based on input resolution, meaning that every resolution is against one of the clauses given in the original statement of the problem (rather than a derived clause). This makes it feasible to compile all the clauses in the original statement of the problem.

The main drawback of PTTP is that the user has to relinquish all control over the search for solutions. Each inference rule is used by the system both in its original form and in the contrapositive form. This can lead to unintuitive searches. For example, consider the rule

$$(f(x, y) = f(a, b)) \Leftarrow (x = a) \wedge (y = b) .$$

As a Prolog rule, this is a reasonable way to prove that two $f$ terms are equal. But PTTP would also generate the contrapositive:

$$(x \neq a) \Leftarrow (f(x, y) \neq f(a, b)) \wedge (y = b) .$$

It seems that this is a wasteful way to prove that any two terms $x$ and $a$ are different.

### Theorem provers as assistants

So far, we have thought of a reasoning system as an independent agent that has to make decisions and act on its own. Another use of theorem provers is as an assistant, providing advice to, say, a mathematician. In this mode the mathematician acts as a supervisor, mapping out the strategy for determining what to do next and asking the theorem prover to fill in the details. This alleviates the problem of semi-decidability to some extent, because the supervisor can cancel a query and try another approach if the query is taking too much time. A theorem prover can also act as a **proof-checker**, where the proof is given by a human as a series of fairly large steps; the individual inferences required to show that each step is sound are filled in by the system.

PROOF-CHECKER

SOCRATIC REASONER

A **Socratic reasoner** is a theorem prover whose ASK function is incomplete, but which can always arrive at a solution if asked the right series of questions. Thus, Socratic reasoners make good assistants, provided that there is a supervisor to make the right series of calls to ASK. ONTIC (McAllester, 1989) is a Socratic reasoning system for mathematics.

### Practical uses of theorem provers

Theorem provers have come up with novel mathematical results. The SAM (Semi-Automated Mathematics) program was the first, proving a lemma in lattice theory (Guard *et al.*, 1969). The AURA program has also answered open questions in several areas of mathematics (Wos and Winker, 1983). The Boyer–Moore theorem prover (Boyer and Moore, 1979) has been used and extended over many years and was used by Natarajan Shankar to give the first fully rigorous formal proof of Gödel's Incompleteness Theorem (Shankar, 1986). The OTTER program is one of the strongest theorem provers; it has been used to solve several open questions in combinatorial logic. The most famous of these concerns **Robbins algebra**. In 1933, Herbert Robbins proposed a simple set of axioms that appeared to define Boolean algebra, but no proof of this could be found (despite serious work by several mathematicians including Alfred Tarski himself). On October 10, 1996, after eight days of computation, EQP (a version of OTTER) found a proof (McCune, 1997).

ROBBINS ALGEBRA

VERIFICATION

SYNTHESIS

Theorem provers can be applied to the problems involved in the **verification** and **synthesis** of both hardware and software, because both domains can be given correct axiomatizations. Thus, theorem proving research is carried out in the fields of hardware design, programming languages, and software engineering—not just in AI. In the case of software, the axioms state the properties of each syntactic element of the programming language. (Reasoning about programs is quite similar to reasoning about actions in the situation calculus.) An algorithm is verified by showing that its outputs meet the specifications for all inputs. The RSA public key encryption algorithm and the Boyer–Moore string-matching algorithm have been verified this way (Boyer and Moore, 1984). In the case of hardware, the axioms describe the interactions between signals and circuit elements. (See Chapter 8 for an example.) The design of a 16-bit adder has been verified by AURA (Wojcik, 1983). Logical reasoners designed specially for verification have been able to verify entire CPUs, including their timing properties (Srivas and Bickford, 1990).

DEDUCTIVE SYNTHESIS

The formal synthesis of algorithms was one of the first uses of theorem provers, as outlined by Cordell Green (1969a), who built on earlier ideas by Simon (1963). The idea is to prove a theorem to the effect that "there exists a program $p$ satisfying a certain specification." If the proof is constrained to be constructive, the program can be extracted. Although fully automated **deductive synthesis**, as it is called, has not yet become feasible for general-purpose programming, hand-guided deductive synthesis has been successful in designing several novel and sophisticated algorithms. Synthesis of special-purpose programs is also an active area of research. In the area of hardware synthesis, the AURA theorem prover has been applied to design circuits that are more compact than any previous design (Wojciechowski and Wojcik, 1983). For many circuit designs, propositional logic is sufficient because the set of interesting propositions is fixed by the set of circuit elements. The application of propositional inference in hardware synthesis is now a standard technique having many large-scale deployments (see, e.g., Nowick *et al.* (1993)).

These same techniques are now starting to be applied to software verification as well, by systems such as the SPIN model checker (Holzmann, 1997). For example, the Remote Agent spacecraft control program was verified before and after flight (Havelund *et al.*, 2000).

## 9.6 SUMMARY

We have presented an analysis of logical inference in first-order logic and a number of algorithms for doing it.

- A first approach uses inference rules for instantiating quantifiers in order to propositionalize the inference problem. Typically, this approach is very slow.
- The use of **unification** to identify appropriate substitutions for variables eliminates the instantiation step in first-order proofs, making the process much more efficient.
- A lifted version of **Modus Ponens** uses unification to provide a natural and powerful inference rule, **generalized Modus Ponens**. The **forward chaining** and **backward chaining** algorithms apply this rule to sets of definite clauses.
- Generalized Modus Ponens is complete for definite clauses, although the entailment problem is **semidecidable**. For **Datalog** programs consisting of function-free definite clauses, entailment is decidable.
- Forward chaining is used in **deductive databases**, where it can be combined with relational database operations. It is also used in **production systems**, which perform efficient updates with very large rule sets.
- Forward chaining is complete for Datalog programs and runs in polynomial time.
- Backward chaining is used in **logic programming systems** such as **Prolog**, which employ sophisticated compiler technology to provide very fast inference.
- Backward chaining suffers from redundant inferences and infinite loops; these can be alleviated by **memoization**.
- The generalized **resolution** inference rule provides a complete proof system for first-order logic, using knowledge bases in conjunctive normal form.
- Several strategies exist for reducing the search space of a resolution system without compromising completeness. Efficient resolution-based theorem provers have been used to prove interesting mathematical theorems and to verify and synthesize software and hardware.

## BIBLIOGRAPHICAL AND HISTORICAL NOTES

SYLLOGISM

Logical inference was studied extensively in Greek mathematics. The type of inference most carefully studied by Aristotle was the **syllogism**, which is a kind of inference rule. Aristotle's syllogisms did include elements of first-order logic, such as quantification, but were restricted to unary predicates. Syllogisms were categorized by "figures" and "moods," depending on the order of the terms (which we would call predicates) in the sentences, the degree of generality (which we would today interpret through quantifiers) applied to each term, and whether each term is negated. The most fundamental syllogism is that of the first mood of the first figure:

All $S$ are $M$.
All $M$ are $P$.
Therefore, all $S$ are $P$.

Aristotle tried to prove the validity of other syllogisms by "reducing" them to those of the first figure. He was much less precise in describing what this "reduction" should involve than he was in characterizing the syllogistic figures and moods themselves.

Gottlob Frege, who developed full first-order logic in 1879, based his system of inference on a large collection of logically valid schemas plus a single inference rule, Modus Ponens. Frege took advantage of the fact that the effect of an inference rule of the form "From $P$, infer $Q$" can be simulated by applying Modus Ponens to $P$ along with a logically valid schema $P \Rightarrow Q$. This "axiomatic" style of exposition, using Modus Ponens plus a number of logically valid schemas, was employed by a number of logicians after Frege; most notably, it was used in *Principia Mathematica* (Whitehead and Russell, 1910).

Inference rules, as distinct from axiom schemas, were the focus of the **natural deduction** approach, introduced by Gerhard Gentzen (1934) and by Stanisław Jaśkowski (1934). Natural deduction is called "natural" because it does not require conversion to (unreadable) normal form and because its inference rules are intended to appear natural to humans. Prawitz (1965) offers a book-length treatment of natural deduction. Gallier (1986) uses Gentzen's approach to expound the theoretical underpinnings of automated deduction.

The invention of clausal form was a crucial step in the development of a deep mathematical analysis of first-order logic. Whitehead and Russell (1910) expounded the so-called *rules of passage* (the actual term is from Herbrand (1930)) that are used to move quantifiers to the front of formulas. Skolem constants and Skolem functions were introduced, appropriately enough, by Thoralf Skolem (1920). The general procedure for skolemization is given by Skolem (1928), along with the important notion of the Herbrand universe.

Herbrand's theorem, named after the French logician Jacques Herbrand (1930), has played a vital role in the development of automated reasoning methods, both before and after Robinson's introduction of resolution. This is reflected in our reference to the "Herbrand universe" rather than the "Skolem universe," even though Skolem really invented the concept. Herbrand can also be regarded as the inventor of unification. Gödel (1930) built on the ideas of Skolem and Herbrand to show that first-order logic has a complete proof procedure. Alan Turing (1936) and Alonzo Church (1936) simultaneously showed, using very different proofs, that validity in first-order logic was not decidable. The excellent text by Enderton (1972) explains all of these results in a rigorous yet moderately understandable fashion.

Although McCarthy (1958) had suggested the use of first-order logic for representation and reasoning in AI, the first such systems were developed by logicians interested in mathematical theorem proving. It was Abraham Robinson who proposed the use of propositionalization and Herbrand's theorem, and Gilmore (1960) who wrote the first program based on this approach. Davis and Putnam (1960) used clausal form and produced a program that attempted to find refutations by substituting members of the Herbrand universe for variables to produce ground clauses and then looking for propositional inconsistencies among the ground clauses. Prawitz (1960) developed the key idea of letting the quest for propositional inconsistency drive the search process, and generating terms from the Herbrand universe only when it was necessary to do so in order to establish propositional inconsistency. After further development by other researchers, this idea led J. A. Robinson (no relation) to develop the resolution method (Robinson, 1965). The so-called inverse method developed at about the same time by the Soviet researcher S. Maslov (1964, 1967), based on somewhat different principles, offers similar computational advantages over propositionalization. Wolfgang Bibel's (1981) **connection method** can be viewed as an extension of this approach.

After the development of resolution, work on first-order inference proceeded in several different directions. In AI, resolution was adopted for question-answering systems by Cordell Green and Bertram Raphael (1968). A somewhat less formal approach was taken by Carl Hewitt (1969). His PLANNER language, although never fully implemented, was a precursor to logic programming and included directives for forward and backward chaining and for negation as failure. A subset known as MICRO-PLANNER (Sussman and Winograd, 1970) was implemented and used in the SHRDLU natural language understanding system (Winograd, 1972). Early AI implementations put a good deal of effort into data structures that would allow efficient retrieval of facts; this work is covered in AI programming texts (Charniak *et al.*, 1987; Norvig, 1992; Forbus and de Kleer, 1993).

By the early 1970s, **forward chaining** was well established in AI as an easily understandable alternative to resolution. It was used in a wide variety of systems, ranging from Nevins's geometry theorem prover (Nevins, 1975) to the R1 expert system for VAX configuration (McDermott, 1982). AI applications typically involved large numbers of rules, so it was important to develop efficient rule-matching technology, particularly for incremental updates. The technology for **production systems** was developed to support such applications. The production system language OPS-5 (Forgy, 1981; Brownston *et al.*, 1985) was used for R1 and for the SOAR cognitive architecture (Laird *et al.*, 1987). OPS-5 incorporated the rete match process (Forgy, 1982). SOAR, which generates new rules to cache the results of previous computations, can handle very large rule sets—over 8,000 rules in the case of the TACAIR-SOAR system for controlling simulated fighter aircraft (Jones *et al.*, 1998). CLIPS (Wygant, 1989) was a C-based production system language developed at NASA that allowed better integration with other software, hardware, and sensor systems and was used for spacecraft automation and several military applications.

The area of research known as **deductive databases** has also contributed a great deal to our understanding of forward inference. It began with a workshop in Toulouse in 1977, organized by Jack Minker, that brought together experts in logical inference and database systems (Gallaire and Minker, 1978). A recent historical survey (Ramakrishnan and Ullman, 1995) says, "Deductive [database] systems are an attempt to adapt Prolog, which has a 'small data' view of the world, to a 'large data' world." Thus, it aims to meld relational database technology, which is designed for retrieving large *sets* of facts, with Prolog-based inference technology, which typically retrieves one fact at a time. Texts on deductive databases include Ullman (1989) and Ceri *et al.* (1990).

Influential work by Chandra and Harel (1980) and Ullman (1985) led to the adoption of Datalog as a standard language for deductive databases. "Bottom-up" inference, or forward chaining, also became the standard—partly because it avoids the problems with nontermination and redundant computation that occur with backward chaining and partly because it has a more natural implementation in terms of the basic relational database operations. The development of the **magic sets** technique for rule rewriting by Bancilhon *et al.* (1986) allowed forward chaining to borrow the advantage of goal-directedness from backward chaining. Equalizing the arms race, tabled logic programming methods (see page 313) borrow the advantage of dynamic programming from forward chaining.

CONJUNCTIVE QUERY

DATA COMPLEXITY

Much of our understanding of the complexity of logical inference has come from the deductive database community. Chandra and Merlin (1977) first showed that matching a single nonrecursive rule (a **conjunctive query** in database terminology) can be NP-hard. Kuper and Vardi (1993) proposed **data complexity**—that is, complexity as a function of database size, viewing rule size as constant—as a suitable measure for query answering. Gottlob *et al.* (1999b) discuss the connection between conjunctive queries and constraint satisfaction, showing how hypertree decomposition can optimize the matching process.

SL-RESOLUTION

SLD-RESOLUTION

As mentioned earlier, **backward chaining** for logical inference appeared in Hewitt's PLANNER language (1969). Logic programming *per se* evolved independently of this effort. A restricted form of linear resolution called **SL-resolution** was developed by Kowalski and Kuehner (1971), building on Loveland's **model elimination** technique (1968); when applied to definite clauses, it becomes **SLD-resolution**, which lends itself to the interpretation of definite clauses as programs (Kowalski, 1974, 1979a, 1979b). Meanwhile, in 1972, the French researcher Alain Colmerauer had developed and implemented **Prolog** for the purpose of parsing natural language—Prolog's clauses were intended initially as context-free grammar rules (Roussel, 1975; Colmerauer *et al.*, 1973). Much of the theoretical background for logic programming was developed by Kowalski, working with Colmerauer. The semantic definition using least fixed points is due to Van Emden and Kowalski (1976). Kowalski (1988) and Cohen (1988) provide good historical overviews of the origins of Prolog. *Foundations of Logic Programming* (Lloyd, 1987) is a theoretical analysis of the underpinnings of Prolog and other logic programming languages.

Efficient Prolog compilers are generally based on the Warren Abstract Machine (WAM) model of computation developed by David H. D. Warren (1983). Van Roy (1990) showed that the application of additional compiler techniques, such as type inference, made Prolog programs competitive with C programs in terms of speed. The Japanese Fifth Generation project, a 10-year research effort beginning in 1982, was based completely on Prolog as the means to develop intelligent systems.

Methods for avoiding unnecessary looping in recursive logic programs were developed independently by Smith *et al.* (1986) and Tamaki and Sato (1986). The latter paper also included memoization for logic programs, a method developed extensively as **tabled logic programming** by David S. Warren. Swift and Warren (1994) show how to extend the WAM to handle tabling, enabling Datalog programs to execute an order of magnitude faster than forward-chaining deductive database systems.

Early theoretical work on constraint logic programming was done by Jaffar and Lassez (1987). Jaffar *et al.* (1992a) developed the CLP(R) system for handling real-valued constraints. Jaffar *et al.* (1992b) generalized the WAM to produce the CLAM (Constraint Logic Abstract Machine) for specifying implementations of CLP. Ait-Kaci and Podelski (1993) describe a sophisticated language called LIFE, which combines CLP with functional programming and with inheritance reasoning. Kohn (1991) describes an ambitious project to use constraint logic programming as the foundation for a real-time control architecture, with applications to fully automatic pilots.

There are a number of textbooks on logic programming and Prolog. *Logic for Problem Solving* (Kowalski, 1979b) is an early text on logic programming in general. Prolog texts include Clocksin and Mellish (1994), Shoham (1994), and Bratko (2001). Marriott and Stuckey (1998) provide excellent coverage of CLP. Until its demise in 2000, the *Journal of Logic Programming* was the journal of record; it has now been replaced by *Theory and Practice of Logic Programming*. Logic programming conferences include the International Conference on Logic Programming (ICLP) and the International Logic Programming Symposium (ILPS).

Research into **mathematical theorem proving** began even before the first complete first-order systems were developed. Herbert Gelernter's Geometry Theorem Prover (Gelernter, 1959) used heuristic search methods combined with diagrams for pruning false subgoals and was able to prove some quite intricate results in Euclidean geometry. Since that time, however, there has not been very much interaction between theorem proving and AI.

Early work concentrated on completeness. Following Robinson's seminal paper, the demodulation and paramodulation rules for equality reasoning were introduced by Wos *et al.* (1967) and Wos and Robinson (1968), respectively. These rules were also developed independently in the context of term rewriting systems (Knuth and Bendix, 1970). The incorporation of equality reasoning into the unification algorithm is due to Gordon Plotkin (1972); it was also a feature of QLISP (Sacerdoti *et al.*, 1976). Jouannaud and Kirchner (1991) survey equational unification from a term rewriting perspective. Efficient algorithms for standard unification were developed by Martelli and Montanari (1976) and Paterson and Wegman (1978).

In addition to equality reasoning, theorem provers have incorporated a variety of special-purpose decision procedures. Nelson and Oppen (1979) proposed an influential scheme for integrating such procedures into a general reasoning system; other methods include Stickel's (1985) "theory resolution" and Manna and Waldinger's (1986) "special relations."

A number of control strategies have been proposed for resolution, beginning with the unit preference strategy (Wos *et al.*, 1964). The set of support strategy was proposed by Wos *et al.* (1965), to provide a degree of goal-directedness in resolution. Linear resolution first appeared in Loveland (1970). Genesereth and Nilsson (1987, Chapter 5) provide a short but thorough analysis of a wide variety of control strategies.

Guard *et al.* (1969) describe the early SAM theorem prover, which helped to solve an open problem in lattice theory. Wos and Winker (1983) give an overview of the contributions of the AURA theorem prover toward solving open problems in various areas of mathematics and logic. McCune (1992) follows up on this, recounting the accomplishments of AURA's successor, OTTER, in solving open problems. Weidenbach (2001) describes SPASS, one of the strongest current theorem provers. *A Computational Logic* (Boyer and Moore, 1979) is the basic reference on the Boyer-Moore theorem prover. Stickel (1988) covers the Prolog Technology Theorem Prover (PTTP), which combines the advantages of Prolog compilation with the completeness of model elimination (Loveland, 1968). SETHEO (Letz *et al.*, 1992) is another widely used theorem prover based on this approach; it can perform several million inferences per second on 2000-model workstations. LEANTAP (Beckert and Posegga, 1995) is an efficient theorem prover implemented in only 25 lines of Prolog.

Early work in automated program synthesis was done by Simon (1963), Green (1969a), and Manna and Waldinger (1971). The transformational system of Burstall and Darlington (1977) used equational reasoning for recursive program synthesis. KIDS (Smith, 1990, 1996) is one of the strongest modern systems; it operates as an expert assistant. Manna and Waldinger (1992) give a tutorial introduction to the current state of the art, with emphasis on their own deductive approach. *Automating Software Design* (Lowry and McCartney, 1991) collects a number of papers in the area. The use of logic in hardware design is surveyed by Kern and Greenstreet (1999); Clarke *et al.* (1999) cover model checking for hardware verification.

*Computability and Logic* (Boolos and Jeffrey, 1989) is a good reference on completeness and undecidability. Many early papers in mathematical logic are to be found in *From Frege to Gödel: A Source Book in Mathematical Logic* (van Heijenoort, 1967). The journal of record for the field of pure mathematical logic (as opposed to automated deduction) is *The Journal of Symbolic Logic*. Textbooks geared toward automated deduction include the classic *Symbolic Logic and Mechanical Theorem Proving* (Chang and Lee, 1973), as well as more recent works by Wos *et al.* (1992), Bibel (1993), and Kaufmann *et al.* (2000). The anthology *Automation of Reasoning* (Siekmann and Wrightson, 1983) includes many important early papers on automated deduction. Other historical surveys have been written by Loveland (1984) and Bundy (1999). The principal journal for the field of theorem proving is the *Journal of Automated Reasoning*; the main conference is the annual Conference on Automated Deduction (CADE). Research in theorem proving is also strongly related to the use of logic in analyzing programs and programming languages, for which the principal conference is Logic in Computer Science.

## EXERCISES

**9.1** Prove from first principles that Universal Instantiation is sound and that Existential Instantiation produces an inferentially equivalent knowledge base.

**9.2** From $Likes(Jerry, IceCream)$ it seems reasonable to infer $\exists x \;\; Likes(x, IceCream)$. Write down a general inference rule, **Existential Introduction**, that sanctions this inference. State carefully the conditions that must be satisfied by the variables and terms involved.

**9.3** Suppose a knowledge base contains just one sentence, $\exists x \;\; AsHighAs(x, Everest)$. Which of the following are legitimate results of applying Existential Instantiation?

**a.** $AsHighAs(Everest, Everest)$.

**b.** $AsHighAs(Kilimanjaro, Everest)$.

**c.** $AsHighAs(Kilimanjaro, Everest) \wedge AsHighAs(BenNevis, Everest)$ (after two applications).

**9.4** For each pair of atomic sentences, give the most general unifier if it exists:

**a.** $P(A, B, B)$, $P(x, y, z)$.
**b.** $Q(y, G(A, B))$, $Q(G(x, x), y)$.
**c.** $Older(Father(y), y)$, $Older(Father(x), John)$.
**d.** $Knows(Father(y), y)$, $Knows(x, x)$.

**9.5** Consider the subsumption lattices shown in Figure 9.2.

**a.** Construct the lattice for the sentence $Employs(Mother(John), Father(Richard))$.
**b.** Construct the lattice for the sentence $Employs(IBM, y)$ ("Everyone works for IBM"). Remember to include every kind of query that unifies with the sentence.
**c.** Assume that STORE indexes each sentence under every node in its subsumption lattice. Explain how FETCH should work when some of these sentences contain variables; use as examples the sentences in (a) and (b) and the query $Employs(x, Father(x))$.

**9.6** Suppose we put into a logical database a segment of the U.S. census data listing the age, city of residence, date of birth, and mother of every person, using social security numbers as identifying constants for each person. Thus, George's age is given by $Age(\text{443-65-1282}, 56)$. Which of the indexing schemes S1–S5 following enable an efficient solution for which of the queries Q1–Q4 (assuming normal backward chaining)?

◇ **S1**: an index for each atom in each position.
◇ **S2**: an index for each first argument.
◇ **S3**: an index for each predicate atom.
◇ **S4**: an index for each *combination* of predicate and first argument.
◇ **S5**: an index for each *combination* of predicate and second argument and an index for each first argument (nonstandard).

◇ **Q1**: $Age(\text{443-44-4321}, x)$
◇ **Q2**: $ResidesIn(x, Houston)$
◇ **Q3**: $Mother(x, y)$
◇ **Q4**: $Age(x, 34) \wedge ResidesIn(x, TinyTownUSA)$

**9.7** One might suppose that we can avoid the problem of variable conflict in unification during backward chaining by standardizing apart all of the sentences in the knowledge base once and for all. Show that, for some sentences, this approach cannot work. (*Hint*: Consider a sentence, one part of which unifies with another.)

**9.8** Explain how to write any given 3-SAT problem of arbitrary size using a single first-order definite clause and no more than 30 ground facts.

**9.9** Write down logical representations for the following sentences, suitable for use with Generalized Modus Ponens:

**a.** Horses, cows, and pigs are mammals.

**b.** An offspring of a horse is a horse.

**c.** Bluebeard is a horse.

**d.** Bluebeard is Charlie's parent.

**e.** Offspring and parent are inverse relations.

**f.** Every mammal has a parent.

**9.10** In this question we will use the sentences you wrote in Exercise 9.9 to answer a question using a backward-chaining algorithm.

**a.** Draw the proof tree generated by an exhaustive backward-chaining algorithm for the query $\exists h \;\; Horse(h)$, where clauses are matched in the order given.

**b.** What do you notice about this domain?

**c.** How many solutions for $h$ actually follow from your sentences?

**d.** Can you think of a way to find all of them? (*Hint*: You might want to consult Smith *et al.* (1986).)

**9.11** A popular children's riddle is "Brothers and sisters have I none, but that man's father is my father's son." Use the rules of the family domain (Chapter 8) to show who that man is. You may apply any of the inference methods described in this chapter. Why do you think that this riddle is difficult?

**9.12** Trace the execution of the backward chaining algorithm in Figure 9.6 when it is applied to solve the crime problem. Show the sequence of values taken on by the *goals* variable, and arrange them into a tree.

**9.13** The following Prolog code defines a predicate `P`:

```
P(X, [X|Y]).
P(X, [Y|Z]) :- P(X,Z).
```

**a.** Show proof trees and solutions for the queries `P(A, [1,2,3])` and `P(2, [1,A,3])`.

**b.** What standard list operation does `P` represent?

**9.14** In this exercise, we will look at sorting in Prolog.

**a.** Write Prolog clauses that define the predicate `sorted(L)`, which is true if and only if list `L` is sorted in ascending order.

**b.** Write a Prolog definition for the predicate `perm(L,M)`, which is true if and only if `L` is a permutation of `M`.

**c.** Define `sort(L,M)` (`M` is a sorted version of `L`) using `perm` and `sorted`.

**d.** Run `sort` on longer and longer lists until you lose patience. What is the time complexity of your program?

**e.** Write a faster sorting algorithm, such as insertion sort or quicksort, in Prolog.

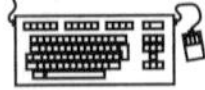

**9.15** In this exercise, we will look at the recursive application of rewrite rules, using logic programming. A rewrite rule (or **demodulator** in OTTER terminology) is an equation with a specified direction. For example, the rewrite rule $x+0 \rightarrow x$ suggests replacing any expression that matches $x + 0$ with the expression $x$. The application of rewrite rules is a central part of equational reasoning systems. We will use the predicate `rewrite(X,Y)` to represent rewrite rules. For example, the earlier rewrite rule is written as `rewrite(X+0,X)`. Some terms are *primitive* and cannot be further simplified; thus, we will write `primitive(0)` to say that 0 is a primitive term.

**a.** Write a definition of a predicate `simplify(X,Y)`, that is true when `Y` is a simplified version of `X`—that is, when no further rewrite rules are applicable to any subexpression of `Y`.

**b.** Write a collection of rules for the simplification of expressions involving arithmetic operators, and apply your simplification algorithm to some sample expressions.

**c.** Write a collection of rewrite rules for symbolic differentiation, and use them along with your simplification rules to differentiate and simplify expressions involving arithmetic expressions, including exponentiation.

**9.16** In this exercise, we will consider the implementation of search algorithms in Prolog. Suppose that `successor(X,Y)` is true when state `Y` is a successor of state `X`; and that `goal(X)` is true when `X` is a goal state. Write a definition for `solve(X,P)`, which means that `P` is a path (list of states) beginning with `X`, ending in a goal state, and consisting of a sequence of legal steps as defined by `successor`. You will find that depth-first search is the easiest way to do this. How easy would it be to add heuristic search control?

**9.17** How can resolution be used to show that a sentence is valid? Unsatisfiable?

**9.18** From "Horses are animals," it follows that "The head of a horse is the head of an animal." Demonstrate that this inference is valid by carrying out the following steps:

**a.** Translate the premise and the conclusion into the language of first-order logic. Use three predicates: $HeadOf(h, x)$ (meaning "$h$ is the head of $x$"), $Horse(x)$, and $Animal(x)$.

**b.** Negate the conclusion, and convert the premise and the negated conclusion into conjunctive normal form.

**c.** Use resolution to show that the conclusion follows from the premise.

**9.19** Here are two sentences in the language of first-order logic:

**(A):** $\forall x \;\; \exists y \;\; (x \geq y)$

**(B):** $\exists y \;\; \forall x \;\; (x \geq y)$

**a.** Assume that the variables range over all the natural numbers $0, 1, 2, \ldots, \infty$ and that the "$\geq$" predicate means "is greater than or equal to." Under this interpretation, translate (A) and (B) into English.

**b.** Is (A) true under this interpretation?

**c.** Is (B) true under this interpretation?

**d.** Does (A) logically entail (B)?

**e.** Does (B) logically entail (A)?

**f.** Using resolution, try to prove that (A) follows from (B). Do this even if you think that (B) does not logically entail (A); continue until the proof breaks down and you cannot proceed (if it does break down). Show the unifying substitution for each resolution step. If the proof fails, explain exactly where, how, and why it breaks down.

**g.** Now try to prove that (B) follows from (A).

**9.20** Resolution can produce nonconstructive proofs for queries with variables, so we had to introduce special mechanisms to extract definite answers. Explain why this issue does not arise with knowledge bases containing only definite clauses.

**9.21** We said in this chapter that resolution cannot be used to generate all logical consequences of a set of sentences. Can any algorithm do this?

# 10 KNOWLEDGE REPRESENTATION

*In which we show how to use first-order logic to represent the most important aspects of the real world, such as action, space, time, mental events, and shopping.*

The last three chapters described the technology for knowledge-based agents: the syntax, semantics, and proof theory of propositional and first-order logic, and the implementation of agents that use these logics. In this chapter we address the question of what *content* to put into such an agent's knowledge base—how to represent facts about the world.

Section 10.1 introduces the idea of a general ontology, which organizes everything in the world into a hierarchy of categories. Section 10.2 covers the basic categories of objects, substances, and measures. Section 10.3 discusses representations for actions, which are central to the construction of knowledge-based agents, and also explains the more general notion of **events**, or space–time chunks. Section 10.4 discusses knowledge about beliefs, and Section 10.5 brings all the knowledge together in the context of an Internet shopping environment. Sections 10.6 and 10.7 cover specialized reasoning systems for representing uncertain and changing knowledge.

## 10.1 ONTOLOGICAL ENGINEERING

In "toy" domains, the choice of representation is not that important; it is easy to come up with a consistent vocabulary. On the other hand, complex domains such as shopping on the Internet or controlling a robot in a changing physical environment require more general and flexible representations. This chapter shows how to create these representations, concentrating on general concepts—such as *Actions, Time, Physical Objects*, and *Beliefs*—that occur in many different domains. Representing these abstract concepts is sometimes called

ONTOLOGICAL ENGINEERING

**ontological engineering**—it is related to the **knowledge engineering** process described in Section 8.4, but operates on a grander scale.

The prospect of representing *everything* in the world is daunting. Of course, we won't actually write a complete description of everything—that would be far too much for even a 1000–page textbook—but we will leave placeholders where new knowledge for any domain can fit in. For example, we will define what it means to be a physical object, and the details

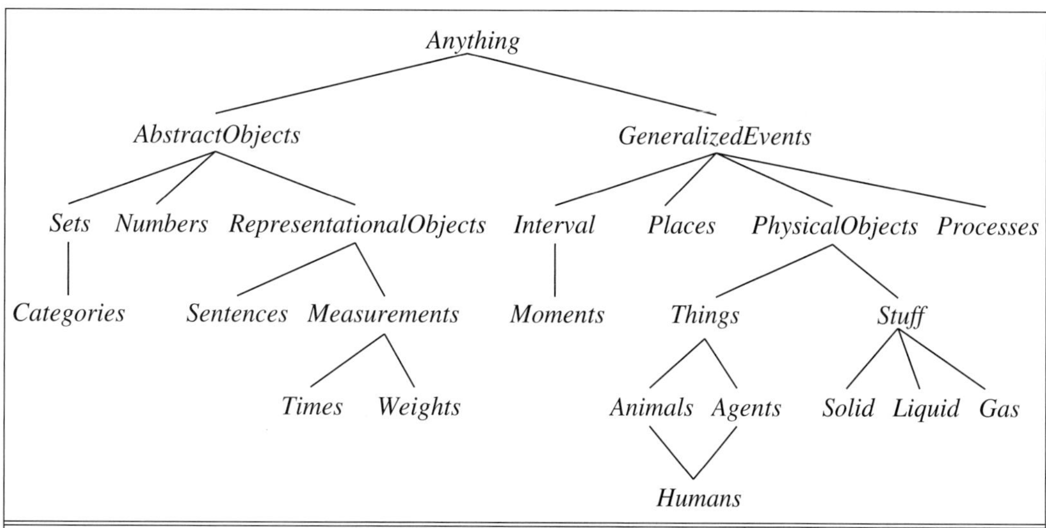


**Figure 10.1** The upper ontology of the world, showing the topics to be covered later in the chapter. Each arc indicates that the lower concept is a specialization of the upper one.

of different types of objects—robots, televisions, books, or whatever—can be filled in later. UPPER ONTOLOGY The general framework of concepts is called an **upper ontology**, because of the convention of drawing graphs with the general concepts at the top and the more specific concepts below them, as in Figure 10.1.

Before considering the ontology further, we should state one important caveat. We have elected to use first-order logic to discuss the content and organization of knowledge. Certain aspects of the real world are hard to capture in FOL. The principal difficulty is that almost all generalizations have exceptions, or hold only to a degree. For example, although "tomatoes are red" is a useful rule, some tomatoes are green, yellow, or orange. Similar exceptions can be found to almost all the general statements in this chapter. The ability to handle exceptions and uncertainty is extremely important, but is orthogonal to the task of understanding the general ontology. For this reason, we will delay the discussion of exceptions until Section 10.6, and the more general topic of uncertain information until Chapter 13.

Of what use is an upper ontology? Consider again the ontology for circuits in Section 8.4. It makes a large number of simplifying assumptions. For example, time is omitted completely. Signals are fixed, and do not propagate. The structure of the circuit remains constant. If we wanted to make this more general, consider signals at particular times, and include the wire lengths and propagation delays. This would allow us to simulate the timing properties of the circuit, and indeed such simulations are often carried out by circuit designers. We could also introduce more interesting classes of gates, for example by describing the technology (TTL, MOS, CMOS, and so on) as well as the input/output specification. If we wanted to discuss reliability or diagnosis, we would include the possibility that the structure of the circuit or the properties of the gates might change spontaneously. To account for stray capacitances, we would need to move from a purely topological representation of connectivity to a more realistic description of geometric properties.

If we look at the wumpus world, similar considerations apply. Although we do include time, it has a very simple structure: Nothing happens except when the agent acts, and all changes are instantaneous. A more general ontology, better suited for the real world, would allow for simultaneous changes extended over time. We also used a $Pit$ predicate to say which squares have pits. We could have allowed for different kinds of pits by having several individuals belonging to the class of pits, each having different properties. Similarly, we might want to allow for other animals besides wumpuses. It might not be possible to pin down the exact species from the available percepts, so we would need to build up a wumpus-world biological taxonomy to help the agent predict behavior from scanty clues.

For any special-purpose ontology, it is possible to make changes like these to move toward greater generality. An obvious question then arises: do all these ontologies converge on a general-purpose ontology? After centuries of philosophical and computational investigation, the answer is "Possibly." In this section, we will present one version, representing a synthesis of ideas from those centuries. There are two major characteristics of general-purpose ontologies that distinguish them from collections of special-purpose ontologies:

- A general-purpose ontology should be applicable in more or less any special-purpose domain (with the addition of domain-specific axioms). This means that, as far as possible, no representational issue can be finessed or brushed under the carpet.
- In any sufficiently demanding domain, different areas of knowledge must be *unified*, because reasoning and problem solving could involve several areas simultaneously. A robot circuit-repair system, for instance, needs to reason about circuits in terms of electrical connectivity and physical layout, and about time, both for circuit timing analysis and estimating labor costs. The sentences describing time therefore must be capable of being combined with those describing spatial layout and must work equally well for nanoseconds and minutes and for angstroms and meters.

After we present the general ontology we use it to describe the Internet shopping domain. This domain is more than adequate to exercise our ontology, and leaves plenty of scope for the reader to do some creative knowledge representation of his or her own. Consider for example that the Internet shopping agent must know about myriad subjects and authors to buy books at Amazon.com, about all sorts of foods to buy groceries at Peapod.com, and about everything one might find at a garage sale to hunt for bargains at Ebay.com.[1]

## 10.2 Categories and Objects

CATEGORIES

The organization of objects into **categories** is a vital part of knowledge representation. Although interaction with the world takes place at the level of individual objects, *much reasoning takes place at the level of categories.* For example, a shopper might have the goal of buying a basketball, rather than a *particular* basketball such as $BB_9$. Categories also serve to make predictions about objects once they are classified. One infers the presence of certain

[1] We apologize if, due to circumstances beyond our control, some of these online stores are no longer functioning by the time you read this.

objects from perceptual input, infers category membership from the perceived properties of the objects, and then uses category information to make predictions about the objects. For example, from its green, mottled skin, large size, and ovoid shape, one can infer that an object is a watermelon; from this, one infers that it would be useful for fruit salad.

There are two choices for representing categories in first-order logic: predicates and objects. That is, we can use the predicate $Basketball(b)$, or we can **reify** the category as an object, $Basketballs$. We could then say $Member(b, Basketballs)$ (which we will abbreviate as $b \in Basketballs$) to say that $b$ is a member of the category of basketballs. We say $Subset(Basketballs, Balls)$ (abbreviated as $Basketballs \subset Balls$) to say that $Basketballs$ is a subcategory, or subset, of $Balls$. So you can think of a category as being the set of its members, or you can think of it as a more complex object that just happens to have the $Member$ and $Subset$ relations defined for it.

INHERITANCE

Categories serve to organize and simplify the knowledge base through **inheritance**. If we say that all instances of the category $Food$ are edible, and if we assert that $Fruit$ is a subclass of $Food$ and $Apples$ is a subclass of $Fruit$, then we know that every apple is edible. We say that the individual apples **inherit** the property of edibility, in this case from their membership in the $Food$ category.

TAXONOMY

Subclass relations organize categories into a **taxonomy**, or **taxonomic hierarchy**. Taxonomies have been used explicitly for centuries in technical fields. For example, systematic biology aims to provide a taxonomy of all living and extinct species; library science has developed a taxonomy of all fields of knowledge, encoded as the Dewey Decimal system; and tax authorities and other government departments have developed extensive taxonomies of occupations and commercial products. Taxonomies are also an important aspect of general commonsense knowledge.

First-order logic makes it easy to state facts about categories, either by relating objects to categories or by quantifying over their members:

- An object is a member of a category. For example:
  $BB_9 \in Basketballs$
- A category is a subclass of another category. For example:
  $Basketballs \subset Balls$
- All members of a category have some properties. For example:
  $x \in Basketballs \Rightarrow Round(x)$
- Members of a category can be recognized by some properties. For example:
  $Orange(x) \land Round(x) \land Diameter(x) = 9.5'' \land x \in Balls \Rightarrow x \in Basketballs$
- A category as a whole has some properties. For example:
  $Dogs \in DomesticatedSpecies$

Notice that because $Dogs$ is a category and is a member of $DomesticatedSpecies$, the latter must be a category of categories. One can even have categories of categories of categories, but they are not much use.

Although subclass and member relations are the most important ones for categories, we also want to be able to state relations between categories that are not subclasses of each other. For example, if we just say that $Males$ and $Females$ are subclasses of $Animals$, then we have not said that a male cannot be a female. We say that two or more categories are **disjoint** if they have no members in common. And even if we know that males and females are disjoint, we will not know that an animal that is not a male must be a female, unless we say that males and females constitute an **exhaustive decomposition** of the animals. A disjoint exhaustive decomposition is known as a **partition**. The following examples illustrate these three concepts:

DISJOINT

EXHAUSTIVE DECOMPOSITION

PARTITION

$$\begin{aligned}
&Disjoint(\{Animals, Vegetables\})\\
&ExhaustiveDecomposition(\{Americans, Canadians, Mexicans\},\\
&\qquad\qquad NorthAmericans)\\
&Partition(\{Males, Females\}, Animals)\ .
\end{aligned}$$

(Note that the $ExhaustiveDecomposition$ of $NorthAmericans$ is not a $Partition$, because some people have dual citizenship.) The three predicates are defined as follows:

$$\begin{aligned}
&Disjoint(s) \Leftrightarrow (\forall c_1, c_2\ \ c_1 \in s \land c_2 \in s \land c_1 \neq c_2 \Rightarrow Intersection(c_1, c_2) = \{\ \})\\
&ExhaustiveDecomposition(s, c) \Leftrightarrow (\forall i\ \ i \in c \Leftrightarrow \exists c_2\ \ c_2 \in s \land i \in c_2)\\
&Partition(s, c) \Leftrightarrow Disjoint(s) \land ExhaustiveDecomposition(s, c)\ .
\end{aligned}$$

Categories can also be *defined* by providing necessary and sufficient conditions for membership. For example, a bachelor is an unmarried adult male:

$$x \in Bachelors \Leftrightarrow Unmarried(x) \land x \in Adults \land x \in Males\ .$$

As we discuss in the sidebar on natural kinds, strict logical definitions for categories are neither always possible nor always necessary.

### Physical composition

The idea that one object can be part of another is a familiar one. One's nose is part of one's head, Romania is part of Europe, and this chapter is part of this book. We use the general $PartOf$ relation to say that one thing is part of another. Objects can be grouped into $PartOf$ hierarchies, reminiscent of the $Subset$ hierarchy:

$$\begin{aligned}
&PartOf(Bucharest, Romania)\\
&PartOf(Romania, EasternEurope)\\
&PartOf(EasternEurope, Europe)\\
&PartOf(Europe, Earth)\ .
\end{aligned}$$

The $PartOf$ relation is transitive and reflexive; that is,

$$\begin{aligned}
&PartOf(x, y) \land PartOf(y, z) \Rightarrow PartOf(x, z)\ .\\
&PartOf(x, x)\ .
\end{aligned}$$

Therefore, we can conclude $PartOf(Bucharest, Earth)$.

COMPOSITE OBJECT

Categories of **composite objects** are often characterized by structural relations among parts. For example, a biped has two legs attached to a body:

$$\begin{aligned}
Biped(a) \Rightarrow\ & \exists l_1, l_2, b\ \ Leg(l_1) \land Leg(l_2) \land Body(b) \land\\
& PartOf(l_1, a) \land PartOf(l_2, a) \land PartOf(b, a) \land\\
& Attached(l_1, b) \land Attached(l_2, b) \land\\
& l_1 \neq l_2 \land [\forall l_3\ \ Leg(l_3) \land PartOf(l_3, a) \Rightarrow (l_3 = l_1 \lor l_3 = l_2)]\ .
\end{aligned}$$

The notation for "exactly two" is a little awkward; we are forced to say that there are two legs, that they are not the same, and that if anyone proposes a third leg, it must be the same as one of the other two. In Section 10.6, we will see how a formalism called description logic makes it easier to represent constraints like "exactly two."

We can define a $PartPartition$ relation analogous to the $Partition$ relation for categories. (See Exercise 10.6.) An object is composed of the parts in its $PartPartition$ and can be viewed as deriving some properties from those parts. For example, the mass of a composite object is the sum of the masses of the parts. Notice that this is not the case with categories, which have no mass, even though their elements might.

It is also useful to define composite objects with definite parts but no particular structure. For example, we might want to say, "The apples in this bag weigh two pounds." The temptation would be to ascribe this weight to the *set* of apples in the bag, but this would be a mistake because the set is an abstract mathematical concept that has elements but does not have weight. Instead, we need a new concept, which we will call a **bunch**. For example, if the apples are $Apple_1$, $Apple_2$, and $Apple_3$, then

BUNCH

$$BunchOf(\{Apple_1, Apple_2, Apple_3\})$$

denotes the composite object with the three apples as parts (not elements). We can then use the bunch as a normal, albeit unstructured, object. Notice that $BunchOf(\{x\}) = x$. Furthermore, $BunchOf(Apples)$ is the composite object consisting of all apples—not to be confused with $Apples$, the category or set of all apples.

We can define $BunchOf$ in terms of the $PartOf$ relation. Obviously, each element of $s$ is part of $BunchOf(s)$:

$$\forall x \;\; x \in s \;\Rightarrow\; PartOf(x, BunchOf(s)) \,.$$

Furthermore, $BunchOf(s)$ *is the smallest object satisfying this condition.* In other words, $BunchOf(s)$ must be part of any object that has all the elements of $s$ as parts:

$$\forall y \;\; [\forall x \;\; x \in s \;\Rightarrow\; PartOf(x, y)] \;\Rightarrow\; PartOf(BunchOf(s), y) \,.$$

LOGICAL MINIMIZATION

These axioms are an example of a general technique called **logical minimization**, which means defining an object as the smallest one satisfying certain conditions.

## Measurements

MEASURES

In both scientific and commonsense theories of the world, objects have height, mass, cost, and so on. The values that we assign for these properties are called **measures**. Ordinary quantitative measures are quite easy to represent. We imagine that the universe includes abstract "measure objects," such as the *length* that is the length of this line segment: ⊢——————————⊣. We can call this length 1.5 inches or 3.81 centimeters. Thus, the same length has different names in our language. Logically, this can be done by combining a **units function** with a number. (An alternative scheme is explored in Exercise 10.8.) If the line segment is called $L_1$, we can write

UNITS FUNCTION

$$Length(L_1) = Inches(1.5) = Centimeters(3.81) \,.$$

Conversion between units is done by equating multiples of one unit to another:

$$Centimeters(2.54 \times d) = Inches(d) \,.$$

### NATURAL KINDS

Some categories have strict definitions: an object is a triangle if and only if it is a polygon with three sides. On the other hand, most categories in the real world have no clear-cut definition; these are called **natural kind** categories. For example, tomatoes tend to be a dull scarlet; roughly spherical; with an indentation at the top where the stem was; about two to four inches in diameter; with a thin but tough skin; and with flesh, seeds, and juice inside. There is, however, variation: some tomatoes are orange, unripe tomatoes are green, some are smaller or larger than average, and cherry tomatoes are uniformly small. Rather than having a complete definition of tomatoes, we have a set of features that serves to identify objects that are clearly typical tomatoes, but might not be able to decide for other objects. (Could there be a tomato that is furry, like a peach?)

This poses a problem for a logical agent. The agent cannot be sure that an object it has perceived is a tomato, and even if it were sure, it could not be certain which of the properties of typical tomatoes this one has. This problem is an inevitable consequence of operating in partially observable environments.

One useful approach is to separate what is true of all instances of a category from what is true only of typical instances. So in addition to the category $Tomatoes$, we will also have the category $Typical(Tomatoes)$. Here, the $Typical$ function maps a category to the subclass that contains only typical instances:

$$Typical(c) \subseteq c \, .$$

Most knowledge about natural kinds will actually be about their typical instances:

$$x \in Typical(Tomatoes) \;\Rightarrow\; Red(x) \land Round(x) \, .$$

Thus, we can write down useful facts about categories without exact definitions.

The difficulty of providing exact definitions for most natural categories was explained in depth by Wittgenstein (1953), in his book *Philosophical Investigations*. He used the example of *games* to show that members of a category shared "family resemblances" rather than necessary and sufficient characteristics.

The utility of the notion of strict definition was also challenged by Quine (1953). He pointed out that even the definition of "bachelor" as an unmarried adult male is suspect; one might, for example, question a statement such as "the Pope is a bachelor." While not strictly *false*, this usage is certainly *infelicitous* because it induces unintended inferences on the part of the listener. The tension could perhaps be resolved by distinguishing between logical definitions suitable for internal knowledge representation and the more nuanced criteria for felicitous linguistic usage. The latter may be achieved by "filtering" the assertions derived from the former. It is also possible that failures of linguistic usage serve as feedback for modifying internal definitions, so that filtering becomes unnecessary.

Similar axioms can be written for pounds and kilograms, seconds and days, and dollars and cents. Measures can be used to describe objects as follows:

$$Diameter(Basketball_{12}) = Inches(9.5) .$$
$$ListPrice(Basketball_{12}) = \$(19) .$$
$$d \in Days \Rightarrow Duration(d) = Hours(24) .$$

Note that $\$(1)$ is *not* a dollar bill! One can have two dollar bills, but there is only one object named $\$(1)$. Note also that, while $Inches(0)$ and $Centimeters(0)$ refer to the same zero length, they are not identical to other zero measures, such as $Seconds(0)$.

Simple, quantitative measures are easy to represent. Other measures present more of a problem, because they have no agreed scale of values. Exercises have difficulty, desserts have deliciousness, and poems have beauty, yet numbers cannot be assigned to these qualities. One might, in a moment of pure accountancy, dismiss such properties as useless for the purpose of logical reasoning; or, still worse, attempt to impose a numerical scale on beauty. This would be a grave mistake, because it is unnecessary. The most important aspect of measures is not the particular numerical values, but the fact that measures can be *ordered.*

Although measures are not numbers, we can still compare them using an ordering symbol such as $>$. For example, we might well believe that Norvig's exercises are tougher than Russell's, and that one scores less on tougher exercises:

$$e_1 \in Exercises \wedge e_2 \in Exercises \wedge Wrote(Norvig, e_1) \wedge Wrote(Russell, e_2) \Rightarrow$$
$$Difficulty(e_1) > Difficulty(e_2) .$$
$$e_1 \in Exercises \wedge e_2 \in Exercises \wedge Difficulty(e_1) > Difficulty(e_2) \Rightarrow$$
$$ExpectedScore(e_1) < ExpectedScore(e_2) .$$

This is enough to allow one to decide which exercises to do, even though no numerical values for difficulty were ever used. (One does, however, have to discover who wrote which exercises.) These sorts of monotonic relationships among measures form the basis for the field of **qualitative physics**, a subfield of AI that investigates how to reason about physical systems without plunging into detailed equations and numerical simulations. Qualitative physics is discussed in the historical notes section.

## Substances and objects

The real world can be seen as consisting of primitive objects (particles) and composite objects built from them. By reasoning at the level of large objects such as apples and cars, we can overcome the complexity involved in dealing with vast numbers of primitive objects individually. There is, however, a significant portion of reality that seems to defy any obvious

INDIVIDUATION

**individuation**—division into distinct objects. We give this portion the generic name **stuff**.

STUFF

For example, suppose I have some butter and an aardvark in front of me. I can say there is one aardvark, but there is no obvious number of "butter-objects," because any part of a butter-object is also a butter-object, at least until we get to very small parts indeed. This is the major distinction between stuff and things. If we cut an aardvark in half, we do not get two aardvarks (unfortunately).

The English language distinguishes clearly between stuff and things. We say "an aardvark," but, except in pretentious California restaurants, one cannot say "a butter." Linguists

COUNT NOUNS

MASS NOUNS

distinguish between **count nouns**, such as aardvarks, holes, and theorems, and **mass nouns**, such as butter, water, and energy. Several competing ontologies claim to handle this distinction. We will describe just one; the others are covered in the historical notes section.

To represent stuff properly, we begin with the obvious. We will need to have as objects in our ontology at least the gross "lumps" of stuff we interact with. For example, we might recognize a lump of butter as the same butter that was left on the table the night before; we might pick it up, weigh it, sell it, or whatever. In these senses, it is an object just like the aardvark. Let us call it $Butter_3$. We will also define the category $Butter$. Informally, its elements will be all those things of which one might say "It's butter," including $Butter_3$. With some caveats about very small parts that we will omit for now, any part of a butter-object is also a butter-object:

$$x \in Butter \wedge PartOf(y, x) \Rightarrow y \in Butter .$$

We can now say that butter melts at around 30 degrees centigrade:

$$x \in Butter \Rightarrow MeltingPoint(x, Centigrade(30)) .$$

We could go on to say that butter is yellow, is less dense than water, is soft at room temperature, has a high fat content, and so on. On the other hand, butter has no particular size, shape, or weight. We can define more specialized categories of butter such as $UnsaltedButter$, which is also a kind of stuff. On the other hand, the category $PoundOfButter$, which includes as members all butter-objects weighing one pound, is not a substance! If we cut a pound of butter in half, we do not, alas, get two pounds of butter.

INTRINSIC

EXTRINSIC

What is actually going on is this: there are some properties that are **intrinsic**: they belong to the very substance of the object, rather than to the object as a whole. When you cut a substance in half, the two pieces retain the same set of intrinsic properties—things like density, boiling point, flavor, color, ownership, and so on. On the other hand, **extrinsic** properties are the opposite: properties such as weight, length, shape, function, and so on are not retained under subdivision.

A class of objects that includes in its definition only *intrinsic* properties is then a substance, or mass noun; a class that includes *any* extrinsic properties in its definition is a count noun. The category *Stuff* is the most general substance category, specifying no intrinsic properties. The category $Thing$ is the most general discrete object category, specifying no extrinsic properties. All physical objects belong to both categories, so the categories are coextensive—they refer to the same entities.

## 10.3 ACTIONS, SITUATIONS, AND EVENTS

Reasoning about the results of actions is central to the operation of a knowledge-based agent. Chapter 7 gave examples of propositional sentences describing how actions affect the wumpus world—for example, Equation (7.3) on page 227 states how the agent's location is changed by forward motion. One drawback of propositional logic is the need to have a different copy of the action description for each time at which the action might be executed. This section describes a representation method that uses first-order logic to avoid that problem.

### The ontology of situation calculus

One obvious way to avoid multiple copies of axioms is simply to quantify over time—to say, "$\forall\, t$, such-and-such is the result at $t + 1$ of doing the action at $t$." Instead of dealing with explicit times like $t + 1$, we will concentrate in this section on *situations*, which denote the states resulting from executing actions. This approach is called **situation calculus** and involves the following ontology:

SITUATION CALCULUS

- As in Chapter 8, actions are logical terms such as $Forward$ and $Turn(Right)$. For now, we will assume that the environment contains only one agent. (If there is more than one, an additional argument can be inserted to say which agent is doing the action.)
- **Situations** are logical terms consisting of the initial situation (usually called $S_0$) and all situations that are generated by applying an action to a situation. The function $Result(a, s)$ (sometimes called $Do$) names the situation that results when action $a$ is executed in situation $s$. Figure 10.2 illustrates this idea.
- **Fluents** are functions and predicates that vary from one situation to the next, such as the location of the agent or the aliveness of the wumpus. The dictionary says a fluent is something that flows, like a liquid. In this use, it means flowing or changing across situations. By convention, the situation is always the last argument of a fluent. For example, $\neg Holding(G_1, S_0)$ says that the agent is not holding the gold $G_1$ in the initial situation $S_0$. $Age(Wumpus, S_0)$ refers to the wumpus's age in $S_0$.
- **Atemporal** or **eternal** predicates and functions are also allowed. Examples include the predicate $Gold(G_1)$ and the function $LeftLegOf(Wumpus)$.

SITUATIONS

FLUENTS

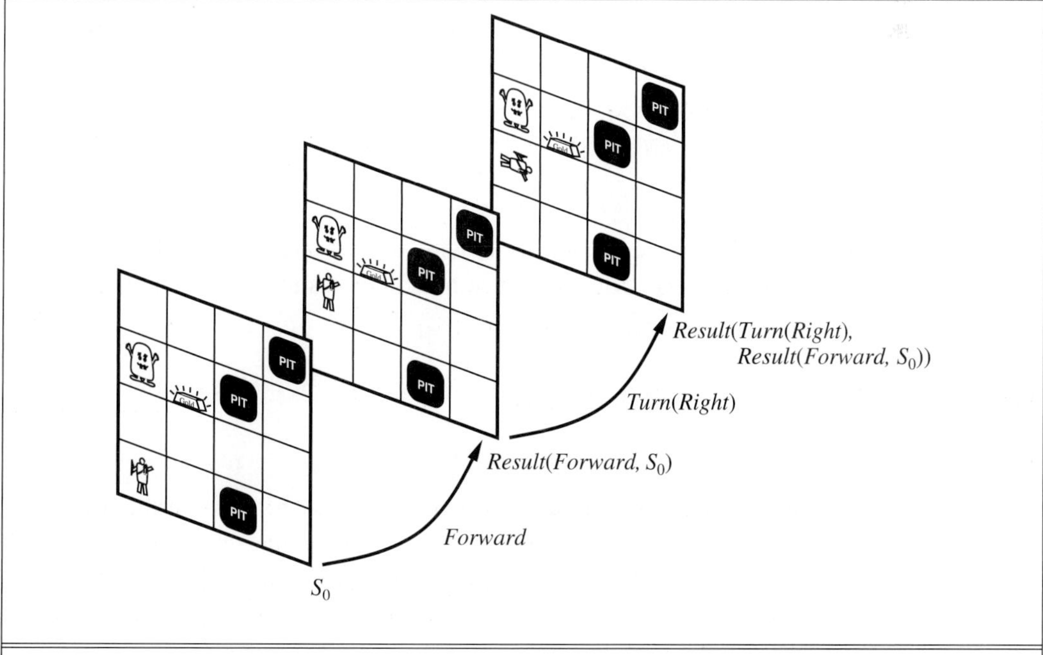


**Figure 10.2** In situation calculus, each situation (except $S_0$) is the result of an action.

In addition to single actions, it is also helpful to reason about action sequences. We can define the results of sequences in terms of the results of individual actions. First, we say that executing an empty sequence leaves the situation unchanged:

$$Result([], s) = s .$$

Executing a nonempty sequence is the same as executing the first action and then executing the rest in the resulting situation:

$$Result([a|seq], s) = Result(seq, Result(a, s)) .$$

PROJECTION

PLANNING

A situation calculus agent should be able to deduce the outcome of a given sequence of actions; this is the **projection** task. With a suitable constructive inference algorithm, it should also be able to *find* a sequence that achieves a desired effect; this is the **planning** task.

We will use an example from a modified version of the wumpus world where we do not worry about the agent's orientation and where the agent can $Go$ from one location to an adjacent one. Suppose the agent is at $[1, 1]$ and the gold is at $[1, 2]$. The aim is to have the gold in $[1, 1]$. The fluent predicates are $At(o, x, s)$ and $Holding(o, s)$. Then the initial knowledge base might include the following description:

$$At(Agent, [1, 1], S_0) \wedge At(G_1, [1, 2], S_0) .$$

This is not quite enough, however, because it doesn't say what *isn't* true in $S_0$. (See page 355 for further discussion of this point.) The complete description is as follows:

$$At(o, x, S_0) \Leftrightarrow [(o = Agent \wedge x = [1, 1]) \vee (o = G_1 \wedge x = [1, 2])] .$$
$$\neg Holding(o, S_0) .$$

We also need to state that $G_1$ is gold and that $[1, 1]$ and $[1, 2]$ are adjacent:

$$Gold(G_1) \wedge Adjacent([1, 1], [1, 2]) \wedge Adjacent([1, 2], [1, 1]) .$$

One would like to be able to prove that the agent achieves its aim by going to $[1, 2]$, grabbing the gold, and returning to $[1, 1]$. That is,

$$At(G_1, [1, 1], Result([Go([1, 1], [1, 2]), Grab(G_1), Go([1, 2], [1, 1])], S_0)) .$$

More interesting is the possibility of constructing a plan to get the gold, which is achieved by answering the query "what sequence of actions results in the gold being at [1,1]?"

$$\exists\, seq \;\; At(G_1, [1, 1], Result(seq, S_0)) .$$

Let us see what has to go into the knowledge base for these queries to be answered.

### Describing actions in situation calculus

POSSIBILITY AXIOM

EFFECT AXIOM

In the simplest version of situation calculus, each action is described by two axioms: a **possibility axiom** that says when it is possible to execute the action, and an **effect axiom** that says what happens when a possible action is executed. We will use $Poss(a, s)$ to mean that it is possible to execute action $a$ in situation $s$. The axioms have the following form:

POSSIBILITY AXIOM: $Preconditions \Rightarrow Poss(a, s)$ .
EFFECT AXIOM: $Poss(a, s) \Rightarrow$ *Changes that result from taking action.*

We will present these axioms for the modified wumpus world. To shorten our sentences, we will omit universal quantifiers whose scope is the entire sentence. We assume that the variable $s$ ranges over situations, $a$ ranges over actions, $o$ over objects (including agents), $g$ over gold, and $x$ and $y$ over locations.

The possibility axioms for this world state that an agent can go between adjacent locations, grab a piece of gold in the current location, and release some gold that it is holding:

$$\begin{aligned} &At(Agent, x, s) \land Adjacent(x, y) &&\Rightarrow Poss(Go(x, y), s) . \\ &Gold(g) \land At(Agent, x, s) \land At(g, x, s) &&\Rightarrow Poss(Grab(g), s) . \\ &Holding(g, s) &&\Rightarrow Poss(Release(g), s) . \end{aligned}$$

The effect axioms state that, if an action is possible, then certain properties (fluents) will hold in the situation that results from executing the action. Going from $x$ to $y$ results in being at $y$, grabbing the gold results in holding the gold, and releasing the gold results in not holding it:

$$\begin{aligned} &Poss(Go(x, y), s) &&\Rightarrow At(Agent, y, Result(Go(x, y), s)) . \\ &Poss(Grab(g), s) &&\Rightarrow Holding(g, Result(Grab(g), s)) . \\ &Poss(Release(g), s) &&\Rightarrow \neg Holding(g, Result(Release(g), s)) . \end{aligned}$$

Having stated these axioms, can we prove that our little plan achieves the goal? Unfortunately not! At first, everything works fine; $Go([1, 1], [1, 2])$ is indeed possible in $S_0$ and the effect axiom for $Go$ allows us to conclude that the agent reaches [1,2]:

$$At(Agent, [1, 2], Result(Go([1, 1], [1, 2]), S_0)) .$$

Now we consider the $Grab(G_1)$ action. We have to show that it is possible in the new situation—that is,

$$At(G_1, [1, 2], Result(Go([1, 1], [1, 2]), S_0)) .$$

Alas, nothing in the knowledge base justifies such a conclusion. Intuitively, we understand that the agent's $Go$ action should have no effect on the gold's location, so it should still be at $[1, 2]$, where it was in $S_0$. *The problem is that the effect axioms say what changes, but don't say what stays the same.*

FRAME PROBLEM

Representing all the things that stay the same is called the **frame problem**. We must find an efficient solution to the frame problem because, in the real world, almost everything stays the same almost all the time. Each action affects only a tiny fraction of all fluents.

FRAME AXIOM

One approach is to write explicit **frame axioms** that *do* say what stays the same. For example, the agent's movements leave other objects stationary unless they are held:

$$At(o, x, s) \land (o \neq Agent) \land \neg Holding(o, s) \Rightarrow At(o, x, Result(Go(y, z), s)) .$$

If there are $F$ fluent predicates and $A$ actions, then we will need $O(AF)$ frame axioms. On the other hand, if each action has at most $E$ effects, where $E$ is typically much less than $F$, then we should be able to represent what happens with a much smaller knowledge base of size $O(AE)$. This is the **representational frame problem**. The closely related **inferential frame problem** is to project the results of a $t$-step sequence of actions in time $O(Et)$, rather than time $O(Ft)$ or $O(AEt)$. We will address each problem in turn. Even then, another problem remains—that of ensuring that *all* necessary conditions for an action's success have been specified. For example, $Go$ fails if the agent dies *en route*. This is the **qualification problem**, for which there is no complete solution.

REPRESENTATIONAL FRAME PROBLEM

INFERENTIAL FRAME PROBLEM

QUALIFICATION PROBLEM

### Solving the representational frame problem

The solution to the representational frame problem involves just a slight change in viewpoint on how to write the axioms. Instead of writing out the effects of each action, we consider how each fluent predicate evolves over time.[3] The axioms we use are called **successor-state axioms**. They have the following form:

SUCCESSOR-STATE AXIOM

SUCCESSOR-STATE AXIOM:
*Action is possible* $\Rightarrow$
(*Fluent is true in result state* $\Leftrightarrow$ *Action's effect made it true*
$\vee$ *It was true before and action left it alone*) .

After the qualification that we are not considering impossible actions, notice that this definition uses $\Leftrightarrow$, not $\Rightarrow$. This means that the axiom says that the fluent will be true if *and only if* the right-hand side holds. Put another way, we are specifying the truth value of each fluent in the next state as a function of the action and the truth value in the current state. This means that the next state is completely specified from the current state and hence that there are no additional frame axioms needed.

The successor-state axiom for the agent's location says that the agent is at $y$ after executing an action either if the action is possible and consists of moving to $y$ or if the agent was already at $y$ and the action is not a move to somewhere else:

$$\begin{aligned}&Poss(a, s) \Rightarrow\\&(At(Agent, y, Result(a, s)) \Leftrightarrow a = Go(x, y)\\&\qquad \vee (At(Agent, y, s) \wedge a \neq Go(y, z))) .\end{aligned}$$

The axiom for $Holding$ says that the agent is holding $g$ after executing an action if the action was a grab of $g$ and the grab is possible or if the agent was already holding $g$, and the action is not releasing it:

$$\begin{aligned}&Poss(a, s) \Rightarrow\\&(Holding(g, Result(a, s)) \Leftrightarrow a = Grab(g)\\&\qquad \vee (Holding(g, s) \wedge a \neq Release(g))) .\end{aligned}$$

*Successor-state axioms solve the representational frame problem* because the total size of the axioms is $O(AE)$ literals: each of the $E$ effects of each of the $A$ actions is mentioned exactly once. The literals are spread over $F$ different axioms, so the axioms have average size $AE/F$.

The astute reader will have noticed that these axioms handle the $At$ fluent for the agent, but not for the gold; thus, we still cannot prove that the three-step plan achieves the goal of having the gold in $[1, 1]$. We need to say that an **implicit effect** of an agent moving from $x$ to $y$ is that any gold it is carrying will move too (as will any ants on the gold, any bacteria on the ants, etc.). Dealing with implicit effects is called the **ramification problem**. We will discuss the problem in general later, but for this specific domain, it can be solved by writing a more general successor-state axiom for $At$. The new axiom, which subsumes the previous version, says that an object $o$ is at $y$ if the agent went to $y$ and $o$ is the agent or something the

IMPLICIT EFFECT

RAMIFICATION PROBLEM

[3] This is essentially the approach we took in building the Boolean circuit-based agent in Chapter 7. Indeed, axioms such as Equation (7.4) and Equation (7.5) can be viewed as successor-state axioms.

agent was holding; or if $o$ was already at $y$ and the agent didn't go elsewhere, with $o$ being the agent or something the agent was holding.

$$\begin{aligned}&Poss(a,s) \Rightarrow \\ &At(o,y,Result(a,s)) \;\Leftrightarrow\; (a = Go(x,y) \land (o = Agent \lor Holding(o,s))) \\ &\qquad \lor (At(o,y,s) \land \neg(\exists z \;\; y \neq z \land a = Go(y,z) \land \\ &\qquad\qquad (o = Agent \lor Holding(o,s)))) \,.\end{aligned}$$

There is one more technicality: an inference process that uses these axioms must be able to prove nonidentities. The simplest kind of nonidentity is between constants—for example, $Agent \neq G_1$. The general semantics of first-order logic allows distinct constants to refer to the same object, so the knowledge base must include an axiom to prevent this. The **unique names axiom** states a disequality for every pair of constants in the knowledge base. When this is assumed by the theorem prover, rather than written down in the knowledge base, it is called a **unique names assumption**. We also need to state disequalities between action terms: $Go([1,1],[1,2])$ is a different action from $Go([1,2],[1,1])$ or $Grab(G_1)$. First, we say that each type of action is distinct—that no $Go$ action is a $Grab$ action. For each pair of action names $A$ and $B$, we would have

UNIQUE NAMES AXIOM

$$A(x_1,\ldots,x_m) \neq B(y_1,\ldots,y_n) \,.$$

Next, we say that two action terms with the same action name refer to the same action only if they involve all the same objects:

$$A(x_1,\ldots,x_m) = A(y_1,\ldots,y_m) \;\Leftrightarrow\; x_1 = y_1 \land \ldots \land x_m = y_m \,.$$

UNIQUE ACTION AXIOMS

These are called, collectively, the **unique action axioms**. The combination of initial state description, successor-state axioms, unique name axiom, and unique action axioms suffices to prove that the proposed plan achieves the goal.

### Solving the inferential frame problem

Successor-state axioms solve the representational frame problem, but not the inferential frame problem. Consider a $t$-step plan $p$ such that $S_t = Result(p, S_0)$. To decide which fluents are true in $S_t$, we need to consider each of the $F$ frame axioms on each of the $t$ time steps. Because the axioms have average size $AE/F$, this gives us $O(AEt)$ inferential work. Most of the work involves copying fluents unchanged from one situation to the next.

To solve the inferential frame problem, we have two possibilities. First, we could discard situation calculus and invent a new formalism for writing axioms. This has been done with formalisms such as the **fluent calculus**. Second, we could alter the inference mechanism to handle frame axioms more efficiently. A hint that this should be possible is that the simple approach is $O(AEt)$; why should it depend on the number of actions, $A$, when we know exactly which one action is executed at each time step? To see how to improve matters, we first look at the format of the frame axioms:

$$\begin{aligned}&Poss(a,s) \Rightarrow \\ &F_i(Result(a,s)) \;\Leftrightarrow\; (a = A_1 \lor a = A_2 \ldots) \\ &\qquad \lor F_i(s) \land (a \neq A_3) \land (a \neq A_4) \ldots\end{aligned}$$

That is, each axiom mentions several actions that can make the fluent true and several actions that can make it false. We can formalize this by introducing the predicate $PosEffect(a, F_i)$, meaning that action $a$ causes $F_i$ to become true, and $NegEffect(a, F_i)$ meaning that $a$ causes $F_i$ to become false. Then we can rewrite the foregoing axiom schema as:

$$
\begin{aligned}
&Poss(a, s) \Rightarrow \\
&\quad F_i(Result(a, s)) \Leftrightarrow PosEffect(a, F_i) \lor [F_i(s) \land \neg NegEffect(a, F_i)] \\
&PosEffect(A_1, F_i) \\
&PosEffect(A_2, F_i) \\
&NegEffect(A_3, F_i) \\
&NegEffect(A_4, F_i)\ .
\end{aligned}
$$

Whether this can be done automatically depends on the exact format of the frame axioms. To make an efficient inference procedure using axioms like this, we need to do three things:

1. Index the $PosEffect$ and $NegEffect$ predicates by their first argument so that when we are given an action that occurs at time $t$, we can find its effects in $O(1)$ time.
2. Index the axioms so that once you know that $F_i$ is an effect of an action, you can find the axiom for $F_i$ in $O(1)$ time. Then you need not even consider the axioms for fluents that are not an effect of the action.
3. Represent each situation as a previous situation plus a delta. Thus, if nothing changes from one step to the next, we need do no work at all. In the old approach, we would need to do $O(F)$ work in generating an assertion for each fluent $F_i(Result(a, s))$ from the preceding $F_i(s)$ assertions.

Thus at each time step, we look at the current action, fetch its effects, and update the set of true fluents. Each time step will have an average of $E$ of these updates, for a total complexity of $O(Et)$. This constitutes a solution to the inferential frame problem.

### Time and event calculus

Situation calculus works well when there is a single agent performing instantaneous, discrete actions. When actions have duration and can overlap with each other, situation calculus becomes somewhat awkward. Therefore, we will cover those topics with an alternative formalism known as **event calculus**, which is based on points in time rather than on situations. (The terms "event" and "action" may be used interchangeably. Informally, "event" connotes a wider class of actions, including ones with no explicit agent. These are easier to handle in event calculus than in situation calculus.)

EVENT CALCULUS

In event calculus, fluents hold at points in time rather than at situations, and the calculus is designed to allow reasoning over intervals of time. The event calculus axiom says that a fluent is true at a point in time if the fluent was initiated by an event at some time in the past and was not terminated by an intervening event. The $Initiates$ and $Terminates$ relations play a role similar to the $Result$ relation in situation calculus; $Initiates(e, f, t)$ means that the occurrence of event $e$ at time $t$ causes fluent $f$ to become true, while $Terminates(w, f, t)$ means that $f$ ceases to be true. We use $Happens(e, t)$ to mean that event $e$ happens at time $t$, and we use $Clipped(f, t, t_2)$ to mean that $f$ is terminated by some event sometime between $t$ and $t_2$. Formally, the axiom is:

EVENT CALCULUS AXIOM:

$$T(f, t_2) \Leftrightarrow \exists\, e, t \;\; Happens(e, t) \wedge Initiates(e, f, t) \wedge (t < t_2) \wedge \neg Clipped(f, t, t_2)$$

$$Clipped(f, t, t_2) \Leftrightarrow \exists\, e, t_1 \;\; Happens(e, t_1) \wedge Terminates(e, f, t_1) \wedge (t < t_1) \wedge (t_1 < t_2)\,.$$

This gives us functionality that is similar to situation calculus, but with the ability to talk about time points and intervals, so we can say $Happens(TurnOff(LightSwitch_1), 1{:}00)$ to say that a lightswitch was turned off at exactly 1:00.

Many extensions to event calculus have been made to address problems of indirect effects, events with duration, concurrent events, continuously changing events, nondeterministic effects, causal constraints, and other complications. We will revisit some of these issues in the next subsection. It is fair to say that, at present, completely satisfactory solutions are not yet available for most of them, but no insuperable obstacles have been encountered.

## Generalized events

So far, we have looked at two main concepts: actions and objects. Now it is time to see how they fit into an encompassing ontology in which both actions and objects can be thought of as aspects of a physical universe. We think of a particular universe as having both a spatial and a temporal dimension. The wumpus world has its spatial component laid out in a two-dimensional grid and has discrete time; our world has three spatial dimensions and one temporal dimension,[3] all continuous. A **generalized event** is composed from aspects of some "space–time chunk"—a piece of this multidimensional space–time universe. This abstraction generalizes most of the concepts we have seen so far, including actions, locations, times, fluents, and physical objects. Figure 10.3 gives the general idea. From now on, we will use the simple term "event" to refer to generalized events.

GENERALIZED EVENT

For example, World War II is an event that took place at various points in space–time, as indicated by the irregularly shaped grey patch. We can break it down into **subevents**:[4]

SUBEVENTS

$$SubEvent(BattleOfBritain, WorldWarII)\,.$$

Similarly, World War II is a subevent of the 20th century:

$$SubEvent(WorldWarII, TwentiethCentury)\,.$$

The 20th century is an *interval* of time. Intervals are chunks of space–time that include all of space between two time points. The function $Period(e)$ denotes the smallest interval enclosing the event $e$. $Duration(i)$ is the length of time occupied by an interval, so we can say $Duration(Period(WorldWarII)) > Years(5)$.

[3] Some physicists studying string theory argue for 10 dimensions or more, and some argue for a discrete world, but 4-D continuous space–time is an adequate representation for commonsense reasoning purposes.

[4] Note that $SubEvent$ is a special case of the $PartOf$ relation and is also transitive and reflexive.

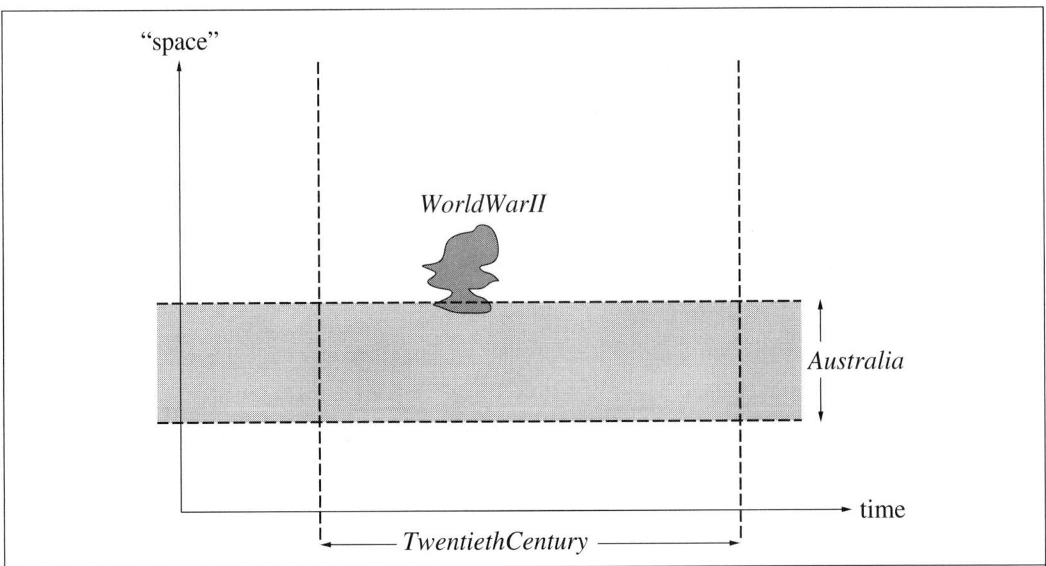


**Figure 10.3** Generalized events. A universe has spatial and temporal dimensions; in this figure we show only a single spatial dimension. All events are *PartOf* the universe. An event, such as $WorldWarII$, occurs in a portion of space–time with somewhat arbitrary and time-varying borders. An $Interval$, such as the $TwentiethCentury$, has a fixed, limited temporal extent and maximal spatial extent, and a $Place$, such as Australia, has a roughly fixed spatial extent and maximal temporal extent.

Australia is a *place*; a chunk with some fixed spatial borders. The borders can vary over time, due to geological or political changes. We use the predicate $In$ to denote the subevent relation that holds when one event's spatial projection is $PartOf$ of another's:

$$In(Sydney, Australia) .$$

The function $Location(e)$ denotes the smallest place that encloses the event $e$.

Like any other sort of object, events can be grouped into categories. For example, $WorldWarII$ belongs to the category $Wars$. To say that a civil war occurred in England in the 1640s, we would say

$$\exists w \;\; w \in CivilWars \land SubEvent(w, 1640s) \land In(Location(w), England) .$$

The notion of a category of events answers a question that we avoided when we described the effects of actions in Section 10.3: what exactly do logical terms such as $Go([1,1],[1,2])$ refer to? Are they events? The answer, perhaps surprisingly, is *no*. We can see this by considering a plan with two "identical" actions, such as

$$[Go([1,1],[1,2]), Go([1,2],[1,1]), Go([1,1],[1,2])] .$$

In this plan, $Go([1,1],[1,2])$ cannot be the name of an event, because there are *two different events* occurring at different times. Instead, $Go([1,1],[1,2])$ is the name of a *category* of events—all those events where the agent goes from $[1,1]$ to $[1,2]$. The three-step plan says that instances of these three event categories will occur.

Notice that this is the first time we have seen categories named by complex terms rather than just constant symbols. This presents no new difficulties; in fact, we can use the argument structure to our advantage. Eliminating arguments creates a more general category:

$$Go(x, y) \subseteq GoTo(y) \qquad\qquad Go(x, y) \subseteq GoFrom(x) .$$

Similarly, we can add arguments to create more specific categories. For example, to describe actions by other agents, we can add an agent argument. Thus, to say that Shankar flew from New York to New Delhi yesterday, we would write:

$$\exists e \;\; e \in Fly(Shankar, NewYork, NewDelhi) \land SubEvent(e, Yesterday) .$$

The form of this formula is so common that we will create an abbreviation for it: $E(c, i)$ will mean that an element of the category of events $c$ is a subevent of the event or interval $i$:

$$E(c, i) \;\Leftrightarrow\; \exists e \;\; e \in c \land SubEvent(e, i) .$$

Thus, we have:

$$E(Fly(Shankar, NewYork, NewDelhi), Yesterday) .$$

## Processes

DISCRETE EVENTS

The events we have seen so far are what we call **discrete events**—they have a definite structure. Shankar's trip has a beginning, middle, and end. If interrupted halfway, the event would be different—it would not be a trip from New York to New Delhi, but instead a trip from New York to somewhere over Europe. On the other hand, the category of events denoted by $Flying(Shankar)$ has a different quality. If we take a small interval of Shankar's flight, say, the third 20-minute segment (while he waits anxiously for a second bag of peanuts), that event is still a member of $Flying(Shankar)$. In fact, this is true for any subinterval.

PROCESS

LIQUID EVENT

Categories of events with this property are called **process** categories or **liquid event** categories. Any subinterval of a process is also a member of the same process category. We can employ the same notation used for discrete events to say that, for example, Shankar was flying at some time yesterday:

$$E(Flying(Shankar), Yesterday) .$$

We often want to say that some process was going on *throughout* some interval, rather than just in some subinterval of it. To do this, we use the predicate $T$:

$$T(Working(Stuart), TodayLunchHour) .$$

$T(c, i)$ means that some event of type $c$ occurred over exactly the interval $i$—that is, the event begins and ends at the same time as the interval.

The distinction between liquid and nonliquid events is exactly analogous to the difference between substances, or *stuff*, and individual objects. In fact, some have called liquid event types **temporal substances**, whereas things like butter are **spatial substances**.

TEMPORAL SUBSTANCES

SPATIAL SUBSTANCES

STATES

As well as describing processes of continuous change, liquid events can describe processes of continuous non-change. These are often called **states**. For example, "Shankar being in New York" is a category of states that we denote by $In(Shankar, NewYork)$. To say he was in New York all day, we would write

$$T(In(Shankar, NewYork), Today) .$$

We can form more complex states and events by combining primitive ones. This approach is called **fluent calculus**. Fluent calculus reifies combinations of fluents, not just individual fluents. We have already seen a way of representing the event of two things happening at once, namely, the function $Both(e_1, e_2)$. In fluent calculus, this is usually abbreviated with the infix notation $e_1 \circ e_2$. For example, to say that someone walked and chewed gum at the same time, we can write

FLUENT CALCULUS

$$\exists p, i \;\; (p \in People) \wedge T(Walk(p) \circ ChewGum(p), i) \; .$$

The "$\circ$" function is commutative and associative, just like logical conjunction. We can also define analogs of disjunction and negation, but we have to be more careful—there are two reasonable ways of interpreting disjunction. When we say "the agent was either walking or chewing gum for the last two minutes" we might mean that the agent was doing one of the actions for the whole interval, or we might mean that the agent was alternating between the two actions. We will use *OneOf* and *Either* to indicate these two possibilities. Figure 10.4 diagrams the complex events.

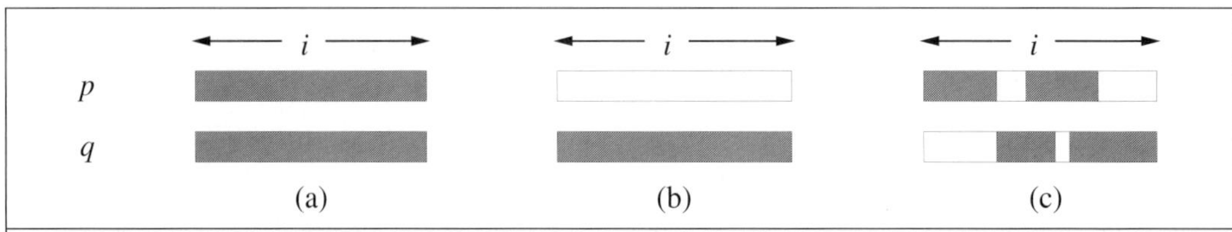


**Figure 10.4** A depiction of complex events. (a) $T(Both(p, q), i)$, also denoted as $T(p \circ q, i)$. (b) $T(OneOf(p, q), i)$. (c) $T(Either(p, q), i)$.

## Intervals

Time is important to any agent that takes action, and there has been much work on the representation of time intervals. We will consider two kinds: moments and extended intervals. The distinction is that only moments have zero duration:

$$Partition(\{Moments, ExtendedIntervals\}, Intervals)$$
$$i \in Moments \;\Leftrightarrow\; Duration(i) = Seconds(0) \; .$$

Next we invent a time scale and associate points on that scale with moments, giving us absolute times. The time scale is arbitrary; we will measure it in seconds and say that the moment at midnight (GMT) on January 1, 1900, has time 0. The functions *Start* and *End* pick out the earliest and latest moments in an interval, and the function *Time* delivers the point on the time scale for a moment. The function *Duration* gives the difference between the end time and the start time.

$$Interval(i) \;\Rightarrow\; Duration(i) = (Time(End(i)) - Time(Start(i))) \; .$$
$$Time(Start(AD1900)) = Seconds(0) \; .$$
$$Time(Start(AD2001)) = Seconds(3187324800) \; .$$
$$Time(End(AD2001)) = Seconds(3218860800) \; .$$
$$Duration(AD2001) = Seconds(31536000) \; .$$

To make these numbers easier to read, we also introduce a function $Date$, which takes six arguments (hours, minutes, seconds, day, month, and year) and returns a time point:

$$Time(Start(AD2001)) = Date(0, 0, 0, 1, Jan, 2001)$$
$$Date(0, 20, 21, 24, 1, 1995) = Seconds(3000000000) .$$

Two intervals $Meet$ if the end time of the first equals the start time of the second. It is possible to define predicates such as $Before$, $After$, $During$, and $Overlap$ solely in terms of $Meet$, but it is more intuitive to define them in terms of points on the time scale. (See Figure 10.5 for a graphical representation.)

$$\begin{array}{lcl}
Meet(i,j) & \Leftrightarrow & Time(End(i)) = Time(Start(j)) . \\
Before(i,j) & \Leftrightarrow & Time(End(i)) < Time(Start(j)) . \\
After(j,i) & \Leftrightarrow & Before(i,j) . \\
During(i,j) & \Leftrightarrow & Time(Start(j)) \leq Time(Start(i)) \\
 & & \wedge\ Time(End(i)) \leq Time(End(j)) . \\
Overlap(i,j) & \Leftrightarrow & \exists k\ \ During(k,i) \wedge During(k,j) .
\end{array}$$

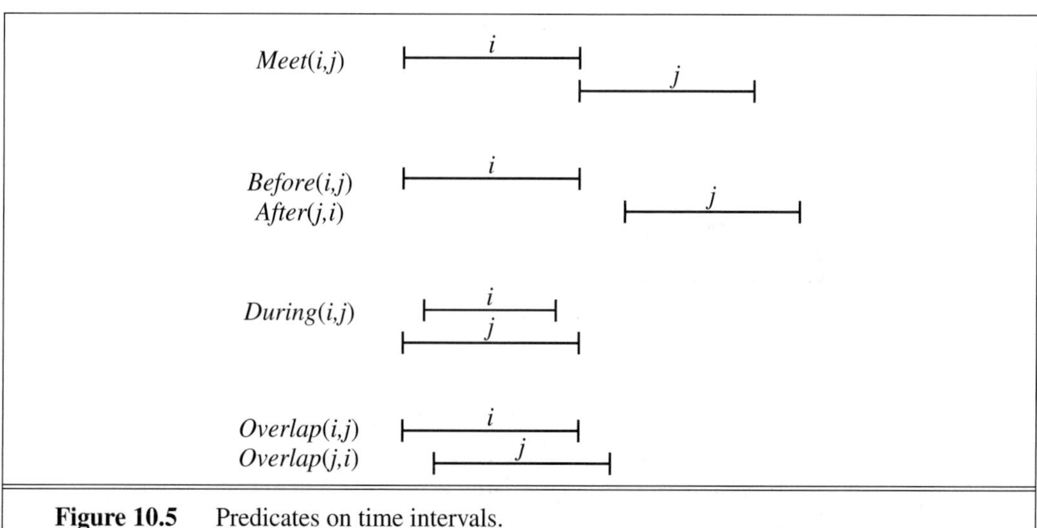


**Figure 10.5** Predicates on time intervals.

For example, to say that the reign of Elizabeth II followed that of George VI, and the reign of Elvis overlapped with the 1950s, we can write the following:

$$After(ReignOf(ElizabethII), ReignOf(GeorgeVI)) .$$
$$Overlap(Fifties, ReignOf(Elvis)) .$$
$$Start(Fifties) = Start(AD1950) .$$
$$End(Fifties) = End(AD1959) .$$

### Fluents and objects

We mentioned that physical objects can be viewed as generalized events, in the sense that a physical object is a chunk of space–time. For example, $USA$ can be thought of as an event that began in, say, 1776 as a union of 13 states and is still in progress today as a union of 50.

We can describe the changing properties of $USA$ using state fluents. For example, we can say that at some point in 1999 its population was 271 million:

$$E(Population(USA, 271000000), AD1999) .$$

Another property of the USA that changes every four or eight years, barring mishaps, is its president. One might propose that $President(USA)$ is a logical term that denotes a different object at different times. Unfortunately, this is not possible, because a term denotes exactly one object in a given model structure. (The term $President(USA, t)$ can denote different objects, depending on the value of $t$, but our ontology keeps time indices separate from fluents.) The only possibility is that $President(USA)$ denotes a single object that consists of different people at different times. It is the object that is George Washington from 1789 to 1796, John Adams from 1796 to 1800, and so on, as in Figure 10.6.

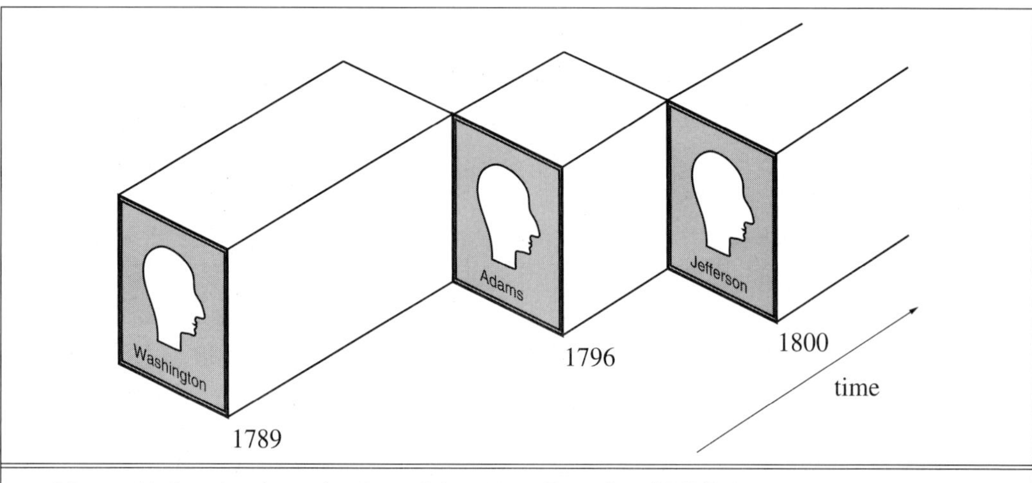


**Figure 10.6** A schematic view of the object $President(USA)$ for the first 15 years of its existence.

To say that George Washington was president throughout 1790, we can write

$$T(President(USA) = GeorgeWashington, AD1790) .$$

We need to be careful, however. In this sentence, "=" must be a function symbol rather than the standard logical operator. The interpretation is *not* that $GeorgeWashington$ and $President(USA)$ are logically identical in 1790; logical identity is not something that can change over time. The logical identity exists between the subevents of each object that are defined by the period 1790.

Don't confuse the physical object $GeorgeWashington$ with a collections of atoms. George Washington is not logically identical to *any* specific collection of atoms, because the set of atoms of which he is constituted varies considerably over time. He has his short lifetime, and each atom has its own very long lifetime. They intersect for some period, during which the temporal slice of the atom is $PartOf$ George, and then they go their separate ways.

## 10.4 Mental Events and Mental Objects

The agents we have constructed so far have beliefs and can deduce new beliefs. Yet none of them has any knowledge *about* beliefs or *about* deduction. For single-agent domains, knowledge about one's own knowledge and reasoning processes is useful for controlling inference. For example, if one knows that one does not know anything about Romanian geography, then one need not expend enormous computational effort trying to calculate the shortest path from Arad to Bucharest. One can also reason about one's own knowledge in order to construct plans that will change it—for example by buying a map of Romania. In multiagent domains, it becomes important for an agent to reason about the mental states of the other agents. For example, a Romanian police officer might well know the best way to get to Bucharest, so the agent might ask for help.

In essence, what we need is a model of the mental objects that are in someone's head (or something's knowledge base) and of the mental processes that manipulate those mental objects. The model should be faithful, but it does not have to be detailed. We do not have to be able to predict how many milliseconds it will take for a particular agent to make a deduction, nor do we have to predict what neurons will fire when an animal is faced with a particular visual stimulus. We will be happy to conclude that the Romanian police officer will tell us how to get to Bucharest if he or she knows the way and believes we are lost.

### A formal theory of beliefs

We begin with the relationships between agents and "mental objects"—relationships such as $Believes$, $Knows$, and $Wants$. Relations of this kind are called **propositional attitudes**, because they describe an attitude that an agent can take toward a proposition. Suppose that Lois believes something—that is, $Believes(Lois, x)$. What kind of thing is $x$? Clearly, $x$ cannot be a logical sentence. If $Flies(Superman)$ is a logical sentence, we can't say $Believes(Lois, Flies(Superman))$, because only terms (not sentences) can be arguments of predicates. But if $Flies$ is a function, then $Flies(Superman)$ is a candidate for being a mental object, and $Believes$ can be a relation between an agent and a propositional fluent. Turning a proposition into an object is called **reification**.[6]

PROPOSITIONAL ATTITUDE

REIFICATION

This appears to give us what we want: the ability for an agent to reason about the beliefs of agents. Unfortunately, there is a problem with that approach: If Clark and Superman are one and the same (i.e., $Clark = Superman$) then Clark's flying and Superman's flying are one and the same event category, i.e., $Flies(Clark) = Flies(Superman)$. Hence, we must conclude that if Lois believes that Superman can fly, she also believes that Clark can fly, *even if she doesn't believe that Clark is Superman*. That is,

$$(Superman = Clark) \models \\ (Believes(Lois, Flies(Superman)) \Leftrightarrow Believes(Lois, Flies(Clark))) .$$

There is a sense in which this is right: Lois does believe of a certain person, who happens

[6] The term "reification" comes from the Latin word *res*, or thing. John McCarthy proposed the term "thingification," but it never caught on.

to be called Clark sometimes, that that person can fly. But there is another sense in which it is wrong: if you asked Lois "Can Clark fly?" she would certainly say no. Reified objects and events work fine for the first sense of *Believes*, but for the second sense we need to reify *descriptions* of those objects and events, so that *Clark* and *Superman* can be different descriptions (even though they refer to the same object).

Technically, the property of being able to substitute a term freely for an equal term is called **referential transparency**. In first-order logic, every relation is referentially transparent. We would like to define *Believes* (and the other propositional attitudes) as relations whose second argument is referentially **opaque**—that is, one cannot substitute an equal term for the second argument without changing the meaning.

REFERENTIAL TRANSPARENCY

OPAQUE

There are two ways to achieve this. The first is to use a different form of logic called **modal logic**, in which propositional attitudes such as *Believes* and *Knows* become **modal operators** that are referentially opaque. This approach is covered in the historical notes section. The second approach, which we will pursue, is to achieve effective opacity within a referentially transparent language using a **syntactic theory** of mental objects. This means that mental objects are represented by **strings**. The result is a crude model of an agent's knowledge base as consisting of strings that represent sentences believed by the agent. A string is just a complex term denoting a list of symbols, so the event *Flies*(*Clark*) can be represented by the list of characters $[F, l, i, e, s, (, C, l, a, r, k, )]$, which we will abbreviate as a quoted string, "*Flies*(*Clark*)". The syntactic theory includes a **unique string axiom** stating that strings are identical if and only if they consist of identical characters. In this way, even if $Clark = Superman$, we still have "$Clark$" $\neq$ "$Superman$".

MODAL LOGIC

MODAL OPERATOR

SYNTACTIC THEORY

STRINGS

UNIQUE STRING AXIOM

Now all we have to do is provide a syntax, semantics, and proof theory for the string representation language, just as we did in Chapter 7. The difference is that we have to define them all in first-order logic. We start by defining *Den* as the function that maps a string to the object that it denotes and *Name* as a function that maps an object to a string that is the name of a constant that denotes the object. For example, the denotation of both "*Clark*" and "*Superman*" is the object referred to by the constant symbol *ManOfSteel*, and the name of that object within the knowledge base could be either "*Superman*", "*Clark*", or some other constant, such as "$X_{11}$":

$$Den(\text{"}Clark\text{"}) = ManOfSteel \land Den(\text{"}Superman\text{"}) = ManOfSteel\ .$$
$$Name(ManOfSteel) = \text{"}X_{11}\text{"}\ .$$

The next step is to define inference rules for logical agents. For example, we might want to say that a logical agent can do Modus Ponens: if it believes $p$ and believes $p \Rightarrow q$, then it will also believe $q$. The first attempt at writing this axiom is

$$LogicalAgent(a) \land Believes(a, p) \land Believes(a, \text{"}p \Rightarrow q\text{"}) \Rightarrow Believes(a, q)\ .$$

But this is not right because the string "$p \Rightarrow q$" contains the letters 'p' and 'q' but has nothing to do with the strings that are the values of the variables $p$ and $q$. The correct formulation is

$$LogicalAgent(a) \land Believes(a, p) \land Believes(a, Concat(p, \text{"}\Rightarrow\text{"}, q)) \\ \Rightarrow Believes(a, q)\ .$$

where *Concat* is a function on strings that concatenates their elements. We will abbreviate $Concat(p, \text{"}\Rightarrow\text{"}, q)$ as "$\underline{p} \Rightarrow \underline{q}$". That is, an occurrence of $\underline{x}$ within a string is **unquoted**,

UNQUOTED

meaning that we are to substitute in the value of the variable $x$. Lisp programmers will recognize this as the comma/backquote operator, and Perl programmers will recognize it as \$-variable interpolation.

Once we add in the other inference rules besides Modus Ponens, we will be able to answer questions of the form "given that a logical agent knows these premises, can it draw that conclusion?" Besides the normal inference rules, we need some rules that are specific to belief. For example, the following rule says that if a logical agent believes something, then it believes that it believes it.

$$LogicalAgent(a) \wedge Believes(a, p) \Rightarrow Believes(a, \text{“}Believes(\underline{Name(a)}, \underline{p})\text{”}) .$$

Now, according to our axioms, an agent can deduce any consequence of its beliefs infallibly. This is called **logical omniscience**. A variety of attempts have been made to define limited rational agents, which can make a limited number of deductions in a limited time. None is completely satisfactory, but these formulations do allow a highly restricted range of predictions about limited agents.

### Knowledge and belief

The relation between believing and knowing has been studied extensively in philosophy. It is commonly said that knowledge is justified true belief. That is, if you believe something for an unassailably good reason, and if it is actually true, then you know it. The "unassailably good reason" is necessary to prevent you from saying "I know this coin flip will come up heads" and being right half the time.

Let $Knows(a, p)$ mean that agent $a$ *knows that* proposition $p$ is true. It is also possible to define other kinds of knowing. For example, here is a definition of "knowing whether":

$$KnowsWhether(a, p) \Leftrightarrow Knows(a, p) \vee Knows(a, \text{“}\neg \underline{p}\text{”}) .$$

Continuing our example, Lois knows whether Clark can fly if she either knows that Clark can fly or knows that he cannot.

The concept of "knowing what" is more complicated. One is tempted to say that an agent knows what Bob's phone number is if there is some $x$ for which the agent knows $PhoneNumber(Bob) = x$. But that is not enough, because the agent might know that Alice and Bob have the same number (i.e., $PhoneNumber(Bob) = PhoneNumber(Alice)$), but if Alice's number is unknown, that isn't much help. A better definition of "knowing what" says that the agent has to be aware of some $x$ that is a string of digits and that is Bob's number:

$$\begin{aligned} &KnowsWhat(a, \text{“}PhoneNumber(\underline{b})\text{”}) \Leftrightarrow \\ &\qquad \exists\, x \;\; Knows(a, \text{“}\underline{x} = PhoneNumber(\underline{b})\text{”}) \wedge x \in DigitStrings . \end{aligned}$$

Of course, for other questions we have different criteria for what is an acceptable answer. For the question "what is the capital of New York," an acceptable answer is a proper name, "Albany," not something like "the city where the state house is." To handle this, we will make $KnowsWhat$ a three-place relation: it takes an agent, a string representing a term, and a category to which the answer must belong. For example, we might have the following:

$$\begin{aligned} &KnowsWhat(Agent, \text{“}Capital(NewYork)\text{”}, ProperNames) . \\ &KnowsWhat(Agent, \text{“}PhoneNumber(Bob)\text{”}, DigitStrings) . \end{aligned}$$

### Knowledge, time, and action

In most real situations, an agent will be dealing with beliefs—its own or those of other agents—that change over time. The agent will also have to make plans that involve changes to its own beliefs, such as buying a map to find out how to get to Bucharest. As with other predicates, we can reify *Believes* and talk about beliefs occurring over some period. For example, to say that Lois believes today that Superman can fly, we write

$$T(Believes(Lois, \text{“}Flies(Superman)\text{”}), Today)\ .$$

If the object of belief is a proposition that can change over time, then it too can be described using the $T$ operator within the string. For example, Lois might believe today that that Superman could fly yesterday:

$$T(Believes(Lois, \text{“}T(Flies(Superman), Yesterday)\text{”}, Today)\ .$$

KNOWLEDGE PRECONDITIONS
KNOWLEDGE EFFECTS

Given a way to describe beliefs over time, we can use the machinery of event calculus to make plans involving beliefs. Actions can have **knowledge preconditions** and **knowledge effects**. For example, the action of dialing a person's number has the precondition of knowing the number, and the action of looking up the number has the effect of knowing the number. We can describe the latter action using the machinery of event calculus:

$$\begin{aligned}&Initiates(Lookup(a, \text{“}PhoneNumber(\underline{b})\text{”}),\\ &\qquad KnowsWhat(a, \text{“}PhoneNumber(\underline{b})\text{”}, DigitStrings), t)\ .\end{aligned}$$

RUNTIME VARIABLES

Plans to gather and use information are often represented using a shorthand notation called **runtime variables**, which is closely related to the unquoted-variable convention described earlier. For example, the plan to look up Bob's number and then dial it can be written as

$$[Lookup(Agent, \text{“}PhoneNumber(Bob)\text{”}, \underline{n}), Dial(\underline{n})]\ .$$

Here, $\underline{n}$ is a runtime variable whose value will be bound by the *Lookup* action and can then be used by the *Dial* action. Plans of this kind occur frequently in partially observable domains. We will see examples in the next section and in Chapter 12.

## 10.5 The Internet Shopping World

In this section we will encode some knowledge related to shopping on the Internet. We will create a shopping research agent that helps a buyer find product offers on the Internet. The shopping agent is given a product description by the buyer and has the task of producing a list of Web pages that offer such a product for sale. In some cases the buyer's product description will be precise, as in *Coolpix 995 digital camera*, and the task is then to find the store(s) with the best offer. In other cases the description will be only partially specified, as in *digital camera for under $300*, and the agent will have to compare different products.

The shopping agent's environment is the entire World Wide Web—not a toy simulated environment, but the same complex, constantly evolving environment that is used by millions of people every day. The agent's percepts are Web pages, but whereas a human Web user would see pages displayed as an array of pixels on a screen, the shopping agent will perceive

**Generic Online Store**

*Select* from our fine line of products:

- Computers
- Cameras
- Books
- Videos
- Music

```
<h1>Generic Online Store</h1>
<i>Select</i> from our fine line of products:
<ul>
<li> <a href="http://gen-store.com/compu">Computers</a>
<li> <a href="http://gen-store.com/camer">Cameras</a>
<li> <a href="http://gen-store.com/books">Books</a>
<li> <a href="http://gen-store.com/video">Videos</a>
<li> <a href="http://gen-store.com/music">Music</a>
</ul>
```

**Figure 10.7** A Web page from a generic online store in the form perceived by the human user of a browser (top), and the corresponding HTML string as perceived by the browser or the shopping agent (bottom). In HTML, characters between < and > are markup directives that specify how the page is displayed. For example, the string `<i>Select</i>` means to switch to italic font, display the word *Select*, and then end the use of italic font. A page identifier such as `http://gen-store.com/books` is called a **uniform resource locator (URL)** or URL. The markup `<a href="`*url*`">`*anchor*`</a>` means to create a hypertext link to *url* with the **anchor text** *anchor*.

a page as a character string consisting of ordinary words interspersed with formatting commands in the HTML markup language. Figure 10.7 shows a Web page and a corresponding HTML character string. The perception problem for the shopping agent involves extracting useful information from percepts of this kind.

Clearly, perception on Web pages is easier than, say, perception while driving a taxi in Cairo. Nonetheless, there are complications to the Internet perception task. The web page in Figure 10.7 is very simple compared to real shopping sites, which include cookies, Java, Javascript, Flash, robot exclusion protocols, malformed HTML, sound files, movies, and text that appears only as part of a JPEG image. An agent that can deal with *all* of the Internet is almost as complex as a robot that can move in the real world. We will concentrate on a simple agent that ignores most of these complications.

The agent's first task is to find relevant product offers (we'll see later how to choose the best of the relevant offers). Let *query* be the product description that the user types in (e.g., "laptops"); then a page is a relevant offer for *query* if the page is relevant and the page is indeed an offer. We will also keep track of the URL associated with the page:

$$RelevantOffer(page, url, query) \Leftrightarrow Relevant(page, url, query) \land Offer(page) .$$

A page with a review of the latest high-end laptop would be relevant, but if it doesn't provide a way to buy, it isn't an offer. For now, we can say a page is an offer if it contains the word "buy" or "price" within an HTML link or form on the page. In other words, if the page contains a string of the form "`<a ...buy ...</a`" then it is an offer; it could also say "`price`" instead of "`buy`" or use "`form`" instead of "`a`". We can write axioms for this:

$$\begin{aligned}
&\mathit{Offer}(\mathit{page}) && \Leftrightarrow && (\mathit{InTag}(\text{“}a\text{”}, \mathit{str}, \mathit{page}) \lor \mathit{InTag}(\text{“}form\text{”}, \mathit{str}, \mathit{page})) \\
& && && \land (\mathit{In}(\text{“}buy\text{”}, \mathit{str}) \lor \mathit{In}(\text{“}price\text{”}, \mathit{str}))\ . \\
&\mathit{InTag}(\mathit{tag}, \mathit{str}, \mathit{page}) && \Leftrightarrow && \mathit{In}(\text{“}<\text{”} + \mathit{tag} + \mathit{str} + \text{“}</\text{”} + \mathit{tag}, \mathit{page})\ . \\
&\mathit{In}(\mathit{sub}, \mathit{str}) && \Leftrightarrow && \exists i\ \ \mathit{str}[i : i + \mathit{Length}(\mathit{sub})] = \mathit{sub}\ .
\end{aligned}$$

Now we need to find relevant pages. The strategy is to start at the home page of an online store and consider all pages that can be reached by following relevant links.[7] The agent will have knowledge of a number of stores, for example:

$$\begin{aligned}
&\mathit{Amazon} \in \mathit{OnlineStores} \land \mathit{Homepage}(\mathit{Amazon}, \text{“}amazon.com\text{”})\ . \\
&\mathit{Ebay} \in \mathit{OnlineStores} \land \mathit{Homepage}(\mathit{Ebay}, \text{“}ebay.com\text{”})\ . \\
&\mathit{GenStore} \in \mathit{OnlineStores} \land \mathit{Homepage}(\mathit{GenStore}, \text{“}gen\text{-}store.com\text{”})\ .
\end{aligned}$$

These stores classify their goods into product categories, and provide links to the major categories from their home page. Minor categories can be reached by following a chain of relevant links, and eventually we will reach offers. In other words, a page is relevant to the query if it can be reached by a chain of relevant category links from a store's home page, and then following one more link to the product offer:

$$\begin{aligned}
&\mathit{Relevant}(\mathit{page}, \mathit{url}, \mathit{query}) \Leftrightarrow \\
&\quad \exists\, \mathit{store}, \mathit{home}\ \ \mathit{store} \in \mathit{OnlineStores} \land \mathit{Homepage}(\mathit{store}, \mathit{home}) \\
&\quad \land \exists\, \mathit{url}_2\ \ \mathit{RelevantChain}(\mathit{home}, \mathit{url}_2, \mathit{query}) \land \mathit{Link}(\mathit{url}_2, \mathit{url}) \\
&\qquad \land \mathit{page} = \mathit{GetPage}(\mathit{url})\ .
\end{aligned}$$

Here the predicate $\mathit{Link}(\mathit{from}, \mathit{to})$ means that there is a hyperlink from the *from* URL to the *to* URL. (See Exercise 10.13.) To define what counts as a *RelevantChain*, we need to follow not just any old hyperlinks, but only those links whose associated anchor text indicates that the link is relevant to the product query. For this, we will use $\mathit{LinkText}(\mathit{from}, \mathit{to}, \mathit{text})$ to mean that there is a link between *from* and *to* with *text* as the anchor text. A chain of links between two URLs, *start* and *end*, is relevant to a description $d$ if the anchor text of each link is a relevant category name for $d$. The existence of the chain itself is determined by a recursive definition, with the empty chain ($\mathit{start} = \mathit{end}$) as the base case:

$$\begin{aligned}
&\mathit{RelevantChain}(\mathit{start}, \mathit{end}, \mathit{query}) \Leftrightarrow (\mathit{start} = \mathit{end}) \\
&\quad \lor (\exists\, u, \mathit{text}\ \ \mathit{LinkText}(\mathit{start}, u, \mathit{text}) \land \mathit{RelevantCategoryName}(\mathit{query}, \mathit{text}) \\
&\qquad \land \mathit{RelevantChain}(u, \mathit{end}, \mathit{query}))\ .
\end{aligned}$$

Now we must define what it means for *text* to be a *RelevantCategoryName* for *query*. First, we need to relate strings to the categories they name. This is done using the predicate $\mathit{Name}(s, c)$, which says that string $s$ is a name for category $c$—for example, we might assert that $\mathit{Name}(\text{“}laptops\text{”}, \mathit{LaptopComputers})$. Some more examples of the *Name* predicate

[7] An alternative to the link-following strategy is to use an Internet search engine; the technology behind Internet search, information retrieval, will be covered in Section 23.2.

| (a) | (b) |
|---|---|
| $Books \subset Products$ | $Name(\text{"books"}, Books)$ |
| $MusicRecordings \subset Products$ | $Name(\text{"music"}, MusicRecordings)$ |
| $MusicCDs \subset MusicRecordings$ | $Name(\text{"CDs"}, MusicCDs)$ |
| $MusicTapes \subset MusicRecordings$ | $Name(\text{"tapes"}, MusicTapes)$ |
| $Electronics \subset Products$ | $Name(\text{"electronics"}, Electronics)$ |
| $DigitalCameras \subset Electronics$ | $Name(\text{"digital cameras"}, DigitalCameras)$ |
| $StereoEquipment \subset Electronics$ | $Name(\text{"stereos"}, StereoEquipment)$ |
| $Computers \subset Electronics$ | $Name(\text{"computers"}, Computers)$ |
| $LaptopComputers \subset Computers$ | $Name(\text{"laptops"}, LaptopComputers)$ |
| $DesktopComputers \subset Computers$ | $Name(\text{"desktops"}, DesktopComputers)$ |
| ... | ... |

**Figure 10.8** (a) Taxonomy of product categories. (b) Referring words for those categories.

appear in Figure 10.8(b). Next, we define relevance. Suppose that *query* is "laptops." Then $RelevantCategoryName(query, text)$ is true when one of the following holds:

- The *text* and *query* name the same category—e.g., "laptop computers" and "laptops."
- The *text* names a supercategory such as "computers."
- The *text* names a subcategory such as "ultralight notebooks."

The logical definition of $RelevantCategoryName$ is as follows:

$$RelevantCategoryName(query, text) \Leftrightarrow$$
$$\exists c_1, c_2 \;\; Name(query, c_1) \wedge Name(text, c_2) \wedge (c_1 \subseteq c_2 \vee c_2 \subseteq c_1) \,. \quad (10.1)$$

Otherwise, the anchor text is irrelevant because it names a category outside this line, such as "mainframe computers" or "lawn & garden."

To follow relevant links, then, it is essential to have a rich hierarchy of product categories. The top part of this hierarchy might look like Figure 10.8(a). It will not be feasible to list *all* possible shopping categories, because a buyer could always come up with some new desire and manufacturers will always come out with new products to satisfy them (electric kneecap warmers?). Nonetheless, an ontology of about a thousand categories will serve as a very useful tool for most buyers.

In addition to the product hierarchy itself, we also need to have a rich vocabulary of names for categories. Life would be much easier if there were a one-to-one correspondence between categories and the character strings that name them. We have already seen the problem of **synonymy**—two names for the same category, such as "laptop computers" and "laptops." There is also the problem of **ambiguity**—one name for two or more different categories. For example, if we add the sentence

$$Name(\text{"CDs"}, CertificatesOfDeposit)$$

to the knowledge base in Figure 10.8(b), then "CDs" will name two different categories.

Synonymy and ambiguity can cause a significant increase in the number of paths that the agent has to follow, and can sometimes make it difficult to determine whether a given page is indeed relevant. A much more serious problem is that there is a very broad range of descriptions that a user can type, or category names that a store can use. For example, the link might say "laptop" when the knowledge base has only "laptops;" or the user might ask for "a computer I can fit on the tray table of an economy-class seat in a Boeing 737." It is impossible to enumerate in advance all the ways a category can be named, so the agent will have to be able to do additional reasoning in some cases to determine if the *Name* relation holds. In the worst case, this requires full natural language understanding, a topic that we will defer to Chapter 22. In practice, a few simple rules—such as allowing "laptop" to match a category named "laptops"—go a long way. Exercise 10.15 asks you to develop a set of such rules after doing some research into online stores.

Given the logical definitions from the preceding paragraphs and suitable knowledge bases of product categories and naming conventions, are we ready to apply an inference algorithm to obtain a set of relevant offers for our query? Not quite! The missing element is the $GetPage(url)$ function, which refers to the HTML page at a given URL. The agent doesn't have the page contents of every URL in its knowledge base; nor does it have explicit rules for deducing what those contents might be. Instead, we can arrange for the right HTTP procedure to be executed whenever a subgoal involves the *GetPage* function. In this way, it appears to the inference engine as if the entire Web is inside the knowledge base. This is an example of a general technique called **procedural attachment**, whereby particular predicates and functions can be handled by special-purpose methods.

PROCEDURAL ATTACHMENT

## Comparing offers

Let us assume that the reasoning processes of the preceding section have produced a set of offer pages for our "laptops" query. To compare those offers, the agent must extract the relevant information—price, speed, disk size, weight, and so on—from the offer pages. This can be a difficult task with real web pages, for all the reasons mentioned previously. A common way of dealing with this problem is to use programs called **wrappers** to extract information from a page. The technology of information extraction is discussed in Section 23.3. For now we assume that wrappers exist, and when given a page and a knowledge base, they add assertions to the knowledge base. Typically a hierarchy of wrappers would be applied to a page: a very general one to extract dates and prices, a more specific one to extract attributes for computer-related products, and if necessary a site-specific one that knows the format of a particular store. Given a page on the gen-store.com site with the text

WRAPPER

```
YVM ThinkBook 970.  Our price:  $1449.00
```

followed by various technical specifications, we would like a wrapper to extract information such as the following:

$$\begin{aligned}&\exists\, lc, offer\;\; lc \in LaptopComputers \land offer \in ProductOffers \land\\ &\;\; ScreenSize(lc, Inches(14)) \land ScreenType(lc, ColorLCD) \land\\ &\;\; MemorySize(lc, Megabytes(512)) \land CPUSpeed(lc, GHz(2.4)) \land\\ &\;\; OfferedProduct(offer, lc) \land Store(offer, GenStore) \land\\ &\;\; URL(offer, \text{“}\texttt{genstore.com/comps/34356.}html\text{”}) \land\\ &\;\; Price(offer, \$(449)) \land Date(offer, Today)\,.\end{aligned}$$

This example illustrates several issues that arise when we take seriously the task of knowledge engineering for commercial transactions. For example, notice that the price is an attribute of the *offer*, not the product itself. This is important because the offer at a given store may change from day to day even for the same individual laptop; for some categories—such as houses and paintings—the same individual object may even be offered simultaneously by different intermediaries at different prices. There are still more complications that we have not handled, such as the possibility that the price depends on method of payment and on the buyer's qualifications for certain discounts. All in all, there is much interesting work to do.

The final task is to compare the offers that have been extracted. For example, consider these three offers:

$$A : \text{2.4 GHz CPU, 512MB RAM, 80 GB disk, DVD, CDRW, \$1695} .$$
$$B : \text{2.0 GHz CPU, 1GB RAM, 120 GB disk, DVD, CDRW, \$1800} .$$
$$C : \text{2.2 GHz CPU, 512MB RAM, 80 GB disk, DVD, CDRW, \$1800} .$$

$C$ is **dominated** by $A$; that is, $A$ is cheaper and faster, and they are otherwise the same. In general, $X$ dominates $Y$ if $X$ has a better value on at least one attribute, and is not worse on any attribute. But neither $A$ nor $B$ dominates the other. To decide which is better we need to know how the buyer weighs CPU speed and price against memory and disk space. The general topic of preferences among multiple attributes is addressed in Section 16.4; for now, our shopping agent will simply return a list of all undominated offers that meet the buyer's description. In this example, both $A$ and $B$ are undominated. Notice that this outcome relies on the assumption that everyone prefers cheaper prices, faster processors, and more storage. Some attributes, such as screen size on a notebook, depend on the user's particular preference (portability versus visibility); for these, the shopping agent will just have to ask the user.

The shopping agent we have described here is a simple one; many refinements are possible. Still, it has enough capability that with the right domain-specific knowledge it can actually be of use to a shopper. Because of its declarative construction, it extends easily to more complex applications. The main point of this section is to show that some knowledge representation—in particular, the product hierarchy—is necessary for an agent like this, and that once we have some knowledge in this form, it is not too hard to do the rest as a knowledge-based agent.

## 10.6 Reasoning Systems for Categories

We have seen that categories are the primary building blocks of any large-scale knowledge representation scheme. This section describes systems specially designed for organizing and reasoning with categories. There are two closely related families of systems: **semantic networks** provide graphical aids for visualizing a knowledge base and efficient algorithms for inferring properties of an object on the basis of its category membership; and **description logics** provide a formal language for constructing and combining category definitions and efficient algorithms for deciding subset and superset relationships between categories.

### Semantic networks

EXISTENTIAL GRAPHS

In 1909, Charles Peirce proposed a graphical notation of nodes and arcs called **existential graphs** that he called "the logic of the future." Thus began a long-running debate between advocates of "logic" and advocates of "semantic networks." Unfortunately, the debate obscured the fact that semantics networks—at least those with well-defined semantics—*are* a form of logic. The notation that semantic networks provide for certain kinds of sentences is often more convenient, but if we strip away the "human interface" issues, the underlying concepts—objects, relations, quantification, and so on—are the same.

There are many variants of semantic networks, but all are capable of representing individual objects, categories of objects, and relations among objects. A typical graphical notation displays object or category names in ovals or boxes, and connects them with labeled arcs. For example, Figure 10.9 has a $MemberOf$ link between $Mary$ and $FemalePersons$, corresponding to the logical assertion $Mary \in FemalePersons$; similarly, the $SisterOf$ link between $Mary$ and $John$ corresponds to the assertion $SisterOf(Mary, John)$. We can connect categories using $SubsetOf$ links, and so on. It is such fun drawing bubbles and arrows that one can get carried away. For example, we know that persons have female persons as mothers, so can we draw a $HasMother$ link from $Persons$ to $FemalePersons$? The answer is no, because $HasMother$ is a relation between a person and his or her mother, and categories do not have mothers.[8] For this reason, we have used a special notation—the double-boxed link—in Figure 10.9. This link asserts that

$$\forall x \;\; x \in Persons \;\Rightarrow\; [\forall y \;\; HasMother(x, y) \;\Rightarrow\; y \in FemalePersons] \,.$$

We might also want to assert that persons have two legs—that is,

$$\forall x \;\; x \in Persons \;\Rightarrow\; Legs(x, 2) \,.$$

As before, we need to be careful not to assert that a category has legs; the single-boxed link in Figure 10.9 is used to assert properties of every member of a category.

The semantic network notation makes it very convenient to perform **inheritance** reasoning of the kind introduced in Section 10.2. For example, by virtue of being a person, Mary inherits the property of having two legs. Thus, to find out how many legs Mary has, the inheritance algorithm follows the $MemberOf$ link from $Mary$ to the category she belongs to, and then follows $SubsetOf$ links up the hierarchy until it finds a category for which there is a boxed $Legs$ link—in this case, the $Persons$ category. The simplicity and efficiency of this inference mechanism, compared with logical theorem proving, has been one of the main attractions of semantic networks.

MULTIPLE INHERITANCE

Inheritance becomes complicated when an object can belong to more than one category or when a category can be a subset of more than one other category; this is called **multiple inheritance**. In such cases, the inheritance algorithm might find two or more conflicting values

[8] Several early systems failed to distinguish between properties of members of a category and properties of the category as a whole. This can lead directly to inconsistencies, as pointed out by Drew McDermott (1976) in his article "Artificial Intelligence Meets Natural Stupidity." Another common problem was the use of $IsA$ links for both subset and membership relations, in correspondence with English usage: "a cat is a mammal" and "Fifi is a cat." See Exercise 10.25 for more on these issues.

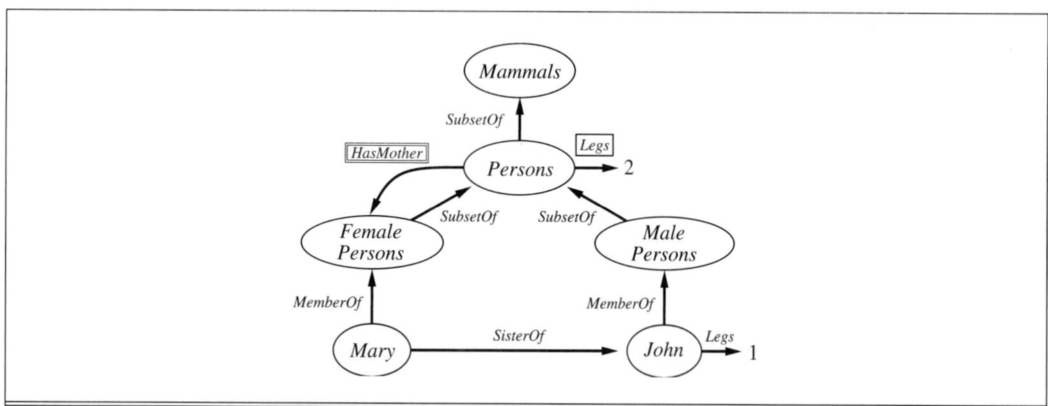


**Figure 10.9** A semantic network with four objects (John, Mary, 1, and 2) and four categories. Relations are denoted by labeled links.

answering the query. For this reason, multiple inheritance is banned in some **object-oriented programming** (OOP) languages, such as Java, that use inheritance in a class hierarchy. It is usually allowed in semantic networks, but we defer discussion of that until Section 10.7.

INVERSE LINK

Another common form of inference is the use of **inverse links**. For example, $HasSister$ is the inverse of $SisterOf$, which means that

$$\forall p, s \;\; HasSister(p, s) \;\Leftrightarrow\; SisterOf(s, p)\,.$$

This sentence can be asserted in a semantic network if links are **reified**—that is, made into objects in their own right. For example, we could have a $SisterOf$ object, connected by an $Inverse$ link to $HasSister$. Given a query asking who is a $SisterOf$ John, the inference algorithm can discover that $HasSister$ is the inverse of $SisterOf$ and can therefore answer the query by following the $HasSister$ link from $John$ to $Mary$. Without the inverse information, it might be necessary to check every female person to see whether that person has a $SisterOf$ link to John. This is because semantic networks provide direct indexing only for objects, categories, and the links emanating from them; in the vocabulary of first-order logic, it is as if the knowledge base were indexed only on the first argument of each predicate.

The reader might have noticed an obvious drawback of semantic network notation, compared to first-order logic: the fact that links between bubbles represent only *binary* relations. For example, the sentence $Fly(Shankar, NewYork, NewDelhi, Yesterday)$ cannot be asserted directly in a semantic network. Nonetheless, we *can* obtain the effect of $n$-ary assertions by reifying the proposition itself as an event (see Section 10.3) belonging to an appropriate event category. Figure 10.10 shows the semantic network structure for this particular event. Notice that the restriction to binary relations forces the creation of a rich ontology of reified concepts; indeed, much of the ontology developed in this chapter originated in semantic network systems.

Reification of propositions makes it possible to represent every ground, function-free atomic sentence of first-order logic in the semantic network notation. Certain kinds of universally quantified sentences can be asserted using inverse links and the singly boxed and doubly boxed arrows applied to categories, but that still leaves us a long way short of full first-order

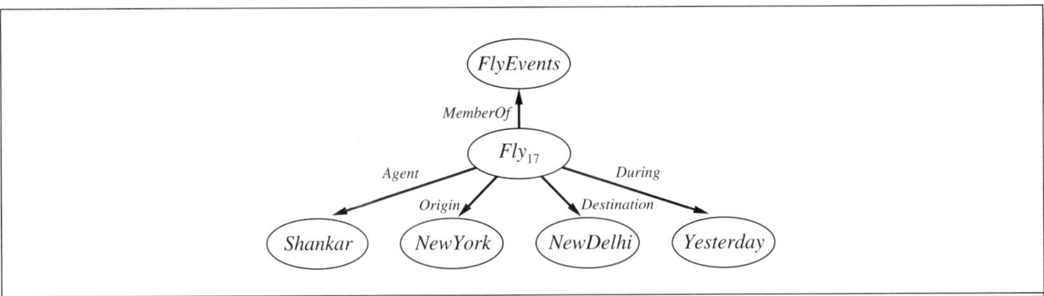


**Figure 10.10** A fragment of a semantic network showing the representation of the logical assertion $Fly(Shankar, NewYork, NewDelhi, Yesterday)$.

logic. Negation, disjunction, nested function symbols, and existential quantification are all missing. Now it is *possible* to extend the notation to make it equivalent to first-order logic—as in Peirce's existential graphs or Hendrix's (1975) partitioned semantic networks—but doing so negates one of the main advantages of semantic networks, which is the simplicity and transparency of the inference processes. Designers can build a large network and still have a good idea about what queries will be efficient, because (a) it is easy to visualize the steps that the inference procedure will go through and (b) in some cases the query language is so simple that difficult queries cannot be posed. In cases where the expressive power proves to be too limiting, many semantic network systems provide for **procedural attachment** to fill in the gaps. Procedural attachment is a technique whereby a query about (or sometimes an assertion of) a certain relation results in a call to a special procedure designed for that relation rather than a general inference algorithm.

DEFAULT VALUES

One of the most important aspects of semantic networks is their ability to represent **default values** for categories. Examining Figure 10.9 carefully, one notices that John has one leg, despite the fact that he is a person and all persons have two legs. In a strictly logical KB, this would be a contradiction, but in a semantic network, the assertion that all persons have two legs has only default status; that is, a person is assumed to have two legs unless this is contradicted by more specific information. The default semantics is enforced naturally by the inheritance algorithm, because it follows links upwards from the object itself (John in this case) and stops as soon as it finds a value. We say that the default is **overridden** by the more specific value. Notice that we could also override the default number of legs by creating a category of $OneLeggedPersons$, a subset of $Persons$ of which $John$ is a member.

OVERRIDING

We can retain a strictly logical semantics for the network if we say that the $Legs$ assertion for $Persons$ includes an exception for John:

$$\forall x \;\; x \in Persons \land x \neq John \;\Rightarrow\; Legs(x, 2) \,.$$

For a *fixed* network, this is semantically adequate, but will be much less concise than the network notation itself if there are lots of exceptions. For a network that will be updated with more assertions, however, such an approach fails—we really want to say that any persons as yet unknown with one leg are exceptions too. Section 10.7 goes into more depth on this issue and on default reasoning in general.

### Description logics

DESCRIPTION LOGICS

The syntax of first-order logic is designed to make it easy to say things about objects. **Description logics** are notations that are designed to make it easier to describe definitions and properties of categories. Description logic systems evolved from semantic networks in response to pressure to formalize what the networks mean while retaining the emphasis on taxonomic structure as an organizing principle.

SUBSUMPTION

CLASSIFICATION

The principal inference tasks for description logics are **subsumption**—checking if one category is a subset of another by comparing their definitions—and **classification**—checking whether an object belongs to a category. Some systems also include **consistency** of a category definition—whether the membership criteria are logically satisfiable.

The CLASSIC language (Borgida *et al.*, 1989) is a typical description logic. The syntax of CLASSIC descriptions is shown in Figure 10.11.[9] For example, to say that bachelors are unmarried adult males we would write

$$Bachelor = And(Unmarried, Adult, Male)\ .$$

The equivalent in first-order logic would be

$$Bachelor(x) \;\Leftrightarrow\; Unmarried(x) \land Adult(x) \land Male(x)\ .$$

Notice that the description logic effectively allows direct logical operations on predicates, rather than having to first create sentences to be joined by connectives. Any description in CLASSIC can be written in first-order logic, but some descriptions are more straightforward in CLASSIC. For example, to describe the set of men with at least three sons who are all unemployed and married to doctors and at most two daughters who are all professors in physics or math departments, we would use

$$\begin{aligned}&And(Man, AtLeast(3, Son), AtMost(2, Daughter),\\ &\quad All(Son, And(Unemployed, Married, All(Spouse, Doctor))),\\ &\quad All(Daughter, And(Professor, Fills(Department, Physics, Math))))\ .\end{aligned}$$

We leave it as an exercise to translate this into first-order logic.

Perhaps the most important aspect of description logics is their emphasis on tractability of inference. A problem instance is solved by describing it and then asking if it is subsumed by one of several possible solution categories. In standard first-order logic systems, predicting the solution time is often impossible. It is frequently left to the user to engineer the representation to detour around sets of sentences that seem to be causing the system to take several weeks to solve a problem. The thrust in description logics, on the other hand, is to ensure that subsumption-testing can be solved in time polynomial in the size of the descriptions.[10]

This sounds wonderful in principle, until one realizes that it can only have one of two consequences: either hard problems cannot be stated at all, or they require exponentially large descriptions! However, the tractability results do shed light on what sorts of constructs cause problems and thus help the user to understand how different representations behave.

[9] Notice that the language does *not* allow one to simply state that one concept, or category, is a subset of another. This is a deliberate policy: subsumption between categories must be derivable from some aspects of the descriptions of the categories. If not, then something is missing from the descriptions.

[10] CLASSIC provides efficient subsumption testing in practice, but the worst-case runtime is exponential.

$$
\begin{array}{rcl}
\mathit{Concept} & \rightarrow & \textbf{Thing} \mid \mathit{ConceptName} \\
& \mid & \textbf{And}(\mathit{Concept}, \ldots) \\
& \mid & \textbf{All}(\mathit{RoleName}, \mathit{Concept}) \\
& \mid & \textbf{AtLeast}(\mathit{Integer}, \mathit{RoleName}) \\
& \mid & \textbf{AtMost}(\mathit{Integer}, \mathit{RoleName}) \\
& \mid & \textbf{Fills}(\mathit{RoleName}, \mathit{IndividualName}, \ldots) \\
& \mid & \textbf{SameAs}(\mathit{Path}, \mathit{Path}) \\
& \mid & \textbf{OneOf}(\mathit{IndividualName}, \ldots) \\
\mathit{Path} & \rightarrow & [\mathit{RoleName}, \ldots]
\end{array}
$$

**Figure 10.11** The syntax of descriptions in a subset of the CLASSIC language.

For example, description logics usually lack *negation* and *disjunction*. Each forces first-order logical systems to go through a potentially exponential case analysis in order to ensure completeness. For the same reason, they are excluded from Prolog. CLASSIC allows only a limited form of disjunction in the $Fills$ and $OneOf$ constructs, which permit disjunction over explicitly enumerated individuals but not over descriptions. With disjunctive descriptions, nested definitions can lead easily to an exponential number of alternative routes by which one category can subsume another.

## 10.7 Reasoning with Default Information

In the preceding section, we saw a simple example of an assertion with default status: people have two legs. This default can be overridden by more specific information, such as that Long John Silver has one leg. We saw that the inheritance mechanism in semantic networks implements the overriding of defaults in a simple and natural way. In this section, we study defaults more generally, with a view toward understanding the *semantics* of defaults rather than just providing a procedural mechanism.

### Open and closed worlds

Suppose you were looking at a bulletin board in a university computer science department and saw a notice saying, "The following courses will be offered: CS 101, CS 102, CS 106, EE 101." Now, how many courses will be offered? If you answered "Four," you would be in agreement with a typical database system. Given a relational database with the equivalent of the four assertions

$$Course(CS, 101),\ Course(CS, 102),\ Course(CS, 106),\ Course(EE, 101), \quad (10.2)$$

the SQL query `count * from Course` returns 4. On the other hand, a first-order logical system would answer "Somewhere between one and infinity," not "four." The reason is that the *Course* assertions do not deny the possibility that other unmentioned courses are also offered, nor do they say that the courses mentioned are different from each other.

This example shows that database systems and human communication conventions differ from first-order logic in at least two ways. First, databases (and people) assume that the information provided is *complete*, so that ground atomic sentences not asserted to be true are assumed to be false. This is called the **closed-world assumption**, or CWA. Second, we usually assume that distinct names refer to distinct objects. This is the **unique names assumption**, or UNA, which we introduced first in the context of action names in Section 10.3.

CLOSED-WORLD ASSUMPTION

First-order logic does not assume these conventions, and thus needs to be more explicit. To say that *only* the four distinct courses are offered, we would write:

$$\begin{aligned} Course(d,n) \;\Leftrightarrow\;\; & [d,n]=[CS,101] \lor [d,n]=[CS,102] \\ & \lor [d,n]=[CS,106] \lor [d,n]=[EE,101]\,. \end{aligned} \qquad (10.3)$$

COMPLETION

Equation 10.3 is called the **completion**[11] of 10.2. In general, the completion will contain a definition—an if-and-only-if sentence—for each predicate, and each definition will contain a disjunct for each definite clause having that predicate in its head.[12] In general, the completion is constructed as follows:

CLARK NORMAL FORM

1. Gather up all the clauses with the same predicate name ($P$) and the same arity ($n$).
2. Translate each clause to **Clark Normal Form**: replace

   $$P(t_1,\ldots,t_n) \leftarrow Body\;,$$

   where $t_i$ are terms, with

   $$P(v_1,\ldots,v_n) \leftarrow \exists\, w_1 \ldots w_m \;\; [v_1,\ldots,v_n] = [t_1,\ldots,t_n] \land Body\;,$$

   where $v_i$ are newly invented variables and $w_i$ are the variables that appear in the original clause. Use the same set of $v_i$ for every clause. This gives us a set of clauses

   $$\begin{aligned} & P(v_1,\ldots,v_n) \leftarrow B_1 \\ & \vdots \\ & P(v_1,\ldots,v_n) \leftarrow B_k\,. \end{aligned}$$

3. Combine these together into one big disjunctive clause:

   $$P(v_1,\ldots,v_n) \leftarrow B_1 \lor \ldots \lor B_k\,.$$

4. Form the completion by replacing the $\leftarrow$ with an equivalence:

   $$P(v_1,\ldots,v_n) \;\Leftrightarrow\; B_1 \lor \ldots \lor B_k\,.$$

Figure 10.12 shows an example of the Clark completion for a knowledge base with both ground facts and rules. To add in the unique names assumption, we simply construct the Clark completion for the equality relation, where the only known facts are that $CS = CS$, $101 = 101$, and so on. This is left as an exercise.

The closed-world assumption allows us to find a **minimal model** of a relation. That is, we can find the model of the relation *Course* with the fewest elements. In Equation (10.2)

[11] Sometimes called "Clark Completion" after the inventor, Keith Clark.

[12] Notice that this is also the form of the successor-state axioms given in Section 10.3.

| **Horn Clauses** | **Clark Completion** |
|---|---|
| $Course(CS, 101)$ | $Course(d, n) \Leftrightarrow [d, n] = [CS, 101]$ |
| $Course(CS, 102)$ | $\lor [d, n] = [CS, 102]$ |
| $Course(CS, 106)$ | $\lor [d, n] = [CS, 106]$ |
| $Course(EE, 101)$ | $\lor [d, n] = [EE, 101]$ |
| $Course(EE, i) \leftarrow Integer(i)$ | $\lor \exists i \;\; [d, n] = [EE, i] \land Integer(i)$ |
| $\land 101 \leq i \land i \leq 130$ | $\land 101 \leq i \land i \leq 130$ |
| $Course(CS, m + 100) \Leftarrow$ | $\lor \exists m \;\; [d, n] = [CS, m + 100]$ |
| $Course(CS, m) \land 100 \leq m$ | $\land Course(CS, m) \land 100 \leq m$ |
| $\land m < 200$ | $\land m < 200$ |

**Figure 10.12** The Clark Completion of a set of Horn clauses. The original Horn program (left) lists four courses explicitly and also asserts that there is an EE class for every integer from 101 to 130, and that for every CS class in the 100 (undergraduate) series, there is a corresponding class in the 200 (graduate) series. The Clark completion (right) says that there are no other classes. With the completion and the unique names assumption (and the obvious definition of the *Integer* predicate), we get the desired conclusion that there are exactly 36 courses: 30 EE courses and 6 CS courses.

the minimal model of *Course* has four elements; any less and we'd have a contradiction. For Horn knowledge bases, there is always a *unique* minimal model. Notice that, with the unique names assumption, this applies to the equality relation too: each term is equal only to itself. Paradoxically, this means that minimal models are maximal in the sense of having as many objects as possible.

It is possible to take a Horn program, generate the Clark completion, and hand that to a theorem prover to do inference. But it is usually more efficient to use a special-purpose inference mechanism such as Prolog, which has the closed world and unique names assumptions built into the inference mechanism.

Those who make the closed-world assumption must be careful about what kind of reasoning they will be doing. For example, in a census database it would be reasonable to make the CWA when reasoning about the current population of cities, but it would be wrong to conclude that no baby will ever be born in the future just because the database contains no entries with future birthdates. The CWA makes the database **complete**, in the sense that every atomic query is answered either positively or negatively; when we are genuinely ignorant of facts (such as future births) we cannot use the CWA. A more sophisticated knowledge representation system might allow the user to specify rules for when to apply the CWA.

### Negation as failure and stable model semantics

We saw in Chapters 7 and 9 than Horn-form knowledge bases have desirable computational properties. In many applications, however, the requirement that every literal in the body of a clause be positive is rather inconvenient. We would like to say "You can go outside if it's not raining," without having to concoct predicates such as *NotRaining*. In this section, we explore the addition of a form of explicit negation to Horn clauses based on the concept of

NEGATION AS FAILURE

**negation as failure**. The idea is that a negative literal, $not\ P$, can be "proved" true just in case the proof of $P$ fails. This is a form of default reasoning closely related to the closed world assumption: we assume something is false if it cannot be proved true. We use "$not$" to distinguish negation as failure from the logical "$\neg$" operator.

Prolog allows the $not$ operator in the body of a clause. For example, consider the following Prolog program:

$$\begin{aligned}&IDEdrive \leftarrow Drive \land not\ SCSIdrive\ .\\&SCSIdrive \leftarrow Drive \land not\ IDEdrive\ .\\&SCSIcontroller \leftarrow SCSIdrive\ .\\&Drive\ .\end{aligned} \tag{10.4}$$

The first rule says that if we have a hard drive on a computer and it is not SCSI, then it must be IDE. The second says if it is not IDE it must be SCSI. The third says that having a SCSI drive implies having a SCSI controller, and the fourth says that we do indeed have a drive. This program has *two* minimal models:

$$\begin{aligned}&M_1 = \{Drive, IDEdrive\}\ ,\\&M_2 = \{Drive, SCSIdrive, SCSIcontroller\}\ .\end{aligned}$$

Minimal models do not capture the intended semantics of programs with negation as failure. Consider the program

$$P \leftarrow not\ Q. \tag{10.5}$$

This has two minimal models, $\{P\}$ and $\{Q\}$. From an FOL point of view this makes sense, since $P \Leftarrow \neg Q$ is equivalent to $P \lor Q$. But from a Prolog point of view it is worrisome: $Q$ never appears on the left hand side of an arrow, so how can it be a consequence?

STABLE MODEL

JUSTIFICATION

REDUCT

An alternative is the idea of a **stable model**, which is a minimal model where every atom in the model has a **justification**: a rule where the head is the atom and where every literal in the body is satisfied. Technically, we say that $M$ is a stable model of a program $H$ if $M$ is the unique minimal model of the **reduct** of $H$ with respect to $M$. The reduct of a program $H$ is defined by first deleting from $H$ any rule that has a literal $not\ A$ in the body, where $A$ is in the model, and then deleting any negative literals in the remaining rules. Since the reduct of $H$ is now a list of Horn clauses, it must have a unique minimal model.

The reduct of $P \leftarrow not\ Q$ with respect to $\{P\}$ is $P$, which has minimal model $\{P\}$. Therefore $\{P\}$ is a stable model. The reduct with respect to $\{Q\}$ is the empty program, which has minimal model $\{\}$. Therefore $\{Q\}$ is not a stable model because $Q$ has no justification in Equation (10.5). As another example, the reduct of 10.4 with respect to $M_1$ is as follows:

$$\begin{aligned}&IDEdrive \leftarrow Drive\ .\\&SCSIcontroller \leftarrow SCSIdrive\ .\\&Drive\ .\end{aligned}$$

ANSWER SET PROGRAMMING

ANSWER SETS

This has minimal model $M_1$, so $M_1$ is a stable model. **Answer set programming** is a kind of logic programming with negation as failure that works by translating the logic program into ground form and then searching for stable models (also known as **answer sets**) using propositional model checking techniques. Thus answer set programming is a descendant both of Prolog and of the fast propositional satisfiability provers such as WALKSAT. Indeed, answer set programming has been successfully applied to problems in planning just as the propositional satisfiability provers have. The advantage of answer set planning over other planners is the degree of flexibility: the planning operators and constraints can be expressed as logic programs and are not bound to the restricted format of a particular planning formalism. The disadvantage of answer set planning is the same as for other propositional techniques: if there are very many objects in the universe, then there can be an exponential slow-down.

### Circumscription and default logic

We have seen two examples where apparently natural reasoning processes violate the **monotonicity** property of logic that was proved in Chapter 7.[13] In the first example, a property inherited by all members of a category in a semantic network could be overridden by more specific information for a subcategory. In the second example, negated literals derived from a closed-world assumption could be overridden by the addition of positive literals.

Simple introspection suggests that these failures of monotonicity are widespread in commonsense reasoning. It seems that humans often "jump to conclusions." For example, when one sees a car parked on the street, one is normally willing to believe that it has four wheels even though only three are visible. (If you feel that the existence of the fourth wheel is dubious, consider also the question as to whether the three visible wheels are real or merely cardboard facsimiles.) Now, probability theory can certainly provide a conclusion that the fourth wheel exists with high probability, yet, for most people, the possibility of the car's not having four wheels *does not arise unless some new evidence presents itself.* Thus, it seems that the four-wheel conclusion is reached *by default*, in the absence of any reason to doubt it. If new evidence arrives—for example, if one sees the owner carrying a wheel and notices that the car is jacked up—then the conclusion can be retracted. This kind of reasoning is said to exhibit **nonmonotonicity**, because the set of beliefs does not grow monotonically over time as new evidence arrives. **Nonmonotonic logics** have been devised with modified notions of truth and entailment in order to capture such behavior. We will look at two such logics that have been studied extensively: circumscription and default logic.

NONMONOTONICITY

NONMONOTONIC LOGICS

CIRCUMSCRIPTION

**Circumscription** can be seen as a more powerful and precise version of the closed-world assumption. The idea is to specify particular predicates that are assumed to be "as false as possible"—that is, false for every object except those for which they are known to be true. For example, suppose we want to assert the default rule that birds fly. We would introduce a predicate, say $Abnormal_1(x)$, and write

$$Bird(x) \land \neg Abnormal_1(x) \;\Rightarrow\; Flies(x) .$$

If we say that $Abnormal_1$ is to be **circumscribed**, a circumscriptive reasoner is entitled to assume $\neg Abnormal_1(x)$ unless $Abnormal_1(x)$ is known to be true. This allows the conclusion $Flies(Tweety)$ to be drawn from the premise $Bird(Tweety)$, but the conclusion no longer holds if $Abnormal_1(Tweety)$ is asserted.

MODEL PREFERENCE

Circumscription can be viewed as an example of a **model preference** logic. In such logics, a sentence is entailed (with default status) if it is true in all *preferred* models of the KB,

[13] Recall that monotonicity requires all entailed sentences to remain entailed after new sentences are added to the KB. That is, if $KB \models \alpha$ then $KB \land \beta \models \alpha$.

as opposed to the requirement of truth in *all* models in classical logic. For circumscription, one model is preferred to another if it has fewer abnormal objects.[14] Let us see how this idea works in the context of multiple inheritance in semantic networks. The standard example for which multiple inheritance is problematic is called the "Nixon diamond." It arises from the observation that Richard Nixon was both a Quaker (and hence by default a pacifist) and a Republican (and hence by default not a pacifist). We can write this as follows:

$$Republican(Nixon) \wedge Quaker(Nixon) .$$
$$Republican(x) \wedge \neg Abnormal_2(x) \Rightarrow \neg Pacifist(x) .$$
$$Quaker(x) \wedge \neg Abnormal_3(x) \Rightarrow Pacifist(x) .$$

If we circumscribe $Abnormal_2$ and $Abnormal_3$, there are two preferred models: one in which $Abnormal_2(Nixon)$ and $Pacifist(Nixon)$ hold and one in which $Abnormal_3(Nixon)$ and $\neg Pacifist(Nixon)$ hold. Thus, the circumscriptive reasoner remains properly agnostic as to whether Nixon is a pacifist. If we wish, in addition, to assert that religious beliefs take precedence over political beliefs, we can use a formalism called **prioritized circumscription** to give preference to models where $Abnormal_3$ is minimized.

PRIORITIZED CIRCUMSCRIPTION

DEFAULT LOGIC

DEFAULT RULES

**Default logic** is a formalism in which **default rules** can be written to generate contingent, nonmonotonic conclusions. A default rule looks like this:

$$Bird(x) : Flies(x)/Flies(x) .$$

This rule means that if $Bird(x)$ is true, and if $Flies(x)$ is consistent with the knowledge base, then $Flies(x)$ may be concluded by default. In general, a default rule has the form

$$P : J_1, \ldots, J_n/C$$

where $P$ is called the prerequisite, $C$ is the conclusion, and $J_i$ are the justifications—if any one of them can be proven false, then the conclusion cannot be drawn. Any variable that appears in $J_i$ or $C$ must also appear in $P$. The Nixon-diamond example can be represented in default logic with one fact and two default rules:

$$Republican(Nixon) \wedge Quaker(Nixon) .$$
$$Republican(x) : \neg Pacifist(x)/\neg Pacifist(x) .$$
$$Quaker(x) : Pacifist(x)/Pacifist(x) .$$

EXTENSION

To interpret what the default rules mean, we define the notion of an **extension** of a default theory to be a maximal set of consequences of the theory. That is, an extension $S$ consists of the original known facts and a set of conclusions from the default rules, such that no additional conclusions can be drawn from $S$ and the justifications of every default conclusion in $S$ are consistent with $S$. As in the case of the preferred models in circumscription, we have two possible extensions for the Nixon diamond: one wherein he is a pacifist and one wherein he is not. Prioritized schemes exist in which some default rules can be given precedence over others, allowing some ambiguities to be resolved.

Since 1980, when nonmonotonic logics were first proposed, a great deal of progress has been made in understanding their mathematical properties. Beginning in the late 1990s,

[14] For the closed-world assumption, one model is preferred to another if it has fewer true atoms—that is, preferred models are **minimal** models. There is a natural connection between the CWA and definite clause KBs, because the fixed point reached by forward chaining on such KBs is the unique minimal model. (See page 219.)

practical systems based on logic programming have shown promise as knowledge representation tools. There are still unresolved questions, however. For example, if "Cars have four wheels" is false, what does it mean to have it in one's knowledge base? What is a good set of default rules to have? If we cannot decide, for each rule separately, whether it belongs in our knowledge base, then we have a serious problem of nonmodularity. Finally, how can beliefs that have default status be used to make decisions? This is probably the hardest issue for default reasoning. Decisions often involve tradeoffs, and one therefore needs to compare the *strengths* of belief in the outcomes of different actions. In cases where the same kinds of decisions are being made repeatedly, it is possible to interpret default rules as "threshold probability" statements. For example, the default rule "My brakes are always OK" really means "The probability that my brakes are OK, given no other information, is sufficiently high that the optimal decision is for me to drive without checking them." When the decision context changes—for example, when one is driving a heavily laden truck down a steep mountain road—the default rule suddenly becomes inappropriate, even though there is no new evidence to suggest that the brakes are faulty. These considerations have led some researchers to consider how to embed default reasoning in probability theory.

## 10.8 Truth Maintenance Systems

The previous section argued that many of the inferences drawn by a knowledge representation system will have only default status, rather than being absolutely certain. Inevitably, some of these inferred facts will turn out to be wrong and will have to be retracted in the face of new information. This process is called **belief revision**.[15] Suppose that a knowledge base $KB$ contains a sentence $P$—perhaps a default conclusion recorded by a forward-chaining algorithm, or perhaps just an incorrect assertion—and we want to execute TELL($KB$, $\neg P$). To avoid creating a contradiction, we must first execute RETRACT($KB$, $P$). This sounds easy enough. Problems arise, however, if any *additional* sentences were inferred from $P$ and asserted in the KB. For example, the implication $P \Rightarrow Q$ might have been used to add $Q$. The obvious "solution"—retracting all sentences inferred from $P$—fails because such sentences may have other justifications besides $P$. For example, if $R$ and $R \Rightarrow Q$ are also in the KB, then $Q$ does not have to be removed after all. **Truth maintenance systems**, or TMSs, are designed to handle exactly these kinds of complications.

BELIEF REVISION

TRUTH MAINTENANCE SYSTEM

One very simple approach to truth maintenance is to keep track of the order in which sentences are told to the knowledge base by numbering them from $P_1$ to $P_n$. When the call RETRACT($KB$, $P_i$) is made, the system reverts to the state just before $P_i$ was added, thereby removing both $P_i$ and any inferences that were derived from $P_i$. The sentences $P_{i+1}$ through $P_n$ can then be added again. This is simple, and it guarantees that the knowledge base will be consistent, but retracting $P_i$ requires retracting and reasserting $n - i$ sentences as well as

[15] Belief revision is often contrasted with **belief update**, which occurs when a knowledge base is revised to reflect a change in the world rather than new information about a fixed world. Belief update combines belief revision with reasoning about time and change; it is also related to the process of **filtering** described in Chapter 15.

undoing and redoing all the inferences drawn from those sentences. For systems to which many facts are being added—such as large commercial databases—this is impractical.

JTMS

JUSTIFICATION

A more efficient approach is the justification-based truth maintenance system, or **JTMS**. In a JTMS, each sentence in the knowledge base is annotated with a **justification** consisting of the set of sentences from which it was inferred. For example, if the knowledge base already contains $P \Rightarrow Q$, then $\text{TELL}(P)$ will cause $Q$ to be added with the justification $\{P,\ P \Rightarrow Q\}$. In general, a sentence can have any number of justifications. Justifications are used to make retraction efficient. Given the call $\text{RETRACT}(P)$, the JTMS will delete exactly those sentences for which $P$ is a member of every justification. So, if a sentence $Q$ had the single justification $\{P,\ P \Rightarrow Q\}$ it would be removed, if it had the additional justification $\{P,\ P \vee R \Rightarrow Q\}$ it would still be removed, but if it also had the justification $\{R,\ P \vee R \Rightarrow Q\}$, then it would be spared. In this way, the time required for retraction of $P$ depends only on the number of sentences derived from $P$ rather than on the number of other sentences added since $P$ entered the knowledge base.

The JTMS assumes that sentences that are considered once will probably be considered again, so rather than deleting a sentence from the knowledge base entirely when it loses all justifications, we merely mark the sentence as being *out* of the knowledge base. If a subsequent assertion restores one of the justifications, then we mark the sentence as being back *in*. In this way, the JTMS retains all of the inference chains that it uses and need not rederive sentences when a justification becomes valid again.

In addition to handling the retraction of incorrect information, TMSs can be used to speed up the analysis of multiple hypothetical situations. Suppose, for example, that the Romanian Olympic Committee is choosing sites for the swimming, athletics, and equestrian events at the 2048 Games to be held in Romania. For example, let the first hypothesis be $Site(Swimming, Pitesti)$, $Site(Athletics, Bucharest)$, and $Site(Equestrian, Arad)$. A great deal of reasoning must then be done to work out the logistical consequences and hence the desirability of this selection. If we want to consider $Site(Athletics, Sibiu)$ instead, the TMS avoids the need to start again from scratch. Instead, we simply retract $Site(Athletics, Bucharest)$ and assert $Site(Athletics, Sibiu)$ and the TMS takes care of the necessary revisions. Inference chains generated from the choice of Bucharest can be reused with Sibiu, provided that the conclusions are the same.

ATMS

An assumption-based truth maintenance system, or **ATMS**, is designed to make this type of context-switching between hypothetical worlds particularly efficient. In a JTMS, the maintenance of justifications allows you to move quickly from one state to another by making a few retractions and assertions, but at any time only one state is represented. An ATMS represents *all* the states that have ever been considered at the same time. Whereas a JTMS simply labels each sentence as being *in* or *out*, an ATMS keeps track, for each sentence, of which assumptions would cause the sentence to be true. In other words, each sentence has a label that consists of a set of assumption sets. The sentence holds just in those cases where all the assumptions in one of the assumption sets hold.

EXPLANATIONS

Truth maintenance systems also provide a mechanism for generating **explanations**. Technically, an explanation of a sentence $P$ is a set of sentences $E$ such that $E$ entails $P$. If the sentences in $E$ are already known to be true, then $E$ simply provides a sufficient ba-

ASSUMPTIONS

sis for proving that $P$ must be the case. But explanations can also include **assumptions**—sentences that are not known to be true, but would suffice to prove $P$ if they were true. For example, one might not have enough information to prove that one's car won't start, but a reasonable explanation might include the assumption that the battery is dead. This, combined with knowledge of how cars operate, explains the observed nonbehavior. In most cases, we will prefer an explanation $E$ that is minimal, meaning that there is no proper subset of $E$ that is also an explanation. An ATMS can generate explanations for the "car won't start" problem by making assumptions (such as "gas in car" or "battery dead") in any order we like, even if some assumptions are contradictory. Then we look at the label for the sentence "car won't start" to read off the sets of assumptions that would justify the sentence.

The exact algorithms used to implement truth maintenance systems are a little complicated, and we do not cover them here. The computational complexity of the truth maintenance problem is at least as great as that of propositional inference—that is, NP-hard. Therefore, you should not expect truth maintenance to be a panacea. When used carefully, however, a TMS can provide a substantial increase in the ability of a logical system to handle complex environments and hypotheses.

## 10.9 Summary

This has been the most detailed chapter of the book so far. By delving into the details of how one represents a variety of knowledge, we hope we have given the reader a sense of how real knowledge bases are constructed. The major points are as follows:

- Large-scale knowledge representation requires a general-purpose ontology to organize and tie together the various specific domains of knowledge.
- A general-purpose ontology needs to cover a wide variety of knowledge and should be capable, in principle, of handling any domain.
- We presented an **upper ontology** based on categories and the event calculus. We covered structured objects, time and space, change, processes, substances, and beliefs.
- Actions, events, and time can be represented either in situation calculus or in more expressive representations such as event calculus and fluent calculus. Such representations enable an agent to construct plans by logical inference.
- The mental states of agents can be represented by strings that denote beliefs.
- We presented a detailed analysis of the Internet shopping domain, exercising the general ontology and showing how the domain knowledge can be used by a shopping agent.
- Special-purpose representation systems, such as **semantic networks** and **description logics**, have been devised to help in organizing a hierarchy of categories. **Inheritance** is an important form of inference, allowing the properties of objects to be deduced from their membership in categories.
- The **closed-world assumption**, as implemented in logic programs, provides a simple way to avoid having to specify lots of negative information. It is best interpreted as a **default** that can be overridden by additional information.

- **Nonmonotonic logics**, such as **circumscription** and **default logic**, are intended to capture default reasoning in general. **Answer set programming** speeds up nonmonotonic inference, much as WALKSAT speeds up propositional inference.
- **Truth maintenance systems** handle knowledge updates and revisions efficiently.

## BIBLIOGRAPHICAL AND HISTORICAL NOTES

There are plausible claims (Briggs, 1985) that formal knowledge representation research began with classical Indian theorizing about the grammar of Shastric Sanskrit, which dates back to the first millennium B.C. In the West, the use of definitions of terms in ancient Greek mathematics can be regarded as the earliest instance. Indeed, the development of technical terminology in any field can be regarded as a form of knowledge representation.

Early discussions of representation in AI tended to focus on "*problem* representation" rather than "*knowledge* representation." (See, for example, Amarel's (1968) discussion of the Missionaries and Cannibals problem.) In the 1970s, AI emphasized the development of "expert systems" (also called "knowledge-based systems") that could, if given the appropriate domain knowledge, match or exceed the performance of human experts on narrowly defined tasks. For example, the first expert system, DENDRAL (Feigenbaum *et al.*, 1971; Lindsay *et al.*, 1980), interpreted the output of a mass spectrometer (a type of instrument used to analyze the structure of organic chemical compounds) as accurately as expert chemists. Although the success of DENDRAL was instrumental in convincing the AI research community of the importance of knowledge representation, the representational formalisms used in DENDRAL are highly specific to the domain of chemistry. Over time, researchers became interested in standardized knowledge representation formalisms and ontologies that could streamline the process of creating new expert systems. In so doing, they ventured into territory previously explored by philosophers of science and of language. The discipline imposed in AI by the need for one's theories to "work" has led to more rapid and deeper progress than was the case when these problems were the exclusive domain of philosophy (although it has at times also led to the repeated reinvention of the wheel).

The creation of comprehensive taxonomies or classifications dates back to ancient times. Aristotle (384–322 B.C.) strongly emphasized classification and categorization schemes. His *Organon*, a collection of works on logic assembled by his students after his death, included a treatise called *Categories* in which he attempted to construct what we would now call an upper ontology. He also introduced the notions of **genus** and **species** for lower-level classification, although not with their modern, specifically biological meaning. Our present system of biological classification, including the use of "binomial nomenclature" (classification via genus and species in the technical sense), was invented by the Swedish biologist Carolus Linnaeus, or Carl von Linne (1707–1778). The problems associated with natural kinds and inexact category boundaries have been addressed by Wittgenstein (1953), Quine (1953), Lakoff (1987), and Schwartz (1977), among others.

Interest in larger-scale ontologies is increasing. The CYC project (Lenat, 1995; Lenat and Guha, 1990) has released a 6,000-concept upper ontology with 60,000 facts, and licenses a much larger global ontology. The IEEE has established subcommittee P1600.1, the Standard Upper Ontology Working Group, and the Open Mind Initiative has enlisted over 7,000 Internet users to enter more than 400,000 facts about commonsense concepts. On the Web, standards such as RDF, XML, and the Semantic Web (Berners-Lee *et al.*, 2001) are emerging, but are not yet widely used. The conferences on *Formal Ontology in Information Systems* (FOIS) contain many interesting papers on both general and domain-specific ontologies.

The taxonomy used in this chapter was developed by the authors and is based in part on their experience in the CYC project and in part on work by Hwang and Schubert (1993) and Davis (1990). An inspirational discussion of the general project of commonsense knowledge representation appears in Hayes's (1978, 1985b) "The Naive Physics Manifesto."

The representation of time, change, actions, and events has been studied extensively in philosophy and theoretical computer science as well as in AI. The oldest approach is **temporal logic**, which is a specialized logic in which each model describes a complete trajectory through time (usually either linear or branching), rather than just a static relational structure. The logic includes **modal operators** that are applied to formulas; $\Box p$ means "$p$ will be true at all times in the future," and $\Diamond p$ means "$p$ will be true at some time in the future." The study of temporal logic was initiated by Aristotle and the Megarian and Stoic schools in ancient Greece. In modern times, Findlay (1941) was the first to suggest a formal calculus for reasoning about time, but the work of Arthur Prior (1967) is considered the most influential. Textbooks on temporal logic include those by Rescher and Urquhart (1971) and van Benthem (1983).

Theoretical computer scientists have long been interested in formalizing the properties of programs, viewed as sequences of computational actions. Burstall (1974) introduced the idea of using modal operators to reason about computer programs. Soon thereafter, Vaughan Pratt (1976) designed **dynamic logic**, in which modal operators indicate the effects of programs or other actions (see also Harel, 1984). For instance, in dynamic logic, if $\alpha$ is the name of a program, then "$[\alpha]p$" means "$p$ would be true in all world states resulting from executing program $\alpha$ in the current world state", and "$\langle\alpha\rangle p$" means "$p$ would be true in at least one world state resulting from executing program $\alpha$ in the current world state." Dynamic logic was applied to the actual analysis of programs by Fischer and Ladner (1977). Pnueli (1977) introduced the idea of using classical temporal logic to reason about programs.

Whereas temporal logic puts time directly into the model theory of the language, representations of time in AI have tended to incorporate axioms about times and events explicitly in the knowledge base, giving time no special status in the logic. This approach can allow for greater clarity and flexibility in some cases. Also, temporal knowledge expressed in first-order logic can be more easily integrated with other knowledge that has been accumulated in that notation.

The earliest treatment of time and action in AI was John McCarthy's (1963) situation calculus. The first AI system to make substantial use of general-purpose reasoning about actions in first-order logic was QA3 (Green, 1969b). Kowalski (1979b) developed the idea of reifying propositions within situation calculus.

The **frame problem** was first recognized by McCarthy and Hayes (1969). Many researchers considered the problem insoluble within first-order logic, and it spurred a great deal of research into nonmonotonic logics. Philosophers from Dreyfus (1972) to Crockett (1994) have cited the frame problem as one symptom of the inevitable failure of the entire AI enterprise. The partial solution of the representational frame problem using successor-state axioms is due to Ray Reiter (1991); a solution of the inferential frame problem can be traced to work by Holldobler and Schneeberger (1990) on what became known as fluent calculus (Thielscher, 1999). The discussion in this chapter is based partly on the analyses by Lin and Reiter (1997) and Thielscher (1999). Books by Shanahan (1997) and Reiter (2001b) give complete, modern treatments of reasoning about action in situation calculus.

COGNITIVE ROBOTICS

The partial resolution of the frame problem has rekindled interest in the declarative approach to reasoning about actions, which had been eclipsed by special-purpose planning systems since the early 1970s. (See Chapter 11.) Under the banner of **cognitive robotics**, much progress has been made on logical representations of action and time. The GOLOG language uses the full expressive power of logic programming to describe actions and plans (Levesque *et al.*, 1997a) and has been extended to handle concurrent actions (Giacomo *et al.*, 2000), stochastic environments (Boutilier *et al.*, 2000), and sensing (Reiter, 2001a).

The event calculus was introduced by Kowalski and Sergot (1986) to handle continuous time, and there have been several variations (Sadri and Kowalski, 1995). Shanahan (1999) presents a good short overview. James Allen introduced time intervals for the same reason (Allen, 1983, 1984), arguing that intervals were much more natural than situations for reasoning about extended and concurrent events. Peter Ladkin (1986a, 1986b) introduced "concave" time intervals (intervals with gaps; essentially, unions of ordinary "convex" time intervals) and applied the techniques of mathematical abstract algebra to time representation. Allen (1991) systematically investigates the wide variety of techniques available for time representation. Shoham (1987) describes the reification of events and sets forth a novel scheme of his own for the purpose. There are significant commonalities between the event-based ontology given in this chapter and an analysis of events due to the philosopher Donald Davidson (1980). The **histories** in Pat Hayes's (1985a) ontology of liquids also have much the same flavor.

The question of the ontological status of substances has a long history. Plato proposed that substances were abstract entities entirely distinct from physical objects; he would say $MadeOf(Butter_3, Butter)$ rather than $Butter_3 \in Butter$. This leads to a substance hierarchy in which, for example, $UnsaltedButter$ is a more specific substance than $Butter$. The position adopted in this chapter, in which substances are categories of objects, was championed by Richard Montague (1973). It has also been adopted in the CYC project. Copeland (1993) mounts a serious, but not invincible, attack. The alternative approach mentioned in the chapter, in which butter is one object consisting of all buttery objects in the universe, was proposed

MEREOLOGY

originally by the Polish logician Leśniewski (1916). His **mereology** (the name is derived from the Greek word for "part") used the part–whole relation as a substitute for mathematical set theory, with the aim of eliminating abstract entities such as sets. A more readable exposition of these ideas is given by Leonard and Goodman (1940), and Goodman's *The Structure of Appearance* (1977) applies the ideas to various problems in knowledge representation. While some aspects of the mereological approach are awkward—for example, the need for a separate inheritance mechanism based on part–whole relations—the approach gained the support of Quine (1960). Harry Bunt (1985) has provided an extensive analysis of its use in knowledge representation.

MODAL LOGIC

Mental objects and states have been the subject of intensive study in philosophy and AI. **Modal logic** is the classical method for reasoning about knowledge in philosophy. Modal logic augments first-order logic with modal operators, such as $B$ (believes) and $K$ (knows), that take *sentences* rather than terms as arguments. The proof theory for modal logic restricts substitution within modal contexts, thereby achieving referential opacity. The modal logic of knowledge was invented by Jaakko Hintikka (1962). Saul Kripke (1963) defined the semantics of the modal logic of knowledge in terms of **possible worlds**. Roughly speaking, a world is possible for an agent if it is consistent with everything the agent knows. From this, one can derive rules of inference involving the $K$ operator. Robert C. Moore relates the modal logic of knowledge to a style of reasoning about knowledge that refers directly to possible worlds in first-order logic (Moore, 1980, 1985). Modal logic can be an intimidatingly arcane field, but it has found significant applications in reasoning about information in distributed computer systems. The book *Reasoning about Knowledge* by Fagin *et al.* (1995) provides a thorough introduction to the modal approach. The biennial conference on *Theoretical Aspects of Reasoning About Knowledge* (TARK) covers applications of the theory of knowledge in AI, economics, and distributed systems.

The syntactic theory of mental objects was first studied in depth by Kaplan and Montague (1960), who showed that it led to paradoxes if not handled carefully. Because it has a natural model in terms of beliefs as physical configurations of a computer or a brain, it has been popular in AI in recent years. Konolige (1982) and Haas (1986) used it to describe inference engines of limited power, and Morgenstern (1987) showed how it could be used to describe knowledge preconditions in planning. The methods for planning observation actions in Chapter 12 are based on the syntactic theory. Ernie Davis (1990) gives an excellent comparison of the syntactic and modal theories of knowledge.

The Greek philosopher Porphyry (c. 234–305 A.D.), commenting on Aristotle's *Categories*, drew what might qualify as the first semantic network. Charles S. Peirce (1909) developed existential graphs as the first semantic network formalism using modern logic. Ross Quillian (1961), driven by an interest in human memory and language processing, initiated work on semantic networks within AI. An influential paper by Marvin Minsky (1975) presented a version of semantic networks called **frames**; a frame was a representation of an object or category, with attributes and relations to other objects or categories. Although the paper served to initiate interest in the field of knowledge representation *per se*, it was criticized as a recycling of earlier ideas developed in object-oriented programming, such as inheritance and the use of default values (Dahl *et al.*, 1970; Birtwistle *et al.*, 1973). It is not clear to what extent the latter papers on object-oriented programming were influenced in turn by early AI work on semantic networks.

The question of semantics arose quite acutely with respect to Quillian's semantic networks (and those of others who followed his approach), with their ubiquitous and very vague "IS-A links," as well as other early knowledge representation formalisms such as that of MERLIN (Moore and Newell, 1973) with its mysterious "flat" and "cover" operations. Woods' (1975) famous article "What's In a Link?" drew the attention of AI researchers to the need for precise semantics in knowledge representation formalisms. Brachman (1979) elaborated on this point and proposed solutions. Patrick Hayes's (1979) "The Logic of Frames" cut even deeper, claiming that "Most of 'frames' is just a new syntax for parts of first-order logic." Drew McDermott's (1978b) "Tarskian Semantics, or, No Notation without Denotation!" argued that the model-theoretic approach to semantics used in first-order logic should be applied to all knowledge representation formalisms. This remains a controversial idea; notably, McDermott himself has reversed his position in "A Critique of Pure Reason" (McDermott, 1987). NETL (Fahlman, 1979) was a sophisticated semantic network system whose IS-A links (called "virtual copy," or VC, links) were based more on the notion of "inheritance" characteristic of frame systems or of object-oriented programming languages than on the subset relation and were much more precisely defined than Quillian's links from the pre-Woods era. NETL is particularly intriguing because it was intended to be implemented in parallel hardware to overcome the difficulty of retrieving information from large semantic networks. David Touretzky (1986) subjects inheritance to rigorous mathematical analysis. Selman and Levesque (1993) discuss the complexity of inheritance with exceptions, showing that in most formulations it is NP-complete.

The development of description logics is the most recent stage in a long line of research aimed at finding useful subsets of first-order logic for which inference is computationally tractable. Hector Levesque and Ron Brachman (1987) showed that certain logical constructs—notably, certain uses of disjunction and negation—were primarily responsible for the intractability of logical inference. Building on the KL-ONE system (Schmolze and Lipkis, 1983), a number of systems have been developed whose designs incorporate the results of theoretical complexity analysis, most notably KRYPTON (Brachman *et al.*, 1983) and Classic (Borgida *et al.*, 1989). The result has been a marked increase in the speed of inference and a much better understanding of the interaction between complexity and expressiveness in reasoning systems. Calvanese *et al.* (1999) summarize the state of the art. Against this trend, Doyle and Patil (1991) have argued that restricting the expressiveness of a language either makes it impossible to solve certain problems or encourages the user to circumvent the language restrictions through nonlogical means.

The three main formalisms for dealing with nonmonotonic inference—circumscription (McCarthy, 1980), default logic (Reiter, 1980), and modal nonmonotonic logic (McDermott and Doyle, 1980)—were all introduced in one special issue of the AI Journal. Answer set programming can be seen as an extension of negation as failure or as a refinement of circumscription; the underlying theory of stable model semantics was introduced by Gelfond and Lifschitz (1988) and the leading answer set programming systems are DLV (Eiter *et al.*, 1998) and SMODELS (Niemelä *et al.*, 2000). The disk drive example comes from the SMODELS user manual (Syrjänen, 2000). Lifschitz (2001) discusses the use of answer set programming for planning. Brewka *et al.* (1997) give a good overview of the various approaches to nonmonotonic logic. Clark (1978) covers the negation-as-failure approach to logic programming and Clark completion. Van Emden and Kowalski (1976) show that every Prolog program without negation has a unique minimal model. Recent years have seen renewed interest in applications of nonmonotonic logics to large-scale knowledge representation systems. The BENINQ systems for handling insurance benefits inquiries was perhaps the first commercially successful application of a nonmonotonic inheritance system (Morgenstern, 1998). Lifschitz (2001) discusses the application of answer set programming to planning. A variety of nonmonotonic reasoning systems based on logic programming are documented in the proceedings of the conferences on *Logic Programming and Nonmonotonic Reasoning* (LPNMR).

The study of truth maintenance systems began with the TMS (Doyle, 1979) and RUP (McAllester, 1980) systems, both of which were essentially JTMSs. The ATMS approach was described in a series of papers by Johan de Kleer (1986a, 1986b, 1986c). *Building Problem Solvers* (Forbus and de Kleer, 1993) explains in depth how TMSs can be used in AI applications. Nayak and Williams (1997) show how an efficient TMS makes it feasible to plan the operations of a NASA spacecraft in real time.

For obvious reasons, this chapter does not cover *every* area of knowledge representation in depth. The three principal topics omitted are the following:

QUALITATIVE PHYSICS

◇ **Qualitative physics**: Qualitative physics is a subfield of knowledge representation concerned specifically with constructing a logical, nonnumeric theory of physical objects and processes. The term was coined by Johan de Kleer (1975), although the enterprise could be said to have started in Fahlman's (1974) BUILD, a sophisticated planner for constructing complex towers of blocks. Fahlman discovered in the process of designing it that most of the effort (80%, by his estimate) went into modeling the physics of the blocks world to calculate the stability of various subassemblies of blocks, rather than into planning per se. He sketches a hypothetical naive-physics-like process to explain why young children can solve BUILD-like problems without access to the high-speed floating-point arithmetic used in BUILD's physical modeling. Hayes (1985a) uses "histories"—four-dimensional slices of space-time similar to Davidson's events—to construct a fairly complex naive physics of liquids. Hayes was the first to prove that a bath with the plug in will eventually overflow if the tap keeps running and that a person who falls into a lake will get wet all over. De Kleer and Brown (1985) and Ken Forbus (1985) attempted to construct something like a general-purpose theory of the physical world, based on qualitative abstractions of physical equations. In recent years, qualitative physics has developed to the point where it is possible to analyze an impressive variety of complex physical systems (Sacks and Joskowicz, 1993; Yip, 1991). Qualitative techniques have been used to construct novel designs for clocks, windscreen wipers, and six-legged walkers (Subramanian, 1993; Subramanian and Wang, 1994). The collection *Readings in Qualitative Reasoning about Physical Systems* (Weld and de Kleer, 1990) provides a good introduction to the field.

SPATIAL REASONING

◇ **Spatial reasoning**: The reasoning necessary to navigate in the wumpus world and shopping world is trivial in comparison to the rich spatial structure of the real world. The earliest serious attempt to capture commonsense reasoning about space appears in the work of Ernest Davis (1986, 1990). The region connection calculus of Cohn *et al.* (1997) supports a form of qualitative spatial reasoning and has led to new kinds of geographical information system. As with qualitative physics, an agent can go a long way, so to speak, without resorting to a full metric representation. When such a representation is necessary, techniques developed in robotics (Chapter 25) can be used.

PSYCHOLOGICAL REASONING

◇ **Psychological reasoning**: Psychological reasoning involves the development of a working *psychology* for artificial agents to use in reasoning about themselves and other agents. This is often based on so-called folk psychology, the theory that humans in general are believed to use in reasoning about themselves and other humans. When AI researchers provide their artificial agents with psychological theories for reasoning about other agents, the theories are frequently based on the researchers' description of the logical agents' own design. Psychological reasoning is currently most useful within the context of natural language understanding, where divining the speaker's intentions is of paramount importance.

The proceedings of the international conferences on *Principles of Knowledge Representation and Reasoning* provide the most up-to-date sources for work in this area. *Readings in Knowledge Representation* (Brachman and Levesque, 1985) and *Formal Theories of the Commonsense World* (Hobbs and Moore, 1985) are excellent anthologies on knowledge representation; the former focuses more on historically important papers in representation languages and formalisms, the latter on the accumulation of the knowledge itself. Davis (1990), Stefik (1995), and Sowa (1999) provide textbook introductions to knowledge representation.

## EXERCISES

**10.1** Write sentences to define the effects of the *Shoot* action in the wumpus world. Describe its effects on the wumpus and remember that shooting uses the agent's arrow.

**10.2** Within situation calculus, write an axiom to associate time 0 with the situation $S_0$ and another axiom to associate the time $t$ with any situation that is derived from $S_0$ by a sequence of $t$ actions.

**10.3** In this exercise, we will consider the problem of planning a route for a robot to take from one city to another. The basic action taken by the robot is $Go(x, y)$, which takes it from city $x$ to city $y$ if there is a direct route between those cities. $DirectRoute(x, y)$ is true if and only if there is a direct route from $x$ to $y$; you can assume that all such facts are already in the KB. (See the map on page 63.) The robot begins in Arad and must reach Bucharest.

**a.** Write a suitable logical description of the initial situation of the robot.

**b.** Write a suitable logical query whose solutions will provide possible paths to the goal.

**c.** Write a sentence describing the *Go* action.

**d.** Now suppose that following the direct route between two cities consumes an amount of fuel equal to the distance between the cities. The robot starts with fuel at full capacity. Augment your representation to include these considerations. Your action description should be such that the query you specified earlier will still result in feasible plans.

**e.** Describe the initial situation, and write a new rule or rules describing the *Go* action.

**f.** Now suppose some of the vertices are also gas stations, at which the robot can fill its tank. Extend your representation and write all the rules needed to describe gas stations, including the *Fillup* action.

**10.4** Investigate ways to extend the event calculus to handle *simultaneous* events. Is it possible to avoid a combinatorial explosion of axioms?

**10.5** Represent the following seven sentences using and extending the representations developed in the chapter:

**a.** Water is a liquid between 0 and 100 degrees.

**b.** Water boils at 100 degrees.

**c.** The water in John's water bottle is frozen.

**d.** Perrier is a kind of water.

**e.** John has Perrier in his water bottle.

**f.** All liquids have a freezing point.

**g.** A liter of water weighs more than a liter of alcohol.

Now repeat the exercise using a representation based on the mereological approach, in which, for example, $Water$ is an object containing as parts all the water in the world.

**10.6** Write definitions for the following:

**a.** $ExhaustivePartDecomposition$

**b.** $PartPartition$

**c.** $PartwiseDisjoint$

These should be analogous to the definitions for $ExhaustiveDecomposition$, $Partition$, and $Disjoint$. Is it the case that $PartPartition(s, BunchOf(s))$? If so, prove it; if not, give a counterexample and define sufficient conditions under which it does hold.

**10.7** Write a set of sentences that allows one to calculate the price of an individual tomato (or other object), given the price per pound. Extend the theory to allow the price of a bag of tomatoes to be calculated.

**10.8** An alternative scheme for representing measures involves applying the units function to an abstract length object. In such a scheme, one would write $Inches(Length(L_1)) = 1.5$. How does this scheme compare with the one in the chapter? Issues include conversion axioms, names for abstract quantities (such as "50 dollars"), and comparisons of abstract measures in different units (50 inches is more than 50 centimeters).

**10.9** Construct a representation for exchange rates between currencies that allows fluctuations on a daily basis.

**10.10** This exercise concerns the relationships between event categories and the time intervals in which they occur.

**a.** Define the predicate $T(c, i)$ in terms of $During$ and $\in$.

**b.** Explain precisely why we do not need two different notations to describe conjunctive event categories.

**c.** Give a formal definition for $T(OneOf(p, q), i)$ and $T(Either(p, q), i)$.

**d.** Explain why it makes sense to have two forms of negation of events, analogous to the two forms of disjunction. Call them $Not$ and $Never$ and give them formal definitions.

**10.11** Define the predicate $Fixed$, where $Fixed(Location(x))$ means that the location of object $x$ is fixed over time.

**10.12** Define the predicates $Before$, $After$, $During$, and $Overlap$, using the predicate $Meet$ and the functions $Start$ and $End$, but not the function $Time$ or the predicate $<$.

**10.13** Section 10.5 used the predicates *Link* and *LinkText* to describe connections between web pages. Using the *InTag* and *GetPage* predicates, among others, write definitions for *Link* and *LinkText*.

**10.14** One part of the shopping process that was not covered in this chapter is checking for compatibility between items. For example, if a customer orders a computer, is it matched with the right peripherals? If a digital camera is ordered, does it have the right memory card and batteries? Write a knowledge base that will decide whether a set of items is compatible and that can be used to suggest replacements or additional items if they are not compatible. Make sure that the knowledge base works with at least one line of products, and is easily extensible to other lines.

**10.15** Add rules to extend the definition of the predicate $Name(s, c)$ so that a string such as "laptop computer" matches against the appropriate category names from a variety of stores. Try to make your definition general. Test it by looking at ten online stores, and at the category names they give for three different categories. For example, for the category of laptops, we found the names "Notebooks," "Laptops," "Notebook Computers," "Notebook," "Laptops and Notebooks," and "Notebook PCs." Some of these can be covered by explicit $Name$ facts, while others could be covered by rules for handling plurals, conjunctions, etc.

**10.16** A complete solution to the problem of inexact matches to the buyer's description in shopping is very difficult and requires a full array of natural language processing and information retrieval techniques. (See Chapters 22 and 23.) One small step is to allow the user to specify minimum and maximum values for various attributes. We will insist that the buyer use the following grammar for product descriptions:

$$
\begin{array}{lcl}
\mathit{Description} & \rightarrow & \mathit{Category}\ [\mathit{Connector}\ \mathit{Modifier}]* \\
\mathit{Connector} & \rightarrow & \text{"}\mathit{with}\text{"} \mid \text{"}\mathit{and}\text{"} \mid \text{","} \\
\mathit{Modifier} & \rightarrow & \mathit{Attribute} \mid \mathit{Attribute}\ \mathit{Op}\ \mathit{Value} \\
\mathit{Op} & \rightarrow & \text{"="} \mid \text{">"} \mid \text{"<"}
\end{array}
$$

Here, $Category$ names a product category, $Attribute$ is some feature such as "CPU" or "price," and $Value$ is the target value for the attribute. So the query "computer with at least a 2.5-GHz CPU for under \$1000" must be re-expressed as "computer with CPU $>$ 2.5 GHz and price $<$ \$1000." Implement a shopping agent that accepts descriptions in this language.

**10.17** Our description of Internet shopping omitted the all-important step of actually *buying* the product. Provide a formal logical description of buying, using event calculus. That is, define the sequence of events that occurs when a buyer submits a credit card purchase and then eventually gets billed and receives the product.

**10.18** Describe the event of trading something for something else. Describe buying as a kind of trading in which one of the objects traded is a sum of money.

**10.19** The two preceding exercises assume a fairly primitive notion of ownership. For example, the buyer starts by *owning* the dollar bills. This picture begins to break down when, for example, one's money is in the bank, because there is no longer any specific collection of dollar bills that one owns. The picture is complicated still further by borrowing, leasing, renting, and bailment. Investigate the various commonsense and legal concepts of ownership, and propose a scheme by which they can be represented formally.

**10.20** You are to create a system for advising computer science undergraduates on what courses to take over an extended period in order to satisfy the program requirements. (Use whatever requirements are appropriate for your institution.) First, decide on a vocabulary for representing all the information, and then represent it; then use an appropriate query to the system, that will return a legal program of study as a solution. You should allow for some tailoring to individual students, in that your system should ask what courses or equivalents the student has already taken, and not generate programs that repeat those courses.

Suggest ways in which your system could be improved—for example to take into account knowledge about student preferences, the workload, good and bad instructors, and so on. For each kind of knowledge, explain how it could be expressed logically. Could your system easily incorporate this information to find the *best* program of study for a student?

**10.21** Figure 10.1 shows the top levels of a hierarchy for everything. Extend it to include as many real categories as possible. A good way to do this is to cover all the things in your everyday life. This includes objects and events. Start with waking up, and proceed in an orderly fashion noting everything that you see, touch, do, and think about. For example, a random sampling produces music, news, milk, walking, driving, gas, Soda Hall, carpet, talking, Professor Fateman, chicken curry, tongue, $7, sun, the daily newspaper, and so on.

You should produce both a single hierarchy chart (on a large sheet of paper) and a listing of objects and categories with the relations satisfied by members of each category. Every object should be in a category, and every category should be in the hierarchy.

**10.22** (Adapted from an example by Doug Lenat.) Your mission is to capture, in logical form, enough knowledge to answer a series of questions about the following simple sentence:

> Yesterday John went to the North Berkeley Safeway supermarket and bought two pounds of tomatoes and a pound of ground beef.

Start by trying to represent the content of the sentence as a series of assertions. You should write sentences that have straightforward logical structure (e.g., statements that objects have certain properties, that objects are related in certain ways, that all objects satisfying one property satisfy another). The following might help you get started:

- Which classes, objects, and relations would you need? What are their parents, siblings and so on? (You will need events and temporal ordering, among other things.)
- Where would they fit in a more general hierarchy?
- What are the constraints and interrelationships among them?
- How detailed must you be about each of the various concepts?

The knowledge base you construct must be capable of answering a list of questions that we will give shortly. Some of the questions deal with the material stated explicitly in the story, but most of them require one to have other background knowledge—to read between the lines. You'll have to deal with what kind of things are at a supermarket, what is involved with purchasing the things one selects, what will purchases be used for, and so on. Try to make your representation as general as possible. To give a trivial example: don't say "People buy food from Safeway," because that won't help you with those who shop at another supermarket. Don't say "Joe made spaghetti with the tomatoes and ground beef," because that won't help you with anything else at all. Also, don't turn the questions into answers; for example, question (c) asks "Did John buy any meat?"—not "Did John buy a pound of ground beef?"

Sketch the chains of reasoning that would answer the questions. In the process of doing so, you will no doubt need to create additional concepts, make additional assertions, and so on. If possible, use a logical reasoning system to demonstrate the sufficiency of your knowledge base. Many of the things you write might be only approximately correct in reality, but don't worry too much; the idea is to extract the common sense that lets you answer these questions at all. A truly complete answer to this question is *extremely* difficult, probably beyond the state of the art of current knowledge representation. But you should be able to put together a consistent set of axioms for the limited questions posed here.

**a**. Is John a child or an adult? [Adult]

**b**. Does John now have at least two tomatoes? [Yes]

**c**. Did John buy any meat? [Yes]

**d**. If Mary was buying tomatoes at the same time as John, did he see her? [Yes]

**e**. Are the tomatoes made in the supermarket? [No]

**f**. What is John going to do with the tomatoes? [Eat them]

**g**. Does Safeway sell deodorant? [Yes]

**h**. Did John bring any money to the supermarket? [Yes]

**i**. Does John have less money after going to the supermarket? [Yes]

**10.23** Make the necessary additions or changes to your knowledge base from the previous exercise so that the questions that follow can be answered. Show that they can indeed be answered by the KB, and include in your report a discussion of the fixes, explaining why they were needed, whether they were minor or major, and so on.

**a**. Are there other people in Safeway while John is there? [Yes—staff!]

**b**. Is John a vegetarian? [No]

**c**. Who owns the deodorant in Safeway? [Safeway Corporation]

**d**. Did John have an ounce of ground beef? [Yes]

**e**. Does the Shell station next door have any gas? [Yes]

**f**. Do the tomatoes fit in John's car trunk? [Yes]

**10.24** Recall that inheritance information in semantic networks can be captured logically by suitable implication sentences. In this exercise, we will consider the efficiency of using such sentences for inheritance.

**a.** Consider the information content in a used-car catalog such as Kelly's Blue Book—for example, that 1973 Dodge Vans are worth $575. Suppose all this information (for 11,000 models) is encoded as logical rules, as suggested in the chapter. Write down three such rules, including that for 1973 Dodge Vans. How would you use the rules to find the value of a *particular* car (e.g., JB, which is a 1973 Dodge Van), given a backward-chaining theorem prover such as Prolog?

**b.** Compare the time efficiency of the backward-chaining method for solving this problem with the inheritance method used in semantic nets.

**c.** Explain how forward chaining allows a logic-based system to solve the same problem efficiently, assuming that the KB contains only the 11,000 rules about prices.

**d.** Describe a situation in which neither forward nor backward chaining on the rules will allow the price query for an individual car to be handled efficiently.

**e.** Can you suggest a solution enabling this type of query to be solved efficiently in all cases in logic systems? [*Hint:* Remember that two cars of the same category have the same price.]

**10.25** One might suppose that the syntactic distinction between unboxed links and singly boxed links in semantic networks is unnecessary, because singly boxed links are always attached to categories; an inheritance algorithm could simply assume that an unboxed link attached to a category is intended to apply to all members of that category. Show that this argument is fallacious, giving examples of errors that would arise.

# 11 PLANNING

*In which we see how an agent can take advantage of the structure of a problem to construct complex plans of action.*

The task of coming up with a sequence of actions that will achieve a goal is called **planning**. We have seen two examples of planning agents so far: the search-based problem-solving agent of Chapter 3 and the logical planning agent of Chapter 10. This chapter is concerned primarily with *scaling up* to complex planning problems that defeat the approaches we have seen so far.

Section 11.1 develops an expressive yet carefully constrained language for representing planning problems, including actions and states. The language is closely related to the propositional and first-order representations of actions in Chapters 7 and 10. Section 11.2 shows how forward and backward search algorithms can take advantage of this representation, primarily through accurate heuristics that can be derived automatically from the structure of the representation. (This is analogous to the way in which effective heuristics were constructed for constraint satisfaction problems in Chapter 5.) Sections 11.3 through 11.5 describe planning algorithms that go beyond forward and backward search, taking advantage of the representation of the problem. In particular, we explore approaches that are not constrained to consider only totally ordered sequences of actions.

CLASSICAL PLANNING

For this chapter, we consider only environments that are fully observable, deterministic, finite, static (change happens only when the agent acts), and discrete (in time, action, objects, and effects). These are called **classical planning** environments. In contrast, nonclassical planning is for partially observable or stochastic environments and involves a different set of algorithms and agent designs, outlined in Chapters 12 and 17.

## 11.1 THE PLANNING PROBLEM

Let us consider what can happen when an ordinary problem-solving agent using standard search algorithms—depth-first, A*, and so on—comes up against large, real-world problems. That will help us design better planning agents.

The most obvious difficulty is that the problem-solving agent can be overwhelmed by irrelevant actions. Consider the task of buying a copy of *AI: A Modern Approach* from an online bookseller. Suppose there is one buying action for each 10-digit ISBN number, for a total of 10 billion actions. The search algorithm would have to examine the outcome states of all 10 billion actions to find one that satisfies the goal, which is to own a copy of ISBN 0137903952. A sensible planning agent, on the other hand, should be able to work back from an explicit goal description such as $Have(ISBN0137903952)$ and generate the action $Buy(ISBN0137903952)$ directly. To do this, the agent simply needs the general knowledge that $Buy(x)$ results in $Have(x)$. Given this knowledge and the goal, the planner can decide in a single unification step that $Buy(ISBN0137903952)$ is the right action.

The next difficulty is finding a good **heuristic function**. Suppose the agent's goal is to buy four different books online. Then there will be $10^{40}$ plans of just four steps, so searching without an accurate heuristic is out of the question. It is obvious to a human that a good heuristic estimate for the cost of a state is the number of books that remain to be bought; unfortunately, this insight is not obvious to a problem-solving agent, because it sees the goal test only as a black box that returns true or false for each state. Therefore, the problem-solving agent lacks autonomy; it requires a human to supply a heuristic function for each new problem. On the other hand, if a planning agent has access to an explicit representation of the goal as a conjunction of subgoals, then it can use a single *domain-independent* heuristic: the number of unsatisfied conjuncts. For the book-buying problem, the goal would be $Have(A) \wedge Have(B) \wedge Have(C) \wedge Have(D)$, and a state containing $Have(A) \wedge Have(C)$ would have cost 2. Thus, the agent automatically gets the right heuristic for this problem, and for many others. We shall see later in the chapter how to construct more sophisticated heuristics that examine the available actions as well as the structure of the goal.

PROBLEM DECOMPOSITION

Finally, the problem solver might be inefficient because it cannot take advantage of **problem decomposition**. Consider the problem of delivering a set of overnight packages to their respective destinations, which are scattered across Australia. It makes sense to find out the nearest airport for each destination and divide the overall problem into several subproblems, one for each airport. Within the set of packages routed through a given airport, whether further decomposition is possible depends on the destination city. We saw in Chapter 5 that the ability to do this kind of decomposition contributes to the efficiency of constraint satisfaction problem solvers. The same holds true for planners: in the worst case, it can take $O(n!)$ time to find the best plan to deliver $n$ packages, but only $O((n/k)! \times k)$ time if the problem can be decomposed into $k$ equal parts.

NEARLY DECOMPOSABLE

As we noted in Chapter 5, perfectly decomposable problems are delicious but rare.[1] The design of many planning systems—particularly the partial-order planners described in Section 11.3—is based on the assumption that most real-world problems are **nearly decomposable**. That is, the planner can work on subgoals independently, but might need to do some additional work to combine the resulting subplans. For some problems, this assump-

[1] Notice that even the delivery of a package is not perfectly decomposable. There may be cases in which it is better to assign packages to a more distant airport if that renders a flight to the nearest airport unnecessary. Nevertheless, most delivery companies prefer the computational and organizational simplicity of sticking with decomposed solutions.

tion breaks down because working on one subgoal is likely to undo another subgoal. These interactions among subgoals are what makes puzzles (like the 8-puzzle) puzzling.

### The language of planning problems

The preceding discussion suggests that the representation of planning problems—states, actions, and goals—should make it possible for planning algorithms to take advantage of the logical structure of the problem. The key is to find a language that is expressive enough to describe a wide variety of problems, but restrictive enough to allow efficient algorithms to operate over it. In this section, we first outline the basic representation language of classical planners, known as the STRIPS language.[2] Later, we point out some of the many possible variations in STRIPS-like languages.

**Representation of states.** Planners decompose the world into logical conditions and represent a state as a conjunction of positive literals. We will consider propositional literals; for example, $Poor \wedge Unknown$ might represent the state of a hapless agent. We will also use first-order literals; for example, $At(Plane_1, Melbourne) \wedge At(Plane_2, Sydney)$ might represent a state in the package delivery problem. Literals in first-order state descriptions must be **ground** and **function-free**. Literals such as $At(x, y)$ or $At(Father(Fred), Sydney)$ are not allowed. The **closed-world assumption** is used, meaning that any conditions that are not mentioned in a state are assumed false.

**Representation of goals.** A goal is a partially specified state, represented as a conjunction of positive ground literals, such as $Rich \wedge Famous$ or $At(P_2, Tahiti)$. A propositional state $s$ **satisfies** a goal $g$ if $s$ contains all the atoms in $g$ (and possibly others). For example, the state $Rich \wedge Famous \wedge Miserable$ satisfies the goal $Rich \wedge Famous$.

GOAL SATISFACTION

**Representation of actions.** An action is specified in terms of the preconditions that must hold before it can be executed and the effects that ensue when it is executed. For example, an action for flying a plane from one location to another is:

$$\begin{array}{l} Action(Fly(p, from, to), \\ \quad \text{PRECOND:} At(p, from) \wedge Plane(p) \wedge Airport(from) \wedge Airport(to) \\ \quad \text{EFFECT:} \neg At(p, from) \wedge At(p, to)) \end{array}$$

ACTION SCHEMA

This is more properly called an **action schema**, meaning that it represents a number of different actions that can be derived by instantiating the variables $p$, $from$, and $to$ to different constants. In general, an action schema consists of three parts:

- The action name and parameter list—for example, $Fly(p, from, to)$—serves to identify the action.

PRECONDITION

- The **precondition** is a conjunction of function-free positive literals stating what must be true in a state before the action can be executed. Any variables in the precondition must also appear in the action's parameter list.

EFFECT

- The **effect** is a conjunction of function-free literals describing how the state changes when the action is executed. A positive literal $P$ in the effect is asserted to be true in

[2] STRIPS stands for STanford Research Institute Problem Solver.

the state resulting from the action, whereas a negative literal $\neg P$ is asserted to be false. Variables in the effect must also appear in the action's parameter list.

ADD LIST

DELETE LIST

To improve readability, some planning systems divide the effect into the **add list** for positive literals and the **delete list** for negative literals.

Having defined the syntax for representations of planning problems, we can now define the semantics. The most straightforward way to do this is to describe how actions affect states. (An alternative method is to specify a direct translation into successor-state axioms, whose semantics comes from first-order logic; see Exercise 11.3.) First, we say that an action is **applicable** in any state that satisfies the precondition; otherwise, the action has no effect. For a first-order action schema, establishing applicability will involve a substitution $\theta$ for the variables in the precondition. For example, suppose the current state is described by

APPLICABLE

$$At(P_1, JFK) \wedge At(P_2, SFO) \wedge Plane(P_1) \wedge Plane(P_2) \\ \wedge Airport(JFK) \wedge Airport(SFO) .$$

This state satisfies the precondition

$$At(p, from) \wedge Plane(p) \wedge Airport(from) \wedge Airport(to)$$

with substitution $\{p/P_1, from/JFK, to/SFO\}$ (among others—see Exercise 11.2). Thus, the concrete action $Fly(P_1, JFK, SFO)$ is applicable.

RESULT

Starting in state $s$, the **result** of executing an applicable action $a$ is a state $s'$ that is the same as $s$ except that any positive literal $P$ in the effect of $a$ is added to $s'$ and any negative literal $\neg P$ is removed from $s'$. Thus, after $Fly(P_1, JFK, SFO)$, the current state becomes

$$At(P_1, SFO) \wedge At(P_2, SFO) \wedge Plane(P_1) \wedge Plane(P_2) \\ \wedge Airport(JFK) \wedge Airport(SFO) .$$

Note that if a positive effect is already in $s$ it is not added twice, and if a negative effect is not in $s$, then that part of the effect is ignored. This definition embodies the so-called STRIPS **assumption**: that every literal not mentioned in the effect remains unchanged. In this way, STRIPS avoids the representational **frame problem** described in Chapter 10.

STRIPS ASSUMPTION

SOLUTION

Finally, we can define the **solution** for a planning problem. In its simplest form, this is just an action sequence that, when executed in the initial state, results in a state that satisfies the goal. Later in the chapter, we will allow solutions to be partially ordered sets of actions, provided that every action sequence that respects the partial order is a solution.

### Expressiveness and extensions

The various restrictions imposed by the STRIPS representation were chosen in the hope of making planning algorithms simpler and more efficient, without making it too difficult to describe real problems. One of the most important restrictions is that literals be *function-free*. With this restriction, we can be sure that any action schema for a given problem can be propositionalized—that is, turned into a finite collection of purely propositional action representations with no variables. (See Chapter 9 for more on this topic.) For example, in the air cargo domain for a problem with 10 planes and five airports, we could translate the $Fly(p, from, to)$ schema into $10 \times 5 \times 5 = 250$ purely propositional actions. The planners

| STRIPS **Language** | ADL **Language** |
|---|---|
| Only positive literals in states: $Poor \land Unknown$ | Positive and negative literals in states: $\neg Rich \land \neg Famous$ |
| Closed World Assumption: Unmentioned literals are false. | Open World Assumption: Unmentioned literals are unknown. |
| Effect $P \land \neg Q$ means add $P$ and delete $Q$. | Effect $P \land \neg Q$ means add $P$ and $\neg Q$ and delete $\neg P$ and $Q$. |
| Only ground literals in goals: $Rich \land Famous$ | Quantified variables in goals: $\exists x\, At(P_1, x) \land At(P_2, x)$ is the goal of having $P_1$ and $P_2$ in the same place. |
| Goals are conjunctions: $Rich \land Famous$ | Goals allow conjunction and disjunction: $\neg Poor \land (Famous \lor Smart)$ |
| Effects are conjunctions. | Conditional effects allowed: **when** $P$: $E$ means $E$ is an effect only if $P$ is satisfied. |
| No support for equality. | Equality predicate $(x = y)$ is built in. |
| No support for types. | Variables can have types, as in $(p : Plane)$. |

**Figure 11.1** Comparison of STRIPS and ADL languages for representing planning problems. In both cases, goals behave as the preconditions of an action with no parameters.

in Sections 11.4 and 11.5 work directly with propositionalized descriptions. If we allow function symbols, then infinitely many states and actions can be constructed.

In recent years, it has become clear that STRIPS is insufficiently expressive for some real domains. As a result, many language variants have been developed. Figure 11.1 briefly describes one important one, the Action Description Language or **ADL**, by comparing it with the basic STRIPS language. In ADL, the $Fly$ action could be written as

ADL

$$\begin{aligned}&Action(Fly(p : Plane, from : Airport, to : Airport),\\&\quad \text{PRECOND:} At(p, from) \land (from \neq to)\\&\quad \text{EFFECT:} \neg At(p, from) \land At(p, to))\ .\end{aligned}$$

The notation $p : Plane$ in the parameter list is an abbreviation for $Plane(p)$ in the precondition; this adds no expressive power, but can be easier to read. (It also cuts down on the number of possible propositional actions that can be constructed.) The precondition $(from \neq to)$ expresses the fact that a flight cannot be made from an airport to itself. This could not be expressed succinctly in STRIPS.

The various planning formalisms used in AI have been systematized within a standard syntax called the Planning Domain Definition Language, or PDDL. This language allows researchers to exchange benchmark problems and compare results. PDDL includes sublanguages for STRIPS, ADL, and the hierarchical task networks we will see in Chapter 12.

$$
\begin{array}{l}
Init(At(C_1,\ SFO) \land At(C_2,\ JFK) \land At(P_1,\ SFO) \land At(P_2,\ JFK) \\
\quad \land Cargo(C_1) \land Cargo(C_2) \land Plane(P_1) \land Plane(P_2) \\
\quad \land Airport(JFK) \land Airport(SFO)) \\
Goal(At(C_1,\ JFK) \land At(C_2,\ SFO)) \\
Action(Load(c,\ p,\ a), \\
\ \ \text{PRECOND: } At(c,\ a) \land At(p,\ a) \land Cargo(c) \land Plane(p) \land Airport(a) \\
\ \ \text{EFFECT: } \neg\, At(c,\ a) \land In(c,\ p)) \\
Action(Unload(c,\ p,\ a), \\
\ \ \text{PRECOND: } In(c,\ p) \land At(p,\ a) \land Cargo(c) \land Plane(p) \land Airport(a) \\
\ \ \text{EFFECT: } At(c,\ a) \land \neg\, In(c,\ p)) \\
Action(Fly(p,\ from,\ to), \\
\ \ \text{PRECOND: } At(p,\ from) \land Plane(p) \land Airport(from) \land Airport(to) \\
\ \ \text{EFFECT: } \neg\, At(p,\ from) \land At(p,\ to))
\end{array}
$$

**Figure 11.2** A STRIPS problem involving transportation of air cargo between airports.

The STRIPS and ADL notations are adequate for many real domains. The subsections that follow show some simple examples. There are still some significant restrictions, however. The most obvious is that they cannot represent in a natural way the **ramifications** of actions. For example, if there are people, packages, or dust motes in the airplane, then they too change location when the plane flies. We can represent these changes as the direct effects of flying, whereas it seems more natural to represent the location of the plane's contents as a logical consequence of the location of the plane. We will see more examples of such

STATE CONSTRAINTS

**state constraints** in Section 11.5. Classical planning systems do not even attempt to address the **qualification** problem: the problem of unrepresented circumstances that could cause an action to fail. We will see how to address qualifications in Chapter 12.

### Example: Air cargo transport

Figure 11.2 shows an air cargo transport problem involving loading and unloading cargo onto and off of planes and flying it from place to place. The problem can be defined with three actions: $Load$, $Unload$, and $Fly$. The actions affect two predicates: $In(c, p)$ means that cargo $c$ is inside plane $p$, and $At(x, a)$ means that object $x$ (either plane or cargo) is at airport $a$. Note that cargo is not $At$ anywhere when it is $In$ a plane, so $At$ really means "available for use at a given location." It takes some experience with action definitions to handle such details consistently. The following plan is a solution to the problem:

$$
\begin{array}{l}
[Load(C_1, P_1, SFO), Fly(P_1, SFO, JFK), Unload(C_1, P_1, JFK), \\
\ Load(C_2, P_2, JFK), Fly(P_2, JFK, SFO), Unload(C_2, P_2, SFO)]\ .
\end{array}
$$

Our representation is pure STRIPS. In particular, it allows a plane to fly to and from the same airport. Inequality literals in ADL could prevent this.

### Example: The spare tire problem

Consider the problem of changing a flat tire. More precisely, the goal is to have a good spare tire properly mounted onto the car's axle, where the initial state has a flat tire on the axle and a good spare tire in the trunk. To keep it simple, our version of the problem is a very abstract one, with no sticky lug nuts or other complications. There are just four actions: removing the spare from the trunk, removing the flat tire from the axle, putting the spare on the axle, and leaving the car unattended overnight. We assume that the car is in a particularly bad neighborhood, so that the effect of leaving it overnight is that the tires disappear.

The ADL description of the problem is shown in Figure 11.3. Notice that it is purely propositional. It goes beyond STRIPS in that it uses a negated precondition, $\neg At(Flat, Axle)$, for the $PutOn(Spare, Axle)$ action. This could be avoided by using $Clear(Axle)$ instead, as we will see in the next example.

$Init(At(Flat, Axle) \wedge At(Spare, Trunk))$
$Goal(At(Spare, Axle))$
$Action(Remove(Spare, Trunk),$
  PRECOND: $At(Spare, Trunk)$
  EFFECT: $\neg At(Spare, Trunk) \wedge At(Spare, Ground))$
$Action(Remove(Flat, Axle),$
  PRECOND: $At(Flat, Axle)$
  EFFECT: $\neg At(Flat, Axle) \wedge At(Flat, Ground))$
$Action(PutOn(Spare, Axle),$
  PRECOND: $At(Spare, Ground) \wedge \neg At(Flat, Axle)$
  EFFECT: $\neg At(Spare, Ground) \wedge At(Spare, Axle))$
$Action(LeaveOvernight,$
  PRECOND:
  EFFECT: $\neg At(Spare, Ground) \wedge \neg At(Spare, Axle) \wedge \neg At(Spare, Trunk)$
    $\wedge \neg At(Flat, Ground) \wedge \neg At(Flat, Axle))$

**Figure 11.3** The simple spare tire problem.

### Example: The blocks world

BLOCKS WORLD

One of the most famous planning domains is known as the **blocks world**. This domain consists of a set of cube-shaped blocks sitting on a table.[3] The blocks can be stacked, but only one block can fit directly on top of another. A robot arm can pick up a block and move it to another position, either on the table or on top of another block. The arm can pick up only one block at a time, so it cannot pick up a block that has another one on it. The goal will always be to build one or more stacks of blocks, specified in terms of what blocks are on top of what other blocks. For example, a goal might be to get block $A$ on $B$ and block $C$ on $D$.

[3] The blocks world used in planning research is much simpler than SHRDLU's version, shown on page 20.

We will use $On(b, x)$ to indicate that block $b$ is on $x$, where $x$ is either another block or the table. The action for moving block $b$ from the top of $x$ to the top of $y$ will be $Move(b, x, y)$. Now, one of the preconditions on moving $b$ is that no other block be on it. In first-order logic, this would be $\neg\exists\, x\ On(x, b)$ or, alternatively, $\forall\, x\ \neg On(x, b)$. These could be stated as preconditions in ADL. We can stay within the STRIPS language, however, by introducing a new predicate, $Clear(x)$, that is true when nothing is on $x$.

The action $Move$ moves a block $b$ from $x$ to $y$ if both $b$ and $y$ are clear. After the move is made, $x$ is clear but $y$ is not. A formal description of $Move$ in STRIPS is

$$\begin{aligned}&Action(Move(b, x, y),\\ &\quad \text{PRECOND:} On(b, x) \wedge Clear(b) \wedge Clear(y),\\ &\quad \text{EFFECT:} On(b, y) \wedge Clear(x) \wedge \neg On(b, x) \wedge \neg Clear(y))\ .\end{aligned}$$

Unfortunately, this action does not maintain $Clear$ properly when $x$ or $y$ is the table. When $x = Table$, this action has the effect $Clear(Table)$, but the table should not become clear, and when $y = Table$, it has the precondition $Clear(Table)$, but the table does not have to be clear to move a block onto it. To fix this, we do two things. First, we introduce another action to move a block $b$ from $x$ to the table:

$$\begin{aligned}&Action(MoveToTable(b, x),\\ &\quad \text{PRECOND:} On(b, x) \wedge Clear(b),\\ &\quad \text{EFFECT:} On(b, Table) \wedge Clear(x) \wedge \neg On(b, x))\ .\end{aligned}$$

Second, we take the interpretation of $Clear(b)$ to be "there is a clear space on $b$ to hold a block." Under this interpretation, $Clear(Table)$ will always be true. The only problem is that nothing prevents the planner from using $Move(b, x, Table)$ instead of $MoveToTable(b, x)$. We could live with this problem—it will lead to a larger-than-necessary search space, but will not lead to incorrect answers—or we could introduce the predicate $Block$ and add $Block(b) \wedge Block(y)$ to the precondition of $Move$.

Finally, there is the problem of spurious actions such as $Move(B, C, C)$, which should be a no-op, but which has contradictory effects. It is common to ignore such problems, because they seldom cause incorrect plans to be produced. The correct approach is add inequality preconditions as shown in Figure 11.4.

## 11.2 PLANNING WITH STATE-SPACE SEARCH

Now we turn our attention to planning algorithms. The most straightforward approach is to use state-space search. Because the descriptions of actions in a planning problem specify both preconditions and effects, it is possible to search in either direction: either forward from the initial state or backward from the goal, as shown in Figure 11.5. We can also use the explicit action and goal representations to derive effective heuristics automatically.

### Forward state-space search

PROGRESSION

Planning with forward state-space search is similar to the problem-solving approach of Chapter 3. It is sometimes called **progression** planning, because it moves in the forward direction.

$Init(On(A, Table) \wedge On(B, Table) \wedge On(C, Table)$
$\quad \wedge\ Block(A) \wedge Block(B) \wedge Block(C)$
$\quad \wedge\ Clear(A) \wedge Clear(B) \wedge Clear(C))$
$Goal(On(A, B) \wedge On(B, C))$
$Action(Move(b, x, y),$
$\quad$ PRECOND: $On(b, x) \wedge Clear(b) \wedge Clear(y) \wedge Block(b) \wedge$
$\qquad (b \neq x) \wedge (b \neq y) \wedge (x \neq y),$
$\quad$ EFFECT: $On(b, y) \wedge Clear(x) \wedge \neg On(b, x) \wedge \neg Clear(y))$
$Action(MoveToTable(b, x),$
$\quad$ PRECOND: $On(b, x) \wedge Clear(b) \wedge Block(b) \wedge (b \neq x),$
$\quad$ EFFECT: $On(b, Table) \wedge Clear(x) \wedge \neg On(b, x))$

**Figure 11.4** A planning problem in the blocks world: building a three-block tower. One solution is the sequence $[Move(B, Table, C), Move(A, Table, B)]$.

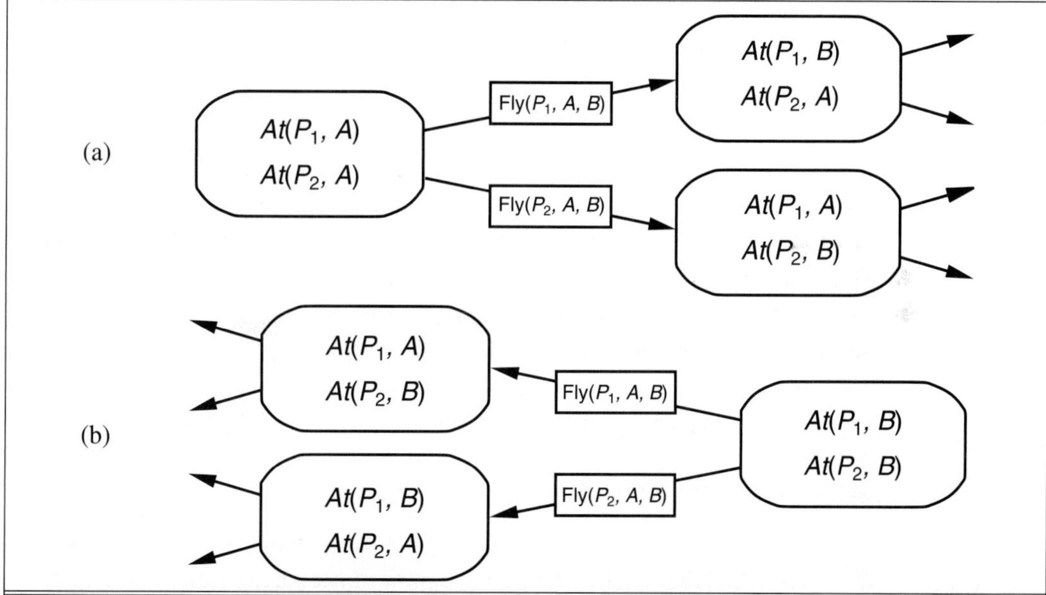


**Figure 11.5** Two approaches to searching for a plan. (a) Forward (progression) state-space search, starting in the initial state and using the problem's actions to search forward for the goal state. (b) Backward (regression) state-space search: a belief-state search (see page 84) starting at the goal state(s) and using the inverse of the actions to search backward for the initial state.

We start in the problem's initial state, considering sequences of actions until we find a sequence that reaches a goal state. The formulation of planning problems as state-space search problems is as follows:

- The **initial state** of the search is the initial state from the planning problem. In general, each state will be a set of positive ground literals; literals not appearing are false.

- The **actions** that are applicable to a state are all those whose preconditions are satisfied. The successor state resulting from an action is generated by adding the positive effect literals and deleting the negative effect literals. (In the first-order case, we must apply the unifier from the preconditions to the effect literals.) Note that a single successor function works for all planning problems—a consequence of using an explicit action representation.
- The **goal test** checks whether the state satisfies the goal of the planning problem.
- The **step cost** of each action is typically 1. Although it would be easy to allow different costs for different actions, this is seldom done by STRIPS planners.

Recall that, in the absence of function symbols, the state space of a planning problem is finite. Therefore, any graph search algorithm that is complete—for example, A*—will be a complete planning algorithm.

From the earliest days of planning research (around 1961) until recently (around 1998) it was assumed that forward state-space search was too inefficient to be practical. It is not hard to come up with reasons why—just refer back to the start of Section 11.1. First, forward search does not address the irrelevant action problem—all applicable actions are considered from each state. Second, the approach quickly bogs down without a good heuristic. Consider an air cargo problem with 10 airports, where each airport has 5 planes and 20 pieces of cargo. The goal is to move all the cargo at airport $A$ to airport $B$. There is a simple solution to the problem: load the 20 pieces of cargo into one of the planes at $A$, fly the plane to $B$, and unload the cargo. But finding the solution can be difficult because the average branching factor is huge: each of the 50 planes can fly to 9 other airports, and each of the 200 packages can be either unloaded (if it is loaded), or loaded into any plane at its airport (if it is unloaded). On average, let's say there are about 1000 possible actions, so the search tree up to the depth of the obvious solution has about $1000^{41}$ nodes. It is clear that a very accurate heuristic will be needed to make this kind of search efficient. We will discuss some possible heuristics after looking at backward search.

### Backward state-space search

Backward state-space search was described briefly as part of bidirectional search in Chapter 3. We noted there that backward search can be difficult to implement when the goal states are described by a set of constraints rather than being listed explicitly. In particular, it is not always obvious how to generate a description of the possible **predecessors** of the set of goal states. We will see that the STRIPS representation makes this quite easy because sets of states can be described by the literals that must be true in those states.

RELEVANCE

The main advantage of backward search is that it allows us to consider only **relevant** actions. An action is relevant to a conjunctive goal if it achieves one of the conjuncts of the goal. For example, the goal in our 10-airport air cargo problem is to have 20 pieces of cargo at airport $B$, or more precisely,

$$At(C_1, B) \land At(C_2, B) \land \ldots \land At(C_{20}, B) .$$

Now consider the conjunct $At(C_1, B)$. Working backwards, we can seek actions that have this as an effect. There is only one: $Unload(C_1, p, B)$, where plane $p$ is unspecified.

Notice that there are many *irrelevant* actions that can also lead to a goal state. For example, we can fly an empty plane from $JFK$ to $SFO$; this action reaches a goal state from a predecessor state in which the plane is at $JFK$ and all the goal conjuncts are satisfied. A backward search that allows irrelevant actions will still be complete, but it will be much less efficient. If a solution exists, it will be found by a backward search that allows only relevant actions. The restriction to relevant actions means that backward search often has a much lower branching factor than forward search. For example, our air cargo problem has about 1000 actions leading forward from the initial state, but only 20 actions working backward from the goal.

REGRESSION

Searching backwards is sometimes called **regression** planning. The principal question in regression planning is this: what are the states from which applying a given action leads to the goal? Computing the description of these states is called **regressing** the goal through the action. To see how to do it, consider the air cargo example. We have the goal

$$At(C_1, B) \land At(C_2, B) \land \ldots \land At(C_{20}, B)$$

and the relevant action $Unload(C_1, p, B)$, which achieves the first conjunct. The action will work only if its preconditions are satisfied. Therefore, any predecessor state must include these preconditions: $In(C_1, p) \land At(p, B)$. Moreover, the subgoal $At(C_1, B)$ should not be true in the predecessor state.[4] Thus, the predecessor description is

$$In(C_1, p) \land At(p, B) \land At(C_2, B) \land \ldots \land At(C_{20}, B)\ .$$

CONSISTENCY

In addition to insisting that actions achieve some desired literal, we must insist that the actions *not undo* any desired literals. An action that satisfies this restriction is called **consistent**. For example, the action $Load(C_2, p)$ would not be consistent with the current goal, because it would negate the literal $At(C_2, B)$.

Given definitions of relevance and consistency, we can describe the general process of constructing predecessors for backward search. Given a goal description $G$, let $A$ be an action that is relevant and consistent. The corresponding predecessor is as follows:

- Any positive effects of $A$ that appear in $G$ are deleted.
- Each precondition literal of $A$ is added, unless it already appears.

Any of the standard search algorithms can be used to carry out the search. Termination occurs when a predecessor description is generated that is satisfied by the initial state of the planning problem. In the first-order case, satisfaction might require a substitution for variables in the predecessor description. For example, the predecessor description in the preceding paragraph is satisfied by the initial state

$$In(C_1, P_{12}) \land At(P_{12}, B) \land At(C_2, B) \land \ldots \land At(C_{20}, B)$$

with substitution $\{p/P_{12}\}$. The substitution must be applied to the actions leading from the state to the goal, producing the solution $[Unload(C_1, P_{12}, B)]$.

[4] If the subgoal were true in the predecessor state, the action would still lead to a goal state. On the other hand, such actions are irrelevant because they do not *make* the goal true.

### Heuristics for state-space search

It turns out that neither forward nor backward search is efficient without a good heuristic function. Recall from Chapter 4 that a heuristic function estimates the distance from a state to the goal; in STRIPS planning, the cost of each action is 1, so the distance is the number of actions. The basic idea is to look at the effects of the actions and at the goals that must be achieved and to guess how many actions are needed to achieve all the goals. Finding the exact number is NP hard, but it is possible to find reasonable estimates most of the time without too much computation. We might also be able to derive an **admissible** heuristic—one that does not overestimate. This could be used with A* search to find optimal solutions.

There are two approaches that can be tried. The first is to derive a **relaxed problem** from the given problem specification, as described in Chapter 4. The optimal solution cost for the relaxed problem—which we hope is very easy to solve—gives an admissible heuristic for the original problem. The second approach is to pretend that a pure divide-and-conquer algorithm will work. This is called the **subgoal independence** assumption: the cost of solving a conjunction of subgoals is approximated by the sum of the costs of solving each subgoal *independently*. The subgoal independence assumption can be optimistic or pessimistic. It is optimistic when there are negative interactions between the subplans for each subgoal—for example, when an action in one subplan deletes a goal achieved by another subplan. It is pessimistic, and therefore inadmissible, when subplans contain redundant actions—for instance, two actions that could be replaced by a single action in the merged plan.

SUBGOAL INDEPENDENCE

Let us consider how to derive relaxed planning problems. Since explicit representations of preconditions and effects are available, the process will work by modifying those representations. (Compare this approach with search problems, where the successor function is a black box.) The simplest idea is to relax the problem by *removing all preconditions* from the actions. Then every action will always be applicable, and any literal can be achieved in one step (if there is an applicable action—if not, the goal is impossible). This almost implies that the number of steps required to solve a conjunction of goals is the number of unsatisfied goals—almost but not quite, because (1) there may be two actions, each of which deletes the goal literal achieved by the other, and (2) some action may achieve multiple goals. If we combine our relaxed problem with the subgoal independence assumption, both of these issues are assumed away and the resulting heuristic is exactly the number of unsatisfied goals.

In many cases, a more accurate heuristic is obtained by considering at least the positive interactions arising from actions that achieve multiple goals. First, we relax the problem further by *removing negative effects* (see Exercise 11.6). Then, we count the minimum number of actions required such that the union of those actions' positive effects satisfies the goal. For example, consider

$$\begin{array}{l} Goal(A \land B \land C) \\ Action(X, \text{EFFECT:}A \land P) \\ Action(Y, \text{EFFECT:}B \land C \land Q) \\ Action(Z, \text{EFFECT:}B \land P \land Q)\ . \end{array}$$

The minimal set cover of the goal $\{A, B, C\}$ is given by the actions $\{X, Y\}$, so the set cover heuristic returns a cost of 2. This improves on the subgoal independence assumption, which gives a heuristic value of 3. There is one minor irritation: the set cover problem is NP-hard. A simple greedy set-covering algorithm is guaranteed to return a value that is within a factor of $\log n$ of the true minimum value, where $n$ is the number of literals in the goal, and usually works much better than this in practice. Unfortunately, the greedy algorithm loses the guarantee of admissibility for the heuristic.

It is also possible to generate relaxed problems by removing negative effects without removing preconditions. That is, if an action has the effect $A \wedge \neg B$ in the original problem, it will have the effect $A$ in the relaxed problem. This means that we need not worry about negative interactions between subplans, because no action can delete the literals achieved by another action. The solution cost of the resulting relaxed problem gives what is called the

EMPTY-DELETE-LIST

**empty-delete-list** heuristic. The heuristic is quite accurate, but computing it involves actually running a (simple) planning algorithm. In practice, the search in the relaxed problem is often fast enough that the cost is worthwhile.

The heuristics described here can be used in either the progression or the regression direction. At the time of writing, progression planners using the empty-delete-list heuristic hold the lead. That is likely to change as new heuristics and new search techniques are explored. Since planning is exponentially hard,[5] no algorithm will be efficient for all problems, but many practical problems can be solved with the heuristic methods in this chapter—far more than could be solved just a few years ago.

## 11.3 PARTIAL-ORDER PLANNING

Forward and backward state-space search are particular forms of *totally ordered* plan search. They explore only strictly linear sequences of actions directly connected to the start or goal. This means that they cannot take advantage of problem decomposition. Rather than work on each subproblem separately, they must always make decisions about how to sequence actions from all the subproblems. We would prefer an approach that works on several subgoals independently, solves them with several subplans, and then combines the subplans.

Such an approach also has the advantage of flexibility in the order in which it *constructs* the plan. That is, the planner can work on "obvious" or "important" decisions first, rather than being forced to work on steps in chronological order. For example, a planning agent that is in Berkeley and wishes to be in Monte Carlo might first try to find a flight from San Francisco to Paris; given information about the departure and arrival times, it can then work on ways to get to and from the airports.

LEAST COMMITMENT

The general strategy of delaying a choice during search is called a **least commitment** strategy. There is no formal definition of least commitment, and clearly some degree of commitment is necessary, lest the search would make no progress. Despite the informality, least commitment is a useful concept for analyzing when decisions should be made in any search problem.

---

[5] Technically, STRIPS-style planning is PSPACE-complete unless actions have only positive preconditions and only one effect literal (Bylander, 1994).

Our first concrete example will be much simpler than planning a vacation. Consider the simple problem of putting on a pair of shoes. We can describe this as a formal planning problem as follows:

$$\begin{array}{l} Goal(RightShoeOn \land LeftShoeOn) \\ Init() \\ Action(RightShoe, \text{PRECOND:}RightSockOn, \text{EFFECT:}RightShoeOn) \\ Action(RightSock, \text{EFFECT:}RightSockOn) \\ Action(LeftShoe, \text{PRECOND:}LeftSockOn, \text{EFFECT:}LeftShoeOn) \\ Action(LeftSock, \text{EFFECT:}LeftSockOn)\ . \end{array}$$

A planner should be able to come up with the two-action sequence *RightSock* followed by *RightShoe* to achieve the first conjunct of the goal and the sequence *LeftSock* followed by *LeftShoe* for the second conjunct. Then the two sequences can be combined to yield the final plan. In doing this, the planner will be manipulating the two subsequences independently, without committing to whether an action in one sequence is before or after an action in the other. Any planning algorithm that can place two actions into a plan without specifying which comes first is called a **partial-order planner**. Figure 11.6 shows the partial-order plan that is the solution to the shoes and socks problem. Note that the solution is represented as a *graph* of actions, not a sequence. Note also the "dummy" actions called *Start* and *Finish*, which mark the beginning and end of the plan. Calling them actions symplifies things, because now every step of a plan is an action. The partial-order solution corresponds to six possible total-order plans; each of these is called a **linearization** of the partial-order plan.

PARTIAL-ORDER PLANNER

LINEARIZATION

Partial-order planning can be implemented as a search in the space of partial-order plans. (From now on, we will just call them "plans.") That is, we start with an empty plan. Then we consider ways of refining the plan until we come up with a complete plan that solves the problem. The actions in this search are not actions in the world, but actions on plans: adding a step to the plan, imposing an ordering that puts one action before another, and so on.

We will define the POP algorithm for partial-order planning. It is traditional to write out the POP algorithm as a stand-alone program, but we will instead formulate partial-order planning as an instance of a search problem. This allows us to focus on the plan refinement steps that can be applied, rather than worrying about how the algorithm explores the space. In fact, a wide variety of uninformed or heuristic search methods can be applied once the search problem is formulated.

Remember that the states of our search problem will be (mostly unfinished) plans. To avoid confusion with the states of the world, we will talk about plans rather than states. Each plan has the following four components, where the first two define the steps of the plan and the last two serve a bookkeeping function to determine how plans can be extended:

- A set of **actions** that make up the steps of the plan. These are taken from the set of actions in the planning problem. The "empty" plan contains just the *Start* and *Finish* actions. *Start* has no preconditions and has as its effect all the literals in the initial state of the planning problem. *Finish* has no effects and has as its preconditions the goal literals of the planning problem.

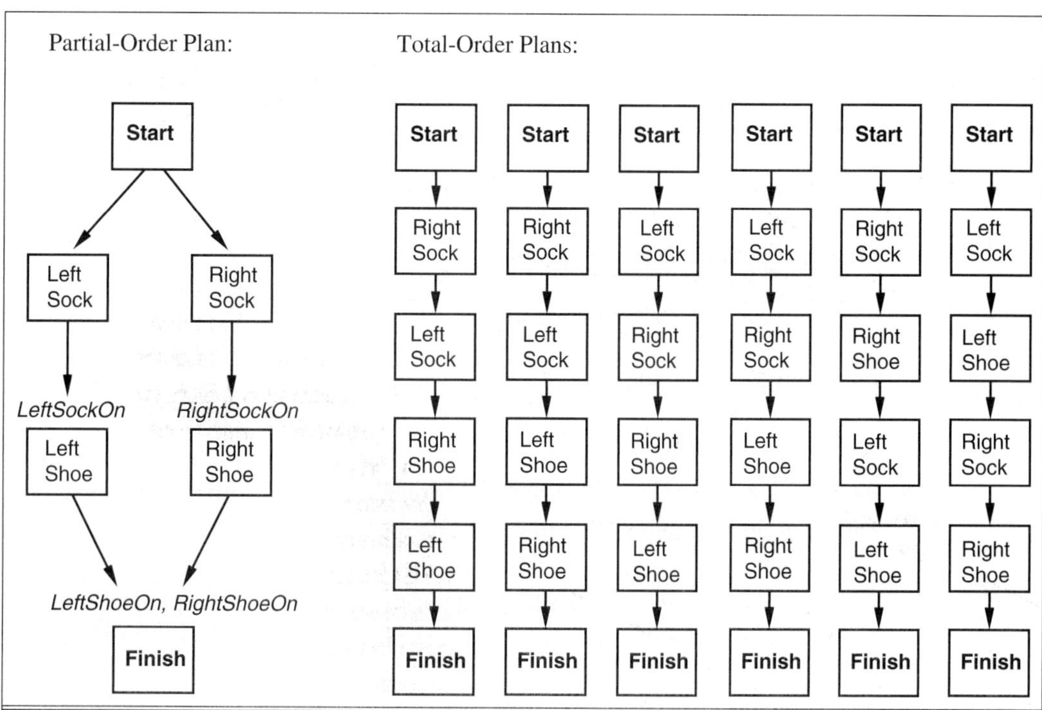


**Figure 11.6** A partial-order plan for putting on shoes and socks, and the six corresponding linearizations into total-order plans.

ORDERING CONSTRAINTS

- A set of **ordering constraints**. Each ordering constraint is of the form $A \prec B$, which is read as "$A$ before $B$" and means that action $A$ must be executed sometime before action $B$, but not necessarily immediately before. The ordering constraints must describe a proper partial order. Any cycle—such as $A \prec B$ and $B \prec A$—represents a contradiction, so an ordering constraint cannot be added to the plan if it creates a cycle.

CAUSAL LINKS

ACHIEVES

- A set of **causal links**. A causal link between two actions $A$ and $B$ in the plan is written as $A \xrightarrow{p} B$ and is read as "$A$ **achieves** $p$ for $B$." For example, the causal link

$$RightSock \xrightarrow{RightSockOn} RightShoe$$

asserts that $RightSockOn$ is an effect of the $RightSock$ action and a precondition of $RightShoe$. It also asserts that $RightSockOn$ must remain true from the time of action $RightSock$ to the time of action $RightShoe$. In other words, the plan may not be extended by adding a new action $C$ that **conflicts** with the causal link. An action $C$ conflicts with $A \xrightarrow{p} B$ if $C$ has the effect $\neg p$ and if $C$ could (according to the ordering constraints) come after $A$ and before $B$. Some authors call causal links **protection intervals**, because the link $A \xrightarrow{p} B$ protects $p$ from being negated over the interval from $A$ to $B$.

CONFLICTS

OPEN PRECONDITIONS

- A set of **open preconditions**. A precondition is open if it is not achieved by some action in the plan. Planners will work to reduce the set of open preconditions to the empty set, without introducing a contradiction.

For example, the final plan in Figure 11.6 has the following components (not shown are the ordering constraints that put every other action after $Start$ and before $Finish$):

Actions:$\{RightSock, RightShoe, LeftSock, LeftShoe, Start, Finish\}$
Orderings:$\{RightSock \prec RightShoe, LeftSock \prec LeftShoe\}$
Links:$\{RightSock \xrightarrow{RightSockOn} RightShoe, LeftSock \xrightarrow{LeftSockOn} LeftShoe,$
$RightShoe \xrightarrow{RightShoeOn} Finish, LeftShoe \xrightarrow{LeftShoeOn} Finish\}$
Open Preconditions:$\{\}$ .

CONSISTENT PLAN

We define a **consistent plan** as a plan in which there are no cycles in the ordering constraints and no conflicts with the causal links. A consistent plan with no open preconditions is a **solution**. A moment's thought should convince the reader of the following fact: *every linearization of a partial-order solution is a total-order solution whose execution from the initial state will reach a goal state.* This means that we can extend the notion of "executing a plan" from total-order to partial-order plans. A partial-order plan is executed by repeatedly choosing *any* of the possible next actions. We will see in Chapter 12 that the flexibility available to the agent as it executes the plan can be very useful when the world fails to cooperate. The flexible ordering also makes it easier to combine smaller plans into larger ones, because each of the small plans can reorder its actions to avoid conflict with the other plans.

Now we are ready to formulate the search problem that POP solves. We will begin with a formulation suitable for propositional planning problems, leaving the first-order complications for later. As usual, the definition includes the initial state, actions, and goal test.

- The initial plan contains $Start$ and $Finish$, the ordering constraint $Start \prec Finish$, and no causal links and has all the preconditions in $Finish$ as open preconditions.
- The successor function arbitrarily picks one open precondition $p$ on an action $B$ and generates a successor plan for every possible consistent way of choosing an action $A$ that achieves $p$. Consistency is enforced as follows:
  1. The causal link $A \xrightarrow{p} B$ and the ordering constraint $A \prec B$ are added to the plan. Action $A$ may be an existing action in the plan or a new one. If it is new, add it to the plan and also add $Start \prec A$ and $A \prec Finish$.
  2. We resolve conflicts between the new causal link and all existing actions and between the action $A$ (if it is new) and all existing causal links. A conflict between $A \xrightarrow{p} B$ and $C$ is resolved by making $C$ occur at some time outside the protection interval, either by adding $B \prec C$ or $C \prec A$. We add successor states for either or both if they result in consistent plans.
- The goal test checks whether a plan is a solution to the original planning problem. Because only consistent plans are generated, the goal test just needs to check that there are no open preconditions.

Remember that the actions considered by the search algorithms under this formulation are plan refinement steps rather than the real actions from the domain itself. The path cost is therefore irrelevant, strictly speaking, because the only thing that matters is the total cost of the real actions in the plan to which the path leads. Nonetheless, it *is* possible to specify a path cost function that reflects the real plan costs: we charge 1 for each real action added to the plan and 0 for all other refinement steps. In this way, $g(n)$, where $n$ is a plan, will be equal to the number of real actions in the plan. A heuristic estimate $h(n)$ can also be used.

At first glance, one might think that the successor function should include successors for *every* open $p$, not just for one of them. This would be redundant and inefficient, however, for the same reason that constraint satisfaction algorithms don't include successors for every possible variable: the order in which we consider open preconditions (like the order in which we consider CSP variables) is commutative. (See page 141.) Thus, we can choose an arbitrary ordering and still have a complete algorithm. Choosing the right ordering can lead to a faster search, but all orderings end up with the same set of candidate solutions.

### A partial-order planning example

Now let's look at how POP solves the spare tire problem from Section 11.1. The problem description is repeated in Figure 11.7.

$Init(At(Flat, Axle) \wedge At(Spare, Trunk))$
$Goal(At(Spare, Axle))$
$Action(Remove(Spare, Trunk),$
  PRECOND: $At(Spare, Trunk)$
  EFFECT: $\neg\, At(Spare, Trunk) \wedge At(Spare, Ground))$
$Action(Remove(Flat, Axle),$
  PRECOND: $At(Flat, Axle)$
  EFFECT: $\neg\, At(Flat, Axle) \wedge At(Flat, Ground))$
$Action(PutOn(Spare, Axle),$
  PRECOND: $At(Spare, Ground) \wedge \neg\, At(Flat, Axle)$
  EFFECT: $\neg\, At(Spare, Ground) \wedge At(Spare, Axle))$
$Action(LeaveOvernight,$
  PRECOND:
  EFFECT: $\neg\, At(Spare, Ground) \wedge \neg\, At(Spare, Axle) \wedge \neg\, At(Spare, Trunk)$
    $\wedge \neg\, At(Flat, Ground) \wedge \neg\, At(Flat, Axle))$

**Figure 11.7** The simple flat tire problem description.

The search for a solution begins with the initial plan, containing a $Start$ action with the effect $At(Spare, Trunk) \wedge At(Flat, Axle)$ and a $Finish$ action with the sole precondition $At(Spare, Axle)$. Then we generate successors by picking an open precondition to work on (irrevocably) and choosing among the possible actions to achieve it. For now, we will not worry about a heuristic function to help with these decisions; we will make seemingly arbitrary choices. The sequence of events is as follows:

1. Pick the only open precondition, $At(Spare, Axle)$ of $Finish$. Choose the only applicable action, $PutOn(Spare, Axle)$.
2. Pick the $At(Spare, Ground)$ precondition of $PutOn(Spare, Axle)$. Choose the only applicable action, $Remove(Spare, Trunk)$ to achieve it. The resulting plan is shown in Figure 11.8.

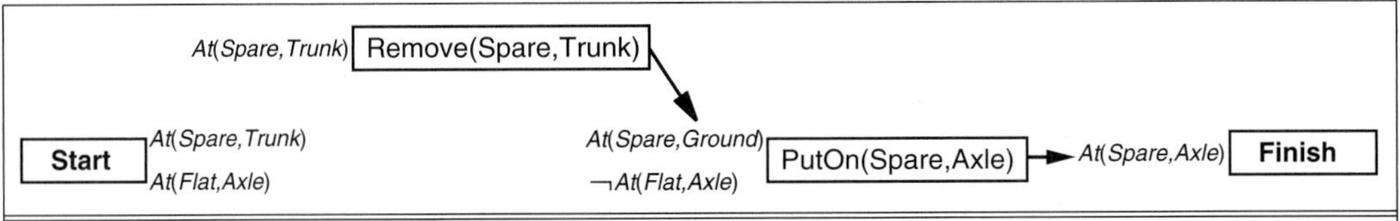


**Figure 11.8** The incomplete partial-order plan for the tire problem, after choosing actions for the first two open preconditions. Boxes represent actions, with preconditions on the left and effects on the right. (Effects are omitted, except for that of the *Start* action.) Dark arrows represent causal links protecting the proposition at the head of the arrow.

3. Pick the $\neg At(Flat, Axle)$ precondition of $PutOn(Spare, Axle)$. Just to be contrary, choose the $LeaveOvernight$ action rather than the $Remove(Flat, Axle)$ action. Notice that $LeaveOvernight$ also has the effect $\neg At(Spare, Ground)$, which means it conflicts with the causal link

$$Remove(Spare, Trunk) \xrightarrow{At(Spare, Ground)} PutOn(Spare, Axle) .$$

To resolve the conflict we add an ordering constraint putting $LeaveOvernight$ before $Remove(Spare, Trunk)$. The resulting plan is shown in Figure 11.9. (Why does this resolve the conflict, and why is there no other way to resolve it?)

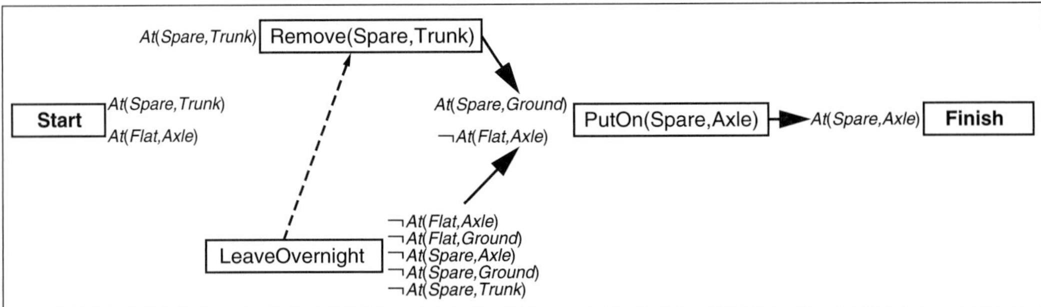


**Figure 11.9** The plan after choosing $LeaveOvernight$ as the action for achieving $\neg At(Flat, Axle)$. To avoid a conflict with the causal link from $Remove(Spare, Trunk)$ that protects $At(Spare, Ground)$, $LeaveOvernight$ is constrained to occur before $Remove(Spare, Trunk)$, as shown by the dashed arrow.

4. The only remaining open precondition at this point is the $At(Spare, Trunk)$ precondition of the action $Remove(Spare, Trunk)$. The only action that can achieve it is the existing $Start$ action, but the causal link from $Start$ to $Remove(Spare, Trunk)$ is in conflict with the $\neg At(Spare, Trunk)$ effect of $LeaveOvernight$. This time there is no way to resolve the conflict with $LeaveOvernight$: we cannot order it before $Start$ (because nothing can come before $Start$), and we cannot order it after $Remove(Spare, Trunk)$ (because there is already a constraint ordering it before $Remove(Spare, Trunk)$). So we are forced to back up, remove the $LeaveOvernight$ action and the last two causal links, and return to the state in Figure 11.8. In essence, the planner has proved that $LeaveOvernight$ doesn't work as a way to change a tire.

5. Consider again the $\neg At(Flat, Axle)$ precondition of $PutOn(Spare, Axle)$. This time, we choose $Remove(Flat, Axle)$.
6. Once again, pick the $At(Spare, Trunk)$ precondition of $Remove(Spare, Trunk)$ and choose $Start$ to achieve it. This time there are no conflicts.
7. Pick the $At(Flat, Axle)$ precondition of $Remove(Flat, Axle)$, and choose $Start$ to achieve it. This gives us a complete, consistent plan—in other words a solution—as shown in Figure 11.10.

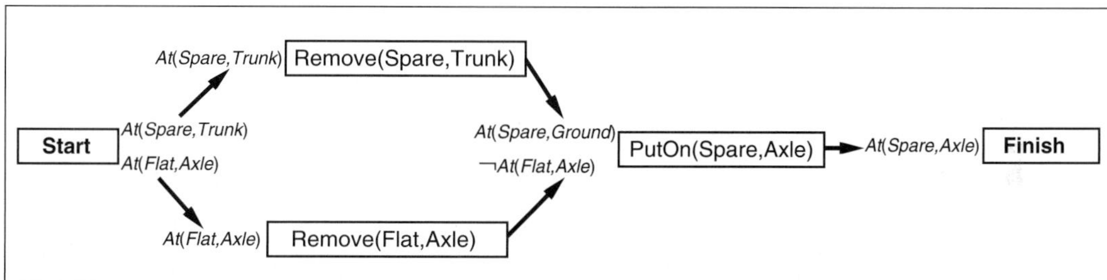


**Figure 11.10** The final solution to the tire problem. Note that $Remove(Spare, Trunk)$ and $Remove(Flat, Axle)$ can be done in either order, as long as they are completed before the $PutOn(Spare, Axle)$ action.

Although this example is very simple, it illustrates some of the strengths of partial-order planning. First, the causal links lead to early pruning of portions of the search space that, because of irresolvable conflicts, contain no solutions. Second, the solution in Figure 11.10 is a partial-order plan. In this case the advantage is small, because there are only two possible linearizations; nonetheless, an agent might welcome the flexibility—for example, if the tire has to be changed in the middle of heavy traffic.

The example also points to some possible improvements that could be made. For example, there is duplication of effort: $Start$ is linked to $Remove(Spare, Trunk)$ before the conflict causes a backtrack and is then unlinked by backtracking even though it is not involved in the conflict. It is then relinked as the search continues. This is typical of chronological backtracking and might be mitigated by dependency-directed backtracking.

### Partial-order planning with unbound variables

In this section, we consider the complications that can arise when POP is used with first-order action representations that include variables. Suppose we have a blocks world problem (Figure 11.4) with the open precondition $On(A, B)$ and the action

$$\begin{aligned}&Action(Move(b, x, y),\\&\quad \text{PRECOND:} On(b, x) \land Clear(b) \land Clear(y),\\&\quad \text{EFFECT:} On(b, y) \land Clear(x) \land \neg On(b, x) \land \neg Clear(y))\ .\end{aligned}$$

This action achieves $On(A, B)$ because the effect $On(b, y)$ unifies with $On(A, B)$ with the substitution $\{b/A, y/B\}$. We then apply this substitution to the action, yielding

$$\begin{aligned}&Action(Move(A, x, B),\\&\quad \text{PRECOND:} On(A, x) \wedge Clear(A) \wedge Clear(B),\\&\quad \text{EFFECT:} On(A, B) \wedge Clear(x) \wedge \neg On(A, x) \wedge \neg Clear(B)) .\end{aligned}$$

This leaves the variable $x$ unbound. That is, the action says to move block $A$ from *somewhere*, without yet saying whence. This is another example of the least commitment principle: we can delay making the choice until some other step in the plan makes it for us. For example, suppose we have $On(A, D)$ in the initial state. Then the $Start$ action can be used to achieve $On(A, x)$, binding $x$ to $D$. This strategy of waiting for more information before choosing $x$ is often more efficient than trying every possible value of $x$ and backtracking for each one that fails.

The presence of variables in preconditions and actions complicates the process of detecting and resolving conflicts. For example, when $Move(A, x, B)$ is added to the plan, we will need a causal link

$$Move(A, x, B) \xrightarrow{On(A,B)} Finish .$$

If there is another action $M_2$ with effect $\neg On(A, z)$, then $M_2$ conflicts only if $z$ is $B$. To accommodate this possibility, we extend the representation of plans to include a set of **inequality constraints** of the form $z \neq X$ where $z$ is a variable and $X$ is either another variable or a constant symbol. In this case, we would resolve the conflict by adding $z \neq B$, which means that future extensions to the plan can instantiate $z$ to any value except $B$. Anytime we apply a substitution to a plan, we must check that the inequalities do not contradict the substitution. For example, a substitution that includes $x/y$ conflicts with the inequality constraint $x \neq y$. Such conflicts cannot be resolved, so the planner must backtrack.

INEQUALITY CONSTRAINTS

A more extensive example of POP planning with variables in the blocks world is given in Section 12.6.

### Heuristics for partial-order planning

Compared with total-order planning, partial-order planning has a clear advantage in being able to decompose problems into subproblems. It also has a disadvantage in that it does not represent states directly, so it is harder to estimate how far a partial-order plan is from achieving a goal. At present, there is less understanding of how to compute accurate heuristics for partial-order planning than for total-order planning.

The most obvious heuristic is to count the number of distinct open preconditions. This can be improved by subtracting the number of open preconditions that match literals in the $Start$ state. As in the total-order case, this overestimates the cost when there are actions that achieve multiple goals and underestimates the cost when there are negative interactions between plan steps. The next section presents an approach that allows us to get much more accurate heuristics from a relaxed problem.

The heuristic function is used to choose which plan to refine. Given this choice, the algorithm generates successors based on the selection of a single open precondition to work on. As in the case of variable selection on constraint satisfaction algorithms, this selection has a large impact on efficiency. The **most-constrained-variable** heuristic from CSPs can be adapted for planning algorithms and seems to work well. The idea is to select the open condition that can be satisfied in the *fewest* number of ways. There are two special cases of this heuristic. First, if an open condition cannot be achieved by any action, the heuristic will select it; this is a good idea because early detection of impossibility can save a great deal of work. Second, if an open condition can be achieved in only one way, then it should be selected because the decision is unavoidable and could provide additional constraints on other choices still to be made. Although full computation of the number of ways to satisfy each open condition is expensive and not always worthwhile, experiments show that handling the two special cases provides very substantial speedups.

## 11.4 PLANNING GRAPHS

All of the heuristics we have suggested for total-order and partial-order planning can suffer from inaccuracies. This section shows how a special data structure called a **planning graph** can be used to give better heuristic estimates. These heuristics can be applied to any of the search techniques we have seen so far. Alternatively, we can extract a solution directly from the planning graph, using a specialized algorithm such as the one called GRAPHPLAN.

PLANNING GRAPH

LEVELS

A planning graph consists of a sequence of **levels** that correspond to time steps in the plan, where level 0 is the initial state. Each level contains a set of literals and a set of actions. Roughly speaking, the literals are all those that *could* be true at that time step, depending on the actions executed at preceding time steps. Also roughly speaking, the actions are all those actions that *could* have their preconditions satisfied at that time step, depending on which of the literals actually hold. We say "roughly speaking" because the planning graph records only a restricted subset of the possible negative interactions among actions; therefore, it might be optimistic about the minimum number of time steps required for a literal to become true. Nonetheless, this number of steps in the planning graph provides a good estimate of how difficult it is to achieve a given literal from the initial state. More importantly, the planning graph is defined in such a way that it can be constructed very efficiently.

Planning graphs work only for propositional planning problems—ones with no variables. As we mentioned in Section 11.1, both STRIPS and ADL representations can be propositionalized. For problems with large numbers of objects, this could result in a very substantial blowup in the number of action schemata. Despite this, planning graphs have proved to be effective tools for solving hard planning problems.

We will illustrate planning graphs with a simple example. (More complex examples lead to graphs that won't fit on the page.) Figure 11.11 shows a problem, and Figure 11.12 shows its planning graph. We start with state level $S_0$, which represents the problem's initial state. We follow that with action level $A_0$, in which we place all the actions whose preconditions are satisfied in the previous level. Each action is connected to its preconditions in $S_0$ and its effects in $S_1$, in this case introducing new literals into $S_1$ that were not in $S_0$.

$Init(Have(Cake))$
$Goal(Have(Cake) \land Eaten(Cake))$
$Action(Eat(Cake)$
  PRECOND: $Have(Cake)$
  EFFECT: $\neg\ Have(Cake) \land Eaten(Cake))$
$Action(Bake(Cake)$
  PRECOND: $\neg\ Have(Cake)$
  EFFECT: $Have(Cake))$

**Figure 11.11** The "have cake and eat cake too" problem.

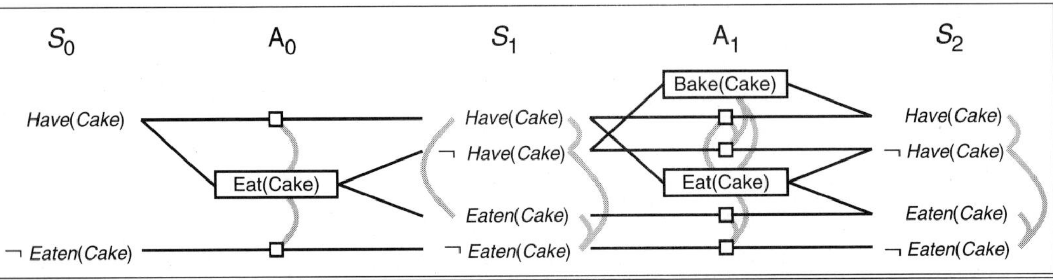


**Figure 11.12** The planning graph for the "have cake and eat cake too" problem up to level $S_2$. Rectangles indicate actions (small squares indicate persistence actions) and straight lines indicate preconditions and effects. Mutex links are shown as curved gray lines.

The planning graph needs a way to represent inaction as well as action. That is, it needs the equivalent of the frame axioms in situation calculus that allow a literal to remain true from one situation to the next if no action alters it. In a planning graph this is done with a set of **persistence actions**. For every positive and negative literal $C$, we add to the problem a persistence action with precondition $C$ and effect $C$. Figure 11.12 shows one "real" action, $Eat(Cake)$ in $A_0$, along with two persistence actions drawn as small square boxes.

PERSISTENCE ACTIONS

Level $A_0$ contains all the actions that *could* occur in state $S_0$, but just as importantly it records conflicts between actions that would prevent them from occurring together. The gray lines in Figure 11.12 indicate **mutual exclusion** (or **mutex**) links. For example, $Eat(Cake)$ is mutually exclusive with the persistence of either $Have(Cake)$ or $\neg Eaten(Cake)$. We shall see shortly how mutex links are computed.

MUTUAL EXCLUSION

MUTEX

Level $S_1$ contains all the literals that could result from picking any subset of the actions in $A_0$. It also contains mutex links (gray lines) indicating literals that could not appear together, regardless of the choice of actions. For example, $Have(Cake)$ and $Eaten(Cake)$ are mutex: depending on the choice of actions in $A_0$, one or the other, but not both, could be the result. In other words, $S_1$ represents multiple states, just as regression state-space search does, and the mutex links are constraints that define the set of possible states.

We continue in this way, alternating between state level $S_i$ and action level $A_i$ until we reach a level where two consecutive levels are identical. At this point, we say that the graph

LEVELED OFF

has **leveled off**. Every subsequent level will be identical, so further expansion is unnecessary.

What we end up with is a structure where every $A_i$ level contains all the actions that are applicable in $S_i$, along with constraints saying which pairs of actions cannot both be executed. Every $S_i$ level contains all the literals that could result from any possible choice of actions in $A_{i-1}$, along with constraints saying which pairs of literals are not possible. It is important to note that the process of constructing the planning graph does *not* require choosing among actions, which would entail combinatorial search. Instead, it just records the impossibility of certain choices using mutex links. The complexity of constructing the planning graph is a low-order polynomial in the number of actions and literals, whereas the state space is exponential in the number of literals.

We now define mutex links for both actions and literals. A mutex relation holds between two *actions* at a given level if any of the following three conditions holds:

- *Inconsistent effects:* one action negates an effect of the other. For example $Eat(Cake)$ and the persistence of $Have(Cake)$ have inconsistent effects because they disagree on the effect $Have(Cake)$.
- *Interference:* one of the effects of one action is the negation of a precondition of the other. For example $Eat(Cake)$ interferes with the persistence of $Have(Cake)$ by negating its precondition.
- *Competing needs:* one of the preconditions of one action is mutually exclusive with a precondition of the other. For example, $Bake(Cake)$ and $Eat(Cake)$ are mutex because they compete on the value of the $Have(Cake)$ precondition.

A mutex relation holds between two *literals* at the same level if one is the negation of the other or if each possible pair of actions that could achieve the two literals is mutually exclusive. This condition is called *inconsistent support*. For example, $Have(Cake)$ and $Eaten(Cake)$ are mutex in $S_1$ because the only way of achieving $Have(Cake)$, the persistence action, is mutex with the only way of achieving $Eaten(Cake)$, namely $Eat(Cake)$. In $S_2$ the two literals are not mutex because there are new ways of achieving them, such as $Bake(Cake)$ and the persistence of $Eaten(Cake)$, that are not mutex.

### Planning graphs for heuristic estimation

A planning graph, once constructed, is a rich source of information about the problem. For example, *a literal that does not appear in the final level of the graph cannot be achieved by any plan.* This observation can be used in backward search as follows: any state containing an unachievable literal has a cost $h(n) = \infty$. Similarly, in partial-order planning, any plan with an unachievable open condition has $h(n) = \infty$.

This idea can be made more general. We can estimate the cost of achieving any goal literal as the level at which it first appears in the planning graph. We will call this the **level cost** of the goal. In Figure 11.12, $Have(Cake)$ has level cost 0 and $Eaten(Cake)$ has level cost 1. It is easy to show (Exercise 11.9) that these estimates are admissible for the individual goals. The estimate might not be very good, however, because planning graphs allow several actions at each level whereas the heuristic counts just the level and not the number of actions. For this reason, it is common to use a **serial planning graph** for computing heuristics. A

LEVEL COST

SERIAL PLANNING GRAPH

serial graph insists that only one action can actually occur at any given time step; this is done by adding mutex links between every pair of actions except persistence actions. Level costs extracted from serial graphs are often quite reasonable estimates of actual costs.

MAX-LEVEL
LEVEL SUM

To estimate the cost of a conjunction of goals, there are three simple approaches. The **max-level** heuristic simply takes the maximum level cost of any of the goals; this is admissible, but not necessarily very accurate. The **level sum** heuristic, following the subgoal independence assumption, returns the sum of the level costs of the goals; this is inadmissible but works very well in practice for problems that are largely decomposable. It is much more accurate than the number-of-unsatisfied-goals heuristic from Section 11.2. For our problem, the heuristic estimate for the conjunctive goal $Have(Cake) \wedge Eaten(Cake)$ will be $0+1 = 1$, whereas the correct answer is 2. Moreover, if we eliminated the $Bake(Cake)$ action, the estimate would still be 1, but the conjunctive goal would be impossible. Finally, the **set-level** heuristic finds the level at which all the literals in the conjunctive goal appear in the planning graph without any pair of them being mutually exclusive. This heuristic gives the correct values of 2 for our original problem and infinity for the problem without $Bake(Cake)$. It dominates the max-level heuristic and works extremely well on tasks in which there is a good deal of interaction among subplans.

SET-LEVEL

As a tool for generating accurate heuristics, we can view the planning graph as a relaxed problem that is efficiently soluble. To understand the nature of the relaxed problem, we need to understand exactly what it means for a literal $g$ to appear at level $S_i$ in the planning graph. Ideally, we would like it to be a guarantee that there exists a plan with $i$ action levels that achieves $g$, and also that if $g$ does not appear that there is no such plan. Unfortunately, making that guarantee is as difficult as solving the original planning problem. So the planning graph makes the second half of the guarantee (if $g$ does not appear, there is no plan), but if $g$ does appear, then all the planning graph promises is that there is a plan that *possibly* achieves $g$ and has no "obvious" flaws. An obvious flaw is defined as a flaw that can be detected by considering two actions or two literals at a time—in other words, by looking at the mutex relations. There could be more subtle flaws involving three, four, or more actions, but experience has shown that it is not worth the computational effort to keep track of these possible flaws. This is similar to the lesson learned from constraint satisfaction problems that it is often worthwhile to compute 2-consistency before searching for a solution, but less often worthwhile to compute 3-consistency or higher. (See Section 5.2.)

### The GRAPHPLAN algorithm

This subsection shows how to extract a plan directly from the planning graph, rather than just using the graph to provide a heuristic. The GRAPHPLAN algorithm (Figure 11.13) has two main steps, which alternate within a loop. First, it checks whether all the goal literals are present in the current level with no mutex links between any pair of them. If this is the case, then a solution *might* exist within the current graph, so the algorithm tries to extract that solution. Otherwise, it expands the graph by adding the actions for the current level and the state literals for the next level. The process continues until either a solution is found or it is learned that no solution exists.

```
function GRAPHPLAN(problem) returns solution or failure

  graph ← INITIAL-PLANNING-GRAPH(problem)
  goals ← GOALS[problem]
  loop do
     if goals all non-mutex in last level of graph then do
        solution ← EXTRACT-SOLUTION(graph, goals, LENGTH(graph))
        if solution ≠ failure then return solution
        else if NO-SOLUTION-POSSIBLE(graph) then return failure
     graph ← EXPAND-GRAPH(graph, problem)
```

**Figure 11.13** The GRAPHPLAN algorithm. GRAPHPLAN alternates between a solution extraction step and a graph expansion step. EXTRACT-SOLUTION looks for whether a plan can be found, starting at the end and searching backwards. EXPAND-GRAPH adds the actions for the current level and the state literals for the next level.

Let us now trace the operation of GRAPHPLAN on the spare tire problem from Section 11.1. The entire graph is shown in Figure 11.14. The first line of GRAPHPLAN initializes the planning graph to a one-level ($S_0$) graph consisting of the five literals from the initial state. The goal literal $At(Spare, Axle)$ is not present in $S_0$, so we need not call EXTRACT-SOLUTION—we are certain that there is no solution yet. Instead, EXPAND-GRAPH adds the three actions whose preconditions exist at level $S_0$ (i.e., all the actions except $PutOn(Spare, Axle)$), along with persistence actions for all the literals in $S_0$. The effects of the actions are added at level $S_1$. EXPAND-GRAPH then looks for mutex relations and adds them to the graph.

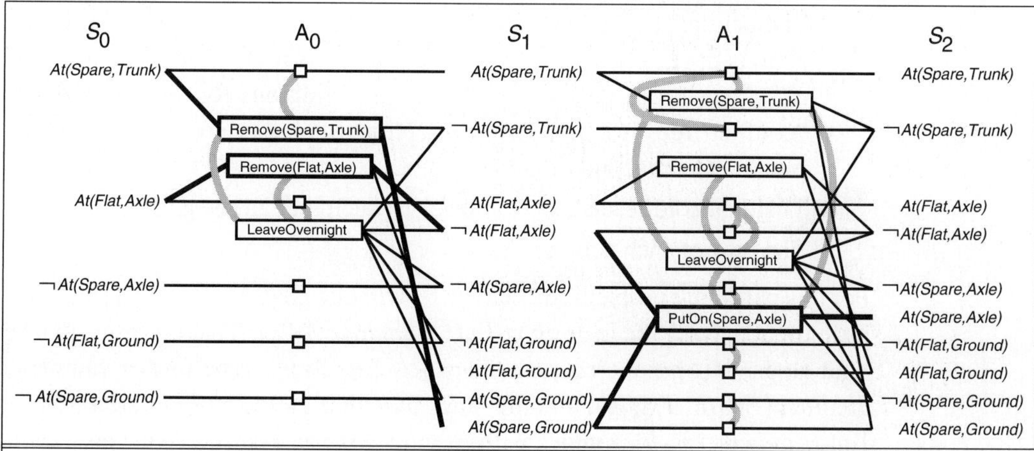


**Figure 11.14** The planning graph for the spare tire problem after expansion to level $S_2$. Mutex links are shown as gray lines. Only some representative mutexes are shown, because the graph would be too cluttered if we showed them all. The solution is indicated by bold lines and outlines.

$At(Spare, Axle)$ is still not present in $S_1$, so again we do not call EXTRACT-SOLUTION. The call to EXPAND-GRAPH gives us the planning graph shown in Figure 11.14. Now that we have the full complement of actions, it is worthwhile to look at some of the examples of mutex relations and their causes:

- *Inconsistent effects:* $Remove(Spare, Trunk)$ is mutex with $LeaveOvernight$ because one has the effect $At(Spare, Ground)$ and the other has its negation.
- *Interference:* $Remove(Flat, Axle)$ is mutex with $LeaveOvernight$ because one has the precondition $At(Flat, Axle)$ and the other has its negation as an effect.
- *Competing needs:* $PutOn(Spare, Axle)$ is mutex with $Remove(Flat, Axle)$ because one has $At(Flat, Axle)$ as a precondition and the other has its negation.
- *Inconsistent support:* $At(Spare, Axle)$ is mutex with $At(Flat, Axle)$ in $S_2$ because the only way of achieving $At(Spare, Axle)$ is by $PutOn(Spare, Axle)$, and that is mutex with the persistence action that is the only way of achieving $At(Flat, Axle)$. Thus, the mutex relations detect the immediate conflict that arises from trying to put two objects in the same place at the same time.

This time, when we go back to the start of the loop, all the literals from the goal are present in $S_2$, and none of them is mutex with any other. That means that a solution might exist, and EXTRACT-SOLUTION will try to find it. In essence, EXTRACT-SOLUTION solves a Boolean CSP whose variables are the actions at each level, and the values for each variable are *in* or *out* of the plan. We can use standard CSP algorithms for this, or we can define EXTRACT-SOLUTION as a search problem, where each state in the search contains a pointer to a level in the planning graph and a set of unsatisfied goals. We define this search problem as follows:

- The initial state is the last level of the planning graph, $S_n$, along with the set of goals from the planning problem.
- The actions available in a state at level $S_i$ are to select any conflict-free subset of the actions in $A_{i-1}$ whose effects cover the goals in the state. The resulting state has level $S_{i-1}$ and has as its set of goals the preconditions for the selected set of actions. By "conflict-free," we mean a set of actions such that no two of them are mutex, and no two of their preconditions are mutex.
- The goal is to reach a state at level $S_0$ such that all the goals are satisfied.
- The cost of each action is 1.

For this particular problem, we start at $S_2$ with the goal $At(Spare, Axle)$. The only choice we have for achieving the goal set is $PutOn(Spare, Axle)$. That brings us to a search state at $S_1$ with goals $At(Spare, Ground)$ and $\neg At(Flat, Axle)$. The former can be achieved only by $Remove(Spare, Trunk)$, and the latter by either $Remove(Flat, Axle)$ or $LeaveOvernight$. But $LeaveOvernight$ is mutex with $Remove(Spare, Trunk)$, so the only solution is to choose $Remove(Spare, Trunk)$ and $Remove(Flat, Axle)$. That brings us to a search state at $S_0$ with the goals $At(Spare, Trunk)$ and $At(Flat, Axle)$. Both of these are present in the state, so we have a solution: the actions $Remove(Spare, Trunk)$ and $Remove(Flat, Axle)$ in level $A_0$, followed by $PutOn(Spare, Axle)$ in $A_1$.

We know that planning is PSPACE-complete and that constructing the planning graph takes polynomial time, so it must be the case that solution extraction is intractable in the worst case. Therefore, we will need some heuristic guidance for choosing among actions during the backward search. One approach that works well in practice is a greedy algorithm based on the level cost of the literals. For any set of goals, we proceed in the following order:

1. Pick first the literal with the highest level cost.
2. To achieve that literal, choose the action with the easiest preconditions first. That is, choose an action such that the sum (or maximum) of the level costs of its preconditions is smallest.

## Termination of GRAPHPLAN

So far, we have skated over the question of termination. If a problem has no solution, can we be sure that GRAPHPLAN will not loop forever, extending the planning graph at each iteration? The answer is yes, but the full proof is beyond the scope of this book. Here, we outline just the main ideas, particularly the ones that shed light on planning graphs in general.

The first step is to notice that certain properties of planning graphs are monotonically increasing or decreasing. "X increases monotonically" means that the set of Xs at level $i + 1$ is a superset (not necessarily proper) of the set at level $i$. The properties are as follows:

- *Literals increase monotonically:* Once a literal appears at a given level, it will appear at all subsequent levels. This is because of the persistence actions; once a literal shows up, persistence actions cause it to stay forever.
- *Actions increase monotonically:* Once an action appears at a given level, it will appear at all subsequent levels. This is a consequence of literals' increasing; if the preconditions of an action appear at one level, they will appear at subsequent levels, and thus so will the action.
- *Mutexes decrease monotonically:* If two actions are mutex at a given level $A_i$, then they will also be mutex for all *previous* levels at which they both appear. The same holds for mutexes between literals. It might not always appear that way in the figures, because the figures have a simplification: they display neither literals that cannot hold at level $S_i$ nor actions that cannot be executed at level $A_i$. We can see that "mutexes decrease monotonically" is true if you consider that these invisible literals and actions are mutex with everything.

  The proof is a little complex, but can be handled by cases: if actions $A$ and $B$ are mutex at level $A_i$, it must be because of one of the three types of mutex. The first two, inconsistent effects and interference, are properties of the actions themselves, so if the actions are mutex at $A_i$, they will be mutex at every level. The third case, competing needs, depends on conditions at level $S_i$: that level must contain a precondition of $A$ that is mutex with a precondition of $B$. Now, these two preconditions can be mutex if they are negations of each other (in which case they would be mutex in every level) or if all actions for achieving one are mutex with all actions for achieving the other. But we already know that the available actions are increasing monotonically, so by induction, the mutexes must be decreasing.

Because the actions and literals increase and the mutexes decrease, and because there are only a finite number of actions and literals, every planning graph will eventually level off—all subsequent levels will be identical. Once a graph has leveled off, if it is missing one of the goals of the problem, or if two of the goals are mutex, then the problem can never be solved, and we can stop the GRAPHPLAN algorithm and return failure. If the graph levels off with all goals present and nonmutex, but EXTRACT-SOLUTION fails to find a solution, then we might have to extend the graph again a finite number of times, but eventually we can stop. This aspect of termination is more complex and is not covered here.

## 11.5 PLANNING WITH PROPOSITIONAL LOGIC

We saw in Chapter 10 that planning can be done by proving a theorem in situation calculus. That theorem says that, given the initial state and the successor-state axioms that describe the effects of actions, the goal will be true in a situation that results from a certain action sequence. As early as 1969, this approach was thought to be too inefficient for finding interesting plans. Recent developments in efficient reasoning algorithms for propositional logic (see Chapter 7) have generated renewed interest in planning as logical reasoning.

The approach we take in this section is based on testing the **satisfiability** of a logical sentence rather than on proving a theorem. We will be finding models of propositional sentences that look like this:

$$\textit{initial state} \wedge \textit{all possible action descriptions} \wedge \textit{goal} .$$

The sentence will contain proposition symbols corresponding to every possible action occurrence; a model that satisfies the sentence will assign $true$ to the actions that are part of a correct plan and $false$ to the others. An assignment that corresponds to an incorrect plan will not be a model, because it will be inconsistent with the assertion that the goal is true. If the planning problem is unsolvable, then the sentence will be unsatisfiable.

### Describing planning problems in propositional logic

The process we will follow to translate STRIPS problems into propositional logic is a textbook example (so to speak) of the knowledge representation cycle: We will begin with what seems to be a reasonable set of axioms, we will find that these axioms allow for spurious unintended models, and we will write more axioms.

Let us begin with a very simple air transport problem. In the initial state (time 0), plane $P_1$ is at $SFO$ and plane $P_2$ is at $JFK$. The goal is to have $P_1$ at $JFK$ and $P_2$ at $SFO$; that is, the planes are to change places. First, we will need distinct proposition symbols for assertions about each time step. We will use superscripts to denote the time step, as in Chapter 7. Thus, the initial state will be written as

$$At(P_1, SFO)^0 \wedge At(P_2, JFK)^0 .$$

(Remember that $At(P_1, SFO)^0$ is an atomic symbol.) Because propositional logic has no closed-world assumption, we must also specify the propositions that are *not* true in the initial state. If some propositions are unknown in the initial state, then they can be left unspecified (the **open world assumption**). In this example we specify:

$$\neg At(P_1, JFK)^0 \wedge \neg At(P_2, SFO)^0 .$$

The goal itself must be associated with a particular time step. Since we do not know *a priori* how many steps it takes to achieve the goal, we can try asserting that the goal is true in the initial state, time $T=0$. That is, we assert $At(P_1, JFK)^0 \wedge At(P_2, SFO)^0$. If that fails, we try again with $T=1$, and so on until we reach the minimum feasible plan length. For each value of $T$, the knowledge base will include only sentences covering the time steps from 0 up to $T$. To ensure termination, an arbitrary upper limit, $T_{\max}$, is imposed. This algorithm is shown in Figure 11.15. An alternative approach that avoids multiple solution attempts is discussed in Exercise 11.17.

```
function SATPLAN(problem, T_max) returns solution or failure
  inputs: problem, a planning problem
          T_max, an upper limit for plan length

  for T = 0 to T_max do
    cnf, mapping ← TRANSLATE-TO-SAT(problem, T)
    assignment ← SAT-SOLVER(cnf)
    if assignment is not null then
      return EXTRACT-SOLUTION(assignment, mapping)
  return failure
```

**Figure 11.15** The SATPLAN algorithm. The planning problem is translated into a CNF sentence in which the goal is asserted to hold at a fixed time step $T$ and axioms are included for each time step up to $T$. (Details of the translation are given in the text.) If the satisfiability algorithm finds a model, then a plan is extracted by looking at those proposition symbols that refer to actions and are assigned *true* in the model. If no model exists, then the process is repeated with the goal moved one step later.

The next issue is how to encode action descriptions in propositional logic. The most straightforward approach is to have one proposition symbol for each action occurrence; for example, $Fly(P_1, SFO, JFK)^0$ is true if plane $P_1$ flies from $SFO$ to $JFK$ at time 0. As in Chapter 7, we write propositional versions of the successor-state axioms developed for the situation calculus in Chapter 10. For example, we have

$$\begin{aligned} At(P_1, JFK)^1 \Leftrightarrow\ & (At(P_1, JFK)^0 \wedge \neg(Fly(P_1, JFK, SFO)^0 \wedge At(P_1, JFK)^0)) \\ & \vee (Fly(P_1, SFO, JFK)^0 \wedge At(P_1, SFO)^0) . \end{aligned} \tag{11.1}$$

That is, plane $P_1$ will be at $JFK$ at time 1 if it was at $JFK$ at time 0 and didn't fly away, or it was at $SFO$ at time 0 and flew to $JFK$. We need one such axiom for each plane, airport, and time step. Moreover, each additional airport adds another way to travel to or from a given airport and hence adds more disjuncts to the right-hand side of each axiom.

With these axioms in place, we can run the satisfiability algorithm to find a plan. There ought to be a plan that achieves the goal at time $T=1$, namely, the plan in which the two planes swap places. Now, suppose the KB is

$$\textit{initial state} \wedge \textit{successor-state axioms} \wedge \textit{goal}^1\ , \tag{11.2}$$

which asserts that the goal is true at time $T = 1$. You can check that the assignment in which

$$Fly(P_1, SFO, JFK)^0 \text{ and } Fly(P_2, JFK, SFO)^0$$

are true and all other action symbols are false is a model of the KB. So far, so good. Are there other possible models that the satisfiability algorithm might return? Indeed, yes. Are all these other models satisfactory plans? Alas, no. Consider the rather silly plan specified by the action symbols

$$Fly(P_1, SFO, JFK)^0 \text{ and } Fly(P_1, JFK, SFO)^0 \text{ and } Fly(P_2, JFK, SFO)^0\ .$$

This plan is silly because plane $P_1$ starts at $SFO$, so the action $Fly(P_1, JFK, SFO)^0$ is infeasible. Nonetheless, the plan *is* a model of the sentence in Equation (11.2)! That is, it is consistent with everything we have said so far about the problem. To understand why, we need to look more carefully at what the successor-state axioms (such as Equation (11.1)) say about actions whose preconditions are not satisfied. The axioms *do* predict correctly that nothing will happen when such an action is executed (see Exercise 11.15), but they do *not* say that the action cannot be executed! To avoid generating plans with illegal actions, we must add **precondition axioms** stating that an action occurrence requires the preconditions to be satisfied.[6] For example, we need

PRECONDITION AXIOMS

$$Fly(P_1, JFK, SFO)^0 \Rightarrow At(P_1, JFK)^0\ .$$

Because $At(P_1, JFK)^0$ is stated to be false in the initial state, this axiom ensures that every model also has $Fly(P_1, JFK, SFO)^0$ set to false. With the addition of precondition axioms, there is exactly one model that satisfies all of the axioms when the goal is to be achieved at time 1, namely the model in which plane $P_1$ flies to $JFK$ and plane $P_2$ flies to $SFO$. Notice that this solution has two parallel actions, just as with GRAPHPLAN or POP.

More surprises emerge when we add a third airport, $LAX$. Now, each plane has two actions that are legal in each state. When we run the satisfiability algorithm, we find that a model with $Fly(P_1, SFO, JFK)^0$ and $Fly(P_2, JFK, SFO)^0$ and $Fly(P_2, JFK, LAX)^0$ satisfies all the axioms. That is, the successor-state and precondition axioms allow a plane to fly to two destinations at once! The preconditions for the two flights by $P_2$ are satisfied in the initial state; the successor-state axioms say that $P_2$ will be at $SFO$ *and* $LAX$ at time 1; so the goal is satisfied. Clearly, we must add more axioms to eliminate these spurious solutions. One approach is to add **action exclusion axioms** that prevent simultaneous actions. For example, we can insist on complete exclusion by adding all possible axioms of the form

ACTION EXCLUSION AXIOMS

$$\neg(Fly(P_2, JFK, SFO)^0 \wedge Fly(P_2, JFK, LAX)^0)\ .$$

These axioms ensure that no two actions can occur at the same time. They eliminate all spurious plans, but also force every plan to be totally ordered. This loses the flexibility of partially ordered plans; also, by increasing the number of time steps in the plan, computation time may be lengthened.

[6] Notice that the addition of precondition axioms means that we need not include preconditions for actions in the successor-state axioms.

Instead of complete exclusion, we can require only partial exclusion—that is, rule out simultaneous actions only if they interfere with each other. The conditions are the same as those for mutex actions: two actions cannot occur simultaneously if one negates a precondition or effect of the other. For example, $Fly(P_2, JFK, SFO)^0$ and $Fly(P_2, JFK, LAX)^0$ cannot both occur, because each negates the precondition of the other; on the other hand, $Fly(P_1, SFO, JFK)^0$ and $Fly(P_2, JFK, SFO)^0$ can occur together because the two planes do not interfere. Partial exclusion eliminates spurious plans without forcing a total ordering.

Exclusion axioms sometimes seem a rather blunt instrument. Instead of saying that a plane cannot fly to two airports at the same time, we might simply insist that no object can be in two places at once:

$$\forall\, p, x, y, t \;\; x \neq y \;\Rightarrow\; \neg(At(p,x)^t \wedge At(p,y)^t)\ .$$

STATE CONSTRAINTS

This fact, combined with the successor-state axioms, *implies* that a plane cannot fly to two airports at the same time. Facts such as this are called **state constraints**. In propositional logic, of course, we have to write out all the ground instances of each state constraint. For the airport problem, the state constraint suffices to rule out all spurious plans. State constraints are often much more compact than action exclusion axioms, but they are not always easy to derive from the original STRIPS description of a problem.

To summarize, planning as satisfiability involves finding models for a sentence containing the initial state, the goal, the successor-state axioms, the precondition axioms, and either the action exclusion axioms or the state constraints. It can be shown that this collection of axioms is sufficient, in the sense that there are no longer any spurious "solutions." Any model satisfying the propositional sentence will be a valid plan for the original problem—that is, every linearization of the plan is a legal sequence of actions that reaches the goal.

### Complexity of propositional encodings

The principal drawback of the propositional approach is the sheer size of the propositional knowledge base that is generated from the original planning problem. For example, the action schema $Fly(p, a_1, a_2)$ becomes $T \times |Planes| \times |Airports|^2$ different proposition symbols. In general, the total number of action symbols is bounded by $T \times |Act| \times |O|^P$, where $|Act|$ is the number of action schemata, $|O|$ is the number of objects in the domain, and $P$ is the maximum arity (number of arguments) of any action schema. The number of clauses is larger still. For example, with 10 time steps, 12 planes, and 30 airports, the complete action exclusion axiom has 583 million clauses.

Because the number of action symbols is exponential in the arity of the action schema, one answer might be to try to reduce the arity. We can do this by borrowing an idea from semantic networks (Chapter 10). Semantic networks use only binary predicates; predicates with more arguments are reduced to a set of binary predicates that describe each argument separately. Applying this idea to an action symbol such as $Fly(P_1, SFO, JFK)^0$, we obtain three new symbols:

$Fly_1(P_1)^0$ : plane $P_1$ flew at time 0
$Fly_2(SFO)^0$ : the origin of the flight was $SFO$
$Fly_3(JFK)^0$ : the destination of the flight was $JFK$ .

SYMBOL SPLITTING

This process, called **symbol splitting**, eliminates the need for an exponential number of symbols. Now we only need $T \times |Act| \times P \times |O|$.

Symbol splitting by itself can reduce the number of symbols, but does not automatically reduce the number of axioms in the KB. That is, if each action symbol in each clause were simply replaced by a conjunction of three symbols, then the total size of the KB would remain roughly the same. Symbol splitting actually does reduce the size of the KB because some of the split symbols will be irrelevant to certain axioms and can be omitted. For example, consider the successor-state axiom in Equation (11.1), modified to include $LAX$ and to omit action preconditions (which will be covered by separate precondition axioms):

$$\begin{aligned} At(P_1, JFK)^1 \;\Leftrightarrow\; & (At(P_1, JFK)^0 \wedge \neg Fly(P_1, JFK, SFO)^0 \wedge \neg Fly(P_1, JFK, LAX)^0) \\ & \vee Fly(P_1, SFO, JFK)^0 \vee Fly(P_1, LAX, JFK)^0 \,. \end{aligned}$$

The first condition says that $P_1$ will be at $JFK$ if it was there at time 0 and didn't fly from $JFK$ to any other city, no matter which one; the second says it will be there if it flew to $JFK$ from another city, no matter which one. Using the split symbols, we can simply omit the argument whose value does not matter:

$$\begin{aligned} At(P_1, JFK)^1 \;\Leftrightarrow\; & (At(P_1, JFK)^0 \wedge \neg(Fly_1(P_1)^0 \wedge Fly_2(JFK)^0)) \\ & \vee (Fly_1(P_1)^0 \wedge Fly_3(JFK)^0) \,. \end{aligned}$$

Notice that $SFO$ and $LAX$ are no longer mentioned in the axiom. More generally, the split action symbols now allow the size of each successor-state axiom to be independent of the number of airports. Similar reductions occur with the precondition axioms and action exclusion axioms (see Exercise 11.16). For the case described earlier with 10 time steps, 12 planes, and 30 airports, the complete action exclusion axiom is reduced from 583 million clauses to 9,360 clauses.

There is one drawback: the split-symbol representation does not allow for parallel actions. Consider the two parallel actions $Fly(P_1, SFO, JFK)^0$ and $Fly(P_2, JFK, SFO)^0$. Converting to the split representation, we have

$$\begin{aligned} & Fly_1(P_1)^0 \wedge Fly_2(SFO)^0 \wedge Fly_3(JFK)^0 \wedge \\ & Fly_1(P_2)^0 \wedge Fly_2(JFK)^0 \wedge Fly_3(SFO)^0 \,. \end{aligned}$$

It is no longer possible to determine what happened! We know that $P_1$ and $P_2$ flew, but we cannot identify the origin and destination of each flight. This means that a complete action exclusion axiom must be used, with the drawbacks noted previously.

Planners based on satisfiability can handle large planning problems—for example, finding optimal 30-step solutions to blocks-world planning problems with dozens of blocks. The size of the propositional encoding and the cost of solution are highly problem-dependent, but in most cases the memory required to store the propositional axioms is the bottleneck. One interesting finding from this work has been that backtracking algorithms such as DPLL are often better at solving planning problems than local search algorithms such as WALKSAT. This is because the majority of the propositional axioms are Horn clauses, which are handled efficiently by the unit propagation technique. This observation has led to the development of hybrid algorithms combining some random search with backtracking and unit propagation.

## 11.6 ANALYSIS OF PLANNING APPROACHES

Planning is an area of great current interest within AI. One reason for this is that it combines the two major areas of AI we have covered so far: *search* and *logic*. That is, a planner can be seen either as a program that searches for a solution or as one that (constructively) proves the existence of a solution. The cross-fertilization of ideas from the two areas has led to both improvements in performance amounting to several orders of magnitude in the last decade and an increased use of planners in industrial applications. Unfortunately, we do not yet have a clear understanding of which techniques work best on which kinds of problems. Quite possibly, new techniques will emerge that dominate existing methods.

Planning is foremost an exercise in controlling combinatorial explosion. If there are $p$ primitive propositions in a domain, then there are $2^p$ states. For complex domains, $p$ can grow quite large. Consider that objects in the domain have properties ($Location$, $Color$, etc.) and relations ($At$, $On$, $Between$, etc.). With $d$ objects in a domain with ternary relations, we get $2^{d^3}$ states. We might conclude that, in the worst case, planning is hopeless.

Against such pessimism, the divide-and-conquer approach can be a powerful weapon. In the best case—full decomposability of the problem—divide-and-conquer offers an exponential speedup. Decomposability is destroyed, however, by negative interactions between actions. Partial-order planners deal with this with causal links, a powerful representational approach, but unfortunately each conflict must be resolved with a choice (put the conflicting action before or after the link), and the choices can multiply exponentially. GRAPHPLAN avoids these choices during the graph construction phase, using mutex links to record conflicts without actually making a choice as to how to resolve them. SATPLAN represents a similar range of mutex relations, but does so by using the general CNF form rather than a specific data structure. How well this works depends on the SAT solver used.

SERIALIZABLE SUBGOALS

Sometimes it is possible to solve a problem efficiently by recognizing that negative interactions can be ruled out. We say that a problem has **serializable subgoals** if there exists an order of subgoals such that the planner can achieve them in that order, without having to undo any of the previously achieved subgoals. For example, in the blocks world, if the goal is to build a tower (e.g., $A$ on $B$, which in turn is on $C$, which in turn is on the $Table$), then the subgoals are serializable bottom to top: if we first achieve $C$ on $Table$, we will never have to undo it while we are achieving the other subgoals. A planner that uses the bottom-to-top trick can solve any problem in the blocks world domain without backtracking (although it might not always find the shortest plan).

As a more complex example, for the Remote Agent planner which commanded NASA's Deep Space One spacecraft, it was determined that the propositions involved in commanding a spacecraft are serializable. This is perhaps not too surprising, because a spacecraft is designed by its engineers to be as easy as possible to control (subject to other constraints). Taking advantage of the serialized ordering of goals, the Remote Agent planner was able to eliminate most of the search. This meant that it was fast enough to control the spacecraft in real time, something previously considered impossible.

There is more than one way to control combinatorial explosions. We saw in Chapter 5 that there are many techniques for controlling backtracking in constraint satisfaction problems (CSPs), such as dependency-directed backtracking. All of these techniques can be applied to planning. For example, extracting a solution from a planning graph can be formulated as a Boolean CSP whose variables state whether a given action should occur at a given time. The CSP can be solved using any of the algorithms in Chapter 5, such as min-conflicts. A closely related method, used in the BLACKBOX system, is to convert the planning graph into a CNF expression and then extract a plan by using a SAT solver. This approach seems to work better than SATPLAN, presumably because the planning graph has already eliminated many of the impossible states and actions from the problem. It also works better than GRAPHPLAN, presumably because a satisfiability search such as WALKSAT has much greater flexibility than the strict backtracking search that GRAPHPLAN uses.

There is no doubt that planners such as GRAPHPLAN, SATPLAN, and BLACKBOX have moved the field of planning forward, both by raising the level of performance of planning systems and by clarifying the representational and combinatorial issues involved. These methods are, however, inherently propositional and thus are limited in the domains they can express. (For example, logistics problems with a few dozen objects and locations can require gigabytes of storage for the corresponding CNF expressions.) It seems likely that first-order representations and algorithms will be required if further progress is to occur, although structures such as planning graphs will continue to be useful as a source of heuristics.

## 11.7 SUMMARY

In this chapter, we defined the problem of planning in deterministic, fully observable environments. We described the principal representations used for planning problems and several algorithmic approaches for solving them. The points to remember are:

- Planning systems are problem-solving algorithms that operate on explicit propositional (or first-order) representations of states and actions. These representations make possible the derivation of effective heuristics and the development of powerful and flexible algorithms for solving problems.
- The STRIPS language describes actions in terms of their preconditions and effects and describes the initial and goal states as conjunctions of positive literals. The ADL language relaxes some of these constraints, allowing disjunction, negation, and quantifiers.
- State-space search can operate in the forward direction (**progression**) or the backward direction (**regression**). Effective heuristics can be derived by making a subgoal independence assumption and by various relaxations of the planning problem.
- Partial-order planning (POP) algorithms explore the space of plans without committing to a totally ordered sequence of actions. They work back from the goal, adding actions to the plan to achieve each subgoal. They are particularly effective on problems amenable to a divide-and-conquer approach.

- A **planning graph** can be constructed incrementally, starting from the initial state. Each layer contains a superset of all the literals or actions that could occur at that time step and encodes mutual exclusion, or **mutex**, relations among literals or actions that cannot co-occur. Planning graphs yield useful heuristics for state-space and partial-order planners and can be used directly in the GRAPHPLAN algorithm.
- The GRAPHPLAN algorithm processes the planning graph, using a backward search to extract a plan. It allows for some partial ordering among actions.
- The SATPLAN algorithm translates a planning problem into propositional axioms and applies a satisfiability algorithm to find a model that corresponds to a valid plan. Several different propositional representations have been developed, with varying degrees of compactness and efficiency.
- Each of the major approaches to planning has its adherents, and there is as yet no consensus on which is best. Competition and cross-fertilization among the approaches have resulted in significant gains in efficiency for planning systems.

## BIBLIOGRAPHICAL AND HISTORICAL NOTES

AI planning arose from investigations into state-space search, theorem proving, and control theory and from the practical needs of robotics, scheduling, and other domains. STRIPS (Fikes and Nilsson, 1971), the first major planning system, illustrates the interaction of these influences. STRIPS was designed as the planning component of the software for the Shakey robot project at SRI. Its overall control structure was modeled on that of GPS, the General Problem Solver (Newell and Simon, 1961), a state-space search system that used means–ends analysis. STRIPS used a version of the QA3 theorem proving system (Green, 1969b) as a subroutine for establishing the truth of preconditions for actions. Lifschitz (1986) offers precise definitions and an analysis of the STRIPS language. Bylander (1992) shows simple STRIPS planning to be PSPACE-complete. Fikes and Nilsson (1993) give a historical retrospective on the STRIPS project and a survey of its relationship to more recent planning efforts.

The action representation used by STRIPS has been far more influential than its algorithmic approach. Almost all planning systems since then have used one variant or another of the STRIPS language. Unfortunately, the proliferation of variants has made comparisons needlessly difficult. With time came a better understanding of the limitations and tradeoffs among formalisms. The Action Description Language, or ADL, (Pednault, 1986) relaxed some of the restrictions in the STRIPS language and made it possible to encode more realistic problems. Nebel (2000) explores schemes for compiling ADL into STRIPS. The Problem Domain Description Language or PDDL (Ghallab *et al.*, 1998) was introduced as a computer-parsable, standardized syntax for representing STRIPS, ADL, and other languages. PDDL has been used as the standard language for the planning competitions at the AIPS conference, beginning in 1998.

Planners in the early 1970s generally worked with totally ordered action sequences. Problem decomposition was achieved by computing a subplan for each subgoal and then

LINEAR PLANNING

stringing the subplans together in some order. This approach, called **linear planning** by Sacerdoti (1975), was soon discovered to be incomplete. It cannot solve some very simple problems, such as the Sussman anomaly (see Exercise 11.11), found by Allen Brown during experimentation with the HACKER system (Sussman, 1975). A complete planner must allow for **interleaving** of actions from different subplans within a single sequence. The notion of serializable subgoals (Korf, 1987) corresponds exactly to the set of problems for which noninterleaved planners are complete.

INTERLEAVING

One solution to the interleaving problem was goal regression planning, a technique in which steps in a totally ordered plan are reordered so as to avoid conflict between subgoals. This was introduced by Waldinger (1975) and also used by Warren's (1974) WARPLAN. WARPLAN is also notable in that it was the first planner to be written in a logic programming language (Prolog) and is one of the best examples of the remarkable economy that can sometimes be gained by using logic programming: WARPLAN is only 100 lines of code, a small fraction of the size of comparable planners of the time. INTERPLAN (Tate, 1975a, 1975b) also allowed arbitrary interleaving of plan steps to overcome the Sussman anomaly and related problems.

The ideas underlying partial-order planning include the detection of conflicts (Tate, 1975a) and the protection of achieved conditions from interference (Sussman, 1975). The construction of partially ordered plans (then called **task networks**) was pioneered by the NOAH planner (Sacerdoti, 1975, 1977) and by Tate's (1975b, 1977) NONLIN system.[7]

Partial-order planning dominated the next 20 years of research, yet for much of that time, the field was not widely understood. TWEAK (Chapman, 1987) was a logical reconstruction and simplification of planning work of this time; his formulation was clear enough to allow proofs of completeness and intractability (NP-hardness and undecidability) of various formulations of the planning problem. Chapman's work led to what was arguably the first simple and readable description of a complete partial-order planner (McAllester and Rosenblitt, 1991). An implementation of McAllester and Rosenblitt's algorithm called SNLP (Soderland and Weld, 1991) was widely distributed and allowed many researchers to understand and experiment with partial-order planning for the first time. The POP algorithm described in this chapter is based on SNLP.

Weld's group also developed UCPOP (Penberthy and Weld, 1992), the first planner for problems expressed in ADL. UCPOP incorporated the number-of-unsatisfied-goals heuristic. It ran somewhat faster than SNLP, but was seldom able to find plans with more than a dozen or so steps. Although improved heuristics were developed for UCPOP (Joslin and Pollack, 1994; Gerevini and Schubert, 1996), partial-order planning fell into disrepute in the 1990s as faster methods emerged. Nguyen and Kambhampati (2001) suggest that a rehabilitation is merited: with accurate heuristics derived from a planning graph, their REPOP planner scales up much better than GRAPHPLAN and is competitive with the fastest state-space planners.

Avrim Blum and Merrick Furst (1995, 1997) revitalized the field of planning with their GRAPHPLAN system, which was orders of magnitude faster than the partial-order planners of

[7] Some confusion exists over terminology. Many authors use the term **nonlinear** to mean partially ordered. This is slightly different from Sacerdoti's original usage referring to interleaved plans.

the time. Other graph planning systems, such as IPP (Koehler *et al.*, 1997), STAN (Fox and Long, 1998) and SGP (Weld *et al.*, 1998), soon followed. A data structure closely resembling the planning graph had been developed slightly earlier by Ghallab and Laruelle (1994), whose IXTET partial-order planner used it to derive accurate heuristics to guide searches. Nguyen *et al.* (2001) give a very thorough analysis of heuristics derived from planning graphs. Our discussion of planning graphs is based partly on this work and on lecture notes by Subbarao Kambhampati. As mentioned in the chapter, a planning graph can be used in many different ways to guide the search for a solution. The winner of the 2002 AIPS planning competition, LPG (Gerevini and Serina, 2002), searched planning graphs using a local search technique inspired by WALKSAT.

Planning as satisfiability and the SATPLAN algorithm were proposed by Kautz and Selman (1992), who were inspired by the surprising success of greedy local search for satisfiability problems. (See Chapter 7.) Kautz *et al.* (1996) also investigated various forms of propositional representations for STRIPS axioms, finding that the most compact forms did not necessarily lead to the fastest solution times. A systematic analysis was carried out by Ernst *et al.* (1997), who also developed an automatic "compiler" for generating propositional representations from PDDL problems. The BLACKBOX planner, which combines ideas from GRAPHPLAN and SATPLAN, was developed by Kautz and Selman (1998).

The resurgence of interest in state-space planning was pioneered by Drew McDermott's UNPOP program (1996), which was the first to suggest a distance heuristic based on a relaxed problem with delete lists ignored. The name UNPOP was a reaction to the overwhelming concentration on partial-order planning at the time; McDermott suspected that other approaches were not getting the attention they deserved. Bonet and Geffner's Heuristic Search Planner (HSP) and its later derivatives (Bonet and Geffner, 1999) were the first to make state-space search practical for large planning problems. The most successful state-space searcher to date is Hoffmann's (2000) FASTFORWARD or FF, winner of the AIPS 2000 planning competition. FF uses a simplified planning graph heuristic with a very fast search algorithm that combines forward and local search in a novel way.

BINARY DECISION DIAGRAMS

Most recently, there has been interest in the representation of plans as **binary decision diagrams**, a compact description of finite automata widely studied in the hardware verification community (Clarke and Grumberg, 1987; McMillan, 1993). There are techniques for proving properties of binary decision diagrams, including the property of being a solution to a planning problem. Cimatti *et al.* (1998) present a planner based on this approach. Other representations have also been used; for example, Vossen *et al.* (2001) survey the use of integer programming for planning.

The jury is still out, but there are now some interesting comparisons of the various approaches to planning. Helmert (2001) analyzes several classes of planning problems, and shows that constraint-based approaches, such as GRAPHPLAN and SATPLAN are best for NP-hard domains, while search-based approaches do better in domains where feasible solutions can be found without backtracking. GRAPHPLAN and SATPLAN have trouble in domains with many objects, because that means they must create many actions. In some cases the problem can be delayed or avoided by generating the propositionalized actions dynamically, only as needed, rather than instantiating them all before the search begins.

Weld (1994, 1999) provides two excellent surveys of modern planning algorithms. It is interesting to see the change in the five years between the two surveys: the first concentrates on partial-order planning, and the second introduces GRAPHPLAN and SATPLAN. *Readings in Planning* (Allen *et al.*, 1990) is a comprehensive anthology of many of the best earlier articles in the field, including several good surveys. Yang (1997) provides a book-length overview of partial-order planning techniques.

Planning research has been central to AI since its inception, and papers on planning are a staple of mainstream AI journals and conferences. There are also specialized conferences such as the International Conference on AI Planning Systems (AIPS), the International Workshop on Planning and Scheduling for Space, and the European Conference on Planning.

## EXERCISES

**11.1** Describe the differences and similarities between problem solving and planning.

**11.2** Given the axioms from Figure 11.2, what are all the applicable concrete instances of $Fly(p, from, to)$ in the state described by

$$At(P_1, JFK) \land At(P_2, SFO) \land Plane(P_1) \land Plane(P_2) \\ \land Airport(JFK) \land Airport(SFO)\ ?$$

**11.3** Let us consider how we might translate a set of STRIPS schemata into the successor-state axioms of situation calculus. (See Chapter 10.)

- Consider the schema for $Fly(p, from, to)$. Write a logical definition for the predicate $FlyPrecond(p, from, to, s)$, which is true if the preconditions for $Fly(p, from, to)$ are satisfied in situation $s$.
- Next, assuming that $Fly(p, from, to)$ is the only action schema available to the agent, write down a successor-state axiom for $At(p, x, s)$ that captures the same information as the action schema.
- Now suppose there is an additional method of travel: $Teleport(p, from, to)$. It has the additional precondition $\neg Warped(p)$ and the additional effect $Warped(p)$. Explain how the situation calculus knowledge base must be modified.
- Finally, develop a general and precisely specified procedure for carrying out the translation from a set of STRIPS schemata to a set of successor-state axioms.

**11.4** The monkey-and-bananas problem is faced by a monkey in a laboratory with some bananas hanging out of reach from the ceiling. A box is available that will enable the monkey to reach the bananas if he climbs on it. Initially, the monkey is at $A$, the bananas at $B$, and the box at $C$. The monkey and box have height $Low$, but if the monkey climbs onto the box he will have height $High$, the same as the bananas. The actions available to the monkey include $Go$ from one place to another, $Push$ an object from one place to another, $ClimbUp$ onto or

*ClimbDown* from an object, and *Grasp* or *Ungrasp* an object. Grasping results in holding the object if the monkey and object are in the same place at the same height.

**a.** Write down the initial state description.

**b.** Write down STRIPS-style definitions of the six actions.

**c.** Suppose the monkey wants to fool the scientists, who are off to tea, by grabbing the bananas, but leaving the box in its original place. Write this as a general goal (i.e., not assuming that the box is necessarily at C) in the language of situation calculus. Can this goal be solved by a STRIPS-style system?

**d.** Your axiom for pushing is probably incorrect, because if the object is too heavy, its position will remain the same when the *Push* operator is applied. Is this an example of the ramification problem or the qualification problem? Fix your problem description to account for heavy objects.

**11.5** Explain why the process for generating predecessors in backward search does not need to add the literals that are negative effects of the action.

**11.6** Explain why dropping negative effects from every action schema in a STRIPS problem results in a relaxed problem.

**11.7** Examine the definition of **bidirectional search** in Chapter 3.

**a.** Would bidirectional state-space search be a good idea for planning?

**b.** What about bidirectional search in the space of partial-order plans?

**c.** Devise a version of partial-order planning in which an action can be added to a plan if its preconditions can be achieved by the effects of actions already in the plan. Explain how to deal with conflicts and ordering constraints. Is the algorithm essentially identical to forward state-space search?

**d.** Consider a partial-order planner that combines the method in part (c) with the standard method of adding actions to achieve open conditions. Would the resulting algorithm be the same as part (b)?

**11.8** Construct levels 0, 1, and 2 of the planning graph for the problem in Figure 11.2.

**11.9** Prove the following assertions about planning graphs:

- A literal that does not appear in the final level of the graph cannot be achieved.
- The level cost of a literal in a serial graph is no greater than the actual cost of an optimal plan for achieving it.

**11.10** We contrasted forward and backward state-space search planners with partial-order planners, saying that the latter is a plan-space searcher. Explain how forward and backward state-space search can also be considered plan-space searchers, and say what the plan refinement operators are.

SUSSMAN ANOMALY

**11.11** Figure 11.16 shows a blocks-world problem known as the **Sussman anomaly**. The problem was considered anomalous because the noninterleaved planners of the early 1970s could not solve it. Write a definition of the problem in STRIPS notation and solve it, either by hand or with a planning program. A noninterleaved planner is a planner that, when given two subgoals $G_1$ and $G_2$, produces either a plan for $G_1$ concatenated with a plan for $G_2$, or vice-versa. Explain why a noninterleaved planner cannot solve this problem.

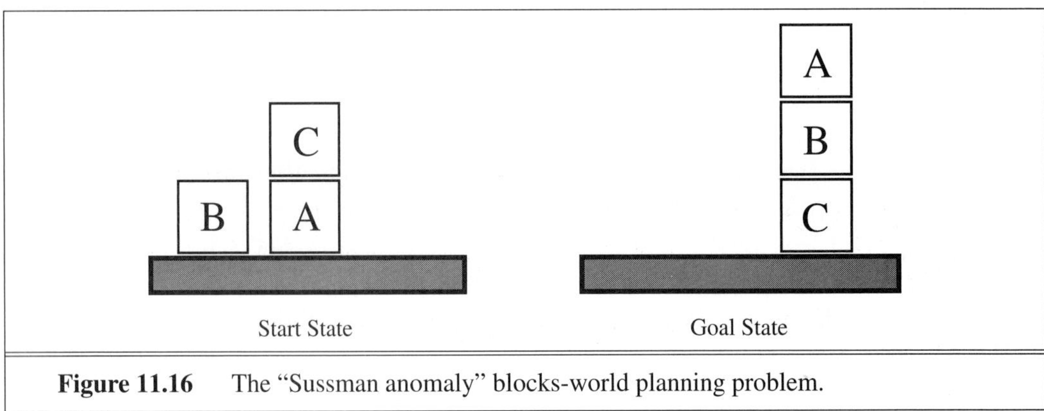


**Figure 11.16** The "Sussman anomaly" blocks-world planning problem.

**11.12** Consider the problem of putting on one's shoes and socks, as defined in Section 11.3. Apply GRAPHPLAN to this problem and show the solution obtained. Now add actions for putting on a coat and a hat. Show the partial order plan that is a solution, and show that there are 180 different linearizations of the partial-order plan. What is the minimum number of different planning graph solutions needed to represent all 180 linearizations?

**11.13** The original STRIPS program was designed to control Shakey the robot. Figure 11.17 shows a version of Shakey's world consisting of four rooms lined up along a corridor, where each room has a door and a light switch.

The actions in Shakey's world include moving from place to place, pushing movable objects (such as boxes), climbing onto and down from rigid objects (such as boxes), and turning light switches on and off. The robot itself was never dexterous enough to climb on a box or toggle a switch, but the STRIPS planner was capable of finding and printing out plans that were beyond the robot's abilities. Shakey's six actions are the following:

- $Go(x, y)$, which requires that Shakey be at $x$ and that $x$ and $y$ are locations in the same room. By convention a door between two rooms is in both of them.
- Push a box $b$ from location $x$ to location $y$ within the same room: $Push(b, x, y)$. We will need the predicate $Box$ and constants for the boxes.
- Climb onto a box: $ClimbUp(b)$; climb down from a box: $ClimbDown(b)$. We will need the predicate $On$ and the constant $Floor$.
- Turn a light switch on: $TurnOn(s)$; turn it off: $TurnOff(s)$. To turn a light on or off, Shakey must be on top of a box at the light switch's location.

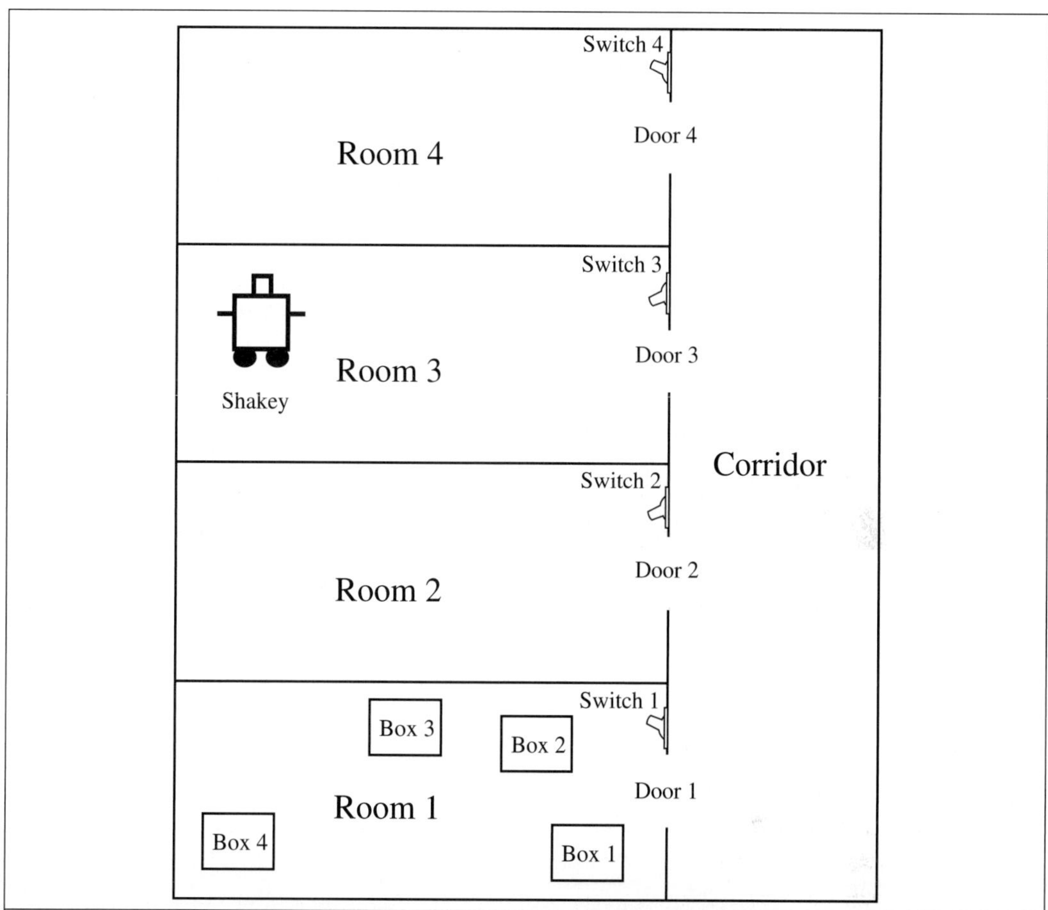


**Figure 11.17** Shakey's world. Shakey can move between landmarks within a room, can pass through the door between rooms, can climb climbable objects and push pushable objects, and can flip light switches.

Describe Shakey's six actions and the initial state from Figure 11.17 in STRIPS notation. Construct a plan for Shakey to get $Box_2$ into $Room_2$.

**11.14** We saw that planning graphs can handle only propositional actions. What if we want to use planning graphs for a problem with variables in the goal, such as $At(P_1, x) \wedge At(P_2, x)$, where $x$ ranges over a finite domain of locations? How could you encode such a problem to work with planning graphs? (Hint: remember the *Finish* action from POP planning. What preconditions should it have?)

**11.15** Up to now we have assumed that actions are only executed in the appropriate situations. Let us see what propositional successor-state axioms such as Equation (11.1) have to say about actions whose preconditions are not satisfied.

**a**. Show that the axioms predict that nothing will happen when an action is executed in a state where its preconditions are not satisifed.

**b**. Consider a plan $p$ that contains the actions required to achieve a goal but also includes illegal actions. Is it the case that

$$\textit{initial state} \wedge \textit{successor-state axioms} \wedge p \models \textit{goal} \ ?$$

**c**. With first-order successor-state axioms in situation calculus (as in Chapter 10), is it possible to prove that a plan containing illegal actions will achieve the goal?

**11.16** Giving examples from the airport domain, explain how symbol-splitting reduces the size of the precondition axioms and the action exclusion axioms. Derive a general formula for the size of each axiom set in terms of the number of time steps, the number of action schemata, their arities, and the number of objects.

**11.17** In the SATPLAN algorithm in Figure 11.15, each call to the satisfiability algorithm asserts a goal $g^T$, where $T$ ranges from 0 to $T_{\max}$. Suppose instead that the satisfiability algorithm is called only once, with the goal $g^0 \vee g^1 \vee \cdots \vee g^{T_{\max}}$.

**a**. Will this always return a plan if one exists with length less than or equal to $T_{\max}$?

**b**. Does this approach introduce any new spurious "solutions"?

**c**. Discuss how one might modify a satisfiability algorithm such as WALKSAT so that it finds short solutions (if they exist) when given a disjunctive goal of this form.

# 12 PLANNING AND ACTING IN THE REAL WORLD

*In which we see how more expressive representations and more interactive agent architectures lead to planners that are useful in the real world.*

The previous chapter introduced the most basic concepts, representations, and algorithms for planning. Planners that are are used in the real world for tasks such as scheduling Hubble Space Telescope observations, operating factories, and handling the logistics for military campaigns are more complex; they extend the basics in terms both of the representation language and of the way the planner interacts with the environment. This chapter shows how. Section 12.1 describes planning and scheduling with time and resource constraints, and Section 12.2 describes planning with predefined subplans. Sections 12.3 to 12.6 present a series of agent architectures designed to deal with uncertain environments. Section 12.7 shows how to plan when the environment contains other agents.

## 12.1 TIME, SCHEDULES, AND RESOURCES

The STRIPS representation talks about *what* actions do, but, because the representation is based on situation calculus, it cannot talk about *how long* an action takes or even about *when* an action occurs, except to say that it is before or after another action. For some domains, we would like to talk about when actions begin and end. For example, in the cargo delivery domain, we might like to know when the plane carrying some cargo will arrive, not just that it will arrive when it is done flying.

JOB SHOP SCHEDULING

Time is of the essence in the general family of applications called **job shop scheduling**. Such tasks require completing a set of jobs, each of which consists of a sequence of actions, where each action has a given duration and might require some resources. The problem is to determine a schedule that minimizes the total time required to complete all the jobs, while respecting the resource constraints.

An example of a job shop scheduling problem is given in Figure 12.1. This is a highly simplified automobile assembly problem. There are two jobs: assembling cars $C_1$ and $C_2$. Each job consists of three actions: adding the engine, adding the wheels, and inspecting the

$Init(Chassis(C_1) \wedge Chassis(C_2)$
$\quad \wedge\ Engine(E_1, C_1, 30) \wedge Engine(E_2, C_2, 60)$
$\quad \wedge\ Wheels(W_1, C_1, 30) \wedge Wheels(W_2, C_2, 15))$
$Goal(Done(C_1) \wedge Done(C_2))$

$Action(AddEngine(e, c),$
$\quad$ PRECOND: $Engine(e, c, d) \wedge Chassis(c) \wedge \neg EngineIn(c),$
$\quad$ EFFECT: $EngineIn(c) \wedge Duration(d))$
$Action(AddWheels(w, c),$
$\quad$ PRECOND: $Wheels(w, c, d) \wedge Chassis(c) \wedge EngineIn(c),$
$\quad$ EFFECT: $WheelsOn(c) \wedge Duration(d))$
$Action(Inspect(c),$ PRECOND: $EngineIn(c) \wedge WheelsOn(c) \wedge Chassis(c),$
$\quad$ EFFECT: $Done(c) \wedge Duration(10))$

**Figure 12.1** A job shop scheduling problem for assembling two cars. The notation $Duration(d)$ means that an action takes $d$ minutes to execute. $Engine(E_1, C_1, 60)$ means that $E_1$ is an engine that fits into chassis $C_1$ and takes 60 minutes to install.

results. The engine must be put in first (because having the front wheels on would inhibit access to the engine compartment) and of course the inspection must be done last.

The problem in Figure 12.1 can be solved by any of the planners we have already seen. Figure 12.2 (if you ignore the numbers) shows the solution that the partial-order planner POP would come up with. To make this a *scheduling* problem rather than a *planning* problem, we must now determine when each action should begin and end, based on the *durations* of actions as well as their ordering. The notation $Duration(d)$ in the effect of an action (where $d$ must be bound to a number) means that the action takes $d$ minutes to complete.

CRITICAL PATH METHOD

Given a partial ordering of actions with durations, as in Figure 12.2, we can apply the **critical path method** (CPM) to determine the possible start and end times of each action. A **path** through a partial-order plan is a linearly ordered sequence of actions beginning with $Start$ and ending with $Finish$. (For example, there are two paths in the partial-order plan in Figure 12.2.)

CRITICAL PATH

The **critical path** is that path whose total duration is longest; the path is "critical" because it determines the duration of the entire plan—shortening other paths doesn't shorten the plan as a whole, but delaying the start of any action on the critical path slows down the whole plan. In the figure, the critical path is shown with bold lines. To complete the whole plan in the minimal total time, the actions on the critical path must be executed with no delay between them. Actions that are off the critical path have some leeway—a window of time in which they can be executed. The window is specified in terms of an earliest possible start time, $ES$, and a latest possible start time, $LS$. The quantity $LS - ES$ is known as the **slack** of an action. We can see in Figure 12.2 that the whole plan will take 85 minutes, that each action on the critical path has 0 slack (this will always be the case) and that each of the actions in the assembly of $C_1$ have a 15-minute window in which they can be started. Together the $ES$ and $LS$ times for all the actions constitute a **schedule** for the problem.

SLACK

SCHEDULE

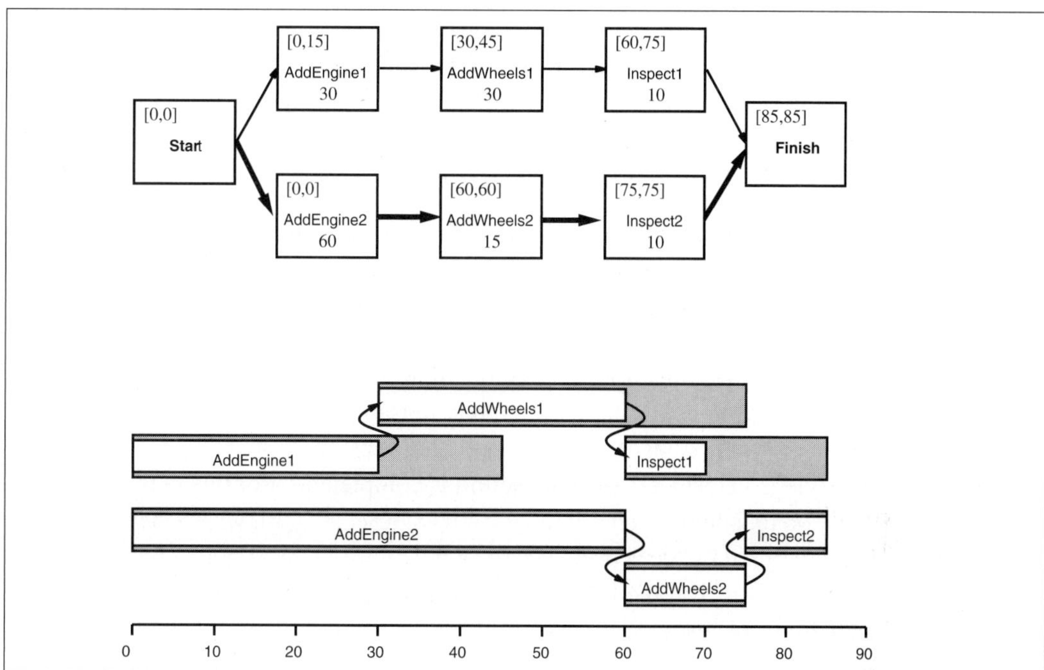


**Figure 12.2** A solution to the job shop scheduling problem from Figure 12.1. At the top, the solution is given as a partial-order plan. The duration of each action is given at the bottom of each rectangle, with the earliest and latest start time listed as $[ES, LS]$ in the upper left. The difference between these two numbers is the slack of an action; actions with zero slack are on the critical path, shown with bold arrows. At the bottom of the figure, the same solution is shown as a timeline. Grey rectangles represent time intervals during which an action may be executed, provided that the ordering constraints are respected. The unoccupied portion of a gray rectangle indicates the slack.

The following formulas serve as a definition for $ES$ and $LS$ and also as the outline of a dynamic programming algorithm to compute them:

$$ES(Start) = 0\ .$$
$$ES(B) = \max_{A \prec B} ES(A) + Duration(A)\ .$$
$$LS(Finish) = ES(Finish)\ .$$
$$LS(A) = \min_{A \prec B} LS(B) - Duration(A)\ .$$

The idea is that we start by assigning $ES(Start)$ to be 0. Then as soon as we get an action $B$ such that all the actions that come immediately before $B$ have $ES$ values assigned, we set $ES(B)$ to be the maximum of the earliest finish times of those immediately preceding actions, where the earliest finish time of an action is defined as the earliest start time plus the duration. This process repeats until every action has been assigned an $ES$ value. The $LS$ values are computed in a similar manner, working backwards from the $Finish$ action. The details are left as an exercise.

The complexity of the critical path algorithm is just $O(Nb)$, where $N$ is the number of actions and $b$ is the maximum branching factor into or out of an action. (To see this, note that the $LS$ and $ES$ computations are done once for each action, and each computation iterates over at most $b$ other actions.) Therefore, the problem of finding a minimum-duration schedule, *given a partial ordering on the actions*, is quite easy to solve.

### Scheduling with resource constraints

RESOURCES

Real scheduling problems are complicated by the presence of constraints on **resources**. For example, adding an engine to a car requires an engine hoist. If there is only one hoist, then we cannot simultaneously add engine $E_1$ to car $C_1$ and engine $E_2$ to car $C_2$; hence, the schedule shown in Figure 12.2 would be infeasible. The engine hoist is an example of a **reusable resource**—a resource that is "occupied" during the action but that becomes available again when the action is finished. Notice that reusable resources cannot be handled in our standard description of actions in terms of preconditions and effects, because the amount of resource available is unchanged after the action is completed.[1] For this reason, we augment our representation to include a field of the form RESOURCE: $R(k)$, which means that $k$ units of resource $R$ are required by the action. The resource requirement is both a prerequisite—the action cannot be performed if the resource is unavailable—and a *temporary* effect, in the sense that the availability of resource $r$ is reduced by $k$ for the duration of the action. Figure 12.3 shows how to extend the engine assembly problem to include three resources: an engine hoist for installing engines, a wheel station for putting on the wheels, and two inspectors. Figure 12.4 shows the solution with the fastest completion time, 115 minutes. This is longer than the 85 minutes required for a schedule without resource constraints. Notice that there is no time at which both inspectors are required, so we can immediately move one of our two inspectors to a more productive position.

REUSABLE RESOURCE

The representation of resources as numerical quantities, such as $Inspectors(2)$, rather than as named entities, such as $Inspector(I_1)$ and $Inspector(I_2)$, is an example of a very general technique called **aggregation**. The central idea of aggregation is to group individual objects into quantities when the objects are all indistinguishable with respect to the purpose at hand. In our assembly problem, it does not matter *which* inspector inspects the car, so there is no need to make the distinction. (The same idea works in the missionaries-and-cannibals problem in Exercise 3.9.) Aggregation is essential for reducing complexity. Consider what happens when a schedule is proposed that has 10 concurrent $Inspect$ actions but only 9 inspectors are available. With inspectors represented as quantities, a failure is detected immediately and the algorithm backtracks to try another schedule. With inspectors represented as individuals, the algorithm backtracks to try all 10! ways of assigning inspectors to $Inspect$ actions, to no avail.

AGGREGATION

Despite their advantages, resource constraints make scheduling problems more complicated by introducing additional interactions among actions. Whereas unconstrained scheduling using the critical-path method is easy, finding a resource-constrained schedule with the earliest possible completion time is NP-hard. This complexity is often seen in practice as well as in theory. A challenge problem posed in 1963—to find the optimal schedule for a

[1] In contrast, **consumable resources**, such as screws for assembling the engine, can be handled within the standard framework; see Exercise 12.2.

$$
\begin{array}{l}
\mathit{Init}(\mathit{Chassis}(C_1) \land \mathit{Chassis}(C_2) \\
\quad \land \mathit{Engine}(E_1, C_1, 30) \land \mathit{Engine}(E_2, C_2, 60) \\
\quad \land \mathit{Wheels}(W_1, C_1, 30) \land \mathit{Wheels}(W_2, C_2, 15) \\
\quad \land \mathit{EngineHoists}(1) \land \mathit{WheelStations}(1) \land \mathit{Inspectors}(2)) \\
\mathit{Goal}(\mathit{Done}(C_1) \land \mathit{Done}(C_2)) \\
\\
\mathit{Action}(\mathit{AddEngine}(e, c), \\
\quad \textsc{Precond}{:}\mathit{Engine}(e, c, d) \land \mathit{Chassis}(c) \land \neg \mathit{EngineIn}(c), \\
\quad \textsc{Effect}{:}\mathit{EngineIn}(c) \land \mathit{Duration}(d), \\
\quad \textsc{Resource}{:}\mathit{EngineHoists}(1)) \\
\mathit{Action}(\mathit{AddWheels}(w, c), \\
\quad \textsc{Precond}{:}\ \mathit{Wheels}(w, c, d) \land \mathit{Chassis}(c) \land \mathit{EngineIn}(c), \\
\quad \textsc{Effect}{:}\ \mathit{WheelsOn}(c) \land \mathit{Duration}(d), \\
\quad \textsc{Resource}{:}\ \mathit{WheelStations}(1)) \\
\mathit{Action}(\mathit{Inspect}(c), \\
\quad \textsc{Precond}{:}\mathit{EngineIn}(c) \land \mathit{WheelsOn}(c), \\
\quad \textsc{Effect}{:}\mathit{Done}(c) \land \mathit{Duration}(10), \\
\quad \textsc{Resource}{:}\mathit{Inspectors}(1))
\end{array}
$$

**Figure 12.3** Job shop scheduling problem for assembling two cars, with resources. The available resources are one engine assembly station, one wheel assembly station, and two inspectors. The notation RESOURCE:$r$ means that the resource $r$ is used during execution of an action, but becomes free again when the action is complete.

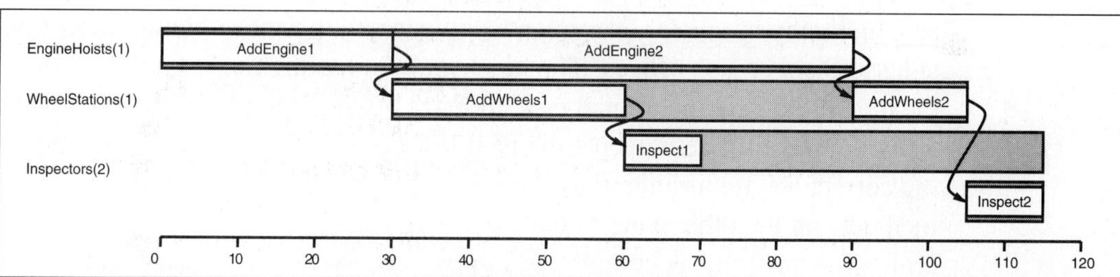


**Figure 12.4** A solution to the job shop scheduling problem with resources from Figure 12.3. The left-hand margin lists the three resources, and actions are shown aligned horizontally with the resources they consume. There are two possible schedules, depending on which assembly uses the engine station first; we've shown the optimal solution, which takes 115 minutes.

problem involving just 10 machines and 10 jobs of 100 actions each—went unsolved for 23 years (Lawler *et al.*, 1993). Many approaches have been tried, including branch-and-bound, simulated annealing, tabu search, constraint satisfaction, and other techniques from Part II. One simple but popular heuristic is the **minimum slack** algorithm. It schedules actions in a greedy fashion. On each iteration, it considers the unscheduled actions that have had all their predecessors scheduled and schedules the one with the least slack for the earliest possible start. It then updates the $ES$ and $LS$ times for each affected action and repeats. The heuristic

MINIMUM SLACK

is based on the same principle as the most-constrained-variable heuristic in constraint satisfaction. It often works well in practice, but for our assembly problem it yields a 130–minute solution, not the 115–minute solution of Figure 12.4.

The approach we have taken in this section is "plan first, schedule later": that is, we divided the overall problem into a *planning* phase in which actions are selected and partially ordered to meet the goals of the problem, and a later *scheduling* phase, in which temporal information is added to the plan to ensure that it meets resource and deadline constraints. This approach is common in real-world manufacturing and logistical settings, where the planning phase is often performed by human experts. When there are severe resource constraints, however, it could be that some legal plans will lead to much better schedules than others. In that case, it makes sense to *integrate* planning and scheduling by taking into account durations and overlaps during the construction of a partial-order plan. Several of the planning algorithms in Chapter 11 can be augmented to handle this information. For example, partial-order planners can detect resource constraint violations in much the same way that they detect conflicts with causal links. Heuristics can be modified to estimate the total completion time of a plan, rather than just the total cost of the actions. This is currently an active area of research.

## 12.2 Hierarchical Task Network Planning

HIERARCHICAL DECOMPOSITION

One of the most pervasive ideas for dealing with complexity is **hierarchical decomposition**. Complex software is created from a hierarchy of subroutines or object classes, armies operate as a hierarchy of units, governments and corporations have hierarchies of departments, subsidiaries, and branch offices. The key benefit of hierarchical structure is that, at each level of the hierarchy, a computational task, military mission, or administrative function is reduced to a *small* number of activities at the next lower level, so that the computational cost of finding the correct way to arrange those activities for the current problem is small. Nonhierarchical methods, on the other hand, reduce a task to a *large* number of individual actions; for large-scale problems, this is completely impractical. In the best case—when high-level solutions always turn out to have satisfactory low-level implementations—hierarchical methods can result in linear-time instead of exponential-time planning algorithms.

HIERARCHICAL TASK NETWORK

This section describes a planning method based on **hierarchical task networks** or HTNs. The approach we take combines ideas from both partial-order planning (Section 11.3) and the area known as "HTN planning." In HTN planning, the initial plan, which describes the problem, is viewed as a very high-level description of what is to be done—for example, building a house. Plans are refined by applying **action decompositions**. Each action decomposition reduces a high-level action to a partially ordered set of lower-level actions. Action decompositions, therefore, embody knowledge about how to implement actions. For example, building a house might be reduced to obtaining a permit, hiring a contractor, doing the construction, and paying the contractor. (Figure 12.5 shows such a decomposition.) The process continues until only **primitive actions** remain in the plan. Typically, the primitive actions will be actions that the agent can execute automatically. For a general contractor,

ACTION DECOMPOSITION

PRIMITIVE ACTION

"install landscaping" might be primitive because it simply involves calling the landscaping contractor. For the landscaping contractor, actions such as "plant rhododendrons here" might be considered primitive.

In "pure" HTN planning, plans are generated *only* by successive action decompositions. The HTN therefore views planning as a process of making an activity description more *concrete*, rather than (as in the case of state-space and partial-order planning) a process of *constructing* an activity description, starting from the empty activity. It turns out that every STRIPS action description can be turned into an action decomposition (see Exercise 12.6), and that partial-order planning can be viewed as a special case of pure HTN planning. For certain tasks, however—especially "novel" conjunctive goals—the pure HTN viewpoint is rather unnatural, and we prefer to take a *hybrid* approach in which action decompositions are used as plan refinements in partial-order planning, in addition to the standard operations of establishing an open condition and resolving conflicts by adding ordering constraints. (Viewing HTN planning as an extension of partial-order planning has the additional advantage that we can use the same notational conventions instead of introducing a whole new set.) We begin by describing action decomposition in more detail. Then we explain how the partial-order planning algorithm must be modified to handle decompositions, and finally we discuss issues of completeness, complexity, and practicality.

### Representing action decompositions

PLAN LIBRARY

General descriptions of action decomposition methods are stored in a **plan library**, from which they are extracted and instantiated to fit the needs of the plan being constructed. Each method is an expression of the form $Decompose(a, d)$. This says that an action $a$ can be decomposed into the plan $d$, which is represented as a partial-order plan, as described in Section 11.3.

Building a house is a nice, concrete example, so we will use it to illustrate the concept of action decomposition. Figure 12.5 depicts one possible decomposition of the $BuildHouse$ action into four lower-level actions. Figure 12.6 shows some of the action descriptions for the domain, as well as the decomposition for $BuildHouse$ as it would appear in the plan library. There might be other possible decompositions in the library.

EXTERNAL PRECONDITIONS

EXTERNAL EFFECT

PRIMARY EFFECT

SECONDARY EFFECT

The $Start$ action of the decomposition supplies all those preconditions of actions in the plan that are not supplied by other actions. We call these the **external preconditions**. In our example, the external preconditions of the decomposition are $Land$ and $Money$. Similarly, the **external effects**, which are the preconditions of $Finish$, are all those effects of actions in the plan that are not negated by other actions. In our example, the external effects of $BuildHouse$ are $House$ and $\neg Money$. Some HTN planners also distinguish between **primary effects**, such as $House$, and **secondary effects**, such as $\neg Money$. Only primary effects may be used to achieve goals, whereas both kinds of effects might cause conflicts with other actions; this can greatly reduce the search space.[2]

[2] It could also prevent the discovery of unexpected plans. For example, a person facing bankruptcy proceedings can eliminate all liquid assets (i.e., achieve $\neg Money$) by buying or building a house. This plan is useful because current law precludes the seizure of a primary residence by creditors.

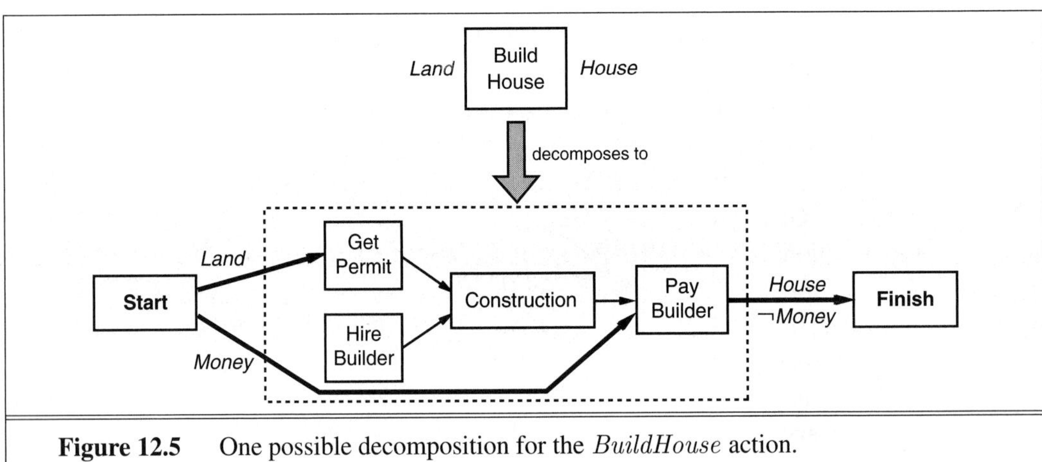


**Figure 12.5** One possible decomposition for the *BuildHouse* action.

$$
\begin{array}{l}
Action(BuyLand,\ \text{PRECOND}{:}Money,\ \text{EFFECT}{:}Land \wedge \neg\ Money)\\
Action(GetLoan,\ \text{PRECOND}{:}GoodCredit,\ \text{EFFECT}{:}Money\ \wedge\ Mortgage)\\
Action(BuildHouse,\ \text{PRECOND}{:}Land,\ \text{EFFECT}{:}House)\\[1ex]
Action(GetPermit,\ \text{PRECOND}{:}Land,\ \text{EFFECT}{:}Permit)\\
Action(HireBuilder,\ \text{EFFECT}{:}\ Contract)\\
Action(Construction,\ \text{PRECOND}{:}Permit\ \wedge\ Contract,\\
\quad \text{EFFECT}{:}HouseBuilt \wedge\ \neg\ Permit)\\
Action(PayBuilder,\ \text{PRECOND}{:}Money\ \wedge\ HouseBuilt,\\
\quad \text{EFFECT}{:}\ \neg\ Money\ \wedge\ House\ \wedge\ \neg\ Contract)\\[1ex]
Decompose(BuildHouse,\\
\quad Plan(\text{STEPS}{:}\ \{S_1 :\ GetPermit,\ S_2 :\ HireBuilder,\\
\qquad\qquad S_3 :\ Construction,\ S_4 :\ PayBuilder\}\\
\qquad \text{ORDERINGS}{:}\ \{Start \prec S_1 \prec S_3 \prec S_4 \prec Finish,\quad Start \prec S_2 \prec S_3\},\\
\qquad \text{LINKS}{:}\ \{Start \xrightarrow{Land} S_1,\ Start \xrightarrow{Money} S_4,\\
\qquad\qquad S_1 \xrightarrow{Permit} S_3,\ S_2 \xrightarrow{Contract} S_3,\ S_3 \xrightarrow{HouseBuilt} S_4,\\
\qquad\qquad S_4 \xrightarrow{House} Finish,\ S_4 \xrightarrow{\neg\ Money} Finish\}))
\end{array}
$$

**Figure 12.6** Action descriptions for the house-building problem and a detailed decomposition for the *BuildHouse* action. The descriptions adopt a simplified view of money and an optimistic view of builders.

A decomposition should be a *correct* implementation of the action. A plan $d$ implements an action $a$ correctly if $d$ is a complete and consistent partial-order plan for the problem of achieving the effects of $a$ given the preconditions of $a$. Obviously, a decomposition will be correct if it is the result of running a sound partial-order planner.

A plan library could contain several decompositions for any given high-level action; for example, there might be another decomposition for *BuildHouse* that describes a process whereby the agent builds a house from rocks and turf with its own bare hands. Each decomposition should be a correct plan, but it could have additional preconditions and effects beyond those stated in the high-level action description. For example, the decomposition for *BuildHouse* in Figure 12.5 requires *Money* in addition to *Land* and has the effect $\neg Money$. The self-build option, on the other hand, doesn't require money, but does require a ready supply of *Rocks* and *Turf*, and could result in a *BadBack*.

Given that a high-level action, such as *BuildHouse*, may have several possible decompositions, it is inevitable that its STRIPS action description will hide some of the preconditions and effects of those decompositions. The preconditions of the high-level action should be the *intersection* of the external preconditions of its decompositions, and the effects should be the intersection of the external effects of the decompositions. Put another way, the high-level preconditions and effects are guaranteed to be a subset of the true preconditions and effects of every primitive implementation.

Two other forms of information hiding should be noted. First, the high-level description completely ignores all **internal effects** of the decompositions. For example, our *BuildHouse* decomposition has temporary internal effects *Permit* and *Contract*.[3] Second, the high-level description does not specify the intervals "inside" the activity during which the high-level preconditions and effects must hold. For example, the *Land* precondition needs to be true (in our very approximate model) only until *GetPermit* is performed, and *House* is true only after *PayBuilder* is performed.

INTERNAL EFFECT

Information hiding of this kind is essential if hierarchical planning is to reduce complexity; we need to be able to reason about high-level actions without worrying about myriad details of the implementations. There is, however, a price to pay. For example, conflicts might exist between internal conditions of one high-level action and internal actions of another, but there is no way to detect this from the high-level descriptions. This issue has significant implications for HTN planning algorithms. In a nutshell, whereas primitive actions can be treated as point events by the planning algorithm, high-level actions have temporal extent within which all sorts of things can be going on.

### Modifying the planner for decompositions

We now show how to modify POP to incorporate HTN planning. We do that by modifying the POP successor function (page 390) to allow decomposition methods to be applied to the current partial plan $P$. The new successor plans are formed by first selecting some nonprimitive action $a'$ in $P$ and then, for any $Decompose(a, d)$ method from the plan library such that $a$ and $a'$ unify with substitution $\theta$, replacing $a'$ with $d' = \text{SUBST}(\theta, d)$.

Figure 12.7 shows an example. At the top, there is a plan $P$ for getting a house. The high-level action, $a' = BuildHouse$, is selected for decomposition. The decomposition $d$ is selected from Figure 12.5, and *BuildHouse* is replaced by this decomposition. An additional step, *GetLoan*, is then introduced to resolve the new open condition, *Money*, that is created by the decomposition step. Replacing an action with its decomposition is a bit like transplant surgery: we have to take the new subplan out of its packaging (the *Start* and *Finish* steps),

[3] *Construction* negates the *Permit*, otherwise the same permit could be used to build many houses. Unfortunately, *Construction* does not terminate the *Contract* because we have to *PayBuilder* first.

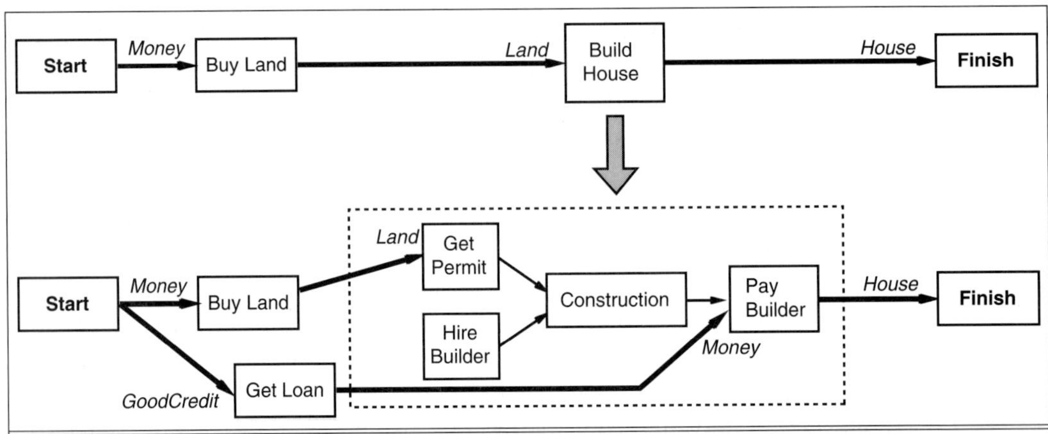


**Figure 12.7** Decomposition of a high-level action within an existing plan. The *BuildHouse* action is replaced by the decomposition from Figure 12.5. The external precondition *Land* is supplied by the existing causal link from *BuyLand*. The external precondition *Money* remains open after the decomposition step, so we add a new action, *GetLoan*.

insert it, and hook everything up properly. There might be several ways to do this. To be more precise, we have for each possible decomposition $d'$,

1. First, the action $a'$ is removed from $P$. Then, for each step $s$ in the decomposition $d'$, we need to choose an action to fill the role of $s$ and add it to the plan. It can be either a new instantiation of $s$ *or an existing step* $s'$ from $P$ that unifies with $s$. For example, the decomposition of a *MakeWine* action might suggest that we *BuyLand*; possibly, we can use the same *BuyLand* action that we already have in the plan. We call this **subtask sharing**.

   SUBTASK SHARING

   In Figure 12.7, there are no sharing opportunities, so new instances of the actions are created. Once the actions have been chosen, all the internal constraints from $d'$ are copied over—for example, that *GetPermit* is ordered before *Construction* and that there is a causal link between these two steps supplying the *Permit* precondition of *Construction*. This completes the task of replacing $a'$ with the instantiation of $d\theta$.

2. The next step is to hook up the ordering constraints for $a'$ in the original plan to the steps in $d'$. First, consider an ordering constraint in $P$ of the form $B \prec a'$. How should $B$ be ordered with respect to the steps in $d'$? The most obvious solution is that $B$ should come before every step in $d'$, and that can be achieved by replacing every constraint of the form $Start \prec s$ in $d'$ with a constraint $B \prec s$. On the other hand, this approach might be too strict! For example, *BuyLand* has to come before *BuildHouse*, but there is no need for *BuyLand* to come before *HireBuilder* in the expanded plan. Imposing an overly strict ordering might prevent some solutions from being found. Therefore, the best solution is for each ordering constraint to record the *reason* for the constraint; then, when a high-level action is expanded, the new ordering constraints can be as relaxed as possible, consistent with the reason for the original constraint. Exactly the same considerations apply when we are replacing constraints of the form $a' \prec C$.

3. The final step is to hook up causal links. If $B \xrightarrow{p} a'$ was a causal link in the original plan, replace it by a set of causal links from $B$ to all the steps in $d'$ with preconditions $p$ that were supplied by the $Start$ step in the decomposition $d$ (i.e., to all the steps in $d'$ for which $p$ is an *external* precondition). In the example, the causal link $BuyLand \xrightarrow{Land} BuildHouse$ is replaced by the link $BuyLand \xrightarrow{Land} Permit$. (The $Money$ precondition for $PayBuilder$ in the decomposition becomes an open condition, because no action in the original plan supplies $Money$ to $BuildHouse$.) Similarly, for each causal link $a' \xrightarrow{p} C$ in the plan, replace it with a set of causal links to $C$ from whichever step in $d'$ supplies $p$ to the $Finish$ step in the decomposition $d$ (i.e., from the step in $d'$ that has $p$ as an *external* effect). In the example, we replace the link $BuildHouse \xrightarrow{House} Finish$ with the link $PayBuilder \xrightarrow{House} Finish$.

This completes the additions required for generating decompositions in the context of the POP planner.[4]

Additional modifications to the POP algorithm are required because of the fact that high-level actions *hide information* about their final primitive implementations. In particular, the original POP algorithm backtracks with failure if the current plan contains an irresolvable conflict—that is, if an action conflicts with a causal link but cannot be ordered either before or after the link. (Figure 11.9 shows an example.) With high-level actions, on the other hand, apparently irresolvable conflicts can sometimes be resolved by *decomposing* the conflicting actions and interleaving their steps. An example is given in Figure 12.8. Thus, it may be the case that a complete and consistent primitive plan can be obtained by decomposition *even when no complete and consistent high-level plan exists.* This possibility means that a complete HTN planner must forgo many pruning opportunities that are available to a standard POP planner. Alternatively, we can prune anyway and hope that no solution is missed.

## Discussion

Let's begin with the bad news: pure HTN planning (where the only allowable plan refinement is decomposition) is undecidable, *even though the underlying state space is finite*! This might seem very depressing, since the point of HTN planning is to gain efficiency. The difficulty arises because action decompositions can be **recursive**—for example, going for a walk can be implemented by taking a step and then going for a walk—so HTN plans can be arbitrarily long. In particular, the shortest HTN solution could be arbitrarily long, so that there is no way to terminate the search after any fixed time. There are, however, at least three ways to look on the bright side:

1. We can rule out recursion, which very few domains require. In that case, all HTN plans are of finite length and can be enumerated.
2. We can bound the length of solutions we care about. Because the state space is finite, a plan that has more steps than there are states in the state space *must* include a loop that visits the same state twice. We would lose little by ruling out HTN solutions of this kind, and we would control the search.

[4] There are some additional minor modifications required for handling conflict resolution with high-level actions; the interested reader can consult the papers cited at the end of the chapter.

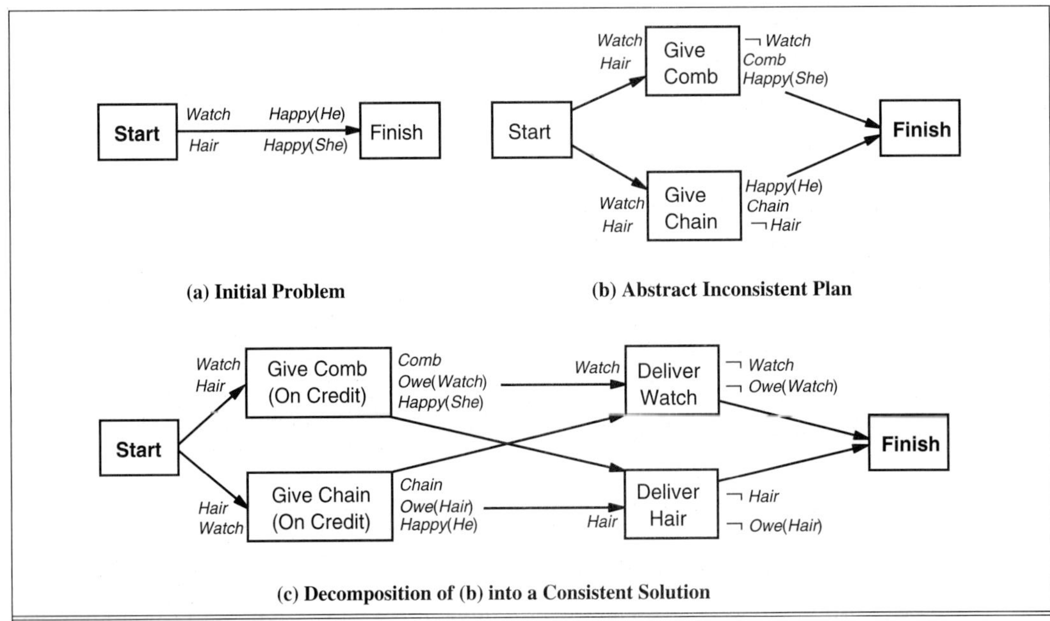


**Figure 12.8** The *Gift of the Magi* problem, taken from the O. Henry story, shows an inconsistent abstract plan that nevertheless can be decomposed into a consistent solution. Part (a) shows the problem: A poor couple has only two prized possessions—he a gold watch and she her beautiful long hair. Each plans to buy a present to make the other happy. He decides to trade his watch to buy a silver comb for her hair, and she decides to sell her hair to get a gold chain for his watch. In (b) the partial plan is inconsistent, because there is no way to order the "Give Comb" and "Give Chain" abstract steps without a conflict. (We assume that the "Give Comb" action has the precondition $Hair$, because if the wife doesn't have her long hair, the action won't have the intended effect of making her happy, and similarly for the "Give Chain" action.) In (c) we decompose the "Give Comb" step with an "installment plan" method. In the first step of the decomposition, the husband takes possession of the comb and gives it to his wife, while agreeing to deliver the watch in payment at a later date. In the second step, the watch is handed over and the obligation is fulfilled. A similar method decomposes the "Give Chain" step. As long as both giving steps are ordered before the delivery steps, this decomposition solves the problem. (Note that it relies on the problem being defined so that the happiness of using the chain with the watch or the comb with the hair persists even after the possessions are surrendered.)

3. We can adopt the hybrid approach that combines POP and HTN planning. Partial-order planning by itself suffices to decide whether a plan exists, so the hybrid problem is clearly decidable.

We need to be a little bit careful with the third answer. POP can string together primitive actions in arbitrary ways, so we might find ourselves with solutions that are very hard to understand and do not have the nice, hierarchical organization of HTN plans. An appropriate compromise is to control the hybrid search so that action decompositions are preferred over adding new actions, although not to such an extent that arbitrarily long HTN plans are generated before any primitive actions can be added. One way to do this is to use a cost function that gives a discount for actions introduced by decomposition; the larger the discount, the more the search will resemble pure HTN planning and the more hierarchical the solution will be. Hierarchical plans are usually much easier to execute in realistic settings, and are easier to fix when things go wrong.

Another important characteristic of HTN plans is the possibility of subtask sharing. Recall that subtask sharing means using the same action to implement two different steps in plan decompositions. If we disallow subtask sharing, then each instantiation of a decomposition $d'$ can be done in only one way, rather than many, thereby greatly pruning the search space. Usually, this pruning saves some time and at worst leads to a solution that is slightly longer than optimal. In some cases, however, it can be more problematic. For example, consider the goal "enjoy a honeymoon and raise a family." The plan library might come up with "get married and go to Hawaii" for the first subgoal and "get married and have two children" for the second. Without subtask sharing, the plan will include two distinct marriage actions, often considered highly undesirable.

An interesting example of the costs and benefits of subtask sharing occurs in optimizing compilers. Consider the problem of compiling the expression $\tan(x) - \sin(x)$. Most compilers accomplish this by merging two separate subroutine calls in a trivial way: all the steps of $\tan$ come before any of the steps of $\sin$. But consider the following Taylor series approximations for $\sin$ and $\tan$:

$$\tan x \approx x + \frac{x^3}{3} + \frac{2x^5}{15} + \frac{17x^7}{315}; \quad \sin x \approx x - \frac{x^3}{6} + \frac{x^5}{120} - \frac{x^7}{5040}.$$

An HTN planner with subtask sharing could generate a more efficient solution, because it could choose to implement many steps of the sin computation with existing steps from $\tan$. Most compilers do not do this kind of interprocedural sharing because it would take too much time to consider all the possible shared plans. Instead, most compilers generate each subplan independently, and then perhaps modify the result with a peephole optimizer.

Given all the additional complications caused by the introduction of action decompositions, why do we believe that HTN planning can be efficient? The actual sources of complexity are hard to analyze in practice, so we consider an idealized case. Suppose, for example, that we want to construct a plan with $n$ actions. For a nonhierarchical, forward state-space planner with $b$ allowable actions at each state, the cost is $O(b^n)$. For an HTN planner, let us suppose a very regular decomposition structure: each nonprimitive action has $d$ possible decompositions, each into $k$ actions at the next lower level. We want to know how many different decomposition trees there are with this structure. Now, if there are $n$ actions at the primitive level, then the number of levels below the root is $\log_k n$, so the number of internal decomposition nodes is $1 + k + k^2 + \cdots + k^{\log_k n - 1} = (n-1)/(k-1)$. Each internal node has $d$ possible decompositions, so there are $d^{(n-1)/(k-1)}$ possible regular decomposition trees that could be constructed. Examining this formula, we see that keeping $d$ small and $k$ large can result in huge savings: essentially we are taking the $k$th root of the nonhierarchical cost, if $b$ and $d$ are comparable. On the other hand, constructing a plan library that has a small number of long decompositions, but nonetheless allows us to solve any problem, is not always possible. Another way of saying this is that long macros that are usable across a wide range of problems are extremely precious.

Another, and perhaps better, reason for believing that HTN planning is efficient is that it works in practice. Almost all planners for large-scale applications are HTN planners, because HTN planning allows the human expert to provide the crucial knowledge about how to perform complex tasks so that large plans can be constructed with little computational effort. For example, O-PLAN (Bell and Tate, 1985), which combines HTN planning with scheduling, has been used to develop production plans for Hitachi. A typical problem involves a product line of 350 different products, 35 assembly machines, and over 2000 different operations. The planner generates a 30-day schedule with three 8-hour shifts a day, involving millions of steps.

The key to HTN planning, then, is the construction of a plan library containing known methods for implementing complex, high-level actions. One method of constructing the library is to *learn* the methods from problem-solving experience. After the excruciating experience of constructing a plan from scratch, the agent can save the plan in the library as a method for implementing the high-level action defined by the task. In this way, the agent can become more and more competent over time as new methods are built on top of old methods. One important aspect of this learning process is the ability to *generalize* the methods that are constructed, eliminating detail that is specific to the problem instance (e.g., the name of the builder or the address of the plot of land) and keeping just the key elements of the plan. Methods for achieving this kind of generalization are described in Chapter 19. It seems to us inconceivable that humans could be as competent as they are without some such mechanism.

## 12.3 PLANNING AND ACTING IN NONDETERMINISTIC DOMAINS

So far we have considered only **classical planning** domains that are fully observable, static, and deterministic. Furthermore, we have assumed that the action descriptions are correct and complete. In these circumstances, an agent can plan first and then execute the plan "with its eyes closed." In an uncertain environment, on the other hand, an agent must use its percepts to discover what is happening while the plan is being executed and possibly modify or replace the plan if something unexpected happens.

Agents have to deal with both *incomplete* and *incorrect* information. Incompleteness arises because the world is partially observable, nondeterministic, or both. For example, the door to the office supply cabinet might or might not be locked; one of my keys might or might not open the door if it is locked; and I might or might not be aware of these kinds of incompleteness in my knowledge. Thus, my model of the world is weak, but correct. On the other hand, incorrectness arises because the world does not necessarily match my model of the world; for example, I might *believe* that my key opens the supply cabinet, but I could be wrong if the locks have been changed. Without the ability to handle incorrect information, an agent can end up being as unintelligent as the dung beetle (page 37), which attempts to plug up its nest with a ball of dung even after the ball has been removed from its grasp.

The possibility of having complete or correct knowledge depends on *how much* indeterminacy there is in the world. With **bounded indeterminacy**, actions can have unpredictable

BOUNDED INDETERMINACY

effects, but the possible effects can be listed in the action description axioms. For example, when we flip a coin, it is reasonable to say that the outcome will be *Heads* or *Tails*. An agent can cope with bounded indeterminacy by making plans that work in all possible circumstances. With **unbounded indeterminacy**, on the other hand, the set of possible preconditions or effects either is unknown or is too large to be enumerated completely. This would be the case in very complex or dynamic domains such as driving, economic planning, and military strategy. An agent can cope with unbounded indeterminacy only if it is prepared to revise its plans and/or its knowledge base. Unbounded indeterminacy is closely related to the **qualification problem** discussed in Chapter 10—the impossibility of listing *all* the preconditions required for a real-world action to have its intended effect.

UNBOUNDED INDETERMINACY

There are four planning methods for handling indeterminacy. The first two are suitable for bounded indeterminacy, and the second two for unbounded indeterminacy:

SENSORLESS PLANNING

◇ **Sensorless planning**: Also called **conformant planning**, this method constructs standard, sequential plans that are to be executed without perception. The sensorless planning algorithm must ensure that the plan achieves the goal *in all possible circumstances*, regardless of the true initial state and the actual action outcomes. Sensorless planning relies on **coercion**—the idea that the world can be forced into a given state even when the agent has only partial information about the current state. Coercion is not always possible, so sensorless planning is often inapplicable. Sensorless problem solving, involving search in belief state space, was described in Chapter 3.

CONDITIONAL PLANNING

SENSING ACTIONS

◇ **Conditional planning**: Also known as **contingency planning**, this approach deals with bounded indeterminacy by constructing a conditional plan with different branches for the different contingencies that could arise. Just as in classical planning, the agent plans first and then executes the plan that was produced. The agent finds out which part of the plan to execute by including **sensing actions** in the plan to test for the appropriate conditions. In the air transport domain, for example, we could have plans that say "check whether SFO airport is operational. If so, fly there; otherwise, fly to Oakland." Conditional planning is covered in Section 12.4.

EXECUTION MONITORING AND REPLANNING

◇ **Execution monitoring and replanning**: In this approach, the agent can use any of the preceding planning techniques (classical, sensorless, or conditional) to construct a plan, but it also uses **execution monitoring** to judge whether the plan has a provision for the actual current situation or need to be revised. **Replanning** occurs when something goes wrong. In this way, the agent can handle unbounded indeterminacy. For example, even if a replanning agent did not envision the possibility of SFO's being closed, it can recognize that situation when it occurs and call the planner again to find a new path to the goal. Replanning agents are covered in Section 12.5.

CONTINUOUS PLANNING

◇ **Continuous planning**: All the planners we have seen so far are designed to achieve a goal and then stop. A continuous planner is designed to persist over a lifetime. It can handle unexpected circumstances in the environment, even if these occur while the agent is in the middle of constructing a plan. It can also handle the abandonment of goals and the creation of additional goals by **goal formulation**. Continuous planning is described in Section 12.6.

Let's consider an example to clarify the differences among the various kinds of agents. The problem is this: given an initial state with a chair, a table, and some cans of paint, with everything of unknown color, achieve the state where the chair and table have the same color.

A **classical planning** agent could not handle this problem, because the initial state is not fully specified—we don't know what color the furniture is.

A **sensorless planning** agent must find a plan that works without requiring any sensors during plan execution. The solution is to open any can of paint and apply it to both chair and table, thus **coercing** them to be the same color (even though the agent doesn't know what the color is). Coercion is most appropriate when propositions are expensive or impossible to perceive. For example, doctors often prescribe a broad-spectrum antibiotic rather than using the conditional plan of doing a blood test, then waiting for the results to come back, and then prescribing a more specific antibiotic. They do this because the delays and costs involved in performing the blood tests are usually too great.

A **conditional planning** agent can generate a better plan: first sense the color of the table and chair; if they are already the same then the plan is done. If not, sense the labels on the paint cans; if there is a can that is the same color as one piece of furniture, then apply the paint to the other piece. Otherwise paint both pieces with any color.

A **replanning** agent could generate the same plan as the conditional planner, or it could generate fewer branches at first and fill in the others at execution time as needed. It could also deal with incorrectness of its action descriptions. For example, suppose that the $Paint(obj, color)$ action is believed to have the deterministic effect $Color(obj, color)$. A conditional planner would just assume that the effect has occurred once the action has been executed, but a replanning agent would check for the effect, and if it were not true (perhaps because the agent was careless and missed a spot), it could then replan to repaint the spot. We will return to this example on page 441.

A **continuous planning** agent, in addition to handling unexpected events, can revise its plans appropriately if, say, we add the goal of having dinner on the table, so that the painting plan must be postponed.

In the real world, agents use a combination of approaches. Car manufacturers sell spare tires and air bags, which are physical embodiments of conditional plan branches designed to handle punctures or crashes; on the other hand, most car drivers never consider these possibilities, so they respond to punctures and crashes as replanning agents. In general, agents create conditional plans only for those contingencies that have important consequences and a nonnegligible chance of going wrong. Thus, a car driver contemplating a trip across the Sahara desert might do well to consider explicitly the possibility of breakdowns, whereas a trip to the supermarket requires less advance planning.

The agents we describe in this chapter are designed to handle indeterminacy, but are not capable of making tradeoffs between the probability of success and the cost of plan construction. Chapter 16 provides additional tools for dealing with these issues.

## 12.4 CONDITIONAL PLANNING

Conditional planning is a way to deal with uncertainty by checking what is actually happening in the environment at predetermined points in the plan. Conditional planning is simplest to explain for fully observable environments, so we will begin with that case. The partially observable case is more difficult, but more interesting.

### Conditional planning in fully observable environments

Full observability means that the agent always knows the current state. If the environment is nondeterministic, however, the agent will not be able to predict the *outcome* of its actions. A conditional planning agent handles nondeterminism by building into the plan (at planning time) conditional steps that will check the state of the environment (at execution time) to decide what to do next. The problem, then, is how to construct these conditional plans.

We will use as our example domain the venerable **vacuum world**, whose state space, for the deterministic case, is laid out on page 65. Recall that the available actions are *Left*, $Right$, and $Suck$. We will need some propositions to define the states: let $AtL$ ($AtR$) be true if the agent is in the left (right) state,[5] and let *CleanL* (*CleanR*) be true if the left (right) state is clean. The first thing we need to do is augment the STRIPS language to allow for nondeterminism. To do this, we allow actions to have **disjunctive effects**, meaning that the action can have two or more different outcomes whenever it is executed. For example, suppose that moving *Left* sometimes fails. Then the normal action description

DISJUNCTIVE EFFECTS

$$Action(Left, \text{PRECOND}{:}AtR, \text{EFFECT}{:}AtL \land \neg AtR)$$

must be modified to include a disjunctive effect:

$$Action(Left, \text{PRECOND}{:}AtR, \text{EFFECT}{:}AtL \lor AtR)\ . \quad (12.1)$$

CONDITIONAL EFFECTS

We will also find it useful to allow actions to have **conditional effects**, wherein the effect of the action depends on the state in which it is executed. Conditional effects appear in the EFFECT slot of an action, and have the syntax "**when** <*condition*>: <*effect*>." For example, to model the $Suck$ action, we would write

$$Action(Suck, \text{PRECOND}{:}, \text{EFFECT}{:}(\textbf{when } AtL{:}\ CleanL) \land (\textbf{when } AtR{:}\ CleanR))].$$

Conditional effects do not introduce indeterminacy, but they can help to model it. For example, suppose we have a devious vacuum cleaner that sometimes dumps dirt on the destination square when it moves, but only if that square is clean. This can be modeled with a description such as

$$Action(Left, \text{PRECOND}{:}AtR, \text{EFFECT}{:}AtL \lor (AtL \land \textbf{when } CleanL{:}\ \neg CleanL)),$$

which is both disjunctive and conditional.[6] To create conditional plans, we need **conditional steps**. We will write these using the syntax "**if** <$test$> **then** $plan\_A$ **else** $plan\_B$," where

CONDITIONAL STEPS

[5] Obviously, $AtR$ is true iff $\neg AtL$ is true, and vice versa. We use two propositions mainly to improve readability.

[6] The conditional effect **when** *CleanL*: $\neg$*CleanL* may look a little odd. Remember, however, that here *CleanL* refers to the situation *before* the action and $\neg$*CleanL* refers to the situation *after* the action.

<*test*> is a Boolean function of the state variables. For example, a conditional step for the vacuum world might be, "**if** $AtL \wedge CleanL$ **then** $Right$ **else** $Suck$." The execution of such a step proceeds in the obvious way. By nesting conditional steps, plans become trees.

We want conditional plans that work *regardless of which action outcomes actually occur*. We have seen this problem before, in a different guise. In two-player games (Chapter 6), we want moves that will win *regardless of which moves the opponent makes*. For this reason, nondeterministic planning problems are often called **games against nature**.

GAMES AGAINST NATURE

Let us consider a specific example in the vacuum world. The initial state has the robot in the right square of a clean world; because the environment is fully observable, the agent knows the full state description, $AtR \wedge CleanL \wedge CleanR$. The goal state has the robot in the left square of a clean world. This would be quite trivial, were it not for the "double Murphy" vacuum cleaner that sometimes deposits dirt when it moves to a clean destination square and sometimes deposits dirt if $Suck$ is applied to a clean square.

A "game tree" for this environment is shown in Figure 12.9. Actions are taken by the robot in the "state" nodes of the tree, and nature decides what the outcome will be at the "chance" nodes, shown as circles. A solution is a subtree that (1) has a goal node at every leaf, (2) specifies one action at each of its "state" nodes, and (3) includes every outcome branch at each of its "chance" nodes. The solution is shown in bold lines in the figure; it corresponds to the plan $[Left,$ **if** $AtL \wedge CleanL \wedge CleanR$ **then** $[\,]$ **else** $Suck]$. (For now, because we are using a state-space planner, the tests in conditional steps will be complete state descriptions.)

For exact solutions of games, we use the **minimax algorithm** (Figure 6.3). For conditional planning, there are typically two modifications. First, MAX and MIN nodes can become

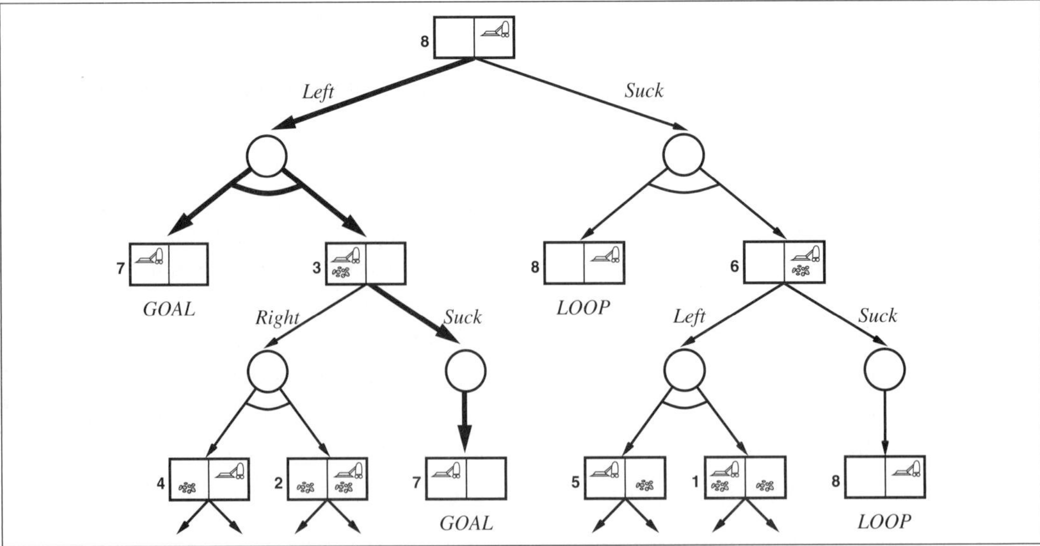


**Figure 12.9** The first two levels of the search tree for the "double Murphy" vacuum world. State nodes are OR nodes where some action must be chosen. Chance nodes, shown as circles, are AND nodes where every outcome must be handled, as indicated by the arc linking the outgoing branches. The solution is shown in bold lines.

```
function AND-OR-GRAPH-SEARCH(problem) returns a conditional plan, or failure
   OR-SEARCH(INITIAL-STATE[problem], problem, [ ])
```

```
function OR-SEARCH(state, problem, path) returns a conditional plan, or failure
   if GOAL-TEST[problem](state) then return the empty plan
   if state is on path then return failure
   for each action, state_set in SUCCESSORS[problem](state) do
      plan ← AND-SEARCH(state_set, problem, [state | path])
      if plan ≠ failure then return [action | plan]
   return failure
```

```
function AND-SEARCH(state_set, problem, path) returns a conditional plan, or failure
   for each s_i in state_set do
      plan_i ← OR-SEARCH(s_i, problem, path)
      if plan = failure then return failure
   return [if s_1 then plan_1 else if s_2 then plan_2 else ... if s_{n-1} then plan_{n-1} else plan_n]
```

**Figure 12.10** An algorithm for searching AND–OR graphs generated by nondeterministic environments. We assume that SUCCESSORS returns a list of actions, each associated with a *set* of possible outcomes. The aim is to find a conditional plan that reaches a goal state in all circumstances.

OR and AND nodes. Intuitively, the plan needs to take *some* action at every state it reaches, but must handle *every* outcome for the action it takes. Second, the algorithm needs to return a conditional plan rather than just a single move. At an OR node, the plan is just the action selected, followed by whatever comes next. At an AND node, the plan is a nested series of if–then–else steps specifying subplans for each outcome; the tests in these steps are the complete state descriptions.[7]

Formally speaking, the search space we have defined is an AND–OR **graph**. In Chapter 7, AND–OR graphs showed up in propositional Horn clause inference. Here, the branches are actions rather than logical inference steps, but the algorithm is the same. Figure 12.10 gives a recursive, depth-first algorithm for AND–OR graph search.

One key aspect of the algorithm is the way in which it deals with cycles, which often arise in nondeterministic planning problems (e.g., if an action sometimes has no effect, or if an unintended effect can be corrected). If the current state is identical to a state on the path from the root, then it returns with failure. This doesn't mean that there is *no* solution from the current state; it simply means that if there *is* a noncyclic solution, it must be reachable from the earlier incarnation of the current state, so the new incarnation can be discarded. With this check, we ensure that the algorithm terminates in every finite state space, because every path must reach a goal, a dead end, or a repeated state. Notice that the algorithm does not check whether the current state is a repetition of a state on some *other* path from the root. Exercise 12.15 investigates this issue.

[7] Such plans could also be written using a **case** construct.

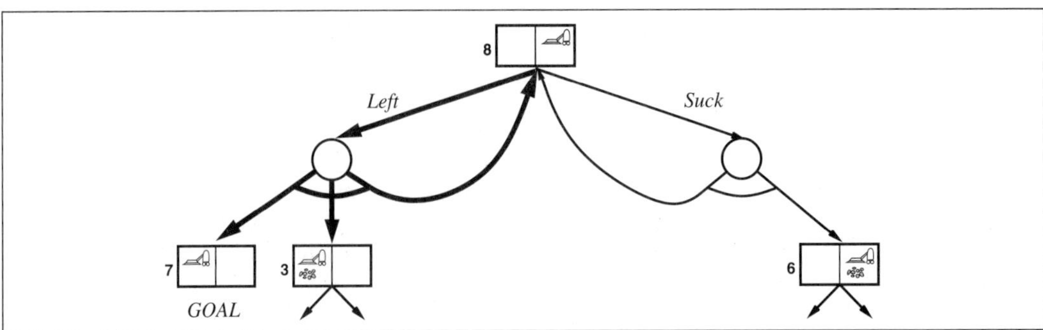


**Figure 12.11** The first level of the search graph for the "triple Murphy" vacuum world, where we have shown cycles explicitly. All solutions for this problem are cyclic plans.

The plans returned by AND-OR-GRAPH-SEARCH contain conditional steps that test the entire state description to decide on a branch. In many cases, we can get away with less exhaustive tests. For example, the solution plan in Figure 12.9 could be written simply as $[Left, \textbf{if } CleanL \textbf{ then } [\,] \textbf{ else } Suck]$. This is because the single test, *CleanL*, suffices to divide the states at the AND-node into two singleton sets, so that after the test the agent knows exactly what state it is in. In fact, a series of if–then–else tests of single variables always suffices to divide a set of states into singletons, *provided* that the state is fully observable. We could, therefore, restrict the tests to be of single variables without loss of generality.

There is one final complication that often arises in nondeterministic domains: things don't always work the first time, and one has to try again. For example, consider the "triple Murphy" vacuum cleaner, which (in addition to its previously stated habits) sometimes fails to move when commanded—for example, *Left* can have the disjunctive effect $AtL \vee AtR$, as in Equation (12.1). Now the plan $[Left, \textbf{if } CleanL \textbf{ then } [\,] \textbf{ else } Suck]$ is no longer guaranteed to work. Figure 12.11 shows part of the the search graph; clearly, there are no longer any acyclic solutions, and AND-OR-GRAPH-SEARCH would return with failure. There is, however, a **cyclic solution**, which is to keep trying *Left* until it works. We can express this solution by adding a **label** to denote some portion of the plan and using that label later instead of repeating the plan itself. Thus, our cyclic solution is

CYCLIC SOLUTION

LABEL

$$[L_1 : \; Left, \textbf{if } AtR \textbf{ then } L_1 \textbf{ else if } CleanL \textbf{ then } [\,] \textbf{ else } Suck] \; .$$

(A better syntax for the looping part of this plan would be "**while** $AtR$ **do** *Left*.") The modifications needed to AND-OR-GRAPH-SEARCH are covered in Exercise 12.16. The key realization is that a loop in the state space back to a state $L$ translates to a loop in the plan back to the point where the subplan for state $L$ is executed.

Now we have the ability to synthesize complex plans that look more like programs, with conditionals and loops. Unfortunately, these loops are, potentially, *infinite* loops. For example, nothing in the action representation for the triple Murphy world says that *Left* will eventually succeed. Cyclic plans are therefore less desirable than acyclic plans, but they may be considered solutions, provided that every leaf is a goal state and a leaf is reachable from every point in the plan.

### Conditional planning in partially observable environments

The preceding section dealt with fully observable environments, which have the advantage that conditional tests can ask any question at all and be sure of getting an answer. In the real world, partial observability is much more common. In the initial state of a partially observable planning problem, the agent knows only a certain amount about the actual state. The simplest way to model this situation is to say that the initial state belongs to a **state set**; the state set is a way of describing the agent's initial **belief state**.[8]

Suppose that a vacuum-world agent knows that it is in the right-hand square and that the square is clean, but it cannot sense the presence or absence of dirt in other squares. Then *as far as it knows* it could be in one of two states: the left-hand square might be either clean or dirty. This belief state is marked $A$ in Figure 12.12. The figure shows part of the AND–OR graph for the "alternate double Murphy" vacuum world, in which dirt can sometimes be left behind when the agent leaves a clean square.[9] If the world were fully observable, the agent could construct a cyclic solution of the form "Keep moving left and right, sucking up dirt whenever it appears, until both squares are clean and I'm in the left square." (See Exercise 12.16.) Unfortunately, with local dirt sensing, this plan is unexecutable, because the truth value of the test "both squares are clean" cannot be determined.

Let us look at how the AND–OR graph is constructed. From belief state $A$, we show the outcome of moving $Left$. (The other actions make no sense.) Because the agent can leave dirt behind, the two possible initial worlds become four possible worlds, as shown in $B$ and $C$. The worlds form two distinct belief states, classified by the available sensor information.[10] In $B$, the agent knows $CleanL$; in $C$ it knows $\neg CleanL$. From $C$, cleaning up the dirt moves the agent to $B$. From $B$, moving $Right$ might or might not leave dirt behind, so there are again four possible worlds, divided according to the agent's knowledge of $CleanR$ (back to $A$) or $\neg CleanR$ (belief state $D$).

In sum, nondeterministic, partially observable environments give us an AND–OR graph of belief states. Conditional plans can be found, therefore, using exactly the same algorithm as in the fully observable case, namely AND-OR-GRAPH-SEARCH. Another way to understand what's going on is to see that the agent's *belief* state is *always* fully observable—it always knows what it knows. "Standard" fully observable problem solving is just a special case in which every belief state is a singleton set containing exactly one physical state.

Are we done? Not quite! We still need to decide how belief states should be represented, how sensing works, and how action descriptions should be written in this new setting.

There are three basic choices for belief states:

1. Sets of full state descriptions. For example, the initial belief state in Figure 12.12 is

$$\{ (AtR \land CleanR \land CleanL),\ (AtR \land CleanR \land \neg CleanL) \}\ .$$

This representation is simple to work with, but very expensive: if there are $n$ Boolean

---

[8] These concepts are introduced in Section 3.6, which the reader might wish to consult before proceeding.

[9] Parents with young children will be familiar with this phenomenon. Apologies to others, as usual.

[10] Notice that they are *not* classified by whether there is dirt left behind when the agent moves. Branching in belief-state space is caused by alternative knowledge outcomes, not alternative physical outcomes.

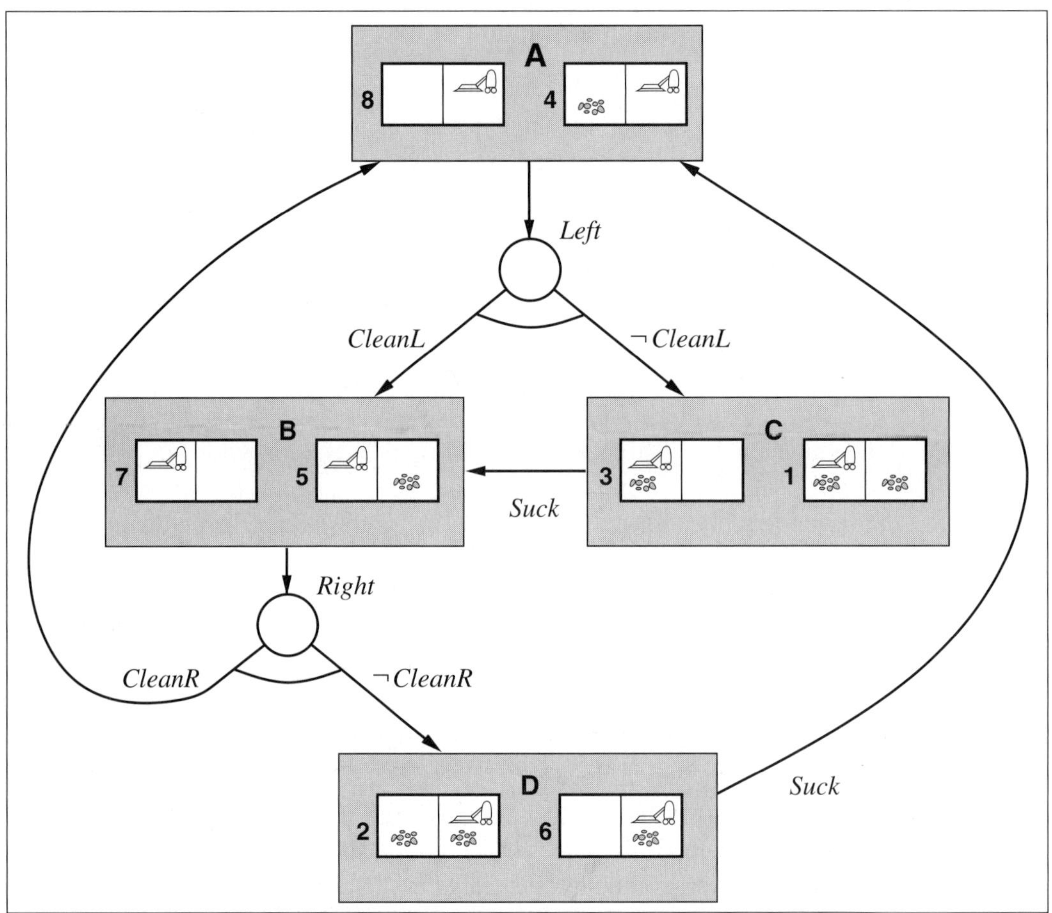


**Figure 12.12** Part of the AND–OR graph for the "alternate double Murphy" vacuum world, in which dirt can sometimes be left behind when the agent leaves a clean square. The agent cannot sense dirt in other squares.

propositions defining the state, then a belief state can contain $O(2^n)$ physical state descriptions, each of size $O(n)$. Exponentially large belief states will occur whenever the agent knows only a fraction of the propositions—the less it knows, the more possible states it might be in.

2. Logical sentences that capture exactly the set of possible worlds in the belief state. For example, the initial state can be written as

$$AtR \wedge CleanR \,.$$

Clearly, every belief state can be captured exactly by a single logical sentence; if we have to, we can use the disjunction of all the conjunctive state descriptions, but our example shows that more compact sentences could exist.

One drawback with general logical sentences is that, because there are many different, logically equivalent sentences that describe the same belief state, repeated state checking in the graph search algorithm can require general theorem proving. For this reason, we would like a *canonical* representation for sentences in which every belief state corresponds to exactly one sentence.[11] One such representation uses a conjunction of literals ordered by proposition name—$AtR \wedge CleanR$ is an example. This is just the standard state representation under the **open-world assumption** from Chapter 11. Not all logical sentences can be written in such form—for example, there is no way to represent $AtL \vee CleanR$—but many domains can be handled.

3. **Knowledge propositions** describing the agent's knowledge. (See also Section 7.7.) For the initial state, we have

   $$K(AtR) \wedge K(CleanR)\ .$$

   Here, $K$ stands for "knows that" and $K(P)$ means that the agent knows that $P$ is true.[12] With knowledge propositions, we use the **closed-world assumption**—if a knowledge proposition does not appear in the list, it is assumed false. For example, $\neg K(CleanL)$ and $\neg K(\neg CleanL)$ are implicit in the sentence above, so it captures the fact that the agent is ignorant of the truth value of $CleanL$.

It turns out that the second and third options are roughly equivalent, but we will use the third option, knowledge propositions, because it gives a more vivid description of sensing and because we already know how to write STRIPS descriptions with the closed-world assumption.

In both options, each proposition symbol can appear in one of three ways: positive, negative, or unknown. Therefore, there are exactly $3^n$ possible belief states that can be described this way. Now, the set of belief states is the powerset (set of all subsets) of the set of physical states. There are $2^n$ physical states, so there are $2^{2^n}$ belief states—far more than $3^n$, so options 2 and 3 are quite restricted as representations of belief states. This currently is believed to be inevitable, because *any scheme capable of representing every possible belief state will require* $O(\log_2(2^{2^n})) = O(2^n)$ *bits to represent each one in the worst case.* Our simple schemes require only $O(n)$ bits to represent each belief state, trading expressiveness for compactness. In particular, if an action occurs, one of whose preconditions is unknown, then the resulting belief state will not be exactly representable and the action outcome becomes unknown.

Now we need to decide how sensing works. There are two choices here. We can have **automatic sensing**, which means that at every time step the agent gets all the available percepts. The example in Figure 12.12 assumes automatic sensing of location and local dirt. Alternatively, we can insist on **active sensing**, which means that percepts are obtained only by executing specific **sensory actions** such as $CheckDirt$ and $CheckLocation$. We will treat each kind of sensing in turn.

AUTOMATIC SENSING

ACTIVE SENSING

SENSORY ACTIONS

Let us now write an action description using knowledge propositions. Suppose the agent moves $Left$ in the alternate-double-Murphy world with automatic local dirt sensing; according to the rules for that world, the agent might or might not leave dirt behind if the square was clean. As a *physical* effect, this would be *disjunctive*; but as a *knowledge* effect, it

[11] The best-known canonical representation for a general propositional sentence is the **binary decision diagram**, or BDD (Bryant, 1992).

[12] This is the same notation used for circuit-based agents in Chapter 7. Some authors use it to mean "knows whether $P$ is true." Translating between the two representations is straightforward.

simply deletes the agent's knowledge of $CleanR$. The agent will also know whether $CleanL$ is true, one way or the other, because of local dirt sensing, and it will know that it is $AtL$:

$$\begin{aligned}&Action(Left, \text{PRECOND:}AtR,\\ &\quad \text{EFFECT:}K(AtL) \wedge \neg K(AtR) \wedge \textbf{when } CleanR\text{: } \neg K(CleanR) \wedge\\ &\qquad \textbf{when } CleanL\text{: } K(CleanL) \wedge\\ &\qquad \textbf{when } \neg CleanL\text{: } K(\neg CleanL))\,.\end{aligned} \tag{12.2}$$

Notice that the preconditions and **when** conditions are plain propositions, not knowledge propositions. This is as it should be, because the outcomes of actions do depend on the actual world, but how do we check the truth of those conditions when all we have is the belief state? If the agent *knows* a proposition, say $K(AtR)$, in the current belief state, then the proposition must be true in the current physical state, and indeed the action is applicable. If the agent doesn't know a proposition—for example, the **when** condition $CleanL$—then the belief state must include worlds in which $CleanL$ is true and worlds in which $CleanL$ is false. It is this that gives rise to multiple belief states resulting from the action. Thus, if the initial state is $(K(AtR) \wedge K(CleanR))$, then after the move $Left$, the two outcome belief states are $(K(AtL) \wedge K(CleanL))$ and $(K(AtL) \wedge K(\neg CleanL))$. In both cases, the truth value of $CleanL$ is known, so the $CleanL$ test can be used in the plan.

With active sensing (as opposed to automatic sensing), the agent gets new percepts only by asking for them. Thus, after moving $Left$, the agent will not know whether the left-hand square is dirty, so the last two conditional effects no longer appear in the action description in Equation (12.2). To find out whether the square is dirty, the agent can $CheckDirt$:

$$\begin{aligned}&Action(CheckDirt, \text{EFFECT:}\textbf{when } AtL \wedge CleanL\text{: } K(CleanL) \wedge\\ &\qquad \textbf{when } AtL \wedge \neg CleanL\text{: } K(\neg CleanL) \wedge\\ &\qquad \textbf{when } AtR \wedge CleanR\text{: } K(CleanR) \wedge\\ &\qquad \textbf{when } AtR \wedge \neg CleanR\text{: } K(\neg CleanR))\,.\end{aligned} \tag{12.3}$$

It is easy to show that $Left$ followed by $CheckDirt$ in the active sensing setting results in the same two belief states as $Left$ did in the automatic sensing setting. With active sensing, it is always the case that physical actions map a belief state into a single successor belief state. Multiple belief states can be introduced only by sensory actions, which provide specific knowledge and hence allow conditional tests to be used in plans.

We have described a general approach to conditional planning based on state-space AND–OR search. The approach has proved to be quite effective on some test problems, but other problems are intractable. Theoretically, it can be shown that conditional planning belongs to a harder complexity class than classical planning. Recall that the definition of the class NP is that a candidate solution can be checked to see whether it really is a solution in polynomial time. This is true for classical plans (at least, for those of polynomial size) so the problem of classical planning is in *NP*. But in conditional planning a candidate must be checked to see whether, for *all* possible states, there exists *some* path through the plan that satisfies the goal. Checking the "all/some" combination cannot be done in polynomial time, so conditional planning is harder than *NP*. The only way out is to ignore some of the possible contingencies during the planning phase and to handle them only when they actually occur. This is the approach we pursue in the next section.

## 12.5 EXECUTION MONITORING AND REPLANNING

An **execution monitoring** agent checks its percepts to see whether everything is going according to plan. Murphy's law tells us that even the best-laid plans of mice, men, and conditional planning agents frequently fail. The problem is unbounded indeterminacy—some unanticipated circumstance will always arise for which the agent's actions descriptions are incorrect. Therefore, execution monitoring is a necessity in realistic environments. We will consider two kinds of execution monitoring: a simple, but weak form called **action monitoring**, whereby the agent checks the environment to verify that the next action will work, and a more complex but more effective form called **plan monitoring**, in which the agent verifies the entire remaining plan.

A **replanning** agent knows what to do when something unexpected happens: call a planner again to come up with a new plan to reach the goal. To avoid spending too much time planning, this is usually done by trying to repair the old plan—to find a way from the current unexpected state back onto the plan.

As an example, let us return to the double Murphy vacuum world in Figure 12.9. In this world, moving into a clean square sometimes deposits dirt in that square; but what if the agent doesn't know that or doesn't worry about it? Then it will come up with a very simple solution: $[Left]$. If no dirt is dumped on arrival when the plan is actually executed, then the agent will detect the achievement of the goal. Otherwise, because the $CleanL$ precondition of the implicit $Finish$ step is not satisfied, the agent will generate a new plan: $[Suck]$. Execution of this plan always succeeds.

Together, execution monitoring and replanning form a general strategy that can be applied to both fully and partially observable environments, and to a variety of planning representations including state-space, partial-order, and conditional plans. One simple approach to state-space planning is shown in Figure 12.13. The planning agent starts with a goal and creates an initial plan to achieve it. The agent then starts executing actions one by one. The replanning agent, unlike our other planning agents, keeps track of both the remaining unexecuted plan segment $plan$ and the complete original plan $whole\_plan$. It uses **action**

ACTION MONITORING

**monitoring**: before carrying out the next action of $plan$, the agent examines its percepts to see whether any preconditions of the plan have unexpectedly become unsatisfied. If they have, the agent will try to get back on track by replanning a sequence of actions that should take it back to some point in the $whole\_plan$.

Figure 12.14 provides a schematic illustration of the process. The replanner notices that the preconditions of the first action in $plan$ are not satisfied by the current state. It then calls the planner to come up with a new subplan called $repair$ that will get from the current situation to some state $s$ on $whole\_plan$. In this example, the state $s$ happens to be one step back from the current remaining $plan$. (That is why we keep track of the whole plan, rather than just the remaining plan.) In general, we choose $s$ to be as close as possible to the current state. The concatenation of $repair$ and the portion of $whole\_plan$ from $s$ onward, which we call $continuation$, makes up the new $plan$, and the agent is ready to resume execution.

```
function REPLANNING-AGENT(percept) returns an action
  static: KB, a knowledge base (includes action descriptions)
          plan, a plan, initially [ ]
          whole_plan, a plan, initially [ ]
          goal, a goal

  TELL(KB, MAKE-PERCEPT-SENTENCE(percept, t))
  current ← STATE-DESCRIPTION(KB, t)
  if plan = [ ] then
     whole_plan ← plan ← PLANNER(current, goal, KB)
  if PRECONDITIONS(FIRST(plan)) not currently true in KB then
     candidates ← SORT(whole_plan, ordered by distance to current)
     find state s in candidates such that
          failure ≠ repair ← PLANNER(current, s, KB)
     continuation ← the tail of whole_plan starting at s
     whole_plan ← plan ← APPEND(repair, continuation)
  return POP(plan)
```

**Figure 12.13** An agent that does action monitoring and replanning. It uses a complete state-space planning algorithm called PLANNER as a subroutine. If the preconditions of the next action are not met, the agent loops through the possible points $p$ in *whole_plan*, trying to find one that PLANNER can plan a path to. This path is called *repair*. If PLANNER succeeds in finding a repair, the agent appends *repair* and the tail of the plan after $p$, to create the new plan. The agent then returns the first step in the plan.

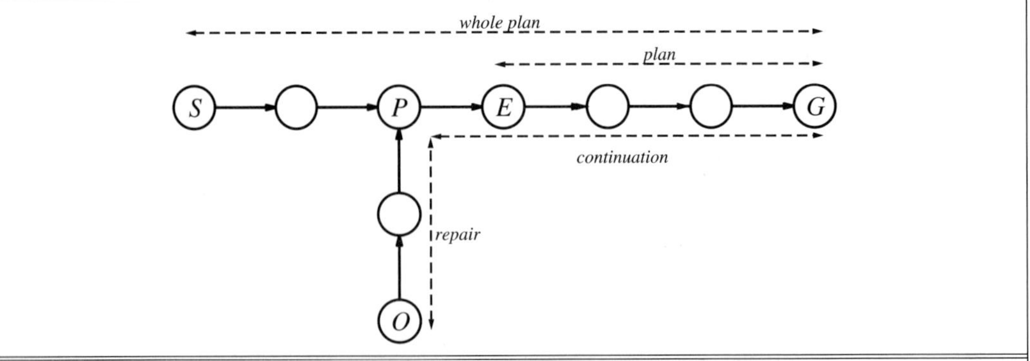


**Figure 12.14** Before execution, the planner comes up with a plan, here called *whole_plan*, to get from $S$ to $G$. The agent executes the plan until the point marked $E$. Before executing the remaining *plan*, it checks preconditions as usual and finds that it is actually in state $O$ rather than state $E$. It then calls its planning algorithm to come up with *repair*, which is a plan to get from $O$ to some point $P$ on the original *whole_plan*. The new *plan* now becomes the concatenation of *repair* and *continuation* (the resumption of the original *whole_plan*).

Now let's return to the example problem of achieving a chair and table of matching color, this time via replanning. We'll assume a fully observable environment. In the initial state the chair is blue, the table is green, and there is a can of blue paint and a can of red paint. That gives us the following problem definition:

$$\begin{aligned}
&Init(Color(Chair, Blue) \land Color(Table, Green) \\
&\quad \land ContainsColor(BC, Blue) \land PaintCan(BC)) \\
&\quad \land ContainsColor(RC, Red) \land PaintCan(RC) \\
&Goal(Color(Chair, x) \land Color(Table, x)) \\
&Action(Paint(object, color), \\
&\quad \text{PRECOND:} HavePaint(color) \\
&\quad \text{EFFECT:} Color(object, color)) \\
&Action(Open(can), \\
&\quad \text{PRECOND:} PaintCan(can) \land ContainsColor(can, color) \\
&\quad \text{EFFECT:} HavePaint(color)
\end{aligned}$$

The agent's PLANNER should come up with the following plan:

$$[Start; Open(BC); Paint(Table, Blue); Finish]$$

Now the agent is ready to execute the plan. Assume that all goes well as the agent opens the blue paint and applies it to the table. The agents from previous sections would declare victory at this point, having completed the steps in the plan. But the execution monitoring agent must first check the precondition of the $Finish$ step, which says that the two pieces must have the same color. Suppose the agent perceives that they do not have the same color, because it missed a spot of green on the table. The agent then needs to figure out a position in $whole\_plan$ to aim for and a repair action sequence to get there. The agent notices that the current state is identical to the precondition before the $Paint$ action, so the agent chooses the empty sequence for $repair$ and makes its $plan$ be the same $[Paint, Finish]$ sequence that it just attempted. With this new plan in place, execution monitoring resumes, and the $Paint$ action is retried. This behavior will loop until the table is perceived to be completely painted. But notice that the loop is created by a process of plan–execute–replan, rather than by an explicit loop in a plan.

Action monitoring is a very simple method of execution monitoring but it can sometimes lead to less than intelligent behavior. For example, suppose that the agent constructs a plan to solve the painting problem by painting the chair and table red. Then it opens the can of red paint and finds that there is only enough paint for the chair. Action monitoring would not detect failure until *after* the chair has been painted, at which point $HavePaint(Red)$ becomes false. What we really need to do is detect failure whenever the state is such that the remaining plan no longer works. **Plan monitoring** achieves this by checking the preconditions for success of the entire remaining plan—that is, the preconditions of each step in the plan, except those preconditions that are achieved by another step in the remaining plan. Plan monitoring cuts off execution of a doomed plan as soon as possible, rather than continuing until the failure actually occurs.[13] In some cases, it can rescue the agent from disaster when the doomed plan would have led to a dead end from which the goal would be unachievable.

PLAN MONITORING

[13] Plan monitoring makes our agent smarter than a dung beetle. (See page 37.) Our agent would notice that the

It is relatively straightforward to modify a planning algorithm so that it annotates the plan at each point with the preconditions for success of the remaining plan. If we extend plan monitoring to check whether the current state satisfies the plan preconditions at any future point, rather than just the current point, then plan monitoring will also be able to take advantage of **serendipity**—that is, accidental success. If someone comes along and paints the table red at the same time that the agent is painting the chair red, then the final plan preconditions are satisfied (the goal has been achieved), and the agent can go home early.

So far, we have described monitoring and replanning in fully observable environments. Things can become much more complicated when the environment is partially observable. First, things can go wrong without the agent's being able to detect it. Second, "checking preconditions" could require the execution of sensing actions, which have to be planned for—either at planning time, which takes us back to conditional planning, or at execution time. In the worst case, the execution of a sensing action could require a complex plan that itself requires monitoring and hence further sensing actions, and so on. If the agent insists on checking every precondition, it might never get around to actually *doing* anything. The agent should prefer to check those variables that are important, have a good chance of going wrong, and are not too expensive to perceive. This allows the agent to respond appropriately to important threats, but not waste time checking to see whether the sky is falling.

Now that we have described a method for monitoring and replanning, we need to ask, "Does it work?" This is a surprisingly tricky question. If we mean, "Can we guarantee that the agent will always achieve the goal, even with unbounded indeterminacy?" then the answer is no, because the agent could inadvertently arrive at a dead end, as described for online search in Section 4.5. For example, the vacuum agent might not know that its batteries can run out. Let's rule out dead ends; that is, let's assume that the agent can construct a plan to reach the goal from *any* state in the environment. If we assume that the environment is really nondeterministic, in the sense that such a plan always has *some* chance of success on any given execution attempt, then the agent will eventually reach the goal. The replanning agent therefore has capabilities analogous to those of the conditional planning agent. In fact, we can modify a conditional planner so that it constructs only a partial solution plan that includes steps of the form "**if** $<test>$ **then** $plan\_A$ **else** $replan$." Under the assumptions we have made, such a plan can be a correct solution to the original problem; it might also be much cheaper to construct than a full conditional plan.

Trouble occurs when the agent's repeated attempts to reach the goal are futile—when they are blocked by some precondition or effect that it doesn't know about. For example, if the agent has the wrong card key to its hotel room, no amount of inserting and removing it is going to open the door.[14] One solution is to choose randomly from among the set of possible repair plans, rather than trying the same one each time. In this case, the repair plan of going to the front desk and getting a card key to the room would be a useful alternative. Given that the agent might not be able to distinguish between the truly nondeterministic case and the futile case, some variation in repairs is a good idea in general.

---

dung ball was missing from its grasp and would replan to get another ball and plug its hole.

[14] Futile repetition of a plan repair is exactly the behavior exhibited by the sphex wasp. (See page 37.)

Another solution to the problem of incorrect action descriptions is **learning**. After a few tries, a learning agent should be able to modify the action description that says that the key opens the door. At that point, the replanner will automatically come up with an alternative plan, such as getting a new key. This kind of learning is described in Chapter 21.

Even with all these potential improvements, the replanning agent still has a few shortcomings. It cannot perform in real-time environments, and there is no bound on the amount of time it will spend replanning and thus no bound on the time it takes to decide on an action. Also, it cannot formulate new goals of its own or accept new goals in addition to its current goals, so it cannot be a long-lived agent in a complex environment. These shortcomings will be addressed in the next section.

## 12.6 CONTINUOUS PLANNING

In this section, we design an agent that persists indefinitely in an environment. Thus it is not a "problem solver" that is given a single goal and then plans and acts until the goal is achieved; rather, it lives through a series of ever-changing goal formulation, planning, and acting phases. Rather than thinking of the planner and execution monitor as separate processes, one of which passes its results to the other, we can think of them as a single process in a **continuous planning agent**.

CONTINUOUS PLANNING AGENT

The agent is thought of as always being *part of the way through* executing a plan—the grand plan of living its life. Its activities include executing some steps of the plan that are ready to be executed, refining the plan to satisfy open preconditions or resolve conflicts, and modifying the plan in the light of additional information obtained during execution. Obviously, when it first formulates a new goal, the agent will have no actions ready to execute, so it will spend a while generating a partial plan. It is quite possible, however, for the agent to begin execution before the plan is complete, especially when it has independent subgoals to achieve. The continuous planning agent monitors the world continuously, updating its world model from new percepts even if its deliberations are still continuing.

We will first go through an example and then describe the agent program, which we will call CONTINUOUS-POP-AGENT because it uses partial-order plans to represent its intended activities. To simplify the presentation, we will assume a fully observable environment. The same techniques can be extended to the partially observable case.

The example we will use is a problem from the blocks world domain (Section 11.1). The start state is shown in Figure 12.15(a). The action we will need is $Move(x, y)$, which moves block $x$ onto block $y$, provided that both are clear. Its action schema is

$$\begin{aligned}&Action(Move(x,y),\\&\quad \text{PRECOND:}Clear(x) \land Clear(y) \land On(x,z),\\&\quad \text{EFFECT:}On(x,y) \land Clear(z) \land \neg On(x,z) \land \neg Clear(y))\ .\end{aligned}$$

The agent first needs to formulate a goal for itself. We won't discuss goal formulation here, but instead we will assume that somehow the agent was told (or decided on its own) to achieve the goal $On(C, D) \land On(D, B)$. The agent starts planning for this goal. Unlike

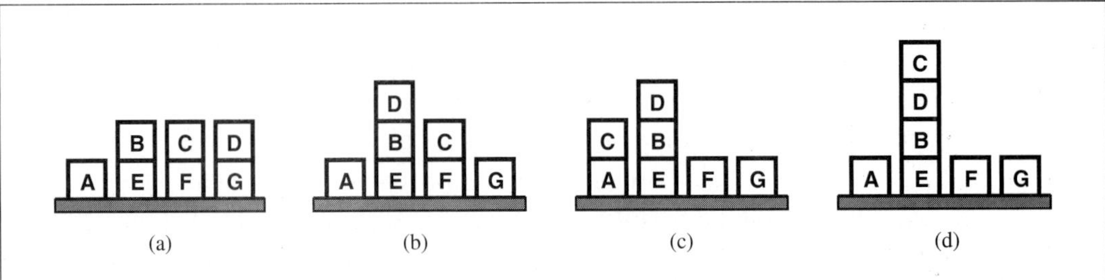


**Figure 12.15** The sequence of states as the continuous planning agent tries to reach the goal state $On(C, D) \wedge On(D, B)$, as shown in (d). The start state is (a). At (b), another agent has interfered, putting $D$ on $B$. At (c), the agent has executed $Move(C, D)$ but has failed, dropping $C$ on $A$ instead. It retries $Move(C, D)$, reaching the goal state (d).

all our other agents, which would shut off their percepts until the planner returns a complete solution to this problem, the continuous planning agent builds the plan incrementally, with each increment taking a bounded amount of time. After each increment, the agent returns $NoOp$ as its action and checks its percepts again. We assume that the percepts don't change and the agent quickly constructs the plan shown in Figure 12.16. Notice that although the preconditions of both actions are satisfied by $Start$, there is an ordering constraint putting $Move(D, B)$ before $Move(C, D)$. This is needed to ensure that $Clear(D)$ remains true until $Move(D, B)$ is completed. Throughout the continuous planning process, $Start$ is always used as the label for the current state. The agent updates the state after each action.

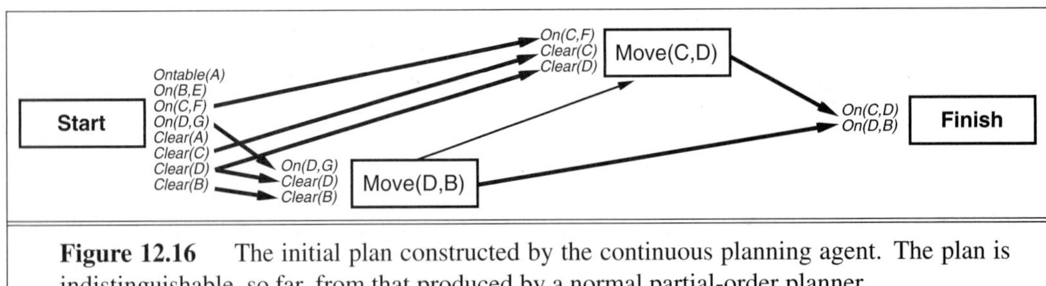


**Figure 12.16** The initial plan constructed by the continuous planning agent. The plan is indistinguishable, so far, from that produced by a normal partial-order planner.

The plan is now ready to be executed, but before the agent can take action, nature intervenes. An external agent (perhaps the agent's teacher getting impatient) moves $D$ onto $B$ and the world is now in the state shown in Figure 12.15(b). The agent perceives this, recognizes that $Clear(B)$ and $On(D, G)$ are no longer true in the current state, and updates its model of the current state accordingly. The causal links that were supplying the preconditions $Clear(B)$ and $On(D, G)$ for the $Move(D, B)$ action become invalid and must be removed from the plan. The new plan is shown in Figure 12.17. At all times, $Start$ represents the current state, so this $Start$ is different from the one in the previous figure. Notice that the plan is now incomplete: two of the preconditions for $Move(D, B)$ are open, and its precondition $On(D, y)$ is now uninstantiated, because there is no longer any reason to assume the that move will be from $G$.

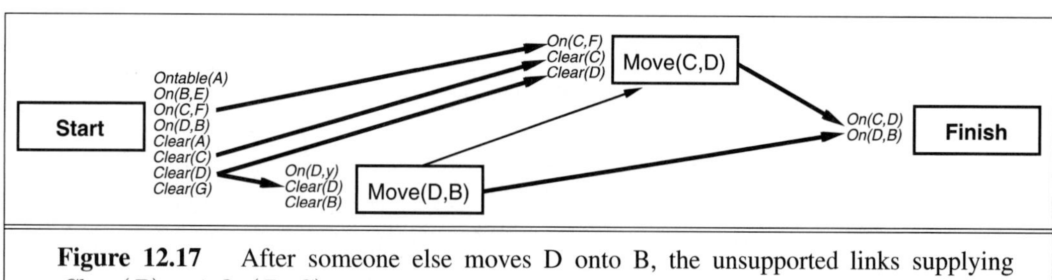


**Figure 12.17** After someone else moves D onto B, the unsupported links supplying $Clear(B)$ and $On(D,G)$ are dropped, producing this plan.

Now the agent can take advantage of the "helpful" interference by noticing that the causal link $Move(D,B) \xrightarrow{On(D,B)} Finish$ can be replaced by a direct link from $Start$ to $Finish$. This process is called **extending** a causal link and is done whenever a condition can be supplied by an earlier step instead of a later one without causing a new conflict.

EXTENSION

Once the old causal link from $Move(D,B)$ to $Finish$ is removed, $Move(D,B)$ no longer supplies any causal links at all. It is now a **redundant step**. All redundant steps, and any links supplying them, are dropped from the plan. This gives the plan in Figure 12.18.

REDUNDANT STEP

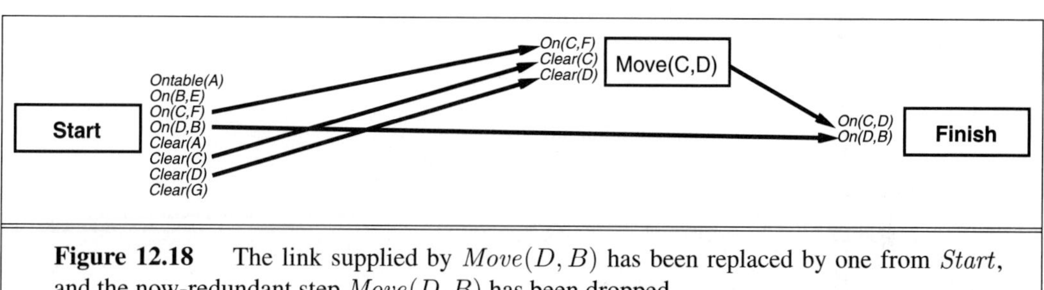


**Figure 12.18** The link supplied by $Move(D,B)$ has been replaced by one from $Start$, and the now-redundant step $Move(D,B)$ has been dropped.

Now the step $Move(C,D)$ is ready to be executed, because all of its preconditions are satisfied by the $Start$ step, no other steps are necessarily before it, and it does not conflict with any other link in the plan. The step is removed from the plan and executed. Unfortunately, the agent is clumsy and drops $C$ onto $A$ instead of $D$, giving the state shown in Figure 12.15(c). The new plan state is shown in Figure 12.19. Notice that although there are now no actions in the plan, there is still an open condition for the $Finish$ step.

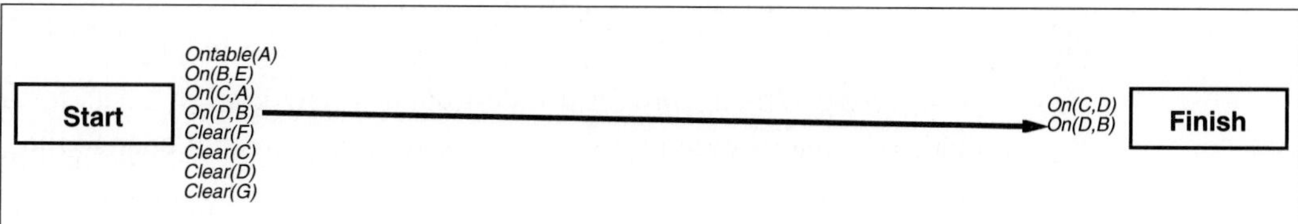


**Figure 12.19** After $Move(C,D)$ is executed and removed from the plan, the effects of the $Start$ step reflect the fact that $C$ ended up on $A$ instead of the intended $D$. The goal precondition $On(C,D)$ is still open.

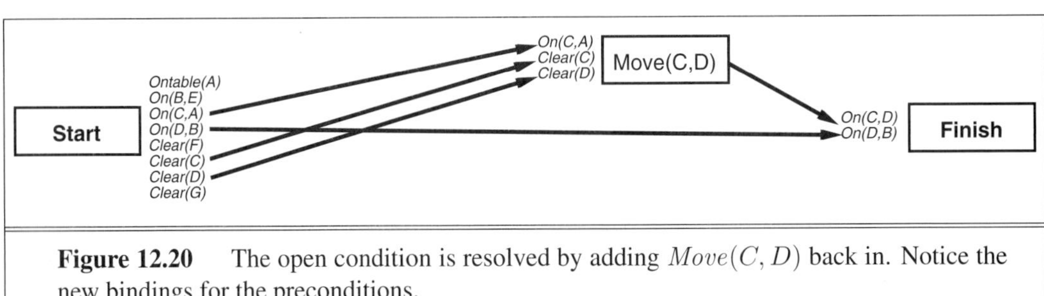


**Figure 12.20** The open condition is resolved by adding $Move(C, D)$ back in. Notice the new bindings for the preconditions.

The agent decides to plan for the open condition. Once again, $Move(C, D)$ will satisfy the goal condition. Its preconditions are satisfied by new causal links from the $Start$ step. The new plan appears in Figure 12.20.

Once again, $Move(C, D)$ is ready for execution. This time it works, resulting in the goal state shown in Figure 12.15(d). Once the step is dropped from the plan, the goal condition $On(C, D)$ becomes open again. Because the $Start$ step is updated to reflect the new world state, however, the goal condition can be satisfied immediately by a link from the $Start$ step. This is the normal course of events when an action is successful. The final plan state is shown in Figure 12.21. Because all the goal conditions are satisfied by the $Start$ step and there are no remaining actions, the agent is now free to remove the goals from $Finish$ and formulate a new goal.

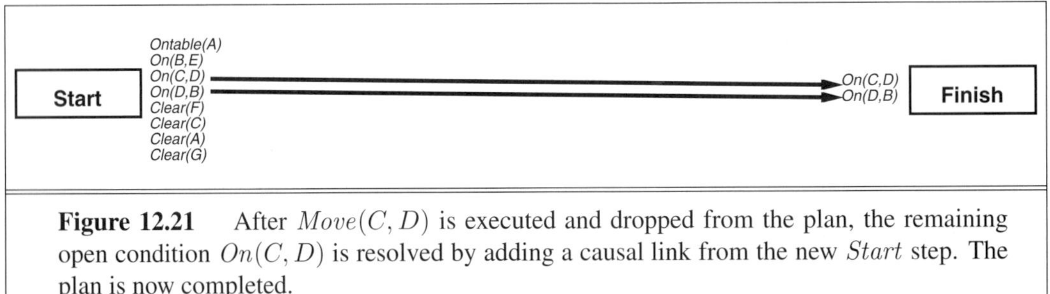


**Figure 12.21** After $Move(C, D)$ is executed and dropped from the plan, the remaining open condition $On(C, D)$ is resolved by adding a causal link from the new $Start$ step. The plan is now completed.

From this example, we can see that continuous planning is quite similar to partial-order planning. On each iteration, the algorithm finds something about the plan that needs fixing—a so-called **plan flaw**—and fixes it. The POP algorithm can be seen as a flaw-removal algorithm where the two flaws are open preconditions and causal conflicts. The continuous planning agent, on the other hand, addresses a much broader range of flaws:

PLAN FLAW

- *Missing goal:* The agent can decide to add a new goal or goals to the $Finish$ state. (Under continuous planning, it might make more sense to change the name of $Finish$ to $Infinity$, and of $Start$ to $Current$, but we will stick with tradition.)
- *Open precondition:* Add a causal link to an open precondition, choosing either a new or an existing action (as in POP).
- *Causal Conflict:* Given a causal link $A \xrightarrow{p} B$ and an action $C$ with effect $\neg p$, choose an ordering constraint or variable constraint to resolve the conflict (as in POP).

- *Unsupported link:* If there is a causal link $Start \xrightarrow{p} A$ where $p$ is no longer true in $Start$, then remove the link. (This prevents us from executing an action whose preconditions are false.)
- *Redundant action:* If an action $A$ supplies no causal links, remove it and its links. (This allows us to take advantage of serendipitous events.)
- *Unexecuted action:* If an action $A$ (other than $Finish$) has its preconditions satisfied in $Start$, has no other actions (besides $Start$) ordered before it, and conflicts with no causal links, then remove $A$ and its causal links and return it as the action to be executed.
- *Unnecessary historical goal:* If there are no open preconditions and no actions in the plan (so that all causal links go directly from $Start$ to $Finish$), then we have achieved the current goal set. Remove the goals and the links to them to allow for new goals.

The CONTINUOUS-POP-AGENT is shown in Figure 12.22. It has a cycle of "perceive, remove flaw, act." It keeps a persistent plan in its knowledge base, and on each turn it removes one flaw from the plan. It then takes an action (although often the action will be $NoOp$) and repeats the loop. This agent can handle many of the problems listed in the discussion of the replanning agent on page 445. In particular, it can act in real time, it handles serendipity, it can formulate its own goals, and it can handle unexpected events that affect future plans.

```
function CONTINUOUS-POP-AGENT(percept) returns an action
  static: plan, a plan, initially with just Start, Finish

  action ← NoOp (the default)
  EFFECTS[Start] = UPDATE(EFFECTS[Start], percept)
  REMOVE-FLAW(plan) // possibly updating action
  return action
```

**Figure 12.22** CONTINUOUS-POP-AGENT, a continuous partial-order planning agent. After receiving a percept, the agent removes a flaw from its constantly updated plan and then returns an action. Often it will take many steps of flaw-removal planning, during which it returns $NoOp$, before it is ready to take a real action.

## 12.7 MULTIAGENT PLANNING

So far we have dealt with **single-agent environments**, in which our agent is alone. When there are other agents in the environment, our agent could simply include them in its model of the environment, without changing its basic algorithms. In many cases, however, that would lead to poor performance because dealing with other agents is not the same as dealing with nature. In particular, nature is (one assumes) indifferent to the agent's intentions,[15] whereas other agents are not. This section introduces multiagent planning to handle these issues.

[15] Residents of the United Kingdom, where the mere act of planning a picnic guarantees rain, might disagree.

$Agents(A, B)$
$Init(At(A, [Left, Baseline]) \wedge At(B, [Right, Net]) \wedge$
$\quad Approaching(Ball, [Right, Baseline])) \wedge Partner(A, B) \wedge Partner(B, A)$
$Goal(Returned(Ball) \wedge At(agent, [x, Net]))$
$Action(Hit(agent, Ball),$
$\quad \text{PRECOND:} Approaching(Ball, [x, y]) \wedge At(agent, [x, y]) \wedge$
$\qquad Partner(agent, partner) \wedge \neg At(partner, [x, y])$
$\quad \text{EFFECT:} Returned(Ball))$
$Action(Go(agent, [x, y]),$
$\quad \text{PRECOND:} At(agent, [a, b]),$
$\quad \text{EFFECT:} At(agent, [x, y]) \wedge \neg At(agent, [a, b]))$

**Figure 12.23** The doubles tennis problem. Two agents are playing together and can be in one of four locations: $[Left, Baseline]$, $[Right, Baseline]$, $[Left, Net]$, and $[Right, Net]$. The ball can be returned if exactly one player is in the right place.

We saw in Chapter 2 that multiagent environments can be **cooperative** or **competitive**. We will begin with a simple cooperative example: team planning in doubles tennis. Plans can be constructed that specify actions for both players on the team; we will describe techniques for constructing such plans efficiently. Efficient plan construction is useful, but does not guarantee success; the agents have to agree to use the same plan! This requires some form of **coordination**, possibly achieved by **communication**.

### Cooperation: Joint goals and plans

Two agents playing on a doubles tennis team have the joint goal of winning the match, which gives rise to various subgoals. Let's suppose that at one point in the game, they have the joint goal of returning the ball that has been hit to them and ensuring that at least one of them is covering the net. We can represent this notion as a **multiagent planning** problem, as shown in Figure 12.23.

MULTIAGENT PLANNING

This notation introduces two new features. First, $Agents(A, B)$ declares that there are two agents, $A$ and $B$, who are participating in the plan. (For this problem the opposing players are not considered agents.) Second, each action explicitly mentions the agent as a parameter, because we need to keep track of which agent does what.

JOINT PLAN

A solution to a multiagent planning problem is a **joint plan** consisting of actions for each agent. A joint plan is a solution if the goal will be achieved when each agent performs its assigned actions. The following plan is a solution to the tennis problem:

PLAN 1:

$$\begin{aligned} A &: [Go(A, [Right, Baseline]), Hit(A, Ball)] \\ B &: [NoOp(B), NoOp(B)] \, . \end{aligned}$$

If both agents have the same knowledge base, and if this is the only solution, then everything would be fine; the agents could each determine the solution and then jointly execute it. Unfortunately for the agents (and we will soon see why it's unfortunate), there is another plan that satisfies the goal just as well as the first:

PLAN 2:

$$A: \ [Go(A, [Left, Net]), NoOp(A)]$$
$$B: \ [Go(B, [Right, baseline]), Hit(B, Ball)] .$$

If $A$ chooses plan 2 and $B$ chooses plan 1, then nobody will return the ball. Conversely, if $A$ chooses 1 and $B$ chooses 2, then they will probably collide with each other; no one returns the ball and the net may remain uncovered. Hence, the existence of correct joint plans does not mean that the goal will be achieved. The agents need a mechanism for **coordination** to reach the *same* joint plan; moreover, it must be common knowledge (see Chapter 10) among the agents that some particular joint plan will be executed.

COORDINATION

## Multibody planning

MULTIBODY PLANNING

This section concentrates on the construction of correct joint plans, deferring the coordination issue for the time being. We call this **multibody planning**; it is essentially the planning problem faced by a single centralized agent that can dictate actions to each of several physical entities. In the truly multiagent case, it enables each agent to figure out what the possible joint plans are that would succeed if executed jointly.

Our approach to multibody planning will be based on partial-order planning, as described in Section 11.3. We will assume full observability, to keep things simple. There is one additional issue that doesn't arise in the single-agent case: the environment is no longer truly **static**, because other agents could act while any particular agent is deliberating. Therefore, we need to be concerned about **synchronization**. For simplicity, we will assume that each action takes the same amount of time and that actions at each point in the joint plan are simultaneous.

SYNCHRONIZATION

At any point in time, each agent is executing exactly one action (perhaps including *NoOp*). This set of concurrent actions is called a **joint action**. For example, a joint action in the tennis domain (page 450) with two agents $A$ and $B$ is $\langle NoOp(A), Hit(B, Ball)\rangle$. A joint plan consists of a partially ordered graph of joint actions. For example, Plan 2 for the tennis problem can be represented as this sequence of joint actions:

JOINT ACTION

$$\langle Go(A, [Left, Net]), Go(B, [Right, baseline])\rangle$$
$$\langle NoOp(A), Hit(B, Ball)\rangle$$

We *could* do planning using the regular POP algorithm, applied to the set of all possible joint actions. The only problem is the size of this set: with 10 actions and 5 agents we get $10^5$ joint actions. It would be tedious to specify the preconditions and effects of each action correctly, and inefficient to do planning with such a large set.

An alternative is to define joint actions implicitly, by describing how each individual action interacts with other possible actions. This will be simpler, because most actions are independent of most others; we need list only the few actions that actually interact. We can do that by augmenting the usual STRIPS or ADL action descriptions with one new feature: a **concurrent action list**. This is similar to the precondition of an action description except that rather than describing state variables, it describes actions that must or must not be executed

CONCURRENT ACTION LIST

concurrently. For example, the $Hit$ action could be described as follows:

$$\begin{aligned}&Action(Hit(A, Ball),\\ &\quad \text{CONCURRENT:}\neg Hit(B, Ball)\\ &\quad \text{PRECOND:}Approaching(Ball, [x, y]) \wedge At(A, [x, y])\\ &\quad \text{EFFECT:}Returned(Ball))\ .\end{aligned}$$

Here, we have the prohibited-concurrency constraint that, during the execution of the $Hit$ action, there can be no other $Hit$ action by another agent. We can also *require* concurrent action, for example when two agents are needed to carry a cooler full of beverages to the tennis court. The description for this action says that agent $A$ cannot execute a $Carry$ action unless there is another agent $B$ who is simultaneously executing a $Carry$ of the same cooler:

$$\begin{aligned}&Action(Carry(A, cooler, here, there),\\ &\quad \text{CONCURRENT:}Carry(B, cooler, here, there)\\ &\quad \text{PRECOND:}At(A, here) \wedge At(cooler, here) \wedge Cooler(cooler)\\ &\quad \text{EFFECT:}At(A, there) \wedge At(cooler, there) \wedge \neg At(A, here) \wedge \neg At(cooler, here)).\end{aligned}$$

With this representation, it is possible to create a planner that is very close to the POP partial-order planner. There are three differences:

1. In addition to the temporal ordering relation $A \prec B$, we allow $A = B$ and $A \preceq B$, meaning "concurrent" and "before or concurrent," respectively.
2. When a new action has required concurrent actions, we must instantiate those actions, using new or existing actions in the plan.
3. Prohibited concurrent actions are an additional source of constraints. Each constraint must be resolved by constraining conflicting actions to be before or after.

This representation gives us the equivalent of POP for multibody domains. We could extend this approach with the refinements of the last two chapters—HTNs, partial observability, conditionals, execution monitoring, and replanning—but that is beyond the scope of this book.

### Coordination mechanisms

CONVENTION

The simplest method by which a group of agents can ensure agreement on a joint plan is to adopt a **convention** prior to engaging in joint activity. A convention is any constraint on the selection of joint plans, beyond the basic constraint that the joint plan must work if all agents adopt it. For example, the convention "stick to your side of the court" would cause the doubles partners to select plan 2, whereas the convention "one player always stays at the net" would lead them to plan 1. Some conventions, such as driving on the proper side of the road, are so widely adopted that they are considered **social laws**. Human languages can also be viewed as conventions.

SOCIAL LAWS

The conventions in the preceding paragraph are domain-specific and can be implemented by constraining the action descriptions to rule out violations of the convention. A more general approach is to use domain-independent conventions. For example, if each agent runs the same multibody planning algorithm with the same inputs, it can follow the convention of executing the first feasible joint plan found, confident that the other agents will come to the same choice. A more robust but more expensive strategy would be to generate all joint plans and then pick the one, say, whose printed representation is alphabetically first.

Conventions can also arise through evolutionary processes. For example, colonies of social insects execute very elaborate joint plans, which are facilitated by the common genetic makeup of the individuals in the colony. Conformity can also be enforced by the fact that deviation from conventions reduces evolutionary fitness, so that any feasible joint plan can become a stable equilibrium. Similar considerations apply to the development of human language, where the important thing is not which language each individual should speak, but the fact that all individuals speak the same language. One final example appears in the flocking behavior of birds. We can obtain a reasonable simulation if each bird agent (sometimes called a birdoid or **boid**) executes the following three rules with some method of combination:

BOID

1. Separation: Steer away from neighbors when you start to get too close.
2. Cohesion: Steer towards the average position of the neighbors.
3. Alignment: Steer towards the average orientation (heading) of the neighbors.

EMERGENT BEHAVIOR

If all the birds execute the same policy, the flock exhibits the **emergent behavior** of flying as a pseudo-rigid body with roughly constant density that does not disperse over time. As with insects, there is no need for each agent to possess the joint plan that models the actions of other agents.

Typically, conventions are adopted to cover a universe of individual multiagent planning problems, rather than being developed anew for each problem. This can lead to inflexibility and breakdown, as can be seen sometimes in doubles tennis when the ball is roughly equidistant between the two partners. In the absence of an applicable convention, agents can use **communication** to achieve common knowledge of a feasible joint plan. For example, a doubles tennis player could shout "Mine!" or "Yours!" to indicate a preferred joint plan. We cover mechanisms for communication in more depth in Chapter 22, where we observe that communication does not necessarily involve a verbal exchange. For example, one player can communicate a preferred joint plan to the other simply by executing the first part of it. In our tennis problem, if agent $A$ heads for the net, then agent $B$ is obliged to go back to the baseline to hit the ball, because plan 2 is the only joint plan that begins with $A$'s heading for the net. This approach to coordination, sometimes called **plan recognition**, works when a single action (or short sequence of actions) is enough to determine a joint plan unambiguously.

PLAN RECOGNITION

The burden for ensuring that the agents arrive at a successful joint plan can be placed either on the agent designers or on the agents themselves. In the former case, before the agents begin to plan, the agent designer should prove that the agents' policies and strategies will be successful. The agents themselves can be reactive if that works for the environment they exist in, and they need not have explicit models about the other agents. In the latter case, the agents are deliberative; they must prove or otherwise demonstrate that their plan will be effective, taking the other agents' reasoning into account. For example, in an environment with two logical agents $A$ and $B$, they could both have the following definition:

$$\forall p, s \;\; Feasible(p, s) \;\Leftrightarrow\; CommonKnowledge(\{A, B\}, Achieves(p, s, Goal))$$

This says that in any situation $s$, the plan $p$ is a feasible joint plan in that situation if it is common knowledge among the agents that $p$ will achieve the goal. We need further axioms

JOINT INTENTION

to establish common knowledge of a **joint intention** to execute a *particular* joint plan; only then can agents begin to act.

### Competition

COMPETITION

Not all multiagent environments involve cooperative agents. Agents with conflicting utility functions are in **competition** with each other. One example of this is two-player zero-sum games, such as chess. We saw in Chapter 6 that a chess-playing agent needs to consider the opponent's possible moves for several steps into the future. That is, an agent in a competitive environment must (a) recognize that there are other agents, (b) compute some of the other agent's possible plans, (c) compute how the other agent's plans interact with its own plans, and (d) decide on the best action in view of these interactions. So competition, like cooperation, requires a model of the other agent's plans. On the other hand, there is no commitment to a joint plan in a competitive environment.

Section 12.4 drew the analogy between games and conditional planning problems. The conditional planning algorithm in Figure 12.10 constructs plans that work under worst-case assumptions about the environment, so it can be applied in competitive situations where the agent is concerned only with success and failure. When the agent and its opponents are concerned about the *cost* of a plan, then minimax is appropriate. As yet, there has been little work on combining minimax with methods, such as POP and HTN planning, that go beyond the state-space search model used in Chapter 6. We will return to the question of competition in Section 17.6, which covers game theory.

## 12.8 SUMMARY

This chapter has addressed some of the complications of planning and acting in the real world. The main points are:

- Many actions consume **resources**, such as money, gas, or raw materials. It is convenient to treat these resources as numeric measures in a pool rather than try to reason about, say, each individual coin and bill in the world. Actions can generate and consume resources, and it is usually cheap and effective to check partial plans for satisfaction of resource constraints before attempting further refinements.
- Time is one of the most important resources. It can be handled by specialized scheduling algorithms, or scheduling can be integrated with planning.
- **Hierarchical task network** (HTN) planning allows the agent to take advice from the domain designer in the form of decomposition rules. This makes it feasible to create the very large plans required by many real-world applications.
- Standard planning algorithms assume complete and correct information and deterministic, fully observable environments. Many domains violate this assumption.
- Incomplete information can be dealt with by planning to use sensing actions to obtain the information needed. **Conditional plans** allow the agent to sense the world during

execution to decide what branch of the plan to follow. In some cases, **sensorless** or **conformant planning** can be used to construct a plan that works without the need for perception. Both sensorless and conditional plans can be constructed by search in the space of **belief states**.

- Incorrect information results in unsatisfied preconditions for actions and plans. **Execution monitoring** detects violations of the preconditions for successful completion of the plan.
- A **replanning agent** uses execution monitoring and splices in repairs as needed.
- A **continuous planning** agent creates new goals as it goes and reacts in real time.
- **Multiagent** planning is necessary when there are other agents in the environment with which to cooperate, compete, or coordinate. **Multibody** planning constructs joint plans, using an efficient decomposition of joint action descriptions, but must be augmented with some form of coordination if two cooperative agents are to agree on which joint plan to execute.

## Bibliographical and Historical Notes

Planning with continuous time was first dealt with by DEVISER (Vere, 1983). The issue of systematic representation of time in plans was addressed by Dean *et al.* (1990) in the FORBIN system. NONLIN+ (Tate and Whiter, 1984) and SIPE (Wilkins, 1988, 1990) could reason about the allocation of limited resources to various plan steps. O-PLAN (Bell and Tate, 1985), an HTN planner, had a uniform, general representation for constraints on time and resources. In addition to the Hitachi application mentioned in the text, O-PLAN has been applied to software procurement planning at Price Waterhouse and back-axle assembly planning at Jaguar Cars. A number of hybrid planning-and-scheduling systems have been deployed: ISIS (Fox *et al.*, 1982; Fox, 1990) has been used for job shop scheduling at Westinghouse, GARI (Descotte and Latombe, 1985) planned the machining and construction of mechanical parts, FORBIN was used for factory control, and NONLIN+ was used for naval logistics planning.

After an initial flurry of theoretical work in the late 1980s, temporal planning made a comeback recently, when new algorithms and increased processing power made it feasible to attack practical applications. The two planners SAPA (Do and Kambhampati, 2001) and T4 (Haslum and Geffner, 2001) both used forward state-space search with sophisticated heuristics to handle actions with durations and resources. An alternative is to use very expressive action languages, but guide them by human-written domain-specific heuristics, as is done by ASPEN (Fukunaga *et al.*, 1997), HSTS (Jonsson *et al.*, 2000), and IxTeT (Ghallab and Laruelle, 1994).

There is a long history of scheduling in aerospace. T-SCHED (Drabble, 1990) was used to schedule mission-command sequences for the UOSAT-II satellite. OPTIMUM-AIV (Aarup *et al.*, 1994) and PLAN-ERS1 (Fuchs *et al.*, 1990), both based on O-PLAN, were used for spacecraft assembly and observation planning, respectively, at the European Space Agency.

SPIKE (Johnston and Adorf, 1992) was used for observation planning at NASA for the Hubble Space Telescope, while the Space Shuttle Ground Processing Scheduling System (Deale *et al.*, 1994) does job-shop scheduling of up to 16,000 worker-shifts. Remote Agent (Muscettola *et al.*, 1998) became the first autonomous planner-scheduler to control a spacecraft when it flew onboard the Deep Space One probe in 1999. The literature on job-shop scheduling in operations research is surveyed by Vaessens *et al.* (1996); theoretical results are presented by Martin and Shmoys (1996).

MACROPS

The facility in the STRIPS program for learning **macrops**—"macro-operators" consisting of a sequence of primitive steps—could be considered the first mechanism for hierarchical planning (Fikes *et al.*, 1972). Hierarchy was also used in the LAWALY system (Siklossy and Dreussi, 1973). The ABSTRIPS system (Sacerdoti, 1974) introduced the idea of an **abstraction hierarchy**, whereby planning at higher levels was permitted to ignore lower-level preconditions of actions in order to derive the general structure of a working plan. Austin Tate's Ph.D. thesis (1975b) and work by Earl Sacerdoti (1977) developed the basic ideas of HTN planning in its modern form. Many practical planners, including O-PLAN and SIPE, are HTN planners. Yang (1990) discusses properties of actions that make HTN planning efficient. Erol, Hendler, and Nau (1994, 1996) present a complete hierarchical decomposition planner as well as a range of complexity results for pure HTN planners. Other authors (Ambros-Ingerson and Steel, 1988; Young *et al.*, 1994; Barrett and Weld, 1994; Kambhampati *et al.*, 1998) have proposed the hybrid approach taken in this chapter, in which decompositions are just another form of refinement that can be used in partial-order planning.

ABSTRACTION HIERARCHY

Beginning with the work on macro-operators in STRIPS, one of the goals of hierarchical planning has been the reuse of previous planning experience in the form of generalized plans. The technique of **explanation-based learning**, described in depth in Chapter 19, has been applied in several systems as a means of generalizing previously computed plans, including SOAR (Laird *et al.*, 1986) and PRODIGY (Carbonell *et al.*, 1989). An alternative approach is to store previously computed plans in their original form and then reuse them to solve new, similar problems by analogy to the original problem. This is the approach taken by the field called **case-based planning** (Carbonell, 1983; Alterman, 1988; Hammond, 1989). Kambhampati (1994) argues that case-based planning should be analyzed as a form of refinement planning and provides a formal foundation for case-based partial-order planning.

CASE-BASED PLANNING

The unpredictability and partial observability of real environments was recognized early on in robotics projects that used planning techniques, including Shakey (Fikes *et al.*, 1972) and FREDDY (Michie, 1974). The problem received more attention after the publication of McDermott's (1978a) influential article, *Planning and Acting*.

Early planners, which lacked conditionals and loops, did not explicitly recognize the concept of conditional planning; but nevertheless they sometimes resorted to a coercive style in response to environmental uncertainty. Sacerdoti's NOAH used coercion in its solution to the "keys and boxes" problem, a planning challenge problem in which the planner knows little about the initial state. Mason (1993) argued that sensing often can and should be dispensed with in robotic planning, and described a sensorless plan that can move a tool into a specific position on a table by a sequence of tilting actions, *regardless* of the initial position. We describe this idea in the context of robotics. (See Figure 25.17.)

Goldman and Boddy (1996) introduced the term **conformant planning** for sensorless planners that handle uncertainty by coercing the world into known states, noting that sensorless plans are often effective even if the agent has sensors. The first moderately efficient conformant planner was Smith and Weld's (1998) Conformant Graphplan or CGP. Ferraris and Giunchiglia (2000) and Rintanen (1999) independently developed SATplan-based conformant planners. Bonet and Geffner (2000) describe a conformant planner based on heuristic search in the space of belief states, drawing on ideas first developed in the 1960s for partially observable Markov decision processes, or POMDPs (see Chapter 17). Currently, the fastest belief-state conformant planners, such as HSCP (Bertoli *et al.*, 2001a), use binary decision diagrams (BDDs) (Bryant, 1992) to represent belief states and are up to five orders of magnitude faster than CGP.

WARPLAN-C (Warren, 1976), a variant of WARPLAN, was one of the earliest planners to use conditional actions. Olawski and Gini (1990) lay out the major issues involved in conditional planning.

The conditional planning approach described in the chapter is based on the efficient search algorithms for cyclic AND–OR graphs developed by Jimenez and Torras (2000) and Hansen and Zilberstein (2001). Bertoli *et al.* (2001b) describe a BDD-based approach that constructs conditional plans with loops. C-BURIDAN (Draper *et al.*, 1994) handles conditional planning for actions with probabilistic outcomes, a problem also addressed under the heading of POMDPs (Chapter 17).

There is a close relation between conditional planning and automated program synthesis; a number of references appear in Chapter 9. The two fields have been pursued separately, because of the enormous difference in cost between execution of machine instructions and execution of actions by robot vehicles or manipulators. Linden (1991) attempts explicit cross-fertilization between the two fields.

In retrospect, it is now possible to see how the major classical planning algorithms led to extended versions for domains involving uncertainty. Search-based techniques led to search in belief space (Bonet and Geffner, 2000); SATPLAN led to stochastic SATPLAN (Majercik and Littman, 1999) and to planning using quantified Boolean logic (Rintanen, 1999); partial order planning led to UWL (Etzioni *et al.*, 1992), CNLP (Peot and Smith, 1992), and CASSANDRA (Pryor and Collins, 1996). GRAPHPLAN led to Sensory Graphplan or SGP (Weld *et al.*, 1998), but a full probabilistic GRAPHPLAN has yet to be developed.

The earliest major treatment of execution monitoring was PLANEX (Fikes *et al.*, 1972), which worked with the STRIPS planner to control the robot Shakey. PLANEX used triangle tables—essentially an efficient storage mechanism for the plan preconditions at each point in the plan—to allow recovery from partial execution failure without complete replanning. Shakey's model of execution is discussed further in Chapter 25. The NASL planner (McDermott, 1978a) treated a planning problem simply as a specification for carrying out a complex action, so that execution and planning were completely unified. It used theorem proving to reason about these complex actions.

SIPE (System for Interactive Planning and Execution monitoring) (Wilkins, 1988, 1990) was the first planner to deal systematically with the problem of replanning. It has been used in demonstration projects in several domains, including planning operations on the flight deck of an aircraft carrier and job-shop scheduling for an Australian beer factory. Another study used SIPE to plan the construction of multistory buildings, one of the most complex domains ever tackled by a planner.

IPEM (Integrated Planning, Execution, and Monitoring) (Ambros-Ingerson and Steel, 1988) was the first system to integrate partial-order planning and execution to yield a continuous planning agent. Our CONTINUOUS-POP-AGENT combines ideas from IPEM, the PUCCINI planner (Golden, 1998), and the CYPRESS system (Wilkins *et al.*, 1995).

In the mid-1980s, it was believed by some that partial-order planning and related techniques could never run fast enough to generate effective behavior for an agent in the real world (Agre and Chapman, 1987). Instead, **reactive planning** systems were proposed; in their basic form, these are reflex agents, possibly with internal state, that can be implemented with any of a variety of representations for condition–action rules. Brooks's (1986) subsumption architecture (see Chapters 7 and 25) used layered finite-state machines in legged and wheeled robots to control their locomotion and avoid obstacles. Pengi (Agre and Chapman, 1987) was able to play a (fully observable) video game using Boolean circuits combined with a "visual" representation of current goals and the agent's internal state.

REACTIVE PLANNING

"Universal plans" (Schoppers, 1987) were developed as a lookup-table method for reactive planning, but turned out to be a rediscovery of the idea of **policies** that had long been used in Markov decision processes. A universal plan (or a policy) contains a mapping from any state to the action that should be taken in that state. Ginsberg (1989) made a spirited attack on universal plans, including intractability results for some formulations of the reactive planning problem. Schoppers (1989) made an equally spirited reply.

POLICIES

As is often the case, a hybrid approach resolves the controversy. Using well-designed hierarchies, HTN planners, such as PRS (Georgeff and Lansky, 1987) and RAP (Firby, 1996), as well as continuous planning agents, can achieve reactive response times and complex long-range planning behavior in many problem domains.

Multiagent planning has leaped in popularity in recent years, although it does have a long history. Konolige (1982) provided a formalization of multiagent planning in first-order logic, while Pednault (1986) gave a STRIPS-style description. The notion of joint intention, which is essential if agents are to execute a joint plan, comes from work on communicative acts (Cohen and Levesque, 1990; Cohen *et al.*, 1990). Our presentation of multibody partial-order planning is based on the work of Boutilier and Brafman (2001).

We have barely skimmed the surface of work on negotiation in multiagent planning. Durfee and Lesser (1989) discuss how tasks can be shared out among agents by negotiation. Kraus *et al.* (1991) describe a system for playing Diplomacy, a board game requiring negotiation, coalition formation and dissolution, and dishonesty. Stone (2000) shows how agents can cooperate as teammates in the competitive, dynamic, partially observable environment of robotic soccer. (Weiss, 1999) is a book-length overview of multiagent systems.

The boid model on page 453 is due to Reynolds (1987), who won an Academy Award for its application to flocks of bats and swarms of penguins in *Batman Returns*.

## EXERCISES

**12.1** Examine carefully the representation of time and resources in Section 12.1.

**a.** Why is it a good idea to have $Duration(d)$ be an effect of an action, rather than having a separate field in the action of the form DURATION: $d$? (*Hint:* Consider conditional effects and disjunctive effects.)

**b.** Why is RESOURCE:$m$ a separate field in the action, rather than being an effect?

CONSUMABLE RESOURCE

**12.2** A **consumable resource** is a resource that is (partially) used up by an action. For example, attaching engines to cars requires screws. The screws, once used, are not available for other attachments.

**a.** Explain how to modify the representation in Figure 12.3 so that there are 100 screws initially, engine $E_1$ requires 40 screws, and engine $E_2$ requires 50 screws. The $+$ and $-$ function symbols may be used in effect literals for resources.

**b.** Explain how the definition of **conflict** between causal links and actions in partial-order planning must be modified to handle consumable resources.

**c.** Some actions—for example, resupplying the factory with screws or refueling a car—can *increase* the availability of resources. A resource is monotonically non-increasing if no action increases it. Explain how to use this property to prune the search space.

**12.3** Give decompositions for the *HireBuilder* and *GetPermit* steps in Figure 12.7, and show how the decomposed subplans connect into the overall plan.

**12.4** Give an example in the house-building domain of two abstract subplans that cannot be merged into a consistent plan without sharing steps. (*Hint:* Places where two physical parts of the house come together are also places where two subplans tend to interact.)

**12.5** Some people say an advantage of HTN planning is that it can solve problems like "take a round trip from Los Angeles to New York and back" that are hard to express in non-HTN notations because the start and goal states would be the same ($At(LA)$). Can you think of a way to represent and solve this problem without HTNs?

**12.6** Show how a standard STRIPS action description can be rewritten as an HTN decomposition, using the notation $Achieve(p)$ to denote the *activity* of achieving the condition $p$.

**12.7** Some of the operations in standard programming languages can be modeled as actions that change the state of the world. For example, the assignment operation copies the contents of a memory location, while the print operation changes the state of the output stream. A program consisting of these operations can also be considered as a plan, whose goal is given by the specification of the program. Therefore, planning algorithms can be used to construct programs that achieve a given specification.

**a.** Write an operator schema for the assignment operator (assigning the value of one variable to another). Remember that the original value will be overwritten!

**b**. Show how object creation can be used by a planner to produce a plan for exchanging the values of two variables using a temporary variable.

**12.8** Consider the following argument: In a framework that allows uncertain initial states, **disjunctive effects** are just a notational convenience, not a source of additional representational power. For any action schema $a$ with disjunctive effect $P \vee Q$, we could always replace it with the conditional effects **when** $R$: $P \wedge$ **when** $\neg R$: $Q$, which in turn can be reduced to two regular actions. The proposition $R$ stands for a random proposition that is unknown in the initial state and for which there are no sensing actions. Is this argument correct? Consider separately two cases, one in which only one instance of action schema $a$ is in the plan, the other in which more than one instance is.

**12.9** Why can't conditional planning deal with unbounded indeterminacy?

**12.10** In the blocks world we were forced to introduce two STRIPS actions, *Move* and *MoveToTable*, in order to maintain the *Clear* predicate properly. Show how conditional effects can be used to represent both of these cases with a single action.

**12.11** Conditional effects were illustrated for the *Suck* action in the vacuum world—which square becomes clean depends on which square the robot is in. Can you think of a new set of propositional variables to define states of the vacuum world, such that *Suck* has an *unconditional* description? Write out the descriptions of *Suck*, *Left*, and *Right*, using your propositions, and demonstrate that they suffice to describe all possible states of the world.

**12.12** Write out the full description of *Suck* for the double Murphy vacuum cleaner that sometimes deposits dirt when it moves to a clean destination square and sometimes deposits dirt if *Suck* is applied to a clean square.

**12.13** Find a suitably dirty carpet, free of obstacles, and vacuum it. Draw the path taken by the vacuum cleaner as accurately as you can. Explain it, with reference to the forms of planning discussed in this chapter.

**12.14** The following quotes are from the backs of shampoo bottles. Identify each as an unconditional, conditional, or execution monitoring plan. (a) "Lather. Rinse. Repeat." (b) "Apply shampoo to scalp and let it remain for several minutes. Rinse and repeat if necessary." (c) "See a doctor if problems persist."

**12.15** The AND-OR-GRAPH-SEARCH algorithm in Figure 12.10 checks for repeated states only on the path from the root to the current state. Suppose that, in addition, the algorithm were to store *every* visited state and check against that list. (See GRAPH-SEARCH in Figure 3.19 for an example.) Determine the information that should be stored and how the algorithm should use that information when a repeated state is found. (*Hint*: You will need to distinguish at least between states for which a successful subplan was constructed previously and states for which no subplan could be found.) Explain how to use **labels** to avoid having multiple copies of subplans.

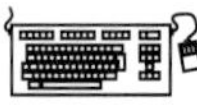

**12.16** Explain precisely how to modify the AND-OR-GRAPH-SEARCH algorithm to generate a cyclic plan if no acyclic plan exists. You will need to deal with three issues: labeling the plan steps so that a cyclic plan can point back to an earlier part of the plan, modifying OR-SEARCH so that it continues to look for acyclic plans after finding a cyclic plan, and augmenting the plan representation to indicate whether a plan is cyclic. Show how your algorithm works on (a) the triple Murphy vacuum world, and (b) the alternate double Murphy vacuum world. You might wish to use a computer implementation to check your results. Can the plan for case (b) be written using standard loop syntax?

**12.17** Specify in full the belief state update procedure for partially observable environments. That is, the method for computing the new belief state representation (as a list of knowledge propositions) from the current belief-state representation and an action description with conditional effects.

**12.18** Write action descriptions, analogous to Equation (12.2), for the $Right$ and $Suck$ actions. Also write a description for $CheckLocation$, analogous to Equation (12.3). Repeat using the alternative set of propositions from Exercise 12.11.

**12.19** Look at the list on page 445 of things that the replanning agent can't do. Sketch an algorithm that can handle one or more of them.

**12.20** Consider the following problem: A patient arrives at the doctor's office with symptoms that could have been caused either by dehydration or by disease $D$ (but not both). There are two possible actions: $Drink$, which unconditionally cures dehydration, and $Medicate$, which cures disease $D$, but has an undesirable side-effect if taken when the patient is dehydrated. Write the problem description in PDDL, and diagram a sensorless plan that solves the problem, enumerating all relevant possible worlds.

**12.21** To the medication problem in the previous exercise, add a $Test$ action that has the conditional effect $CultureGrowth$ when $Disease$ is true and in any case has the perceptual effect $Known(CultureGrowth)$. Diagram a conditional plan that solves the problem and minimizes the use of the $Medicate$ action.

# 13 UNCERTAINTY

*In which we see what an agent should do when not all is crystal clear.*

## 13.1 ACTING UNDER UNCERTAINTY

The logical agents described in Parts III and IV make the epistemological commitment that propositions are true, false, or unknown. When an agent knows enough facts about its environment, the logical approach enables it to derive plans that are guaranteed to work. This is a good thing. Unfortunately, *agents almost never have access to the whole truth about their environment.* Agents must, therefore, act under **uncertainty**. For example, an agent in the wumpus world of Chapter 7 has sensors that report only local information; most of the world is not immediately observable. A wumpus agent often will find itself unable to discover which of two squares contains a pit. If those squares are *en route* to the gold, then the agent might have to take a chance and enter one of the two squares.

UNCERTAINTY

The real world is far more complex than the wumpus world. For a logical agent, it might be impossible to construct a complete and correct description of how its actions will work. Suppose, for example, that the agent wants to drive someone to the airport to catch a flight and is considering a plan, $A_{90}$, that involves leaving home 90 minutes before the flight departs and driving at a reasonable speed. Even though the airport is only about 15 miles away, the agent will not be able to conclude with certainty that "Plan $A_{90}$ will get us to the airport in time." Instead, it reaches the weaker conclusion "Plan $A_{90}$ will get us to the airport in time, as long as my car doesn't break down or run out of gas, and I don't get into an accident, and there are no accidents on the bridge, and the plane doesn't leave early, and . . . ." None of these conditions can be deduced, so the plan's success cannot be inferred. This is an example of the **qualification problem** mentioned in Chapter 10.

If a logical agent cannot conclude that any particular course of action achieves its goal, then it will be unable to act. Conditional planning can overcome uncertainty to some extent, but only if the agent's sensing actions can obtain the required information and only if there are not too many different contingencies. Another possible solution would be to endow the agent with a simple but incorrect theory of the world that *does* enable it to derive a plan;

presumably, such plans will work *most* of the time, but problems arise when events contradict the agent's theory. Moreover, handling the tradeoff between the accuracy and usefulness of the agent's theory seems itself to require reasoning about uncertainty. In sum, no purely logical agent will be able to conclude that plan $A_{90}$ is the right thing to do.

Nonetheless, let us suppose that $A_{90}$ *is* in fact the right thing to do. What do we mean by saying this? As we discussed in Chapter 2, we mean that out of all the plans that could be executed, $A_{90}$ is expected to maximize the agent's performance measure, given the information it has about the environment. The performance measure includes getting to the airport in time for the flight, avoiding a long, unproductive wait at the airport, and avoiding speeding tickets along the way. The information the agent has cannot guarantee any of these outcomes for $A_{90}$, but it can provide some degree of belief that they will be achieved. Other plans, such as $A_{120}$, might increase the agent's belief that it will get to the airport on time, but also increase the likelihood of a long wait. *The right thing to do—the* ***rational decision****—therefore depends on both the relative importance of various goals and the likelihood that, and degree to which, they will be achieved.* The remainder of this section hones these ideas, in preparation for the development of the general theories of uncertain reasoning and rational decisions that we present in this and subsequent chapters.

## Handling uncertain knowledge

In this section, we look more closely at the nature of uncertain knowledge. We will use a simple diagnosis example to illustrate the concepts involved. Diagnosis—whether for medicine, automobile repair, or whatever—is a task that almost always involves uncertainty. Let us try to write rules for dental diagnosis using first-order logic, so that we can see how the logical approach breaks down. Consider the following rule:

$$\forall p \;\; Symptom(p, Toothache) \;\Rightarrow\; Disease(p, Cavity)\,.$$

The problem is that this rule is wrong. Not all patients with toothaches have cavities; some of them have gum disease, an abscess, or one of several other problems:

$$\forall p \;\; Symptom(p, Toothache) \;\Rightarrow$$
$$Disease(p, Cavity) \lor Disease(p, GumDisease) \lor Disease(p, Abscess) \ldots$$

Unfortunately, in order to make the rule true, we have to add an almost unlimited list of possible causes. We could try turning the rule into a causal rule:

$$\forall p \;\; Disease(p, Cavity) \;\Rightarrow\; Symptom(p, Toothache)\,.$$

But this rule is not right either; not all cavities cause pain. The only way to fix the rule is to make it logically exhaustive: to augment the left-hand side with all the qualifications required for a cavity to cause a toothache. Even then, for the purposes of diagnosis, one must also take into account the possibility that the patient might have a toothache and a cavity that are unconnected.

Trying to use first-order logic to cope with a domain like medical diagnosis thus fails for three main reasons:

LAZINESS

◇ **Laziness**: It is too much work to list the complete set of antecedents or consequents needed to ensure an exceptionless rule and too hard to use such rules.

THEORETICAL IGNORANCE

◇ **Theoretical ignorance**: Medical science has no complete theory for the domain.

PRACTICAL IGNORANCE

◇ **Practical ignorance**: Even if we know all the rules, we might be uncertain about a particular patient because not all the necessary tests have been or can be run.

DEGREE OF BELIEF

PROBABILITY THEORY

The connection between toothaches and cavities is just not a logical consequence in either direction. This is typical of the medical domain, as well as most other judgmental domains: law, business, design, automobile repair, gardening, dating, and so on. The agent's knowledge can at best provide only a **degree of belief** in the relevant sentences. Our main tool for dealing with degrees of belief will be **probability theory**, which assigns to each sentence a numerical degree of belief between 0 and 1. (Some alternative methods for uncertain reasoning are covered in Section 14.7.)

*Probability provides a way of* **summarizing** *the uncertainty that comes from our laziness and ignorance.* We might not know for sure what afflicts a particular patient, but we believe that there is, say, an 80% chance—that is, a probability of 0.8—that the patient has a cavity if he or she has a toothache. That is, we expect that out of all the situations that are indistinguishable from the current situation as far as the agent's knowledge goes, the patient will have a cavity in 80% of them. This belief could be derived from statistical data—80% of the toothache patients seen so far have had cavities—or from some general rules, or from a combination of evidence sources. The 80% summarizes those cases in which all the factors needed for a cavity to cause a toothache are present and other cases in which the patient has both toothache and cavity but the two are unconnected. The missing 20% summarizes all the other possible causes of toothache that we are too lazy or ignorant to confirm or deny.

Assigning a probability of 0 to a given sentence corresponds to an unequivocal belief that the sentence is false, while assigning a probability of 1 corresponds to an unequivocal belief that the sentence is true. Probabilities between 0 and 1 correspond to intermediate degrees of belief in the truth of the sentence. The sentence itself is *in fact* either true or false. It is important to note that a degree of belief is different from a degree of truth. A probability of 0.8 does not mean "80% true" but rather an 80% degree of belief—that is, a fairly strong expectation. Thus, probability theory makes the same ontological commitment as logic—namely, that facts either do or do not hold in the world. Degree of truth, as opposed to degree of belief, is the subject of **fuzzy logic**, which is covered in Section 14.7.

EVIDENCE

In logic, a sentence such as "The patient has a cavity" is true or false depending on the interpretation and the world; it is true just when the fact it refers to is the case. In probability theory, a sentence such as "The probability that the patient has a cavity is 0.8" is about the agent's beliefs, not directly about the world. These beliefs depend on the percepts that the agent has received to date. These percepts constitute the **evidence** on which probability assertions are based. For example, suppose that the agent has drawn a card from a shuffled pack. Before looking at the card, the agent might assign a probability of $1/52$ to its being the ace of spades. After looking at the card, an appropriate probability for the same proposition would be 0 or 1. Thus, an assignment of probability to a proposition is analogous to saying whether a given logical sentence (or its negation) is entailed by the knowledge base, rather than whether or not it is true. Just as entailment status can change when more sentences are added to the knowledge base, probabilities can change when more evidence is acquired.[1]

All probability statements must therefore indicate the evidence with respect to which the probability is being assessed. As the agent receives new percepts, its probability assessments are updated to reflect the new evidence. Before the evidence is obtained, we talk about **prior** or **unconditional** probability; after the evidence is obtained, we talk about **posterior** or **conditional** probability. In most cases, an agent will have some evidence from its percepts and will be interested in computing the posterior probabilities of the outcomes it cares about.

### Uncertainty and rational decisions

The presence of uncertainty radically changes the way an agent makes decisions. A logical agent typically has a goal and executes any plan that is guaranteed to achieve it. An action can be selected or rejected on the basis of whether it achieves the goal, regardless of what other actions might achieve. When uncertainty enters the picture, this is no longer the case. Consider again the $A_{90}$ plan for getting to the airport. Suppose it has a 95% chance of succeeding. Does this mean it is a rational choice? Not necessarily: There might be other plans, such as $A_{120}$, with higher probabilities of success. If it is vital not to miss the flight, then it is worth risking the longer wait at the airport. What about $A_{1440}$, a plan that involves leaving home 24 hours in advance? In most circumstances, this is not a good choice, because, although it almost guarantees getting there on time, it involves an intolerable wait.

PREFERENCES

OUTCOMES

UTILITY THEORY

To make such choices, an agent must first have **preferences** between the different possible **outcomes** of the various plans. A particular outcome is a completely specified state, including such factors as whether the agent arrives on time and the length of the wait at the airport. We will be using **utility theory** to represent and reason with preferences. (The term **utility** is used here in the sense of "the quality of being useful," not in the sense of the electric company or water works.) Utility theory says that every state has a degree of usefulness, or utility, to an agent and that the agent will prefer states with higher utility.

The utility of a state is relative to the agent whose preferences the utility function is supposed to represent. For example, the payoff functions for games in Chapter 6 are utility functions. The utility of a state in which White has won a game of chess is obviously high for the agent playing White, but low for the agent playing Black. Or again, some players (including the authors) might be happy with a draw against the world champion, whereas other players (including the former world champion) might not. There is no accounting for taste or preferences: you might think that an agent who prefers jalapeño bubble-gum ice cream to chocolate chocolate chip is odd or even misguided, but you could not say the agent is irrational. A utility function can even account for altruistic behavior, simply by including the welfare of others as one of the factors contributing to the agent's own utility.

DECISION THEORY

Preferences, as expressed by utilities, are combined with probabilities in the general theory of rational decisions called **decision theory**:

$$\textit{Decision theory} = \textit{probability theory} + \textit{utility theory}\ .$$

[1] This is quite different from a sentence's becoming true or false as the world changes. Handling a changing world via probabilities requires the same kinds of mechanisms—situations, intervals, and events—that we used in Chapter 10 for logical representations. These mechanisms are discussed in Chapter 15.

The fundamental idea of decision theory is that *an agent is rational if and only if it chooses the action that yields the highest expected utility, averaged over all the possible outcomes of the action.* This is called the principle of **Maximum Expected Utility** (MEU). We saw this principle in action in Chapter 6 when we touched briefly on optimal decisions in backgammon. We will see that it is in fact a completely general principle.

### Design for a decision-theoretic agent

Figure 13.1 sketches the structure of an agent that uses decision theory to select actions. The agent is identical, at an abstract level, to the logical agent described in Chapter 7. The primary difference is that the decision-theoretic agent's knowledge of the current state is uncertain; the agent's **belief state** is a representation of the probabilities of all possible actual states of the world. As time passes, the agent accumulates more evidence and its belief state changes. Given the belief state, the agent can make probabilistic predictions of action outcomes and hence select the action with highest expected utility. This chapter and the next concentrate on the task of representing and computing with probabilistic information in general. Chapter 15 deals with methods for the specific tasks of representing and updating the belief state and predicting the environment. Chapter 16 covers utility theory in more depth, and Chapter 17 develops algorithms for making complex decisions.

BELIEF STATE

```
function DT-AGENT(percept) returns an action
   static: belief_state, probabilistic beliefs about the current state of the world
           action, the agent's action

   update belief_state based on action and percept
   calculate outcome probabilities for actions,
      given action descriptions and current belief_state
   select action with highest expected utility
      given probabilities of outcomes and utility information
   return action
```

**Figure 13.1** A decision-theoretic agent that selects rational actions. The steps will be fleshed out in the next five chapters.

## 13.2 Basic Probability Notation

Now that we have set up the general framework for a rational agent, we will need a formal language for representing and reasoning with uncertain knowledge. Any notation for describing degrees of belief must be able to deal with two main issues: the nature of the sentences to which degrees of belief are assigned and the dependence of the degree of belief on the agent's experience. The version of probability theory we present uses an extension of propositional logic for its sentences. The dependence on experience is reflected in the syntactic distinction between prior probability statements, which apply before any evidence is obtained, and conditional probability statements, which include the evidence explicitly.

### Propositions

Degrees of belief are always applied to **propositions**—assertions that such-and-such is the case. So far we have seen two formal languages—propositional logic and first-order logic—for stating propositions. Probability theory typically uses a language that is slightly more expressive than propositional logic. This section describes that language. (Section 14.6 discusses ways to ascribe degrees of belief to assertions in first-order logic.)

RANDOM VARIABLE

The basic element of the language is the **random variable**, which can be thought of as referring to a "part" of the world whose "status" is initially unknown. For example, $Cavity$ might refer to whether my lower left wisdom tooth has a cavity. Random variables play a role similar to that of CSP variables in constraint satisfaction problems and that of proposition symbols in propositional logic. We will always capitalize the names of random variables. (However, we still use lowercase, single-letter names to represent an unknown random variable, for example: $P(a) = 1 - P(\neg a)$.)

DOMAIN

Each random variable has a **domain** of values that it can take on. For example, the domain of $Cavity$ might be $\langle true, false \rangle$.[2] (We will use lowercase for the names of values.) The simplest kind of proposition asserts that a random variable has a particular value drawn from its domain. For example, $Cavity = true$ might represent the proposition that I do in fact have a cavity in my lower left wisdom tooth.

As with CSP variables, random variables are typically divided into three kinds, depending on the type of the domain:

BOOLEAN RANDOM VARIABLES

◇ **Boolean random variables**, such as $Cavity$, have the domain $\langle true, false \rangle$. We will often abbreviate a proposition such as $Cavity = true$ simply by the lowercase name $cavity$. Similarly, $Cavity = false$ would be abbreviated by $\neg cavity$.

DISCRETE RANDOM VARIABLES

◇ **Discrete random variables**, which include Boolean random variables as a special case, take on values from a *countable* domain. For example, the domain of $Weather$ might be $\langle sunny, rainy, cloudy, snow \rangle$. The values in the domain must be mutually exclusive and exhaustive. Where no confusion arises, we will use, for example, $snow$ as an abbreviation for $Weather = snow$.

CONTINUOUS RANDOM VARIABLES

◇ **Continuous random variables** take on values from the real numbers. The domain can be either the entire real line or some subset such as the interval [0,1]. For example, the proposition $X = 4.02$ asserts that the random variable $X$ has the exact value 4.02. Propositions concerning continuous random variables can also be inequalities, such as $X \leq 4.02$

With some exceptions, we will be concentrating on the discrete case.

Elementary propositions, such as $Cavity = true$ and $Toothache = false$, can be combined to form complex propositions using all the standard logical connectives. For example,

---

[2] One might expect the domain to be written as a set: $\{true, false\}$. We write it as a tuple because it will be convenient later to impose an ordering on the values.

$Cavity = true \land Toothache = false$ is a proposition to which one may ascribe a degree of (dis)belief. As explained in the previous paragraph, this proposition may also be written as $cavity \land \neg toothache$.

## Atomic events

ATOMIC EVENT

The notion of an **atomic event** is useful in understanding the foundations of probability theory. An atomic event is a *complete* specification of the state of the world about which the agent is uncertain. It can be thought of as an assignment of particular values to all the variables of which the world is composed. For example, if my world consists of only the Boolean variables $Cavity$ and $Toothache$, then there are just four distinct atomic events; the proposition $Cavity = false \land Toothache = true$ is one such event.[3]

Atomic events have some important properties:

- They are *mutually exclusive*—at most one can actually be the case. For example, $cavity \land toothache$ and $cavity \land \neg toothache$ cannot both be the case.
- The set of all possible atomic events is *exhaustive*—at least one must be the case. That is, the disjunction of all atomic events is logically equivalent to $true$.
- Any particular atomic event entails the truth or falsehood of every proposition, whether simple or complex. This can be seen by using the standard semantics for logical connectives (Chapter 7). For example, the atomic event $cavity \land \neg toothache$ entails the truth of $cavity$ and the falsehood of $cavity \Rightarrow toothache$.
- Any proposition is logically equivalent to the disjunction of all atomic events that entail the truth of the proposition. For example, the proposition $cavity$ is equivalent to disjunction of the atomic events $cavity \land toothache$ and $cavity \land \neg toothache$.

Exercise 13.4 asks you to prove some of these properties.

## Prior probability

UNCONDITIONAL

PRIOR PROBABILITY

The **unconditional** or **prior probability** associated with a proposition $a$ is the degree of belief accorded to it *in the absence of any other information*; it is written as $P(a)$. For example, if the prior probability that I have a cavity is 0.1, then we would write

$$P(Cavity = true) = 0.1 \quad \text{or} \quad P(cavity) = 0.1 \,.$$

It is important to remember that $P(a)$ can be used only when there is no other information. As soon as some new information is known, we must reason with the *conditional* probability of $a$ given that new information. Conditional probabilities are covered in the next section.

Sometimes, we will want to talk about the probabilities of all the possible values of a random variable. In that case, we will use an expression such as $\mathbf{P}(Weather)$, which denotes a *vector* of values for the probabilities of each individual state of the weather. Thus, instead

[3] Many standard formulations of probability theory take atomic events, also known as **sample points**, as primitive and define a random variable as a function taking an atomic event as input and returning a value from the appropriate domain. Such an approach is perhaps more general, but also less intuitive.

of writing the four equations

$$P(Weather = sunny) = 0.7$$
$$P(Weather = rain) = 0.2$$
$$P(Weather = cloudy) = 0.08$$
$$P(Weather = snow) = 0.02 .$$

we may simply write

$$\mathbf{P}(Weather) = \langle 0.7, 0.2, 0.08, 0.02 \rangle .$$

PROBABILITY DISTRIBUTION

This statement defines a prior **probability distribution** for the random variable $Weather$.

We will also use expressions such as $\mathbf{P}(Weather, Cavity)$ to denote the probabilities of all combinations of the values of a set of random variables.[4] In that case, $\mathbf{P}(Weather, Cavity)$ can be represented by a $4 \times 2$ table of probabilities. This is called the **joint probability distribution** of $Weather$ and $Cavity$.

JOINT PROBABILITY DISTRIBUTION

Sometimes it will be useful to think about the complete set of random variables used to describe the world. A joint probability distribution that covers this complete set is called the **full joint probability distribution**. For example, if the world consists of just the variables $Cavity$, $Toothache$, and $Weather$, then the full joint distribution is given by

FULL JOINT PROBABILITY DISTRIBUTION

$$\mathbf{P}(Cavity, Toothache, Weather).$$

This joint distribution can be represented as a $2 \times 2 \times 4$ table with 16 entries. A full joint distribution specifies the probability of every atomic event and is therefore a complete specification of one's uncertainty about the world in question. We will see in Section 13.4 that any probabilistic query can be answered from the full joint distribution.

For continuous variables, it is not possible to write out the entire distribution as a table, because there are infinitely many values. Instead, one usually defines the probability that a random variable takes on some value $x$ as a parameterized function of $x$. For example, let the random variable $X$ denote tomorrow's maximum temperature in Berkeley. Then the sentence

$$P(X = x) = U[18, 26](x)$$

expresses the belief that $X$ is distributed uniformly between 18 and 26 degrees Celsius. (Several useful continuous distributions are defined in Appendix A.) Probability distributions for continuous variables are called **probability density functions**. Density functions differ in meaning from discrete distributions. For example, using the temperature distribution given earlier, we find that $P(X = 20.5) = U[18, 26](20.5) = 0.125/C$. This does *not* mean that there's a 12.5% chance that the maximum temperature will be *exactly* 20.5 degrees tomorrow; the probability that this will happen is of course zero. The technical meaning is that the probability that the temperature is in a small region around 20.5 degrees is equal, in the limit, to 0.125 divided by the width of the region in degrees Celsius:

PROBABILITY DENSITY FUNCTIONS

$$\lim_{dx \to 0} P(20.5 \leq X \leq 20.5 + dx)/dx = 0.125/C .$$

[4] The general notational rule is that the distribution covers all values of the variables that are capitalized. Thus, the expression $\mathbf{P}(Weather, cavity)$ is a four-element vector of probabilities for the conjunction of each weather type with $Cavity = true$.

Some authors use different symbols for discrete distributions and density functions; we use $P$ in both cases, since confusion seldom arises and the equations are usually identical. Note that probabilities are unitless numbers, whereas density functions are measured with a unit, in this case reciprocal degrees.

### Conditional probability

CONDITIONAL PROBABILITY
POSTERIOR PROBABILITY

Once the agent has obtained some evidence concerning the previously unknown random variables making up the domain, prior probabilities are no longer applicable. Instead, we use **conditional** or **posterior** probabilities. The notation used is $P(a|b)$, where $a$ and $b$ are any propositions.[5] This is read as "the probability of $a$, given that *all we know* is $b$." For example,

$$P(cavity|toothache) = 0.8$$

indicates that if a patient is observed to have a toothache and no other information is yet available, then the probability of the patient's having a cavity will be 0.8. A prior probability, such as $P(cavity)$, can be thought of as a special case of the conditional probability $P(cavity|\ )$, where the probability is conditioned on no evidence.

Conditional probabilities can be defined in terms of unconditional probabilities. The defining equation is

$$P(a|b) = \frac{P(a \wedge b)}{P(b)} \tag{13.1}$$

which holds whenever $P(b) > 0$. This equation can also be written as

$$P(a \wedge b) = P(a|b)P(b)$$

PRODUCT RULE

which is called the **product rule**. The product rule is perhaps easier to remember: it comes from the fact that, for $a$ and $b$ to be true, we need $b$ to be true, and we also need $a$ to be true given $b$. We can also have it the other way around:

$$P(a \wedge b) = P(b|a)P(a) .$$

In some cases, it is easier to reason in terms of prior probabilities of conjunctions, but for the most part, we will use conditional probabilities as our vehicle for probabilistic inference.

We can also use the **P** notation for conditional distributions. $\mathbf{P}(X|Y)$ gives the values of $P(X = x_i|Y = y_j)$ for each possible $i$, $j$. As an example of how this makes our notation more concise, consider applying the product rule to each case where the propositions $a$ and $b$ assert particular values of $X$ and $Y$ respectively. We obtain the following equations:

$$P(X = x_1 \wedge Y = y_1) = P(X = x_1|Y = y_1)P(Y = y_1) .$$
$$P(X = x_1 \wedge Y = y_2) = P(X = x_1|Y = y_2)P(Y = y_2) .$$
$$\vdots$$

We can combine all these into the single equation

$$\mathbf{P}(X, Y) = \mathbf{P}(X|Y)\mathbf{P}(Y) .$$

Remember that this denotes a set of equations relating the corresponding individual entries in the tables, *not* a matrix multiplication of the tables.

5 The "|" operator has the lowest possible precedence, so $P(a \wedge b|c \vee d)$ means $P((a \wedge b)|(c \vee d))$.

It is tempting, but wrong, to view conditional probabilities as if they were logical implications with uncertainty added. For example, the sentence $P(a|b) = 0.8$ *cannot* be interpreted to mean "whenever $b$ holds, conclude that $P(a)$ is 0.8." Such an interpretation would be wrong on two counts: first, $P(a)$ always denotes the prior probability of $a$, not the posterior probability given some evidence; second, the statement $P(a|b) = 0.8$ is immediately relevant just when $b$ is the *only* available evidence. When additional information $c$ is available, the degree of belief in $a$ is $P(a|b \wedge c)$, which might have little relation to $P(a|b)$. For example, $c$ might tell us directly whether $a$ is true or false. If we examine a patient who complains of toothache, and discover a cavity, then we have additional evidence $cavity$, and we conclude (trivially) that $P(cavity|toothache \wedge cavity) = 1.0$.

## 13.3 The Axioms of Probability

So far, we have defined a syntax for propositions and for prior and conditional probability statements about those propositions. Now we must provide some sort of semantics for probability statements. We begin with the basic axioms that serve to define the probability scale and its endpoints:

1. All probabilities are between 0 and 1. For any proposition $a$,

$$0 \leq P(a) \leq 1 \,.$$

2. Necessarily true (i.e., valid) propositions have probability 1, and necessarily false (i.e., unsatisfiable) propositions have probability 0.

$$P(\mathit{true}) = 1 \qquad\qquad P(\mathit{false}) = 0 \,.$$

Next, we need an axiom that connects the probabilities of logically related propositions. The simplest way to do this is to define the probability of a disjunction as follows:

3. The probability of a disjunction is given by

$$P(a \vee b) = P(a) + P(b) - P(a \wedge b) \,.$$

This rule is easily remembered by noting that the cases where $a$ holds, together with the cases where $b$ holds, certainly cover all the cases where $a \vee b$ holds; but summing the two sets of cases counts their intersection twice, so we need to subtract $P(a \wedge b)$.

KOLMOGOROV'S AXIOMS

These three axioms are often called **Kolmogorov's axioms** in honor of the Russian mathematician Andrei Kolmogorov, who showed how to build up the rest of probability theory from this simple foundation. Notice that the axioms deal only with prior probabilities rather than conditional probabilities; this is because we have already defined the latter in terms of the former via Equation (13.1).

## Where Do Probabilities Come From?

There has been endless debate over the source and status of probability numbers. The **frequentist** position is that the numbers can come only from *experiments*: if we test 100 people and find that 10 of them have a cavity, then we can say that the probability of a cavity is approximately 0.1. In this view, the assertion "the probability of a cavity is 0.1" means that 0.1 is the fraction that would be observed in the limit of infinitely many samples. From any finite sample, we can estimate the true fraction and also calculate how accurate our estimate is likely to be.

The **objectivist** view is that probabilities are real aspects of the universe—propensities of objects to behave in certain ways—rather than being just descriptions of an observer's degree of belief. For example, that a fair coin comes up heads with probability 0.5 is a propensity of the coin itself. In this view, frequentist measurements are attempts to observe these propensities. Most physicists agree that quantum phenomena are objectively probabilistic, but uncertainty at the macroscopic scale—e.g., in coin tossing—usually arises from ignorance of initial conditions and does not seem consistent with the propensity view.

The **subjectivist** view describes probabilities as a way of characterizing an agent's beliefs, rather than as having any external physical significance. This allows the doctor or analyst to make the numbers up—to say, "In my opinion, I expect the probability of a cavity to be about 0.1." Several more reliable techniques, such as the betting systems described on page 474, have also been developed for eliciting probability assessments from humans.

In the end, even a strict frequentist position involves subjective analysis, so the difference probably has little practical importance. The **reference class** problem illustrates the intrusion of subjectivity. Suppose that a frequentist doctor wants to know the chances that a patient has a particular disease. The doctor wants to consider other patients who are similar in important ways—age, symptoms, perhaps sex—and see what proportion of them had the disease. But if the doctor considered everything that is known about the patient—weight to the nearest gram, hair color, mother's maiden name, etc.—the result would be that there are no other patients who are exactly the same and thus no reference class from which to collect experimental data. This has been a vexing problem in the philosophy of science.

Laplace's **principle of indifference** (1816) states that propositions that are syntactically "symmetric" with respect to the evidence should be accorded equal probability. Various refinements have been proposed, culminating in the attempt by Carnap and others to develop a rigorous **inductive logic**, capable of computing the correct probability for any proposition from any collection of observations. Currently, it is believed that no unique inductive logic exists; rather, any such logic rests on a subjective prior probability distribution whose effect is diminished as more observations are collected.

### Using the axioms of probability

We can derive a variety of useful facts from the basic axioms. For example, the familiar rule for negation follows by substituting $\neg a$ for $b$ in axiom 3, giving us:

$$\begin{aligned} P(a \lor \neg a) &= P(a) + P(\neg a) - P(a \land \neg a) && \text{(by axiom 3 with } b = \neg a) \\ P(true) &= P(a) + P(\neg a) - P(false) && \text{(by logical equivalence)} \\ 1 &= P(a) + P(\neg a) && \text{(by axiom 2)} \\ P(\neg a) &= 1 - P(a) && \text{(by algebra).} \end{aligned}$$

The third line of this derivation is itself a useful fact and can be extended from the Boolean case to the general discrete case. Let the discrete variable $D$ have the domain $\langle d_1, \ldots, d_n \rangle$. Then it is easy to show (Exercise 13.2) that

$$\sum_{i=1}^{n} P(D = d_i) = 1 \,.$$

That is, any probability distribution on a single variable must sum to 1.[6] It is also true that any *joint* probability distribution on any *set* of variables must sum to 1: this can be seen simply by creating a single megavariable whose domain is the cross product of the domains of the the original variables.

Recall that any proposition $a$ is equivalent to the disjunction of all the atomic events in which $a$ holds; call this set of events $\mathbf{e}(a)$. Recall also that atomic events are mutually exclusive, so the probability of any conjunction of atomic events is zero, by axiom 2. Hence, from axiom 3, we can derive the following simple relationship: *The probability of a proposition is equal to the sum of the probabilities of the atomic events in which it holds;* that is,

$$P(a) = \sum_{e_i \in \mathbf{e}(a)} P(e_i) \,. \tag{13.2}$$

This equation provides a simple method for computing the probability of any proposition, given a full joint distribution that specifies the probabilities of all atomic events. (See Section 13.4.) In subsequent sections we will derive additional rules for manipulating probabilities. First, however, we will examine the foundation for the axioms themselves.

### Why the axioms of probability are reasonable

The axioms of probability can be seen as restricting the set of probabilistic beliefs that an agent can hold. This is somewhat analogous to the logical case, where a logical agent cannot simultaneously believe $A$, $B$, and $\neg(A \land B)$, for example. There is, however, an additional complication. In the logical case, the semantic definition of conjunction means that at least one of the three beliefs just mentioned *must be false in the world*, so it is unreasonable for an agent to believe all three. With probabilities, on the other hand, statements refer not to the world directly, but to the agent's own state of knowledge. Why, then, can an agent not hold the following set of beliefs, which clearly violates axiom 3?

$$\begin{aligned} P(a) &= 0.4 & \qquad P(a \land b) &= 0.0 \\ P(b) &= 0.3 & \qquad P(a \lor b) &= 0.8 \end{aligned} \tag{13.3}$$

[6] For continuous variables, the summation is replaced by an integral: $\int_{-\infty}^{\infty} P(X = x)\, dx = 1$.

This kind of question has been the subject of decades of intense debate between those who advocate the use of probabilities as the only legitimate form for degrees of belief and those who advocate alternative approaches. Here, we give one argument for the axioms of probability, first stated in 1931 by Bruno de Finetti.

The key to de Finetti's argument is the connection between degree of belief and actions. The idea is that if an agent has some degree of belief in a proposition $a$, then the agent should be able to state odds at which it is indifferent to a bet for or against $a$. Think of it as a game between two agents: Agent 1 states "my degree of belief in event $a$ is 0.4." Agent 2 is then free to choose whether to bet for or against $a$, at stakes that are consistent with the stated degree of belief. That is, Agent 2 could choose to bet that $a$ will occur, betting \$4 against Agent 1's \$6. Or Agent 2 could bet \$6 against \$4 that $A$ will not occur.[7] If an agent's degrees of belief do not accurately reflect the world, then you would expect that it would tend to lose money over the long run to an opposing agent whose beliefs more accurately reflect the state of the world.

But de Finetti proved something much stronger: *If Agent 1 expresses a set of degrees of belief that violate the axioms of probability theory then there is a combination of bets by Agent 2 that* **guarantees** *that Agent 1 will lose money* **every** *time.* So if you accept the idea that an agent should be willing to "put its money where its probabilities are," then you should accept that it is irrational to have beliefs that violate the axioms of probability.

One might think that this betting game is rather contrived. For example, what if one refuses to bet? Does that end the argument? The answer is that the betting game is an abstract model for the decision-making situation in which every agent is *unavoidably* involved at every moment. Every action (including inaction) is a kind of bet, and every outcome can be seen as a payoff of the bet. Refusing to bet is like refusing to allow time to pass.

We will not provide the proof of de Finetti's theorem, but we will show an example. Suppose that Agent 1 has the set of degrees of belief from Equation (13.3). Figure 13.2 shows that if Agent 2 chooses to bet \$4 on $a$, \$3 on $b$, and \$2 on $\neg(a \vee b)$, then Agent 1 always loses money, regardless of the outcomes for $a$ and $b$.

| Agent 1 | | Agent 2 | | Outcome for Agent 1 | | | |
|---|---|---|---|---|---|---|---|
| Proposition | Belief | Bet | Stakes | $a \wedge b$ | $a \wedge \neg b$ | $\neg a \wedge b$ | $\neg a \wedge \neg b$ |
| $a$ | 0.4 | $a$ | 4 to 6 | –6 | –6 | 4 | 4 |
| $b$ | 0.3 | $b$ | 3 to 7 | –7 | 3 | –7 | 3 |
| $a \vee b$ | 0.8 | $\neg(a \vee b)$ | 2 to 8 | 2 | 2 | 2 | –8 |
| | | | | –11 | –1 | –1 | –1 |

**Figure 13.2** Because Agent 1 has inconsistent beliefs, Agent 2 is able to devise a set of bets that guarantees a loss for Agent 1, no matter what the outcome of $a$ and $b$.

[7] One might argue that the agent's preferences for different bank balances are such that the possibility of losing \$1 is not counterbalanced by an equal possibility of winning \$1. One possible response is to make the bet amounts small enough to avoid this problem. Savage's analysis (1954) circumvents the issue altogether.

Other strong philosophical arguments have been put forward for the use of probabilities, most notably those of Cox (1946) and Carnap (1950). The world being the way it is, however, practical demonstrations sometimes speak louder than proofs. The success of reasoning systems based on probability theory has been much more effective in making converts. We now look at how the axioms can be deployed to make inferences.

## 13.4 INFERENCE USING FULL JOINT DISTRIBUTIONS

PROBABILISTIC INFERENCE

In this section we will describe a simple method for **probabilistic inference**—that is, the computation from observed evidence of posterior probabilities for query propositions. We will use the full joint distribution as the "knowledge base" from which answers to all questions may be derived. Along the way we will also introduce several useful techniques for manipulating equations involving probabilities.

We begin with a very simple example: a domain consisting of just the three Boolean variables $Toothache$, $Cavity$, and $Catch$ (the dentist's nasty steel probe catches in my tooth). The full joint distribution is a $2 \times 2 \times 2$ table as shown in Figure 13.3.

| | $toothache$ | | $\neg toothache$ | |
|---|---|---|---|---|
| | $catch$ | $\neg catch$ | $catch$ | $\neg catch$ |
| $cavity$ | 0.108 | 0.012 | 0.072 | 0.008 |
| $\neg cavity$ | 0.016 | 0.064 | 0.144 | 0.576 |

**Figure 13.3** A full joint distribution for the $Toothache$, $Cavity$, $Catch$ world.

Notice that the probabilities in the joint distribution sum to 1, as required by the axioms of probability. Notice also that Equation (13.2) gives us a direct way to calculate the probability of any proposition, simple or complex: We simply identify those atomic events in which the proposition is true and add up their probabilities. For example, there are six atomic events in which $cavity \lor toothache$ holds:

$$P(cavity \lor toothache) = 0.108 + 0.012 + 0.072 + 0.008 + 0.016 + 0.064 = 0.28 \,.$$

One particularly common task is to extract the distribution over some subset of variables or a single variable. For example, adding the entries in the first row gives the unconditional or

MARGINAL PROBABILITY

**marginal probability**[8] of $cavity$:

$$P(cavity) = 0.108 + 0.012 + 0.072 + 0.008 = 0.2 \,.$$

MARGINALIZATION

This process is called **marginalization**, or **summing out**—because the variables other than $Cavity$ are summed out. We can write the following general marginalization rule for any sets of variables $\mathbf{Y}$ and $\mathbf{Z}$:

$$\mathbf{P}(\mathbf{Y}) = \sum_{\mathbf{z}} \mathbf{P}(\mathbf{Y}, \mathbf{z}) \,. \tag{13.4}$$

[8] So called because of a common practice among actuaries of writing the sums of observed frequencies in the margins of insurance tables.

That is, a distribution over $\mathbf{Y}$ can be obtained by summing out all the other variables from any joint distribution containing $\mathbf{Y}$. A variant of this rule involves conditional probabilities instead of joint probabilities, using the product rule:

$$\mathbf{P}(\mathbf{Y}) = \sum_{\mathbf{z}} \mathbf{P}(\mathbf{Y}|\mathbf{z})P(\mathbf{z}) . \tag{13.5}$$

CONDITIONING

This rule is called **conditioning**. Marginalization and conditioning will turn out to be useful rules for all kinds of derivations involving probability expressions.

In most cases, we will be interested in computing *conditional* probabilities of some variables, given evidence about others. Conditional probabilities can be found by first using Equation (13.1) to obtain an expression in terms of unconditional probabilities and then evaluating the expression from the full joint distribution. For example, we can compute the probability of a cavity, given evidence of a toothache, as follows:

$$\begin{aligned} P(cavity|toothache) &= \frac{P(cavity \land toothache)}{P(toothache)} \\ &= \frac{0.108 + 0.012}{0.108 + 0.012 + 0.016 + 0.064} = 0.6 . \end{aligned}$$

Just to check, we can also compute the probability that there is no cavity, given a toothache:

$$\begin{aligned} P(\neg cavity|toothache) &= \frac{P(\neg cavity \land toothache)}{P(toothache)} \\ &= \frac{0.016 + 0.064}{0.108 + 0.012 + 0.016 + 0.064} = 0.4 . \end{aligned}$$

NORMALIZATION

Notice that in these two calculations the term $1/P(toothache)$ remains constant, no matter which value of $Cavity$ we calculate. In fact, it can be viewed as a **normalization** constant for the distribution $\mathbf{P}(Cavity|toothache)$, ensuring that it adds up to 1. Throughout the chapters dealing with probability, we will use $\alpha$ to denote such constants. With this notation, we can write the two preceding equations in one:

$$\begin{aligned} &\mathbf{P}(Cavity|toothache) = \alpha\, \mathbf{P}(Cavity, toothache) \\ &\quad = \alpha\, [\mathbf{P}(Cavity, toothache, catch) + \mathbf{P}(Cavity, toothache, \neg catch)] \\ &\quad = \alpha\, [\langle 0.108, 0.016\rangle + \langle 0.012, 0.064\rangle] = \alpha\, \langle 0.12, 0.08\rangle = \langle 0.6, 0.4\rangle . \end{aligned}$$

Normalization will turn out to be a useful shortcut in many probability calculations.

From the example, we can extract a general inference procedure. We will stick to the case in which the query involves a single variable. We will need some notation: let $X$ be the query variable ($Cavity$ in the example), let $\mathbf{E}$ be the set of evidence variables (just $Toothache$ in the example), let $\mathbf{e}$ be the observed values for them, and let $\mathbf{Y}$ be the remaining unobserved variables (just $Catch$ in the example). The query is $\mathbf{P}(X|\mathbf{e})$ and can be evaluated as

$$\mathbf{P}(X|\mathbf{e}) = \alpha\, \mathbf{P}(X, \mathbf{e}) = \alpha \sum_{\mathbf{y}} \mathbf{P}(X, \mathbf{e}, \mathbf{y}) , \tag{13.6}$$

where the summation is over all possible $\mathbf{y}$s (i.e., all possible combinations of values of the unobserved variables $\mathbf{Y}$). Notice that together the variables $X$, $\mathbf{E}$, and $\mathbf{Y}$ constitute the complete set of variables for the domain, so $\mathbf{P}(X, \mathbf{e}, \mathbf{y})$ is simply a subset of probabilities from the full joint distribution. The algorithm is shown in Figure 13.4. It loops over the values

```
function ENUMERATE-JOINT-ASK(X, e, P) returns a distribution over X
  inputs: X, the query variable
          e, observed values for variables E
          P, a joint distribution on variables {X} ∪ E ∪ Y   /* Y = hidden variables */

  Q(X) ← a distribution over X, initially empty
  for each value x_i of X do
     Q(x_i) ← ENUMERATE-JOINT(x_i, e, Y, [], P)
  return NORMALIZE(Q(X))
```

```
function ENUMERATE-JOINT(x, e, vars, values, P) returns a real number
  if EMPTY?(vars) then return P(x, e, values)
  Y ← FIRST(vars)
  return Σ_y ENUMERATE-JOINT(x, e, REST(vars), [y|values], P)
```

**Figure 13.4** An algorithm for probabilistic inference by enumeration of the entries in a full joint distribution.

of $X$ and the values of $Y$ to enumerate all possible atomic events with **e** fixed, adds up their probabilities from the joint table, and normalizes the results.

Given the full joint distribution to work with, ENUMERATE-JOINT-ASK is a complete algorithm for answering probabilistic queries for discrete variables. It does not scale well, however: For a domain described by $n$ Boolean variables, it requires an input table of size $O(2^n)$ and takes $O(2^n)$ time to process the table. In a realistic problem, there might be hundreds or thousands of random variables to consider, not just three. It quickly becomes completely impractical to define the vast numbers of probabilities required—the experience needed in order to estimate each of the table entries separately simply cannot exist.

For these reasons, the full joint distribution in tabular form is not a practical tool for building reasoning systems (although the historical notes at the end of the chapter includes one real-world application of this method). Instead, it should be viewed as the theoretical foundation on which more effective approaches may be built. The remainder of this chapter introduces some of the basic ideas required in preparation for the development of realistic systems in Chapter 14.

## 13.5 INDEPENDENCE

Let us expand the full joint distribution in Figure 13.3 by adding a fourth variable, *Weather*. The full joint distribution then becomes $\mathbf{P}(Toothache, Catch, Cavity, Weather)$, which has 32 entries (because *Weather* has four values). It contains four "editions" of the table shown in Figure 13.3, one for each kind of weather. It seems natural to ask what relationship these editions have to each other and to the original three-variable table. For example, how are $P(toothache, catch, cavity, Weather = cloudy)$ and $P(toothache, catch, cavity)$ related?

One way to answer this question is to use the product rule:

$$P(toothache, catch, cavity, Weather = cloudy)$$
$$= P(Weather = cloudy | toothache, catch, cavity) P(toothache, catch, cavity) .$$

Now, unless one is in the deity business, one should not imagine that one's dental problems influence the weather. Therefore, the following assertion seems reasonable:

$$P(Weather = cloudy | toothache, catch, cavity) = P(Weather = cloudy) . \quad (13.7)$$

From this, we can deduce

$$P(toothache, catch, cavity, Weather = cloudy)$$
$$= P(Weather = cloudy) P(toothache, catch, cavity) .$$

A similar equation exists for *every entry* in $\mathbf{P}(Toothache, Catch, Cavity, Weather)$. In fact, we can write the general equation

$$\mathbf{P}(Toothache, Catch, Cavity, Weather) = \mathbf{P}(Toothache, Catch, Cavity)\mathbf{P}(Weather) .$$

Thus, the 32-element table for four variables can be constructed from one 8-element table and one four-element table. This decomposition is illustrated schematically in Figure 13.5(a).

INDEPENDENCE

The property we used in writing Equation (13.7) is called **independence** (also **marginal independence** and **absolute independence**). In particular, the weather is independent of one's dental problems. Independence between propositions $a$ and $b$ can be written as

$$P(a|b) = P(a) \quad \text{or} \quad P(b|a) = P(b) \quad \text{or} \quad P(a \wedge b) = P(a)P(b) . \quad (13.8)$$

All these forms are equivalent (Exercise 13.7). Independence between variables $X$ and $Y$ can be written as follows (again, these are all equivalent):

$$\mathbf{P}(X|Y) = \mathbf{P}(X) \quad \text{or} \quad \mathbf{P}(Y|X) = \mathbf{P}(Y) \quad \text{or} \quad \mathbf{P}(X, Y) = \mathbf{P}(X)\mathbf{P}(Y) .$$

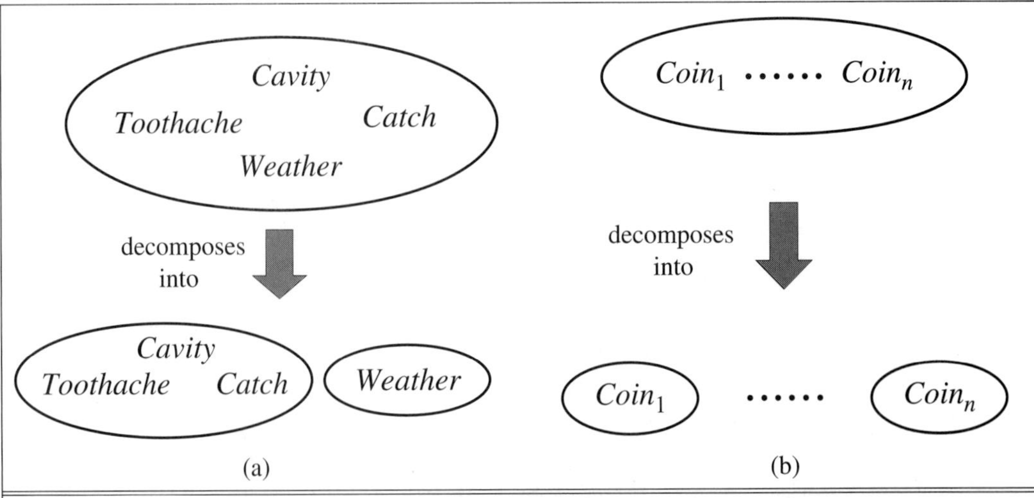


**Figure 13.5** Two examples of factoring a large joint distribution into smaller distributions, using absolute independence. (a) Weather and dental problems are independent. (b) Coin flips are independent.

Independence assertions are usually based on knowledge of the domain. As we have seen, they can dramatically reduce the amount of information necessary to specify the full joint distribution. If the complete set of variables can be divided into independent subsets, then the full joint can be *factored* into separate joint distributions on those subsets. For example, the joint distribution on the outcome of $n$ independent coin flips, $\mathbf{P}(C_1, \ldots, C_n)$, can be represented as the product of $n$ single-variable distributions $\mathbf{P}(C_i)$. In a more practical vein, the independence of dentistry and meteorology is a good thing, because otherwise the practice of dentistry might require intimate knowledge of meteorology and *vice versa*.

When they are available, then, independence assertions can help in reducing the size of the domain representation and the complexity of the inference problem. Unfortunately, clean separation of entire sets of variables by independence is quite rare. Whenever a connection, however indirect, exists between two variables, independence will fail to hold. Moreover, even independent subsets can be quite large—for example, dentistry might involve dozens of diseases and hundreds of symptoms, all of which are interrelated. To handle such problems, we will need more subtle methods than the straightforward concept of independence.

## 13.6 Bayes' Rule and Its Use

On page 470, we defined the **product rule** and pointed out that it can be written in two forms because of the commutativity of conjunction:

$$P(a \wedge b) = P(a|b)P(b)$$
$$P(a \wedge b) = P(b|a)P(a) .$$

Equating the two right-hand sides and dividing by $P(a)$, we get

$$P(b|a) = \frac{P(a|b)P(b)}{P(a)} . \quad (13.9)$$

BAYES' RULE

This equation is known as **Bayes' rule** (also Bayes' law or Bayes' theorem).[9] This simple equation underlies all modern AI systems for probabilistic inference. The more general case of multivalued variables can be written in the **P** notation as

$$\mathbf{P}(Y|X) = \frac{\mathbf{P}(X|Y)\mathbf{P}(Y)}{\mathbf{P}(X)} ,$$

where again this is to be taken as representing a set of equations, each dealing with specific values of the variables. We will also have occasion to use a more general version conditionalized on some background evidence **e**:

$$\mathbf{P}(Y|X, \mathbf{e}) = \frac{\mathbf{P}(X|Y, \mathbf{e})\mathbf{P}(Y|\mathbf{e})}{\mathbf{P}(X|\mathbf{e})} . \quad (13.10)$$

[9] According to rule 1 on page 1 of Strunk and White's *The Elements of Style*, it should be Bayes's rather than Bayes'. The latter is, however, more commonly used.

### Applying Bayes' rule: The simple case

On the surface, Bayes' rule does not seem very useful. It requires three terms—a conditional probability and two unconditional probabilities—just to compute one conditional probability.

Bayes' rule is useful in practice because there are many cases where we do have good probability estimates for these three numbers and need to compute the fourth. In a task such as medical diagnosis, we often have conditional probabilities on causal relationships and want to derive a diagnosis. A doctor knows that the disease meningitis causes the patient to have a stiff neck, say, 50% of the time. The doctor also knows some unconditional facts: the prior probability that a patient has meningitis is 1/50,000, and the prior probability that any patient has a stiff neck is 1/20. Letting $s$ be the proposition that the patient has a stiff neck and $m$ be the proposition that the patient has meningitis, we have

$$\begin{aligned} P(s|m) &= 0.5 \\ P(m) &= 1/50000 \\ P(s) &= 1/20 \\ P(m|s) &= \frac{P(s|m)P(m)}{P(s)} = \frac{0.5 \times 1/50000}{1/20} = 0.0002 \,. \end{aligned}$$

That is, we expect only 1 in 5000 patients with a stiff neck to have meningitis. Notice that, even though a stiff neck is quite strongly indicated by meningitis (with probability 0.5), the probability of meningitis in the patient remains small. This is because the prior probability on stiff necks is much higher than that on meningitis.

Section 13.4 illustrated a process by which one can avoid assessing the probability of the evidence (here, $P(s)$) by instead computing a posterior probability for each value of the query variable (here, $m$ and $\neg m$) and then normalizing the results. The same process can be applied when using Bayes' rule. We have

$$\mathbf{P}(M|s) = \alpha \, \langle P(s|m)P(m), P(s|\neg m)P(\neg m) \rangle \,.$$

Thus, in order to use this approach we need to estimate $P(s|\neg m)$ instead of $P(s)$. There is no free lunch—sometimes this is easier, sometimes it is harder. The general form of Bayes' rule with normalization is

$$\mathbf{P}(Y|X) = \alpha \, \mathbf{P}(X|Y)\mathbf{P}(Y) \,, \qquad (13.11)$$

where $\alpha$ is the normalization constant needed to make the entries in $\mathbf{P}(Y|X)$ sum to 1.

One obvious question to ask about Bayes' rule is why one might have available the conditional probability in one direction, but not the other. In the meningitis domain, perhaps the doctor knows that a stiff neck implies meningitis in 1 out of 5000 cases; that is, the doctor has quantitative information in the **diagnostic** direction from symptoms to causes. Such a doctor has no need to use Bayes' rule. Unfortunately, *diagnostic knowledge is often more fragile than causal knowledge.* If there is a sudden epidemic of meningitis, the unconditional probability of meningitis, $P(m)$, will go up. The doctor who derived the diagnostic probability $P(m|s)$ directly from statistical observation of patients before the epidemic will have no idea how to update the value, but the doctor who computes $P(m|s)$ from the other three values will see that $P(m|s)$ should go up proportionately with $P(m)$. Most importantly, the

causal information $P(s|m)$ is *unaffected* by the epidemic, because it simply reflects the way meningitis works. The use of this kind of direct causal or model-based knowledge provides the crucial robustness needed to make probabilistic systems feasible in the real world.

### Using Bayes' rule: Combining evidence

We have seen that Bayes' rule can be useful for answering probabilistic queries conditioned on one piece of evidence—for example, the stiff neck. In particular, we have argued that probabilistic information is often available in the form $P(\mathit{effect}|\mathit{cause})$. What happens when we have two or more pieces of evidence? For example, what can a dentist conclude if her nasty steel probe catches in the aching tooth of a patient? If we know the full joint distribution (Figure 13.3), one can read off the answer:

$$\mathbf{P}(\mathit{Cavity}|\mathit{toothache} \wedge \mathit{catch}) = \alpha \langle 0.108, 0.016 \rangle \approx \langle 0.871, 0.129 \rangle \, .$$

We know, however, that such an approach will not scale up to larger numbers of variables.

We can try using Bayes' rule to reformulate the problem:

$$\mathbf{P}(\mathit{Cavity}|\mathit{toothache} \wedge \mathit{catch}) = \alpha \mathbf{P}(\mathit{toothache} \wedge \mathit{catch}|\mathit{Cavity})\mathbf{P}(\mathit{Cavity}) \, . \quad (13.12)$$

For this reformulation to work, we need to know the conditional probabilities of the conjunction $\mathit{toothache} \wedge \mathit{catch}$ for each value of $\mathit{Cavity}$. That might be feasible for just two evidence variables, but again it will not scale up. If there are $n$ possible evidence variables (X rays, diet, oral hygiene, etc.), then there are $2^n$ possible combinations of observed values for which we would need to know conditional probabilities. We might as well go back to using the full joint distribution. This is what first led researchers away from probability theory toward approximate methods for evidence combination that, while giving incorrect answers, require fewer numbers to give any answer at all.

Rather than taking this route, we need to find some additional assertions about the domain that will enable us to simplify the expressions. The notion of **independence** in Section 13.5 provides a clue, but needs refining. It would be nice if $\mathit{Toothache}$ and $\mathit{Catch}$ were independent, but they are not: if the probe catches in the tooth, it probably has a cavity and that probably causes a toothache. These variables *are* independent, however, *given the presence or the absence of a cavity*. Each is directly caused by the cavity, but neither has a direct effect on the other: toothache depends on the state of the nerves in the tooth, whereas the probe's accuracy depends on the dentist's skill, to which the toothache is irrelevant.[10] Mathematically, this property is written as

$$\mathbf{P}(\mathit{toothache} \wedge \mathit{catch}|\mathit{Cavity}) = \mathbf{P}(\mathit{toothache}|\mathit{Cavity})\mathbf{P}(\mathit{catch}|\mathit{Cavity}) \, . \quad (13.13)$$

This equation expresses the **conditional independence** of $\mathit{toothache}$ and $\mathit{catch}$ given $\mathit{Cavity}$. We can plug it into Equation (13.12) to obtain the probability of a cavity:

$$\mathbf{P}(\mathit{Cavity}|\mathit{toothache} \wedge \mathit{catch}) = \alpha \, \mathbf{P}(\mathit{toothache}|\mathit{Cavity})\mathbf{P}(\mathit{catch}|\mathit{Cavity})\mathbf{P}(\mathit{Cavity}) .$$

Now the information requirements are the same as for inference using each piece of evidence separately: the prior probability $\mathbf{P}(\mathit{Cavity})$ for the query variable and the conditional probability of each effect, given its cause.

[10] We assume that the patient and dentist are distinct individuals.

The general definition of conditional independence of two variables $X$ and $Y$, given a third variable $Z$ is

$$\mathbf{P}(X, Y|Z) = \mathbf{P}(X|Z)\mathbf{P}(Y|Z) .$$

In the dentist domain, for example, it seems reasonable to assert conditional independence of the variables *Toothache* and *Catch*, given *Cavity*:

$$\mathbf{P}(Toothache, Catch|Cavity) = \mathbf{P}(Toothache|Cavity)\mathbf{P}(Catch|Cavity) . \quad (13.14)$$

Notice that this assertion is somewhat stronger than Equation (13.13), which asserts independence only for specific values of *Toothache* and *Catch*. As with absolute independence in Equation (13.8), the equivalent forms

$$\mathbf{P}(X|Y, Z) = \mathbf{P}(X|Z) \quad \text{and} \quad \mathbf{P}(Y|X, Z) = \mathbf{P}(Y|Z)$$

can also be used.

Section 13.5 showed that absolute independence assertions allow a decomposition of the full joint distribution into much smaller pieces. It turns out that the same is true for conditional independence assertions. For example, given the assertion in Equation (13.14), we can derive a decomposition as follows:

$$\begin{aligned}&\mathbf{P}(Toothache, Catch, Cavity)\\ &\quad = \mathbf{P}(Toothache, Catch|Cavity)\mathbf{P}(Cavity) \quad \text{(product rule)}\\ &\quad = \mathbf{P}(Toothache|Cavity)\mathbf{P}(Catch|Cavity)\mathbf{P}(Cavity) \quad \text{[using (13.14)].}\end{aligned}$$

In this way, the original large table is decomposed into three smaller tables. The original table has seven independent numbers ($2^3 - 1$, because the numbers must sum to 1). The smaller tables contain five independent numbers ($2 \times (2^1 - 1)$ for each conditional probability distribution and $2^1 - 1$ for the prior on *Cavity*). This might not seem to be a major triumph, but the point is that, for $n$ symptoms that are all conditionally independent given *Cavity*, the size of the representation grows as $O(n)$ instead of $O(2^n)$. Thus, *conditional independence assertions can allow probabilistic systems to scale up; moreover, they are much more commonly available than absolute independence assertions.* Conceptually, *Cavity* **separates** *Toothache* and *Catch* because it is a direct cause of both of them. The decomposition of large probabilistic domains into weakly connected subsets via conditional independence is one of the most important developments in the recent history of AI.

SEPARATION

The dentistry example illustrates a commonly occurring pattern in which a single cause directly influences a number of effects, all of which are conditionally independent, given the cause. The full joint distribution can be written as

$$\mathbf{P}(Cause, Effect_1, \ldots, Effect_n) = \mathbf{P}(Cause)\prod_i \mathbf{P}(Effect_i|Cause) .$$

NAIVE BAYES

Such a probability distribution is called a **naive Bayes** model—"naive" because it is often used (as a simplifying assumption) in cases where the "effect" variables are *not* conditionally independent given the cause variable. (The naive Bayes model is sometimes called a **Bayesian classifier**, a somewhat careless usage that has prompted true Bayesians to call it the **idiot Bayes** model.) In practice, naive Bayes systems can work surprisingly well, even when the independence assumption is not true. Chapter 20 describes methods for learning naive Bayes distributions from observations.

IDIOT BAYES

## 13.7 THE WUMPUS WORLD REVISITED

We can combine many of the ideas in this chapter to solve probabilistic reasoning problems in the wumpus world. (See Chapter 7 for a complete description of the wumpus world.) Uncertainty arises in the wumpus world because the agent's sensors give only partial, local information about the world. For example, Figure 13.6 shows a situation in which each of the three reachable squares—[1,3], [2,2], and [3,1]—might contain a pit. Pure logical inference can conclude nothing about which square is most likely to be safe, so a logical agent might be forced to choose randomly. We will see that a probabilistic agent can do much better than the logical agent.

Our aim will be to calculate the probability that each of the three squares contains a pit. (For the purposes of this example, we will ignore the wumpus and the gold.) The relevant properties of the wumpus world are that (1) a pit causes breezes in all neighboring squares, and (2) each square other than [1,1] contains a pit with probability 0.2. The first step is to identify the set of random variables we need:

- As in the propositional logic case, we want one Boolean variable $P_{ij}$ for each square, which is true iff square $[i,j]$ actually contains a pit.
- We also have Boolean variables $B_{ij}$ that are true iff square $[i,j]$ is breezy; we include these variables only for the observed squares—in this case, [1,1], [1,2], and [2,1].

The next step is to specify the full joint distribution, $\mathbf{P}(P_{1,1},\ldots,P_{4,4},B_{1,1},B_{1,2},B_{2,1})$. Applying the product rule, we have

$$\mathbf{P}(P_{1,1},\ldots,P_{4,4},B_{1,1},B_{1,2},B_{2,1}) = \mathbf{P}(B_{1,1},B_{1,2},B_{2,1} \mid P_{1,1},\ldots,P_{4,4})\mathbf{P}(P_{1,1},\ldots,P_{4,4}) .$$

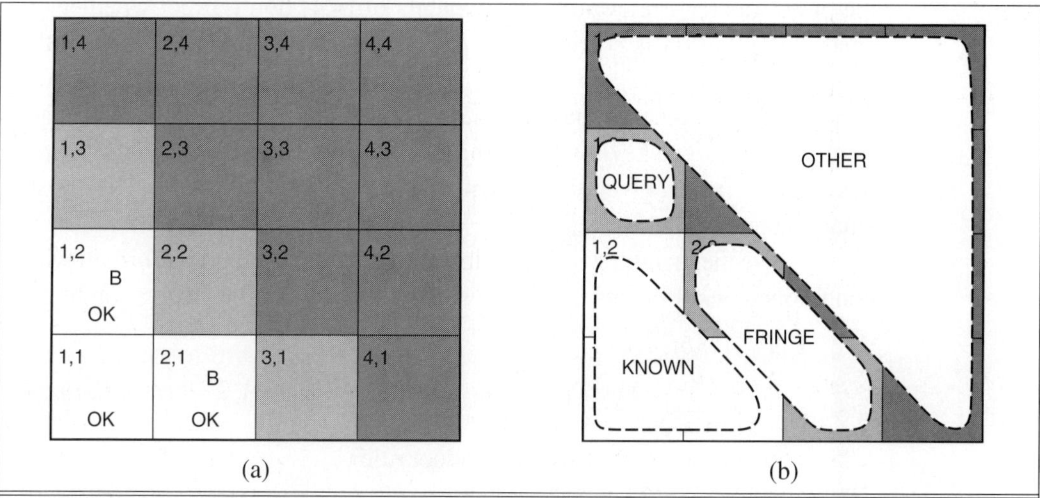


**Figure 13.6** (a) After finding a breeze in both [1,2] and [2,1], the agent is stuck—there is no safe place to explore. (b) Division of the squares into *Known*, *Fringe*, and *Other*, for a query about [1,3].

This decomposition makes it very easy to see what the joint probability values should be. The first term is the conditional probability of a breeze configuration, given a pit configuration; this is 1 if the breezes are adjacent to the pits and 0 otherwise. The second term is the prior probability of a pit configuration. Each square contains a pit with probability 0.2, independently of the other squares; hence,

$$\mathbf{P}(P_{1,1}, \ldots, P_{4,4}) = \prod_{i,j=1,1}^{4,4} \mathbf{P}(P_{i,j}) . \tag{13.15}$$

For a configuration with $n$ pits, this is just $0.2^n \times 0.8^{16-n}$.

In the situation in Figure 13.6(a), the evidence consists of the observed breeze (or its absence) in each square that is visited, combined with the fact that each such square contains no pit. We'll abbreviate these facts as $b = \neg b_{1,1} \wedge b_{1,2} \wedge b_{2,1}$ and $known = \neg p_{1,1} \wedge \neg p_{1,2} \wedge \neg p_{2,1}$. We are interested in answering queries such as $\mathbf{P}(P_{1,3}|known, b)$: how likely is it that [1,3] contains a pit, given the observations so far?

To answer this query, we can follow the standard approach suggested by Equation (13.6) and implemented in the ENUMERATE-JOINT-ASK, namely, summing over entries from the full joint distribution. Let *Unknown* be a composite variable consisting of the $P_{i,j}$ variables for squares other than the *Known* squares and the query square [1,3]. Then, by Equation (13.6), we have

$$\mathbf{P}(P_{1,3}|known, b) = \alpha \sum_{unknown} \mathbf{P}(P_{1,3}, unknown, known, b) .$$

The full joint probabilities have already been specified, so we are done—that is, unless we care about computation. There are 12 unknown squares; hence the summation contains $2^{12} = 4096$ terms. In general, the summation grows exponentially with the number of squares.

Intuition suggests that we are missing something here. Surely, one might ask, aren't the other squares irrelevant? The contents of [4,4] don't affect whether [1,3] has a pit! Indeed, this intuition is correct. Let *Fringe* be the variables (other than the query variable) that are adjacent to visited squares, in this case just [2,2] and [3,1]. Also, let *Other* be the variables for the other unknown squares; in this case, there are 10 other squares, as shown in Figure 13.6(b). The key insight is that the observed breezes are *conditionally independent* of the other variables, given the known, fringe, and query variables. The rest is, as they say, a small matter of algebra.

To use the insight, we manipulate the query formula into a form in which the breezes are conditioned on all the other variables, and then we simplify using conditional independence:

$$\begin{aligned}
&\mathbf{P}(P_{1,3}|known, b)\\
&= \alpha \sum_{unknown} \mathbf{P}(b|P_{1,3}, known, unknown)\mathbf{P}(P_{1,3}, known, unknown)\\
&\qquad \text{(by the product rule)}\\
&= \alpha \sum_{fringe} \sum_{other} \mathbf{P}(b|known, P_{1,3}, fringe, other)\mathbf{P}(P_{1,3}, known, fringe, other)\\
&= \alpha \sum_{fringe} \sum_{other} \mathbf{P}(b|known, P_{1,3}, fringe)\mathbf{P}(P_{1,3}, known, fringe, other) ,
\end{aligned}$$

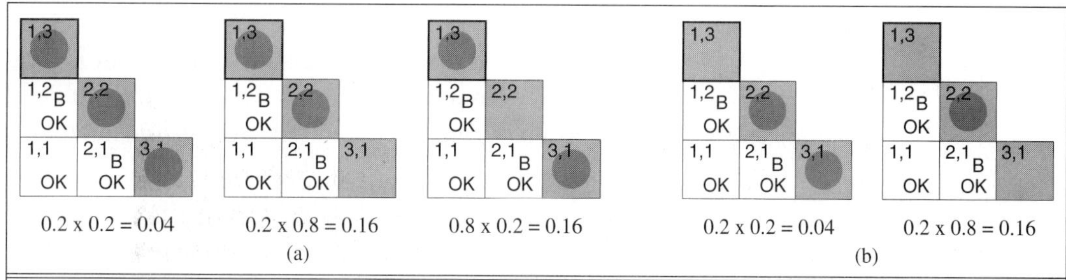


**Figure 13.7** Consistent models for the fringe variables $P_{2,2}$ and $P_{3,1}$, showing $P(fringe)$ for each model: (a) three models with $P_{1,3} = true$ showing two or three pits, and (b) two models with $P_{1,3} = false$ showing one or two pits.

where the final step uses conditional independence. Now, the first term in this expression does not depend on the other variables, so we can move the summation inwards:

$$\begin{aligned}
&\mathbf{P}(P_{1,3}|known, b) \\
&= \alpha \sum_{fringe} \mathbf{P}(b|known, P_{1,3}, fringe) \sum_{other} \mathbf{P}(P_{1,3}, known, fringe, other) .
\end{aligned}$$

By independence, as in Equation (13.15), the prior term can be factored, and then the terms can be reordered:

$$\begin{aligned}
&\mathbf{P}(P_{1,3}|known, b) \\
&= \alpha \sum_{fringe} \mathbf{P}(b|known, P_{1,3}, fringe) \sum_{other} \mathbf{P}(P_{1,3}) P(known) P(fringe) P(other) \\
&= \alpha\, P(known) \mathbf{P}(P_{1,3}) \sum_{fringe} \mathbf{P}(b|known, P_{1,3}, fringe) P(fringe) \sum_{other} P(other) \\
&= \alpha' \, \mathbf{P}(P_{1,3}) \sum_{fringe} \mathbf{P}(b|known, P_{1,3}, fringe) P(fringe) ,
\end{aligned}$$

where the last step folds $P(known)$ into the normalizing constant and uses the fact that $\sum_{other} P(other)$ equals 1.

Now, there are just four terms in the summation over the fringe variables $P_{2,2}$ and $P_{3,1}$. The use of independence and conditional independence has completely eliminated the other squares from consideration. Notice that the expression $\mathbf{P}(b|known, P_{1,3}, fringe)$ is 1 when the fringe is consistent with the breeze observations and 0 otherwise. Thus, for each value of $P_{1,3}$, we sum over the *logical models* for the fringe variables that are consistent with the known facts. (Compare with the enumeration over models in Figure 7.5.) The models and their associated prior probabilities—$P(fringe)$—are shown in Figure 13.7. We have

$$\mathbf{P}(P_{1,3}|known, b) = \alpha' \langle 0.2(0.04 + 0.16 + 0.16),\ 0.8(0.04 + 0.16) \rangle \approx \langle 0.31, 0.69 \rangle .$$

That is, [1,3] (and [3,1] by symmetry) contains a pit with roughly 31% probability. A similar calculation, which the reader might wish to perform, shows that [2,2] contains a pit with roughly 86% probability. The wumpus agent should definitely avoid [2,2]!

What this section has shown is that even seemingly complicated problems can be formulated precisely in probability theory and solved using simple algorithms. To get *efficient* solutions, independence and conditional independence relationships can be used to simplify the summations required. These relationships often correspond to our natural understanding of how the problem should be decomposed. In the next chapter, we will develop formal representations for such relationships as well as algorithms that operate on those representations to perform probabilistic inference efficiently.

## 13.8 SUMMARY

This chapter has argued that probability is the right way to reason about uncertainty.

- Uncertainty arises because of both laziness and ignorance. It is inescapable in complex, dynamic, or inaccessible worlds.
- Uncertainty means that many of the simplifications that are possible with deductive inference are no longer valid.
- Probabilities express the agent's inability to reach a definite decision regarding the truth of a sentence. Probabilities summarize the agent's beliefs.
- Basic probability statements include **prior probabilities** and **conditional probabilities** over simple and complex propositions.
- The **full joint probability distribution** specifies the probability of each complete assignment of values to random variables. It is usually too large to create or use in its explicit form.
- The axioms of probability constrain the possible assignments of probabilities to propositions. An agent that violates the axioms will behave irrationally in some circumstances.
- When the full joint distribution is available, it can be used to answer queries simply by adding up entries for the atomic events corresponding to the query propositions.
- **Absolute independence** between subsets of random variables might allow the full joint distribution to be factored into smaller joint distributions. This could greatly reduce complexity, but seldom occurs in practice.
- **Bayes' rule** allows unknown probabilities to be computed from known conditional probabilities, usually in the causal direction. Applying Bayes' rule with many pieces of evidence will in general run into the same scaling problems as does the full joint distribution.
- **Conditional independence** brought about by direct causal relationships in the domain might allow the full joint distribution to be factored into smaller, conditional distributions. The **naive Bayes** model assumes the conditional independence of all effect variables, given a single cause variable, and grows linearly with the number of effects.
- A wumpus-world agent can calculate probabilities for unobserved aspects of the world and use them to make better decisions than a purely logical agent makes.

## Bibliographical and Historical Notes

Although games of chance date back at least to around 300 B.C., the mathematical analysis of odds and probability appears to be much more recent. Some work done by Mahaviracarya in India is dated to roughly the ninth century A.D. In Europe, the first attempts date only to the Italian Renaissance, beginning around 1500 A.D. The first significant systematic analyses were produced by Girolamo Cardano around 1565, but they remained unpublished until 1663. By that time, the discovery by Blaise Pascal (in correspondence with Pierre Fermat in 1654) of a systematic way of calculating probabilities had for the first time established probability as a mathematical discipline. The first published textbook on probability was *De Ratiociniis in Ludo Aleae* (Huygens, 1657). Pascal also introduced conditional probability, which is covered in Huygens's textbook. The Rev. Thomas Bayes (1702–1761) introduced the rule for reasoning about conditional probabilities that was named after him. It was published posthumously (Bayes, 1763). Kolmogorov (1950, first published in German in 1933) presented probability theory in a rigorously axiomatic framework for the first time. Rényi (1970) later gave an axiomatic presentation that took conditional probability, rather than absolute probability, as primitive.

Pascal used probability in ways that required both the objective interpretation, as a property of the world based on symmetry or relative frequency, and the subjective interpretation, based on degree of belief—the former in his analyses of probabilities in games of chance, the latter in the famous "Pascal's wager" argument about the possible existence of God. However, Pascal did not clearly realize the distinction between these two interpretations. The distinction was first drawn clearly by James Bernoulli (1654–1705).

Leibniz introduced the "classical" notion of probability as a proportion of enumerated, equally probable cases, which was also used by Bernoulli, although it was brought to prominence by Laplace (1749–1827). This notion is ambiguous between the frequency interpretation and the subjective interpretation. The cases can be thought to be equally probable either because of a natural, physical symmetry between them, or simply because we do not have any knowledge that would lead us to consider one more probable than another. The use of this latter, subjective consideration to justify assigning equal probabilities is known as the *principle of indifference* (Keynes, 1921).

The debate between objectivists and subjectivists became sharper in the 20th century. Kolmogorov (1963), R. A. Fisher (1922), and Richard von Mises (1928) were advocates of the relative frequency interpretation. Karl Popper's (1959, first published in German in 1934) "propensity" interpretation traces relative frequencies to an underlying physical symmetry. Frank Ramsey (1931), Bruno de Finetti (1937), R. T. Cox (1946), Leonard Savage (1954), and Richard Jeffrey (1983) interpreted probabilities as the degrees of belief of specific individuals. Their analyses of degree of belief were closely tied to utilities and to behavior—specifically, to the willingness to place bets. Rudolf Carnap, following Leibniz and Laplace, offered a different kind of subjective interpretation of probability—not as any actual individual's degree of belief, but as the degree of belief that an idealized individual *should* have in a particular proposition $a$, given a particular body of evidence **e**. Carnap attempted to go further

CONFIRMATION

INDUCTIVE LOGIC

than Leibniz or Laplace by making this notion of degree of **confirmation** mathematically precise, as a logical relation between $a$ and **e**. The study of this relation was intended to constitute a mathematical discipline called **inductive logic**, analogous to ordinary deductive logic (Carnap, 1948, 1950). Carnap was not able to extend his inductive logic much beyond the propositional case, and Putnam (1963) showed that some fundamental difficulties would prevent a strict extension to languages capable of expressing arithmetic.

The question of reference classes is closely tied to the attempt to find an inductive logic. The approach of choosing the "most specific" reference class of sufficient size was formally proposed by Reichenbach (1949). Various attempts have been made, notably by Henry Kyburg (1977, 1983), to formulate more sophisticated policies in order to avoid some obvious fallacies that arise with Reichenbach's rule, but such approaches remain somewhat *ad hoc*. More recent work by Bacchus, Grove, Halpern, and Koller (1992) extends Carnap's methods to first-order theories, thereby avoiding many of the difficulties associated with the straightfoward reference-class method.

Bayesian probabilistic reasoning has been used in AI since the 1960s, especially in medical diagnosis. It was used not only to make a diagnosis from available evidence, but also to select further questions and tests using the theory of information value (Section 16.6) when available evidence was inconclusive (Gorry, 1968; Gorry *et al.*, 1973). One system outperformed human experts in the diagnosis of acute abdominal illnesses (de Dombal *et al.*, 1974). These early Bayesian systems suffered from a number of problems, however. Because they lacked any theoretical model of the conditions they were diagnosing, they were vulnerable to unrepresentative data occurring in situations for which only a small sample was available (de Dombal *et al.*, 1981). Even more fundamentally, because they lacked a concise formalism (such as the one to be described in Chapter 14) for representing and using conditional independence information, they depended on the acquisition, storage, and processing of enormous tables of probabilistic data. Because of these difficulties, probabilistic methods for coping with uncertainty fell out of favor in AI from the 1970s to the mid-1980s. Developments since the late 1980s are described in the next chapter.

The naive Bayes representation for joint distributions has been studied extensively in the pattern recognition literature since the 1950s (Duda and Hart, 1973). It has also been used, often unwittingly, in text retrieval, beginning with the work of Maron (1961). The probabilistic foundations of this technique, described further in Exercise 13.18, were elucidated by Robertson and Sparck Jones (1976). Domingos and Pazzani (1997) provide an explanation for the surprising success of naive Bayesian reasoning even in domains where the independence assumptions are clearly violated.

There are many good introductory textbooks on probability theory, including those by Chung (1979) and Ross (1988). Morris DeGroot (1989) offers a combined introduction to probability and statistics from a Bayesian standpoint, as well as a more advanced text (1970). Richard Hamming's (1991) textbook gives a mathematically sophisticated introduction to probability theory from the standpoint of a propensity interpretation based on physical symmetry. Hacking (1975) and Hald (1990) cover the early history of the concept of probability. Bernstein (1996) gives an entertaining popular account of the story of risk.

## EXERCISES

**13.1** Show from first principles that $P(a|b \wedge a) = 1$.

**13.2** Using the axioms of probability, prove that any probability distribution on a discrete random variable must sum to 1.

**13.3** Would it be rational for an agent to hold the three beliefs $P(A) = 0.4$, $P(B) = 0.3$, and $P(A \vee B) = 0.5$? If so, what range of probabilities would be rational for the agent to hold for $A \wedge B$? Make up a table like the one in Figure 13.2, and show how it supports your argument about rationality. Then draw another version of the table where $P(A \vee B) = 0.7$. Explain why it is rational to have this probability, even though the table shows one case that is a loss and three that just break even. (*Hint:* what is Agent 1 committed to about the probability of each of the four cases, especially the case that is a loss?)

**13.4** This question deals with the properties of atomic events, as discussed on page 468.

**a.** Prove that the disjunction of all possible atomic events is logically equivalent to $true$. [*Hint:* Use a proof by induction on the number of random variables.]

**b.** Prove that any proposition is logically equivalent to the disjunction of the atomic events that entail its truth.

**13.5** Consider the domain of dealing 5-card poker hands from a standard deck of 52 cards, under the assumption that the dealer is fair.

**a.** How many atomic events are there in the joint probability distribution (i.e., how many 5-card hands are there)?

**b.** What is the probability of each atomic event?

**c.** What is the probability of being dealt a royal straight flush? Four of a kind?

**13.6** Given the full joint distribution shown in Figure 13.3, calculate the following:

**a.** $P(toothache)$

**b.** $\mathbf{P}(Cavity)$

**c.** $\mathbf{P}(Toothache|cavity)$

**d.** $\mathbf{P}(Cavity|toothache \vee catch)$.

**13.7** Show that the three forms of independence in Equation (13.8) are equivalent.

**13.8** After your yearly checkup, the doctor has bad news and good news. The bad news is that you tested positive for a serious disease and that the test is 99% accurate (i.e., the probability of testing positive when you do have the disease is 0.99, as is the probability of testing negative when you don't have the disease). The good news is that this is a rare disease, striking only 1 in 10,000 people of your age. Why is it good news that the disease is rare? What are the chances that you actually have the disease?

**13.9** It is quite often useful to consider the effect of some specific propositions in the context of some general background evidence that remains fixed, rather than in the complete absence of information. The following questions ask you to prove more general versions of the product rule and Bayes' rule, with respect to some background evidence **e**:

**a.** Prove the conditionalized version of the general product rule:

$$\mathbf{P}(X, Y|\mathbf{e}) = \mathbf{P}(X|Y, \mathbf{e})\mathbf{P}(Y|\mathbf{e}) .$$

**b.** Prove the conditionalized version of Bayes' rule in Equation (13.10).

**13.10** Show that the statement

$$\mathbf{P}(A, B|C) = \mathbf{P}(A|C)\mathbf{P}(B|C)$$

is equivalent to either of the statements

$$\mathbf{P}(A|B, C) = \mathbf{P}(A|C) \quad \text{and} \quad \mathbf{P}(B|A, C) = \mathbf{P}(B|C) .$$

**13.11** Suppose you are given a bag containing $n$ unbiased coins. You are told that $n - 1$ of these coins are normal, with heads on one side and tails on the other, whereas one coin is a fake, with heads on both sides.

**a.** Suppose you reach into the bag, pick out a coin uniformly at random, flip it, and get a head. What is the (conditional) probability that the coin you chose is the fake coin?

**b.** Suppose you continue flipping the coin for a total of $k$ times after picking it and see $k$ heads. Now what is the conditional probability that you picked the fake coin?

**c.** Suppose you wanted to decide whether the chosen coin was fake by flipping it $k$ times. The decision procedure returns FAKE if all $k$ flips come up heads, otherwise it returns NORMAL. What is the (unconditional) probability that this procedure makes an error?

**13.12** In this exercise, you will complete the normalization calculation for the meningitis example. First, make up a suitable value for $P(S|\neg M)$, and use it to calculate unnormalized values for $P(M|S)$ and $P(\neg M|S)$ (i.e., ignoring the $P(S)$ term in the Bayes' rule expression). Now normalize these values so that they add to 1.

**13.13** This exercise investigates the way in which conditional independence relationships affect the amount of information needed for probabilistic calculations.

**a.** Suppose we wish to calculate $P(h|e_1, e_2)$ and we have no conditional independence information. Which of the following sets of numbers are sufficient for the calculation?

(i) $\mathbf{P}(E_1, E_2), \mathbf{P}(H), \mathbf{P}(E_1|H), \mathbf{P}(E_2|H)$
(ii) $\mathbf{P}(E_1, E_2), \mathbf{P}(H), \mathbf{P}(E_1, E_2|H)$
(iii) $\mathbf{P}(H), \mathbf{P}(E_1|H), \mathbf{P}(E_2|H)$

**b.** Suppose we know that $\mathbf{P}(E_1|H, E_2) = \mathbf{P}(E_1|H)$ for all values of $H$, $E_1$, $E_2$. Now which of the three sets are sufficient?

**13.14** Let $X$, $Y$, $Z$ be Boolean random variables. Label the eight entries in the joint distribution $\mathbf{P}(X, Y, Z)$ as $a$ through $h$. Express the statement that $X$ and $Y$ are conditionally independent given $Z$ as a set of equations relating $a$ through $h$. How many *nonredundant* equations are there?

**13.15** (Adapted from Pearl (1988).) Suppose you are a witness to a nighttime hit-and-run accident involving a taxi in Athens. All taxis in Athens are blue or green. You swear, under oath, that the taxi was blue. Extensive testing shows that, under the dim lighting conditions, discrimination between blue and green is 75% reliable. Is it possible to calculate the most likely color for the taxi? (*Hint:* distinguish carefully between the proposition that the taxi *is* blue and the proposition that it *appears* blue.)

What about now, given that 9 out of 10 Athenian taxis are green?

**13.16** (Adapted from Pearl (1988).) Three prisoners, *A*, *B*, and *C*, are locked in their cells. It is common knowledge that one of them will be executed the next day and the others pardoned. Only the governor knows which one will be executed. Prisoner *A* asks the guard a favor: "Please ask the governor who will be executed, and then take a message to one of my friends *B* or *C* to let him know that he will be pardoned in the morning." The guard agrees, and comes back later and tells *A* that he gave the pardon message to *B*.

What are *A*'s chances of being executed, given this information? (Answer this *mathematically*, not by energetic waving of hands.)

**13.17** Write out a general algorithm for answering queries of the form $\mathbf{P}(Cause|\mathbf{e})$, using a naive Bayes distribution. You should assume that the evidence $\mathbf{e}$ may assign values to *any subset* of the effect variables.

**13.18** Text categorization is the task of assigning a given document to one of a fixed set of categories, on the basis of the text it contains. Naive Bayes models are often used for this task. In these models, the query variable is the document category, and the "effect" variables are the presence or absence of each word in the language; the assumption is that words occur independently in documents, with frequencies determined by the document category.

**a.** Explain precisely how such a model can be constructed, given as "training data" a set of documents that have been assigned to categories.

**b.** Explain precisely how to categorize a new document.

**c.** Is the independence assumption reasonable? Discuss.

**13.19** In our analysis of the wumpus world, we used the fact that each square contains a pit with probability 0.2, independently of the contents of the other squares. Suppose instead that exactly $N/5$ pits are scattered uniformly at random among the $N$ squares other than [1,1]. Are the variables $P_{i,j}$ and $P_{k,l}$ still independent? What is the joint distribution $\mathbf{P}(P_{1,1}, \ldots, P_{4,4})$ now? Redo the calculation for the probabilities of pits in [1,3] and [2,2].

# 14 PROBABILISTIC REASONING

*In which we explain how to build network models to reason under uncertainty according to the laws of probability theory.*

Chapter 13 gave the syntax and semantics of probability theory. We remarked on the importance of independence and conditional independence relationships in simplifying probabilistic representations of the world. This chapter introduces a systematic way to represent such relationships explicitly in the form of **Bayesian networks**. We define the syntax and semantics of these networks and show how they can be used to capture uncertain knowledge in a natural and efficient way. We then show how probabilistic inference, although computationally intractable in the worst case, can be done efficiently in many practical situations. We also describe a variety of approximate inference algorithms that are often applicable when exact inference is infeasible. We explore ways in which probability theory can be applied to worlds with objects and relations—that is, to *first-order*, as opposed to *propositional*, representations. Finally, we survey alternative approaches to uncertain reasoning.

## 14.1 REPRESENTING KNOWLEDGE IN AN UNCERTAIN DOMAIN

In Chapter 13, we saw that the full joint probability distribution can answer any question about the domain, but can become intractably large as the number of variables grows. Furthermore, specifying probabilities for atomic events is rather unnatural and can be very difficult unless a large amount of data is available from which to gather statistical estimates.

BAYESIAN NETWORK

We also saw that independence and conditional independence relationships among variables can greatly reduce the number of probabilities that need to be specified in order to define the full joint distribution. This section introduces a data structure called a **Bayesian network**[1] to represent the dependencies among variables and to give a concise specification of *any* full joint probability distribution.

[1] This is the most common name, but there are many others, including **belief network**, **probabilistic network**, **causal network**, and **knowledge map**. In statistics, the term **graphical model** refers to a somewhat broader class that includes Bayesian networks. An extension of Bayesian networks called a **decision network** or **influence diagram** will be covered in Chapter 16.

A Bayesian network is a directed graph in which each *node* is annotated with quantitative probability information. The full specification is as follows:

1. A set of random variables makes up the nodes of the network. Variables may be discrete or continuous.
2. A set of directed links or arrows connects pairs of nodes. If there is an arrow from node $X$ to node $Y$, $X$ is said to be a *parent* of $Y$.
3. Each node $X_i$ has a conditional probability distribution $P(X_i|Parents(X_i))$ that quantifies the effect of the parents on the node.
4. The graph has no directed cycles (and hence is a directed, acyclic graph, or DAG).

The topology of the network—the set of nodes and links—specifies the conditional independence relationships that hold in the domain, in a way that will be made precise shortly. The *intuitive* meaning of an arrow in a properly constructed network is usually that $X$ has a *direct influence* on $Y$. It is usually easy for a domain expert to decide what direct influences exist in the domain—much easier, in fact, than actually specifying the probabilities themselves. Once the topology of the Bayesian network is laid out, we need only specify a conditional probability distribution for each variable, given its parents. We will see that the combination of the topology and the conditional distributions suffices to specify (implicitly) the full joint distribution for all the variables.

Recall the simple world described in Chapter 13, consisting of the variables $Toothache$, $Cavity$, $Catch$, and $Weather$. We argued that $Weather$ is independent of the other variables; furthermore, we argued that $Toothache$ and $Catch$ are conditionally independent, given $Cavity$. These relationships are represented by the Bayesian network structure shown in Figure 14.1. Formally, the conditional independence of $Toothache$ and $Catch$ given $Cavity$ is indicated by the *absence* of a link between $Toothache$ and $Catch$. Intuitively, the network represents the fact that $Cavity$ is a direct cause of $Toothache$ and $Catch$, whereas no direct causal relationship exists between $Toothache$ and $Catch$.

Now consider the following example, which is just a little more complex. You have a new burglar alarm installed at home. It is fairly reliable at detecting a burglary, but also responds on occasion to minor earthquakes. (This example is due to Judea Pearl, a resident of Los Angeles—hence the acute interest in earthquakes.) You also have two neighbors, John and Mary, who have promised to call you at work when they hear the alarm. John always calls

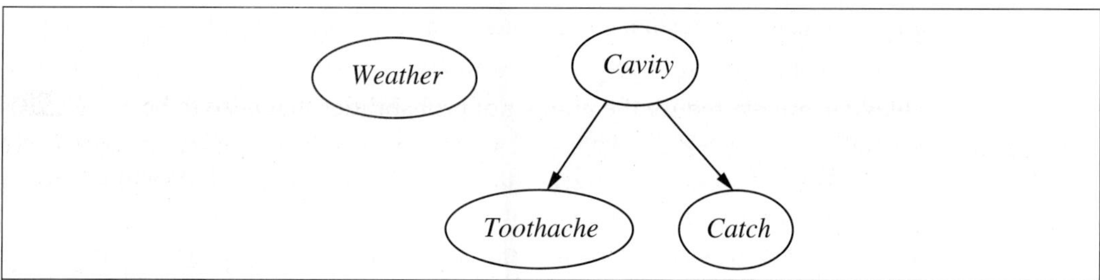


**Figure 14.1** A simple Bayesian network in which $Weather$ is independent of the other three variables and $Toothache$ and $Catch$ are conditionally independent, given $Cavity$.

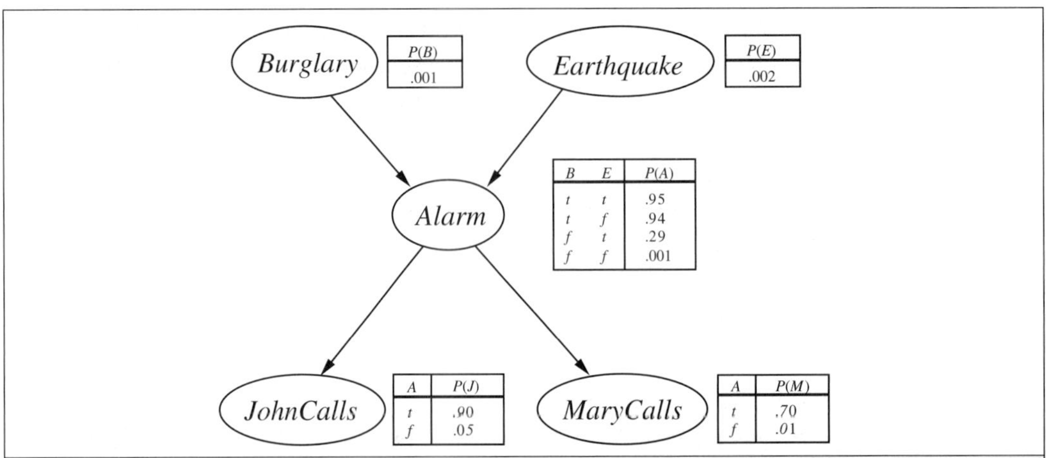


**Figure 14.2** A typical Bayesian network, showing both the topology and the conditional probability tables (CPTs). In the CPTs, the letters $B$, $E$, $A$, $J$, and $M$ stand for $Burglary$, $Earthquake$, $Alarm$, $JohnCalls$, and $MaryCalls$, respectively.

when he hears the alarm, but sometimes confuses the telephone ringing with the alarm and calls then, too. Mary, on the other hand, likes rather loud music and sometimes misses the alarm altogether. Given the evidence of who has or has not called, we would like to estimate the probability of a burglary. The Bayesian network for this domain appears in Figure 14.2.

For the moment, let us ignore the conditional distributions in the figure and concentrate on the topology of the network. In the case of the burglary network, the topology shows that burglary and earthquakes directly affect the probability of the alarm's going off, but whether John and Mary call depends only on the alarm. The network thus represents our assumptions that they do not perceive any burglaries directly, they do not notice the minor earthquakes, and they do not confer before calling.

Notice that the network does not have nodes corresponding to Mary's currently listening to loud music or to the telephone ringing and confusing John. These factors are summarized in the uncertainty associated with the links from $Alarm$ to $JohnCalls$ and $MaryCalls$. This shows both laziness and ignorance in operation: it would be a lot of work to find out why those factors would be more or less likely in any particular case, and we have no reasonable way to obtain the relevant information anyway. The probabilities actually summarize a *potentially infinite* set of circumstances in which the alarm might fail to go off (high humidity, power failure, dead battery, cut wires, a dead mouse stuck inside the bell, etc.) or John or Mary might fail to call and report it (out to lunch, on vacation, temporarily deaf, passing helicopter, etc.). In this way, a small agent can cope with a very large world, at least approximately. The degree of approximation can be improved if we introduce additional relevant information.

Now let us turn to the conditional distributions shown in Figure 14.2. In the figure, each distribution is shown as a **conditional probability table**, or CPT. (This form of table can be used for discrete variables; other representations, including those suitable for continuous variables, are described in Section 14.2.) Each row in a CPT contains the conditional probability of each node value for a **conditioning case**. A conditioning case is just a possible

CONDITIONAL PROBABILITY TABLE

CONDITIONING CASE

combination of values for the parent nodes—a miniature atomic event, if you like. Each row must sum to 1, because the entries represent an exhaustive set of cases for the variable. For Boolean variables, once you know that the probability of a true value is $p$, the probability of false must be $1 - p$, so we often omit the second number, as in Figure 14.2. In general, a table for a Boolean variable with $k$ Boolean parents contains $2^k$ independently specifiable probabilities. A node with no parents has only one row, representing the prior probabilities of each possible value of the variable.

## 14.2 THE SEMANTICS OF BAYESIAN NETWORKS

The previous section described what a network is, but not what it means. There are two ways in which one can understand the semantics of Bayesian networks. The first is to see the network as a representation of the joint probability distribution. The second is to view it as an encoding of a collection of conditional independence statements. The two views are equivalent, but the first turns out to be helpful in understanding how to *construct* networks, whereas the second is helpful in designing inference procedures.

### Representing the full joint distribution

A Bayesian network provides a complete description of the domain. Every entry in the full joint probability distribution (hereafter abbreviated as "joint") can be calculated from the information in the network. A generic entry in the joint distribution is the probability of a conjunction of particular assignments to each variable, such as $P(X_1 = x_1 \wedge \ldots \wedge X_n = x_n)$. We use the notation $P(x_1, \ldots, x_n)$ as an abbreviation for this. The value of this entry is given by the formula

$$P(x_1, \ldots, x_n) = \prod_{i=1}^{n} P(x_i | parents(X_i)) , \tag{14.1}$$

where $parents(X_i)$ denotes the specific values of the variables in $Parents(X_i)$. Thus, each entry in the joint distribution is represented by the product of the appropriate elements of the conditional probability tables (CPTs) in the Bayesian network. The CPTs therefore provide a decomposed representation of the joint distribution.

To illustrate this, we can calculate the probability that the alarm has sounded, but neither a burglary nor an earthquake has occurred, and both John and Mary call. We use single-letter names for the variables:

$$\begin{aligned} &P(j \wedge m \wedge a \wedge \neg b \wedge \neg e) \\ &= P(j|a)P(m|a)P(a|\neg b \wedge \neg e)P(\neg b)P(\neg e) \\ &= 0.90 \times 0.70 \times 0.001 \times 0.999 \times 0.998 = 0.00062 . \end{aligned}$$

Section 13.4 explained that the full joint distribution can be used to answer any query about the domain. If a Bayesian network is a representation of the joint distribution, then it too can be used to answer any query, by summing all the relevant joint entries. Section 14.4 explains how to do this, but also describes methods that are much more efficient.

### A method for constructing Bayesian networks

Equation (14.1) defines what a given Bayesian network means. It does not, however, explain how to *construct* a Bayesian network in such a way that the resulting joint distribution is a good representation of a given domain. We will now show that Equation (14.1) implies certain conditional independence relationships that can be used to guide the knowledge engineer in constructing the topology of the network. First, we rewrite the joint distribution in terms of a conditional probability, using the product rule (see Chapter 13):

$$P(x_1, \ldots, x_n) = P(x_n|x_{n-1}, \ldots, x_1)P(x_{n-1}, \ldots, x_1) .$$

Then we repeat the process, reducing each conjunctive probability to a conditional probability and a smaller conjunction. We end up with one big product:

$$\begin{aligned} P(x_1, \ldots, x_n) &= P(x_n|x_{n-1}, \ldots, x_1)P(x_{n-1}|x_{n-2}, \ldots, x_1) \cdots P(x_2|x_1)P(x_1) \\ &= \prod_{i=1}^{n} P(x_i|x_{i-1}, \ldots, x_1) . \end{aligned}$$

CHAIN RULE

This identity holds true for any set of random variables and is called the **chain rule**. Comparing it with Equation (14.1), we see that the specification of the joint distribution is equivalent to the general assertion that, for every variable $X_i$ in the network,

$$\mathbf{P}(X_i|X_{i-1}, \ldots, X_1) = \mathbf{P}(X_i|Parents(X_i)) , \qquad (14.2)$$

provided that $Parents(X_i) \subseteq \{X_{i-1}, \ldots, X_1\}$. This last condition is satisfied by labeling the nodes in any order that is consistent with the partial order implicit in the graph structure.

What Equation (14.2) says is that the Bayesian network is a correct representation of the domain only if each node is conditionally independent of its predecessors in the node ordering, given its parents. Hence, in order to construct a Bayesian network with the correct structure for the domain, we need to choose parents for each node such that this property holds. Intuitively, the parents of node $X_i$ should contain all those nodes in $X_1, \ldots, X_{i-1}$ that *directly influence* $X_i$. For example, suppose we have completed the network in Figure 14.2 except for the choice of parents for $MaryCalls$. $MaryCalls$ is certainly influenced by whether there is a $Burglary$ or an $Earthquake$, but not *directly* influenced. Intuitively, our knowledge of the domain tells us that these events influence Mary's calling behavior only through their effect on the alarm. Also, given the state of the alarm, whether John calls has no influence on Mary's calling. Formally speaking, we believe that the following conditional independence statement holds:

$$\mathbf{P}(MaryCalls|JohnCalls, Alarm, Earthquake, Burglary) = \mathbf{P}(MaryCalls|Alarm) .$$

### Compactness and node ordering

As well as being a complete and nonredundant representation of the domain, a Bayesian network can often be far more *compact* than the full joint distribution. This property is what makes it feasible to handle domains with many variables. The compactness of Bayesian networks is an example of a very general property of **locally structured** (also called **sparse**) systems. In a locally structured system, each subcomponent interacts directly with only a bounded number of other components, regardless of the total number of components. Local

LOCALLY STRUCTURED

SPARSE

structure is usually associated with linear rather than exponential growth in complexity. In the case of Bayesian networks, it is reasonable to suppose that in most domains each random variable is directly influenced by at most $k$ others, for some constant $k$. If we assume $n$ Boolean variables for simplicity, then the amount of information needed to specify each conditional probability table will be at most $2^k$ numbers, and the complete network can be specified by $n2^k$ numbers. In contrast, the joint distribution contains $2^n$ numbers. To make this concrete, suppose we have $n = 30$ nodes, each with five parents ($k = 5$). Then the Bayesian network requires 960 numbers, but the full joint distribution requires over a billion.

There are domains in which each variable can be influenced directly by all the others, so that the network is fully connected. Then specifying the conditional probability tables requires the same amount of information as specifying the joint distribution. In some domains, there will be slight dependencies that should strictly be included by adding a new link. But if these dependencies are very tenuous, then it may not be worth the additional complexity in the network for the small gain in accuracy. For example, one might object to our burglary network on the grounds that if there is an earthquake, then John and Mary would not call even if they heard the alarm, because they assume that the earthquake is the cause. Whether to add the link from $Earthquake$ to $JohnCalls$ and $MaryCalls$ (and thus enlarge the tables) depends on comparing the importance of getting more accurate probabilities with the cost of specifying the extra information.

Even in a locally structured domain, constructing a locally structured Bayesian network is not a trivial problem. We require not only that each variable be directly influenced by only a few others, but also that the network topology actually reflect those direct influences with the appropriate set of parents. Because of the way that the construction procedure works, the "direct influencers" will have to be added to the network first if they are to become parents of the node they influence. Therefore, *the correct order in which to add nodes is to add the "root causes" first, then the variables they influence,* and so on, until we reach the "leaves," which have no direct causal influence on the other variables.

What happens if we happen to choose the wrong order? Let us consider the burglary example again. Suppose we decide to add the nodes in the order $MaryCalls$, $JohnCalls$, $Alarm$, $Burglary$, $Earthquake$. Then we get the somewhat more complicated network shown in Figure 14.3(a). The process goes as follows:

- Adding $MaryCalls$: No parents.
- Adding $JohnCalls$: If Mary calls, that probably means the alarm has gone off, which of course would make it more likely that John calls. Therefore, $JohnCalls$ needs $MaryCalls$ as a parent
- Adding $Alarm$: Clearly, if both call, it is more likely that the alarm has gone off than if just one or neither call, so we need both $MaryCalls$ and $JohnCalls$ as parents.
- Adding $Burglary$: If we know the alarm state, then the call from John or Mary might give us information about our phone ringing or Mary's music, but not about burglary:

$$\mathbf{P}(Burglary|Alarm, JohnCalls, MaryCalls) = \mathbf{P}(Burglary|Alarm) .$$

  Hence we need just $Alarm$ as parent.

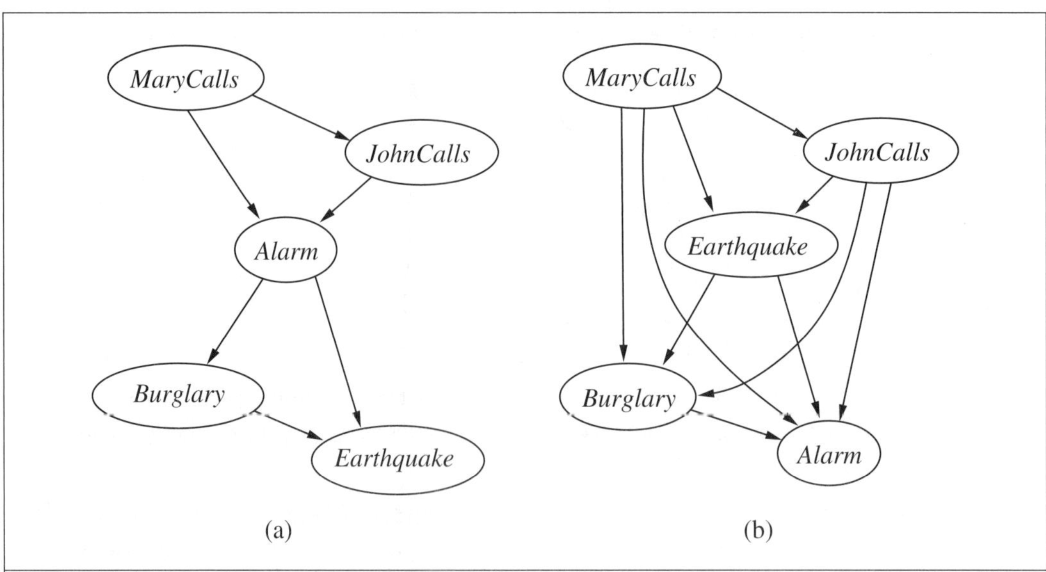


**Figure 14.3** Network structure depends on order of introduction. In each network, we have introduced nodes in top-to-bottom order.

- Adding *Earthquake*: if the alarm is on, it is more likely that there has been an earthquake. (The alarm is an earthquake detector of sorts.) But if we know that there has been a burglary, then that explains the alarm, and the probability of an earthquake would be only slightly above normal. Hence, we need both *Alarm* and *Burglary* as parents.

The resulting network has two more links than the original network in Figure 14.2 and requires three more probabilities to be specified. What's worse, some of the links represent tenuous relationships that require difficult and unnatural probability judgments, such as assessing the probability of *Earthquake*, given *Burglary* and *Alarm*. This phenomenon is quite general and is related to the distinction between causal and diagnostic models introduced in Chapter 8. If we try to build a diagnostic model with links from symptoms to causes (as from *MaryCalls* to *Alarm* or *Alarm* to *Burglary*), we end up having to specify additional dependencies between otherwise independent causes (and often between separately occurring symptoms as well). *If we stick to a causal model, we end up having to specify fewer numbers, and the numbers will often be easier to come up with.* In the domain of medicine, for example, it has been shown by Tversky and Kahneman (1982) that expert physicians prefer to give probability judgments for causal rules rather than for diagnostic ones.

Figure 14.3(b) shows a very bad node ordering: *MaryCalls*, *JohnCalls*, *Earthquake*, *Burglary*, *Alarm*. This network requires 31 distinct probabilities to be specified—exactly the same as the full joint distribution. It is important to realize, however, that any of the three networks can represent *exactly the same joint distribution*. The last two versions simply fail to represent all the conditional independence relationships and hence end up specifying a lot of unnecessary numbers instead.

### Conditional independence relations in Bayesian networks

We have provided a "numerical" semantics for Bayesian networks in terms of the representation of the full joint distribution, as in Equation (14.1). Using this semantics to derive a method for constructing Bayesian networks, we were led to the consequence that a node is conditionally independent of its predecessors, given its parents. It turns out that we can also go in the other direction. We can start from a "topological" semantics that specifies the conditional independence relationships encoded by the graph structure, and from these we can derive the "numerical" semantics. The topological semantics is given by either of the following specifications, which are equivalent:[2]

DESCENDANTS

1. A node is conditionally independent of its non-**descendants**, given its parents. For example, in Figure 14.2, *JohnCalls* is independent of *Burglary* and *Earthquake*, given the value of *Alarm*.

MARKOV BLANKET

2. A node is conditionally independent of all other nodes in the network, given its parents, children, and children's parents—that is, given its **Markov blanket**. For example, *Burglary* is independent of *JohnCalls* and *MaryCalls*, given *Alarm* and *Earthquake*.

These specifications are illustrated in Figure 14.4. From these conditional independence assertions and the CPTs, the full joint distribution can be reconstructed; thus, the "numerical" semantics and the "topological" semantics are equivalent.

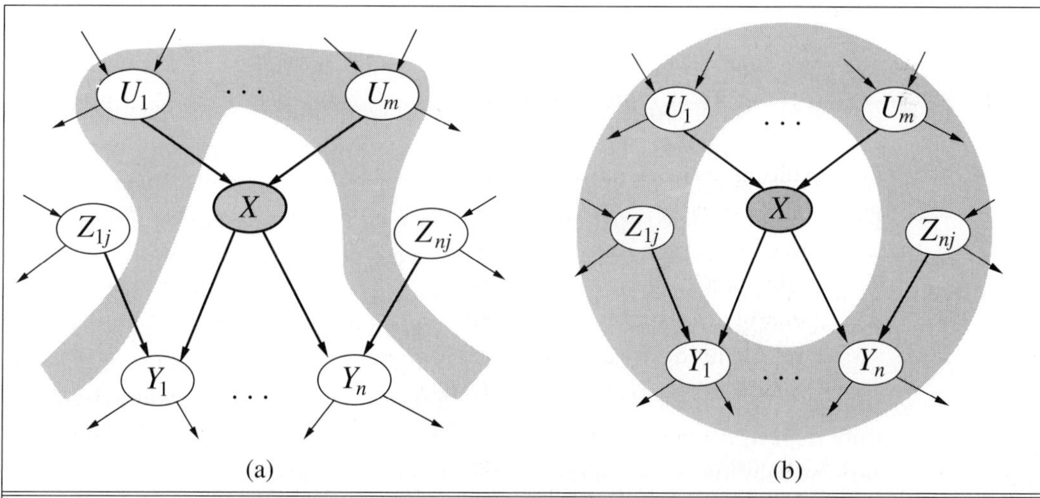


**Figure 14.4** (a) A node $X$ is conditionally independent of its non-descendants (e.g., the $Z_{ij}$s) given its parents (the $U_i$s shown in the gray area). (b) A node $X$ is conditionally independent of all other nodes in the network given its Markov blanket (the gray area).

[2] There is also a general topological criterion called **d-separation** for deciding whether a set of nodes **X** is independent of another set **Y**, given a third set **Z**. The criterion is rather complicated and is not needed for deriving the algorithms in this chapter, so we omit it. Details may be found in Russell and Norvig (1995) or Pearl (1988). Shachter (1998) gives a more intuitive method of ascertaining d-separation.

## 14.3 EFFICIENT REPRESENTATION OF CONDITIONAL DISTRIBUTIONS

Even if the maximum number of parents $k$ is smallish, filling in the CPT for a node requires up to $O(2^k)$ numbers and perhaps a great deal of experience with all the possible conditioning cases. In fact, this is a worst-case scenario in which the relationship between the parents and the child is completely arbitrary. Usually, such relationships are describable by a **canonical distribution** that fits some standard pattern. In such cases, the complete table can be specified by naming the pattern and perhaps supplying a few parameters—much easier than supplying an exponential number of parameters.

CANONICAL DISTRIBUTION

DETERMINISTIC NODES

The simplest example is provided by **deterministic nodes**. A deterministic node has its value specified exactly by the values of its parents, with no uncertainty. The relationship can be a logical one: for example, the relationship between the parent nodes $Canadian$, $US$, $Mexican$ and the child node $NorthAmerican$ is simply that the child is the disjunction of the parents. The relationship can also be numerical: for example, if the parent nodes are the prices of a particular model of car at several dealers, and the child node is the price that a bargain hunter ends up paying, then the child node is the minimum of the parent values; or if the parent nodes are the inflows (rivers, runoff, precipitation) into a lake and the outflows (rivers, evaporation, seepage) from the lake and the child is the change in the water level of the lake, then the value of the child is the difference between the inflow parents and the outflow parents.

NOISY-OR

LEAK NODE

Uncertain relationships can often be characterized by so-called "noisy" logical relationships. The standard example is the **noisy-OR** relation, which is a generalization of the logical OR. In propositional logic, we might say that $Fever$ is true if and only if $Cold$, $Flu$, or $Malaria$ is true. The noisy-OR model allows for uncertainty about the ability of each parent to cause the child to be true—the causal relationship between parent and child may be *inhibited*, and so a patient could have a cold, but not exhibit a fever. The model makes two assumptions. First, it assumes that all the possible causes are listed. (This is not as strict as it seems, because we can always add a so-called **leak node** that covers "miscellaneous causes.") Second, it assumes that inhibition of each parent is independent of inhibition of any other parents: for example, whatever inhibits $Malaria$ from causing a fever is independent of whatever inhibits $Flu$ from causing a fever. Given these assumptions, $Fever$ is *false* if and only if all its *true* parents are inhibited, and the probability of this is the product of the inhibition probabilities for each parent. Let us suppose these individual inhibition probabilities are as follows:

$$P(\neg fever|cold, \neg flu, \neg malaria) = 0.6 ,$$
$$P(\neg fever|\neg cold, flu, \neg malaria) = 0.2 ,$$
$$P(\neg fever|\neg cold, \neg flu, malaria) = 0.1 .$$

Then, from this information and the noisy-OR assumptions, the entire CPT can be built. The following table shows how:

| $Cold$ | $Flu$ | $Malaria$ | $P(Fever)$ | $P(\neg Fever)$ |
|---|---|---|---|---|
| F | F | F | 0.0 | 1.0 |
| F | F | T | 0.9 | **0.1** |
| F | T | F | 0.8 | **0.2** |
| F | T | T | 0.98 | $0.02 = 0.2 \times 0.1$ |
| T | F | F | 0.4 | **0.6** |
| T | F | T | 0.94 | $0.06 = 0.6 \times 0.1$ |
| T | T | F | 0.88 | $0.12 = 0.6 \times 0.2$ |
| T | T | T | 0.988 | $0.012 = 0.6 \times 0.2 \times 0.1$ |

In general, noisy logical relationships in which a variable depends on $k$ parents can be described using $O(k)$ parameters instead of $O(2^k)$ for the full conditional probability table. This makes assessment and learning much easier. For example, the CPCS network (Pradhan *et al.*, 1994) uses noisy-OR and noisy-MAX distributions to model relationships among diseases and symptoms in internal medicine. With 448 nodes and 906 links, it requires only 8,254 values instead of 133,931,430 for a network with full CPTs.

### Bayesian nets with continuous variables

Many real-world problems involve continuous quantities, such as height, mass, temperature, and money; in fact, much of statistics deals with random variables whose domains are continuous. By definition, continuous variables have an infinite number of possible values, so it is impossible to specify conditional probabilities explicitly for each value. One possible way to handle continuous variables is to avoid them by using **discretization**—that is, dividing up the possible values into a fixed set of intervals. For example, temperatures could be divided into (<0°C), (0°C−100°C), and (>100°C). Discretization is sometimes an adequate solution, but often results in a considerable loss of accuracy and very large CPTs. The other solution is to define standard families of probability density functions (see Appendix A) that are specified by a finite number of **parameters**. For example, a Gaussian (or normal) distribution $N(\mu, \sigma^2)(x)$ has the mean $\mu$ and the variance $\sigma^2$ as parameters.

DISCRETIZATION

PARAMETERS

A network with both discrete and continuous variables is called a **hybrid Bayesian network**. To specify a hybrid network, we have to specify two new kinds of distributions: the conditional distribution for a continuous variable given discrete or continuous parents; and the conditional distribution for a discrete variable given continuous parents. Consider the simple example in Figure 14.5, in which a customer buys some fruit depending on its cost, which depends in turn on the size of the harvest and whether the government's subsidy scheme is operating. The variable $Cost$ is continuous and has continuous and discrete parents; the variable $Buys$ is discrete and has a continuous parent.

HYBRID BAYESIAN NETWORK

For the $Cost$ variable, we need to specify $\mathbf{P}(Cost|Harvest, Subsidy)$. The discrete parent is handled by explicit enumeration—that is, specifying both $P(Cost|Harvest, subsidy)$ and $P(Cost|Harvest, \neg subsidy)$. To handle $Harvest$, we specify how the distribution over the cost $c$ depends on the continuous value $h$ of $Harvest$. In other words, we specify the *parameters* of the cost distribution as a function of $h$. The most common choice is the **linear**

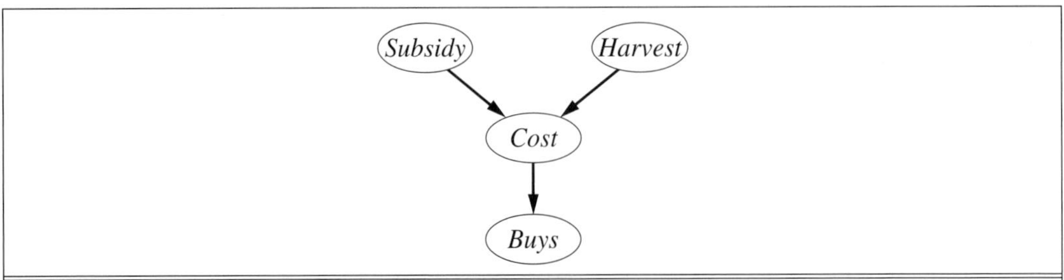


**Figure 14.5** A simple network with discrete variables ($Subsidy$ and $Buys$) and continuous variables ($Harvest$ and $Cost$).

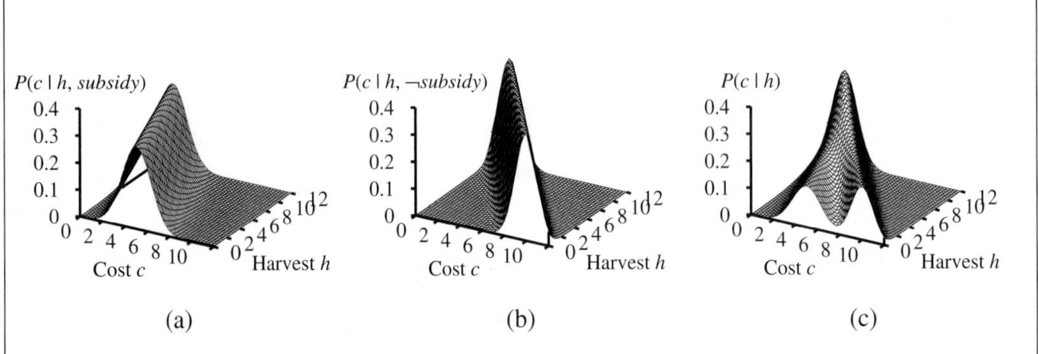


**Figure 14.6** The graphs in (a) and (b) show the probability distribution over $Cost$ as a function of $Harvest$ size, with $Subsidy$ true and false respectively. Graph (c) shows the distribution $P(Cost|Harvest)$, obtained by summing over the two subsidy cases.

LINEAR GAUSSIAN

**Gaussian** distribution, in which the child has a Gaussian distribution whose mean $\mu$ varies linearly with the value of the parent and whose standard deviation $\sigma$ is fixed. We need two distributions, one for $subsidy$ and one for $\neg subsidy$, with different parameters:

$$P(c|h, subsidy) = N(a_t h + b_t, \sigma_t^2)(c) = \frac{1}{\sigma_t\sqrt{2\pi}} e^{-\frac{1}{2}\left(\frac{c-(a_t h+b_t)}{\sigma_t}\right)^2}$$

$$P(c|h, \neg subsidy) = N(a_f h + b_f, \sigma_f^2)(c) = \frac{1}{\sigma_f\sqrt{2\pi}} e^{-\frac{1}{2}\left(\frac{c-(a_f h+b_f)}{\sigma_f}\right)^2}$$

For this example, then, the conditional distribution for $Cost$ is specified by naming the linear Gaussian distribution and providing the parameters $a_t$, $b_t$, $\sigma_t$, $a_f$, $b_f$, and $\sigma_f$. Figures 14.6(a) and (b) show these two relationships. Notice that in each case the slope is negative, because price decreases as supply increases. (Of course, the assumption of linearity implies that the price becomes negative at some point; the linear model is reasonable only if the harvest size is limited to a narrow range.) Figure 14.6(c) shows the distribution $P(c|h)$, averaging over the two possible values of $Subsidy$ and assuming that each has prior probability 0.5. This shows that even with very simple models, quite interesting distributions can be represented.

The linear Gaussian conditional distribution has some special properties. A network containing only continuous variables with linear Gaussian distributions has a joint distribu-

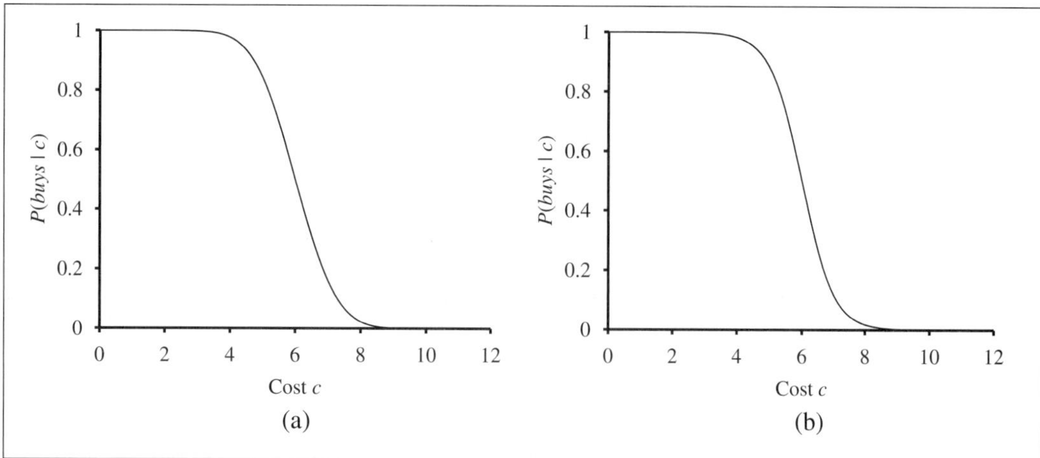


**Figure 14.7** (a) A probit distribution for the probability of $Buys$ given $Cost$, with $\mu = 6.0$ and $\sigma = 1.0$. (b) A logit distribution with the same parameters.

tion that is a multivariate Gaussian distribution over all the variables (Exercise 14.5).[3] (A multivariate Gaussian distribution is a surface in more than one dimension that has a peak at the mean (in $n$ dimensions) and drops off on all sides.) When discrete variables are added (provided that no discrete variable is a child of a continuous variable), the network defines a **conditional Gaussian**, or CG, distribution: given any assignment to the discrete variables, the distribution over the continuous variables is a multivariate Gaussian.

CONDITIONAL GAUSSIAN

Now we turn to the distributions for discrete variables with continuous parents. Consider, for example, the $Buys$ node in Figure 14.5. It seems reasonable to assume that the customer will buy if the cost is low and will not buy if it is high and that the probability of buying varies smoothly in some intermediate region. In other words, the conditional distribution is like a "soft" threshold function. One way to make soft thresholds is to use the *integral* of the standard normal distribution:

$$\Phi(x) = \int_{-\infty}^{x} N(0,1)(x)dx \; .$$

Then the probability of $Buys$ given $Cost$ might be

$$P(buys \mid Cost = c) = \Phi((-c + \mu)/\sigma)$$

which means that the cost threshold occurs around $\mu$, the width of the threshold region is proportional to $\sigma$, and the probability of buying decreases as cost increases.

PROBIT DISTRIBUTION

This **probit distribution** is illustrated in Figure 14.7(a). The form can be justified by proposing that the underlying decision process has a hard threshold, but that the precise location of the threshold is subject to random Gaussian noise. An alternative to the probit model is the **logit distribution**, which uses the **sigmoid function** to produce a soft threshold:

LOGIT DISTRIBUTION

SIGMOID FUNCTION

$$P(buys \mid Cost = c) = \frac{1}{1 + exp(-2\frac{-c+\mu}{\sigma})} \; .$$

[3] It follows that inference in linear Gaussian networks takes only $O(n^3)$ time in the worst case, regardless of the network topology. In Section 14.4, we will see that inference for networks of discrete variables is NP-hard.

This is illustrated in Figure 14.7(b). The two distributions look similar, but the logit actually has much longer "tails." The probit is often a better fit to real situations, but the logit is sometimes easier to deal with mathematically. It is used widely in neural networks (Chapter 20). Both probit and logit can be generalized to handle multiple continuous parents by taking a linear combination of the parent values. Extensions for a multivalued discrete child are explored in Exercise 14.6.

## 14.4 EXACT INFERENCE IN BAYESIAN NETWORKS

EVENT

HIDDEN VARIABLES

The basic task for any probabilistic inference system is to compute the posterior probability distribution for a set of **query variables**, given some observed **event**—that is, some assignment of values to a set of **evidence variables**. We will use the notation introduced in Chapter 13: $X$ denotes the query variable; $\mathbf{E}$ denotes the set of evidence variables $E_1, \ldots, E_m$, and $\mathbf{e}$ is a particular observed event; $\mathbf{Y}$ will denote the nonevidence variables $Y_1, \ldots, Y_l$ (sometimes called the **hidden variables**). Thus, the complete set of variables $\mathbf{X} = \{X\} \cup \mathbf{E} \cup \mathbf{Y}$. A typical query asks for the posterior probability distribution $\mathbf{P}(X|\mathbf{e})$.[4]

In the burglary network, we might observe the event in which $JohnCalls = true$ and $MaryCalls = true$. We could then ask for, say, the probability that a burglary has occurred:

$$\mathbf{P}(Burglary|JohnCalls = true, MaryCalls = true) = \langle 0.284, 0.716 \rangle \; .$$

In this section we will discuss exact algorithms for computing posterior probabilities and will consider the complexity of this task. It turns out that the general case is intractable, so Section 14.5 covers methods for approximate inference.

### Inference by enumeration

Chapter 13 explained that any conditional probability can be computed by summing terms from the full joint distribution. More specifically, a query $\mathbf{P}(X|\mathbf{e})$ can be answered using Equation (13.6), which we repeat here for convenience:

$$\mathbf{P}(X|\mathbf{e}) = \alpha\, \mathbf{P}(X, \mathbf{e}) = \alpha \sum_{\mathbf{y}} \mathbf{P}(X, \mathbf{e}, \mathbf{y}) \; .$$

Now, a Bayesian network gives a complete representation of the full joint distribution. More specifically, Equation (14.1) shows that the terms $P(x, \mathbf{e}, \mathbf{y})$ in the joint distribution can be written as products of conditional probabilities from the network. Therefore, *a query can be answered using a Bayesian network by computing sums of products of conditional probabilities from the network.*

In Figure 13.4, an algorithm, ENUMERATE-JOINT-ASK, was given for inference by enumeration from the full joint distribution. The algorithm takes as input a full joint distribution $\mathbf{P}$ and looks up values therein. It is a simple matter to modify the algorithm so that it takes

4 We will assume that the query variable is not among the evidence variables; if it is, then the posterior distribution for $X$ simply gives probability 1 to the observed value. For simplicity, we have also assumed that the query is just a single variable. Our algorithms can be extended easily to handle a joint query over several variables.

as input a Bayesian network $bn$ and "looks up" joint entries by multiplying the corresponding CPT entries from $bn$.

Consider the query $\mathbf{P}(Burglary|JohnCalls = true, MaryCalls = true)$. The hidden variables for this query are $Earthquake$ and $Alarm$. From Equation (13.6), using initial letters for the variables in order to shorten the expressions, we have[5]

$$\mathbf{P}(B|j,m) = \alpha\,\mathbf{P}(B,j,m) = \alpha \sum_{e}\sum_{a} \mathbf{P}(B,e,a,j,m)\,.$$

The semantics of Bayesian networks (Equation (14.1)) then gives us an expression in terms of CPT entries. For simplicity, we will do this just for $Burglary = true$:

$$P(b|j,m) = \alpha \sum_{e}\sum_{a} P(b)P(e)P(a|b,e)P(j|a)P(m|a)\,.$$

To compute this expression, we have to add four terms, each computed by multiplying five numbers. In the worst case, where we have to sum out almost all the variables, the complexity of the algorithm for a network with $n$ Boolean variables is $O(n2^n)$.

An improvement can be obtained from the following simple observations: the $P(b)$ term is a constant and can be moved outside the summations over $a$ and $e$, and the $P(e)$ term can be moved outside the summation over $a$. Hence, we have

$$P(b|j,m) = \alpha\, P(b) \sum_{e} P(e) \sum_{a} P(a|b,e)P(j|a)P(m|a)\,. \tag{14.3}$$

This expression can be evaluated by looping through the variables in order, multiplying CPT entries as we go. For each summation, we also need to loop over the variable's possible values. The structure of this computation is shown in Figure 14.8. Using the numbers from Figure 14.2, we obtain $P(b|j,m) = \alpha \times 0.00059224$. The corresponding computation for $\neg b$ yields $\alpha \times 0.0014919$; hence

$$\mathbf{P}(B|j,m) = \alpha\,\langle 0.00059224, 0.0014919\rangle \approx \langle 0.284, 0.716\rangle\,.$$

That is, the chance of a burglary, given calls from both neighbors, is about 28%.

The evaluation process for the expression in Equation (14.3) is shown as an expression tree in Figure 14.8. The ENUMERATION-ASK algorithm in Figure 14.9 evaluates such trees using depth-first recursion. Thus, the space complexity of ENUMERATION-ASK is only linear in the number of variables—effectively, the algorithm sums over the full joint distribution without ever constructing it explicitly. Unfortunately, its time complexity for a network with $n$ Boolean variables is always $O(2^n)$—better than the $O(n2^n)$ for the simple approach described earlier, but still rather grim. One thing to note about the tree in Figure 14.8 is that it makes explicit the *repeated subexpressions* that are evaluated by the algorithm. The products $P(j|a)P(m|a)$ and $P(j|\neg a)P(m|\neg a)$ are computed twice, once for each value of $e$. The next section describes a general method that avoids such wasted computations.

---

[5] An expression such as $\sum_e P(a,e)$ means to sum $P(A = a, E = e)$ for all possible values of $e$. There is an ambiguity in that $P(e)$ is used to mean both $P(E = true)$ and $P(E = e)$, but it should be clear from context which is intended; in particular, in the context of a sum the latter is intended.

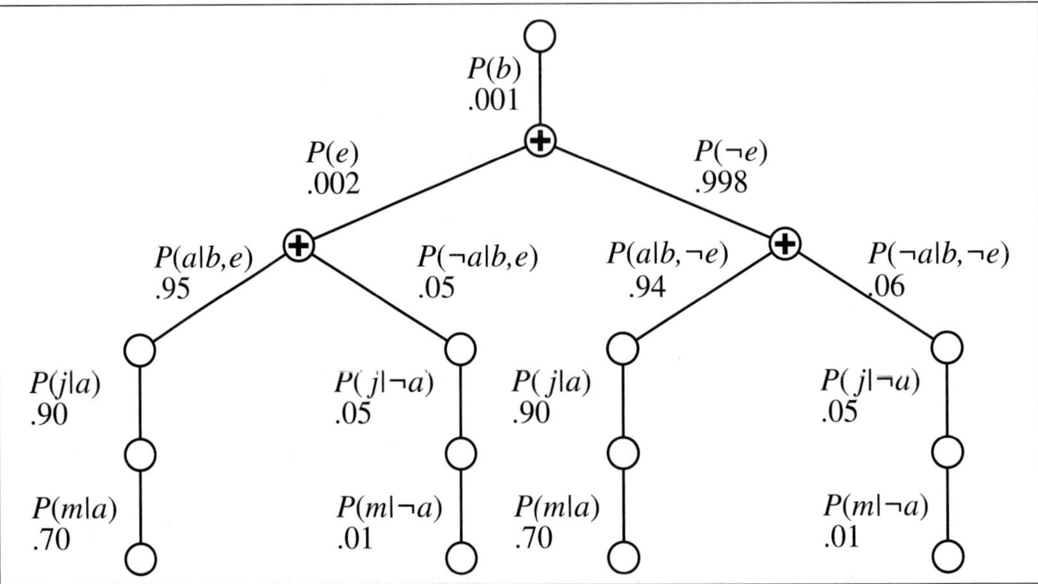


**Figure 14.8** The structure of the expression shown in Equation (14.3). The evaluation proceeds top-down, multiplying values along each path and summing at the "+" nodes. Notice the repetition of the paths for $j$ and $m$.

```
function ENUMERATION-ASK(X, e, bn) returns a distribution over X
  inputs: X, the query variable
          e, observed values for variables E
          bn, a Bayes net with variables {X} ∪ E ∪ Y   /* Y = hidden variables */

  Q(X) ← a distribution over X, initially empty
  for each value x_i of X do
     extend e with value x_i for X
     Q(x_i) ← ENUMERATE-ALL(VARS[bn], e)
  return NORMALIZE(Q(X))
```

```
function ENUMERATE-ALL(vars, e) returns a real number
  if EMPTY?(vars) then return 1.0
  Y ← FIRST(vars)
  if Y has value y in e
     then return P(y | parents(Y)) × ENUMERATE-ALL(REST(vars), e)
     else return Σ_y P(y | parents(Y)) × ENUMERATE-ALL(REST(vars), e_y)
        where e_y is e extended with Y = y
```

**Figure 14.9** The enumeration algorithm for answering queries on Bayesian networks.

## The variable elimination algorithm

The enumeration algorithm can be improved substantially by eliminating repeated calculations of the kind illustrated in Figure 14.8. The idea is simple: do the calculation once and save the results for later use. This is a form of dynamic programming. There are several versions of this approach; we present the **variable elimination** algorithm, which is the simplest. Variable elimination works by evaluating expressions such as Equation (14.3) in *right-to-left* order (that is, *bottom-up* in Figure 14.8). Intermediate results are stored, and summations over each variable are done only for those portions of the expression that depend on the variable.

VARIABLE ELIMINATION

Let us illustrate this process for the burglary network. We evaluate the expression

$$\mathbf{P}(B|j,m) = \alpha \underbrace{\mathbf{P}(B)}_{B} \sum_e \underbrace{P(e)}_{E} \sum_a \underbrace{\mathbf{P}(a|B,e)}_{A} \underbrace{P(j|a)}_{J} \underbrace{P(m|a)}_{M} .$$

Notice that we have annotated each part of the expression with the name of the associated variable; these parts are called **factors**. The steps are as follows:

FACTORS

- The factor for $M$, $P(m|a)$, does not require summing over $M$ (because $M$'s value is already fixed). We store the probability, given each value of $a$, in a two-element vector,

$$\mathbf{f}_M(A) = \begin{pmatrix} P(m|a) \\ P(m|\neg a) \end{pmatrix} .$$

  (The $\mathbf{f}_M$ means that $M$ was used to produce $\mathbf{f}$.)
- Similarly, we store the factor for $J$ as the two-element vector $\mathbf{f}_J(A)$.
- The factor for $A$ is $\mathbf{P}(a|B,e)$, which will be a $2 \times 2 \times 2$ matrix $\mathbf{f}_A(A,B,E)$.
- Now we must sum out $A$ from the product of these three factors. This will give us a $2 \times 2$ matrix whose indices range over just $B$ and $E$. We put a bar over $A$ in the name of the matrix to indicate that $A$ has been summed out:

$$\begin{aligned} \mathbf{f}_{\bar{A}JM}(B,E) &= \sum_a \mathbf{f}_A(a,B,E) \times \mathbf{f}_J(a) \times \mathbf{f}_M(a) \\ &= \mathbf{f}_A(a,B,E) \times \mathbf{f}_J(a) \times \mathbf{f}_M(a) \\ &\quad + \mathbf{f}_A(\neg a,B,E) \times \mathbf{f}_J(\neg a) \times \mathbf{f}_M(\neg a) . \end{aligned}$$

  POINTWISE PRODUCT

  The multiplication process used here is called a **pointwise product** and will be described shortly.
- We process $E$ in the same way: sum out $E$ from the product of $\mathbf{f}_E(E)$ and $\mathbf{f}_{\bar{A}JM}(B,E)$:

$$\begin{aligned} \mathbf{f}_{\bar{E}\bar{A}JM}(B) &= \mathbf{f}_E(e) \times \mathbf{f}_{\bar{A}JM}(B,e) \\ &\quad + \mathbf{f}_E(\neg e) \times \mathbf{f}_{\bar{A}JM}(B,\neg e) . \end{aligned}$$

- Now we can compute the answer simply by multiplying the factor for $B$ (i.e., $\mathbf{f}_B(B) = \mathbf{P}(B)$), by the accumulated matrix $\mathbf{f}_{\bar{E}\bar{A}JM}(B)$:

$$\mathbf{P}(B|j,m) = \alpha\, \mathbf{f}_B(B) \times \mathbf{f}_{\bar{E}\bar{A}JM}(B) .$$

Exercise 14.7(a) asks you to check that this process yields the correct answer.

Examining this sequence of steps, we see that there are two basic computational operations required: pointwise product of a pair of factors, and summing out a variable from a product of factors.

The pointwise product is not matrix multiplication, nor is it element-by-element multiplication. The pointwise product of two factors $\mathbf{f}_1$ and $\mathbf{f}_2$ yields a new factor $\mathbf{f}$ whose variables are the *union* of the variables in $\mathbf{f}_1$ and $\mathbf{f}_2$. Suppose the two factors have variables $Y_1, \ldots, Y_k$ in common. Then we have

$$\mathbf{f}(X_1 \ldots X_j, Y_1 \ldots Y_k, Z_1 \ldots Z_l) = \mathbf{f}_1(X_1 \ldots X_j, Y_1 \ldots Y_k)\, \mathbf{f}_2(Y_1 \ldots Y_k, Z, \ldots Z_l).$$

If all the variables are binary, then $\mathbf{f}_1$ and $\mathbf{f}_2$ have $2^{j+k}$ and $2^{k+l}$ entries respectively, and the pointwise product has $2^{j+k+l}$ entries. For example, given two factors $\mathbf{f}_1(A, B)$ and $\mathbf{f}_2(B, C)$ with probability distributions shown below, the pointwise product $\mathbf{f}_1 \times \mathbf{f}_2$ is given as $\mathbf{f}_3(A, B, C)$:

| $A$ | $B$ | $\mathbf{f}_1(A,B)$ | $B$ | $C$ | $\mathbf{f}_2(B,C)$ | $A$ | $B$ | $C$ | $\mathbf{f}_3(A,B,C)$ |
|---|---|---|---|---|---|---|---|---|---|
| T | T | .3 | T | T | .2 | T | T | T | $.3 \times .2$ |
| T | F | .7 | T | F | .8 | T | T | F | $.3 \times .8$ |
| F | T | .9 | F | T | .6 | T | F | T | $.7 \times .6$ |
| F | F | .1 | F | F | .4 | T | F | F | $.7 \times .4$ |
| | | | | | | F | T | T | $.9 \times .2$ |
| | | | | | | F | T | F | $.9 \times .8$ |
| | | | | | | F | F | T | $.1 \times .6$ |
| | | | | | | F | F | F | $.1 \times .4$ |

Summing out a variable from a product of factors is also a straightforward computation. The only trick is to notice that any factor that does *not* depend on the variable to be summed out can be moved outside the summation process. For example,

$$\begin{aligned}&\textstyle\sum_e \mathbf{f}_E(e) \times \mathbf{f}_A(A, B, e) \times \mathbf{f}_J(A) \times \mathbf{f}_M(A) = \\ &\qquad \mathbf{f}_J(A) \times \mathbf{f}_M(A) \times \textstyle\sum_e \mathbf{f}_E(e) \times \mathbf{f}_A(A, B, e)\,.\end{aligned}$$

Now the pointwise product inside the summation is computed, and the variable is summed out of the resulting matrix:

$$\mathbf{f}_J(A) \times \mathbf{f}_M(A) \times \sum_e \mathbf{f}_E(e) \times \mathbf{f}_A(A, B, e) = \mathbf{f}_J(A) \times \mathbf{f}_M(A) \times \mathbf{f}_{\bar{E},A}(A, B)\,.$$

Notice that matrices are *not* multiplied until we need to sum out a variable from the accumulated product. At that point, we multiply just those matrices that include the variable to be summed out. Given routines for pointwise product and summing out, the variable elimination algorithm itself can be written quite simply, as shown in Figure 14.10.

Let us consider one more query: $P(JohnCalls|Burglary = true)$. As usual, the first step is to write out the nested summation:

$$P(J|b) = \alpha\, P(b) \sum_e P(e) \sum_a P(a|b, e) P(J|a) \sum_m P(m|a)\,.$$

If we evaluate this expression from right to left, we notice something interesting: $\sum_m P(m|a)$ is equal to 1 by definition! Hence, there was no need to include it in the first place; the variable $M$ is *irrelevant* to this query. Another way of saying this is that the result of the query $P(JohnCalls|Burglary = true)$ is unchanged if we remove $MaryCalls$ from the network altogether. In general, we can remove any leaf node that is not a query variable or an evidence

```
function ELIMINATION-ASK(X, e, bn) returns a distribution over X
  inputs: X, the query variable
          e, evidence specified as an event
          bn, a Bayesian network specifying joint distribution P(X_1, ..., X_n)

  factors ← [ ]; vars ← REVERSE(VARS[bn])
  for each var in vars do
     factors ← [MAKE-FACTOR(var, e)|factors]
     if var is a hidden variable then factors ← SUM-OUT(var, factors)
  return NORMALIZE(POINTWISE-PRODUCT(factors))
```

**Figure 14.10** The variable elimination algorithm for answering queries on Bayesian networks.

variable. After its removal, there may be some more leaf nodes, and these too may be irrelevant. Continuing this process, we eventually find that *every variable that is not an ancestor of a query variable or evidence variable is irrelevant to the query.* A variable elimination algorithm can therefore remove all these variables before evaluating the query.

## The complexity of exact inference

We have argued that variable elimination is more efficient than enumeration because it avoids repeated computations (as well as dropping irrelevant variables). The time and space requirements of variable elimination are dominated by the size of the largest factor constructed during the operation of the algorithm. This in turn is determined by the order of elimination of variables and by the structure of the network.

The burglary network of Figure 14.2 belongs to the family of networks in which there is at most one undirected path between any two nodes in the network. These are called **singly connected** networks or **polytrees**, and they have a particularly nice property: *The time and space complexity of exact inference in polytrees is linear in the size of the network.* Here, the size is defined as the number of CPT entries; if the number of parents of each node is bounded by a constant, then the complexity will also be linear in the number of nodes. These results hold for any ordering consistent with the topological ordering of the network (Exercise 14.7).

SINGLY CONNECTED

POLYTREES

MULTIPLY CONNECTED

For **multiply connected** networks, such as that of Figure 14.11(a), variable elimination can have exponential time and space complexity in the worst case, even when the number of parents per node is bounded. This is not surprising when one considers that, *because it includes inference in propositional logic as a special case, inference in Bayesian networks is NP-hard.* In fact, it can be shown (Exercise 14.8) that the problem is as hard as that of computing the *number* of satisfying assignments for a propositional logic formula. This means that it is #P-hard ("number-P hard")—that is, strictly harder than NP-complete problems.

There is a close connection between the complexity of Bayesian network inference and the complexity of constraint satisfaction problems (CSPs). As we discussed in Chapter 5, the difficulty of solving a discrete CSP is related to how "tree-like" its constraint graph is.

Measures such as **hypertree width**, which bound the complexity of solving a CSP, can also be applied directly to Bayesian networks. Moreover, the variable elimination algorithm can be generalized to solve CSPs as well as Bayesian networks.

### Clustering algorithms

The variable elimination algorithm is simple and efficient for answering individual queries. If we want to compute posterior probabilities for all the variables in a network, however, it can be less efficient. For example, in a polytree network, one would need to issue $O(n)$ queries costing $O(n)$ each, for a total of $O(n^2)$ time. Using **clustering** algorithms (also known as **join tree** algorithms), the time can be reduced to $O(n)$. For this reason, these algorithms are widely used in commercial Bayesian network tools.

CLUSTERING

JOIN TREE

The basic idea of clustering is to join individual nodes of the network to form cluster nodes in such a way that the resulting network is a polytree. For example, the multiply connected network shown in Figure 14.11(a) can be converted into a polytree by combining the $Sprinkler$ and $Rain$ node into a cluster node called $Sprinkler+Rain$, as shown in Figure 14.11(b). The two Boolean nodes are replaced by a meganode that takes on four possible values: $TT$, $TF$, $FT$, and $FF$. The meganode has only one parent, the Boolean variable $Cloudy$, so there are two conditioning cases.

Once the network is in polytree form, a special-purpose inference algorithm is applied. Essentially, the algorithm is a form of constraint propagation (see Chapter 5) where the constraints ensure that neighboring clusters agree on the posterior probability of any variables that they have in common. With careful bookkeeping, this algorithm is able to compute posterior probabilities for all the nonevidence nodes in the network in time $O(n)$, where $n$ is now the size of the modified network. However, the NP-hardness of the problem has not disappeared: if a network requires exponential time and space with variable elimination, then the CPTs in the clustered network will require exponential time and space to construct.

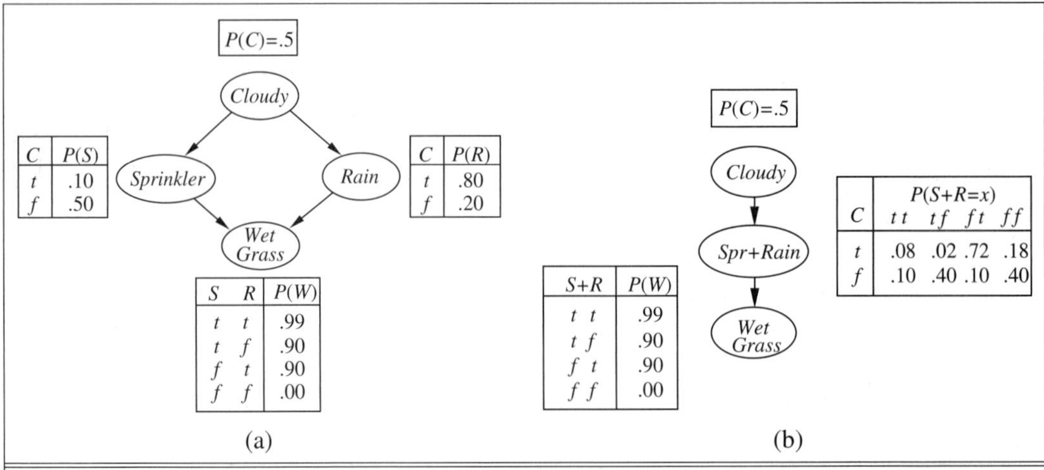


**Figure 14.11** (a) A multiply connected network with conditional probability tables. (b) A clustered equivalent of the multiply connected network.

## 14.5 APPROXIMATE INFERENCE IN BAYESIAN NETWORKS

Given the intractability of exact inference in large, multiply connected networks, it is essential to consider approximate inference methods. This section describes randomized sampling algorithms, also called **Monte Carlo** algorithms, that provide approximate answers whose accuracy depends on the number of samples generated. In recent years, Monte Carlo algorithms have become widely used in computer science to estimate quantities that are difficult to calculate exactly. For example, the simulated annealing algorithm described in Chapter 4 is a Monte Carlo method for optimization problems. In this section, we are interested in sampling applied to the computation of posterior probabilities. We describe two families of algorithms: direct sampling and Markov chain sampling. Two other approaches—variational methods and loopy propagation—are mentioned in the notes at the end of the chapter.

MONTE CARLO

### Direct sampling methods

The primitive element in any sampling algorithm is the generation of samples from a known probability distribution. For example, an unbiased coin can be thought of as a random variable $Coin$ with values $\langle heads, tails\rangle$ and a prior distribution $\mathbf{P}(Coin) = \langle 0.5, 0.5\rangle$. Sampling from this distribution is exactly like flipping the coin: with probability 0.5 it will return $heads$, and with probability 0.5 it will return $tails$. Given a source of random numbers in the range $[0,1]$, it is a simple matter to sample any distribution on a single variable. (See Exercise 14.9.)

The simplest kind of random sampling process for Bayesian networks generates events from a network that has no evidence associated with it. The idea is to sample each variable in turn, in topological order. The probability distribution from which the value is sampled is conditioned on the values already assigned to the variable's parents. This algorithm is shown in Figure 14.12. We can illustrate its operation on the network in Figure 14.11(a), assuming an ordering $[Cloudy, Sprinkler, Rain, WetGrass]$:

1. Sample from $\mathbf{P}(Cloudy) = \langle 0.5, 0.5\rangle$; suppose this returns $true$.
2. Sample from $\mathbf{P}(Sprinkler \mid Cloudy = true) = \langle 0.1, 0.9\rangle$; suppose this returns $false$.
3. Sample from $\mathbf{P}(Rain \mid Cloudy = true) = \langle 0.8, 0.2\rangle$; suppose this returns $true$.
4. Sample from $\mathbf{P}(WetGrass \mid Sprinkler = false, Rain = true) = \langle 0.9, 0.1\rangle$; suppose this returns $true$.

In this case, PRIOR-SAMPLE returns the event $[true, false, true, true]$.

It is easy to see that PRIOR-SAMPLE generates samples from the prior joint distribution specified by the network. First, let $S_{PS}(x_1, \ldots, x_n)$ be the probability that a specific event is generated by the PRIOR-SAMPLE algorithm. *Just looking at the sampling process*, we have

$$S_{PS}(x_1 \ldots x_n) = \prod_{i=1}^{n} P(x_i \mid parents(X_i))$$

because each sampling step depends only on the parent values. This expression should look

**function** PRIOR-SAMPLE($bn$) **returns** an event sampled from the prior specified by $bn$
**inputs**: $bn$, a Bayesian network specifying joint distribution $\mathbf{P}(X_1, \ldots, X_n)$

$\mathbf{x} \leftarrow$ an event with $n$ elements
**for** $i = 1$ **to** $n$ **do**
$x_i \leftarrow$ a random sample from $\mathbf{P}(X_i \mid parents(X_i))$
**return x**

**Figure 14.12** A sampling algorithm that generates events from a Bayesian network.

familiar, because it is also the probability of the event according to the Bayesian net's representation of the joint distribution, as stated in Equation (14.1). That is, we have

$$S_{PS}(x_1 \ldots x_n) = P(x_1 \ldots x_n) .$$

This simple fact makes it very easy to answer questions by using samples.

In any sampling algorithm, the answers are computed by counting the actual samples generated. Suppose there are $N$ total samples, and let $N(x_1, \ldots, x_n)$ be the frequency of the specific event $x_1, \ldots, x_n$. We expect this frequency to converge, in the limit, to its expected value according to the sampling probability:

$$\lim_{N \to \infty} \frac{N_{PS}(x_1, \ldots, x_n)}{N} = S_{PS}(x_1, \ldots, x_n) = P(x_1, \ldots, x_n) . \qquad (14.4)$$

For example, consider the event produced earlier: $[true, false, true, true]$. The sampling probability for this event is

$$S_{PS}(true, false, true, true) = 0.5 \times 0.9 \times 0.8 \times 0.9 = 0.324 .$$

Hence, in the limit of large $N$, we expect 32.4% of the samples to be of this event.

Whenever we use an approximate equality ("$\approx$") in what follows, we mean it in exactly this sense—that the estimated probability becomes exact in the large-sample limit. Such an estimate is called **consistent**. For example, one can produce a consistent estimate of the probability of any partially specified event $x_1, \ldots, x_m$, where $m \leq n$, as follows:

CONSISTENT

$$P(x_1, \ldots, x_m) \approx N_{PS}(x_1, \ldots, x_m)/N . \qquad (14.5)$$

That is, the probability of the event can be estimated as the fraction of all complete events generated by the sampling process that match the partially specified event. For example, if we generate 1000 samples from the sprinkler network, and 511 of them have $Rain = true$, then the estimated probability of rain, written as $\hat{P}(Rain = true)$, is 0.511.

### Rejection sampling in Bayesian networks

REJECTION SAMPLING

**Rejection sampling** is a general method for producing samples from a hard-to-sample distribution given an easy-to-sample distribution. In its simplest form, it can be used to compute conditional probabilities—that is, to determine $P(X|\mathbf{e})$. The REJECTION-SAMPLING algorithm is shown in Figure 14.13. First, it generates samples from the prior distribution specified

```
function REJECTION-SAMPLING(X, e, bn, N) returns an estimate of P(X|e)
  inputs: X, the query variable
          e, evidence specified as an event
          bn, a Bayesian network
          N, the total number of samples to be generated
  local variables: N, a vector of counts over X, initially zero

  for j = 1 to N do
     x ← PRIOR-SAMPLE(bn)
     if x is consistent with e then
        N[x] ← N[x]+1 where x is the value of X in x
  return NORMALIZE(N[X])
```

**Figure 14.13** The rejection sampling algorithm for answering queries given evidence in a Bayesian network.

by the network. Then, it rejects all those that do not match the evidence. Finally, the estimate $\hat{P}(X=x|\mathbf{e})$ is obtained by counting how often $X=x$ occurs in the remaining samples.

Let $\hat{\mathbf{P}}(X|\mathbf{e})$ be the estimated distribution that the algorithm returns. From the definition of the algorithm, we have

$$\hat{\mathbf{P}}(X|\mathbf{e}) = \alpha\,\mathbf{N}_{PS}(X,\mathbf{e}) = \frac{\mathbf{N}_{PS}(X,\mathbf{e})}{N_{PS}(\mathbf{e})} .$$

From Equation (14.5), this becomes

$$\hat{\mathbf{P}}(X|\mathbf{e}) \approx \frac{\mathbf{P}(X,\mathbf{e})}{P(\mathbf{e})} = \mathbf{P}(X|\mathbf{e}) .$$

That is, rejection sampling produces a consistent estimate of the true probability.

Continuing with our example from Figure 14.11(a), let us assume that we wish to estimate $\mathbf{P}(Rain|Sprinkler=true)$, using 100 samples. Of the 100 that we generate, suppose that 73 have $Sprinkler=false$ and are rejected, while 27 have $Sprinkler=true$; of the 27, 8 have $Rain=true$ and 19 have $Rain=false$. Hence,

$$\mathbf{P}(Rain|Sprinkler=true) \approx \text{NORMALIZE}(\langle 8,19\rangle) = \langle 0.296, 0.704\rangle .$$

The true answer is $\langle 0.3, 0.7\rangle$. As more samples are collected, the estimate will converge to the true answer. The standard deviation of the error in each probability will be proportional to $1/\sqrt{n}$, where $n$ is the number of samples used in the estimate.

The biggest problem with rejection sampling is that it rejects so many samples! The fraction of samples consistent with the evidence **e** drops exponentially as the number of evidence variables grows, so the procedure is simply unusable for complex problems.

Notice that rejection sampling is very similar to the estimation of conditional probabilities directly from the real world. For example, to estimate $\mathbf{P}(Rain|RedSkyAtNight=true)$, one can simply count how often it rains after a red sky is observed the previous evening—ignoring those evenings when the sky is not red. (Here, the world itself plays the role of the sample generation algorithm.) Obviously, this could take a long time if the sky is very seldom red, and that is the weakness of rejection sampling.

### Likelihood weighting

LIKELIHOOD WEIGHTING

**Likelihood weighting** avoids the inefficiency of rejection sampling by generating only events that are consistent with the evidence **e**. We begin by describing how the algorithm works; then we show that it works correctly—that is, generates consistent probability estimates.

LIKELIHOOD-WEIGHTING (see Figure 14.14) fixes the values for the evidence variables **E** and samples only the remaining variables $X$ and **Y**. This guarantees that each event generated is consistent with the evidence. Not all events are equal, however. Before tallying the counts in the distribution for the query variable, each event is weighted by the *likelihood* that the event accords to the evidence, as measured by the product of the conditional probabilities for each evidence variable, given its parents. Intuitively, events in which the actual evidence appears unlikely should be given less weight.

Let us apply the algorithm to the network shown in Figure 14.11(a), with the query $\mathbf{P}(Rain|Sprinkler = true, WetGrass = true)$. The process goes as follows: First, the weight $w$ is set to 1.0. Then an event is generated:

1. Sample from $\mathbf{P}(Cloudy) = \langle 0.5, 0.5\rangle$; suppose this returns $true$.
2. $Sprinkler$ is an evidence variable with value $true$. Therefore, we set
$$w \leftarrow w \times P(Sprinkler = true|Cloudy = true) = 0.1\ .$$
3. Sample from $\mathbf{P}(Rain|Cloudy = true) = \langle 0.8, 0.2\rangle$; suppose this returns $true$.
4. $WetGrass$ is an evidence variable with value $true$. Therefore, we set
$$w \leftarrow w \times P(WetGrass = true|Sprinkler = true, Rain = true) = 0.099\ .$$

Here WEIGHTED-SAMPLE returns the event $[true, true, true, true]$ with weight 0.099, and this is tallied under $Rain = true$. The weight is low because the event describes a cloudy day, which makes the sprinkler unlikely to be on.

To understand why likelihood weighting works, we start by examining the sampling distribution $S_{WS}$ for WEIGHTED-SAMPLE. Remember that the evidence variables **E** are fixed with values **e**. We will call the other variables **Z**, that is, $\mathbf{Z} = \{X\} \cup \mathbf{Y}$. The algorithm samples each variable in **Z** given its parent values:

$$S_{WS}(\mathbf{z}, \mathbf{e}) = \prod_{i=1}^{l} P(z_i|parents(Z_i))\ . \qquad (14.6)$$

Notice that $Parents(Z_i)$ can include both hidden variables and evidence variables. Unlike the prior distribution $P(\mathbf{z})$, the distribution $S_{WS}$ pays some attention to the evidence: the sampled values for each $Z_i$ will be influenced by evidence among $Z_i$'s ancestors. On the other hand, $S_{WS}$ pays less attention to the evidence than does the true posterior distribution $P(\mathbf{z}|\mathbf{e})$, because the sampled values for each $Z_i$ *ignore* evidence among $Z_i$'s non-ancestors.[6]

[6] Ideally, we would like to use a sampling distribution equal to the true posterior $P(\mathbf{z}|\mathbf{e})$, to take all the evidence into account. This cannot be done effi ciently, however. If it could, then we could approximate the desired probability to arbitrary accuracy with a polynomial number of samples. It can be shown that no such polynomial-time approximation scheme can exist.

```
function LIKELIHOOD-WEIGHTING(X, e, bn, N) returns an estimate of P(X|e)
  inputs: X, the query variable
          e, evidence specified as an event
          bn, a Bayesian network
          N, the total number of samples to be generated
  local variables: W, a vector of weighted counts over X, initially zero

  for j = 1 to N do
     x, w ← WEIGHTED-SAMPLE(bn, e)
     W[x] ← W[x] + w where x is the value of X in x
  return NORMALIZE(W[X])
```

```
function WEIGHTED-SAMPLE(bn, e) returns an event and a weight

  x ← an event with n elements; w ← 1
  for i = 1 to n do
     if X_i has a value x_i in e
        then w ← w × P(X_i = x_i | parents(X_i))
        else x_i ← a random sample from P(X_i | parents(X_i))
  return x, w
```

**Figure 14.14** The likelihood weighting algorithm for inference in Bayesian networks.

The likelihood weight $w$ makes up for the difference between the actual and desired sampling distributions. The weight for a given sample **x**, composed from **z** and **e**, is the product of the likelihoods for each evidence variable given its parents (some or all of which may be among the $Z_i$s):

$$w(\mathbf{z}, \mathbf{e}) = \prod_{i=1}^{m} P(e_i|parents(E_i)) \ . \tag{14.7}$$

Multiplying Equations (14.6) and (14.7), we see that the *weighted* probability of a sample has the particularly convenient form

$$\begin{aligned} S_{WS}(\mathbf{z}, \mathbf{e})w(\mathbf{z}, \mathbf{e}) &= \prod_{i=1}^{l} P(z_i|parents(Z_i)) \prod_{i=1}^{m} P(e_i|parents(E_i)) \\ &= P(\mathbf{z}, \mathbf{e}) \ , \end{aligned} \tag{14.8}$$

because the two products cover all the variables in the network, allowing us to use Equation (14.1) for the joint probability.

Now it is easy to show that likelihood weighting estimates are consistent. For any particular value $x$ of $X$, the estimated posterior probability can be calculated as follows:

$$\begin{aligned} \hat{P}(x|\mathbf{e}) &= \alpha \sum_{\mathbf{y}} N_{WS}(x, \mathbf{y}, \mathbf{e})w(x, \mathbf{y}, \mathbf{e}) && \text{from LIKELIHOOD-WEIGHTING} \\ &\approx \alpha' \sum_{\mathbf{y}} S_{WS}(x, \mathbf{y}, \mathbf{e})w(x, \mathbf{y}, \mathbf{e}) && \text{for large } N \end{aligned}$$

$$= \alpha' \sum_{\mathbf{y}} P(x, \mathbf{y}, \mathbf{e}) \qquad \text{by Equation (14.8)}$$
$$= \alpha' P(x, \mathbf{e}) = P(x|\mathbf{e}) .$$

Hence, likelihood weighting returns consistent estimates.

Because likelihood weighting uses all the samples generated, it can be much more efficient than rejection sampling. It will, however, suffer a degradation in performance as the number of evidence variables increases. This is because most samples will have very low weights and hence the weighted estimate will be dominated by the tiny fraction of samples that accord more than an infinitesimal likelihood to the evidence. The problem is exacerbated if the evidence variables occur late in the variable ordering, because then the samples will be simulations that bear little resemblance to the reality suggested by the evidence.

### Inference by Markov chain simulation

MARKOV CHAIN MONTE CARLO

In this section, we describe the **Markov chain Monte Carlo** (MCMC) algorithm for inference in Bayesian networks. We will first describe what the algorithm does, then we will explain why it works and why it has such a complicated name.

#### The MCMC algorithm

Unlike the other two sampling algorithms, which generate each event from scratch, MCMC generates each event by making a random change to the preceding event. It is therefore helpful to think of the network as being in a particular *current state* specifying a value for every variable. The next state is generated by randomly sampling a value for one of the nonevidence variables $X_i$, *conditioned on the current values of the variables in the Markov blanket of* $X_i$. (Recall from page 499 that the Markov blanket of a variable consists of its parents, children, and children's parents.) MCMC therefore wanders randomly around the state space—the space of possible complete assignments—flipping one variable at a time, but keeping the evidence variables fixed.

Consider the query $\mathbf{P}(Rain|Sprinkler = true, WetGrass = true)$ applied to the network in Figure 14.11(a). The evidence variables $Sprinkler$ and $WetGrass$ are fixed to their observed values and the hidden variables $Cloudy$ and $Rain$ are initialized randomly—let us say to $true$ and $false$ respectively. Thus, the initial state is $[true, true, false, true]$. Now the following steps are executed repeatedly:

1. $Cloudy$ is sampled, given the current values of its Markov blanket variables: in this case, we sample from $\mathbf{P}(Cloudy|Sprinkler = true, Rain = false)$. (Shortly, we will show how to calculate this distribution.) Suppose the result is $Cloudy = false$. Then the new current state is $[false, true, false, true]$.
2. $Rain$ is sampled, given the current values of its Markov blanket variables: in this case, we sample from $\mathbf{P}(Rain|Cloudy = false, Sprinkler = true, WetGrass = true)$. Suppose this yields $Rain = true$. The new current state is $[false, true, true, true]$.

Each state visited during this process is a sample that contributes to the estimate for the query variable $Rain$. If the process visits 20 states where $Rain$ is true and 60 states where $Rain$ is

```
function MCMC-ASK(X, e, bn, N) returns an estimate of P(X|e)
   local variables: N[X], a vector of counts over X, initially zero
                    Z, the nonevidence variables in bn
                    x, the current state of the network, initially copied from e

   initialize x with random values for the variables in Z
   for j = 1 to N do
      for each Z_i in Z do
         sample the value of Z_i in x from P(Z_i|mb(Z_i)) given the values of MB(Z_i) in x
         N[x] ← N[x] + 1 where x is the value of X in x
   return NORMALIZE(N[X])
```

**Figure 14.15** The MCMC algorithm for approximate inference in Bayesian networks.

false, then the answer to the query is NORMALIZE($\langle 20, 60 \rangle$) $= \langle 0.25, 0.75 \rangle$. The complete algorithm is shown in Figure 14.15.

### Why MCMC works

We will now show that MCMC returns consistent estimates for posterior probabilities. The material in this section is quite technical, but the basic claim is straightforward: *the sampling process settles into a "dynamic equilibrium" in which the long-run fraction of time spent in each state is exactly proportional to its posterior probability.* This remarkable property follows from the specific **transition probability** with which the process moves from one state to another, as defined by the conditional distribution given the Markov blanket of the variable being sampled.

TRANSITION PROBABILITY

Let $q(\mathbf{x} \to \mathbf{x}')$ be the probability that the process makes a transition from state $\mathbf{x}$ to state $\mathbf{x}'$. This transition probability defines what is called a **Markov chain** on the state space. (Markov chains will also figure prominently in Chapters 15 and 17.) Now suppose that we run the Markov chain for $t$ steps, and let $\pi_t(\mathbf{x})$ be the probability that the system is in state $\mathbf{x}$ at time $t$. Similarly, let $\pi_{t+1}(\mathbf{x}')$ be the probability of being in state $\mathbf{x}'$ at time $t+1$. Given $\pi_t(\mathbf{x})$, we can calculate $\pi_{t+1}(\mathbf{x}')$ by summing, for all states the system could be in at time $t$, the probability of being in that state times the probability of making the transition to $\mathbf{x}'$:

MARKOV CHAIN

$$\pi_{t+1}(\mathbf{x}') = \sum_{\mathbf{x}} \pi_t(\mathbf{x}) q(\mathbf{x} \to \mathbf{x}') .$$

We will say that the chain has reached its **stationary distribution** if $\pi_t = \pi_{t+1}$. Let us call this stationary distribution $\pi$; its defining equation is therefore

STATIONARY DISTRIBUTION

$$\pi(\mathbf{x}') = \sum_{\mathbf{x}} \pi(\mathbf{x}) q(\mathbf{x} \to \mathbf{x}') \qquad \text{for all } \mathbf{x}' . \tag{14.9}$$

Under certain standard assumptions about the transition probability distribution $q$,[7] there is exactly one distribution $\pi$ satisfying this equation for any given $q$.

[7] The Markov chain defined by $q$ must be **ergodic**—that is, essentially, every state must be reachable from every other, and there can be no strictly periodic cycles.

Equation (14.9) can be read as saying that the expected "outflow" from each state (i.e., its current "population") is equal to the expected "inflow" from all the states. One obvious way to satisfy this relationship is if the expected flow between any pair of states is the same in both directions. This is the property of **detailed balance**:

DETAILED BALANCE

$$\pi(\mathbf{x})q(\mathbf{x} \rightarrow \mathbf{x}') = \pi(\mathbf{x}')q(\mathbf{x}' \rightarrow \mathbf{x}) \qquad \text{for all } \mathbf{x},\ \mathbf{x}' . \tag{14.10}$$

We can show that detailed balance implies stationarity simply by summing over $\mathbf{x}$ in Equation (14.10). We have

$$\sum_{\mathbf{x}} \pi(\mathbf{x})q(\mathbf{x} \rightarrow \mathbf{x}') = \sum_{\mathbf{x}} \pi(\mathbf{x}')q(\mathbf{x}' \rightarrow \mathbf{x}) = \pi(\mathbf{x}') \sum_{\mathbf{x}} q(\mathbf{x}' \rightarrow \mathbf{x}) = \pi(\mathbf{x}')$$

where the last step follows because a transition from $\mathbf{x}'$ is guaranteed to occur.

Now we will show that the transition probability $q(\mathbf{x} \rightarrow \mathbf{x}')$ defined by the sampling step in MCMC-ASK satisfies the detailed balance equation with a stationary distribution equal to $P(\mathbf{x}|\mathbf{e})$, (the true posterior distribution on the hidden variables). We will do this in two steps. First, we will define a Markov chain in which each variable is sampled conditionally on the current values of *all* the other variables, and we will show that this satisfies detailed balance. Then, we will simply observe that, for Bayesian networks, doing that is equivalent to sampling conditionally on the variable's Markov blanket (see page 499).

Let $X_i$ be the variable to be sampled, and let $\overline{\mathbf{X}_i}$ be all the hidden variables *other than* $X_i$. Their values in the current state are $x_i$ and $\overline{\mathbf{x}_i}$. If we sample a new value $x_i'$ for $X_i$ conditionally on all the other variables, including the evidence, we have

$$q(\mathbf{x} \rightarrow \mathbf{x}') = q((x_i, \overline{\mathbf{x}_i}) \rightarrow (x_i', \overline{\mathbf{x}_i})) = P(x_i'|\overline{\mathbf{x}_i}, \mathbf{e}) .$$

GIBBS SAMPLER

This transition probability is called the **Gibbs sampler** and is a particularly convenient form of MCMC. Now we show that the Gibbs sampler is in detailed balance with the true posterior:

$$\begin{aligned}
\pi(\mathbf{x})q(\mathbf{x} \rightarrow \mathbf{x}') &= P(\mathbf{x}|\mathbf{e})P(x_i'|\overline{\mathbf{x}_i}, \mathbf{e}) = P(x_i, \overline{\mathbf{x}_i}|\mathbf{e})P(x_i'|\overline{\mathbf{x}_i}, \mathbf{e}) \\
&= P(x_i|\overline{\mathbf{x}_i}, \mathbf{e})P(\overline{\mathbf{x}_i}|\mathbf{e})P(x_i'|\overline{\mathbf{x}_i}, \mathbf{e}) \qquad \text{(using the chain rule on the first term)} \\
&= P(x_i|\overline{\mathbf{x}_i}, \mathbf{e})P(x_i', \overline{\mathbf{x}_i}|\mathbf{e}) \qquad \text{(using the chain rule backwards)} \\
&= \pi(\mathbf{x}')q(\mathbf{x}' \rightarrow \mathbf{x}) .
\end{aligned}$$

As stated on page 499, a variable is independent of all other variables given its Markov blanket; hence,

$$P(x_i'|\overline{\mathbf{x}_i}, \mathbf{e}) = P(x_i'|mb(X_i))$$

where $mb(X_i)$ denotes the values of the variables in $X_i$'s Markov blanket, $MB(X_i)$. As shown in Exercise 14.10, the probability of a variable given its Markov blanket is proportional to the probability of the variable given its parents times the probability of each child given its respective parents:

$$P(x_i'|mb(X_i)) = \alpha\, P(x_i'|parents(X_i)) \times \prod_{Y_j \in Children(X_i)} P(y_j|parents(Y_j)) . \tag{14.11}$$

Hence, to flip each variable $X_i$, the number of multiplications required is equal to the number of $X_i$'s children.

We have discussed here only one simple variant of MCMC, namely the Gibbs sampler. In its most general form, MCMC is a powerful method for computing with probability models and many variants have been developed, including the simulated annealing algorithm presented in Chapter 4, the stochastic satisfiability algorithms in Chapter 7, and the Metropolis–Hastings sampler in Chapter 15.

## 14.6 EXTENDING PROBABILITY TO FIRST-ORDER REPRESENTATIONS

In Chapter 8, we explained the representational advantages possessed by first-order logic in comparison to propositional logic. First-order logic commits to the existence of objects and relations among them and can express facts about *some* or *all* of the objects in a domain. This often results in representations that are vastly more concise than the equivalent propositional descriptions. Now, Bayesian networks are essentially propositional: the set of variables is fixed and finite, and each has a fixed domain of possible values. This fact limits the applicability of Bayesian networks. *If we can find a way to combine probability theory with the expressive power of first-order representations, we expect to be able to increase dramatically the range of problems that can be handled.*

The basic insight required to achieve this goal is the following: In the propositional context, a Bayesian network specifies probabilities over atomic events, each of which specifies a value for each variable in the network. Thus, an atomic event is a **model** or **possible world**, in the terminology of propositional logic. In the first-order context, a model (with its interpretation) specifies a domain of objects, the relations that hold among those objects, and a mapping from the constants and predicates of the knowledge base to the objects and relations in the model. Therefore, *a first-order probabilistic knowledge base should specify probabilities for all possible first-order models.* Let $\mu(M)$ be the probability assigned to model $M$ by the knowledge base. For any first-order sentence $\phi$, the probability $P(\phi)$ is given in the usual way by summing over the possible worlds where $\phi$ is true:

$$P(\phi) = \sum_{M:\phi \text{ is true in } M} \mu(M) . \tag{14.12}$$

So far, so good. There is, however, a problem: the set of first-order models is infinite. This means that (1) the summation could be infeasible, and (2) specifying a complete, consistent distribution over an infinite set of worlds could be very difficult.

Let us scale back our ambition, at least temporarily. In particular, let us devise a restricted language for which there are only finitely many models of interest. There are several ways to do this. Here, we present **relational probability models**, or RPMs, which borrow ideas from semantic networks (Chapter 10) and from object-relational databases. Other approaches are discussed in the bibliographical and historical notes.

RELATIONAL PROBABILITY MODEL

RPMs allow constant symbols that name objects. For example, let $ProfSmith$ be the name of a professor, and let $Jones$ be the name of a student. Each object is an instance of a class; for example, $ProfSmith$ is a $Professor$ and $Jones$ is a $Student$. We assume that the class of every constant symbol is known.

SIMPLE FUNCTION

Our function symbols will be divided into two kinds. The first kind, **simple functions**, maps an object not to another structured object, but to a value from a fixed domain of values, just like a random variable. For example, $Intelligence(Jones)$ and $Funding(ProfSmith)$ might be $hi$ or $lo$; $Success(Jones)$ and $Fame(ProfSmith)$ may be $true$ or $false$. Function symbols must not be applied to values such as $true$ and $false$, so it is not possible to have nesting of simple functions. In this way, we avoid one source of infinities. The value of a simple function applied to a given object may be observed or unknown; these will be the basic random variables of our representation.[8]

COMPLEX FUNCTION

We also allow **complex functions**, which map objects to other objects. For example, $Advisor(Jones)$ may be $ProfSmith$. Each complex function has a specified domain and range, which are classes. For example, the domain of $Advisor$ is $Student$ and the range is $Professor$. Functions apply only to objects of the right class; for instance, the $Advisor$ of $ProfSmith$ is undefined. Complex functions may be nested: $DeptHead(Advisor(Jones))$ could be $ProfMoore$. We will assume (for now) that the values of all complex functions are known for all constant symbols. Because the KB is finite, this implies that every chain of complex function applications leads to one of a finite number of objects.[9]

The last element we need is the probabilistic information. For each simple function, we specify a set of parents, just as in Bayesian networks. The parents can be other simple functions of the same object; for example, the $Funding$ of a $Professor$ might depend on his or her $Fame$. The parents can also be simple functions of *related* objects—for example, the $Success$ of a student could depend on the $Intelligence$ of the student and the $Fame$ of the student's advisor. These are really *universally quantified* assertions about the parents of all the objects in a class. Thus, we could write

$$\begin{aligned}&\forall x \;\; x \in Student \Rightarrow \\ &\quad Parents(Success(x)) = \{Intelligence(x), Fame(Advisor(x))\} .\end{aligned}$$

(Less formally, we can draw diagrams like Figure 14.16(a).) Now we specify the conditional probability distribution for the child, given its parents. For example, we might say that

$$\begin{aligned}&\forall x \;\; x \in Student \Rightarrow \\ &\quad P(Success(x) = true | Intelligence(x) = hi, Fame(Advisor(x)) = true) = 0.95 .\end{aligned}$$

Just as in semantic networks, we can attach the conditional distribution to the class itself, so that the instances **inherit** the dependencies and conditional probabilities from the class.

The semantics for the RPM language assumes that every constant symbol refers to a distinct object—the **unique names assumption** described in Chapter 10. Given this assumption and the restrictions listed previously, it can be shown that every RPM generates a fixed, finite set of random variables, each of which is a simple function applied to a constant symbol. Then, provided that the parent–child dependencies are *acyclic*, we can construct an equivalent Bayesian network. That is, the RPM and the Bayesian network specify identical probabili-

8 They play a role very similar to that of the ground atomic sentences generated in the propositionalization process described in Section 9.1.

9 This restriction means that we cannot use complex functions such as $Father$ and $Mother$, which lead to potentially infinite chains that would have to end with an unknown object. We revisit this restriction later.

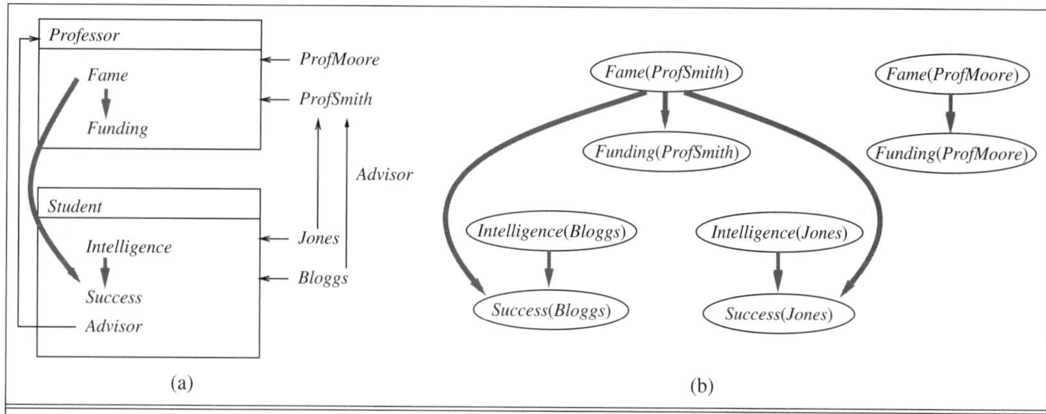


**Figure 14.16** (a) An RPM describing two classes: *Professor* and *Student*. There are two professors and two students, and *ProfSmith* is the advisor of both students. (b) The Bayesian network equivalent to the RPM in (a).

ties for each possible world. Figure 14.16(b) shows the Bayesian network corresponding to the RPM in Figure 14.16(a). Notice that the $Advisor$ links in the RPM are absent in the Bayesian network. This is because they are fixed and known. They appear *implicitly* in the network topology, however; for example, $Success(Jones)$ has $Fame(ProfSmith)$ as a parent because $Advisor(Jones)$ is $ProfSmith$. In general, the relations that hold among the objects determine the pattern of dependencies among the properties of those objects.

RECURSIVE DEPENDENCY

There are several ways to increase the expressive power of RPMs. We can allow **recursive dependencies** among variables to capture certain kinds of recurring relationships. For example, suppose that addiction to fast food is caused by the $McGene$. Then, for any $x$, $McGene(x)$ depends on $McGene(Father(x))$ and $McGene(Mother(x))$, which depend in turn on $McGene(Father(Father(x)))$, $McGene(Mother(Father(x)))$, and so on. Even though such knowledge bases correspond to Bayesian networks with infinitely many random variables, solutions can sometimes be obtained from fixed-point equations. For example, the equilibrium distribution of the $McGene$ can be calculated, given the conditional probability of inheritance. Another very important family of recursive knowledge bases consists of the **temporal probability models** described in Chapter 15. In these models, properties of the state at time $t$ depend on properties of the state at time $t-1$, and so on.

RELATIONAL UNCERTAINTY

RPMs can also be extended to allow for **relational uncertainty**—that is, uncertainty about the values of complex functions. For example, we may not know who $Advisor(Jones)$ is. $Advisor(Jones)$ then becomes a random variable, with possible values $ProfSmith$ and $ProfMoore$. The corresponding network is shown in Figure 14.17.

IDENTITY UNCERTAINTY

There can also be **identity uncertainty**; for example, we might not know whether $Mary$ and $ProfSmith$ are the same person. With identity uncertainty, the number of objects and propositions can vary across possible worlds. A world where $Mary$ and $ProfSmith$ are the same person has one fewer object than a world in which they are different people. This makes the inference process more complicated, but the basic principle established in Equation (14.12) still holds: the probability of any sentence is well defined and can be calculated.

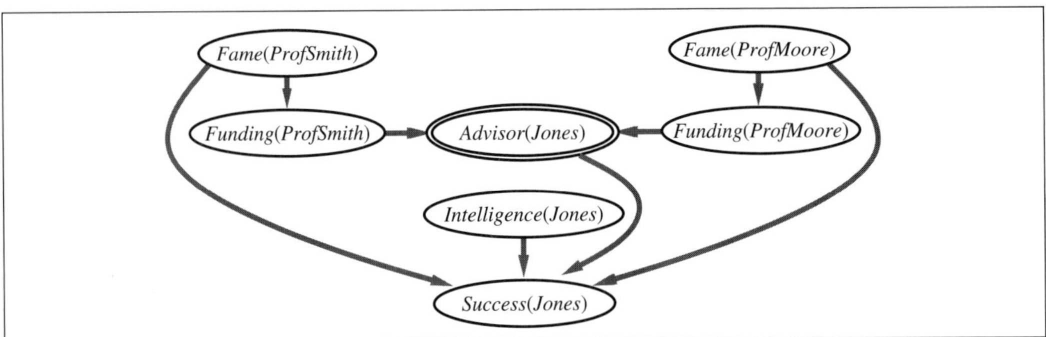


**Figure 14.17** Part of the Bayesian network corresponding to an RPM in which $Advisor(Jones)$ is unknown, but is either $ProfSmith$ or $ProfMoore$. The choice of advisor depends on how much funding each professor has. Notice that $Success(Jones)$ will now depend on the $Fame$ of *both* professors, although the value of $Advisor(Jones)$ determines which one actually has an influence.

Identity uncertainty is particularly important for robots and for embedded sensor systems that must keep track of multiple objects. We return to this problem in Chapter 15.

Let us now examine the question of inference. Clearly, inference can be done in the equivalent Bayesian network, provided that we restrict the RPM language so that the equivalent network is finite and has a fixed structure. This is analogous to the way in which first-order logical inference can be done via propositional inference on the equivalent propositional knowledge base. (See Section 9.1.) As in the logical case, the equivalent network could be too large to construct, let alone evaluate. Dense interconnections are also a problem. (See Exercise 14.12.) Approximation algorithms. such as MCMC (Section 14.5), are therefore very useful for RPM inference.

When MCMC is applied to the equivalent Bayesian network for a simple RPM knowledge base with no relational or identity uncertainty, the algorithm samples from the space of possible worlds defined by the values of simple functions of the objects. It is easy to see that this approach can be extended to handle relational and identity uncertainty as well. In that case, a transition between possible worlds might change the value of a simple function or it might change a complex function, and so lead to a change in the dependency structure. Transitions might also change the identity relations among the constant symbols. Thus, MCMC seems to be an elegant way to handle inference for quite expressive first-order probabilistic knowledge bases.

Research in this area is still at an early stage, but already it is becoming clear that first-order probabilistic reasoning yields a tremendous increase in the effectiveness of AI systems at handling uncertain information. Potential applications include computer vision, natural language understanding, information retrieval, and situation assessment. In all of these areas, the set of objects—and hence the set of random variables—is not known in advance, so purely "propositional" methods, such as Bayesian networks, are incapable of representing the situation completely. They have been augmented by search over the space of model, but RPMs allow reasoning about this uncertainty in a single model.

## 14.7 OTHER APPROACHES TO UNCERTAIN REASONING

Other sciences (e.g., physics, genetics, and economics) have long favored probability as a model for uncertainty. In 1819, Pierre Laplace said "Probability theory is nothing but common sense reduced to calculation." In 1850, James Maxwell said "the true logic for this world is the calculus of Probabilities, which takes account of the magnitude of the probability which is, or ought to be, in a reasonable man's mind."

Given this long tradition, it is perhaps surprising that AI has considered many alternatives to probability. The earliest expert systems of the 1970s ignored uncertainty and used strict logical reasoning, but it soon became clear that this was impractical for most real-world domains. The next generation of expert systems (especially in medical domains) used probabilistic techniques. Initial results were promising, but they did not scale up because of the exponential number of probabilities required in the full joint distribution. (Efficient Bayesian network algorithms were unknown then.) As a result, probabilistic approaches fell out of favor from roughly 1975 to 1988, and a variety of alternatives to probability were tried for a variety of reasons:

- One common view is that probability theory is essentially numerical, whereas human judgmental reasoning is more "qualitative." Certainly, we are not consciously aware of doing numerical calculations of degrees of belief. (Neither are we aware of doing unification, yet we seem to be capable of some kind of logical reasoning.) It might be that we have some kind of numerical degrees of belief encoded directly in strengths of connections and activations in our neurons. In that case, the difficulty of conscious access to those strengths is not surprising. One should also note that qualitative reasoning mechanisms can be built directly on top of probability theory, so that the "no numbers" argument against probability has little force. Nonetheless, some qualitative schemes have a good deal of appeal in their own right. One of the best studied is **default reasoning**, which treats conclusions not as "believed to a certain degree," but as "believed until a better reason is found to believe something else." Default reasoning is covered in Chapter 10.
- **Rule-based** approaches to uncertainty also have been tried. Such approaches hope to build on the success of logical rule-based systems, but add a sort of "fudge factor" to each rule to accommodate uncertainty. These methods were developed in the mid-1970s and formed the basis for a large number of expert systems in medicine and other areas.
- One area that we have not addressed so far is the question of **ignorance**, as opposed to uncertainty. Consider the flipping of a coin. If we know that the coin is fair, then a probability of 0.5 for heads is reasonable. If we know that the coin is biased, but we do not know which way, then 0.5 is the only reasonable probability. Obviously, the two cases are different, yet probability seems not to distinguish them. The **Dempster–Shafer theory** uses **interval-valued** degrees of belief to represent an agent's knowledge of the probability of a proposition. Other methods using second-order probabilities are also discussed.

- Probability makes the same ontological commitment as logic: that events are true or false in the world, even if the agent is uncertain as to which is the case. Researchers in **fuzzy logic** have proposed an ontology that allows **vagueness**: that an event can be "sort of" true. Vagueness and uncertainty are in fact orthogonal issues, as we will see.

The next three subsections treat some of these approaches in slightly more depth. We will not provide detailed technical material, but we cite references for further study.

### Rule-based methods for uncertain reasoning

Rule-based systems emerged from early work on practical and intuitive systems for logical inference. Logical systems in general, and logical rule-based systems in particular, have three desirable properties:

LOCALITY

◇ **Locality**: In logical systems, whenever we have a rule of the form $A \Rightarrow B$, we can conclude $B$, given evidence $A$, *without worrying about any other rules.* In probabilistic systems, we need to consider all the evidence in the Markov blanket.

DETACHMENT

◇ **Detachment**: Once a logical proof is found for a proposition $B$, the proposition can be used regardless of how it was derived. That is, it can be **detached** from its justification. In dealing with probabilities, on the other hand, the source of the evidence for a belief is important for subsequent reasoning.

TRUTH-FUNCTIONALITY

◇ **Truth-functionality**: In logic, the truth of complex sentences can be computed from the truth of the components. Probability combination does not work this way, except under strong global independence assumptions.

There have been several attempts to devise uncertain reasoning schemes that retain these advantages. The idea is to attach degrees of belief to propositions and rules and to devise purely local schemes for combining and propagating those degrees of belief. The schemes are also truth-functional; for example, the degree of belief in $A \vee B$ is a function of the belief in $A$ and the belief in $B$.

The bad news for rule-based systems is that the properties of *locality, detachment, and truth-functionality are simply not appropriate for uncertain reasoning.* Let us look at truth-functionality first. Let $H_1$ be the event that a fair coin flip comes up heads, let $T_1$ be the event that the coin comes up tails on that same flip, and let $H_2$ be the event that the coin comes up heads on a second flip. Clearly, all three events have the same probability, 0.5, and so a truth-functional system must assign the same belief to the disjunction of any two of them. But we can see that the probability of the disjunction depends on the events themselves and not just on their probabilities:

| $P(A)$ | $P(B)$ | $P(A \vee B)$ |
|---|---|---|
| | $P(H_1) = 0.5$ | $P(H_1 \vee H_1) = 0.50$ |
| $P(H_1) = 0.5$ | $P(T_1) = 0.5$ | $P(H_1 \vee T_1) = 1.00$ |
| | $P(H_2) = 0.5$ | $P(H_1 \vee H_2) = 0.75$ |

It gets worse when we chain evidence together. Truth-functional systems have **rules** of the form $A \mapsto B$ that allow us to compute the belief in $B$ as a function of the belief in the rule and the belief in $A$. Both forward- and backward-chaining systems can be devised. The belief in the rule is assumed to be constant and is usually specified by the knowledge engineer—for example, as $A \mapsto_{0.9} B$.

Consider the wet-grass situation from Figure 14.11(a). If we wanted to be able to do both causal and diagnostic reasoning, we would need the two rules

$$Rain \mapsto WetGrass \qquad \text{and} \qquad WetGrass \mapsto Rain\ .$$

These two rules form a feedback loop: evidence for $Rain$ increases the belief in $WetGrass$, which in turn increases the belief in $Rain$ even more. Clearly, uncertain reasoning systems need to keep track of the paths along which evidence is propagated.

Intercausal reasoning (or explaining away) is also tricky. Consider what happens when we have the two rules

$$Sprinkler \mapsto WetGrass \qquad \text{and} \qquad WetGrass \mapsto Rain\ .$$

Suppose we see that the sprinkler is on. Chaining forward through our rules, this increases the belief that the grass will be wet, which in turn increases the belief that it is raining. But this is ridiculous: the fact that the sprinkler is on explains away the wet grass and should *reduce* the belief in rain. A truth-functional system acts as if it also believes $Sprinkler \mapsto Rain$.

Given these difficulties, how is it possible that truth-functional systems were ever considered useful? The answer lies in restricting the task and in carefully engineering the rule base so that undesirable interactions do not occur. The most famous example of a truth-functional system for uncertain reasoning is the **certainty factors** model, which was developed for the MYCIN medical diagnosis program and was widely used in expert systems of the late 1970s and 1980s. Almost all uses of certainty factors involved rule sets that were either purely diagnostic (as in MYCIN) or purely causal. Furthermore, evidence was entered only at the "roots" of the rule set, and most rule sets were singly connected. Heckerman (1986) has shown that, under these circumstances, a minor variation on certainty-factor inference was exactly equivalent to Bayesian inference on polytrees. In other circumstances, certainty factors could yield disastrously incorrect degrees of belief through overcounting of evidence. As rule sets became larger, undesirable interactions between rules became more common, and practitioners found that the certainty factors of many other rules had to be "tweaked" when new rules were added. Needless to say, the approach is no longer recommended.

CERTAINTY FACTORS

### Representing ignorance: Dempster–Shafer theory

DEMPSTER–SHAFER

The **Dempster–Shafer** theory is designed to deal with the distinction between **uncertainty** and **ignorance**. Rather than computing the probability of a proposition, it computes the probability that the evidence supports the proposition. This measure of belief is called a **belief function**, written $Bel(X)$.

BELIEF FUNCTION

We return to coin flipping for an example of belief functions. Suppose a shady character comes up to you and offers to bet you \$10 that his coin will come up heads on the next flip. Given that the coin might or might not be fair, what belief should you ascribe to the event that it comes up heads? Dempster–Shafer theory says that because you have no evidence either way, you have to say that the belief $Bel(Heads) = 0$ and also that $Bel(\neg Heads) = 0$.

This makes Dempster–Shafer reasoning systems skeptical in a way that has some intuitive appeal. Now suppose you have an expert at your disposal who testifies with 90% certainty that the coin is fair (i.e., he is 90% sure that $P(Heads) = 0.5$). Then Dempster–Shafer theory gives $Bel(Heads) = 0.9 \times 0.5 = 0.45$ and likewise $Bel(\neg Heads) = 0.45$. There is still a 10 percentage point "gap" that is not accounted for by the evidence. "Dempster's rule" (Dempster, 1968) shows how to combine evidence to give new values for $Bel$, and Shafer's work extends this into a complete computational model.

As with default reasoning, there is a problem in connecting beliefs to actions. With probabilities, decision theory says that if $P(Heads) = P(\neg Heads) = 0.5$, then (assuming that winning \$10 and losing \$10 are considered equal magnitude opposites) the reasoner will be indifferent between the action of accepting and declining the bet. A Dempster–Shafer reasoner has $Bel(\neg Heads) = 0$ and thus no reason to accept the bet, but then it also has $Bel(Heads) = 0$ and thus no reason to decline it. Thus, it seems that the Dempster–Shafer reasoner comes to the same conclusion about how to act in this case. Unfortunately, Dempster–Shafer theory allows no definite decision in many other cases where probabilistic inference does yield a specific choice. In fact, the notion of utility in the Dempster–Shafer model is not yet well understood.

One interpretation of Dempster—Shafer theory is that it defines a probability interval: the interval for $Heads$ is $[0, 1]$ before our expert testimony and $[0.45, 0.55]$ after. The width of the interval might be an aid in deciding when we need to acquire more evidence: it can tell you that the expert's testimony will help you if you do not know whether the coin is fair, but will not help you if you have already learned that the coin is fair. However, there are no clear guidelines for how to do this, because there is no clear meaning for what the width of an interval means. In the Bayesian approach, this kind of reasoning can be done easily by examining how much one's belief would change if one were to acquire more evidence. For example, knowing whether the coin is fair would have a significant impact on the belief that it will come up heads, and detecting an asymmetric weight would have an impact on the belief that the coin is fair. A complete Bayesian model would include probability estimates for factors such as these, allowing us to express our "ignorance" in terms of how our beliefs would change in the face of future information gathering.

### Representing vagueness: Fuzzy sets and fuzzy logic

FUZZY SET THEORY

**Fuzzy set theory** is a means of specifying how well an object satisfies a vague description. For example, consider the proposition "Nate is tall." Is this true, if Nate is $5'\ 10''$? Most people would hesitate to answer "true" or "false," preferring to say, "sort of." Note that this is not a question of uncertainty about the external world—we are sure of Nate's height. The issue is that the linguistic term "tall" does not refer to a sharp demarcation of objects into two classes—there are *degrees* of tallness. For this reason, *fuzzy set theory is not a method for uncertain reasoning at all.* Rather, fuzzy set theory treats $Tall$ as a fuzzy predicate and says that the truth value of $Tall(Nate)$ is a number between 0 and 1, rather than being just $true$ or $false$. The name "fuzzy set" derives from the interpretation of the predicate as implicitly defining a set of its members—a set that does not have sharp boundaries.

FUZZY LOGIC

**Fuzzy logic** is a method for reasoning with logical expressions describing membership in fuzzy sets. For example, the complex sentence $Tall(Nate) \wedge Heavy(Nate)$ has a fuzzy truth value that is a function of the truth values of its components. The standard rules for evaluating the fuzzy truth, $T$, of a complex sentence are

$$T(A \wedge B) = \min(T(A), T(B))$$
$$T(A \vee B) = \max(T(A), T(B))$$
$$T(\neg A) = 1 - T(A) .$$

Fuzzy logic is therefore a truth-functional system—a fact that causes serious difficulties. For example, suppose that $T(Tall(Nate)) = 0.6$ and $T(Heavy(Nate)) = 0.4$. Then we have $T(Tall(Nate) \wedge T(Heavy(Nate)) = 0.4$, which seems reasonable, but we also get the result $T(Tall(Nate) \wedge \neg Tall(Nate)) = 0.4$, which does not. Clearly, the problem arises from the inability of a truth-functional approach to take into account the correlations or anticorrelations among the component propositions.

FUZZY CONTROL

**Fuzzy control** is a methodology for constructing control systems in which the mapping between real-valued input and output parameters is represented by fuzzy rules. Fuzzy control has been very successful in commercial products such as automatic transmissions, video cameras, and electric shavers. Critics (see, e.g., Elkan, 1993) argue that these applications are successful because they have small rule bases, no chaining of inferences, and tunable parameters that can be adjusted to improve the system's performance. The fact that they are implemented with fuzzy operators might be incidental to their success; the key is simply to provide a concise and intuitive way to specify a smoothly interpolated, real-valued function.

There have been attempts to provide an explanation of fuzzy logic in terms of probability theory. One idea is to view assertions such as "Nate is Tall" as discrete observations made concerning a continuous hidden variable, Nate's actual $Height$. The probability model specifies $P(\text{Observer says Nate is tall} \mid Height)$, perhaps using a **probit distribution** as described on page 503. A posterior distribution over Nate's height can then be calculated in the usual way, for example if the model is part of a hybrid Bayesian network. Such an approach is not truth-functional, of course. For example, the conditional distribution

$$P(\text{Observer says Nate is tall and heavy} \mid Height, Weight)$$

allows for interactions between height and weight in the causing of the observation. Thus, someone who is eight feet tall and weighs 190 pounds is very unlikely to be called "tall and heavy," even though "eight feet" counts as "tall" and "190 pounds" counts as "heavy."

RANDOM SETS

Fuzzy predicates can also be given a probabilistic interpretation in terms of **random sets**—that is, random variables whose possible values are sets of objects. For example, $Tall$ is a random set whose possible values are sets of people. The probability $P(Tall = S_1)$, where $S_1$ is some particular set of people, is the probability that exactly that set would be identified as "tall" by an observer. Then the probability that "Nate is tall" is the sum of the probabilities of all the sets of which Nate is a member.

Both the hybrid Bayesian network approach and the random sets approach appear to capture aspects of fuzziness without introducing degrees of truth. Nonetheless, there remain many open issues concerning the proper representation of linguistic observations and continuous quantities—issues that have been neglected by most outside the fuzzy community.

## 14.8 SUMMARY

This chapter has described **Bayesian networks**, a well-developed representation for uncertain knowledge. Bayesian networks play a role roughly analogous to that of propositional logic for definite knowledge.

- A Bayesian network is a directed acyclic graph whose nodes correspond to random variables; each node has a conditional distribution for the node, given its parents.
- Bayesian networks provide a concise way to represent **conditional independence** relationships in the domain.
- A Bayesian network specifies a full joint distribution; each joint entry is defined as the product of the corresponding entries in the local conditional distributions. A Bayesian network is often exponentially smaller than the full joint distribution.
- Many conditional distributions can be represented compactly by canonical families of distributions. **Hybrid Bayesian networks**, which include both discrete and continuous variables, use a variety of canonical distributions.
- Inference in Bayesian networks means computing the probability distribution of a set of query variables, given a set of evidence variables. Exact inference algorithms, such as **variable elimination**, evaluate sums of products of conditional probabilities as efficiently as possible.
- In **polytrees** (singly connected networks), exact inference takes time linear in the size of the network. In the general case, the problem is intractable.
- Stochastic approximation techniques such as **likelihood weighting** and **Markov chain Monte Carlo** can give reasonable estimates of the true posterior probabilities in a network and can cope with much larger networks than can exact algorithms.
- Probability theory can be combined with representational ideas from first-order logic to produce very powerful systems for reasoning under uncertainty. **Relational probability models** (RPMs) include representational restrictions that guarantee a well-defined probability distribution that can be expressed as an equivalent Bayesian network.
- Various alternative systems for reasoning under uncertainty have been suggested. Generally speaking, **truth-functional** systems are not well suited for such reasoning.

## BIBLIOGRAPHICAL AND HISTORICAL NOTES

The use of networks to represent probabilistic information began early in the 20th century, with the work of Sewall Wright on the probabilistic analysis of genetic inheritance and animal growth factors (Wright, 1921, 1934). One of his networks appears on the cover of this book. I. J. Good (1961), in collaboration with Alan Turing, developed probabilistic representations and Bayesian inference methods that could be regarded as a forerunner of modern Bayesian networks—although the paper is not often cited in this context.[10] The same paper is the original source for the noisy-OR model.

The **influence diagram** representation for decision problems, which incorporated a DAG representation for random variables, was used in decision analysis in the late 1970s (see Chapter 16), but only enumeration was used for evaluation. Judea Pearl developed the message-passing method for carrying out inference in tree networks (Pearl, 1982a) and polytree networks (Kim and Pearl, 1983) and explained the importance of constructing causal rather than diagnostic probability models, in contrast to the certainty-factor systems then in vogue. The first expert system using Bayesian networks was CONVINCE (Kim, 1983; Kim and Pearl, 1987). More recent systems include the MUNIN system for diagnosing neuromuscular disorders (Andersen *et al.*, 1989) and the PATHFINDER system for pathology (Heckerman, 1991). By far the most widely used Bayesian network systems have been the diagnosis-and-repair modules (e.g., the Printer Wizard) in Microsoft Windows (Breese and Heckerman, 1996) and the Office Assistant in Microsoft Office (Horvitz *et al.*, 1998).

Pearl (1986) developed a clustering algorithm for exact inference in general Bayesian networks, utilizing a conversion to a directed polytree of clusters in which message passing was used to achieve consistency over variables shared between clusters. A similar approach, developed by the statisticians David Spiegelhalter and Steffen Lauritzen (Spiegelhalter, 1986; Lauritzen and Spiegelhalter, 1988), is based on conversion to an undirected (Markov) network. This approach is implemented in the HUGIN system, an efficient and widely used tool for uncertain reasoning (Andersen *et al.*, 1989). Ross Shachter, working in the influence diagram community, developed an exact method based on goal-directed reduction of the network, using posterior-preserving transformations (Shachter, 1986).

The variable elimination method described in the chapter is closest in spirit to Shachter's method, from which emerged the symbolic probabilistic inference (SPI) algorithm (Shachter *et al.*, 1990). SPI attempts to optimize the evaluation of expression trees such as that shown in Figure 14.8. The algorithm we describe is closest to that developed by Zhang and Poole (1994, 1996). Criteria for pruning irrelevant variables were developed by Geiger *et al.* (1990) and by Lauritzen *et al.* (1990); the criterion we give is a simple special case of these. Rina Dechter (1999) shows how the variable elimination idea is essentially identical to **nonserial dynamic programming** (Bertele and Brioschi, 1972), an algorithmic approach that can be applied to solve a range of inference problems in Bayesian networks—for example, finding the **most probable explanation** for a set of observations. This connects Bayesian network algorithms to related methods for solving CSPs and gives a direct measure of the complexity of exact inference in terms of the **hypertree width** of the network.

NONSERIAL DYNAMIC PROGRAMMING

The inclusion of continuous random variables in Bayesian networks was considered by Pearl (1988) and Shachter and Kenley (1989); these papers discussed networks containing only continuous variables with linear Gaussian distributions. The inclusion of discrete variables has been investigated by Lauritzen and Wermuth (1989) and implemented in the

[10] I. J. Good was chief statistician for Turing's code-breaking team in World War II. In *2001: A Space Odyssey* (Clarke, 1968a), Good and Minsky are credited with making the breakthrough that led to the development of the HAL 9000 computer.

cHUGIN system (Olesen, 1993). The probit distribution was studied first by Finney (1947), who called it the sigmoid distribution. It has been used widely for modeling discrete choice phenomena and can be extended to handle more than two choices (Daganzo, 1979). Bishop (1995) gives a justification for the use of the logit distribution.

Cooper (1990) showed that the general problem of inference in unconstrained Bayesian networks is NP-hard, and Paul Dagum and Mike Luby (1993) showed the corresponding approximation problem to be NP-hard. Space complexity is also a serious problem in both clustering and variable elimination methods. The method of **cutset conditioning**, which was developed for CSPs in Chapter 5, avoids the construction of exponentially large tables. In a Bayesian network, a cutset is a set of nodes that, when instantiated, reduces the remaining nodes to a polytree that can be solved in linear time and space. The query is answered by summing over all the instantiations of the cutset, so the overall space requirement is still linear (Pearl, 1988). Darwiche (2001) describes a recursive conditioning algorithm that allows a complete range of space/time tradeoffs.

The development of fast approximation algorithms for Bayesian network inference is a very active area, with contributions from statistics, computer science, and physics. The rejection sampling method is a general technique that is long known to statisticians; it was first applied to Bayesian networks by Max Henrion (1988), who called it **logic sampling**. Likelihood weighting, which was developed by Fung and Chang (1989) and Shachter and Peot (1989), is an example of the well-known statistical method of **importance sampling**. A large-scale application of likelihood weighting to medical diagnosis appears in Shwe and Cooper (1991). Cheng and Druzdzel (2000) describe an adaptive version of likelihood weighting that works well even when the evidence has very low prior likelihood.

Markov chain Monte Carlo (MCMC) algorithms began with the Metropolis algorithm, due to Metropolis *et al.* (1953), which was also the source of the simulated annealing algorithm described in Chapter 4. The Gibbs sampler was devised by Geman and Geman (1984) for inference in undirected Markov networks. The application of MCMC to Bayesian networks is due to Pearl (1987). The papers collected by Gilks *et al.* (1996) cover a wide variety of applications of MCMC, several of which were developed in the well-known BUGS package (Gilks *et al.*, 1994).

VARIATIONAL APPROXIMATION

VARIATIONAL PARAMETERS

MEAN FIELD

There are two very important families of approximation methods that we did not cover in the chapter. The first is the family of **variational approximation** methods, which can be used to simplify complex calculations of all kinds. The basic idea is to propose a reduced version of the original problem that is simple to work with, but that resembles the original problem as closely as possible. The reduced problem is described by some **variational parameters** $\boldsymbol{\lambda}$ that are adjusted to minimize a distance function $D$ between the original and the reduced problem, often by solving the system of equations $\partial D/\partial\boldsymbol{\lambda} = 0$. In many cases, strict upper and lower bounds can be obtained. Variational methods have long been used in statistics (Rustagi, 1976). In statistical physics, the **mean field** method is a particular variational approximation in which the individual variables making up the model are assumed to be completely independent. This idea was applied to solve large undirected Markov networks (Peterson and Anderson, 1987; Parisi, 1988). Saul *et al.* (1996) developed the mathematical foundations for applying variational methods to Bayesian networks and obtained accurate lower-bound approximations for sigmoid networks with the use of mean-field methods. Jaakkola and Jordan (1996) extended the methodology to obtain both lower and upper bounds. Variational approaches are surveyed by Jordan *et al.* (1999).

A second important family of approximation algorithms is based on Pearl's polytree message-passing algorithm (1982a). This algorithm can be applied to general networks, as suggested by Pearl (1988). The results might be incorrect, or the algorithm might fail to terminate, but in many cases, the values obtained are close to the true values. Little attention was paid to this so-called **belief propagation** (or **loopy propagation**) approach until McEliece *et al.* (1998) observed that message passing in a multiply-connected Bayesian network was exactly the computation performed by the **turbo decoding** algorithm (Berrou *et al.*, 1993), which provided a major breakthrough in the design of efficient error-correcting codes. The implication is that loopy propagation is both fast and accurate on the very large and very highly connected networks used for decoding and might therefore be useful more generally. Murphy *et al.* (1999) present an empirical study of where it does work. Yedidia *et al.* (2001) make further connections between loopy propagation and ideas from statistical physics.

BELIEF PROPAGATION

TURBO DECODING

The connection between probability and first-order languages was first studied by Carnap (1950). Gaifman (1964) and Scott and Krauss (1966) defined a language in which probabilities could be associated with first-order sentences and for which models were probability measures on possible worlds. Within AI, this idea was developed for propositional logic by Nilsson (1986) and for first-order logic by Halpern (1990). The first extensive investigation of knowledge representation issues in such languages was carried out by Bacchus (1990), and the paper by Wellman *et al.* (1992) surveys early implementation approaches based on the construction of equivalent propositional Bayesian networks. More recently, researchers have come to understand the importance of *complete* knowledge bases—that is, knowledge bases that, like Bayesian networks, define a unique joint distribution over all possible worlds. Methods for doing this have been based on probabilistic versions of logic programming (Poole, 1993; Sato and Kameya, 1997) or semantic networks (Koller and Pfeffer, 1998). Relational probability models of the kind described in this chapter are investigated in depth by Pfeffer (2000). Pasula and Russell (2001) examine both issues of relational and identity uncertainty within RPMs and the use of MCMC inference.

As explained in Chapter 13, early probabilistic systems fell out of favor in the early 1970s, leaving a partial vacuum to be filled by alternative methods. Certainty factors were invented for use in the medical expert system MYCIN (Shortliffe, 1976), which was intended both as an engineering solution and as a model of human judgment under uncertainty. The collection *Rule-Based Expert Systems* (Buchanan and Shortliffe, 1984) provides a complete overview of MYCIN and its descendants (see also Stefik, 1995). David Heckerman (1986) showed that a slightly modified version of certainty factor calculations gives correct probabilistic results in some cases, but results in serious overcounting of evidence in other cases. The PROSPECTOR expert system (Duda *et al.*, 1979) used a rule-based approach in which the rules were justified by a (seldom tenable) global independence assumption.

Dempster–Shafer theory originates with a paper by Arthur Dempster (1968) proposing a generalization of probability to interval values and a combination rule for using them. Later work by Glenn Shafer (1976) led to the Dempster-Shafer theory's being viewed as a competing approach to probability. Ruspini *et al.* (1992) analyze the relationship between the Dempster-Shafer theory and standard probability theory. Shenoy (1989) has proposed a method for decision making with Dempster–Shafer belief functions.

Fuzzy sets were developed by Lotfi Zadeh (1965) in response to the perceived difficulty of providing exact inputs to intelligent systems. The text by Zimmermann (2001) provides a thorough introduction to fuzzy set theory; papers on fuzzy applications are collected in Zimmermann (1999). As we mentioned in the text, fuzzy logic has often been perceived incorrectly as a direct competitor to probability theory, whereas in fact it addresses a different set of issues. POSSIBILITY THEORY **Possibility theory** (Zadeh, 1978) was introduced to handle uncertainty in fuzzy systems and has much in common with probability. Dubois and Prade (1994) provide a thorough survey of the connections between possibility theory and probability theory.

The resurgence of probability depended mainly on the discovery of Bayesian networks as a method for representing and using conditional independence information. This resurgence did not come without a fight; Peter Cheeseman's (1985) pugnacious "In Defense of Probability," and his later article "An Inquiry into Computer Understanding" (Cheeseman, 1988, with commentaries) give something of the flavor of the debate. One of the principal objections of the logicists was that the numerical calculations that probability theory was thought to require were not apparent to introspection and presumed an unrealistic level of precision in our uncertain knowledge. The development of **qualitative probabilistic networks** (Wellman, 1990a) provided a purely qualitative abstraction of Bayesian networks, using the notion of positive and negative influences between variables. Wellman shows that in many cases such information is sufficient for optimal decision making without the need for the precise specification of probability values. Work by Adnan Darwiche and Matt Ginsberg (1992) extracts the basic properties of conditioning and evidence combination from probability theory and shows that they can also be applied in logical and default reasoning.

The heart disease treatment system described in the chapter is due to Lucas (1996). Other fielded applications of Bayesian networks include the work at Microsoft on inferring computer user goals from their actions (Horvitz *et al.*, 1998) and on filtering junk email (Sahami *et al.*, 1998), the Electric Power Research Institute's work on monitoring power generators (Morjaria *et al.*, 1995), and NASA's work on displaying time-critical information at Mission Control in Houston (Horvitz and Barry, 1995).

Some important early papers on uncertain reasoning methods in AI are collected in the anthologies *Readings in Uncertain Reasoning* (Shafer and Pearl, 1990) and *Uncertainty in Artificial Intelligence* (Kanal and Lemmer, 1986). The most important single publication in the growth of Bayesian networks was undoubtedly the text *Probabilistic Reasoning in Intelligent Systems* (Pearl, 1988). Several excellent texts, including Lauritzen (1996), Jensen (2001) and Jordan (2003), contain more recent material. New research on probabilistic reasoning appears both in mainstream AI journals such as *Artificial Intelligence* and the *Journal of AI Research*, and in more specialized journals, such as the *International Journal of Approximate Reasoning*. Many papers on **graphical models**, which include Bayesian networks, appear in statistical journals. The proceedings of the conferences on Uncertainty in Artificial Intelligence (UAI), Neural Information Processing Systems (NIPS), and Artificial Intelligence and Statistics (AISTATS) are excellent sources for current research.

## EXERCISES

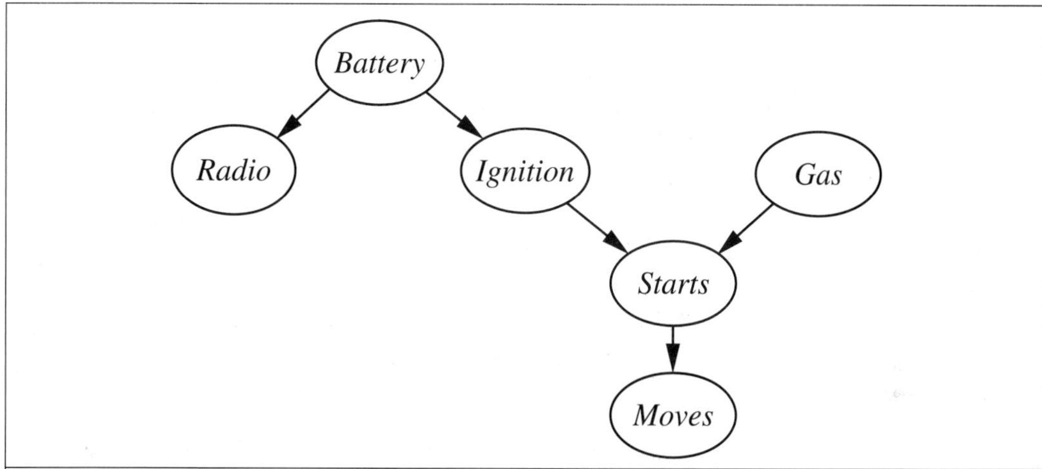


**Figure 14.18** A Bayesian network describing some features of a car's electrical system and engine. Each variable is Boolean, and the *true* value indicates that the corresponding aspect of the vehicle is in working order.

**14.1** Consider the network for car diagnosis shown in Figure 14.18.

**a.** Extend the network with the Boolean variables *IcyWeather* and *StarterMotor*.

**b.** Give reasonable conditional probability tables for all the nodes.

**c.** How many independent values are contained in the joint probability distribution for eight Boolean nodes, assuming that no conditional independence relations are known to hold among them?

**d.** How many independent probability values do your network tables contain?

**e.** The conditional distribution for *Starts* could be described as a **noisy-AND** distribution. Define this family in general and relate it to the noisy-OR distribution.

**14.2** In your local nuclear power station, there is an alarm that senses when a temperature gauge exceeds a given threshold. The gauge measures the temperature of the core. Consider the Boolean variables $A$ (alarm sounds), $F_A$ (alarm is faulty), and $F_G$ (gauge is faulty) and the multivalued nodes $G$ (gauge reading) and $T$ (actual core temperature).

**a.** Draw a Bayesian network for this domain, given that the gauge is more likely to fail when the core temperature gets too high.

**b.** Is your network a polytree?

**c.** Suppose there are just two possible actual and measured temperatures, normal and high; the probability that the gauge gives the correct temperature is $x$ when it is working, but $y$ when it is faulty. Give the conditional probability table associated with $G$.

**d.** Suppose the alarm works correctly unless it is faulty, in which case it never sounds. Give the conditional probability table associated with $A$.

**e.** Suppose the alarm and gauge are working and the alarm sounds. Calculate an expression for the probability that the temperature of the core is too high, in terms of the various conditional probabilities in the network.

**14.3** Two astronomers in different parts of the world make measurements $M_1$ and $M_2$ of the number of stars $N$ in some small region of the sky, using their telescopes. Normally, there is a small possibility $e$ of error by up to one star in each direction. Each telescope can also (with a much smaller probability $f$) be badly out of focus (events $F_1$ and $F_2$), in which case the scientist will undercount by three or more stars (or, if $N$ is less than 3, fail to detect any stars at all). Consider the three networks shown in Figure 14.19.

**a.** Which of these Bayesian networks are correct (but not necessarily efficient) representations of the preceding information?

**b.** Which is the best network? Explain.

**c.** Write out a conditional distribution for $\mathbf{P}(M_1|N)$, for the case where $N \in \{1,2,3\}$ and $M_1 \in \{0,1,2,3,4\}$. Each entry in the conditional distribution should be expressed as a function of the parameters $e$ and/or $f$.

**d.** Suppose $M_1 = 1$ and $M_2 = 3$. What are the *possible* numbers of stars if we assume no prior constraint on the values of $N$?

**e.** What is the *most likely* number of stars, given these observations? Explain how to compute this, or, if it is not possible to compute, explain what additional information is needed and how it would affect the result.

**14.4** Consider the network shown in Figure 14.19(ii), and assume that the two telescopes work identically. $N \in \{1,2,3\}$ and $M_1, M_2 \in \{0,1,2,3,4\}$, with the symbolic CPTs as described in Exercise 14.3. Using the enumeration algorithm, calculate the probability distribution $\mathbf{P}(N|M_1=2, M_2=2)$.

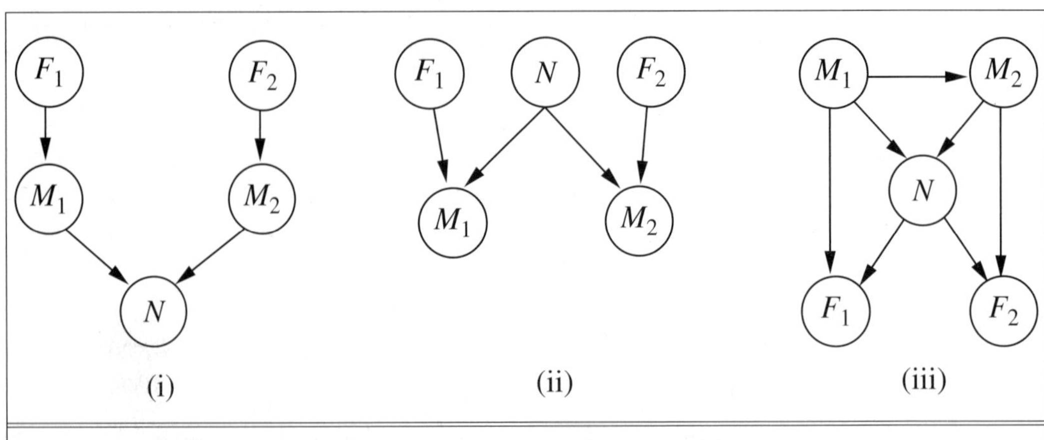


**Figure 14.19** Three possible networks for the telescope problem.

**14.5** Consider the family of linear Gaussian networks, as illustrated on page 502.

**a.** In a two-variable network, let $X_1$ be the parent of $X_2$, let $X_1$ have a Gaussian prior, and let $\mathbf{P}(X_2|X_1)$ be a linear Gaussian distribution. Show that the joint distribution $P(X_1, X_2)$ is a multivariate Gaussian, and calculate its covariance matrix.

**b.** Prove by induction that the joint distribution for a general linear Gaussian network on $X_1, \ldots, X_n$ is also a multivariate Gaussian.

**14.6** The probit distribution defined on page 503 describes the probability distribution for a Boolean child, given a single continuous parent.

**a.** How might the definition be extended to cover multiple continuous parents?

**b.** How might it be extended to handle a *multivalued* child variable? Consider both cases where the child's values are ordered (as in selecting a gear while driving, depending on speed, slope, desired acceleration, etc.) and cases where they are unordered (as in selecting bus, train, or car to get to work). [*Hint*: Consider ways to divide the possible values into two sets, to mimic a Boolean variable.]

**14.7** This exercise is concerned with the variable elimination algorithm in Figure 14.10.

**a.** Section 14.4 applies variable elimination to the query

$$\mathbf{P}(Burglary|JohnCalls = true, MaryCalls = true)\ .$$

Perform the calculations indicated and check that the answer is correct.

**b.** Count the number of arithmetic operations performed, and compare it with the number performed by the enumeration algorithm.

**c.** Suppose a network has the form of a *chain*: a sequence of Boolean variables $X_1, \ldots, X_n$ where $Parents(X_i) = \{X_{i-1}\}$ for $i = 2, \ldots, n$. What is the complexity of computing $\mathbf{P}(X_1|X_n = true)$ using enumeration? Using variable elimination?

**d.** Prove that the complexity of running variable elimination on a polytree network is linear in the size of the tree for any variable ordering consistent with the network structure.

**14.8** Investigate the complexity of exact inference in general Bayesian networks:

**a.** Prove that any 3-SAT problem can be reduced to exact inference in a Bayesian network constructed to represent the particular problem and hence that exact inference is NP-hard. [*Hint*: Consider a network with one variable for each proposition symbol, one for each clause, and one for the conjunction of clauses.]

**b.** The problem of counting the number of satisfying assignments for a 3-SAT problem is #P-complete. Show that exact inference is at least as hard as this.

**14.9** Consider the problem of generating a random sample from a specified distribution on a single variable. You can assume that a random number generator is available that returns a random number uniformly distributed between 0 and 1.

CUMULATIVE DISTRIBUTION

**a.** Let $X$ be a discrete variable with $P(X = x_i) = p_i$ for $i \in \{1, \ldots, k\}$. The **cumulative distribution** of $X$ gives the probability that $X \in \{x_1, \ldots, x_j\}$ for each possible $j$. Explain how to calculate the cumulative distribution in $O(k)$ time and how to generate a single sample of $X$ from it. Can the latter be done in less than $O(k)$ time?

**b.** Now suppose we want to generate $N$ samples of $X$, where $N \gg k$. Explain how to do this with an expected runtime per sample that is *constant* (i.e., independent of $k$).

**c.** Now consider a continuous-valued variable with a parametrized distribution (e.g., Gaussian). How can samples be generated from such a distribution?

**d.** Suppose you want to query a continuous-valued variable and you are using a sampling algorithm such as LIKELIHOODWEIGHTING to do the inference. How would you have to modify the query-answering process?

**14.10** The **Markov blanket** of a variable is defined on page 499.

**a.** Prove that a variable is independent of all other variables in the network, given its Markov blanket.

**b.** Derive Equation (14.11).

**14.11** Consider the query $\mathbf{P}(Rain|Sprinkler = true, WetGrass = true)$ in Figure 14.11(a) and how MCMC can answer it.

**a.** How many states does the Markov chain have?

**b.** Calculate the **transition matrix Q** containing $q(\mathbf{y} \rightarrow \mathbf{y}')$ for all $\mathbf{y}$, $\mathbf{y}'$.

**c.** What does $\mathbf{Q}^2$, the square of the transition matrix, represent?

**d.** What about $\mathbf{Q}^n$ as $n \rightarrow \infty$?

**e.** Explain how to do probabilistic inference in Bayesian networks, assuming that $\mathbf{Q}^n$ is available. Is this a practical way to do inference?

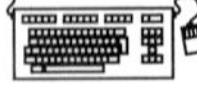

**14.12** Three soccer teams $A$, $B$, and $C$, play each other once. Each match is between two teams, and can be won, drawn, or lost. Each team has a fixed, unknown degree of quality—an integer ranging from 0 to 3—and the outcome of a match depends probabilistically on the difference in quality between the two teams.

**a.** Construct a relational probability model to describe this domain, and suggest numerical values for all the necessary probability distributions.

**b.** Construct the equivalent Bayesian network.

**c.** Suppose that in the first two matches $A$ beats $B$ and draws with $C$. Using an exact inference algorithm of your choice, compute the posterior distribution for the outcome of the third match.

**d.** Suppose there are $n$ teams in the league and we have the results for all but the last match. How does the complexity of predicting the last game vary with $n$?

**e.** Investigate the application of MCMC to this problem. How quickly does it converge in practice and how well does it scale?

# 15 PROBABILISTIC REASONING OVER TIME

*In which we try to interpret the present, understand the past, and perhaps predict the future, even when very little is crystal clear.*

Agents in uncertain environments must be able to keep track of the current state of the environment, just as logical agents must. The task is made more difficult by partial and noisy percepts and uncertainty about how the environment changes over time. At best, the agent will be able to obtain only a probabilistic assessment of the current situation. This chapter describes the representations and inference algorithms that make that assessment possible, building on the ideas introduced in Chapter 14.

The basic approach is described in Section 15.1: a changing world is modeled using a random variable for each aspect of the world state *at each point in time*. The relations among these variables describe how the state evolves. Section 15.2 defines the basic inference tasks and describes the general structure of inference algorithms for temporal models. Then we describe three specific kinds of models: **hidden Markov models**, **Kalman filters**, and **dynamic Bayesian networks** (which include hidden Markov models and Kalman filters as special cases). Finally, Section 15.6 explains how temporal probability models form the core of modern speech recognition systems. Learning plays a central role in the construction of all these models, but a detailed investigation of learning algorithms is left until Part VI.

## 15.1 Time and Uncertainty

We have developed our techniques for probabilistic reasoning in the context of **static** worlds, in which each random variable has a single fixed value. For example, when repairing a car, we assume that whatever is broken remains broken during the process of diagnosis; our job is to infer the state of the car from observed evidence, which also remains fixed.

Now consider a slightly different problem: treating a diabetic patient. As in the case of car repair, we have evidence such as recent insulin doses, food intake, blood sugar measurements, and other physical signs. The task is to assess the current state of the patient, including the actual blood sugar level and insulin level. Given this information, the doctor (or patient) makes a decision about the patient's food intake and insulin dose. Unlike the case of car repair, here the *dynamic* aspects of the problem are essential. Blood sugar levels and measurements thereof can change rapidly over time, depending on one's recent food intake and insulin doses, one's metabolic activity, the time of day, and so on. To assess the current state from the history of evidence and to predict the outcomes of treatment actions, we must model these changes.

The same considerations arise in many other contexts, ranging from tracking the economic activity of a nation, given approximate and partial statistics, to understanding a sequence of spoken words, given noisy and ambiguous acoustic measurements. How can dynamic situations like these be modeled?

### States and observations

The basic approach we will adopt is similar to the idea underlying situation calculus, as described in Chapter 10: the process of change can be viewed as a series of snapshots, each of which describes the state of the world at a particular time. Each snapshot, or **time slice**, contains a set of random variables, some of which are observable and some of which are not. For simplicity, we will assume that the same subset of variables is observable in each slice (although this is not strictly necessary in anything that follows). We will use $\mathbf{X}_t$ to denote the set of unobservable state variables at time $t$ and $\mathbf{E}_t$ to denote the set of observable evidence variables. The observation at time $t$ is $\mathbf{E}_t = \mathbf{e}_t$ for some set of values $\mathbf{e}_t$.

TIME SLICE

Consider the following oversimplified example: Suppose you are the security guard at some secret underground installation. You want to know whether it's raining today, but your only access to the outside world occurs each morning when you see the director coming in with, or without, an umbrella. For each day $t$, the set $\mathbf{E}_t$ thus contains a single evidence variable $U_t$ (whether the umbrella appears), and the set $\mathbf{X}_t$ contains a single state variable $R_t$ (whether it is raining). Other problems can involve larger sets of variables. In the diabetes example, we might have evidence variables such as $MeasuredBloodSugar_t$ and $PulseRate_t$, and state variables such as $BloodSugar_t$ and $StomachContents_t$.[1]

The interval between time slices also depends on the problem. For diabetes monitoring, a suitable interval might be an hour rather than a day. In this chapter, we will generally assume a fixed, finite interval; this means that times can be labeled by integers. We will assume that the state sequence starts at $t=0$; for various uninteresting reasons, we will assume that evidence starts arriving at $t=1$ rather than $t=0$. Hence, our umbrella world is represented by state variables $R_0, R_1, R_2, \ldots$ and evidence variables $U_1, U_2, \ldots$. We will use the notation $a{:}b$ to denote the sequence of integers from $a$ to $b$ (inclusive), and the notation $\mathbf{X}_{a:b}$ to denote the corresponding set of variables from $\mathbf{X}_a$ to $\mathbf{X}_b$. For example, $U_{1:3}$ corresponds to the variables $U_1, U_2, U_3$.

### Stationary processes and the Markov assumption

With the set of state and evidence variables for a given problem decided on, the next step is to specify the dependencies among the variables. We could follow the procedure laid down

[1] Notice that $BloodSugar_t$ and $MeasuredBloodSugar_t$ are not the same variable; this is how we deal with noisy measurements of actual quantities.

in Chapter 14, placing the variables in some order and asking questions about conditional independence of predecessors, given some set of parents. One obvious choice is to order the variables in their natural temporal order, since cause usually precedes effect and we prefer to add the variables in causal order.

We would quickly run into an obstacle, however: the set of variables is unbounded, because it includes the state and evidence variables for every time slice. This actually creates two problems: first, we might have to specify an unbounded number of conditional probability tables, one for each variable in each slice; second, each one might involve an unbounded number of parents.

STATIONARY PROCESS

The first problem is solved by assuming that changes in the world state are caused by a **stationary process**—that is, a process of change that is governed by laws that do not themselves change over time. (Don't confuse *stationary* with *static*: in a *static* process, the state itself does not change.) In the umbrella world, then, the conditional probability that the umbrella appears, $\mathbf{P}(U_t|Parents(U_t))$, is the same for all $t$. Given the assumption of stationarity, therefore, we need specify conditional distributions only for the variables within a "representative" time slice.

MARKOV ASSUMPTION

MARKOV PROCESSES

FIRST-ORDER MARKOV PROCESS

The second problem, that of handling the potentially infinite number of parents, is solved by making what is called a **Markov assumption**—that is, that the current state depends on only a *finite* history of previous states. Processes satisfying this assumption were first studied in depth by the Russian statistician Andrei Markov and are called **Markov processes** or **Markov chains**. They come in various flavors; the simplest is the **first-order Markov process**, in which the current state depends only on the previous state and not on any earlier states. In other words, a state is the information you need to make the future independent of the past given the state. Using our notation, the corresponding conditional independence assertion states that, for all $t$,

$$\mathbf{P}(\mathbf{X}_t|\mathbf{X}_{0:t-1}) = \mathbf{P}(\mathbf{X}_t|\mathbf{X}_{t-1}) \,. \tag{15.1}$$

Hence, in a first-order Markov process, the laws describing how the state evolves over time are contained entirely within the conditional distribution $\mathbf{P}(\mathbf{X}_t|\mathbf{X}_{t-1})$, which we call the **transition model** for first-order processes.[2] The transition model for a second-order Markov process is the conditional distribution $\mathbf{P}(\mathbf{X}_t|\mathbf{X}_{t-2}, \mathbf{X}_{t-1})$. Figure 15.1 shows the Bayesian network structures corresponding to first-order and second-order Markov processes.

In addition to restricting the parents of the state variables $\mathbf{X}_t$, we must restrict the parents of the evidence variables $\mathbf{E}_t$. Typically, we will assume that the evidence variables at time $t$ depend only on the current state:

$$\mathbf{P}(\mathbf{E}_t|\mathbf{X}_{0:t}, \mathbf{E}_{0:t-1}) = \mathbf{P}(\mathbf{E}_t|\mathbf{X}_t) \,. \tag{15.2}$$

SENSOR MODEL

The conditional distribution $\mathbf{P}(\mathbf{E}_t|\mathbf{X}_t)$ is called the **sensor model** (or sometimes the **observation model**), because it describes how the "sensors"—that is, the evidence variables—are affected by the actual state of the world. Notice the direction of the dependence: the "arrow" goes from state to sensor values because the state of the world *causes* the sensors to take on

[2] The transition model is the probabilistic analog of the Boolean update circuits in Chapter 7 and the successor-state axioms in Chapter 10.

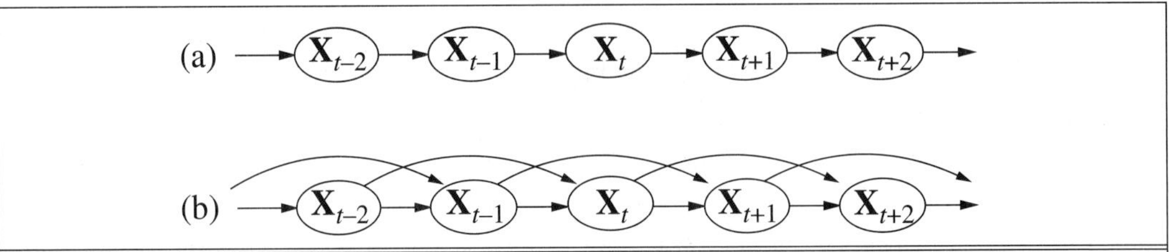


**Figure 15.1** (a) Bayesian network structure corresponding to a first-order Markov process with state defined by the variables $\mathbf{X}_t$. (b) A second-order Markov process.

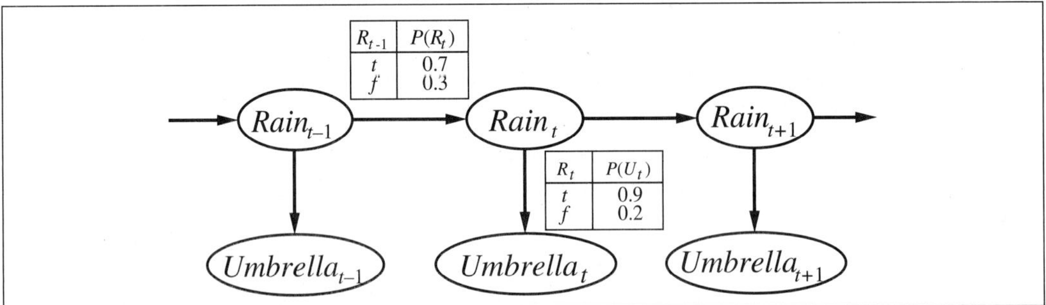


**Figure 15.2** Bayesian network structure and conditional distributions describing the umbrella world. The transition model is $P(Rain_t|Rain_{t-1})$ and the sensor model is $P(Umbrella_t|Rain_t)$.

particular values. In the umbrella world, for example, the rain *causes* the umbrella to appear. (The inference process, of course, goes in the other direction; the distinction between the direction of modeled dependencies and the direction of inference is one of the principal advantages of Bayesian networks.)

In addition to the transition model and sensor model, we need to specify a prior probability $\mathbf{P}(\mathbf{X}_0)$ over the states at time 0. These three distributions, combined with the conditional independence assertions in Equations (15.1) and (15.2), give us a specification of the complete joint distribution over all the variables. For any finite $t$, we have

$$\mathbf{P}(\mathbf{X}_0, \mathbf{X}_1, \ldots, \mathbf{X}_t, \mathbf{E}_1, \ldots, \mathbf{E}_t) = \mathbf{P}(\mathbf{X}_0) \prod_{i=1}^{t} \mathbf{P}(\mathbf{X}_i|\mathbf{X}_{i-1})\mathbf{P}(\mathbf{E}_i|\mathbf{X}_i) .$$

The independence assumptions correspond to a very simple structure for the Bayesian network describing the whole system. Figure 15.2 shows the network structure for the umbrella example, including the conditional distributions for the transition and sensor models.

The structure in the figure assumes a first-order Markov process, because the probability of rain is assumed to depend only on whether it rained the previous day. Whether such an assumption is reasonable depends on the domain itself. The first-order Markov assumption says that the state variables contain *all* the information needed to characterize the probability distribution for the next time slice. Sometimes the assumption is exactly true—for example, if a particle is executing a **random walk** along the $x$-axis, changing its position by $\pm 1$ at each time step, then using the $x$-coordinate as the state gives a first-order Markov process.

RANDOM WALK

Sometimes the assumption is only approximate, as in the case of predicting rain only on the basis of whether it rained the previous day. There are two possible fixes if the approximation proves too inaccurate:

1. Increasing the order of the Markov process model. For example, we could make a second-order model by adding $Rain_{t-2}$ as a parent of $Rain_t$, which might give slightly more accurate predictions (for example, in Palo Alto it very rarely rains more than two days in a row).
2. Increasing the set of state variables. For example, we could add $Season_t$ to allow us to incorporate historical records of rainy seasons, or we could add $Temperature_t$, $Humidity_t$ and $Pressure_t$ to allow us to use a physical model of rainy conditions.

Exercise 15.1 asks you to show that the first solution—increasing the order—can always be reformulated as an increase in the set of state variables, keeping the order fixed. Notice that adding state variables might improve the system's predictive power but also increases the prediction *requirements*: we now have to predict the new variables as well. Thus, we are looking for a "self-sufficient" set of variables, which really means that we have to understand the "physics" of the process being modeled. The requirement for accurate modeling of the process is obviously lessened if we can add new sensors (e.g., measurements of temperature and pressure) that provide information directly about the new state variables.

Consider, for example, the problem of tracking a robot wandering randomly on the X–Y plane. One might propose that the position and velocity are a sufficient set of state variables: one can simply use Newton's laws to calculate the new position, and the velocity may change unpredictably. If the robot is battery-powered, however, then battery exhaustion would tend to have a systematic effect on the change in velocity. Because this in turn depends on how much power was used by all previous maneuvers, the Markov property is violated. We can restore the Markov property by including the charge level $Battery_t$ as one of the state variables that make up $\mathbf{X}_t$. This helps in predicting the motion of the robot, but in turn requires a model for predicting $Battery_t$ from $Battery_{t-1}$ and the velocity. In some cases, that can be done reliably; accuracy would be improved by *adding a new sensor* for the battery level

## 15.2 INFERENCE IN TEMPORAL MODELS

Having set up the structure of a generic temporal model, we can formulate the basic inference tasks that must be solved:

FILTERING
MONITORING
BELIEF STATE

◇ **Filtering** or **monitoring**: This is the task of computing the **belief state**—the posterior distribution over the current state, given all evidence to date. That is, we wish to compute $\mathbf{P}(\mathbf{X}_t|\mathbf{e}_{1:t})$, assuming that evidence arrives in a continuous stream beginning at $t=1$. In the umbrella example, this would mean computing the probability of rain today, given all the observations of the umbrella carrier made so far. Filtering is what a rational agent needs to do in order to keep track of the current state so that rational decisions can be made. (See Chapter 17.) It turns out that an almost identical calculation provides the **likelihood** of the evidence sequence, $P(\mathbf{e}_{1:t})$.

PREDICTION

◇ **Prediction**: This is the task of computing the posterior distribution over the *future* state, given all evidence to date. That is, we wish to compute $\mathbf{P}(\mathbf{X}_{t+k}|\mathbf{e}_{1:t})$ for some $k > 0$. In the umbrella example, this might mean computing the probability of rain three days from now, given all the observations of the umbrella-carrier made so far. Prediction is useful for evaluating possible courses of action.

SMOOTHING

HINDSIGHT

◇ **Smoothing**, or **hindsight**: This is the task of computing the posterior distribution over a *past* state, given all evidence up to the present. That is, we wish to compute $\mathbf{P}(\mathbf{X}_k|\mathbf{e}_{1:t})$ for some $k$ such that $0 \leq k < t$. In the umbrella example, it might mean computing the probability that it rained last Wednesday, given all the observations of the umbrella carrier made up to today. Hindsight provides a better estimate of the state than was available at the time, because it incorporates more evidence.

◇ **Most likely explanation**: Given a sequence of observations, we might wish to find the sequence of states that is most likely to have generated those observations. That is, we wish to compute $\operatorname{argmax}_{\mathbf{x}_{1:t}} P(\mathbf{x}_{1:t}|\mathbf{e}_{1:t})$. For example, if the umbrella appears on each of the first three days and is absent on the fourth, then the most likely explanation is that it rained on the first three days and did not rain on the fourth. Algorithms for this task are useful in many applications, including speech recognition—where the aim is to find the most likely sequence of words, given a series of sounds—and the reconstruction of bit strings transmitted over a noisy channel.

In addition to these tasks, methods are needed for *learning* the transition and sensor models from observations. Just as with static Bayesian networks, dynamic Bayes net learning can be done as a by-product of inference. Inference provides an estimate of what transitions actually occurred and of what states generated the sensor readings, and these estimates can be used to update the models. The updated models provide new estimates, and the process iterates to convergence. The overall process is an instance of the expectation-maximization or **EM algorithm**. (See Section 20.3.) One point to note is that learning requires the full smoothing inference, rather than filtering, because it provides better estimates of the states of the process. Learning with filtering can fail to converge correctly; consider, for example, the problem of learning to solve murders: hindsight is *always* required to infer what happened at the murder scene from the observable variables.

Algorithms for the four inference tasks listed in the preceding paragraph can be described first at a generic level, independently of the particular kind of model employed. Improvements specific to each model will be described in the corresponding sections.

### Filtering and prediction

Let us begin with filtering. We will show that this can be done in a simple online fashion: given the result of filtering up to time $t$, one can easily compute the result for $t+1$ from the new evidence $\mathbf{e}_{t+1}$. That is,

$$\mathbf{P}(\mathbf{X}_{t+1}|\mathbf{e}_{1:t+1}) = f(\mathbf{e}_{t+1}, \mathbf{P}(\mathbf{X}_t|\mathbf{e}_{1:t}))\ .$$

RECURSIVE ESTIMATION

for some function $f$. This process is often called **recursive estimation**. We can view the calculation as actually being composed of two parts: first, the current state distribution is projected forward from $t$ to $t + 1$; then it is updated using the new evidence $\mathbf{e}_{t+1}$. This two-part process emerges quite simply:

$$\mathbf{P}(\mathbf{X}_{t+1}|\mathbf{e}_{1:t+1}) = \mathbf{P}(\mathbf{X}_{t+1}|\mathbf{e}_{1:t}, \mathbf{e}_{t+1}) \quad \text{(dividing up the evidence)}$$
$$= \alpha\, \mathbf{P}(\mathbf{e}_{t+1}|\mathbf{X}_{t+1}, \mathbf{e}_{1:t})\mathbf{P}(\mathbf{X}_{t+1}|\mathbf{e}_{1:t}) \quad \text{(using Bayes' rule)}$$
$$= \alpha\, \mathbf{P}(\mathbf{e}_{t+1}|\mathbf{X}_{t+1})\mathbf{P}(\mathbf{X}_{t+1}|\mathbf{e}_{1:t}) \quad \text{(by the Markov property of evidence).}$$

Here and throughout this chapter, $\alpha$ is a normalizing constant used to make probabilities sum up to 1. The second term, $\mathbf{P}(\mathbf{X}_{t+1}|\mathbf{e}_{1:t})$ represents a one-step prediction of the next state, and the first term updates this with the new evidence; notice that $\mathbf{P}(\mathbf{e}_{t+1}|\mathbf{X}_{t+1})$ is obtainable directly from the sensor model. Now we obtain the one-step prediction for the next state by conditioning on the current state $\mathbf{X}_t$:

$$\mathbf{P}(\mathbf{X}_{t+1}|\mathbf{e}_{1:t+1}) = \alpha\, \mathbf{P}(\mathbf{e}_{t+1}|\mathbf{X}_{t+1}) \sum_{\mathbf{x}_t} \mathbf{P}(\mathbf{X}_{t+1}|\mathbf{x}_t, \mathbf{e}_{1:t})P(\mathbf{x}_t|\mathbf{e}_{1:t})$$
$$= \alpha\, \mathbf{P}(\mathbf{e}_{t+1}|\mathbf{X}_{t+1}) \sum_{\mathbf{x}_t} \mathbf{P}(\mathbf{X}_{t+1}|\mathbf{x}_t)P(\mathbf{x}_t|\mathbf{e}_{1:t}) \quad \text{(using the Markov property).} \quad (15.3)$$

Within the summation, the first factor is simply the transition model and the second is the current state distribution. Hence, we have the desired recursive formulation. We can think of the filtered estimate $\mathbf{P}(\mathbf{X}_t|\mathbf{e}_{1:t})$ as a "message" $\mathbf{f}_{1:t}$ that is propagated forward along the sequence, modified by each transition and updated by each new observation. The process is

$$\mathbf{f}_{1:t+1} = \alpha\, \text{FORWARD}(\mathbf{f}_{1:t}, \mathbf{e}_{t+1})$$

where FORWARD implements the update described in Equation (15.3).

When all the state variables are discrete, the time for each update is constant (i.e., independent of $t$), and the space required is also constant. (The constants depend, of course, on the size of the state space and the specific type of the temporal model in question.) *The time and space requirements for updating must be constant if an agent with limited memory is to keep track of the current state distribution over an unbounded sequence of observations.*

Let us illustrate the filtering process for two steps in the basic umbrella example. (See Figure 15.2.) We assume that our security guard has some prior belief about whether it rained on day 0, just before the observation sequence begins. Let's suppose this is $\mathbf{P}(R_0) = \langle 0.5, 0.5\rangle$. Now we process the two observations as follows:

- On day 1, the umbrella appears, so $U_1 = true$. The prediction from $t=0$ to $t=1$ is

$$\mathbf{P}(R_1) = \sum_{r_0} \mathbf{P}(R_1|r_0)P(r_0)$$
$$= \langle 0.7, 0.3\rangle \times 0.5 + \langle 0.3, 0.7\rangle \times 0.5 = \langle 0.5, 0.5\rangle\ ,$$

  and updating it with the evidence for $t=1$ gives

$$\mathbf{P}(R_1|u_1) = \alpha\, \mathbf{P}(u_1|R_1)\mathbf{P}(R_1) = \alpha\, \langle 0.9, 0.2\rangle\langle 0.5, 0.5\rangle$$
$$= \alpha\, \langle 0.45, 0.1\rangle \approx \langle 0.818, 0.182\rangle\ .$$

- On day 2, the umbrella appears, so $U_2 = true$. The prediction from $t=1$ to $t=2$ is

$$\mathbf{P}(R_2|u_1) = \sum_{r_1} \mathbf{P}(R_2|r_1)P(r_1|u_1)$$
$$= \langle 0.7, 0.3\rangle \times 0.818 + \langle 0.3, 0.7\rangle \times 0.182 \approx \langle 0.627, 0.373\rangle\ ,$$

and updating it with the evidence for $t = 2$ gives

$$\begin{aligned}\mathbf{P}(R_2|u_1, u_2) &= \alpha\, \mathbf{P}(u_2|R_2)\mathbf{P}(R_2|u_1) = \alpha\, \langle 0.9, 0.2 \rangle \langle 0.627, 0.373 \rangle \\ &= \alpha\, \langle 0.565, 0.075 \rangle \approx \langle 0.883, 0.117 \rangle\ .\end{aligned}$$

Intuitively, the probability of rain increases from day 1 to day 2 because rain persists. Exercise 15.2(a) asks you to investigate this tendency further.

The task of **prediction** can be seen simply as filtering without the addition of new evidence. In fact, the filtering process already incorporates a one-step prediction, and it is easy to derive the following recursive computation for predicting the state at $t + k + 1$ from a prediction for $t + k$:

$$\mathbf{P}(\mathbf{X}_{t+k+1}|\mathbf{e}_{1:t}) = \sum_{\mathbf{x}_{t+k}} \mathbf{P}(\mathbf{X}_{t+k+1}|\mathbf{x}_{t+k}) P(\mathbf{x}_{t+k}|\mathbf{e}_{1:t})\ . \tag{15.4}$$

Naturally, this computation involves only the transition model and not the sensor model.

It is interesting to consider what happens as we try to predict further and further into the future. As Exercise 15.2(b) shows, the predicted distribution for rain converges to a fixed point $\langle 0.5, 0.5 \rangle$, after which it remains constant for all time. This is the **stationary distribution** of the Markov process defined by the transition model. (See also page 517.) A great deal is known about the properties of such distributions and about the **mixing time**—roughly, the time taken to reach the fixed point. In practical terms, this dooms to failure any attempt to predict the *actual* state for a number of steps that is more than a small fraction of the mixing time. The more uncertainty there is in the transition model, the shorter will be the mixing time and the more the future is obscured.

MIXING TIME

In addition to filtering and prediction, we can use a forward recursion to compute the **likelihood** of the evidence sequence, $P(\mathbf{e}_{1:t})$. This is a useful quantity if we want to compare different temporal models that might have produced the same evidence sequence; for example, in Section 15.6, we compare different words that might have produced the same sound sequence. For this recursion, we use a likelihood message $\boldsymbol{\ell}_{1:t} = \mathbf{P}(\mathbf{X}_t, \mathbf{e}_{1:t})$. It is a simple exercise to show that

$$\boldsymbol{\ell}_{1:t+1} = \text{FORWARD}(\boldsymbol{\ell}_{1:t}, \mathbf{e}_{t+1})\ .$$

Having computed $\boldsymbol{\ell}_{1:t}$, we obtain the actual likelihood by summing out $\mathbf{X}_t$:

$$L_{1:t} = P(\mathbf{e}_{1:t}) = \sum_{\mathbf{x}_t} \boldsymbol{\ell}_{1:t}(\mathbf{x}_t)\ . \tag{15.5}$$

### Smoothing

As we said earlier, **smoothing** is the process of computing the distribution over past states given evidence up to the present; that is, $\mathbf{P}(\mathbf{X}_k|\mathbf{e}_{1:t})$ for $1 \leq k < t$. (See Figure 15.3.) This is done most conveniently in two parts—the evidence up to $k$ and the evidence from $k + 1$ to $t$,

$$\begin{aligned}\mathbf{P}(\mathbf{X}_k|\mathbf{e}_{1:t}) &= \mathbf{P}(\mathbf{X}_k|\mathbf{e}_{1:k}, \mathbf{e}_{k+1:t}) \\ &= \alpha\, \mathbf{P}(\mathbf{X}_k|\mathbf{e}_{1:k})\mathbf{P}(\mathbf{e}_{k+1:t}|\mathbf{X}_k, \mathbf{e}_{1:k}) \quad \text{(using Bayes' rule)} \\ &= \alpha\, \mathbf{P}(\mathbf{X}_k|\mathbf{e}_{1:k})\mathbf{P}(\mathbf{e}_{k+1:t}|\mathbf{X}_k) \quad \text{(using conditional independence)} \\ &= \alpha\, \mathbf{f}_{1:k} \mathbf{b}_{k+1:t}\ ,\end{aligned} \tag{15.6}$$

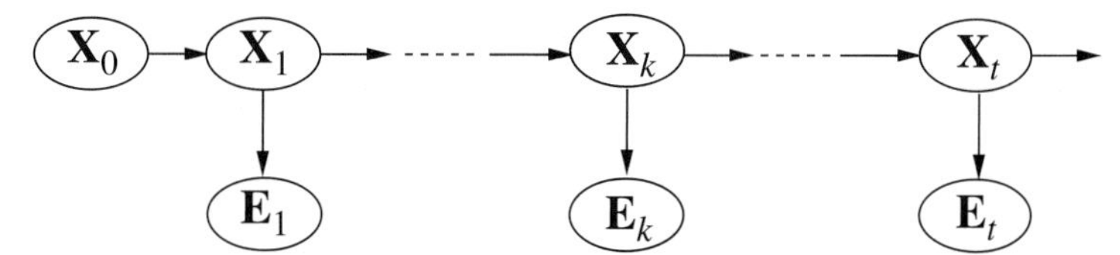


**Figure 15.3** Smoothing computes $\mathbf{P}(\mathbf{X}_k|\mathbf{e}_{1:t})$, the posterior distribution of the state at some past time $k$ given a complete sequence of observations from 1 to $t$.

where we have defined a "backward" message $\mathbf{b}_{k+1:t} = \mathbf{P}(\mathbf{e}_{k+1:t}|\mathbf{X}_k)$, analogous to the forward message $\mathbf{f}_{1:k}$. The forward message $\mathbf{f}_{1:k}$ can be computed by filtering forward from 1 to $k$, as given by Equation (15.3). It turns out that the backward message $\mathbf{b}_{k+1:t}$ can be computed by a recursive process that runs *backwards* from $t$:

$$\begin{aligned}
\mathbf{P}(\mathbf{e}_{k+1:t}|\mathbf{X}_k) &= \sum_{\mathbf{x}_{k+1}} \mathbf{P}(\mathbf{e}_{k+1:t}|\mathbf{X}_k, \mathbf{x}_{k+1})\mathbf{P}(\mathbf{x}_{k+1}|\mathbf{X}_k) \quad \text{(conditioning on } \mathbf{X}_{k+1}\text{)} \\
&= \sum_{\mathbf{x}_{k+1}} P(\mathbf{e}_{k+1:t}|\mathbf{x}_{k+1})\mathbf{P}(\mathbf{x}_{k+1}|\mathbf{X}_k) \quad \text{(by conditional independence)} \\
&= \sum_{\mathbf{x}_{k+1}} P(\mathbf{e}_{k+1}, \mathbf{e}_{k+2:t}|\mathbf{x}_{k+1})\mathbf{P}(\mathbf{x}_{k+1}|\mathbf{X}_k) \\
&= \sum_{\mathbf{x}_{k+1}} P(\mathbf{e}_{k+1}|\mathbf{x}_{k+1})P(\mathbf{e}_{k+2:t}|\mathbf{x}_{k+1})\mathbf{P}(\mathbf{x}_{k+1}|\mathbf{X}_k)\,, \qquad (15.7)
\end{aligned}$$

where the last step follows by the conditional independence of $\mathbf{e}_{k+1}$ and $\mathbf{e}_{k+2:t}$, given $\mathbf{X}_{k+1}$. Of the three factors in this summation, the first and third are obtained directly from the model, and the second is the "recursive call." Using the message notation, we have

$$\mathbf{b}_{k+1:t} = \text{BACKWARD}(\mathbf{b}_{k+2:t}, \mathbf{e}_{k+1:t})$$

where BACKWARD implements the update described in Equation (15.7). As with the forward recursion, the time and space needed for each update are constant and thus independent of $t$.

We can now see that the two terms in Equation (15.6) can both be computed by recursions through time, one running forward from 1 to $k$ and using the filtering equation (15.3) and the other running backward from $t$ to $k+1$ and using Equation (15.7). Note that the backward phase is initialized with $\mathbf{b}_{t+1:t} = \mathbf{P}(\mathbf{e}_{t+1:t}|\mathbf{X}_t) = \mathbf{1}$, where $\mathbf{1}$ is a vector of ones. (Because $\mathbf{e}_{t+1:t}$ is an empty sequence, the probability of observing it is 1.)

Let us now apply this algorithm to the umbrella example, computing the smoothed estimate for the probability of rain at $t = 1$, given the umbrella observations on days 1 and 2. From Equation (15.6), this is given by

$$\mathbf{P}(R_1|u_1, u_2) = \alpha\, \mathbf{P}(R_1|u_1)\, \mathbf{P}(u_2|R_1)\,. \qquad (15.8)$$

The first term we already know to be $\langle .818, .182\rangle$, from the forward filtering process described earlier. The second term can be computed by applying the backward recursion in Equation (15.7):

$$\begin{aligned}
\mathbf{P}(u_2|R_1) &= \sum_{r_2} P(u_2|r_2)P(\;|r_2)\mathbf{P}(r_2|R_1) \\
&= (0.9 \times 1 \times \langle 0.7, 0.3\rangle) + (0.2 \times 1 \times \langle 0.3, 0.7\rangle) = \langle 0.69, 0.41\rangle\,.
\end{aligned}$$

Plugging this into Equation (15.8), we find that the smoothed estimate for rain on day 1 is

$$\mathbf{P}(R_1|u_1, u_2) = \alpha \langle 0.818, 0.182 \rangle \times \langle 0.69, 0.41 \rangle \approx \langle 0.883, 0.117 \rangle .$$

Thus, the smoothed estimate is *higher* than the filtered estimate (0.818) in this case. This is because the umbrella on day 2 makes it more likely to have rained on day 2; in turn, because rain tends to persist, that makes it more likely to have rained on day 1.

Both the forward and backward recursions take a constant amount of time per step; hence, the time complexity of smoothing with respect to evidence $\mathbf{e}_{1:t}$ is $O(t)$. This is the complexity for smoothing at a particular time step $k$. If we want to smooth the whole sequence, one obvious method is simply to run the whole smoothing process once for each time step to be smoothed. This results in a time complexity of $O(t^2)$. A better approach uses a very simple application of dynamic programming to reduce the complexity to $O(t)$. A clue appears in the preceding analysis of the umbrella example, where we were able to reuse the results of the forward filtering phase. The key to the linear-time algorithm is to *record the results* of forward filtering over the whole sequence. Then we run the backward recursion from $t$ down to 1, computing the smoothed estimate at each step $k$ from the computed backward message $\mathbf{b}_{k+1:t}$ and the stored forward message $\mathbf{f}_{1:k}$. The algorithm, aptly called the **forward–backward algorithm**, is shown in Figure 15.4.

The alert reader will have spotted that the Bayesian network structure shown in Figure 15.3 is a **polytree** in the terminology of Chapter 14. This means that a straightforward application of the clustering algorithm also yields a linear-time algorithm that computes smoothed estimates for the entire sequence. It is now understood that the forward–backward algorithm is in fact a special case of the polytree propagation algorithm used with clustering methods (although the two were developed independently).

```
function FORWARD-BACKWARD(ev, prior) returns a vector of probability distributions
  inputs: ev, a vector of evidence values for steps 1,...,t
          prior, the prior distribution on the initial state, P(X_0)
  local variables: fv, a vector of forward messages for steps 0,...,t
                   b, a representation of the backward message, initially all 1s
                   sv, a vector of smoothed estimates for steps 1,...,t

  fv[0] ← prior
  for i = 1 to t do
     fv[i] ← FORWARD(fv[i − 1], ev[i])
  for i = t downto 1 do
     sv[i] ← NORMALIZE(fv[i] × b)
     b ← BACKWARD(b, ev[i])
  return sv
```

**Figure 15.4** The forward–backward algorithm for computing posterior probabilities of a sequence of states given a sequence of observations. The FORWARD and BACKWARD operators are defined by Equations (15.3) and (15.7), respectively.

The forward–backward algorithm forms the backbone of the computational methods employed in many applications that deal with sequences of noisy observations, ranging from speech recognition to radar tracking of aircraft. As described, it has two practical drawbacks. The first is that its space complexity can be too high for applications where the state space is large and the sequences are long. It uses $O(|\mathbf{f}|t)$ space where $|\mathbf{f}|$ is the size of the representation of the forward message. The space requirement can be reduced to $O(|\mathbf{f}| \log t)$ with a concomitant increase in the time complexity by a factor of $\log t$, as shown in Exercise 15.3. In some cases (see Section 15.3), a constant-space algorithm can be used with no time penalty.

FIXED-LAG SMOOTHING

The second drawback of the basic algorithm is that it needs to be modified to work in an *online* setting where smoothed estimates must be computed for earlier time slices as new observations are continuously added to the end of the sequence. The most common requirement is for **fixed-lag smoothing**, which requires computing the smoothed estimate $\mathbf{P}(\mathbf{X}_{t-d}|\mathbf{e}_{1:t})$ for fixed $d$. That is, smoothing is done for the time slice $d$ steps behind the current time $t$; as $t$ increases, the smoothing has to keep up. Obviously, we can run the forward–backward algorithm over the $d$-step "window" as each new observation is added, but this seems inefficient. In Section 15.3, we will see that fixed-lag smoothing can, in some cases, be done in constant time per update, independently of the lag $d$.

### Finding the most likely sequence

Suppose that $[true, true, false, true, true]$ is the umbrella sequence for the security guard's first five days on the job. What is the weather sequence most likely to explain this? Does the absence of the umbrella on day 3 mean that it wasn't raining, or did the director forget to bring it? If it didn't rain on day 3, perhaps (because weather tends to persist) it didn't rain on day 4 either, but the director brought the umbrella just in case. In all, there are $2^5$ possible weather sequences we could pick. Is there a way to find the most likely one, short of enumerating all of them?

One approach we could try is the following linear-time procedure: use the smoothing algorithm to find the posterior distribution for the weather at each time step; then construct the sequence, using at each step the weather most likely according to the posterior. Such an approach should set off alarm bells in the reader's head, because the posteriors computed by smoothing are distributions over *single* time steps, whereas to find the most likely *sequence* we must consider *joint* probabilities over all the time steps. The results can in fact be quite different. (See Exercise 15.4.)

There *is* a linear-time algorithm for finding the most likely sequence, but it requires a little more thought. It relies on the same Markov property that yielded efficient algorithms for filtering and smoothing. The easiest way to think about the problem is to view each sequence as a *path* through a graph whose nodes are the possible *states* at each time step. Such a graph is shown for the umbrella world in Figure 15.5(a). Now consider the task of finding the most likely path through this graph, where the likelihood of any path is the product of the transition probabilities along the path and the probabilities of the given observations at each state. Let's focus in particular on paths that reach the state $Rain_5 = true$. Because of the Markov property, it follows that the most likely path to the state $Rain_5 = true$ consists of

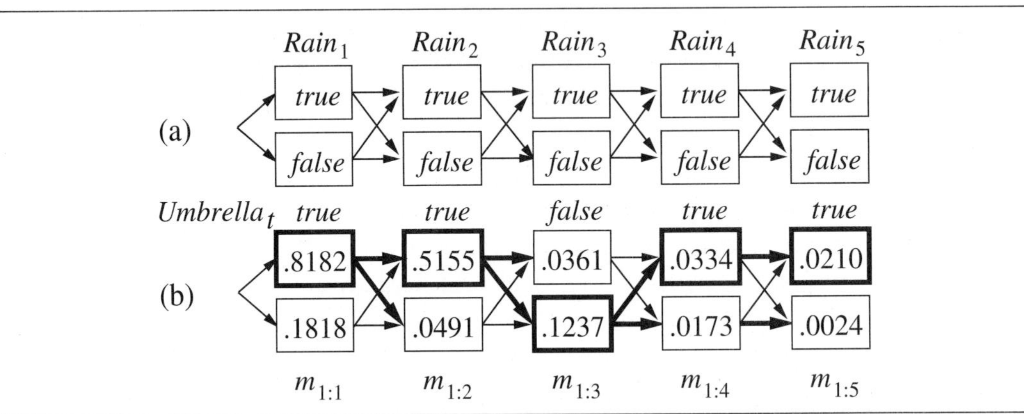


**Figure 15.5** (a) Possible state sequences for $Rain_t$ can be viewed as paths through a graph of the possible states at each time step. (States are shown as rectangles to avoid confusion with nodes in a Bayes net.) (b) Operation of the Viterbi algorithm for the umbrella observation sequence $[true, true, false, true, true]$. For each $t$, we have shown the values of the message $\mathbf{m}_{1:t}$, which gives the probability of the best sequence reaching each state at time $t$. Also, for each state, the bold arrow leading into it indicates its best predecessor as measured by the product of the preceding sequence probability and the transition probability. Following the bold arrows back from the most likely state in $\mathbf{m}_{1:5}$ gives the most likely sequence.

the most likely path to *some* state at time 4 followed by a transition to $Rain_5 = true$; and the state at time 4 that will become part of the path to $Rain_5 = true$ is whichever maximizes the likelihood of that path. In other words, *there is a recursive relationship between most likely paths to each state* $\mathbf{x}_{t+1}$ *and most likely paths to each state* $\mathbf{x}_t$. We can write this relationship as an equation connecting the probabilities of the paths:

$$\max_{\mathbf{x}_1 \ldots \mathbf{x}_t} \mathbf{P}(\mathbf{x}_1, \ldots, \mathbf{x}_t, \mathbf{X}_{t+1} | \mathbf{e}_{1:t+1})$$
$$= \alpha \, \mathbf{P}(\mathbf{e}_{t+1} | \mathbf{X}_{t+1}) \max_{\mathbf{x}_t} \left( \mathbf{P}(\mathbf{X}_{t+1} | \mathbf{x}_t) \max_{\mathbf{x}_1 \ldots \mathbf{x}_{t-1}} P(\mathbf{x}_1, \ldots, \mathbf{x}_{t-1}, \mathbf{x}_t | \mathbf{e}_{1:t}) \right) . \quad (15.9)$$

Equation (15.9) is *identical* to the filtering equation (15.3) except that

1. The forward message $\mathbf{f}_{1:t} = \mathbf{P}(\mathbf{X}_t | \mathbf{e}_{1:t})$ is replaced by the message

   $$\mathbf{m}_{1:t} = \max_{\mathbf{x}_1 \ldots \mathbf{x}_{t-1}} \mathbf{P}(\mathbf{x}_1, \ldots, \mathbf{x}_{t-1}, \mathbf{X}_t | \mathbf{e}_{1:t}) ,$$

   that is, the probabilities of the most likely path to each state $\mathbf{x}_t$; and
2. the summation over $\mathbf{x}_t$ in Equation (15.3) is replaced by the maximization over $\mathbf{x}_t$ in Equation (15.9).

Thus, the algorithm for computing the most likely sequence is similar to filtering: it runs forward along the sequence, computing the **m** message at each time step, using Equation (15.9). The progress of this computation is shown in Figure 15.5(b). At the end, it will have the probability for the most likely sequence reaching *each* of the final states. One can thus easily select the most likely sequence overall (the state outlined in bold). In order to identify the actual sequence, as opposed to just computing its probability, the algorithm will also need to keep pointers from each state back to the best state that leads to it (shown in bold); the sequence is identified by following the pointers back from the best final state.

VITERBI ALGORITHM

The algorithm we have just described is called the **Viterbi algorithm**, after its inventor. Like the filtering algorithm, its complexity is linear in $t$, the length of the sequence. Unlike filtering, however, its space requirement is also linear in $t$. This is because the Viterbi algorithm needs to keep the pointers that identify the best sequence leading to each state.

## 15.3 HIDDEN MARKOV MODELS

The preceding section developed algorithms for temporal probabilistic reasoning using a general framework that was independent of the specific form of the transition and sensor models. In this and the next two sections, we discuss more concrete models and applications that illustrate the power of the basic algorithms and in some cases allow further improvements.

HIDDEN MARKOV MODEL

We begin with the **hidden Markov model**, or **HMM**. An HMM is a temporal probabilistic model in which the state of the process is described by a *single discrete* random variable. The possible values of the variable are the possible states of the world. The umbrella example described in the preceding section is therefore an HMM, since it has just one state variable: $Rain_t$. Additional state variables can be added to a temporal model while staying within the HMM framework, but only by combining all the state variables into a single "megavariable" whose values are all possible tuples of values of the individual state variables. We will see that the restricted structure of HMMs allows for a very simple and elegant matrix implementation of all the basic algorithms.[3] Section 15.6 shows how HMMs are used for speech recognition.

### Simplified matrix algorithms

With a single, discrete state variable $X_t$, we can give concrete form to the representations of the transition model, the sensor model, and the forward and backward messages. Let the state variable $X_t$ have values denoted by integers $1, \ldots, S$, where $S$ is the number of possible states. The transition model $\mathbf{P}(X_t|X_{t-1})$ becomes an $S \times S$ matrix $\mathbf{T}$, where

$$\mathbf{T}_{ij} = P(X_t = j | X_{t-1} = i) .$$

That is, $\mathbf{T}_{ij}$ is the probability of a transition from state $i$ to state $j$. For example, the transition matrix for the umbrella world is

$$\mathbf{T} = \mathbf{P}(X_t|X_{t-1}) = \begin{pmatrix} 0.7 & 0.3 \\ 0.3 & 0.7 \end{pmatrix} .$$

We also put the sensor model in matrix form. In this case, because the value of the evidence variable $E_t$ is known to be, say, $e_t$, we need use only that part of the model specifying the probability that $e_t$ appears. For each time step $t$, we construct a diagonal matrix $\mathbf{O}_t$ whose

[3] The reader unfamiliar with basic operations on vectors and matrices might wish to consult Appendix A before proceeding with this section.

diagonal entries are given by the values $P(e_t | X_t = i)$ and whose other entries are 0. For example, on day 1 in the umbrella world, $U_1 = true$, so, from Figure 15.2, we have

$$\mathbf{O}_1 = \begin{pmatrix} 0.9 & 0 \\ 0 & 0.2 \end{pmatrix} .$$

Now, if we use column vectors to represent the forward and backward messages, the computations become simple matrix–vector operations. The forward equation (15.3) becomes

$$\mathbf{f}_{1:t+1} = \alpha \, \mathbf{O}_{t+1} \mathbf{T}^{\top} \mathbf{f}_{1:t} \qquad (15.10)$$

and the backward equation (15.7) becomes

$$\mathbf{b}_{k+1:t} = \mathbf{T} \mathbf{O}_{k+1} \mathbf{b}_{k+2:t} . \qquad (15.11)$$

From these equations, we can see that the time complexity of the forward–backward algorithm (Figure 15.4) applied to a sequence of length $t$ is $O(S^2 t)$, because each step requires multiplying an $S$-element vector by an $S \times S$ matrix. The space requirement is $O(St)$, because the forward pass stores $t$ vectors of size $S$.

Besides providing an elegant description of the filtering and smoothing algorithms for HMMs, the matrix formulation reveals opportunities for improved algorithms. The first is a simple variation on the forward–backward algorithm that allows smoothing to be carried out in *constant* space, independently of the length of the sequence. The idea is that smoothing for any particular time slice $k$ requires the simultaneous presence of both the forward and backward messages, $\mathbf{f}_{1:k}$ and $\mathbf{b}_{k+1:t}$, according to Equation (15.6). The forward–backward algorithm achieves this by storing the **f**s computed on the forward pass so that they are available during the backward pass. Another way to achieve this is with a single pass that propagates both **f** and **b** in the same direction. For example, the "forward" message **f** can be propagated backwards if we manipulate Equation (15.10) to work in the other direction:

$$\mathbf{f}_{1:t} = \alpha' (\mathbf{T}^{\top})^{-1} \mathbf{O}_{t+1}^{-1} \mathbf{f}_{1:t+1} .$$

The modified smoothing algorithm works by first running the standard forward pass to compute $\mathbf{f}_{t:t}$ (forgetting all the intermediate results) and then running the backward pass for both **b** and **f** together, using them to compute the smoothed estimate at each step. Since only one copy of each message is needed, the storage requirements are constant (i.e. independent of $t$, the length of the sequence). There is one significant restriction on this algorithm: it requires that the transition matrix be invertible and that the sensor model have no zeroes—that is, every observation is possible in every state.

A second area in which the matrix formulation reveals an improvement is in *online* smoothing with a fixed lag. The fact that smoothing can be done in constant space suggests that there should exist an efficient recursive algorithm for online smoothing—that is, an algorithm whose time complexity is independent of the length of the lag. Let us suppose that the lag is $d$; that is, we are smoothing at time slice $t - d$, where the current time is $t$. By Equation (15.6), we need to compute

$$\alpha \, \mathbf{f}_{1:t-d} \mathbf{b}_{t-d+1:t}$$

for slice $t - d$. Then, when a new observation arrives, we need to compute

$$\alpha \, \mathbf{f}_{1:t-d+1} \mathbf{b}_{t-d+2:t+1}$$

for slice $t-d+1$. How can this be done incrementally? First, we can compute $\mathbf{f}_{1:t-d+1}$ from $\mathbf{f}_{1:t-d}$, using the standard filtering process, Equation (15.3).

Computing the backward message incrementally is more tricky, because there is no simple relationship between the old backward message $\mathbf{b}_{t-d+1:t}$ and the new backward message $\mathbf{b}_{t-d+2:t+1}$. Instead, we will examine the relationship between the old backward message $\mathbf{b}_{t-d+1:t}$ and the backward message at the front of the sequence, $\mathbf{b}_{t+1:t}$. To do this, we apply Equation (15.11) $d$ times to get

$$\mathbf{b}_{t-d+1:t} = \left( \prod_{i=t-d+1}^{t} \mathbf{T}\mathbf{O}_i \right) \mathbf{b}_{t+1:t} = \mathbf{B}_{t-d+1:t}\mathbf{1}\,, \tag{15.12}$$

where the matrix $\mathbf{B}_{t-d+1:t}$ is the product of the sequence of $\mathbf{T}$ and $\mathbf{O}$ matrices. $\mathbf{B}$ can be thought of as a "transformation operator" that transforms a later backward message into an earlier one. A similar equation holds for the new backward messages *after* the next observation arrives:

$$\mathbf{b}_{t-d+2:t+1} = \left( \prod_{i=t-d+2}^{t+1} \mathbf{T}\mathbf{O}_i \right) \mathbf{b}_{t+2:t+1} = \mathbf{B}_{t-d+2:t+1}\mathbf{1}\,. \tag{15.13}$$

Examining the product expressions in Equations (15.12) and (15.13), we see that they have a simple relationship: to get the second product, "divide" the first product by the first element $\mathbf{T}\mathbf{O}_{t-d+1}$, and multiply by the new last element $\mathbf{T}\mathbf{O}_{t+1}$. In matrix language, then, there is a simple relationship between the old and new $\mathbf{B}$ matrices:

$$\mathbf{B}_{t-d+2:t+1} = \mathbf{O}_{t-d+1}^{-1}\mathbf{T}^{-1}\mathbf{B}_{t-d+1:t}\mathbf{T}\mathbf{O}_{t+1}\,. \tag{15.14}$$

This equation provides an incremental update for the $\mathbf{B}$ matrix, which in turn (through Equation (15.13)) allows us to compute the new backward message $\mathbf{b}_{t-d+2:t+1}$. The complete algorithm, which requires storing and updating $\mathbf{f}$ and $\mathbf{B}$, is shown in Figure 15.6.

## 15.4 Kalman Filters

Imagine watching a small bird flying through dense jungle foliage at dusk: you glimpse brief, intermittent flashes of motion; you try hard to guess where the bird is and where it will appear next so that you don't lose it. Or imagine that you are a World War II radar operator peering at a faint, wandering blip that appears once every 10 seconds on the screen. Or, going back further still, imagine you are Kepler trying to reconstruct the motions of the planets from a collection of highly inaccurate angular observations taken at irregular and imprecisely measured intervals. In all these cases, you are trying to estimate the state (position and velocity, for example) of a physical system from noisy observations over time. The problem can be formulated as inference in a temporal probability model, where the transition model describes the physics of motion and the sensor model describes the measurement process. This section examines the special representations and inference algorithms that have been developed to solve these sorts of problems; the method we will cover is called **Kalman filtering**, after its inventor, Rudolf E. Kalman.

KALMAN FILTERING

```
function FIXED-LAG-SMOOTHING(e_t, hmm, d) returns a distribution over X_{t-d}
  inputs: e_t, the current evidence for time step t
          hmm, a hidden Markov model with S × S transition matrix T
          d, the length of the lag for smoothing
  static: t, the current time, initially 1
          f, a probability distribution, the forward message P(X_t|e_{1:t}), initially PRIOR[hmm]
          B, the d-step backward transformation matrix, initially the identity matrix
          e_{t-d:t}, double-ended list of evidence from t − d to t, initially empty
  local variables: O_{t-d}, O_t, diagonal matrices containing the sensor model information

  add e_t to the end of e_{t-d:t}
  O_t ← diagonal matrix containing P(e_t|X_t)
  if t > d then
     f ← FORWARD(f, e_t)
     remove e_{t-d-1} from the beginning of e_{t-d:t}
     O_{t-d} ← diagonal matrix containing P(e_{t-d}|X_{t-d})
     B ← O_{t-d}^{-1} T^{-1} B T O_t
  else B ← B T O_t
  t ← t + 1
  if t > d then return NORMALIZE(f × B1) else return null
```

**Figure 15.6** An algorithm for smoothing with a fixed time lag of $d$ steps, implemented as an online algorithm that outputs the new smoothed estimate given the observation for a new time step.

Clearly, we will need several *continuous* variables to specify the state of the system. For example, the bird's flight might be specified by position $(X, Y, Z)$ and velocity $(\dot{X}, \dot{Y}, \dot{Z})$ at each point in time. We will also need suitable conditional densities to represent the transition and sensor models; as in Chapter 14, we will use **linear Gaussian** distributions. This means that the next state $\mathbf{X}_{t+1}$ must be a linear function of the current state $\mathbf{X}_t$, plus some Gaussian noise, a condition that turns out to be quite reasonable in practice. Consider, for example, the $X$-coordinate of the bird, ignoring the other coordinates for now. Let the interval between observations be $\Delta$, and let us assume constant velocity; then the position update is given by

$$X_{t+\Delta} = X_t + \dot{X}\,\Delta\,.$$

If we add Gaussian noise then we have a linear Gaussian transition model:

$$P(X_{t+\Delta} = x_{t+\Delta} | X_t = x_t, \dot{X}_t = \dot{x}_t) = N(x_t + \dot{x}_t\,\Delta, \sigma)(x_{t+\Delta})\,.$$

The Bayesian network structure for a system with position $\mathbf{X}_t$ and velocity $\dot{\mathbf{X}}_t$ is shown in Figure 15.7. Note that this is a very specific form of linear Gaussian model; the general form will be described later in this section and covers a vast array of applications beyond the simple motion examples of the first paragraph. The reader might wish to consult Appendix A for some of the mathematical properties of Gaussian distributions; for our immediate purposes, the most important is that a **multivariate Gaussian** distribution for $d$ variables is specified by a $d$-element mean $\boldsymbol{\mu}$ and a $d \times d$ covariance matrix $\boldsymbol{\Sigma}$.

MULTIVARIATE GAUSSIAN

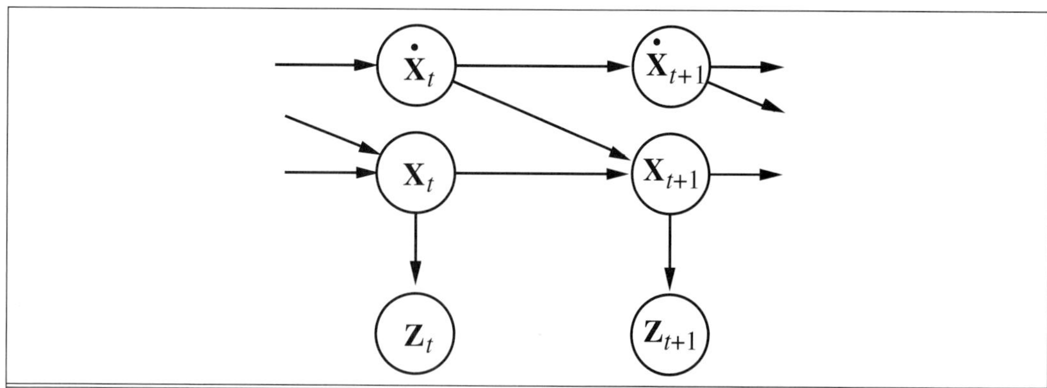


**Figure 15.7** Bayesian network structure for a linear dynamical system with position $\mathbf{X}_t$, velocity $\dot{\mathbf{X}}_t$, and position measurement $\mathbf{Z}_t$.

### Updating Gaussian distributions

In Chapter 14, we alluded to a key property of the linear Gaussian family of distributions: it remains closed under the standard Bayesian network operations. Here, we make this claim precise in the context of filtering in a temporal probability model. The required properties correspond to the two-step filtering calculation in Equation (15.3):

1. If the current distribution $\mathbf{P}(\mathbf{X}_t|\mathbf{e}_{1:t})$ is Gaussian and the transition model $\mathbf{P}(\mathbf{X}_{t+1}|\mathbf{x}_t)$ is linear Gaussian, then the one-step predicted distribution given by

$$\mathbf{P}(\mathbf{X}_{t+1}|\mathbf{e}_{1:t}) = \int_{\mathbf{x}_t} \mathbf{P}(\mathbf{X}_{t+1}|\mathbf{x}_t)P(\mathbf{x}_t|\mathbf{e}_{1:t})\,d\mathbf{x}_t \qquad (15.15)$$

is also a Gaussian distribution.

2. If the predicted distribution $\mathbf{P}(\mathbf{X}_{t+1}|\mathbf{e}_{1:t})$ is Gaussian and sensor model $\mathbf{P}(\mathbf{e}_{t+1}|\mathbf{X}_{t+1})$ is linear Gaussian, then, after conditioning on the new evidence, the updated distribution

$$\mathbf{P}(\mathbf{X}_{t+1}|\mathbf{e}_{1:t+1}) = \alpha\,\mathbf{P}(\mathbf{e}_{t+1}|\mathbf{X}_{t+1})\mathbf{P}(\mathbf{X}_{t+1}|\mathbf{e}_{1:t}) \qquad (15.16)$$

is also a Gaussian distribution.

Thus, the FORWARD operator for Kalman filtering takes a Gaussian forward message $\mathbf{f}_{1:t}$, specified by a mean $\boldsymbol{\mu}_t$ and covariance matrix $\boldsymbol{\Sigma}_t$, and produces a new multivariate Gaussian forward message $\mathbf{f}_{1:t+1}$, specified by a mean $\boldsymbol{\mu}_{t+1}$ and covariance matrix $\boldsymbol{\Sigma}_{t+1}$. So, if we start with a Gaussian prior $\mathbf{f}_{1:0} = \mathbf{P}(\mathbf{X}_0) = N(\boldsymbol{\mu}_0, \boldsymbol{\Sigma}_0)$, filtering with a linear Gaussian model produces a Gaussian state distribution for all time.

This seems to be a nice, elegant result, but why is it so important? The reason is that, except for a few special cases such as this, *filtering with continuous or hybrid (discrete and continuous) networks generates state distributions whose representation grows without bound over time.* This statement is not easy to prove in general, but Exercise 15.5 shows what happens for a simple example.

### A simple one-dimensional example

We have said that the FORWARD operator for the Kalman filter maps a Gaussian into a new Gaussian. This translates into computing a new mean and covariance matrix from the previous mean and covariance matrix. Deriving the update rule in the general (multivariate) case requires rather a lot of linear algebra, so we will stick to a very simple univariate case for now; later we will give the results for the general case. Even for the univariate case, the calculations are somewhat tedious, but we feel that they are worth seeing because the usefulness of the Kalman filter is tied so intimately to the mathematical properties of Gaussian distributions.

The temporal model we will consider describes a **random walk** of a single continuous state variable $X_t$ with a noisy observation $Z_t$. An example might be the "consumer confidence" index, which can be modeled as undergoing a random Gaussian-distributed change each month and is measured by a random consumer survey that also introduces Gaussian sampling noise. The prior distribution is assumed to be Gaussian with variance $\sigma_0^2$:

$$P(x_0) = \alpha\, e^{-\frac{1}{2}\left(\frac{(x_0-\mu_0)^2}{\sigma_0^2}\right)} .$$

(For simplicity, we will use the same symbol $\alpha$ for all normalizing constants in this section.) The transition model simply adds a Gaussian perturbation of constant variance $\sigma_x^2$ to the current state:

$$P(x_{t+1}|x_t) = \alpha\, e^{-\frac{1}{2}\left(\frac{(x_{t+1}-x_t)^2}{\sigma_x^2}\right)} .$$

The sensor model then assumes Gaussian noise with variance $\sigma_z^2$:

$$P(z_t|x_t) = \alpha\, e^{-\frac{1}{2}\left(\frac{(z_t-x_t)^2}{\sigma_z^2}\right)} .$$

Now, given the prior $P(X_0)$, we can compute the one-step predicted distribution using Equation (15.15):

$$\begin{aligned} P(x_1) &= \int_{-\infty}^{\infty} P(x_1|x_0)P(x_0)\, dx_0 = \alpha \int_{-\infty}^{\infty} e^{-\frac{1}{2}\left(\frac{(x_1-x_0)^2}{\sigma_x^2}\right)} e^{-\frac{1}{2}\left(\frac{(x_0-\mu_0)^2}{\sigma_0^2}\right)}\, dx_0 \\ &= \alpha \int_{-\infty}^{\infty} e^{-\frac{1}{2}\left(\frac{\sigma_0^2(x_1-x_0)^2+\sigma_x^2(x_0-\mu_0)^2}{\sigma_0^2\sigma_x^2}\right)}\, dx_0 . \end{aligned}$$

This integral looks rather complicated. The key to progress is to notice that the exponent is the sum of two expressions that are *quadratic* in $x_0$ and hence is itself a quadratic in $x_0$. A simple trick known as **completing the square** allows the rewriting of any quadratic $ax_0^2 + bx_0 + c$ as the sum of a squared term $a(x_0 - \frac{-b}{2a})^2$ and a residual term $c - \frac{b^2}{4a}$ that is independent of $x_0$. The residual term can be taken outside the integral, giving us

COMPLETING THE SQUARE

$$P(x_1) = \alpha\, e^{-\frac{1}{2}\left(c-\frac{b^2}{4a}\right)} \int_{-\infty}^{\infty} e^{-\frac{1}{2}\left(a(x_0-\frac{-b}{2a})^2\right)}\, dx_0 .$$

Now the integral is just the integral of a Gaussian over its full range, which is simply 1. Thus, we are left with only the residual term from the quadratic.

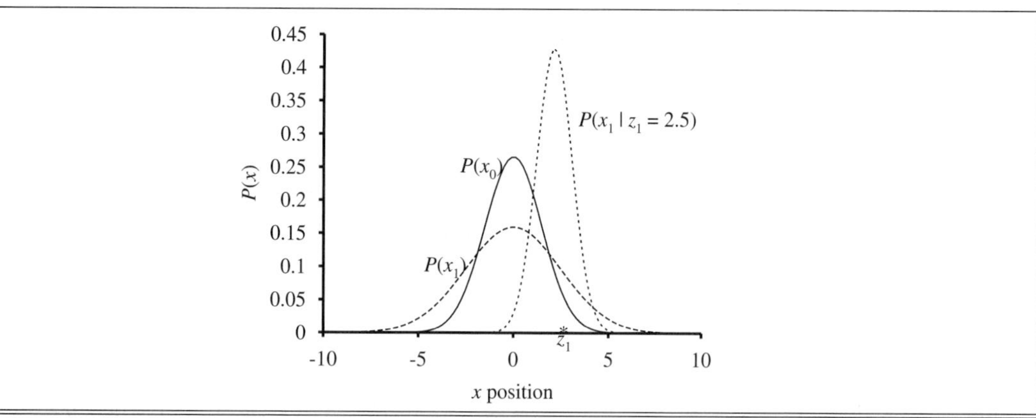


**Figure 15.8** Stages in the Kalman filter update cycle for a random walk with a prior given by $\mu_0 = 0.0$ and $\sigma_0 = 1.0$, transition noise given by $\sigma_x = 2.0$, sensor noise given by $\sigma_z = 1.0$, and a first observation $z_1 = 2.5$ (marked on the $x$-axis). Notice how the prediction $P(x_1)$ is flattened out, relative to $P(x_0)$, by the transition noise. Notice also that the mean of the posterior $P(x_1|z_1)$ is slightly to the left of the observation $z_1$ because the mean is a weighted average of the prediction and the observation.

The second key step is to notice that the residual term has to be a quadratic in $x_1$; in fact, after simplification, we obtain

$$P(x_1) = \alpha\, e^{-\frac{1}{2}\left(\frac{(x_1-\mu_0)^2}{\sigma_0^2+\sigma_x^2}\right)} .$$

That is, the one-step predicted distribution is a Gaussian with the same mean $\mu_0$ and a variance equal to the sum of the original variance $\sigma_0^2$ and the transition variance $\sigma_x^2$. A momentary exercise of intuition reveals that this is intuitively reasonable.

To complete the update step, we need to condition on the observation at the first time step, namely, $z_1$. From Equation (15.16), this is given by

$$\begin{aligned} P(x_1|z_1) &= \alpha\, P(z_1|x_1)P(x_1) \\ &= \alpha\, e^{-\frac{1}{2}\left(\frac{(z_1-x_1)^2}{\sigma_z^2}\right)} e^{-\frac{1}{2}\left(\frac{(x_1-\mu_0)^2}{\sigma_0^2+\sigma_x^2}\right)} . \end{aligned}$$

Once again, we combine the exponents and complete the square (Exercise 15.6), obtaining

$$P(x_1|z_1) = \alpha\, e^{-\frac{1}{2}\left(\frac{(x_1-\frac{(\sigma_0^2+\sigma_x^2)z_1+\sigma_z^2\mu_0}{\sigma_0^2+\sigma_x^2+\sigma_z^2})^2}{(\sigma_0^2+\sigma_x^2)\sigma_z^2/(\sigma_0^2+\sigma_x^2+\sigma_z^2)}\right)} . \tag{15.17}$$

Thus, after one update cycle, we have a new Gaussian distribution for the state variable.

From the Gaussian formula in Equation (15.17), we see that the new mean and standard deviation can be calculated from the old mean and standard deviation as follows:

$$\begin{aligned} \mu_{t+1} &= \frac{(\sigma_t^2+\sigma_x^2)z_{t+1}+\sigma_z^2\mu_t}{\sigma_t^2+\sigma_x^2+\sigma_z^2} \\ \sigma_{t+1}^2 &= \frac{(\sigma_t^2+\sigma_x^2)\sigma_z^2}{\sigma_t^2+\sigma_x^2+\sigma_z^2} . \end{aligned} \tag{15.18}$$

Figure 15.8 shows one update cycle for particular values of the transition and sensor models.

The preceding pair of equations plays exactly the same role as the general filtering equation (15.3) or the HMM filtering equation (15.10). Because of the special nature of Gaussian distributions, however, the equations have some interesting additional properties. First, we can interpret the calculation for the new mean $\mu_{t+1}$ as simply a *weighted mean* of the new observation $z_{t+1}$ and the old mean $\mu_t$. If the observation is unreliable, then $\sigma_z^2$ is large and we pay more attention to the old mean; if the old mean is unreliable ($\sigma_t^2$ is large) or the process is highly unpredictable ($\sigma_x^2$ is large), then we pay more attention to the observation. Second, notice that the update for the variance $\sigma_{t+1}^2$ is *independent of the observation.* We can therefore compute in advance what the sequence of variance values will be. Third, the sequence of variance values converges quickly to a fixed value that depends only on $\sigma_x^2$ and $\sigma_z^2$, thereby substantially simplifying the subsequent calculations. (See Exercise 15.7.)

### The general case

The preceding derivation illustrates the key property of Gaussian distributions that allows Kalman filtering to work: the fact that the exponent is a quadratic form. This is true not just for the univariate case; the full multivariate Gaussian distribution has the form

$$N(\boldsymbol{\mu}, \boldsymbol{\Sigma})(\mathbf{x}) = \alpha\, e^{-\frac{1}{2}\left((\mathbf{x}-\boldsymbol{\mu})^\top \boldsymbol{\Sigma}^{-1}(\mathbf{x}-\boldsymbol{\mu})\right)} .$$

Multiplying out the terms in the exponent makes it clear that the exponent is also a quadratic function of the random variables $x_i$ in $\mathbf{x}$. As in the univariate case, the filtering update preserves the Gaussian nature of the state distribution.

Let us first define the general temporal model used with Kalman filtering. Both the transition model and the sensor model allow for a *linear* transformation with additive Gaussian noise. Thus, we have

$$\begin{aligned} P(\mathbf{x}_{t+1}|\mathbf{x}_t) &= N(\mathbf{F}\mathbf{x}_t, \boldsymbol{\Sigma}_x)(\mathbf{x}_{t+1}) \\ P(\mathbf{z}_t|\mathbf{x}_t) &= N(\mathbf{H}\mathbf{x}_t, \boldsymbol{\Sigma}_z)(\mathbf{z}_t) , \end{aligned} \qquad (15.19)$$

where $\mathbf{F}$ and $\boldsymbol{\Sigma}_x$ are matrices describing the linear transition model and transition noise covariance and $\mathbf{H}$ and $\boldsymbol{\Sigma}_z$ are the corresponding matrices for the sensor model. Now the update equations for the mean and covariance, in their full, hairy horribleness, are

$$\begin{aligned} \boldsymbol{\mu}_{t+1} &= \mathbf{F}\boldsymbol{\mu}_t + \mathbf{K}_{t+1}(\mathbf{z}_{t+1} - \mathbf{H}\mathbf{F}\boldsymbol{\mu}_t) \\ \boldsymbol{\Sigma}_{t+1} &= (\mathbf{I} - \mathbf{K}_{t+1})(\mathbf{F}\boldsymbol{\Sigma}_t\mathbf{F}^\top + \boldsymbol{\Sigma}_x) \end{aligned} \qquad (15.20)$$

KALMAN GAIN MATRIX

where $\mathbf{K}_{t+1} = (\mathbf{F}\boldsymbol{\Sigma}_t\mathbf{F}^\top + \boldsymbol{\Sigma}_x)\mathbf{H}^\top(\mathbf{H}(\mathbf{F}\boldsymbol{\Sigma}_t\mathbf{F}^\top + \boldsymbol{\Sigma}_x)\mathbf{H}^\top + \boldsymbol{\Sigma}_z)^{-1}$ is called the **Kalman gain matrix**. Believe it or not, these equations make some intuitive sense. For example, consider the update for the mean state estimate $\boldsymbol{\mu}$. The term $\mathbf{F}\boldsymbol{\mu}_t$ is the *predicted* state at $t+1$, so $\mathbf{H}\mathbf{F}\boldsymbol{\mu}_t$ is the *predicted* observation. Therefore, the term $\mathbf{z}_{t+1} - \mathbf{H}\mathbf{F}\boldsymbol{\mu}_t$ represents the error in the predicted observation. This is multiplied by $\mathbf{K}_{t+1}$ to correct the predicted state; hence $\mathbf{K}_{t+1}$ is a measure of *how seriously to take the new observation* relative to the prediction. As in Equation (15.18), we also have the property that the variance update is independent of the observations. The sequence of values for $\boldsymbol{\Sigma}_t$ and $\mathbf{K}_t$ can therefore be computed offline, and the actual calculations required during online tracking are quite modest.

To illustrate these equations at work, we have applied them to the problem of tracking an object moving on the $X$–$Y$ plane. The state variables are $\mathbf{X} = (X, Y, \dot{X}, \dot{Y})^\top$ so $\mathbf{F}$, $\mathbf{\Sigma}_x$, $\mathbf{H}$, and $\mathbf{\Sigma}_z$ are $4 \times 4$ matrices. Figure 15.9(a) shows the true trajectory, a series of noisy observations, and the trajectory estimated by Kalman filtering, along with the covariances indicated by the one-standard-deviation contours. The filtering process does a good job of tracking the actual motion, and, as expected, the variance quickly reaches a fixed point.

We can also derive equations for *smoothing* as well as filtering with linear Gaussian models. The smoothing results are shown in Figure 15.9(b). Notice how the variance in the position estimate is sharply reduced, except at the ends of the trajectory (why?), and that the estimated trajectory is much smoother.

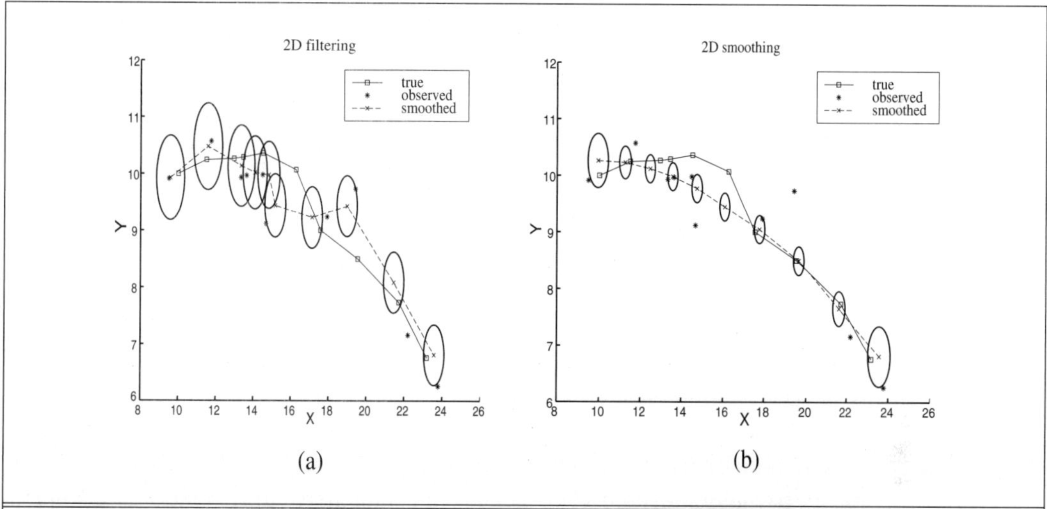


**Figure 15.9** (a) Results of Kalman filtering for an object moving on the $X$–$Y$ plane, showing the true trajectory (left to right), a series of noisy observations, and the trajectory estimated by Kalman filtering. Variance in the position estimate is indicated by the ovals. (b) The results of Kalman smoothing for the same observation sequence.

## Applicability of Kalman filtering

The Kalman filter and its elaborations are used in a vast array of applications. The "classical" application is in radar tracking of aircraft and missiles. Related applications include acoustic tracking of submarines and ground vehicles and visual tracking of vehicles and people. In a slightly more esoteric vein, Kalman filters are used to reconstruct particle trajectories from bubble-chamber photographs and ocean currents from satellite surface measurements. The range of application is much larger than just the tracking of motion: any system characterized by continuous state variables and noisy measurements will do. Such systems include pulp mills, chemical plants, nuclear reactors, plant ecosystems, and national economies.

The fact that Kalman filtering can be applied to a system does not mean that the results will be valid or useful. The assumptions made—a linear Gaussian transition and sensor models—are very strong. The **extended Kalman filter (EKF)** attempts to overcome nonlin-

EXTENDED KALMAN FILTER (EKF)

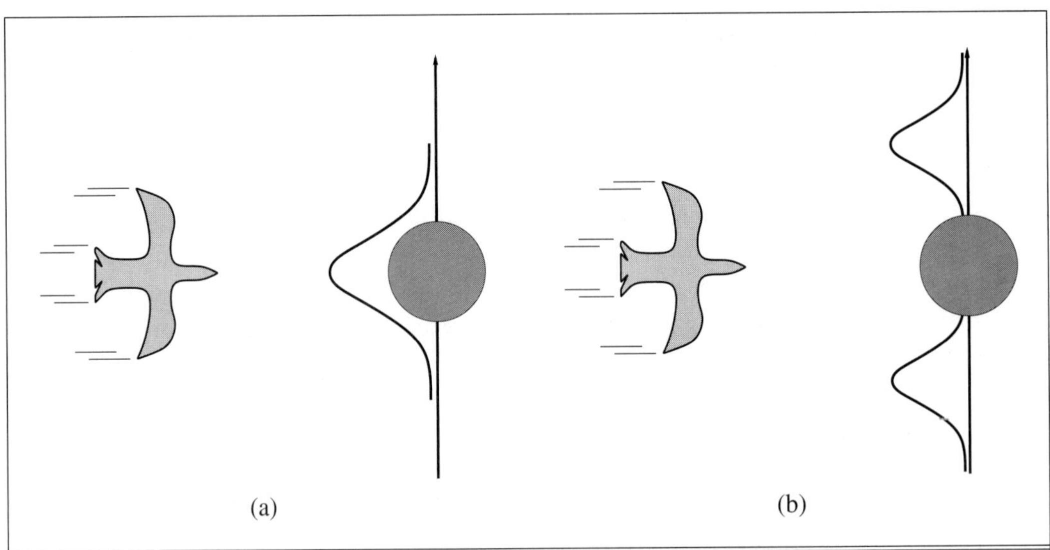


**Figure 15.10** A bird flying toward a tree (top views). (a) A Kalman filter will predict the location of the bird using a single Gaussian centered on the obstacle. (b) A more realistic model allows for the bird's evasive action, predicting that it will fly to one side or the other.

earities in the system being modeled. A system is nonlinear if the transition model cannot be described as a matrix multiplication of the state vector, as in Equation (15.19). The EKF works by modeling the system as *locally* linear in $\mathbf{x}_t$ in the region of $\mathbf{x}_t = \boldsymbol{\mu}_t$, the mean of the current state distribution. This works well for smooth, well-behaved systems and allows the tracker to maintain and update a Gaussian state distribution that is a reasonable approximation to the true posterior.

What does it mean for a system to be "unsmooth" or "poorly behaved"? Technically, it means that there is significant nonlinearity in system response within the region that is "close" (according to the covariance $\boldsymbol{\Sigma}_t$) to the current mean $\boldsymbol{\mu}_t$. To understand this idea in nontechnical terms, consider the example of trying to track a bird as it flies through the jungle. The bird appears to be heading at high speed straight for a tree trunk. The Kalman filter, whether regular or extended, can make only a Gaussian prediction of the location of the bird, and the mean of this Gaussian will be centered on the trunk, as shown in Figure 15.10(a). A reasonable model of the bird, on the other hand, would predict evasive action to one side or the other, as shown in Figure 15.10(b). Such a model is highly nonlinear, because the bird's decision varies sharply depending on its precise location relative to the trunk.

In order to handle examples like these, we clearly need a more expressive language for representing the behavior of the system being modeled. Within the control theory community, for which problems such as evasive maneuvering by aircraft raise the same kinds of difficulties, the standard solution is the **switching Kalman filter**. In this approach, multiple Kalman filters run in parallel, each using a different model of the system—for example, one for straight flight, one for sharp left turns, and one for sharp right turns. A weighted sum of predictions is used, where the weight depends on how well each filter fits the current data. We

SWITCHING KALMAN FILTER

will see in the next section that this is simply a special case of the general dynamic Bayesian network model, obtained by adding a discrete "maneuver" state variable to the network shown in Figure 15.7. Switching Kalman filters are discussed further in Exercise 15.5.

## 15.5 DYNAMIC BAYESIAN NETWORKS

DYNAMIC BAYESIAN NETWORK

A **dynamic Bayesian network**, or **DBN**, is a Bayesian network that represents a temporal probability model of the kind described in Section 15.1. We have already seen examples of DBNs: the umbrella network in Figure 15.2 and the Kalman filter network in Figure 15.7. In general, each slice of a DBN can have any number of state variables $\mathbf{X}_t$ and evidence variables $\mathbf{E}_t$. For simplicity, we will assume that the variables and their links are exactly replicated from slice to slice and that the DBN represents a first-order Markov process, so that each variable can have parents only in its own slice or the immediately preceding slice.

It should be clear that every hidden Markov model can be represented as a DBN with a single state variable and a single evidence variable. It is also the case that every discrete-variable DBN can be represented as an HMM; as explained in Section 15.3, we can combine all the state variables in the DBN into a single state variable whose values are all possible tuples of values of the individual state variables. Now, if every HMM is a DBN and every DBN can be translated into an HMM, what's the difference? The difference is that, *by decomposing the state of a complex system into its constituent variables, the DBN is able to take advantage of* sparseness *in the temporal probability model.* Suppose, for example, that a DBN has 20 Boolean state variables, each of which has three parents in the preceding slice. Then the DBN transition model has $20 \times 2^3 = 160$ probabilities, whereas the corresponding HMM has $2^{20}$ states and therefore $2^{40}$, or roughly a trillion, probabilities in the transition matrix. This is bad for at least three reasons: first, the HMM itself requires much more space; second, the huge transition matrix makes HMM inference much more expensive; and third, the problem of learning such a huge number of parameters makes the pure HMM model unsuitable for large problems. The relationship between DBNs and HMMs is roughly analogous to the relationship between ordinary Bayesian networks and full tabulated joint distributions.

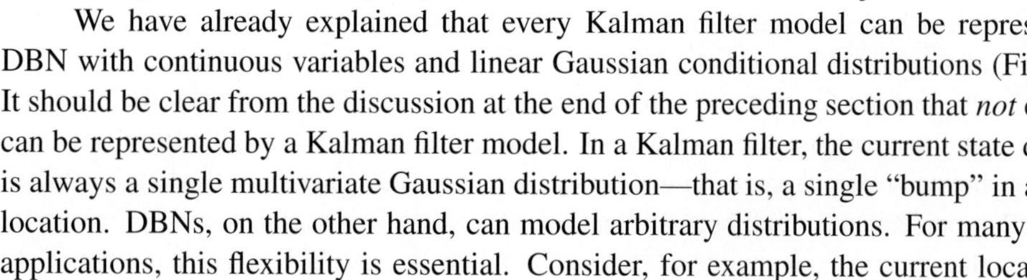

We have already explained that every Kalman filter model can be represented in a DBN with continuous variables and linear Gaussian conditional distributions (Figure 15.7). It should be clear from the discussion at the end of the preceding section that *not* every DBN can be represented by a Kalman filter model. In a Kalman filter, the current state distribution is always a single multivariate Gaussian distribution—that is, a single "bump" in a particular location. DBNs, on the other hand, can model arbitrary distributions. For many real-world applications, this flexibility is essential. Consider, for example, the current location of my keys. They might be in my pocket, on the bedside table, on the kitchen counter, or dangling from the front door. A single Gaussian bump that included all these places would have to allocate significant probability to the keys being in mid-air in the front hall. Aspects of the real world such as purposive agents, obstacles, and pockets introduce "nonlinearities" that require combinations of discrete and continuous variables in order to get reasonable models.

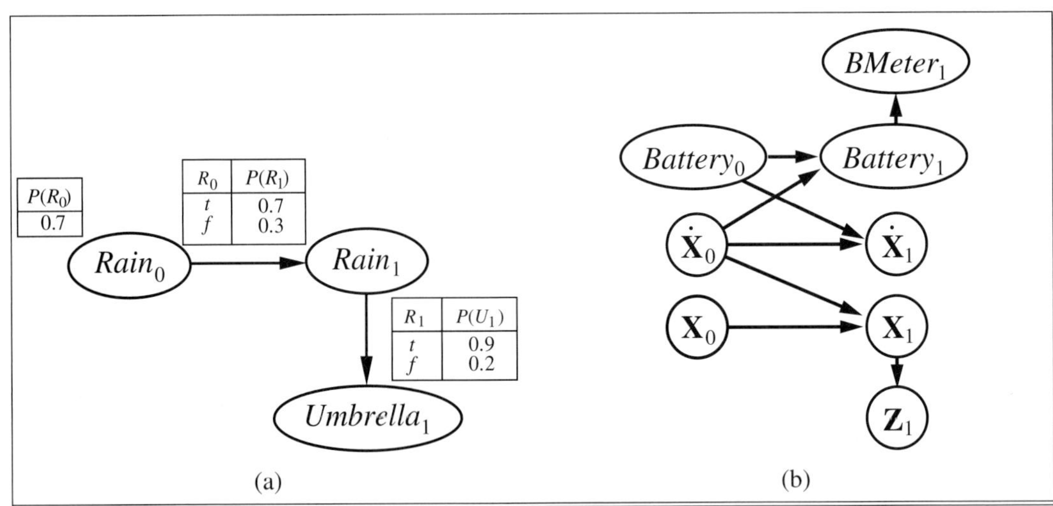


**Figure 15.11** (a) Specification of the prior, transition model, and sensor model for the umbrella DBN. All subsequent slices are assumed to be copies of slice 1. (b) A simple DBN for robot motion in the X–Y plane.

### Constructing DBNs

To construct a DBN, one must specify three kinds of information: the prior distribution over the state variables, $\mathbf{P}(\mathbf{X}_0)$; the transition model $\mathbf{P}(\mathbf{X}_{t+1}|\mathbf{X}_t)$; and the sensor model $\mathbf{P}(\mathbf{E}_t|\mathbf{X}_t)$. To specify the transition and sensor models, one must also specify the topology of the connections between successive slices and between the state and evidence variables. Because the transition and sensor models are assumed to be stationary—the same for all $t$—it is most convenient simply to specify them for the first slice. For example, the complete DBN specification for the umbrella world is given by the three-node network shown in Figure 15.11(a). From this specification, the complete (semi-infinite) DBN can be constructed as needed by copying the first slice.

Let us now consider a more interesting example: monitoring a battery-powered robot moving in the X–Y plane, as introduced in Section 15.1. First, we need state variables, which will include both $\mathbf{X}_t = (X_t, Y_t)$ for position and $\dot{\mathbf{X}}_t = (\dot{X}_t, \dot{Y}_t)$ for velocity. We will assume some method of measuring position—perhaps a fixed camera or onboard GPS (Global Positioning System)—yielding measurements $\mathbf{Z}_t$. The position at the next time step depends on the current position and velocity, as in the standard Kalman filter model. The velocity at the next step depends on the current velocity and the state of the battery. We add $Battery_t$ to represent the actual battery charge level, which has as parents the previous battery level and the velocity, and we add $BMeter_t$, which measures the battery charge level. This gives us the basic model shown in Figure 15.11(b).

It is worth looking in more depth at the nature of the sensor model for $BMeter_t$. Let us suppose, for simplicity, that both $Battery_t$ and $BMeter_t$ can take on discrete values 0 through 5—rather like the battery meter on a typical laptop computer. If the meter is always accurate, then the CPT $\mathbf{P}(BMeter_t|Battery_t)$ should have probabilities of 1.0 "along the diagonal" and probabilities of 0.0 elsewhere. In reality, noise always creeps into measurements. For continuous measurements, a Gaussian distribution with a small variance might be used instead.[4] For our discrete variables, we can approximate a Gaussian using a distribution in which the probability of error drops off in the appropriate way, so that the probability of a large error is very small. We will use the term **Gaussian error model** to cover both the continuous and discrete versions.

GAUSSIAN ERROR MODEL

Anyone with hands-on experience of robotics, computerized process control, or other forms of automatic sensing will readily testify to the fact that small amounts of measurement noise are often the least of one's problems. Real sensors *fail*. When a sensor fails, it does not necessarily send a signal saying, "Oh, by the way, the data I'm about to send you is a load of nonsense." Instead, it simply sends the nonsense. The simplest kind of failure is called a **transient failure**, where the sensor occasionally decides to send some nonsense. For example, the battery level sensor might have a habit of sending a zero when someone bumps the robot, even if the battery is fully charged.

TRANSIENT FAILURE

Let's see what happens when a transient failure occurs with a Gaussian error model that doesn't accommodate such failures. Suppose, for example, that the robot is sitting quietly and observes 20 consecutive battery readings of 5. Then the battery meter has a temporary seizure and the next reading is $BMeter_{21} = 0$. What will the simple Gaussian error model lead us to believe about $Battery_{21}$? According to Bayes' rule, the answer depends on both the sensor model $\mathbf{P}(BMeter_{21} = 0 | Battery_{21})$ and the prediction $\mathbf{P}(Battery_{21} | BMeter_{1:20})$. If the probability of a large sensor error is significantly less likely than the probability of a transition to $Battery_{21} = 0$, even if the latter is very unlikely, then the posterior distribution will assign a high probability to the battery's being empty. A second reading of zero at $t = 22$ will make this conclusion almost certain. If the transient failure then disappears and the reading returns to 5 from $t = 23$ onwards, the estimate for the battery level will quickly return to 5, as if by magic. This course of events is illustrated in the upper curve of Figure 15.12(a), which shows the expected value of $Battery_t$ over time using a discrete Gaussian error model.

Despite the recovery, there is a time ($t = 22$) when the robot is convinced that its battery is empty; presumably, then, it should send out a mayday signal and shut down. Alas, its oversimplified sensor model has led it astray. How can this be fixed? Consider a familiar example from everyday human driving: on sharp curves or steep hills, one's "fuel tank empty" warning light sometimes turns on. Rather than looking for the emergency phone, one simply recalls that the fuel gauge sometimes gives a very large error when the fuel is sloshing around in the tank. The moral of the story is the following: *in order for the system to handle sensor failure properly, the sensor model must include the possibility of failure.*

The simplest kind of failure model for a sensor allows a certain probability that the sensor will return some completely incorrect value, regardless of the true state of the world. For example, if the battery meter fails by returning 0, we might say that

$$P(BMeter_t = 0 | Battery_t = 5) = 0.03 ,$$

which is presumably much larger than the probability assigned by the simple Gaussian error

[4] Strictly speaking, a Gaussian distribution is problematic because it assigns nonzero probability to large negative charge levels. The **beta distribution** is sometimes a better choice for a variable whose range is restricted.

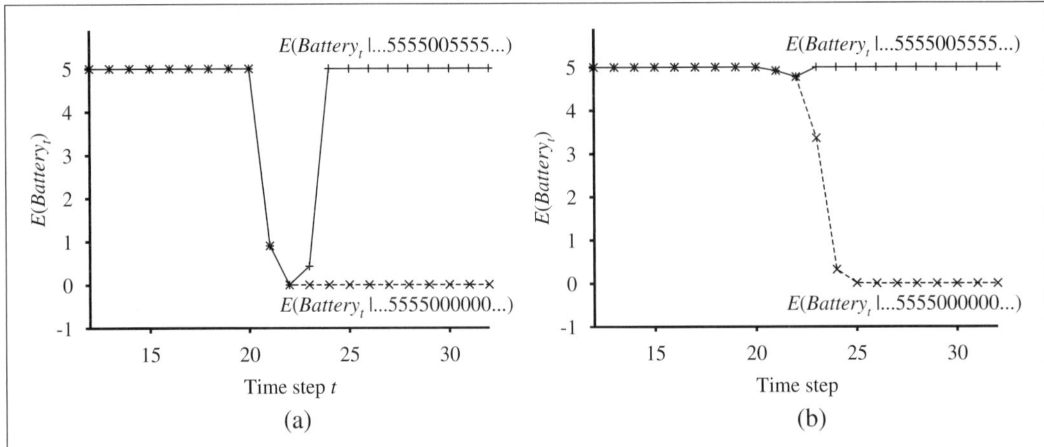


**Figure 15.12** (a) Upper curve: trajectory of the expected value of $Battery_t$ for an observation sequence consisting of all 5s except for 0s at $t=21$ and $t=22$, using a simple Gaussian error model. Lower curve: trajectory when the observation remains at 0 from $t=21$ onwards. (b) The same experiment run with the transient failure model. Notice that the transient failure is handled well, but the persistent failure results in excessive pessimism.

TRANSIENT FAILURE MODEL

model. Let's call this the **transient failure model**. How does it help when we are faced with a reading of 0? Provided that the *predicted* probability of an empty battery, according to the readings so far, is much less than 0.03, then the best explanation of the observation $BMeter_{21}=0$ is that the sensor has temporarily failed. Intuitively, we can think of the belief about the battery level as having a certain amount of "inertia" that helps to overcome temporary blips in the meter reading. The upper curve in Figure 15.12(b) shows that the transient failure model can handle transient failures without a catastrophic change in beliefs.

So much for temporary blips. What about a persistent sensor failure? Sadly, failures of this kind are all too common. If the sensor returns 20 readings of 5 followed by 20 readings of 0, then the transient sensor failure model described in the preceding paragraph will result in the robot gradually coming to believe that its battery is empty when in fact it may be that the meter has failed. The lower curve in Figure 15.12(b) shows the belief "trajectory" for this case. By $t=25$—five readings of 0—the robot is convinced that its battery is empty. Obviously, we would prefer the robot to believe that its battery meter is broken—if indeed this is the more likely event.

PERSISTENT FAILURE MODEL

Unsurprisingly, to handle persistent failure, we will need a **persistent failure model** that describes how the sensor behaves under normal conditions and after failure. To do this, we need to augment the hidden state of the system with an additional variable, say $BMBroken$, that describes the status of the battery meter. The persistence of failure must be modeled by an arc linking $BMBroken_0$ to $BMBroken_1$. This **persistence arc** has a CPT that gives a small probability of failure in any given time step, say 0.001, but specifies that the sensor stays broken once it breaks. When the sensor is OK, the sensor model for $BMeter$ is identical to the transient failure model; when the sensor is broken, it says $BMeter$ is always 0, regardless of the actual battery charge.

PERSISTENCE ARC

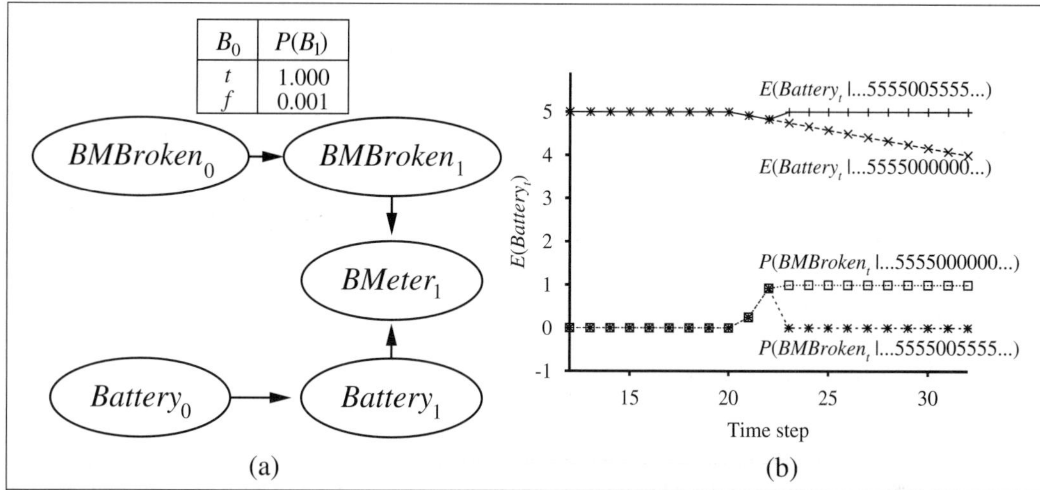


**Figure 15.13** (a) A DBN fragment showing the sensor status variable required for modeling persistent failure of the battery sensor. (b) Upper curves: trajectories of the expected value of $Battery_t$ for the "transient failure" and "permanent failure" observations sequences. Lower curves: probability trajectories for $BMBroken$ given the two observation sequences.

The persistent failure model for the battery sensor is shown in Figure 15.13(a). Its performance on the two data sequences (temporary blip and persistent failure) is shown in Figure 15.13(b). There are several things to notice about these curves. First, in the case of the temporary blip, the probability that the sensor is broken rises significantly after the second 0 reading, but immediately drops back to zero once a 5 is observed. Second, in the case of persistent failure, the probability that the sensor is broken rises quickly to almost 1 and stays there. Finally, once the sensor is known to be broken, the robot can only assume that its battery discharges at the "normal" rate, as shown by the gradually descending level of $E(Battery_t|\ldots)$.

So far, we have merely scratched the surface of the problem of representing complex processes. The variety of transition models is huge, encompassing topics as disparate as modeling the human endocrine system and modeling multiple vehicles driving on a freeway. Sensor modeling is also a vast subfield in itself, but even subtle phenomena, such as sensor drift, sudden decalibration, and the effects of exogenous conditions (such as weather) on sensor readings, can be handled by explicit representation within dynamic Bayesian networks.

## Exact inference in DBNs

Having sketched some ideas for representing complex processes as DBNs, we now turn to the question of inference. In a sense, this question has already been answered: dynamic Bayesian networks *are* Bayesian networks, and we already have algorithms for inference in Bayesian networks. Given a sequence of observations, one can construct the full Bayesian network representation of a DBN by replicating slices until the network is large enough to accommodate the observations, as in Figure 15.14. This technique is called **unrolling**. (Technically, the DBN is equivalent to the semi-infinite network obtained by unrolling forever. Slices added

UNROLLING

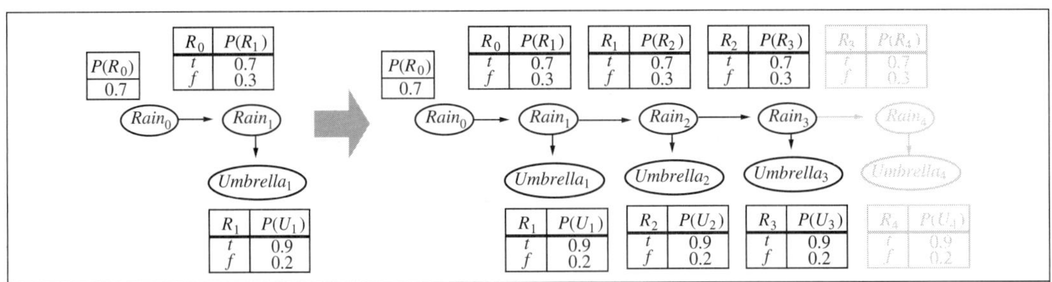


**Figure 15.14** Unrolling a dynamic Bayesian network: slices are replicated to accommodate the observation sequence (shaded nodes). Further slices have no effect on inferences within the observation period.

beyond the last observation have no effect on inferences within the observation period and can be omitted.) Once the DBN is unrolled, one can use any of the inference algorithms—variable elimination, join-tree methods, and so on—described in Chapter 14.

Unfortunately, a naive application of unrolling would not be particularly efficient. If we want to perform filtering or smoothing with a long sequence of observations $\mathbf{e}_{1:t}$, the unrolled network would require $O(t)$ space and would thus grow without bound as more observations were added. Moreover, if we simply run the inference algorithm anew each time an observation is added, the inference time per update will also increase as $O(t)$.

Looking back to Section 15.2, we see that constant time and space per filtering update can be achieved if the computation can be done in a recursive fashion. Essentially, the filtering update in Equation (15.3) works by *summing out* the state variables of the previous time step to get the distribution for the new time step. Summing out variables is exactly what the **variable elimination** (Figure 14.10) algorithm does, and it turns out that running variable elimination with the variables in temporal order exactly mimics the operation of the recursive filtering update in Equation (15.3). The modified algorithm keeps at most two slices in memory at any one time: starting with slice 0, we add slice 1, then sum out slice 0, then add slice 2, then sum out slice 1, and so on. In this way, we can achieve constant space and time per filtering update. (The same performance can be achieved by making suitable modifications to the join tree algorithm.) Exercise 15.10 asks you to verify this fact for the umbrella network.

So much for the good news; now for the bad news: It turns out that the "constant" for the per-update time and space complexity is, in almost all cases, exponential in the number of state variables. What happens is that, as the variable elimination proceeds, the factors grow to include all the state variables (or, more precisely, all those state variables that have parents in the previous time slice). The maximum factor size is $O(d^{n+1})$ and the update cost is $O(d^{n+2})$.

Of course, this is much less than the cost of HMM updating, which is $O(d^{2n})$, but it is still infeasible for large numbers of variables. This grim fact is somewhat hard to accept. What it means is that *even though we can use DBNs to* represent *very complex temporal processes with many sparsely connected variables, we cannot* reason *efficiently and exactly about those processes.* The DBN model itself, which represents the prior joint distribution over all the variables, is factorable into its constituent CPTs, but the posterior joint distribution conditioned on an observation sequence—that is, the forward message—is generally *not* factorable. So far, no one has found a way around this problem, despite the fact that many important areas of science and engineering would benefit enormously from its solution. Thus, we must fall back on approximate methods.

### Approximate inference in DBNs

Chapter 14 described two approximation algorithms: likelihood weighting (Figure 14.14) and Markov chain Monte Carlo (MCMC, Figure 14.15). Of the two, the former is most easily adapted to the DBN context. We will see, however, that several improvements are required over the standard likelihood weighting algorithm before a practical method emerges.

Recall that likelihood weighting works by sampling the non-evidence nodes of the network in topological order, weighting each sample by the likelihood it accords to the observed evidence variables. As with the exact algorithms, we could apply likelihood weighting directly to an unrolled DBN, but this would suffer from the same problems in terms of increasing time and space requirements per update as the observation sequence grows. The problem is that the standard algorithm runs each sample in turn, all the way through the network. Instead, we can simply run all $N$ samples together through the DBN, one slice at a time. The modified algorithm fits the general pattern of filtering algorithms, with the set of $N$ samples as the forward message. The first key innovation, then, is to *use the samples themselves as an approximate representation of the current state distribution.* This meets the requirement of a "constant" time per update, although the constant depends on the number of samples required to maintain a reasonable approximation to the true posterior distribution. There is also no need to unroll the DBN, because we need to have in memory only the current slice and the next slice.

In our discussion of likelihood weighting in Chapter 14, we pointed out that the algorithm's accuracy suffers if the evidence variables are "downstream" from the variables being sampled, because in that case the samples are generated without any influence from the evidence. Looking at the typical structure of a DBN—say, the umbrella DBN in Figure 15.14—we see that indeed the early state variables will be sampled without the benefit of the later evidence. In fact, looking more carefully, we see that *none* of the state variables has *any* evidence variables among its ancestors! Hence, although the weight of each sample will depend on the evidence, the actual set of samples generated will be *completely independent* of the evidence. For example, even if the boss brings in the umbrella every day, the sampling process could still hallucinate endless days of sunshine. What this means in practice is that the fraction of samples that remain reasonably close to the actual series of events drops exponentially with $t$, the length of the observation sequence; in other words, to maintain a given level of accuracy, we need to increase the number of samples exponentially with $t$. Given that a filtering algorithm that works in real time can only use a fixed number of samples, what happens in practice is that the error blows up after a very small number of update steps.

Clearly, we need a better solution. The second key innovation is to *focus the set of samples on the high-probability regions of the state space.* This can be done by throwing away samples that have very low weight, according to the observations, while multiplying

```
function PARTICLE-FILTERING(e, N, dbn) returns a set of samples for the next time step
  inputs: e, the new incoming evidence
          N, the number of samples to be maintained
          dbn, a DBN with prior P(X0), transition model P(X1|X0), and sensor model P(E1|X1)
  static: S, a vector of samples of size N, initially generated from P(X0)
  local variables: W, a vector of weights of size N

  for i = 1 to N do
      S[i] ← sample from P(X1|X0 = S[i])
      W[i] ← P(e|X1 = S[i])
  S ← WEIGHTED-SAMPLE-WITH-REPLACEMENT(N, S, W)
  return S
```

**Figure 15.15** The particle filtering algorithm implemented as a recursive update operation with state (the set of samples). Each of the sampling steps involves sampling the relevant slice variables in topological order, much as in PRIOR-SAMPLE. The WEIGHTED-SAMPLE-WITH-REPLACEMENT operation can be implemented to run in $O(N)$ expected time.

those that have high weight. In that way, the population of samples will stay reasonably close to reality. If we think of samples as a resource for modeling the posterior distribution, then it makes sense to use more samples in regions of the state space where the posterior is higher.

PARTICLE FILTERING

A family of algorithms called **particle filtering** is designed to do just that. Particle filtering works as follows: First, a population of $N$ samples is created by sampling from the prior distribution at time 0, $\mathbf{P}(\mathbf{X}_0)$. Then the update cycle is repeated for each time step:

- Each sample is propagated forward by sampling the next state value $\mathbf{x}_{t+1}$ given the current value $\mathbf{x}_t$ for the sample, and using the transition model $\mathbf{P}(\mathbf{X}_{t+1}|\mathbf{x}_t)$.
- Each sample is weighted by the likelihood it assigns to the new evidence, $P(\mathbf{e}_{t+1}|\mathbf{x}_{t+1})$.
- The population is *resampled* to generate a new population of $N$ samples. Each new sample is selected from the current population; the probability that a particular sample is selected is proportional to its weight. The new samples are unweighted.

The algorithm is shown in detail in Figure 15.15, and its operation for the umbrella DBN is illustrated in Figure 15.16.

We can show that this algorithm is consistent—gives the correct probabilities as $N$ tends to infinity—by considering what happens during one update cycle. We will assume that the sample population starts with a correct representation of the forward message $\mathbf{f}_{1:t}$ at time $t$. Writing $N(\mathbf{x}_t|\mathbf{e}_{1:t})$ for the number of samples occupying state $\mathbf{x}_t$ after observations $\mathbf{e}_{1:t}$ have been processed, we therefore have

$$N(\mathbf{x}_t|\mathbf{e}_{1:t})/N = P(\mathbf{x}_t|\mathbf{e}_{1:t}) \tag{15.21}$$

for large $N$. Now we propagate each sample forward by sampling the state variables at $t+1$, given the values for the sample at $t$. The number of samples reaching state $\mathbf{x}_{t+1}$ from each

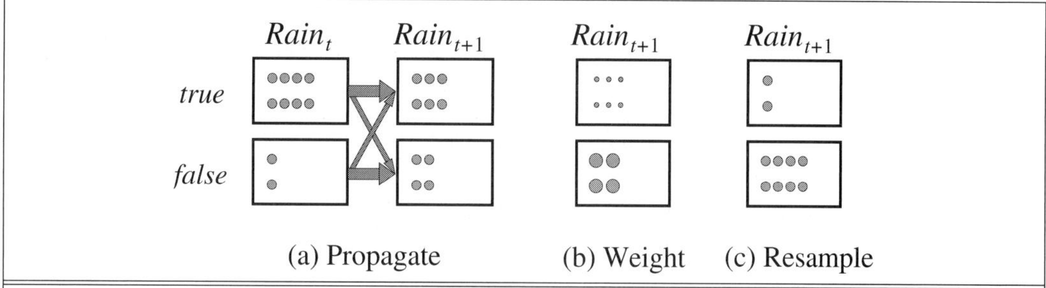


**Figure 15.16** The particle filtering update cycle for the umbrella DBN with $N = 10$, showing the sample populations of each state. (a) At time $t$, 8 samples indicate $Rain$ and 2 indicate $\neg Rain$. Each is propagated forward by sampling the next state via the transition model. At time $t + 1$, 6 samples indicate $Rain$ and 4 indicate $\neg Rain$. (b) $\neg Umbrella$ is observed at $t + 1$. Each sample is weighted by its likelihood for the observation, as indicated by the size of the circles. (c) A new set of 10 samples is generated by weighted random selection from the current set, resulting in 2 samples that indicate $Rain$ and 8 that indicate $\neg Rain$.

$\mathbf{x}_t$ is the transition probability times the population of $\mathbf{x}_t$; hence, the total number of samples reaching $\mathbf{x}_{t+1}$ is

$$N(\mathbf{x}_{t+1}|\mathbf{e}_{1:t}) = \sum_{\mathbf{x}_t} P(\mathbf{x}_{t+1}|\mathbf{x}_t)N(\mathbf{x}_t|\mathbf{e}_{1:t}) \ .$$

Now we weight each sample by its likelihood for the evidence at $t + 1$. A sample in state $\mathbf{x}_{t+1}$ receives weight $P(\mathbf{e}_{t+1}|\mathbf{x}_{t+1})$. The total weight of the samples in $\mathbf{x}_{t+1}$ after seeing $\mathbf{e}_{t+1}$ is therefore

$$W(\mathbf{x}_{t+1}|\mathbf{e}_{1:t+1}) = P(\mathbf{e}_{t+1}|\mathbf{x}_{t+1})N(\mathbf{x}_{t+1}|\mathbf{e}_{1:t}) \ .$$

Now for the resampling step. Since each sample is replicated with probability proportional to its weight, the number of samples in state $\mathbf{x}_{t+1}$ after resampling is proportional to the total weight in $\mathbf{x}_{t+1}$ before resampling:

$$\begin{aligned}
N(\mathbf{x}_{t+1}|\mathbf{e}_{1:t+1})/N &= \alpha\, W(\mathbf{x}_{t+1}|\mathbf{e}_{1:t+1}) \\
&= \alpha\, P(\mathbf{e}_{t+1}|\mathbf{x}_{t+1})N(\mathbf{x}_{t+1}|\mathbf{e}_{1:t}) \\
&= \alpha\, P(\mathbf{e}_{t+1}|\mathbf{x}_{t+1})\sum_{\mathbf{x}_t} P(\mathbf{x}_{t+1}|\mathbf{x}_t)N(\mathbf{x}_t|\mathbf{e}_{1:t}) \\
&= \alpha\, NP(\mathbf{e}_{t+1}|\mathbf{x}_{t+1})\sum_{\mathbf{x}_t} P(\mathbf{x}_{t+1}|\mathbf{x}_t)P(\mathbf{x}_t|\mathbf{e}_{1:t}) \quad \text{(by 15.21)} \\
&= \alpha' P(\mathbf{e}_{t+1}|\mathbf{x}_{t+1})\sum_{\mathbf{x}_t} P(\mathbf{x}_{t+1}|\mathbf{x}_t)P(\mathbf{x}_t|\mathbf{e}_{1:t}) \\
&= P(\mathbf{x}_{t+1}|\mathbf{e}_{1:t+1}) \quad \text{(by 15.3).}
\end{aligned}$$

Therefore the sample population after one update cycle correctly represents the forward message at time $t + 1$.

Particle filtering is *consistent*, therefore, but is it *efficient*? In practice, it seems that the answer is yes: particle filtering seems to maintain a good approximation to the true posterior using a constant number of samples. There are, as yet, no theoretical guarantees; particle filtering is currently an area of intensive study. Many variants and improvements have been proposed, and the set of applications is growing rapidly. Because it is a sampling algorithm, particle filtering can be used easily with hybrid and continuous DBNs, allowing it to be applied to areas such as tracking complex motion patterns in video (Isard and Blake, 1996) and predicting the stock market (de Freitas *et al.*, 2000).

## 15.6 Speech Recognition

SPEECH RECOGNITION

In this section, we look at one of the most important applications of temporal probability models—**speech recognition**. The task is to identify a sequence of words uttered by a speaker, given the acoustic signal. Speech is the dominant modality for communication between humans, and reliable speech recognition by machines would be immensely useful. Still more useful would be **speech understanding**—the identification of the *meaning* of the utterance. For this, we must wait until Chapter 22.

Speech provides our first contact with the raw, unwashed world of real sensor data. These data are *noisy*, quite literally: there can be background noise as well as artifacts introduced by the digitization process; there is variation in the way that words are pronounced, even by the same speaker; different words can sound the same; and so on. For these reasons, speech recognition has come to be viewed as a problem of probabilistic inference.

At the most general level, we can define the probabilistic inference problem as follows. Let $Words$ be a random variable ranging over all possible sequences of words that might be uttered, and let $signal$ be the observed acoustic signal sequence. Then the most likely interpretation of the utterance is the value of $Words$ that maximizes $P(words|signal)$. As is often the case, applying Bayes' rule is helpful:

$$P(words|signal) = \alpha\, P(signal|words)P(words)\ .$$

ACOUSTIC MODEL

$P(signal|words)$ is the **acoustic model**. It describes the sounds of words—that "ceiling" begins with a soft "c" and sounds the same as "sealing." (Words that sound the same are called **homophones**.) $P(words)$ is known as the **language model**. It specifies the prior probability of each utterance—for example, that "high ceiling" is a much more likely word sequence than "high sealing."

HOMOPHONES

The language models used in speech recognition systems are usually very simple. The **bigram model** that we describe later in this section gives the probability of each word following each other word. The acoustic model is much more complex. At its heart is an important discovery made in the field of **phonology** (the study of how language sounds), namely, that all human languages use a limited repertoire of about 40 or 50 sounds, called **phones**. Roughly speaking, a phone is the sound that corresponds to a single vowel or consonant, but there are some complications: combinations of letters, such as "th" and "ng" produce single phones, and some letters produce different phones in different contexts (e.g., the "a" in *rat* and *rate*. Figure 15.17 lists phones that are used in English with an example of each. A **phoneme** is the smallest unit of sound that has a distinct meaning to speakers of a particular language. For example, in English the "t" phone in "stick" is the same phoneme as the "t" phone in "tick,"

PHONOLOGY

PHONES

PHONEME

| Vowels | | Consonants B–N | | Consonants P–Z | |
|---|---|---|---|---|---|
| Phone | Example | Phone | Example | Phone | Example |
| [iy] | b**ea**t | [b] | **b**et | [p] | **p**et |
| [ih] | b**i**t | [ch] | **Ch**et | [r] | **r**at |
| [eh] | b**e**t | [d] | **d**ebt | [s] | **s**et |
| [æ] | b**a**t | [f] | **f**at | [sh] | **sh**oe |
| [ah] | b**u**t | [g] | **g**et | [t] | **t**en |
| [ao] | b**ough**t | [hh] | **h**at | [th] | **th**ick |
| [ow] | b**oa**t | [hv] | **h**igh | [dh] | **th**at |
| [uh] | b**oo**k | [jh] | **j**et | [dx] | bu**tt**er |
| [ey] | b**ai**t | [k] | **k**ick | [v] | **v**et |
| [er] | B**er**t | [l] | **l**et | [w] | **w**et |
| [ay] | b**uy** | [el] | bott**le** | [wh] | **wh**ich |
| [oy] | b**oy** | [m] | **m**et | [y] | **y**et |
| [axr] | din**er** | [em] | bott**om** | [z] | **z**oo |
| [aw] | d**ow**n | [n] | **n**et | [zh] | mea**s**ure |
| [ax] | **a**bout | [en] | butt**on** | | |
| [ix] | ros**e**s | [ng] | si**ng** | | |
| [aa] | c**o**t | [eng] | wash**ing** | [-] | *silence* |

**Figure 15.17** The DARPA phonetic alphabet, or **ARPAbet**, listing all the phones used in American English. There are several alternative notations, including an International Phonetic Alphabet (IPA), which contains the phones in all known languages.

but in Thai they are distinguishable as two separate phonemes.

The existence of phones makes it possible to divide the acoustic model into two parts. PRONUNCIATION The first part deals with **pronunciation** and specifies, for each word, a probability distribution over possible phone sequences. For example, "ceiling" is pronounced [s iy l ih ng], or sometimes [s iy l ix ng], or sometimes even [s iy l en]. The phones are not directly observable, so, roughly speaking, speech is represented as a hidden Markov model whose state variable $X_t$ specifies which phone is being uttered at time $t$.

The second part of the acoustic model deals with the way that phones are realized as acoustic signals: that is, the evidence variable $E_t$ for the hidden Markov model gives the observed features of the acoustic signal at time $t$, and the acoustic model specifies $P(E_t|X_t)$, where $X_t$ is the current phone. The model must allow for variations in pitch, speed, and SIGNAL PROCESSING volume, and relies on techniques from **signal processing** to provide signal descriptions that are reasonably robust against these kinds of variations.

The remainder of the section describes the models and algorithms from the bottom up, beginning with acoustic signals and phones, then individual words, and finally entire sentences. We conclude with a description of how all these models are trained and how well the resulting systems work.

### Speech sounds

Sound waves are periodic changes in pressure that propagate through the air. Sound can be measured by a microphone whose diaphragm is displaced by the pressure changes and generates a continuously varying current. An analog-to-digital converter measures the size of the current—which corresponds to the amplitude of the sound wave—at discrete intervals determined by the **sampling rate**. For speech, a sampling rate between 8 and 16 kHz (i.e., 8 to 16,000 times per second) is typical. (High-quality music recordings sample at a rate of 44 kHz or more.) The precision of each measurement is determined by the **quantization factor**; speech recognizers typically keep 8 to 12 bits. That means that a low-end system, sampling at 8 kHz with 8-bit quantization, would require nearly half a megabyte per minute of speech. It would be impractical to construct and manipulate $P(signal|phone)$ distributions with so much signal information; therefore, we need to develop more concise descriptions of the acoustic signal.

SAMPLING RATE

QUANTIZATION FACTOR

First, we observe that although the sound frequencies in speech may be several kHz, the *changes* in the content of the signal occur much less often, perhaps at no more than 100 Hz. Therefore, speech systems summarize the properties of the signal over extended intervals called **frames**. A frame length of about 10 msecs (i.e., 80 samples at 8 kHz) is short enough to ensure that few short-duration phenomena will be smudged out by the summarization process. Within each frame, we represent what is happening with a vector of **features**. For example, we might want to characterize the amount of energy at each of several frequency ranges. Other important features include the overall energy in a frame and the difference from the previous frame. Picking out features from a speech signal is like listening to an orchestra and saying "here the French horns are playing loudly and the violins are playing softly." Figure 15.18 shows the sequence of transformations from the raw sound to a sequence of frames. Note that the frames overlap; this prevents us from losing information if an important acoustic event just happens to fall on a frame boundary.

FRAMES

FEATURES

In our example, we have shown frames with just three features. Real systems have tens or even hundreds of features. If there are $n$ features and each has, say, 256 possible values, then a frame is described by a point in $n$-dimensional space and there are $256^n$ possible

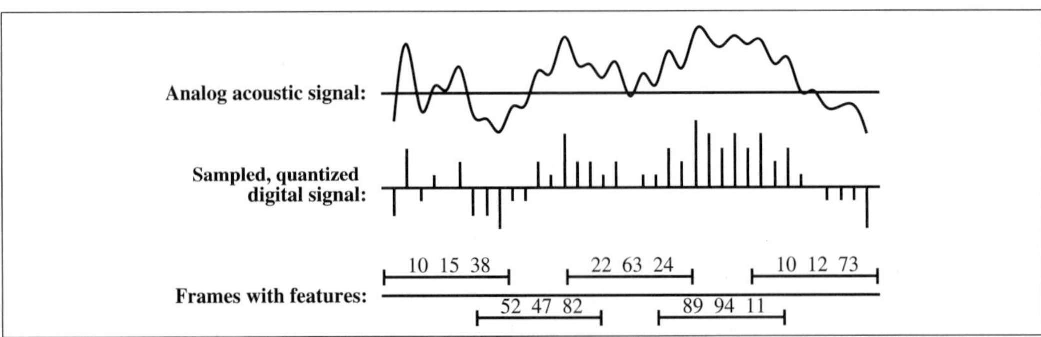


**Figure 15.18** Translating the acoustic signal into a sequence of frames; each frame is described by the values of three acoustic features.

frames. For $n > 2$ it would be impractical to represent the distribution $P(features|phone)$ as an explicit table, so we need further compression. There are two possible approaches:

VECTOR QUANTIZATION

- The method of **vector quantization**, or VQ, divides the $n$-dimensional space into, say, 256 regions labeled C1 through C256. Each frame can then be represented with a single label rather than a vector of $n$ numbers. Thus, the tabulated distribution $P(VQ|phone)$ has 256 probabilities specified for each phone. Vector quantization is no longer popular in large-scale systems.
- Instead of discretizing the feature space, we can use a parameterized continuous distribution to describe $P(features|phone)$. For example, we could use a Gaussian distribution with a different mean and covariance matrix for each phone. This works well if the acoustic realizations of each phone are clustered in a single region of feature space. In practice, the sounds can be spread over several regions, and a **mixture of Gaussians** must be used. A mixture is a weighted sum of $k$ individual distributions, so $P(features|phone)$ has $k$ weights, $k$ mean vectors of size $n$, and $k$ covariance matrices of size $n^2$—that is, $O(kn^2)$ parameters for each phone.

Of course, some information is lost in going from the full speech signal to a VQ label or a set of mixture parameters. The art of signal processing lies in choosing features and regions (or Gaussians) so that the loss of *useful* information is minimized. A given speech sound can be pronounced so many ways: loud or soft, fast or slow, high pitched or low, against a background of silence or of noise, and by any of millions of different speakers, each with a different accent and vocal tract. Signal processing hopes to eliminate the variations while keeping the commonalities that define the sound.[5]

There are two more refinements we need to make to the simple model we have described so far. The first deals with the temporal structure of phones. In normal speech, most phones have a duration of 50–100 milliseconds, or 5–10 frames. The probability model $P(features|phone)$ is the same for all these frames, whereas most phones have a good deal of internal structure. For example, [t] is one of several **stop consonants**, in which the flow of air is cut off for a short period before a sharp release. Examining the acoustic signal, we find that [t] has a silent beginning, a small explosion in the middle, and (usually) a hissing at the end. This internal structure of phones can be captured by the **three-state phone** model; each phone has Onset, Mid, and End states, and each state has its own distribution over features.

STOP CONSONANTS

THREE-STATE PHONE

The second refinement deals with the context in which the phone is uttered. The sound of a given phone can be changed by the surrounding phones.[6] Remember that speech sounds are produced by moving the lips, tongue, and jaw and forcing air through the vocal tract. To coordinate these complex movements at the rate of five or more phones per second, the brain initiates action for a second phone before the first is completed, thereby altering one or both phones. For example, in pronouncing "sweet" the lips are rounded during the production of [s] in anticipation of the following [w]. These **coarticulation effects** are partially captured

COARTICULATION EFFECTS

[5] The complementary problem, **speaker identification**, eliminates the commonalities and keeps the individual differences, and then tries to match the differences to models of individual speakers.

[6] In this sense, the "phone model" of speech should be thought of as a useful approximation rather than an immutable law.

TRIPHONE

by the **triphone** model, in which the acoustic model for each phone is allowed to depend on the preceding and succeeding phones. Thus, the [w] in "sweet is written [w(s,iy)], i.e., [w] with left-context [s] and right-context [iy].

The combined effect of the three-state and triphone models is to increase the number of possible states of the temporal process from $n$ phones in the original phone alphabet ($n \approx 50$ for the ARPAbet) to $3n^3$. Experience shows that the improved accuracy more than offsets the extra expense in terms of inference and learning.

### Words

We can think of each word as specifying a distinct probability distribution $\mathbf{P}(X_{1:t}|word)$, where $X_i$ specifies the phone state in the $i$th frame. Typically, we separate this distribution into two parts. The **pronunciation model** gives a distribution over phone sequences (ignoring metric time and frames), while the **phone model** describes how a phone maps into a sequence of frames.

Consider the word "tomato." According to Gershwin (1937), you say [t ow m ey t ow] and I say [t ow m aa t ow]. The top of Figure 15.19 shows a transition model that provides for this variation. There are only two possible paths through the model, one corresponding to the phone sequence [t ow m ey t ow] and the other to [t ow m aa t ow]. The probability of a path is the product of the probabilities on the arcs that make up the path:

$$P([towmeytow]|\text{"tomato"}) = P([towmaatow]|\text{"tomato"}) = 0.5\ .$$

The second source of phonetic variation is **coarticulation**. For example, the [t] phone is produced with the tongue at the top of the mouth, whereas the [ow] has the tongue near the bottom. When spoken quickly, the tongue often goes to an intermediate position, and we get [t ah] rather than [t ow]. The bottom half of Figure 15.19 gives a more complicated pronunciation model for "tomato" that takes this coarticulation effect into account. In this model, there are four distinct paths, and we have

$$P([towmeytow]|\text{"tomato"}) = P([towmaatow]|\text{"tomato"}) = 0.1\ ,$$
$$P([tahmeytow]|\text{"tomato"}) = P([tahmaatow]|\text{"tomato"}) = 0.4\ .$$

Similar models can be constructed for every word we want to be able to recognize.

The model for a three-state phone is shown as a state transition diagram in Figure 15.20. The model is for a particular phone, [m], but all phones will have models with similar topology. For each phone state, we show the associated acoustic model, assuming that the signal is represented by a VQ label. For example, the model asserts that $P(E_t = C_1 | X_t = [\text{m}]_{\text{Onset}}) = 0.5$. Notice the self-loops in the figure; for instance, the $[\text{m}]_{\text{Mid}}$ state persists with probability 0.9, which means that the $[\text{m}]_{\text{Mid}}$ state has an expected duration of 10 frames. In the model we have, the duration of each phone is independent of the duration of other phones; a more sophisticated model could distinguish between fast and slow speech.

We can construct similar models for each phone, possibly depending on the triphone context. Each word model, when combined with the phone models, gives a complete specification of an HMM. The model specifies the transition probabilities between phone states from frame to frame, as well as the acoustic feature probabilities for each phone state.

(a) Word model with dialect variation:

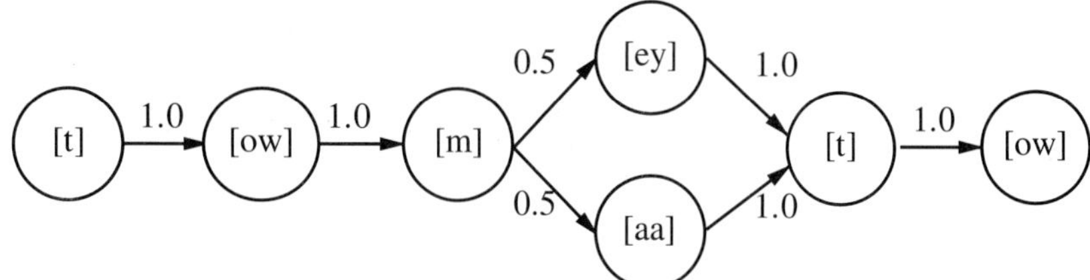


(b) Word model with coarticulation and dialect variations

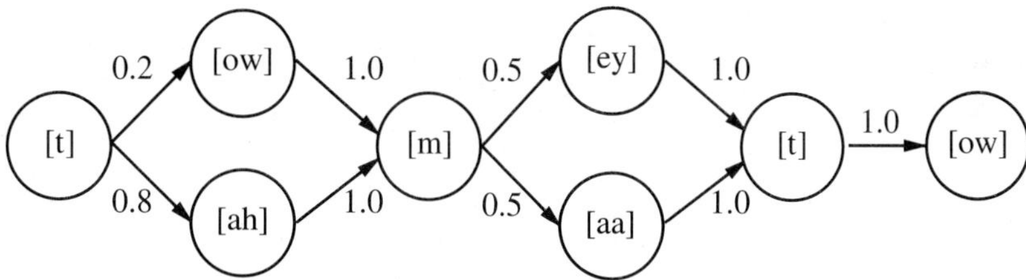


**Figure 15.19** Two pronunciation models of the word "tomato." Each model is shown as a transition diagram with states as circles and arrows showing allowed transitions with their associated probabilities. (a) A model allowing for dialect differences. The 0.5 numbers are estimates based on the two authors' preferred pronunciations. (b) A model with a coarticulation effect on the first vowel, allowing either the [ow] or the [ah] phone.

Phone HMM for [m]:

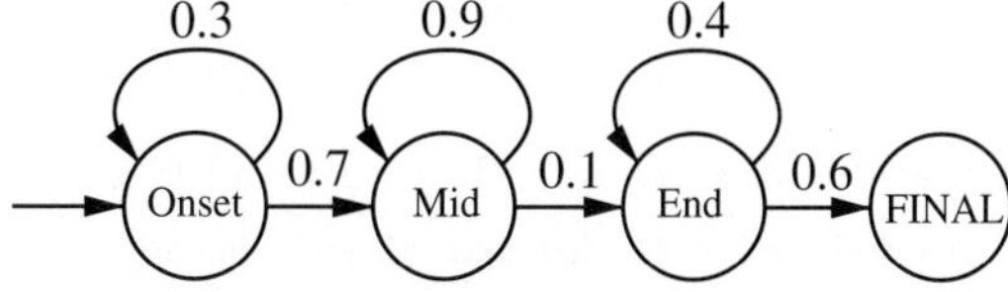


Output probabilities for the phone HMM:

| Onset: | Mid: | End: |
|---|---|---|
| $C_1$: 0.5 | $C_3$: 0.2 | $C_4$: 0.1 |
| $C_2$: 0.2 | $C_4$: 0.7 | $C_6$: 0.5 |
| $C_3$: 0.3 | $C_5$: 0.1 | $C_7$: 0.4 |

**Figure 15.20** An HMM for the three-state phone [m]. Each state has several possible outputs, each with its own probability. The VQ labels $C_1$ through $C_7$ are arbitrary.

ISOLATED WORDS

If we want to recognized **isolated words**—that is, words spoken without any surrounding context and with clear boundaries—then we need to find the word that maximizes

$$P(word|e_{1:t}) = \alpha\, P(e_{1:t}|word)P(word)\ .$$

The prior probability $P(word)$ can be obtained from actual text data. $P(e_{1:t}|word)$ is the likelihood of the sequence of acoustic features according to the word model. Section 15.2 covered the computation of such likelihoods; in particular, Equation (15.5) gives a simple recursive computation whose cost is linear in $t$ and in the number of states of the Markov chain. To find the most likely word, we can perform this calculation for each possible word model, multiply by the prior, and select the best word accordingly.

### Sentences

CONTINUOUS SPEECH

To have a conversation with a human, a machine needs to be able to recognize **continuous speech** rather than just isolated words. One might think that continuous speech is nothing more than a sequence of words, to each of which we can apply the algorithm from the previous section. This approach fails for two reasons. First, we have already seen (page 547) that the sequence of most likely words is not the most likely sequence of words. For example, in the movie *Take the Money and Run*, a bank teller interprets Woody Allen's sloppily written hold-up note as saying "I have a gub." A good language model would suggest "I have a gun" as a much more likely sequence, even though the last word looks more like "gub" than "gun." The second issue we must face with continuous speech is **segmentation**—the problem of deciding where one word ends and the next begins. Anyone who has tried to learn a foreign language will appreciate this problem: at first all the words seem to run together. Gradually, one learns to pick out words from the jumble of sounds. In this case, first impressions are correct; a spectrographic analysis shows that in fluent speech, the words really *do* run together with no silence between them. We learn to identify word boundaries despite the lack of silence.

SEGMENTATION

Let us begin with the language model, whose job in speech recognition is to specify the probability of each possible sequence of words. Using the notation $w_1 \cdots w_n$ to denote a string of $n$ words and $w_i$ to denote the $i$th word of the string, we can write an expression for the probability of a string with the use of the chain rule as follows:[7]

$$\begin{aligned} P(w_1 \cdots w_n) &= P(w_1)\, P(w_2|w_1)\, P(w_3|w_1 w_2) \cdots\ P(w_n|w_1 \cdots w_{n-1}) \\ &= \textstyle\prod_{i=1}^{n} P(w_i|w_1 \cdots w_{i-1})\ . \end{aligned}$$

Most of these terms are quite complex and difficult to estimate or compute. Fortunately, we can approximate this formula with something simpler and still capture a large part of the language model. One simple, popular, and effective approach is the **bigram** model. This model approximates $P(w_i|w_1 \cdots w_{i-1})$ with $P(w_i|w_{i-1})$. In other words, it makes a first-order Markov assumption for word sequences.

BIGRAM

A big advantage of the bigram model is that it is easy to train the model by counting the number of times each word pair occurs in a representative corpus of strings and using the

[7] Strictly speaking, the probability of a word sequence depends strongly on the *context* of the utterance; for example, "I have a gun" is much more common on notes passed to a bank teller than it is in, say, the *Wall Street Journal*. Few speech recognizers handle context, other than by training a special-purpose language model for a particular task.

| Word | Unigram count | Previous words | | | | | | | |
|---|---|---|---|---|---|---|---|---|---|
| | | of | in | is | on | to | from | model | agent |
| the | 33508 | 3833 | 2479 | 832 | 944 | 1365 | 597 | 28 | 24 |
| on | 2573 | 1 | 0 | 33 | 2 | 1 | 0 | 0 | 6 |
| of | 15474 | 0 | 0 | 29 | 1 | 0 | 0 | 88 | 7 |
| to | 11527 | 0 | 4 | 450 | 21 | 4 | 16 | 9 | 82 |
| is | 10566 | 3 | 6 | 1 | 4 | 2 | 1 | 47 | 127 |
| model | 752 | 8 | 1 | 0 | 1 | 14 | 0 | 6 | 4 |
| agent | 2100 | 10 | 3 | 3 | 2 | 3 | 0 | 0 | 36 |
| idea | 241 | 0 | 0 | 0 | 0 | 0 | 0 | 0 | 0 |

**Figure 15.21** A partial table of unigram and bigram counts for the words in this book. "The" is the most common single word with a count of 33,508 (out of 513,893 total words). The bigram "of the" is the most common, at 3,833. Some counts are higher than expected (e.g. 4 for "on is") because the bigram counts ignore punctuation: one sentence might end with "on" and the next begin with "is."

counts to estimate the probabilities. For example, if "a" appears 10,000 times in the training corpus and it is followed by "gun" 37 times, then $\hat{P}(gun_i|a_{i-1}) = 37/10,000$, where by $\hat{P}$ we mean the estimated probability. After such training one would expect "I have" and "a gun" to have high estimated probabilities, while "I has" and "an gun" would have low probabilities. Figure 15.21 shows some bigram counts derived from the words in this book.

TRIGRAM

It is possible to go to a **trigram** model that provides values for $P(w_i|w_{i-1}w_{i-2})$. This is a more powerful language model, capable of judging that "ate a banana" is more likely than "ate a bandanna." For trigram models and to a lesser extent for bigram and unigram models, there is a problem with counts of zero: We wouldn't want to say that a combination of words is impossible just because they didn't happen to appear in the training corpus. The process of **smoothing** gives a small non-zero probability to such combinations. It is discussed on page 835.

Bigram or trigram models are not as sophisticated as some of the grammar models we will see in Chapters 22 and 23, but they account for local context-sensitive effects better and manage to capture some local syntax. For example, the fact that the word pairs "I has" and "man have" get low scores is reflective of subject–verb agreement. The problem is that these relationships can be detected only locally: "the man have" gets a low score, but "the man with the yellow hat have" is not penalized.

Now we consider how to combine the language model with the word models, so that we can handle word sequences properly. We'll assume a bigram language model for simplicity. With such a model, we can combine all the word models (which are composed in turn of pronunciation models and phone models) into one large HMM model. A state in a single-word HMM is a frame labeled by the current phone and phone state (for example, $[\mathrm{m}]_{\mathrm{Onset}}$); a state in a continuous-speech HMM is also labeled with a word, as in $[\mathrm{m}]^{\mathrm{tomato}}_{Onset}$. If each word has an average of $p$ three-state phones in its pronunciation model, and there are $W$

words, then the continuous-speech HMM has $3pW$ states. Transitions can occur between phone states within a given phone, between phones in a given word, and between the final state of one word and the initial state of another. The transitions between words occur with probabilities specified by the bigram model.

Once we have constructed the combined HMM, we can use it to analyze the continuous speech signal. In particular, the Viterbi algorithm embodied in Equation (15.9) can be used to find the most likely state sequence. From this state sequence, we can then extract a word sequence simply by reading the word labels from the states. Thus, the Viterbi algorithm solves the word segmentation problem by using dynamic programming to consider (in effect) all possible word sequences and word boundaries simultaneously.

Notice that we didn't say "we can extract *the most likely* word sequence." The most likely word sequence is not necessarily the one that contains the most likely state sequence. This is because the probability of a word sequence is the sum of the probabilities over all possible state sequences consistent with that word sequence. Comparing two word sequences, say, "a back" and "aback," it might be that case that there are ten alternative state sequences for "a back," each with probability 0.03, but just one state sequence for "aback," with probability 0.20. Viterbi chooses "aback," but "a back" is actually more likely.

A* DECODER

In practice, this difficulty is not life-threatening, but it is serious enough that other approaches have been tried. The most common is the **A* decoder**, which makes ingenious use of A* search (see Chapter 4) to find the most likely word sequence. The idea is to view each word sequence as a path through a graph whose nodes are labeled with words. The successors of a node are all the words that can come next; thus, the graph for all sentences of length $n$ or less has $n$ layers, each of width at most $W$, where $W$ is the number of possible words. With a bigram model, the cost $g(w_1, w_2)$ of an arc between nodes labeled $w_1$ to $w_2$ is given by $-\log P(w_2|w_1)$; in this way, the total path cost of a sequence is

$$Cost(w_1 \cdots w_n) = \sum_{i=1}^{n} -\log P(w_i|w_{i-1}) = -\log \prod_{i=1}^{n} P(w_i|w_{i-1}) .$$

With this definition of path cost, finding the shortest path is exactly equivalent to finding the most likely word sequence. For the process to be efficient, we also need a good heuristic $h(w_i)$ to estimate the cost of completing the word sequence. Obviously, this has something to do with how much of the speech signal is not yet covered by the words on the current path. As yet, no especially interesting heuristics have been devised for this problem.

### Building a speech recognizer

The quality of a speech recognition system depends on the quality of all of its components—the language model, the word pronunciation models, the phone models, and the signal processing algorithms used to extract spectral features from the acoustic signal. We have discussed how the language model can be constructed, and we leave the details of signal processing to other textbooks. We are left with the pronunciation and phone models. The *structure* of the pronunciation models—such as the tomato models in Figure 15.19—is usually developed by hand. Large pronunciation dictionaries are now available for English and other languages, although their accuracy varies greatly. The structure of the three-state phone models is the same for all phones, as shown in Figure 15.20. That leaves the probabilities themselves. How are these to be obtained, given that the models could require hundreds of thousands or millions of parameters?

The only plausible method is to learn the models from actual speech data, of which there is certainly no shortage. The next question is how to do the learning. We give the answer in full in Chapter 20, but we can present the main ideas here. Consider the bigram language model; we explained how to learn it by looking at frequencies of word pairs in actual text. Can we do the same for, say, phone transition probabilities in the pronunciation model? The answer is yes, but only if someone goes to the trouble of annotating every occurrence of each word with the right phone sequence. This is a difficult and error-prone task, but it has been carried out for some standard data sets containing several hours of speech. If we know the phone sequences, we can estimate transition probabilities for the pronunciation models from frequencies of phone pairs. Similarly, if we are given the phone state for each frame—an even more excruciating manual labeling task—then we can estimate transition probabilities for the phone models. Given the phone state and the acoustic features in each frame, we can also estimate the acoustic model, either directly from frequencies (for VQ models) or by using statistical fitting methods (for mixture-of-Gaussian models; see Chapter 20).

The cost and rarity of hand-labeled data, and the fact that the available hand-labeled data sets might not represent the kinds of speakers and acoustic conditions found in a new recognition context, could doom this approach to failure. *Fortunately, the* ***expectation–maximization*** *or EM algorithm learns HMM transition and sensor models without the need for labeled data.* Estimates derived from hand-labeled data can be used to initialize the models; after that, EM takes over and trains the models for the task at hand. The idea is simple: given an HMM and an observation sequence, we can use the smoothing algorithms from Sections 15.2 and 15.3 to compute the probability of each state at each time step and, by a simple extension, the probability of each state–state pair at consecutive time steps. These probabilities can be viewed as *uncertain labels*. From the uncertain labels, we can estimate new transition and sensor probabilities, and the EM procedure repeats. The method is guaranteed to increase the fit between model and data on each iteration, and it generally converges to a much better set of parameter values than those provided by the initial, hand-labeled estimates.

State-of-the-art speech systems use enormous data sets and massive computational resources to train their models. For isolated word recognition under good acoustic conditions (no background noise or reverberation) with a vocabulary of a few thousand words and a single speaker, accuracy can be over 99%. For unrestricted continuous speech with a variety of speakers, 60–80% accuracy is common, even with good acoustic conditions. With background noise and telephone transmission, accuracy degrades further. Although fielded systems have improved continuously for decades, there is still room for many new ideas.

## 15.7 SUMMARY

This chapter has addressed the general problem of representing and reasoning about probabilistic temporal processes. The main points are as follows:

- The changing state of the world is handled by using a set of random variables to represent the state at each point in time.
- Representations can be designed to satisfy the **Markov property**, so that the future is independent of the past given the present. Combined with the assumption that the process is **stationary**—that is, the dynamics do not change over time—this greatly simplifies the representation.
- A temporal probability model can be thought of as containing a **transition model** describing the evolution and a **sensor model** describing the observation process.
- The principal inference tasks in temporal models are **filtering**, **prediction**, **smoothing**, and computing the **most likely explanation**. Each of these can be achieved using simple, recursive algorithms whose runtime is linear in the length of the sequence.
- Three families of temporal models were studied in more depth: **hidden Markov models**, **Kalman filters**, and **dynamic Bayesian networks** (which include the other two as special cases).
- **Speech recognition** and **tracking** are two important applications for temporal probability models.
- Unless special assumptions are made, as in Kalman filters, exact inference with many state variables appears to be intractable. In practice, the **particle filtering** algorithm seems to be an effective approximation algorithm.

## BIBLIOGRAPHICAL AND HISTORICAL NOTES

Many of the basic ideas for estimating the state of dynamical systems came from the mathematician C. F. Gauss (1809), who formulated a deterministic least-squares algorithm for the problem of estimating orbits from astronomical observations. The Russian mathematician A. A. Markov (1913) developed what was later called the **Markov assumption** in his analysis of stochastic processes; he estimated a first-order Markov chain on letters from the text of *Eugene Onegin*. Significant classified work on filtering was done during World War II by Wiener (1942) for continuous-time processes and by Kolmogorov (1941) for discrete-time processes. Although this work led to important technological developments over the next 20 years, its use of a frequency-domain representation made many calculations quite cumbersome. Direct state-space modeling of the stochastic process turned out to be simpler, as shown by Swerling (1959) and Kalman (1960). The latter paper introduced what is now known as the Kalman filter for forward inference in linear systems with Gaussian noise. Important results on smoothing were derived by Rauch *et al.* (1965), and the impressively named Rauch–Tung–Striebel smoother is still a standard technique today. Many early results are gathered in Gelb (1974). Bar-Shalom and Fortmann (1988) give a more modern treatment with a Bayesian flavor, as well as many references to the vast literature on the subject. Chatfield (1989) covers the "classical" approach to time series analysis.

In many applications of Kalman filtering, one must deal not only with uncertain sensing and dynamics, but also with uncertain *identity*; that is, if there are multiple objects being monitored, the system must determine which observations were generated by which objects before it can update each of the state estimates. This is the problem of **data association** (Bar-Shalom and Fortmann, 1988; Bar-Shalom, 1992). With $n$ observations and $n$ tracks (a fairly benign case), there are $n!$ possible assignments of observations to tracks; a proper probabilistic treatment must take all of them into account, and this can be shown to be NP-hard (Cox, 1993; Cox and Hingorani, 1994). Polynomial-time approximation methods based on MCMC appear to work well in practice (Pasula *et al.*, 1999). It is interesting to note that the data association problem is an instance of probabilistic inference in a *first-order* language; unlike most probabilistic inference problems, which are purely propositional, data association involves *objects* as well as the *identity relation*. It is therefore intimately connected to the first-order probabilistic languages that were mentioned in Chapter 14. Recent work has shown that reasoning about identity in general, and data association in particular, can be carried out within the first-order probabilistic framework (Pasula and Russell, 2001).

DATA ASSOCIATION

The hidden Markov model and associated algorithms for inference and learning, including the forward–backward algorithm, were developed by Baum and Petrie (1966). Similar ideas also appeared independently in the Kalman filtering community (Rauch *et al.*, 1965). The forward–backward algorithm was one of the main precursors of the general formulation of the EM algorithm (Dempster *et al.*, 1977); see also Chapter 20. Constant-space smoothing appears in Binder *et al.* (1997b), as does the divide-and-conquer algorithm developed in Exercise 15.3.

Dynamic Bayesian networks (DBNs) can be viewed as a sparse encoding of a Markov process and were first used in AI by Dean and Kanazawa (1989b), Nicholson (1992), and Kjaerulff (1992). The last work includes a generic extension to the HUGIN belief net system to provide the necessary facilities for dynamic Bayesian network generation and compilation. Dynamic Bayesian networks have become popular for modeling a variety of complex motion processes in computer vision (Huang *et al.*, 1994; Intille and Bobick, 1999). The link between HMMs and DBNs, and between the forward–backward algorithm and Bayesian network propagation, was made explicitly by Smyth *et al.* (1997). A further unification with Kalman filters (and other statistical models) appears in Roweis and Ghahramani (1999).

The particle filtering algorithm described in Section 15.5 has a particularly interesting history. The first sampling algorithms for filtering were developed in the control theory community by Handschin and Mayne (1969), and the resampling idea that is the core of particle filtering appeared in a Russian control journal (Zaritskii *et al.*, 1975). It was later reinvented in statistics as **sequential importance-sampling resampling**, or **SIR** (Rubin, 1988; Liu and Chen, 1998), in control theory as particle filtering (Gordon *et al.*, 1993; Gordon, 1994), in AI as **survival of the fittest** (Kanazawa *et al.*, 1995), and in computer vision as **condensation** (Isard and Blake, 1996). The paper by Kanazawa *et al.* (1995) includes an improvement called **evidence reversal** whereby the state at time $t + 1$ is sampled conditional on both the state at time $t$ *and the evidence at time* $t + 1$. This allows the evidence to influence sample generation directly and was proved by Doucet (1997) to reduce the approximation error.

Other methods for approximate filtering include the **decayed MCMC** algorithm (Marthi *et al.*, 2002) and the factored approximation method of Boyen *et al.* (1999). Both of these methods have the important property that the approximation error does not diverge over time. Variational techniques (see Chapter 14) have also been developed for temporal models. Ghahramani and Jordan (1997) discuss an approximation algorithm for the **factorial HMM**, a DBN in which two or more independently evolving Markov chains are linked by a shared observation stream. Jordan *et al.* (1998) cover a number of other applications. Properties of mixing times are discussed by Pak (2001) and by (Luby and Vigoda, 1999).

The prehistory of speech recognition began in the 1920s with Radio Rex, a voice-activated toy dog. Rex jumped in response to sound frequencies near 500 Hz, which corresponds to the [eh] vowel in "Rex!" Somewhat more serious work began after World War II. At AT&T Bell Labs, a system was built for recognizing isolated digits (Davis *et al.*, 1952) by means of simple pattern matching of acoustic features. Phone transition probabilities were first used in a system built at University College, London, by Fry (1959) and Denes (1959). Starting in 1971, the Defense Advanced Research Projects Agency (DARPA) of the United States Department of Defense funded four competing five-year projects to develop high-performance speech recognition systems. The winner, and the only system to meet the goal of 90% accuracy with a 1000-word vocabulary, was the HARPY system at CMU (Lowerre, 1976; Lowerre and Reddy, 1980).[8] The final version of HARPY was derived from a system called DRAGON built by CMU graduate student James Baker (1975); DRAGON was the first to use HMMs for speech. Almost simultaneously, Jelinek (1976) at IBM had developed another HMM-based system. From that point onwards, probabilistic methods in general, and HMMs in particular, came to dominate speech recognition research and development. Recent years have been characterized by incremental progress, larger data sets and models, and more rigorous competitions on more realistic speech tasks. Some researchers have explored the possibility of using DBNs instead of HMMs for speech, with the aim of using the greater expressive power of DBNs to capture more of the complex hidden state of the speech apparatus (Zweig and Russell, 1998; Richardson *et al.*, 2000).

Several good textbooks on speech recognition are available (Rabiner and Juang, 1993; Jelinek, 1997; Gold and Morgan, 2000; Huang *et al.*, 2001). Waibel and Lee (1990) collect important papers in the area, including some tutorial ones. The presentation in this chapter drew on the survey by Kay, Gawron, and Norvig (1994) and on the textbook by Jurafsky and Martin (2000). Speech recognition research is published in *Computer Speech and Language*, *Speech Communications*, and the IEEE *Transactions on Acoustics, Speech, and Signal Processing* and at the DARPA Workshops on Speech and Natural Language Processing and the Eurospeech, ICSLP, and ASRU conferences.

---

[8] The second-ranked system in the competition, HEARSAY-II (Erman *et al.*, 1980), had a great deal of influence on other branches of AI research because of its use of the **blackboard architecture**. It was a rule-based expert system with a number of more or less independent, modular **knowledge sources** that communicated via a common **blackboard** from which they could write and read. Blackboard systems are the foundation of modern user interface architectures.

## EXERCISES

**15.1** Show that any second-order Markov process can be rewritten as a first-order Markov process with an augmented set of state variables. Can this always be done *parsimoniously*; that is, without increasing the number of parameters needed to specify the transition model?

**15.2** In this exercise, we examine what happens to the probabilities in the umbrella world in the limit of long time sequences.

**a.** Suppose we observe an unending sequence of days on which the umbrella appears. Show that, as the days go by, the probability of rain on the current day increases monotonically towards a fixed point. Calculate this fixed point.

**b.** Now consider *forecasting* further and further into the future, given just the first two umbrella observations. First, compute the probability $P(r_{2+k}|u_1, u_2)$ for $k = 1 \ldots 20$ and plot the results. You should see that the probability converges towards a fixed point. Calculate the exact value of this fixed point.

**15.3** This exercise develops a space-efficient variant of the forward–backward algorithm described in Figure 15.4. We wish to compute $\mathbf{P}(\mathbf{X}_k|\mathbf{e}_{1:t})$ for $k = 1, \ldots, t$. This will be done with a divide-and-conquer approach.

**a.** Suppose, for simplicity, that $t$ is odd, and let the halfway point be $h = (t + 1)/2$. Show that $\mathbf{P}(\mathbf{X}_k|\mathbf{e}_{1:t})$ can be computed for $k = 1, \ldots, h$ given just the initial forward message $\mathbf{f}_{1:0}$, the backward message $\mathbf{b}_{h+1:t}$, and the evidence $\mathbf{e}_{1:h}$.

**b.** Show a similar result for the second half of the sequence.

**c.** Given the results of (a) and (b), a recursive divide-and-conquer algorithm can be constructed by first running forward along the sequence and then backwards from the end, storing just the required messages at the middle and the ends. Then the algorithm is called on each half. Write out the algorithm in detail.

**d.** Compute the time and space complexity of the algorithm as a function of $t$, the length of the sequence. How does this change if we divide the input into more than two pieces?

**15.4** On page 547, we outlined a flawed procedure for finding the most likely state sequence, given an observation sequence. The procedure involves finding the most likely state at each time step, using smoothing, and returning the sequence composed of these states. Show that, for some temporal probability models and observation sequences, this procedure returns an impossible state sequence (i.e., the posterior probability of the sequence is zero).

**15.5** Often, we wish to monitor a continuous-state system whose behavior switches unpredictably among a set of $k$ distinct "modes." For example, an aircraft trying to evade a missile can execute a series of distinct maneuvers that the missile may attempt to track. A Bayesian network representation of such a **switching Kalman filter** model is shown in Figure 15.22.

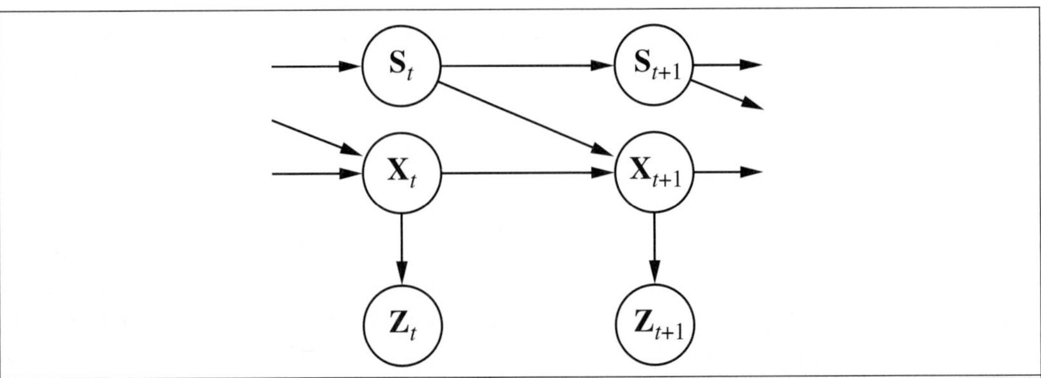


**Figure 15.22** A Bayesian network representation of a switching Kalman filter. The switching variable $S_t$ is a discrete state variable whose value determines the transition model for the continuous state variables $\mathbf{X}_t$. For any discrete state $i$, the transition model $\mathbf{P}(\mathbf{X}_{t+1}|\mathbf{X}_t, S_t = i)$ is a linear Gaussian model, just as in a regular Kalman filter. The transition model for the discrete state, $\mathbf{P}(S_{t+1}|S_t)$, can be thought of as a matrix, as in a hidden Markov model.

**a.** Suppose that the discrete state $S_t$ has $k$ possible values and that the prior continuous state estimate $\mathbf{P}(\mathbf{X}_0)$ is a multivariate Gaussian distribution. Show that the prediction $\mathbf{P}(\mathbf{X}_1)$ is a **mixture of Gaussians**—that is, a weighted sum of Gaussians such that the weights sum to 1.

**b.** Show that if the current continuous state estimate $\mathbf{P}(\mathbf{X}_t|\mathbf{e}_{1:t})$ is a mixture of $m$ Gaussians, then in the general case the updated state estimate $\mathbf{P}(\mathbf{X}_{t+1}|\mathbf{e}_{1:t+1})$ will be a mixture of $km$ Gaussians.

**c.** What aspect of the temporal process do the weights in the Gaussian mixture represent?

Together, the results in (a) and (b) show that the representation of the posterior grows without limit even for switching Kalman filters, which are the simplest hybrid dynamic models.

**15.6** Complete the missing step in the derivation of Equation (15.17), the first update step for the one-dimensional Kalman filter.

**15.7** Let us examine the behavior of the variance update in Equation (15.18).

**a.** Plot the value of $\sigma_t^2$ as a function of $t$, given various values for $\sigma_x^2$ and $\sigma_z^2$.

**b.** Show that the update has a fixed point $\sigma^2$ such that $\sigma_t^2 \to \sigma^2$ as $t \to \infty$, and calculate the value of $\sigma^2$.

**c.** Give a qualitative explanation for what happens as $\sigma_x^2 \to 0$ and as $\sigma_z^2 \to 0$.

**15.8** Show how to represent an HMM as a recursive relational probabilistic model, as suggested in Section 14.6.

**15.9** In this exercise, we analyze in more detail the persistent-failure model for the battery sensor in Figure 15.13(a).

**a.** Figure 15.13(b) stops at $t = 32$. Describe qualitatively what should happen as $t \to \infty$ if the sensor continues to read 0.

**b.** Suppose that the external temperature affects the battery sensor in such a way that transient failures become more likely as temperature increases. Show how to augment the DBN structure in Figure 15.13(a), and explain any required changes to the CPTs.

**c.** Given the new network structure, can battery readings be used by the robot to infer the current temperature?

**15.10** Consider applying the variable elimination algorithm to the umbrella DBN unrolled for three slices, where the query is $\mathbf{P}(R_3|U_1, U_2, U_3)$. Show that the complexity of the algorithm—the size of the largest factor—is the same, regardless of whether the rain variables are eliminated in forward or backward order.

**15.11** The model of "tomato" in Figure 15.19 allows for a coarticulation on the first vowel by giving two possible phones. An alternative approach is to use a triphone model in which the [ow(t,m)] phone automatically includes the change in vowel sound. Draw a complete triphone model for "tomato," including the dialect variation.

**15.12** Calculate the most probable path through the HMM in Figure 15.20 for the output sequence $[C_1, C_2, C_3, C_4, C_4, C_6, C_7]$. Also give its probability.

# 16 MAKING SIMPLE DECISIONS

*In which we see how an agent should make decisions so that it gets what it wants—on average, at least.*

In this chapter, we return to the idea of utility theory that was introduced in Chapter 13 and show how it is combined with probability theory to yield a decision-theoretic agent—an agent that can make rational decisions based on what it believes and what it wants. Such an agent can make decisions in contexts where uncertainty and conflicting goals leave a logical agent with no way to decide. In effect, a goal-based agent has a binary distinction between good (goal) and bad (non-goal) states, while a decision-theoretic agent has a continuous measure of state quality.

Section 16.1 introduces the basic principle of decision theory: the maximization of expected utility. Section 16.2 shows that the behavior of any rational agent can be captured by supposing a utility function that is being maximized. Section 16.3 discusses the nature of utility functions in more detail, and in particular their relation to individual quantities such as money. Section 16.4 shows how to handle utility functions that depend on several quantities. In Section 16.5, we describe the implementation of decision-making systems. In particular, we introduce a formalism called **decision networks** (also known as **influence diagrams**) that extends Bayesian networks by incorporating actions and utilities. The remainder of the chapter discusses issues that arise in applications of decision theory to expert systems.

## 16.1 COMBINING BELIEFS AND DESIRES UNDER UNCERTAINTY

In the *Port-Royal Logic*, written in 1662, the French philosopher Arnauld stated

> To judge what one must do to obtain a good or avoid an evil, it is necessary to consider not only the good and the evil in itself, but also the probability that it happens or does not happen; and to view geometrically the proportion that all these things have together.

Modern texts talk of utility rather than good and evil, but the principle is exactly the same. An agent's preferences between world states are captured by a **utility function**, which assigns a single number to express the desirability of a state. Utilities are combined with outcome probabilities of actions to give an expected utility for each action.

We will use the notation $U(S)$ to denote the utility of state $S$ according to the agent that is making the decisions. For now, we will consider states as complete snapshots of the world, similar to the **situations** of Chapter 10. This will simplify our initial discussions, but it can become rather cumbersome to specify the utility of each possible state separately. In Section 16.4, we will see how states can be decomposed under some circumstances for the purpose of assigning utilities.

A nondeterministic action $A$ will have possible outcome states $Result_i(A)$, where the index $i$ ranges over the different outcomes. Prior to the execution of $A$, the agent assigns probability $P(Result_i(A)|Do(A), E)$ to each outcome, where $E$ summarizes the agent's available evidence about the world and $Do(A)$ is the proposition that action $A$ is executed in the current state. Then we can calculate the **expected utility** of the action given the evidence, $EU(A|E)$, using the following formula:

EXPECTED UTILITY

$$EU(A|E) = \sum_i P(Result_i(A)|Do(A), E)\, U(Result_i(A)) \,. \tag{16.1}$$

MAXIMUM EXPECTED UTILITY

The principle of **maximum expected utility** (MEU) says that a rational agent should choose an action that maximizes the agent's expected utility. If we wanted to choose the best sequence of actions using this equation we would have to enumerate all action sequences and choose the best; this is clearly infeasible for long sequences. Therefore, this chapter will focus on simple decisions (usually a single action) and the next chapter will introduce new techniques for efficiently dealing with action sequences.

In a sense, the MEU principle could be seen as defining all of AI. All an intelligent agent has to do is calculate the various quantities, maximize utility over its actions, and away it goes. But this does not mean that the AI problem is *solved* by the definition!

Although the MEU principle defines the right action to take in any decision problem, the computations involved can be prohibitive, and it is sometimes difficult even to formulate the problem completely. Knowing the initial state of the world requires perception, learning, knowledge representation, and inference. Computing $P(Result_i(A)|Do(A), E)$ requires a complete causal model of the world and, as we saw in Chapter 14, NP-hard inference in Bayesian networks. Computing the utility of each state, $U(Result_i(A))$, often requires searching or planning, because an agent does not know how good a state is until it knows where it can get to from that state. So, decision theory is not a panacea that solves the AI problem. On the other hand, it does provide a framework into which we can see where all the components of an AI system fit.

The MEU principle has a clear relation to the idea of performance measures introduced in Chapter 2. The basic idea is very simple. Consider the environments that could lead to an agent having a given percept history, and consider the different agents that we could design.

*If an agent maximizes a utility function that correctly reflects the performance measure by which its behavior is being judged, then it will achieve the highest possible performance score if we average over the environments in which the agent could be placed.* This is the central justification for the MEU principle itself. While the claim may seem tautological, it does in fact embody a very important transition from a global, external criterion of rationality—the performance measure over environment histories—to a local, internal criterion involving the maximization of a utility function applied to the next state.

ONE-SHOT DECISIONS

In this chapter, we will be concerned only with single or **one-shot decisions**, whereas Chapter 2 defined performance measures over environment histories, which usually involve many decisions. In the next chapter, which covers the case of **sequential decisions**, we will show how these two views can be reconciled.

## 16.2 THE BASIS OF UTILITY THEORY

Intuitively, the principle of Maximum Expected Utility (MEU) seems like a reasonable way to make decisions, but it is by no means obvious that it is the *only* rational way. After all, why should maximizing the *average* utility be so special? Why not try to maximize the sum of the cubes of the possible utilities, or try to minimize the worst possible loss? Also, couldn't an agent act rationally just by expressing preferences between states, without giving them numeric values? Finally, why should a utility function with the required properties exist at all? Perhaps a rational agent can have a preference structure that is too complex to be captured by something as simple as a single real number for each state.

### Constraints on rational preferences

These questions can be answered by writing down some constraints on the preferences that a rational agent should have and then showing that the MEU principle can be derived from the constraints. We use the following notation to describe an agent's preferences:

$A \succ B$ $A$ is preferred to $B$.

$A \sim B$ the agent is indifferent between $A$ and $B$.

$A \succsim B$ the agent prefers $A$ to $B$ or is indifferent between them.

LOTTERIES

Now the obvious question is, what sorts of things are $A$ and $B$? If the agent's actions are deterministic, then $A$ and $B$ will typically be the concrete, fully specified outcome states of those actions. In the more general, nondeterministic case, $A$ and $B$ will be **lotteries**. A lottery is essentially a probability distribution over a set of actual outcomes (the "prizes" of the lottery). A lottery $L$ with possible outcomes $C_1, \ldots, C_n$ that can occur with probabilities $p_1, \ldots, p_n$ is written

$$L = [p_1, C_1;\ p_2, C_2;\ \ldots\ p_n, C_n] .$$

(A lottery with only one outcome can be written either as $A$ or as $[1, A]$.) In general, each outcome of a lottery can be either an atomic state or another lottery. The primary issue for utility theory is to understand how preferences between complex lotteries are related to preferences between the underlying states in those lotteries.

To do this, we impose reasonable constraints on the preference relation, much as we imposed rationality constraints on degrees of belief in order to obtain the axioms of probability in Chapter 13. One reasonable constraint is that preference should be **transitive**: that is, if $A \succ B$ and $B \succ C$, then we would expect that $A \succ C$. We argue for transitivity by showing that an agent whose preferences do not respect transitivity would behave irrationally. Suppose, for example, that an agent has the nontransitive preferences $A \succ B \succ C \succ A$, where $A$, $B$, and $C$ are goods that can be freely exchanged. If the agent currently has $A$, then we could offer to trade $C$ for $A$ and some cash. The agent prefers $C$, and so would be willing to give up some amount of cash to make this trade. We could then offer to trade $B$ for $C$, extracting more cash, and finally trade $A$ for $B$. This brings us back where we started from, except that the agent has less money (Figure 16.1(a)). We can keep going around the cycle until the agent has no money at all. Clearly, this case the agent has not acted rationally.

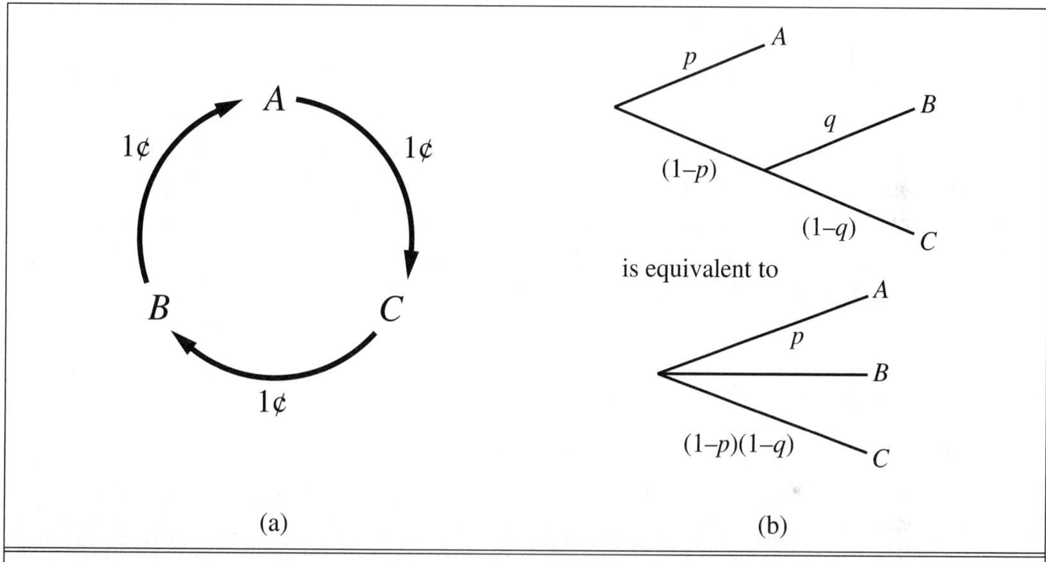


**Figure 16.1** (a) A cycle of exchanges showing that the nontransitive preferences $A \succ B \succ C \succ A$ result in irrational behavior. (b) The decomposability axiom.

The following six constraints are known as the axioms of utility theory. They specify the most obvious semantic constraints on preferences and lotteries.

ORDERABILITY

◇ **Orderability**: Given any two states, a rational agent must either prefer one to the other or else rate the two as equally preferable. That is, the agent cannot avoid deciding. As we said on page 474, refusing to bet is like refusing to allow time to pass.

$$(A \succ B) \vee (B \succ A) \vee (A \sim B) .$$

TRANSITIVITY

◇ **Transitivity**: Given any three states, if an agent prefers $A$ to $B$ and prefers $B$ to $C$, then the agent must prefer $A$ to $C$.

$$(A \succ B) \wedge (B \succ C) \Rightarrow (A \succ C) .$$

CONTINUITY

◇ **Continuity**: If some state $B$ is between $A$ and $C$ in preference, then there is some probability $p$ for which the rational agent will be indifferent between getting $B$ for sure and the lottery that yields $A$ with probability $p$ and $C$ with probability $1 - p$.

$$A \succ B \succ C \Rightarrow \exists p \; [p, A;\; 1 - p, C] \sim B .$$

SUBSTITUTABILITY

◇ **Substitutability**: If an agent is indifferent between two lotteries, $A$ and $B$, then the agent is indifferent between two more complex lotteries that are the same except that $B$ is substituted for $A$ in one of them. This holds regardless of the probabilities and the other outcome(s) in the lotteries.

$$A \sim B \Rightarrow [p, A;\ 1-p, C] \sim [p, B; 1-p, C]\ .$$

MONOTONICITY

◇ **Monotonicity**: Suppose there are two lotteries that have the same two outcomes, $A$ and $B$. If an agent prefers $A$ to $B$, then the agent must prefer the lottery that has a higher probability for $A$ (and vice versa).

$$A \succ B \Rightarrow (p \geq q \Leftrightarrow [p, A;\ 1-p, B] \succsim [q, A;\ 1-q, B])\ .$$

DECOMPOSABILITY

◇ **Decomposability**: Compound lotteries can be reduced to simpler ones using the laws of probability. This has been called the "no fun in gambling" rule because it says that two consecutive lotteries can be compressed into a single equivalent lottery, as shown in Figure 16.1(b).[1]

$$[p, A;\ 1-p, [q, B;\ 1-q, C]] \sim [p, A;\ (1-p)q, B;\ (1-p)(1-q), C]\ .$$

### And then there was Utility

Notice that the axioms of utility theory do not say anything about utility: They talk only about preferences. Preference is assumed to be a basic property of rational agents. The existence of a utility function *follows* from the axioms of utility:

1. **Utility principle**
   If an agent's preferences obey the axioms of utility, then there exists a real-valued function $U$ that operates on states such that $U(A) > U(B)$ if and only if $A$ is preferred to $B$, and $U(A) = U(B)$ if and only if the agent is indifferent between $A$ and $B$.

$$U(A) > U(B) \Leftrightarrow A \succ B\ ;$$
$$U(A) = U(B) \Leftrightarrow A \sim B\ .$$

2. **Maximum Expected Utility principle**
   The utility of a lottery is the sum of the probability of each outcome times the utility of that outcome.

$$U([p_1, S_1; \ldots ; p_n, S_n]) = \sum_i p_i U(S_i)\ .$$

In other words, once the probabilities and utilities of the possible outcome states are specified, the utility of a compound lottery involving those states is completely determined. Because the outcome of a nondeterministic action is a lottery, this gives us the MEU decision rule from Equation (16.1).

It is important to remember that the existence of a utility function that describes an agent's preference behavior does not necessarily mean that the agent is *explicitly* maximizing that utility function in its own deliberations. As we showed in Chapter 2, rational behavior can be generated in any number of ways, some of which are more efficient than explicit

[1] We can account for the enjoyment of gambling by encoding gambling events into the state description; for example, "Have \$10 and gambled" could be preferred to "Have \$10 and didn't gamble."

utility maximization. By observing a rational agent's preferences, however, it is possible to construct the utility function that represents what it is that the agent's actions are actually trying to achieve.

## 16.3 Utility Functions

Utility is a function that maps from states to real numbers. Is that all we can say about utility functions? Strictly speaking, that is it. Beyond the constraints listed earlier, an agent can have any preferences it likes. For example, an agent might prefer to have a prime number of dollars in its bank account; in which case, if it had \$16 it would give away \$3. It might prefer a dented 1973 Ford Pinto to a shiny new Mercedes. Preferences can also interact: for example, it might only prefer prime numbers of dollars when it owns the Pinto, but when it owns the Mercedes, it might prefer more dollars to less.

If all utility functions were as arbitrary as this, however, then utility theory would not be of much help because we would have to observe the agent's preferences in every possible combination of circumstances before being able to make any predictions about its behavior. Fortunately, the preferences of real agents are usually more systematic. Conversely, there are systematic ways of designing utility functions that, when installed in an artificial agent, cause it to generate the kinds of behavior we want.

### The utility of money

Utility theory has its roots in economics, and economics provides one obvious candidate for a utility measure: money (or more specifically, an agent's total net assets). The almost universal exchangeability of money for all kinds of goods and services suggests that money plays a significant role in human utility functions. (In fact, most people think of economics as the study of money, when actually the root of the word *economy* refers to management, and its current emphasis is on the management of choice.)

If we restrict our attention to actions that only affect the amount of money that an agent has, then it will usually be the case that the agent prefers more money to less, all other things being equal. We say that the agent exhibits a **monotonic preference** for definite amounts of money. This is not, however, sufficient to guarantee that money behaves as a utility function, because it says nothing about preferences between *lotteries* involving money.

MONOTONIC PREFERENCE

Suppose you have triumphed over the other competitors in a television game show. The host now offers you a choice: either you can take the \$1,000,000 prize or you can gamble it on the flip of a coin. If the coin comes up heads, you end up with nothing, but if it comes up tails, you get \$3,000,000. If you're like most people, you would decline the gamble and pocket the million. Are you being irrational?

EXPECTED MONETARY VALUE

Assuming you believe that the coin is fair, the **expected monetary value** (EMV) of the gamble is $\frac{1}{2}(\$0) + \frac{1}{2}(\$3{,}000{,}000) = \$1{,}500{,}000$, and the EMV of taking the original prize is of course \$1,000,000, which is less. But that does not necessarily mean that accepting the gamble is a better decision. Suppose we use $S_n$ to denote the state of possessing total wealth $\$n$, and that your current wealth is $\$k$. Then the expected utilities of the two actions of accepting and declining the gamble are

$$\begin{aligned} EU(Accept) &= \tfrac{1}{2}U(S_k) + \tfrac{1}{2}U(S_{k+3{,}000{,}000}) , \\ EU(Decline) &= U(S_{k+1{,}000{,}000}) . \end{aligned}$$

To determine what to do, we need to assign utilities to the outcome states. Utility is not directly proportional to monetary value, because the utility—the positive change in lifestyle—for your first million is very high (or so we are told), whereas the utility for an additional million is much smaller. Suppose you assign a utility of 5 to your current financial status ($S_k$), a 10 to the state $S_{k+3{,}000{,}000}$, and an 8 to the state $S_{k+1{,}000{,}000}$. Then the rational action would be to decline, because the expected utility of accepting is only 7.5 (less than the 8 for declining). On the other hand, suppose that you happen to have $500,000,000 in the bank already (and appear on game shows just for fun, one assumes). In this case, the gamble is probably acceptable, because the additional benefit of the 503rd million is probably about the same as that of the 501st million.

In a pioneering study of actual utility functions, Grayson (1960) found that the utility of money was almost exactly proportional to the *logarithm* of the amount. (This idea was first suggested by Bernoulli (1738); see Exercise 16.3.) One particular curve, for a certain Mr. Beard, is shown in Figure 16.2(a). The data obtained for Mr. Beard's preferences are consistent with a utility function

$$U(S_{k+n}) = -263.31 + 22.09 \log(n + 150,000)$$

for the range between $n = -\$150,000$ and $n = \$800,000$.

We should not assume that this is the definitive utility function for monetary value, but it is likely that most people have a utility function that is concave for positive wealth. Going into debt is usually considered disastrous, but preferences between different levels of debt can display a reversal of the concavity associated with positive wealth. For example,

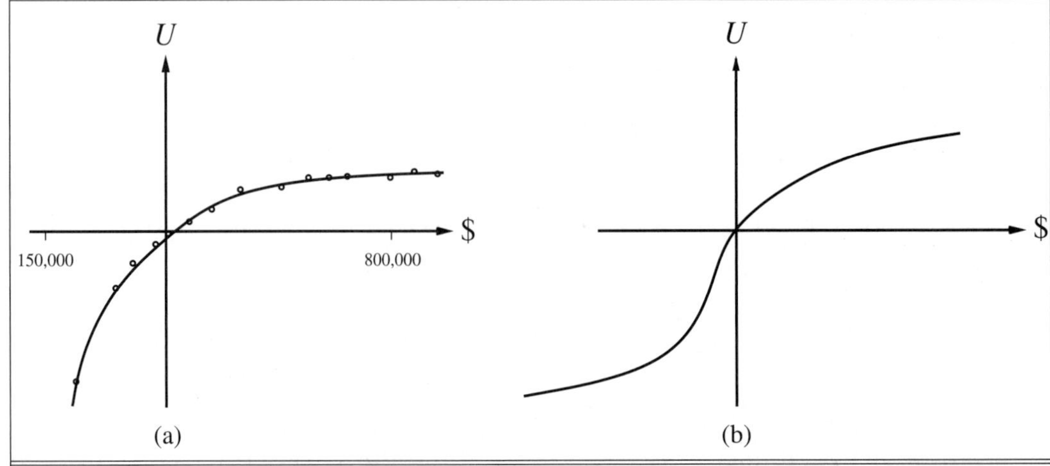


**Figure 16.2** The utility of money. (a) Empirical data for Mr. Beard over a limited range. (b) A typical curve for the full range.

someone already \$10,000,000 in debt might well accept a gamble on a fair coin with a gain of \$10,000,000 for heads and a loss of \$20,000,000 for tails.[2] This yields the S-shaped curve shown in Figure 16.2(b).

If we restrict our attention to the positive part of the curves, where the slope is decreasing, then for any lottery $L$, the utility of being faced with that lottery is less than the utility of being handed the expected monetary value of the lottery as a sure thing:

$$U(L) < U(S_{EMV(L)}) .$$

RISK-AVERSE

RISK-SEEKING

CERTAINTY EQUIVALENT

INSURANCE PREMIUM

That is, agents with curves of this shape are **risk-averse**: they prefer a sure thing with a payoff that is less than the expected monetary value of a gamble. On the other hand, in the "desperate" region at large negative wealth in Figure 16.2(b), the behavior is **risk-seeking**. The value an agent will accept in lieu of a lottery is called the **certainty equivalent** of the lottery. Studies have shown that most people will accept about \$400 in lieu of a gamble that gives \$1000 half the time and \$0 the other half—that is, the certainty equivalent of the lottery is \$400. The difference between the expected monetary value of a lottery and its certainty equivalent is called the **insurance premium**. Risk aversion is the basis for the insurance industry, because it means that insurance premiums are positive. People would rather pay a small insurance premium than gamble the price of their house against the chance of a fire. From the insurance company's point of view, the price of the house is very small compared with the firm's total reserves. This means that the insurer's utility curve is approximately linear over such a small region, and the gamble costs the company almost nothing.

RISK-NEUTRAL

Notice that for *small* changes in wealth relative to the current wealth, almost any curve will be approximately linear. An agent that has a linear curve is said to be **risk-neutral**. For gambles with small sums, therefore, we expect risk neutrality. In a sense, this justifies the simplified procedure that proposed small gambles to assess probabilities and to justify the axioms of probability in Chapter 13.

### Utility scales and utility assessment

The axioms of utility do not specify a unique utility function for an agent, given its preference behavior. For example, we can transform a utility function $U(S)$ into

$$U'(S) = k_1 + k_2 U(S) ,$$

where $k_1$ is a constant and $k_2$ is any *positive* constant. Clearly, this linear transformation leaves the agent's behavior unchanged.

VALUE FUNCTION

ORDINAL UTILITY FUNCTION

In *deterministic* contexts, where there are states but no lotteries, behavior is unchanged by any *monotonic* transformation. For example, we can take the cube root of all the utilities without affecting the preference ordering on actions. An agent in a deterministic environment is said to have a **value function** or **ordinal utility function**; the function really provides just rankings of states rather than meaningful numerical values. We saw this distinction in Chapter 6 for games: evaluation functions in deterministic games such as chess are value functions, whereas evaluation functions in nondeterministic games like backgammon are true utility functions.

---

[2] Such behavior might be called desperate, but it is rational if one is already in a desperate situation.

### HUMAN JUDGMENT AND FALLIBILITY

Decision theory is a **normative** theory: it describes how a rational agent *should* act. The application of economic theory would be greatly enhanced if it were also a **descriptive** theory of actual human decision making. However, there is experimental evidence indicating that people systematically violate the axioms of utility theory. An example is given by the psychologists Tversky and Kahneman (1982), based on an example by the economist Allais (1953). Subjects in this experiment are given a choice between lotteries $A$ and $B$ and then between $C$ and $D$:

$$A: \ 80\% \text{ chance of } \$4000 \qquad C: \ 20\% \text{ chance of } \$4000$$
$$B: \ 100\% \text{ chance of } \$3000 \qquad D: \ 25\% \text{ chance of } \$3000\,.$$

The majority of subjects choose $B$ over $A$ and $C$ over $D$. But if we assign $U(\$0) = 0$, then the first of these choices implies that $0.8U(\$4000) < U(\$3000)$, whereas the second choice implies exactly the reverse. In other words, there seems to be no utility function that is consistent with these choices. One possible conclusion is that humans are simply irrational by the standards of our utility axioms. An alternative view is that the analysis does not take into account **regret**—the feeling that humans know they would experience if they gave up a certain reward ($B$) for an 80% chance at a higher reward and then lost. In other words, if $A$ is chosen, there is a 20% chance of getting no money *and feeling like a complete idiot.*

Kahneman and Tversky go on to develop a descriptive theory that explains how people are risk-averse with high-probability events, but are willing to take more risks with unlikely payoffs. The connection between this finding and AI is that the choices our agents can make are only as good as the preferences they are based on. If our human informants insist on contradictory preference judgments, there is nothing our agent can do to be consistent with them.

Fortunately, preference judgments made by humans are often open to revision in the light of further consideration. In early work at Harvard Business School on assessing the utility of money, Keeney and Raiffa (1976, p. 210) found the following:

> A great deal of empirical investigation has shown that there is a serious deficiency in the assessment protocol. Subjects tend to be too risk-averse in the small and therefore ... the fitted utility functions exhibit unacceptably large risk premiums for lotteries with a large spread. ... Most of the subjects, however, can reconcile their inconsistencies and feel that they have learned an important lesson about how they want to behave. As a consequence, some subjects cancel their automobile collision insurance and take out more term insurance on their lives.

Even today, human (ir)rationality is the subject of intensive investigation.

NORMALIZED UTILITIES

STANDARD LOTTERY

One procedure for assessing utilities is to establish a scale with a "best possible prize" at $U(S) = u_\top$ and a "worst possible catastrophe" at $U(S) = u_\perp$. **Normalized utilities** use a scale with $u_\perp = 0$ and $u_\top = 1$. Utilities of intermediate outcomes are assessed by asking the agent to indicate a preference between the given outcome state $S$ and a **standard lottery** $[p, u_\top;\ (1-p), u_\perp]$. The probability $p$ is adjusted until the agent is indifferent between $S$ and the standard lottery. Assuming normalized utilities, the utility of $S$ is given by $p$.

In medical, transportation, and environmental decision problems, among others, people's lives are at stake. In such cases, $u_\perp$ is the value assigned to immediate death (or perhaps many deaths). *Although nobody feels comfortable with putting a value on human life, it is a fact that tradeoffs are made all the time.* Aircraft are given a complete overhaul at intervals determined by trips and miles flown, rather than after every trip. Car bodies are made with relatively thin sheet metal to reduce costs, despite the decrease in accident survival rates. Leaded fuel is still widely used even though it has known health hazards. Paradoxically, a refusal to "put a monetary value on life" means that life is often *undervalued.* Ross Shachter relates an experience with a government agency that commissioned a study on removing asbestos from schools. The study assumed a particular dollar value for the life of a school-age child, and argued that the rational choice under that assumption was to remove the asbestos. The government agency, morally outraged, rejected the report out of hand. It then decided against asbestos removal.

MICROMORT

QALY

Some attempts have been made to find out the value that people place on their own lives. Two common "currencies" used in medical and safety analysis are the **micromort** (a one in a million chance of death) and the **QALY**, or quality-adjusted life year (equivalent to a year in good health with no infirmities). A number of studies across a wide range of individuals have shown that a micromort is worth about \$20 (1980 dollars). We have already seen that utility functions need not be linear, so this does not imply that a decision maker would kill himself for \$20 million. Again, the local linearity of any utility curve means that micromort and QALY values are most appropriate for small incremental risks and rewards.

## 16.4 Multiattribute Utility Functions

MULTIATTRIBUTE UTILITY THEORY

Decision making in the field of public policy involves both millions of dollars and life and death. For example, in deciding what levels of a carcinogenic substance to allow into the environment, policy makers must weigh the prevention of deaths against the economic hardship that might result from the elimination of certain products and processes. Siting a new airport requires consideration of the disruption caused by construction; the cost of land; the distance from centers of population; the noise of flight operations; safety issues arising from local topography and weather conditions; and so on. Problems like these, in which outcomes are characterized by two or more attributes, are handled by **multiattribute utility theory**.

We will call the attributes $\mathbf{X} = X_1, \ldots, X_n$; a complete vector of assignments will be $\mathbf{x} = \langle x_1, \ldots, x_n \rangle$. Each attribute is generally assumed to have discrete or continuous scalar values. For simplicity, we will assume that each attribute is defined in such a way that, all other things being equal, higher values of the attribute correspond to higher utilities. For example, if we choose *AbsenceOfNoise* as an attribute in the airport problem then the greater its value, the better the solution. In some cases, it may be necessary to subdivide the range of values so that utility varies monotonically within each range.

We begin by examining cases in which decisions can be made *without* combining the attribute values into a single utility value. Then we look at cases where the utilities of attribute combinations can be specified very concisely.

### Dominance

Suppose that airport site $S_1$ costs less, generates less noise pollution, and is safer than site $S_2$. One would not hesitate to reject $S_2$. We then say that there is **strict dominance** of $S_1$ over $S_2$. In general, if an option is of lower value on all attributes than some other option, it need not be considered further. Strict dominance is often very useful in narrowing down the field of choices to the real contenders, although it seldom yields a unique choice. Figure 16.3(a) shows a schematic diagram for the two-attribute case.

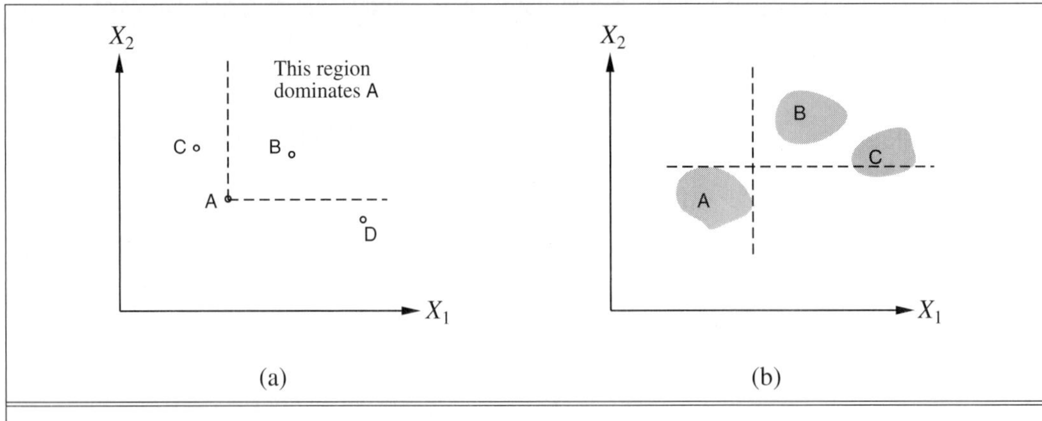


**Figure 16.3** Strict dominance. (a) Deterministic: Option A is strictly dominated by B but not by C or D. (b) Uncertain: A is strictly dominated by B but not by C.

That is fine for the deterministic case, in which the attribute values are known for sure. What about the general case, where the action outcomes are uncertain? A direct analog of strict dominance can be constructed, where, despite the uncertainty, all possible concrete outcomes for $S_1$ strictly dominate all possible outcomes for $S_2$. (See Figure 16.3(b).) Of course, this will probably occur even less often than in the deterministic case.

Fortunately, there is a more useful generalization called **stochastic dominance**, which occurs very frequently in real problems. Stochastic dominance is easiest to understand in the context of a single attribute. Suppose we believe that the cost of siting the airport at $S_1$ is uniformly distributed between \$2.8 billion and \$4.8 billion and that the cost at $S_2$ is uniformly distributed between \$3 billion and \$5.2 billion. Figure 16.4(a) shows these distributions, with cost plotted as a negative value. Then, given only the information that utility decreases with cost, we can say that $S_1$ stochastically dominates $S_2$ (i.e., $S_2$ can be discarded). It is important

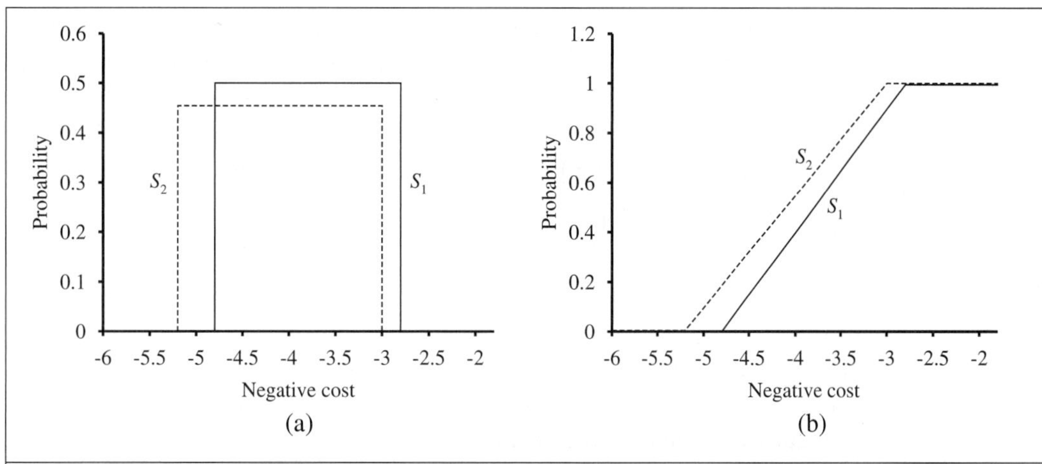


**Figure 16.4** Stochastic dominance. (a) $S_1$ stochastically dominates $S_2$ on cost. (b) Cumulative distributions for the negative cost of $S_1$ and $S_2$.

to note that this does *not* follow from comparing the expected costs. For example, if we knew the cost of $S_1$ to be *exactly* \$3.8 billion, then we would be *unable* to make a decision without additional information on the utility of money.[3]

The exact relationship between the attribute distributions needed to establish stochastic dominance is best seen by examining the *cumulative* distributions, shown in Figure 16.4(b). The cumulative distribution measures the probability that the cost is less than or equal to any given amount—that is, it integrates the original distribution. If the cumulative distribution for $S_1$ is always to the right of the cumulative distribution for $S_2$, then, stochastically speaking, $S_1$ is cheaper than $S_2$. Formally, if two actions $A_1$ and $A_2$ lead to probability distributions $p_1(x)$ and $p_2(x)$ on attribute $X$, then $A_1$ stochastically dominates $A_2$ on $X$ if

$$\forall\, x \quad \int_{-\infty}^{x} p_1(x')\, dx' \le \int_{-\infty}^{x} p_2(x')\, dx' \,.$$

The relevance of this definition to the selection of optimal decisions comes from the following property: *if $A_1$ stochastically dominates $A_2$, then for any monotonically nondecreasing utility function $U(x)$, the expected utility of $A_1$ is at least as high as the expected utility of $A_2$.* Hence, if an action is stochastically dominated by another action on all attributes, then it can be discarded.

The stochastic dominance condition might seem rather technical and perhaps not so easy to evaluate without extensive probability calculations. In fact, it can be decided very easily in many cases. Suppose, for example, that the construction cost depends on the distance to centers of population. The cost itself is uncertain, but the greater the distance, the greater the cost. If $S_1$ is less remote than $S_2$, then $S_1$ will dominate $S_2$ on cost. Although we will not

[3] It might seem odd that *more* information on the cost of $S_1$ could make the agent *less* able to decide. The paradox is resolved by noting that the decision reached in the absence of exact cost information is less likely to have the highest utility payoff.

QUALITATIVE PROBABILISTIC NETWORKS

present them here, there exist algorithms for propagating this kind of qualitative information among uncertain variables in **qualitative probabilistic networks**, enabling a system to make rational decisions based on stochastic dominance, without using any numeric values.

### Preference structure and multiattribute utility

Suppose we have $n$ attributes, each of which has $d$ distinct possible values. To specify the complete utility function $U(x_1, \ldots, x_n)$, we need $d^n$ values in the worst case. Now, the worst case corresponds to a situation in which the agent's preferences have no regularity at all. Multiattribute utility theory is based on the supposition that the preferences of typical agents have much more structure than that. The basic approach is to identify regularities in the preference behavior we would expect to see and to use what are called **representation theorems** to show that an agent with a certain kind of preference structure has a utility function

REPRESENTATION THEOREMS

$$U(x_1, \ldots, x_n) = f[f_1(x_1), \ldots, f_n(x_n)\ ,]$$

where $f$ is, we hope, a simple function such as addition. Notice the similarity to the use of Bayesian networks to decompose the joint probability of several random variables.

#### Preferences without uncertainty

Let us begin with the deterministic case. Remember that for deterministic environments the agent has a value function $V(x_1, \ldots, x_n)$; the aim is to represent this function concisely. The basic regularity that arises in deterministic preference structures is called **preference independence**. Two attributes $X_1$ and $X_2$ are preferentially independent of a third attribute $X_3$ if the preference between outcomes $\langle x_1, x_2, x_3\rangle$ and $\langle x'_1, x'_2, x_3\rangle$ does not depend on the particular value $x_3$ for attribute $X_3$.

PREFERENCE INDEPENDENCE

Going back to the airport example, where we have (among other attributes) $Noise$, $Cost$, and $Deaths$ to consider, one may propose that $Noise$ and $Cost$ are preferentially independent of $Deaths$. For example, if we prefer a state with 20,000 people residing in the flight path and a construction cost of \$4 billion to a state with 70,000 people residing in the flight path and a cost of \$3.7 billion when the safety level is 0.06 deaths per million passenger miles in both cases, then we would have the same preference when the safety level is 0.13 or 0.01; and the same independence would hold for preferences between any other pair of values for $Noise$ and $Cost$. It is also apparent that $Cost$ and $Deaths$ are preferentially independent of $Noise$ and that $Noise$ and $Deaths$ are preferentially independent of $Cost$. We say that the set of attributes $\{Noise, Cost, Deaths\}$ exhibits **mutual preferential independence** (MPI). MPI says that, whereas each attribute may be important, it does not affect the way in which one trades off the other attributes against each other.

MUTUAL PREFERENTIAL INDEPENDENCE

Mutual preferential independence is something of a mouthful, but thanks to a remarkable theorem due to the economist Debreu (1960), we can derive from it a very simple form for the agent's value function: *If attributes $X_1, \ldots, X_n$ are mutually preferentially independent, then the agent's preference behavior can be described as maximizing the function*

$$V(x_1, \ldots, x_n) = \sum_i V_i(x_i)\ ,$$

*where each $V_i$ is a value function referring only to the attribute $X_i$.* For example, it might well be the case that the airport decision can be made using a value function

$$V(noise, cost, deaths) = -noise \times 10^4 - cost - deaths \times 10^{12} .$$

ADDITIVE VALUE FUNCTION

A value function of this type is called an **additive value function**. Additive functions are an extremely natural way to describe an agent's value function and are valid in many real-world situations. Even when MPI does not strictly hold, as might be the case at extreme values of the attributes, an additive value function might still provide a good approximation to the agent's preferences. This is especially true when the violations of MPI occur in portions of the attribute ranges that are unlikely to occur in practice.

### Preferences with uncertainty

When uncertainty is present in the domain, we will also need to consider the structure of preferences between lotteries and to understand the resulting properties of utility functions, rather than just value functions. The mathematics of this problem can become quite complicated, so we will present just one of the main results to give a flavor of what can be done. The reader is referred to Keeney and Raiffa (1976) for a thorough survey of the field.

UTILITY INDEPENDENCE

The basic notion of **utility independence** extends preference independence to cover lotteries: a set of attributes $\mathbf{X}$ is utility-independent of a set of attributes $\mathbf{Y}$ if preferences between lotteries on the attributes in $\mathbf{X}$ are independent of the particular values of the attributes in $\mathbf{Y}$. A set of attributes is **mutually utility-independent** (MUI) if each of its subsets is utility-independent of the remaining attributes. Again, it seems reasonable to propose that the airport attributes are MUI.

MUTUALLY UTILITY-INDEPENDENT

MULTIPLICATIVE UTILITY FUNCTION

MUI implies that the agent's behavior can be described using a **multiplicative utility function** (Keeney, 1974). The general form of a multiplicative utility function is best seen by looking at the case for three attributes. For conciseness, we will use $U_i$ to mean $U_i(x_i)$:

$$\begin{aligned} U = {} & k_1U_1 + k_2U_2 + k_3U_3 + k_1k_2U_1U_2 + k_2k_3U_2U_3 + k_3k_1U_3U_1 \\ & + k_1k_2k_3U_1U_2U_3 . \end{aligned}$$

Although this does not look very simple, it contains just three single-attribute utility functions and three constants. In general, an $n$-attribute problem exhibiting MUI can be modeled using $n$ single-attribute utilities and $n$ constants. Each of the single-attribute utility functions can be developed independently of the other attributes, and this combination will be guaranteed to generate the correct overall preferences. Additional assumptions are required to obtain a purely additive utility function.

## 16.5 DECISION NETWORKS

INFLUENCE DIAGRAM

DECISION NETWORK

In this section, we will look at a general mechanism for making rational decisions. The notation is often called an **influence diagram** (Howard and Matheson, 1984), but we will use the more descriptive term **decision network**. Decision networks combine Bayesian networks with additional node types for actions and utilities. We will use airport siting as an example.

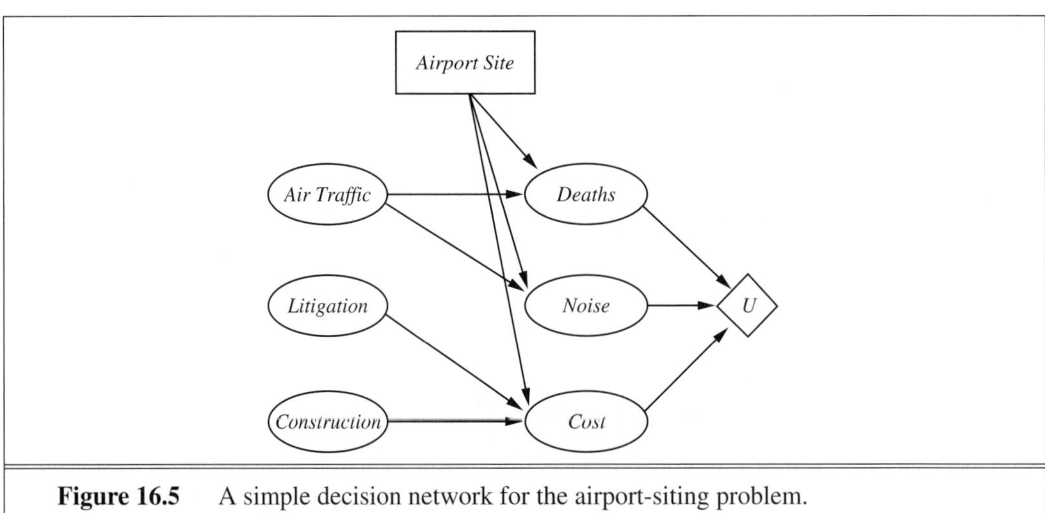


**Figure 16.5** A simple decision network for the airport-siting problem.

### Representing a decision problem with a decision network

In its most general form, a decision network represents information about the agent's current state, its possible actions, the state that will result from the agent's action, and the utility of that state. It therefore provides a substrate for implementing utility-based agents of the type first introduced in Section 2.4. Figure 16.5 shows a decision network for the airport siting problem. It illustrates the three types of nodes used:

CHANCE NODES

◇ **Chance nodes** (ovals) represent random variables, just as they do in Bayes nets. The agent could be uncertain about the construction cost, the level of air traffic and the potential for litigation, and the $Deaths$, $Noise$, and total $Cost$ variables, each of which also depends on the site chosen. Each chance node has associated with it a conditional distribution that is indexed by the state of the parent nodes. In decision networks, the parent nodes can include decision nodes as well as chance nodes. Note that each of the current-state chance nodes could be part of a large Bayes net for assessing construction costs, air traffic levels, or litigation potentials.

DECISION NODES

◇ **Decision nodes** (rectangles) represent points where the decision-maker has a choice of actions. In this case, the $AirportSite$ action can take on a different value for each site under consideration. The choice influences the cost, safety, and noise that will result. In this chapter, we will assume that we are dealing with a single decision node. Chapter 17 deals with cases where more than one decision must be made.

UTILITY NODES

◇ **Utility nodes** (diamonds) represent the agent's utility function.[4] The utility node has as parents all variables describing the outcome that directly affect utility. Associated with the utility node is a description of the agent's utility as a function of the parent attributes. The description could be just a tabulation of the function, or it might be a parameterized additive or multilinear function.

---

[4] These nodes are often called **value nodes** in the literature. We prefer to maintain the distinction between utility and value functions, as discussed earlier, because the outcome state may represent a lottery.

A simplified form is also used in many cases. The notation remains identical, but the chance nodes describing the outcome state are omitted. Instead, the utility node is connected directly to the current-state nodes and the decision node. In this case, rather than representing a utility function on states, the utility node represents the *expected* utility associated with each action, as defined in Equation (16.1). We therefore call such tables **action-utility tables**. Figure 16.6 shows the action-utility representation of the airport problem.

ACTION-UTILITY TABLES

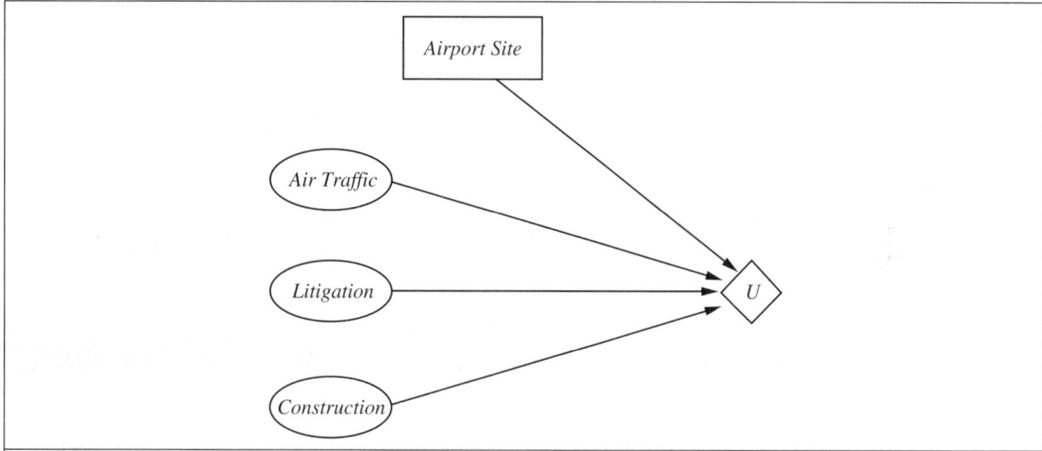


**Figure 16.6** A simplified representation of the airport-siting problem. Chance nodes corresponding to outcome states have been factored out.

Notice that, because the $Noise$, $Deaths$, and $Cost$ chance nodes in Figure 16.5 refer to future states, they can never have their values set as evidence variables. Thus, the simplified version that omits these nodes can be used whenever the more general form can be used. Although the simplified form contains fewer nodes, the omission of an explicit description of the outcome of the siting decision means that it is less flexible with respect to changes in circumstances. For example, in Figure 16.5, a change in aircraft noise levels can be reflected by a change in the conditional probability table associated with the $Noise$ node, whereas a change in the weight accorded to noise pollution in the utility function can be reflected by a change in the utility table. In the action-utility diagram, Figure 16.6, on the other hand, all such changes have to be reflected by changes to the action-utility table. Essentially, the action-utility formulation is a *compiled* version of the original formulation.

## Evaluating decision networks

Actions are selected by evaluating the decision network for each possible setting of the decision node. Once the decision node is set, it behaves exactly like a chance node that has been set as an evidence variable. The algorithm for evaluating decision networks is the following:

1. Set the evidence variables for the current state.
2. For each possible value of the decision node;
   (a) Set the decision node to that value.

(b) Calculate the posterior probabilities for the parent nodes of the utility node, using a standard probabilistic inference algorithm.

(c) Calculate the resulting utility for the action.

3. Return the action with the highest utility.

This is a straightforward extension of the Bayes net algorithm and can be incorporated directly into the agent design given in Figure 13.1. We will see in Chapter 17 that the possibility of executing several actions in sequence makes the problem much more interesting.

## 16.6 THE VALUE OF INFORMATION

In the preceding analysis, we have assumed that all relevant information, or at least all available information, is provided to the agent before it makes its decision. In practice, this is hardly ever the case. *One of the most important parts of decision making is knowing what questions to ask.* For example, a doctor cannot expect to be provided with the results of *all possible* diagnostic tests and questions at the time a patient first enters the consulting room.[5] Tests are often expensive and sometimes hazardous (both directly and because of associated delays). Their importance depends on two factors: whether the test results would lead to a significantly better treatment plan, and how likely the various test results are.

INFORMATION VALUE THEORY

This section describes **information value theory**, which enables an agent to choose what information to acquire. The acquisition of information is achieved by **sensing actions**, as described in Chapter 12. Because the agent's utility function seldom refers to the contents of the agent's internal state, whereas the whole purpose of sensing actions is to affect the internal state, we must evaluate sensing actions by their effect on the agent's subsequent "real" actions. Thus, information value theory involves a form of sequential decision making.

### A simple example

Suppose an oil company is hoping to buy one of $n$ indistinguishable blocks of ocean drilling rights. Let us assume further that exactly one of the blocks contains oil worth $C$ dollars and that the price of each block is $C/n$ dollars. If the company is risk-neutral, then it will be indifferent between buying a block and not buying one.

Now suppose that a seismologist offers the company the results of a survey of block number 3, which indicates definitively whether the block contains oil. How much should the company be willing to pay for the information? The way to answer this question is to examine what the company would do if it had the information:

- With probability $1/n$, the survey will indicate oil in block 3. In this case, the company will buy block 3 for $C/n$ dollars and make a profit of $C - C/n = (n-1)C/n$ dollars.
- With probability $(n-1)/n$, the survey will show that the block contains no oil, in which case the company will buy a different block. Now the probability of finding oil in one

[5] In the United States, the only question that is always asked beforehand is whether the patient has insurance.

of the other blocks changes from $1/n$ to $1/(n-1)$, so the company makes an expected profit of $C/(n-1) - C/n = C/n(n-1)$ dollars.

Now we can calculate the expected profit, given the survey information:

$$\frac{1}{n} \times \frac{(n-1)C}{n} + \frac{n-1}{n} \times \frac{C}{n(n-1)} = C/n \,.$$

Therefore, the company should be willing to pay the seismologist up to $C/n$ dollars for the information: the information is worth as much as the block itself.

The value of information derives from the fact that *with* the information, one's course of action can be changed to suit the *actual* situation. One can discriminate according to the situation, whereas without the information, one has to do what's best on average over the possible situations. In general, the value of a given piece of information is defined to be the difference in expected value between best actions before and after information is obtained.

## A general formula

It is simple to derive a general mathematical formula for the value of information. Usually, we assume that exact evidence is obtained about the value of some random variable $E_j$, so the phrase **value of perfect information** (VPI) is used.[6] Let the agent's current knowledge be $E$. Then the value of the current best action $\alpha$ is defined by

VALUE OF PERFECT INFORMATION

$$EU(\alpha|E) = \max_A \sum_i U(Result_i(A))\ P(Result_i(A)|Do(A), E)$$

and the value of the new best action (after the new evidence $E_j$ is obtained) will be

$$EU(\alpha_{E_j}|E, E_j) = \max_A \sum_i U(Result_i(A))\ P(Result_i(A)|Do(A), E, E_j) \,.$$

But $E_j$ is a random variable whose value is *currently* unknown, so we must average over all possible values $e_{jk}$ that we might discover for $E_j$, using our *current* beliefs about its value. The value of discovering $E_j$, given current information $E$, is then defined as

$$VPI_E(E_j) = \left(\sum_k P(E_j = e_{jk}|E) EU(\alpha_{e_{jk}}|E, E_j = e_{jk})\right) - EU(\alpha|E) \,.$$

In order to get some intuition for this formula, consider the simple case where there are only two actions, $A_1$ and $A_2$, from which to choose. Their current expected utilities are $U_1$ and $U_2$. The information $E_j$ will yield some new expected utilities $U_1'$ and $U_2'$ for the actions, but before we obtain $E_j$, we will have some probability distributions over the possible values of $U_1'$ and $U_2'$ (which we will assume are independent).

Suppose that $A_1$ and $A_2$ represent two different routes through a mountain range in winter. $A_1$ is a nice, straight highway through a low pass, and $A_2$ is a winding dirt road over the top. Just given this information, $A_1$ is clearly preferable, because it is quite likely that the second route is blocked by avalanches, whereas it is quite unlikely that the first route is blocked by traffic. $U_1$ is therefore clearly higher than $U_2$. It is possible to obtain satellite

---

[6] Imperfect information about a variable $X$ can be modeled as perfect information about a variable $Y$ that is probabilistically related to $X$. See Exercise 16.11 for an example of this.

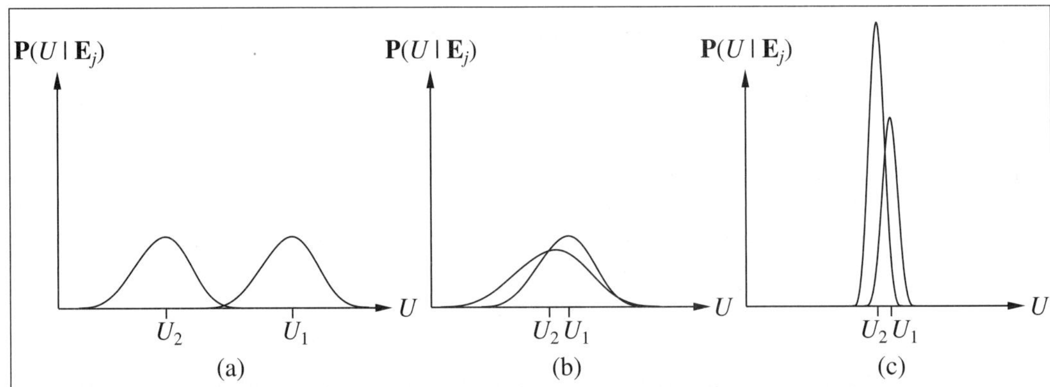


**Figure 16.7** Three generic cases for the value of information. In (a), $A_1$ will almost certainly remain superior to $A_2$, so the information is not needed. In (b), the choice is unclear and the information is crucial. In (c), the choice is unclear but because it makes little difference, the information is less valuable.

reports $E_j$ on the actual state of each road that would give new expectations, $U_1'$ and $U_2'$, for the two crossings. The distributions for these expectations are shown in Figure 16.7(a). Obviously, in this case, it is not worth the expense of obtaining satellite reports, because it is unlikely that the information derived from them will change the plan. With no change, information has no value.

Now suppose that we are choosing between two different winding dirt roads of slightly different lengths and we are carrying a seriously injured passenger. Then, even when $U_1$ and $U_2$ are quite close, the distributions of $U_1'$ and $U_2'$ are very broad. There is a significant possibility that the second route will turn out to be clear while the first is blocked, and in this case the difference in utilities will be very high. The VPI formula indicates that it might be worthwhile getting the satellite reports. Such a situation is shown in Figure 16.7(b).

Now suppose that we are choosing between the two dirt roads in summertime, when blockage by avalanches is unlikely. In this case, satellite reports might show one route to be more scenic than the other because of flowering alpine meadows, or perhaps wetter because of errant streams. It is therefore quite likely that we would change our plan if we had the information. But in this case, the difference in value between the two routes is still likely to be very small, so we will not bother to obtain the reports. This situation is shown in Figure 16.7(c).

In sum, *information has value to the extent that it is likely to cause a change of plan and to the extent that the new plan will be significantly better than the old plan.*

### Properties of the value of information

One might ask whether it is possible for information to be deleterious: can it actually have negative expected value? Intuitively, one should expect this to be impossible. After all, one could in the worst case just ignore the information and pretend that one has never received it. This is confirmed by the following theorem, which applies to any decision-theoretic agent:

*The value of information is nonnegative:*

$$\forall j, E \;\; VPI_E(E_j) \geq 0 \, .$$

The theorem follows directly from the definition of VPI, and we leave the proof as an exercise (Exercise 16.12). It is important to remember that VPI depends on the current state of information, which is why it is subscripted. It can change as more information is acquired. In the extreme case, it will become zero if the variable in question already has a known value. Thus, VPI is not additive. That is,

$$VPI_E(E_j, E_k) \neq VPI_E(E_j) + VPI_E(E_k) \qquad \text{(in general)} \, .$$

VPI is, however, order-independent, which should be intuitively obvious. That is,

$$VPI_E(E_j, E_k) = VPI_E(E_j) + VPI_{E,E_j}(E_k) = VPI_E(E_k) + VPI_{E,E_k}(E_j) \, .$$

Order independence distinguishes sensing actions from ordinary actions and simplifies the problem of calculating the value of a sequence of sensing actions.

### Implementing an information-gathering agent

A sensible agent should ask questions of the user in a reasonable order, should avoid asking questions that are irrelevant, should take into account the importance of each piece of information in relation to its cost, and should stop asking questions when that is appropriate. All of these capabilities can be achieved by using the value of information as a guide.

Figure 16.8 shows the overall design of an agent that can gather information intelligently before acting. For now, we will assume that with each observable evidence variable $E_j$, there is an associated cost, $Cost(E_j)$, which reflects the cost of obtaining the evidence through tests, consultants, questions, or whatever. The agent requests what appears to be the most valuable piece of information, compared with its cost. We assume that the result of the action $Request(E_j)$ is that the next percept provides the value of $E_j$. If no observation is worth its cost, the agent selects a "real" action.

MYOPIC

The agent algorithm we have described implements a form of information gathering that is called **myopic**. This is because it uses the VPI formula shortsightedly, calculating

```
function INFORMATION-GATHERING-AGENT(percept) returns an action
  static: D, a decision network

  integrate percept into D
  j ← the value that maximizes VPI(E_j) − Cost(E_j)
  if VPI(E_j) > Cost(E_j)
     then return REQUEST(E_j)
  else return the best action from D
```

**Figure 16.8** Design of a simple information-gathering agent. The agent works by repeatedly selecting the observation with the highest information value, until the cost of the next observation is greater than its expected benefit.

the value of information as if only a single evidence variable will be acquired. If there is no single evidence variable that will help a lot, a myopic agent might hastily take an action when it would have been better to request two or more variables first and then take action. Myopic control is based on the same heuristic idea as greedy search and often works well in practice. (For example, it has been shown to outperform expert physicians in selecting diagnostic tests.) However, a perfectly rational information-gathering agent should consider all possible sequences of information requests terminating in an external action and all possible outcomes of those requests. Because the value of the second request depends on the outcome of the first request, the agent needs to explore the space of **conditional plans**, as described in Chapter 12.

## 16.7 Decision-Theoretic Expert Systems

DECISION ANALYSIS

The field of **decision analysis**, which evolved in the 1950s and 1960s, studies the application of decision theory to actual decision problems. It is used to help make rational decisions in important domains where the stakes are high, such as business, government, law, military strategy, medical diagnosis and public health, engineering design, and resource management. The process involves a careful study of the possible actions and outcomes, as well as the preferences placed on each outcome. It is traditional in decision analysis to talk about two roles: the **decision maker** states preferences between outcomes, and the **decision analyst** enumerates the possible actions and outcomes and elicits preferences from the decision maker to determine the best course of action. Until the early 1980s, the main purpose of decision analysis was to help humans make decisions that actually reflect their own preferences. In the current day, more and more decision processes are automated, and decision analysis is used to make sure that the automated processes are behaving as desired.

DECISION MAKER

DECISION ANALYST

As we discussed in Chapter 14, early expert system research concentrated on answering questions, rather than on making decisions. Those systems that did recommend actions rather than providing opinions on matters of fact generally did so using condition-action rules, rather than with explicit representations of outcomes and preferences. The emergence of Bayesian networks in the late 1980s made it possible to build large-scale systems that generated sound probabilistic inferences from evidence. The addition of decision networks means that expert systems can be developed that recommend optimal decisions, reflecting the preferences of the user as well as the available evidence.

A system that incorporates utilities can avoid one of the most common pitfalls associated with the consultation process: confusing likelihood and importance. A common strategy in early medical expert systems, for example, was to rank possible diagnoses in order of likelihood and report the most likely. Unfortunately, this can be disastrous! For the majority of patients in general practice, the two most *likely* diagnoses are usually "There's nothing wrong with you" and "You have a bad cold," but if the third-most-likely diagnosis for a given patient is lung cancer, that's a serious matter. Obviously, a testing or treatment plan should depend both on probabilities and utilities.

We will now describe the knowledge engineering process for decision-theoretic expert systems. As an example we will consider the problem of selecting a medical treatment for a kind of congenital heart disease in children (see Lucas, 1996).

AORTIC COARCTATION

About 0.8% of children are born with a heart anomaly, the most common being **aortic coarctation** (a constriction of the aorta). It can be treated with surgery, angioplasty (expanding the aorta with a balloon placed inside the artery) or medication. The problem is to decide what treatment to use and when to do it: the younger the infant the greater the risks of certain treatments, but one mustn't wait too long. A decision-theoretic expert system for this problem can be created by a team consisting of at least one domain expert (a pediatric cardiologist) and one knowledge engineer. The process can be broken down into the following steps (which you can compare to the steps in developing a logic-based system in Section 8.4).

**Create a causal model**. Determine what are the possible symptoms, disorders, treatments, and outcomes. Then draw arcs between them, indicating what disorders cause what symptoms, and what treatments alleviate what disorders. Some of this will be well known to the domain expert, and some will come from the literature. Often the model will match well with the informal graphical descriptions given in medical textbooks.

**Simplify to a qualitative decision model**. Since we are using the model to make treatment decisions and not for other purposes (such as determining the joint probability of certain symptom/disorder combinations), we can often simplify by removing variables that are not involved in treatment decisions. Sometimes variables will have to be split or joined to match the expert's intuitions. For example, the original aortic coarctation model had a *Treatment* variable with values *surgery*, *angioplasty* and *medication*, and a separate variable for *Timing* of the treatment. But the expert had a hard time thinking of these separately, so they were combined, with *Treatment* taking on values such as *surgery in 1 month*. This gives us the model of Figure 16.9.

**Assign probabilities**. Probabilities can come from patient databases, literature studies, or the expert's subjective assessments. In cases where the wrong kinds of probabilities are given in the literature, techniques such as Bayes' rule and marginalization can be used to compute the desired probabilities. It has been found that experts are best able to assess the probability of an effect given a cause (e.g. $P(dyspnoea|heartfailure)$) rather than the other way around.

**Assign utilities**. When there are a small number of possible outcomes, they can be enumerated and evaluated individually. We would create a scale from best to worst outcome and give each a numeric value, for example -1000 for death and 0 for complete recovery. We would then place the other outcomes on this scale. This can be done by the expert, but it is better if the patient (or in the case of infants, the patient's parents) can be involved, because different people have different preferences. If there are exponentially many outcomes, we need some way to combine them using multiattribute utility functions. For example, we may say that the negative utility of various complications is additive.

GOLD STANDARD

**Verify and refine the model**. To evaluate the system we will need a set of correct (input, output) pairs; a so-called **gold standard** to compare against. For medical expert systems this usually means assembling the best available doctors, presenting them with a few cases, and asking them for their diagnosis and recommended treatment plan. We then see

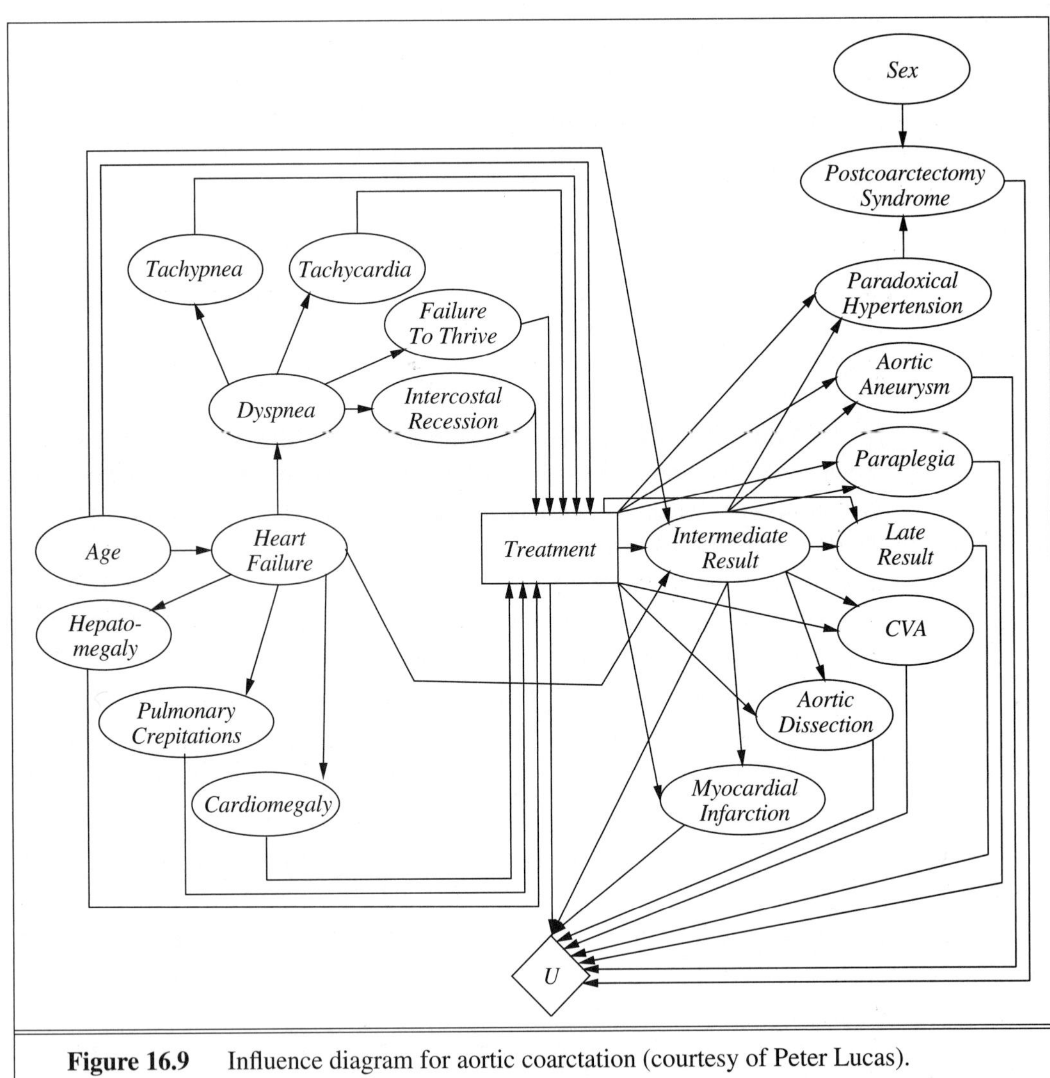


**Figure 16.9** Influence diagram for aortic coarctation (courtesy of Peter Lucas).

how well the system matches their recommendations. If it does poorly, we try to isolate the parts that are going wrong and fix them. It can be useful to run the system "backwards." Instead of presenting the system with symptoms and asking for a diagnosis, we can present it with a diagnosis such as "heart failure," examine the predicted probability of symptoms such as tachycardia, and compare to the medical literature.

**Perform sensitivity analysis**. This important step checks whether the best decision is sensitive to small changes in the assigned probabilities and utilities by systematically varying those parameters and running the evaluation again. If small changes lead to significantly different decisions, then it could be worthwhile to spend more resources to collect better data. If all variations lead to the same decision, then the user will have more confidence that it is the right decision. Sensitivity analysis is particularly important, because one of the main criticisms of probabilistic approaches to expert systems is that it is too difficult to assess the numerical probabilities required. Sensitivity analysis often reveals that many of the numbers need be specified only very approximately. For example, we might be uncertain about the prior probability $P(tachycardia)$, but if we try many different values for this probability and in each case the recommended action of the influence diagram is the same then we can be less concerned about our ignorance.

## 16.8 Summary

This chapter shows how to combine utility theory with probability to enable an agent to select actions that will maximize its expected performance.

- **Probability theory** describes what an agent should believe on the basis of evidence, **utility theory** describes what an agent wants, and **decision theory** puts the two together to describe what an agent should do.
- We can use decision theory to build a system that makes decisions by considering all possible actions and choosing the one that leads to the best expected outcome. Such a system is known as a **rational agent**.
- Utility theory shows that an agent whose preferences between lotteries are consistent with a set of simple axioms can be described as possessing a utility function; furthermore, the agent selects actions as if maximizing its expected utility.
- **Multiattribute utility theory** deals with utilities that depend on several distinct attributes of states. **Stochastic dominance** is a particularly useful technique for making unambiguous decisions, even without precise utility values for attributes.
- **Decision networks** provide a simple formalism for expressing and solving decision problems. They are a natural extension of Bayesian networks, containing decision and utility nodes in addition to chance nodes.
- Sometimes, solving a problem involves finding more information before making a decision. The **value of information** is defined as the expected improvement in utility compared with making a decision without the information.
- **Expert systems** that incorporate utility information have additional capabilities compared with pure inference systems. In addition to being able to make decisions, they can use the value of information to decide whether to acquire it and they can calculate the sensitivity of their decisions to small changes in probability and utility assessments.

## Bibliographical and Historical Notes

One of the earliest applications of the principle of maximum expected utility (although a deviant one involving infinite utilities) was Pascal's wager, first published as part of the *Port-Royal Logic* (Arnauld, 1662). Daniel Bernoulli (1738), investigating the St. Petersburg paradox (see Exercise 16.3), was the first to realize the importance of preference measurement for lotteries, writing "the *value* of an item must not be based on its *price*, but rather on the *utility* that it yields" (italics his). Jeremy Bentham (1823) proposed the **hedonic calculus** for weighing "pleasures" and "pains," arguing that all decisions (not just monetary ones) could be reduced to utility comparisons.

The derivation of numerical utilities from preferences was first carried out by Ramsey (1931); the axioms for preference in the present text are closer in form to those rediscovered in *Theory of Games and Economic Behavior* (von Neumann and Morgenstern, 1944). A good presentation of these axioms, in the course of a discussion on risk preference, is given by Howard (1977). Ramsey had derived subjective probabilities (not just utilities) from an agent's preferences; Savage (1954) and Jeffrey (1983) carry out more recent constructions of this kind. Von Winterfeldt and Edwards (1986) provide a modern perspective on decision analysis and its relationship to human preference structures. The micromort utility measure is discussed by Howard (1989). A 1994 survey by the *Economist* set the value of a life at between $750,000 and $2.6 million. However, Richard Thaler (1992) found irrational variation in the price one is willing to pay to avoid a risk of death versus the price one is willing to be paid to accept a risk. For a 1/1000 chance, a respondent wouldn't pay more than $200 to remove the risk, but wouldn't accept $50,000 to take on the risk.

QALYs are much more widely used in medical and social policy decision making than are micromorts; see (Russell, 1990) for a typical example of an argument for a major change in public health policy on grounds of increased expected utility measured in QALYs.

The book *Decisions with Multiple Objectives: Preferences and Value Tradeoffs* (Keeney and Raiffa, 1976) gives a thorough introduction to multiattribute utility theory. It describes early computer implementations of methods for eliciting the necessary parameters for a multiattribute utility function and includes extensive accounts of real applications of the theory. In AI, the principal reference for MAUT is Wellman's (1985) paper, which includes a system called URP (Utility Reasoning Package) that can use a collection of statements about preference independence and conditional independence to analyze the structure of decision problems. The use of stochastic dominance together with qualitative probability models was investigated extensively by Wellman (1988, 1990a). Wellman and Doyle (1992) provide a preliminary sketch of how a complex set of utility-independence relationships might be used to provide a structured model of a utility function, in much the same way that Bayesian networks provide a structured model of joint probability distributions. Bacchus and Grove (1995, 1996) and La Mura and Shoham (1999) give further results along these lines.

Decision theory has been a standard tool in economics, finance, and management science since the 1950s. Until the 1980s, decision trees were the main tool used for representing simple decision problems. Smith (1988) gives an overview of the methodology of decision analysis. Decision networks or influence diagrams were introduced by Howard and Matheson (1984), based on earlier work by a group (including Howard and Matheson) at SRI (Miller *et al.*, 1976). Howard and Matheson's method involved the derivation of a decision tree from a decision network, but in general the tree is of exponential size. Shachter (1986) developed a method for making decisions based directly on a decision network, without the creation of an intermediate decision tree. This algorithm was also one of the first to provide complete inference for multiply connected Bayesian networks. Recent work by Nilsson and

Lauritzen (2000) links algorithms for decision networks to ongoing developments in clustering algorithms for Bayesian networks. The collection by Oliver and Smith (1990) has a number of useful articles on decision networks, as does the 1990 special issue of the journal *Networks*. Papers on decision networks and utility modeling also appear regularly in the journal *Management Science*.

Information value theory was first analyzed by Ron Howard (1966). His paper ends with the remark "If information value theory and associated decision theoretic structures do not in the future occupy a large part of the education of engineers, then the engineering profession will find that its traditional role of managing scientific and economic resources for the benefit of man has been forfeited to another profession." To date, the implied revolution in managerial methods has not occurred, although this may change as the use of information value theory in Bayesian expert systems becomes more widespread.

Surprisingly few AI researchers adopted decision-theoretic tools after the early applications in medical decision making described in Chapter 13. One of the few exceptions was Jerry Feldman, who applied decision theory to problems in vision (Feldman and Yakimovsky, 1974) and planning (Feldman and Sproull, 1977). After the resurgence of interest in probabilistic methods in AI in the 1980s, decision-theoretic expert systems gained widespread acceptance (Horvitz *et al.*, 1988). In fact, from 1991 onward, the cover design of the journal *Artificial Intelligence* has depicted a decision network, although some artistic license appears to have been taken with the direction of the arrows.

## EXERCISES

**16.1** (Adapted from David Heckerman.) This exercise concerns the **Almanac Game**, which is used by decision analysts to calibrate numeric estimations. For each of the questions that follow, give your best guess of the answer, that is, a number that you think is as likely to be too high as it is to be too low. Also give your guess at a 25th percentile estimate, that is, a number that you think has a 25% chance of being too high, and a 75% chance of being too low. Do the same for the 75th percentile. (Thus, you should give three estimates in all—low, median, and high—for each question.)

**a.** Number of passengers who flew between New York and Los Angeles in 1989.

**b.** Population of Warsaw in 1992.

**c.** Year in which Coronado discovered the Mississippi River.

**d.** Number of votes received by Jimmy Carter in the 1976 presidential election.

**e.** Age of the oldest living tree, as of 2002.

**f.** Height of the Hoover Dam in feet.

**g.** Number of eggs produced in Oregon in 1985.

**h.** Number of Buddhists in the world in 1992.

**i.** Number of deaths due to AIDS in the United States in 1981.

**j.** Number of U.S. patents granted in 1901.

The correct answers appear after the last exercise of this chapter. From the point of view of decision analysis, the interesting thing is not how close your median guesses came to the real answers, but rather how often the real answer came within your 25% and 75% bounds. If it was about half the time, then your bounds are accurate. But if you're like most people, you will be more sure of yourself than you should be, and fewer than half the answers will fall within the bounds. With practice, you can calibrate yourself to give realistic bounds, and thus be more useful in supplying information for decision making. Try this second set of questions and see if there is any improvement:

**a.** Year of birth of Zsa Zsa Gabor.

**b.** Maximum distance from Mars to the sun in miles.

**c.** Value in dollars of exports of whcat from the United States in 1992.

**d.** Tons handled by the port of Honolulu in 1991.

**e.** Annual salary in dollars of the governor of California in 1993.

**f.** Population of San Diego in 1990.

**g.** Year in which Roger Williams founded Providence, Rhode Island.

**h.** Height of Mt. Kilimanjaro in feet.

**i.** Length of the Brooklyn Bridge in feet.

**j.** Number of deaths due to automobile accidents in the United States in 1992.

**16.2** Tickets to a lottery cost \$1. There are two possible prizes: a \$10 payoff with probability 1/50, and a \$1,000,000 payoff with probability 1/2,000,000. What is the expected monetary value of a lottery ticket? When (if ever) is it rational to buy a ticket? Be precise—show an equation involving utilities. You may assume current wealth of $\$k$ and that $U(S_k) = 0$. You may also assume that $U(S_{k+10}) = 10 \times U(S_{k+1}))$, but you may not make any assumptions about $U(S_{k+1,000,000})$. Sociological studies show that people with lower income buy a disproportionate number of lottery tickets. Do you think this is because they are worse decision makers or because they have a different utility function?

**16.3** In 1738, J. Bernoulli investigated the St. Petersburg paradox, which works as follows. You have the opportunity to play a game in which a fair coin is tossed repeatedly until it comes up heads. If the first heads appears on the $n$th toss, you win $2^n$ dollars.

**a.** Show that the expected monetary value of this game is infinite.

**b.** How much would you, personally, pay to play the game?

**c.** Bernoulli resolved the apparent paradox by suggesting that the utility of money is measured on a logarithmic scale (i.e., $U(S_n) = a \log_2 n + b$, where $S_n$ is the state of having \$n). What is the expected utility of the game under this assumption?

**d.** What is the maximum amount that it would be rational to pay to play the game, assuming that one's initial wealth is $\$k$ ?

**16.4** Assess your own utility for different incremental amounts of money by running a series of preference tests between some definite amount $M_1$ and a lottery $[p, M_2; (1-p), 0]$. Choose different values of $M_1$ and $M_2$, and vary $p$ until you are indifferent between the two choices. Plot the resulting utility function.

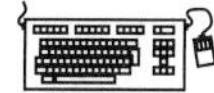

**16.5** Write a computer program to automate the process in Exercise 16.4. Try your program out on several people of different net worth and political outlook. Comment on the consistency of your results, both for an individual and across individuals.

**16.6** How much is a micromort worth to you? Devise a protocol to determine this. Ask questions based both on paying to avoid risk and being paid to accept risk.

**16.7** Show that if $X_1$ and $X_2$ are preferentially independent of $X_3$, and $X_2$ and $X_3$ are preferentially independent of $X_1$, then $X_3$ and $X_1$ are preferentially independent of $X_2$.

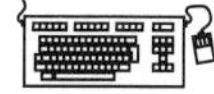

**16.8** This exercise completes the analysis of the airport-siting problem in Figure 16.5.

**a**. Provide reasonable variable domains, probabilities, and utilities for the network, assuming that there are three possible sites.

**b**. Solve the decision problem.

**c**. What happens if changes in technology mean that each aircraft generates half as much noise?

**d**. What if noise avoidance becomes three times more important?

**e**. Calculate the VPI for *AirTraffic*, *Litigation*, and *Construction* in your model.

**16.9** Repeat Exercise 16.8, using the action-utility representation shown in Figure 16.6.

**16.10** For either of the airport-siting diagrams from Exercises 16.8 and 16.9, to which conditional probability table entry is the utility most sensitive, given the available evidence?

**16.11** (Adapted from Pearl (1988).) A used-car buyer can decide to carry out various tests with various costs (e.g., kick the tires, take the car to a qualified mechanic) and then, depending on the outcome of the tests, decide which car to buy. We will assume that the buyer is deciding whether to buy car $c_1$, that there is time to carry out at most one test, and that $t_1$ is the test of $c_1$ and costs \$50.

A car can be in good shape (quality $q^+$) or bad shape (quality $q^-$), and the tests might help to indicate what shape the car is in. Car $c_1$ costs \$1,500, and its market value is \$2,000 if it is in good shape; if not, \$700 in repairs will be needed to make it in good shape. The buyer's estimate is that $c_1$ has a 70% chance of being in good shape.

**a**. Draw the decision network that represents this problem.

**b**. Calculate the expected net gain from buying $c_1$, given no test.

**c**. Tests can be described by the probability that the car will pass or fail the test given that the car is in good or bad shape. We have the following information:
$P(pass(c_1, t_1)|q^+(c_1)) = 0.8$
$P(pass(c_1, t_1)|q^-(c_1)) = 0.35$
Use Bayes' theorem to calculate the probability that the car will pass (or fail) its test and hence the probability that it is in good (or bad) shape given each possible test outcome.

**d.** Calculate the optimal decisions given either a pass or a fail, and their expected utilities.

**e.** Calculate the value of information of the test, and derive an optimal conditional plan for the buyer.

**16.12** Prove that the value of information is nonnegative and order-independent, as stated in Section 16.6. Explain how it is that one can make a worse decision after receiving information than one would have made before receiving it.

**16.13** Modify and extend the Bayesian network code in the code repository to provide for creation and evaluation of decision networks and the calculation of information value.

The answers to Exercise 16.1 (where M stands for million): First set: 3M, 1.6M, 1541, 41M, 4768, 221, 649M, 295M, 132, 25,546. Second set: 1917, 155M, 4,500M, 11M, 120,000, 1.1M, 1,636, 19,340, 1,595, 41,710.

# 17 MAKING COMPLEX DECISIONS

*In which we examine methods for deciding what to do today, given that we may decide again tomorrow.*

In this chapter, we address the computational issues involved in making decisions. Whereas Chapter 16 was concerned with one-shot or episodic decision problems, in which the utility of each action's outcome was well known, we will be concerned here with **sequential decision problems**, in which the agent's utility depends on a sequence of decisions. Sequential decision problems, which include utilities, uncertainty, and sensing, generalize the search and planning problems described in Parts II and IV. Section 17.1 explains how sequential decision problems are defined, and Sections 17.2 and 17.3 explain how they can be solved to produce optimal behavior that balances the risks and rewards of acting in an uncertain environment. Section 17.4 extends these ideas to the case of partially observable environments, and Section 17.5 develops a complete design for decision-theoretic agents in partially observable environments, combining dynamic Bayesian networks from Chapter 15 with decision networks from Chapter 16.

SEQUENTIAL DECISION PROBLEMS

The second part of the chapter covers environments with multiple agents. In such environments, the notion of optimal behavior becomes much more complicated by the interactions among the agents. Section 17.6 introduces the main ideas of **game theory**, including the idea that rational agents might need to behave randomly. Section 17.7 looks at how multiagent systems can be designed so that multiple agents can achieve a common goal.

## 17.1 SEQUENTIAL DECISION PROBLEMS

### An example

Suppose that an agent is situated in the $4 \times 3$ environment shown in Figure 17.1(a). Beginning in the start state, it must choose an action at each time step. The interaction with the environment terminates when the agent reaches one of the goal states, marked +1 or –1. In each location, the available actions are called *Up*, *Down*, *Left*, and *Right*. We will assume for now that the environment is **fully observable**, so that the agent always knows where it is.

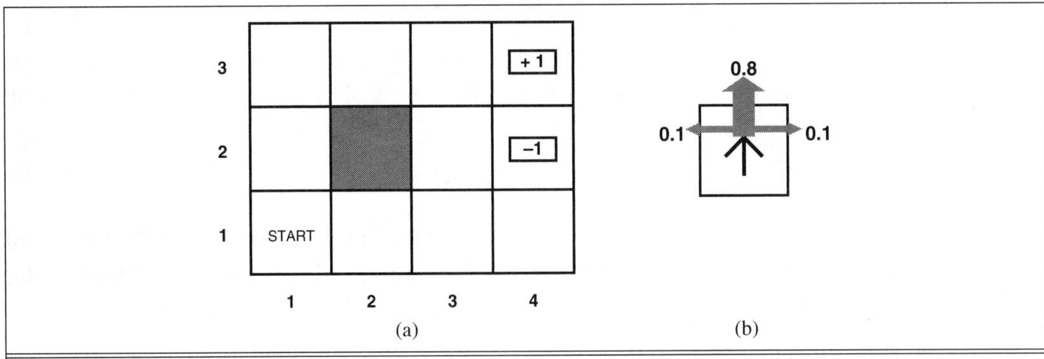


**Figure 17.1** (a) A simple $4 \times 3$ environment that presents the agent with a sequential decision problem. (b) Illustration of the transition model of the environment: the "intended" outcome occurs with probability 0.8, but with probability 0.2 the agent moves at right angles to the intended direction. A collision with a wall results in no movement. The two terminal states have reward +1 and –1, respectively, and all other states have a reward of –0.04.

If the environment were deterministic, a solution would be easy: [*Up, Up, Right, Right, Right*]. Unfortunately, the environment won't always go along with this solution, because the actions are unreliable. The particular model of stochastic motion that we adopt is illustrated in Figure 17.1(b). Each action achieves the intended effect with probability 0.8, but the rest of the time, the action moves the agent at right angles to the intended direction. Furthermore, if the agent bumps into a wall, it stays in the same square. For example, from the start square (1,1), the action *Up* moves the agent to (1,2) with probability 0.8, but with probability 0.1, it moves right to (2,1), and with probability 0.1, it moves left, bumps into the wall, and stays in (1,1). In such an environment, the sequence $[Up, Up, Right, Right, Right]$ goes up around the barrier and reaches the goal state at (4,3) with probability $0.8^5 = 0.32768$. There is also a small chance of accidentally reaching the goal by going the other way around with probability $0.1^4 \times 0.8$, for a grand total of 0.32776. (See also Exercise 17.1.)

A specification of the outcome probabilities for each action in each possible state is called a **transition model** (or just "model," whenever no confusion can arise). We will use $T(s, a, s')$ to denote the probability of reaching state $s'$ if action $a$ is done in state $s$. We will assume that transitions are **Markovian** in the sense of Chapter 15, that is, the probability of reaching $s'$ from $s$ depends only on $s$ and not on the history of earlier states. For now, you can think of $T(s, a, s')$ as a big three-dimensional table containing probabilities. Later, in Section 17.5, we will see that the transition model can be represented as a **dynamic Bayesian network**, just as in Chapter 15.

TRANSITION MODEL

To complete the definition of the task environment, we must specify the utility function for the agent. Because the decision problem is sequential, the utility function will depend on a sequence of states—an **environment history**—rather than on a single state. Later in this section, we will investigate how such utility functions can be specified in general; for now, we will simply stipulate that in each state $s$, the agent receives a **reward** $R(s)$, which may be positive or negative, but must be bounded. For our particular example, the reward is $-0.04$ in all states except the terminal states (which have rewards +1 and –1). The utility of

REWARD

an environment history is just (for now) the *sum* of the rewards received. For example, if the agent reaches the +1 state after 10 steps, its total utility will be 0.6. The negative reward of –0.04 gives the agent an incentive to reach (4,3) quickly, so our environment is a stochastic generalization of the search problems of Chapter 3. Another way of saying this is that the agent does not enjoy living in this environment and so wants to get out of the game as soon as possible.

MARKOV DECISION PROCESS

The specification of a sequential decision problem for a fully observable environment with a Markovian transition model and additive rewards is called a **Markov decision process**, or **MDP**. An MDP is defined by the following three components:

Initial State: $S_0$

Transition Model: $T(s, a, s')$

Reward Function:[1] $R(s)$

The next question is, what does a solution to the problem look like? We have seen that any fixed action sequence won't solve the problem, because the agent might end up in a state other than the goal. Therefore, a solution must specify what the agent should do for *any* state that the agent might reach. A solution of this kind is called a **policy**. We usually denote a policy by $\pi$, and $\pi(s)$ is the action recommended by the policy $\pi$ for state $s$. If the agent has a complete policy, then no matter what the outcome of any action, the agent will always know what to do next.

POLICY

Each time a given policy is executed starting from the initial state, the stochastic nature of the environment will lead to a different environment history. The quality of a policy is therefore measured by the *expected* utility of the possible environment histories generated by that policy. An **optimal policy** is a policy that yields the highest expected utility. We use $\pi^*$ to denote an optimal policy. Given $\pi^*$, the agent decides what to do by consulting its current percept, which tells it the current state $s$, and then executing the action $\pi^*(s)$. A policy represents the agent function explicitly and is therefore a description of a simple reflex agent, computed from the information used for a utility-based agent.

OPTIMAL POLICY

An optimal policy for the world of Figure 17.1 is shown in Figure 17.2(a). Notice that, because the cost of taking a step is fairly small compared with the penalty for ending up in (4,2) by accident, the optimal policy for the state (3,1) is conservative. The policy recommends taking the long way round, rather than taking the short cut and thereby risking entering (4,2).

The balance of risk and reward changes depends on the value of $R(s)$ for the nonterminal states. Figure 17.2(b) shows optimal policies for four different ranges of $R(s)$. When $R(s) \leq -1.6284$, life is so painful that the agent heads straight for the nearest exit, even if the exit is worth –1. When $-0.4278 \leq R(s) \leq -0.0850$, life is quite unpleasant; the agent takes the shortest route to the +1 state and is willing to risk falling into the –1 state by accident. In particular, the agent takes the shortcut from (3,1). When life is only slightly dreary ($-0.0221 < R(s) < 0$), the optimal policy takes *no risks at all.* In (4,1) and (3,2), the agent

[1] Some definitions of MDPs allow the reward to depend on the action and outcome too, so the reward function is $R(s, a, s')$. This simplifies the description of some environments but does not change the problem in any fundamental way.

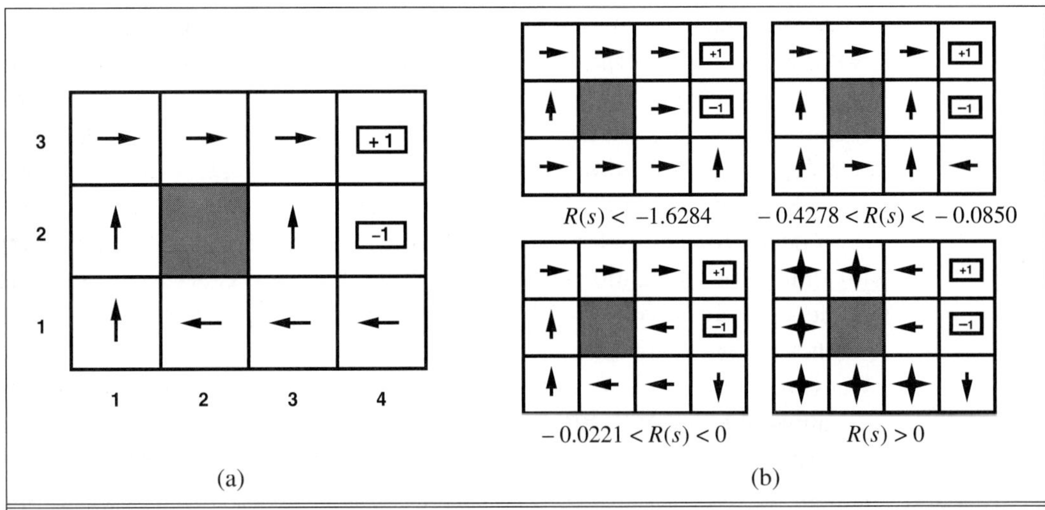


**Figure 17.2** (a) An optimal policy for the stochastic environment with $R(s) = -0.04$ in the nonterminal states. (b) Optimal policies for four different ranges of $R(s)$.

heads directly away from the –1 state so that it cannot fall in by accident, even though this means banging its head against the wall quite a few times. Finally, if $R(s) > 0$, then life is positively enjoyable and the agent avoids *both* exits. As long as the actions in (4,1), (3,2), and (3,3) are as shown, every policy is optimal, and the agent obtains infinite total reward because it never enters a terminal state. Surprisingly, it turns out that there are six other optimal policies for various ranges of $R(s)$; Exercise 17.7 asks you to find them.

The careful balancing of risk and reward is a characteristic of MDPs that does not arise in deterministic search problems; moreover, it is a characteristic of many real-world decision problems. For this reason, MDPs have been studied in several fields, including AI, operations research, economics, and control theory. Dozens of algorithms have been proposed for calculating optimal policies. In sections 17.2 and 17.3 we will describe two of the most important algorithm families. First, however, we must complete our investigation of utilities and policies for sequential decision problems.

### Optimality in sequential decision problems

In the MDP example in Figure 17.1, the performance of the agent was measured by a sum of rewards for the states visited. This choice of performance measure is not arbitrary, but it is not the only possibility. This section investigates the possible choices for the performance measure—that is, choices for the utility function on environment histories, which we will write as $U_h([s_0, s_1, \ldots, s_n])$. The section draws on ideas from Chapter 16 and is somewhat technical; the main points are summarized at the end.

FINITE HORIZON
INFINITE HORIZON

The first question to answer is whether there is a **finite horizon** or an **infinite horizon** for decision making. A finite horizon means that there is a *fixed* time $N$ after which nothing matters—the game is over, so to speak. Thus, $U_h([s_0, s_1, \ldots, s_{N+k}]) = U_h([s_0, s_1, \ldots, s_N])$ for all $k > 0$. For example, suppose an agent starts at (3,1) in the $4 \times 3$ world of Figure 17.1, and suppose that $N = 3$. Then, to have any chance of reaching the +1 state, the agent must head directly for it, and the optimal action is to go *Up*. On the other hand, if $N = 100$ then there is plenty of time to take the safe route by going *Left*. *So, with a finite horizon, the optimal action in a given state could change over time.* We say that the optimal policy for a finite horizon is **nonstationary**. With no fixed time limit, on the other hand, there is no reason to behave differently in the same state at different times. Hence, the optimal action depends only on the current state, and the optimal policy is **stationary**. Policies for the infinite-horizon case are therefore simpler than those for the finite-horizon case, and we will deal mainly with the infinite-horizon case in this chapter.[2] Note that "infinite horizon" does not necessarily mean that all state sequences are infinite; it just means that there is no fixed deadline. In particular, there can be finite state sequences in an infinite-horizon MDP containing a terminal state.

NONSTATIONARY POLICY

STATIONARY POLICY

The next question we must decide is how to calculate the utility of state sequences. We can view this as a question in **multiattribute utility theory** (see Section 16.4), where each state $s_i$ is viewed as an attribute of the state sequence $[s_0, s_1, s_2 \ldots]$. To obtain a simple expression in terms of the attributes, we will need to make some sort of preference independence assumption. The most natural assumption is that the agent's preferences between state sequences are **stationary**. Stationarity for preferences means the following: if two state sequences $[s_0, s_1, s_2, \ldots]$ and $[s'_0, s'_1, s'_2, \ldots]$ begin with the same state (i.e., $s_0 = s'_0$) then the two sequences should be preference-ordered the same way as the sequences $[s_1, s_2, \ldots]$ and $[s'_1, s'_2, \ldots]$. In English, this means that if you prefer one future to another starting tomorrow, then you should still prefer that future if it were to start today. Stationarity is a fairly innocuous-looking assumption with very strong consequences: it turns out that under stationarity there are just two ways to assign utilities to sequences:

STATIONARY PREFERENCE

ADDITIVE REWARDS

1. **Additive rewards**: The utility of a state sequence is

$$U_h([s_0, s_1, s_2, \ldots]) = R(s_0) + R(s_1) + R(s_2) + \cdots .$$

The $4 \times 3$ world in Figure 17.1 uses additive rewards. Notice that additivity was used implicitly in our use of path cost functions in heuristic search algorithms (Chapter 4).

DISCOUNTED REWARDS

2. **Discounted rewards**: The utility of a state sequence is

$$U_h([s_0, s_1, s_2, \ldots]) = R(s_0) + \gamma R(s_1) + \gamma^2 R(s_2) + \cdots ,$$

DISCOUNT FACTOR

where the **discount factor** $\gamma$ is a number between 0 and 1. The discount factor describes the preference of an agent for current rewards over future rewards. When $\gamma$ is close to 0, rewards in the distant future are viewed as insignificant. When $\gamma$ is 1, discounted rewards are exactly equivalent to additive rewards, so additive rewards are a special case of discounted rewards. Discounting appears to be a good model of both animal and human preferences over time. A discount factor of $\gamma$ is equivalent to an interest rate of $(1/\gamma) - 1$.

For reasons that will shortly become clear, we will assume discounted rewards in the remainder of the chapter, although sometimes we will allow $\gamma = 1$.

---

[2] This is for completely observable environments. We will see later that for partially observable environments, the infinite-horizon case is not so simple.

Lurking beneath our choice of infinite horizons is a problem: if the environment does not contain a terminal state, or if the agent never reaches one, then all environment histories will be infinitely long, and utilities with additive rewards will generally be infinite. Now, we can agree that $+\infty$ is better than $-\infty$, but comparing two state sequences, both having $+\infty$ utility is more difficult. There are three solutions, two of which we have seen already:

1. With discounted rewards, the utility of an infinite sequence is *finite*. In fact, if rewards are bounded by $R_{\max}$ and $\gamma < 1$, we have

$$U_h([s_0, s_1, s_2, \ldots]) = \sum_{t=0}^{\infty} \gamma^t R(s_t) \leq \sum_{t=0}^{\infty} \gamma^t R_{\max} = R_{\max}/(1-\gamma)\,, \qquad (17.1)$$

using the standard formula for the sum of an infinite geometric series.

2. If the environment contains terminal states *and if the agent is guaranteed to get to one eventually*, then we will never need to compare infinite sequences. A policy that is guaranteed to reach a terminal state is called a **proper policy**. With proper policies, we can use $\gamma = 1$ (i.e., additive rewards). The first three policies shown in Figure 17.2(b) are proper, but the fourth is improper. It gains infinite total reward by staying away from the terminal states when the reward for the nonterminal states is positive. The existence of improper policies can cause the standard algorithms for solving MDPs to fail with additive rewards, and so provides a good reason for using discounted rewards.

PROPER POLICY

3. Another possibility is to compare infinite sequences in terms of the **average reward** obtained per time step. Suppose that square (1,1) in the $4 \times 3$ world has a reward of 0.1 while the other nonterminal states have a reward of 0.01. Then a policy that does its best to stay in (1,1) will have higher average reward than one that stays elsewhere. Average reward is a useful criterion for some problems, but the analysis of average-reward algorithms is beyond the scope of this book.

AVERAGE REWARD

In sum, the use of discounted rewards presents the fewest difficulties in evaluating state sequences. The final step is to show how to choose between policies, bearing in mind that a given policy $\pi$ generates not one state sequence, but a whole range of possible state sequences, each with a specific probability determined by the transition model for the environment. Thus, the value of a policy is the *expected* sum of discounted rewards obtained, where the expectation is taken over all possible state sequences that could occur, given that the policy is executed. An optimal policy $\pi^*$ satisfies

$$\pi^* = \operatorname*{argmax}_{\pi} E\left[\sum_{t=0}^{\infty} \gamma^t R(s_t) \mid \pi\right]. \qquad (17.2)$$

The next two sections describe algorithms for finding optimal policies.

## 17.2 Value Iteration

VALUE ITERATION

In this section, we present an algorithm, called **value iteration**, for calculating an optimal policy. The basic idea is to calculate the utility of each *state* and then use the state utilities to select an optimal action in each state.

### Utilities of states

The utility of states is defined in terms of the utility of state sequences. Roughly speaking, the utility of a state is the expected utility of the state sequences that might follow it. Obviously, the state sequences depend on the policy that is executed, so we begin by defining the utility $U^{\pi}(s)$ with respect to a specific policy $\pi$. If we let $s_t$ be the state the agent is in after executing $\pi$ for $t$ steps (note that $s_t$ is a random variable), then we have

$$U^{\pi}(s) = E\left[\sum_{t=0}^{\infty} \gamma^t R(s_t) \mid \pi, s_0 = s\right] . \tag{17.3}$$

Given this definition, the true utility of a state, which we write as $U(s)$, is just $U^{\pi^*}(s)$—that is, the expected sum of discounted rewards if the agent executes an optimal policy. Notice that $U(s)$ and $R(s)$ are quite different quantities; $R(s)$ is the "short-term" reward for being *in* $s$, whereas $U(s)$ is the "long-term" total reward from $s$ onwards. Figure 17.3 shows the utilities for the $4 \times 3$ world. Notice that the utilities are higher for states closer to the +1 exit, because fewer steps are required to reach the exit.

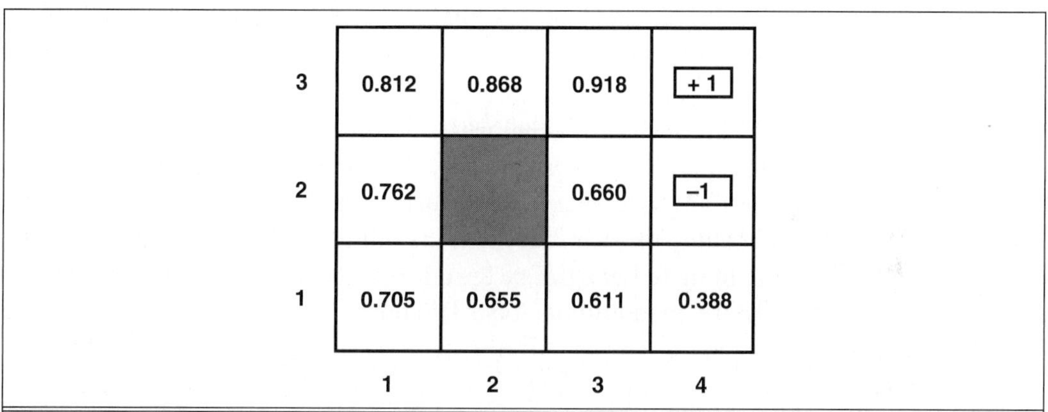


**Figure 17.3** The utilities of the states in the $4 \times 3$ world, calculated with $\gamma = 1$ and $R(s) = -0.04$ for nonterminal states.

The utility function $U(s)$ allows the agent to select actions by using the Maximum Expected Utility principle from Chapter 16—that is, choose the action that maximizes the expected utility of the subsequent state:

$$\pi^*(s) = \operatorname*{argmax}_a \sum_{s'} T(s, a, s')U(s') . \tag{17.4}$$

Now, if the utility of a state is the expected sum of discounted rewards from that point onwards, then there is a direct relationship between the utility of a state and the utility of its neighbors: *the utility of a state is the immediate reward for that state plus the expected discounted utility of the next state, assuming that the agent chooses the optimal action.* That is, the utility of a state is given by

$$U(s) = R(s) + \gamma \max_a \sum_{s'} T(s, a, s')U(s') . \tag{17.5}$$

BELLMAN EQUATION

Equation (17.5) is called the **Bellman equation**, after Richard Bellman (1957). The utilities of the states—defined by Equation (17.3) as the expected utility of subsequent state sequences—are solutions of the set of Bellman equations. In fact, they are the *unique* solutions, as we show in the next two sections.

Let us look at one of the Bellman equations for the $4 \times 3$ world. The equation for the state (1,1) is

$$\begin{aligned} U(1,1) = -0.04 + \gamma \max\{ \ & 0.8U(1,2) + 0.1U(2,1) + 0.1U(1,1), && (Up) \\ & 0.9U(1,1) + 0.1U(1,2), && (Left) \\ & 0.9U(1,1) + 0.1U(2,1), && (Down) \\ & 0.8U(2,1) + 0.1U(1,2) + 0.1U(1,1) \ \} && (Right) \end{aligned}$$

When we plug in the numbers from Figure 17.3, we find that *Up* is the best action.

### The value iteration algorithm

The Bellman equation is the basis of the value iteration algorithm for solving MDPs. If there are $n$ possible states, then there are $n$ Bellman equations, one for each state. The $n$ equations contain $n$ unknowns—the utilities of the states. So we would like to solve these simultaneous equations to find the utilities. There is one problem: the equations are *nonlinear*, because the "$\max$" operator is not a linear operator. Whereas systems of linear equations can be solved quickly using linear algebra techniques, systems of nonlinear equations are more problematic. One thing to try is an *iterative* approach. We start with arbitrary initial values for the utilities, calculate the right-hand side of the equation, and plug it into the left-hand side—thereby updating the utility of each state from the utilities of its neighbors. We repeat this until we reach an equilibrium. Let $U_i(s)$ be the utility value for state $s$ at the $i$th iteration. The iteration step, called a **Bellman update**, looks like this:

BELLMAN UPDATE

$$U_{i+1}(s) \leftarrow R(s) + \gamma \max_a \sum_{s'} T(s,a,s')U_i(s') . \qquad (17.6)$$

If we apply the Bellman update infinitely often, we are guaranteed to reach an equilibrium (see the next subsection), in which case the final utility values must be solutions to the Bellman equations. In fact, they are also the *unique* solutions, and the corresponding policy (obtained using Equation (17.4)) is optimal. The algorithm, called VALUE-ITERATION, is shown in Figure 17.4.

We can apply value iteration to the $4 \times 3$ world in Figure 17.1(a). Starting with initial values of zero, the utilities evolve as shown in Figure 17.5(a). Notice how the states at different distances from (4,3) accumulate negative reward until, at some point, a path is found to (4,3) whereupon the utilities start to increase. We can think of the value iteration algorithm as *propagating information* through the state space by means of local updates.

### Convergence of value iteration

We said that value iteration eventually converges to a unique set of solutions of the Bellman equations. In this section, we explain why this happens. We introduce some useful mathematical ideas along the way, and we obtain some methods for assessing the error in the utility

```
function VALUE-ITERATION(mdp, ε) returns a utility function
  inputs: mdp, an MDP with states S, transition model T, reward function R, discount γ
          ε, the maximum error allowed in the utility of any state
  local variables: U, U′, vectors of utilities for states in S, initially zero
                   δ, the maximum change in the utility of any state in an iteration

  repeat
    U ← U′; δ ← 0
    for each state s in S do
      U′[s] ← R[s] + γ max_a Σ_s′ T(s, a, s′) U[s′]
      if |U′[s] − U[s]| > δ then δ ← |U′[s] − U[s]|
  until δ < ε(1 − γ)/γ
  return U
```

**Figure 17.4** The value iteration algorithm for calculating utilities of states. The termination condition is from Equation (17.8).

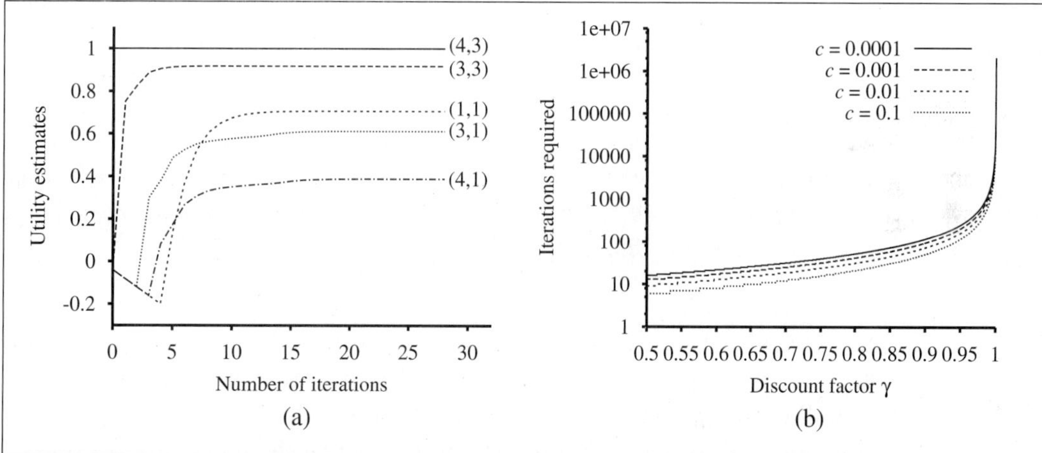


**Figure 17.5** (a) Graph showing the evolution of the utilities of selected states using value iteration. (b) The number of value iterations $k$ required to guarantee an error of at most $\epsilon = c \cdot R_{\max}$, for different values of $c$, as a function of the discount factor $\gamma$.

function returned when the algorithm is terminated early; this is useful because it means that we don't have to run forever. The section is quite technical.

CONTRACTION

The basic concept used in showing that value iteration converges is the notion of a **contraction**. Roughly speaking, a contraction is a function of one argument that, when applied to two different inputs in turn, produces two output values that are "closer together," by at least some constant amount, than the original arguments. For example, the function "divide by two" is a contraction, because, after we divide any two numbers by two, their difference is halved. Notice that the "divide by two" function has a fixed point, namely zero, that is unchanged by the application of the function. From this example, we can discern two important properties of contractions:

- A contraction has only one fixed point; if there were two fixed points they would not get closer together when the function was applied, so it would not be a contraction.
- When the function is applied to any argument, the value must get closer to the fixed point (because the fixed point does not move), so repeated application of a contraction always reaches the fixed point in the limit.

Now, suppose we view the Bellman update (Equation (17.6)) as an operator $B$ that is applied simultaneously to update the utility of every state. Let $U_i$ denote the vector of utilities for all the states at the $i$th iteration. Then the Bellman update equation can be written as

$$U_{i+1} \leftarrow B\,U_i\,.$$

MAX NORM

Next, we need a way to measure distances between utility vectors. We will use the **max norm**, which measures the length of a vector by the length of its biggest component:

$$||U|| = \max_s |U(s)|\,.$$

With this definition, the "distance" between two vectors, $||U - U'||$, is the maximum difference between any two corresponding elements. The main result of this section is the following: *Let $U_i$ and $U_i'$ be any two utility vectors. Then we have*

$$||B\,U_i - B\,U_i'|| \leq \gamma\,||U_i - U_i'||\,. \tag{17.7}$$

*That is, the Bellman update is a contraction by a factor of $\gamma$ on the space of utility vectors.* Hence, value iteration always converges to a unique solution of the Bellman equations.

In particular, we can replace $U_i'$ in Equation (17.7) with the *true* utilities $U$, for which $B\,U = U$. Then we obtain the inequality

$$||B\,U_i - U|| \leq \gamma\,||U_i - U||\,.$$

So, if we view $||U_i - U||$ as the *error* in the estimate $U_i$, we see that the error is reduced by a factor of at least $\gamma$ on each iteration. This means that value iteration converges exponentially fast. We can calculate the number of iterations required to reach a specified error bound $\epsilon$ as follows: First, recall from Equation (17.1) that the utilities of all states are bounded by $\pm R_{\max}/(1-\gamma)$. This means that the maximum initial error $||U_0 - U|| \leq 2R_{\max}/(1-\gamma)$. Suppose we run for $N$ iterations to reach an error of at most $\epsilon$. Then, because the error is reduced by at least $\gamma$ each time, we require $\gamma^N \cdot 2R_{\max}/(1-\gamma) \leq \epsilon$. Taking logs, we find

$$N = \lceil \log(2R_{\max}/\epsilon(1-\gamma))/\log(1/\gamma) \rceil$$

iterations suffice. Figure 17.5(b) shows how $N$ varies with $\gamma$, for different values of the ratio $\epsilon/R_{\max}$. The good news is that, because of the exponentially fast convergence, $N$ does not depend much on the ratio $\epsilon/R_{\max}$. The bad news is that $N$ grows rapidly as $\gamma$ becomes close to 1. We can get fast convergence if we make $\gamma$ small, but this effectively gives the agent a short horizon and could miss the long-term effects of the agent's actions.

The error bound in the preceding paragraph gives some idea of the factors influencing the runtime of the algorithm, but is sometimes overly conservative as a method of deciding when to stop the iteration. For the latter purpose, we can use a bound relating the error to the size of the Bellman update on any given iteration. From the contraction property (Equation (17.7)), it can be shown that if the update is small (i.e., no state's utility changes by much), then the error, compared with the true utility function, also is small. More precisely,

$$\text{if} \quad ||U_{i+1} - U_i|| < \epsilon(1-\gamma)/\gamma \quad \text{then} \quad ||U_{i+1} - U|| < \epsilon \,. \tag{17.8}$$

This is the termination condition used in the VALUE-ITERATION algorithm of Figure 17.4.

So far, we have analyzed the error in the utility function returned by the value iteration algorithm. *What the agent really cares about, however, is how well it will do if it makes its decisions on the basis of this utility function.* Suppose that after $i$ iterations of value iteration, the agent has an estimate $U_i$ of the true utility $U$ and obtains the MEU policy $\pi_i$ based on one-step look-ahead using $U_i$ (as in Equation (17.4)). Will the resulting behavior be nearly as good as the optimal behavior? This is a crucial question for any real agent, and it turns out that the answer is yes. $U^{\pi_i}(s)$ is the utility obtained if $\pi_i$ is executed starting in $s$, and the

POLICY LOSS

**policy loss** $||U^{\pi_i} - U||$ is the most the agent can lose by executing $\pi_i$ instead of the optimal policy $\pi^*$. The policy loss of $\pi_i$ is connected to the error in $U_i$ by the following inequality:

$$\text{if} \quad ||U_i - U|| < \epsilon \quad \text{then} \quad ||U^{\pi_i} - U|| < 2\epsilon\gamma/(1-\gamma) \,. \tag{17.9}$$

In practice, it often occurs that $\pi_i$ becomes optimal long before $U_i$ has converged. Figure 17.6 shows how the maximum error in $U_i$ and the policy loss approach zero as the value iteration process proceeds for the $4 \times 3$ environment with $\gamma = 0.9$. The policy $\pi_i$ is optimal when $i = 4$, even though the maximum error in $U_i$ is still 0.46.

Now we have everything we need to use value iteration in practice. We know that it converges to the correct utilities, we can bound the error in the utility estimates if we stop after a finite number of iterations, and we can bound the policy loss that results from executing the corresponding MEU policy. As a final note, all of the results in this section depend on discounting with $\gamma < 1$. If $\gamma = 1$ and the environment contains terminal states, then a similar set of convergence results and error bounds can be derived whenever certain technical conditions are satisfied.

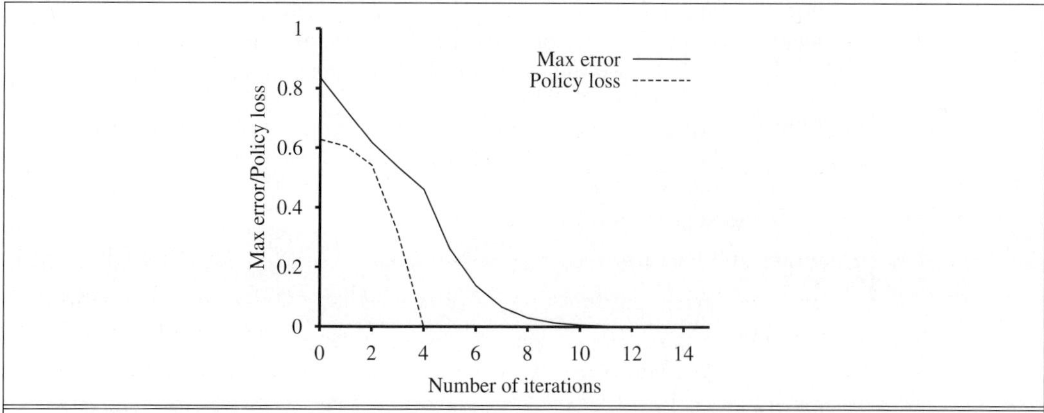


**Figure 17.6** The maximum error $||U_i - U||$ of the utility estimates and the policy loss $||U^{\pi_i} - U||$ compared with the optimal policy, as a function of the number of iterations of value iteration.

## 17.3 POLICY ITERATION

In the previous section, we observed that it is possible to get an optimal policy even when the utility function estimate is inaccurate. If one action is clearly better than all others, then the exact magnitude of the utilities on the states involved need not be precise. This insight suggests an alternative way to find optimal policies. The **policy iteration** algorithm alternates the following two steps, beginning from some initial policy $\pi_0$:

POLICY ITERATION

POLICY EVALUATION

- **Policy evaluation**: given a policy $\pi_i$, calculate $U_i = U^{\pi_i}$, the utility of each state if $\pi_i$ were to be executed.

POLICY IMPROVEMENT

- **Policy improvement**: Calculate a new MEU policy $\pi_{i+1}$, using one-step look-ahead based on $U_i$ (as in Equation (17.4)).

The algorithm terminates when the policy improvement step yields no change in the utilities. At this point, we know that the utility function $U_i$ is a fixed point of the Bellman update, so it is a solution to the Bellman equations, and $\pi_i$ must be an optimal policy. Because there are only finitely many policies for a finite state space, and each iteration can be shown to yield a better policy, policy iteration must terminate. The algorithm is shown in Figure 17.7.

The policy improvement step is obviously straightforward, but how do we implement the POLICY-EVALUATION routine? It turns out that doing so is much simpler than solving the standard Bellman equations (which is what value iteration does), because the action in each state is fixed by the policy. At the $i$th iteration, the policy $\pi_i$ specifies the action $\pi_i(s)$ in state $s$. This means that we have a simplified version of the Bellman equation (17.5) relating

```
function POLICY-ITERATION(mdp) returns a policy
  inputs: mdp, an MDP with states S, transition model T
  local variables: U, a vector of utilities for states in S, initially zero
                   π, a policy vector indexed by state, initially random

  repeat
     U ← POLICY-EVALUATION(π, U, mdp)
     unchanged? ← true
     for each state s in S do
        if max_a Σ_{s'} T(s, a, s') U[s'] > Σ_{s'} T(s, π[s], s') U[s'] then
           π[s] ← argmax_a Σ_{s'} T(s, a, s') U[s']
           unchanged? ← false
  until unchanged?
  return π
```

**Figure 17.7** The policy iteration algorithm for calculating an optimal policy.

the utility of $s$ (under $\pi_i$) to the utilities of its neighbors:

$$U_i(s) = R(s) + \gamma \sum_{s'} T(s, \pi_i(s), s') U_i(s') . \qquad (17.10)$$

For example, suppose $\pi_i$ is the policy shown in Figure 17.2(a). Then we have $\pi_i(1,1) = Up$, $\pi_i(1,2) = Up$, and so on, and the simplified Bellman equations are

$$\begin{aligned} U_i(1,1) &= -0.04 + 0.8U_i(1,2) + 0.1U_i(1,1) + 0.1U_i(2,1) , \\ U_i(1,2) &= -0.04 + 0.8U_i(1,3) + 0.2U_i(1,2) , \\ &\vdots \end{aligned}$$

The important point is that these equations are *linear*, because the "max" operator has been removed. For $n$ states, we have $n$ linear equations with $n$ unknowns, which can be solved exactly in time $O(n^3)$ by standard linear algebra methods.

For small state spaces, policy evaluation using exact solution methods is often the most efficient approach. For large state spaces, $O(n^3)$ time might be prohibitive. Fortunately, it is not necessary to do *exact* policy evaluation. Instead, we can perform some number of simplified value iteration steps (simplified because the policy is fixed) to give a reasonably good approximation of the utilities. The simplified Bellman update for this process is

$$U_{i+1}(s) \leftarrow R(s) + \gamma \sum_{s'} T(s, \pi_i(s), s') U_i(s')$$

and this is repeated $k$ times to produce the next utility estimate. The resulting algorithm is called **modified policy iteration**. It is often much more efficient than standard policy iteration or value iteration.

MODIFIED POLICY ITERATION

The algorithms we have described so far require updating the utility or policy for all states at once. It turns out that this is not strictly necessary. In fact, on each iteration, we can pick *any subset* of states and apply *either* kind of updating (policy improvement or simplified value iteration) to that subset. This very general algorithm is called **asynchronous policy iteration**. Given certain conditions on the initial policy and utility function, asynchronous policy iteration is guaranteed to converge to an optimal policy. The freedom to choose any states to work on means that we can design much more efficient heuristic algorithms—for example, algorithms that concentrate on updating the values of states that are likely to be reached by a good policy. This makes a lot of sense in real life: if one has no intention of throwing oneself off a cliff, one should not spend time worrying about the exact value of the resulting states.

ASYNCHRONOUS POLICY ITERATION

## 17.4 PARTIALLY OBSERVABLE MDPS

The description of Markov decision processes in Section 17.1 assumed that the environment was **fully observable**. With this assumption, the agent always knows which state it is in. This, combined with the Markov assumption for the transition model, means that the optimal policy depends only on the current state. When the environment is only **partially observable**, the situation is, one might say, much less clear. The agent does not necessarily know which state it is in, so it cannot execute the action $\pi(s)$ recommended for that state. Furthermore, the utility of a state $s$ and the optimal action in $s$ depend not just on $s$, but also on *how much the agent knows* when it is in $s$. For these reasons, **partially observable MDPs** (or POMDPs—pronounced "pom-dee-pees") are usually viewed as much more difficult than ordinary MDPs. We cannot avoid POMDPs, however, because the real world is one.

PARTIALLY OBSERVABLE MDP

As an example, consider again the $4 \times 3$ world of Figure 17.1, but now let's suppose that the agent has *no sensors whatsoever* and has *no idea where it is*. More precisely, let's suppose the agent's initial state is equally likely to be any of the nine nonterminal states (Figure 17.8(a)). Clearly, if the agent *knew* it was in (3,3), it would move *Right*; if it *knew* it was in (1,1), it would move *Up*; but since it could be anywhere, what should it do? One possible answer is that the agent should first act so as to reduce its uncertainty, and only then should it try heading for the +1 exit. For example, if the agent moves *Left* five times, then it is quite likely to be at the left wall (Figure 17.8(b)). Then, if it moves *Up* five times, it is quite likely to be at the top, probably in the top left corner (Figure 17.8(c)). Finally, if it moves *Right* five times, it has a good chance—about 77.5%—of reaching the +1 exit (Figure 17.8(d)). Continuing to move right thereafter increases its chances to 81.8%. This policy is therefore surprisingly safe, but under it, the agent is rather slow to reach the exit, and has an expected utility of only about 0.08. The optimal policy, which we will describe shortly, does much better.

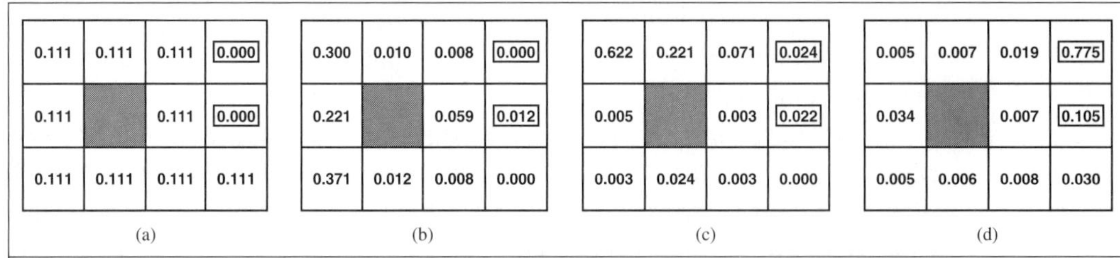


**Figure 17.8** (a) The initial probability distribution for the agent's location. (b) After moving *Left* five times. (c) After moving *Up* five times. (d) After moving *Right* five times.

To get a handle on POMDPs, we must first define them properly. A POMDP has the same elements as an MDP—the transition model $T(s, a, s')$ and the reward function $R(s)$—but it also has an **observation model** $O(s, o)$ that specifies the probability of perceiving the observation $o$ in state $s$.[3] For example, our agent with no sensors has only one possible observation (the empty observation), and this occurs with probability 1 in every state.

OBSERVATION MODEL

In Chapters 3 and 12, we studied nondeterministic and partially observable planning problems and identified the **belief state**—the set of actual states the agent might be in—as a key concept for describing and calculating solutions. In POMDPs, the concept is refined somewhat. A belief state $b$ is now a *probability distribution* over all possible states. For example, the initial belief state in Figure 17.8(a) could be written as $\langle \frac{1}{9}, \frac{1}{9}, \frac{1}{9}, \frac{1}{9}, \frac{1}{9}, \frac{1}{9}, \frac{1}{9}, \frac{1}{9}, \frac{1}{9}, 0, 0 \rangle$.

[3] The observation model is essentially identical to the **sensor model** for temporal processes, as described in Chapter 15. As with the reward function for MDPs, the observation model can also depend on the action and outcome state, but again this change is not fundamental.

We will write $b(s)$ for the probability assigned to the actual state $s$ by belief state $b$. The agent can calculate its current belief state as the conditional probability distribution over the actual states given the sequence of observations and actions so far. This is essentially the **filtering** task. (See Chapter 15.) The basic recursive filtering equation (15.3 on page 543) shows how to calculate the new belief state from the previous belief state and the new observation. For POMDPs, we also have an action to consider and a slightly different notation, but the result is essentially the same. If $b(s)$ was the previous belief state, and the agent does action $a$ and perceives observation $o$, then the new belief state is given by

$$b'(s') = \alpha\, O(s', o) \sum_s T(s, a, s')b(s) \tag{17.11}$$

where $\alpha$ is a normalizing constant that makes the belief state sum to 1. We can abbreviate this equation as $b' = \text{FORWARD}(b, a, o)$.

The fundamental insight required to understand POMDPs is this: *the optimal action depends only on the agent's current belief state.* That is, the optimal policy can be described by a mapping $\pi^*(b)$ from belief states to actions. It does *not* depend on the *actual* state the agent is in. This is a good thing, because the agent does not know its actual state; all it knows is the belief state. Hence, the decision cycle of a POMDP agent is this:

1. Given the current belief state $b$, execute the action $a = \pi^*(b)$.
2. Receive observation $o$.
3. Set the current belief state to $\text{FORWARD}(b, a, o)$ and repeat.

Now we can think of POMDPs as requiring a search in belief state space, just like the methods for sensorless and contingency problems in Chapter 3. The main difference is that the POMDP belief state space is *continuous*, because a POMDP belief state is a probability distribution. For example, a belief state for the $4 \times 3$ world is a point in an 11-dimensional continuous space. An action changes the belief state, not just the physical state, so it is evaluated according to the information the agent acquires as a result. POMDPs therefore include the value of information (Section 16.6) as one component of the decision problem.

Let's look more carefully at the outcome of actions. In particular, let's calculate the probability that an agent in belief state $b$ reaches belief state $b'$ after executing action $a$. Now, if we knew the action *and the subsequent observation*, then Equation (17.11) would provide a *deterministic* update to the belief state: $b' = \text{FORWARD}(b, a, o)$. Of course, the subsequent observation is not yet known, so the agent might arrive in one of several possible belief states $b'$, depending on the observation that occurs. The probability of perceiving $o$, given that $a$ was performed starting in belief state $b$, is given by summing over all the actual states $s'$ that the agent might reach:

$$\begin{aligned}
P(o|a,b) &= \sum_{s'} P(o|a,s',b)P(s'|a,b) \\
&= \sum_{s'} O(s',o)P(s'|a,b) \\
&= \sum_{s'} O(s',o) \sum_s T(s,a,s')b(s)\,.
\end{aligned}$$

Let us write the probability of reaching $b'$ from $b$, given action $a$, as $\tau(b, a, b')$. Then that gives us

$$\begin{aligned}\tau(b,a,b') &= P(b'|a,b) = \sum_o P(b'|o,a,b)P(o|a,b) \\ &= \sum_o P(b'|o,a,b) \sum_{s'} O(s',o) \sum_s T(s,a,s')b(s) \,, \end{aligned} \quad (17.12)$$

where $P(b'|o, a, b)$ is 1 if $b' = \text{FORWARD}(b, a, o)$ and 0 otherwise.

Equation (17.12) can be viewed as defining a transition model for the belief state space. We can also define a reward function for belief states (i.e., the expected reward for the actual states the agent might be in):

$$\rho(b) = \sum_s b(s)R(s) \,.$$

So it seems that $\tau(b, a, b')$ and $\rho(b)$ together define an *observable* MDP on the space of belief states. Furthermore, it can be shown that an optimal policy for this MDP, $\pi^*(b)$, is also an optimal policy for the original POMDP. In other words, *solving a POMDP on a physical state space can be reduced to solving an MDP on the corresponding belief state space.* This fact is perhaps less surprising if we remember that the belief state is always observable to the agent, by definition.

Notice that, although we have reduced POMDPs to MDPs, the MDP we obtain has a continuous (and usually high-dimensional) state space. None of the MDP algorithms described in Sections 17.2 and 17.3 applies directly to such MDPs. It turns out that we *can* develop versions of value and policy iteration that apply to continuous-state MDPs. The basic idea is that a policy $\pi(b)$ can be represented as a set of *regions* of belief state space, each of which is associated with a particular optimal action.[4] The value function associates a distinct *linear* function of $b$ with each region. Each value- or policy-iteration step refines the boundaries of the regions and might introduce new regions.

The details of the algorithms are beyond the scope of this book, but we will report the solution for the sensorless $4 \times 3$ world. The optimal policy is the following:

$$[\mathit{Left}, \mathit{Up}, \mathit{Up}, \mathit{Right}, \mathit{Up}, \mathit{Up}, \mathit{Right}, \mathit{Up}, \mathit{Up}, \mathit{Right}, \mathit{Up}, \mathit{Right}, \mathit{Up}, \mathit{Right}, \mathit{Up}, \ldots] \,.$$

The policy is a sequence because this problem is *deterministic* in belief state space—there are no observations. The "trick" it embodies is to have the agent move *Left* once to ensure that it's *not* in (4,1), so that it's then fairly safe to keep moving *Up* and *Right* to reach the +1 exit. The agent reaches the +1 exit 86.6% of the time and does so much faster than the policy given earlier in the section, so its expected utility is 0.38 compared with 0.08.

For more complex POMDPs with observations, finding approximately optimal policies is very difficult (PSPACE-hard, in fact—i.e., very hard indeed). Problems with a few dozen states are often infeasible. The next section describes a different, approximate method for solving POMDPs, one based on look-ahead search.

[4] For some POMDPs, the optimal policy has infinitely many regions, so the simple list-of-regions approach fails and more ingenious methods are needed to find even an approximation.

## 17.5 DECISION-THEORETIC AGENTS

In this section, we outline a comprehensive approach to agent design for partially observable, stochastic environments. The basic elements of the design are already familiar:

- The transition and observation models are represented by a **dynamic Bayesian network** (as described in Chapter 15).
- The dynamic Bayesian network is extended with decision and utility nodes, as used in **decision networks** in Chapter 16. The resulting model is called a **dynamic decision network** or DDN.

DYNAMIC DECISION NETWORK

- A filtering algorithm is used to incorporate each new percept and action and to update the belief state representation.
- cisions are made by projecting forward possible action sequences and choosing the
st one.

ary advantage of using a dynamic Bayesian network to represent the transition and
odels is that it decomposes the state description into a set of random variables, much
ing algorithms use logical representations to decompose the state space used by
lgorithms. The agent design is therefore a practical implementation of the **utility-**
**gent** sketched in Chapter 2.

cause we are using dynamic Bayesian networks, we will revert to the notation of
15, where $\mathbf{X}_t$ referred to the set of state variables for time $t$ and $\mathbf{E}_t$ referred to the evidence variables. Thus, where we have used $s_t$ (the state at time $t$) so far in this chapter, we will now use $\mathbf{X}_t$. We will use $A_t$ to refer to the action at time $t$, so the transition model $T(s, a, s')$ is the same as $\mathbf{P}(\mathbf{X}_{t+1}|\mathbf{X}_t, A_t)$ and the observation model $O(s, o)$ is the same as $\mathbf{P}(\mathbf{E}_t|\mathbf{X}_t)$. We will use $R_t$ to refer to the reward received at time $t$ and $U_t$ to refer to the utility of the state at time $t$. With this notation, a dynamic decision network looks like the one shown in Figure 17.9.

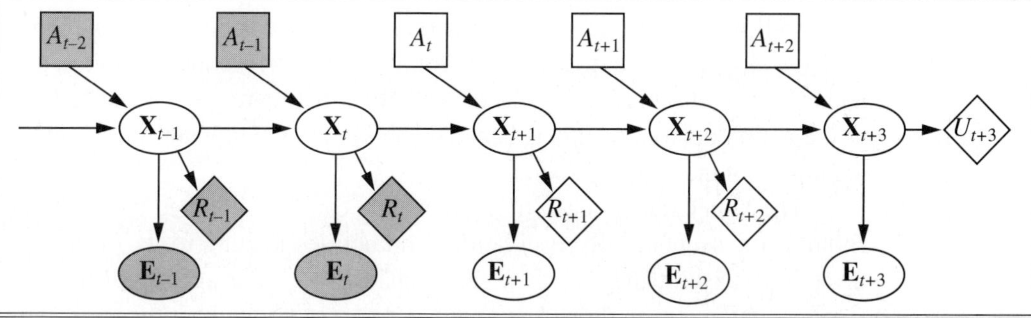


**Figure 17.9** The generic structure of a dynamic decision network. Variables with known values are shaded. The current time is $t$ and the agent must decide what to do—that is, choose a value for $A_t$. The network has been unrolled into the future for three steps and represents future rewards, as well as the utility of the state at the look-ahead horizon.

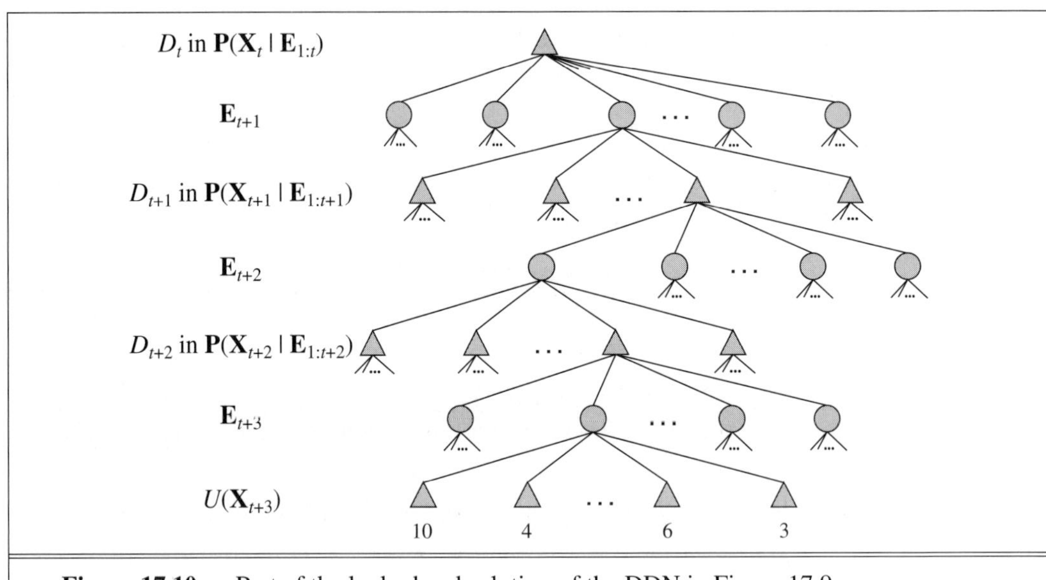


**Figure 17.10** Part of the look-ahead solution of the DDN in Figure 17.9.

Dynamic decision networks provide a concise representation for large POMDPs, so they can be used as inputs for any POMDP algorithm including those for value- and policy-iteration methods. In this section, we will focus on look-ahead methods that project action sequences forward from the current belief state in much the same way as do the game-playing algorithms of Chapter 6. The network in Figure 17.9 has been projected three steps into the future; the current and future decisions and the future observations and rewards are all unknown. Notice that the network includes nodes for the *rewards* for $\mathbf{X}_{t+1}$ and $\mathbf{X}_{t+2}$, but the *utility* for $\mathbf{X}_{t+3}$. This is because the agent must maximize the (discounted) sum of all future rewards, and $U(\mathbf{X}_{t+3})$ represents the reward for $\mathbf{X}_{t+3}$ and all subsequent rewards. As in Chapter 6, we assume that $U$ is available only in some approximate form: if exact utility values were available, there would be no need for look-ahead beyond depth 1.

Figure 17.10 shows part of the search tree corresponding to the three-step look-ahead DDN in Figure 17.9. Each of the triangular nodes is a belief state in which the agent makes a decision $A_{t+i}$ for $i = 0, 1, 2, \ldots$. The round nodes correspond to choices by the environment, namely, what observation $\mathbf{E}_{t+i}$ occurs. Notice that there are no chance nodes corresponding to the action outcomes; this is because the belief state update for an action is deterministic regardless of the actual outcome.

The belief state at each triangular node can be computed by applying a filtering algorithm to the sequence of observations and actions leading to it. In this way, the algorithm takes into account the fact that, for decision $A_{t+i}$, the agent *will* have available percepts $\mathbf{E}_{t+1}, \ldots, \mathbf{E}_{t+i}$, even though at time $t$ it does not know what those percepts will be. In this way, a decision-theoretic agent automatically takes into account the value of information and will execute information-gathering actions where appropriate.

A decision can be extracted from the search tree by backing up the utility values from the leaves, taking an average at the chance nodes and taking the maximum at the decision nodes. This is similar to the EXPECTIMINIMAX algorithm for game trees with chance nodes, except that (1) there can also be rewards at non-leaf states and (2) the decision nodes correspond to belief states rather than actual states. The time complexity of an exhaustive search to depth $d$ is $O(|D|^d \cdot |\mathbf{E}|^d)$, where $|D|$ is the number of available actions and $\mathbf{E}$ is the number of possible observations. For problems in which the discount factor $\gamma$ is not too close to 1, a shallow search is often good enough to give near-optimal decisions. It is also possible to approximate the averaging step at the chance nodes, by sampling from the set of possible observations instead of summing over all possible observations. There are various other ways of finding good approximate solutions quickly, but we defer them to Chapter 21.

Decision-theoretic agents based on dynamic decision networks have a number of advantages compared with other, simpler agent designs presented in earlier chapters. In particular, they handle partially observable, uncertainty environments and can easily revise their "plans" to handle unexpected observations. With appropriate sensor models, they can handle sensor failure and can plan to gather information. They exhibit "graceful degradation" under time pressure and in complex environments, using various approximation techniques. So what is missing? The most important defect of our DDN-based algorithm is its reliance on forward search, just like the state-space search algorithms of Part II. In Part IV, we explained how the ability to consider partially ordered, abstract plans via goal-directed search provided a massive increase in problem-solving power, particularly when combined with plan libraries. There have been attempts to extend these methods into the probabilistic domain, but so far they have proven to be inefficient. A second, related problem is the basically propositional nature of the DDN language. We would like to be able to extend some of the ideas for first-order probabilistic languages in Section 14.6 to the problem of decision making. Current research has shown that this extension is possible and has significant benefits, as discussed in the notes at the end of the chapter.

## 17.6 DECISIONS WITH MULTIPLE AGENTS: GAME THEORY

This chapter has concentrated on making decisions in uncertain environments. But what if the uncertainty is due to other agents and the decisions they make? And what if the decisions of those agents are in turn influenced by our decisions? We addressed this question once before, when we studied games in Chapter 6. There, however, we were concerned with turn-taking games with perfect information, for which minimax search can be used to find optimal moves. In this section we study the aspects of **game theory** that can be used to analyze games with simultaneous moves. To simplify matters, we will look first at games that are only one move long. The word "game" and the simplification to single moves might make this seem trivial, but in fact, game theory is used in very serious decision making situations including bankruptcy proceedings, the auctioning of wireless frequency spectrums, product development and pricing decisions, and national defense, situations involving billions of dollars and hundreds of thousands of lives. Game theory can be used in at least two ways:

GAME THEORY

1. **Agent design**: Game theory can analyze the agent's decisions, and compute the expected utility for each decision (under the assumption that other agents are acting optimally according to game theory). For example, in the game **two-finger Morra**, two players, $O$ and $E$, simultaneously display one or two fingers. Let the total number of fingers be $f$. If $f$ is odd, $O$ collects $f$ dollars from $E$, and if $f$ is even, $E$ collects $f$ dollars from $O$. Game theory can determine the best strategy against a rational player and the expected return for each player.[5]
2. **Mechanism Design**: When an environment is inhabited by many agents, it might be possible to define the rules of the environment (i.e., the game that the agents must play) so that the collective good of all agents is maximized when each agent adopts the game-theoretic solution that maximizes its own utility. For example, game theory can help design the protocols for a collection of Internet traffic routers so that each router has an incentive to act in such a way that global throughput is maximized. Mechanism design can also be used to construct intelligent **multiagent systems** that solve complex problems in a distributed fashion without the need for each agent to know about the whole problem being solved.

A game in game theory is defined by the following components:

PLAYERS

- **Players** or agents who will be making decisions. Two-player games have received the most attention, although $n$-player games for $n > 2$ are also common. We will give players capitalized names, like *Alice* and *Bob* or $O$ and $E$.

ACTIONS

- **Actions** that the players can choose. We will give actions lowercase names, like $one$ or $testify$. The players may or may not have the same set of actions available.

PAYOFF MATRIX

- A **payoff matrix** that gives the utility to each player for each combination of actions by all the players. The payoff matrix for two-finger Morra is as follows:

| | *O: one* | *O: two* |
|---|---|---|
| *E: one* | $E = 2, O = -2$ | $E = -3, O = 3$ |
| *E: two* | $E = -3, O = 3$ | $E = 4, O = -4$ |

For example, the lower-right corner shows that when $O$ chooses action *two* and $E$ also chooses *two*, the payoff is 4 for $E$ and $-4$ for $O$.

PURE STRATEGY

MIXED STRATEGY

STRATEGY PROFILE

OUTCOME

Each player in a game must adopt and then execute a **strategy** (which is the name used in game theory for a policy). A **pure strategy** is a deterministic policy specifying a particular action to take in each situation; for a one-move game, a pure strategy is just a single action. The analysis of games leads to the idea of a **mixed strategy**, which is a randomized policy that selects particular actions according to a specific probability distribution over actions. The mixed strategy that chooses action $a$ with probability $p$ and action $b$ otherwise is written $[p\colon a; (1-p)\colon b]$. For example, a mixed strategy for two-finger Morra might be $[0.5\colon one; 0.5\colon two]$. A **strategy profile** is an assignment of a strategy to each player; given the strategy profile, the game's **outcome** is a numeric value for each player.

5 Morra is a recreational version of an **inspection game**. In such games, an inspector chooses a day to inspect a facility (such as a restaurant or a biological weapons plant), and the facility operator chooses a day to hide all the nasty stuff. The inspector wins if the days are different and the facility operator wins if they are the same.

SOLUTION

A **solution** to a game is a strategy profile in which each player adopts a rational strategy. We will see that the most important issue in game theory is to define what "rational" means when each agent chooses only part of the strategy profile that determines the outcome. It is important to realize that outcomes are actual results of playing a game, while solutions are theoretical constructs used to analyze a game. We will see that some games only have a solution in mixed strategies. But that does not mean that a player must literally be adopting a mixed strategy to be rational.

PRISONER'S DILEMMA

Consider the following story: Two alleged burglars, Alice and Bob, are caught red-handed near the scene of a burglary and are interrogated separately by the police. Both know that if they both confess to the crime, they will each serve 5 years in prison for burglary, but if both refuse to confess, they will serve only 1 year each for the lesser charge of possessing stolen property. However, the police separately offer each a deal: if you testify against your partner as the leader of a burglary ring, you'll go free, while the partner will serve 10 years. Now Alice and Bob face the so-called **prisoner's dilemma**: should they testify or refuse? Being rational agents, Alice and Bob each want to maximize their own expected utility. Let's assume that Alice is callously unconcerned about her partner's fate, so her utility decreases in proportion to the number of years she will spend in prison, regardless of what happens to Bob. Bob feels exactly the same way. To help reach a rational decision, they both construct the following payoff matrix:

| | $Alice$:$testify$ | $Alice$:$refuse$ |
|---|---|---|
| $Bob$:$testify$ | $A = -5, B = -5$ | $A = -10, B = 0$ |
| $Bob$:$refuse$ | $A = 0, B = -10$ | $A = -1, B = -1$ |

Alice analyzes the payoff matrix as follows: Suppose Bob testifies. Then I get 5 years if I testify and 10 years if I don't, so in that case testifying is better. On the other hand, if Bob refuses, then I get 0 years if I testify and 1 year if I refuse, so in that case as well testifying is better. So in either case, it's better for me to testify, so that's what I must do.

DOMINANT STRATEGY

STRONGLY DOMINATES

WEAKLY DOMINATES

Alice has discovered that $testify$ is a **dominant strategy** for the game. We say that a strategy $s$ for player $p$ **strongly dominates** strategy $s'$ if the outcome for $s$ is better for $p$ than the outcome for $s'$, for every choice of strategies by the other players. Strategy $s$ **weakly dominates** $s'$ if $s$ is better than $s'$ on at least one strategy profile and no worse on any other. A dominant strategy is a strategy that dominates all others. It is irrational to play a strongly dominated strategy, and irrational not to play a dominant strategy if one exists. Being rational, Alice chooses the dominant strategy. We need just a bit more terminology before we go on: we say that an outcome is **Pareto optimal**[6] if there is no other outcome that all players would prefer. An outcome is **Pareto dominated** by another outcome if all players would prefer the other outcome.

PARETO OPTIMAL

PARETO DOMINATED

If Alice is clever as well as rational, she will continue to reason as follows: Bob's dominant strategy is also to testify. Therefore, he will testify and we will both get five years. When each player has a dominant strategy, the combination of those strategies is called a **dominant strategy equilibrium**. In general, a strategy profile forms an **equilibrium** if no

DOMINANT STRATEGY EQUILIBRIUM

EQUILIBRIUM

[6] Pareto optimality is named after the economist Vilfredo Pareto (1848–1923).

player can benefit by switching strategies, given that every other player sticks with the same strategy. An equilibrium is essentially a **local optimum** in the space of policies; it is the top of a peak that slopes downward along every dimension, where a dimension corresponds to a player's strategy choices.

The *dilemma* in the prisoner's dilemma is that the outcome of the equilibrium point is worse for both players than the outcome they would get if they both refused to testify. In other words, the outcome for the equilibrium solution is Pareto dominated by the (-1, -1) outcome of $(refuse, refuse)$.

Is there any way for Alice and Bob to arrive at the (-1, -1) outcome? It is certainly an *allowable* option for both of them to refuse to testify, but is is an *unlikely* option. Either player contemplating playing $refuse$ will realize that he or she would do better by playing $testify$. That is the attractive power of an equilibrium point.

NASH EQUILIBRIUM

The mathematician John Nash (1928–) proved that *every game has an equilibrium of the type defined here.* It is now called a **Nash equilibrium** in his honor. Clearly, a dominant strategy equilibrium is a Nash equilibrium (Exercise 17.9), but not all games have dominant strategies. Nash's theorem means that there are equilibrium strategies even when there is no dominant strategy.

For the prisoner's dilemma, only the strategy profile $(testify, testify)$ is a Nash equilibrium. It is hard to see how rational players can avoid this outcome, because in any proposed non-equilibrium solution at least one of the players will be tempted to change strategies. Game theorists agree that being a Nash equilibrium is a necessary condition for being a solution—although they disagree whether it is a sufficient condition.

It is easy enough to avoid the $(testify, testify)$ solution if we change the game (or the players) in some way. For example, we could change to an iterated game in which the players know that they will meet again (but crucially, they must be uncertain about how many times they will meet again). Or if the agents have moral beliefs that encourage cooperation and fairness, we could change the payoff matrix to reflect the utility to each agent of cooperating with the other. We will see later that changing the agents to have limited computational powers, rather than the ability to reason absolutely rationally, can also affect the outcome, as can telling one agent that the other has limited rationality.

Now, let's look at a game that has no dominant strategy. Acme, a video game hardware manufacturer, has to decide whether its next game machine will use DVDs or CDs. Meanwhile, the video game software producer Best needs to decide whether to produce its next game on DVD or CD. The profits for both will be positive if they agree and negative if they disagree, as shown in the following payoff matrix:

| | $Acme{:}dvd$ | $Acme{:}cd$ |
|---|---|---|
| $Best{:}dvd$ | $A = 9, B = 9$ | $A = -4, B = -1$ |
| $Best{:}cd$ | $A = -3, B = -1$ | $A = 5, B = 5$ |

There is no dominant strategy equilibrium for this game, but there are *two* Nash equilibria: (*dvd, dvd*) and (*cd, cd*). We know these are Nash equilibria because, if either player unilaterally moves to a different strategy, that player will be worse off. Now the agents have a problem: *there are multiple acceptable solutions, but if each agent chooses a different*

*solution then the resulting strategy profile won't be a solution at all and both agents will suffer.* How can they agree on a solution? One answer is that both should choose the Pareto-optimal solution (*dvd, dvd*); that is, we can restrict the definition of "solution" to the unique Pareto-optimal Nash equilibrium *provided that one exists*. Every game has at least one Pareto-optimal solution, but a game might have several, or they might not be equilibrium points. For example, we could set the payoffs for (*dvd, dvd*) to 5 instead of 9. In that case, there are two equal Pareto-optimal equilibrium points. To choose between them the agents can either guess or *communicate*, which can be done either by establishing a convention that orders the solutions before the game begins or by negotiating to reach a mutually beneficial solution during the game (which would mean including communicative actions as part of a multimove game). Communication thus arises in game theory for exactly the same reasons that it arose in multiagent planning in Chapter 12. Games in which players need to communicate like this are called **coordination games**.

COORDINATION GAME

We have seen that a game can have more than one Nash equilibrium; how do we know that every game must have at least one? It can be that a game has no *pure-strategy* Nash equilibria. Consider, for example, any pure strategy profile for two-finger Morra (page 632). If the total number of fingers is even then $O$ will want to switch; if the total is odd then $E$ will want to switch. Therefore no pure strategy profile can be an equilibrium and we must look to mixed strategies.

But *which* mixed strategy? In 1928, von Neumann developed a method for finding the *optimal* mixed strategy for two-player, **zero-sum games**. A zero-sum game is a game in which the payoffs in each cell of the payoff matrix sum to zero.[7] Clearly, Morra is such a game. For two-player, zero-sum games, we know that the payoffs are equal and opposite, so we need consider the payoffs of only one player, who will be the maximizer (just as in Chapter 6). For Morra, we pick the even player $E$ to be the maximizer, so we can define the payoff matrix by the values $U_E(e, o)$—the payoff to $E$ if $E$ does $e$ and $O$ does $o$.

ZERO-SUM GAME

Von Neumann's method is called the the **maximin** technique, and it works as follows:

MAXIMIN

- Suppose we change the rules to force $E$ to reveal his or her strategy first, followed by $O$. Then we have a turn-taking game to which we can apply the standard **minimax** algorithm from Chapter 6. Let's suppose this gives an outcome $U_{E,O}$. Clearly, this game favors $O$, so the true utility $U$ of the game (from $E$'s point of view) is *at least* $U_{E,O}$. For example, if we just look at pure strategies, the minimax game tree has a root value of $-3$ (see Figure 17.11(a)), so we know that $U \geq -3$.

- Now suppose we change the rules to force $O$ to reveal his or her strategy first, followed by $E$. Then the minimax value of this game is $U_{O,E}$, and because this game favors $E$ we know that $U$ is *at most* $U_{O,E}$. With pure strategies, the value is $+2$ (see Figure 17.11(b)), so we know $U \leq +2$.

[7] More general is the concept of **constant-sum games**, in which the sum of every cell in the game adds up to a constant, $c$. An $n$-person constant-sum game can be turned into a zero-sum game by subtracting $c/n$ from every payoff. Thus chess, with traditional payoff of 1 for a win, 1/2 for a draw, and 0 for a loss, is technically a constant-sum game with $c = 1$, but can easily be transformed into a zero-sum game by subtracting 1/2 from every payoff.

Combining these two arguments, we see that the true utility $U$ of the solution must satisfy

$$U_{E,O} \leq U \leq U_{O,E} \qquad \text{or in this case,} \qquad -3 \leq U \leq 2 \,.$$

To pinpoint the value of $U$, we need to turn our analysis to mixed strategies. First, observe the following: *once the first player has revealed his or her strategy, the second player cannot lose by playing a pure strategy.* The reason is simple: if the second player plays a mixed strategy, $[p\colon one; (1-p)\colon two]$, its expected utility is a linear combination $(p \cdot u_{one} + (1-p) \cdot u_{two})$ of the utilities of the pure strategies, $u_{one}$ and $u_{two}$. This linear combination can never be better than the best of $u_{one}$ and $u_{two}$, so the second player might as well play a pure strategy.

With this observation in mind, the minimax trees can be thought of as having infinitely many branches at the root, corresponding to the infinitely many mixed strategies the first player can choose. Each of these leads to a node with two branches corresponding to the pure strategies for the second player. We can depict these infinite trees finitely by having one "parameterized" choice at the root:

- If $E$ moves first, the situation is as shown in Figure 17.11(c). $E$ plays $[p\colon one; (1-p)\colon two]$ at the root, and then $O$ chooses a move given the value of $p$. If $O$ chooses $one$, the expected payoff (to $E$) is $2p - 3(1-p) = 5p - 3$; if $O$ chooses $two$, the expected payoff is $-3p + 4(1-p) = 4 - 7p$. We can draw these two payoffs as straight lines on a graph, where $p$ ranges from 0 to 1 on the $x$-axis, as shown in Figure 17.11(e). $O$, the minimizer, will always choose the lower of the two lines, as shown by the heavy lines in the figure. Therefore, the best that $E$ can do at the root is to choose $p$ to be at the intersection point, which is where

  $$5p - 3 = 4 - 7p \qquad \Rightarrow \qquad p = 7/12 \,.$$

  The utility for $E$ at this point is $U_{E,O} = -1/12$.
- If $O$ moves first, the situation is as shown in Figure 17.11(d). $O$ plays $[q\colon one; (1-q)\colon two]$ at the root, and then $E$ chooses a move given the value of $q$. The payoffs are $2q - 3(1-q) = 5q - 3$ and $-3q + 4(1-q) = 4 - 7q$.[8] Again, Figure 17.11(f) shows that the best $O$ can do at the root is to choose the intersection point:

  $$5q - 3 = 4 - 7q \qquad \Rightarrow \qquad q = 7/12 \,.$$

  The utility for $E$ at this point is $U_{O,E} = -1/12$.

MAXIMIN EQUILIBRIUM

Now we know that the true utility of the game lies between $-1/12$ and $-1/12$, that is, it is exactly $-1/12$! (The moral is that it is better to be $O$ than $E$ if you are playing this game.) Furthermore, the true utility is attained by the mixed strategy $[7/12\colon one; 5/12\colon two]$, which should be played by both players. This strategy is called the **maximin equilibrium** of the game, and is a Nash equilibrium. Note that each component strategy in an equilibrium mixed strategy has the same expected utility. In this case, both $one$ and $two$ have the same expected utility, $-1/12$, as the mixed strategy itself.

Our result for two-finger Morra is an example of the general result by von Neumann: *every two-player zero-sum game has a maximin equilibrium when you allow mixed strategies.*

---

[8] It is a coincidence that these equations are the same as those for $p$; the coincidence arises because $U_E(one, two) = U_E(two, one) = -3$. This also explains why the optimal strategy is the same for both players.

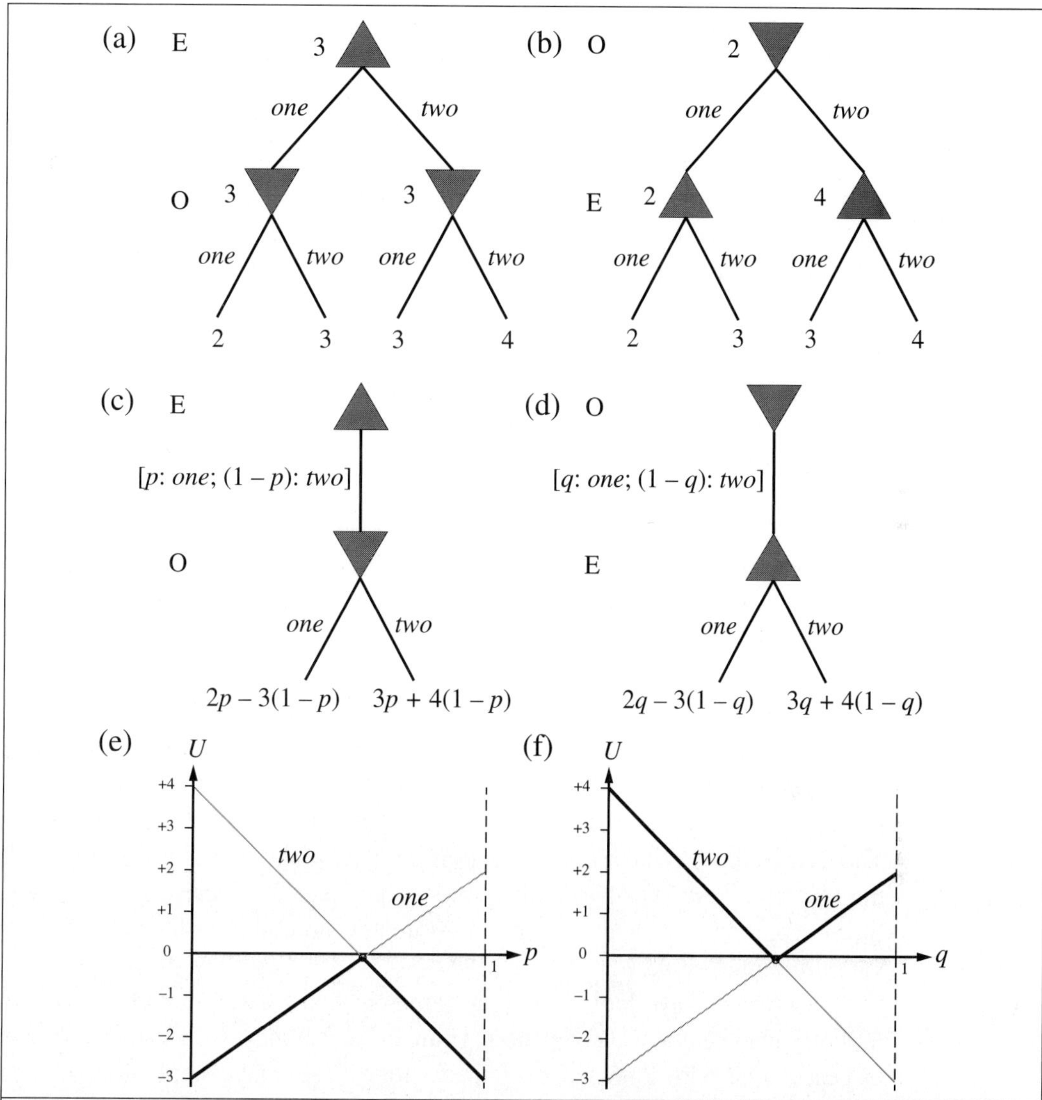


**Figure 17.11** (a) and (b): Minimax game trees for two-finger Morra if the players take turns playing pure strategies. (c) and (d): Parameterized game trees where the first player plays a mixed strategy. The payoffs depend on the probability parameter ($p$ or $q$) in the mixed strategy. (e) and (f): For any particular value of the probability parameter, the second player will choose the "better" of the two actions, so the value of the first player's mixed strategy is given by the heavy lines. The first player will choose the probability parameter for the mixed strategy at the intersection point.

Furthermore, every Nash equilibrium in a zero-sum game is a maximin for both players. The general algorithm for finding maximin equilibria in zero-sum games is somewhat more involved than Figures 17.11(e) and (f) might suggest. When there are $n$ possible actions, a mixed strategy is a point in $n$-dimensional space and the lines become hyperplanes. It's also possible for some pure strategies for the second player to be dominated by others, so that they are not optimal against *any* strategy for the first player. After removing all such strategies (which might have to be done repeatedly), the optimal choice at the root is the highest (or lowest) intersection point of the remaining hyperplanes. Finding this choice is an example of a **linear programming** problem: maximizing an objective function subject to linear constraints. Such problems can be solved by standard techniques in time polynomial in the number of actions (and in the number of bits used to specify the reward function, if you want to get technical).

The question remains, what should a rational agent actually *do* in playing a single game of Morra? The rational agent will have derived the fact that $[7/12\colon one; 5/12\colon two]$ is the maximin equilibrium strategy, and will assume that this is mutual knowledge with a rational opponent. The agent could use a 12-sided die or a random number generator to pick randomly according to this mixed strategy, in which case the expected payoff would be -1/12 for $E$. Or the agent could just decide to play $one$, or $two$. In either case, the expected payoff remains -1/12 for $E$. Curiously, unilaterally choosing a particular action does not harm one's expected payoff, but allowing the other agent to know that one has made such a unilateral decision *does* affect the expected payoff, because then the opponent can adjust his strategy accordingly.

Finding solutions to non-zero-sum finite games (i.e., Nash equilibria) is somewhat more complicated. The general approach has two steps: (1) Enumerate all possible subsets of actions that might form mixed strategies. For example, first try all strategy profiles where each player uses a single action, then those where each player uses either one or two actions, and so on. This is exponential in the number of actions, and so only applies to relatively small games. (2) For each strategy profile enumerated in (1), check to see if it is an equilibrium. This is done by solving a set of equations and inequalities that are similar to the ones used in the zero-sum case. For two players these equations are linear and can be solved with basic linear programming techniques, but for three or more players they are nonlinear and may be very difficult to solve.

REPEATED GAME

So far we have looked only at games that last a single move. The simplest kind of multiple-move game is the **repeated game**, in which players face the same choice repeatedly, but each time with knowledge of the history of all players' previous choices. A strategy profile for a repeated game specifies an action choice for each player at each time step for every possible history of previous choices. As with MDPs, payoffs are additive over time.

Let's consider the repeated version of the prisoner's dilemma. Will Alice and Bob work together and refuse to testify, knowing that they will meet again? The answer depends on the details of the engagement. For example, suppose Alice and Bob know that they must play exactly 100 rounds of prisoner's dilemma. Then they both know that the 100th round will not be a repeated game—that is, its outcome can have no effect on future rounds—and therefore they will both choose the dominant strategy, $testify$, in that round. But once the 100th round is determined, the 99th round can have no effect on subsequent rounds, so it too will have a dominant strategy equilibrium at $(testify, testify)$. By induction, both players will choose $testify$ on every round, earning a total jail sentence of 500 years each.

We can get different solutions by changing the rules of the interaction. For example, suppose that after each round there is a 99% chance that the players will meet again. Then the expected number of rounds is still 100, but neither player knows for sure which round will be the last. Under these conditions, more cooperative behavior is possible. For example, one equilibrium strategy is for each player to *refuse* unless the other player has ever played *testify*. This strategy could be called **perpetual punishment**. Suppose both players have adopted this strategy, and this is mutual knowledge. Then as long as neither player has played *testify*, then at any point in time the expected future total payoff for each player is

PERPETUAL PUNISHMENT

$$\sum_{t=0}^{\infty} 0.99^t \cdot (-1) = -100 \,.$$

A player who chooses *testify* will gain a score of 0 rather than $-1$ on the very next move, but his or her total expected future payoff becomes

$$0 + \sum_{t=1}^{\infty} 0.99^t \cdot (-10) = -999 \,.$$

Therefore, at every step, there is no incentive to deviate from (*refuse*, *refuse*). Perpetual punishment is the "mutually assured destruction" strategy of the prisoner's dilemma: once either player decides to *testify*, it assures that both players suffer a great deal. But it only works as a deterrent if the other player believes you have adopted this strategy—or at least that you might have adopted it.

There are other strategies that are more forgiving. The most famous, called **tit-for-tat**, calls for starting with *refuse* and then echoing the other player's previous move on all subsequent moves. So Alice would refuse as long as Bob refuses and would testify the move after Bob testified, but would go back to refusing if Bob did. Although very simple, this strategy has proven to be highly robust and effective against a wide variety of strategies.

TIT-FOR-TAT

We can also get different solutions by changing the agents, rather than changing the rules of engagement. Suppose the agents are finite-state machines with $n$ states and they are playing a game with $m > n$ total steps. The agents are thus incapable of representing the number of remaining steps, and must treat it as an unknown. Therefore they cannot do the induction, and are free to arrive at the more favorable (*refuse, refuse*) equilibrium. In this case, ignorance *is* bliss—or rather, having your opponent believe that you are ignorant is bliss. Your success in these repeated games depends on the other player's *perception* of you as a bully or a simpleton, and not on your actual characteristics.

Repeated games in full generality are beyond the scope of this book, but they arise in many settings. For example, we can construct a sequential game by putting two agents in the $4 \times 3$ world of Figure 17.1. If we specify that no movement occurs when the two agents try to move into the same square simultaneously (a common problem at many traffic intersections), then certain pure strategies can get stuck forever. One solution is for each agent to randomize its choice between moving forward and staying put; the stalemate will be resolved quickly and both agents will be happy. This is exactly what is done to resolve packet collisions in Ethernet networks.

Currently known solution methods for repeated games resemble those for turn-taking games in Chapter 6, in that a game tree can be constructed from the root downwards and solved from the leaves upwards. The main difference is that, instead of simply taking the maximum or minimum of the child values, the algorithm must solve a game in mixed strategies at each level, assuming that the child nodes have been solved and have well-defined values to work with.

PARTIAL INFORMATION

Repeated games in *partially observable* environments are called games of **partial information**. Examples include card games such as poker and bridge, wherein each player can see only a subset of the cards, and more serious "games" such as abstractions of nuclear war, where neither side knows the location of all its opponent's weapons. Games of partial information are solved by considering a tree of belief states, as in POMDPs. (See Section 17.4.) One important difference is that, while one's own belief state is observable, the opponent's belief state is not. Only recently have practical algorithms been developed for such games. Some simplified versions of poker have been solved, proving that bluffing is indeed a rational choice, as part of a well balanced mixed strategy. One important insight to emerge from such studies is that mixed strategies are useful not just for making one's actions unpredictable, but also for minimizing the amount of information that one's opponent can learn from observing one's actions. It is interesting that, although designers of programs for playing bridge are well aware of the importance of gathering and hiding information, none has yet proposed the use of randomized strategies.

BAYES–NASH EQUILIBRIUM

So far, there have been some barriers that have prevented game theory from being widely used in agent design. First, note that in a Nash equilibrium solution, a player is assuming that the opponents will definitely play the equilibrium strategy. This means that the player is unable to incorporate any beliefs it might have about how the other players are likely to act, and therefore that it might be wasting some of its value defending against threats that will never materialize. The notion of a **Bayes–Nash equilibrium** partially addresses this point: it is an equilibrium with respect to a player's prior probability distribution over the other players' strategies—in other words, it expresses a player's beliefs about the other players' likely strategies. Second, there is currently no good way to combine game theoretic and POMDP control strategies. Because of these and other problems, game theory has been used primarily to *analyze* environments that are at equilibrium, rather than to *control* agents within an environment. We shall soon see how it can help *design* environments.

## 17.7 MECHANISM DESIGN

MECHANISM DESIGN

In the previous section, we looked at the question "Given a game, what is a rational strategy?" In this section, we ask "Given that agents are rational, what game should we design?" More specifically, we would like to design a game whose solutions, consisting of each agent pursuing its own rational strategy, result in the maximization of some global utility function. This problem is called **mechanism design**, or sometimes **inverse game theory**. Mechanism design is a staple of economics and political science. For collections of agents, it holds the possibility of using game-theoretic mechanisms to construct smart systems out of a collection of more limited systems—even noncooperative systems—in much the same way that teams of humans can achieve goals far beyond the reach of any individual.

Examples of mechanism design include auctioning off cheap airline tickets, routing TCP packets between computers, deciding how medical interns will be assigned to hospitals, and deciding how robotic soccer players will cooperate with their teammates. Mechanism design became more than an academic subject in the 1990s when several nations, faced with the problem of auctioning off licenses to broadcast in various frequency bands, lost hundreds of millions of dollars in potential revenue as a result of poor mechanism design. Formally, a **mechanism** consists of (1) a language for describing the (possibly infinite) set of allowable strategies that agents may adopt and (2) an outcome rule $G$ that determines the payoffs to the agents given a strategy profile of allowable strategies.

MECHANISM

At first sight, the mechanism design problem can seem trivial. Suppose that the global utility function $U$ is decomposed into any set of individual agent utility functions $U_i$, such that $U = \sum_i U_i$. Then, one might say, if each agent maximizes its own utility, surely that will lead automatically to the maximization of the global utility. (For example, Capitalism 101 says that if everyone tries to get rich, the total wealth of society will increase.) Unfortunately, this doesn't work. The actions of each agent could affect the well-being of other agents in ways that decrease global utility. One example of this is the **tragedy of the commons**, a situation in which individual farmers all bring their livestock to graze for free on the town commons, with the result being the destruction of the commons and a negative utility for all the farmers. Each farmer individually acted rationally, reasoning that the use of the commons was free and that, although using the commons could lead to its destruction, refraining from using it would not help (because the others would use it anyway). Similar arguments apply to the use of the atmosphere and the oceans for free dumping of pollutants.

TRAGEDY OF THE COMMONS

A standard approach in mechanism design for dealing with such problems is to charge each agent for using the commons. More generally, we need to ensure that all **externalities**—effects on global utility that are not recognized in the individual agents' transactions—are made explicit. Setting the prices correctly is the difficult part. In the limit, this approach amounts to creating a mechanism in which each agent is effectively required to maximize global utility. This is an impossibly difficult task for the agent, who can neither assess the current state of the world nor observe the effects of its actions on all other agents. Mechanism design therefore concentrates on finding mechanisms for which the decision problem for the individual agents is straightforward.

EXTERNALITIES

Let's consider auctions first. In the most common form, an auction is a mechanism for selling some goods to members of a pool of bidders. The strategies are the bids and the outcome determines who gets the goods and how much they pay. One example of where auctions can come into play within AI is when a collection of agents are deciding whether to cooperate on a joint plan. Hunsberger and Grosz (2000) show that this can be accomplished efficiently with an auction in which the agents bid for roles in the joint plan.

For now, we'll consider auctions wherein (1) there is a single good, (2) each bidder has a utility value $v_i$ for the good, and (3) these values are known only to the bidder. Bidders make bids $b_i$, and the highest bid wins the goods, but the mechanism determines how the bids are made and the price paid by the winner (it need not be $b_i$). The best-known type of auction is the **English auction**, in which the auctioneer increments the price of the goods, checking whether bidders are still interested, until only one bidder is left. This mechanism

ENGLISH AUCTION

has the property that the bidder with the highest value $v_i$ gets the goods at a price of $b_m + d$, where $b_m$ is the highest bid among all the other players and $d$ is the auctioneer's increment between bids.[9] The English auction also has the property that bidders have a simple dominant strategy: keep bidding as long as the current cost is below your personal value. Recall that "dominant" means that the strategy works against all other strategies, which in turn means that a player can adopt it without regard for the other strategies. Therefore, players don't have to waste time and energy contemplating other players' possible strategies. A mechanism where players have a dominant strategy that involves revealing their true incentives is called a **strategy-proof** mechanism.

STRATEGY-PROOF

One negative property of the English auction is its high communication costs, so either the auction takes place in one room or all bidders have to have high-speed, secure communication lines. An alternative mechanism that requires much less communication is the **sealed bid auction**. Here, each bidder makes a single bid and communicates it to the auctioneer, and the highest bid wins. With this mechanism, the strategy of bidding your true value is no longer dominant. If your value is $v_i$ and you believe that the maximum of all the other players' bids will be $b_m$, then you should bid the lower of $v_i$ and $b_m + \epsilon$. Two drawbacks of the sealed bid auction are that the player with the highest $v_i$ might not get the goods and that players must spend effort contemplating the other players' strategies.

SEALED BID AUCTION

A small change in the rules for sealed bid auctions produces the **sealed bid second-price auction**, also known as a **Vickrey auction.**[10] In such auctions, the winner pays the price of the *second* highest bid, rather than paying his own bid. This simple modification completely eliminates the complex deliberations required for standard (or **first-price**) sealed bid auctions, because the dominant strategy is now to bid your actual value. To see that, we note that any player can think of the auction as a two-player game, ignoring all players except himself and the highest bidder among the other players. The utility of player $i$ in terms of his bid $b_i$, his value $v_i$, and the best bid among the other players, $b_m$, is

SEALED BID SECOND-PRICE AUCTION

VICKREY AUCTION

$$u_i(b_i, b_m) = \begin{cases} (v_i - b_m) & \text{if } b_i > b_m \\ 0 & \text{otherwise.} \end{cases}$$

To see that $b_i = v_i$ is a dominant strategy, note that when $(v_i - b_m)$ is positive, any bid that wins the auction is optimal, and bidding $v_i$ in particular wins the auction. On the other hand, when $(v_i - b_m)$ is negative, any bid that loses the auction is optimal, and bidding $v_i$ in particular loses the auction. So bidding $v_i$ is optimal for all possible values of $b_m$, and in fact, $v_i$ is the only bid that has this property. Because of its simplicity and the minimal computation requirements for both seller and bidders, the Vickrey auction is widely used in constructing distributed AI systems.

Now let's consider the Internet routing problem. The players correspond to edges in the graph of network connections. Each player knows the cost $c_i$ of sending a message along its own edge; the cost of not having a message to send is 0. The goal is to find the cheapest path for a message to travel from origin to destination, where the cost of the whole route

9 There is actually a small chance that the player with highest $v_i$ fails to get the goods, in the case where $b_m < v_i < b_m + d$. The chance of this happening can be made arbitrarily small by decreasing the increment $d$.

10 Named after William Vickrey (1914–1996), winner of the 1996 Nobel prize in economics.

is the sum of the individual edge costs. Chapter 4 gives several algorithms for computing the shortest path, given the edge costs, so all we have to do is get each agent to report its true cost, $c_i$. Unfortunately, if we just ask each agent, it will report costs that are high, to encourage us to send traffic elsewhere. We need to develop a strategy-proof mechanism. One such mechanism is to pay each player a payoff $p_i$ equal to the length of the shortest path that does not contain the $i$th edge minus the length of the shortest path (as computed by a search algorithm) where the cost of the $i$th edge is assumed to be 0:

$$p_i = \text{LENGTH}(\text{path with } c_i = \infty) - \text{LENGTH}(\text{path with } c_i = 0) .$$

We can show that, under this mechanism, the dominant strategy for each player is to report $c_i$ truthfully and that doing so will result in a cheapest path. Despite this desirable property, the mechanism outlined here is not used in practice, because of the high communication and central computation cost. The mechanism designer must communicate with all $n$ players and then must solve the optimization problem. This might be worth it if the costs could be amortized over many messages, but in a real network the costs $c_i$ would fluctuate constantly, because of traffic congestion and because some machines will crash and others will come online. No completely satisfactory solution has yet been devised.

## 17.8 SUMMARY

This chapter shows how to use knowledge about the world to make decisions even when the outcomes of an action are uncertain and the rewards for acting might not be reaped until many actions have passed. The main points are as follows:

- Sequential decision problems in uncertain environments, also called **Markov decision processes**, or MDPs, are defined by a **transition model** specifying the probabilistic outcomes of actions and a **reward function** specifying the reward in each state.
- The utility of a state sequence is the sum of all the rewards over the sequence, possibly discounted over time. The solution of an MDP is a **policy** that associates a decision with every state that the agent might reach. An optimal policy maximizes the utility of the state sequences encountered when it is executed.
- The utility of a state is the expected utility of the state sequences encountered when an optimal policy is executed, starting in that state. The **value iteration** algorithm for solving MDPs works by iteratively solving the equations relating the utilities of each state to that of its neighbors.
- **Policy iteration** alternates between calculating the utilities of states under the current policy and improving the current policy with respect to the current utilities.
- Partially observable MDPs, or POMDPs, are much more difficult to solve than are MDPs. They can be solved by conversion to an MDP in the continuous space of belief states. Optimal behavior in POMDPs includes information gathering to reduce uncertainty and therefore make better decisions in the future.

- A decision-theoretic agent can be constructed for POMDP environments. The agent uses a **dynamic decision network** to represent the transition and observation models, to update its belief state, and to project forward possible action sequences.
- **Game theory** describes rational behavior for agents in situations where multiple agents interact simultaneously. Solutions of games are **Nash equilibria**—strategy profiles in which no agent has an incentive to deviate from the specified strategy.
- **Mechanism design** can be used to set the rules by which agents will interact, in order to maximize some global utility through the operation of individually rational agents. Sometimes, mechanisms exist that achieve this goal without requiring each agent to consider the choices made by other agents.

We shall return to the world of MDPs and POMDP in Chapter 21, when we study **reinforcement learning** methods that allow an agent to improve its behavior from experience in sequential, uncertain environments.

## BIBLIOGRAPHICAL AND HISTORICAL NOTES

Richard Bellman (1957) initiated the modern approach to sequential decision problems and proposed the dynamic programming approach in general and the value iteration algorithm in particular. Ron Howard's Ph.D. thesis (1960) introduced policy iteration and the idea of average reward for solving infinite-horizon problems. Several additional results were introduced by Bellman and Dreyfus (1962). Modified policy iteration is due to van Nunen (1976) and Puterman and Shin (1978). Asynchronous policy iteration was analyzed by Williams and Baird (1993), who also proved the policy loss bound in Equation (17.9). The analysis of discounting in terms of stationary preferences is due to Koopmans (1972). The texts by Bertsekas (1987), Puterman (1994), and Bertsekas and Tsitsiklis (1996) provide a rigorous introduction to sequential decision problems. Papadimitriou and Tsitsiklis (1987) describe results on the computational complexity of MDPs.

Seminal work by Sutton (1988) and Watkins (1989) on reinforcement learning methods for solving MDPs played a significant role in introducing MDPs into the AI community, as did the later survey by Barto *et al.* (1995). (Earlier work by Werbos (1977) contained many similar ideas, but was not taken up to the same extent.) The connection between MDPs and AI planning problems was made first by Sven Koenig (1991), who showed how probabilistic STRIPS operators provide a compact representation for transition models. (See also Wellman (1990b).) Work by Dean *et al.* (1993) and Tash and Russell (1994) attempted to overcome the combinatorics of large state spaces by using a limited search horizon and abstract states. Heuristics based on the value of information can be used to select areas of the state space where a local expansion of the horizon will yield a significant improvement in decision quality. Agents using this approach can tailor their effort to handle time pressure and generate some interesting behaviors such as using familiar "beaten paths" to find their way around the state space quickly without having to recompute optimal decisions at each point. Recent work by Boutilier and others (Boutilier *et al.*, 2000, 2001) has focused on dynamic programming using *symbolic* representations of both transition models and value functions, based on propositional and first-order formulæ.

The observation that a partially observable MDP can be transformed into a regular MDP by using the belief states is due to Astrom (1965). The first complete algorithm for the exact solution of partially-observable Markov decision processes (POMDPs) was proposed by Edward Sondik (1971) in his Ph.D. thesis. (A later journal paper by Smallwood and Sondik (1973) contains some errors, but is more accessible.) Lovejoy (1991) surveys the state of the art in POMDPs. The first significant contribution within AI was the Witness algorithm (Cassandra *et al.*, 1994; Kaelbling *et al.*, 1998), an improved version of POMDP value iteration. Other algorithms soon followed, including an approach due to Hansen (1998) that constructs a policy incrementally in the form of a finite-state automaton. In this policy representation, the belief state corresponds directly to a particular state in the automaton. Approximately optimal policies for POMDPs can be constructed by forward search combined with sampling of possible observations and action outcomes (Kearns *et al.*, 2000; Ng and Jordan, 2000). Additional work on POMDP algorithms is covered in Chapter 21.

The basic ideas for an agent architecture using dynamic decision networks were proposed by Dean and Kanazawa (1989a). The book *Planning and Control* by Dean and Wellman (1991) goes into much greater depth, making connections between DBN/DDN models and the classical control literature on filtering. Tatman and Shachter (1990) showed how to apply dynamic programming algorithms to DDN models. Russell (1998) explains various ways in which such agents can be scaled up and identifies a number of open research issues.

The early roots of game theory can be traced back to proposals made in the 17th century by Christiaan Huygens and Gottfried Leibniz to study competitive and cooperative human interactions scientifically and mathematically. Throughout the 19th century, several leading economists created simple mathematical examples to analyze particular examples of competitive situations. The first formal results in game theory are due to Zermelo (1913) (who had, the year before, suggested a form of minimax search for games, albeit an incorrect one). Emile Borel (1921) introduced the notion of a mixed strategy. John von Neumann (1928) proved that every two-person, zero-sum game has a maximin equilibrium in mixed strategies and a well-defined value. Von Neumann's collaboration with the economist Oskar Morgenstern led to the publication in 1944 of the *Theory of Games and Economic Behavior*, the defining book for game theory. Publication of the book was delayed by the wartime paper shortage until a member of the Rockefeller family personally subsidized its publication.

In 1950, at the age of 21, John Nash published his ideas concerning equilibria in general games. His definition of an equilibrium solution, although originating in the work of Cournot (1838), became known as Nash equilibrium. After a long delay due to the schizophrenia he suffered from 1959 onwards, Nash was awarded the Nobel prize in Economics (along with Reinhart Selten and John Harsanyi) in 1994.

The Bayes–Nash equilibrium is described by Harsanyi (1967) and discussed by Kadane and Larkey (1982). Some issues in the use of game theory for agent control are covered by Binmore (1982).

The prisoner's dilemma was invented as a classroom exercise by Albert W. Tucker in 1950 and is covered extensively by Axelrod (1985). Repeated games were introduced by

Luce and Raiffa (1957) as were games of partial information by Kuhn (1953). The first practical algorithm for partial information games was developed within AI by Koller *et al.* (1996); the paper by Koller and Pfeffer (1997) provides a readable introduction to the general area and describes a working system for representing and solving sequential games. Game theory and MDPs are combined in the theory of Markov games (Littman, 1994). Shapley (1953) actually described the value iteration algorithm before Bellman, but his results were not widely appreciated, perhaps because they were presented in the context of Markov games. Textbooks on game theory include those by Myerson (1991), Fudenberg and Tirole (1991), and Osborne and Rubinstein (1994).

The tragedy of the commons, a motivating problem for the field of mechanism design, was presented by Hardin (1968). Hurwicz (1973) created a mathematical foundation for mechanism design. Milgrom (1997) writes about the multibillion-dollar spectrum auction mechanism he designed. Auctions can also be used in planning (Hunsberger and Grosz, 2000) and scheduling (Rassenti *et al.*, 1982). Varian (1995) gives a brief overview with connections to the computer science literature, and Rosenschein and Zlotkin (1994) present a book-length treatment with applications to distributed AI. Related work on distributed AI also goes under other names, including Collective Intelligence (Tumer and Wolpert, 2000) and market-based control (Clearwater, 1996). Papers on computational issues in auctions often appear in the ACM Conferences on Electronic Commerce.

## EXERCISES

**17.1** For the $4 \times 3$ world shown in Figure 17.1, calculate which squares can be reached from (1,1) by the action sequence $[Up, Up, Right, Right, Right]$ and with what probabilities. Explain how this computation is related to the task of projecting a hidden Markov model.

**17.2** Suppose that we define the utility of a state sequence to be the *maximum* reward obtained in any state in the sequence. Show that this utility function does not result in stationary preferences between state sequences. Is it still possible to define a utility function on states such that MEU decision making gives optimal behavior?

**17.3** Can any finite search problem be translated exactly into a Markov decision problem such that an optimal solution of the latter is also an optimal solution of the former? If so, explain *precisely* how to translate the problem and how to translate the solution back; if not, explain *precisely* why not (i.e., give a counterexample).

**17.4** Consider an undiscounted MDP having three states, (1, 2, 3), with rewards $-1$, $-2$, 0 respectively. State 3 is a terminal state. In states 1 and 2 there are two possible actions: $a$ and $b$. The transition model is as follows:

- In state 1, action $a$ moves the agent to state 2 with probability 0.8 and makes the agent stay put with probability 0.2.
- In state 2, action $a$ moves the agent to state 1 with probability 0.8 and makes the agent stay put with probability 0.2.

- In either state 1 or state 2, action $b$ moves the agent to state 3 with probability 0.1 and makes the agent stay put with probability 0.9.

Answer the following questions:

**a.** What can be determined *qualitatively* about the optimal policy in states 1 and 2?

**b.** Apply policy iteration, showing each step in full, to determine the optimal policy and the values of states 1 and 2. Assume that the initial policy has action $b$ in both states.

**c.** What happens to policy iteration if the initial policy has action $a$ in both states? Does discounting help? Does the optimal policy depend on the discount factor?

**17.5** Sometimes MDPs are formulated with a reward function $R(s, a)$ that depends on the action taken or a reward function $R(s, a, s')$ that also depends on the outcome state.

**a.** Write the Bellman equations for these formulations.

**b.** Show how an MDP with reward function $R(s, a, s')$ can be transformed into a different MDP with reward function $R(s, a)$, such that optimal policies in the new MDP correspond exactly to optimal policies in the original MDP.

**c.** Now do the same to convert MDPs with $R(s, a)$ into MDPs with $R(s)$.

**17.6** Consider the $4 \times 3$ world shown in Figure 17.1.

**a.** Implement an environment simulator for this environment, such that the specific geography of the environment is easily altered. Some code for doing this is already in the online code repository.

**b.** Create an agent that uses policy iteration, and measure its performance in the environment simulator from various starting states. Perform several experiments from each starting state, and compare the average total reward received per run with the utility of the state, as determined by your algorithm.

**c.** Experiment with increasing the size of the environment. How does the runtime for policy iteration vary with the size of the environment?

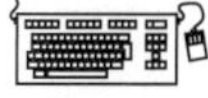

**17.7** For the environment shown in Figure 17.1, find all the threshold values for $R(s)$ such that the optimal policy changes when the threshold is crossed. You will need a way to calculate the optimal policy and its value for fixed $R(s)$. [*Hint*: Prove that the value of any fixed policy varies linearly with $R(s)$.]

**17.8** In this exercise we will consider two-player MDPs that correspond to zero-sum, turn-taking games like those in Chapter 6. Let the players be $A$ and $B$, and let $R(s)$ be the reward for player $A$ in $s$. (The reward for $B$ is always equal and opposite.)

**a.** Let $U_A(s)$ be the utility of state $s$ when it is $A$'s turn to move in $s$, and let $U_B(s)$ be the utility of state $s$ when it is $B$'s turn to move in $s$. All rewards and utilities are calculated from $A$'s point of view (just as in a minimax game tree). Write down Bellman equations defining $U_A(s)$ and $U_B(s)$.

**b.** Explain how to do two-player value iteration with these equations, and define a suitable stopping criterion.

**c.** Consider the game described in Figure 6.14 on page 190. Draw the state space (rather than the game tree), showing the moves by $A$ as solid lines and moves by $B$ as dashed lines. Mark each state with $R(s)$. You will find it helpful to arrange the states $(s_A, s_B)$ on a two-dimensional grid, using $s_A$ and $s_B$ as "coordinates."

**d.** Now apply two-player value iteration to solve this game, and derive the optimal policy.

**17.9** Show that a dominant strategy equilibrium is a Nash equilibrium, but not *vice versa*.

**17.10** In the children's game of rock–paper–scissors each player reveals at the same time a choice of rock, paper, or scissors. Paper wraps rock, rock blunts scissors, and scissors cut paper. In the extended version rock–paper–scissors–fire–water, fire beats rock, paper and scissors; rock, paper and scissors beat water, and water beats fire. Write out the payoff matrix and find a mixed-strategy solution to this game.

**17.11** Solve the game of *three*-finger Morra.

**17.12** Prior to 1999, teams in the National Hockey League received 2 points for a win, 1 for a tie, and 0 for a loss. Is this a constant-sum game? In 1999, the rules were amended so that a team receives 1 point for a loss in overtime. The winning team still gets 2 points. How does this modification change the answers to the questions above? If it were legal to do so, when would it be rational for the two teams to secretly agree to end regulation play in a tie and then battle it out in overtime? Assume that the utility to each team is the number of points it receives, and that there is a mutually known prior probability $p$ that the first team will win in overtime. For what values of $p$ would both teams agree to this arrangement?

**17.13** The following payoff matrix, from Blinder (1983) by way of Bernstein (1996), shows a game between politicians and the Federal Reserve.

| | Fed: contract | Fed: do nothing | Fed: expand |
|---|---|---|---|
| Pol: contract | $F = 7, P = 1$ | $F = 9, P = 4$ | $F = 6, P = 6$ |
| Pol: do nothing | $F = 8, P = 2$ | $F = 5, P = 5$ | $F = 4, P = 9$ |
| Pol: expand | $F = 3, P = 3$ | $F = 2, P = 7$ | $F = 1, P = 8$ |

Politicians can expand or contract fiscal policy, while the Fed can expand or contract monetary policy. (And of course either side can choose to do nothing.) Each side also has preferences for who should do what—neither side wants to look like the bad guys. The payoffs shown are simply the rank orderings: 9 for first choice through 1 for last choice. Find the Nash equilibrium of the game in pure strategies. Is this a Pareto optimal solution? The reader might wish to analyze the policies of recent administrations in this light.

# 18 LEARNING FROM OBSERVATIONS

*In which we describe agents that can improve their behavior through diligent study of their own experiences.*

The idea behind learning is that percepts should be used not only for acting, but also for improving the agent's ability to act in the future. Learning takes place as the agent observes its interactions with the world and its own decision-making processes. Learning can range from trivial memorization of experience, as exhibited by the wumpus-world agent in Chapter 10, to the creation of entire scientific theories, as exhibited by Albert Einstein. This chapter describes **inductive learning** from observations. In particular, we describe how to learn simple theories in propositional logic. We also give a theoretical analysis that explains why inductive learning works.

## 18.1 FORMS OF LEARNING

In Chapter 2, we saw that a learning agent can be thought of as containing a **performance element** that decides what actions to take and a **learning element** that modifies the performance element so that it makes better decisions. (See Figure 2.15.) Machine learning researchers have come up with a large variety of learning elements. To understand them, it will help to see how their design is affected by the context in which they will operate. The design of a learning element is affected by three major issues:

- Which *components* of the performance element are to be learned.
- What *feedback* is available to learn these components.
- What *representation* is used for the components.

We now analyze each of these issues in turn. We have seen that there are many ways to build the performance element of an agent. Chapter 2 described several agent designs (Figures 2.9, 2.11, 2.13, and 2.14). The components of these agents include the following:

1. A direct mapping from conditions on the current state to actions.
2. A means to infer relevant properties of the world from the percept sequence.

3. Information about the way the world evolves and about the results of possible actions the agent can take.
4. Utility information indicating the desirability of world states.
5. Action-value information indicating the desirability of actions.
6. Goals that describe classes of states whose achievement maximizes the agent's utility.

Each of these components can be learned from appropriate feedback. Consider, for example, an agent training to become a taxi driver. Every time the instructor shouts "Brake!" the agent can learn a condition–action rule for when to brake (component 1). By seeing many camera images that it is told contain buses, it can learn to recognize them (2). By trying actions and observing the results—for example, braking hard on a wet road—it can learn the effects of its actions (3). Then, when it receives no tip from passengers who have been thoroughly shaken up during the trip, it can learn a useful component of its overall utility function (4).

The *type of feedback* available for learning is usually the most important factor in determining the nature of the learning problem that the agent faces. The field of machine learning usually distinguishes three cases: **supervised**, **unsupervised**, and **reinforcement** learning.

SUPERVISED LEARNING

The problem of **supervised learning** involves learning a *function* from examples of its inputs and outputs. Cases (1), (2), and (3) are all instances of supervised learning problems. In (1), the agent learns condition–action rule for braking—this is a function from states to a Boolean output (to brake or not to brake), In (2), the agent learns a function from images to a Boolean output (whether the image contains a bus). In (3), the theory of braking is a function from states and braking actions to, say, stopping distance in feet. Notice that in cases (1) and (2), a teacher provided the correct output value of the examples; in the third, the output value was available directly from the agent's percepts. For fully observable environments, it will always be the case that an agent can observe the effects of its actions and hence can use supervised learning methods to learn to predict them. For partially observable environments, the problem is more difficult, because the immediate effects might be invisible.

UNSUPERVISED LEARNING

The problem of **unsupervised learning** involves learning patterns in the input when no specific output values are supplied. For example, a taxi agent might gradually develop a concept of "good traffic days" and "bad traffic days" without ever being given labelled examples of each. A purely unsupervised learning agent cannot learn what to do, because it has no information as to what constitutes a correct action or a desirable state. We will study unsupervised learning primarily in the context of probabilistic reasoning systems (Chapter 20).

REINFORCEMENT LEARNING

The problem of **reinforcement learning**, which we cover in Chapter 21, is the most general of the three categories. Rather than being told what to do by a teacher, a reinforcement learning agent must learn from **reinforcement**.[1] For example, the lack of a tip at the end of the journey (or a hefty bill for rear-ending the car in front) gives the agent some indication that its behavior is undesirable. Reinforcement learning typically includes the subproblem of learning how the environment works.

REINFORCEMENT

The *representation of the learned information* also plays a very important role in determining how the learning algorithm must work. Any of the components of an agent can be represented using any of the representation schemes in this book. We have seen sev-

[1] The term **reward** as used in Chapter 17 is a synonym for **reinforcement**.

eral examples: linear weighted polynomials for utility functions in game-playing programs; propositional and first-order logical sentences for all of the components in a logical agent; and probabilistic descriptions such as Bayesian networks for the inferential components of a decision-theoretic agent. Effective learning algorithms have been devised for all of these. This chapter will cover methods for propositional logic, Chapter 19 describes methods for first-order logic, and Chapter 20 covers methods for Bayesian networks and for neural networks (which include linear polynomials as a special case).

The last major factor in the design of learning systems is the *availability of prior knowledge*. The majority of learning research in AI, computer science, and psychology has studied the case in which the agent begins with no knowledge at all about what it is trying to learn. It has access only to the examples presented by its experience. Although this is an important special case, it is by no means the general case. Most human learning takes place in the context of a good deal of background knowledge. Some psychologists and linguists claim that even newborn babies exhibit knowledge of the world. Whatever the truth of this claim, there is no doubt that prior knowledge can help enormously in learning. A physicist examining a stack of bubble-chamber photographs might be able to induce a theory positing the existence of a new particle of a certain mass and charge; but an art critic examining the same stack might learn nothing more than that the "artist" must be some sort of abstract expressionist. Chapter 19 shows several ways in which learning is helped by the use of existing knowledge; it also shows how knowledge can be *compiled* in order to speed up decision making. Chapter 20 shows how prior knowledge helps in the learning of probabilistic theories.

## 18.2 INDUCTIVE LEARNING

An algorithm for deterministic supervised learning is given as input the correct value of the unknown function for particular inputs and must try to recover the unknown function or something close to it. More formally, we say that an **example** is a pair $(x, f(x))$, where $x$ is the input and $f(x)$ is the output of the function applied to $x$. The task of **pure inductive inference** (or **induction**) is this:

EXAMPLE

PURE INDUCTIVE INFERENCE

Given a collection of examples of $f$, return a function $h$ that approximates $f$.

HYPOTHESIS

GENERALIZATION

PROBLEM OF INDUCTION

The function $h$ is called a **hypothesis**. The reason that learning is difficult, from a conceptual point of view, is that it is not easy to tell whether any particular $h$ is a good approximation of $f$. A good hypothesis will **generalize** well—that is, will predict unseen examples correctly. This is the fundamental **problem of induction**. The problem has been studied for centuries; Section 18.5 provides a partial solution.

HYPOTHESIS SPACE

CONSISTENT

Figure 18.1 shows a familiar example: fitting a function of a single variable to some data points. The examples are $(x, f(x))$ pairs, where both $x$ and $f(x)$ are real numbers. We choose the **hypothesis space H**—the set of hypotheses we will consider—to be the set of polynomials of degree at most $k$, such as $3x^2 + 2$, $x^{17} - 4x^3$, and so on. Figure 18.1(a) shows some data with an exact fit by a straight line (a polynomial of degree 1). The line is called a **consistent** hypothesis because it agrees with all the data. Figure 18.1(b) shows a

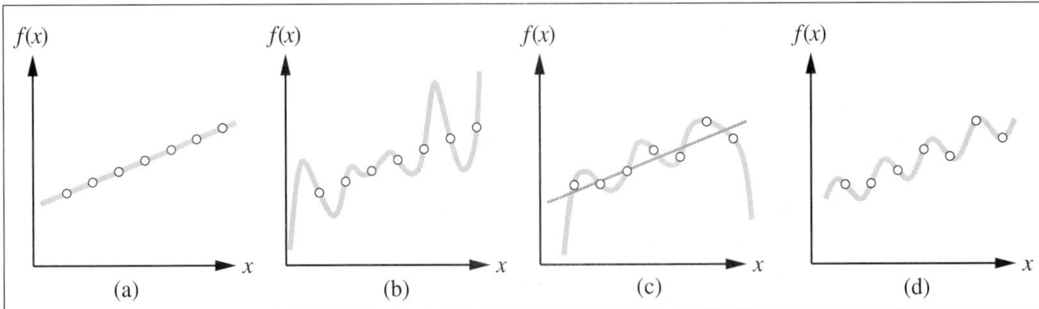


**Figure 18.1** (a) Example $(x, f(x))$ pairs and a consistent, linear hypothesis. (b) A consistent, degree-7 polynomial hypothesis for the same data set. (c) A different data set that admits an exact degree-6 polynomial fit or an approximate linear fit. (d) A simple, exact sinusoidal fit to the same data set.

OCKHAM'S RAZOR

high-degree polynomial that is also consistent with the same data. This illustrates the first issue in inductive learning: *how do we choose from among multiple consistent hypotheses?* One answer is **Ockham's**[2] **razor**: prefer the *simplest* hypothesis consistent with the data. Intuitively, this makes sense, because hypotheses that are no simpler than the data themselves are failing to extract any *pattern* from the data. Defining simplicity is not easy, but it seems reasonable to say that a degree-1 polynomial is simpler than a degree-12 polynomial.

Figure 18.1(c) shows a second data set. There is no consistent straight line for this data set; in fact, it requires a degree-6 polynomial (with 7 parameters) for an exact fit. There are just 7 data points, so the polynomial has as many parameters as there are data points; thus, it does not seem to be finding any pattern in the data and we do not expect it to generalize well. It might be better to fit a simple straight line that is not exactly consistent but might make reasonable predictions. This amounts to accepting the possibility that the true function is not deterministic (or, roughly equivalently, that the true inputs are not fully observed). *For nondeterministic functions, there is an inevitable tradeoff between the complexity of the hypothesis and the degree of fit to the data.* Chapter 20 explains how to make this tradeoff using probability theory.

One should keep in mind that the possibility or impossibility of finding a simple, consistent hypothesis depends strongly on the hypothesis space chosen. Figure 18.1(d) shows that the data in (c) can be fit exactly by a simple function of the form $ax + b + c \sin x$. This example shows the importance of the choice of hypothesis space. A hypothesis space consisting of polynomials of finite degree cannot represent sinusoidal functions accurately, so a learner using that hypothesis space will not be able to learn from sinusoidal data. We say that a learning problem is **realizable** if the hypothesis space contains the true function; otherwise, it is **unrealizable**. Unfortunately, we cannot always tell whether a given learning problem is realizable, because the true function is not known. One way to get around this barrier is to use *prior knowledge* to derive a hypothesis space in which we know the true function must lie. This topic is covered in Chapter 19.

REALIZABLE

UNREALIZABLE

[2] Named after the 14th-century English philosopher, William of Ockham. The name is often misspelled as "Occam," perhaps from the French rendering, "Guillaume d'Occam."

Another approach is to use the largest possible hypothesis space. For example, why not let **H** be the class of all Turing machines? After all, every computable function can be represented by some Turing machine, and that is the best we can do. The problem with this idea is that it does not take into account the *computational complexity* of learning. *There is a tradeoff between the expressiveness of a hypothesis space and the complexity of finding simple, consistent hypotheses within that space.* For example, fitting straight lines to data is very easy; fitting high-degree polynomials is harder; and fitting Turing machines is very hard indeed because determining whether a given Turing machine is consistent with the data is not even decidable in general. A second reason to prefer simple hypothesis spaces is that the resulting hypotheses may be simpler to use—that is, it is faster to compute $h(x)$ when $h$ is a linear function than when it is an arbitrary Turing machine program.

For these reasons, most work on learning has focused on relatively simple representations. In this chapter, we concentrate on propositional logic and related languages. Chapter 19 looks at learning theories in first-order logic. We will see that the expressiveness–complexity tradeoff is not as simple as it first seems: it is often the case, as we saw in Chapter 8, that an expressive language makes it possible for a *simple* theory to fit the data, whereas restricting the expressiveness of the language means that any consistent theory must be very complex. For example, the rules of chess can be written in a page or two of first-order logic, but require thousands of pages when written in propositional logic. In such cases, it should be possible to learn much faster by using the more expressive language.

## 18.3 Learning Decision Trees

Decision tree induction is one of the simplest, and yet most successful forms of learning algorithm. It serves as a good introduction to the area of inductive learning, and is easy to implement. We first describe the performance element, and then show how to learn it. Along the way, we will introduce ideas that appear in all areas of inductive learning.

### Decision trees as performance elements

DECISION TREE
ATTRIBUTES
CLASSIFICATION
REGRESSION
POSITIVE
NEGATIVE

A **decision tree** takes as input an object or situation described by a set of **attributes** and returns a "decision"—the predicted output value for the input. The input attributes can be discrete or continuous. For now, we assume discrete inputs. The output value can also be discrete or continuous; learning a discrete-valued function is called **classification** learning; learning a continuous function is called **regression**. We will concentrate on *Boolean* classification, wherein each example is classified as true (**positive**) or false (**negative**).

A decision tree reaches its decision by performing a sequence of tests. Each internal node in the tree corresponds to a test of the value of one of the properties, and the branches from the node are labeled with the possible values of the test. Each leaf node in the tree specifies the value to be returned if that leaf is reached. The decision tree representation seems to be very natural for humans; indeed, many "How To" manuals (e.g., for car repair) are written entirely as a single decision tree stretching over hundreds of pages.

GOAL PREDICATE

A somewhat simpler example is provided by the problem of whether to wait for a table at a restaurant. The aim here is to learn a definition for the **goal predicate** $WillWait$. In setting this up as a learning problem, we first have to state what attributes are available to describe examples in the domain. In Chapter 19, we will see how to automate this task; for now, let's suppose we decide on the following list of attributes:

1. *Alternate*: whether there is a suitable alternative restaurant nearby.
2. *Bar*: whether the restaurant has a comfortable bar area to wait in.
3. *Fri/Sat*: true on Fridays and Saturdays.
4. *Hungry*: whether we are hungry.
5. *Patrons*: how many people are in the restaurant (values are $None$, $Some$, and $Full$).
6. *Price*: the restaurant's price range ($, $$, $$$).
7. *Raining*: whether it is raining outside.
8. *Reservation*: whether we made a reservation.
9. *Type*: the kind of restaurant (French, Italian, Thai, or burger).
10. *WaitEstimate*: the wait estimated by the host (0–10 minutes, 10–30, 30–60, >60).

The decision tree usually used by one of us (SR) for this domain is shown in Figure 18.2. Notice that the tree does not use the $Price$ and $Type$ attributes, in effect considering them to be irrelevant. Examples are processed by the tree starting at the root and following the appropriate branch until a leaf is reached. For instance, an example with $Patrons = Full$ and $WaitEstimate = 0\text{–}10$ will be classified as positive (i.e., yes, we will wait for a table).

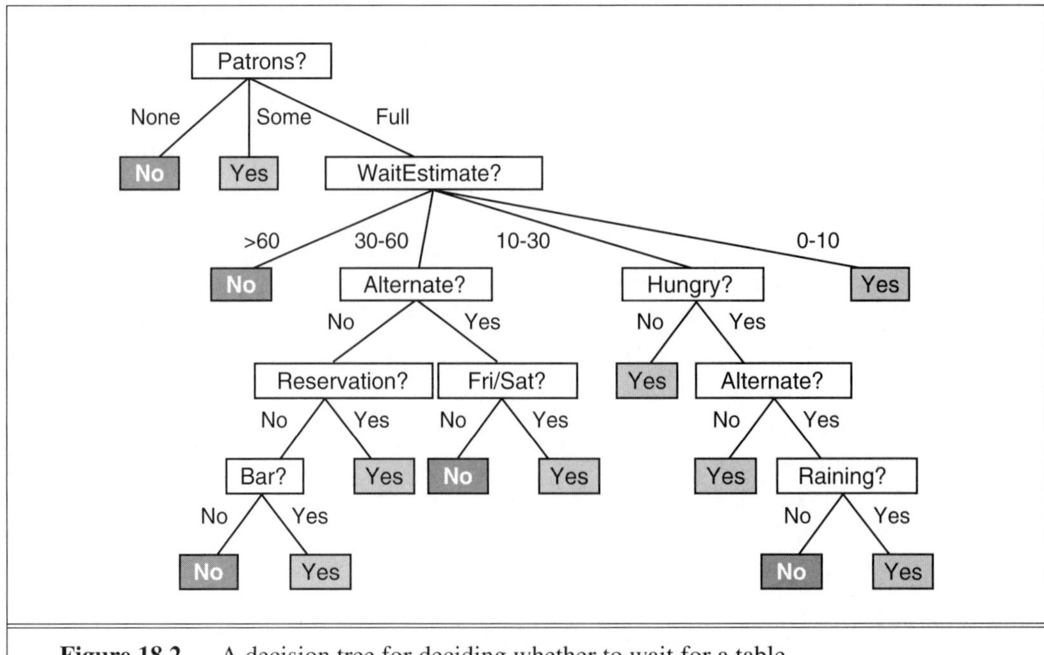


**Figure 18.2** A decision tree for deciding whether to wait for a table.

### Expressiveness of decision trees

Logically speaking, any particular decision tree hypothesis for the $WillWait$ goal predicate can be seen as an assertion of the form

$$\forall s \ WillWait(s) \Leftrightarrow (P_1(s) \lor P_2(s) \lor \cdots \lor P_n(s)) ,$$

where each condition $P_i(s)$ is a conjunction of tests corresponding to a path from the root of the tree to a leaf with a positive outcome. Although this looks like a first-order sentence, it is, in a sense, propositional, because it contains just one variable and all the predicates are unary. The decision tree is really describing a relationship between $WillWait$ and some logical combination of attribute values. We cannot use decision trees to represent tests that refer to two or more different objects—for example,

$$\exists r_2 \ Nearby(r_2, r) \land Price(r, p) \land Price(r_2, p_2) \land Cheaper(p_2, p)$$

(is there a cheaper restaurant nearby?). Obviously, we could add another Boolean attribute with the name $CheaperRestaurantNearby$, but it is intractable to add *all* such attributes. Chapter 19 will delve further into the problem of learning in first-order logic proper.

Decision trees *are* fully expressive within the class of propositional languages; that is, any Boolean function can be written as a decision tree. This can be done trivially by having each row in the truth table for the function correspond to a path in the tree. This would yield an exponentially large decision tree representation because the truth table has exponentially many rows. Clearly, decision trees can represent many functions with much smaller trees.

For some kinds of functions, however, this is a real problem. For example, if the function is the **parity function**, which returns 1 if and only if an even number of inputs are 1, then an exponentially large decision tree will be needed. It is also difficult to use a decision tree to represent a **majority function**, which returns 1 if more than half of its inputs are 1.

PARITY FUNCTION

MAJORITY FUNCTION

In other words, decision trees are good for some kinds of functions and bad for others. Is there *any* kind of representation that is efficient for *all* kinds of functions? Unfortunately, the answer is no. We can show this in a very general way. Consider the set of all Boolean functions on $n$ attributes. How many different functions are in this set? This is just the number of different truth tables that we can write down, because the function is defined by its truth table. The truth table has $2^n$ rows, because each input case is described by $n$ attributes. We can consider the "answer" column of the table as a $2^n$-bit number that defines the function. No matter what representation we use for functions, some of the functions (almost all of them, in fact) are going to require at least that many bits to represent.

If it takes $2^n$ bits to define the function, then there are $2^{2^n}$ different functions on $n$ attributes. This is a scary number. For example, with just six Boolean attributes, there are $2^{2^6} = 18,446,744,073,709,551,616$ different functions to choose from. We will need some ingenious algorithms to find consistent hypotheses in such a large space.

### Inducing decision trees from examples

An example for a Boolean decision tree consists of a vector of input attributes, $X$, and a single Boolean output value $y$. A set of examples $(X_1, y_1) \ldots, (X_{12}, y_{12})$ is shown in Figure 18.3.

| Example | Attributes | | | | | | | | | | Goal |
|---|---|---|---|---|---|---|---|---|---|---|---|
| | *Alt* | *Bar* | *Fri* | *Hun* | *Pat* | *Price* | *Rain* | *Res* | *Type* | *Est* | *WillWait* |
| $X_1$ | *Yes* | *No* | *No* | *Yes* | *Some* | *$$$* | *No* | *Yes* | *French* | *0–10* | *Yes* |
| $X_2$ | *Yes* | *No* | *No* | *Yes* | *Full* | *$* | *No* | *No* | *Thai* | *30–60* | *No* |
| $X_3$ | *No* | *Yes* | *No* | *No* | *Some* | *$* | *No* | *No* | *Burger* | *0–10* | *Yes* |
| $X_4$ | *Yes* | *No* | *Yes* | *Yes* | *Full* | *$* | *Yes* | *No* | *Thai* | *10–30* | *Yes* |
| $X_5$ | *Yes* | *No* | *Yes* | *No* | *Full* | *$$$* | *No* | *Yes* | *French* | *>60* | *No* |
| $X_6$ | *No* | *Yes* | *No* | *Yes* | *Some* | *$$* | *Yes* | *Yes* | *Italian* | *0–10* | *Yes* |
| $X_7$ | *No* | *Yes* | *No* | *No* | *None* | *$* | *Yes* | *No* | *Burger* | *0–10* | *No* |
| $X_8$ | *No* | *No* | *No* | *Yes* | *Some* | *$$* | *Yes* | *Yes* | *Thai* | *0–10* | *Yes* |
| $X_9$ | *No* | *Yes* | *Yes* | *No* | *Full* | *$* | *Yes* | *No* | *Burger* | *>60* | *No* |
| $X_{10}$ | *Yes* | *Yes* | *Yes* | *Yes* | *Full* | *$$$* | *No* | *Yes* | *Italian* | *10–30* | *No* |
| $X_{11}$ | *No* | *No* | *No* | *No* | *None* | *$* | *No* | *No* | *Thai* | *0–10* | *No* |
| $X_{12}$ | *Yes* | *Yes* | *Yes* | *Yes* | *Full* | *$* | *No* | *No* | *Burger* | *30–60* | *Yes* |

**Figure 18.3** Examples for the restaurant domain.

The positive examples are the ones in which the goal $WillWait$ is true $(X_1, X_3, \ldots)$; the negative examples are the ones in which it is false $(X_2, X_5, \ldots)$. The complete set of examples is called the **training set**.

TRAINING SET

The problem of finding a decision tree that agrees with the training set might seem difficult, but in fact there is a trivial solution. We could simply construct a decision tree that has one path to a leaf for each example, where the path tests each attribute in turn and follows the value for the example and the leaf has the classification of the example. When given the same example again,[3] the decision tree will come up with the right classification. Unfortunately, it will not have much to say about any other cases!

The problem with this trivial tree is that it just memorizes the observations. It does not extract any pattern from the examples, so we cannot expect it to be able to extrapolate to examples it has not seen. Applying Ockham's razor, we should find instead the *smallest* decision tree that is consistent with the examples. Unfortunately, for any reasonable definition of "smallest," finding the smallest tree is an intractable problem. With some simple heuristics, however, we can do a good job of finding a "smallish" one. The basic idea behind the DECISION-TREE-LEARNING algorithm is to test the most important attribute first. By "most important," we mean the one that makes the most difference to the classification of an example. That way, we hope to get to the correct classification with a small number of tests, meaning that all paths in the tree will be short and the tree as a whole will be small.

Figure 18.4 shows how the algorithm gets started. We are given 12 training examples, which we classify into positive and negative sets. We then decide which attribute to use as the first test in the tree. Figure 18.4(a) shows that *Type* is a poor attribute, because it leaves us with four possible outcomes, each of which has the same number of positive and negative examples. On the other hand, in Figure 18.4(b) we see that *Patrons* is a fairly important

3 The same example *or an example with the same description*—this distinction is very important, and we will return to it in Chapter 19.

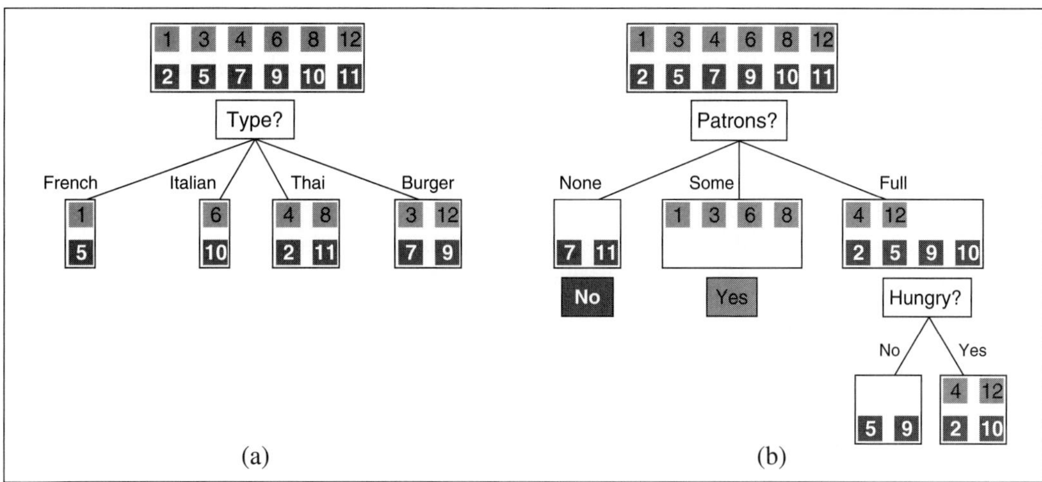


**Figure 18.4** Splitting the examples by testing on attributes. (a) Splitting on *Type* brings us no nearer to distinguishing between positive and negative examples. (b) Splitting on *Patrons* does a good job of separating positive and negative examples. After splitting on *Patrons*, *Hungry* is a fairly good second test.

attribute, because if the value is *None* or *Some*, then we are left with example sets for which we can answer definitively (*No* and *Yes*, respectively). If the value is *Full*, we are left with a mixed set of examples. In general, after the first attribute test splits up the examples, each outcome is a new decision tree learning problem in itself, with fewer examples and one fewer attribute. There are four cases to consider for these recursive problems:

1. If there are some positive and some negative examples, then choose the best attribute to split them. Figure 18.4(b) shows *Hungry* being used to split the remaining examples.
2. If all the remaining examples are positive (or all negative), then we are done: we can answer *Yes* or *No*. Figure 18.4(b) shows examples of this in the *None* and *Some* cases.
3. If there are no examples left, it means that no such example has been observed, and we return a default value calculated from the majority classification at the node's parent.
4. If there are no attributes left, but both positive and negative examples, we have a problem. It means that these examples have exactly the same description, but different classifications. This happens when some of the data are incorrect; we say there is **noise** in the data. It also happens either when the attributes do not give enough information to describe the situation fully, or when the domain is truly nondeterministic. One simple way out of the problem is to use a majority vote.

NOISE

The DECISION-TREE-LEARNING algorithm is shown in Figure 18.5. The details of the method for CHOOSE-ATTRIBUTE are given in the next subsection.

The final tree produced by the algorithm applied to the 12-example data set is shown in Figure 18.6. The tree is clearly different from the original tree shown in Figure 18.2, despite the fact that the data were actually generated from an agent using the original tree. One might conclude that the learning algorithm is not doing a very good job of learning the correct

**function** DECISION-TREE-LEARNING(*examples*, *attribs*, *default*) **returns** a decision tree
  **inputs**: *examples*, set of examples
    *attribs*, set of attributes
    *default*, default value for the goal predicate

  **if** *examples* is empty **then return** *default*
  **else if** all *examples* have the same classification **then return** the classification
  **else if** *attribs* is empty **then return** MAJORITY-VALUE(*examples*)
  **else**
    *best* ← CHOOSE-ATTRIBUTE(*attribs*, *examples*)
    *tree* ← a new decision tree with root test *best*
    $m$ ← MAJORITY-VALUE(*examples*)
    **for each** value $v_i$ of *best* **do**
      $examples_i \leftarrow \{$elements of *examples* with $best = v_i\}$
      *subtree* ← DECISION-TREE-LEARNING($examples_i$, $attribs - best$, $m$)
      add a branch to *tree* with label $v_i$ and subtree *subtree*
    **return** *tree*

**Figure 18.5** The decision tree learning algorithm.

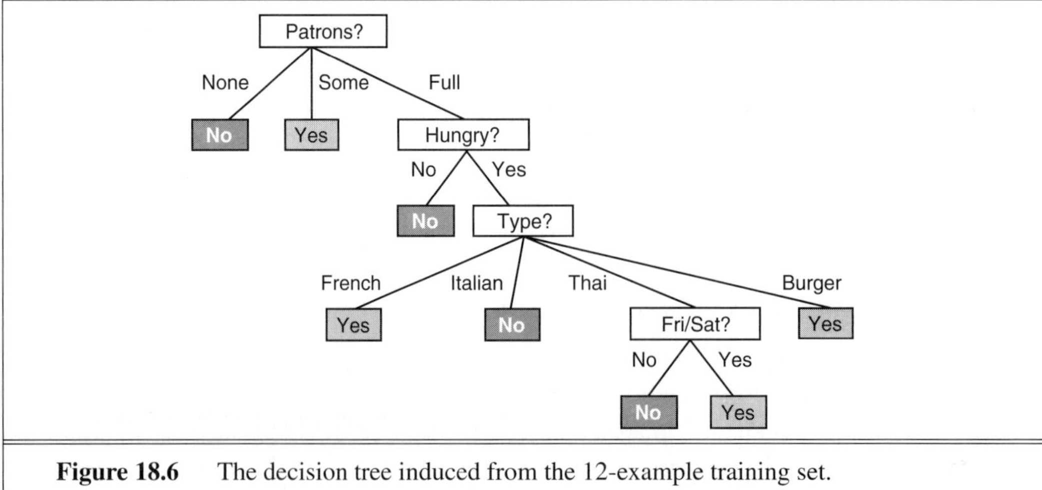


**Figure 18.6** The decision tree induced from the 12-example training set.

function. This would be the wrong conclusion to draw, however. The learning algorithm looks at the *examples*, not at the correct function, and in fact, its hypothesis (see Figure 18.6) not only agrees with all the examples, but is considerably simpler than the original tree. The learning algorithm has no reason to include tests for *Raining* and *Reservation*, because it can classify all the examples without them. It has also detected an interesting and previously unsuspected pattern: the first author will wait for Thai food on weekends.

Of course, if we were to gather more examples, we might induce a tree more similar to the original. The tree in Figure 18.6 is bound to make a mistake; for example, it has never seen a case where the wait is 0–10 minutes but the restaurant is full. For a case where

*Hungry* is false, the tree says not to wait, but I (SR) would certainly wait. This raises an obvious question: if the algorithm induces a consistent, but incorrect, tree from the examples, how incorrect will the tree be? We will show how to analyze this question experimentally, after we explain the details of the attribute selection step.

### Choosing attribute tests

The scheme used in decision tree learning for selecting attributes is designed to minimize the depth of the final tree. The idea is to pick the attribute that goes as far as possible toward providing an exact classification of the examples. A perfect attribute divides the examples into sets that are all positive or all negative. The *Patrons* attribute is not perfect, but it is fairly good. A really useless attribute, such as *Type*, leaves the example sets with roughly the same proportion of positive and negative examples as the original set.

All we need, then, is a formal measure of "fairly good" and "really useless" and we can implement the CHOOSE-ATTRIBUTE function of Figure 18.5. The measure should have its maximum value when the attribute is perfect and its minimum value when the attribute is of no use at all. One suitable measure is the expected amount of **information** provided by the attribute, where we use the term in the mathematical sense first defined in Shannon and Weaver (1949). To understand the notion of information, think about it as providing the answer to a question—for example, whether a coin will come up heads. The amount of information contained in the answer depends on one's prior knowledge. The less you know, the more information is provided. Information theory measures information content in **bits**. One bit of information is enough to answer a yes/no question about which one has no idea, such as the flip of a fair coin. In general, if the possible answers $v_i$ have probabilities $P(v_i)$, then the information content $I$ of the actual answer is given by

INFORMATION

$$I(P(v_1), \ldots, P(v_n)) = \sum_{i=1}^{n} -P(v_i) \log_2 P(v_i) .$$

To check this equation, for the tossing of a fair coin, we get

$$I\left(\tfrac{1}{2}, \tfrac{1}{2}\right) = -\tfrac{1}{2} \log_2 \tfrac{1}{2} - \tfrac{1}{2} \log_2 \tfrac{1}{2} = 1 \text{ bit.}$$

If the coin is loaded to give 99% heads, we get $I\,(1/100, 99/100) = 0.08$ bits, and as the probability of heads goes to 1, the information of the actual answer goes to 0.

For decision tree learning, the question that needs answering is; for a given example, what is the correct classification? A correct decision tree will answer this question. An estimate of the probabilities of the possible answers before any of the attributes have been tested is given by the proportions of positive and negative examples in the training set. Suppose the training set contains $p$ positive examples and $n$ negative examples. Then an estimate of the information contained in a correct answer is

$$I\left(\tfrac{p}{p+n}, \tfrac{n}{p+n}\right) = -\tfrac{p}{p+n} \log_2 \tfrac{p}{p+n} - \tfrac{n}{p+n} \log_2 \tfrac{n}{p+n} .$$

The restaurant training set in Figure 18.3 has $p = n = 6$, so we need 1 bit of information.

Now a test on a single attribute $A$ will not usually tell us this much information, but it will give us some of it. We can measure exactly how much by looking at how much information we still need *after* the attribute test. Any attribute $A$ divides the training set $E$ into subsets $E_1, \ldots, E_v$ according to their values for $A$, where $A$ can have $v$ distinct values. Each subset $E_i$ has $p_i$ positive examples and $n_i$ negative examples, so if we go along that branch, we will need an additional $I\left(p_i/(p_i+n_i), n_i/(p_i+n_i)\right)$ bits of information to answer the question. A randomly chosen example from the training set has the $i$th value for the attribute with probability $(p_i+n_i)/(p+n)$, so on average, after testing attribute $A$, we will need

$$Remainder(A) = \sum_{i=1}^{v} \frac{p_i+n_i}{p+n} I\left(\frac{p_i}{p_i+n_i}, \frac{n_i}{p_i+n_i}\right)$$

INFORMATION GAIN

bits of information to classify the example. The **information gain** from the attribute test is the difference between the original information requirement and the new requirement:

$$Gain(A) = I\left(\frac{p}{p+n}, \frac{n}{p+n}\right) - Remainder(A) .$$

The heuristic used in the CHOOSE-ATTRIBUTE function is just to choose the attribute with the largest gain. Returning to the attributes considered in Figure 18.4, we have

$$Gain(Patrons) = 1 - \left[\tfrac{2}{12}I(0,1) + \tfrac{4}{12}I(1,0) + \tfrac{6}{12}I\left(\tfrac{2}{6}, \tfrac{4}{6}\right)\right] \approx 0.541 \text{ bits.}$$

$$Gain(Type) = 1 - \left[\tfrac{2}{12}I\left(\tfrac{1}{2}, \tfrac{1}{2}\right) + \tfrac{2}{12}I\left(\tfrac{1}{2}, \tfrac{1}{2}\right) + \tfrac{4}{12}I\left(\tfrac{2}{4}, \tfrac{2}{4}\right) + \tfrac{4}{12}I\left(\tfrac{2}{4}, \tfrac{2}{4}\right)\right] = 0.$$

confirming our intuition that $Patrons$ is a better attribute to split on. In fact, $Patrons$ has the highest gain of any of the attributes and would be chosen by the decision-tree learning algorithm as the root.

### Assessing the performance of the learning algorithm

A learning algorithm is good if it produces hypotheses that do a good job of predicting the classifications of unseen examples. In Section 18.5, we will see how prediction quality can be estimated in advance. For now, we will look at a methodology for assessing prediction quality after the fact.

Obviously, a prediction is good if it turns out to be true, so we can assess the quality of a hypothesis by checking its predictions against the correct classification once we know it. We

TEST SET

do this on a set of examples known as the **test set**. If we train on all our available examples, then we will have to go out and get some more to test on, so often it is more convenient to adopt the following methodology:

1. Collect a large set of examples.
2. Divide it into two disjoint sets: the **training set** and the **test set**.
3. Apply the learning algorithm to the training set, generating a hypothesis $h$.
4. Measure the percentage of examples in the test set that are correctly classified by $h$.
5. Repeat steps 2 to 4 for different sizes of training sets and different randomly selected training sets of each size.

The result of this procedure is a set of data that can be processed to give the average prediction quality as a function of the size of the training set. This function can be plotted on a graph,

LEARNING CURVE

giving what is called the **learning curve** for the algorithm on the particular domain. The

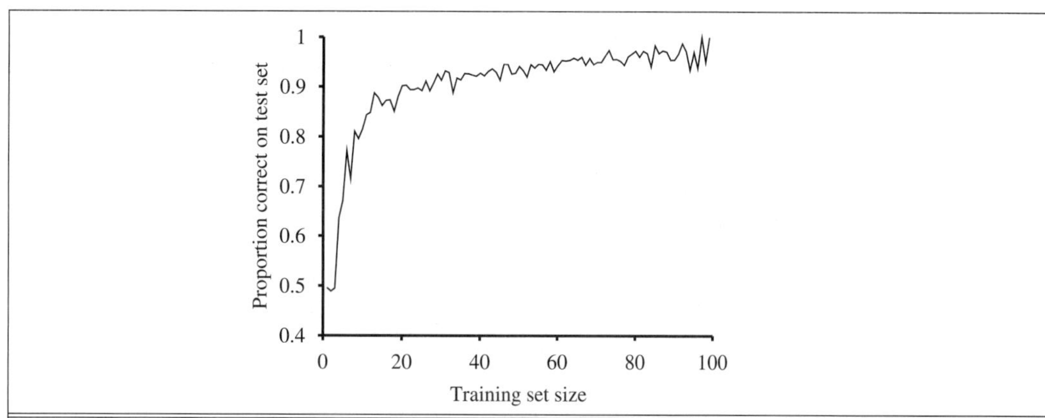


**Figure 18.7** A learning curve for the decision tree algorithm on 100 randomly generated examples in the restaurant domain. The graph summarizes 20 trials.

learning curve for DECISION-TREE-LEARNING with the restaurant examples is shown in Figure 18.7. Notice that, as the training set grows, the prediction quality increases. (For this reason, such curves are also called **happy graphs**.) This is a good sign that there is indeed some pattern in the data and the learning algorithm is picking it up.

PEEKING

Obviously, the learning algorithm must not be allowed to "see" the test data before the learned hypothesis is tested on them. Unfortunately, it is all too easy to fall into the trap of **peeking** at the test data. Peeking typically happens as follows: A learning algorithm can have various "knobs" that can be twiddled to tune its behavior—for example, various different criteria for choosing the next attribute in decision tree learning. We generate hypotheses for various different settings of the knobs, measure their performance on the test set, and report the prediction performance of the best hypothesis. Alas, peeking has occurred! The reason is that the hypothesis was selected *on the basis of its test set performance*, so information about the test set has leaked into the learning algorithm. The moral of this tale is that any process that involves comparing the performance of hypotheses on a test set must use a *new* test set to measure the performance of the hypothesis that is finally selected. In practice, this is too difficult, so people continue to run experiments on tainted sets of examples.

### Noise and overfitting

We saw earlier that if there are two or more examples with the same description (in terms of the attributes) but different classifications, then the DECISION-TREE-LEARNING algorithm must fail to find a decision tree consistent with all the examples. The solution we mentioned before is to have each leaf node report either the majority classification for its set of examples, if a deterministic hypothesis is required, or report the estimated probabilities of each classification using the relative frequencies. Unfortunately, this is far from the whole story. It is quite possible, and in fact likely, that even when vital information is missing, the decision tree learning algorithm will find a decision tree that is consistent with all the examples. This is because the algorithm can use the *irrelevant* attributes, if any, to make spurious distinctions among the examples.

Consider the problem of trying to predict the roll of a die. Suppose that experiments are carried out during an extended period of time with various dice and that the attributes describing each training example are as follows:

1. *Day*: the day on which the die was rolled (Mon, Tue, Wed, Thu).
2. *Month*: the month in which the die was rolled (Jan or Feb).
3. *Color*: the color of the die (Red or Blue).

As long as no two examples have identical descriptions, DECISION-TREE-LEARNING will find an exact hypothesis. The more attributes there are, the more likely it is that an exact hypothesis will be found. Any such hypothesis will be totally spurious. What we would like is that DECISION-TREE-LEARNING return a single leaf node with probabilities close to 1/6 for each roll, once it has seen enough examples.

Whenever there is a large set of possible hypotheses, one has to be careful not to use the resulting freedom to find meaningless "regularity" in the data. This problem is called **overfitting**. A very general phenomenon, overfitting occurs even when the target function is not at all random. It afflicts every kind of learning algorithm, not just decision trees.

OVERFITTING

A complete mathematical treatment of overfitting is beyond the scope of this book. Here we present a simple technique called **decision tree pruning** to deal with the problem. Pruning works by preventing recursive splitting on attributes that are not clearly relevant, even when the data at that node in the tree are not uniformly classified. The question is, how do we detect an irrelevant attribute?

DECISION TREE PRUNING

Suppose we split a set of examples using an irrelevant attribute. Generally speaking, we would expect the resulting subsets to have roughly the same proportions of each class as the original set. In this case, the information gain will be close to zero.[4] Thus, the information gain is a good clue to irrelevance. Now the question is, how large a gain should we require in order to split on a particular attribute?

SIGNIFICANCE TEST

NULL HYPOTHESIS

We can answer this question by using a statistical **significance test**. Such a test begins by assuming that there is no underlying pattern (the so-called **null hypothesis**). Then the actual data are analyzed to calculate the extent to which they deviate from a perfect absence of pattern. If the degree of deviation is statistically unlikely (usually taken to mean a 5% probability or less), then that is considered to be good evidence for the presence of a significant pattern in the data. The probabilities are calculated from standard distributions of the amount of deviation one would expect to see in random sampling.

In this case, the null hypothesis is that the attribute is irrelevant and, hence, that the information gain for an infinitely large sample would be zero. We need to calculate the probability that, under the null hypothesis, a sample of size $v$ would exhibit the observed deviation from the expected distribution of positive and negative examples. We can measure the deviation by comparing the actual numbers of positive and negative examples in each subset, $p_i$ and $n_i$, with the expected numbers, $\hat{p}_i$ and $\hat{n}_i$, assuming true irrelevance:

$$\hat{p}_i = p \times \frac{p_i + n_i}{p + n} \qquad \hat{n}_i = n \times \frac{p_i + n_i}{p + n}.$$

[4] In fact, the gain will be positive unless the proportions are all exactly the same. (See Exercise 18.10.)

A convenient measure of the total deviation is given by

$$D = \sum_{i=1}^{v} \frac{(p_i - \hat{p}_i)^2}{\hat{p}_i} + \frac{(n_i - \hat{n}_i)^2}{\hat{n}_i} .$$

Under the null hypothesis, the value of $D$ is distributed according to the $\chi^2$ (chi-squared) distribution with $v - 1$ degrees of freedom. The probability that the attribute is really irrelevant can be calculated with the help of standard $\chi^2$ tables or with statistical software. Exercise 18.11 asks you to make the appropriate changes to DECISION-TREE-LEARNING to implement this form of pruning, which is known as $\chi^2$ **pruning**.

$\chi^2$ PRUNING

With pruning, noise can be tolerated: classification errors give a linear increase in prediction error, whereas errors in the descriptions of examples have an asymptotic effect that gets worse as the tree shrinks down to smaller sets. Trees constructed with pruning perform significantly better than trees constructed without pruning when the data contain a large amount of noise. The pruned trees are often much smaller and hence easier to understand.

CROSS-VALIDATION

**Cross-validation** is another technique that reduces overfitting. It can be applied to any learning algorithm, not just decision tree learning. The basic idea is to estimate how well each hypothesis will predict unseen data. This is done by setting aside some fraction of the known data and using it to test the prediction performance of a hypothesis induced from the remaining data. $K$-fold cross-validation means that you run $k$ experiments, each time setting aside a different $1/k$ of the data to test on, and average the results. Popular values for $k$ are 5 and 10. The extreme is $k = n$, also known as leave-one-out cross-validation. Cross-validation can be used in conjunction with any tree-construction method (including pruning) in order to select a tree with good prediction performance. To avoid peeking, we must then measure this performance with a new test set.

## Broadening the applicability of decision trees

In order to extend decision tree induction to a wider variety of problems, a number of issues must be addressed. We will briefly mention each, suggesting that a full understanding is best obtained by doing the associated exercises:

◇ **Missing data**: In many domains, not all the attribute values will be known for every example. The values might have gone unrecorded, or they might be too expensive to obtain. This gives rise to two problems: First, given a complete decision tree, how should one classify an object that is missing one of the test attributes? Second, how should one modify the information gain formula when some examples have unknown values for the attribute? These questions are addressed in Exercise 18.12.

◇ **Multivalued attributes**:When an attribute has many possible values, the information gain measure gives an inappropriate indication of the attribute's usefulness. In the extreme case, we could use an attribute, such as *RestaurantName*, that has a different value for every example. Then each subset of examples would be a singleton with a unique classification, so the information gain measure would have its highest value for this attribute. Nonetheless, the attribute could be irrelevant or useless. One solution is to use the **gain ratio** (Exercise 18.13).

GAIN RATIO

SPLIT POINT

REGRESSION TREE

◇ **Continuous and integer-valued input attributes**: Continuous or integer-valued attributes such as $Height$ and $Weight$, have an infinite set of possible values. Rather than generate infinitely many branches, decision-tree learning algorithms typically find the **split point** that gives the highest information gain. For example, at a given node in the tree, it might be the case that testing on $Weight > 160$ gives the most information. Efficient dynamic programming methods exist for finding good split points, but it is still by far the most expensive part of real-world decision tree learning applications.

◇ **Continuous-valued output attributes**: If we are trying to predict a numerical value, such as the price of a work of art, rather than a discrete classification, then we need a **regression tree**. Such a tree has at each leaf a linear function of some subset of numerical attributes, rather than a single value. For example, the branch for hand-colored engravings might end with a linear function of area, age, and number of colors. The learning algorithm must decide when to stop splitting and begin applying linear regression using the remaining attributes (or some subset thereof).

A decision-tree learning system for real-world applications must be able to handle all of these problems. Handling continuous-valued variables is especially important, because both physical and financial processes provide numerical data. Several commercial packages have been built that meet these criteria, and they have been used to develop several hundred fielded systems. In many areas of industry and commerce, decision trees are usually the first method tried when a classification method is to be extracted from a data set. One important property of decision trees is that it is possible for a human to understand the output of the learning algorithm. (Indeed, this is a *legal requirement* for financial decisions that are subject to anti-discrimination laws.) This is a property not shared by neural networks (see Chapter 20).

## 18.4 ENSEMBLE LEARNING

ENSEMBLE LEARNING

So far we have looked at learning methods in which a single hypothesis, chosen from a hypothesis space, is used to make predictions. The idea of **ensemble learning** methods is to select a whole collection, or **ensemble**, of hypotheses from the hypothesis space and combine their predictions. For example, we might generate a hundred different decision trees from the same training set and have them vote on the best classification for a new example.

The motivation for ensemble learning is simple. Consider an ensemble of $M = 5$ hypotheses and suppose that we combine their predictions using simple majority voting. For the ensemble to misclassify a new example, *at least three of the five hypotheses have to misclassify it.* The hope is that this is much less likely than a misclassification by a single hypothesis. Suppose we assume that each hypothesis $h_i$ in the ensemble has an error of $p$—that is, the probability that a randomly chosen example is misclassified by $h_i$ is $p$. Furthermore, suppose we assume that the errors made by each hypothesis are *independent.* In that case, if $p$ is small, then the probability of a large number of misclassifications occurring is minuscule. For example, a simple calculation (Exercise 18.14) shows that using an ensemble of five hypotheses reduces an error rate of 1 in 10 down to an error rate of less than 1 in 100. Now, obviously

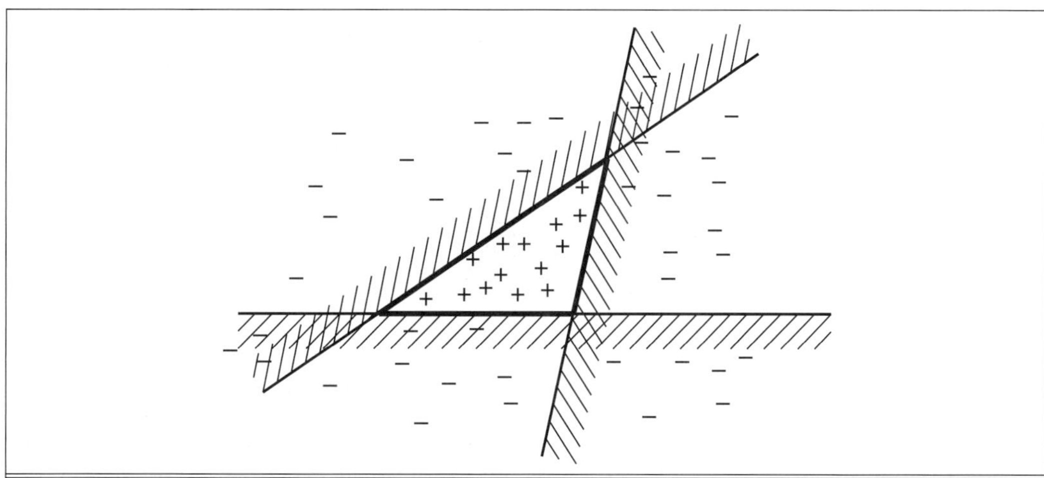

**Figure 18.8** Illustration of the increased expressive power obtained by ensemble learning. We take three linear threshold hypotheses, each of which classifies positively on the non-shaded side, and classify as positive any example classified positively by all three. The resulting triangular region is a hypothesis not expressible in the original hypothesis space.

the assumption of independence is unreasonable, because hypotheses are likely to be misled in the same way by any misleading aspects of the training data. But if the hypotheses are at least a little bit different, thereby reducing the correlation between their errors, then ensemble learning can be very useful.

Another way to think about the ensemble idea is as a generic way of enlarging the hypothesis space. That is, think of the ensemble itself as a hypothesis and the new hypothesis space as the set of all possible ensembles constructible from hypotheses in the original space. Figure 18.8 shows how this can result in a more expressive hypothesis space. If the original hypothesis space allows for a simple and efficient learning algorithm, then the ensemble method provides a way to learn a much more expressive class of hypotheses without incurring much additional computational or algorithmic complexity.

BOOSTING

WEIGHTED TRAINING SET

The most widely used ensemble method is called **boosting**. To understand how it works, we need first to explain the idea of a **weighted training set**. In such a training set, each example has an associated weight $w_j \geq 0$. The higher the weight of an example, the higher is the importance attached to it during the learning of a hypothesis. It is straightforward to modify the learning algorithms we have seen so far to operate with weighted training sets.[5]

Boosting starts with $w_j = 1$ for all the examples (i.e., a normal training set). From this set, it generates the first hypothesis, $h_1$. This hypothesis will classify some of the training examples correctly and some incorrectly. We would like the next hypothesis to do better on the misclassified examples, so we increase their weights while decreasing the weights of the correctly classified examples. From this new weighted training set, we generate hypothesis $h_2$. The process continues in this way until we have generated $M$ hypotheses, where $M$ is

[5] For learning algorithms in which this is not possible, one can instead create a **replicated training set** where the $i$th example appears $w_j$ times, using randomization to handle fractional weights.

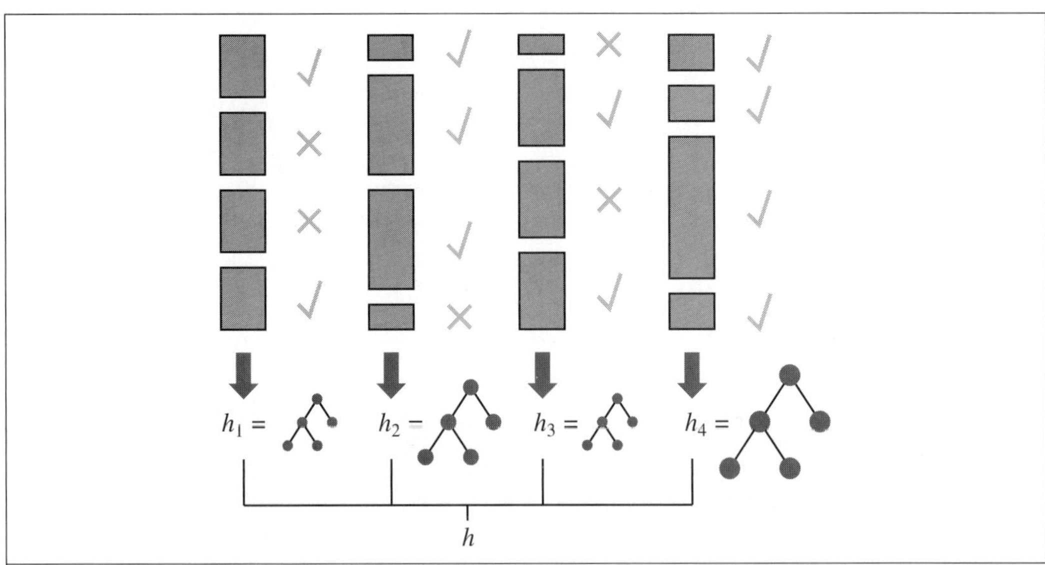


**Figure 18.9** How the boosting algorithm works. Each shaded rectangle corresponds to an example; the height of the rectangle corresponds to the weight. The ticks and crosses indicate whether the example was classified correctly by the current hypothesis. The size of the decision tree indicates the weight of that hypothesis in the final ensemble.

an input to the boosting algorithm. The final ensemble hypothesis is a weighted-majority combination of all the $M$ hypotheses, each weighted according to how well it performed on the training set. Figure 18.9 shows how the algorithm works conceptually. There are many variants of the basic boosting idea with different ways of adjusting the weights and combining the hypotheses. One specific algorithm, called ADABOOST, is shown in Figure 18.10. While the details of the weight adjustments are not so important, ADABOOST does have a very important property: if the input learning algorithm $L$ is a **weak learning** algorithm—which means that $L$ always returns a hypothesis with weighted error on the training set that is slightly better than random guessing (i.e., 50% for Boolean classification)—then ADABOOST will return a hypothesis that *classifies the training data perfectly* for large enough $M$. Thus, the algorithm *boosts* the accuracy of the original learning algorithm on the training data. This result holds no matter how inexpressive the original hypothesis space and no matter how complex the function being learned.

WEAK LEARNING

Let us see how well boosting does on the restaurant data. We will choose as our original hypothesis space the class of **decision stumps**, which are decision trees with just one test at the root. The lower curve in Figure 18.11(a) shows that unboosted decision stumps are not very effective for this data set, reaching a prediction performance of only 81% on 100 training examples. When boosting is applied (with $M = 5$), the performance is better, reaching 93% after 100 examples.

DECISION STUMP

An interesting thing happens as the ensemble size $M$ increases. Figure 18.11(b) shows the training set performance (on 100 examples) as a function of $M$. Notice that the error reaches zero (as the boosting theorem tells us) when $M$ is 20; that is, a weighted-majority

```
function ADABOOST(examples, L, M) returns a weighted-majority hypothesis
  inputs: examples, set of N labelled examples (x_1, y_1), ..., (x_N, y_N)
          L, a learning algorithm
          M, the number of hypotheses in the ensemble
  local variables: w, a vector of N example weights, initially 1/N
                   h, a vector of M hypotheses
                   z, a vector of M hypothesis weights

  for m = 1 to M do
     h[m] ← L(examples, w)
     error ← 0
     for j = 1 to N do
        if h[m](x_j) ≠ y_j then error ← error + w[j]
     for j = 1 to N do
        if h[m](x_j) = y_j then w[j] ← w[j] · error/(1 − error)
     w ← NORMALIZE(w)
     z[m] ← log (1 − error)/error
  return WEIGHTED-MAJORITY(h, z)
```

**Figure 18.10** The ADABOOST variant of the boosting method for ensemble learning. The algorithm generates hypotheses by successively reweighting the trainng examples. The function WEIGHTED-MAJORITY generates a hypothesis that returns the output value with the highest vote from the hypotheses in **h**, with votes weighted by **z**.

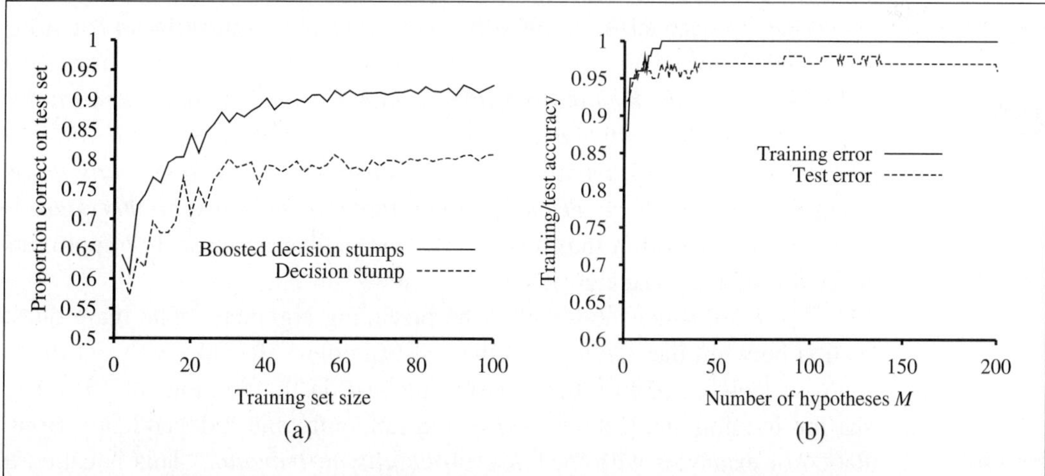


**Figure 18.11** (a) Graph showing the performance of boosted decision stumps with $M = 5$ versus decision stumps on the restaurant data. (b) The proportion correct on the training set and the test set as a function of $M$, the number of hypotheses in the ensemble. Notice that the test set accuracy improves slightly even after the training accuracy reaches 1, i.e., after the ensemble fits the data exactly.

combination of 20 decision stumps suffices to fit the 100 examples exactly. As more stumps are added to the ensemble, the error remains at zero. The graph also shows that *the test set performance continues to increase long after the training set error has reached zero.* At $M = 20$, the test performance is 0.95 (or 0.05 error), and the performance increases to 0.98 as late as $M = 137$, before gradually dropping to 0.95.

This finding, which is quite robust across data sets and hypothesis spaces, came as quite a surprise when it was first noticed. Ockham's razor tells us not to make hypotheses more complex than necessary, but the graph tells us that the predictions *improve* as the ensemble hypothesis gets more complex! Various explanations have been proposed for this. One view is that boosting approximates **Bayesian learning** (see Chapter 20), which can be shown to be an optimal learning algorithm, and the approximation improves as more hypotheses are added. Another possible explanation is that the addition of further hypotheses enables the ensemble to be *more definite* in its distinction between positive and negative examples, which helps it when it comes to classifying new examples.

## 18.5 WHY LEARNING WORKS: COMPUTATIONAL LEARNING THEORY

The main unanswered question posed in Section 18.2 was this: how can one be sure that one's learning algorithm has produced a theory that will correctly predict the future? In formal terms, how do we know that the hypothesis $h$ is close to the target function $f$ if we don't know what $f$ is? These questions have been pondered for several centuries. Until we find answers, machine learning will, at best, be puzzled by its own success.

COMPUTATIONAL LEARNING THEORY

The approach taken in this section is based on **computational learning theory**, a field at the intersection of AI, statistics, and theoretical computer science. The underlying principle is the following: *any hypothesis that is seriously wrong will almost certainly be "found out" with high probability after a small number of examples, because it will make an incorrect prediction. Thus, any hypothesis that is consistent with a sufficiently large set of training examples is unlikely to be seriously wrong: that is, it must be* ***probably approximately correct****.* Any learning algorithm that returns hypotheses that are probably approximately correct is called a **PAC-learning** algorithm.

PROBABLY APPROXIMATELY CORRECT

PAC-LEARNING

There are some subtleties in the preceding argument. The main question is the connection between the training and the test examples; after all, we want the hypothesis to be approximately correct on the test set, not just on the training set. The key assumption is that the training and test sets are drawn randomly and independently from the same population of examples with the *same probability distribution*. This is called the **stationarity** assumption. Without the stationarity assumption, the theory can make no claims at all about the future, because there would be no necessary connection between future and past. The stationarity assumption amounts to supposing that the process that selects examples is not malevolent. Obviously, if the training set consists only of weird examples—two-headed dogs, for instance—then the learning algorithm cannot help but make unsuccessful generalizations about how to recognize dogs.

STATIONARITY

### How many examples are needed?

In order to put these insights into practice, we will need some notation:

- Let **X** be the set of all possible examples.
- Let $D$ be the distribution from which examples are drawn.
- Let **H** be the set of possible hypotheses.
- Let $N$ be the number of examples in the training set.

Initially, we will assume that the true function $f$ is a member of **H**. Now we can define the **error** of a hypothesis $h$ with respect to the true function $f$ given a distribution $D$ over the examples as the probability that $h$ is different from $f$ on an example:

ERROR

$$\text{error}(h) = P(h(x) \neq f(x) | x \text{ drawn from } D) .$$

This is the same quantity being measured experimentally by the learning curves shown earlier.

A hypothesis $h$ is called **approximately correct** if $\text{error}(h) \leq \epsilon$, where $\epsilon$ is a small constant. The plan of attack is to show that after seeing $N$ examples, with high probability, all consistent hypotheses will be approximately correct. One can think of an approximately correct hypothesis as being "close" to the true function in hypothesis space: it lies inside what is called the **$\epsilon$-ball** around the true function $f$. Figure 18.12 shows the set of all hypotheses **H**, divided into the $\epsilon$-ball around $f$ and the remainder, which we call $\mathbf{H}_{\text{bad}}$.

$\epsilon$-BALL

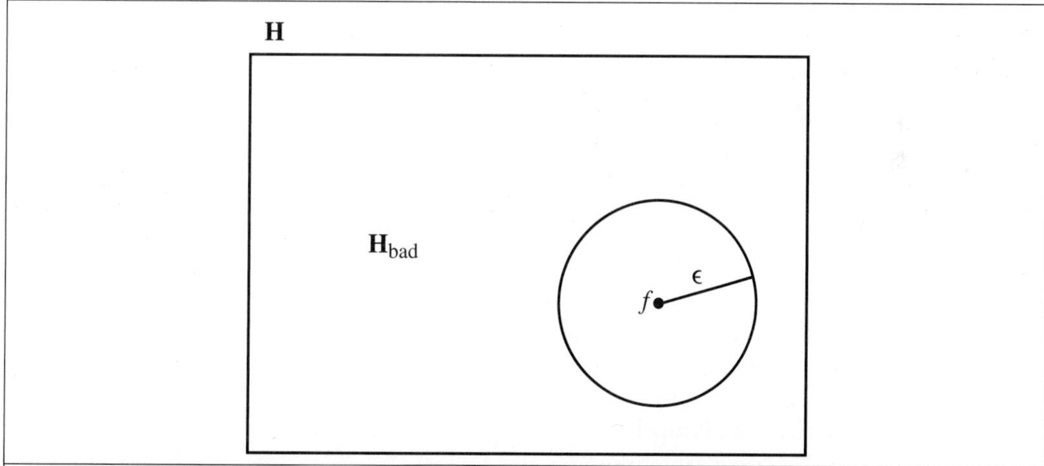


**Figure 18.12** Schematic diagram of hypothesis space, showing the "$\epsilon$-ball" around the true function $f$.

We can calculate the probability that a "seriously wrong" hypothesis $h_b \in \mathbf{H}_{\text{bad}}$ is consistent with the first $N$ examples as follows. We know that $\text{error}(h_b) > \epsilon$. Thus, the probability that it agrees with a given example is at least $1 - \epsilon$. The bound for $N$ examples is

$$P(h_b \text{ agrees with } N \text{ examples}) \leq (1 - \epsilon)^N .$$

The probability that $\mathbf{H}_{\text{bad}}$ contains at least one consistent hypothesis is bounded by the sum of the individual probabilities:

$$P(\mathbf{H}_{\text{bad}} \text{ contains a consistent hypothesis}) \leq |\mathbf{H}_{\text{bad}}|(1 - \epsilon)^N \leq |\mathbf{H}|(1 - \epsilon)^N ,$$

where we have used the fact that $|\mathbf{H}_{\text{bad}}| \leq |\mathbf{H}|$. We would like to reduce the probability of this event below some small number $\delta$:

$$|\mathbf{H}|(1-\epsilon)^N \leq \delta\,.$$

Given that $1-\epsilon \leq e^{-\epsilon}$, we can achieve this if we allow the algorithm to see

$$N \geq \frac{1}{\epsilon}\left(\ln\frac{1}{\delta} + \ln|\mathbf{H}|\right) \tag{18.1}$$

examples. Thus, if a learning algorithm returns a hypothesis that is consistent with this many examples, then with probability at least $1-\delta$, it has error at most $\epsilon$. In other words, it is probably approximately correct. The number of required examples, as a function of $\epsilon$ and $\delta$, is called the **sample complexity** of the hypothesis space.

SAMPLE COMPLEXITY

It appears, then, that the key question is the size of the hypothesis space. As we saw earlier, if $\mathbf{H}$ is the set of all Boolean functions on $n$ attributes, then $|\mathbf{H}| = 2^{2^n}$. Thus, the sample complexity of the space grows as $2^n$. Because the number of possible examples is also $2^n$, this says that any learning algorithm for the space of all Boolean functions will do no better than a lookup table if it merely returns a hypothesis that is consistent with all known examples. Another way to see this is to observe that for any unseen example, the hypothesis space will contain as many consistent hypotheses that predict a positive outcome as it does hypotheses that predict a negative outcome.

The dilemma we face, then, is that unless we restrict the space of functions the algorithm can consider, it will not be able to learn; but if we do restrict the space, we might eliminate the true function altogether. There are two ways to "escape" this dilemma. The first way is to insist that the algorithm return not just any consistent hypothesis, but preferably a simple one (as is done in decision tree learning). The theoretical analysis of such algorithms is beyond the scope of this book, but in cases where finding simple consistent hypotheses is tractable, the sample complexity results are generally better than for analyses based only on consistency. The second escape, which we pursue here, is to focus on learnable subsets of the entire set of Boolean functions. The idea is that in most cases we do not need the full expressive power of Boolean functions, and can get by with more restricted languages. We now examine one such restricted language in more detail.

## Learning decision lists

DECISION LIST

A **decision list** is a logical expression of a restricted form. It consists of a series of tests, each of which is a conjunction of literals. If a test succeeds when applied to an example description, the decision list specifies the value to be returned. If the test fails, processing continues with the next test in the list.[6] Decision lists resemble decision trees, but their overall structure is simpler. In contrast, the individual tests are more complex. Figure 18.13 shows a decision list that represents the following hypothesis:

$$\forall x\ \ \mathit{WillWait}(x)\ \Leftrightarrow\ \mathit{Patrons}(x, \mathit{Some}) \lor (\mathit{Patrons}(x, \mathit{Full}) \land \mathit{Fri/Sat}(x))\,.$$

If we allow tests of arbitrary size, then decision lists can represent any Boolean function (Exercise 18.15). On the other hand, if we restrict the size of each test to at most $k$ literals,

[6] A decision list is therefore identical in structure to a COND statement in Lisp.

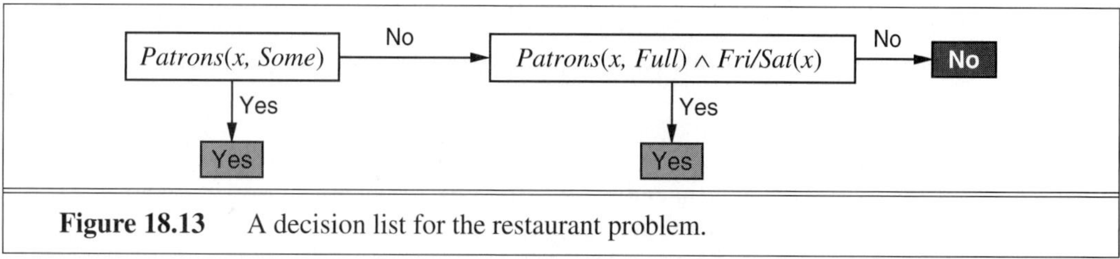


**Figure 18.13** A decision list for the restaurant problem.

then it is possible for the learning algorithm to generalize successfully from a small number of examples. We call this language **$k$-DL**. The example in Figure 18.13 is in 2-DL. It is easy to show (Exercise 18.15) that $k$-DL includes as a subset the language **$k$-DT**, the set of all decision trees of depth at most $k$. It is important to remember that the particular language referred to by $k$-DL depends on the attributes used to describe the examples. We will use the notation $k\text{-DL}(n)$ to denote a $k$-DL language using $n$ Boolean attributes.

The first task is to show that $k$-DL is learnable—that is, that any function in $k$-DL can be approximated accurately after training on a reasonable number of examples. To do this, we need to calculate the number of hypotheses in the language. Let the language of tests—conjunctions of at most $k$ literals using $n$ attributes—be $Conj(n, k)$. Because a decision list is constructed of tests, and because each test can be attached to either a *Yes* or a *No* outcome or can be absent from the decision list, there are at most $3^{|Conj(n,k)|}$ distinct sets of component tests. Each of these sets of tests can be in any order, so

$$|k\text{-DL}(n)| \leq 3^{|Conj(n,k)|} |Conj(n,k)|! \,.$$

The number of conjunctions of $k$ literals from $n$ attributes is given by

$$|Conj(n,k)| = \sum_{i=0}^{k} \binom{2n}{i} = O(n^k) \,.$$

Hence, after some work, we obtain

$$|k\text{-DL}(n)| = 2^{O(n^k \log_2(n^k))} \,.$$

We can plug this into Equation (18.1) to show that the number of examples needed for PAC-learning a $k$-DL function is polynomial in $n$:

$$N \geq \frac{1}{\epsilon}\left(\ln\frac{1}{\delta} + O(n^k \log_2(n^k))\right) \,.$$

Therefore, any algorithm that returns a consistent decision list will PAC-learn a $k$-DL function in a reasonable number of examples, for small $k$.

The next task is to find an efficient algorithm that returns a consistent decision list. We will use a greedy algorithm called DECISION-LIST-LEARNING that repeatedly finds a test that agrees exactly with some subset of the training set. Once it finds such a test, it adds it to the decision list under construction and removes the corresponding examples. It then constructs the remainder of the decision list, using just the remaining examples. This is repeated until there are no examples left. The algorithm is shown in Figure 18.14.

This algorithm does not specify the method for selecting the next test to add to the decision list. Although the formal results given earlier do not depend on the selection method,

```
function DECISION-LIST-LEARNING(examples) returns a decision list, or failure

  if examples is empty then return the trivial decision list No
  t ← a test that matches a nonempty subset examples_t of examples
       such that the members of examples_t are all positive or all negative
  if there is no such t then return failure
  if the examples in examples_t are positive then o ← Yes else o ← No
  return a decision list with initial test t and outcome o and remaining tests given by
         DECISION-LIST-LEARNING(examples − examples_t)
```

**Figure 18.14** An algorithm for learning decision lists.

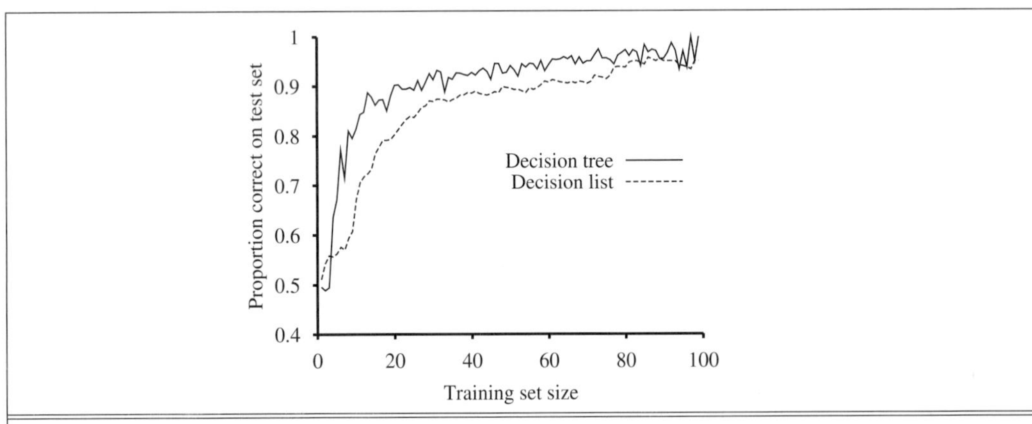


**Figure 18.15** Learning curve for DECISION-LIST-LEARNING algorithm on the restaurant data. The curve for DECISION-TREE-LEARNING is shown for comparison.

it would seem reasonable to prefer small tests that match large sets of uniformly classified examples, so that the overall decision list will be as compact as possible. The simplest strategy is to find the smallest test $t$ that matches any uniformly classified subset, regardless of the size of the subset. Even this approach works quite well, as Figure 18.15 suggests.

### Discussion

IDENTIFICATION IN THE LIMIT

Computational learning theory has generated a new way of looking at the problem of learning. In the early 1960s, the theory of learning focused on the problem of **identification in the limit**. According to this notion, an identification algorithm must return a hypothesis that exactly matches the true function. One way to do that is as follows: First, order all the hypotheses in **H** according to some measure of simplicity. Then, choose the simplest hypothesis consistent with all the examples so far. As new examples arrive, the method will abandon a simpler hypothesis that is invalidated and adopt a more complex one instead. Once it reaches the true function, it will never abandon it. Unfortunately, in many hypothesis spaces, the number of examples and the computation time required to reach the true function are enormous. Thus, computational learning theory does not insist that the learning agent find the "one true law" governing its environment, but instead that it find a hypothesis with a certain degree of predictive accuracy. Computational learning theory also brings sharply into focus the tradeoff between the expressiveness of the hypothesis language and the complexity of learning, and has led directly to an important class of learning algorithms called support vector machines.

The PAC-learning results we have shown are worst-case complexity results and do not necessarily reflect the average-case sample complexity as measured by the learning curves we have shown. An average-case analysis must also make assumptions about the distribution of examples and the distribution of true functions that the algorithm will have to learn. As these issues become better understood, computational learning theory continues to provide valuable guidance to machine learning researchers who are interested in predicting or modifying the learning ability of their algorithms. Besides decision lists, results have been obtained for almost all known subclasses of Boolean functions, for sets of first-order logical sentences (see Chapter 19), and for neural networks (see Chapter 20). The results show that the pure inductive learning problem, where the agent begins with no prior knowledge about the target function, is generally very hard. As we show in Chapter 19, the use of prior knowledge to guide inductive learning makes it possible to learn quite large sets of sentences from reasonable numbers of examples, even in a language as expressive as first-order logic.

## 18.6 SUMMARY

This chapter has concentrated on inductive learning of deterministic functions from examples. The main points were as follows:

- Learning takes many forms, depending on the nature of the performance element, the component to be improved, and the available feedback.
- If the available feedback, either from a teacher or from the environment, provides the correct value for the examples, the learning problem is called **supervised learning**. The task, also called **inductive learning**, is then to learn a function from examples of its inputs and outputs. Learning a discrete-valued function is called **classification**; learning a continuous function is called **regression**.
- Inductive learning involves finding a **consistent** hypothesis that agrees with the examples. **Ockham's razor** suggests choosing the simplest consistent hypothesis. The difficulty of this task depends on the chosen representation.
- **Decision trees** can represent all Boolean functions. The **information gain** heuristic provides an efficient method for finding a simple, consistent decision tree.
- The performance of a learning algorithm is measured by the **learning curve**, which shows the prediction accuracy on the **test set** as a function of the **training set** size.
- Ensemble methods such as **boosting** often perform better than individual methods.
- **Computational learning theory** analyzes the sample complexity and computational complexity of inductive learning. There is a tradeoff between the expressiveness of the hypothesis language and the ease of learning.

## Bibliographical and Historical Notes

Chapter 1 outlined the history of philosophical investigations into inductive learning. William of Ockham (1280–1349), the most influential philosopher of his century and a major contributer to medieval epistemology, logic, and metaphysics, is credited with a statement called "Ockham's Razor"—in Latin, *Entia non sunt multiplicanda praeter necessitatem*, and in English, "Entities are not to be multiplied beyond necessity." Unfortunately, this laudable piece of advice is nowhere to be found in his writings in precisely these words.

EPAM, the "Elementary Perceiver And Memorizer" (Feigenbaum, 1961), was one of the earliest systems to use decision trees (or **discrimination nets**). EPAM was intended as a cognitive-simulation model of human concept learning. CLS (Hunt *et al.*, 1966) used a heuristic look-ahead method to construct decision trees. ID3 (Quinlan, 1979) added the crucial idea of using information content to provide the heuristic function. Information theory itself was developed by Claude Shannon to aid in the study of communication (Shannon and Weaver, 1949). (Shannon also contributed one of the earliest examples of machine learning, a mechanical mouse named Theseus that learned to navigate through a maze by trial and error.) The $\chi^2$ method of tree pruning was described by Quinlan (1986). C4.5, an industrial-strength decision tree package, can be found in Quinlan (1993). An independent tradition of decision tree learning exists in the statistical literature. *Classification and Regression Trees* (Breiman *et al.*, 1984), known as the "CART book," is the principal reference.

Many other algorithmic approaches to learning have been tried. The **current-best-hypothesis** approach maintains a single hypothesis, specializing it when it proves too broad and generalizing it when it proves too narrow. This is an old idea in philosophy (Mill, 1843). Early work in cognitive psychology also suggested that it is a natural form of concept learning in humans (Bruner *et al.*, 1957). In AI, the approach is most closely associated with the work of Patrick Winston, whose Ph.D. thesis (Winston, 1970) addressed the problem of learning descriptions of complex objects. The **version space** method (Mitchell, 1977, 1982) takes a different approach, maintaining the set of *all* consistent hypotheses and eliminating those found to be inconsistent with new examples. The approach was used in the Meta-DENDRAL expert system for chemistry (Buchanan and Mitchell, 1978), and later in Mitchell's (1983) LEX system, which learns to solve calculus problems. A third influential thread was formed by the work of Michalski and colleagues on the AQ series of algorithms, which learned sets of logical rules (Michalski, 1969; Michalski *et al.*, 1986b).

Ensemble learning is an increasingly popular technique for improving the performance of learning algorithms. BAGGING **Bagging** (Breiman, 1996), the first effective method, combines hypotheses learned from multiple **bootstrap** data sets, each generated by subsampling the original data set. The **boosting** method described in the chapter originated with theoretical work by Schapire (1990). The ADABOOST algorithm was developed by Freund and Schapire (1996) and analyzed theoretically by Schapire (1999). Friedman *et al.* (2000) explain boosting from a statistician's viewpoint.

Theoretical analysis of learning algorithms began with the work of Gold (1967) on **identification in the limit**. This approach was motivated in part by models of scientific discovery from the philosophy of science (Popper, 1962), but has been applied mainly to the problem of learning grammars from example sentences (Osherson *et al.*, 1986).

KOLMOGOROV COMPLEXITY

Whereas the identification-in-the-limit approach concentrates on eventual convergence, the study of **Kolmogorov complexity** or **algorithmic complexity**, developed independently by Solomonoff (1964) and Kolmogorov (1965), attempts to provide a formal definition for the notion of simplicity used in Ockham's razor. To escape the problem that simplicity depends on the way in which information is represented, it is proposed that simplicity be measured by the length of the shortest program for a universal Turing machine that correctly reproduces the observed data. Although there are many possible universal Turing machines, and hence many possible "shortest" programs, these programs differ in length by at most a constant that is independent of the amount of data. This beautiful insight, which essentially shows that *any* initial representation bias will eventually be overcome by the data itself, is marred only by the undecidability of computing the length of the shortest program. Approximate measures such as the **minimum description length**, or MDL (Rissanen, 1984) can be used instead and have produced excellent results in practice. The text by Li and Vitanyi (1993) is the best source for Kolmogorov complexity.

MINIMUM DESCRIPTION LENGTH

Computational learning theory—that is, the theory of PAC-learning—was inaugurated by Leslie Valiant (1984). Valiant's work stressed the importance of computational and sample complexity. With Michael Kearns (1990), Valiant showed that several concept classes cannot be PAC-learned tractably, even though sufficient information is available in the examples. Some positive results were obtained for classes such as decision lists (Rivest, 1987).

UNIFORM CONVERGENCE THEORY

VC DIMENSION

An independent tradition of sample complexity analysis has existed in statistics, beginning with the work on **uniform convergence theory** (Vapnik and Chervonenkis, 1971). The so-called **VC dimension** provides a measure roughly analogous to, but more general than, the $\ln |\mathbf{H}|$ measure obtained from PAC analysis. The VC dimension can be applied to continuous function classes, to which standard PAC analysis does not apply. PAC-learning theory and VC theory were first connected by the "four Germans" (none of whom actually is German): Blumer, Ehrenfeucht, Haussler, and Warmuth (1989). Subsequent developments in VC theory led to the invention of the **support vector machine** or SVM (Boser *et al.*, 1992; Vapnik, 1998), which we describe in Chapter 20.

A large number of important papers on machine learning have been collected in *Readings in Machine Learning* (Shavlik and Dietterich, 1990). The two volumes *Machine Learning 1* (Michalski *et al.*, 1983) and *Machine Learning 2* (Michalski *et al.*, 1986a) also contain many important papers, as well as huge bibliographies. Weiss and Kulikowski (1991) provide a broad introduction to function-learning methods from machine learning, statistics, and neural networks. The STATLOG project (Michie *et al.*, 1994) is by far the most exhaustive investigation into the comparative performance of learning algorithms. Good current research in machine learning is published in the annual proceedings of the International Conference on Machine Learning and the conference on Neural Information Processing Systems, in *Machine Learning* and the *Journal of Machine Learning Research*, and in mainstream AI journals. Work in computational learning theory also appears in the annual ACM Workshop on Computational Learning Theory (COLT), and is described in the texts by Kearns and Vazirani (1994) and Anthony and Bartlett (1999).

## EXERCISES

**18.1** Consider the problem faced by an infant learning to speak and understand a language. Explain how this process fits into the general learning model, identifying each of the components of the model as appropriate.

**18.2** Repeat Exercise 18.1 for the case of learning to play tennis (or some other sport with which you are familiar). Is this supervised learning or reinforcement learning?

**18.3** Draw a decision tree for the problem of deciding whether to move forward at a road intersection, given that the light has just turned green.

**18.4** We never test the same attribute twice along one path in a decision tree. Why not?

**18.5** Suppose we generate a training set from a decision tree and then apply decision-tree learning to that training set. Is it the case that the learning algorithm will eventually return the correct tree as the training set size goes to infinity? Why or why not?

**18.6** A good "straw man" learning algorithm is as follows: create a table out of all the training examples. Identify which output occurs most often among the training examples; call it $d$. Then when given an input that is not in the table, just return $d$. For inputs that *are* in the table, return the output associated with it (or the most frequent output, if there is more than one). Implement this algorithm and see how well it does on the restaurant domain. This should give you an idea of the baseline for the domain—the minimal performance that any algorithm should be able to obtain.

**18.7** Suppose you are running a learning experiment on a new algorithm. You have a data set consisting of 25 examples of each of two classes. You plan to use leave-one-out cross-validation. As a baseline, you run your experimental setup on a simple majority classifier. (A majority classifier is given a set of training data and then always outputs the class that is in the majority in the training set, regardless of the input.) You expect the majority classifier to score about 50% on leave-one-out cross-validation, but to your surprise, it scores zero. Can you explain why?

**18.8** In the recursive construction of decision trees, it sometimes happens that a mixed set of positive and negative examples remains at a leaf node, even after all the attributes have been used. Suppose that we have $p$ positive examples and $n$ negative examples.

**a.** Show that the solution used by DECISION-TREE-LEARNING, which picks the majority classification, minimizes the absolute error over the set of examples at the leaf.

CLASS PROBABILITY

**b.** Show that the **class probability** $p/(p+n)$ minimizes the sum of squared errors.

**18.9** Suppose that a learning algorithm is trying to find a consistent hypothesis when the classifications of examples are actually random. There are $n$ Boolean attributes, and examples are drawn uniformly from the set of $2^n$ possible examples. Calculate the number of examples required before the probability of finding a contradiction in the data reaches 0.5.

**18.10** Suppose that an attribute splits the set of examples $E$ into subsets $E_i$ and that each subset has $p_i$ positive examples and $n_i$ negative examples. Show that the attribute has strictly positive information gain unless the ratio $p_i/(p_i + n_i)$ is the same for all $i$.

**18.11** Modify DECISION-TREE-LEARNING to include $\chi^2$-pruning. You might wish to consult Quinlan (1986) for details.

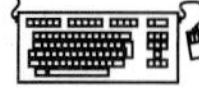

**18.12** The standard DECISION-TREE-LEARNING algorithm described in the chapter does not handle cases in which some examples have missing attribute values.

**a.** First, we need to find a way to classify such examples, given a decision tree that includes tests on the attributes for which values can be missing. Suppose that an example $X$ has a missing value for attribute $A$ and that the decision tree tests for $A$ at a node that $X$ reaches. One way to handle this case is to pretend that the example has *all* possible values for the attribute, but to weight each value according to its frequency among all of the examples that reach that node in the decision tree. The classification algorithm should follow all branches at any node for which a value is missing and should multiply the weights along each path. Write a modified classification algorithm for decision trees that has this behavior.

**b.** Now modify the information gain calculation so that in any given collection of examples $C$ at a given node in the tree during the construction process, the examples with missing values for any of the remaining attributes are given "as-if" values according to the frequencies of those values in the set $C$.

**18.13** In the chapter, we noted that attributes with many different possible values can cause problems with the gain measure. Such attributes tend to split the examples into numerous small classes or even singleton classes, thereby appearing to be highly relevant according to the gain measure. The **gain ratio** criterion selects attributes according to the ratio between their gain and their intrinsic information content—that is, the amount of information contained in the answer to the question, "What is the value of this attribute?" The gain ratio criterion therefore tries to measure how efficiently an attribute provides information on the correct classification of an example. Write a mathematical expression for the information content of an attribute, and implement the gain ratio criterion in DECISION-TREE-LEARNING.

**18.14** Consider an ensemble learning algorithm that uses simple majority voting among $M$ learned hypotheses. Suppose that each hypothesis has error $\epsilon$ and that the errors made by each hypothesis are independent of the others'. Calculate a formula for the error of the ensemble algorithm in terms of $M$ and $\epsilon$, and evaluate it for the cases where $M = 5$, 10, and 20 and $\epsilon = 0.1$, 0.2, and 0.4. If the independence assumption is removed, is it possible for the ensemble error to be *worse* than $\epsilon$?

**18.15** This exercise concerns the expressiveness of decision lists (Section 18.5).

**a.** Show that decision lists can represent any Boolean function, if the size of the tests is not limited.

**b.** Show that if the tests can contain at most $k$ literals each, then decision lists can represent any function that can be represented by a decision tree of depth $k$.

# 19 KNOWLEDGE IN LEARNING

*In which we examine the problem of learning when you know something already.*

In all of the approaches to learning described in the previous three chapters, the idea is to construct a function that has the input/output behavior observed in the data. In each case, the learning methods can be understood as searching a hypothesis space to find a suitable function, starting from only a very basic assumption about the form of the function, such as "second degree polynomial" or "decision tree" and a bias such as "simpler is better." Doing this amounts to saying that before you can learn something new, you must first forget (almost) everything you know. In this chapter, we study learning methods that can take advantage of **prior knowledge** about the world. In most cases, the prior knowledge is represented as general first-order logical theories; thus for the first time we bring together the work on knowledge representation and learning.

PRIOR KNOWLEDGE

## 19.1 A LOGICAL FORMULATION OF LEARNING

Chapter 18 defined pure inductive learning as a process of finding a hypothesis that agrees with the observed examples. Here, we specialize this definition to the case where the hypothesis is represented by a set of logical sentences. Example descriptions and classifications will also be logical sentences, and a new example can be classified by inferring a classification sentence from the hypothesis and the example description. This approach allows for incremental construction of hypotheses, one sentence at a time. It also allows for prior knowledge, because sentences that are already known can assist in the classification of new examples. The logical formulation of learning may seem like a lot of extra work at first, but it turns out to clarify many of the issues in learning. It enables us to go well beyond the simple learning methods of Chapter 18 by using the full power of logical inference in the service of learning.

### Examples and hypotheses

Recall from Chapter 18 the restaurant learning problem: learning a rule for deciding whether to wait for a table. Examples were described by **attributes** such as $Alternate$, $Bar$, $Fri/Sat$, and so on. In a logical setting, an example is an object that is described by a logical sentence; the attributes become unary predicates. Let us generically call the $i$th example $X_i$. For instance, the first example from Figure 18.3 is described by the sentences

$$Alternate(X_1) \land \neg Bar(X_1) \land \neg Fri/Sat(X_1) \land Hungry(X_1) \land \ldots$$

We will use the notation $D_i(X_i)$ to refer to the description of $X_i$, where $D_i$ can be any logical expression taking a single argument. The classification of the object is given by the sentence

$$WillWait(X_1) .$$

We will use the generic notation $Q(X_i)$ if the example is positive, and $\neg Q(X_i)$ if the example is negative. The complete training set is then just the conjunction of all the description and classification sentences.

The aim of inductive learning in the logical setting is to find an equivalent logical expression for the goal predicate $Q$ that we can use to classify examples correctly. Each hypothesis proposes such an expression, which we call a **candidate definition** of the goal predicate. Using $C_i$ to denote the candidate definition, each hypothesis $H_i$ is a sentence of the form $\forall x \;\; Q(x) \;\Leftrightarrow\; C_i(x)$. For example, a decision tree asserts that the goal predicate is true of an object if only if one of the branches leading to *true* is satisfied. Thus, the Figure 18.6 expresses the following logical definition (which we will call $H_r$ for future reference):

CANDIDATE DEFINITION

$$\begin{aligned} \forall r \;\; WillWait(r) \Leftrightarrow\; & Patrons(r, Some) \\ \lor\; & Patrons(r, Full) \land Hungry(r) \land Type(r, French) \\ \lor\; & Patrons(r, Full) \land Hungry(r) \land Type(r, Thai) \\ & \quad \land Fri/Sat(r) \\ \lor\; & Patrons(r, Full) \land Hungry(r) \land Type(r, Burger) . \end{aligned} \tag{19.1}$$

EXTENSION

Each hypothesis predicts that a certain set of examples—namely, those that satisfy its candidate definition—will be examples of the goal predicate. This set is called the **extension** of the predicate. Two hypotheses with different extensions are therefore logically inconsistent with each other, because they disagree on their predictions for at least one example. If they have the same extension, they are logically equivalent.

The hypothesis space **H** is the set of all hypotheses $\{H_1, \ldots, H_n\}$ that the learning algorithm is designed to entertain. For example, the DECISION-TREE-LEARNING algorithm can entertain any decision tree hypothesis defined in terms of the attributes provided; its hypothesis space therefore consists of all these decision trees. Presumably, the learning algorithm believes that one of the hypotheses is correct; that is, it believes the sentence

$$H_1 \lor H_2 \lor H_3 \lor \ldots \lor H_n . \tag{19.2}$$

As the examples arrive, hypotheses that are not **consistent** with the examples can be ruled out. Let us examine this notion of consistency more carefully. Obviously, if hypothesis $H_i$ is consistent with the entire training set, it has to be consistent with each example. What would it mean for it to be inconsistent with an example? This can happen in one of two ways:

FALSE NEGATIVE

- An example can be a **false negative** for the hypothesis, if the hypothesis says it should be negative but in fact it is positive. For instance, the new example $X_{13}$ described by $Patrons(X_{13}, Full) \land Wait(X_{13}, 0\text{-}10) \land \neg Hungry(X_{13}) \land \ldots \land WillWait(X_{13})$

would be a false negative for the hypothesis $H_r$ given earlier. From $H_r$ and the example description, we can deduce both $WillWait(X_{13})$, which is what the example says, and $\neg WillWait(X_{13})$, which is what the hypothesis predicts. The hypothesis and the example are therefore logically inconsistent.

FALSE POSITIVE

- An example can be a **false positive** for the hypothesis, if the hypothesis says it should be positive but in fact it is negative.[1]

If an example is a false positive or false negative for a hypothesis, then the example and the hypothesis are logically inconsistent with each other. Assuming that the example is a correct observation of fact, then the hypothesis can be ruled out. Logically, this is exactly analogous to the resolution rule of inference (see Chapter 9), where the disjunction of hypotheses corresponds to a clause and the example corresponds to a literal that resolves against one of the literals in the clause. An ordinary logical inference system therefore could, in principle, learn from the example by eliminating one or more hypotheses. Suppose, for example, that the example is denoted by the sentence $I_1$, and the hypothesis space is $H_1 \lor H_2 \lor H_3 \lor H_4$. Then if $I_1$ is inconsistent with $H_2$ and $H_3$, the logical inference system can deduce the new hypothesis space $H_1 \lor H_4$.

We therefore can characterize inductive learning in a logical setting as a process of gradually eliminating hypotheses that are inconsistent with the examples, narrowing down the possibilities. Because the hypothesis space is usually vast (or even infinite in the case of first-order logic), we do not recommend trying to build a learning system using resolution-based theorem proving and a complete enumeration of the hypothesis space. Instead, we will describe two approaches that find logically consistent hypotheses with much less effort.

### Current-best-hypothesis search

CURRENT-BEST-HYPOTHESIS

The idea behind **current-best-hypothesis** search is to maintain a single hypothesis, and to adjust it as new examples arrive in order to maintain consistency. The basic algorithm was described by John Stuart Mill (1843), and may well have appeared even earlier.

Suppose we have some hypothesis such as $H_r$, of which we have grown quite fond. As long as each new example is consistent, we need do nothing. Then along comes a false negative example, $X_{13}$. What do we do? Figure 19.1(a) shows $H_r$ schematically as a region: everything inside the rectangle is part of the extension of $H_r$. The examples that have actually been seen so far are shown as "+" or "–", and we see that $H_r$ correctly categorizes all the examples as positive or negative examples of $WillWait$. In Figure 19.1(b), a new example (circled) is a false negative: the hypothesis says it should be negative but it is actually positive. The extension of the hypothesis must be increased to include it. This is called **generalization**; one possible generalization is shown in Figure 19.1(c). Then in Figure 19.1(d), we see a false positive: the hypothesis says the new example (circled) should be positive, but it actually is negative. The extension of the hypothesis must be decreased to exclude the example. This is called **specialization**; in Figure 19.1(e) we see one possible specialization of the hypothesis.

GENERALIZATION

SPECIALIZATION

[1] The terms "false positive" and "false negative" are used in medicine to describe erroneous results from lab tests. A result is a false positive if it indicates that the patient has the disease when in fact no disease is present.

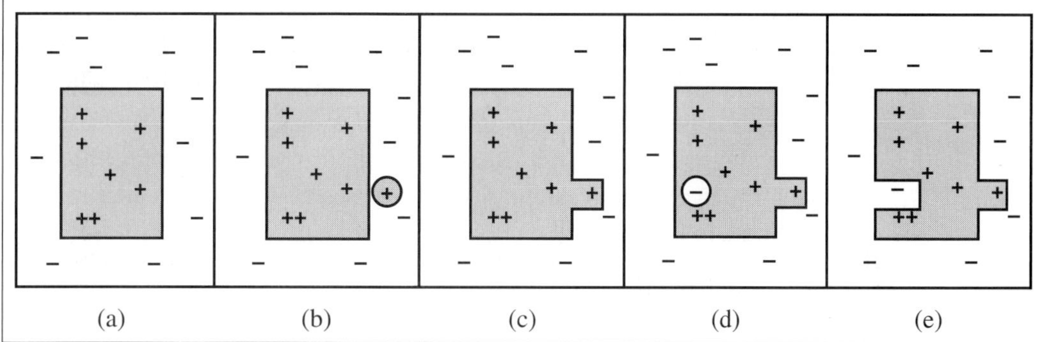


**Figure 19.1** (a) A consistent hypothesis. (b) A false negative. (c) The hypothesis is generalized. (d) A false positive. (e) The hypothesis is specialized.

The "more general than" and "more specific than" relations between hypotheses provide the logical structure on the hypothesis space that makes efficient search possible.

We can now specify the CURRENT-BEST-LEARNING algorithm, shown in Figure 19.2. Notice that each time we consider generalizing or specializing the hypothesis, we must check for consistency with the other examples, because an arbitrary increase/decrease in the extension might include/exclude previously seen negative/positive examples.

```
function CURRENT-BEST-LEARNING(examples) returns a hypothesis

  H ← any hypothesis consistent with the first example in examples
  for each remaining example in examples do
     if e is false positive for H then
        H ← choose a specialization of H consistent with examples
     else if e is false negative for H then
        H ← choose a generalization of H consistent with examples
     if no consistent specialization/generalization can be found then fail
  return H
```

**Figure 19.2** The current-best-hypothesis learning algorithm. It searches for a consistent hypothesis and backtracks when no consistent specialization/generalization can be found.

We have defined generalization and specialization as operations that change the *extension* of a hypothesis. Now we need to determine exactly how they can be implemented as syntactic operations that change the candidate definition associated with the hypothesis, so that a program can carry them out. This is done by first noting that generalization and specialization are also *logical* relationships between hypotheses. If hypothesis $H_1$, with definition $C_1$, is a generalization of hypothesis $H_2$ with definition $C_2$, then we must have

$$\forall x \;\; C_2(x) \;\Rightarrow\; C_1(x) \; .$$

Therefore in order to construct a generalization of $H_2$, we simply need to find a definition $C_1$ that is logically implied by $C_2$. This is easily done. For example, if $C_2(x)$ is

DROPPING CONDITIONS

$Alternate(x) \wedge Patrons(x, Some)$, then one possible generalization is given by $C_1(x) \equiv Patrons(x, Some)$. This is called **dropping conditions**. Intuitively, it generates a weaker definition and therefore allows a larger set of positive examples. There are a number of other generalization operations, depending on the language being operated on. Similarly, we can specialize a hypothesis by adding extra conditions to its candidate definition or by removing disjuncts from a disjunctive definition. Let us see how this works on the restaurant example, using the data in Figure 18.3.

- The first example $X_1$ is positive. $Alternate(X_1)$ is true, so let the initial hypothesis be
$$H_1: \ \forall x \ \ WillWait(x) \ \Leftrightarrow \ Alternate(x) \ .$$
- The second example $X_2$ is negative. $H_1$ predicts it to be positive, so it is a false positive. Therefore, we need to specialize $H_1$. This can be done by adding an extra condition that will rule out $X_2$. One possibility is
$$H_2: \ \forall x \ \ WillWait(x) \ \Leftrightarrow \ Alternate(x) \wedge Patrons(x, Some) \ .$$
- The third example $X_3$ is positive. $H_2$ predicts it to be negative, so it is a false negative. Therefore, we need to generalize $H_2$. We drop the *Alternate* condition, yielding
$$H_3: \ \forall x \ \ WillWait(x) \ \Leftrightarrow \ Patrons(x, Some) \ .$$
- The fourth example $X_4$ is positive. $H_3$ predicts it to be negative, so it is a false negative. We therefore need to generalize $H_3$. We cannot drop the *Patrons* condition, because that would yield an all-inclusive hypothesis that would be inconsistent with $X_2$. One possibility is to add a disjunct:
$$H_4: \ \forall x \ \ WillWait(x) \ \Leftrightarrow \ Patrons(x, Some) \\ \qquad \vee (Patrons(x, Full) \wedge Fri/Sat(x)) \ .$$

Already, the hypothesis is starting to look reasonable. Obviously, there are other possibilities consistent with the first four examples; here are two of them:

$$H_4': \ \forall x \ \ WillWait(x) \ \Leftrightarrow \ \neg WaitEstimate(x, 30\text{-}60) \ .$$

$$H_4'': \ \forall x \ \ WillWait(x) \ \Leftrightarrow \ Patrons(x, Some) \\ \qquad \vee (Patrons(x, Full) \wedge WaitEstimate(x, 10\text{-}30)) \ .$$

The CURRENT-BEST-LEARNING algorithm is described nondeterministically, because at any point, there may be several possible specializations or generalizations that can be applied. The choices that are made will not necessarily lead to the simplest hypothesis, and may lead to an unrecoverable situation where no simple modification of the hypothesis is consistent with all of the data. In such cases, the program must backtrack to a previous choice point.

The CURRENT-BEST-LEARNING algorithm and its variants have been used in many machine learning systems, starting with Patrick Winston's (1970) "arch-learning" program. With a large number of instances and a large space, however, some difficulties arise:

1. Checking all the previous instances over again for each modification is very expensive.
2. The search process may involve a great deal of backtracking. As we saw in Chapter 18, hypothesis space can be a doubly exponentially large place.

### Least-commitment search

Backtracking arises because the current-best-hypothesis approach has to *choose* a particular hypothesis as its best guess even though it does not have enough data yet to be sure of the choice. What we can do instead is to keep around all and only those hypotheses that are consistent with all the data so far. Each new instance will either have no effect or will get rid of some of the hypotheses. Recall that the original hypothesis space can be viewed as a disjunctive sentence

$$H_1 \lor H_2 \lor H_3 \ldots \lor H_n \,.$$

As various hypotheses are found to be inconsistent with the examples, this disjunction shrinks, retaining only those hypotheses not ruled out. Assuming that the original hypothesis space does in fact contain the right answer, the reduced disjunction must still contain the right answer because only incorrect hypotheses have been removed. The set of hypotheses remaining is called the **version space**, and the learning algorithm (sketched in Figure 19.3) is called the version space learning algorithm (also the **candidate elimination** algorithm).

VERSION SPACE

CANDIDATE ELIMINATION

```
function VERSION-SPACE-LEARNING(examples) returns a version space
  local variables: V, the version space: the set of all hypotheses

  V ← the set of all hypotheses
  for each example e in examples do
     if V is not empty then V ← VERSION-SPACE-UPDATE(V, e)
  return V
```

```
function VERSION-SPACE-UPDATE(V, e) returns an updated version space
  V ← {h ∈ V : h is consistent with e}
```

**Figure 19.3** The version space learning algorithm. It finds a subset of $V$ that is consistent with the *examples*.

One important property of this approach is that it is *incremental*: one never has to go back and reexamine the old examples. All remaining hypotheses are guaranteed to be consistent with them anyway. It is also a **least-commitment** algorithm because it makes no arbitrary choices (cf. the partial-order planning algorithm in Chapter 11). But there is an obvious problem. We already said that the hypothesis space is enormous, so how can we possibly write down this enormous disjunction?

The following simple analogy is very helpful. How do you represent all the real numbers between 1 and 2? After all, there is an infinite number of them! The answer is to use an interval representation that just specifies the boundaries of the set: [1,2]. It works because we have an *ordering* on the real numbers.

We also have an ordering on the hypothesis space, namely, generalization/specialization. This is a partial ordering, which means that each boundary will not be a point but rather a set of hypotheses called a **boundary set**. The great thing is that we can represent the entire

BOUNDARY SET

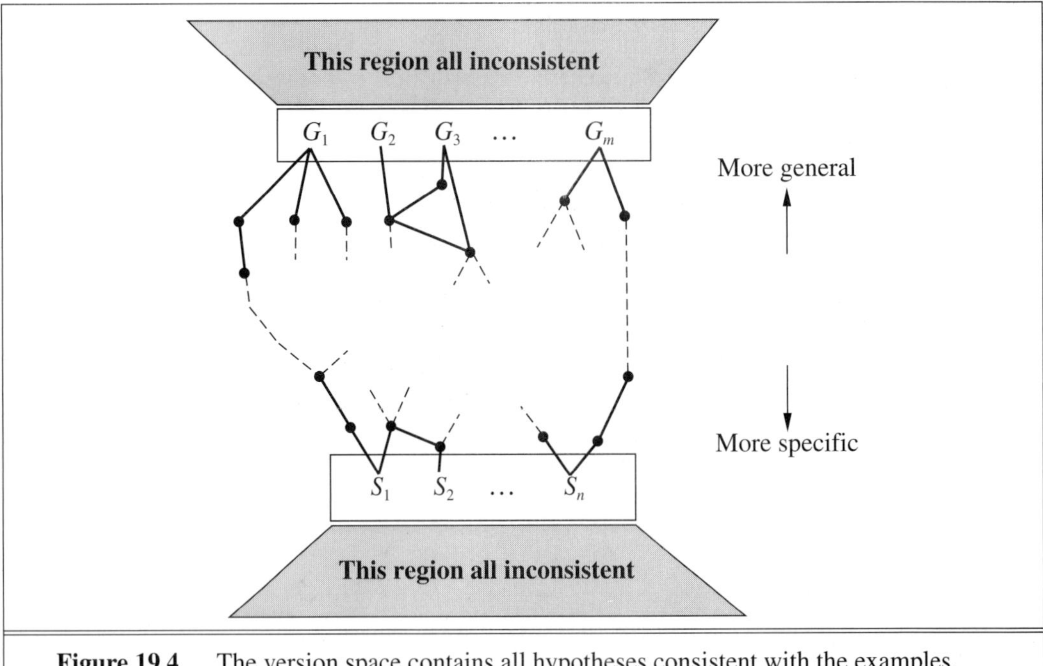


**Figure 19.4** The version space contains all hypotheses consistent with the examples.

G-SET
S-SET

version space using just two boundary sets: a most general boundary (the **G-set**) and a most specific boundary (the **S-set**). *Everything in between is guaranteed to be consistent with the examples.* Before we prove this, let us recap:

- The current version space is the set of hypotheses consistent with all the examples so far. It is represented by the S-set and G-set, each of which is a set of hypotheses.
- Every member of the S-set is consistent with all observations so far, and there are no consistent hypotheses that are more specific.
- Every member of the G-set is consistent with all observations so far, and there are no consistent hypotheses that are more general.

We want the initial version space (before any examples have been seen) to represent all possible hypotheses. We do this by setting the G-set to contain $True$ (the hypothesis that contains everything), and the S-set to contain $False$ (the hypothesis whose extension is empty).

Figure 19.4 shows the general structure of the boundary set representation of the version space. To show that the representation is sufficient, we need the following two properties:

1. Every consistent hypothesis (other than those in the boundary sets) is more specific than some member of the G-set, and more general than some member of the S-set. (That is, there are no "stragglers" left outside.) This follows directly from the definitions of $S$ and $G$. If there were a straggler $h$, then it would have to be no more specific than any member of $G$, in which case it belongs in $G$; or no more general than any member of $S$, in which case it belongs in $S$.
2. Every hypothesis more specific than some member of the G-set and more general than some member of the S-set is a consistent hypothesis. (That is, there are no "holes" be-

tween the boundaries.) Any $h$ between $S$ and $G$ must reject all the negative examples rejected by each member of $G$ (because it is more specific), and must accept all the positive examples accepted by any member of $S$ (because it is more general). Thus, $h$ must agree with all the examples, and therefore cannot be inconsistent. Figure 19.5 shows the situation: there are no known examples outside $S$ but inside $G$, so any hypothesis in the gap must be consistent.

We have therefore shown that *if* $S$ and $G$ are maintained according to their definitions, then they provide a satisfactory representation of the version space. The only remaining problem is how to *update* $S$ and $G$ for a new example (the job of the VERSION-SPACE-UPDATE function). This may appear rather complicated at first, but from the definitions and with the help of Figure 19.4, it is not too hard to reconstruct the algorithm.

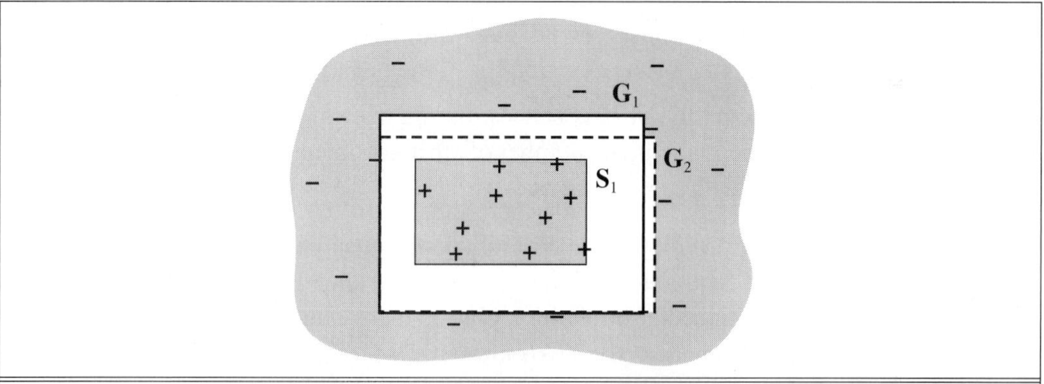


**Figure 19.5** The extensions of the members of $G$ and $S$. No known examples lie in between the two sets of boundaries.

We need to worry about the members $S_i$ and $G_i$ of the S- and G-sets. For each one, the new instance may be a false positive or a false negative.

1. False positive for $S_i$: This means $S_i$ is too general, but there are no consistent specializations of $S_i$ (by definition), so we throw it out of the S-set.
2. False negative for $S_i$: This means $S_i$ is too specific, so we replace it by all its immediate generalizations, provided they are more specific than some member of $G$.
3. False positive for $G_i$: This means $G_i$ is too general, so we replace it by all its immediate specializations, provided they are more general than some member of $S$.
4. False negative for $G_i$: This means $G_i$ is too specific, but there are no consistent generalizations of $G_i$ (by definition) so we throw it out of the G-set.

We continue these operations for each new instance until one of three things happens:

1. We have exactly one concept left in the version space, in which case we return it as the unique hypothesis.
2. The version space *collapses*—either S or G becomes empty, indicating that there are no consistent hypotheses for the training set. This is the same case as the failure of the simple version of the decision tree algorithm.

3. We run out of examples with several hypotheses remaining in the version space. This means the version space represents a disjunction of hypotheses. For any new example, if all the disjuncts agree, then we can return their classification of the example. If they disagree, one possibility is to take the majority vote.

We leave as an exercise the application of the VERSION-SPACE-LEARNING algorithm to the restaurant data.

There are two principal drawbacks to the version-space approach:

- If the domain contains noise or insufficient attributes for exact classification, the version space will always collapse.
- If we allow unlimited disjunction in the hypothesis space, the S-set will always contain a single most-specific hypothesis, namely, the disjunction of the descriptions of the positive examples seen to date. Similarly, the G-set will contain just the negation of the disjunction of the descriptions of the negative examples.
- For some hypothesis spaces, the number of elements in the S-set of G-set may grow exponentially in the number of attributes, even though efficient learning algorithms exist for those hypothesis spaces.

To date, no completely successful solution has been found for the problem of noise. The problem of disjunction can be addressed by allowing limited forms of disjunction or by including a **generalization hierarchy** of more general predicates. For example, instead of using the disjunction $WaitEstimate(x, 30\text{-}60) \vee WaitEstimate(x, >60)$, we might use the single literal $LongWait(x)$. The set of generalization and specialization operations can be easily extended to handle this.

GENERALIZATION HIERARCHY

The pure version space algorithm was first applied in the Meta-DENDRAL system, which was designed to learn rules for predicting how molecules would break into pieces in a mass spectrometer (Buchanan and Mitchell, 1978). Meta-DENDRAL was able to generate rules that were sufficiently novel to warrant publication in a journal of analytical chemistry—the first real scientific knowledge generated by a computer program. It was also used in the elegant LEX system (Mitchell *et al.*, 1983), which was able to learn to solve symbolic integration problems by studying its own successes and failures. Although version space methods are probably not practical in most real-world learning problems, mainly because of noise, they provide a good deal of insight into the logical structure of hypothesis space.

## 19.2 KNOWLEDGE IN LEARNING

The preceding section described the simplest setting for inductive learning. To understand the role of prior knowledge, we need to talk about the logical relationships among hypotheses, example descriptions, and classifications. Let *Descriptions* denote the conjunction of all the example descriptions in the training set, and let *Classifications* denote the conjunction of all the example classifications. Then a *Hypothesis* that "explains the observations" must satisfy the following property (recall that $\models$ means "logically entails"):

$$Hypothesis \wedge Descriptions \models Classifications . \qquad (19.3)$$

ENTAILMENT CONSTRAINT

We call this kind of relationship an **entailment constraint**, in which *Hypothesis* is the "unknown." Pure inductive learning means solving this constraint, where *Hypothesis* is drawn from some predefined hypothesis space. For example, if we consider a decision tree as a logical formula (see Equation (19.1) on page 679), then a decision tree that is consistent with all the examples will satisfy Equation (19.3). If we place *no* restrictions on the logical form of the hypothesis, of course, then $Hypothesis = Classifications$ also satisfies the constraint. Ockham's razor tells us to prefer *small*, consistent hypotheses, so we try to do better than simply memorizing the examples.

This simple knowledge-free picture of inductive learning persisted until the early 1980s. The modern approach is to design agents that *already know something* and are trying to learn some more. This may not sound like a terrifically deep insight, but it makes quite a difference to the way we design agents. It might also have some relevance to our theories about how science itself works. The general idea is shown schematically in Figure 19.6.

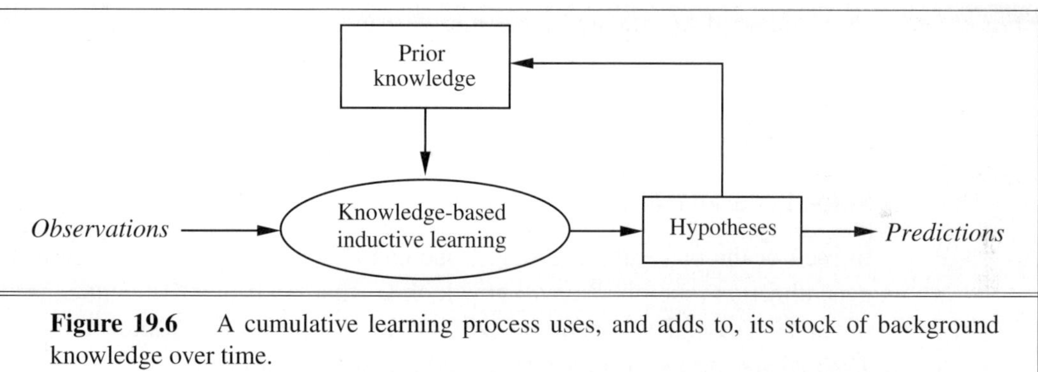


**Figure 19.6** A cumulative learning process uses, and adds to, its stock of background knowledge over time.

If we want to build an autonomous learning agent that uses background knowledge, the agent must have some method for obtaining the background knowledge in the first place, in order for it to be used in the new learning episodes. This method must itself be a learning process. The agent's life history will therefore be characterized by *cumulative*, or *incremental*, development. Presumably, the agent could start out with nothing, performing inductions *in vacuo* like a good little pure induction program. But once it has eaten from the Tree of Knowledge, it can no longer pursue such naive speculations and should use its background knowledge to learn more and more effectively. The question is then how to actually do this.

### Some simple examples

Let us consider some commonsense examples of learning with background knowledge. Many apparently rational cases of inferential behavior in the face of observations clearly do not follow the simple principles of pure induction.

- Sometimes one leaps to general conclusions after only one observation. Gary Larson once drew a cartoon in which a bespectacled caveman, Zog, is roasting his lizard on the end of a pointed stick. He is watched by an amazed crowd of his less intellectual contemporaries, who have been using their bare hands to hold their victuals over the fire. This enlightening experience is enough to convince the watchers of a general principle of painless cooking.

- Or consider the case of the traveller to Brazil meeting her first Brazilian. On hearing him speak Portuguese, she immediately concludes that Brazilians speak Portuguese, yet on discovering that his name is Fernando, she does not conclude that all Brazilians are called Fernando. Similar examples appear in science. For example, when a freshman physics student measures the density and conductance of a sample of copper at a particular temperature, she is quite confident in generalizing those values to all pieces of copper. Yet when she measures its mass, she does not even consider the hypothesis that all pieces of copper have that mass. On the other hand, it would be quite reasonable to make such a generalization over all pennies.
- Finally, consider the case of a pharmacologically ignorant but diagnostically sophisticated medical student observing a consulting session between a patient and an expert internist. After a series of questions and answers, the expert tells the patient to take a course of a particular antibiotic. The medical student infers the general rule that that particular antibiotic is effective for a particular type of infection.

These are all cases in which *the use of background knowledge allows much faster learning than one might expect from a pure induction program.*

### Some general schemes

In each of the preceding examples, one can appeal to prior knowledge to try to justify the generalizations chosen. We will now look at what kinds of entailment constraints are operating in each case. The constraints will involve the $Background$ knowledge, in addition to the $Hypothesis$ and the observed $Descriptions$ and $Classifications$.

In the case of lizard toasting, the cavemen generalize by *explaining* the success of the pointed stick: it supports the lizard while keeping the hand away from the fire. From this explanation, they can infer a general rule: that any long, rigid, sharp object can be used to toast small, soft-bodied edibles. This kind of generalization process has been called **explanation-based learning**, or **EBL**. Notice that the general rule *follows logically* from the background knowledge possessed by the cavemen. Hence, the entailment constraints satisfied by EBL are the following:

$$Hypothesis \wedge Descriptions \models Classifications$$
$$Background \models Hypothesis\ .$$

Because EBL uses Equation (19.3), it was initially thought to be a better way to learn from examples. But because it requires that the background knowledge be sufficient to explain the $Hypothesis$, which in turn explains the observations, *the agent does not actually learn anything factually new from the instance.* The agent *could have* derived the example from what it already knew, although that might have required an unreasonable amount of computation. EBL is now viewed as a method for converting first-principles theories into useful, special-purpose knowledge. We describe algorithms for EBL in Section 19.3.

The situation of our traveler in Brazil is quite different, for she cannot necessarily explain why Fernando speaks the way he does, unless she knows her Papal bulls. Moreover, the same generalization would be forthcoming from a traveler entirely ignorant of colonial history. The relevant prior knowledge in this case is that, within any given country, most people tend to speak the same language; on the other hand, Fernando is not assumed to be the name of all Brazilians because this kind of regularity does not hold for names. Similarly, the freshman physics student also would be hard put to explain the particular values that she discovers for the conductance and density of copper. She does know, however, that the material of which an object is composed and its temperature together determine its conductance.

RELEVANCE

In each case, the prior knowledge $Background$ concerns the **relevance** of a set of features to the goal predicate. This knowledge, *together with the observations*, allows the agent to infer a new, general rule that explains the observations:

$$\begin{aligned} &Hypothesis \land Descriptions \models Classifications\ , \\ &Background \land Descriptions \land Classifications \models Hypothesis\ . \end{aligned} \quad (19.4)$$

RELEVANCE-BASED LEARNING

We call this kind of generalization **relevance-based learning**, or **RBL** (although the name is not standard). Notice that whereas RBL does make use of the content of the observations, it does not produce hypotheses that go beyond the logical content of the background knowledge and the observations. It is a *deductive* form of learning and cannot by itself account for the creation of new knowledge starting from scratch.

In the case of the medical student watching the expert, we assume that the student's prior knowledge is sufficient to infer the patient's disease $D$ from the symptoms. This is not, however, enough to explain the fact that the doctor prescribes a particular medicine $M$. The student needs to propose another rule, namely, that $M$ generally is effective against $D$. Given this rule and the student's prior knowledge, the student can now explain why the expert prescribes $M$ in this particular case. We can generalize this example to come up with the entailment constraint:

$$Background \land Hypothesis \land Descriptions \models Classifications\ . \quad (19.5)$$

That is, *the background knowledge and the new hypothesis combine to explain the examples.* As with pure inductive learning, the learning algorithm should propose hypotheses that are as simple as possible, consistent with this constraint. Algorithms that satisfy constraint (19.5) are called **knowledge-based inductive learning**, or **KBIL**, algorithms.

KNOWLEDGE-BASED INDUCTIVE LEARNING

INDUCTIVE LOGIC PROGRAMMING

KBIL algorithms, which are described in detail in Section 19.5, have been studied mainly in the field of **inductive logic programming**, or **ILP**. In ILP systems, prior knowledge plays two key roles in reducing the complexity of learning:

1. Because any hypothesis generated must be consistent with the prior knowledge as well as with the new observations, the effective hypothesis space size is reduced to include only those theories that are consistent with what is already known.
2. For any given set of observations, the size of the hypothesis required to construct an explanation for the observations can be much reduced, because the prior knowledge will be available to help out the new rules in explaining the observations. The smaller the hypothesis, the easier it is to find.

In addition to allowing the use of prior knowledge in induction, ILP systems can formulate hypotheses in general first-order logic, rather than in the restricted attribute-based language of Chapter 18. This means that they can learn in environments that cannot be understood by simpler systems.

## 19.3 EXPLANATION-BASED LEARNING

As we explained in the introduction to this chapter, explanation-based learning is a method for extracting general rules from individual observations. As an example, consider the problem of differentiating and simplifying algebraic expressions (Exercise 9.15). If we differentiate an expression such as $X^2$ with respect to $X$, we obtain $2X$. (Notice that we use a capital letter for the arithmetic unknown $X$, to distinguish it from the logical variable $x$.) In a logical reasoning system, the goal might be expressed as $\text{ASK}(Derivative(X^2, X) = d,\ KB)$, with solution $d = 2X$.

Anyone who knows differential calculus can see this solution "by inspection" as a result of practice in solving such problems. A student encountering such problems for the first time, or a program with no experience, will have a much more difficult job. Application of the standard rules of differentiation eventually yields the expression $1 \times (2 \times (X^{(2-1)}))$, and eventually this simplifies to $2X$. In the authors' logic programming implementation, this takes 136 proof steps, of which 99 are on dead-end branches in the proof. After such an experience, we would like the program to solve the same problem much more quickly the next time it arises..

MEMOIZATION

The technique of **memoization** has long been used in computer science to speed up programs by saving the results of computation. The basic idea of memo functions is to accumulate a database of input/output pairs; when the function is called, it first checks the database to see whether it can avoid solving the problem from scratch. Explanation-based learning takes this a good deal further, by creating *general* rules that cover an entire class of cases. In the case of differentiation, memoization would remember that the derivative of $X^2$ with respect to $X$ is $2X$, but would leave the agent to calculate the derivative of $Z^2$ with respect to $Z$ from scratch. We would like to be able to extract the general rule[2] that for any arithmetic unknown $u$, the derivative of $u^2$ with respect to $u$ is $2u$. In logical terms, this is expressed by the rule

$$ArithmeticUnknown(u) \Rightarrow Derivative(u^2, u) = 2u\ .$$

If the knowledge base contains such a rule, then any new case that is an instance of this rule can be solved immediately.

This is, of course, merely a trivial example of a very general phenomenon. Once something is understood, it can be generalized and reused in other circumstances. It becomes an "obvious" step and can then be used as a building block in solving problems still more complex. Alfred North Whitehead (1911), co-author with Bertrand Russell of *Principia Mathe-*

[2] Of course, a general rule for $u^n$ can also be produced, but the current example suffices to make the point.

*matica*, wrote *"Civilization advances by extending the number of important operations that we can do without thinking about them,"* perhaps himself applying EBL to his understanding of events such as Zog's discovery. If you have understood the basic idea of the differentiation example, then your brain is already busily trying to extract the general principles of explanation-based learning from it. Notice that you hadn't *already* invented EBL before you saw the example. Like the cavemen watching Zog, you (and we) needed an example before we could generate the basic principles. This is because *explaining why* something is a good idea is much easier than coming up with the idea in the first place.

### Extracting general rules from examples

The basic idea behind EBL is first to construct an explanation of the observation using prior knowledge, and then to establish a definition of the class of cases for which the same explanation structure can be used. This definition provides the basis for a rule covering all of the cases in the class. The "explanation" can be a logical proof, but more generally it can be any reasoning or problem-solving process whose steps are well defined. The key is to be able to identify the necessary conditions for those same steps to apply to another case.

We will use for our reasoning system the simple backward-chaining theorem prover described in Chapter 9. The proof tree for $Derivative(X^2, X) = 2X$ is too large to use as an example, so we will use a simpler problem to illustrate the generalization method. Suppose our problem is to simplify $1 \times (0 + X)$. The knowledge base includes the following rules:

$$\begin{array}{l} Rewrite(u, v) \land Simplify(v, w) \Rightarrow Simplify(u, w) . \\ Primitive(u) \Rightarrow Simplify(u, u) . \\ ArithmeticUnknown(u) \Rightarrow Primitive(u) . \\ Number(u) \Rightarrow Primitive(u) . \\ Rewrite(1 \times u, u) . \\ Rewrite(0 + u, u) . \\ \quad\vdots \end{array}$$

The proof that the answer is $X$ is shown in the top half of Figure 19.7. The EBL method actually constructs two proof trees simultaneously. The second proof tree uses a *variabilized* goal in which the constants from the original goal are replaced by variables. As the original proof proceeds, the variabilized proof proceeds in step, using *exactly the same rule applications*. This could cause some of the variables to become instantiated. For example, in order to use the rule $Rewrite(1 \times u, u)$, the variable $x$ in the subgoal $Rewrite(x \times (y + z), v)$ must be bound to 1. Similarly, $y$ must be bound to 0 in the subgoal $Rewrite(y + z, v')$ in order to use the rule $Rewrite(0 + u, u)$. Once we have the generalized proof tree, we take the leaves (with the necessary bindings) and form a general rule for the goal predicate:

$$\begin{array}{l} Rewrite(1 \times (0 + z), 0 + z) \land Rewrite(0 + z, z) \land ArithmeticUnknown(z) \\ \quad \Rightarrow Simplify(1 \times (0 + z), z) . \end{array}$$

Notice that the first two conditions on the left-hand side are true *regardless of the value of $z$*. We can therefore drop them from the rule, yielding

$$ArithmeticUnknown(z) \Rightarrow Simplify(1 \times (0 + z), z) .$$

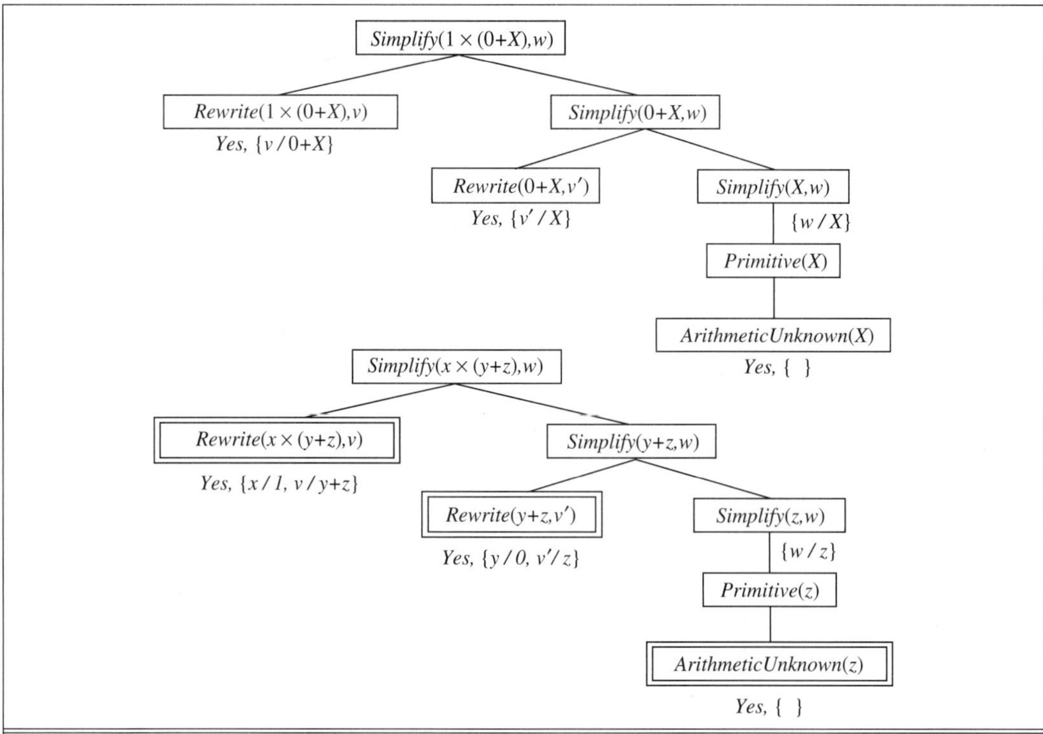


**Figure 19.7** Proof trees for the simplification problem. The first tree shows the proof for the original problem instance, from which we can derive

$$ArithmeticUnknown(z) \Rightarrow Simplify(1 \times (0 + z), z) .$$

The second shows the proof for a problem instance with all constants replaced by variables, from which we can derive a variety of other rules.

In general, conditions can be dropped from the final rule if they impose no constraints on the variables on the right-hand side of the rule, because the resulting rule will still be true and will be more efficient. Notice that we cannot drop the condition $ArithmeticUnknown(z)$, because not all possible values of $z$ are arithmetic unknowns. Values other than arithmetic unknowns might require different forms of simplification: for example, if $z$ were $2 \times 3$, then the correct simplification of $1 \times (0 + (2 \times 3))$ would be 6 and not $2 \times 3$.

To recap, the basic EBL process works as follows:

1. Given an example, construct a proof that the goal predicate applies to the example using the available background knowledge.
2. In parallel, construct a generalized proof tree for the variabilized goal using the same inference steps as in the original proof.
3. Construct a new rule whose left-hand side consists of the leaves of the proof tree and whose right-hand side is the variabilized goal (after applying the necessary bindings from the generalized proof).
4. Drop any conditions that are true regardless of the values of the variables in the goal.

### Improving efficiency

The generalized proof tree in Figure 19.7 actually yields more than one generalized rule. For example, if we terminate, or **prune**, the growth of the right-hand branch in the proof tree when it reaches the *Primitive* step, we get the rule

$$Primitive(z) \Rightarrow Simplify(1 \times (0 + z), z) .$$

This rule is as valid as, but *more general* than, the rule using $ArithmeticUnknown$, because it covers cases where $z$ is a number. We can extract a still more general rule by pruning after the step $Simplify(y + z, w)$, yielding the rule

$$Simplify(y + z, w) \Rightarrow Simplify(1 \times (y + z), w) .$$

In general, a rule can be extracted from *any partial subtree* of the generalized proof tree. Now we have a problem: which of these rules do we choose?

The choice of which rule to generate comes down to the question of efficiency. There are three factors involved in the analysis of efficiency gains from EBL:

1. Adding large numbers of rules can slow down the reasoning process, because the inference mechanism must still check those rules even in cases where they do not yield a solution. In other words, it increases the **branching factor** in the search space.
2. To compensate for the slowdown in reasoning, the derived rules must offer significant increases in speed for the cases that they do cover. These increases come about mainly because the derived rules avoid dead ends that would otherwise be taken, but also because they shorten the proof itself.
3. Derived rules should be as general as possible, so that they apply to the largest possible set of cases.

OPERATIONALITY

A common approach to ensuring that derived rules are efficient is to insist on the **operationality** of each subgoal in the rule. A subgoal is operational if it is "easy" to solve. For example, the subgoal $Primitive(z)$ is easy to solve, requiring at most two steps, whereas the subgoal $Simplify(y + z, w)$ could lead to an arbitrary amount of inference, depending on the values of $y$ and $z$. If a test for operationality is carried out at each step in the construction of the generalized proof, then we can prune the rest of a branch as soon as an operational subgoal is found, keeping just the operational subgoal as a conjunct of the new rule.

Unfortunately, there is usually a tradeoff between operationality and generality. More specific subgoals are generally easier to solve but cover fewer cases. Also, operationality is a matter of degree: one or 2 steps is definitely operational, but what about 10 or 100? Finally, the cost of solving a given subgoal depends on what other rules are available in the knowledge base. It can go up or down as more rules are added. Thus, EBL systems really face a very complex optimization problem in trying to maximize the efficiency of a given initial knowledge base. It is sometimes possible to derive a mathematical model of the effect on overall efficiency of adding a given rule and to use this model to select the best rule to add. The analysis can become very complicated, however, especially when recursive rules are involved. One promising approach is to address the problem of efficiency empirically, simply by adding several rules and seeing which ones are useful and actually speed things up.

Empirical analysis of efficiency is actually at the heart of EBL. What we have been calling loosely the "efficiency of a given knowledge base" is actually the average-case complexity on a distribution of problems. *By generalizing from past example problems, EBL makes the knowledge base more efficient for the kind of problems that it is reasonable to expect.* This works as long as the distribution of past examples is roughly the same as for future examples—the same assumption used for PAC-learning in Section 18.5. If the EBL system is carefully engineered, it is possible to obtain significant speedups. For example, a very large Prolog-based natural language system designed for speech-to-speech translation between Swedish and English was able to achieve real-time performance only by the application of EBL to the parsing process (Samuelsson and Rayner, 1991).

## 19.4 Learning Using Relevance Information

Our traveler in Brazil seems to be able to make a confident generalization concerning the language spoken by other Brazilians. The inference is sanctioned by her background knowledge, namely, that people in a given country (usually) speak the same language. We can express this in first-order logic as follows:[3]

$$Nationality(x,n) \wedge Nationality(y,n) \wedge Language(x,l) \Rightarrow Language(y,l)\ . \quad (19.6)$$

(Literal translation: "If $x$ and $y$ have the same nationality $n$ and $x$ speaks language $l$, then $y$ also speaks it.") It is not difficult to show that, from this sentence and the observation that

$$Nationality(Fernando, Brazil) \wedge Language(Fernando, Portuguese)\ ,$$

the following conclusion is entailed (see Exercise 19.1):

$$Nationality(x, Brazil) \Rightarrow Language(x, Portuguese)\ .$$

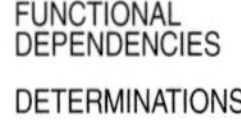

FUNCTIONAL DEPENDENCIES

DETERMINATIONS

Sentences such as (19.6) express a strict form of relevance: given nationality, language is fully determined. (Put another way: language is a function of nationality.) These sentences are called **functional dependencies** or **determinations**. They occur so commonly in certain kinds of applications (e.g., defining database designs) that a special syntax is used to write them. We adopt the notation of Davies (1985):

$$Nationality(x,n) \succ Language(x,l)\ .$$

As usual, this is simply a syntactic sugaring, but it makes it clear that the determination is really a relationship between the predicates: nationality determines language. The relevant properties determining conductance and density can be expressed similarly:

$$Material(x,m) \wedge Temperature(x,t) \succ Conductance(x,\rho)\ ;$$
$$Material(x,m) \wedge Temperature(x,t) \succ Density(x,d)\ .$$

The corresponding generalizations follow logically from the determinations and observations.

[3] We assume for the sake of simplicity that a person speaks only one language. Clearly, the rule also would have to be amended for countries such as Switzerland and India.

### Determining the hypothesis space

Although the determinations sanction general conclusions concerning all Brazilians, or all pieces of copper at a given temperature, they cannot, of course, yield a general predictive theory for *all* nationalities, or for *all* temperatures and materials, from a single example. Their main effect can be seen as limiting the space of hypotheses that the learning agent need consider. In predicting conductance, for example, one need consider only material and temperature and can ignore mass, ownership, day of the week, the current president, and so on. Hypotheses can certainly include terms that are in turn determined by material and temperature, such as molecular structure, thermal energy, or free-electron density. *Determinations specify a sufficient basis vocabulary from which to construct hypotheses concerning the target predicate.* This statement can be proven by showing that a given determination is logically equivalent to a statement that the correct definition of the target predicate is one of the set of all definitions expressible using the predicates on the left-hand side of the determination.

Intuitively, it is clear that a reduction in the hypothesis space size should make it easier to learn the target predicate. Using the basic results of computational learning theory (Section 18.5), we can quantify the possible gains. First, recall that for Boolean functions, $\log(|\mathbf{H}|)$ examples are required to converge to a reasonable hypothesis, where $|\mathbf{H}|$ is the size of the hypothesis space. If the learner has $n$ Boolean features with which to construct hypotheses, then, in the absence of further restrictions, $|\mathbf{H}| = O(2^{2^n})$, so the number of examples is $O(2^n)$. If the determination contains $d$ predicates in the left-hand side, the learner will require only $O(2^d)$ examples, a reduction of $O(2^{n-d})$. For biased hypothesis spaces, such as a conjunctively biased space, the reduction will be less dramatic, but still significant.

### Learning and using relevance information

As we stated in the introduction to this chapter, prior knowledge is useful in learning, but it too has to be learned. In order to provide a complete story of relevance-based learning, we must therefore provide a learning algorithm for determinations. The learning algorithm we now present is based on a straightforward attempt to find the simplest determination consistent with the observations. A determination $P \succ Q$ says that if any examples match on $P$, then they must also match on $Q$. A determination is therefore consistent with a set of examples if every pair that matches on the predicates on the left-hand side also matches on the target predicate—that is, has the same classification. For example, suppose we have the following examples of conductance measurements on material samples:

| Sample | Mass | Temperature | Material | Size | Conductance |
|---|---|---|---|---|---|
| S1 | 12 | 26 | Copper | 3 | 0.59 |
| S1 | 12 | 100 | Copper | 3 | 0.57 |
| S2 | 24 | 26 | Copper | 6 | 0.59 |
| S3 | 12 | 26 | Lead | 2 | 0.05 |
| S3 | 12 | 100 | Lead | 2 | 0.04 |
| S4 | 24 | 26 | Lead | 4 | 0.05 |

```
function MINIMAL-CONSISTENT-DET(E, A) returns a set of attributes
  inputs: E, a set of examples
          A, a set of attributes, of size n

  for i ← 0, ..., n do
     for each subset A_i of A of size i do
        if CONSISTENT-DET?(A_i, E) then return A_i
```

```
function CONSISTENT-DET?(A, E) returns a truth-value
  inputs: A, a set of attributes
          E, a set of examples
  local variables: H, a hash table

  for each example e in E do
     if some example in H has the same values as e for the attributes A
        but a different classification then return false
     store the class of e in H, indexed by the values for attributes A of the example e
  return true
```

**Figure 19.8** An algorithm for finding a minimal consistent determination.

The minimal consistent determination is $Material \land Temperature \succ Conductance$. There is a nonminimal but consistent determination, namely, $Mass \land Size \land Temperature \succ Conductance$. This is consistent with the examples because mass and size determine density and, in our data set, we do not have two different materials with the same density. As usual, we would need a larger sample set in order to eliminate a nearly correct hypothesis.

There are several possible algorithms for finding minimal consistent determinations. The most obvious approach is to conduct a search through the space of determinations, checking all determinations with one predicate, two predicates, and so on, until a consistent determination is found. We will assume a simple attribute-based representation, like that used for decision-tree learning in Chapter 18. A determination $d$ will be represented by the set of attributes on the left-hand side, because the target predicate is assumed fixed. The basic algorithm is outlined in Figure 19.8.

The time complexity of this algorithm depends on the size of the smallest consistent determination. Suppose this determination has $p$ attributes out of the $n$ total attributes. Then the algorithm will not find it until searching the subsets of $A$ of size $p$. There are $\binom{n}{p} = O(n^p)$ such subsets; hence the algorithm is exponential in the size of the minimal determination. It turns out that the problem is NP-complete, so we cannot expect to do better in the general case. In most domains, however, there will be sufficient local structure (see Chapter 14 for a definition of locally structured domains) that $p$ will be small.

Given an algorithm for learning determinations, a learning agent has a way to construct a minimal hypothesis within which to learn the target predicate. For example, we can combine MINIMAL-CONSISTENT-DET with the DECISION-TREE-LEARNING algorithm. This yields a relevance-based decision-tree learning algorithm RBDTL that first identifies a minimal

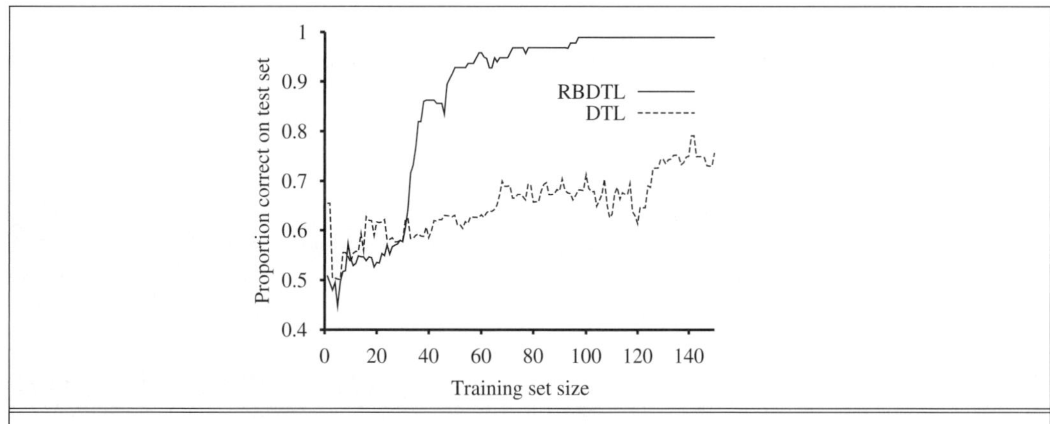


**Figure 19.9** A performance comparison between RBDTL and DECISION-TREE-LEARNING on randomly generated data for a target function that depends on only 5 of 16 attributes.

set of relevant attributes and then passes this set to the decision tree algorithm for learning. Unlike DECISION-TREE-LEARNING, RBDTL simultaneously learns and uses relevance information in order to minimize its hypothesis space. We expect that RBDTL will learn faster than DECISION-TREE-LEARNING, and this is in fact the case. Figure 19.9 shows the learning performance for the two algorithms on randomly generated data for a function that depends on only 5 of 16 attributes. Obviously, in cases where all the available attributes are relevant, RBDTL will show no advantage.

DECLARATIVE BIAS

This section has only scratched the surface of the field of **declarative bias**, which aims to understand how prior knowledge can be used to identify the appropriate hypothesis space within which to search for the correct target definition. There are many unanswered questions:

- How can the algorithms be extended to handle noise?
- Can we handle continuous-valued variables?
- How can other kinds of prior knowledge be used, besides determinations?
- How can the algorithms be generalized to cover any first-order theory, rather than just an attribute-based representation?

Some of these questions are addressed in the next section.

## 19.5 INDUCTIVE LOGIC PROGRAMMING

Inductive logic programming (ILP) combines inductive methods with the power of first-order representations, concentrating in particular on the representation of theories as logic programs.[4] It has gained popularity for three reasons. First, ILP offers a rigorous approach to

[4] It might be appropriate at this point for the reader to refer to Chapter 9 for some of the underlying concepts, including Horn clauses, conjunctive normal form, unification, and resolution.

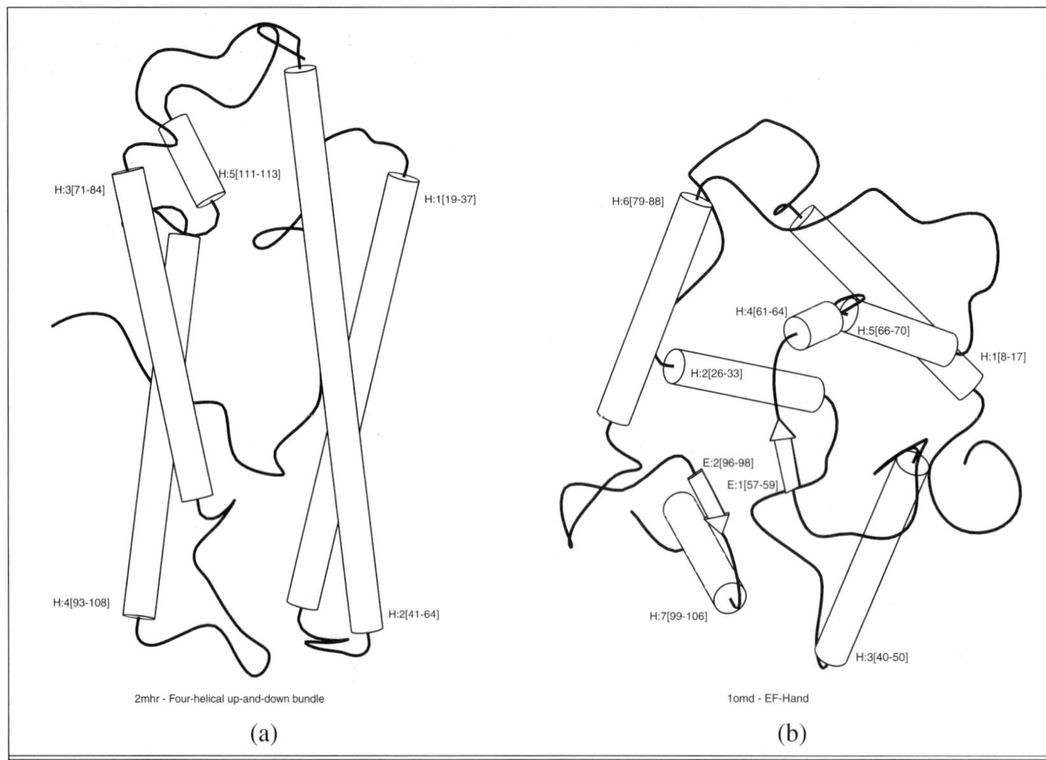


(a) (b)

**Figure 19.10** (a) and (b) show positive and negative examples, respectively, of the "four-helical up-and-down bundle" concept in the domain of protein folding. Each example structure is coded into a logical expression of about 100 conjuncts such as $TotalLength(D2mhr, 118) \wedge NumberHelices(D2mhr, 6) \wedge \ldots$. From these descriptions and from classifications such as $Fold(\text{FOUR-HELICAL-UP-AND-DOWN-BUNDLE}, D2mhr)$, the inductive logic programming system PROGOL (Muggleton, 1995) learned the following rule:

$$\begin{aligned} &Fold(\text{FOUR-HELICAL-UP-AND-DOWN-BUNDLE}, p) \Leftarrow \\ &\quad Helix(p, h_1) \wedge Length(h_1, \text{HIGH}) \wedge Position(p, h_1, n) \\ &\quad \wedge (1 \le n \le 3) \wedge Adjacent(p, h_1, h_2) \wedge Helix(p, h_2) \,. \end{aligned}$$

This kind of rule could not be learned, or even represented, by an attribute-based mechanism such as we saw in previous chapters. The rule can be translated into English as

> The protein $P$ has fold class "Four helical up and down bundle" if it contains a long helix $h_1$ at a secondary structure position between 1 and 3 and $h_1$ is next to a second helix.

the general knowledge-based inductive learning problem. Second, it offers complete algorithms for inducing general, first-order theories from examples, which can therefore learn successfully in domains where attribute-based algorithms are hard to apply. An example is in learning how protein structures fold (Figure 19.10). The three-dimensional configuration of a protein molecule cannot be represented reasonably by a set of attributes, because the configuration inherently refers to *relationships* between objects, not to attributes of a single object. First-order logic is an appropriate language for describing the relationships. Third, inductive logic programming produces hypotheses that are (relatively) easy for humans to read. For example, the English translation in Figure 19.10 can be scrutinized and criticized by working biologists. This means that inductive logic programming systems can participate in the scientific cycle of experimentation, hypothesis generation, debate, and refutation. Such participation would not be possible for systems that generate "black-box" classifiers, such as neural networks.

### An example

Recall from Equation (19.5) that the general knowledge-based induction problem is to "solve" the entailment constraint

$$Background \land Hypothesis \land Descriptions \models Classifications$$

for the unknown $Hypothesis$, given the $Background$ knowledge and examples described by $Descriptions$ and $Classifications$. To illustrate this, we will use the problem of learning family relationships from examples. The descriptions will consist of an extended family tree, described in terms of $Mother$, $Father$, and $Married$ relations and $Male$ and $Female$ properties. As an example, we will use the family tree from Exercise 8.11, shown here in Figure 19.11. The corresponding descriptions are as follows:

$$\begin{array}{lll} Father(Philip, Charles) & Father(Philip, Anne) & \ldots \\ Mother(Mum, Margaret) & Mother(Mum, Elizabeth) & \ldots \\ Married(Diana, Charles) & Married(Elizabeth, Philip) & \ldots \\ Male(Philip) & Male(Charles) & \ldots \\ Female(Beatrice) & Female(Margaret) & \ldots \end{array}$$

The sentences in $Classifications$ depend on the target concept being learned. We might want to learn $Grandparent$, $BrotherInLaw$, or $Ancestor$, for example. For $Grandparent$, the complete set of $Classifications$ contains $20 \times 20 = 400$ conjuncts of the form

$$\begin{array}{lll} Grandparent(Mum, Charles) & Grandparent(Elizabeth, Beatrice) & \ldots \\ \neg Grandparent(Mum, Harry) & \neg Grandparent(Spencer, Peter) & \ldots \end{array}$$

We could of course learn from a subset of this complete set.

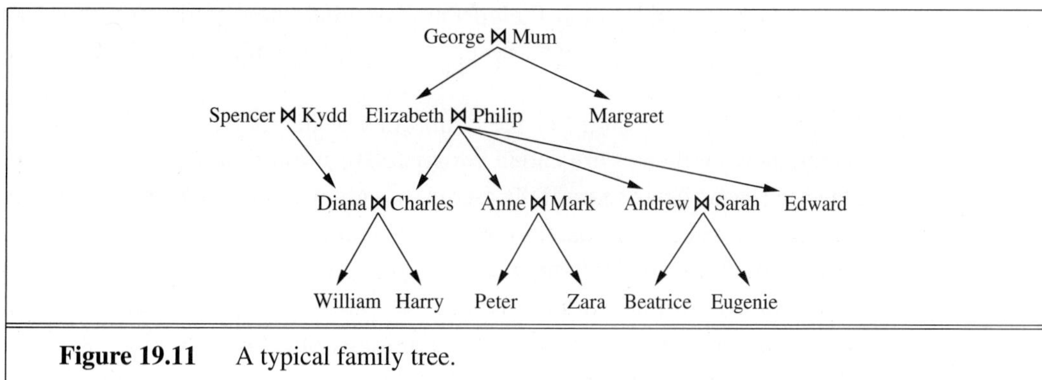


**Figure 19.11** A typical family tree.

The object of an inductive learning program is to come up with a set of sentences for the *Hypothesis* such that the entailment constraint is satisfied. Suppose, for the moment, that the agent has no background knowledge: *Background* is empty. Then one possible solution for *Hypothesis* is the following:

$$\begin{aligned} Grandparent(x,y) \;\Leftrightarrow\;& [\exists z\;\; Mother(x,z) \land Mother(z,y)] \\ \lor\;& [\exists z\;\; Mother(x,z) \land Father(z,y)] \\ \lor\;& [\exists z\;\; Father(x,z) \land Mother(z,y)] \\ \lor\;& [\exists z\;\; Father(x,z) \land Father(z,y)] \,. \end{aligned}$$

Notice that an attribute-based learning algorithm, such as DECISION-TREE-LEARNING, will get nowhere in solving this problem. In order to express *Grandparent* as an attribute (i.e., a unary predicate), we would need to make *pairs* of people into objects:

$$Grandparent(\langle Mum, Charles\rangle)\ldots$$

Then we get stuck in trying to represent the example descriptions. The only possible attributes are horrible things such as

$$FirstElementIsMotherOfElizabeth(\langle Mum, Charles\rangle)\,.$$

The definition of *Grandparent* in terms of these attributes simply becomes a large disjunction of specific cases that does not generalize to new examples at all. *Attribute-based learning algorithms are incapable of learning relational predicates.* Thus, one of the principal advantages of ILP algorithms is their applicability to a much wider range of problems, including relational problems.

The reader will certainly have noticed that a little bit of background knowledge would help in the representation of the *Grandparent* definition. For example, if *Background* included the sentence

$$Parent(x,y) \;\Leftrightarrow\; [Mother(x,y) \lor Father(x,y)]\,,$$

then the definition of *Grandparent* would be reduced to

$$Grandparent(x,y) \;\Leftrightarrow\; [\exists z\;\; Parent(x,z) \land Parent(z,y)]\,.$$

This shows how background knowledge can dramatically reduce the size of hypotheses required to explain the observations.

It is also possible for ILP algorithms to *create* new predicates in order to facilitate the expression of explanatory hypotheses. Given the example data shown earlier, it is entirely reasonable for the ILP program to propose an additional predicate, which we would call "*Parent*," in order to simplify the definitions of the target predicates. Algorithms that can generate new predicates are called **constructive induction** algorithms. Clearly, constructive induction is a necessary part of the picture of cumulative learning sketched in the introduction. It has been one of the hardest problems in machine learning, but some ILP techniques provide effective mechanisms for achieving it.

CONSTRUCTIVE INDUCTION

In the rest of this chapter, we will study the two principal approaches to ILP. The first uses a generalization of decision-tree methods, and the second uses techniques based on inverting a resolution proof.

must include *at least one* variable from an earlier literal or from the head of the clause. Literals such as $Mother(z, u)$, $Married(z, z)$, $\neg Male(y)$, and $Grandfather(v, x)$ are allowed, whereas $Married(u, v)$ is not. Notice that the use of the predicate from the head of the clause allows FOIL to learn *recursive* definitions.

2. *Equality and inequality literals*: these relate variables already appearing in the clause. For example, we might add $z \neq x$. These literals can also include user-specified constants. For learning arithmetic we might use 0 and 1, and for learning list functions we might use the empty list [].
3. *Arithmetic comparisons*: when dealing with functions of continuous variables, literals such as $x > y$ and $y \leq z$ can be added. As in decision-tree learning, a constant threshold value can be chosen to maximize the discriminatory power of the test.

The resulting branching factor in this search space is very large (see Exercise 19.6), but FOIL can also use type information to reduce it. For example, if the domain included numbers as well as people, type restrictions would prevent NEW-LITERALS from generating literals such as $Parent(x, n)$, where $x$ is a person and $n$ is a number.

CHOOSE-LITERAL uses a heuristic somewhat similar to information gain (see page 660) to decide which literal to add. The exact details are not so important here, and a number of different variations have been tried. One interesting additional feature of FOIL is the use of Ockham's razor to eliminate some hypotheses. If a clause becomes longer (according to some metric) than the total length of the positive examples that the clause explains, that clause is not considered as a potential hypothesis. This technique provides a way to avoid overcomplex clauses that fit noise in the data. For an explanation of the connection between noise and clause length, see page 715.

FOIL and its relatives have been used to learn a wide variety of definitions. One of the most impressive demonstrations (Quinlan and Cameron-Jones, 1993) involved solving a long sequence of exercises on list-processing functions from Bratko's (1986) Prolog textbook. In each case, the program was able to learn a correct definition of the function from a small set of examples, using the previously learned functions as background knowledge.

### Inductive learning with inverse deduction

The second major approach to ILP involves inverting the normal deductive proof process. INVERSE RESOLUTION **Inverse resolution** is based on the observation that if the example *Classifications* follow from $Background \wedge Hypothesis \wedge Descriptions$, then one must be able to prove this fact by resolution (because resolution is complete). If we can "run the proof backward," then we can find a *Hypothesis* such that the proof goes through. The key, then, is to find a way to invert the resolution process.

We will show a backward proof process for inverse resolution that consists of individual backward steps. Recall that an ordinary resolution step takes two clauses $C_1$ and $C_2$ and resolves them to produce the **resolvent** $C$. An inverse resolution step takes a resolvent $C$ and produces two clauses $C_1$ and $C_2$, such that $C$ is the result of resolving $C_1$ and $C_2$. Alternatively, it may take a resolvent $C$ and clause $C_1$ and produce a clause $C_2$ such that $C$ is the result of resolving $C_1$ and $C_2$.

The early steps in an inverse resolution process are shown in Figure 19.13, where we focus on the positive example $Grandparent(George, Anne)$. The process begins at the end of the proof (shown at the bottom of the figure). We take the resolvent $C$ to be empty clause (i.e. a contradiction) and $C_2$ to be $\neg Grandparent(George, Anne)$, which is the negation of the goal example. The first inverse step takes $C$ and $C_2$ and generates the clause $Grandparent(George, Anne)$ for $C_1$. The next step takes this clause as $C$ and the clause $Parent(Elizabeth, Anne)$ as $C_2$, and generates the clause

$$\neg Parent(Elizabeth, y) \vee Grandparent(George, y)$$

as $C_1$. The final step treats this clause as the resolvent. With $Parent(George, Elizabeth)$ as $C_2$, one possible clause $C_1$ is the hypothesis

$$Parent(x, z) \wedge Parent(z, y) \Rightarrow Grandparent(x, y) .$$

Now we have a resolution proof that the hypothesis, descriptions, and background knowledge entail the classification $Grandparent(George, Anne)$.

Clearly, inverse resolution involves a search. Each inverse resolution step is nondeterministic, because for any $C$, there can be many or even an infinite number of clauses $C_1$ and $C_2$ that resolve to $C$. For example, instead of choosing $\neg Parent(Elizabeth, y) \vee Grandparent(George, y)$ for $C_1$ in the last step of Figure 19.13, the inverse resolution step might have chosen any of the following sentences:

$$\neg Parent(Elizabeth, Anne) \vee Grandparent(George, Anne) .$$
$$\neg Parent(z, Anne) \vee Grandparent(George, Anne) .$$
$$\neg Parent(z, y) \vee Grandparent(George, y) .$$
$$\vdots$$

(See Exercises 19.4 and 19.5.) Furthermore, the clauses that participate in each step can be chosen from the $Background$ knowledge, from the example $Descriptions$, from the negated

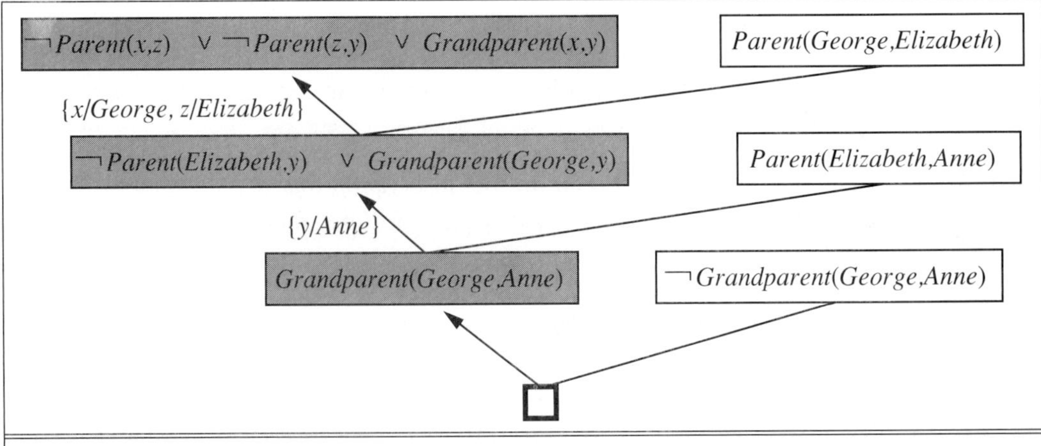


**Figure 19.13** Early steps in an inverse resolution process. The shaded clauses are generated by inverse resolution steps from the clause to the right and the clause below. The unshaded clauses are from the *Descriptions* and *Classifications*.

*Classifications*, or from hypothesized clauses that have already been generated in the inverse resolution tree. The large number of possibilities means a large branching factor (and therefore an inefficient search) without additional controls. A number of approaches to taming the search have been tried in implemented ILP systems:

1. Redundant choices can be eliminated—for example, by generating only the most specific hypotheses possible and by requiring that all the hypothesized clauses be consistent with each other, and with the observations. This last criterion would rule out the clause $\neg Parent(z, y) \lor Grandparent(George, y)$, listed before.
2. The proof strategy can be restricted. For example, we saw in Chapter 9 that **linear resolution** is a complete, restricted strategy that allows proof trees to have only a linear branching structure (as in Figure 19.13).
3. The representation language can be restricted, for example by eliminating function symbols or by allowing only Horn clauses. For instance, PROGOL operates with Horn clauses using **inverse entailment**. The idea is to change the entailment constraint

INVERSE ENTAILMENT

   $$Background \land Hypothesis \land Descriptions \models Classifications$$

   to the logically equivalent form

   $$Background \land Descriptions \land \neg Classifications \models \neg Hypothesis .$$

   From this, one can use a process similar to the normal Prolog Horn-clause deduction, with negation-as-failure to derive *Hypothesis*. Because it is restricted to Horn clauses, this is an incomplete method, but it can be more efficient than full resolution. It is also possible to apply complete inference with inverse entailment Inoue (2001).
4. Inference can be done with model checking rather than theorem proving. The PROGOL system (Muggleton, 1995) uses a form of model checking to limit the search. That is, like answer set programming, it generates possible values for logical variables, and checks for consistency.
5. Inference can be done with ground propositional clauses rather than in first-order logic. The LINUS system (Lavrač and Džeroski, 1994) works by translating first-order theories into propositional logic, solving them with a propositional learning system, and then translating back. Working with propositional formulas can be more efficient on some problems, as we saw with SATPLAN in Chapter 11.

### Making discoveries with inductive logic programming

An inverse resolution procedure that inverts a complete resolution strategy is, in principle, a complete algorithm for learning first-order theories. That is, if some unknown *Hypothesis* generates a set of examples, then an inverse resolution procedure can generate *Hypothesis* from the examples. This observation suggests an interesting possibility: Suppose that the available examples include a variety of trajectories of falling bodies. Would an inverse resolution program be theoretically capable of inferring the law of gravity? The answer is clearly yes, because the law of gravity allows one to explain the examples, given suitable background mathematics. Similarly, one can imagine that electromagnetism, quantum mechanics, and the theory of relativity are also within the scope of ILP programs. Of course, they are also within the scope of a monkey with a typewriter; we still need better heuristics and new ways to structure the search space.

One thing that inverse resolution systems *will* do for you is invent new predicates. This ability is often seen as somewhat magical, because computers are often thought of as "merely working with what they are given." In fact, new predicates fall directly out of the inverse resolution step. The simplest case arises in hypothesizing two new clauses $C_1$ and $C_2$, given a clause $C$. The resolution of $C_1$ and $C_2$ eliminates a literal that the two clauses share; hence, it is quite possible that the eliminated literal contained a predicate that does not appear in $C$. Thus, when working backward, one possibility is to generate a new predicate from which to reconstruct the missing literal.

Figure 19.14 shows an example in which the new predicate $P$ is generated in the process of learning a definition for $Ancestor$. Once generated, $P$ can be used in later inverse resolution steps. For example, a later step might hypothesize that $Mother(x,y) \Rightarrow P(x,y)$. Thus, the new predicate $P$ has its meaning constrained by the generation of hypotheses that involve it. Another example might lead to the constraint $Father(x,y) \Rightarrow P(x,y)$. In other words, the predicate $P$ is what we usually think of as the $Parent$ relationship. As we mentioned earlier, the invention of new predicates can significantly reduce the size of the definition of the goal predicate. Hence, by including the ability to invent new predicates, inverse resolution systems can often solve learning problems that are infeasible with other techniques.

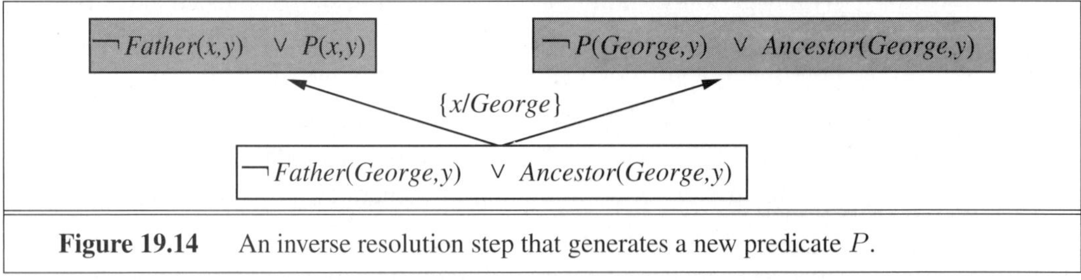


**Figure 19.14** An inverse resolution step that generates a new predicate $P$.

Some of the deepest revolutions in science come from the invention of new predicates and functions—for example, Galileo's invention of acceleration or Joule's invention of thermal energy. Once these terms are available, the discovery of new laws becomes (relatively) easy. The difficult part lies in realizing that some new entity, with a specific relationship to existing entities, will allow an entire body of observations to be explained with a much simpler and more elegant theory than previously existed.

As yet, ILP systems have not made discoveries on the level of Galileo or Joule, but their discoveries have been deemed publishable in the scientific literature. For example, in the *Journal of Molecular Biology*, Turcotte *et al.* (2001) describe the automated discovery of rules for protein folding by the ILP program PROGOL. Many of the rules discovered by PROGOL could have been derived from known principles, but most had not been previously published as part of a standard biological database. (See Figure 19.10 for an example.). In related work, Srinivasan *et al.* (1994) dealt with the problem of discovering molecular-structure-based rules for the mutagenicity of nitroaromatic compounds. These compounds are found in automobile exhaust fumes. For 80% of the compounds in a standard database, it is possible to identify four important features, and linear regression on these features outperforms ILP. For the remaining 20%, the features alone are not predictive, and ILP identifies relationships which allow it to outperform linear regression, neural nets, and decision trees. King *et al.* (1992) showed how to predict the therapeutic efficacy of various drugs from their molecular structures. For all these examples it appears that both the ability to represent relations and to use background knowledge contribute to ILP's high performance. The fact that the rules found by ILP can be interpreted by humans contributes to the acceptance of these techniques in biology journals rather than just computer science journals.

ILP has made contributions to other sciences besides biology. One of the most important is natural language processing, where ILP has been used to extract complex relational information from text. These results are summarized in Chapter 23.

## 19.6 SUMMARY

This chapter has investigated various ways in which prior knowledge can help an agent to learn from new experiences. Because much prior knowledge is expressed in terms of relational models rather than attribute-based models, we have also covered systems that allow learning of relational models. The important points are:

- The use of prior knowledge in learning leads to a picture of **cumulative learning**, in which learning agents improve their learning ability as they acquire more knowledge.
- Prior knowledge helps learning by eliminating otherwise consistent hypotheses and by "filling in" the explanation of examples, thereby allowing for shorter hypotheses. These contributions often result in faster learning from fewer examples.
- Understanding the different logical roles played by prior knowledge, as expressed by **entailment constraints**, helps to define a variety of learning techniques.
- **Explanation-based learning** (EBL) extracts general rules from single examples by *explaining* the examples and generalizing the explanation. It provides a deductive method turning first-principles knowledge into useful, efficient, special-purpose expertise.
- **Relevance-based learning** (RBL) uses prior knowledge in the form of determinations to identify the relevant attributes, thereby generating a reduced hypothesis space and speeding up learning. RBL also allows deductive generalizations from single examples.
- **Knowledge-based inductive learning** (KBIL) finds inductive hypotheses that explain sets of observations with the help of background knowledge.
- **Inductive logic programming** (ILP) techniques perform KBIL on knowledge that is expressed in first-order logic. ILP methods can learn relational knowledge that is not expressible in attribute-based systems.
- ILP can be done with a top-down approach of refining a very general rule or through a bottom-up approach of inverting the deductive process.
- ILP methods naturally generate new predicates with which concise new theories can be expressed and show promise as general-purpose scientific theory formation systems.

## Bibliographical and Historical Notes

Although the use of prior knowledge in learning would seem to be a natural topic for philosophers of science, little formal work was done until quite recently. *Fact, Fiction, and Forecast*, by the philosopher Nelson Goodman (1954), refuted the earlier supposition that induction was simply a matter of seeing enough examples of some universally quantified proposition and then adopting it as a hypothesis. Consider, for example, the hypothesis "All emeralds are grue," where **grue** means "green if observed before time $t$, but blue if observed thereafter." At any time up to $t$, we might have observed millions of instances confirming the rule that emeralds are grue, and no disconfirming instances, and yet we are unwilling to adopt the rule. This can be explained only by appeal to the role of relevant prior knowledge in the induction process. Goodman proposes a variety of different kinds of prior knowledge that might be useful, including a version of determinations called **overhypotheses**. Unfortunately, Goodman's ideas were never pursued in machine learning.

GRUE

EBL had its roots in the techniques used by the STRIPS planner (Fikes *et al.*, 1972). When a plan was constructed, a generalized version of it was saved in a plan library and used in later planning as a **macro-operator**. Similar ideas appeared in Anderson's ACT* architecture, under the heading of **knowledge compilation** (Anderson, 1983), and in the SOAR architecture, as **chunking** (Laird *et al.*, 1986). **Schema acquisition** (DeJong, 1981), **analytical generalization** (Mitchell, 1982), and **constraint-based generalization** (Minton, 1984) were immediate precursors of the rapid growth of interest in EBL stimulated by the papers of Mitchell *et al.* (1986) and DeJong and Mooney (1986). Hirsh (1987) introduced the EBL algorithm described in the text, showing how it could be incorporated directly into a logic programming system. Van Harmelen and Bundy (1988) explain EBL as a variant of the **partial evaluation** method used in program analysis systems (Jones *et al.*, 1993).

More recently, rigorous analysis has led to a better understanding of the potential costs and benefits of EBL in terms of problem-solving speed. Minton (1988) showed that, without extensive extra work, EBL could easily slow down a program significantly. Tambe *et al.* (1990) found a similar problem with chunking and proposed a reduction in the expressive power of the rule language in order to minimize the cost of matching rules against working memory. This work has strong parallels with recent results on the complexity of inference in restricted versions of first-order logic. (See Chapter 9.) Formal probabilistic analysis of the expected payoff of EBL can be found in Greiner (1989) and Subramanian and Feldman (1990). An excellent survey appears in Dietterich (1990).

ANALOGICAL REASONING

Instead of using examples as foci for generalization, one can use them directly to solve new problems, in a process known as **analogical reasoning**. This form of reasoning ranges from a form of plausible reasoning based on degree of similarity (Gentner, 1983), through a form of deductive inference based on determinations but requiring the participation of the example (Davies and Russell, 1987), to a form of "lazy" EBL that tailors the direction of generalization of the old example to fit the needs of the new problem. This latter form of analogical reasoning is found most commonly in **case-based reasoning** (Kolodner, 1993) and **derivational analogy** (Veloso and Carbonell, 1993).

Relevance information in the form of functional dependencies was first developed in the database community, where it is used to structure large sets of attributes into manageable subsets. Functional dependencies were used for analogical reasoning by Carbonell and Collins (1973) and were given a more logical flavor by Bobrow and Raphael (1974). Dependencies were independently rediscovered and given a full logical analysis by Davies and Russell (Davies, 1985; Davies and Russell, 1987). They were used for declarative bias by Russell and Grosof (1987). The equivalence of determinations to a restricted-vocabulary hypothesis space was proved in Russell (1988). Learning algorithms for determinations and the improved performance obtained by RBDTL were first shown in the FOCUS algorithm in Almuallim and Dietterich (1991). Tadepalli (1993) describes an ingenious algorithm for learning with determinations that shows large improvements in learning speed.

The idea that inductive learning can be performed by inverse deduction can be traced to W. S. Jevons (1874), who wrote, "The study both of Formal Logic and of the Theory of Probabilities has led me to adopt the opinion that there is no such thing as a distinct method of induction as contrasted with deduction, but that induction is simply an inverse employment of deduction." Computational investigations began with the remarkable Ph.D. thesis by Gordon Plotkin (1971) at Edinburgh. Although Plotkin developed many of the theorems and methods that are in current use in ILP, he was discouraged by some undecidability results for certain subproblems in induction. MIS (Shapiro, 1981) reintroduced the problem of learning logic programs, but was seen mainly as a contribution to the theory of automated debugging. Work on rule induction, such as the ID3 (Quinlan, 1986) and CN2 (Clark and Niblett, 1989) systems, led to FOIL (Quinlan, 1990), which for the first time allowed practical induction of relational rules. The field of relational learning was reinvigorated by Muggleton and Buntine (1988), whose CIGOL program incorporated a slightly incomplete version of inverse resolution and was capable of generating new predicates.[5] Wirth and O'Rorke (1991) also cover predicate invention. The next major system was GOLEM (Muggleton and Feng, 1990), which uses a covering algorithm based on Plotkin's concept of relative least general generalization. Where FOIL was top-down, CIGOL and GOLEM worked bottom-up. ITOU (Rouveirol and Puget, 1989) and CLINT (De Raedt, 1992) were other systems of that era. More recently, PROGOL (Muggleton, 1995) has taken a hybrid (top-down and bottom-up) approach to inverse entailment and has been applied to a number of practical problems, particularly in biology and natural language processing. Muggleton (2000) describes an extension of PROGOL to handle uncertainty in the form of stochastic logic programs.

A formal analysis of ILP methods appears in Muggleton (1991), a large collection of papers in Muggleton (1992), and a collection of techniques and applications in the book by Lavrač and Džeroski (1994). Page and Srinivasan (2002) give a more recent overview of the field's history and challenges for the future. Early complexity results by Haussler (1989) suggested that learning first-order sentences was hopelessly complex. However, with better understanding of the importance of various kinds of syntactic restrictions on clauses, positive results have been obtained even for clauses with recursion (Dzeroski *et al.*, 1992). Learnability results for ILP are surveyed by Kietz and Dzeroski (1994) and Cohen and Page (1995).

[5] The inverse resolution method also appears in (Russell, 1986), with a simple algorithm given in a footnote.

DISCOVERY SYSTEMS

Although ILP now seems to be the dominant approach to constructive induction, it has not been the only approach taken. So-called **discovery systems** aim to model the process of scientific discovery of new concepts, usually by a direct search in the space of concept definitions. Doug Lenat's Automated Mathematician, or AM, (Davis and Lenat, 1982) used discovery heuristics expressed as expert system rules to guide its search for concepts and conjectures in elementary number theory. Unlike most systems designed for mathematical reasoning, AM lacked a concept of proof and could only make conjectures. It rediscovered Goldbach's conjecture and the Unique Prime Factorization theorem. AM's architecture was generalized in the EURISKO system (Lenat, 1983) by adding a mechanism capable of rewriting the system's own discovery heuristics. EURISKO was applied in a number of areas other than mathematical discovery, although with less success than AM. The methodology of AM and EURISKO has been controversial (Ritchie and Hanna, 1984; Lenat and Brown, 1984).

Another class of discovery systems aims to operate with real scientific data to find new laws. The systems DALTON, GLAUBER, and STAHL (Langley *et al.*, 1987) are rule-based systems that look for quantitative relationships in experimental data from physical systems; in each case, the system has been able to recapitulate a well-known discovery from the history of science. Discovery systems based on probabilistic techniques—especially clustering algorithms that discover new categories—are discussed in Chapter 20.

## EXERCISES

**19.1** Show, by translating into conjunctive normal form and applying resolution, that the conclusion drawn on page 694 concerning Brazilians is sound.

**19.2** For each of the following determinations, write down the logical representation and explain why the determination is true (if it is):

**a.** Zip code determines the state (U.S.).

**b.** Design and denomination determine the mass of a coin.

**c.** For a given program, input determines output.

**d.** Climate, food intake, exercise, and metabolism determine weight gain and loss.

**e.** Baldness is determined by the baldness (or lack thereof) of one's maternal grandfather.

**19.3** Would a probabilistic version of determinations be useful? Suggest a definition.

**19.4** Fill in the missing values for the clauses $C_1$ or $C_2$ (or both) in the following sets of clauses, given that $C$ is the resolvent of $C_1$ and $C_2$:

**a.** $C = \mathit{True} \Rightarrow P(A,B), C_1 = P(x,y) \Rightarrow Q(x,y), C_2 = ??.$

**b.** $C = \mathit{True} \Rightarrow P(A,B), C_1 = ??, C_2 = ??.$

**c.** $C = P(x,y) \Rightarrow P(x,f(y)), C_1 = ??, C_2 = ??.$

If there is more than one possible solution, provide one example of each different kind.

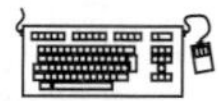

**19.5** Suppose one writes a logic program that carries out a resolution inference step. That is, let $Resolve(c_1, c_2, c)$ succeed if $c$ is the result of resolving $c_1$ and $c_2$. Normally, $Resolve$ would be used as part of a theorem prover by calling it with $c_1$ and $c_2$ instantiated to particular clauses, thereby generating the resolvent $c$. Now suppose instead that we call it with $c$ instantiated and $c_1$ and $c_2$ uninstantiated. Will this succeed in generating the appropriate results of an inverse resolution step? Would you need any special modifications to the logic programming system for this to work?

**19.6** Suppose that FOIL is considering adding a literal to a clause using a binary predicate $P$ and that previous literals (including the head of the clause) contain five different variables.

**a.** How many functionally different literals can be generated? Two literals are functionally identical if they differ only in the names of the *new* variables that they contain.

**b.** Can you find a general formula for the number of different literals with a predicate of arity $r$ when there are $n$ variables previously used?

**c.** Why does FOIL not allow literals that contain no previously used variables?

**19.7** Using the data from the family tree in Figure 19.11, or a subset thereof, apply the FOIL algorithm to learn a definition for the $Ancestor$ predicate.

# 20 STATISTICAL LEARNING METHODS

*In which we view learning as a form of uncertain reasoning from observations.*

Part V pointed out the prevalence of uncertainty in real environments. Agents can handle uncertainty by using the methods of probability and decision theory, but first they must learn their probabilistic theories of the world from experience. This chapter explains how they can do that. We will see how to formulate the learning task itself as a process of probabilistic inference (Section 20.1). We will see that a Bayesian view of learning is extremely powerful, providing general solutions to the problems of noise, overfitting, and optimal prediction. It also takes into account the fact that a less-than-omniscient agent can never be certain about which theory of the world is correct, yet must still make decisions by using some theory of the world.

We describe methods for learning probability models—primarily Bayesian networks—in Sections 20.2 and 20.3. Section 20.4 looks at learning methods that store and recall specific instances. Section 20.5 covers **neural network** learning and Section 20.6 introduces **kernel machines**. Some of the material in this chapter is fairly mathematical (requiring a basic understanding of multivariate calculus), although the general lessons can be understood without plunging into the details. It may benefit the reader at this point to review the material in Chapters 13 and 14 and to peek at the mathematical background in Appendix A.

## 20.1 STATISTICAL LEARNING

The key concepts in this chapter, just as in Chapter 18, are **data** and **hypotheses**. Here, the data are **evidence**—that is, instantiations of some or all of the random variables describing the domain. The hypotheses are probabilistic theories of how the domain works, including logical theories as a special case.

Let us consider a *very* simple example. Our favorite Surprise candy comes in two flavors: cherry (yum) and lime (ugh). The candy manufacturer has a peculiar sense of humor and wraps each piece of candy in the same opaque wrapper, regardless of flavor. The candy is sold in very large bags, of which there are known to be five kinds—again, indistinguishable from the outside:

$h_1$: 100% cherry
$h_2$: 75% cherry + 25% lime
$h_3$: 50% cherry + 50% lime
$h_4$: 25% cherry + 75% lime
$h_5$: 100% lime

Given a new bag of candy, the random variable $H$ (for *hypothesis*) denotes the type of the bag, with possible values $h_1$ through $h_5$. $H$ is not directly observable, of course. As the pieces of candy are opened and inspected, data are revealed—$D_1$, $D_2$, ..., $D_N$, where each $D_i$ is a random variable with possible values $cherry$ and $lime$. The basic task faced by the agent is to predict the flavor of the next piece of candy.[1] Despite its apparent triviality, this scenario serves to introduce many of the major issues. The agent really does need to infer a theory of its world, albeit a very simple one.

BAYESIAN LEARNING

**Bayesian learning** simply calculates the probability of each hypothesis, given the data, and makes predictions on that basis. That is, the predictions are made by using *all* the hypotheses, weighted by their probabilities, rather than by using just a single "best" hypothesis. In this way, learning is reduced to probabilistic inference. Let **D** represent all the data, with observed value **d**; then the probability of each hypothesis is obtained by Bayes' rule:

$$P(h_i|\mathbf{d}) = \alpha P(\mathbf{d}|h_i)P(h_i) . \tag{20.1}$$

Now, suppose we want to make a prediction about an unknown quantity $X$. Then we have

$$\mathbf{P}(X|\mathbf{d}) = \sum_i \mathbf{P}(X|\mathbf{d}, h_i)\mathbf{P}(h_i|\mathbf{d}) = \sum_i \mathbf{P}(X|h_i)P(h_i|\mathbf{d}) , \tag{20.2}$$

where we have assumed that each hypothesis determines a probability distribution over $X$. This equation shows that predictions are weighted averages over the predictions of the individual hypotheses. The hypotheses themselves are essentially "intermediaries" between the raw data and the predictions. The key quantities in the Bayesian approach are the **hypothesis prior**, $P(h_i)$, and the **likelihood** of the data under each hypothesis, $P(\mathbf{d}|h_i)$.

HYPOTHESIS PRIOR

LIKELIHOOD

For our candy example, we will assume for the time being that the prior distribution over $h_1, \ldots, h_5$ is given by $\langle 0.1, 0.2, 0.4, 0.2, 0.1 \rangle$, as advertised by the manufacturer. The likelihood of the data is calculated under the assumption that the observations are **i.i.d.**—that is, independently and identically distributed—so that

I.I.D.

$$P(\mathbf{d}|h_i) = \prod_j P(d_j|h_i) . \tag{20.3}$$

For example, suppose the bag is really an all-lime bag ($h_5$) and the first 10 candies are all lime; then $P(\mathbf{d}|h_3)$ is $0.5^{10}$, because half the candies in an $h_3$ bag are lime.[2] Figure 20.1(a) shows how the posterior probabilities of the five hypotheses change as the sequence of 10 lime candies is observed. Notice that the probabilities start out at their prior values, so $h_3$ is initially the most likely choice and remains so after 1 lime candy is unwrapped. After 2

[1] Statistically sophisticated readers will recognize this scenario as a variant of the **urn-and-ball** setup. We find urns and balls less compelling than candy; furthermore, candy lends itself to other tasks, such as deciding whether to trade the bag with a friend—see Exercise 20.3.

[2] We stated earlier that the bags of candy are very large; otherwise, the i.i.d. assumption fails to hold. Technically, it is more correct (but less hygienic) to rewrap each candy after inspection and return it to the bag.

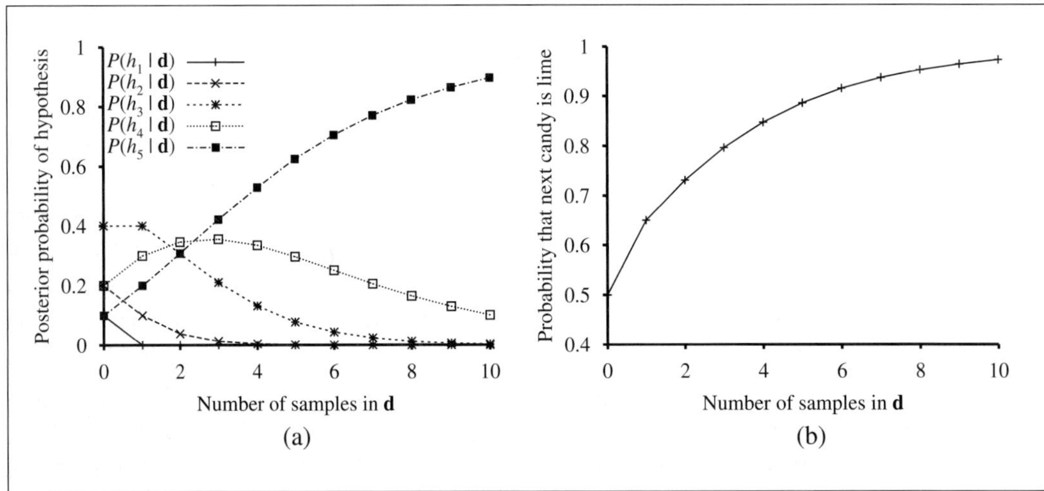


**Figure 20.1** (a) Posterior probabilities $P(h_i|d_1, \ldots, d_N)$ from Equation (20.1). The number of observations $N$ ranges from 1 to 10, and each observation is of a lime candy. (b) Bayesian prediction $P(d_{N+1} = lime|d_1, \ldots, d_N)$ from Equation (20.2).

lime candies are unwrapped, $h_4$ is most likely; after 3 or more, $h_5$ (the dreaded all-lime bag) is the most likely. After 10 in a row, we are fairly certain of our fate. Figure 20.1(b) shows the predicted probability that the next candy is lime, based on Equation (20.2). As we would expect, it increases monotonically toward 1.

The example shows that *the true hypothesis eventually dominates the Bayesian prediction.* This is characteristic of Bayesian learning. For any fixed prior that does not rule out the true hypothesis, the posterior probability of any false hypothesis will eventually vanish, simply because the probability of generating "uncharacteristic" data indefinitely is vanishingly small. (This point is analogous to one made in the discussion of PAC learning in Chapter 18.) More importantly, the Bayesian prediction is *optimal*, whether the data set be small or large. Given the hypothesis prior, any other prediction will be correct less often.

The optimality of Bayesian learning comes at a price, of course. For real learning problems, the hypothesis space is usually very large or infinite, as we saw in Chapter 18. In some cases, the summation in Equation (20.2) (or integration, in the continuous case) can be carried out tractably, but in most cases we must resort to approximate or simplified methods.

A very common approximation—one that is usually adopted in science—is to make predictions based on a single *most probable* hypothesis—that is, an $h_i$ that maximizes $P(h_i|\mathbf{d})$. This is often called a **maximum a posteriori** or MAP (pronounced "em-ay-pee") hypothesis. Predictions made according to an MAP hypothesis $h_{\text{MAP}}$ are approximately Bayesian to the extent that $\mathbf{P}(X|\mathbf{d}) \approx \mathbf{P}(X|h_{\text{MAP}})$. In our candy example, $h_{\text{MAP}} = h_5$ after three lime candies in a row, so the MAP learner then predicts that the fourth candy is lime with probability 1.0—a much more dangerous prediction than the Bayesian prediction of 0.8 shown in Figure 20.1. As more data arrive, the MAP and Bayesian predictions become closer, because the competitors to the MAP hypothesis become less and less probable. Although our example doesn't show it, finding MAP hypotheses is often much easier than Bayesian learn-

MAXIMUM A POSTERIORI

ing, because it requires solving an optimization problem instead of a large summation (or integration) problem. We will see examples of this later in the chapter.

In both Bayesian learning and MAP learning, the hypothesis prior $P(h_i)$ plays an important role. We saw in Chapter 18 that **overfitting** can occur when the hypothesis space is too expressive, so that it contains many hypotheses that fit the data set well. Rather than placing an arbitrary limit on the hypotheses to be considered, Bayesian and MAP learning methods use the prior to *penalize complexity*. Typically, more complex hypotheses have a lower prior probability—in part because there are usually many more complex hypotheses than simple hypotheses. On the other hand, more complex hypotheses have a greater capacity to fit the data. (In the extreme case, a lookup table can reproduce the data exactly with probability 1.) Hence, the hypothesis prior embodies a trade-off between the complexity of a hypothesis and its degree of fit to the data.

We can see the effect of this trade-off most clearly in the logical case, where $H$ contains only *deterministic* hypotheses. In that case, $P(\mathbf{d}|h_i)$ is 1 if $h_i$ is consistent and 0 otherwise. Looking at Equation (20.1), we see that $h_{\text{MAP}}$ will then be the *simplest logical theory that is consistent with the data.* Therefore, maximum *a posteriori* learning provides a natural embodiment of Ockham's razor.

Another insight into the trade-off between complexity and degree of fit is obtained by taking the logarithm of Equation (20.1). Choosing $h_{\text{MAP}}$ to maximize $P(\mathbf{d}|h_i)P(h_i)$ is equivalent to minimizing

$$-\log_2 P(\mathbf{d}|h_i) - \log_2 P(h_i)\ .$$

Using the connection between information encoding and probability that we introduced in Chapter 18, we see that the $-\log_2 P(h_i)$ term equals the number of bits required to specify the hypothesis $h_i$. Furthermore, $-\log_2 P(\mathbf{d}|h_i)$ is the additional number of bits required to specify the data, given the hypothesis. (To see this, consider that no bits are required if the hypothesis predicts the data exactly—as with $h_5$ and the string of lime candies—and $\log_2 1 = 0$.) Hence, MAP learning is choosing the hypothesis that provides maximum *compression* of the data. The same task is addressed more directly by the **minimum description length**, or MDL, learning method, which attempts to minimize the size of hypothesis and data encodings rather than work with probabilities.

MINIMUM DESCRIPTION LENGTH

A final simplification is provided by assuming a **uniform** prior over the space of hypotheses. In that case, MAP learning reduces to choosing an $h_i$ that maximizes $P(\mathbf{d}|H_i)$. This is called a **maximum-likelihood** (ML) hypothesis, $h_{\text{ML}}$. Maximum-likelihood learning is very common in statistics, a discipline in which many researchers distrust the subjective nature of hypothesis priors. It is a reasonable approach when there is no reason to prefer one hypothesis over another *a priori*—for example, when all hypotheses are equally complex. It provides a good approximation to Bayesian and MAP learning when the data set is large, because the data swamps the prior distribution over hypotheses, but it has problems (as we shall see) with small data sets.

MAXIMUM-LIKELIHOOD

## 20.2 LEARNING WITH COMPLETE DATA

PARAMETER LEARNING

COMPLETE DATA

Our development of statistical learning methods begins with the simplest task: **parameter learning** with **complete data**. A parameter learning task involves finding the numerical parameters for a probability model whose structure is fixed. For example, we might be interested in learning the conditional probabilities in a Bayesian network with a given structure. Data are complete when each data point contains values for every variable in the probability model being learned. Complete data greatly simplify the problem of learning the parameters of a complex model. We will also look briefly at the problem of learning structure.

### Maximum-likelihood parameter learning: Discrete models

Suppose we buy a bag of lime and cherry candy from a new manufacturer whose lime–cherry proportions are completely unknown—that is, the fraction could be anywhere between 0 and 1. In that case, we have a continuum of hypotheses. The **parameter** in this case, which we call $\theta$, is the proportion of cherry candies, and the hypothesis is $h_\theta$. (The proportion of limes is just $1-\theta$.) If we assume that all proportions are equally likely *a priori*, then a maximum-likelihood approach is reasonable. If we model the situation with a Bayesian network, we need just one random variable, *Flavor* (the flavor of a randomly chosen candy from the bag). It has values *cherry* and *lime*, where the probability of *cherry* is $\theta$ (see Figure 20.2(a)). Now suppose we unwrap $N$ candies, of which $c$ are cherries and $\ell = N - c$ are limes. According to Equation (20.3), the likelihood of this particular data set is

$$P(\mathbf{d}|h_\theta) = \prod_{j=1}^{N} P(d_j|h_\theta) = \theta^c \cdot (1-\theta)^\ell .$$

LOG LIKELIHOOD

The maximum-likelihood hypothesis is given by the value of $\theta$ that maximizes this expression. The same value is obtained by maximizing the **log likelihood**,

$$L(\mathbf{d}|h_\theta) = \log P(\mathbf{d}|h_\theta) = \sum_{j=1}^{N} \log P(d_j|h_\theta) = c\log\theta + \ell\log(1-\theta) .$$

(By taking logarithms, we reduce the product to a sum over the data, which is usually easier to maximize.) To find the maximum-likelihood value of $\theta$, we differentiate $L$ with respect to $\theta$ and set the resulting expression to zero:

$$\frac{dL(\mathbf{d}|h_\theta)}{d\theta} = \frac{c}{\theta} - \frac{\ell}{1-\theta} = 0 \qquad \Rightarrow \qquad \theta = \frac{c}{c+\ell} = \frac{c}{N} .$$

In English, then, the maximum-likelihood hypothesis $h_{\mathrm{ML}}$ asserts that the actual proportion of cherries in the bag is equal to the observed proportion in the candies unwrapped so far!

It appears that we have done a lot of work to discover the obvious. In fact, though, we have laid out one standard method for maximum-likelihood parameter learning:

1. Write down an expression for the likelihood of the data as a function of the parameter(s).
2. Write down the derivative of the log likelihood with respect to each parameter.
3. Find the parameter values such that the derivatives are zero.

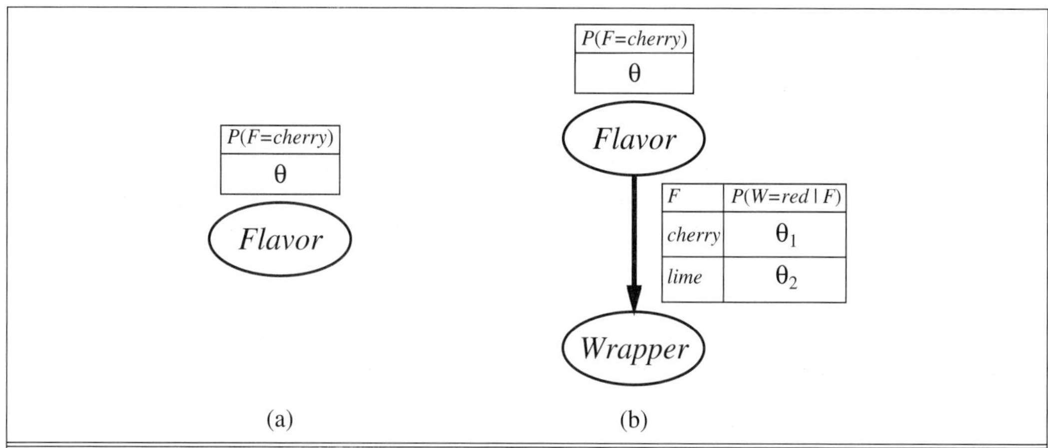


**Figure 20.2** (a) Bayesian network model for the case of candies with an unknown proportion of cherries and limes. (b) Model for the case where the wrapper color depends (probabilistically) on the candy flavor.

The trickiest step is usually the last. In our example, it was trivial, but we will see that in many cases we need to resort to iterative solution algorithms or other numerical optimization techniques, as described in Chapter 4. The example also illustrates a significant problem with maximum-likelihood learning in general: *when the data set is small enough that some events have not yet been observed—for instance, no cherry candies—the maximum likelihood hypothesis assigns zero probability to those events.* Various tricks are used to avoid this problem, such as initializing the counts for each event to 1 instead of zero.

Let us look at another example. Suppose this new candy manufacturer wants to give a little hint to the consumer and uses candy wrappers colored red and green. The *Wrapper* for each candy is selected *probabilistically*, according to some unknown conditional distribution, depending on the flavor. The corresponding probability model is shown in Figure 20.2(b). Notice that it has three parameters: $\theta$, $\theta_1$, and $\theta_2$. With these parameters, the likelihood of seeing, say, a cherry candy in a green wrapper can be obtained from the standard semantics for Bayesian networks (page 495):

$$\begin{aligned} & P(Flavor = cherry, Wrapper = green|h_{\theta,\theta_1,\theta_2}) \\ &= P(Flavor = cherry|h_{\theta,\theta_1,\theta_2})P(Wrapper = green|Flavor = cherry, h_{\theta,\theta_1,\theta_2}) \\ &= \theta \cdot (1-\theta_1) . \end{aligned}$$

Now, we unwrap $N$ candies, of which $c$ are cherries and $\ell$ are limes. The wrapper counts are as follows: $r_c$ of the cherries have red wrappers and $g_c$ have green, while $r_\ell$ of the limes have red and $g_\ell$ have green. The likelihood of the data is given by

$$P(\mathbf{d}|h_{\theta,\theta_1,\theta_2}) = \theta^c(1-\theta)^\ell \cdot \theta_1^{r_c}(1-\theta_1)^{g_c} \cdot \theta_2^{r_\ell}(1-\theta_2)^{g_\ell} .$$

This looks pretty horrible, but taking logarithms helps:

$$L = [c\log\theta + \ell\log(1-\theta)] + [r_c\log\theta_1 + g_c\log(1-\theta_1)] + [r_\ell\log\theta_2 + g_\ell\log(1-\theta_2)] .$$

The benefit of taking logs is clear: the log likelihood is the sum of three terms, each of which contains a single parameter. When we take derivatives with respect to each parameter and set them to zero, we get three independent equations, each containing just one parameter:

$$\begin{aligned}
\frac{\partial L}{\partial \theta} &= \frac{c}{\theta} - \frac{\ell}{1-\theta} = 0 & \Rightarrow \quad \theta &= \frac{c}{c+\ell} \\
\frac{\partial L}{\partial \theta_1} &= \frac{r_c}{\theta_1} - \frac{g_c}{1-\theta_1} = 0 & \Rightarrow \quad \theta_1 &= \frac{r_c}{r_c+g_c} \\
\frac{\partial L}{\partial \theta_2} &= \frac{r_\ell}{\theta_2} - \frac{g_\ell}{1-\theta_2} = 0 & \Rightarrow \quad \theta_2 &= \frac{r_\ell}{r_\ell+g_\ell} .
\end{aligned}$$

The solution for $\theta$ is the same as before. The solution for $\theta_1$, the probability that a cherry candy has a red wrapper, is the observed fraction of cherry candies with red wrappers, and similarly for $\theta_2$.

These results are very comforting, and it is easy to see that they can be extended to any Bayesian network whose conditional probabilities are represented as tables. The most important point is that, *with complete data, the maximum-likelihood parameter learning problem for a Bayesian network decomposes into separate learning problems, one for each parameter.*[3] The second point is that the parameter values for a variable, given its parents, are just the observed frequencies of the variable values for each setting of the parent values. As before, we must be careful to avoid zeroes when the data set is small.

### Naive Bayes models

Probably the most common Bayesian network model used in machine learning is the **naive Bayes** model. In this model, the "class" variable $C$ (which is to be predicted) is the root and the "attribute" variables $X_i$ are the leaves. The model is "naive" because it assumes that the attributes are conditionally independent of each other, given the class. (The model in Figure 20.2(b) is a naive Bayes model with just one attribute.) Assuming Boolean variables, the parameters are

$$\theta = P(C = true), \theta_{i1} = P(X_i = true|C = true), \theta_{i2} = P(X_i = true|C = \mathit{false}).$$

The maximum-likelihood parameter values are found in exactly the same way as for Figure 20.2(b). Once the model has been trained in this way, it can be used to classify new examples for which the class variable $C$ is unobserved. With observed attribute values $x_1, \ldots, x_n$, the probability of each class is given by

$$\mathbf{P}(C|x_1, \ldots, x_n) = \alpha\, \mathbf{P}(C) \prod_i \mathbf{P}(x_i|C) .$$

A deterministic prediction can be obtained by choosing the most likely class. Figure 20.3 shows the learning curve for this method when it is applied to the restaurant problem from Chapter 18. The method learns fairly well but not as well as decision-tree learning; this is presumably because the true hypothesis—which is a decision tree—is not representable exactly using a naive Bayes model. Naive Bayes learning turns out to do surprisingly well in a wide range of applications; the boosted version (Exercise 20.5) is one of the most effective general-purpose learning algorithms. Naive Bayes learning scales well to very large problems: with $n$ Boolean attributes, there are just $2n + 1$ parameters, and *no search is required to find $h_{\mathrm{ML}}$, the maximum-likelihood naive Bayes hypothesis.* Finally, naive Bayes learning has no difficulty with noisy data and can give probabilistic predictions when appropriate.

[3] See Exercise 20.7 for the nontabulated case, where each parameter affects several conditional probabilities.

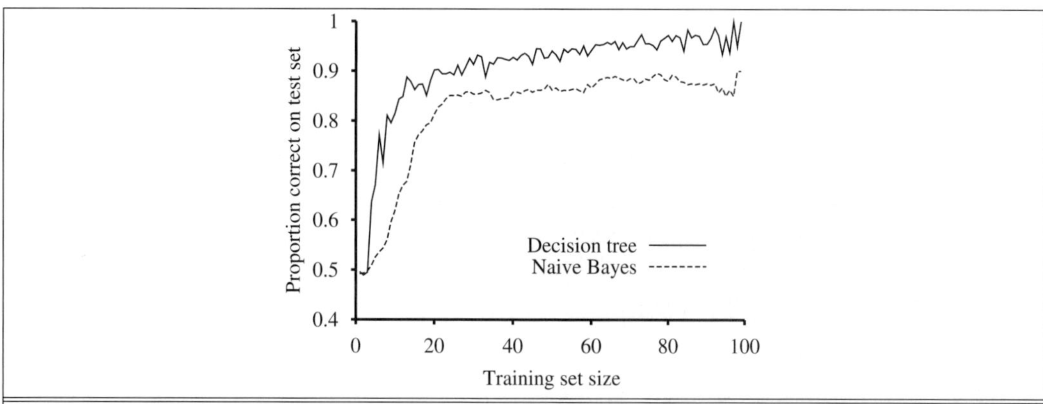


**Figure 20.3** The learning curve for naive Bayes learning applied to the restaurant problem from Chapter 18; the learning curve for decision-tree learning is shown for comparison.

## Maximum-likelihood parameter learning: Continuous models

Continuous probability models such as the **linear-Gaussian** model were introduced in Section 14.3. Because continuous variables are ubiquitous in real-world applications, it is important to know how to learn continuous models from data. The principles for maximum-likelihood learning are identical to those of the discrete case.

Let us begin with a very simple case: learning the parameters of a Gaussian density function on a single variable. That is, the data are generated as follows:

$$P(x) = \frac{1}{\sqrt{2\pi}\sigma} e^{-\frac{(x-\mu)^2}{2\sigma^2}} .$$

The parameters of this model are the mean $\mu$ and the standard deviation $\sigma$. (Notice that the normalizing "constant" depends on $\sigma$, so we cannot ignore it.) Let the observed values be $x_1, \ldots, x_N$. Then the log likelihood is

$$L = \sum_{j=1}^{N} \log \frac{1}{\sqrt{2\pi}\sigma} e^{-\frac{(x_j-\mu)^2}{2\sigma^2}} = N(-\log\sqrt{2\pi} - \log\sigma) - \sum_{j=1}^{N} \frac{(x_j-\mu)^2}{2\sigma^2} .$$

Setting the derivatives to zero as usual, we obtain

$$\begin{aligned} \frac{\partial L}{\partial \mu} &= -\frac{1}{\sigma^2}\sum_{j=1}^{N}(x_j-\mu) = 0 & \Rightarrow \quad \mu &= \frac{\sum_j x_j}{N} \\ \frac{\partial L}{\partial \sigma} &= -\frac{N}{\sigma} + \frac{1}{\sigma^3}\sum_{j=1}^{N}(x_j-\mu)^2 = 0 & \Rightarrow \quad \sigma &= \sqrt{\frac{\sum_j (x_j-\mu)^2}{N}} . \end{aligned} \tag{20.4}$$

That is, the maximum-likelihood value of the mean is the sample average and the maximum-likelihood value of the standard deviation is the square root of the sample variance. Again, these are comforting results that confirm "commonsense" practice.

Now consider a linear Gaussian model with one continuous parent $X$ and a continuous child $Y$. As explained on page 502, $Y$ has a Gaussian distribution whose mean depends linearly on the value of $X$ and whose standard deviation is fixed. To learn the conditional

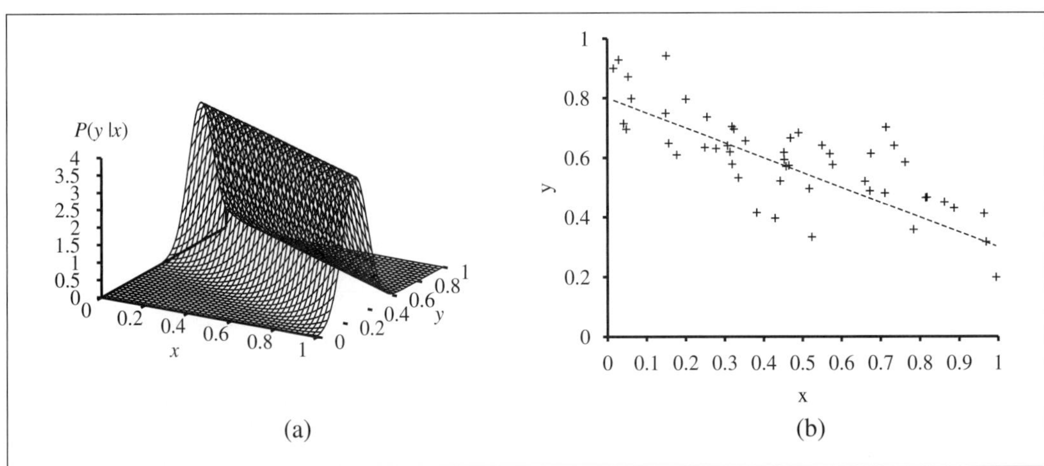


**Figure 20.4** (a) A linear Gaussian model described as $y = \theta_1 x + \theta_2$ plus Gaussian noise with fixed variance. (b) A set of 50 data points generated from this model.

distribution $P(Y|X)$, we can maximize the conditional likelihood

$$P(y|x) = \frac{1}{\sqrt{2\pi}\sigma} e^{-\frac{(y-(\theta_1 x+\theta_2))^2}{2\sigma^2}} . \tag{20.5}$$

Here, the parameters are $\theta_1$, $\theta_2$, and $\sigma$. The data are a collection of $(x_j, y_j)$ pairs, as illustrated in Figure 20.4. Using the usual methods (Exercise 20.6), we can find the maximum-likelihood values of the parameters. Here, we want to make a different point. If we consider just the parameters $\theta_1$ and $\theta_2$ that define the linear relationship between $x$ and $y$, it becomes clear that maximizing the log likelihood with respect to these parameters is the same as *minimizing* the numerator in the exponent of Equation (20.5):

$$E = \sum_{j=1}^{N} (y_j - (\theta_1 x_j + \theta_2))^2 .$$

ERROR

SUM OF SQUARED ERRORS

LINEAR REGRESSION

The quantity $(y_j - (\theta_1 x_j + \theta_2))$ is the **error** for $(x_j, y_j)$—that is, the difference between the actual value $y_j$ and the predicted value $(\theta_1 x_j + \theta_2)$—so $E$ is the well-known **sum of squared errors**. This is the quantity that is minimized by the standard **linear regression** procedure. Now we can understand why: minimizing the sum of squared errors gives the maximum-likelihood straight-line model, *provided that the data are generated with Gaussian noise of fixed variance.*

## Bayesian parameter learning

Maximum-likelihood learning gives rise to some very simple procedures, but it has some serious deficiencies with small data sets. For example, after seeing one cherry candy, the maximum-likelihood hypothesis is that the bag is 100% cherry (i.e., $\theta = 1.0$). Unless one's hypothesis prior is that bags must be either all cherry or all lime, this is not a reasonable conclusion. The Bayesian approach to parameter learning places a hypothesis prior over the possible values of the parameters and updates this distribution as data arrive.

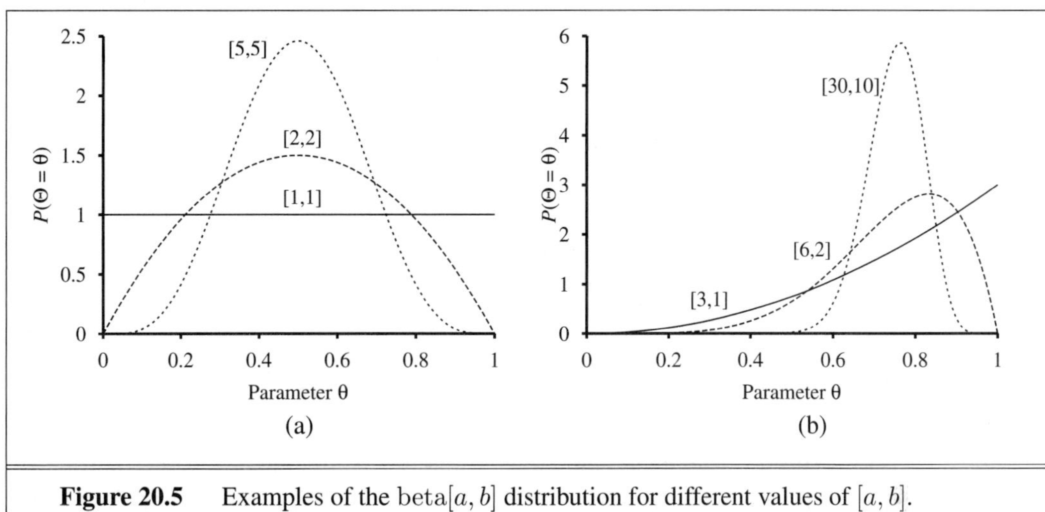


**Figure 20.5** Examples of the $\text{beta}[a, b]$ distribution for different values of $[a, b]$.

The candy example in Figure 20.2(a) has one parameter, $\theta$: the probability that a randomly selected piece of candy is cherry flavored. In the Bayesian view, $\theta$ is the (unknown) value of a random variable $\Theta$; the hypothesis prior is just the prior distribution $\mathbf{P}(\Theta)$. Thus, $P(\Theta = \theta)$ is the prior probability that the bag has a fraction $\theta$ of cherry candies.

If the parameter $\theta$ can be any value between 0 and 1, then $\mathbf{P}(\Theta)$ must be a continuous distribution that is nonzero only between 0 and 1 and that integrates to 1. The uniform density $P(\theta) = U[0, 1](\theta)$ is one candidate. (See Chapter 13.) It turns out that the uniform density is a member of the family of **beta distributions**. Each beta distribution is defined by two **hyperparameters**[4] $a$ and $b$ such that

BETA DISTRIBUTIONS

HYPERPARAMETER

$$\text{beta}[a, b](\theta) = \alpha\, \theta^{a-1}(1-\theta)^{b-1}\,, \tag{20.6}$$

for $\theta$ in the range $[0, 1]$. The normalization constant $\alpha$ depends on $a$ and $b$. (See Exercise 20.8.) Figure 20.5 shows what the distribution looks like for various values of $a$ and $b$. The mean value of the distribution is $a/(a + b)$, so larger values of $a$ suggest a belief that $\Theta$ is closer to 1 than to 0. Larger values of $a + b$ make the distribution more peaked, suggesting greater certainty about the value of $\Theta$. Thus, the beta family provides a useful range of possibilities for the hypothesis prior.

Besides its flexibility, the beta family has another wonderful property: if $\Theta$ has a prior $\text{beta}[a, b]$, then, after a data point is observed, the posterior distribution for $\Theta$ is also a beta distribution. The beta family is called the **conjugate prior** for the family of distributions for a Boolean variable.[5] Let's see how this works. Suppose we observe a cherry candy; then

CONJUGATE PRIOR

$$\begin{aligned} P(\theta | D_1 = \mathit{cherry}) &= \alpha\, P(D_1 = \mathit{cherry} | \theta) P(\theta) \\ &= \alpha'\, \theta \cdot \text{beta}[a, b](\theta) = \alpha'\, \theta \cdot \theta^{a-1}(1-\theta)^{b-1} \\ &= \alpha'\, \theta^{a}(1-\theta)^{b-1} = \text{beta}[a+1, b](\theta)\,. \end{aligned}$$

[4] They are called hyperparameters because they parameterize a distribution over $\theta$, which is itself a parameter.

[5] Other conjugate priors include the **Dirichlet** family for the parameters of a discrete multivalued distribution and the **Normal–Wishart** family for the parameters of a Gaussian distribution. See Bernardo and Smith (1994).

Thus, after seeing a cherry candy, we simply increment the $a$ parameter to get the posterior; similarly, after seeing a lime candy, we increment the $b$ parameter. Thus, we can view the $a$ and $b$ hyperparameters as **virtual counts**, in the sense that a prior $\mathrm{beta}[a, b]$ behaves exactly as if we had started out with a uniform prior $\mathrm{beta}[1, 1]$ and seen $a - 1$ actual cherry candies and $b - 1$ actual lime candies.

VIRTUAL COUNTS

By examining a sequence of beta distributions for increasing values of $a$ and $b$, keeping the proportions fixed, we can see vividly how the posterior distribution over the parameter $\Theta$ changes as data arrive. For example, suppose the actual bag of candy is 75% cherry. Figure 20.5(b) shows the sequence $\mathrm{beta}[3, 1]$, $\mathrm{beta}[6, 2]$, $\mathrm{beta}[30, 10]$. Clearly, the distribution is converging to a narrow peak around the true value of $\Theta$. For large data sets, then, Bayesian learning (at least in this case) converges to give the same results as maximum-likelihood learning.

The network in Figure 20.2(b) has three parameters, $\theta$, $\theta_1$, and $\theta_2$, where $\theta_1$ is the probability of a red wrapper on a cherry candy and $\theta_2$ is the probability of a red wrapper on a lime candy. The Bayesian hypothesis prior must cover all three parameters—that is, we need to specify $\mathbf{P}(\Theta, \Theta_1, \Theta_2)$. Usually, we assume **parameter independence**:

PARAMETER INDEPENDENCE

$$\mathbf{P}(\Theta, \Theta_1, \Theta_2) = \mathbf{P}(\Theta)\mathbf{P}(\Theta_1)\mathbf{P}(\Theta_2) .$$

With this assumption, each parameter can have its own beta distribution that is updated separately as data arrive.

Once we have the idea that unknown parameters can be represented by random variables such as $\Theta$, it is natural to incorporate them into the Bayesian network itself. To do this, we also need to make copies of the variables describing each instance. For example, if we have observed three candies then we need $Flavor_1$, $Flavor_2$, $Flavor_3$ and $Wrapper_1$, $Wrapper_2$, $Wrapper_3$. The parameter variable $\Theta$ determines the probability of each $Flavor_i$ variable:

$$P(Flavor_i = cherry|\Theta = \theta) = \theta .$$

Similarly, the wrapper probabilities depend on $\Theta_1$ and $\Theta_2$, For example,

$$P(Wrapper_i = red|Flavor_i = cherry, \Theta_1 = \theta_1) = \theta_1 .$$

Now, the entire Bayesian learning process can be formulated as an *inference* problem in a suitably constructed Bayes net, as shown in Figure 20.6. Prediction for a new instance is done simply by adding new instance variables to the network, some of which are queried. This formulation of learning and prediction makes it clear that Bayesian learning requires no extra "principles of learning." Furthermore, *there is, in essence, just one learning algorithm,* i.e., the inference algorithm for Bayesian networks.

## Learning Bayes net structures

So far, we have assumed that the structure of the Bayes net is given and we are just trying to learn the parameters. The structure of the network represents basic causal knowledge about the domain that is often easy for an expert, or even a naive user, to supply. In some cases, however, the causal model may be unavailable or subject to dispute—for example, certain corporations have long claimed that smoking does not cause cancer—so it is important to

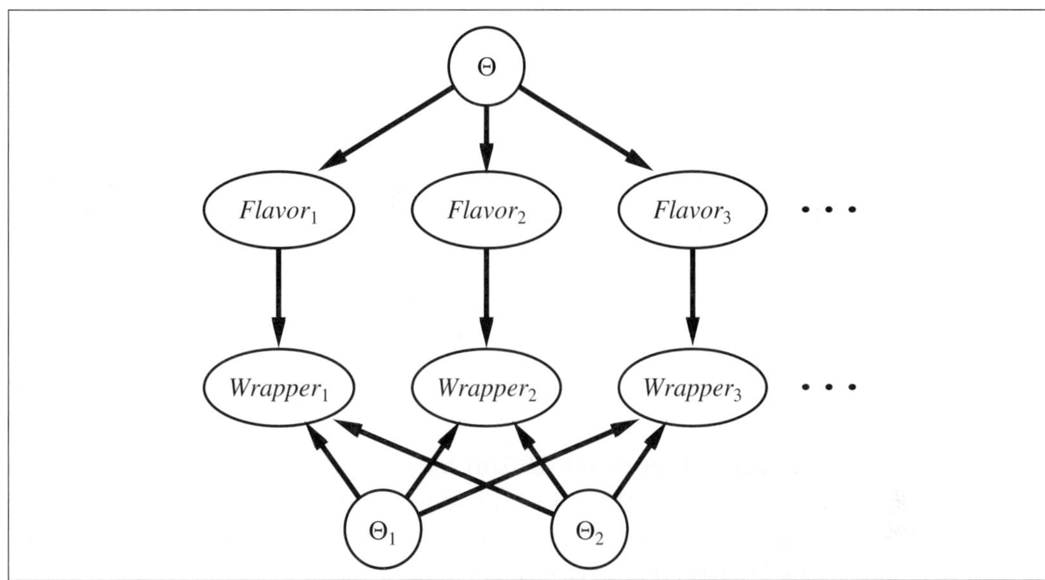


**Figure 20.6** A Bayesian network that corresponds to a Bayesian learning process. Posterior distributions for the parameter variables $\Theta$, $\Theta_1$, and $\Theta_2$ can be inferred from their prior distributions and the evidence in the $Flavor_i$ and $Wrapper_i$ variables.

understand how the structure of a Bayes net can be learned from data. At present, structural learning algorithms are in their infancy, so we will give only a brief sketch of the main ideas.

The most obvious approach is to *search* for a good model. We can start with a model containing no links and begin adding parents for each node, fitting the parameters with the methods we have just covered and measuring the accuracy of the resulting model. Alternatively, we can start with an initial guess at the structure and use hill-climbing or simulated annealing search to make modifications, retuning the parameters after each change in the structure. Modifications can include reversing, adding, or deleting arcs. We must not introduce cycles in the process, so many algorithms assume that an ordering is given for the variables, and that a node can have parents only among those nodes that come earlier in the ordering (just as in the construction process Chapter 14). For full generality, we also need to search over possible orderings.

There are two alternative methods for deciding when a good structure has been found. The first is to test whether the conditional independence assertions implicit in the structure are actually satisfied in the data. For example, the use of a naive Bayes model for the restaurant problem assumes that

$$\mathbf{P}(Fri/Sat, Bar|\,WillWait) = \mathbf{P}(Fri/Sat|\,WillWait)\mathbf{P}(Bar|\,WillWait)$$

and we can check in the data that the same equation holds between the corresponding conditional frequencies. Now, even if the structure describes the true causal nature of the domain, statistical fluctuations in the data set mean that the equation will never be satisfied *exactly*, so we need to perform a suitable statistical test to see if there is sufficient evidence that the independence hypothesis is violated. The complexity of the resulting network will depend on the threshold used for this test—the stricter the independence test, the more links will be added and the greater the danger of overfitting.

An approach more consistent with the ideas in this chapter is to the degree to which the proposed model explains the data (in a probabilistic sense). We must be careful how we measure this, however. If we just try to find the maximum-likelihood hypothesis, we will end up with a fully connected network, because adding more parents to a node cannot decrease the likelihood (Exercise 20.9). We are forced to penalize model complexity in some way. The MAP (or MDL) approach simply subtracts a penalty from the likelihood of each structure (after parameter tuning) before comparing different structures. The Bayesian approach places a joint prior over structures and parameters. There are usually far too many structures to sum over (superexponential in the number of variables), so most practitioners use MCMC to sample over structures.

Penalizing complexity (whether by MAP or Bayesian methods) introduces an important connection between the optimal structure and the nature of the representation for the conditional distributions in the network. With tabular distributions, the complexity penalty for a node's distribution grows exponentially with the number of parents, but with, say, noisy-OR distributions, it grows only linearly. This means that learning with noisy-OR (or other compactly parameterized) models tends to produce learned structures with more parents than does learning with tabular distributions.

## 20.3 LEARNING WITH HIDDEN VARIABLES: THE EM ALGORITHM

The preceding section dealt with the fully observable case. Many real-world problems have **hidden variables** (sometimes called **latent variables**) which are not observable in the data that are available for learning. For example, medical records often include the observed symptoms, the treatment applied, and perhaps the outcome of the treatment, but they seldom contain a direct observation of the disease itself![6] One might ask, "If the disease is not observed, why not construct a model without it?" The answer appears in Figure 20.7, which shows a small, fictitious diagnostic model for heart disease. There are three observable predisposing factors and three observable symptoms (which are too depressing to name). Assume that each variable has three possible values (e.g., $none$, $moderate$, and $severe$). Removing the hidden variable from the network in (a) yields the network in (b); the total number of parameters increases from 78 to 708. Thus, *latent variables can dramatically reduce the number of parameters required to specify a Bayesian network.* This, in turn, can dramatically reduce the amount of data needed to learn the parameters.

LATENT VARIABLES

Hidden variables are important, but they do complicate the learning problem. In Figure 20.7(a), for example, it is not obvious how to learn the conditional distribution for $HeartDisease$, given its parents, because we do not know the value of $HeartDisease$ in each case; the same problem arises in learning the distributions for the symptoms. This section

[6] Some records contain the diagnosis suggested by the physician, but this is a causal consequence of the symptoms, which are in turn caused by the disease.

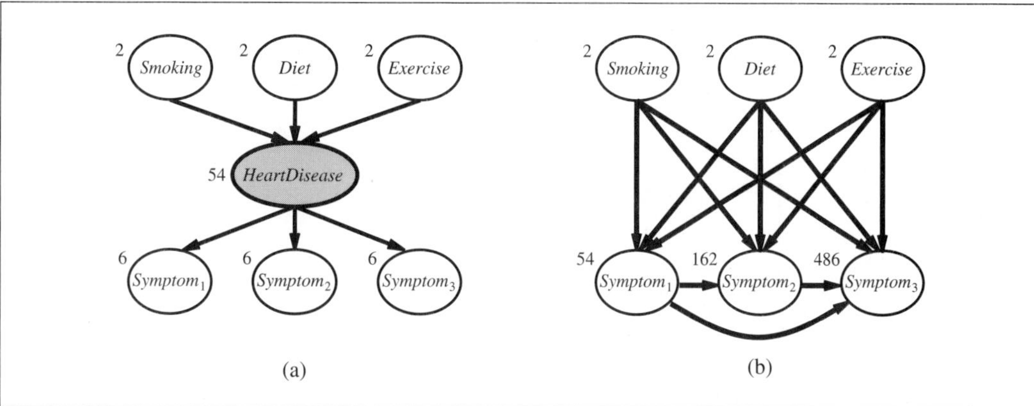


**Figure 20.7** (a) A simple diagnostic network for heart disease, which is assumed to be a hidden variable. Each variable has three possible values and is labeled with the number of independent parameters in its conditional distribution; the total number is 78. (b) The equivalent network with $HeartDisease$ removed. Note that the symptom variables are no longer conditionally independent given their parents. This network requires 708 parameters.

EXPECTATION–MAXIMIZATION

describes an algorithm called **expectation–maximization**, or EM, that solves this problem in a very general way. We will show three examples and then provide a general description. The algorithm seems like magic at first, but once the intuition has been developed, one can find applications for EM in a huge range of learning problems.

### Unsupervised clustering: Learning mixtures of Gaussians

UNSUPERVISED CLUSTERING

**Unsupervised clustering** is the problem of discerning multiple categories in a collection of objects. The problem is unsupervised because the category labels are not given. For example, suppose we record the spectra of a hundred thousand stars; are there different *types* of stars revealed by the spectra, and, if so, how many and what are their characteristics? We are all familiar with terms such as "red giant" and "white dwarf," but the stars do not carry these labels on their hats—astronomers had to perform unsupervised clustering to identify these categories. Other examples include the identification of species, genera, orders, and so on in the Linnæan taxonomy of organisms and the creation of natural kinds to categorize ordinary objects (see Chapter 10).

MIXTURE DISTRIBUTION

COMPONENT

Unsupervised clustering begins with data. Figure 20.8(a) shows 500 data points, each of which specifies the values of two continuous attributes. The data points might correspond to stars, and the attributes might correspond to spectral intensities at two particular frequencies. Next, we need to understand what kind of probability distribution might have generated the data. Clustering presumes that the data are generated from a **mixture distribution**, $P$. Such a distribution has $k$ **components**, each of which is a distribution in its own right. A data point is generated by first choosing a component and then generating a sample from that component. Let the random variable $C$ denote the component, with values $1, \ldots, k$; then the mixture

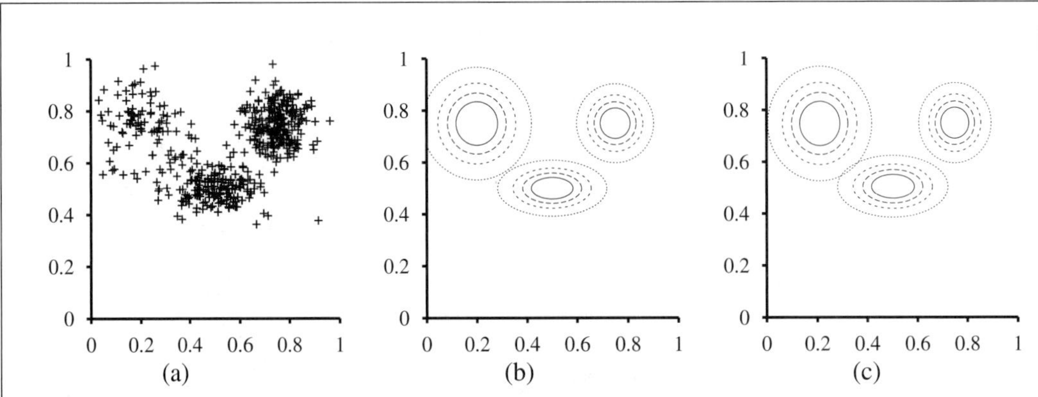


**Figure 20.8** (a) 500 data points in two dimensions, suggesting the presence of three clusters. (b) A Gaussian mixture model with three components; the weights (left-to-right) are 0.2, 0.3, and 0.5. The data in (a) were generated from this model. (c) The model reconstructed by EM from the data in (b).

distribution is given by

$$P(\mathbf{x}) = \sum_{i=1}^{k} P(C=i)\ P(\mathbf{x}|C=i)\ ,$$

where **x** refers to the values of the attributes for a data point. For continuous data, a natural choice for the component distributions is the multivariate Gaussian, which gives the so-called **mixture of Gaussians** family of distributions. The parameters of a mixture of Gaussians are $w_i = P(C=i)$ (the weight of each component), $\boldsymbol{\mu}_i$ (the mean of each component), and $\boldsymbol{\Sigma}_i$ (the covariance of each component). Figure 20.8(b) shows a mixture of three Gaussians; this mixture is in fact the source of the data in (a).

MIXTURE OF GAUSSIANS

The unsupervised clustering problem, then, is to recover a mixture model like the one in Figure 20.8(b) from raw data like that in Figure 20.8(a). Clearly, if we *knew* which component generated each data point, then it would be easy to recover the component Gaussians: we could just select all the data points from a given component and then apply (a multivariate version of) Equation (20.4) for fitting the parameters of a Gaussian to a set of data. On the other hand, if we *knew* the parameters of each component, then we could, at least in a probabilistic sense, assign each data point to a component. The problem is that we know neither the assignments nor the parameters.

The basic idea of EM in this context is to *pretend* that we know the the parameters of the model and then to infer the probability that each data point belongs to each component. After that, we refit the components to the data, where each component is fitted to the entire data set with each point weighted by the probability that it belongs to that component. The process iterates until convergence. Essentially, we are "completing" the data by inferring probability distributions over the hidden variables—which component each data point belongs to—based on the current model. For the mixture of Gaussians, we initialize the mixture model parameters arbitrarily and then iterate the following two steps:

1. E-step: Compute the probabilities $p_{ij} = P(C = i|\mathbf{x}_j)$, the probability that datum $\mathbf{x}_j$ was generated by component $i$. By Bayes' rule, we have $p_{ij} = \alpha P(\mathbf{x}_j|C = i)P(C = i)$. The term $P(\mathbf{x}_j|C = i)$ is just the probability at $\mathbf{x}_j$ of the $i$th Gaussian, and the term $P(C = i)$ is just the weight parameter for the $i$th Gaussian. Define $p_i = \sum_j p_{ij}$.
2. M-step: Compute the new mean, covariance, and component weights as follows:

$$\boldsymbol{\mu}_i \leftarrow \sum_j p_{ij}\mathbf{x}_j/p_i$$

$$\boldsymbol{\Sigma}_i \leftarrow \sum_j p_{ij}(\mathbf{x}_j - \boldsymbol{\mu}_i)(\mathbf{x}_j - \boldsymbol{\mu}_i)^\top/p_i$$

$$w_i \leftarrow p_i \,.$$

INDICATOR VARIABLE

The E-step, or *expectation* step, can be viewed as computing the expected values $p_{ij}$ of the hidden **indicator variables** $Z_{ij}$, where $Z_{ij}$ is 1 if datum $\mathbf{x}_j$ was generated by the $i$th component and 0 otherwise. The M-step, or *maximization* step, finds the new values of the parameters that maximize the log likelihood of the data, given the expected values of the hidden indicator variables.

The final model that EM learns when it is applied to the data in Figure 20.8(a) is shown in Figure 20.8(c); it is virtually indistinguishable from the original model from which the data were generated. Figure 20.9(a) plots the log likelihood of the data according to the current model as EM progresses. There are two points to notice. First, the log likelihood for the final learned model slightly *exceeds* that of the original model, from which the data were generated. This might seem surprising, but it simply reflects the fact that the data were generated randomly and might not provide an exact reflection of the underlying model. The second point is that *EM increases the log likelihood of the data at every iteration.* This fact can be proved in general. Furthermore, under certain conditions, EM can be proven to reach a local maximum in likelihood. (In rare cases, it could reach a saddle point or even a local minimum.) In this sense, EM resembles a gradient-based hill-climbing algorithm, but notice that it has no "step size" parameter!

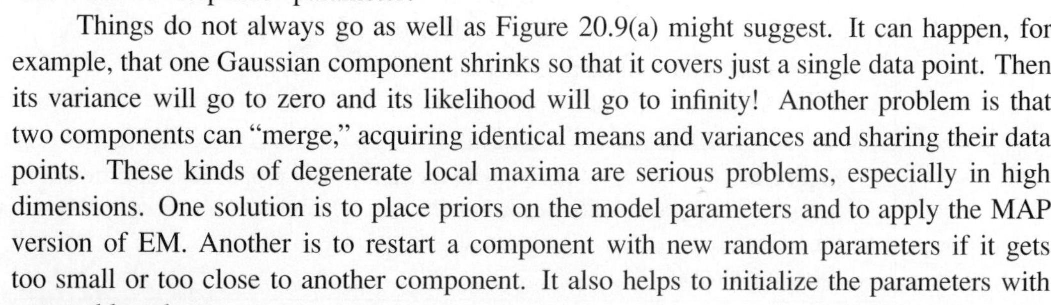

Things do not always go as well as Figure 20.9(a) might suggest. It can happen, for example, that one Gaussian component shrinks so that it covers just a single data point. Then its variance will go to zero and its likelihood will go to infinity! Another problem is that two components can "merge," acquiring identical means and variances and sharing their data points. These kinds of degenerate local maxima are serious problems, especially in high dimensions. One solution is to place priors on the model parameters and to apply the MAP version of EM. Another is to restart a component with new random parameters if it gets too small or too close to another component. It also helps to initialize the parameters with reasonable values.

### Learning Bayesian networks with hidden variables

To learn a Bayesian network with hidden variables, we apply the same insights that worked for mixtures of Gaussians. Figure 20.10 represents a situation in which there are two bags of candies that have been mixed together. Candies are described by three features: in addition to the *Flavor* and the *Wrapper*, some candies have a *Hole* in the middle and some do not.

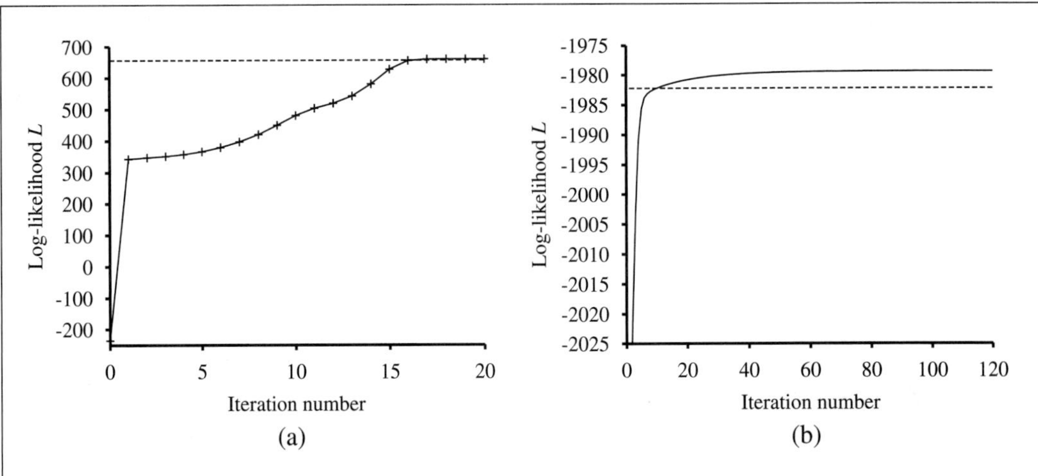


**Figure 20.9** Graphs showing the log-likelihood of the data, $L$, as a function of the EM iteration. The horizontal line shows the log-likelihood according to the true model. (a) Graph for the Gaussian mixture model in Figure 20.8. (b) Graph for the Bayesian network in Figure 20.10(a).

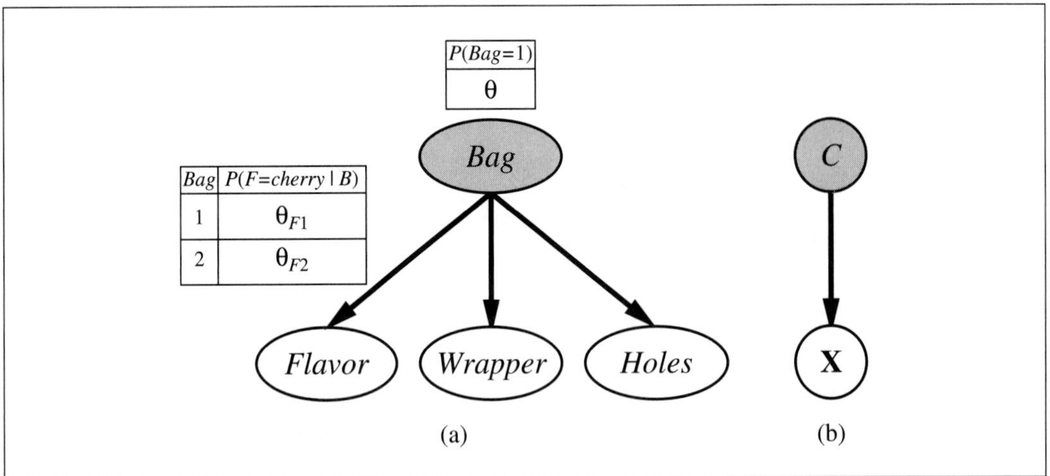


**Figure 20.10** (a) A mixture model for candy. The proportions of different flavors, wrappers, and numbers of holes depend on the bag, which is not observed. (b) Bayesian network for a Gaussian mixture. The mean and covariance of the observable variables **X** depend on the component $C$.

The distribution of candies in each bag is described by a **naive Bayes** model: the features are independent, given the bag, but the conditional probability distribution for each feature depends on the bag. The parameters are as follows: $\theta$ is the prior probability that a candy comes from Bag 1; $\theta_{F1}$ and $\theta_{F2}$ are the probabilities that the flavor is cherry, given that the candy comes from Bag 1 and Bag 2 respectively; $\theta_{W1}$ and $\theta_{W2}$ give the probabilities that the wrapper is red; and $\theta_{H1}$ and $\theta_{H2}$ give the probabilities that the candy has a hole. Notice that the overall model is a mixture model. (In fact, we can also model the mixture of Gaussians as a Bayesian network, as shown in Figure 20.10(b).) In the figure, the bag is is a hidden variable because, once the candies have been mixed together, we no longer know which bag each candy came from. In such a case, can we recover the descriptions of the two bags by observing candies from the mixture?

Let us work through an iteration of EM for this problem. First, let's look at the data. We generated 1000 samples from a model whose true parameters are

$$\theta = 0.5,\ \theta_{F1} = \theta_{W1} = \theta_{H1} = 0.8, \theta_{F2} = \theta_{W2} = \theta_{H2} = 0.3\,. \tag{20.7}$$

That is, the candies are equally likely to come from either bag; the first is mostly cherries with red wrappers and holes; the second is mostly limes with green wrappers and no holes. The counts for the eight possible kinds of candy are as follows:

| | $W = red$ | | $W = green$ | |
|---|---|---|---|---|
| | $H = 1$ | $H = 0$ | $H = 1$ | $H = 0$ |
| $F = cherry$ | 273 | 93 | 104 | 90 |
| $F = lime$ | 79 | 100 | 94 | 167 |

We start by initializing the parameters. For numerical simplicity, we will choose[7]

$$\theta^{(0)} = 0.6,\ \theta_{F1}^{(0)} = \theta_{W1}^{(0)} = \theta_{H1}^{(0)} = 0.6, \theta_{F2}^{(0)} = \theta_{W2}^{(0)} = \theta_{H2}^{(0)} = 0.4\,. \tag{20.8}$$

First, let us work on the $\theta$ parameter. In the fully observable case, we would estimate this directly from the *observed* counts of candies from bags 1 and 2. Because the bag is a hidden variable, we calculate the *expected* counts instead. The expected count $\hat{N}(Bag = 1)$ is the sum, over all candies, of the probability that the candy came from bag 1:

$$\theta^{(1)} = \hat{N}(Bag = 1)/N = \sum_{j=1}^{N} P(Bag = 1 | flavor_j, wrapper_j, holes_j)/N\,.$$

These probabilities can be computed by any inference algorithm for Bayesian networks. For a naive Bayes model such as the one in our example, we can do the inference "by hand," using Bayes' rule and applying conditional independence:

$$\theta^{(1)} = \frac{1}{N} \sum_{j=1}^{N} \frac{P(flavor_j | Bag = 1) P(wrapper_j | Bag = 1) P(holes_j | Bag = 1) P(Bag = 1)}{\sum_i P(flavor_j | Bag = i) P(wrapper_j | Bag = i) P(holes_j | Bag = i) P(Bag = i)}\,.$$

(Notice that the normalizing constant also depends on the parameters.) Applying this formula to, say, the 273 red-wrapped cherry candies with holes, we get a contribution of

$$\frac{273}{1000} \cdot \frac{\theta_{F1}^{(0)} \theta_{W1}^{(0)} \theta_{H1}^{(0)} \theta^{(0)}}{\theta_{F1}^{(0)} \theta_{W1}^{(0)} \theta_{H1}^{(0)} \theta^{(0)} + \theta_{F2}^{(0)} \theta_{W2}^{(0)} \theta_{H2}^{(0)} (1 - \theta^{(0)})} \approx 0.22797\,.$$

Continuing with the other seven kinds of candy in the table of counts, we obtain $\theta^{(1)} = 0.6124$.

[7] It is better in practice to choose them randomly, to avoid local maxima due to symmetry.

Now let us consider the other parameters, such as $\theta_{F1}$. In the fully observable case, we would estimate this directly from the *observed* counts of cherry and lime candies from bag 1. The *expected* count of cherry candies from bag 1 is given by

$$\sum_{j:Flavor_j = cherry} P(Bag = 1 | Flavor_j = cherry, wrapper_j, holes_j) .$$

Again, these probabilities can be calculated by any Bayes net algorithm. Completing this process, we obtain the new values of all the parameters:

$$\begin{aligned} &\theta^{(1)} = 0.6124,\ \theta^{(1)}_{F1} = 0.6684,\ \theta^{(1)}_{W1} = 0.6483,\ \theta^{(1)}_{H1} = 0.6558, \\ &\theta^{(1)}_{F2} = 0.3887, \theta^{(1)}_{W2} = 0.3817,\ \theta^{(1)}_{H2} = 0.3827 . \end{aligned} \qquad (20.9)$$

The log likelihood of the data increases from about $-2044$ initially to about $-2021$ after the first iteration, as shown in Figure 20.9(b). That is, the update improves the likelihood itself by a factor of about $e^{23} \approx 10^{10}$. By the tenth iteration, the learned model is a better fit than the original model ($L = -1982.214$). Thereafter, progress becomes very slow. This is not uncommon with EM, and many practical systems combine EM with a gradient-based algorithm such as Newton–Raphson (see Chapter 4) for the last phase of learning.

The general lesson from this example is that *the parameter updates for Bayesian network learning with hidden variables are directly available from the results of inference on each example. Moreover, only* local *posterior probabilities are needed for each parameter.* For the general case in which we are learning the conditional probability parameters for each variable $X_i$, given its parents —that is, $\theta_{ijk} = P(X_i = x_{ij} | Pa_i = pa_{ik})$—the update is given by the normalized expected counts as follows:

$$\theta_{ijk} \leftarrow \hat{N}(X_i = x_{ij}, Pa_i = pa_{ik}) / \hat{N}(Pa_i = pa_{ik}) .$$

The expected counts are obtained by summing over the examples, computing the probabilities $P(X_i = x_{ij}, Pa_i = pa_{ik})$ for each by using any Bayes net inference algorithm. For the exact algorithms—including variable elimination—all these probabilities are obtainable directly as a by-product of standard inference, with no need for extra computations specific to learning. Moreover, the information needed for learning is available *locally* for each parameter.

### Learning hidden Markov models

Our final application of EM involves learning the transition probabilities in hidden Markov models (HMMs). Recall from Chapter 15 that a hidden Markov model can be represented by a dynamic Bayes net with a single discrete state variable, as illustrated in Figure 20.11. Each data point consists of an observation *sequence* of finite length, so the problem is to learn the transition probabilities from a set of observation sequences (or possibly from just one long sequence).

We have already worked out how to learn Bayes nets, but there is one complication: in Bayes nets, each parameter is distinct; in a hidden Markov model, on the other hand, the individual transition probabilities from state $i$ to state $j$ at time $t$, $\theta_{ijt} = P(X_{t+1} = j | X_t = i)$, are *repeated* across time—that is, $\theta_{ijt} = \theta_{ij}$ for all $t$. To estimate the transition probability

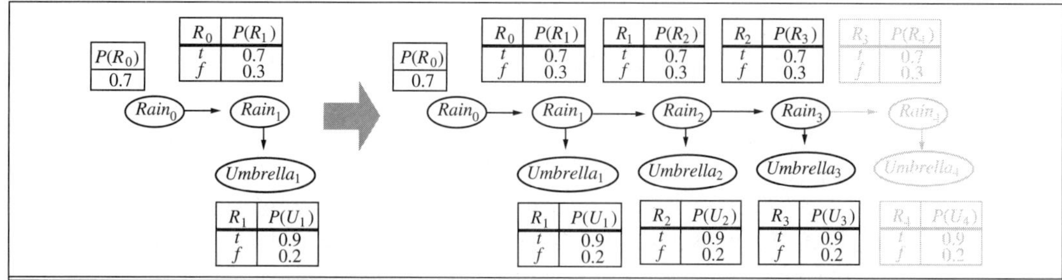


**Figure 20.11** An unrolled dynamic Bayesian network that represents a hidden Markov model (repeat of Figure 15.14).

from state $i$ to state $j$, we simply calculate the expected proportion of times that the system undergoes a transition to state $j$ when in state $i$:

$$\theta_{ij} \leftarrow \sum_t \hat{N}(X_{t+1}=j, X_{t=i}) / \sum_t \hat{N}(X_{t=i}) .$$

Again, the expected counts are computed by any HMM inference algorithm. The **forward–backward** algorithm shown in Figure 15.4 can be modified very easily to compute the necessary probabilities. One important point is that the probabilities required are those obtained by **smoothing** rather than **filtering**; that is, we need to pay attention to subsequent evidence in estimating the probability that a particular transition occurred. As we said in Chapter 15, the evidence in a murder case is usually obtained *after* the crime (i.e., the transition from state $i$ to state $j$) occurs.

## The general form of the EM algorithm

We have seen several instances of the EM algorithm. Each involves computing expected values of hidden variables for each example and then recomputing the parameters, using the expected values as if they were observed values. Let $\mathbf{x}$ be all the observed values in all the examples, let $\mathbf{Z}$ denote all the hidden variables for all the examples, and let $\boldsymbol{\theta}$ be all the parameters for the probability model. Then the EM algorithm is

$$\boldsymbol{\theta}^{(i+1)} = \underset{\boldsymbol{\theta}}{\operatorname{argmax}} \sum_{\mathbf{z}} P(\mathbf{Z}=\mathbf{z}|\mathbf{x}, \boldsymbol{\theta}^{(i)}) L(\mathbf{x}, \mathbf{Z}=\mathbf{z}|\boldsymbol{\theta}) .$$

This equation is the EM algorithm in a nutshell. The E-step is the computation of the summation, which is the expectation of the log likelihood of the "completed" data with respect to the distribution $P(\mathbf{Z}=\mathbf{z}|\mathbf{x}, \boldsymbol{\theta}^{(i)})$, which is the posterior over the hidden variables, given the data. The M-step is the maximization of this expected log likelihood with respect to the parameters. For mixtures of Gaussians, the hidden variables are the $Z_{ij}$s, where $Z_{ij}$ is 1 if example $j$ was generated by component $i$. For Bayes nets, the hidden variables are the values of the unobserved variables for each example. For HMMs, the hidden variables are the $i \rightarrow j$ transitions. Starting from the general form, it is possible to derive an EM algorithm for a specific application once the appropriate hidden variables have been identified.

As soon as we understand the general idea of EM, it becomes easy to derive all sorts of variants and improvements. For example, in many cases the E-step—the computation of posteriors over the hidden variables—is intractable, as in large Bayes nets. It turns out that one can use an *approximate* E-step and still obtain an effective learning algorithm. With a sampling algorithm such as MCMC (see Section 14.5), the learning process is very intuitive: each state (configuration of hidden and observed variables) visited by MCMC is treated exactly as if it were a complete observation. Thus, the parameters can be updated directly after each MCMC transition. Other forms of approximate inference, such as variational and loopy methods, have also proven effective for learning very large networks.

### Learning Bayes net structures with hidden variables

In Section 20.2, we discussed the problem of learning Bayes net structures with complete data. When hidden variables are taken into consideration, things get more difficult. In the simplest case, the hidden variables are listed along with the observed variables; although their values are not observed, the learning algorithm is told that they exist and must find a place for them in the network structure. For example, an algorithm might try to learn the structure shown in Figure 20.7(a), given the information that $HeartDisease$ (a three-valued variable) should be included in the model. If the learning algorithm is not told this information, then there are two choices: either pretend that the data is really complete—which forces the algorithm to learn the parameter-intensive model in Figure 20.7(b)—or *invent* new hidden variables in order to simplify the model. The latter approach can be implemented by including new modification choices in the structure search: in addition to modifying links, the algorithm can add or delete a hidden variable or change its arity. Of course, the algorithm will not know that the new variable it has invented is called $HeartDisease$; nor will it have meaningful names for the values. Fortunately, newly invented hidden variables will usually be connected to pre-existing variables, so a human expert can often inspect the local conditional distributions involving the new variable and ascertain its meaning.

As in the complete-data case, pure maximum-likelihood structure learning will result in a completely connected network (moreover, one with no hidden variables), so some form of complexity penalty is required. We can also apply MCMC to approximate Bayesian learning. For example, we can learn mixtures of Gaussians with an unknown number of components by sampling over the number; the approximate posterior distribution for the number of Gaussians is given by the sampling frequencies of the MCMC process.

So far, the process we have discussed has an outer loop that is a structural search process and an inner loop that is a parametric optimization process. For the complete-data case, the inner loop is very fast—just a matter of extracting conditional frequencies from the data set. When there are hidden variables, the inner loop may involve many iterations of EM or a gradient-based algorithm, and each iteration involves the calculation of posteriors in a Bayes net, which is itself an NP-hard problem. To date, this approach has proved impractical for learning complex models. One possible improvement is the so-called **structural EM** algorithm, which operates in much the same way as ordinary (parametric) EM except that the algorithm can update the structure as well as the parameters. Just as ordinary EM uses the current parameters to compute the expected counts in the E-step and then applies those counts in the M-step to choose new parameters, structural EM uses the current structure to compute

STRUCTURAL EM

expected counts and then applies those counts in the M-step to evaluate the likelihood for potential new structures. (This contrasts with the outer-loop/inner-loop method, which computes new expected counts for each potential structure.) In this way, structural EM may make several structural alterations to the network without once recomputing the expected counts, and is capable of learning nontrivial Bayes net structures. Nonetheless, much work remains to be done before we can say that the structure learning problem is solved.

## 20.4 INSTANCE-BASED LEARNING

So far, our discussion of statistical learning has focused primarily on fitting the parameters of a *restricted* family of probability models to an *unrestricted* data set. For example, unsupervised clustering using mixtures of Gaussians assumes that the data are explained by the *sum* of a *fixed* number of *Gaussian* distributions. We call such methods **parametric learning**. Parametric learning methods are often simple and effective, but assuming a particular restricted family of models often oversimplifies what's happening in the real world, from where the data come. Now, it is true when we have very little data, we cannot hope to learn a complex and detailed model, but it seems silly to keep the hypothesis complexity fixed even when the data set grows very large!

PARAMETRIC LEARNING

In contrast to parametric learning, **nonparametric learning** methods allow the hypothesis complexity to grow with the data. The more data we have, the wigglier the hypothesis can be. We will look at two very simple families of nonparametric **instance-based learning** (or **memory-based learning**) methods, so called because they construct hypotheses directly from the training instances themselves.

NONPARAMETRIC LEARNING

INSTANCE-BASED LEARNING

### Nearest-neighbor models

NEAREST-NEIGHBOR

The key idea of **nearest-neighbor** models is that the properties of any particular input point $\mathbf{x}$ are likely to be similar to those of points in the neighborhood of $\mathbf{x}$. For example, if we want to do **density estimation**—that is, estimate the value of an unknown probability density at $\mathbf{x}$—then we can simply measure the density with which points are scattered in the neighborhood of $\mathbf{x}$. This sounds very simple, until we realize that we need to specify exactly what we mean by "neighborhood." If the neighborhood is too small, it won't contain any data points; too large, and it may include *all* the data points, resulting in a density estimate that is the same everywhere. One solution is to define the neighborhood to be just big enough to include $k$ points, where $k$ is large enough to ensure a meaningful estimate. For fixed $k$, the size of the neighborhood varies—where data are sparse, the neighborhood is large, but where data are dense, the neighborhood is small. Figure 20.12(a) shows an example for data scattered in two dimensions. Figure 20.13 shows the results of $k$-nearest-neighbor density estimation from these data with $k = 3$, 10, and 40 respectively. For $k = 3$, the density estimate at any point is based on only 3 neighboring points and is highly variable. For $k = 10$, the estimate provides a good reconstruction of the true density shown in Figure 20.12(b). For $k = 40$, the neighborhood becomes too large and structure of the data is altogether lost. In practice, using

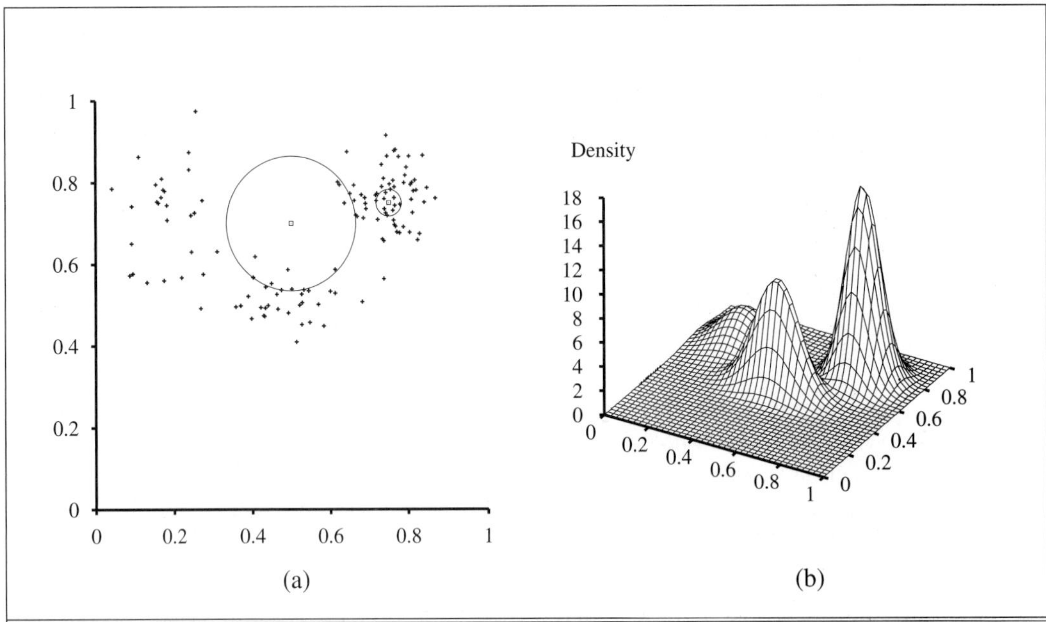


**Figure 20.12** (a) A 128-point subsample of the data shown in Figure 20.8(a), together with two query points and their 10-nearest-neighborhoods. (b) A 3-D plot of the mixture of Gaussians from which the data were generated.

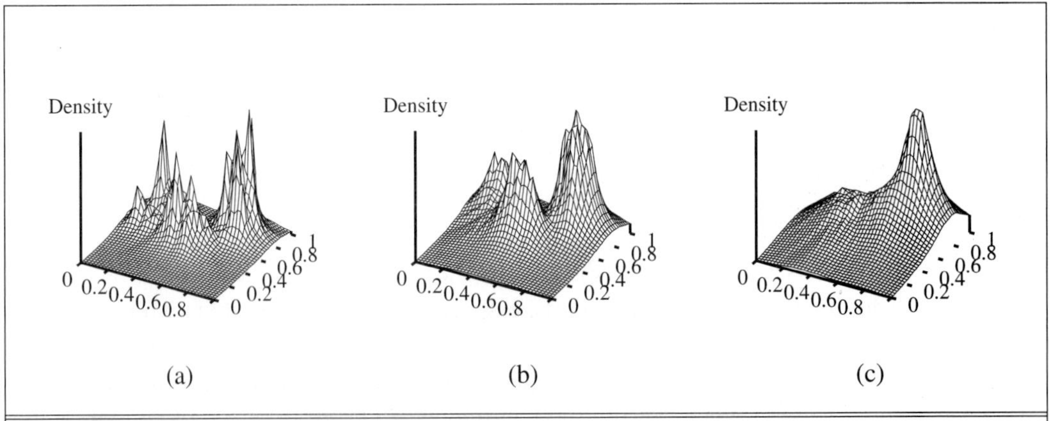


**Figure 20.13** Density estimation using $k$-nearest-neighbors, applied to the data in Figure 20.12(a), for $k = 3$, 10, and 40 respectively.

a value of $k$ somewhere between 5 and 10 gives good results for most low-dimensional data sets. A good value of $k$ can also be chosen by using cross-validation.

To identify the nearest neighbors of a query point, we need a distance metric, $D(\mathbf{x}_1, \mathbf{x}_2)$. The two-dimensional example in Figure 20.12 uses Euclidean distance. This is inappropriate when each dimension of the space is measuring something different—for example, height and weight—because changing the scale of one dimension would change the set of nearest neighbors. One solution is to standardize the scale for each dimension. To do this, we measure the standard deviation of each feature over the whole data set and express feature values as multiples of the standard deviation for that feature. (This is a special case of the **Mahalanobis distance**, which takes into account the covariance of the features as well.) Finally, for discrete features we can use the **Hamming distance**, which defines $D(\mathbf{x}_1, \mathbf{x}_2)$ to be the number of features on which $\mathbf{x}_1$ and $\mathbf{x}_2$ differ.

MAHALANOBIS DISTANCE

HAMMING DISTANCE

Density estimates like those shown in Figure 20.13 define joint distributions over the input space. Unlike a Bayesian network, however, an instance-based representation cannot contain hidden variables, which means that we cannot perform unsupervised clustering as we did with the mixture-of-Gaussians model. We can still use the density estimate to predict a target value $y$ given input feature values $\mathbf{x}$ by calculating $P(y|\mathbf{x}) = P(y, \mathbf{x})/P(\mathbf{x})$, provided that the training data include values for the target feature.

It is also possible to use the nearest-neighbor idea for direct supervised learning. Given a test example with input $\mathbf{x}$, the output $y = h(\mathbf{x})$ is obtained from the $y$-values of the $k$ nearest neighbors of $\mathbf{x}$. In the discrete case, we can obtain a single prediction by majority vote. In the continuous case, we can average the $k$ values or do local linear regression, fitting a hyperplane to the $k$ points and predicting the value at $\mathbf{x}$ according to the hyperplane.

The $k$-nearest-neighbor learning algorithm is very simple to implement, requires little in the way of tuning, and often performs quite well. It is a good thing to try first on a new learning problem. For large data sets, however, we require an efficient mechanism for finding the nearest neighbors of a query point $\mathbf{x}$—simply calculating the distance to every point would take far too long. A variety of ingenious methods have been proposed to make this step efficient by preprocessing the training data. Unfortunately, most of these methods do not scale well with the dimension of the space (i.e., the number of features).

High-dimensional spaces pose an additional problem, namely that nearest neighbors in such spaces are usually a long way away! Consider a data set of size $N$ in the $d$-dimensional unit hypercube, and assume hypercubic neighborhoods of side $b$ and volume $b^d$. (The same argument works with hyperspheres, but the formula for the volume of a hypersphere is more complicated.) To contain $k$ points, the average neighborhood must occupy a fraction $k/N$ of the entire volume, which is 1. Hence, $b^d = k/N$, or $b = (k/N)^{1/d}$. So far, so good. Now let the number of features $d$ be 100 and let $k$ be 10 and $N$ be 1,000,000. Then we have $b \approx 0.89$—that is, the neighborhood has to span almost the entire input space! This suggests that nearest-neighbor methods cannot be trusted for high-dimensional data. In low dimensions there is no problem; with $d = 2$ we have $b = 0.003$.

### Kernel models

KERNEL MODEL

KERNEL FUNCTION

In a **kernel model**, we view each training instance as generating a little density function—a **kernel function**—of its own. The density estimate as a whole is just the normalized sum of all the little kernel functions. A training instance at $\mathbf{x}_i$ will generate a kernel function $K(\mathbf{x}, \mathbf{x}_i)$ that assigns a probability to each point $\mathbf{x}$ in the space. Thus, the density estimate is

$$P(\mathbf{x}) = \frac{1}{N} \sum_{i=1}^{N} K(\mathbf{x}, \mathbf{x}_i) .$$

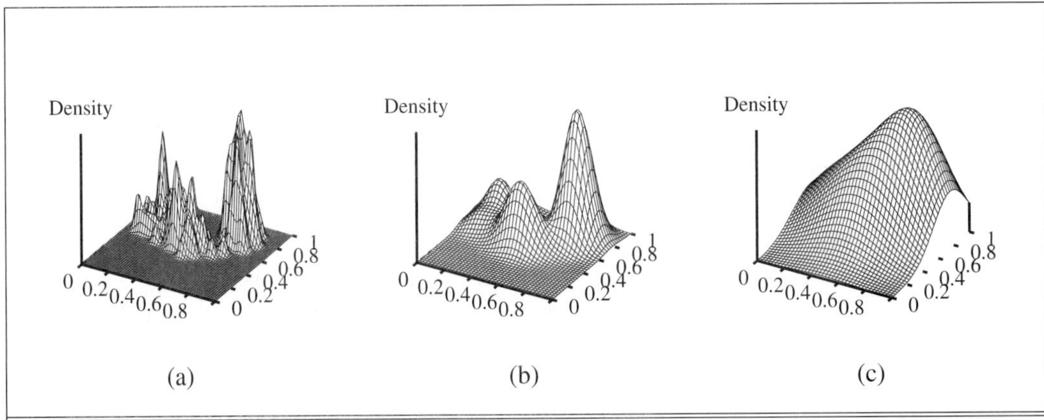


**Figure 20.14** Kernel density estimation for the data in Figure 20.12(a), using Gaussian kernels with $w = 0.02$, $0.07$, and $0.20$ respectively.

The kernel function normally depends only on the *distance* $D(\mathbf{x}, \mathbf{x}_i)$ from **x** to the instance $\mathbf{x}_i$. The most popular kernel function is (of course) the Gaussian. For simplicity, we will assume spherical Gaussians with standard deviation $w$ along each axis, i.e.,

$$K(\mathbf{x}, \mathbf{x}_i) = \frac{1}{(w^2\sqrt{2\pi})^d} e^{-\frac{D(\mathbf{x},\mathbf{x}_i)^2}{2w^2}} ,$$

where $d$ is the number of dimensions in **x**. We still have the problem of choosing a suitable value for $w$; as before, making the neighborhood too small gives a very spiky estimate—see Figure 20.14(a). In (b), a medium value of $w$ gives a very good reconstruction. In (c), too large a neighborhood results in losing the structure altogether. A good value of $w$ can be chosen by using cross-validation.

Supervised learning with kernels is done by taking a *weighted* combination of *all* the predictions from the training instances. (Compare this with $k$-nearest-neighbor prediction, which takes an unweighted combination of the nearest $k$ instances.) The weight of the $i$th instance for a query point **x** is given by the value of the kernel $K(\mathbf{x}, \mathbf{x}_i)$. For a discrete prediction, we can take a weighted vote; for a continuous prediction, we can take weighted average or a weighted linear regression. Notice that making predictions with kernels requires looking at *every* training instance. It is possible to combine kernels with nearest-neighbor indexing schemes to make weighted predictions from just the nearby instances.

## 20.5 Neural Networks

A **neuron** is a cell in the brain whose principal function is the collection, processing, and dissemination of electrical signals. Figure 1.2 on page 11 showed a schematic diagram of a typical neuron. The brain's information-processing capacity is thought to emerge primarily from *networks* of such neurons. For this reason, some of the earliest AI work aimed to create

NEURAL NETWORKS

artificial **neural networks**. (Other names for the field include **connectionism**, **parallel dis-**

**tributed processing**, and **neural computation**.) Figure 20.15 shows a simple mathematical model of the neuron devised by McCulloch and Pitts (1943). Roughly speaking, it "fires" when a linear combination of its inputs exceeds some threshold. Since 1943, much more detailed and realistic models have been developed, both for neurons and for larger systems in the brain, leading to the modern field of **computational neuroscience**. On the other hand, researchers in AI and statistics became interested in the more abstract properties of neural networks, such as their ability to perform distributed computation, to tolerate noisy inputs, and to learn. Although we understand now that other kinds of systems—including Bayesian networks—have these properties, neural networks remain one of the most popular and effective forms of learning system and are worthy of study in their own right.

COMPUTATIONAL NEUROSCIENCE

## Units in neural networks

UNITS LINKS ACTIVATION WEIGHT

Neural networks are composed of nodes or **units** (see Figure 20.15) connected by directed **links**. A link from unit $j$ to unit $i$ serves to propagate the **activation** $a_j$ from $j$ to $i$. Each link also has a numeric **weight** $W_{j,i}$ associated with it, which determines the strength and sign of the connection. Each unit $i$ first computes a weighted sum of its inputs:

$$in_i = \sum_{j=0}^{n} W_{j,i} a_j \ .$$

ACTIVATION FUNCTION

Then it applies an **activation function** $g$ to this sum to derive the output:

$$a_i = g(in_i) = g\left(\sum_{j=0}^{n} W_{j,i} a_j\right) \ . \qquad (20.10)$$

BIAS WEIGHT

Notice that we have included a **bias weight** $W_{0,i}$ connected to a fixed input $a_0 = -1$. We will explain its role in a moment.

The activation function $g$ is designed to meet two desiderata. First, we want the unit to be "active" (near +1) when the "right" inputs are given, and "inactive" (near 0) when the "wrong" inputs are given. Second, the activation needs to be *nonlinear*, otherwise the entire neural network collapses into a simple linear function (see Exercise 20.17). Two choices for $g$

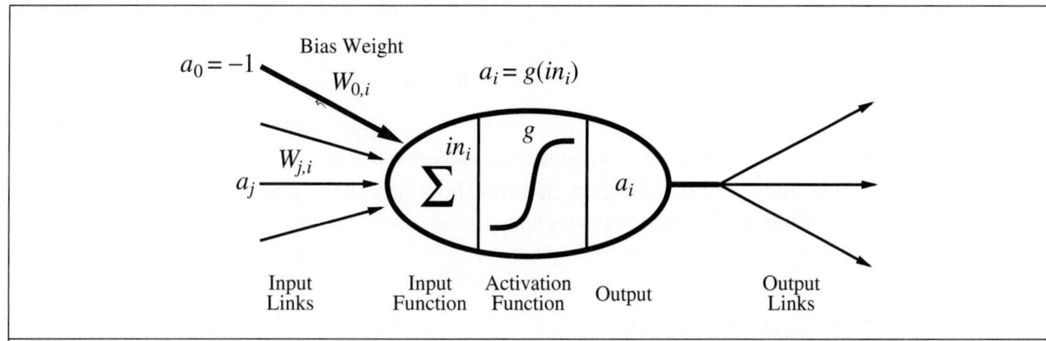


**Figure 20.15** A simple mathematical model for a neuron. The unit's output activation is $a_i = g(\sum_{j=0}^{n} W_{j,i} a_j)$, where $a_j$ is the output activation of unit $j$ and $W_{j,i}$ is the weight on the link from unit $j$ to this unit.

THRESHOLD
SIGMOID FUNCTION
LOGISTIC FUNCTION

are shown in Figure 20.16: the **threshold** function and the **sigmoid function** (also known as the **logistic function**). The sigmoid function has the advantage of being differentiable, which we will see later is important for the weight-learning algorithm. Notice that both functions have a threshold (either hard or soft) at zero; the bias weight $W_{0,i}$ sets the *actual* threshold for the unit, in the sense that the unit is activated when the weighted sum of "real" inputs $\sum_{j=1}^{n} W_{j,i} a_j$ (i.e., excluding the bias input) exceeds $W_{0,i}$.

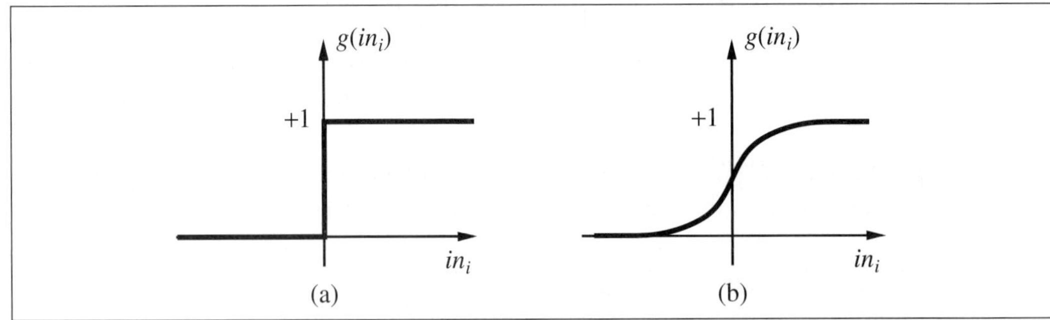


**Figure 20.16** (a) The **threshold** activation function, which outputs 1 when the input is positive and 0 otherwise. (Sometimes the **sign** function is used instead, which outputs $\pm 1$ depending on the sign of the input.) (b) The **sigmoid** function $1/(1+e^{-x})$.

We can get a feel for the operation of individual units by comparing them with logic gates. One of the original motivations for the design of individual units (McCulloch and Pitts, 1943) was their ability to represent basic Boolean functions. Figure 20.17 shows how the Boolean functions AND, OR, and NOT can be represented by threshold units with suitable weights. This is important because it means we can use these units to build a network to compute any Boolean function of the inputs.

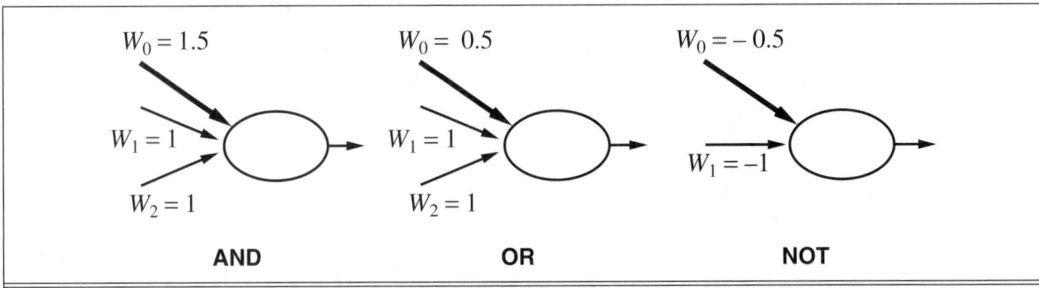


**Figure 20.17** Units with a threshold activation function can act as logic gates, given appropriate input and bias weights.

## Network structures

There are two main categories of neural network structures: acyclic or **feed-forward networks** and cyclic or **recurrent networks**. A feed-forward network represents a function of its current input; thus, it has no internal state other than the weights themselves. A recurrent network, on the other hand, feeds its outputs back into its own inputs. This means that the activation levels of the network form a dynamical system that may reach a stable state or exhibit oscillations or even chaotic behavior. Moreover, the response of the network to a given input depends on its initial state, which may depend on previous inputs. Hence, recurrent networks (unlike feed-forward networks) can support short-term memory. This makes them more interesting as models of the brain, but also more difficult to understand. This section will concentrate on feed-forward networks; some pointers for further reading on recurrent networks are given at the end of the chapter.

Let us look more closely into the assertion that a feed-forward network represents a function of its inputs. Consider the simple network shown in Figure 20.18, which has two input units, two **hidden units**, and an output unit. (To keep things simple, we have omitted the bias units in this example.) Given an input vector $\mathbf{x} = (x_1, x_2)$, the activations of the input units are set to $(a_1, a_2) = (x_1, x_2)$ and the network computes

HIDDEN UNITS

$$\begin{aligned} a_5 &= g(W_{3,5}a_3 + W_{4,5}a_4) \\ &= g(W_{3,5}g(W_{1,3}a_1 + W_{2,3}a_2) + W_{4,5}g(W_{1,4}a_1 + W_{2,4}a_2)) . \end{aligned} \quad (20.11)$$

That is, by expressing the output of each hidden unit as a function of *its* inputs, we have shown that output of the network as a whole, $a_5$, is a function of the network's inputs. Furthermore, we see that the weights in the network act as *parameters* of this function; writing $\mathbf{W}$ for the parameters, the network computes a function $h_{\mathbf{W}}(\mathbf{x})$. By adjusting the weights, we change the function that the network represents. This is how learning occurs in neural networks.

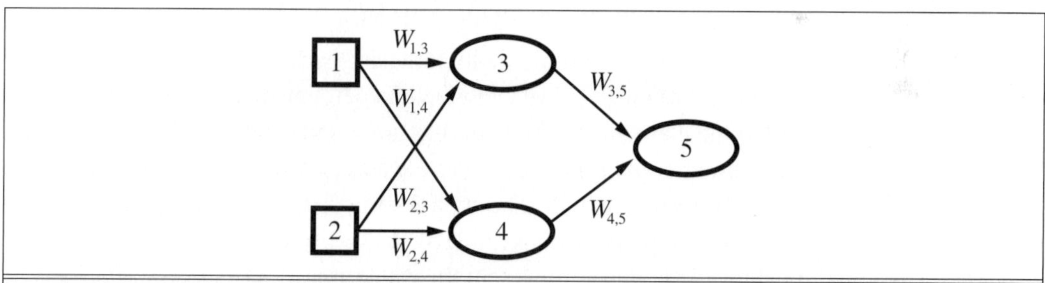


**Figure 20.18** A very simple neural network with two inputs, one hidden layer of two units, and one output.

A neural network can be used for classification or regression. For Boolean classification with continuous outputs (e.g., with sigmoid units), it is traditional to have a single output unit, with a value over 0.5 interpreted as one class and a value below 0.5 as the other. For $k$-way classification, one could divide the single output unit's range into $k$ portions, but it is more common to have $k$ separate output units, with the value of each one representing the relative likelihood of that class given the current input.

LAYERS

Feed-forward networks are usually arranged in **layers**, such that each unit receives input only from units in the immediately preceding layer. In the next two subsections, we will look at single layer networks, which have no hidden units, and multilayer networks, which have one or more layers of hidden units.

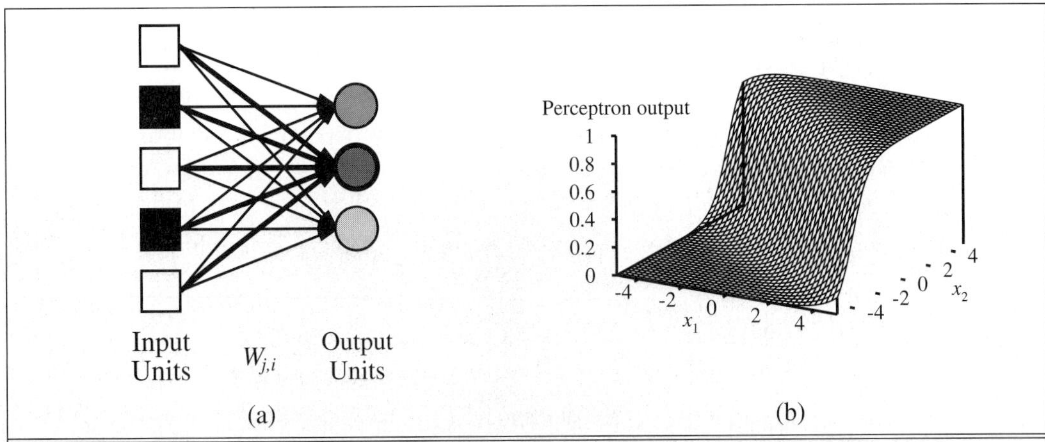


**Figure 20.19** (a) A perceptron network consisting of three perceptron output units that share five inputs. Looking at a particular output unit (say the second one, outlined in bold), we see that the weights on its incoming links have no effect on the other output units. (b) A graph of the output of a two-input perceptron unit with a sigmoid activation function.

### Single layer feed-forward neural networks (perceptrons)

SINGLE-LAYER NEURAL NETWORK

PERCEPTRON

A network with all the inputs connected directly to the outputs is called a **single-layer neural network**, or a **perceptron** network. Since each output unit is independent of the others—each weight affects only one of the outputs—we can limit our study to perceptrons with a single output unit, as explained in Figure 20.19(a).

Let us begin by examining the hypothesis space that a perceptron can represent. With a threshold activation function, we can view the perceptron as representing a Boolean function. In addition to the elementary Boolean functions AND, OR, and NOT (Figure 20.17), a perceptron can represent some quite "complex" Boolean functions very compactly. For example, the **majority function**, which outputs a 1 only if more than half of its $n$ inputs are 1, can be represented by a perceptron with each $W_j = 1$ and threshold $W_0 = n/2$. A decision tree would need $O(2^n)$ nodes to represent this function.

Unfortunately, there are many Boolean functions that the threshold perceptron cannot represent. Looking at Equation (20.10), we see that the threshold perceptron returns 1 if and only if the weighted sum of its inputs (including the bias) is positive:

$$\sum_{j=0}^{n} W_j x_j > 0 \qquad \text{or} \qquad \mathbf{W} \cdot \mathbf{x} > 0\,.$$

LINEAR SEPARATOR

Now, the equation $\mathbf{W} \cdot \mathbf{x} = 0$ defines a *hyperplane* in the input space, so the perceptron returns 1 if and only if the input is on one side of that hyperplane. For this reason, the threshold perceptron is called a **linear separator**. Figure 20.20(a) and (b) show this hyperplane (a line, in two dimensions) for the perceptron representations of the AND and OR functions of two inputs. Black dots indicate a point in the input space where the value of the function is 1, and white dots indicate a point where the value is 0. The perceptron can represent these functions because there is some line that separates all the white dots from all the black

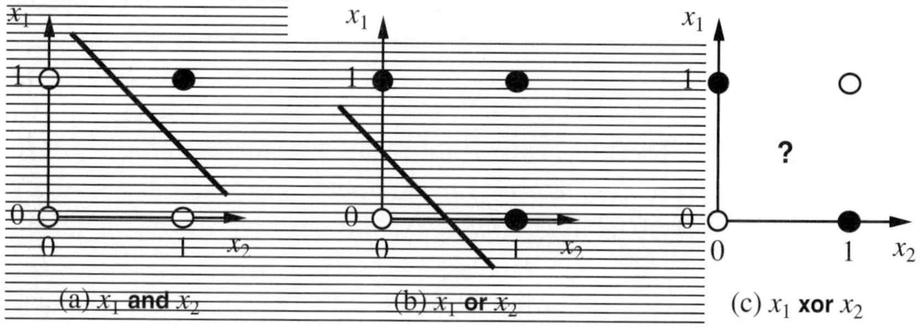

**Figure 20.20** Linear separability in threshold perceptrons. Black dots indicate a point in the input space where the value of the function is 1, and white dots indicate a point where the value is 0. The perceptron returns 1 on the region on the non-shaded side of the line. In (c), no such line exists that correctly classifies the inputs.

LINEARLY SEPARABLE

dots. Such functions are called **linearly separable**. Figure 20.20(c) shows an example of a function that is *not* linearly separable—the XOR function. Clearly, there is no way for a threshold perceptron to learn this function. In general, *threshold perceptrons can represent only linearly separable functions.* These constitute just a small fraction of all functions; Exercise 20.14 asks you to quantify this fraction. Sigmoid perceptrons are similarly limited, in the sense that they represent only "soft" linear separators. (See Figure 20.19(b).)

Despite their limited expressive power, threshold perceptrons have some advantages. In particular, *there is a simple learning algorithm that will fit a threshold perceptron to any linearly separable training set.* Rather than present this algorithm, we will *derive* a closely related algorithm for learning in sigmoid perceptrons.

WEIGHT SPACE

The idea behind this algorithm, and indeed behind most algorithms for neural network learning, is to adjust the weights of the network to minimize some measure of the error on the training set. Thus, learning is formulated as an optimization search in **weight space**.[8] The "classical" measure of error is the **sum of squared errors**, which we used for linear regression on page 720. The squared error for a single training example with input $\mathbf{x}$ and true output $y$ is written as

$$E = \frac{1}{2}Err^2 \equiv \frac{1}{2}(y - h_{\mathbf{W}}(\mathbf{x}))^2 ,$$

where $h_{\mathbf{W}}(\mathbf{x})$ is the output of the perceptron on the example.

We can use gradient descent to reduce the squared error by calculating the partial derivative of $E$ with respect to each weight. We have

$$\begin{aligned} \frac{\partial E}{\partial W_j} &= Err \times \frac{\partial Err}{\partial W_j} \\ &= Err \times \frac{\partial}{\partial W_j}\left(y - g\left(\sum_{j=0}^{n} W_j x_j\right)\right) \\ &= -Err \times g'(in) \times x_j , \end{aligned}$$

[8] See Section 4.4 for general optimization techniques applicable to continuous spaces.

where $g'$ is the derivative of the activation function.[9] In the gradient descent algorithm, where we want to *reduce* $E$, we update the weight as follows:

$$W_j \leftarrow W_j + \alpha \times Err \times g'(in) \times x_j \,, \qquad (20.12)$$

where $\alpha$ is the **learning rate**. Intuitively, this makes a lot of sense. If the error $Err = y - h_{\mathbf{W}}(\mathbf{x})$ is positive, then the network output is too small and so the weights are *increased* for the positive inputs and *decreased* for the negative inputs. The opposite happens when the error is negative.[10]

The complete algorithm is shown in Figure 20.21. It runs the training examples through the net one at a time, adjusting the weights slightly after each example to reduce the error.

EPOCH

Each cycle through the examples is called an **epoch**. Epochs are repeated until some stopping criterion is reached—typically, that the weight changes have become very small. Other methods calculate the gradient for the whole training set by adding up all the gradient contributions in Equation (20.12) before updating the weights. The **stochastic gradient** method selects examples randomly from the training set rather than cycling through them.

STOCHASTIC GRADIENT

**function** PERCEPTRON-LEARNING($examples$, $network$) **returns** a perceptron hypothesis
  **inputs**: $examples$, a set of examples, each with input $\mathbf{x} = x_1, \ldots, x_n$ and output $y$
    $network$, a perceptron with weights $W_j$, $j = 0 \ldots n$, and activation function $g$

  **repeat**
    **for each** $e$ **in** $examples$ **do**
      $in \leftarrow \sum_{j=0}^{n} W_j \, x_j[e]$
      $Err \leftarrow y[e] - g(in)$
      $W_j \leftarrow W_j + \alpha \times Err \times g'(in) \times x_j[e]$
  **until** some stopping criterion is satisfied
  **return** NEURAL-NET-HYPOTHESIS($network$)

**Figure 20.21** The gradient descent learning algorithm for perceptrons, assuming a differentiable activation function $g$. For threshold perceptrons, the factor $g'(in)$ is omitted from the weight update. NEURAL-NET-HYPOTHESIS returns a hypothesis that computes the network output for any given example.

Figure 20.22 shows the learning curve for a perceptron on two different problems. On the left, we show the curve for learning the majority function with 11 Boolean inputs (i.e., the function outputs a 1 if 6 or more inputs are 1). As we would expect, the perceptron learns the function quite quickly, because the majority function is linearly separable. On the other hand, the decision-tree learner makes no progress, because the majority function is very hard (although not impossible) to represent as a decision tree. On the right, we have the restaurant

[9] For the sigmoid, this derivative is given by $g' = g(1-g)$.

[10] For threshold perceptrons, where $g'(in)$ is undefined, the original **perceptron learning rule** developed by Rosenblatt (1957) is identical to Equation (20.12) except that $g'(in)$ is omitted. Since $g'(in)$ is the same for all weights, its omission changes only the magnitude and not the direction of the overall weight update for each example.

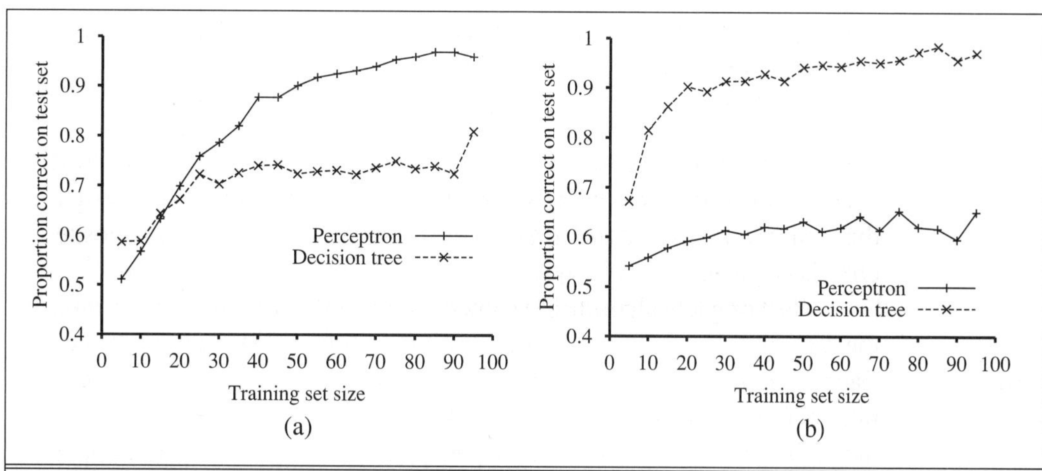


**Figure 20.22** Comparing the performance of perceptrons and decision trees. (a) Perceptrons are better at learning the majority function of 11 inputs. (b) Decision trees are better at learning the *WillWait* predicate in the restaurant example.

example. The solution problem is easily represented as a decision tree, but is not linearly separable. The best plane through the data correctly classifies only 65%.

So far, we have treated perceptrons as deterministic functions with possibly erroneous outputs. It is also possible to interpret the output of a sigmoid perceptron as a *probability*—specifically, the probability that the true output is 1 given the inputs. With this interpretation, one can use the sigmoid as a canonical representation for conditional distributions in Bayesian networks (see Section 14.3). One can also derive a learning rule using the standard method of maximizing the (conditional) log likelihood of the data, as described earlier in this chapter. Let's see how this works.

Consider a single training example with true output value $T$, and let $p$ be the probability returned by the perceptron for this example. If $T=1$, the conditional probability of the datum is $p$, and if $T=0$, the conditional probability of the datum is $(1-p)$. Now we can use a simple trick to write the log likelihood in a form that is differentiable. The trick is that a 0/1

INDICATOR VARIABLE

variable in the *exponent* of an expression acts as an **indicator variable**: $p^T$ is $p$ if $T=1$ and 1 otherwise; similarly $(1-p)^{(1-T)}$ is $(1-p)$ if $T=0$ and 1 otherwise. Hence, we can write the log likelihood of the datum as

$$L = \log p^T (1-p)^{(1-T)} = T \log p + (1-T) \log(1-p)\,. \tag{20.13}$$

Thanks to the properties of the sigmoid function, the gradient reduces to a very simple formula (Exercise 20.16):

$$\frac{\partial L}{\partial W_j} = Err \times x_j\,.$$

Notice that *the weight-update vector for maximum likelihood learning in sigmoid perceptrons is essentially identical to the update vector for squared error minimization.* Thus, we could say that perceptrons have a probabilistic interpretation even when the learning rule is derived from a deterministic viewpoint.

### Multilayer feed-forward neural networks

Now we will consider networks with hidden units. The most common case involves a single hidden layer,[11] as in Figure 20.24. The advantage of adding hidden layers is that it enlarges the space of hypotheses that the network can represent. Think of each hidden unit as a perceptron that represents a soft threshold function in the input space, as shown in Figure 20.19(b). Then, think of an output unit as as a soft-thresholded linear combination of several such functions. For example, by adding two opposite-facing soft threshold functions and thresholding the result, we can obtain a "ridge" function as shown in Figure 20.23(a). Combining two such ridges at right angles to each other (i.e., combining the outputs from four hidden units), we obtain a "bump" as shown in Figure 20.23(b).

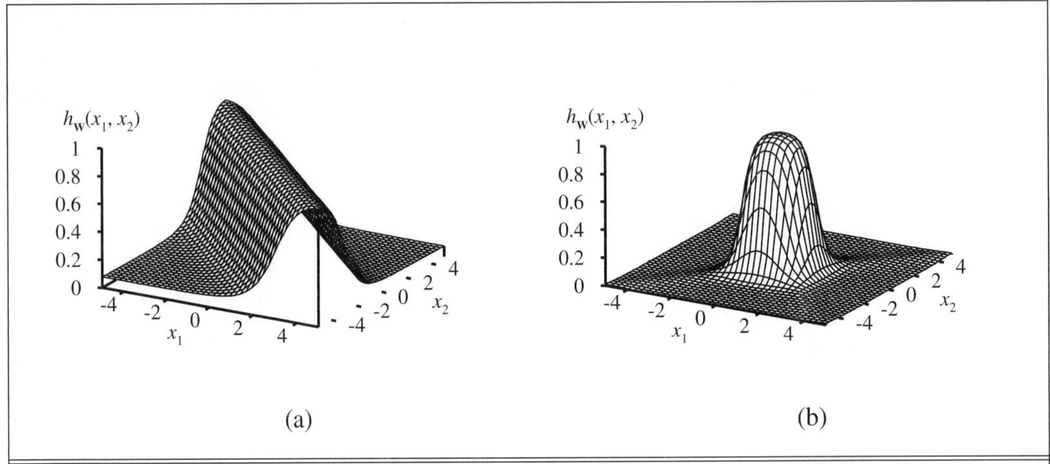


**Figure 20.23** (a) The result of combining two opposite-facing soft threshold functions to produce a ridge. (b) The result of combining two ridges to produce a bump.

With more hidden units, we can produce more bumps of different sizes in more places. In fact, with a single, sufficiently large hidden layer, it is possible to represent any continuous function of the inputs with arbitrary accuracy; with two layers, even discontinuous functions can be represented.[12] Unfortunately, for any *particular* network structure, it is harder to characterize exactly which functions can be represented and which ones cannot.

Suppose we want to construct a hidden layer network for the restaurant problem. We have 10 attributes describing each example, so we will need 10 input units. How many hidden units are needed? In Figure 20.24, we show a network with four hidden units. This turns out to be about right for this problem. The problem of choosing the right number of hidden units in advance is still not well understood. (See page 748.)

Learning algorithms for multilayer networks are similar to the perceptron learning algorithm show in Figure 20.21. One minor difference is that we may have several outputs, so

[11] Some people call this a three-layer network, and some call it a two-layer network (because the inputs aren't "real" units). We will avoid confusion and call it a "single-hidden-layer network."

[12] The proof is complex, but the main point is that the required number of hidden units grows exponentially with the number of inputs. For example, $2^n/n$ hidden units are needed to encode all Boolean functions of $n$ inputs.

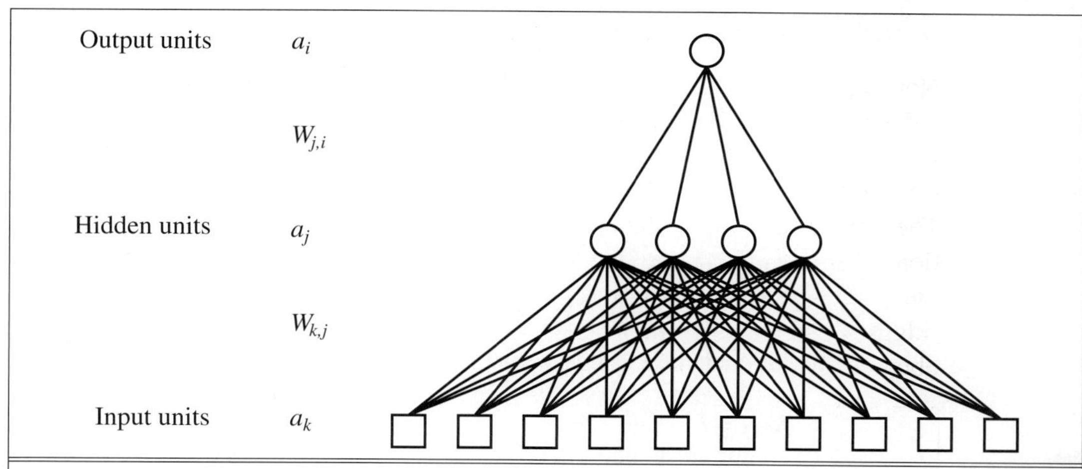


**Figure 20.24** A multilayer neural network with one hidden layer and 10 inputs, suitable for the restaurant problem.

we have an output vector $\mathbf{h_W}(\mathbf{x})$ rather than a single value, and each example has an output vector $\mathbf{y}$. The major difference is that, whereas the error $\mathbf{y} - \mathbf{h_W}$ at the output layer is clear, the error at the hidden layers seems mysterious because the training data does not say what value the hidden nodes should have. It turns out that we can **back-propagate** the error from the output layer to the hidden layers. The back-propagation process emerges directly from a derivation of the overall error gradient. First, we will describe the process with an intuitive justification; then, we will show the derivation.

BACK-PROPAGATION

At the output layer, the weight-update rule is identical to Equation (20.12). We have multiple output units, so let $Err_i$ be $i$th component of the error vector $\mathbf{y} - \mathbf{h_W}$. We will also find it convenient to define a modified error $\Delta_i = Err_i \times g'(in_i)$, so that the weight-update rule becomes

$$W_{j,i} \leftarrow W_{j,i} + \alpha \times a_j \times \Delta_i \ . \qquad (20.14)$$

To update the connections between the input units and the hidden units, we need to define a quantity analogous to the error term for output nodes. Here is where we do the error back-propagation. The idea is that hidden node $j$ is "responsible" for some fraction of the error $\Delta_i$ in each of the output nodes to which it connects. Thus, the $\Delta_i$ values are divided according to the strength of the connection between the hidden node and the output node and are propagated back to provide the $\Delta_j$ values for the hidden layer. The propagation rule for the $\Delta$ values is the following:

$$\Delta_j = g'(in_j) \sum_i W_{j,i} \Delta_i \ . \qquad (20.15)$$

Now the weight-update rule for the weights between the inputs and the hidden layer is almost identical to the update rule for the output layer:

$$W_{k,j} \leftarrow W_{k,j} + \alpha \times a_k \times \Delta_j \ .$$

The back-propagation process can be summarized as follows:

```
function BACK-PROP-LEARNING(examples, network) returns a neural network
  inputs: examples, a set of examples, each with input vector x and output vector y
          network, a multilayer network with L layers, weights W_{j,i}, activation function g

  repeat
     for each e in examples do
        for each node j in the input layer do a_j ← x_j[e]
        for ℓ = 2 to L do
           in_i ← Σ_j W_{j,i} a_j
           a_i ← g(in_i)
        for each node i in the output layer do
           Δ_i ← g'(in_i) × (y_i[e] − a_i)
        for ℓ = L − 1 to 1 do
           for each node j in layer ℓ do
              Δ_j ← g'(in_j) Σ_i W_{j,i} Δ_i
              for each node i in layer ℓ + 1 do
                 W_{j,i} ← W_{j,i} + α × a_j × Δ_i
  until some stopping criterion is satisfied
  return NEURAL-NET-HYPOTHESIS(network)
```

**Figure 20.25** The back-propagation algorithm for learning in multilayer networks.

- Compute the $\Delta$ values for the output units, using the observed error.
- Starting with output layer, repeat the following for each layer in the network, until the earliest hidden layer is reached:
  - Propagate the $\Delta$ values back to the previous layer.
  - Update the weights between the two layers.

The detailed algorithm is shown in Figure 20.25.

For the mathematically inclined, we will now derive the back-propagation equations from first principles. The squared error on a single example is defined as

$$E = \frac{1}{2}\sum_i (y_i - a_i)^2 ,$$

where the sum is over the nodes in the output layer. To obtain the gradient with respect to a specific weight $W_{j,i}$ in the output layer, we need only expand out the activation $a_i$ as all other terms in the summation are unaffected by $W_{j,i}$:

$$\begin{aligned}\frac{\partial E}{\partial W_{j,i}} &= -(y_i - a_i)\frac{\partial a_i}{\partial W_{j,i}} = -(y_i - a_i)\frac{\partial g(in_i)}{\partial W_{j,i}} \\ &= -(y_i - a_i)g'(in_i)\frac{\partial in_i}{\partial W_{j,i}} = -(y_i - a_i)g'(in_i)\frac{\partial}{\partial W_{j,i}}\left(\sum_j W_{j,i}a_j\right) \\ &= -(y_i - a_i)g'(in_i)a_j = -a_j\Delta_i ,\end{aligned}$$

with $\Delta_i$ defined as before. To obtain the gradient with respect to the $W_{k,j}$ weights connecting the input layer to the hidden layer, we have to keep the entire summation over $i$ because each output value $a_i$ may be affected by changes in $W_{k,j}$. We also have to expand out the activations $a_j$. We will show the derivation in gory detail because it is interesting to see how the derivative operator propagates back through the network:

$$\begin{aligned}
\frac{\partial E}{\partial W_{k,j}} &= -\sum_i (y_i - a_i)\frac{\partial a_i}{\partial W_{k,j}} = -\sum_i (y_i - a_i)\frac{\partial g(in_i)}{\partial W_{k,j}} \\
&= -\sum_i (y_i - a_i) g'(in_i)\frac{\partial in_i}{\partial W_{k,j}} = -\sum_i \Delta_i \frac{\partial}{\partial W_{k,j}}\left(\sum_j W_{j,i} a_j\right) \\
&= -\sum_i \Delta_i W_{j,i}\frac{\partial a_j}{\partial W_{k,j}} = -\sum_i \Delta_i W_{j,i}\frac{\partial g(in_j)}{\partial W_{k,j}} \\
&= -\sum_i \Delta_i W_{j,i} g'(in_j)\frac{\partial in_j}{\partial W_{k,j}} \\
&= -\sum_i \Delta_i W_{j,i} g'(in_j)\frac{\partial}{\partial W_{k,j}}\left(\sum_k W_{k,j} a_k\right) \\
&= -\sum_i \Delta_i W_{j,i} g'(in_j) a_k = -a_k \Delta_j \, ,
\end{aligned}$$

where $\Delta_j$ is defined as before. Thus, we obtain the update rules obtained earlier from intuitive considerations. It is also clear that the process can be continued for networks with more than one hidden layer, which justifies the general algorithm given in Figure 20.25.

Having made it through (or skipped over) all the mathematics, let's see how a single-hidden-layer network performs on the restaurant problem. In Figure 20.26, we show two

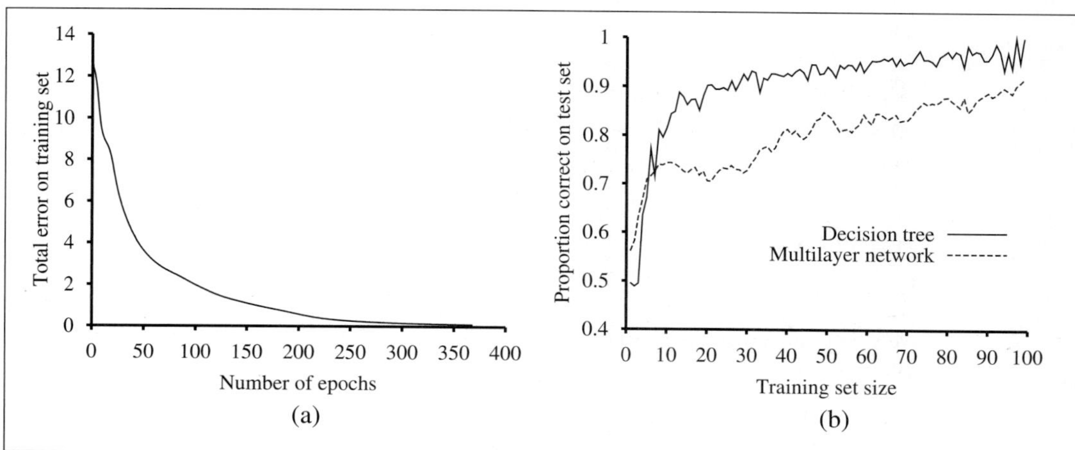


**Figure 20.26** (a) Training curve showing the gradual reduction in error as weights are modified over several epochs, for a given set of examples in the restaurant domain. (b) Comparative learning curves showing that decision-tree learning does slightly better than back-propagation in a multilayer network.

TRAINING CURVE

curves. The first is a **training curve**, which shows the mean squared error on a given training set of 100 restaurant examples during the weight-updating process. This demonstrates that the network does indeed converge to a perfect fit to the training data. The second curve is the standard learning curve for the restaurant data. The neural network does learn well, although not quite as fast as decision-tree learning; this is perhaps not surprising, because the data were generated from a simple decision tree in the first place.

Neural networks are capable of far more complex learning tasks of course, although it must be said that a certain amount of twiddling is needed to get the network structure right and to achieve convergence to something close to the global optimum in weight space. There are literally tens of thousands of published applications of neural networks. Section 20.7 looks at one such application in more depth.

### Learning neural network structures

So far, we have considered the problem of learning weights, given a fixed network structure; just as with Bayesian networks, we also need to understand how to find the best network structure. If we choose a network that is too big, it will be able to memorize all the examples by forming a large lookup table, but will not necessarily generalize well to inputs that have not been seen before.[13] In other words, like all statistical models, neural networks are subject to **overfitting** when there are too many parameters in the model. We saw this in Figure 18.1 (page 652), where the high-parameter models in (b) and (c) fit all the data, but might not generalize as well as the low-parameter models in (a) and (d).

If we stick to fully connected networks, the only choices to be made concern the number of hidden layers and their sizes. The usual approach is to try several and keep the best. The **cross-validation** techniques of Chapter 18 are needed if we are to avoid **peeking** at the test set. That is, we choose the network architecture that gives the highest prediction accuracy on the validation sets.

OPTIMAL BRAIN DAMAGE

If we want to consider networks that are not fully connected, then we need to find some effective search method through the very large space of possible connection topologies. The **optimal brain damage** algorithm begins with a fully connected network and removes connections from it. After the network is trained for the first time, an information-theoretic approach identifies an optimal selection of connections that can be dropped. The network is then retrained, and if its performance has not decreased then the process is repeated. In addition to removing connections, it is also possible to remove units that are not contributing much to the result.

TILING

Several algorithms have been proposed for growing a larger network from a smaller one. One, the **tiling** algorithm, resembles decision-list learning. The idea is to start with a single unit that does its best to produce the correct output on as many of the training examples as possible. Subsequent units are added to take care of the examples that the first unit got wrong. The algorithm adds only as many units as are needed to cover all the examples.

[13] It has been observed that very large networks *do* generalize well *as long as the weights are kept small.* This restriction keeps the activation values in the *linear* region of the sigmoid function $g(x)$ where $x$ is close to zero. This, in turn, means that the network behaves like a linear function (Exercise 20.17) with far fewer parameters.

## 20.6 KERNEL MACHINES

Our discussion of neural networks left us with a dilemma. Single-layer networks have a simple and efficient learning algorithm, but have very limited expressive power—they can learn only linear decision boundaries in the input space. Multilayer networks, on the other hand, are much more expressive—they can represent general nonlinear functions—but are very hard to train because of the abundance of local minima and the high dimensionality of the weight space. In this section, we will explore a relatively new family of learning methods called **support vector machines** (SVMs) or, more generally, **kernel machines**. To some extent, kernel machines give us the best of both worlds. That is, these methods use an efficient training algorithm *and* can represent complex, nonlinear functions.

SUPPORT VECTOR MACHINE

KERNEL MACHINE

The full treatment of kernel machines is beyond the scope of the book, but we can illustrate the main idea through an example. Figure 20.27(a) shows a two-dimensional input space defined by attributes $\mathbf{x} = (x_1, x_2)$, with positive examples ($y = +1$) inside a circular region and negative examples ($y = -1$) outside. Clearly, there is no linear separator for this problem. Now, suppose we re-express the input data using some computed features—i.e., we map each input vector $\mathbf{x}$ to a new vector of feature values, $F(\mathbf{x})$. In particular, let us use the three features

$$f_1 = x_1^2 , \qquad f_2 = x_2^2 , \qquad f_3 = \sqrt{2}x_1x_2 . \tag{20.16}$$

We will see shortly where these came from, but, for now, just look at what happens. Figure 20.27(b) shows the data in the new, three-dimensional space defined by the three features; the data are *linearly separable* in this space! This phenomenon is actually fairly general: if data are mapped into a space of sufficiently high dimension, then they will always be linearly separable. Here, we used only three dimensions,[14] but if we have $N$ data points then, except in special cases, they will always be separable in a space of $N-1$ dimensions or more (Exercise 20.21).

So, is that it? Do we just produce loads of computed features and then find a linear separator in the corresponding high-dimensional space? Unfortunately, it's not that easy. Remember that a linear separator in a space of $d$ dimensions is defined by an equation with $d$ parameters, so we are in serious danger of overfitting the data if $d \approx N$, the number of data points. (This is like overfitting data with a high-degree polynomial, which we discussed in Chapter 18.) For this reason, kernel machines usually find the *optimal* linear separator—the one that has the largest **margin** between it and the positive examples on one side and the negative examples on the other. (See Figure 20.28.) It can be shown, using arguments from computational learning theory (Section 18.5), that this separator has desirable properties in terms of robust generalization to new examples.

MARGIN

QUADRATIC PROGRAMMING

Now, how do we find this separator? It turns out that this is a **quadratic programming** optimization problem. Suppose we have examples $\mathbf{x}_i$ with classifications $y_i = \pm 1$ and we want to find an optimal separator in the input space; then the quadratic programming problem

[14] The reader may notice that we could have used just $f_1$ and $f_2$, but the 3D mapping illustrates the idea better.

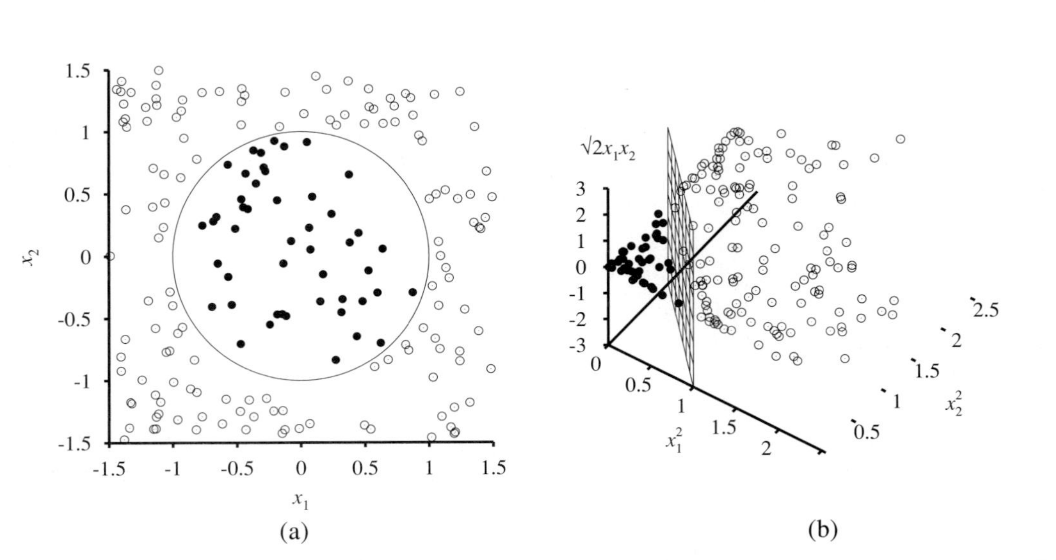


**Figure 20.27** (a) A two-dimensional training set with positive examples as black circles and negative examples as white circles. The true decision boundary, $x_1^2 + x_2^2 \leq 1$, is also shown. (b) The same data after mapping into a three-dimensional input space $(x_1^2, x_2^2, \sqrt{2}x_1x_2)$. The circular decision boundary in (a) becomes a linear decision boundary in three dimensions.

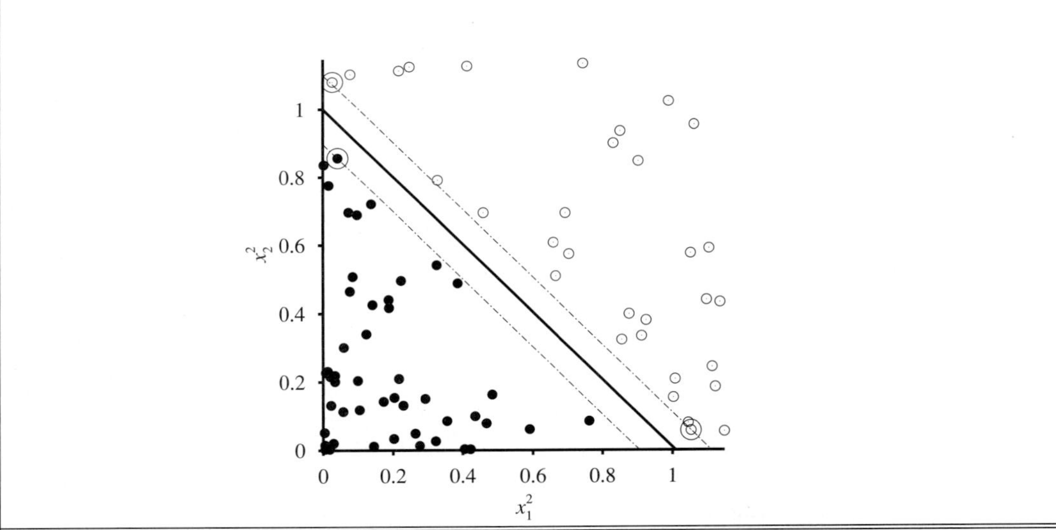


**Figure 20.28** A close-up, projected onto the first two dimensions, of the optimal separator shown in Figure 20.27(b). The separator is shown as a heavy line, with the closest points—the **support vectors**—marked with circles. The **margin** is the separation between the positive and negative examples.

is to find values of the parameters $\alpha_i$ that maximize the expression

$$\sum_i \alpha_i - \frac{1}{2}\sum_{i,j} \alpha_i \alpha_j y_i y_j (\mathbf{x}_i \cdot \mathbf{x}_j) \tag{20.17}$$

subject to the constraints $\alpha_i \geq 0$ and $\sum_i \alpha_i y_i = 0$. Although the derivation of this expression is not crucial to the story, it does have two important properties. First, the expression has a single global maximum that can be found efficiently. Second, *the data enter the expression only in the form of dot products of pairs of points.* This second property is also true of the equation for the separator itself; once the optimal $\alpha_i$s have been calculated, it is

$$h(\mathbf{x}) = \text{sign}\left(\sum_i \alpha_i y_i (\mathbf{x} \cdot \mathbf{x}_i)\right) . \tag{20.18}$$

SUPPORT VECTOR

A final important property of the optimal separator defined by this equation is that the weights $\alpha_i$ associated with each data point are *zero* except for those points closest to the separator—the so-called **support vectors**. (They are called this because they "hold up" the separating plane.) Because there are usually many fewer support vectors than data points, the effective number of parameters defining the optimal separator is usually much less than $N$.

Now, we would not usually expect to find a linear separator in the input space $\mathbf{x}$, but it is easy to see that we can find linear separators in the high-dimensional feature space $F(\mathbf{x})$ simply by replacing $\mathbf{x}_i \cdot \mathbf{x}_j$ in Equation (20.17) with $F(\mathbf{x}_i) \cdot F(\mathbf{x}_j)$. This by itself is not remarkable—replacing $\mathbf{x}$ by $F(\mathbf{x})$ in *any* learning algorithm has the required effect—but the dot product has some special properties. It turns out that $F(\mathbf{x}_i) \cdot F(\mathbf{x}_j)$ can often be computed without first computing $F$ for each point. In our three-dimensional feature space defined by Equation (20.16), a little bit of algebra shows that

$$F(\mathbf{x}_i) \cdot F(\mathbf{x}_j) = (\mathbf{x}_i \cdot \mathbf{x}_j)^2 .$$

The expression $(\mathbf{x}_i \cdot \mathbf{x}_j)^2$ is called a **kernel function**, usually written as $K(\mathbf{x}_i, \mathbf{x}_j)$. In the kernel machine context, this means a function that can be applied to pairs of input data to evaluate dot products in some corresponding feature space. So, we can restate the claim at the beginning of this paragraph as follows: we can find linear separators in the high-dimensional feature space $F(\mathbf{x})$ simply by replacing $\mathbf{x}_i \cdot \mathbf{x}_j$ in Equation (20.17) with a kernel function $K(\mathbf{x}_i, \mathbf{x}_j)$. Thus, we can learn in the high-dimensional space but we compute only kernel functions rather than the full list of features for each data point.

MERCER'S THEOREM

POLYNOMIAL KERNEL

The next step, which should by now be obvious, is to see that there's nothing special about the kernel $K(\mathbf{x}_i, \mathbf{x}_j) = (\mathbf{x}_i \cdot \mathbf{x}_j)^2$. It corresponds to a particular higher-dimensional feature space, but other kernel functions correspond to other feature spaces. A venerable result in mathematics, **Mercer's theorem** (1909), tells us that any "reasonable" [15] kernel function corresponds to *some* feature space. These feature spaces can be very large, even for innocuous-looking kernels. For example, the **polynomial kernel**, $K(\mathbf{x}_i, \mathbf{x}_j) = (1 + \mathbf{x}_i \cdot \mathbf{x}_j)^d$, corresponds to a feature space whose dimension is exponential in $d$. Using such kernels in Equation (20.17), then, *optimal linear separators can be found efficiently in feature spaces with billions (or, in some cases, infinitely many) dimensions.* The resulting linear separators,

[15] Here, "reasonable" means that the matrix $\mathbf{K}_{ij} = K(\mathbf{x}_i, \mathbf{x}_j)$ is positive definite; see Appendix A.

when mapped back to the original input space, can correspond to arbitrarily wiggly, nonlinear boundaries between the positive and negative examples.

We mentioned in the preceding section that kernel machines excel at handwritten digit recognition; they are rapidly being adopted for other applications—especially those with many input features. As part of this process, many new kernels have been designed that work with strings, trees, and other non-numerical data types. It has also been observed that the kernel method can be applied not only with learning algorithms that find optimal linear separators, but also with any other algorithm that can be reformulated to work only with dot products of pairs of data points, as in Equations 20.17 and 20.18. Once this is done, the dot product is replaced by a kernel function and we have a **kernelized** version of the algorithm. This can be done easily for $k$-nearest-neighbor and perceptron learning, among others.

KERNELIZATION

## 20.7 CASE STUDY: HANDWRITTEN DIGIT RECOGNITION

Recognizing handwritten digits is an important problem with many applications, including automated sorting of mail by postal code, automated reading of checks and tax returns, and data entry for hand-held computers. It is an area where rapid progress has been made, in part because of better learning algorithms and in part because of the availability of better training sets. The United States National Institute of Science and Technology (**NIST**) has archived a database of 60,000 labeled digits, each $20 \times 20 = 400$ pixels with 8-bit grayscale values. It has become one of the standard benchmark problems for comparing new learning algorithms. Some example digits are shown in Figure 20.29.

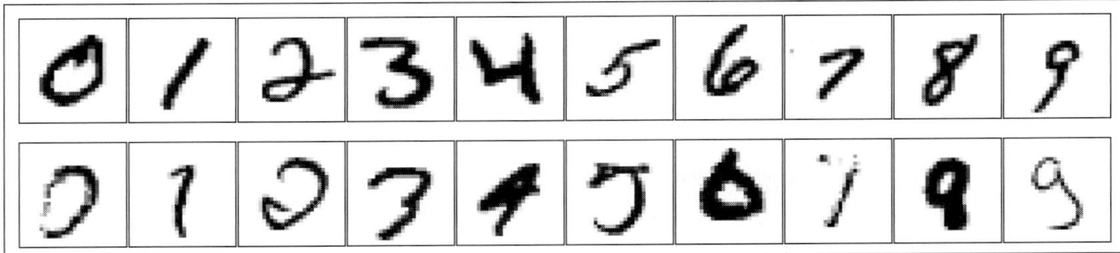

**Figure 20.29** Examples from the NIST database of handwritten digits. Top row: examples of digits 0–9 that are easy to identify. Bottom row: more difficult examples of the same digits.

Many different learning approaches have been tried. One of the first, and probably the simplest, is the **3-nearest-neighbor** classifier, which also has the advantage of requiring no training time. As a memory-based algorithm, however, it must store all 60,000 images, and its runtime performance is slow. It achieved a test error rate of 2.4%.

A **single-hidden-layer neural network** was designed for this problem with 400 input units (one per pixel) and 10 output units (one per class). Using cross-validation, it was found that roughly 300 hidden units gave the best performance. With full interconnections between layers, there were a total of 123,300 weights. This network achieved a 1.6% error rate.

A series of **specialized neural networks** called LeNet were devised to take advantage of the structure of the problem—that the input consists of pixels in a two–dimensional array, and that small changes in the position or slant of an image are unimportant. Each network had an input layer of $32 \times 32$ units, onto which the $20 \times 20$ pixels were centered so that each input unit is presented with a local neighborhood of pixels. This was followed by three layers of hidden units. Each layer consisted of several planes of $n \times n$ arrays, where $n$ is smaller than the previous layer so that the network is down-sampling the input, and where the weights of every unit in a plane are constrained to be identical, so that the plane is acting as a feature detector: it can pick out a feature such as a long vertical line or a short semi-circular arc. The output layer had 10 units. Many versions of this architecture were tried; a representative one had hidden layers with 768, 192, and 30 units, respectively. The training set was augmented by applying affine transformations to the actual inputs: shifting, slightly rotating, and scaling the images. (Of course, the transformations have to be small, or else a 6 will be transformed into a 9!) The best error rate achieved by LeNet was 0.9%.

A **boosted neural network** combined three copies of the LeNet architecture, with the second one trained on a mix of patterns that the first one got 50% wrong, and the third one trained on patterns for which the first two disagreed. During testing, the three nets voted with their weights for each of the ten digits, and the scores are added to determine the winner. The test error rate was 0.7%.

A **support vector machine** (see Section 20.6) with 25,000 support vectors achieved an error rate of 1.1%. This is remarkable because the SVM technique, like the simple nearest-neighbor approach, required almost no thought or iterated experimentation on the part of the developer, yet it still came close to the performance of LeNet, which had had years of development. Indeed, the support vector machine makes no use of the structure of the problem, and would perform just as well if the pixels were presented in a permuted order.

VIRTUAL SUPPORT VECTOR MACHINE

A **virtual support vector machine** starts with a regular SVM and then improves it with a technique that is designed to take advantage of the structure of the problem. Instead of allowing products of all pixel pairs, this approach concentrates on kernels formed from pairs of nearby pixels. It also augments the training set with transformations of the examples, just as LeNet did. A virtual SVM achieved the best error rate recorded to date, 0.56%.

**Shape matching** is a technique from computer vision used to align corresponding parts of two different images of objects. (See Chapter 24.) The idea is to pick out a set of points in each of the two images, and then compute, for each point in the first image, which point in the second image it corresponds to. From this alignment, we then compute a transformation between the images. The transformation gives us a measure of the distance between the images. This distance measure is better motivated than just counting the number of differing pixels, and it turns out that a 3–nearest neighbor algorithm using this distance measure performs very well. Training on only 20,000 of the 60,000 digits, and using 100 sample points per image extracted from a Canny edge detector, a shape matching classifier achieved 0.63% test error.

**Humans** are estimated to have an error rate of about 0.2% on this problem. This figure is somewhat suspect because humans have not been tested as extensively as have machine learning algorithms. On a similar data set of digits from the United States Postal Service, human errors were at 2.5%.

The following figure summarizes the error rates, runtime performance, memory requirements, and amount of training time for the seven algorithms we have discussed. It also adds another measure, the percentage of digits that must be rejected to achieve 0.5% error. For example, if the SVM is allowed to reject 1.8% of the inputs—that is, pass them on for someone else to make the final judgment—then its error rate on the remaining 98.2% of the inputs is reduced from 1.1% to 0.5%.

The following table summarizes the error rate and some of the other characteristics of the seven techniques we have discussed.

| | 3 NN | 300 Hidden | LeNet | Boosted LeNet | SVM | Virtual SVM | Shape Match |
|---|---|---|---|---|---|---|---|
| Error rate (pct.) | 2.4 | 1.6 | 0.9 | 0.7 | 1.1 | 0.56 | 0.63 |
| Runtime (millisec/digit) | 1000 | 10 | 30 | 50 | 2000 | 200 | |
| Memory requirements (Mbyte) | 12 | .49 | .012 | .21 | 11 | | |
| Training time (days) | 0 | 7 | 14 | 30 | 10 | | |
| % rejected to reach 0.5% error | 8.1 | 3.2 | 1.8 | 0.5 | 1.8 | | |

## 20.8 SUMMARY

Statistical learning methods range from simple calculation of averages to the construction of complex models such as Bayesian networks and neural networks. They have applications throughout computer science, engineering, neurobiology, psychology, and physics. This chapter has presented some of the basic ideas and given a flavor of the mathematical underpinnings. The main points are as follows:

- **Bayesian learning** methods formulate learning as a form of probabilistic inference, using the observations to update a prior distribution over hypotheses. This approach provides a good way to implement Ockham's razor, but quickly becomes intractable for complex hypothesis spaces.
- **Maximum a posteriori** (MAP) learning selects a single most likely hypothesis given the data. The hypothesis prior is still used and the method is often more tractable than full Bayesian learning.
- **Maximum likelihood** learning simply selects the hypothesis that maximizes the likelihood of the data; it is equivalent to MAP learning with a uniform prior. In simple cases such as linear regression and fully observable Bayesian networks, maximum likelihood solutions can be found easily in closed form. **Naive Bayes** learning is a particularly effective technique that scales well.
- When some variables are hidden, local maximum likelihood solutions can be found using the EM algorithm. Applications include clustering using mixtures of Gaussians, learning Bayesian networks, and learning hidden Markov models.

- Learning the structure of Bayesian networks is an example of **model selection**. This usually involves a discrete search in the space of structures. Some method is required for trading off model complexity against degree of fit.
- **Instance-based models** represent a distribution using the collection of training instances. Thus, the number of parameters grows with the training set. **Nearest-neighbor** methods look at the instances nearest to the point in question, whereas **kernel** methods form a distance-weighted combination of all the instances.
- **Neural networks** are complex nonlinear functions with many parameters. Their parameters can be learned from noisy data and they have been used for thousands of applications.
- A **perceptron** is a feed-forward neural network with no hidden units that can represent only **linearly separable** functions. If the data are linearly separable, a simple weight-update rule can be used to fit the data exactly.
- **Multilayer feed-forward** neural networks can represent any function, given enough units. The **back-propagation** algorithm implements a gradient descent in parameter space to minimize the output error.

Statistical learning continues to be a very active area of research. Enormous strides have been made in both theory and practice, to the point where it is possible to learn almost any model for which exact or approximate inference is feasible.

## BIBLIOGRAPHICAL AND HISTORICAL NOTES

The application of statistical learning techniques in AI was an active area of research in the early years (see Duda and Hart, 1973) but became separated from mainstream AI as the latter field concentrated on symbolic methods. It continued in various forms—some explicitly probabilistic, others not—in areas such as **pattern recognition** (Devroye *et al.*, 1996) and **information retrieval** (Salton and McGill, 1983). A resurgence of interest occurred shortly after the introduction of Bayesian network models in the late 1980s; at roughly the same time, a statistical view of neural network learning began to emerge. In the late 1990s, there was a noticeable convergence of interests in machine learning, statistics, and neural networks, centered on methods for creating large probabilistic models from data.

The naive Bayes model is one of the oldest and simplest forms of Bayesian network, dating back to the 1950s. Its origins were mentioned in Chapter 13. Its surprising success is partially explained by Domingos and Pazzani (1997). A boosted form of naive Bayes learning won the first KDD Cup data mining competition (Elkan, 1997). Heckerman (1998) gives an excellent introduction to the general problem of Bayes net learning. Bayesian parameter learning with Dirichlet priors for Bayesian networks was discussed by Spiegelhalter *et al.* (1993). The BUGS software package (Gilks *et al.*, 1994) incorporates many of these ideas and provides a very powerful tool for formulating and learning complex probability models. The first algorithms for learning Bayes net structures used conditional independence tests (Pearl, 1988; Pearl and Verma, 1991). Spirtes *et al.* (1993) developed a comprehensive approach and the TETRAD package for Bayes net learning using similar ideas. Algorithmic improvements since then led to a clear victory in the 2001 KDD Cup data mining competition for a Bayes net learning method (Cheng *et al.*, 2002). (The specific task here was a bioinformatics problem with 139,351 features!) A structure-learning approach based on maximizing likelihood was developed by Cooper and Herskovits (1992) and improved by Heckerman *et al.* (1994). Friedman and Goldszmidt (1996) pointed out the influence of the representation of local conditional distributions on the learned structure.

The general problem of learning probability models with hidden variables and missing data was addressed by the EM algorithm (Dempster *et al.*, 1977), which was abstracted from several existing methods including the Baum–Welch algorithm for HMM learning (Baum and Petrie, 1966). (Dempster himself views EM as a schema rather than an algorithm, since a good deal of mathematical work may be required before it can be applied to a new family of distributions.) EM is now one of the most widely used algorithms in science, and McLachlan and Krishnan (1997) devote an entire book to the algorithm and its properties. The specific problem of learning mixture models, including mixtures of Gaussians, is covered by Titterington *et al.* (1985). Within AI, the first successful system that used EM for mixture modeling was AUTOCLASS (Cheeseman *et al.*, 1988; Cheeseman and Stutz, 1996). AUTOCLASS has been applied to a number of real-world scientific classification tasks, including the discovery of new types of stars from spectral data (Goebel *et al.*, 1989) and new classes of proteins and introns in DNA/protein sequence databases (Hunter and States, 1992).

An EM algorithm for learning Bayes nets with hidden variables was developed by Lauritzen (1995). Gradient-based techniques have also proved effective for Bayes nets as well as dynamic Bayes nets (Russell *et al.*, 1995; Binder *et al.*, 1997a). The structural EM algorithm was developed by (Friedman, 1998). The ability to learn the structure of Bayesian networks is closely connected to the issue of recovering *causal* information from data. That is, is it possible to learn Bayes nets in such a way that the recovered network structure indicates real causal influences? For many years, statisticians avoided this question, believing that observational data (as opposed to data generated from experimental trials) could yield only correlational information—after all, any two variables that appear related might in fact be influenced by third, unknown causal factor rather than influencing each other directly. Pearl (2000) has presented convincing arguments to the contrary, showing that there are in fact many cases where causality can be ascertained and developing the **causal network** formalism to express causes and the effects of intervention as well as ordinary conditional probabilities.

CAUSAL NETWORK

Nearest-neighbor models date back at least to (Fix and Hodges, 1951) and have been a standard tool in statistics and pattern recognition ever since. Within AI, they were popularized by (Stanfill and Waltz, 1986), who investigated methods for adapting the distance metric to the data. Hastie and Tibshirani (1996) developed a way to localize the metric to each point in the space, depending on the distribution of data around that point. Efficient indexing schemes for finding nearest neighbors are studied within the algorithms community (see, e.g., Indyk, 2000). Kernel density estimation, also called **Parzen window** density estimation, was investigated initially by Rosenblatt (1956) and Parzen (1962). Since that time, a huge literature has developed investigating the properties of various estimators. Devroye (1987) gives a thorough introduction.

The literature on neural networks is rather too large (approximately 100,000 papers to date) to cover in detail. Cowan and Sharp (1988b, 1988a) survey the early history, beginning with the work of McCulloch and Pitts (1943). Norbert Wiener, a pioneer of cybernetics and control theory (Wiener, 1948), worked with McCulloch and Pitts and influenced a number of young researchers including Marvin Minsky, who may have been the first to develop a working neural network in hardware in 1951 (see Minsky and Papert, 1988, pp. ix–x). Meanwhile, in Britain, W. Ross Ashby (also a pioneer of cybernetics; see Ashby, 1940), Alan Turing, Grey Walter, and others formed the Ratio Club for "those who had Wiener's ideas before Wiener's book appeared." Ashby's *Design for a Brain* (1948, 1952) put forth the idea that intelligence could be created by the use of **homeostatic** devices containing appropriate feedback loops to achieve stable adaptive behavior. Turing (1948) wrote a research report titled *Intelligent Machinery* that begins with the sentence "I propose to investigate the question as to whether it is possible for machinery to show intelligent behaviour" and goes on to describe a recurrent neural network architecture he called "B-type unorganized machines" and an approach to training them. Unfortunately, the report went unpublished until 1969, and was all but ignored until recently.

Frank Rosenblatt (1957) invented the modern "perceptron" and proved the perceptron convergence theorem (1960), although it had been foreshadowed by purely mathematical work outside the context of neural networks (Agmon, 1954; Motzkin and Schoenberg, 1954). Some early work was also done on multilayer networks, including **Gamba perceptrons** (Gamba *et al.*, 1961) and **madalines** (Widrow, 1962). *Learning Machines* (Nilsson, 1965) covers much of this early work and more. The subsequent demise of early perceptron research efforts was hastened (or, the authors later claimed, merely explained) by the book *Perceptrons* (Minsky and Papert, 1969), which lamented the field's lack of mathematical rigor. The book pointed out that single-layer perceptrons could represent only linearly separable concepts and noted the lack of effective learning algorithms for multilayer networks.

The papers in (Hinton and Anderson, 1981), based on a conference in San Diego in 1979, can be regarded as marking the renaissance of connectionism. The two-volume "PDP" (Parallel Distributed Processing) anthology (Rumelhart *et al.*, 1986a) and a short article in *Nature* (Rumelhart *et al.*, 1986b) attracted a great deal of attention—indeed, the number of papers on "neural networks" multiplied by a factor of 200 between 1980–84 and 1990–94. The analysis of neural networks using the physical theory of magnetic spin glasses (Amit *et al.*, 1985) tightened the links between statistical mechanics and neural network theory—providing not only useful mathematical insights but also *respectability*. The back-propagation technique had been invented quite early (Bryson and Ho, 1969) but it was rediscovered several times (Werbos, 1974; Parker, 1985).

Support vector machines were originated in the 1990s (Cortes and Vapnik, 1995) and are now the subject of a fast-growing literature, including textbooks such as Cristianini and Shawe-Taylor (2000). They have proven to be very popular and effective for tasks such as text categorization (Joachims, 2001), bioinformatics research (Brown *et al.*, 2000), and natural language processing, such as the handwritten digit recognition of DeCoste and Scholkopf (2002). A related technique that also uses the "kernel trick" to implicitly represent an exponential feature space is the voted perceptron (Collins and Duffy, 2002).

The probabilistic interpretation of neural networks has several sources, including Baum and Wilczek (1988) and Bridle (1990). The role of the sigmoid function is discussed by Jordan (1995). Bayesian parameter learning for neural networks was proposed by MacKay (1992) and is explored further by Neal (1996). The capacity of neural networks to represent functions was investigated by Cybenko (1988, 1989), who showed that two hidden layers are enough to represent any function and a single layer is enough to represent any *continuous* function. The "optimal brain damage" method for removing useless connections is by LeCun et al. (1989), and Sietsma and Dow (1988) show how to remove useless units. The tiling algorithm for growing larger structures is due to Mézard and Nadal (1989). LeCun *et al.* (1995) survey a number of algorithms for handwritten digit recognition. Improved error rates since then were reported by Belongie *et al.* (2002) for shape matching and DeCoste and Schölkopf (2002) for virtual support vectors.

The complexity of neural network learning has been investigated by researchers in computational learning theory. Early computational results were obtained by Judd (1990), who showed that the general problem of finding a set of weights consistent with a set of examples is NP-complete, even under very restrictive assumptions. Some of the first sample complexity results were obtained by Baum and Haussler (1989), who showed that the number of examples required for effective learning grows as roughly $W \log W$, where $W$ is the number of weights.[16] Since then, a much more sophisticated theory has been developed (Anthony and Bartlett, 1999), including the important result that the representational capacity of a network depends on the *size* of the weights as well as on their number.

RADIAL BASIS FUNCTION

The most popular kind of neural network that we did not cover is the **radial basis function**, or RBF, network. A radial basis function combines a weighted collection of kernels (usually Gaussians, of course) to do function approximation. RBF networks can be trained in two phases: first, an unsupervised clustering approach is used to train the parameters of the Gaussians—the means and variances—are trained, as in Section 20.3. In the second phase, the relative weights of the Gaussians are determined. This is a system of linear equations, which we know how to solve directly. Thus, both phases of RBF training have a nice benefit: the first phase is unsupervised, and thus does not require labelled training data, and the second phase, although supervised, is efficient. See Bishop (1995) for more details.

HOPFIELD NETWORKS

ASSOCIATIVE MEMORY

**Recurrent networks**, in which units are linked in cycles, were mentioned in the chapter but not explored in depth. **Hopfield networks** (Hopfield, 1982) are probably the best-understood class of recurrent networks. They use *bidirectional* connections with *symmetric* weights (i.e., $W_{i,j} = W_{j,i}$), all of the units are both input and output units, the activation function $g$ is the sign function, and the activation levels can only be $\pm 1$. A Hopfield network functions as an **associative memory**: after the network trains on a set of examples, a new stimulus will cause it to settle into an activation pattern corresponding to the example in the training set that *most closely resembles* the new stimulus. For example, if the training set consists of a set of photographs, and the new stimulus is a small piece of one of the photographs, then the network activation levels will reproduce the photograph from which the piece was

[16] This approximately confirmed "Uncle Bernie's rule." The rule was named after Bernie Widrow, who recommended using roughly ten times as many examples as weights.

taken. Notice that the original photographs are not stored separately in the network; each weight is a partial encoding of all the photographs. One of the most interesting theoretical results is that Hopfield networks can reliably store up to $0.138N$ training examples, where $N$ is the number of units in the network.

BOLTZMANN MACHINES

**Boltzmann machines** (Hinton and Sejnowski, 1983, 1986) also use symmetric weights, but include hidden units. In addition, they use a *stochastic* activation function, such that the probability of the output being 1 is some function of the total weighted input. Boltzmann machines therefore undergo state transitions that resemble a simulated annealing search (see Chapter 4) for the configuration that best approximates the training set. It turns out that Boltzmann machines are very closely related to a special case of Bayesian networks evaluated with a stochastic simulation algorithm. (See Section 14.5.)

The first application of the ideas underlying kernel machines was by Aizerman *et al.* (1964), but the full development of the theory, under the heading of support vector machines, is due to Vladimir Vapnik and colleagues (Boser *et al.*, 1992; Vapnik, 1998). Cristianini and Shawe-Taylor (2000) and Schölkopf and Smola (2002) provide rigorous introductions; a friendlier exposition appears in the *AI Magazine* article by Cristianini and Schölkopf (2002).

The material in this chapter brings together work from the fields of statistics, pattern recognition, and neural networks, so the story has been told many times in many ways. Good texts on Bayesian statistics include those by DeGroot (1970), Berger (1985), and Gelman *et al.* (1995). Hastie *et al.* (2001) provide an excellent introduction to statistical learning methods. For pattern classification, the classic text for many years has been Duda and Hart (1973), now updated (Duda *et al.*, 2001). For neural nets, Bishop (1995) and Ripley (1996) are the leading texts. The field of computational neuroscience is covered by Dayan and Abbott (2001). The most important conference on neural networks and related topics is the annual NIPS (Neural Information Processing Conference) conference, whose proceedings are published as the series *Advances in Neural Information Processing Systems*. Papers on learning Bayesian networks also appear in the *Uncertainty in AI* and *Machine Learning* conferences and in several statistics conferences. Journals specific to neural networks include *Neural Computation*, *Neural Networks*, and the *IEEE Transactions on Neural Networks*.

## EXERCISES

**20.1** The data used for Figure 20.1 can be viewed as being generated by $h_5$. For each of the other four hypotheses, generate a data set of length 100 and plot the corresponding graphs for $P(h_i|d_1,\ldots,d_m)$ and $P(D_{m+1} = \mathit{lime}|d_1,\ldots,d_m)$. Comment on your results.

**20.2** Repeat Exercise 20.1, this time plotting the values of $P(D_{m+1} = \mathit{lime}|h_{\mathrm{MAP}})$ and $P(D_{m+1} = \mathit{lime}|h_{\mathrm{ML}})$.

**20.3** Suppose that Ann's utilities for cherry and lime candies are $c_A$ and $\ell_A$, whereas Bob's utilities are $c_B$ and $\ell_B$. (But once Ann has unwrapped a piece of candy, Bob won't buy it.) Presumably, if Bob likes lime candies much more than Ann, it would be wise for Ann to sell her bag of candies once she is sufficiently sure of its lime content. On the other hand, if Ann unwraps too many candies in the process, the bag will be worth less. Discuss the problem of determining the optimal point at which to sell the bag. Determine the expected utility of the optimal procedure, given the prior distribution from Section 20.1.

**20.4** Two statisticians go to the doctor and are both given the same prognosis: A 40% chance that the problem is the deadly disease $A$, and a 60% chance of the fatal disease $B$. Fortunately, there are anti-$A$ and anti-$B$ drugs that are inexpensive, 100% effective, and free of side-effects. The statisticians have the choice of taking one drug, both, or neither. What will the first statistician (an avid Bayesian) do? How about the second statistician, who always uses the maximum likelihood hypothesis?

The doctor does some research and discovers that disease $B$ actually comes in two versions, dextro-$B$ and levo-$B$, which are equally likely and equally treatable by the anti-$B$ drug. Now that there are three hypotheses, what will the two statisticians do?

**20.5** Explain how to apply the boosting method of Chapter 18 to naive Bayes learning. Test the performance of the resulting algorithm on the restaurant learning problem.

**20.6** Consider $m$ data points $(x_j, y_j)$, where the $y_j$s are generated from the $x_j$s according to the linear Gaussian model in Equation (20.5). Find the values of $\theta_1$, $\theta_2$, and $\sigma$ that maximize the conditional log likelihood of the data.

**20.7** Consider the noisy-OR model for fever described in Section 14.3. Explain how to apply maximum-likelihood learning to fit the parameters of such a model to a set of complete data. (*Hint*: use the chain rule for partial derivatives.)

**20.8** This exercise investigates properties of the Beta distribution defined in Equation (20.6).

**a.** By integrating over the range $[0, 1]$, show that the normalization constant for the distribution $\text{beta}[a, b]$ is given by $\alpha = \Gamma(a + b)/\Gamma(a)\Gamma(b)$ where $\Gamma(x)$ is the **Gamma function**, defined by $\Gamma(x+1) = x \cdot \Gamma(x)$ and $\Gamma(1) = 1$. (For integer $x$, $\Gamma(x+1) = x!$.)

GAMMA FUNCTION

**b.** Show that the mean is $a/(a + b)$.

**c.** Find the mode(s) (the most likely value(s) of $\theta$).

**d.** Describe the distribution $\text{beta}[\epsilon, \epsilon]$ for very small $\epsilon$. What happens as such a distribution is updated?

**20.9** Consider an arbitrary Bayesian network, a complete data set for that network, and the likelihood for the data set according to the network. Give a simple proof that the likelihood of the data cannot decrease if we add a new link to the network and recompute the maximum-likelihood parameter values.

**20.10** Consider the application of EM to learn the parameters for the network in Figure 20.10(a), given the true parameters in Equation (20.7).

**a.** Explain why the EM algorithm would not work if there were just two attributes in the model rather than three.

**b.** Show the calculations for the first iteration of EM starting from Equation (20.8).

**c.** What happens if we start with all the parameters set to the same value $p$? (*Hint*: you may find it helpful to investigate this empirically before deriving the general result.)

**d.** Write out an expression for the log likelihood of the tabulated candy data on page 729 in terms of the parameters, calculate the partial derivatives with respect to each parameter, and investigate the nature of the fixed point reached in part (c).

**20.11** Construct by hand a neural network that computes the XOR function of two inputs. Make sure to specify what sort of units you are using.

**20.12** Construct a support vector machine that computes the XOR function. It will be convenient to use values of 1 and –1 instead of 1 and 0 for the inputs and for the outputs. So an example looks like $([-1, 1], 1)$ or $([-1, -1], -1)$. It is typical to map an input $\mathbf{x}$ into a space consisting of five dimensions, the two original dimensions $x_1$ and $x_2$, and the three combination $x_1^2$, $x_2^2$ and $x_1\, x_2$. But for this exercise we will consider only the two dimensions $x_1$ and $x_1\, x_2$. Draw the four input points in this space, and the maximal margin separator. What is the margin? Now draw the separating line back in the original Euclidean input space.

**20.13** A simple perceptron cannot represent XOR (or, generally, the parity function of its inputs). Describe what happens to the weights of a four-input, step-function perceptron, beginning with all weights set to 0.1, as examples of the parity function arrive.

**20.14** Recall from Chapter 18 that there are $2^{2^n}$ distinct Boolean functions of $n$ inputs. How many of these are representable by a threshold perceptron?

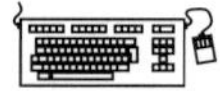

**20.15** Consider the following set of examples, each with six inputs and one target output:

| | | | | | | | | | | | | | | |
|---|---|---|---|---|---|---|---|---|---|---|---|---|---|---|
| $I_1$ | 1 | 1 | 1 | 1 | 1 | 1 | 1 | 0 | 0 | 0 | 0 | 0 | 0 | 0 |
| $I_2$ | 0 | 0 | 0 | 1 | 1 | 0 | 0 | 1 | 1 | 0 | 1 | 0 | 1 | 1 |
| $I_3$ | 1 | 1 | 1 | 0 | 1 | 0 | 0 | 1 | 1 | 0 | 0 | 0 | 1 | 1 |
| $I_4$ | 0 | 1 | 0 | 0 | 1 | 0 | 0 | 1 | 0 | 1 | 1 | 1 | 0 | 1 |
| $I_5$ | 0 | 0 | 1 | 1 | 0 | 1 | 1 | 0 | 1 | 1 | 0 | 0 | 1 | 0 |
| $I_6$ | 0 | 0 | 0 | 1 | 0 | 1 | 0 | 1 | 1 | 0 | 1 | 1 | 1 | 0 |
| $T$ | 1 | 1 | 1 | 1 | 1 | 1 | 0 | 1 | 0 | 0 | 0 | 0 | 0 | 0 |

**a.** Run the perceptron learning rule on these data and show the final weights.

**b.** Run the decision tree learning rule, and show the resulting decision tree.

**c.** Comment on your results.

**20.16** Starting from Equation (20.13), show that $\partial L/\partial W_j = Err \times x_j$.

**20.17** Suppose you had a neural network with linear activation functions. That is, for each unit the output is some constant $c$ times the weighted sum of the inputs.

**a.** Assume that the network has one hidden layer. For a given assignment to the weights $\mathbf{W}$, write down equations for the value of the units in the output layer as a function of $\mathbf{W}$ and the input layer $\mathbf{I}$, without any explicit mention to the output of the hidden layer. Show that there is a network with no hidden units that computes the same function.

**b**. Repeat the calculation in part (a), this time for a network with any number of hidden layers. What can you conclude about linear activation functions?

**20.18** Implement a data structure for layered, feed-forward neural networks, remembering to provide the information needed for both forward evaluation and backward propagation. Using this data structure, write a function NEURAL-NETWORK-OUTPUT that takes an example and a network and computes the appropriate output values.

**20.19** Suppose that a training set contains only a single example, repeated 100 times. In 80 of the 100 cases, the single output value is 1; in the other 20, it is 0. What will a back-propagation network predict for this example, assuming that it has been trained and reaches a global optimum? (*Hint:* to find the global optimum, differentiate the error function and set to zero.)

**20.20** The network in Figure 20.24 has four hidden nodes. This number was chosen somewhat arbitrarily. Run systematic experiments to measure the learning curves for networks with different numbers of hidden nodes. What is the optimal number? Would it be possible to use a cross-validation method to find the best network before the fact?

**20.21** Consider the problem of separating $N$ data points into positive and negative examples using a linear separator. Clearly, this can always be done for $N=2$ points on a line of dimension $d=1$, regardless of how the points are labelled or where they are located (unless the points are in the same place).

**a**. Show that it can always be done for $N=3$ points on a plane of dimension $d=2$, unless they are collinear.

**b**. Show that it cannot always be done for $N=4$ points on a plane of dimension $d=2$.

**c**. Show that it can always be done for $N=4$ points in a space of dimension $d=3$, unless they are coplanar.

**d**. Show that it cannot always be done for $N=5$ points in a space of dimension $d=3$.

**e**. The ambitious student may wish to prove that $N$ points in general position (but not $N+1$ are linearly separable in a space of dimension $N-1$. From this it follows that the **VC dimension** (see Chapter 18) of linear halfspaces in dimension $N-1$ is $N$.

# 21 REINFORCEMENT LEARNING

*In which we examine how an agent can learn from success and failure, from reward and punishment.*

## 21.1 INTRODUCTION

Chapters 18 and 20 covered learning methods that learn functions and probability models from example. In this chapter, we will study how agents can learn *what to do*, particularly when there is no teacher telling the agent what action to take in each circumstance.

For example, we know an agent can learn to play chess by supervised learning—by being given examples of game situations along with the best moves for those situations. But if there is no friendly teacher providing examples, what can the agent do? By trying random moves, the agent can eventually build a predictive model of its environment: what the board will be like after it makes a given move and even how the opponent is likely to reply in a given situation. The problem is this: *without some feedback about what is good and what is bad, the agent will have no grounds for deciding which move to make.* The agent needs to know that something good has happened when it wins and that something bad has happened when it loses. This kind of feedback is called a **reward**, or **reinforcement**. In games like chess, the reinforcement is received only at the end of the game. In other environments, the rewards come more frequently. In ping-pong, each point scored can be considered a reward; when learning to crawl, any forward motion is an achievement. Our framework for agents regards the reward as *part* of the input percept, but the agent must be "hardwired" to recognize that part as a reward rather than as just another sensory input. Thus, animals seem to be hardwired to recognize pain and hunger as negative rewards and pleasure and food intake as positive rewards. Reinforcement has been carefully studied by animal psychologists for over 60 years.

Rewards were introduced in Chapter 17, where they served to define optimal policies in **Markov decision processes** (MDPs). An optimal policy is a policy that maximizes the expected total reward. The task of **reinforcement learning** is to use observed rewards to learn an optimal (or nearly optimal) policy for the environment. Whereas in Chapter 17 the agent has a complete model of the environment and knows the reward function, here we assume no prior knowledge of either. Imagine playing a new game whose rules you don't know; after a hundred or so moves, your opponent announces, "You lose." This is reinforcement learning in a nutshell.

In many complex domains, reinforcement learning is the only feasible way to train a program to perform at high levels. For example, in game playing, it is very hard for a human to provide accurate and consistent evaluations of large numbers of positions, which would be needed to train an evaluation function directly from examples. Instead, the program can be told when it has won or lost, and it can use this information to learn an evaluation function that gives reasonably accurate estimates of the probability of winning from any given position. Similarly, it is extremely difficult to program an agent to fly a helicopter; yet given appropriate negative rewards for crashing, wobbling, or deviating from a set course, an agent can learn to fly by itself.

Reinforcement learning might be considered to encompass all of AI: an agent is placed in an environment and must learn to behave successfully therein. To keep the chapter manageable, we will concentrate on simple settings and simple agent designs. For the most part, we will assume a fully observable environment, so that the current state is supplied by each percept. On the other hand, we will assume that the agent does not know how the environment works or what its actions do, and we will allow for probabilistic action outcomes. We will consider three of the agent designs first introduced in Chapter 2:

- A **utility-based agent** learns a utility function on states and uses it to select actions that maximize the expected outcome utility.
- Q-LEARNING ACTION-VALUE A **Q-learning** agent learns an **action-value** function, or $Q$-function, giving the expected utility of taking a given action in a given state.
- A **reflex agent** learns a policy that maps directly from states to actions.

A utility-based agent must also have a model of the environment in order to make decisions, because it must know the states to which its actions will lead. For example, in order to make use of a backgammon evaluation function, a backgammon program must know what its legal moves are *and how they affect the board position*. Only in this way can it apply the utility function to the outcome states. A $Q$-learning agent, on the other hand, can compare the values of its available choices without needing to know their outcomes, so it does not need a model of the environment. On the other hand, because they do not know where their actions lead, $Q$-learning agents cannot look ahead; this can seriously restrict their ability to learn, as we shall see.

PASSIVE LEARNING

We begin in Section 21.2 with **passive learning**, where the agent's policy is fixed and the task is to learn the utilities of states (or state–action pairs); this could also involve learning a model of the environment. Section 21.3 covers **active learning**, where the agent must also learn what to do. The principal issue is **exploration**: an agent must experience as much as possible of its environment in order to learn how to behave in it. Section 21.4 discusses how an agent can use inductive learning to learn much faster from its experiences. Section 21.5 covers methods for learning direct policy representations in reflex agents. An understanding of Markov decision processes (Chapter 17) is essential for this chapter.

ACTIVE LEARNING

EXPLORATION

## 21.2 PASSIVE REINFORCEMENT LEARNING

To keep things simple, we start with the case of a passive learning agent using a state-based representation in a fully observable environment. In passive learning, the agent's policy $\pi$ is fixed: in state $s$, it always executes the action $\pi(s)$. Its goal is simply to learn how good the policy is—that is, to learn the utility function $U^{\pi}(s)$. We will use as our example the $4 \times 3$ world introduced in Chapter 17. Figure 21.1 shows a policy for that world and the corresponding utilities. Clearly, the passive learning task is similar to the **policy evaluation** task, part of the **policy iteration** algorithm described in Section 17.3. The main difference is that the passive learning agent does not know the **transition model** $T(s, a, s')$, which specifies the probability of reaching state $s'$ from state $s$ after doing action $a$; nor does it know the **reward function** $R(s)$, which specifies the reward for each state.

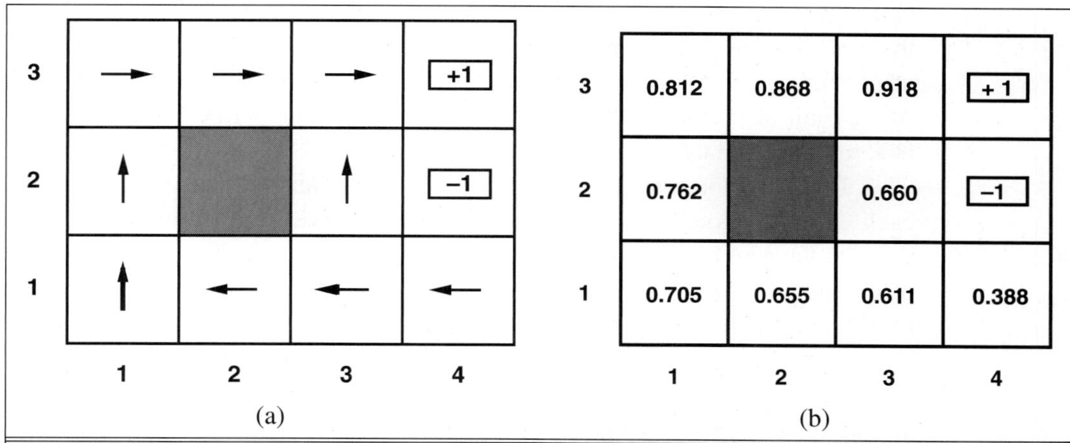


**Figure 21.1** (a) A policy $\pi$ for the $4 \times 3$ world; this policy happens to be optimal with rewards of $R(s) = -0.04$ in the nonterminal states and no discounting. (b) The utilities of the states in the $4 \times 3$ world, given policy $\pi$.

TRIAL The agent executes a set of **trials** in the environment using its policy $\pi$. In each trial, the agent starts in state (1,1) and experiences a sequence of state transitions until it reaches one of the terminal states, (4,2) or (4,3). Its percepts supply both the current state and the reward received in that state. Typical trials might look like this:

$$(1,1)_{\text{-.04}} \rightarrow (1,2)_{\text{-.04}} \rightarrow (1,3)_{\text{-.04}} \rightarrow (1,2)_{\text{-.04}} \rightarrow (1,3)_{\text{-.04}} \rightarrow (2,3)_{\text{-.04}} \rightarrow (3,3)_{\text{-.04}} \rightarrow (4,3)_{\text{+1}}$$
$$(1,1)_{\text{-.04}} \rightarrow (1,2)_{\text{-.04}} \rightarrow (1,3)_{\text{-.04}} \rightarrow (2,3)_{\text{-.04}} \rightarrow (3,3)_{\text{-.04}} \rightarrow (3,2)_{\text{-.04}} \rightarrow (3,3)_{\text{-.04}} \rightarrow (4,3)_{\text{+1}}$$
$$(1,1)_{\text{-.04}} \rightarrow (2,1)_{\text{-.04}} \rightarrow (3,1)_{\text{-.04}} \rightarrow (3,2)_{\text{-.04}} \rightarrow (4,2)_{\text{-1}} \,.$$

Note that each state percept is subscripted with the reward received. The object is to use the information about rewards to learn the expected utility $U^{\pi}(s)$ associated with each nonterminal state $s$. The utility is defined to be the expected sum of (discounted) rewards obtained if policy $\pi$ is followed. As in Equation (17.3) on page 619, this is written as

$$U^\pi(s) = E\left[\sum_{t=0}^{\infty} \gamma^t R(s_t) \mid \pi, s_0 = s\right] . \tag{21.1}$$

We will include a **discount factor** $\gamma$ in all of our equations, but for the $4 \times 3$ world we will set $\gamma = 1$.

### Direct utility estimation

DIRECT UTILITY ESTIMATION

ADAPTIVE CONTROL THEORY

A simple method for **direct utility estimation** was invented in the late 1950s in the area of **adaptive control theory** by Widrow and Hoff (1960). The idea is that the utility of a state is the expected total reward from that state onward, and each trial provides a *sample* of this value for each state visited. For example, the first trial in the set of three given earlier provides a sample total reward of 0.72 for state (1,1), two samples of 0.76 and 0.84 for (1,2), two samples of 0.80 and 0.88 for (1,3), and so on. Thus, at the end of each sequence, the algorithm calculates the observed reward-to-go for each state and updates the estimated utility for that state accordingly, just by keeping a running average for each state in a table. In the limit of infinitely many trials, the sample average will converge to the true expectation in Equation (21.1).

It is clear that direct utility estimation is just an instance of supervised learning where each example has the state as input and the observed reward-to-go as output. This means that we have reduced reinforcement learning to a standard inductive learning problem, as discussed in Chapter 18. Section 21.4 discusses the use of more powerful kinds of representations for the utility function, such as neural networks. Learning techniques for those representations can be applied directly to the observed data.

Direct utility estimation succeeds in reducing the reinforcement learning problem to an inductive learning problem, about which much is known. Unfortunately, it misses a very important source of information, namely, the fact that the utilities of states are not independent! *The utility of each state equals its own reward plus the expected utility of its successor states.* That is, the utility values obey the Bellman equations for a fixed policy (see also Equation (17.10)):

$$U^\pi(s) = R(s) + \gamma \sum_{s'} T(s, \pi(s), s') U^\pi(s') . \tag{21.2}$$

By ignoring the connections between states, direct utility estimation misses opportunities for learning. For example, the second of the three trials given earlier reaches the state (3,2), which has not previously been visited. The next transition reaches (3,3), which is known from the first trial to have a high utility. The Bellman equation suggests immediately that (3,2) is also likely to have a high utility, because it leads to (3,3), but direct utility estimation learns nothing until the end of the trial. More broadly, we can view direct utility estimation as searching in a hypothesis space for $U$ that is much larger than it needs to be, in that it includes many functions that violate the Bellman equations. For this reason, the algorithm often converges very slowly.

### Adaptive dynamic programming

ADAPTIVE DYNAMIC PROGRAMMING

In order to take advantage of the constraints between states, an agent must learn how states are connected. An **adaptive dynamic programming** (or **ADP**) agent works by learning the transition model of the environment as it goes along and solving the corresponding Markov decision process using a dynamic programming method. For a passive learning agent, this means plugging the learned transition model $T(s, \pi(s), s')$ and the observed rewards $R(s)$ into the Bellman equations (21.2) to calculate the utilities of the states. As we remarked in our discussion of policy iteration in Chapter 17, these equations are linear (no maximization involved) so they can be solved using any linear algebra package. Alternatively, we can adopt the approach of **modified policy iteration** (see page 625), using a simplified value iteration process to update the utility estimates after each change to the learned model. Because the model usually changes only slightly with each observation, the value iteration process can use the previous utility estimates as initial values and should converge quite quickly.

The process of learning the model itself is easy, because the environment is fully observable. This means that we have a supervised learning task where the input is a state–action pair and the output is the resulting state. In the simplest case, we can represent the transition model as a table of probabilities. We keep track of how often each action outcome occurs and estimate the transition probability $T(s, a, s')$ from the frequency with which $s'$ is reached when executing $a$ in $s$.[1] For example, in the three traces given on page 765, *Right* is executed three times in (1,3) and two out of three times the resulting state is (2,3), so $T((1,3), Right, (2,3))$ is estimated to be 2/3.

The full agent program for a passive ADP agent is shown in Figure 21.2. Its performance on the $4 \times 3$ world is shown in Figure 21.3. In terms of how quickly its value estimates improve, the ADP agent does as well as possible, subject to its ability to learn the transition model. In this sense, it provides a standard against which to measure other reinforcement learning algorithms. It is, however, somewhat intractable for large state spaces. In backgammon, for example, it would involve solving roughly $10^{50}$ equations in $10^{50}$ unknowns.

### Temporal difference learning

It is possible to have (almost) the best of both worlds; that is, one can approximate the constraint equations shown earlier without solving them for all possible states. *The key is to use the observed transitions to adjust the values of the observed states so that they agree with the constraint equations.* Consider, for example, the transition from (1,3) to (2,3) in the second trial on page 765. Suppose that, as a result of the first trial, the utility estimates are $U^{\pi}(1,3) = 0.84$ and $U^{\pi}(2,3) = 0.92$. Now, if this transition occurred all the time, we would expect the utilities to obey

$$U^{\pi}(1,3) = -0.04 + U^{\pi}(2,3) ,$$

so $U^{\pi}(1,3)$ would be 0.88. Thus, its current estimate of 0.84 might be a little low and should be increased. More generally, when a transition occurs from state $s$ to state $s'$, we apply the

[1] This is the maximum likelihood estimate, as discussed in Chapter 20. A Bayesian update with a Dirichlet prior might work better.

```
function PASSIVE-ADP-AGENT(percept) returns an action
  inputs: percept, a percept indicating the current state s′ and reward signal r′
  static: π, a fixed policy
          mdp, an MDP with model T, rewards R, discount γ
          U, a table of utilities, initially empty
          N_sa, a table of frequencies for state-action pairs, initially zero
          N_sas′, a table of frequencies for state-action-state triples, initially zero
          s, a, the previous state and action, initially null

  if s′ is new then do U[s′] ← r′; R[s′] ← r′
  if s is not null then do
      increment N_sa[s, a] and N_sas′[s, a, s′]
      for each t such that N_sas′[s, a, t] is nonzero do
          T[s, a, t] ← N_sas′[s, a, t] / N_sa[s, a]
  U ← POLICY-EVALUATION(π, U, mdp)
  if TERMINAL?[s′] then s, a ← null else s, a ← s′, π[s′]
  return a
```

**Figure 21.2** A passive reinforcement learning agent based on adaptive dynamic programming. To simplify the code, we have assumed that each percept can be divided into a perceived state and a reward signal.

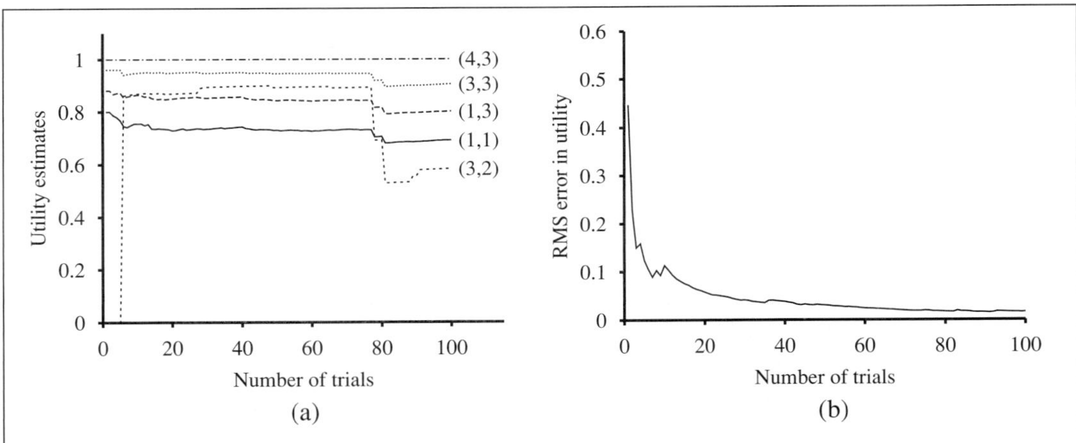


**Figure 21.3** The passive ADP learning curves for the $4 \times 3$ world, given the optimal policy shown in Figure 21.1. (a) The utility estimates for a selected subset of states, as a function of the number of trials. Notice the large changes occurring around the 78th trial—this is the first time that the agent falls into the $-1$ terminal state at (4,2). (b) The root-mean-square error in the estimate for $U(1,1)$, averaged over 20 runs of 100 trials each.

```
function PASSIVE-TD-AGENT(percept) returns an action
  inputs: percept, a percept indicating the current state s' and reward signal r'
  static: π, a fixed policy
          U, a table of utilities, initially empty
          N_s, a table of frequencies for states, initially zero
          s, a, r, the previous state, action, and reward, initially null

  if s' is new then U[s'] ← r'
  if s is not null then do
     increment N_s[s]
     U[s] ← U[s] + α(N_s[s])(r + γ U[s'] − U[s])
  if TERMINAL?[s'] then s, a, r ← null else s, a, r ← s', π[s'], r'
  return a
```

**Figure 21.4** A passive reinforcement learning agent that learns utility estimates using temporal differences.

following update to $U^\pi(s)$:

$$U^\pi(s) \leftarrow U^\pi(s) + \alpha(R(s) + \gamma U^\pi(s') - U^\pi(s)) \,. \tag{21.3}$$

Here, $\alpha$ is the **learning rate** parameter. Because this update rule uses the difference in utilities between successive states, it is often called the **temporal-difference**, or **TD**, equation.

The basic idea of all temporal-difference methods is, first to define the conditions that hold locally when the utility estimates are correct, and then, to write an update equation that moves the estimates toward this ideal "equilibrium" equation. In the case of passive learning, the equilibrium is given by Equation (21.2). Now Equation (21.3) does in fact cause the agent to reach the equilibrium given by Equation (21.2), but there is some subtlety involved. First, notice that the update involves only the observed successor $s'$, whereas the actual equilibrium conditions involve all possible next states. One might think that this causes an improperly large change in $U^\pi(s)$ when a very rare transition occurs; but, in fact, because rare transitions occur only rarely, the *average value* of $U^\pi(s)$ will converge to the correct value. Furthermore, if we change $\alpha$ from a fixed parameter to a function that decreases as the number of times a state has been visited increases, then $U(s)$ itself will converge to the correct value.[2] This gives us the agent program shown in Figure 21.4. Figure 21.5 illustrates the performance of the passive TD agent on the $4 \times 3$ world. It does not learn quite as fast as the ADP agent and shows much higher variability, but it is much simpler and requires much less computation per observation. Notice that *TD does not need a model to perform its updates.* The environment supplies the connection between neighboring states in the form of observed transitions.

The ADP approach and the TD approach are actually closely related. Both try to make local adjustments to the utility estimates in order to make each state "agree" with its successors. One difference is that TD adjusts a state to agree with its *observed* successor (Equa-

[2] Technically, we require that $\sum_{n=1}^{\infty} \alpha(n) = \infty$ and $\sum_{n=1}^{\infty} \alpha^2(n) < \infty$. The decay $\alpha(n) = 1/n$ satisfies these conditions. In Figure 21.5 we have used $\alpha(n) = 60/(59 + n)$.

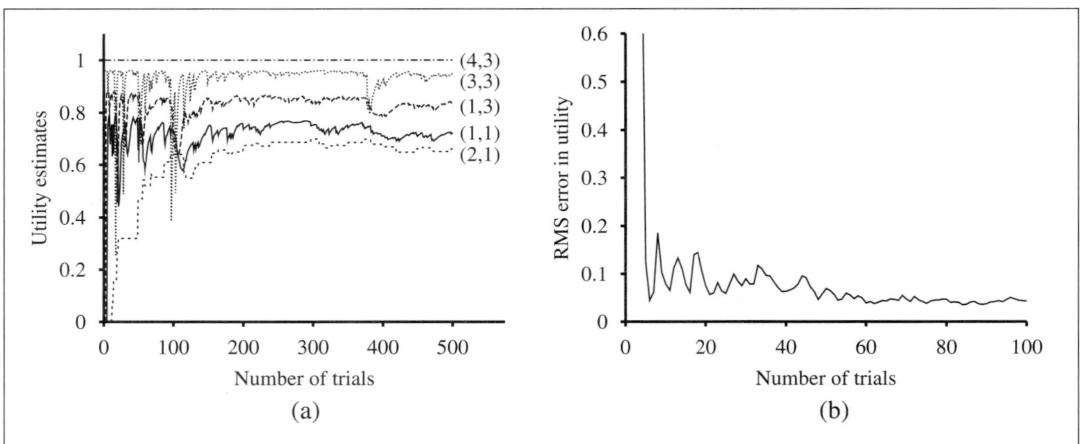


**Figure 21.5** The TD learning curves for the $4 \times 3$ world. (a) The utility estimates for a selected subset of states, as a function of the number of trials. (b) The root-mean-square error in the estimate for $U(1,1)$, averaged over 20 runs of 500 trials each. Only the first 100 trials are shown to enable comparison with Figure 21.3.

tion (21.3)), whereas ADP adjusts the state to agree with *all* of the successors that might occur, weighted by their probabilities (Equation (21.2)). This difference disappears when the effects of TD adjustments are averaged over a large number of transitions, because the frequency of each successor in the set of transitions is approximately proportional to its probability. A more important difference is that whereas TD makes a single adjustment per observed transition, ADP makes as many as it needs to restore consistency between the utility estimates $U$ and the environment model $T$. Although the observed transition makes only a local change in $T$, its effects might need to be propagated throughout $U$. Thus, TD can be viewed as a crude but efficient first approximation to ADP.

Each adjustment made by ADP could be seen, from the TD point of view, as a result of a "pseudo-experience" generated by simulating the current environment model. It is possible to extend the TD approach to use an environment model to generate several pseudo-experiences—transitions that the TD agent can imagine *might* happen, given its current model. For each observed transition, the TD agent can generate a large number of imaginary transitions. In this way, the resulting utility estimates will approximate more and more closely those of ADP—of course, at the expense of increased computation time.

In a similar vein, we can generate more efficient versions of ADP by directly approximating the algorithms for value iteration or policy iteration. Recall that full value iteration can be intractable when the number of states is large. Many of the adjustment steps, however, are extremely tiny. One possible approach to generating reasonably good answers quickly is to bound the number of adjustments made after each observed transition. One can also use a heuristic to rank the possible adjustments so as to carry out only the most significant ones.

The **prioritized sweeping** heuristic prefers to make adjustments to states whose *likely* successors have just undergone a *large* adjustment in their own utility estimates. Using heuristics like this, approximate ADP algorithms usually can learn roughly as fast as full ADP, in terms of the number of training sequences, but can be several orders of magnitude more efficient in terms of computation. (See Exercise 21.3.) This enables them to handle state spaces that are far too large for full ADP. Approximate ADP algorithms have an additional advantage: in the early stages of learning a new environment, the environment model $T$ often will be far from correct, so there is little point in calculating an exact utility function to match it. An approximation algorithm can use a minimum adjustment size that decreases as the environment model becomes more accurate. This eliminates the very long value iterations that can occur early in learning due to large changes in the model.

## 21.3 ACTIVE REINFORCEMENT LEARNING

A passive learning agent has a fixed policy that determines its behavior. An active agent must decide what actions to take. Let us begin with the adaptive dynamic programming agent and consider how it must be modified to handle this new freedom.

First, the agent will need to learn a complete model with outcome probabilities for all actions, rather than just the model for the fixed policy. The simple learning mechanism used by PASSIVE-ADP-AGENT will do just fine for this. Next, we need to take into account the fact that the agent has a choice of actions. The utilities it needs to learn are those defined by the *optimal* policy; they obey the Bellman equations given on page 619, which we repeat here:

$$U(s) = R(s) + \gamma \max_{a} \sum_{s'} T(s, a, s')U(s') . \tag{21.4}$$

These equations can be solved to obtain the utility function $U$ using the value iteration or policy iteration algorithms from Chapter 17. The final issue is what to do at each step. Having obtained a utility function $U$ that is optimal for the learned model, the agent can extract an optimal action by one-step look-ahead to maximize the expected utility; alternatively, if it uses policy iteration, the optimal policy is already available, so it should simply execute the action the optimal policy recommends. Or should it?

### Exploration

Figure 21.6 shows the results of one sequence of trials for an ADP agent that follows the recommendation of the optimal policy for the learned model at each step. The agent *does not* learn the true utilities or the true optimal policy! What happens instead is that, in the 39th trial, it finds a policy that reaches the +1 reward along the lower route via (2,1), (3,1), (3,2), and (3,3). (See Figure 21.6.) After experimenting with minor variations, from the 276th trial onward it sticks to that policy, never learning the utilities of the other states and never finding the optimal route via (1,2), (1,3), and (2,3). We call this agent the **greedy agent**. Repeated experiments show that the greedy agent *very seldom* converges to the optimal policy for this environment and sometimes converges to really horrendous policies.

GREEDY AGENT

How can it be that choosing the optimal action leads to suboptimal results? The answer is that the learned model is not the same as the true environment; what is optimal in the

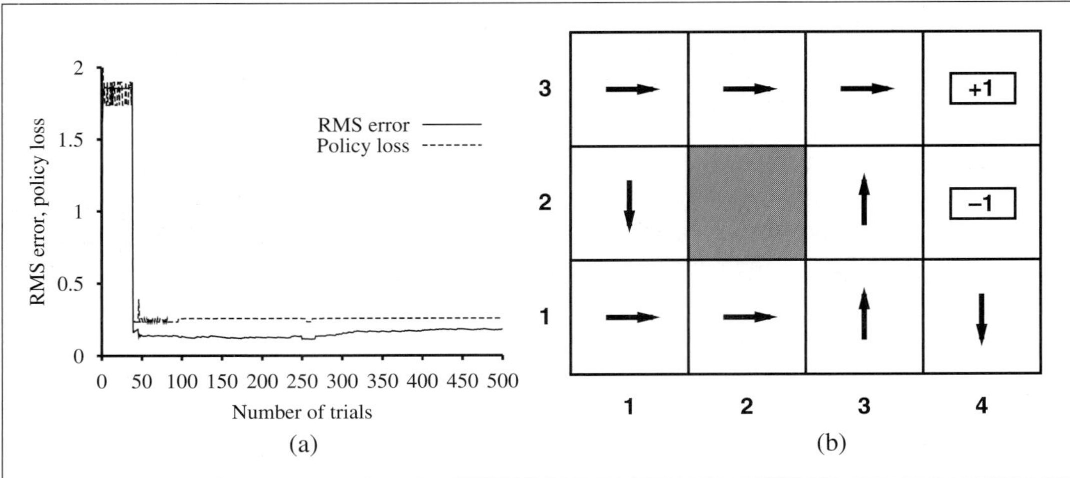


**Figure 21.6** Performance of a greedy ADP agent that executes the action recommended by the optimal policy for the learned model. (a) RMS error in the utility estimates averaged over the nine nonterminal squares. (b) The suboptimal policy to which the greedy agent converges in this particular sequence of trials.

learned model can therefore be suboptimal in the true environment. Unfortunately, the agent does not know what the true environment is, so it cannot compute the optimal action for the true environment. What, then, is to be done?

What the greedy agent has overlooked is that actions do more than provide rewards according to the current learned model; they also contribute to learning the true model by affecting the percepts that are received. By improving the model, the agent will receive greater rewards in the future.[3] An agent therefore must make a trade-off between **exploitation** to maximize its reward—as reflected in its current utility estimates—and **exploration** to maximize its long-term well-being. Pure exploitation risks getting stuck in a rut. Pure exploration to improve one's knowledge is of no use if one never puts that knowledge into practice. In the real world, one constantly has to decide between continuing in a comfortable existence and striking out into the unknown in the hopes of discovering a new and better life. With greater understanding, less exploration is necessary.

EXPLOITATION

EXPLORATION

Can we be a little more precise than this? Is there an *optimal* exploration policy? It turns out that this question has been studied in depth in the subfield of statistical decision theory that deals with so-called **bandit problems**. (See sidebar.)

BANDIT PROBLEMS

Although bandit problems are extremely difficult to solve exactly to obtain an *optimal* exploration method, it is nonetheless possible to come up with a *reasonable* scheme that will eventually lead to optimal behavior by the agent. Technically, any such scheme needs to be greedy in the limit of infinite exploration, or **GLIE**. A GLIE scheme must try each action in each state an unbounded number of times to avoid having a finite probability that an optimal action is missed because of an unusually bad series of outcomes. An ADP agent

GLIE

[3] Notice the direct analogy to the theory of information value in Chapter 16.

### EXPLORATION AND BANDITS

In Las Vegas, a *one-armed bandit* is a slot machine. A gambler can insert a coin, pull the lever, and collect the winnings (if any). An $n$**-armed bandit** has $n$ levers. The gambler must choose which lever to play on each successive coin—the one that has paid off best, or maybe one that has not been tried?

The $n$-armed bandit problem is a formal model for real problems in many vitally important areas, such as deciding on the annual budget for AI research and development. Each arm corresponds to an action (such as allocating $20 million for the development of new AI textbooks), and the payoff from pulling the arm corresponds to the benefits obtained from taking the action (immense). Exploration, whether it is exploration of a new research field or exploration of a new shopping mall, is risky, is expensive, and has uncertain payoffs; on the other hand, failure to explore at all means that one never discovers *any* actions that are worthwhile.

To formulate a bandit problem properly, one must define exactly what is meant by optimal behavior. Most definitions in the literature assume that the aim is to maximize the expected total reward obtained over the agent's lifetime. These definitions require that the expectation be taken over the possible worlds that the agent could be in, as well as over the possible results of each action sequence in any given world. Here, a "world" is defined by the transition model $T(s, a, s')$. Thus, in order to act optimally, the agent needs a prior distribution over the possible models. The resulting optimization problems are usually wildly intractable.

In some cases—for example, when the payoff of each machine is independent and discounted rewards are used—it is possible to calculate a **Gittins index** for each slot machine (Gittins, 1989). The index is a function only of the number of times the slot machine has been played and how much it has paid off. The index for each machine indicates how worthwhile it is to invest more, based on a combination of expected return and expected value of information. Choosing the machine with the highest index value gives an optimal exploration policy. Unfortunately, no way has been found to extend Gittins indices to sequential decision problems.

One can use the theory of $n$-armed bandits to argue for the reasonableness of the selection strategy in genetic algorithms. (See Chapter 4.) If you consider each arm in an $n$-armed bandit problem to be a possible string of genes, and the investment of a coin in one arm to be the reproduction of those genes, then genetic algorithms allocate coins optimally, given an appropriate set of independence assumptions.

using such a scheme will eventually learn the true environment model. A GLIE scheme must also eventually become greedy, so that the agent's actions become optimal with respect to the learned (and hence the true) model.

There are several GLIE schemes; one of the simplest is to have the agent choose a random action a fraction $1/t$ of the time and to follow the greedy policy otherwise. While this does eventually converge to an optimal policy, it can be extremely slow. A more sensible approach would give some weight to actions that the agent has not tried very often, while tending to avoid actions that are believed to be of low utility. This can be implemented by altering the constraint equation (21.4) so that it assigns a higher utility estimate to relatively unexplored state–action pairs. Essentially, this amounts to an optimistic prior over the possible environments and causes the agent to behave initially as if there were wonderful rewards scattered all over the place. Let us use $U^+(s)$ to denote the optimistic estimate of the utility (i.e., the expected reward-to-go) of the state $s$, and let $N(a, s)$ be the number of times action $a$ has been tried in state $s$. Suppose we are using value iteration in an ADP learning agent; then we need to rewrite the update equation (i.e., Equation (17.6)) to incorporate the optimistic estimate. The following equation does this:

$$U^+(s) \leftarrow R(s) + \gamma \max_a f\left(\sum_{s'} T(s,a,s')U^+(s'),\ N(a,s)\right) . \tag{21.5}$$

EXPLORATION FUNCTION

Here, $f(u, n)$ is called the **exploration function**. It determines how greed (preference for high values of $u$) is traded off against curiosity (preference for low values of $n$—actions that have not been tried often). The function $f(u, n)$ should be increasing in $u$ and decreasing in $n$. Obviously, there are many possible functions that fit these conditions. One particularly simple definition is

$$f(u,n) = \begin{cases} R^+ & \text{if } n < N_e \\ u & \text{otherwise} \end{cases}$$

where $R^+$ is an optimistic estimate of the best possible reward obtainable in any state and $N_e$ is a fixed parameter. This will have the effect of making the agent try each action–state pair at least $N_e$ times.

The fact that $U^+$ rather than $U$ appears on the right-hand side of Equation (21.5) is very important. As exploration proceeds, the states and actions near the start state might well be tried a large number of times. If we used $U$, the more pessimistic utility estimate, then the agent would soon become disinclined to explore further afield. The use of $U^+$ means that the benefits of exploration are propagated back from the edges of unexplored regions, so that actions that lead *toward* unexplored regions are weighted more highly, rather than just actions that are themselves unfamiliar. The effect of this exploration policy can be seen clearly in Figure 21.7, which shows a rapid convergence toward optimal performance, unlike that of the greedy approach. A very nearly optimal policy is found after just 18 trials. Notice that the utility estimates themselves do not converge as quickly. This is because the agent stops exploring the unrewarding parts of the state space fairly soon, visiting them only "by accident" thereafter. However, it makes perfect sense for the agent not to care about the exact utilities of states that it knows are undesirable and can be avoided.

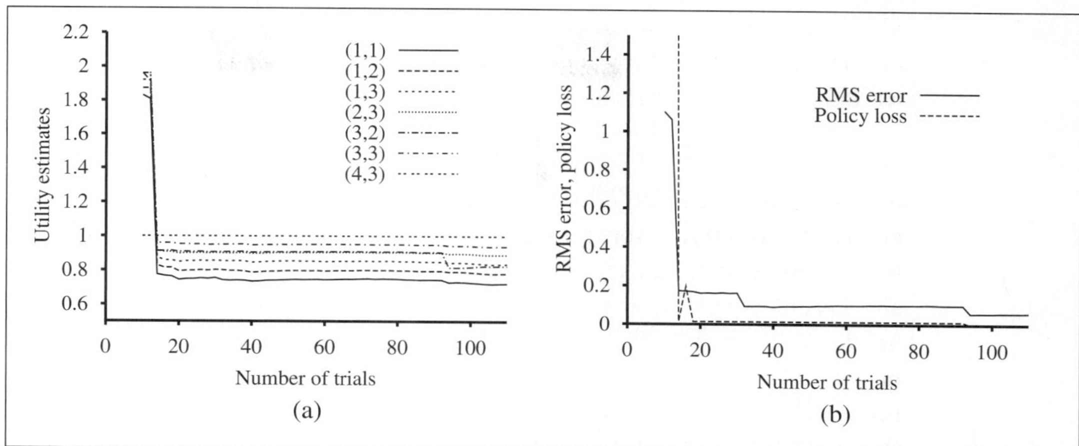


**Figure 21.7** Performance of the exploratory ADP agent. using $R^+ = 2$ and $N_e = 5$. (a) Utility estimates for selected states over time. (b) The RMS error in utility values and the associated policy loss.

## Learning an Action-Value Function

Now that we have an active ADP agent, let us consider how to construct an active temporal-difference learning agent. The most obvious change from the passive case is that the agent is no longer equipped with a fixed policy, so, if it learns a utility function $U$, it will need to learn a model in order to be able to choose an action based on $U$ via one-step look-ahead. The model acquisition problem for the TD agent is identical to that for the ADP agent. What of the TD update rule itself? Perhaps surprisingly, the update rule (21.3) remains unchanged. This might seem odd, for the following reason: Suppose the agent takes a step that normally leads to a good destination, but because of nondeterminism in the environment the agent ends up in a catastrophic state. The TD update rule will take this as seriously as if the outcome had been the normal result of the action, whereas one might suppose that, because the outcome was a fluke, the agent should not worry about it too much. In fact, of course, the unlikely outcome will occur only infrequently in a large set of training sequences; hence in the long run its effects will be weighted proportionally to its probability, as we would hope. Once again, it can be shown that the TD algorithm will converge to the same values as ADP as the number of training sequences tends to infinity.

There is an alternative TD method called **$Q$-learning** that learns an action-value representation instead of learning utilities. We will use the notation $Q(a, s)$ to denote the value of doing action $a$ in state $s$. Q-values are directly related to utility values as follows:

$$U(s) = \max_a Q(a, s) . \tag{21.6}$$

$Q$-functions may seem like just another way of storing utility information, but they have a very important property: *a TD agent that learns a $Q$-function does not need a model for either learning or action selection.* For this reason, $Q$-learning is called a **model-free** method. As with utilities, we can write a constraint equation that must hold at equilibrium when the

MODEL-FREE

```
function Q-LEARNING-AGENT(percept) returns an action
  inputs: percept, a percept indicating the current state s' and reward signal r'
  static: Q, a table of action values index by state and action
          N_sa, a table of frequencies for state-action pairs
          s, a, r, the previous state, action, and reward, initially null

  if s is not null then do
     increment N_sa[s, a]
     Q[a, s] ← Q[a, s] + α(N_sa[s, a])(r + γ max_a' Q[a', s'] − Q[a, s])
  if TERMINAL?[s'] then s, a, r ← null
  else s, a, r ← s', argmax_a' f(Q[a', s'], N_sa[s', a']), r'
  return a
```

**Figure 21.8** An exploratory $Q$-learning agent. It is an active learner that learns the value $Q(a, s)$ of each action in each situation. It uses the same exploration function $f$ as the exploratory ADP agent, but avoids having to learn the transition model because the $Q$-value of a state can be related directly to those of its neighbors.

$Q$-values are correct:

$$Q(a, s) = R(s) + \gamma \sum_{s'} T(s, a, s') \max_{a'} Q(a', s') \;. \tag{21.7}$$

As in the ADP learning agent, we can use this equation directly as an update equation for an iteration process that calculates exact $Q$-values, given an estimated model. This does, however, require that a model also be learned because the equation uses $T(s, a, s')$. The temporal-difference approach, on the other hand, requires no model. The update equation for TD $Q$-learning is

$$Q(a, s) \leftarrow Q(a, s) + \alpha(R(s) + \gamma \max_{a'} Q(a', s') - Q(a, s)) \;, \tag{21.8}$$

which is calculated whenever action $a$ is executed in state $s$ leading to state $s'$.

The complete agent design for an exploratory $Q$-learning agent using TD is shown in Figure 21.8. Notice that it uses exactly the same exploration function $f$ as that used by the exploratory ADP agent—hence the need to keep statistics on actions taken (the table $N$). If a simpler exploration policy is used—say, acting randomly on some fraction of steps, where the fraction decreases over time—then we can dispense with the statistics.

The $Q$-learning agent learns the optimal policy for the $4 \times 3$ world, but does so at a much slower rate than the ADP agent. This is because TD does not enforce consistency among values via the model. The comparison raises a general question: is it better to learn a model and a utility function or to learn an action-value function with no model? In other words, what is the best way to represent the agent function? This is an issue at the foundations of artificial intelligence. As we stated in Chapter 1, one of the key historical characteristics of much of AI research is its (often unstated) adherence to the **knowledge-based** approach. This amounts to an assumption that the best way to represent the agent function is to build a representation of some aspects of the environment in which the agent is situated.

Some researchers, both inside and outside AI, have claimed that the availability of model-free methods such as $Q$-learning means that the knowledge-based approach is unnecessary. There is, however, little to go on but intuition. Our intuition, for what it's worth, is that as the environment becomes more complex, the advantages of a knowledge-based approach become more apparent. This is borne out even in games such as chess, checkers (draughts), and backgammon (see next section), where efforts to learn an evaluation function by means of a model have met with more success than $Q$-learning methods.

## 21.4 GENERALIZATION IN REINFORCEMENT LEARNING

So far, we have assumed that the utility functions and $Q$-functions learned by the agents are represented in tabular form with one output value for each input tuple. Such an approach works reasonably well for small state spaces, but the time to convergence and (for ADP) the time per iteration increase rapidly as the space gets larger. With carefully controlled, approximate ADP methods, it might be possible to handle 10,000 states or more. This suffices for two-dimensional maze-like environments, but more realistic worlds are out of the question. Chess and backgammon are tiny subsets of the real world, yet their state spaces contain on the order of $10^{50}$ to $10^{120}$ states. It would be absurd to suppose that one must visit all these states in order to learn how to play the game!

FUNCTION APPROXIMATION

One way to handle such problems is to use **function approximation**, which simply means using any sort of representation for the function other than a table. The representation is viewed as approximate because it might not be the case that the *true* utility function or $Q$-function can be represented in the chosen form. For example, in Chapter 6 we described an **evaluation function** for chess that is represented as a weighted linear function of a set of **features** (or **basis functions**) $f_1, \ldots, f_n$:

BASIS FUNCTIONS

$$\hat{U}_\theta(s) = \theta_1\, f_1(s) + \theta_2\, f_2(s) + \cdots + \theta_n\, f_n(s)\ .$$

A reinforcement learning algorithm can learn values for the parameters $\theta = \theta_1, \ldots, \theta_n$ such that the evaluation function $\hat{U}_\theta$ approximates the true utility function. Instead of, say, $10^{120}$ values in a table, this function approximator is characterized by, say, $n = 20$ parameters—an *enormous* compression. Although no one knows the true utility function for chess, no one believes that it can be represented exactly in 20 numbers. If the approximation is good enough, however, the agent might still play excellent chess.[4]

Function approximation makes it practical to represent utility functions for very large state spaces, but that is not its principal benefit. *The compression achieved by a function approximator allows the learning agent to generalize from states it has visited to states it has not visited.* That is, the most important aspect of function approximation is not that it

[4] We do know that the exact utility function can be represented in a page or two of Lisp, Java, or C++. That is, it can be represented by a program that solves the game exactly every time it is called. We are interested only in function approximators that use a *reasonable* amount of computation. It might in fact be better to learn a very simple function approximator and combine it with a certain amount of look-ahead search. The trade-offs involved are currently not well understood.

requires less space, but that it allows for inductive generalization over input states. To give you some idea of the power of this effect: by examining only one in every $10^{44}$ of the possible backgammon states, it is possible to learn a utility function that allows a program to play as well as any human (Tesauro, 1992).

On the flip side, of course, there is the problem that there could fail to be any function in the chosen hypothesis space that approximates the true utility function sufficiently well. As in all inductive learning, there is a trade-off between the size of the hypothesis space and the time it takes to learn the function. A larger hypothesis space increases the likelihood that a good approximation can be found, but also means that convergence is likely to be delayed.

Let us begin with the simplest case, which is direct utility estimation. (See Section 21.2.) With function approximation, this is an instance of **supervised learning**. For example, suppose we represent the utilities for the $4 \times 3$ world using a simple linear function. The features of the squares are just their $x$ and $y$ coordinates, so we have

$$\hat{U}_\theta(x, y) = \theta_0 + \theta_1 x + \theta_2 y \; . \tag{21.9}$$

Thus, if $(\theta_0, \theta_1, \theta_2) = (0.5, 0.2, 0.1)$, then $\hat{U}_\theta(1, 1) = 0.8$. Given a collection of trials, we obtain a set of sample values of $\hat{U}_\theta(x, y)$, and we can find the best fit, in the sense of minimizing the squared error, using standard linear regression. (See Chapter 20.)

For reinforcement learning, it makes more sense to use an *online* learning algorithm that updates the parameters after each trial. Suppose we run a trial and the total reward obtained starting at (1,1) is 0.4. This suggests that $\hat{U}_\theta(1, 1)$, currently 0.8, is too large and must be reduced. How should the parameters be adjusted to achieve this? As with neural network learning, we write an error function and compute its gradient with respect to the parameters. If $u_j(s)$ is the observed total reward from state $s$ onward in the $j$th trial, then the error is defined as (half) the squared difference of the predicted total and the actual total: $E_j(s) = (\hat{U}_\theta(s) - u_j(s))^2/2$. The rate of change of the error with respect to each parameter $\theta_i$ is $\partial E_j/\partial \theta_i$, so to move the parameter in the direction of decreasing the error, we want

$$\theta_i \leftarrow \theta_i - \alpha \frac{\partial E_j(s)}{\partial \theta_i} = \theta_i + \alpha \, (u_j(s) - \hat{U}_\theta(s)) \frac{\partial \hat{U}_\theta(s)}{\partial \theta_i} \; . \tag{21.10}$$

WIDROW–HOFF RULE

DELTA RULE

This is called the **Widrow–Hoff rule**, or the **delta rule**, for online least-squares. For the linear function approximator $\hat{U}_\theta(s)$ in Equation (21.9), we get three simple update rules:

$$\begin{aligned}
\theta_0 &\leftarrow \theta_0 + \alpha \, (u_j(s) - \hat{U}_\theta(s)) \; , \\
\theta_1 &\leftarrow \theta_1 + \alpha \, (u_j(s) - \hat{U}_\theta(s)) x \; , \\
\theta_2 &\leftarrow \theta_2 + \alpha \, (u_j(s) - \hat{U}_\theta(s)) y \; .
\end{aligned}$$

We can apply these rules to the example where $\hat{U}_\theta(1, 1)$ is 0.8 and $u_j(1, 1)$ is 0.4. $\theta_0$, $\theta_1$, and $\theta_2$ are all decreased by $0.4\alpha$, which reduces the error for (1,1). Notice that changing the $\theta_i$s *also changes the values of* $\hat{U}_\theta$ *for every other state*! This is what we mean by saying that function approximation allows a reinforcement learner to generalize from its experiences.

We expect that the agent will learn faster if it uses a function approximator, provided that the hypothesis space is not too large, but includes some functions that are a reasonably good fit to the true utility function. Exercise 21.7 asks you to evaluate the performance of direct utility estimation, both with and without function approximation. The improvement in the $4 \times 3$ world is noticeable but not dramatic, because this is a very small state space to begin with. The improvement is much greater in a $10 \times 10$ world with a +1 reward at (10,10). This world is well suited for a linear utility function because the true utility function is smooth and nearly linear. (See Exercise 21.10.) If we put the +1 reward at (5,5), the true utility is more like a pyramid and the function approximator in Equation (21.9) will fail miserably. All is not lost, however! Remember that what matters for linear function approximation is that the function be linear in the *parameters*—the features themselves can be arbitrary nonlinear functions of the state variables. Hence, we can include a term such as $\theta_3\sqrt{(x - x_g)^2 + (y - y_g)^2}$ that measures the distance to the goal.

We can apply these ideas equally well to temporal-difference learners. All we need do is adjust the parameters to try to reduce the temporal difference between successive states. The new versions of the TD and $Q$-learning equations (21.3 and 21.8) are

$$\theta_i \leftarrow \theta_i + \alpha\,[R(s) + \gamma\,\hat{U}_\theta(s') - \hat{U}_\theta(s)]\frac{\partial \hat{U}_\theta(s)}{\partial \theta_i} \tag{21.11}$$

for utilities and

$$\theta_i \leftarrow \theta_i + \alpha\,[R(s) + \gamma\,\max_{a'} \hat{Q}_\theta(a', s') - \hat{Q}_\theta(a, s)]\frac{\partial \hat{Q}_\theta(a, s)}{\partial \theta_i} \tag{21.12}$$

for $Q$-values. These update rules can be shown to converge to the closest possible[5] approximation to the true function when the function approximator is *linear* in the parameters. Unfortunately, all bets are off when *nonlinear* functions—such as neural networks—are used. There are some very simple cases in which the parameters can go off to infinity even though there are good solutions in the hypothesis space. There are more sophisticated algorithms that can avoid these problems, but at present reinforcement learning with general function approximators remains a delicate art.

Function approximation can also be very helpful for learning a model of the environment. Remember that learning a model for an *observable* environment is a *supervised* learning problem, because the next percept gives the outcome state. Any of the supervised learning methods in Chapter 18 can be used, with suitable adjustments for the fact that we need to predict a complete state description rather than just a Boolean classification or a single real value. For example, if the state is defined by $n$ Boolean variables, we will need to learn $n$ Boolean functions to predict all the variables. For a *partially observable* environment, the learning problem is much more difficult. If we know what the hidden variables are and how they are causally related to each other and to the observable variables, then we can fix the structure of a dynamic Bayesian network and use the EM algorithm to learn the parameters, as was described in Chapter 20. Inventing the hidden variables and learning the model structure are still open problems.

We now turn to examples of large-scale applications of reinforcement learning. We will see that, in cases where a utility function (and hence a model) is used, the model is usually taken as given. For example, in learning an evaluation function for backgammon, it is normally assumed that the legal moves and their effects are known in advance.

---

[5] The defi nition of distance between utility functions is rather technical; see Tsitsiklis and Van Roy (1997).

### Applications to game-playing

The first significant application of reinforcement learning was also the first significant learning program of any kind—the checker-playing program written by Arthur Samuel (1959, 1967). Samuel first used a weighted linear function for the evaluation of positions, using up to 16 terms at any one time. He applied a version of Equation (21.11) to update the weights. There were some significant differences, however, between his program and current methods. First, he updated the weights using the difference between the current state and the backed-up value generated by full look-ahead in the search tree. This works fine, because it amounts to viewing the state space at a different granularity. A second difference was that the program did *not* use any observed rewards! That is, the values of terminal states were ignored. This means that it is quite possible for Samuel's program not to converge, or to converge on a strategy designed to lose rather than to win. He managed to avoid this fate by insisting that the weight for material advantage should always be positive. Remarkably, this was sufficient to direct the program into areas of weight space corresponding to good checker play.

Gerry Tesauro's TD-Gammon system (1992) forcefully illustrates the potential of reinforcement learning techniques. In earlier work (Tesauro and Sejnowski, 1989), Tesauro tried learning a neural network representation of $Q(a, s)$ directly from examples of moves labeled with relative values by a human expert. This approach proved extremely tedious for the expert. It resulted in a program, called NEUROGAMMON, that was strong by computer standards, but not competitive with human experts. The TD-Gammon project was an attempt to learn from self-play alone. The only reward signal was given at the end of each game. The evaluation function was represented by a fully connected neural network with a single hidden layer containing 40 nodes. Simply by repeated application of Equation (21.11), TD-Gammon learned to play considerably better than Neurogammon, even though the input representation contained just the raw board position with no computed features. This took about 200,000 training games and two weeks of computer time. Although that may seem like a lot of games, it is only a vanishingly small fraction of the state space. When precomputed features were added to the input representation, a network with 80 hidden units was able, after 300,000 training games, to reach a standard of play comparable to that of the top three human players worldwide. Kit Woolsey, a top player and analyst, said that "There is no question in my mind that its positional judgment is far better than mine."

### Application to robot control

CART–POLE

INVERTED PENDULUM

The setup for the famous **cart–pole** balancing problem, also known as the **inverted pendulum**, is shown in Figure 21.9. The problem is to control the position $x$ of the cart so that the pole stays roughly upright ($\theta \approx \pi/2$), while staying within the limits of the cart track as shown. Over two thousand papers in reinforcement learning and control theory have been published on this seemingly simple problem. The cart–pole problem differs from the problems described earlier in that the state variables $x$, $\theta$, $\dot{x}$, and $\dot{\theta}$ are continuous. The actions are usually discrete: jerk left or jerk right, the so-called **bang-bang control** regime.

BANG-BANG CONTROL

The earliest work on learning for this problem was carried out by Michie and Chambers (1968). Their BOXES algorithm was able to balance the pole for over an hour after only

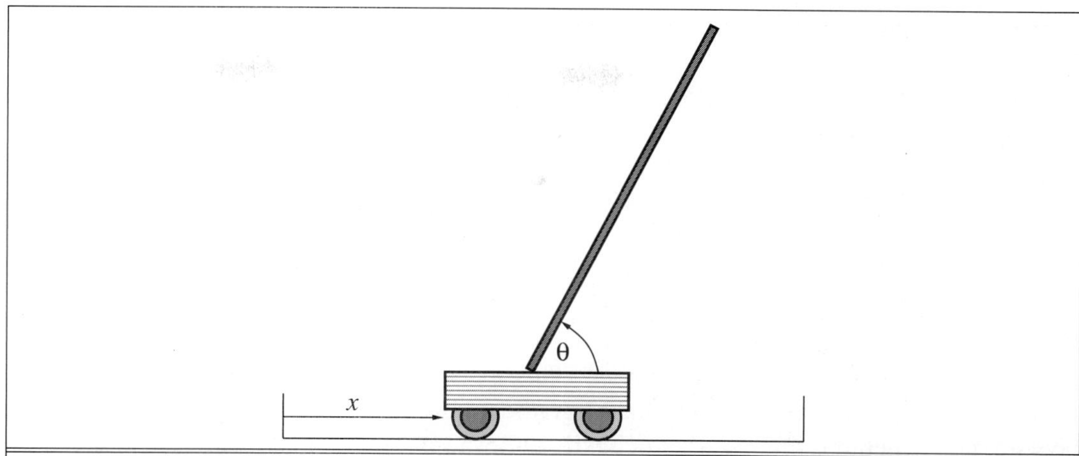


**Figure 21.9** Setup for the problem of balancing a long pole on top of a moving cart. The cart can be jerked left or right by a controller that observes $x$, $\theta$, $\dot{x}$, and $\dot{\theta}$.

about 30 trials. Moreover, unlike many subsequent systems, BOXES was implemented with a real cart and pole, not a simulation. The algorithm first discretized the four-dimensional state space into boxes—hence the name. It then ran trials until the pole fell over or the cart hit the end of the track. Negative reinforcement was associated with the final action in the final box and then propagated back through the sequence. It was found that the discretization caused some problems when the apparatus was initialized in a position different from those used in training, suggesting that generalization was not perfect. Improved generalization and faster learning can be obtained using an algorithm that *adaptively* partitions the state space according to the observed variation in the reward. Nowadays, balancing a *triple* inverted pendulum is a common exercise—a feat far beyond the capabilities of most humans.

## 21.5 POLICY SEARCH

POLICY SEARCH

The final approach we will consider for reinforcement learning problems is called **policy search**. In some ways, policy search is the simplest of all the methods in this chapter: the idea is to keep twiddling the policy as long as its performance improves, then stop.

Let us begin with the policies themselves. Remember that a policy $\pi$ is a function that maps states to actions. We are interested primarily in *parameterized* representations of $\pi$ that have far fewer parameters than there are states in the state space (just as in the preceding section). For example, we could represent $\pi$ by a collection of parameterized $Q$-functions, one for each action, and take the action with the highest predicted value:

$$\pi(s) = \max_a \hat{Q}_\theta(a, s) . \tag{21.13}$$

Each $Q$-function could be a linear function of the parameters $\theta$, as in Equation (21.9), or it could be a nonlinear function such as a neural network. Policy search will then adjust the parameters $\theta$ to improve the policy. Notice that if the policy is represented by $Q$-functions,

then policy search results in a process that learns $Q$-functions. *This process is not the same as $Q$-learning!* In $Q$-learning with function approximation, the algorithm finds a value of $\theta$ such that $\hat{Q}_\theta$ is "close" to $Q^*$, the optimal $Q$-function. Policy search, on the other hand, finds a value of $\theta$ that results in good performance; the values found may differ very substantially.[6] Another clear example of the difference is the case where $\pi(s)$ is calculated using, say, depth-10 look-ahead search with an approximate utility function $\hat{U}_\theta$. The value of $\theta$ that gives good play may be a long way from making $\hat{U}_\theta$ resemble the true utility function.

One problem with policy representations of the kind given in Equation (21.13) is that the policy is a *discontinuous* function of the parameters when the actions are discrete.[7] That is, there will be values of $\theta$ such that an infinitesimal change in $\theta$ causes the policy to switch from one action to another. This means that the value of the policy may also change discontinuously, which makes gradient-based search difficult. For this reason, policy search methods often use a **stochastic policy** representation $\pi_\theta(s, a)$, which specifies the *probability* of selecting action $a$ in state $s$. One popular representation is the **softmax function**:

STOCHASTIC POLICY

SOFTMAX FUNCTION

$$\pi_\theta(s, a) = \exp(\hat{Q}_\theta(a, s)) / \sum_{a'} \exp(\hat{Q}_\theta(a', s)) .$$

Softmax becomes nearly deterministic if one action is much better than the others, but it always gives a differentiable function of $\theta$; hence, the value of the policy (which depends in a continuous fashion on the action selection probabilities) is a differentiable function of $\theta$.

Now let us look at methods for improving the policy. We start with the simplest case: a deterministic policy and a deterministic environment. In this case, evaluating the policy is trivial: we simply execute it and observe the accumulated reward; this gives us the **policy value** $\rho(\theta)$. Improving the policy is just a standard optimization problem, as described in Chapter 4. We can follow the **policy gradient** vector $\nabla_\theta \rho(\theta)$ provided $\rho(\theta)$ is differentiable. Alternatively, we can follow the **empirical gradient** by hillclimbing—i.e., evaluating the change in policy for small increments in each parameter value. With the usual caveats, this process will converge to a local optimum in policy space.

POLICY VALUE

POLICY GRADIENT

When the environment (or the policy) is stochastic, things get more difficult. Suppose we are trying to do hillclimbing, which requires comparing $\rho(\theta)$ and $\rho(\theta + \Delta\theta)$ for some small $\Delta\theta$. The problem is that the total reward on each trial may vary widely, so estimates of the policy value from a small number of trials will be quite unreliable; trying to compare two such estimates will be even more unreliable. One solution is simply to run lots of trials, measuring the sample variance and using it to determine that enough trials have been run to get a reliable indication of the direction of improvement for $\rho(\theta)$. Unfortunately, this is impractical for many real problems where each trial may be expensive, time-consuming, and perhaps even dangerous.

For the case of a stochastic policy $\pi_\theta(s, a)$, it is possible to obtain an unbiased estimate of the gradient at $\theta$, $\nabla_\theta \rho(\theta)$, directly from the results of trials executed at $\theta$. For simplicity, we will derive this estimate for the simple case of a nonsequential environment in which the

---

6 Trivially, the approximate $Q$-function defined by $\hat{Q}_\theta(a, s) = Q^*(a, s)/10$ gives optimal performance, even though it is not at all close to $Q^*$.

7 For a continuous action space, the policy can be a smooth function of the parameters.

reward is obtained immediately after acting in the start state $s_0$. In this case, the policy value is just the expected value of the reward, and we have

$$\nabla_\theta \rho(\theta) = \nabla_\theta \sum_a \pi_\theta(s_0, a) R(a) = \sum_a (\nabla_\theta \pi_\theta(s_0, a)) R(a) .$$

Now we perform a simple trick so that this summation can be approximated by samples generated from the probability distribution defined by $\pi_\theta(s_0, a)$. Suppose that we have $N$ trials in all and the action taken on the $j$th trial is $a_j$. Then

$$\nabla_\theta \rho(\theta) = \sum_a \pi_\theta(s_0, a) \cdot \frac{(\nabla_\theta \pi_\theta(s_0, a)) R(a)}{\pi_\theta(s_0, a)} \approx \frac{1}{N} \sum_{j=1}^{N} \frac{(\nabla_\theta \pi_\theta(s_0, a_j)) R(a_j)}{\pi_\theta(s_0, a_j)} .$$

Thus, the true gradient of the policy value is approximated by a sum of terms involving the gradient of the action selection probability in each trial. For the sequential case, this generalizes to

$$\nabla_\theta \rho(\theta) \approx \frac{1}{N} \sum_{j=1}^{N} \frac{(\nabla_\theta \pi_\theta(s, a_j)) R_j(s)}{\pi_\theta(s, a_j)}$$

for each state $s$ visited, where $a_j$ is executed in $s$ on the $j$th trial and $R_j(s)$ is the total reward received from state $s$ onwards in the $j$th trial. The resulting algorithm is called REINFORCE (Williams, 1992); it is usually much more effective than hillclimbing using lots of trials at each value of $\theta$. It is still much slower than necessary, however.

Consider the following task: given two blackjack[8] programs, determine which is best. One way to do this is to have each play against a standard "dealer" for a certain number of hands and then to measure their respective winnings. The problem with this, as we have seen, is that the winnings of each program fluctuate widely depending on whether it receives good or bad cards. An obvious solution is to generate a certain number of hands in advance and *have each program play the same set of hands*. In this way, we eliminate the measurement error due to differences in the cards received. This is the idea behind the PEGASUS algorithm (Ng and Jordan, 2000). The algorithm is applicable to domains for which a simulator is available so that the "random" outcomes of actions can be repeated. The algorithm works by generating in advance $N$ sequences of random numbers, each of which can be used to run a trial of any policy. Policy search is carried out by evaluating each candidate policy using the *same* set of random sequences to determine the action outcomes. It can be shown that the number of random sequences required to ensure that the value of *every* policy is well-estimated depends only on the complexity of the policy space, and not at all on the complexity of the underlying domain. The PEGASUS algorithm has been used to develop effective policies for several domains, including autonomous helicopter flight (see Figure 21.10).

[8] Also known as twenty-one or pontoon.

**Figure 21.10** Superimposed time-lapse images of an autonomous helicopter performing a very difficult "nose-in circle" maneuver. The helicopter is under the control of a policy developed by the PEGASUS policy search algorithm. A simulator model was developed by observing the effects of various control manipulations on the real helicopter; then the algorithm was run on the simulator model overnight. A variety of controllers were developed for different maneuvers. In all cases, performance far exceeded that of an expert human pilot using remote control. (Image courtesy of Andrew Ng.)

## 21.6 SUMMARY

This chapter has examined the reinforcement learning problem: how an agent can become proficient in an unknown environment, given only its percepts and occasional rewards. Reinforcement learning can be viewed as a microcosm for the entire AI problem, but it is studied in a number of simplified settings to facilitate progress. The major points are:

- The overall agent design dictates the kind of information that must be learned. The three main designs we covered were the model-based design, using a model $T$ and a utility function $U$; the model-free design, using an action-value function $Q$; and the reflex design, using a policy $\pi$.
- Utilities can be learned using three approaches:
  1. **Direct utility estimation** uses the total observed reward-to-go for a given state as direct evidence for learning its utility.
  2. **Adaptive dynamic programming** (ADP) learns a model and a reward function from observations and then uses value or policy iteration to obtain the utilities or an optimal policy. ADP makes optimal use of the local constraints on utilities of states imposed through the neighborhood structure of the environment.
  3. **Temporal-difference** (TD) methods update utility estimates to match those of successor states. They can be viewed as simple approximations to the ADP approach

that require no model for the learning process. Using a learned model to generate pseudoexperiences can, however, result in faster learning.

- Action-value functions, or Q-functions, can be learned by an ADP approach or a TD approach. With TD, Q-learning requires no model in either the learning or action-selection phase. This simplifies the learning problem but potentially restricts the ability to learn in complex environments, because the agent cannot simulate the results of possible courses of action.
- When the learning agent is responsible for selecting actions while it learns, it must trade off the estimated value of those actions against the potential for learning useful new information. An exact solution of the exploration problem is infeasible, but some simple heuristics do a reasonable job.
- In large state spaces, reinforcement learning algorithms must use an approximate functional representation in order to generalize over states. The temporal-difference signal can be used directly to update parameters in representations such as neural networks.
- **Policy search** methods operate directly on a representation of the policy, attempting to improve it based on observed performance. The variance in the performance in a stochastic domain is a serious problem; for simulated domains this can be overcome by fixing the randomness in advance.

Because of its potential for eliminating hand coding of control strategies, reinforcement learning continues to be one of the most active areas of machine learning research. Applications in robotics promise to be particularly valuable; these will require methods for handling *continuous, high-dimensional, partially observable* environments in which successful behaviors may consist of thousands or even millions of primitive actions.

## Bibliographical and Historical Notes

Turing (1948, 1950) proposed the reinforcement learning approach, although he was not convinced of its effectiveness, writing, "the use of punishments and rewards can at best be a part of the teaching process." Arthur Samuel's work (1959) was probably the earliest successful machine learning research. Although this work was informal and had a number of flaws, it contained most of the modern ideas in reinforcement learning, including temporal differencing and function approximation. Around the same time, researchers in adaptive control theory (Widrow and Hoff, 1960), building on work by Hebb (1949), were training simple networks using the delta rule. (This early connection between neural networks and reinforcement learning may have led to the persistent misperception that the latter is a subfield of the former.) The cart–pole work of Michie and Chambers (1968) can also be seen as a reinforcement learning method with a function approximator. The psychological literature on reinforcement learning is much older; Hilgard and Bower (1975) provide a good survey. Direct evidence for the operation of reinforcement learning in animals has been provided by investigations into the foraging behavior of bees; there is a clear neural correlate of the reward signal in the form of a large neuron mapping from the nectar intake sensors directly to the motor cortex (Montague *et al.*, 1995). Research using single-cell recording suggests that the dopamine system in primate brains implements something resembling value function learning (Schultz *et al.*, 1997).

The connection between reinforcement learning and Markov decision processes was first made by Werbos (1977), but the development of reinforcement learning in AI stems from work at the University of Massachusetts in the early 1980s (Barto *et al.*, 1981). The paper by Sutton (1988) provides a good historical overview. Equation (21.3) in this chapter is a special case for $\lambda = 0$ of Sutton's general TD($\lambda$) algorithm. TD($\lambda$) updates the values of all states in a sequence leading up to each transition by an amount that drops off as $\lambda^t$ for states $t$ steps in the past. TD(1) is identical to the Widrow–Hoff or delta rule. Boyan (2002), building on work by Bradtke and Barto (1996), argues that TD($\lambda$) and related algorithms make inefficient use of experiences; essentially, they are online regression algorithms that converge much more slowly than offline regression. His LSTD($\lambda$) is an online algorithm that gives the same results as offline regression.

The combination of temporal difference learning with the model-based generation of simulated experiences was proposed in Sutton's DYNA architecture (Sutton, 1990). The idea of prioritized sweeping was introduced independently by Moore and Atkeson (1993) and Peng and Williams (1993). $Q$-learning was developed in Watkins's Ph.D. thesis (1989).

Bandit problems, which model the problem of exploration for nonsequential decisions, are analyzed in depth by Berry and Fristedt (1985). Optimal exploration strategies for several settings are obtainable using the technique called **Gittins indices** (Gittins, 1989). A variety of exploration methods for sequential decision problems are discussed by Barto *et al.* (1995). Kearns and Singh (1998) and Brafman and Tennenholtz (2000) describe algorithms that explore unknown environments and are guaranteed to converge on near-optimal policies in polynomial time.

Function approximation in reinforcement learning goes back to the work of Samuel, who used both linear and nonlinear evaluation functions and also used feature selection methods to reduce the feature space. Later methods include the **CMAC** (Cerebellar Model Articulation Controller) (Albus, 1975), which is essentially a sum of overlapping local kernel functions, and the associative neural networks of Barto *et al.* (1983). Neural networks are currently the most popular form of function approximator. The best known application is TD-Gammon (Tesauro, 1992, 1995), which was discussed in the chapter. One significant problem exhibited by neural-network-based TD learners is that they tend to forget earlier experiences, especially those in parts of the state space that are avoided once competence is achieved. This can result in catastrophic failure if such circumstances reappear. Function approximation based on **instance-based learning** can avoid this problem (Ormoneit and Sen, 2002; Forbes, 2002).

CMAC

The convergence of reinforcement learning algorithms using function approximation is an extremely technical subject. Results for TD learning have been progressively strengthened for the case of linear function approximators (Sutton, 1988; Dayan, 1992; Tsitsiklis and Van Roy, 1997), but several examples of divergence have been presented for nonlinear functions (see Tsitsiklis and Van Roy, 1997, for a discussion). Papavassiliou and Russell (1999) describe a new type of reinforcement learning that converges with any form of function approximator, provided that a best-fit approximation can be found for the observed data.

Policy search methods were brought to the fore by Williams (1992), who developed the REINFORCE family of algorithms. Later work by Marbach and Tsitsiklis (1998), Sutton *et al.* (2000), and Baxter and Bartlett (2000) strengthened and generalized the convergence results for policy search. The PEGASUS algorithm is due to Ng and Jordan (2000) although similar techniques appear in Van Roy's PhD thesis (1998). As we mentioned in the chapter, the performance of a *stochastic* policy is a continuous function of its parameters, which helps with gradient-based search methods. This is not the only benefit: Jaakkola *et al.* (1995) argue that stochastic policies actually work better than deterministic policies in partially observable environments, if both are limited to acting based on the current percept. (One reason is that the stochastic policy is less likely to get "stuck" because of some unseen hindrance.) Now, in Chapter 17 we pointed out that optimal policies in partially observable MDPs are deterministic functions of the *belief state* rather than the current percept, so we would expect still better results by keeping track of the belief state using the **filtering** methods of Chapter 15. Unfortunately, belief state space is high-dimensional and continuous, and effective algorithms have not yet been developed for reinforcement learning with belief states.

Real-world environments also exhibit enormous complexity in terms of the number of primitive actions required to achieve significant reward. For example, a robot playing soccer might make a hundred thousand individual leg motions before scoring a goal. One common method, used originally in animal training, is called **reward shaping**. This involves supplying the agent with additional rewards for "making progress." For soccer, these might be given for making contact with the ball or for kicking it toward the goal. Such rewards can speed up learning enormously, and are very simple to provide, but there is a risk that the agent will learn to maximize the pseudorewards rather than the true rewards; for example, standing next to the ball and "vibrating" causes many contacts with the ball. Ng *et al.* (1999) show that the agent will still learn the optimal policy provided that the pseudoreward $F(s, a, s')$ satisfies $F(s, a, s') = \gamma\Phi(s') - \Phi(s)$, where $\Phi$ is an arbitrary function of state. $\Phi$ can be constructed to reflect any desirable aspects of the state, such as achievement of subgoals or distance to a goal state.

REWARD SHAPING

The generation of complex behaviors can also be facilitated by **hierarchical reinforcement learning** methods, which attempt to solve problems at multiple levels of abstraction—much like the **HTN planning** methods of Chapter 12. For example, "scoring a goal" can be broken down into "obtain possession," "dribble towards the goal," and "shoot;" and each of these can be broken down further into lower-level motor behaviors. The fundamental result in this area is due to Forestier and Varaiya (1978), who proved that lower-level behaviors of arbitrary complexity can be treated just like primitive actions (albeit ones that can take varying amounts of time) from the point of view of the higher-level behavior that invokes them. Current approaches (Parr and Russell, 1998; Dietterich, 2000; Sutton *et al.*, 2000; Andre and Russell, 2002) build on this result to develop methods for supplying an agent with a **partial program** that constrains the agent's behavior to have a particular hierarchical structure. Reinforcement learning is then applied to learn the best behavior consistent with the partial program. The combination of function approximation, shaping, and hierarchical reinforcement learning may enable large-scale problems to be tackled successfully.

HIERARCHICAL REINFORCEMENT LEARNING

PARTIAL PROGRAM

The survey by Kaelbling *et al.* (1996) provides a good entry point to the literature. The text by Sutton and Barto (1998), two of the field's pioneers, focuses on architectures and algorithms, showing how reinforcement learning weaves together the ideas of learning, planning, and acting. The somewhat more technical work by Bertsekas and Tsitsiklis (1996) gives a rigorous grounding in the theory of dynamic programming and stochastic convergence. Reinforcement learning papers are published frequently in *Machine Learning*, in the *Journal of Machine Learning Research*, and in the International Conferences on Machine Learning and the Neural Information Processing Systems meetings.

## EXERCISES

**21.1** Implement a passive learning agent in a simple environment, such as the $4 \times 3$ world. For the case of an initially unknown environment model, compare the learning performance of the direct utility estimation, TD, and ADP algorithms. Do the comparison for the optimal policy and for several random policies. For which do the utility estimates converge faster? What happens when the size of the environment is increased? (Try environments with and without obstacles.)

**21.2** Chapter 17 defined a **proper policy** for an MDP as one that is guaranteed to reach a terminal state. Show that it is possible for a passive ADP agent to learn a transition model for which its policy $\pi$ is improper even if $\pi$ is proper for the true MDP; with such models, the value determination step may fail if $\gamma = 1$. Show that this problem cannot arise if value determination is applied to the learned model only at the end of a trial.

**21.3** Starting with the passive ADP agent, modify it to use an approximate ADP algorithm as discussed in the text. Do this in two steps:

**a**. Implement a priority queue for adjustments to the utility estimates. Whenever a state is adjusted, all of its predecessors also become candidates for adjustment and should be added to the queue. The queue is initialized with the state from which the most recent transition took place. Allow only a fixed number of adjustments.

**b**. Experiment with various heuristics for ordering the priority queue, examining their effect on learning rates and computation time.

**21.4** The direct utility estimation method in Section 21.2 uses distinguished terminal states to indicate the end of a trial. How could it be modified for environments with discounted rewards and no terminal states?

**21.5** How can the value determination algorithm be used to calculate the expected loss experienced by an agent using a given set of utility estimates $U$ and an estimated model $M$, compared with an agent using correct values?

**21.6** Adapt the vacuum world (Chapter 2) for reinforcement learning by including rewards for picking up each piece of dirt and for getting home and switching off. Make the world accessible by providing suitable percepts. Now experiment with different reinforcement learning agents. Is function approximation necessary for success? What sort of approximator works for this application?

**21.7** Implement an exploring reinforcement learning agent that uses direct utility estimation. Make two versions—one with a tabular representation and one using the function approximator in Equation (21.9). Compare their performance in three environments:

**a.** The $4 \times 3$ world described in the chapter.

**b.** A $10 \times 10$ world with no obstacles and a +1 reward at (10,10).

**c.** A $10 \times 10$ world with no obstacles and a +1 reward at (5,5).

**21.8** Write out the parameter update equations for TD learning with

$$\hat{U}(x, y) = \theta_0 + \theta_1 x + \theta_2 y + \theta_3 \sqrt{(x - x_g)^2 + (y - y_g)^2} \,.$$

**21.9** Devise suitable features for stochastic grid worlds (generalizations of the $4 \times 3$ world) that contain multiple obstacles and multiple terminal states with $+1$ or $-1$ rewards.

**21.10** Compute the true utility function and the best linear approximation in $x$ and $y$ (as in Equation (21.9)) for the following environments:

**a.** A $10 \times 10$ world with a single $+1$ terminal state at (10,10).

**b.** As in (a), but add a $-1$ terminal state at (10,1).

**c.** As in (b), but add obstacles in 10 randomly selected squares.

**d.** As in (b), but place a wall stretching from (5,2) to (5,9).

**e.** As in (a), but with the terminal state at (5,5).

The actions are deterministic moves in the four directions. In each case, compare the results using three-dimensional plots. For each environment, propose additional features (besides $x$ and $y$) that would improve the approximation and show the results.

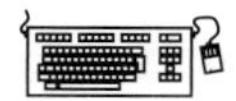

**21.11** Extend the standard game-playing environment (Chapter 6) to incorporate a reward signal. Put two reinforcement learning agents into the environment (they may, of course, share the agent program) and have them play against each other. Apply the generalized TD update rule (Equation (21.11)) to update the evaluation function. You might wish to start with a simple linear weighted evaluation function and a simple game, such as tic-tac-toe.

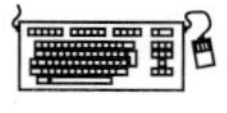

**21.12** Implement the REINFORCE and PEGASUS algorithms and apply them to the $4 \times 3$ world, using a policy family of your own choosing. Comment on the results.

**21.13** Investigate the application of reinforcement learning ideas to the modeling of human and animal behavior.

**21.14** Is reinforcement learning an appropriate abstract model for evolution? What connection exists, if any, between hardwired reward signals and evolutionary fitness?

# 22 COMMUNICATION

*In which we see why agents might want to exchange information-carrying messages with each other and how they can do so.*

It is dusk in the savanna woodlands of Amboseli National Park near the base of Kilimanjaro. A group of vervet monkeys are foraging for food when one lets out a loud barking call. The others in the group recognize this as the leopard warning call (distinct from the short cough used to warn of eagles, or the chutter for snakes) and scramble for the trees. The vervet has successfully communicated with the group.

COMMUNICATION

SIGNS

**Communication** is the intentional exchange of information brought about by the production and perception of **signs** drawn from a shared system of conventional signs. Most animals use signs to represent important messages: food here, predator nearby, approach, withdraw, let's mate. In a partially observable world, communication can help agents be successful because they can learn information that is observed or inferred by others.

LANGUAGE

What sets humans apart from other animals is the complex system of structured messages known as **language** that enables us to communicate most of what we know about the world. Although chimpanzees, dolphins, and other mammals have shown vocabularies of hundreds of signs and some aptitude for stringing them together, only humans can reliably communicate an unbounded number of qualitatively different messages.

Of course, there are other attributes that are uniquely human: no other species wears clothes, creates representational art, or watches three hours of television a day. But when Turing proposed his test (see Section 1.1), he based it on language, because language is intimately tied to thinking. In this chapter, we will both explain how a communicating agent works and describe a fragment of English.

## 22.1 COMMUNICATION AS ACTION

SPEECH ACT

One of the actions available to an agent is to produce language. This is called a **speech act**. "Speech" is used in the same sense as in "free speech," not "talking," so e-mailing, skywriting, and using sign language all count as speech acts. English has no neutral word for an agent that produces language by any means, so we will use **speaker**, **hearer**, and **utterance** as generic

SPEAKER

HEARER

UTTERANCE

WORD

terms referring to any mode of communication. We will also use the term **word** to refer to any kind of conventional communicative sign.

Why would an agent bother to perform a speech act when it could be doing a "regular" action? We saw in Chapter 12 that agents in a multiagent environment can use communication to help arrive at joint plans. For example, a group of agents exploring the wumpus world together gains an advantage (collectively and individually) by being able to do the following:

- **Query** other agents about particular aspects of the world. This is typically done by asking questions: *Have you smelled the wumpus anywhere?*
- **Inform** each other about the world. This is done by making representative statements: *There's a breeze here in 3 4.* Answering a question is another kind of informing.
- **Request** other agents to perform actions: *Please help me carry the gold.* Sometimes an **indirect speech act** (a request in the form of a statement or question) is considered more polite: *I could use some help carrying this.* An agent with authority can give commands (*Alpha go right; Bravo and Charlie go left*), and an agent with power can make a threat (*Give me the gold, or else*). Together, these kinds of speech acts are called **directives**.
- **Acknowledge** requests: *OK.*
- **Promise** or commit to a plan: *I'll shoot the wumpus; you grab the gold.*

INDIRECT SPEECH ACT

All speech acts affect the world by making air molecules vibrate (or the equivalent effect in some other medium) and thereby changing the mental state and eventually the future actions of other agents. Some kinds of speech acts transfer information to the hearer, assuming that the hearer's decision making will be suitably affected by that information. Others are aimed more directly at making the hearer take some action. Another class of speech act, the **declarative**, appears to have a more direct effect on the world, as in *I now pronounce you man and wife* or *Strike three, you're out*. Of course, the effect is achieved by creating or confirming a complex web of mental states among the agents involved: being married and being out are states characterized primarily by convention rather than by "physical" properties of the world.

DECLARATIVE

The communicating agent's task is to decide *when* a speech act of some kind is called for and *which* speech act, out of all the possibilities, is the right one. The problem of understanding speech acts is much like other **understanding** problems, such as understanding images or diagnosing illnesses. We are given a set of ambiguous inputs, and from them we have to work backwards to decide what state of the world could have created these inputs. However, because speech is a planned action, understanding it also involves plan recognition.

UNDERSTANDING

### Fundamentals of language

FORMAL LANGUAGE

STRINGS

TERMINAL SYMBOLS

NATURAL LANGUAGES

A **formal language** is defined as a (possibly infinite) set of **strings**. Each string is a concatenation of **terminal symbols**, sometimes called words. For example, in the language of first-order logic, the terminal symbols include $\land$ and $P$, and a typical string is "$P \land Q$." The string "$P\ Q \land$" is not a member of the language. Formal languages such as first-order logic and Java have strict mathematical definitions. This is in contrast to **natural languages**, such as Chinese, Danish, and English, that have no strict definition but are used by a community of speakers. For this chapter we will attempt to treat natural languages as if they were formal languages, although we recognize the match will not be perfect.

GRAMMAR

A **grammar** is a finite set of rules that specifies a language. Formal languages always have an official grammar, specified in manuals or books. Natural languages have no official grammar, but linguists strive to discover properties of the language by a process of scientific inquiry and then to codify their discoveries in a grammar. To date, no linguist has succeeded completely. Note that linguists are scientists, attempting to define a language as it *is*. There are also prescriptive grammarians who try to dictate how a language *should be*. They create rules such as "Don't split infinitives" which are sometimes printed in style guides, but have little relevance to actual language usage.

PRAGMATICS

Both formal and natural languages associate a meaning or **semantics** to each valid string. For example, in the language of arithmetic, we would have a rule saying that if "$X$" and "$Y$" are expressions, then "$X + Y$" is also an expression, and its semantics is the sum of $X$ and $Y$. In natural languages, it is also important to understand the **pragmatics** of a string: the actual meaning of the string as it is spoken in a given situation. The meaning is not just in the words themselves, but in the interpretation of the words *in situ*.

PHRASE STRUCTURE

NOUN PHRASE

VERB PHRASE

SENTENCE

Most grammar rule formalisms are based on the idea of **phrase structure**—that strings are composed of substrings called **phrases**, which come in different categories. For example, the phrases "the wumpus," "the king," and "the agent in the corner" are all examples of the category **noun phrase**, or $NP$. There are two reasons for identifying phrases in this way. First, phrases usually correspond to natural semantic elements from which the meaning of an utterance can be constructed; for example, noun phrases refer to objects in the world. Second, categorizing phrases helps us to describe the allowable strings of the language. We can say that any of the noun phrases can combine with a **verb phrase** (or $VP$) such as "is dead" to form a phrase of category **sentence** (or $S$). Without the intermediate notions of noun phrase and verb phrase, it would be difficult to explain why "the wumpus is dead" is a sentence whereas "wumpus the dead is" is not.

NONTERMINAL SYMBOLS

REWRITE RULES

Category names such as $NP$, $VP$, and $S$ are called **nonterminal symbols**. Grammars define nonterminals using **rewrite rules**. We will adopt the Backus–Naur form (BNF) notation for rewrite rules, which is described in Appendix B on page 984. In this notation, the meaning of a rule such as

$$S \rightarrow NP\ VP$$

is that an $S$ may consist of any $NP$ followed by any $VP$.

### The component steps of communication

A typical communication episode, in which speaker $S$ wants to inform hearer $H$ about proposition $P$ using words $W$, is composed of seven processes:

INTENTION

**Intention**. Somehow, speaker $S$ decides that there is some proposition $P$ that is worth saying to hearer $H$. For our example, the speaker has the intention of having the hearer know that the wumpus is no longer alive.

GENERATION

**Generation**. The speaker plans how to turn the proposition $P$ into an utterance that makes it likely that the hearer, upon perceiving the utterance in the current situation, can infer

## Generative Capacity

Grammatical formalisms can be classified by their **generative capacity**: the set of languages they can represent. Chomsky (1957) describes four classes of grammatical formalisms that differ only in the form of the rewrite rules. The classes can be arranged in a hierarchy, where each class can be used to describe all the languages that can be described by a less powerful class, as well as some additional languages. Here we list the hierarchy, most powerful class first:

**Recursively enumerable** grammars use unrestricted rules: both sides of the rewrite rules can have any number of terminal and nonterminal symbols, as in the rule $A\ B \ \rightarrow \ C$. These grammars are equivalent to Turing machines in their expressive power.

**Context-sensitive grammars** are restricted only in that the right-hand side must contain at least as many symbols as the left-hand side. The name "context-sensitive" comes from the fact that a rule such as $A\ S\ B \ \rightarrow \ A\ X\ B$ says that an $S$ can be rewritten as an $X$ in the context of a preceding $A$ and a following $B$. Context-sensitive grammars can represent languages such as $a^n b^n c^n$ (a sequence of $n$ copies of $a$ followed by the same number of $b$s and then $c$s).

In **context-free grammars** (or **CFG**s), the left-hand side consists of a single nonterminal symbol. Thus, each rule licenses rewriting the nonterminal as the right-hand side in *any* context. CFGs are popular for natural language and programming language grammars, although it is now widely accepted that at least some natural languages have constructions that are not context-free (Pullum, 1991). Context-free grammars can represent $a^n b^n$, but not $a^n b^n c^n$.

**Regular** grammars are the most restricted class. Every rule has a single nonterminal on the left-hand side and a terminal symbol optionally followed by a nonterminal on the right-hand side. Regular grammars are equivalent in power to finite-state machines. They are poorly suited for programming languages, because they cannot represent constructs such as balanced opening and closing parentheses (a variation of the $a^n b^n$ language). The closest they can come is representing $a^* b^*$, a sequence of any number of $a$s followed by any number of $b$s.

The grammars higher up in the hierarchy have more expressive power, but the algorithms for dealing with them are less efficient. Up to the mid 1980s, linguists focused on context-free and context-sensitive languages. Since then, there has been increased emphasis on regular grammars, brought about by the need to process megabytes and gigabytes of online text very quickly, even at the cost of a less complete analysis. As Fernando Pereira put it, "The older I get, the further down the Chomsky hierarchy I go." To see what he means, compare Pereira and Warren (1980) with Mohri, Pereira, and Riley (2002).

the meaning $P$ (or something close to it). Assume that the speaker is able to come up with the words "The wumpus is dead," and call this $W$.

SYNTHESIS

**Synthesis**. The speaker produces the physical realization $W'$ of the words $W$. This can be via ink on paper, vibrations in air, or some other medium. In Figure 22.1, we show the agent synthesizing a string of sounds $W'$ written in the phonetic alphabet defined on page 569: "[thaxwahmpaxsihzdehd]." The words are run together; this is typical of quickly spoken speech.

PERCEPTION

**Perception**. $H$ perceives the physical realization $W'$ as $W_2'$ and decodes it as the words $W_2$. When the medium is speech, the perception step is called **speech recognition**; when it is printing, it is called **optical character recognition**. Both moved from being esoteric to being commonplace in the 1990s, due largely to increased desktop computing power.

ANALYSIS

PARSING

PARSE TREE

SEMANTIC INTERPRETATION

PRAGMATIC INTERPRETATION

**Analysis**. $H$ infers that $W_2$ has possible meanings $P_1, \ldots, P_n$. We divide analysis into three main parts: syntactic interpretation (or parsing), semantic interpretation, and pragmatic interpretation. **Parsing** is the process of building a **parse tree** for an input string, as shown in Figure 22.1. The interior nodes of the parse tree represent phrases and the leaf nodes represent words. **Semantic interpretation** is the process of extracting the meaning of an utterance as an expression in some representation language. Figure 22.1 shows two possible semantic interpretations: that the wumpus is not alive and that it is tired (a colloquial meaning of *dead*). Utterances with several possible interpretations are said to be **ambiguous**. **Pragmatic interpretation** takes into account the fact that the same words can have different meanings in

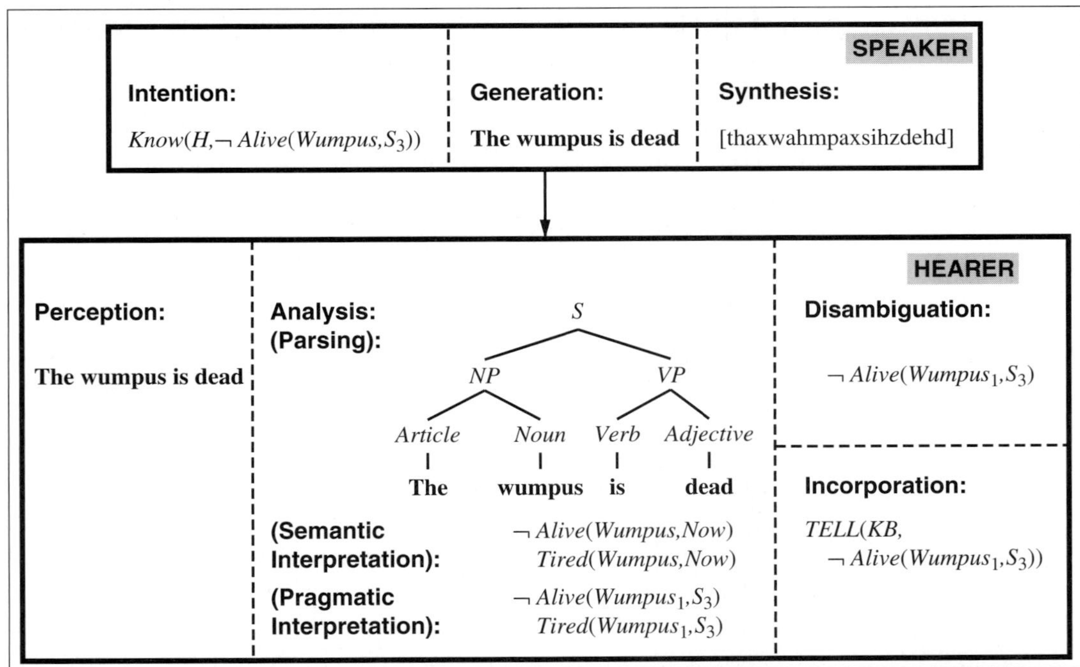


**Figure 22.1** Seven processes involved in communication, using the example sentence "The wumpus is dead."

different situations. Whereas syntactic interpretation is a function of one argument, the string, pragmatic interpretation is a function of the utterance and the context or situation in which it is uttered. In the example, pragmatics does two things: replace the constant *Now* with the constant $S_3$, which stands for the current situation, and replace $Wumpus$ with $Wumpus_1$, which stands for the single Wumpus that is known to be in this cave. In general, pragmatics can contribute much more to the final interpretation of an utterance; consider "I'm looking at the diamond" when spoken by a jeweler or by a baseball player. In Section 22.7, we will see that pragmatics allows us to interpret "It is dead" as meaning that the wumpus is dead if we are in a situation where the wumpus is salient.

DISAMBIGUATION

**Disambiguation.** $H$ infers that $S$ intended to convey $P_i$ (where ideally $P_i = P$). Most speakers are not intentionally ambiguous, but most utterances have several feasible interpretations. Communication works because the hearer does the work of figuring out which interpretation is the one the speaker probably meant to convey. Notice that this is the first time we have used the word *probably*, and disambiguation is the first process that depends heavily on uncertain reasoning. Analysis generates possible interpretations; if more than one interpretation is found, then disambiguation chooses the one that is best.

INCORPORATION

**Incorporation.** $H$ decides to believe $P_i$ (or not). A totally naive agent might believe everything it hears, but a sophisticated agent treats the speech act as evidence for $P_i$, not confirmation of it.

Putting it all together, we get the agent program shown in Figure 22.2. Here the agent acts as a robot slave that can be commanded by a master. On each turn, the slave will answer a question or obey a command if the master has made one, and it will believe any statements made by the master. It will also comment (once) on the current situation if it has nothing more pressing to do, and it will plan its own action if left alone. Here is a typical dialog:

| ROBOT SLAVE | MASTER |
|---|---|
| I feel a breeze. | Go to 1 2. |
| Nothing is here. | Go north. |
| I feel a breeze and I smell a stench | |
| and I see a glitter. | Grab the gold. |

## 22.2 A FORMAL GRAMMAR FOR A FRAGMENT OF ENGLISH

In this section, we define a formal grammar for a small fragment of English that is suitable for making statements about the wumpus world. We will call this language $\mathcal{E}_0$. Later sections will improve on $\mathcal{E}_0$ to make it somewhat closer to real English. We are unlikely ever to devise a complete grammar for English, if only because no two persons would agree entirely on what constitutes valid English.

### The Lexicon of $\mathcal{E}_0$

LEXICON

First we define the **lexicon**, or list of allowable words. The words are grouped into the categories or parts of speech familiar to dictionary users: nouns, pronouns, and names to denote

```
function NAIVE-COMMUNICATING-AGENT(percept) returns action
   static: KB, a knowledge base
           state, the current state of the environment
           action, the most recent action, initially none

   state ← UPDATE-STATE(state, action, percept)
   words ← SPEECH-PART(percept)
   semantics ← DISAMBIGUATE(PRAGMATICS(SEMANTICS(PARSE(words))))
   if words = None and action is not a SAY then /* Describe the state */
      return SAY(GENERATE-DESCRIPTION(state))
   else if TYPE[semantics] = Command then /* Obey the command */
      return CONTENTS[semantics]
   else if TYPE[semantics] = Question then /* Answer the question */
      answer ← ASK(KB, semantics)
      return SAY(GENERATE-DESCRIPTION(answer))
   else if TYPE[semantics] = Statement then /* Believe the statement */
      TELL(KB, CONTENTS[semantics])
   /* If we fall through to here, do a "regular" action */
   return FIRST(PLANNER(KB, state))
```

**Figure 22.2** A communicating agent that accepts commands, questions, and statements. The agent can also describe the current state or perform a "regular" non-speech-act action when there is nothing to say.

things, verbs to denote events, adjectives to modify nouns, and adverbs to modify verbs. Categories that are perhaps less familiar to some readers are articles (such as *the*), prepositions (*in*), and conjunctions (*and*). Figure 22.3 shows a small lexicon.

Each of the categories ends in . . . to indicate that there are other words in the category. However, it should be noted that there are two distinct reasons for the missing words. For nouns, verbs, adjectives, and adverbs, it is in principle infeasible to list them all. Not only are there tens of thousands of members in each class, but new ones–like *MP3* or *anime*—are being added constantly. These four categories are called **open classes**. The other categories (pronoun, article, preposition, and conjunction) are called **closed classes**. They have a small number of words (a few to a few dozen) that can in principle be enumerated in full. Closed classes change over the course of centuries, not months. For example, "thee" and "thou" were commonly used pronouns in the 17th century, were on the decline in the 19th, and are seen today only in poetry and some regional dialects.

OPEN CLASSES

CLOSED CLASSES

### The Grammar of $\mathcal{E}_0$

The next step is to combine the words into phrases. We will use five nonterminal symbols to define the different kinds of phrases: sentence ($S$), noun phrase ($NP$), verb phrase ($VP$),

| | | |
|---|---|---|
| *Noun* | → | **stench** \| **breeze** \| **glitter** \| **nothing** \| **agent** |
| | | \| **wumpus** \| **pit** \| **pits**\| **gold** \| **east** \| ... |
| *Verb* | → | **is** \| **see** \| **smell** \| **shoot** \| **feel** \| **stinks** |
| | | \| **go** \| **grab** \| **carry** \| **kill** \| **turn** \| ... |
| *Adjective* | → | **right** \| **left** \| **east** \| **dead** \| **back** \| **smelly** \| ... |
| *Adverb* | → | **here** \| **there** \| **nearby** \| **ahead** |
| | | \| **right** \| **left** \| **east** \| **south** \| **back** \| ... |
| *Pronoun* | → | **me** \| **you** \| **I** \| **it** \| ... |
| *Name* | → | **John** \| **Mary** \| **Boston** \| **Aristotle** \| ... |
| *Article* | → | **the** \| **a** \| **an** \| ... |
| *Preposition* | → | **to** \| **in** \| **on** \| **near** \| ... |
| *Conjunction* | → | **and** \| **or** \| **but** \| ... |
| *Digit* | → | **0**\| **1**\| **2**\| **3**\| **4**\| **5**\| **6**\| **7**\| **8**\| **9** |

**Figure 22.3** The lexicon for $\mathcal{E}_0$.

| | | | |
|---|---|---|---|
| *S* | → | *NP VP* | I + feel a breeze |
| | \| | *S Conjunction S* | I feel a breeze + and + I smell a wumpus |
| *NP* | → | *Pronoun* | I |
| | \| | *Name* | John |
| | \| | *Noun* | pits |
| | \| | *Article Noun* | the + wumpus |
| | \| | *Digit Digit* | 3 4 |
| | \| | *NP PP* | the wumpus + to the east |
| | \| | *NP RelClause* | the wumpus + that is smelly |
| *VP* | → | *Verb* | stinks |
| | \| | *VP NP* | feel + a breeze |
| | \| | *VP Adjective* | is + smelly |
| | \| | *VP PP* | turn + to the east |
| | \| | *VP Adverb* | go + ahead |
| *PP* | → | *Preposition NP* | to + the east |
| *RelClause* | → | **that** *VP* | that + is smelly |

**Figure 22.4** The grammar for $\mathcal{E}_0$, with example phrases for each rule.

prepositional phrase ($PP$), and relative clause ($RelClause$).[1] Figure 22.4 shows a grammar for $\mathcal{E}_0$, with an example for each rewrite rule. $\mathcal{E}_0$ generates good English sentences such as the following:

John is in the pit
The wumpus that stinks is in 2 2
Mary is in Boston and John stinks

OVERGENERATION

UNDERGENERATION

Unfortunately, the grammar **overgenerates**: that is, it generates sentences that are not grammatical, such as "Me go Boston" and "I smell pit gold wumpus nothing east." It also **undergenerates**: there are many sentences of English that it rejects, such as "I think the wumpus is smelly." (Another shortcoming is that the grammar does not capitalize the first word of a sentence, nor add punctuation at the end. That is because it is designed primarily for speech, not writing.)

## 22.3 SYNTACTIC ANALYSIS (PARSING)

We have already defined **parsing** as the process of finding a parse tree for a given input string. That is, a call to the parsing function PARSE, such as

PARSE("the wumpus is dead", $\mathcal{E}_0$, $S$)

should return a parse tree with root $S$ whose leaves are "the wumpus is dead" and whose internal nodes are nonterminal symbols from the grammar $\mathcal{E}_0$. You can see such a tree in Figure 22.1. In linear text, we write the tree as

$$[S\text{: } [NP\text{: } [Article\text{: } \textbf{the}][Noun\text{: } \textbf{wumpus}]] \quad [VP\text{: } [Verb\text{: } \textbf{is}][Adjective\text{: } \textbf{dead}]]] .$$

TOP-DOWN PARSING

BOTTOM-UP PARSING

*Parsing can be seen as a process of searching for a parse tree.* There are two extreme ways of specifying the search space (and many variants in between). First, we can start with the $S$ symbol and search for a tree that has the words as its leaves. This is called **top-down parsing** (because the $S$ is drawn at the top of the tree). Second, we could start with the words and search for a tree with root $S$. This is called **bottom-up parsing**.[2] Top-down parsing can be precisely defined as a search problem as follows:

- The **initial state** is a parse tree consisting of the root $S$ and unknown children: $[S\text{: } ?]$. In general, each state in the search space is a parse tree.
- The **successor function** selects the leftmost node in the tree with unknown children. It then looks in the grammar for rules that have the root label of the node on the left-hand side. For each such rule, it creates a successor state where the ? is replaced by a list corresponding to the right-hand side of the rule. For example, in $\mathcal{E}_0$ there are two rules for $S$, so the tree $[S\text{: } ?]$ would be replaced by the following two successors:

---

[1] A relative clause follows and modifies a noun phrase. It consists of a relative pronoun (such as "who" or "that") followed by a verb phrase. (Another kind of relative clause is discussed in exercise 22.12.) An example of a relative clause is *that stinks* in "The wumpus *that stinks* is in 2 2."

[2] The reader might notice that top-down and bottom-up parsing are analogous to backward and forward chaining, respectively, as described in Chapter 7. We will see shortly that the analogy is exact.

$[S: [S: ?]\ [Conjunction: ?]\ [S: ?]]$
$[S: [NP: ?]\ [VP: ?]]$

The second of these has seven successors, one for each rewrite rule of $NP$.

- The **goal test** checks that the leaves of the parse tree correspond exactly to the input string, with no unknowns and no uncovered inputs.

One big problem for top-down parsing is dealing with so-called **left-recursive rules**—that is, rules of the form $X \rightarrow X \ldots$. With a depth-first search, such a rule would lead us to keep replacing $X$ with $[X: X \ldots]$ in an infinite loop. With a breadth-first search we would successfully find parses for valid sentences, but when given an invalid sentence, we would get stuck in an infinite search space.

The formulation of bottom-up parsing as a search is as follows:

- The **initial state** is a list of the words in the input string, each viewed as a parse tree that is just a single leaf node—for example; [**the**, **wumpus**, **is**, **dead**]. In general, each state in the search space is a list of parse trees.
- The **successor function** looks at every position $i$ in the list of trees and at every right-hand side of a rule in the grammar. If the subsequence of the list of trees starting at $i$ matches the right-hand side, then the subsequence is replaced by a new tree whose category is the left-hand side of the rule and whose children are the subsequence. By "matches," we mean that the category of the node is the same as the element in the right-hand side. For example, the rule $Article \rightarrow$ **the** matches the subsequence consisting of the first node in the list [**the**, **wumpus**, **is**, **dead**], so a successor state would be [[$Article$: **the**], **wumpus**, **is**, **dead**].
- The **goal test** checks for a state consisting of a single tree with root $S$.

See Figure 22.5 for an example of bottom-up parsing.

| *step* | *list of nodes* | *subsequence* | *rule* |
|---|---|---|---|
| INIT | **the wumpus is dead** | **the** | Article → **the** |
| 2 | *Article* **wumpus is dead** | **wumpus** | Noun → **wumpus** |
| 3 | *Article Noun* **is dead** | *Article Noun* | *NP* → *Article Noun* |
| 4 | *NP* **is dead** | **is** | *Verb* → **is** |
| 5 | *NP Verb* **dead** | **dead** | *Adjective* → **dead** |
| 6 | *NP Verb Adjective* | *Verb* | *VP* → *Verb* |
| 7 | *NP VP Adjective* | *VP Adjective* | *VP* → *VP Adjective* |
| 8 | *NP VP* | *NP VP* | *S* → *NP VP* |
| GOAL | *S* | | |

**Figure 22.5** Trace of a bottom up parse on the string "The wumpus is dead." We start with a list of nodes consisting of words. Then we replace subsequences that match the right-hand side of a rule with a new node whose root is the left-hand side. For example, in the third line the *Article* and *Noun* nodes are replaced by an *NP* node that has those two nodes as children. The top-down parse would produce a similar trace, but in the opposite direction.

Both top-down and bottom-up parsing can be inefficient, because of the multiplicity of ways in which multiple parses for different phrases can be combined. Both can waste time searching irrelevant portions of the search space. Top-down parsing can generate intermediate nodes that could never be latched by the words, and bottom-up parsing can generate partial parses of the words that could not appear in an $S$.

Even if we had a perfect heuristic function that allowed us to search without any irrelevant digressions, these algorithms would still be inefficient, because some sentences have *exponentially many* parse trees. The next subsection shows what to do about that.

### Efficient parsing

Consider the following two sentences:

> Have the students in section 2 of Computer Science 101 take the exam.
> Have the students in section 2 of Computer Science 101 taken the exam?

Even though they share the first 10 words, these sentences have very different parses, because the first is a command and the second is a question. A left-to-right parsing algorithm would have to guess whether the first word is part of a command or a question and will not be able to tell if the guess is correct until at least the eleventh word, *take* or *taken*. If the algorithm guesses wrong, it will have to backtrack all the way to the first word. This kind of backtracking is inevitable, but if our parsing algorithm is to be efficient, it must avoid reanalyzing "the students in section 2 of Computer Science 101" as an $NP$ each time it backtracks.

In this section, we will develop a parsing algorithm that avoids this source of inefficiency. The basic idea is an example of **dynamic programming**: *every time we analyze a substring, store the results so we won't have to re-analyze it later.* For example, once we discover that "the students in section 2 of Computer Science 101" is an $NP$, we can record that result in a data structure known as a **chart**. Algorithms that do this are called **chart parsers**. Because we are dealing with context-free grammars, any phrase that was found in the context of one branch of the search space can work just as well in any other branch of the search space.

CHART

VERTICES

EDGES

The chart for an $n$-word sentence consists of $n+1$ **vertices** and a number of **edges** that connect vertices. Figure 22.6 shows a chart with six vertices (circles) and three edges (lines). For example, the edge labeled

$$[0, 5,\ S \ \rightarrow \ NP\ VP\ \bullet]$$

means that an $NP$ followed by a $VP$ combine to make an $S$ that spans the string from 0 to 5. The symbol $\bullet$ in an edge separates what has been found so far from what remains to be found.[3] Edges with $\bullet$ at the end are called **complete edges**. The edge

$$[0, 2,\ S \ \rightarrow \ NP\ \bullet\ VP]$$

says that an $NP$ spans the string from 0 to 2 (the first two words) and that if we could find a $VP$ to follow it, then we would have an $S$. Edges like this with the dot before the end are called incomplete edges, and we say that the edge is looking for a $VP$.

[3] It is because of the $\bullet$ that edges are sometimes called **dotted rules**.

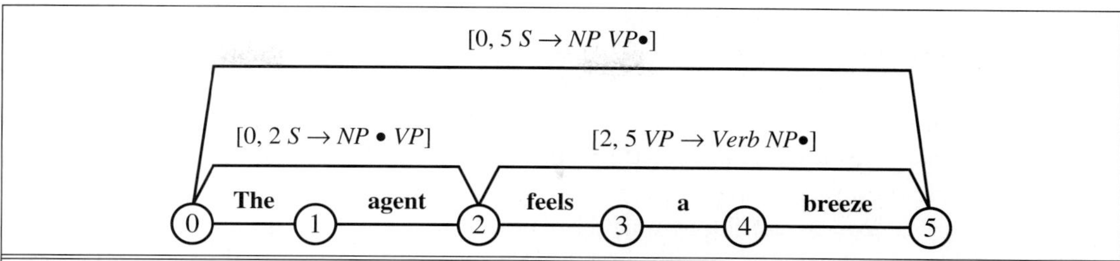


**Figure 22.6** Part of the chart for the sentence "The agent feels a breeze." All six vertices are shown, but only three of the edges that would make up a complete parse.

```
function CHART-PARSE(words, grammar) returns chart

  chart ← array[0... LENGTH(words)] of empty lists
  ADD-EDGE([0, 0, S' → • S])
  for i ← from 0 to LENGTH(words) do
     SCANNER(i, words[i])
  return chart

procedure ADD-EDGE(edge)
   /* Add edge to chart, and see if it extends or predicts another edge. */
   if edge not in chart[END(edge)] then
      append edge to chart[END(edge)]
      if edge has nothing after the dot then EXTENDER(edge)
      else PREDICTOR(edge)

procedure SCANNER(j, word)
   /* For each edge expecting a word of this category here, extend the edge. */
   for each [i, j, A → α • B β] in chart[j] do
      if word is of category B then
         ADD-EDGE([i, j+1, A → α B • β])

procedure PREDICTOR([i, j, A → α • B β])
   /* Add to chart any rules for B that could help extend this edge */
   for each (B → γ) in REWRITES-FOR(B, grammar) do
      ADD-EDGE([j, j, B → • γ])

procedure EXTENDER([j, k, B → γ •])
   /* See what edges can be extended by this edge */
   e_B ← the edge that is the input to this procedure
   for each [i, j, A → α • B' β] in chart[j] do
      if B = B' then
         ADD-EDGE([i, k, A → α e_B • β])
```

**Figure 22.7** The chart-parsing algorithm. $S$ is the start symbol and $S'$ is a new nonterminal symbol. $chart[j]$ is the list of edges that end at vertex $j$. The Greek letters match a string of zero or more symbols.

Figure 22.7 shows the chart-parsing algorithm. The main idea is to combine the best of top-down and bottom-up parsing. The procedure PREDICTOR is top-down: it makes entries into the chart that say what symbols are desired at what locations. SCANNER is the bottom-up procedure that starts from the words, but it will use a word only to extend an existing chart entry. Similarly, EXTENDER builds constituents bottom-up, but only to extend an existing chart entry.

We use a trick to start the whole algorithm: we add the edge $[0, 0,\ S' \rightarrow \bullet\ S]$ to the chart, where $S$ is the grammar's start symbol, and $S'$ is a new symbol that we just invented. The call to ADD-EDGE causes the PREDICTOR to add edges for the rules that can yield an $S$—that is, $[S \rightarrow NP\ VP]$. Then we look at the first constituent of that rule, $NP$, and add rules for every way to yield an $NP$. Eventually, the predictor adds, in a top-down fashion, all possible edges that could be used in the service of creating the final $S$.

When the predictor for $S'$ is finished, we enter a loop that calls SCANNER for each word in the sentence. If the word at position $j$ is a member of a category $B$ that some edge is looking for at $j$, then we extend that edge, noting the word as an instance of $B$. Notice that each call to SCANNER can end up calling PREDICTOR and EXTENDER recursively, thereby interleaving the top-down and bottom-up processing.

The other bottom-up component, EXTENDER,[4] takes a complete edge with left hand side $B$ and uses it to extend any incomplete rule in the chart that ends where the complete edge starts if the incomplete rule is looking for a $B$.

Figures 22.8 and 22.9 show a chart and trace of the algorithm parsing the sentence "I feel it" (which is an answer to the question "Do you feel a breeze?"). Thirteen edges (labeled a–m) are recorded in the chart, including five complete edges (shown above the vertices of the chart) and eight incomplete ones (below the vertices). Note the cycle of predictor, scanner, and extender actions. For example, the predictor uses the fact that edge (a) is looking for an $S$ to license the prediction of an $NP$ (edge b) and then a $Pronoun$ (edge c). Then the scanner recognizes that there is a $Pronoun$ in the right place (edge d), and the extender combines the incomplete edge b with the complete edge d to yield a new edge, e.

The chart-parsing algorithm avoids building a large class of edges that would have been examined by the simple bottom-up procedure. Consider the sentence "The ride the horse gave was wild." A bottom-up parse would label "ride the horse" as a $VP$ and then discard the parse tree when it is found not to fit into a larger $S$. But $\mathcal{E}_0$ does not allow a $VP$ to follow "the," so the chart-parsing algorithm will never predict a $VP$ at that point and thus will avoid wasting time building the $VP$ constituent there. Algorithms that work from left to right and avoid building these impossible constituents are called **left-corner** parsers, because they build up a parse tree that starts with the grammar's start symbol and extends down to the leftmost word in the sentence (the left corner). An edge is added to the chart only if it can serve to extend this parse tree. (See Figure 22.10 for an example.)

LEFT-CORNER

The chart parser uses only polynomial time and space. It requires $O(kn^2)$ space to store the edges, where $n$ is the number of words in the sentence and $k$ is a constant that depends

[4] Traditionally, our EXTENDER procedure has been called COMPLETER. This name is misleading, because the procedure does not complete edges: it takes a complete edge as input and extends incomplete edges.

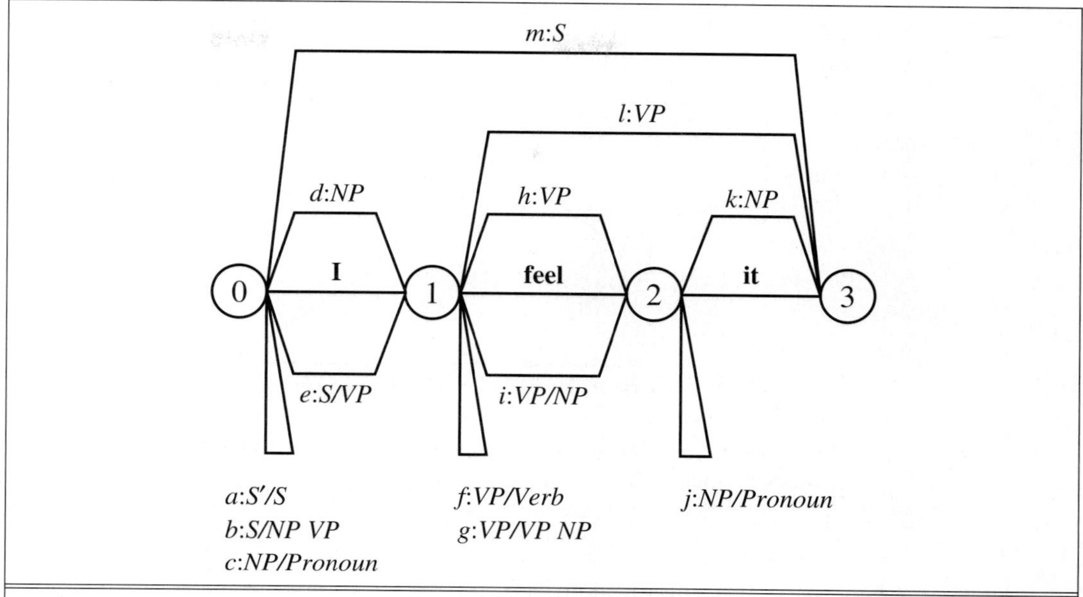


**Figure 22.8** Chart for a parse of "$_0$ I $_1$ feel $_2$ it $_3$." The notation *m:S* means that edge $m$ has an $S$ on the left-hand side, while the notation *f:VP/Verb* means that edge $f$ has a $VP$ on the left-hand side, but is looking for a $Verb$. There are five complete edges above the vertices and eight incomplete edges below.

| Edge | Procedure | Derivation |
|---|---|---|
| a | INITIALIZER | $[0,0,\ S' \rightarrow \bullet S]$ |
| b | PREDICTOR(a) | $[0,0,\ S \rightarrow \bullet NP\ VP]$ |
| c | PREDICTOR(b) | $[0,0,\ NP \rightarrow \bullet Pronoun]$ |
| d | SCANNER(c) | $[0,1,\ NP \rightarrow Pronoun \bullet]$ |
| e | EXTENDER(b,d) | $[0,1,\ S \rightarrow NP \bullet VP]$ |
| f | PREDICTOR(e) | $[1,1,\ VP \rightarrow \bullet Verb]$ |
| g | PREDICTOR(e) | $[1,1,\ VP \rightarrow \bullet VP\ NP]$ |
| h | SCANNER(f) | $[1,2,\ VP \rightarrow Verb \bullet]$ |
| i | EXTENDER(g,h) | $[1,2,\ VP \rightarrow VP \bullet NP]$ |
| j | PREDICTOR(g) | $[2,2,\ NP \rightarrow \bullet Pronoun]$ |
| k | SCANNER(j) | $[2,3,\ NP \rightarrow Pronoun \bullet]$ |
| l | EXTENDER(i,k) | $[1,3,\ VP \rightarrow VP\ NP \bullet]$ |
| m | EXTENDER(e,l) | $[0,3,\ S \rightarrow NP\ VP \bullet]$ |

**Figure 22.9** Trace of a parse of "$_0$ I $_1$ feel $_2$ it $_3$." For each edge a-m, we show the procedure used to derive the edge from other edges already in the chart. Some edges were omitted for brevity.

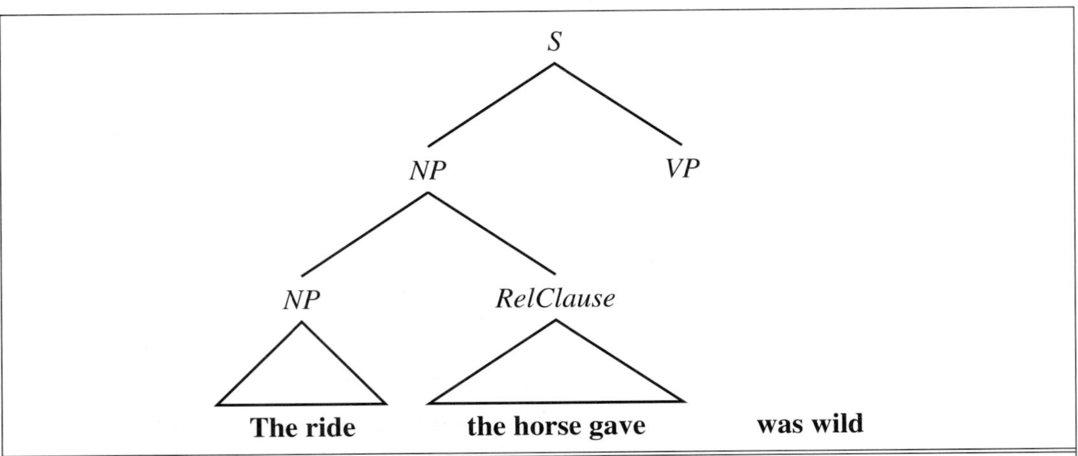


**Figure 22.10** A left-corner parsing algorithm avoids predicting a $VP$ starting with "ride," but does predict a $VP$ starting with "was," because the grammar expects a $VP$ following an $NP$. The triangle over "the horse gave" means that the words have a parse as a $RelClause$, but with additional intermediate constituents that are not shown.

on the grammar. When it can build no more edges it stops, so we know that the algorithm terminates (even when there are left-recursive rules). In fact, it takes time $O(n^3)$ in the worst case, which is the best that can be achieved for context-free grammars. The bottleneck for CHART-PARSE is EXTENDER, which must try to extend each of $O(n)$ incomplete edges ending at position $j$ with each of $O(n)$ complete edges starting at $j$, for each of $n+1$ different values of $j$. Multiplying these together, we get $O(n^3)$. This gives us something of a paradox: how can an $O(n^3)$ algorithm return an answer that might contain an exponential number of parse trees? Consider an example: the sentence

"Fall leaves fall and spring leaves spring"

is ambiguous because each word (except "and") can be either a noun or a verb, and "fall" and "spring" can be adjectives as well. Altogether, the sentence has four parses:[5]

[$S$: [$S$: [$NP$: Fall leaves] fall] and [$S$: [$NP$: spring leaves] spring] ;
[$S$: [$S$: [$NP$: Fall leaves] fall] and [$S$: spring [$VP$: leaves spring]] ;
[$S$: [$S$: Fall [$VP$: leaves fall]] and [$S$: [$NP$: spring leaves] spring] ;
[$S$: [$S$: Fall [$VP$: leaves fall]] and [$S$: spring [$VP$: leaves spring]] .

If we had $n$ ambiguous conjoined subsentences, we would have $2^n$ ways of choosing parses for the subsentences.[6] How does the chart parser avoid exponential processing time? There are actually two answers. First, the CHART-PARSE algorithm itself is actually a *recognizer*, not a parser. If there is a complete edge of the form $[0, n,\ S \ \rightarrow \ \alpha \ \bullet]$ in the chart, then we have recognized an $S$. Recovering the parse tree from this edge is not considered part of

5 The parse [$S$: Fall [$VP$: leaves fall]] is equivalent to "Autumn abandons autumn."

6 There also would be $O(n!)$ ambiguity in the way the components conjoin with each other—for example, ($X$ and ($Y$ and $Z$)) versus (($X$ and $Y$) and $Z$). But that is another story, one that is told quite well by Church and Patil (1982).

CHART-PARSE's job, but it can be done. Note, in the last line of EXTENDER, that we build up $\alpha$ as a list of edges, $e_B$, not just a list of category names. So to convert an edge into a parse tree, simply look recursively at the component edges, converting each $[i, j,\ X \ \rightarrow\ \alpha\ \bullet]$ into the tree $[X : \alpha]$. This is straightforward, but it gives us only *one* parse tree.

The second answer is that if you want all possible parses, you'll have to dig deeper into the chart. While we're converting the edge $[i, j,\ X \ \rightarrow\ \alpha\ \bullet]$ into the tree $[X : \alpha]$, we'll also look to see whether there are any other edges of the form $[i, j,\ X \ \rightarrow\ \beta\ \bullet]$. If there are, these edges will generate additional parses. Now we have a choice of what to do with them. We could enumerate all the possibilities, and that means that the paradox would be resolved and we would require an exponential amount of time to list the parses. Or we could prolong

PACKED FOREST

the mystery a little longer and represent the parses with a structure called a **packed forest**, which looks like this:

$$[S\text{: } [S\text{: } \left\{ \begin{array}{l} [NP\text{: Fall leaves}]\,[VP\text{: fall}] \\ [NP\text{: Fall}]\,[VP\text{: leaves fall}] \end{array} \right\} ] \text{ and } [S\text{: } \left\{ \begin{array}{l} [NP\text{: spring leaves}]\,[VP\text{: spring}] \\ [NP\text{: spring}]\,[VP\text{: leaves spring}] \end{array} \right\} ]]$$

The idea is that each node can be either a regular parse tree node or a set of tree nodes. This enables us to return a representation of an exponential number of parses in a polynomial amount of space and time. Of course, when $n = 2$, there is not much difference between $2^n$ and $2n$, but for large $n$, such a representation offers considerable saving. Unfortunately, this simple packed forest approach won't handle all the $O(n!)$ ambiguity in how the conjunctions associate. Maxwell and Kaplan (1995) show how a more complex representation based on the principles of truth maintenance systems can pack the trees even tighter.

$$\begin{array}{rcl}
S & \rightarrow & NP_S\ VP \mid \ \ldots \\
NP_S & \rightarrow & Pronoun_S \mid Name \mid Noun \mid \ldots \\
NP_O & \rightarrow & Pronoun_O \mid Name \mid Noun \mid \ldots \\
VP & \rightarrow & VP\ NP_O \mid \ \ldots \\
PP & \rightarrow & Preposition\ NP_O \\
Pronoun_S & \rightarrow & \mathbf{I} \mid \mathbf{you} \mid \mathbf{he} \mid \mathbf{she} \mid \mathbf{it} \mid \ \ldots \\
Pronoun_O & \rightarrow & \mathbf{me} \mid \mathbf{you} \mid \mathbf{him} \mid \mathbf{her} \mid \mathbf{it} \mid \ \ldots
\end{array}$$

$$\begin{array}{rcl}
S & \rightarrow & NP(Subjective)\ VP \mid \ldots \\
NP(case) & \rightarrow & Pronoun(case) \mid Name \mid Noun \mid \ldots \\
VP & \rightarrow & VP\ NP(Objective) \mid \ldots \\
PP & \rightarrow & Preposition\ NP(Objective) \\
Pronoun(Subjective) & \rightarrow & \mathbf{I} \mid \mathbf{you} \mid \mathbf{he} \mid \mathbf{she} \mid \mathbf{it} \mid \ \ldots \\
Pronoun(Objective) & \rightarrow & \mathbf{me} \mid \mathbf{you} \mid \mathbf{him} \mid \mathbf{her} \mid \mathbf{it} \mid \ \ldots
\end{array}$$

**Figure 22.11** Top: A BNF grammar for the language $\mathcal{E}_1$, which handles subjective and objective cases in noun phrases and thus does not over-generate quite so badly. The portions that are identical to $\mathcal{E}_0$ have been omitted. Bottom: A definite clause grammar (DCG) of $\mathcal{E}_1$.

## 22.4 AUGMENTED GRAMMARS

We saw in Section 22.2 that the simple grammar for $\mathcal{E}_0$ generates "I smell a stench" and many other sentences of English. Unfortunately, it also generates many non-sentences such as "Me smell a stench." To avoid this problem, our grammar would have to know that "me" is not a valid $NP$ when it is the subject of a sentence. Linguists say that the pronoun "I" is in the subjective case, and "me" is in the objective case.[7] When we take case into account, we realize that the $\mathcal{E}_0$ grammar is not context-free: it is not true that any $NP$ is equal to any other regardless of context. We can fix the problem by introducing new categories such as $NP_S$ and $NP_O$, to stand for noun phrases in the subjective and objective case, respectively. We would also need to split the category $Pronoun$ into the two categories $Pronoun_S$ (which includes "I") and $Pronoun_O$ (which includes "me"). The top part of Figure 22.11 shows the complete BNF grammar for case agreement; we call the resulting language $\mathcal{E}_1$. Notice that all the $NP$ rules must be duplicated, once for $NP_S$ and once for $NP_O$.

AGREEMENT

Unfortunately, $\mathcal{E}_1$ still overgenerates. English and many other languages require **agreement** between the subject and main verb of a sentence. For example, if "I" is the subject, then "I smell" is grammatical, but "I smells" is not. If "it" is the subject, we get the reverse. In English, the agreement distinctions are minimal: most verbs have one form for third-person singular subjects (he, she, or it), and a second form for all other combinations of person and number. There is one exception: "I am / you are / he is" has three forms. If we multiply these three distinctions by the two distinctions of $NP_S$ and $NP_O$, we end up with six forms of $NP$. As we discover more distinctions, we end up with an exponential number.

AUGMENT

The alternative is to **augment** the existing rules of the grammar instead of introducing new rules. We will first give an example of what we would like an augmented rule to look like (see the bottom half of Figure 22.11) and then formally define how to interpret the rules. Augmented rules allow for *parameters* on nonterminal categories. Figure 22.11 shows how to describe $\mathcal{E}_1$ using augmented rules. The categories $NP$ and $Pronoun$ have a parameter indicating their case. (Nouns do not have case in English, although they do in many other languages.) In the rule for $S$, the $NP$ must be in the subjective case, whereas in the rules for $VP$ and $PP$, the $NP$ must be in the objective case. The rule for $NP$ takes a variable, *case*, as its argument. The intent is that the $NP$ can have any case, but if the $NP$ is rewritten as a $Pronoun$, then it must have the same case. This use of a variable—avoiding a decision where the distinction is not important—is what keeps the size of the rule set from growing exponentially with the number of features.

DEFINITE CLAUSE GRAMMAR

This formalism for augmentations is called **definite clause grammar** or DCG, because each grammar rule can be interpreted as a definite clause in Horn logic.[8] First we will show how a normal, unaugmented rule can be interpreted as a definite clause. We consider each

---

7 The subjective case is also sometimes called the nominative case and the objective case is sometimes called the accusative case. Many languages also have a dative case for words in the indirect object position.

8 Recall that a definite clause, when written as an implication, has exactly one atom in its consequent, and a conjunction of zero or more atoms in its antecedent. Two examples are $A \land B \Rightarrow C$ and just $C$.

category symbol to be a predicate on strings, so that $NP(s)$ is true if the string $s$ forms an $NP$. The CFG rule

$$S \rightarrow NP\ VP$$

is shorthand for the definite clause

$$NP(s_1) \land VP(s_2) \Rightarrow S(s_1 + s_2) .$$

Here $s_1 + s_2$ denotes the concatenation of two strings, so this rule says that if the string $s_1$ is an $NP$ and the string $s_2$ is a $VP$, then their concatenation is an $S$, which is exactly how we were already interpreting the CFG rule. It is important to note that *DCGs allow us to talk about parsing as logical inference.* This makes it possible to reason about languages and strings in many different ways. For example, it means we can do bottom-up parsing using forward chaining or top-down parsing using backward chaining. We will see that it also means that we can use the same grammar for both parsing and generation.

The real benefit of the DCG approach is that we can *augment* the category symbols with additional arguments other than the string argument. For example, the rule

$$NP(case) \rightarrow Pronoun(case)$$

is shorthand for the definite clause

$$Pronoun(case, s_1) \Rightarrow NP(case, s_1) .$$

This says that if the string $s_1$ is a $Pronoun$ with case specified by the variable *case*, then $s_1$ is also an $NP$ with the same case. In general, we can augment a category symbol with any number of arguments, and the arguments are parameters that are subject to unification as in regular Horn clause inference.

There is a price to pay for this convenience: we are providing the grammar writer with the full power of a theorem-prover, so we give up the guarantees of $O(n^3)$ syntactic parsing; parsing with augmentations can be NP-complete or even undecidable, depending on the augmentations.

A few more tricks are necessary to make DCG work; for example, we need a way to specify terminal symbols, and it is convenient to have a way *not* to add the automatic string argument. Putting everything together, we define definite clause grammar as follows:

- The notation $X \rightarrow Y\ Z\ \ldots$ translates as $Y(s_1) \land Z(s_2) \land \ldots \Rightarrow X(s_1 + s_2 + \ldots)$.
- The notation $X \rightarrow Y \mid Z \mid \ldots$ translates as $Y(s) \lor Z(s) \lor \ldots \Rightarrow X(s)$.
- In either of the preceding rules, any nonterminal symbol $Y$ can be augmented with one or more arguments. Each argument can be a variable, a constant, or a function of arguments. In the translation, these arguments precede the string argument (e.g., $NP(case)$ translates as $NP(case, s_1)$).
- The notation $\{P(\ldots)\}$ can appear on the right-hand side of a rule and translates verbatim into $P(\ldots)$. This allows the grammar writer to insert a test for $P(\ldots)$ without having the automatic string argument added.
- The notation $X \rightarrow$ **word** translates as $X([word])$.

The problem of subject–verb agreement could also be handled with augmentations, but we defer that to Exercise 22.2. Instead, we address a harder problem: verb subcategorization.

| Verb | Subcats | Example Verb Phrase |
|---|---|---|
| give | $[NP, PP]$<br>$[NP, NP]$ | give the gold in 3 3 to me<br>give me the gold |
| smell | $[NP]$<br>$[Adjective]$<br>$[PP]$ | smell a wumpus<br>smell awful<br>smell like a wumpus |
| is | $[Adjective]$<br>$[PP]$<br>$[NP]$ | is smelly<br>is in 2 2<br>is a pit |
| died | $[]$ | died |
| believe | $[S]$ | believe the wumpus is dead |

**Figure 22.12** Examples of verbs with their subcategorization lists.

### Verb subcategorization

$\mathcal{E}_1$ is an improvement over $\mathcal{E}_0$, but the $\mathcal{E}_1$ grammar still overgenerates. One problem is in the way verb phrases are put together. We want to accept verb phrases like "give me the gold" and "go to 1 2." All these are in $\mathcal{E}_1$, but unfortunately so are "go me the gold" and "give to 1 2." The language $\mathcal{E}_2$ eliminates these $VP$s by stating explicitly which phrases can follow which verbs. We call this list the **subcategorization** list for the verb. The idea is that the category $Verb$ is broken into subcategories—one for verbs that have no object, one for verbs that take a single object, and so on.

SUBCATEGORIZATION

SUBCATEGORIZATION LIST

COMPLEMENTS

To implement this idea, we give each verb a **subcategorization list** that lists the verb's **complements**. A complement is an obligatory phrase that follows the verb within the verb phrase. So in "Give the gold to me," the $NP$ "the gold" and the $PP$ "to me" are complements of "give."[9] We would write this as

$$Verb([NP, PP]) \rightarrow \textbf{give} \mid \textbf{hand} \mid \ldots$$

It is possible for a verb to have several different subcategorizations, just as it is possible for a word to belong to several different categories. In fact, "give" also has the subcategorization list $[NP, NP]$, as in "Give me the gold." We can treat this like any other kind of ambiguity. Figure 22.12 gives some examples of verbs and their subcategorization lists (or **subcats** for short).

To integrate verb subcategorization into the grammar, we take three steps. The first step is to augment the category $VP$ to take a subcategorization argument, $VP(subcat)$, that indicates the list of complements that are needed to form a complete $VP$. For example, "give" can be made into a complete $VP$ by adding $[NP, PP]$, "give the gold" can be made complete by adding $[PP]$, and "give the gold to me" is already a complete $VP$; therefore its

[9] This is one definition of *complement*, but other authors have different terminology. Some say that the subject of the verb is also a complement. Others say that only the prepositional phrase is a complement and that the noun phrase should be called an **argument**.

subcategorization list is the empty list, [ ]. That gives us these rules for $VP$:

$$\begin{aligned} VP(subcat) \;\rightarrow\; & Verb(subcat) \\ \mid\; & VP(subcat + [NP])\; NP(Objective) \\ \mid\; & VP(subcat + [Adjective])\; Adjective \\ \mid\; & VP(subcat + [PP])\; PP\ . \end{aligned}$$

The last line can be read as "A $VP$ with a given subcat list, $subcat$, can be formed by an embedded $VP$ followed by a $PP$, as long as the embedded $VP$ has a subcat list that starts with the elements of the list $subcat$ and ends with the symbol $PP$." For example, a $VP([\,])$ is formed by a $VP([PP])$ followed by a $PP$. The first line says that a $VP$ with subcategorization list *subcat* can be formed by a $Verb$ with the same subcategorization list. For example, a $VP([NP])$ can be formed by a $Verb([NP])$. One example of such a verb is "grab," so "grab the gold" is a $VP([\,])$.

The second step is to change the rule for $S$ to say that it requires a verb phrase that has all its complements and thus has the subcat list [ ]. This means that "I grab the gold" is a legal sentence, but "You give" is not. The new rule,

$$S \;\rightarrow\; NP(Subjective)\; VP([\,])\ ,$$

can be read as "A sentence can be composed of a $NP$ in the subjective case, followed by a $VP$ that has a null subcat list." Figure 22.13 shows a parse tree using this grammar.

ADJUNCTS

The third step is to remember that, in addition to complements, verb phrases (and other phrases) can also take **adjuncts**, which are phrases that are not licensed by the individual verb but rather may appear in any verb phrase. Phrases representing time and place are adjuncts, because almost any action or event can have a time or place. For example, the adverb "now" in "I smell a wumpus now" and the $PP$ "on Tuesday" in "give me the gold on Tuesday" are adjuncts. Here are two rules that allow propositional and adverbial adjuncts on any $VP$:

$$\begin{aligned} VP(subcat) \;\rightarrow\; & VP(subcat)\; PP \\ \mid\; & VP(subcat)\; Adverb\ . \end{aligned}$$

### Generative capacity of augmented grammars

RULE SCHEMA

Each augmented rule is a **rule schema**, that stands for a set of rules, one for each possible combination of values for the augmented constituents. The generative capacity of augmented grammars depends on the number of combinations. If there is a finite number, then the augmented grammar is equivalent to a context-free grammar: the rule schema could be replaced with individual context-free rules. But if there are an infinite number of values, then augmented grammars can represent non-context-free languages. For example, the context-sensitive language $a^n b^n c^n$ can be represented as:

$$\begin{array}{llll} S(n) \rightarrow A(n)\; B(n)\; C(n) & & & \\ A(1) \rightarrow \mathbf{a} & & A(n+1) \rightarrow \mathbf{a}\; A(n) & \\ B(1) \rightarrow \mathbf{b} & & B(n+1) \rightarrow \mathbf{b}\; B(n) & \\ C(1) \rightarrow \mathbf{c} & & C(n+1) \rightarrow \mathbf{c}\; C(n) & \end{array}$$

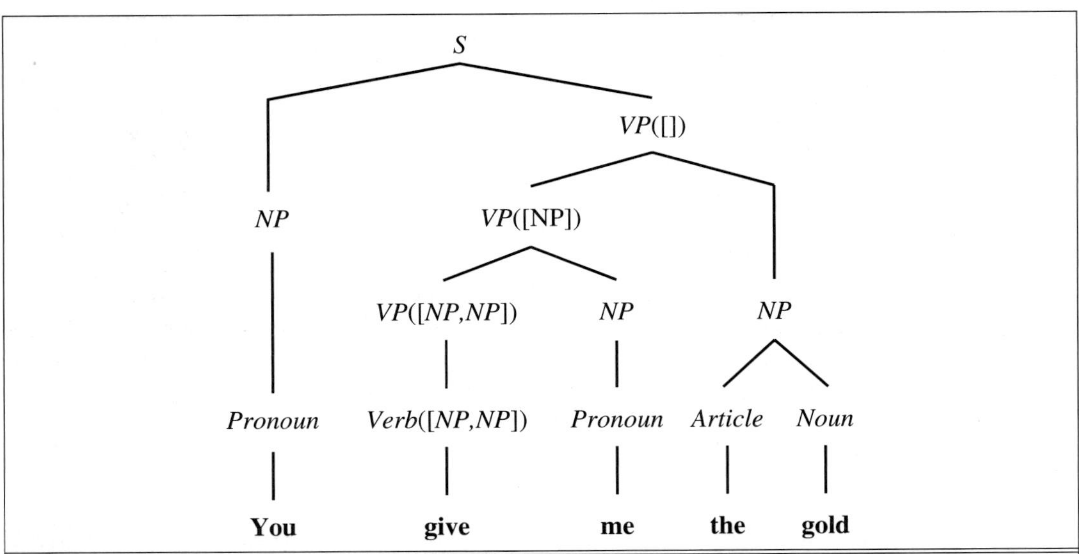


**Figure 22.13** Parse tree for "You give me the gold" showing subcategorization of the verb and verb phrase.

## 22.5 SEMANTIC INTERPRETATION

So far, we have only looked at the syntactic analysis of language. In this section, we turn to the **semantics**—the extraction of the *meaning* of utterances. For this chapter we are using first-order logic as our representation language, so semantic interpretation is the process of associating an FOL expression with a phrase. Intuitively, the meaning of the phrase "the wumpus" is the big, hairy beast that we represent in logic as the logical term $Wumpus_1$, and the meaning of "the wumpus is dead" is the logical sentence $Dead(Wumpus_1)$. This section will make that intuition more precise. We'll start with a simple example: a rule for describing grid locations:

$$NP \rightarrow Digit\ Digit\ .$$

We will augment the rule by adding to each constituent an argument representing the semantics of the constituent. We get

$$NP([x, y]) \rightarrow Digit(x)\ Digit(y)\ .$$

This says that a string consisting of a digit with semantics $x$ followed by another digit with semantics $y$ forms an $NP$ with semantics $[x, y]$, which is our notation for a square in the grid.

COMPOSITIONAL SEMANTICS

Notice that the semantics of the whole $NP$ is composed largely of the semantics of the constituent parts. We have seen this idea of **compositional semantics** before: in logic, the meaning of $P \wedge Q$ is determined by the meaning of $P$, $Q$, and $\wedge$; in arithmetic, the meaning of $x + y$ is determined by the meaning of $x$, $y$, and $+$. Figure 22.14 shows how DCG notation can be used to augment a grammar for arithmetic expressions with semantics and Figure 22.15

$$
\begin{array}{lll}
Exp(x) & \rightarrow & Exp(x_1)\ Operator(op)\ Exp(x_2)\ \{x = Apply(op, x_1, x_2)\} \\
Exp(x) & \rightarrow & (\ Exp(x)\ ) \\
Exp(x) & \rightarrow & Number(x) \\
Number(x) & \rightarrow & Digit(x) \\
Number(x) & \rightarrow & Number(x_1)\ Digit(x_2)\ \{x = 10 \times x_1 + x_2\} \\
Digit(x) & \rightarrow & x\ \{0 \leq x \leq 9\} \\
Operator(x) & \rightarrow & x\ \{x \in \{+, -, \div, \times\}\}
\end{array}
$$

**Figure 22.14** A grammar for arithmetic expressions, augmented with semantics. Each variable $x_i$ represents the semantics of a constituent. Note the use of the $\{test\}$ notation to define logical predicates that must be satisfied, but that are not constituents.

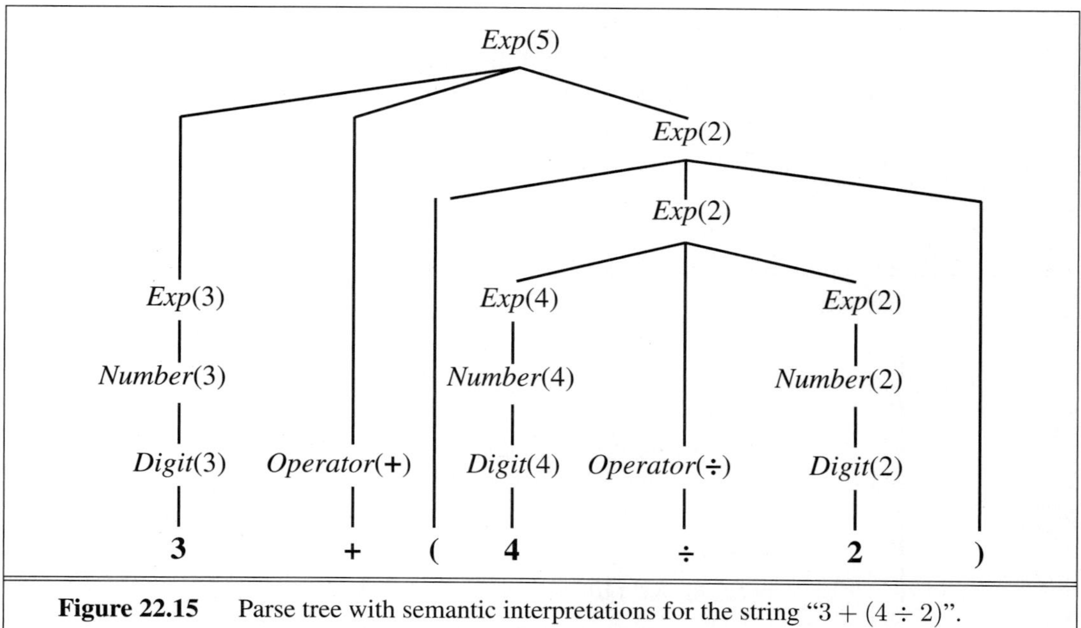


**Figure 22.15** Parse tree with semantic interpretations for the string "$3 + (4 \div 2)$".

shows the parse tree for $3 + (4 \div 2)$ according to this grammar. The root of the parse tree is $Exp(5)$, an expression whose semantic interpretation is 5.

## The semantics of an English fragment

We are now ready to write the semantic augmentations for a fragment of English. We start by determining what semantic representations we want to associate with what phrases. We will use the simple example sentence "John loves Mary." The *NP* "John" should have as its semantic interpretation the logical term $John$, and the sentence as a whole should have as its interpretation the logical sentence $Loves(John, Mary)$. That much seems clear. The complicated part is the *VP* "loves Mary." The semantic interpretation of this phrase is neither a logical term nor a complete logical sentence. Intuitively, "loves Mary" is a description that might or might not apply to a particular person. (In this case, it applies to John.) This means that "loves Mary" is a **predicate** that, when combined with a term that represents a person (the person doing the loving), yields a complete logical sentence. Using the $\lambda$-notation (see page 248), we can represent "loves Mary" as the predicate

$$\lambda x \; Loves(x, Mary) \; .$$

Now we need a rule that says "an $NP$ with semantics $obj$ followed by a $VP$ with semantics $rel$ yields a sentence whose semantics is the result of applying $rel$ to $obj$:"

$$S(rel(obj)) \;\rightarrow\; NP(obj) \; VP(rel) \; .$$

The rule tells us that the semantic interpretation of "John loves Mary" is

$$(\lambda x \; Loves(x, Mary))(John) \; ,$$

which is equivalent to $Loves(John, Mary)$.

The rest of the semantics follows in a straightforward way from the choices we have made so far. Because $VP$s are represented as predicates, it is a good idea to be consistent and represent verbs as predicates as well. The verb "loves" is represented as $\lambda y \; \lambda x \; Loves(x, y)$, the predicate that, when given the argument $Mary$, returns the predicate $\lambda x \; Loves(x, Mary)$.

The $VP \;\rightarrow\; Verb \; NP$ rule applies the predicate that is the semantic interpretation of the verb to the object that is the semantic interpretation of the $NP$ to get the semantic interpretation of the whole $VP$. We end up with the grammar shown in Figure 22.16 and the parse tree shown in Figure 22.17.

$$S(rel(obj)) \;\rightarrow\; NP(obj) \; VP(rel)$$
$$VP(rel(obj)) \;\rightarrow\; Verb(rel) \; NP(obj)$$
$$NP(obj) \;\rightarrow\; Name(obj)$$

$Name(John) \;\rightarrow\;$ **John**
$Name(Mary) \;\rightarrow\;$ **Mary**
$Verb(\lambda y \; \lambda x \; Loves(x, y)) \;\rightarrow\;$ **loves**

**Figure 22.16** A grammar that can derive a parse tree and semantic interpretation for "John loves Mary" (and three other sentences). Each category is augmented with a single argument representing the semantics.

### Time and tense

Now suppose we want to represent the difference between "John loves Mary" and "John loved Mary." English uses verb tenses (past, present, and future) to indicate the relative time of an event. One good choice to represent the time of events is the event calculus notation of Section 10.3. In event calculus, our two sentences have the following interpretations:

$$e \in Loves(John, Mary) \land During(Now, e) \; ;$$
$$e \in Loves(John, Mary) \land After(Now, e) \; .$$

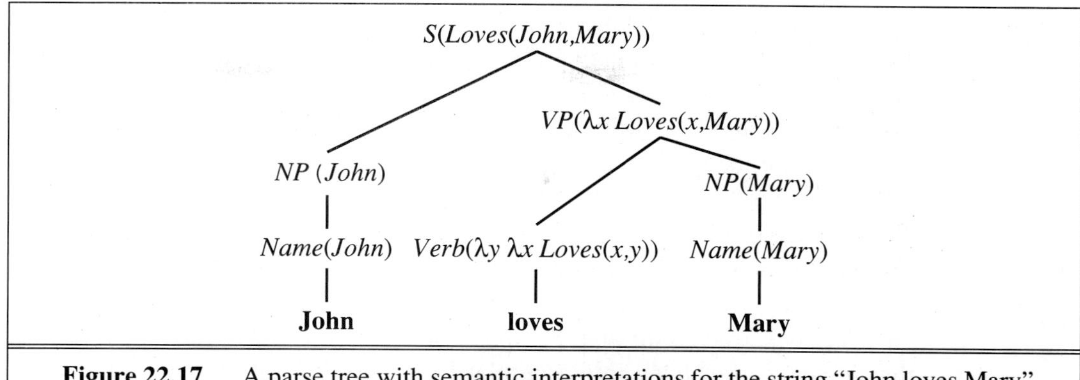


**Figure 22.17** A parse tree with semantic interpretations for the string "John loves Mary".

This suggests that our two lexical rules for the words "loves" and "loved" should be these:

$$Verb(\lambda y\ \lambda x\ e \in Loves(John, Mary) \wedge During(Now, e)) \rightarrow \textbf{loves}\ ;$$
$$Verb(\lambda y\ \lambda x\ e \in Loves(x, y) \wedge After(Now, e)) \rightarrow \textbf{loved}\ .$$

Other than this change, everything else about the grammar remains the same, which is encouraging news; it suggests we are on the right track if we can so easily add a complication like the tense of verbs (although we have just scratched the surface of a complete grammar for time and tense). With this success as a warm-up, we are now ready to tackle a much harder representation problem.

### Quantification

Consider the sentence "Every agent smells a wumpus." The sentence is actually ambiguous; the preferred meaning is that the agents might be smelling different wumpuses, but an alternative meaning is that there is a single wumpus that everyone smells.[10] The two interpretations can be represented as follows:

$$\begin{aligned}&\forall\, a\ \ a \in Agents \ \Rightarrow\\ &\qquad \exists\, w\ \ w \in Wumpuses \wedge \exists\, e\ \ e \in Smell(a, w) \wedge During(Now, e)\ ;\\ &\exists\, w\ \ w \in Wumpuses\ \forall\, a\ \ a \in Agents \ \Rightarrow\\ &\qquad \exists\, e\ \ e \in Smell(a, w) \wedge During(Now, e)\ .\end{aligned}$$

We will defer the problem of ambiguity and for now look only at the first interpretation. We'll try to analyze it compositionally, breaking it into the $NP$ and $VP$ components:

Every agent $\quad NP(\forall\, a\ \ a \in Agents \ \Rightarrow\ P)$
smells a wumpus $\quad VP(\exists\, w\ \ w \in Wumpuses \wedge$
$\qquad\qquad\qquad\qquad \exists\, e\ \ (e \in Smell(a, w) \wedge During(Now, e))\ .$

Right away, there are two difficulties. First, the semantics of the entire sentence appears to be the semantics of the $NP$, with the semantics of the $VP$ filling in the $P$ part. That means that we cannot form the semantics of the sentence with $rel(obj)$. We could do it with $obj(rel)$, which seems a little odd (at least at first glance). The second problem is that we need to get

[10] If this interpretation seems unlikely, consider 'Every Protestant believes in a just God."

the variable $a$ as an argument of the relation $Smell$. In other words, the semantics of the sentence is formed by plugging the semantics of the $VP$ into the correct argument slot of the $NP$, while also plugging the variable $a$ from the $NP$ into the correct argument slot of the semantics of the $VP$. It looks as if we need two functional compositions and promises to be rather confusing. The complexity stems from the fact that the semantic structure is very different from the syntactic structure.

INTERMEDIATE FORM

To avoid this confusion, many modern grammars take a different tack. They define an **intermediate form** to mediate between syntax and semantics. The intermediate form has two key properties. First, it is structurally similar to the syntax of the sentence and thus can be easily constructed through compositional means. Second, it contains enough information that it can be translated into a regular first-order logical sentence. Because it sits between the syntactic and logical forms, it is called a **quasi-logical form**.[11] In this section, we will use a quasi-logical form that includes all of first-order logic and is augmented by lambda expressions and one new construction, which we will call a **quantified term**. The quantified term that is the semantic interpretation of "every agent" is written

QUASI-LOGICAL FORM

QUANTIFIED TERM

$$[\forall\, a\;\; a \in Agents]\;.$$

This looks like a logical sentence, but it is used in the same way that a logical term is used. The interpretation of "Every agent smells a wumpus" in quasi-logical form is

$$\exists\, e\;\; (e \in Smell([\forall\, a\;\; a \in Agents], [\exists\, w\;\; w \in Wumpuses]) \land During(Now, e))\;.$$

To generate quasi-logical form, many of our rules remain unchanged. The rule for $S$ still creates the semantics of the $S$ with $rel(obj)$. Some rules do change; the lexical rule for "a" is

$$Article(\exists) \;\rightarrow\; \mathbf{a}$$

and the rule for combining an article with a noun is

$$NP([q\, x\;\; sem(x)]) \;\rightarrow\; Article(q)\;\; Noun(sem)\;.$$

This says that the semantics of the $NP$ is a quantified term, with a quantifier specified by the article, with a new variable $x$, and with a proposition formed by applying the semantics of the noun to the variable $x$. The other rules for $NP$ are similar. Figure 22.18 shows the semantic types and example forms for each syntactic category under the quasi-logical form approach. Figure 22.19 shows the parse of "every agent smells a wumpus" using this approach, and Figure 22.20 shows the complete grammar.

Now we need to convert the quasi-logical form into real first-order logic by turning quantified terms into real terms. This is done by a simple rule: For each quantified term $[q\, x\;\; P(x)]$ within a quasi-logical form *QLF*, replace the quantified term with $x$, and replace *QLF* with $q\, x\;\; P(x)\;\; op\;\; QLF$, where $op$ is $\Rightarrow$ when $q$ is $\forall$ and is $\land$ when $q$ is $\exists$ or $\exists!$. For example, the sentence "Every dog has a day" has the quasi-logical form:

$$\exists\, e\;\; (e \in Has([\forall\, d\;\; d \in Dogs], [\exists\, a\;\; a \in Days], Now))\;.$$

[11] Some quasi-logical forms have the third property that they can succinctly represent ambiguities that could be represented in logical form only by a long disjunction.

| Category | Semantic Type | Example | Quasi-Logical Form |
|---|---|---|---|
| $S$ | $sentence$ | I sleep. | $\exists e\ \ e \in Sleep(Speaker) \wedge During(Now, e)$ |
| $NP$ | $object$ | a dog | $[\exists d\ Dog(d)]$ |
| $PP$ | $object^2 \rightarrow sentence$ | in [2,2] | $\lambda x\ In(x, [2,2])$ |
| $RelClause$ | $object \rightarrow sentence$ | that sees me | $\lambda x\ \exists e\ \ e \in Sees(x, Speaker) \wedge During(Now, e)$ |
| $VP$ | $object^n \rightarrow sentence$ | sees me | $\lambda x\ \exists e\ \ e \in Sees(x, Speaker) \wedge During(Now, e)$ |
| $Adjective$ | $object \rightarrow sentence$ | smelly | $\lambda x\ Smelly(x)$ |
| $Adverb$ | $event \rightarrow sentence$ | today | $\lambda e\ During(e, Today)$ |
| $Article$ | $quantifier$ | the | $\exists!$ |
| $Conjunction$ | $sentence^2 \rightarrow sentence$ | and | $\lambda p, q\ (p \wedge q)$ |
| $Digit$ | $object$ | 7 | 7 |
| $Noun$ | $object \rightarrow sentence$ | wumpus | $\lambda x\ x \in Wumpuses$ |
| $Preposition$ | $object^2 \rightarrow sentence$ | in | $\lambda x\ \lambda y\ In(x, y)$ |
| $Pronoun$ | $object$ | I | $Speaker$ |
| $Verb$ | $object^n \rightarrow sentence$ | eats | $\lambda y\ \lambda x\ \exists e\ \ e \in Eats(x, y) \wedge During(Now, e)$ |

**Figure 22.18** Table showing the type of quasi-logical form expression for each syntactic category. The notation $t \rightarrow r$ denotes a function that takes an argument of type $t$ and returns a result of type $r$. For example, the semantic type for *Preposition* is $object^2 \rightarrow sentence$, which means that the semantics of a preposition is a function that, when applied to two logical objects, will yield a logical sentence.

We did not specify which of the two quantified terms gets pulled out first, so there are actually two possible logical interpretations:

$$\forall d\ \ d \in Dogs\ \Rightarrow\ \exists a\ \ a \in Days \wedge \exists e\ \ e \in Has(d, a, Now)\ ;$$
$$\exists a\ \ a \in Days \wedge \forall d\ \ d \in Dogs\ \Rightarrow\ \exists e\ \ e \in Has(d, a, Now)\ .$$

The first one says that each dog has his own day, while the second says that there is a special day that all dogs share. Choosing between them is a job for disambiguation. Often, the left-to-right order of the quantified terms matches the left-to-right order of the quantifiers, but other factors come into play. The advantage of quasi-logical form is that it succinctly represents all the possibilities. The disadvantage is that it doesn't help you choose between them; for that we need the full power of disambiguation using all sources of evidence.

## Pragmatic Interpretation

We have shown how an agent can perceive a string of words and use a grammar to derive a set of possible semantic interpretations. Now we address the problem of completing the interpretation by adding context-dependent information about the current situation to each candidate interpretation.

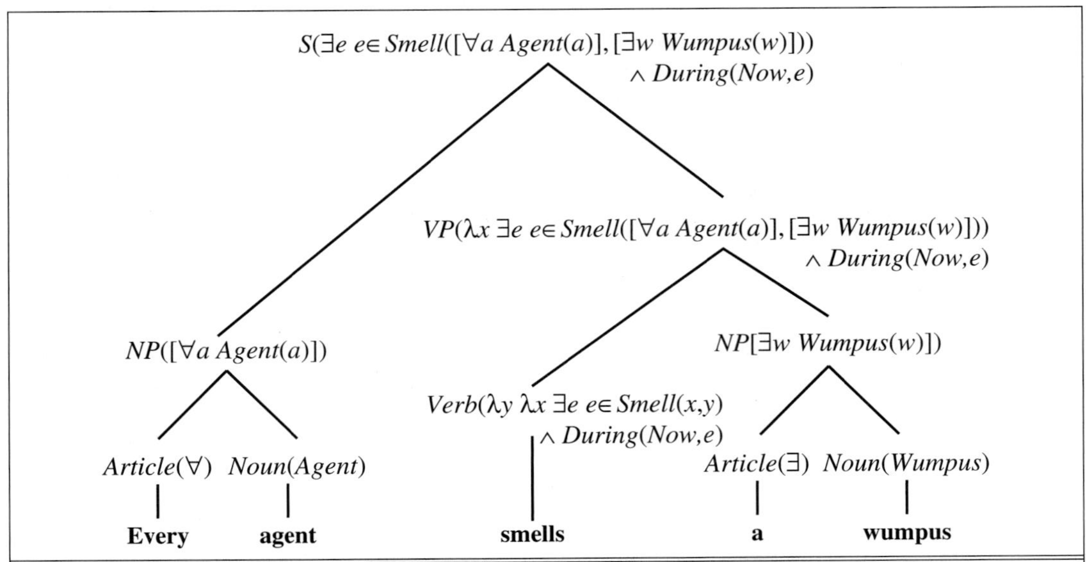


**Figure 22.19** Parse tree for the sentence "Every agent smells a wumpus," showing both syntactic structure and semantic interpretations.

$S(rel(obj)) \rightarrow NP(obj)\ VP(rel)$
$S(conj(sem_1, sem_2)) \rightarrow S(sem_1)\ Conjunction(conj)\ S(sem_2)$

$NP(sem) \rightarrow Pronoun(sem)$
$NP(sem) \rightarrow Name(sem)$
$NP([q\,x\ sem(x)]) \rightarrow Article(q)\ Noun(sem)$
$NP([q\,x\ obj \wedge rel(x)]) \rightarrow NP([q\,x\ obj])\ PP(rel)$
$NP([q\,x\ obj \wedge rel(x)]) \rightarrow NP([q\,x\ obj])\ RelClause(rel)$
$NP([sem_1, sem_2]) \rightarrow Digit(sem_1)\ Digit(sem_2)$

$VP(sem) \rightarrow Verb(sem)$
$VP(rel(obj)) \rightarrow VP(rel)\ NP(obj)$
$VP(sem_1(sem_2) \rightarrow VP(sem_1)\ Adjective(sem_2)$
$VP(sem_1(sem_2)) \rightarrow VP(sem_1)\ PP(sem_2)$

$RelClause(sem) \rightarrow$ **that** $VP(sem)$

$PP(\lambda x\ rel(x, obj)) \rightarrow Preposition(rel)\ NP(obj)$

**Figure 22.20** A grammar with semantics in quasi-logical form.

INDEXICALS

The most obvious need for pragmatic information is in resolving the meaning of **indexicals**, which are phrases that refer directly to the current situation. For example, in the sentence "I am in Boston today," the interpretations of the indexicals "I" and "today" depend on who uttered the sentence when. We represent indexicals by "constants" (such as $Speaker$) which actually are **fluents**—that is, they depend on the situation. The hearer who perceives a speech act should also perceive who the speaker is and use this information to resolve the indexical. For example, the hearer might know $T((Speaker = Agent_B), Now)$.

A command such as "go to 2 2" implicitly refers to the hearer. So far, our grammar for $S$ covers only declarative sentences. We can easily extend it to cover commands.[12]

A command can be formed from a $VP$, where the subject is implicitly the hearer. We need to distinguish commands from statements, so we alter the rules for $S$ to include the type of speech act as part of the quasi-logical form:

$$S(Statement(Speaker, rel(obj))) \rightarrow NP(obj)\ VP(rel)$$
$$S(Command(Speaker, rel(Hearer))) \rightarrow VP(rel)\ .$$

So the quasi-logical form for "Go to 2 2" is[13]

$$Command(\exists e\ \ e \in Go(Hearer, [2, 2]))\ .$$

## Language generation with DCGs

So far, we have concentrated on *parsing* language, not on generating it. Generation is a topic of similar richness. Choosing the right utterance to express a proposition involves many of the same choices that parsing the utterance does.

Remember that a DCG is a logical programming system that specifies constraints between a string and the parse of a string. We know that a logic programming definition of the $Append$ predicate can be used both to tell us that in $Append([1, 2], [3], x)$ we have $x = [1, 2, 3]$ and to enumerate the values of $x$ and $y$ that make $Append(x, y, [1, 2, 3])$ true. In the same way, we can write a definition of $S$ that can be used in two ways: to parse, we ask $S(sem, [John, Loves, Mary])$ and get back $sem = Loves(John, Mary)$; to generate, we ask $S(Loves(John, Mary), words)$ and get back $words = [John, Loves, Mary]$. We can also test a grammar by asking $S(sem, words)$ and getting back as an answer a stream of $[sem, words]$ pairs that are generated by the grammar.

This approach works for the simple grammars in this chapter, but there can be difficulties in scaling up to larger grammars. The search strategy used by the logical inference engine is important; depth-first strategies can lead to infinite loops. Some care must be taken in the

---

[12] To implement a complete communicating agent we would also need a grammar of questions. Questions are beyond the scope of this book because they impose **long-distance dependencies** between constituents. For example, in "Whom did the agent tell you to give the gold to?" the final word "to" should be parsed as a $PP$ with a missing $NP$; the missing $NP$ is licensed by the first word of the sentence, "who." A complex system of augmentations is used to make sure that the missing $NP$s match up with the licensing words.

[13] Note that the quasi-logical form for a command does not include the time of the event (e.g., $During(Now, e)$). That is because the "go" is actually the untensed version of the word, not the present tense version. You can't tell the difference with "go," but observe that the correct form of a command is "Be good!" (using the untensed form "be"), not "Are good!" To ensure the correct tense is used, we could augment $VP$s with a tense argument and write $VP(rel, untensed)$ on the right-hand side of the command rule.

exact details of the semantic form. It could be that a given grammar has no way to express the logical form $X \wedge Y$ for some values of $X$ and $Y$, but can express $Y \wedge X$; this suggests that we need a way to canonicalize semantic forms, or we need to extend the unification routine so that $X \wedge Y$ can unify with $Y \wedge X$.

Serious work in generation tends to use more complex generation models that are distinct from the parsing grammar and offer more control over exactly how components of the semantics are expressed. Systemic grammar is one approach that makes it easy to put emphasis on the most important parts of the semantic form.

## 22.6 AMBIGUITY AND DISAMBIGUATION

In some cases, hearers are consciously aware of ambiguity in an utterance. Here are some examples taken from newspaper headlines:

Squad helps dog bite victim.
Helicopter powered by human flies.
Once-sagging cloth diaper industry saved by full dumps.
Portable toilet bombed; police have nothing to go on.
British left waffles on Falkland Islands.
Teacher strikes idle kids.
Milk drinkers are turning to powder.
Drunk gets nine months in violin case.

But most of the time the language we hear seems unambiguous. Thus, when researchers first began to use computers to analyze language in the 1960s they were quite surprised to learn that *almost every utterance is highly ambiguous, even though the alternative interpretations might not be apparent to a native speaker.* A system with a large grammar and lexicon might find thousands of interpretations for a perfectly ordinary sentence. Consider "The batter hit the ball," which seems to have an unambiguous interpretation in which a baseball player strikes a baseball. But we get a different interpretation if the previous sentence is "The mad scientist unleashed a tidal wave of cake mix towards the ballroom." This example relies on **lexical ambiguity**, in which a word has more than one meaning. Lexical ambiguity is quite common; "back" can be an adverb (go back), an adjective (back door), a noun (the back of the room) or a verb (back up your files). "Jack" can be a name, a noun (a playing card, a six-pointed metal game piece, a nautical flag, a fish, a male donkey, a socket, or a device for raising heavy objects), or a verb (to jack up a car, to hunt with a light, or to hit a baseball hard).

LEXICAL AMBIGUITY

**Syntactic ambiguity** (also known as **structural ambiguity**) can occur with or without lexical ambiguity. For example, the string "I smelled a wumpus in 2,2" has two parses: one where the prepositional phrase "in 2,2" modifies the noun and one where it modifies the verb. The syntactic ambiguity leads to a **semantic ambiguity**, because one parse means that the wumpus is in 2,2 and the other means that a stench is in 2,2. In this case, getting the wrong interpretation could be a deadly mistake.

SYNTACTIC AMBIGUITY

SEMANTIC AMBIGUITY

Semantic ambiguity can occur even in phrases with no lexical or syntactic ambiguity. For example, the noun phrase "cat person" can be someone who likes felines or the lead of the movie *Attack of the Cat People.* A "coast road" can be a road that follows the coast or one that leads to it.

Finally, there can be ambiguity between literal and figurative meanings. Figures of speech are important in poetry, but are surprisingly common in everyday speech as well. A

METONYMY

**metonymy** is a figure of speech in which one object is used to stand for another. When we hear "Chrysler announced a new model," we do not interpret it as saying that companies can talk; rather we understand that a spokesperson representing the company made the announcement. Metonymy is common and is often interpreted unconsciously by human hearers. Unfortunately, our grammar as it is written is not so facile. To handle the semantics of metonymy properly, we need to introduce a whole new level of ambiguity. We do this by providing *two* objects for the semantic interpretation of every phrase in the sentence: one for the object that the phrase literally refers to (Chrysler) and one for the metonymic reference (the spokesperson). We then have to say that there is a relation between the two. In our current grammar, "Chrysler announced" gets interpreted as

$$\exists\, x, e \;\; x = Chrysler \land e \in Announce(x) \land After(Now, e)\;.$$

We need to change that to

$$\exists\, m, x, e \;\; x = Chrysler \land e \in Announce(m) \land After(Now, e) \\ \land\, Metonymy(m, x)\;.$$

This says that there is one entity $x$ that is equal to Chrysler, and another entity $m$ that did the announcing, and that the two are in a metonymy relation. The next step is to define what kinds of metonymy relations can occur. The simplest case is when there is no metonymy at all—the literal object $x$ and the metonymic object $m$ are identical:

$$\forall\, m, x \;\; (m = x) \;\Rightarrow\; Metonymy(m, x)\;.$$

For the Chrysler example, a reasonable generalization is that an organization can be used to stand for a spokesperson of that organization:

$$\forall\, m, x \;\; x \in Organizations \land Spokesperson(m, x) \;\Rightarrow\; Metonymy(m, x)\;.$$

Other metonymies include the author for the works (I read *Shakespeare*) or more generally the producer for the product (I drive a *Honda*) and the part for the whole (The Red Sox need a strong *arm*). Some examples of metonymy, such as "The *ham sandwich* on Table 4 wants another beer," are more novel and are interpreted with respect to a situation.

The rules we have outlined here allow us to construct an explanation for "Chrysler announced a new model," but the explanation doesn't follow by logical deduction. We need to use probabilistic or nonmonotonic reasoning to come up with candidate explanations.

METAPHOR

A **metaphor** is a figure of speech in which a phrase with one literal meaning is used to suggest a different meaning by way of an analogy. Most people think of metaphor as a tool used by poets that does not play a large role in everyday text. However, a number of basic metaphors are so common that we do not even recognize them as such. One such metaphor is the idea that *more is up*. This metaphor allows us to say that prices have risen, climbed, or skyrocketed, that the temperature has dipped or fallen, that one's confidence has plummeted, or that a celebrity's popularity has jumped or soared.

There are two ways to approach metaphors like this. One is to compile all knowledge of the metaphor into the lexicon—to add new senses of the words "rise," "fall," "climb," and so on, that describe them as dealing with quantities on any scale rather than just altitude. This approach suffices for many applications, but it does not capture the generative character of the metaphor that allows humans to use new instances such as "nosedive" or "blasting through the roof" without fear of misunderstanding. The second approach is to include explicit knowledge of common metaphors and use them to interpret new uses as they are read. For example, suppose the system knows the "more is up" metaphor. That is, it knows that logical expressions that refer to a point on a vertical scale can be interpreted as being about corresponding points on a quantity scale. Then the expression "sales are high" would get a literal interpretation along the lines of $Altitude(Sales, High)$, which could be interpreted metaphorically as $Quantity(Sales, Much)$.

## Disambiguation

As we said before, *disambiguation is a question of diagnosis.* The speaker's intent to communicate is an unobserved cause of the words in the utterance, and the hearer's job is to work backwards from the words and from knowledge of the situation to recover the most likely intent of the speaker. In other words, the hearer is solving for

$$\operatorname*{argmax}_{intent} Likelihood(intent | words, situation) ,$$

where $Likelihood$ can either be probability or any numeric measure of preference. Some sort of preference is needed because syntactic and semantic interpretation rules alone cannot identify a unique correct interpretation of a phrase or sentence. So we divide the work: syntactic and semantic interpretation is responsible for enumerating a set of candidate interpretations, and the disambiguation process chooses the best one.

Note that we talk about the intent of the speech act, not just the actual proposition that the speaker is proclaiming. For example, after hearing a politician say, "I am not a crook," we might assign a probability of only 50% to the proposition that the politician is not a criminal, and 99.999% to the proposition that the speaker is not a hooked shepherd's staff. Still, we assign a higher probability to the interpretation

$$Assert(Speaker, \neg(Speaker \in Criminals))$$

because this is a more likely thing to say.

Consider again the ambiguous example "I smelled a wumpus in 2,2." One preference heuristic is the rule of **right association**, which says that when it is time to decide where in the parse tree to place the $PP$ "in 2,2," we should prefer to attach it to the rightmost existing constituent, which in this case is the $NP$ "a wumpus." Of course, this is only a heuristic; for the sentence "I smelled a wumpus with my nose," the heuristic would be outweighed by the fact that the $NP$ "a wumpus with my nose" is unlikely.

RIGHT ASSOCIATION

Disambiguation is made possible by combining evidence, using all the techniques for knowledge representation and uncertain reasoning that we have seen throughout this book.

We can break the knowledge down into four models:

1. The **world model**: the likelihood that a proposition occurs in the world.
2. The **mental model**: the likelihood that the speaker forms the intention of communicating a certain fact to the hearer, given that it occurs. This approach combines models of what the speaker believes, what the speaker believes the hearer believes, and so on.
3. The **language model**: the likelihood that a certain string of words will be chosen, given that the speaker has the intention of communicating a certain fact. The CFG and DCG models presented in this chapter have a Boolean model of likelihood: either a string can have a certain interpretation or it cannot. In the next chapter, we will see a probabilistic version of CFG that makes for a more informed language model for disambiguation.
4. The **acoustic model**: the likelihood that a particular sequence of sounds will be generated, given that the speaker has chosen a given string of words. Section 15.6 covered speech recognition.

## 22.7 DISCOURSE UNDERSTANDING

DISCOURSE

A **discourse** is any string of language—usually one that is more than one sentence long. Textbooks, novels, weather reports and conversations are all discourses. So far we have largely ignored the problems of discourse, preferring to dissect language into individual sentences that can be studied *in vitro*. This section studies sentences in their native habitat. We will look at two particular subproblems: reference resolution and coherence.

### Reference resolution

**Reference resolution** is the interpretation of a pronoun or a definite noun phrase that refers to an object in the world.[14] The resolution is based on knowledge of the world and of the previous parts of the discourse. Consider the passage

> "John flagged down the waiter. He ordered a ham sandwich."

To understand that "he" in the second sentence refers to John, we need to have understood that the first sentence mentions two people and that John is playing the role of a customer and hence is likely to order, whereas the waiter is not. Usually, reference resolution is a matter of selecting a referent from a list of candidates, but sometimes it involves the creation of new candidates. Consider the following sentence:

> "After John proposed to Marsha, they found a preacher and got married. For the honeymoon, they went to Hawaii."

Here, the definite noun phrase "the honeymoon" refers to something that was only implicitly alluded to by the verb "married." The pronoun "they" refers to a group that was not explicitly mentioned before: John and Marsha (but *not* the preacher).

[14] In linguistics, reference to something that has already been introduced is called **anaphoric** reference. Reference to something yet to be introduced is called **cataphoric** reference, as with the pronoun "he" in "When he won his first tournament, Tiger was 20."

Choosing the best referent is a process of disambiguation that relies on combining a variety of syntactic, semantic, and pragmatic information. Some clues are in the form of constraints. For example, pronouns must agree in gender and number with their antecedents: "he" can refer to John, but not Marsha; "they" can refer to a group, but not a single person. Pronouns must also obey syntactic constraints for reflexivity. For example, in "He saw him in the mirror" the two pronouns must refer to different people, whereas in "He saw himself," they must refer to the same person. There are also constraints for semantic consistency. In "He ate it," the pronoun "he" must refer to something that eats and "it" to something that can be eaten.

Some clues are preferences that do not always hold. For example, when adjacent sentences have a parallel structure, it is preferable for pronominal reference to follow that structure. So in

> Marsha flew to San Francisco from New York. John flew there from Boston.

we prefer for "there" to refer to San Francisco because it plays the same syntactic role. Absent a parallel structure, there is a preference for subjects over objects as antecedents. Thus, in

> Marsha gave Sally the homework assignment. Then she left.

"Marsha," the subject of the first sentence, is the preferred antecedent for "she." Another preference is for the entity that has been discussed most prominently. Considered in isolation, the pair of sentences

> Dana dropped the cup on the plate. It broke.

poses a problem: it is not clear whether the cup or the plate is the referent of "it." But in a larger context the ambiguity is resolved:

> Dana was quite fond of the blue cup. The cup had been a present from a close friend. Unfortunately, one day while setting the table. Dana dropped the cup on the plate. It broke.

Here, the cup is the focus of attention and hence is the preferred referent.

A variety of reference resolution algorithms have been devised. One of the first (Hobbs, 1978) is remarkable because it underwent a degree of statistical verification that was unusual for the time. Using three different genres of text, Hobbs reports an accuracy of 92%. This assumed that a correct parse was generated by a parser; not having one available, Hobbs constructed the parses by hand. The Hobbs algorithm works as a search: it searches sentences starting from the current sentence and going backwards. This technique ensures that more recent candidates will be considered first. Within a sentence it searches breadth first, from left to right. This ensures that subjects will be considered before objects. The algorithm chooses the first candidate that satisfies the constraints just outlined.

### The structure of coherent discourse

Open up this book to 10 random pages, and copy down the first sentence from each page. The result is bound to be incoherent. Similarly, if you take a coherent 10-sentence passage and permute the sentences, the result is incoherent. This demonstrates that sentences in natural

- **Enable** or **cause:** $S_1$ brings about a change of state (which may be implicit) that causes or enables $S_2$. Example: "I went outside. I drove to school." (Going outside enables the implicit getting into a car.)
- **Explanation:** The reverse of enablement: $S_2$ causes or enables $S_1$ and thus is an explanation for it. Example: "I was late for school. I overslept."
- **Ground-Figure:** $S_1$ describes a setting or background for $S_2$. Example: "It was a dark and stormy night. *Rest of story.*"
- **Evaluation:** From $S_2$ infer that $S_1$ is part of the speaker's plan for executing the segment as a speech act. Example: "A funny thing happened. *Rest of story.*"
- **Exemplification:** $S_2$ is an example of the general principle in $S_1$. Example: "This algorithm reverses a list. The input $[A, B, C]$ is mapped to $[C, B, A]$."
- **Generalization:** $S_1$ is an example of the general principle in $S_2$. Example: "$[A, B, C]$ is mapped to $[C, B, A]$. In general, the algorithm reverses a list."
- **Violated Expectation:** Infer $\neg P$ from $S_2$, negating the normal inference of $P$ from $S_1$. Example: "This paper is weak. On the other hand, it is interesting."

**Figure 22.21** A list of coherence relations, taken from Hobbs (1990). Each relation holds between two adjacent text segments, $S_1$ and $S_2$.

language discourse are quite different from sentences in logic. In logic, if we TELL sentences $A$, $B$ and $C$ to a knowledge base, in any order, we end up with the conjunction $A \wedge B \wedge C$. In natural language, sentence order matters; consider the difference between "Go two blocks. Turn right." and "Turn right. Go two blocks."

A discourse has structure above the level of a sentence. We can examine this structure with the help of a grammar of discourse:

$$Segment(x) \rightarrow S(x)$$
$$Segment(CoherenceRelation(x, y)) \rightarrow Segment(x)\ Segment(y)\ .$$

This grammar says that a discourse is composed of segments, where each segment is either a sentence or a group of sentences and where segments are joined by **coherence relations**. In the text "Go two blocks. Turn right," the coherence relation is that the first sentence *enables* the second: the listener should turn right only after traveling two blocks. Different researchers have proposed different inventories of coherence relations; Figure 22.21 lists a representative set. Now consider the following story:

(1) A funny thing happened yesterday.
(2) John went to a fancy restaurant.
(3) He ordered the duck.
(4) The bill came to \$50.
(5) John got a shock when he realized he had no money.
(6) He had left his wallet at home.
(7) The waiter said it was all right to pay later.
(8) He was very embarrassed by his forgetfulness.

Here, sentence (1) stands in the *Evaluation* relation to the rest of the discourse; (1) is the speaker's metacomment on the discourse. Sentence (2) enables (3), and together the (2–3) pair cause (4), with the implicit intermediate state that John ate the duck. Now (2–4) serve as the ground for the rest of the discourse. Sentence (6) is an explanation of (5), and (5–6) enable (7). Note that this is an *Enable* and not a *Cause*, because the waiter might have had a different reaction. Together, (5–7) cause (8). Exercise 22.13 asks you to draw the parse tree for this discourse.

Coherence relations serve to bind a discourse together. They guide the speaker in deciding what to say and what to leave implicit, and they guide the hearer in recovering the speaker's intent. Coherence relations can serve as a filter on the ambiguity of sentences: individually, the sentences might be ambiguous, but most of these ambiguous interpretations do not fit together into a coherent discourse.

So far we have looked at reference resolution and discourse structure separately. But the two are actually intertwined. The theory of Grosz and Sidner (1986), for example, accounts for where the speaker's and hearer's attention is focused during the discourse. Their theory includes a pushdown stack of **focus spaces**. Certain utterances cause the focus to shift by pushing or popping elements off the stack. For example, in the restaurant story, the sentence "John went to a fancy restaurant" pushes a new focus onto the stack. Within that focus, the speaker can use a definite *NP* to refer to "the waiter" (rather than "a waiter"). If the story continued with "John went home," then the focus space would be popped from the stack and the discourse could no longer refer to the waiter with "the waiter" or "he."

FOCUS SPACES

## 22.8 GRAMMAR INDUCTION

GRAMMAR INDUCTION

**Grammar induction** is the task of learning a grammar from data. It is an obvious task to attempt, given that it has proven to be so difficult to construct a grammar by hand and that billions of example utterances are available for free on the Internet. It is a difficult task because the space of possible grammars is infinite and because verifying that a given grammar generates a set of sentences is computationally expensive.

One interesting model is the SEQUITUR system (Nevill-Manning and Witten, 1997). It requires no input except a single text (which does not need to be predivided into sentences). It produces a grammar of a very specialized form: a grammar that generates only a single string, namely, the original text. Another way to look at this is that SEQUITUR learns just enough grammar to parse the text. Here is the bracketing it discovers for one sentence within a larger text of news stories:

[Most Labour] [sentiment [[would still] [favor the] abolition]] [[of [the House]] [of Lords]]

It has correctly picked out constituents such as the *PP* "of the House of Lords," although it also goes against traditional analysis in, for example, grouping "the" with the preceding verb rather than the following noun.

SEQUITUR is based on the idea that a good grammar is a compact grammar. In particular, it enforces the following two constraints: (1) No pair of adjacent symbols should appear more than once in the grammar. If the symbol pair $A\ B$ appears on the right-hand side of several rules, then we should replace the pair with a new nonterminal that we will call $C$ and add the rule $C \rightarrow A\ B$. (2) Every rule should be used at least twice. If a nonterminal $C$ appears only once in the grammar, then we should eliminate the rule for $C$ and replace its single use with the rule's right-hand side. These two constraints are applied in a greedy search that scans the input text from left to right, incrementally building a grammar as it goes, and imposing the constraints as soon as possible. Figure 22.22 shows the algorithm in operation on the input text "*abcdbcabcd*." The algorithm recovers an optimally compact grammar for the text.

| | Input | Grammar | Comments |
|---|---|---|---|
| 1 | $a$ | $S \rightarrow a$ | |
| 2 | $ab$ | $S \rightarrow ab$ | |
| 3 | $abc$ | $S \rightarrow abc$ | |
| 4 | $abcd$ | $S \rightarrow abcd$ | |
| 5 | $abcdb$ | $S \rightarrow abcdb$ | |
| 6 | $abcdbc$ | $S \rightarrow abcdbc$ | $bc$ twice |
| | | $S \rightarrow aAdA;\ A \rightarrow bc$ | |
| 7 | $abcdbca$ | $S \rightarrow aAdAa;\ A \rightarrow bc$ | |
| 8 | $abcdbcab$ | $S \rightarrow aAdAab;\ A \rightarrow bc$ | |
| 9 | $abcdbcabc$ | $S \rightarrow aAdAabc;\ A \rightarrow bc$ | $bc$ twice |
| | | $S \rightarrow aAdAaA;\ A \rightarrow bc$ | $aA$ twice |
| | | $S \rightarrow BdAB;\ A \rightarrow bc;\ B \rightarrow aA$ | |
| 10 | $abcdbcabcd$ | $S \rightarrow BdABd;\ A \rightarrow bc;\ B \rightarrow aA$ | $Bd$ twice |
| | | $S \rightarrow CAC;\ A \rightarrow bc;\ B \rightarrow aA;\ C \rightarrow Bd$ | $B$ only once |
| | | $S \rightarrow CAC;\ A \rightarrow bc;\ C \rightarrow aAd$ | |

**Figure 22.22** A trace of SEQUITUR inducing a grammar for the input text "*abcdbcabcd*." We start with a rule for $S$ and add each symbol to the end of this rule in turn. After adding the sixth symbol, we have the first occurrence of a repeated pair: $bc$. So we replace both occurrences of $bc$ with the new nonterminal $A$ and add the rule $A \rightarrow bc$. After three more symbols are added, the ninth causes another repetition of $bc$, so again we replace it with $A$. This leads to two occurrences of $aA$, so we replace them with a new nonterminal, $B$. After adding the tenth and last terminal symbol we get two occurrences of $Bd$, so we replace them with the new nonterminal $C$. But now $B$ appears only once, in the right-hand side of the $C$ rule, so we replace $B$ by its expansion, $aA$.

In the next chapter, we will see other grammar induction algorithms that work with probabilistic context-free grammars. But now we turn to the problem of learning a grammar that is augmented with semantics. Since an augmented grammar is a Horn clause logic program, the techniques of inductive logic programming are appropriate. CHILL (Zelle and Mooney, 1996) is an inductive logic programming (ILP) program that learns a grammar and a specialized parser for that grammar from examples. The target domain is natural language database queries. The training examples consist of pairs of word strings and corresponding queries—for example;

What is the capital of the state with the largest population?
$Answer(c, Capital(s, c) \wedge Largest(p, State(s) \wedge Population(s, p)))$

CHILL's task is to learn a predicate $Parse(words, query)$ that is consistent with the examples and, hopefully, generalizes well to other examples. Applying ILP directly to learn this predicate results in poor performance: the induced parser has only about 20% accuracy. Fortunately, ILP learners can improve by adding knowledge. In this case, most of the $Parse$ predicate was defined as a logic program, and CHILL's task was reduced to inducing the control rules that guide the parser to select one parse over another. With this additional background knowledge, CHILL achieves 70% to 85% accuracy on various database query tasks.

## 22.9 Summary

Natural language understanding is one of the most important subfields of AI. It draws on ideas from philosophy and linguistics, as well as on techniques of logical and probabilistic knowledge representation and reasoning. Unlike other areas of AI, natural language understanding requires an empirical investigation of actual human behavior—which turns out to be complex and interesting.

- Agents send signals to each other to achieve certain purposes: to inform, to warn, to elicit help, to share knowledge, or to promise something. Sending a signal in this way is called a **speech act**. Ultimately, all speech acts are an attempt to get another agent to believe something or do something.
- Language consists of conventional **signs** that convey meaning. Many animals use signs in this sense. Humans appear to be the only animals that use **grammar** to produce an unbounded variety of structured messages.
- Communication involves three steps by the speaker: the intention to convey an idea, the mental generation of words, and their physical synthesis. The hearer then has four steps: perception, analysis, disambiguation, and incorporation of the meaning. All language use is **situated**, in the sense that the meaning of an utterance can depend on the situation in which it is produced.
- Formal language theory and **phrase structure** grammars (and in particular, **context-free** grammar) are useful tools for dealing with some aspects of natural language.
- Sentences in a context-free language can be parsed in $O(n^3)$ time by a **chart parser**.
- It is convenient to **augment** a grammar to handle such problems as subject–verb agreement and pronoun case. **Definite clause grammar** (DCG) is a formalism that allows for augmentations. With DCG, parsing and semantic interpretation (and even generation) can be done using logical inference.
- **Semantic interpretation** can also be handled by an augmented grammar. A quasi-logical form can be a useful intermediate between syntactic trees and semantics.

- **Ambiguity** is a very important problem in natural language understanding; most sentences have many possible interpretations, but usually only one is appropriate. Disambiguation relies on knowledge about the world, about the current situation, and about language use.
- Most language exists in the context of multiple sentences, not just a single one. **Discourse** is the study of connected texts. We saw how to resolve pronominal references across sentences and how sentences are joined into coherent segments.
- **Grammar induction** can learn a grammar from examples, although there are limitations on how well the grammar will generalize.

## BIBLIOGRAPHICAL AND HISTORICAL NOTES

SEMIOTICS

The study of signs and symbols as elements of language was named **semiotics** by John Locke (1690), although it was not developed until the 20th century (Peirce, 1902; de Saussure, 1993). Recent overview texts include Eco's (1979) and Cobley's (1997).

The idea of language as action stems from 20th-century linguistically oriented philosophy (Wittgenstein, 1953; Grice, 1957; Austin, 1962) and particularly from the book *Speech Acts* (Searle, 1969). A precursor to the idea of speech acts was Protagoras's (c. 430 B.C.) identification of four types of sentence: prayer, question, answer, and injunction. A plan-based model of speech acts was suggested first by Cohen and Perrault (1979). Connecting language to action by using plan recognition to understand stories was studied by Wilensky (1983). Cohen, Morgan, and Pollack (1990) collect more recent work in this area.

ATTRIBUTE GRAMMAR

Like semantic networks, context-free grammars (also known as phrase structure grammars) are a reinvention of a technique first used by ancient Indian grammarians (especially Panini, c. 350 B.C.) studying Shastric Sanskrit (Ingerman, 1967). They were reinvented by Noam Chomsky (1956) for the analysis of English syntax and independently by John Backus for the analysis of Algol-58 syntax. Naur (1963) extended Backus's notation and is now credited (Backus, 1996) with the "N" in BNF, which originally stood for "Backus Normal Form." Knuth (1968) defined a kind of augmented grammar called **attribute grammar** that is useful for programming languages. Definite clause grammars were introduced by Colmerauer (1975) and developed and popularized by Pereira and Warren (1980). The Prolog programming language was invented by Alain Colmerauer specifically for the problem of parsing the French language. Colmerauer actually introduced a formalism called metamorphosis grammar that went beyond definite clauses, but DCG followed soon after.

There have been many attempts to write formal grammars of natural languages, both in "pure" linguistics and in computational linguistics. Machine-oriented grammars include those developed in the Linguistic String Project at New York University (Sager, 1981) and the XTAG project at the University of Pennsylvania (Doran *et al.*, 1994). A good example of a modern DCG system is the Core Language Engine (Alshawi, 1992). There are several comprehensive but informal grammars of English (Jespersen, 1965; Quirk *et al.*, 1985; McCawley, 1988; Huddleston and Pullum, 2002). Good textbooks on linguistics include Sag and

Wasow's (1999) introduction to syntax and the semantics texts by Chierchia and McConnell-Ginet (1990) and by Heim and Kratzer (1998). McCawley's (1993) text concentrates on logic for linguists.

Since the mid-1980s, there has been a trend toward putting more information in the lexicon and less in the grammar. Lexical-functional grammar, or LFG, (Bresnan, 1982) was the first major grammar formalism to be highly lexicalized. If we carry lexicalization to an extreme, we end up with **categorial grammar**, in which there can be as few as two grammar rules, or **dependency grammar** (Melćuk and Polguere, 1988), in which there are no phrases, only words. Sleator and Temperley (1993) describe a popular parser that uses dependency grammar. Tree-Adjoining Grammar, or TAG, (Joshi, 1985) is not strictly lexical, but it is gaining popularity in its lexicalized form (Schabes *et al.*, 1988). Wordnet (Fellbaum, 2001) is a publicly-available dictionary of about 100,000 words and phrases, categorized into parts of speech and linked by semantic relations such as synonym, antonym, and part-of.

The first computerized parsing algorithms were demonstrated by Yngve (1955). Efficient algorithms were developed in the late 1960s, with a few twists since then (Kasami, 1965; Younger, 1967; Graham *et al.*, 1980). Our chart parser is closest to Earley's (1970). A good summary appears in the text on parsing and compiling by Aho and Ullman (1972). Maxwell and Kaplan (1993) show how chart parsing with augmentations can be made efficient in the average case. Church and Patil (1982) address the resolution of syntactic ambiguity.

Formal semantic interpretation of natural languages originates within philosophy and formal logic and is especially closely related to Alfred Tarski's (1935) work on the semantics of formal languages. Bar-Hillel was the first to consider the problems of pragmatics and propose that they could be handled by formal logic. For example, he introduced C. S. Peirce's (1902) term *indexical* into linguistics (Bar-Hillel, 1954). Richard Montague's essay "English as a formal language" (1970) is a kind of manifesto for the logical analysis of language, but the book by Dowty *et al.* (1991) and the article by Lewis (1972) are more readable. A complete collection of Montague's contributions has been edited by Thomason (1974). In artificial intelligence, the work of McAllester and Givan (1992) continues the Montagovian tradition, adding many new technical insights.

The idea of an intermediate or quasi-logical form to handle problems such as quantifier scoping goes back to Woods (1978) and is present in many recent systems (Alshawi, 1992; Hwang and Schubert, 1993).

The first NLP system to solve an actual task was probably the BASEBALL question answering system (Green *et al.*, 1961), which handled questions about a database of baseball statistics. Close after that was Woods's (1973) LUNAR, which answered questions about the rocks brought back by the Apollo program. Roger Schank and his students built a series of programs (Schank and Abelson, 1977; Wilensky, 1978; Schank and Riesbeck, 1981; Dyer, 1983) that all had the task of understanding language. The emphasis, however, was less on language *per se* and more on representation and reasoning. The problems included representing stereotypical situations (Cullingford, 1981), describing human memory organization (Rieger, 1976; Kolodner, 1983), and understanding plans and goals (Wilensky, 1983).

Natural language generation was considered from the earliest days of machine translation in the 1950s, but it didn't appear as a monolingual concern until the 1970s. The work by Simmons and Slocum (1972) and Goldman (1975) are representative. PENMAN (Bateman *et al.*, 1989) was one of the first full-scale generation systems, based on Systemic Grammar (Kasper, 1988). In the 1990s, two important public-domain generation systems, KPML (Bateman, 1997) and FUF (Elhadad, 1993), became available. Important books on generation include McKeown (1985), Hovy (1988), Patten (1988) and Reiter and Dale (2000).

Some of the earliest work on disambiguation was Wilks's (1975) theory of **preference semantics**, which tried to find interpretations that minimize the number of semantic anomalies. Hirst (1987) describes a system with similar aims that is closer to the compositional semantics described in this chapter. Hobbs *et al.* (1993) describes a quantitative framework for measuring the quality of a syntactic and semantic interpretation. Since then, it has become more common to use an explicitly Bayesian framework (Charniak and Goldman, 1992; Wu, 1993). In linguistics, optimality theory (Linguistics) (Kager, 1999) is based on the idea of building soft constraints into the grammar, giving a natural ranking to interpretations, rather than having the grammar generate all possibilities with equal rank. Norvig (1988) discusses the problems of considering multiple simultaneous interpretations, rather than settling for a single maximum likelihood interpretation. Literary critics (Empson, 1953; Hobbs, 1990) have been ambiguous about whether ambiguity is something to be resolved or cherished.

Nunberg (1979) outlines a formal model of metonymy. Lakoff and Johnson (1980) give an engaging analysis and catalog of common metaphors in English. Ortony (1979) presents a collection of articles on metaphor; Martin (1990) offers a computational approach to metaphor interpretation.

Our treatment of reference resolution follows Hobbs (1978). A more complex model by Lappin and Leass (1994) is based on a quantitative scoring mechanism. More recent work (Kehler, 1997; Ge *et al.*, 1998) has used machine learning to tune the quantitative parameters. Two excellent surveys of reference resolution are the books by Hirst (1981) and Mitkov (2002).

In 1758, David Hume's *Enquiry Concerning the Human Understanding* argued that discourse is connected by "three principles of connexion among ideas, namely *Resemblance*, *Contiguity* in time or place, and *Cause* or *Effect*." So began a long history of trying to define coherence relations. Hobbs (1990) gives us the set used in this chapter; Mann and Thompson (1983) provide a more elaborate set that includes solutionhood, evidence, justification, motivation, reason, sequence, enablement, elaboration, restatement, condition, circumstance, cause, concession, background, and thesis–antithesis. That model evolved into rhetorical structure theory (RST), which is perhaps the most prominent theory today (Mann and Thompson, 1988). This chapter borrows some of the examples from the chapter in Jurafsky and Martin (2000) written by Andrew Kehler.

Grosz and Sidner (1986) present a theory of discourse coherence based on shifting one's focus of attention, and Grosz *et al.* (1995) offer a related theory based on the notion of centering. Joshi, Webber, and Sag (1981) collect important early work on discourse. Webber presents a model of the interacting constraints of syntax and discourse on what can be said at any point in the discourse (1983) and of the way verb tense interacts with discourse (1988).

The first important result on **grammar induction** was a negative one: Gold (1967) showed that it is not possible to reliably learn a correct context-free grammar, given a set of strings from that grammar. Essentially, the idea is that, given a set of strings $s_1, s_2 \ldots s_n$, the correct grammar could be all-inclusive ($S \rightarrow word*$), or it could be a copy of the input ($S \rightarrow s_1 \mid s_2 \mid \ldots \mid s_n$), or anywhere in between. Prominent linguists, such as Chomsky (1957, 1980) and Pinker (1989, 2000), have used Gold's result to argue that there must be an innate **universal grammar** that all children have from birth. The so-called *Poverty of the Stimulus* argument is that children have no language inputs other than positive examples: their parents and peers produce mostly accurate examples of their language, and very rarely correct mistakes. Therefore, because Gold proved that learning a CFG from positive examples is impossible, the children must already "know" the grammar and be merely tuning some of its parameters of this innate grammar and learning vocabulary. While this argument continues to hold sway throughout much of Chomskian linguistics, it has been dismissed by some other linguists (Pullum, 1996; Elman *et al.*, 1997) and most computer scientists. As early as 1969, Horning showed that it *is* possible to learn, in the sense of PAC learning, a *probabilistic* context-free grammar. Since then there have been many convincing empirical demonstrations of learning from positive examples alone, such as the ILP work of Mooney (1999) and Muggleton and De Raedt (1994) and the remarkable Ph.D. theses of Schütze (1995) and de Marcken (1996). It is possible to learn other grammar formalisms, such as regular languages (Oncina and Garcia, 1992; Denis, 2001), and regular tree languages (Carrasco *et al.*, 1998), and finite state automata (Parekh and Honavar, 2001).

UNIVERSAL GRAMMAR

The SEQUITUR system is due to Nevill-Manning and Witten (1997). Interestingly, they, as well as de Marcken, remark that their grammar induction schemes are also good compression schemes. This is in accordance with the principle of minimal description length encoding: a good grammar is a grammar that minimizes the sum of two lengths: the length of the grammar and the length of the parse tree of the text.

Inductive Logic Programming work for language learning includes the CHILL system by Zelle and Mooney (1996) and a program by Mooney and Califf (1995) that learned rules for the past tense of verbs better than past neural net or decision tree systems. Cussens and Dzeroski (2000) edited a collection of papers on learning language in logic.

The Association for Computational Linguistics (ACL) holds regular conferences and publishes the journal *Computational Linguistics*. There is also an International Conference on Computational Linguistics (COLING). *Readings in Natural Language Processing* (Grosz *et al.*, 1986) is an anthology containing many important early papers. Dale *et al.* (2000) emphasize practical tools for building NLP systems. The textbook by Jurafsky and Martin (2000) gives a comprehensive introduction to the field. Allen (1995) is a slightly older treatment. Pereira and Sheiber (1987) and Covington (1994) offer concise overviews of syntactic processing based on implementations in Prolog. The *Encyclopedia of AI* has many useful articles on the field; see especially the entries "Computational Linguistics" and "Natural Language Understanding."

## EXERCISES

**22.1** Read the following text once for understanding, and remember as much of it as you can. There will be a test later.

> The procedure is actually quite simple. First you arrange things into different groups. Of course, one pile may be sufficient depending on how much there is to do. If you have to go somewhere else due to lack of facilities that is the next step, otherwise you are pretty well set. It is important not to overdo things. That is, it is better to do too few things at once than too many. In the short run this may not seem important but complications can easily arise. A mistake is expensive as well. At first the whole procedure will seem complicated. Soon, however, it will become just another facet of life. It is difficult to foresee any end to the necessity for this task in the immediate future, but then one can never tell. After the procedure is completed one arranges the material into different groups again. Then they can be put into their appropriate places. Eventually they will be used once more and the whole cycle will have to be repeated. However, this is part of life.

**22.2** Using DCG notation, write a grammar for a language that is just like $\mathcal{E}_1$, except that it enforces agreement between the subject and verb of a sentence and thus does not generate "I smells the wumpus."

**22.3** Augment the $\mathcal{E}_1$ grammar so that it handles article–noun agreement. That is, make sure that "agents" is an $NP$, but "agent" and "an agents" are not.

**22.4** Outline the major differences between Java (or any other computer language with which you are familiar) and English, commenting on the "understanding" problem in each case. Think about such things as grammar, syntax, semantics, pragmatics, compositionality, context-dependence, lexical ambiguity, syntactic ambiguity, reference finding (including pronouns), background knowledge, and what it means to "understand" in the first place.

**22.5** Which of the following are reasons for introducing a quasi-logical form?

**a.** To make it easier to write simple compositional grammar rules.
**b.** To extend the expressiveness of the semantic representation language.
**c.** To be able to represent quantifier scoping ambiguities (among others) in a succinct form.
**d.** To make it easier to do semantic disambiguation.

**22.6** Determine what semantic interpretation would be given to the following sentences by the grammar in this chapter:

**a.** It is a wumpus.
**b.** The wumpus is dead.
**c.** The wumpus is in 2,2.

Would it be a good idea to have the semantic interpretation for "It is a wumpus" be simply $\exists x \;\; x \in Wumpuses$? Consider alternative sentences such as "It was a wumpus."

**22.7** Without looking back at Exercise 22.1, answer the following questions:

**a.** What are the four steps that are mentioned?

**b.** What step is left out?

**c.** What is "the material" that is mentioned in the text?

**d.** What kind of mistake would be expensive?

**e.** Is it better to do too few or too many? Why?

**22.8** This exercise concerns grammars for very simple languages.

**a.** Write a context-free grammar for the language $a^n b^n$.

**b.** Write a context-free grammar for the palindrome language: the set of all strings whose second half is the reverse of the first half.

**c.** Write a context-sensitive grammar for the duplicate language: the set of all strings whose second half is the same as the first half.

**22.9** Consider the sentence "Someone walked slowly to the supermarket" and the following lexicon:

| | |
|---|---|
| $Pronoun \rightarrow$ **someone** | $V \rightarrow$ **walked** |
| $Adv \rightarrow$ **slowly** | $Prep \rightarrow$ **to** |
| $Det \rightarrow$ **the** | $Noun \rightarrow$ **supermarket** |

Which of the following three grammars, combined with the lexicon, generates the given sentence? Show the corresponding parse tree(s).

| (A): | (B): | (C): |
|---|---|---|
| $S \rightarrow NP\ VP$ | $S \rightarrow NP\ VP$ | $S \rightarrow NP\ VP$ |
| $NP \rightarrow Pronoun$ | $NP \rightarrow Pronoun$ | $NP \rightarrow Pronoun$ |
| $NP \rightarrow Article\ Noun$ | $NP \rightarrow Noun$ | $NP \rightarrow Article\ NP$ |
| $VP \rightarrow VP\ PP$ | $NP \rightarrow Article\ NP$ | $VP \rightarrow Verb\ Adv$ |
| $VP \rightarrow VP\ Adv\ Adv$ | $VP \rightarrow Verb\ Vmod$ | $Adv \rightarrow Adv\ Adv$ |
| $VP \rightarrow Verb$ | $Vmod \rightarrow Adv\ Vmod$ | $Adv \rightarrow PP$ |
| $PP \rightarrow Prep\ NP$ | $Vmod \rightarrow Adv$ | $PP \rightarrow Prep\ NP$ |
| $NP \rightarrow Noun$ | $Adv \rightarrow PP$ | $NP \rightarrow Noun$ |
| | $PP \rightarrow Prep\ NP$ | |

For each of the preceding three grammars, write down three sentences of English and three sentences of non-English generated by the grammar. Each sentence should be significantly different, should be at least six words long, and should be based on an entirely new set of lexical entries (which you should define). Suggest ways to improve each grammar to avoid generating the non-English sentences.

**22.10** Implement a version of the chart-parsing algorithm that returns a packed tree of all edges that span the entire input.

**22.11** Implement a version of the chart-parsing algorithm that returns a packed tree for the longest leftmost edge, and then if that edge does not span the whole input, continues the parse from the end of that edge. Show why you will need to call PREDICT before continuing. The final result is a list of packed trees such that the list as a whole spans the input.

**22.12** (Derived from Barton *et al.* (1987).) This exercise concerns a language we call *Buffalo*$^n$, which is very much like English (or at least $\mathcal{E}_0$), except that the only word in its lexicon is *buffalo*. Here are two sentences from the language:

Buffalo buffalo buffalo Buffalo buffalo.

Buffalo Buffalo buffalo buffalo buffalo Buffalo buffalo.

In case you don't believe these are sentences, here are two English sentences with corresponding syntactic structure:

Dallas cattle bewilder Denver cattle.

Chefs London critics admire cook French food.

Write a grammar for *Buffalo*$^n$. The lexical categories are city, plural noun, and (transitive) verb, and there should be one grammar rule for sentence, one for verb phrase, and three for noun phrase: plural noun, noun phrase preceded by a city as a modifier, and noun phrase followed by a reduced relative clause. A reduced relative clause is a clause that is missing the relative pronoun. In addition, the clause consists of a subject noun phrase followed by a verb without an object. An example reduced relative clause is "London critics admire" in the example above. Tabulate the number of possible parses for *Buffalo*$^n$ for $n$ up to 10. Extra credit: Carl de Marcken calculated that there are 121,030,872,213,055,159,681,184,485 *Buffalo*$^n$ sentences of length 200 (for the grammar he used). How did he do that?

**22.13** Draw a discourse parse tree for the story on page 823 about John going to a fancy restaurant. Use to the two grammar rules for $Segment$, giving the proper $CoherenceRelation$ for each node. (You needn't show the parse for individual sentences.) Now do the same for a 5 to 10–sentence discourse of your choosing.

**22.14** We forgot to mention that the text in Exercise 22.1 is entitled "Washing Clothes." Reread the text and answer the questions in Exercise 22.7. Did you do better this time? Bransford and Johnson (1973) used this text in a better controlled experiment and found that the title helped significantly. What does this tell you about discourse comprehension?

# 23 PROBABILISTIC LANGUAGE PROCESSING

*In which we see how simple, statistically trained language models can be used to process collections of millions of words, rather than just single sentences.*

In Chapter 22, we saw how an agent could communicate with another agent (human or software), using utterances in a common language. Complete syntactic and semantic analysis of the utterances is *necessary* to extract the full meaning of the utterances, and is *possible* because the utterances are short and restricted to a limited domain.

CORPUS-BASED

In this chapter, we consider the **corpus-based** approach to language understanding. A corpus (plural *corpora*) is a large collection of text, such as the billions of pages that make up the World Wide Web. The text is written by and for humans, and the task of the software is to make it easier for the human to find the right information. This approach implies the use of statistics and learning to take advantage of the corpus, and it usually entails probabilistic language models that can be learned from data and that are simpler than the augmented DCGs of Chapter 22. For most tasks, the volume of data more than makes up for the simpler language model. We will look at three specific tasks: information retrieval (Section 23.2), information extraction (Section 23.3), and machine translation (Section 23.4). But first we present an overview of probabilistic language models.

## 23.1 PROBABILISTIC LANGUAGE MODELS

Chapter 22 gave us a *logical* model of language: we used CFGs and DCGs to characterize a string as either a member or a nonmember of a language. In this section, we will introduce several *probabilistic* models. Probabilistic models have several advantages. They can conveniently be trained from data: learning is just a matter of counting occurrences (with some allowances for the errors of relying on a small sample size). Also, they are more robust (because they can accept *any* string, albeit with a low probability), they reflect the fact that not 100% of speakers agree on which sentences are actually part of a language, and they can be used for disambiguation: probability can be used to choose the most likely interpretation.

PROBABILISTIC LANGUAGE MODEL

A **probabilistic language model** defines a probability distribution over a (possibly infinite) set of strings. Example models that we have already seen are the bigram and trigram language models used in speech recognition (Section 15.6). A unigram model assigns a probability $P(w)$ to each word in the lexicon. The model assumes that words are chosen independently, so the probability of a string is just the product of the probability of its words, given by $\prod_i P(w_i)$. The following 20-word sequence was generated at random from a unigram model of the words in this book:

> logical are as are confusion a may right tries agent goal the was diesel more object then information-gathering search is

A bigram model assigns a probability $P(w_i|w_{i-1})$ to each word, given the previous word. Figure 15.21 listed some of these bigram probabilities. A bigram model of this book generates the following random sequence:

> planning purely diagnostic expert systems are very similar computational approach would be represented compactly using tic tac toe a predicate

In general, an $n$-gram model conditions on the previous $n-1$ words, assigning a probability for $P(w_i|w_{i-(n-1)} \dots w_{i-1})$. A trigram model of this book generates this random sequence:

> planning and scheduling are integrated the success of naive bayes model is just a possible prior source by that time

Even with this small sample, it should be clear that the trigram model is better than the bigram model (which is better than the unigram model), both for approximating the English language and for approximating the subject matter of an AI textbook. The models themselves agree: the trigram model assigns its random string a probability of $10^{-10}$, the bigram $10^{-29}$, and the unigram $10^{-59}$.

At half a million words, this book does not contain enough data to produce a good bigram model, let alone a trigram model. There are about 15,000 different words in the lexicon of this book, so the bigram model includes $15,000^2 = 225$ million word pairs. Clearly, at least 99.8% of these pairs will have a count of zero, but we don't want our model to say that all these pairs are impossible. We need some way of **smoothing** over the zero counts. The simplest way to do this is called **add-one smoothing**: we add one to the count of every possible bigram. So if there are $N$ words in the corpus and $B$ possible bigrams, then each bigram with an actual count of $c$ is assigned a probability estimate of $(c+1)/(N+B)$. This method eliminates the problem of zero-probability $n$-grams, but the assumption that every count should be incremented by exactly one is dubious and can lead to poor estimates.

SMOOTHING

ADD-ONE SMOOTHING

LINEAR INTERPOLATION SMOOTHING

Another approach is **linear interpolation smoothing**, which combines trigram, bigram, and unigram models by linear interpolation. We define our probability estimate as

$$\hat{P}(w_i|w_{i-2}w_{i-1}) = c_3 P(w_i|w_{i-2}w_{i-1}) + c_2 P(w_i|w_{i-1}) + c_1 P(w_i) ,$$

where $c_3 + c_2 + c_1 = 1$. The parameters $c_i$ can be fixed, or they can be trained with an EM algorithm. It is possible to have values of $c_i$ that are dependent on the $n$-gram counts, so that we place a higher weight on the probability estimates that are derived from higher counts.

One method for *evaluating* a language model is as follows: First, split your corpus into a training corpus and a test corpus. Determine the parameters of the model from the training data. Then calculate the probability assigned to the test corpus by the model; the higher the probability the better. One problem with this approach is that $P(words)$ is quite small for long strings; the numbers could cause floating point underflow, or could just be hard to read. So instead of probability we can compute the **perplexity** of a model on a test string of words:

PERPLEXITY

$$Perplexity(words) = 2^{-\log_2(P(words))/N} ,$$

where $N$ is the number of $words$. The lower the perplexity, the better the model. An $n$-gram model that assigns every word a probability of $1/k$ will have perplexity $k$; you can think of perplexity as the average branching factor.

SEGMENTATION

As an example of what $n$-gram models can do, consider the task of **segmentation**: finding the words boundaries in a text with no spaces. This task is necessary in Japanese and Chinese, languages that are written with no spaces between words, but we assume that most readers will be more comfortable with English. The sentence

Itiseasytoreadwordswithoutspaces

is in fact easy for us to read. You might think that is because we have our full knowledge of English syntax, semantics, and pragmatics. We will show that the sentence can be decoded easily by a simple unigram word model.

Earlier we saw how the Viterbi equation (15.9), can be used to solve the problem of finding the most probable sequence through a lattice of word possibilities. Figure 23.1 shows a version of the Viterbi algorithm specifically designed for the segmentation problem. It takes as input a unigram word probability distribution, $P(word)$, and a string. Then, for each position $i$ in the string, it stores in $best[i]$ the probability of the most probable string spanning from the start up to $i$. It also stores in $words[i]$ the word ending at position $i$ that yielded the best probability. Once it has built up the $best$ and $words$ arrays in a dynamic programming fashion, it then works backwards through $words$ to find the best path. In this case, with the unigram model from the book, the best sequence of words is indeed "It is easy to read words without spaces," with probability $10^{-25}$. Comparing subparts of the sequence, we see for example that "easy" has unigram probability $2.6 \times 10^{-4}$, whereas the alternative "e as y" has a much lower probability, $9.8 \times 10^{-12}$, despite the fact that the words $e$ and $y$ are fairly common in equations in the book. Similarly, we have

$$P(\text{"without"}) = 0.0004 ;$$
$$P(\text{"with"}) = 0.005; \; P(\text{"out"}) = 0.0008 ;$$
$$P(\text{"with out"}) = 0.005 \times 0.0008 = 0.000004 .$$

Hence, "without" is 100 times more likely than "with out," according to the unigram model.

In this section we have discussed $n$-gram models over words, but there are also many uses of $n$-gram models over other units, such as characters or parts of speech.

### Probabilistic context-free grammars

PROBABILISTIC CONTEXT-FREE GRAMMAR

$n$-gram models take advantage of co-occurrence statistics in the corpora, but they have no notion of grammar at distances greater than $n$. An alternative language model is the **probabilistic context-free grammar**, or PCFG,[1] which consists of a CFG wherein each rewrite

[1] PCFGs are also known as stochastic context-free grammars or SCFGs.

```
function VITERBI-SEGMENTATION(text, P) returns best words and their probabilities
  inputs: text, a string of characters with spaces removed
          P, a unigram probability distribution over words

  n ← LENGTH(text)
  words ← empty vector of length n + 1
  best ← vector of length n + 1, initially all 0.0
  best[0] ← 1.0
  /* Fill in the vectors best, words via dynamic programming */
  for i = 0 to n do
    for j = 0 to i − 1 do
      word ← text[j:i]
      w ← LENGTH(word)
      if P[word] × best[i - w] ≥ best[i] then
        best[i] ← P[word] × best[i − w]
        words[i] ← word
  /* Now recover the sequence of best words */
  sequence ← the empty list
  i ← n
  while i > 0 do
    push words[i] onto front of sequence
    i ← i − LENGTH(words[i])
  /* Return sequence of best words and overall probability of sequence */
  return sequence, best[i]
```

**Figure 23.1** A Viterbi-based word segmentation algorithm. Given a string of words with spaces removed, it recovers the most probable segmentation into words.

rule has an associated probability. The sum of the probabilities across all rules with the same left-hand side is 1. Figure 23.2 shows a PCFG for a portion of the $\mathcal{E}_0$ grammar.

In the PCFG model, the probability of a string, $P(words)$, is just the sum of the probabilities of its parse trees. The probability of a given tree is the product of the probabilities of all the rules that make up the nodes of the tree. Figure 23.3 shows how to compute the probability of a sentence. It is possible to compute this probability by using a CFG chart parser to enumerate the possible parses and then simply adding up the probabilities. However, if we are interested only in the most probable parse then enumerating the unlikely ones is wasteful. We can use a variation of the Viterbi algorithm to find the most probable parse efficiently, or we can use a best-first search technique (such as A*).

The problem with PCFGs is that they are context-free. That means that the difference between $P$("eat a banana") and $P$("eat a bandanna") depends only on $P$("banana") versus $P$("bandanna") and not on the relation between "eat" and the respective objects. To get at that kind of relationship, we will need some kind of context-sensitive model, such as a **lexicalized PCFG**, in which the head of a phrase[2] can play a role in the probability of a

[2] The *head* of a phrase is the most important word, e.g., the noun of a noun phrase.

$$
\begin{array}{rcl}
S & \rightarrow & NP\ VP\ [1.00] \\
\\
NP & \rightarrow & Pronoun\ [0.10] \\
 & | & Name\ [0.10] \\
 & | & Noun\ [0.20] \\
 & | & Article\ Noun\ [0.50] \\
 & | & NP\ PP\ [0.10] \\
\\
VP & \rightarrow & Verb\ [0.60] \\
 & | & VP\ NP\ [0.20] \\
 & | & VP\ PP\ [0.20] \\
\\
PP & \rightarrow & Preposition\ NP\ [1.00] \\
\\
Noun & \rightarrow & \textbf{breeze}\ [0.10] \mid \textbf{wumpus}\ [0.15] \mid \textbf{agent}\ [0.05] \mid \ldots \\
Verb & \rightarrow & \textbf{sees}\ [0.15] \mid \textbf{smells}\ [0.10] \mid \textbf{goes}\ [0.25] \mid \ldots \\
Pronoun & \rightarrow & \textbf{me}\ [0.05] \mid \textbf{you}\ [0.10] \mid \textbf{I}\ [0.25] \mid \textbf{it}\ [0.20] \mid \ldots \\
Article & \rightarrow & \textbf{the}\ [0.30] \mid \textbf{a}\ [0.35] \mid \textbf{every}\ [0.05] \mid \ldots \\
Preposition & \rightarrow & \textbf{to}\ [0.30] \mid \textbf{in}\ [0.25] \mid \textbf{on}\ [0.05] \mid \ldots
\end{array}
$$

**Figure 23.2** A probabilistic context-free grammar (PCFG) and lexicon for a portion of the $\mathcal{E}_0$ grammar. The numbers in square brackets indicate the probability that a left-hand-side symbol will be rewritten with the corresponding rule.

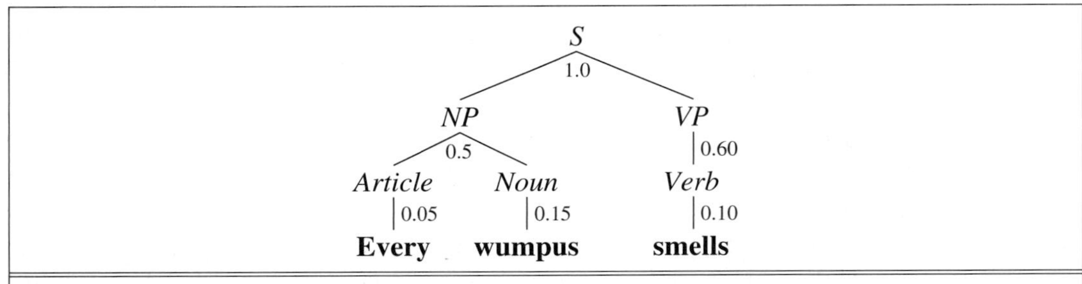


**Figure 23.3** Parse tree for the sentence "Every wumpus smells," showing the probabilities of each subtree. The probability of the tree as a whole is $1.0 \times 0.5 \times 0.05 \times 0.15 \times 0.60 \times 0.10 = 0.000225$. Since this tree is the only parse of the sentence, that number is also the probability of the sentence.

containing phrase. With enough training data, we could have the rule for $VP \rightarrow VP\ NP$ be conditioned on the head of the embedded $VP$ (eat) and on the head of the $NP$ (banana). Lexicalized PCFGs thus capture some of the co-occurrence restrictions of $n$-gram models, along with the grammatical restrictions of CFG models.

One more problem is that PCFGs tend to have too strong a preference for shorter sentences. In a corpus such as the *Wall Street Journal*, the average length of a sentence is about

25 words. But a PCFG will usually end up assigning a fairly high probability to rules such as $S \rightarrow NP\ VP$ and $NP \rightarrow Pronoun$ and $VP \rightarrow Verb$. This means that the PCFG will assign fairly high probability to many short sentences, such as "He slept," whereas in the *Journal* we're more likely to see something like "It has been reported by a reliable government source that the allegation that he slept is credible." It seems that the phrases in the *Journal* really are not context-free; instead the writers have an idea of the expected sentence length and use that length as a soft global constraint on their sentences. This is hard to reflect in a PCFG.

### Learning probabilities for PCFGs

To create a PCFG, we have all the difficulty of constructing a CFG, combined with the problem of setting the probabilities for each rule. This suggests that **learning** the grammar from data might be better than a knowledge engineering approach. Just as with speech recognition, there are two types of data we might be given: parsed and unparsed. The task is considerably easier if we have data that have been parsed into trees by linguists (or at least by trained native speakers). Creating such a corpus is a big investment, and the largest ones contain "only" about a million words. Given a corpus of trees, we can create a PCFG just by counting (and smoothing): For each nonterminal symbol, just look at all the nodes with that symbol as root, and create rules for each different combination of children in those nodes. For example, if the symbol $NP$ appears 100,000 times, and there are 20,000 instances of $NP$ with the list of children $[NP, PP]$, then create the rule

$$NP \rightarrow NP\ PP\ [0.20]\ .$$

The task is much harder if all we have is unparsed text. First of all, we actually have two problems: learning the structure of the grammar rules and learning the probabilities associated with each rule. (We have the same distinction in learning neural nets or Bayes nets.)

For the moment we will assume that the structure of the rules is given and that we are just trying to learn the probabilities. We can use an expectation–maximization (EM) approach, just as we did in learning HMMs. The parameters we are trying to learn are the rule probabilities. The hidden variables are the parse trees: we don't know whether a string of words $w_i \ldots w_j$ is or is not generated by a rule $X \rightarrow \alpha$. The E step estimates the probability that each subsequence is generated by each rule. The M step then estimates the probability of each rule. The whole computation can be done in a dynamic programming fashion with an algorithm called the **inside–outside algorithm** in analogy to the forward–backward algorithm for HMMs.

INSIDE–OUTSIDE ALGORITHM

The inside–outside algorithm seems magical in that it induces a grammar from unparsed text. But it has several drawbacks. First, it is slow: $O(n^3t^3)$, where $n$ is the number of words in a sentence and $t$ is the number of nonterminal symbols. Second, the space of probability assignments is very large, and empirically it seems that getting stuck in local maxima is a severe problem. Alternatives such as simulated annealing can be tried, at a cost of even more computation. Third, the parses that are assigned by the resulting grammars are often difficult to understand and unsatisfying to linguists. This makes it hard to combine handcrafted knowledge with automated induction.

### Learning rule structure for PCFGs

Now suppose the structure of the grammar rules is not known. Our first problem is that the space of possible rule sets is infinite, so we don't know how many rules to consider nor how long each rule can be. One way to sidestep this problem is to learn a grammar in **Chomsky normal form**, which means that every rule is in one of the two forms

CHOMSKY NORMAL FORM

$$X \rightarrow Y\ Z$$
$$X \rightarrow \mathbf{t}\,,$$

where $X$, $Y$ and $Z$ are nonterminals and **t** is a terminal. Any context-free grammar can be rewritten as a Chomsky normal form grammar that recognizes the exact same language. We can then arbitrarily restrict ourself to $n$ non-terminal symbols, thus yielding $n^3 + nv$ rules, where $v$ is the number of terminal symbols. In practice, this approach has proven effective only for small grammars. An alternative approach called **Bayesian model merging** is similar to the SEQUITUR model (Section 22.8). The approach starts by building local models (grammars) of each sentence and then uses minimum description length to merge models.

BAYESIAN MODEL MERGING

## 23.2 INFORMATION RETRIEVAL

INFORMATION RETRIEVAL

**Information retrieval** is the task of finding documents that are relevant to a user's need for information. The best-known examples of information retrieval systems are search engines on the World Wide Web. A Web user can type a query such as [AI book] into a search engine and see a list of relevant pages. In this section, we will see how such systems are built. An information retrieval (henceforth IR) system can be characterized by:

1. **A document collection.** Each system must decide what it wants to treat as a document: a paragraph, a page, or a multi-page text.

QUERY

QUERY LANGUAGE

2. **A query posed in a query language**. The query specifies what the user wants to know. The query language can be just a list of words, such as [AI book]; or it can specify a phrase of words that must be adjacent, as in ["AI book"]; it can contain Boolean operators as in [AI *AND* book]; it can include non-Boolean operators such as [AI *NEAR* book] or [AI book *SITE:*www.aaai.org].

RESULT SET

RELEVANT

3. **A result set.** This is the subset of documents that the IR system judges to be **relevant** to the query. By *relevant*, we mean likely to be of use to the person who asked the query, for the particular information need expressed in the query.

PRESENTATION

4. **A presentation of the result set.** This can be as simple as a ranked list of document titles or as complex as a rotating color map of the result set projected onto a three-dimensional space.

After reading the previous chapter, one might suppose that an information retrieval system could be built by parsing the document collection into a knowledge base of logical sentences and then parsing each query and ASKing the knowledge base for answers. Unfortunately, no one has ever succeeded in building a large-scale IR system that way. It is just too difficult to build a lexicon and grammar that cover a large document collection, so all IR systems use simpler language models.

BOOLEAN KEYWORD MODEL

The earliest IR systems worked on a **Boolean keyword model**. Each word in the document collection is treated as a Boolean feature that is true of a document if the word occurs in the document and false if it does not. So the feature "retrieval" is true for the current chapter but false for Chapter 15. The query language is the language of Boolean expressions over features. A document is relevant only if the expression evaluates to true. For example, the query [information *AND* retrieval] is true for the current chapter and false for Chapter 15.

This model has the advantage of being simple to explain and implement. However, it has some disadvantages. First, the degree of relevance of a document is a single bit, so there is no guidance as to how to order the relevant documents for presentation. Second, Boolean expressions might be unfamiliar to users who are not programmers or logicians. Third, it can be hard to formulate an appropriate query, even for a skilled user. Suppose we try [information *AND* retrieval *AND* models *AND* optimization] and get an empty result set. We could try [information *OR* retrieval *OR* models *OR* optimization], but if that returns too many results, it is difficult to know what to try next.

Most IR systems use models based on the statistics of word counts (and sometimes other low-level features). We will explain a probabilistic framework that fits in well with the language models we have covered. The key idea is that, given a query, we want to find the documents that are most likely to be relevant. In other words, we want to compute

$$P(R = true|D, Q)$$

where $D$ is a document, $Q$ is a query, and $R$ is a Boolean random variable indicating relevance. Once we have this, we can apply the probability ranking principle, which says that if we have to present the result set as an ordered list, we should do it in decreasing probability of relevance.

LANGUAGE MODELING

There are several ways to decompose the joint distribution $P(R = true|D, Q)$. We will show the one known as the **language modeling** approach, which estimates a language model for each document and then, for each query, computes the probability of the query, given the document's language model. Using $r$ to denote the value $R = true$, we can rewrite the probability as follows:

$$\begin{aligned} P(r|D,Q) &= P(D,Q|r)P(r)/P(D,Q) && \text{(by Bayes' rule)} \\ &= P(Q|D,r)P(D|r)P(r)/P(D,Q) && \text{(by chain rule)} \\ &= \alpha\, P(Q|D,r)P(r|D)/P(D,Q) && \text{(by Bayes' rule, for fixed } D\text{)}\,. \end{aligned}$$

We said we were trying to maximize $P(r|D, Q)$, but, equivalently, we can maximize the odds ratio $P(r|D, Q)/P(\neg r|D, Q)$. That is, we can rank documents based on the score:

$$\frac{P(r|D,Q)}{P(\neg r|D,Q)} = \frac{P(Q|D,r)P(r|D)}{P(Q|D,\neg r)P(\neg r|D)}\,.$$

This has the advantage of canceling out the $P(D, Q)$ term. Now we will make the assumption that for irrelevant documents, the document is independent of the query. In other words, if a document is irrelevant to a query, then knowing the document won't help you figure out what the query is. This assumption can be expressed by

$$P(D, Q|\neg r) = P(D|\neg r)P(Q|\neg r)\,.$$

With the assumption, we get

$$\frac{P(r|D,Q)}{P(\neg r|D,Q)} = P(Q|D,r) \times \frac{P(r|D)}{P(\neg r|D)} .$$

The factor $P(r|D)/P(\neg r|D)$ is the query-independent odds that the document is relevant. This is a measure of document quality; some documents are more likely to be relevant to *any* query, because the document is just inherently of high quality. For academic journal articles we can estimate the quality by the number of citations, and for web pages we can use the number of hyperlinks to the page. In either case, we might give more weight to high-quality referrers. The age of a document might also be a factor in estimating its query-independent relevance.

The first factor, $P(Q|D,r)$, is the probability of a query given a relevant document. To estimate this probability we must choose a language model of how queries are related to relevant documents. One popular choice is to represent documents with a unigram word model. This is also known as the **bag of words** model in IR, because what matters is the frequency of each word in the document, not their order. In this model the (very short) documents "man bites dog" and "dog bites man" will behave identically. Clearly, they *mean* different things, but it is true that they are both relevant to queries about dogs and biting. Now to calculate the probability of a query given a relevant document, we just multiply the probabilities of the words in the query, according to the document unigram model. This is a **naive Bayes** model of the query. Using $Q_j$ to indicate the $j$th word in the query, we have

BAG OF WORDS

$$P(Q|D,r) = \prod_j P(Q_j|D,r) .$$

This allows us to make the simplification

$$\frac{P(r|D,Q)}{P(\neg r|D,Q)} = \prod_j P(Q_j|D,r)\frac{P(r|D)}{P(\neg r|D)} .$$

At last, we are ready to apply these mathematical models to an example. Figure 23.4 shows unigram statistics for the words in the query [Bayes information retrieval model] over a document collection consisting of five selected chapters from this book. We assume that the chapters are of uniform quality, so we are interested only in computing the probability of the query given the document, for each document. We do this two times, once using an unsmoothed maximum likelihood estimator $D_i$ and once using a model $D_i'$ with add-one-smoothing. One would expect that the current chapter should be ranked highest for this query, and in fact in either model it is.

The smoothed model has the advantage that it is less susceptible to noise and that it can assign a nonzero probability of relevance to a document that doesn't contain all the words. The unsmoothed model has the advantage that it is easier to compute for collections with many documents: if we create an index that lists which documents mention each word, then we can quickly generate a result set by intersecting these lists, and we need to compute $P(Q|D_i)$ only for those documents in the intersection, rather than for every document.

## Evaluating IR systems

How do we know whether an IR system is performing well? We undertake an experiment in which the system is given a set of queries and the result sets are scored with respect to human

| Words | Query | Chapter 1 Intro | Chapter 13 Uncertainty | Chapter 15 Time | Chapter 22 NLP | Chapter 23 Current |
|---|---|---|---|---|---|---|
| Bayes | 1 | 5 | 32 | 38 | 0 | 7 |
| information | 1 | 15 | 18 | 8 | 12 | 39 |
| retrieval | 1 | 1 | 1 | 0 | 0 | 17 |
| model | 1 | 9 | 7 | 160 | 9 | 63 |
| $N$ | 4 | 14680 | 10941 | 18186 | 16397 | 12574 |
| $P(Q\|D_i, r)$ | | $1.5 \times 10^{-14}$ | $2.8 \times 10^{-13}$ | 0 | 0 | $1.2 \times 10^{-11}$ |
| $P(Q\|D'_i, r)$ | | $4.1 \times 10^{-14}$ | $7.0 \times 10^{-13}$ | $5.2 \times 10^{-13}$ | $1.7 \times 10^{-15}$ | $1.5 \times 10^{-11}$ |

**Figure 23.4** A probabilistic IR model for the query [Bayes information retrieval model] over a document collection consisting of five chapters from this book. We give the word counts for each document–word pair and the total word count $N$ for each document. We use two document models—$D_i$ is an unsmoothed unigram word model of the $i$th document, and $D'_i$ is the same model with add-one smoothing—and compute the probability of the query given each document for both models. The current chapter (23) is the clear winner, over 200 times more likely than any other chapter under either model.

relevance judgments. Traditionally there have been two measures used in the scoring: recall and precision. We will explain them with the help of an example. Imagine that an IR system has returned a result set for a single query, for which we know which documents are and are not relevant, out of a corpus of 100 documents. The document counts in each category are given in the following table:

| | In result set | Not in result set |
|---|---|---|
| Relevant | 30 | 20 |
| Not relevant | 10 | 40 |

PRECISION

**Precision** measures the proportion of documents in the result set that are actually relevant. In our example, the precision is $30/(30+10) = .75$. The false positive rate is $1 - .75 = .25$.

RECALL

**Recall** measures the proportion of all the relevant documents in the collection that are in the result set. In our example, recall is $30/(30+20) = .60$. The false negative rate is $1 - .60 = .40$. In a very large document collection, such as the World Wide Web, recall is difficult to compute, because there is no easy way to examine every page on the web for relevance. The best we can do is either to estimate recall by sampling or to ignore recall completely and just judge precision.

A system can trade off precision against recall. In the extreme, a system that returns every document in the document collection as its result set is guaranteed a recall of 100%, but will have low precision. Alternately, a system could return a single document and have low recall, but a decent chance at 100% precision. One way to summarize this tradeoff is

ROC CURVE

with an **ROC curve**. "ROC" stands for "receiver operating characteristic" (which is not very enlightening). It is a graph measuring the false negative rate on the $y$ axis and false positive rate on the $x$ axis, for various tradeoff points. The area under the curve is a summary of the effectiveness of an IR system.

Recall and precision were defined when IR searches were done primarily by librarians who were interested in thorough, scholarly results. Today, most queries (hundreds of millions per day) are done by Internet users who are less interested in thoroughness and more interested in finding an immediate answer. For them, one good measure is the average **reciprocal rank** of the first relevant result. That is, if a system's first result is relevant, it gets a score of 1 on the query, and if the first two are not relevant, but the third is, it gets a score of $1/3$. An alternative measure is **time to answer**, which measures how long it takes a user to find the desired answer to a problem. This gets closest to what we really want to measure, but it has the disadvantage that each experiment requires a fresh batch of human test subjects.

RECIPROCAL RANK

TIME TO ANSWER

## IR refinements

The unigram word model treats all words as completely independent, but we know that some words are correlated: "couch" is closely related to both "couches" and "sofa." Many IR systems attempt to account for these correlations.

For example, if the query is [couch], it would be a shame to exclude from the result set those documents that mention "COUCH" or "couches" but not "couch." Most IR systems do **case folding** of "COUCH" to "couch," and many use a **stemming** algorithm to reduce "couches" to the stem form "couch." This typically yields a small increase in recall (on the order of 2% for English). However, it can harm precision. For example, stemming "stocking" to "stock" will tend to decrease precision for queries about either foot coverings or financial instruments, although it could improve recall for queries about warehousing. Stemming algorithms based on rules (e.g. remove "-ing") cannot avoid this problem, but newer algorithms based on dictionaries (don't remove "-ing" if the word is already listed in the dictionary) can. While stemming has a small effect in English, it is more important in other languages. In German, for example, it is not uncommon to see words like "Lebensversicherungsgesellschaftsangestellter" (life insurance company employee). Languages such as Finnish, Turkish, Inuit, and Yupik have recursive morphological rules that in principle generate words of unbounded length.

CASE FOLDING

STEMMING

The next step is to recognize **synonyms**, such as "sofa" for "couch." As with stemming, this has the potential for small gains in recall, but with a danger of decreasing precision if applied too aggressively. Those interested in football player Tim Couch would not want to wade through results about sofas. The problem is that "languages abhor absolute synonymy just as nature abhors a vacuum" (Cruse, 1986). That is, anytime there are two words that mean the same thing, speakers of the language conspire to modify the meanings to remove the confusion.

SYNONYMS

Many IR systems use word **bigrams** to some extent, although few implement a complete probabilistic bigram model. **Spelling correction** routines can be used to correct for errors in both documents and queries.

SPELLING CORRECTION

As a final refinement, IR can be improved by considering **metadata**—data outside of the text of the document. Examples include human-supplied keywords and hypertext links between documents.

METADATA

### Presentation of result sets

The probability ranking principle says to take a result set and present it to the user as a list ordered by probability of relevance. This makes sense if a user is interested in finding all the relevant documents as quickly as possible. But it runs into trouble because it doesn't consider *utility*. For example, if there are two copies of the most relevant document in the collection, then once you have seen the first, the second has equal relevance, but zero utility. Many IR systems have mechanisms for eliminating results that are too similar to previous results.

RELEVANCE FEEDBACK

One of the most powerful ways to improve the performance of an IR system is to allow for **relevance feedback**—feedback from the user saying which documents from an initial result set are relevant. The system can then present a second result set of documents that are similar to those.

DOCUMENT CLASSIFICATION

DOCUMENT CLUSTERING

An alternative approach is to present the result set as a *labeled tree* rather than an ordered list. With **document classification**, the results are classified into a preexisting taxonomy of topics. For example, a collection of news stories might be classified into World News, Local news, Business, Entertainment, and Sports. With **document clustering**, the tree of categories is created from scratch for each result set. Classification is appropriate when there are a small number of topics in a collection, and clustering is appropriate for broader collections such as the World Wide Web. In either case, when the user issues a query, the result set is shown organized into folders based on the categories.

Classification is a supervised learning problem, and as such, it can be attacked with any of the methods from Chapter 18. One popular approach is decision trees. Given a training set of documents labeled with the correct categories, we could build a single decision tree whose leaves assign the document to the proper category. This works well when there are only a few categories, but for larger category sets we will build one decision tree for each category, with the leaves labeling the document as either a member or a nonmember of the category. Usually, the features tested at each node are individual words. For example, a node in the decision tree for the "Sports" category might test for the presence of the word "basketball." Boosted decision trees, naive Bayes models, and support vector machines have all been used to classify text; in many cases accuracy is in the 90–98% range for Boolean classification.

Clustering is an unsupervised learning problem. In Section 20.3 we saw how the EM algorithm can be used to improve an initial estimate of a clustering, based on a mixture of Gaussians model. The task of clustering documents is harder because we don't know that the data were generated by a nice Gaussian model and because we are dealing with a much higher dimensional space. A number of approaches have been developed.

AGGLOMERATIVE CLUSTERING

**Agglomerative clustering** creates a tree of clusters going all the way down to individual documents. The tree can be pruned at any level to yield a smaller number of categories, but that is considered outside the algorithm. We begin by considering each document as a separate cluster. Then we find the two clusters that are closest to each other according to some distance measure and merge these two clusters into one. We repeat the process until one cluster remains. The distance measure between two documents is some measure of the overlap between the words in the documents. For example, we could represent a document by a vector of word counts, and define the distance as the Euclidean distance between two vectors. The distance measure between two clusters can be the distance to the median of the cluster, or it can take into account the average distance between members of the clusters. Agglomerative clustering takes time $O(n^2)$, where $n$ is the number of documents.

K-MEANS CLUSTERING

**K-means clustering** creates a flat set of exactly $k$ categories. It works as follows:

1. Pick $k$ documents at random to represent the $k$ categories.
2. Assign every document to the closest category.
3. Compute the mean of each cluster and use the $k$ means to represent the new values of the $k$ categories.
4. Repeat steps (2) and (3) until convergence.

K-means takes time $O(n)$, giving it one advantage over agglomerative clustering. It is often reported to be less accurate than agglomerative clustering, although some have reported that it can do almost as well (Steinbach *et al.*, 2000).

Regardless of the clustering algorithm used, there is one more task before a clustering can be used to present a result set: finding a good way of describing the cluster. In classification, the category names are already defined (e.g. "Earnings"), but in clustering we need to invent the category names. One way to do that is to choose a list of words that are representative of the cluster. Another option is to choose the title of one or more documents near the center of the cluster.

### Implementing IR systems

So far, we have defined how IR systems work in the abstract, but we haven't explained how to make them efficient so that a Web search engine can return the top results from a multi-billion-page collection in a tenth of a second. The two key data structures for any IR system are the lexicon, which lists all the words in the document collection, and the inverted index, which lists all the places where each word appears in the document collection.

The **lexicon** is a data structure that supports one operation: given a word, it returns the location in the inverted index that stores the occurrences of the word. In some implementations it also returns the total number of documents that contain the word. The lexicon should be implemented with a hash table or similar data structure that allows this lookup to be fast. Sometimes a set of common words with little information content will be omitted from the lexicon. These **stop words** ("the," "of," "to," "be," "a," etc.) take up space in the index and don't improve the scoring of results. The only good reason for keeping them in the lexicon is for systems that support phrase queries: an index of stop words is necessary to efficiently retrieve hits for queries such as "to be or not to be."

STOP WORDS

INVERTED INDEX

HIT LISTS

The **inverted index**,[3] like the index in the back of this book, consists of a set of **hit lists**: places where each word occurs. For the Boolean keyword model, a hit list is just a list of documents. For the unigram model, it is a list of (document, count) pairs. To support phrase search, the hit list must also include the positions within each document where the word occurs.

---

[3] The term "inverted index" is redundant; a better term would be just "index." It is inverted in the sense that it is in a different order than the words in the text, but that is what all indices are like. But "inverted index" is the traditional term in IR.

When the query is a single word (26% of the time, according to Silverstein *et al.* (1998)), processing is very fast. We make a single lookup in the lexicon to get the address of the hit list, and then we create an empty priority queue. After that, we go through the hit list one document at a time and check the count for the document. If the priority queue has fewer than $R$ elements (where $R$ is the size of the desired result set), we add the (document, count) pair to the queue. Otherwise, if the count is larger than that of the lowest entry in the priority queue, we delete the lowest entry and add the new (document, count) pair. Thus, answering the query takes time $O(H + R \log R)$, where $H$ is the number of documents in the hit list. When the query has $n$ words, we have to merge $n$ hit lists, which can be done in time $O(nH + R \log R)$.

VECTOR SPACE MODEL

We have presented our theoretical overview of IR using the probabilistic model because that model makes use of the ideas we have already covered for other topics. But actual IR systems in practice are more likely to use a different approach called the **vector space model**. This model uses the same bag-of-words approach as the probability model. Each document is represented as a vector of unigram word frequencies. The query too is represented in the exact same way; the query [Bayes information retrieval model] is represented as the vector

$$[0, \ldots, 1, 0, \ldots, 1, 0, \ldots, 1, 0, \ldots, 1, 0, \ldots]$$

where the idea is that there is one dimension for every word in the document collection and the query gets a score of 0 on every dimension except the four that actually appear in the query. Relevant documents are selected by finding the document vectors that are nearest neighbors to the query vector in vector space. One measure of similarity is the dot product between query vector and document vector; the larger this is, the closer the two vectors. Algebraically, this gives high scores for words that appear frequently in both document and query. Geometrically, the dot product between two vectors is equal to the cosine of the angle between the vectors; maximizing the cosine of two such vectors (in the same quadrant) means that the angle between them is close to 0.

There is much more to the vector space model than this. In practice, it has grown to accommodate a wide variety of extra features, refinements, corrections, and additions. The basic idea of ranking documents by their similarity in a vector space makes it possible to fold in new ideas into the numeric ranking system. Some argue that a probabilistic model would allow these same manipulations to be done in a more principled way, but IR researchers are unlikely to change unless they can see a clear performance advantage to another model.

To get an idea of the magnitude of the indexing problem for a typical IR task, consider a standard document collection from the TREC (Text REtrieval Conference) collection consisting of 750,000 documents totaling 2 GB (gigabytes) of text. The lexicon contains roughly 500,000 words after stemming and case folding; these words can be stored in 7 to 10 MB. The inverted index with (document, count) pairs takes 324 MB, although one can use compression techniques to get it down to 83 MB. Compression saves space, at the cost of slightly increased processing requirements. However, if compression allows you to keep the whole index in memory rather than storing it on disk, then it will yield a substantial net increase in performance. Support for phrase queries increases the size to about 1,200 MB uncompressed or 600 MB with compression. Web search engines work on a scale about 3000 times larger than this. Many of the issues are the same, but because it is impractical to deal with terabytes of data on a single computer, the index is divided into $k$ segments, with each segment stored on a different computer. A query is sent to all of the computers in parallel, and then the $k$ result sets are merged into a single result set that is shown to the user. Web search engines also have to deal with thousands of queries per second, so they need $n$ copies of the $k$ computers. Values of $k$ and $n$ continue to grow over time.

## 23.3 INFORMATION EXTRACTION

INFORMATION EXTRACTION

**Information extraction** is the process of creating database entries by skimming a text and looking for occurrences of a particular class of object or event and for relationships among those objects and events. We could be trying to extract instances of addresses from web pages, with database fields for street, city, state, and zip code; or instances of storms from weather reports, with fields for temperature, wind speed, and precipitation. Information extraction systems are mid-way between information retrieval systems and full-text parsers, in that they need to do more than consider a document as a bag of words, but less than completely analyze every sentence.

The simplest type of information extraction system is called an *attribute-based* system because it assumes that the entire text refers to a single object and the task is to extract attributes of that object. For example, we mentioned in Section 10.5 the problem of extracting from the text "17in SXGA Monitor for only \$249.99" the database relations given by

$$\exists m \;\; m \in ComputerMonitors \land Size(m, Inches(17)) \land Price(m, \$(249.99)) \\ \land Resolution(m, 1280 \times 1024) \ .$$

REGULAR EXPRESSIONS

Some of this information can be handled with the help of **regular expressions**, which define a regular grammar in a single text string. Regular expressions are used in Unix commands such as grep, in programming languages such as Perl, and in word processors such as Microsoft Word. The details vary slightly from one tool to another and so are best learned from the appropriate manual, but here we show how to build up a regular expression for prices in dollars, demonstrating common subexpressions:

| | |
|---|---|
| `[0-9]` | matches any digit from 0 to 9 |
| `[0-9]+` | matches one or more digits |
| `.[0-9][0-9]` | matches a period followed by two digits |
| `(.[0-9][0-9])?` | matches a period followed by two digits, or nothing |
| `$[0-9]+(.[0-9][0-9])?` | matches \$249.99 or \$1.23 or \$1000000 or ... |

Attribute-based extraction systems can be built as a series of regular expressions, one for each attribute. If a regular expression matches the text exactly once, then we can pull out the portion of the text that is the value of the attribute. If there is no match there's nothing more we can do, but if there are several matches, we need a process to choose among them. One strategy is to have several regular expressions for each attribute, ordered by priority. So, for example, the top priority regular expression for price might look for the string "our price:" immediately preceding the dollar sign; if that is not found, we fall back on a less reliable regular expression. Another strategy is to take all the matches and find some way to choose between them. For example, we could take the lowest price that is within 50% of the highest price. This will handle texts like "List price \$99.00, special sale price \$78.00, shipping \$3.00."

One step up from attribute-based extraction systems are *relational-based* extraction systems, which have to worry about more than one object and the relations between them. Thus, when these systems see the text "\$249.99," they need to determine not just that it is a price, but also which object has that price. A typical relational-based extraction system is FASTUS, which handles news stories about corporate mergers and acquisitions. It can read the story:

> Bridgestone Sports Co. said Friday it has set up a joint venture in Taiwan with a local concern and a Japanese trading house to produce golf clubs to be shipped to Japan.

and generate a database record like

$$e \in JointVentures \wedge Product(e, \text{“}golf\ clubs\text{”}) \wedge Date(e, \text{“}Friday\text{”})$$
$$\wedge\ Entity(e, \text{“}Bridgestone\ Sports\ Co\text{”}) \wedge Entity(e, \text{“}a\ local\ concern\text{”})$$
$$\wedge\ Entity(e, \text{“}a\ Japanese\ trading\ house\text{”})\ .$$

Relational extraction systems often are built by using **cascaded finite-state transducers**. That is, they consist of a series of finite-state automata (FSAs), where each automaton receives text as input, transduces the text into a different format, and passes it along to the next automaton. This is appropriate because each FSA can be efficient and because together they can extract the necessary information. A typical system is FASTUS, which consists of the following five stages:

1. Tokenization
2. Complex word handling
3. Basic group handling
4. Complex phrase handling
5. Structure merging

FASTUS's first stage is **tokenization**, which segments the stream of characters into tokens (words, numbers, and punctuation). For English, tokenization can be fairly simple; just separating characters at white space or punctuation does a fairly good job. For Japanese, tokenization would need to do segmentation, using something like the Viterbi segmentation algorithm. (See Figure 23.1.) Some tokenizers also deal with markup languages such as HTML, SGML, and XML.

The second stage handles **complex words**, including collocations such as "set up" and "joint venture," as well as proper names such as "Prime Minister Tony Blair" and "Bridgestone Sports Co." These are recognized by a combination of lexical entries and finite-state grammar rules. For example, a company name might be recognized by the rule

> CapitalizedWord+ ("Company" | "Co" | "Inc" | "Ltd")

These rules should be constructed with care and tested for recall and precision. One commercial system recognized "Intel Chairman Andy Grove" as a place rather than a person because of a rule of the form

> CapitalizedWord+ ("Grove" | "Forest" | "Village" | ...)

The third stage handles **basic groups**, meaning noun groups and verb groups. The idea is to chunk these into units that will be managed by the later stages. A noun group consists of a head noun, optionally preceded by determiners and other modifiers. Because the noun group does not include the full complexity of the $NP$ in $\mathcal{E}_1$ we do not need recursive context-free grammar rules: the regular grammar rules allowed in finite state automata suffice. The verb group consists of a verb and its attached auxiliaries and adverbs, but without the direct and indirect object and prepositional phrases. The example sentence would emerge from this stage as follows:

```
1 NG: Bridgestone Sports Co.| 10 NG: a local concern
2 VG: said                  | 11 CJ: and
3 NG: Friday                | 12 NG: a Japanese trading house
4 NG: it                    | 13 VG: to produce
5 VG: had set up            | 14 NG: golf clubs
6 NG: a joint venture       | 15 VG: to be shipped
7 PR: in                    | 16 PR: to
8 NG: Taiwan                | 17 NG: Japan
9 PR: with
```

Here NG means noun group, VG is verb group, PR is preposition, and CJ is conjunction.

The fourth stage combines the basic groups into **complex phrases**. Again, the aim is to have rules that are finite-state and thus can be processed quickly, and that result in unambiguous (or nearly unambiguous) output phrases. One type of combination rule deals with domain-specific events. For example, the rule

Company+ SetUp JointVenture ("with" Company+)?

captures one way to describe the formation of a joint venture. This stage is the first one in the cascade where the output is placed into a database template as well as being placed in the output stream.

The final stage **merges structures** that were built up in the previous step. If the next sentence says "The joint venture will start production in January," then this step will notice that there are two reference to a joint venture, and that they should be merged into one.

In general, information extraction works well for a restricted domain in which it is possible to predetermine what subjects will be discussed, and how they will be mentioned. It has proven useful in a number of domains, but is not a substitute for full-scale natural language processing.

## 23.4 MACHINE TRANSLATION

Machine translation is the automatic translation of text from one natural language (the source) to another (the target). This process has proven to be useful for a number of tasks, including the following:

1. **Rough translation**, in which the goal is just to get the gist of a passage. Ungrammatical and inelegant sentences are tolerated as long as the meaning is clear. For example, in

Web surfing, a user is often happy with a rough translation of a foreign web page. Sometimes a monolingual human can post-edit the output without having to read the source. This type of machine-assisted translation saves money because such editors can be paid less than bilingual translators.

2. **Restricted-source translation**, in which the subject matter and format of the source text are severely limited. One of the most successful examples is the TAUM-METEO system, which translates weather reports from English to French. It works because the language used in weather reports is highly stylized and regular.
3. **Preedited translation**, in which a human preedits the source document to make it conform to a restricted subset of English (or whatever the original language is) before machine translation. This approach is particularly cost-effective when there is a need to translate one document into many languages, as is the case for legal documents in the European Community or for companies that sell the same product in many countries. Restricted languages are sometimes called "Caterpillar English," because Caterpillar Corp. was the first firm to try writing its manuals in this form. Xerox defined a language for its maintenance manuals which was simple enough that it could be translated by machine into all the languages Xerox deals with. As an added benefit, the original English manuals became clearer as well.
4. **Literary translation**, in which all the nuances of the source text are preserved. This is currently beyond the state of the art for machine translation.

As an example of rough translation, the SYSTRAN translation service translated the first paragraph of this chapter into Italian and back to English as follows:

| **Italian:** In capitolo 22 abbiamo visto come un agente potrebbe comunicare con un altro agente (essere umano o software) che usando le espressioni in un linguaggio reciprocamente accordato. Completare sintattico e l'analisi semantica delle espressioniè necessaria da estrarre il significato completo del utterances ed è possibile perché le espressioni sono corte e limitate ad un settore limitato. | **English:** In chapter 22 we have seen as an agent could communicate with an other agent (to be human or software) that using the expressions in a language mutual come to an agreement. Complete syntactic and the semantic analysis of the expressions is necessary to extract the complete meant one of the utterances and is possible because the expressions short and are limited to a dominion. |
|---|---|

Translation is difficult because, in the general case, it requires in-depth understanding of the text, and that in turn requires in-depth understanding of the situation that is being communicated. This is true even for very simple texts—even "texts" of one word. Consider the word "Open" on the door of a store.[4] It communicates the idea that the store is accepting customers at the moment. Now consider the same word "Open" on a large banner outside a newly constructed store. It means that the store is now in daily operation, but readers of this sign would not feel misled if the store closed at night without removing the banner. The two

[4] This example is due to Martin Kay.

signs use the identical word to convey different meanings. In German, on the other hand, the sign on the door would be "Offen" while the banner would read "Neu Eröffnet."

The problem is that different languages categorize the world differently. For example, the French word "doux" covers a wide range of meanings corresponding approximately to the English words "soft," "sweet," and "gentle." Similarly, the English word "hard" covers virtually all uses of the German word "hart" (physically recalcitrant, cruel) and some uses of the word "schwierig" (difficult). The German verb "heilen" covers the medical uses of the English word "cure," as well as the transitive and intransitive uses of "heal." Therefore, representing the meaning of a sentence is more difficult for translation than it is for single-language understanding. A single-language parsing system could use predicates like $Open(x)$, but for translation, the representation language would have to make more distinctions, perhaps with $Open_1(x)$ representing the "Offen" sense and $Open_2(x)$ representing the "Neu Eröffnet" sense. A representation language that makes all the distinctions necessary for a set of languages is called an **interlingua**.

INTERLINGUA

To do fluent translation, a translator (human or machine) must read the original text, understand the situation to which it is referring, and find a corresponding text in the target language that does a good job of describing the same or a similar situation. Often, this involves a choice. For example, the English word "you," when referring to a single person, can be translated into French as either the formal "vous" or the informal "tu." There is just no way that one can refer to the concept of "you" in French without also making a choice of formal or informal. Translators (both machine and human) sometimes find it difficult to make this choice.

## Machine translation systems

Machine translation systems vary in the level to which they analyze the text. Some systems attempt to analyze the input text all the way into an interlingua representation (as we did in Chapter 22) and then generate sentences in the target language from that representation. This is difficult because it includes the complete language understanding problem as a subproblem, to which is added the difficulty of dealing with an interlingua. It is brittle because if the analysis fails, there is no output. It does have the advantage that there is no part of the system that relies on knowledge of two languages at once. That means that one can build an interlingua system to translate among $n$ languages with $O(n)$ work instead of $O(n^2)$.

TRANSFER

Other systems are based on a **transfer**. They keep a data base of translation rules (or examples), and whenever the rule (or example) matches, they translate directly. Transfer can occur at the lexical, syntactic, or semantic level. For example, a strictly syntactic rule maps English [*Adjective Noun*] to French [*Noun Adjective*]. A mixed syntactic and lexical rule maps French [$S_1$ "et puis" $S_2$] to English [$S_1$ "and then" $S_2$]. A transfer that goes directly from one sentence to another is called a **memory-based translation** method, because it relies on memorizing a large set of (English, French) pairs. The transfer method is robust in that it will always generate *some* output, and at least some of the words are bound to be right. Figure 23.5 diagrams the various transfer points.

MEMORY-BASED TRANSLATION

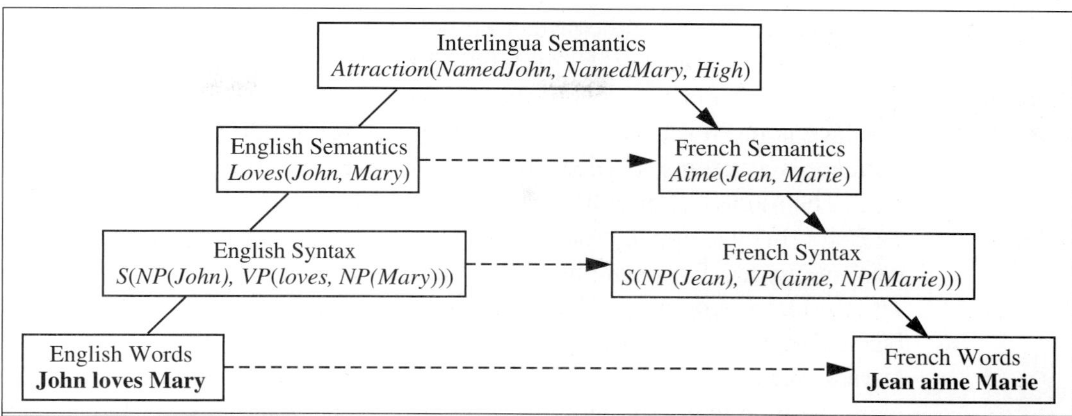


**Figure 23.5** A schematic diagram of the choices for a machine translation system. We start with English text at the top. An interlingua-based system follows the solid lines, parsing English first into a syntactic form, then into a semantic representation and an interlingua representation, and then through generation to a semantic, syntactic, and lexical form in French. A transfer-based system uses the dashed lines as a shortcut. Different systems make the transfer at different points; some make it at multiple points.

### Statistical machine translation

In the early 1960s, there was great hope that computers would be able to translate from one natural language to another, just as Turing's project "translated" coded German messages into intelligible German. By 1966, it became clear that fluent translation requires an understanding of the meaning of the message, whereas code breaking does not.

In the last decade, there has been a move towards statistically based machine translation systems. Of course, any of the steps in Figure 23.5 could benefit from the application of statistical data and from a clear probabilistic model of what constitutes a good analysis or transfer. But "statistical machine translation" has come to denote an approach to the whole translation problem that is based on finding the most probable translation of a sentence, using data gathered from a bilingual corpus. As an example of a bilingual corpus, **Hansard**[5] is a record of parliamentary debate. Canada, Hong Kong, and other countries produce bilingual Hansards, the European Union publishes its official documents in 11 languages, and the United Nations publishes multilingual documents. These have proven to be invaluable resources for statistical machine translation.

HANSARD

We can express the problem of translating an English sentence $E$ into, say, a French[6] sentence $F$ by the following application of Bayes' rule:

$$\begin{aligned}\text{argmax}_F\, P(F|E) &= \text{argmax}_F\, P(E|F)P(F)/P(E)\\ &= \text{argmax}_F\, P(E|F)P(F)\,.\end{aligned}$$

[5] Named after William Hansard, who first published the British parliamentary debates in 1811.

[6] Throughout this section we consider the problem of translating from English to French. Do not be confused by the fact that Bayes' rule leads us to consider $P(E|F)$ rather than $P(F|E)$, making it seem as if we were translating French to English.

This rule says we should consider all possible French sentences $F$ and choose the one that maximizes the product $P(E|F)P(F)$. The factor $P(E)$ can be ignored because it is the same for every $F$. The factor $P(F)$ is the **language model** for French; it says how probable a given sentence is in French. $P(E|F)$ is the **translation model**; it says how probable an English sentence is as a translation, given a French sentence.

LANGUAGE MODEL

TRANSLATION MODEL

The astute reader will wonder what we have gained from defining $P(F|E)$ in terms of $P(E|F)$. In other applications of Bayes' rule, we made this reversal because we wanted to use a causal model. For example, we use the causal model $P(Symptoms|Disease)$ to compute $P(Disease|Symptoms)$. With translation, however, neither direction is more causal than the other. The reason for applying Bayes' rule in this case is that we believe we will be able to learn a language model $P(F)$ that is more accurate than the translation model $P(E|F)$ (and more accurate than estimating $P(F|E)$ directly). Essentially, we have divided the problem into two parts: first we use the translation model $P(F|E)$ to find candidate French sentences that mention the right concepts from the English sentence, but that might not be fluent French; then we use the language model $P(F)$ (for which we have much better probability estimates) to pick out the best candidate.

The **language model** $P(F)$ can be any model that gives a probability to a sentence. With a *very* large corpus, we could estimate $P(F)$ directly by counting how many times each sentence appears in the corpus. For example, we use the Web to collect 100 million French sentences, and if the sentence "Clique ici" appears 50,000 times, then $P(\text{Clique ici})$ is .0005. But even with 100 million examples, most sentence counts will be zero.[7] Therefore, we will use the familiar bigram language model, in which the probability of a French sentence consisting of the words $f_1 \ldots f_n$ is

$$P(f_1 \cdots f_n) = \prod_{i=1}^{n} P(f_i|f_{i-1}) .$$

We will need to know bigram probabilities such as $P(\text{Eiffel}|\text{tour}) = .02$. This captures only a very local notion of syntax, where a word depends on just the previous word. However, for rough translation that is often sufficient.[8]

The **translation model**, $P(E|F)$, is more difficult to come by. For one thing, we don't have a ready collection of (English, French) sentence pairs from which to train. For another, the complexity of the model is greater, because it considers the cross product of sentences rather than just individual sentences. We will start with an overly simplistic translation model and build up to something approximating the "IBM Model 3" (Brown *et al.*, 1993) which might still seem overly simplistic, but has proven to generate acceptable translations roughly half the time.

The overly simplistic model is "to translate a sentence, just translate each word individually and independently, in left-to-right order." This is a unigram word choice model. It

[7] If there are just 100,000 words in the lexicon, then 99.99999% of the three-word sentences have a count of zero in the 100 million sentence corpus. It gets worse for longer sentences.

[8] For the finer points of translation, $P(f_i|f_{i-1})$ is clearly not enough. As a famous example, Marcel Proust's 3500 page novel *A la récherche du temps perdu* begins and ends with the same word, so some translators have decided to do the same, thus basing the translation of a word on one that appeared roughly 2 million words earlier.

makes it easy to compute the probability of a translation:

$$P(E|F) = \prod_{i=1}^{n} P(E_i|F_i) .$$

In a few cases this model works fine. For example, consider

$$P(\text{the dog}|\text{le chien}) = P(\text{the}|\text{le}) \times P(\text{dog}|\text{chien}) .$$

Under any reasonable set of probability values, "the dog" would be the maximum likelihood translation of "le chien." In most cases, however, the model fails. One problem is word order. In French, "dog" is "chien" and "brown" is "brun," but "brown dog" is "chien brun." Another problem is that word choice is not a one-to-one mapping. The English word "home" is often translated as "à la maison," a one-to-three mapping (or three-to-one in the other direction). Despite these problems, IBM Model 3 stubbornly sticks to a basically unigram model, but adds a few complications to patch it up.

FERTILITY

To handle the fact that words are not translated one for one, the model introduces the notion of the **fertility** of a word. A word with fertility $n$ gets copied over $n$ times, and then each of those $n$ copies gets translated independently. The model contains parameters for $P(\mathit{Fertility} = n|\mathit{word})$ for each French word. To translate "à la maison" to "home," the model would choose fertility 0 for "a" and "la" and fertility 1 for "maison" and then use the unigram translation model to translate "maison" to "home." This seems reasonable enough: "à" and "la" are low-content words that could reasonably translate to nothing. Translating in the other direction is more dubious. The word "home" would be assigned fertility 3, giving us "home home home." The first "home" would translate to "à," the second to "la" and the third to "maison." In terms of the translation model, "à la maison" would get the exact same probability as "maison la à." (That's the dubious part.) It would be up to the language model to decide which is better. It might seem to make more sense to make "home" translate directly to "à la maison," rather than indirectly via "home home home," but that would require many more parameters, and they would be hard to obtain from the available corpus.

The final part of the translation model is to permute the words into the right positions. This is done by a model of the offsets by which a word moves from its original position to its final position. For example, in translating "chien brun" to "brown dog," the word "brown" gets an offset of $+1$ (it is moved one position to the right) and "dog" gets an offset of $-1$. You might imagine that the offset should be dependent on the word: adjectives like "brown" would tend to have a positive offset because French tends to put the adjectives after the noun. But IBM Model 3 decided that making offsets dependent on the word would require too many parameters, so the offset is independent of the word and dependent only on the position within the sentence, and the length of the sentences in both languages. That is, the model estimates the parameters

$$P(\mathit{Offset} = o|\mathit{Position} = p, \mathit{EngLen} = m, \mathit{FrLen} = n) .$$

So to determine the offset for "brown" in "brown dog," we consult $P(\mathit{Offset}|1, 2, 2)$, which might give us, say, $+1$ with probability .3 and 0 with probability .7. The offset model seems even *more* dubious, as if it had been concocted by someone more familiar with moving magnetic words around on a refrigerator than with actually speaking a natural language. We will see shortly that it was designed that way not because it is a good model of language, but because it makes reasonable use of the available data. In any case, it serves to remind us vividly that a mediocre translation model can be saved by a good French language model. Here is an example showing all the steps in translating a sentence:

| | | | | | | | | | | |
|---|---|---|---|---|---|---|---|---|---|---|
| Source French: | Le | chien | brun | n' | est | pas | allé | à | la | maison |
| Fertility model: | 1 | 1 | 1 | 1 | 1 | 0 | 1 | 0 | 0 | 1 |
| Transformed French: | Le | chien | brun | n' | est | | allé | | | maison |
| Word choice model: | The | dog | brown | not | did | | go | | | home |
| Offset model: | 0 | $+1$ | $-1$ | $+1$ | $-1$ | | 0 | | | 0 |
| Target English: | The | brown | dog | did | not | | go | | | home |

Now, we know how to compute the probability $P(F|E)$ for any pair of (French, English) sentences. But what we really want to do is, given an English sentence, find the French sentence which maximizes that probability. We can't just enumerate sentences; with $10^5$ words in French, there are $10^{5n}$ sentences of length $n$, and many alignments for each one. Even if we consider only the 10 most frequent word-to-word translations for each word, and only consider offsets of 0 or $\pm 1$, we still get about $2^{n/2}10^n$ sentences, which means that we could enumerate them all for $n=5$, but not for $n=10$. Instead, we need to *search* for the best solution. A version of $A^*$ search has proven effective; see Germann *et al.* (2001).

## Learning probabilities for machine translation

We have outlined a model for $P(F|E)$ that involves four sets of parameters:

Language model: $P(word_i|word_{i-1})$
Fertility model: $P(Fertility = n|word_F)$
Word choice model: $P(word_E|word_F)$
Offset model: $P(Offset = o|pos, len_E, len_F)$

Even with a modest vocabulary of 1,000 words, this model requires millions of parameters. Obviously, we will have to learn them from data. We will assume that the only data available to us is a bilingual corpus. Here is how to use it:

**Segment into sentences**: The unit of translation is a sentence, so we will have to break the corpus into sentences. Periods are strong indicators of the end of a sentence, but consider "Dr. J. R. Smith of Rodeo Dr. arrived."; only the final period ends a sentence. Sentence segmentation can be done with about 98% accuracy.

**Estimate the French language model** $P(word_i|word_{i-1})$: Considering just the French half of the corpus, count the frequencies of word pairs and do smoothing to give an estimate of $P(word_i|word_{i-1})$. For example we might have $P(\text{Eiffel}|\text{tour}) = .02$.

**Align sentences**: For each sentence in the English version, determine what sentence(s) it corresponds to in the French version. Usually, the next sentence of English corresponds to the next sentence of French in a 1:1 match, but sometimes there is variation: one sentence in one language will be split into a 2:1 match, or the order of two sentences will be swapped, resulting in a 2:2 match. By looking at the sentence lengths alone, it is possible to align them (1:1, 1:2, or 2:2, etc.) with accuracy in the 90% to 99% range using a variation on the Viterbi segmentation algorithm (Figure 23.1). Even better alignment can be achieved by using landmarks that are common to both languages, such as numbers or proper names, or words that we know have an unambiguous translation from a bilingual dictionary.

Now we are ready to estimate the parameters of the translation model. We will do that by first making a poor initial guess and then improving it.

**Estimate the initial fertility model** $P(Fertility = n | word_F)$: Given a French sentence of length $m$ that is aligned to an English sentence of length $n$, consider this as evidence that each French word has fertility $n/m$. Consider all the evidence over all sentences to get a fertility probability distribution for each word.

**Estimate the initial word choice model** $P(word_E | word_F)$: Look at all the French sentences that contain, say, "brun." The words that appear most frequently in the English sentences aligned with these sentences are the likely word-to-word translations of "brun."

**Estimate the initial offset model** $P(Offset = o | pos, len_E, len_F)$: Now that we have the word choice model, use it to estimate the offset model. For an English sentence of length $n$ that is aligned to a French sentence of length $m$, look at each French word in the sentence (at position $i$) and at each English word in the sentence (at position $j$) that is a likely word choice for the French word, and consider that as evidence for $P(Offset = i - j | i, n, m)$.

WORD ALIGNMENT VECTOR

**Improve all the estimates**: Use EM (expectation–maximization) to improve the estimates. The hidden variable will be a **word alignment vector** between sentence-aligned sentence pairs. The vector gives, for each English word, the position in the French sentence of the corresponding French word. For example, we might have the following:

| Source French: | Le | chien | brun | n' | est | pas | allé | à | la | maison |
|---|---|---|---|---|---|---|---|---|---|---|
| Target English: | The | brown | dog | did | not | | go | | | home |
| Word alignment: | 1 | 3 | 2 | 5 | 4 | | 7 | | | 10 |

First, using the current estimates of the parameters, create a word alignment vector for each sentence pair. This will allow us to make better estimates. The fertility model is estimated by counting how many times a member of the word alignment vector goes to multiple words or to zero words. The word choice model now can look only at words that are aligned to each other, rather than at all words in the sentence, and the offset model can look at each position in the sentence to see how often it moves according to the word alignment vector. Unfortunately, we don't know for sure what the correct alignment is, and there are too many of them to enumerate. So we are forced to search for a few high-probability alignments and weight them by their probabilities when we collect evidence for the new parameter estimates. That is all we need for the EM algorithm. From the initial parameters we compute alignments and from the alignments we improve the parameter estimates. Repeat until convergence.

## 23.5 SUMMARY

The main points of this chapter are:

1. Probabilistic language models based on $n$-grams recover a surprising amount of information about a language.

2. CFGs can be extended to probabilistic CFGs, making it easier to learn them from data and easier to do disambiguation.
3. **Information retrieval** systems use a very simple language model based on bags of words, yet still manage to perform well in terms of **recall** and **precision** on very large corpora of text.
4. **Information extraction** systems use a more complex model that includes limited notions of syntax and semantics. They are often implemented using a cascade of finite state automata.
5. **Machine translation** systems have been implemented using a range of techniques, from full syntactic and semantic analysis to statistical techniques based on word frequencies.
6. In building a statistical language system, it is best to devise a model that can make good use of available data, even if the model seems overly simplistic.

## BIBLIOGRAPHICAL AND HISTORICAL NOTES

$n$-gram letter models for language modeling were proposed by Markov (1913). Claude Shannon (Shannon and Weaver, 1949) was the first to generate $n$-gram word models of English. Chomsky (1956, 1957) pointed out the limitations of finite-state models compared with context-free models, concluding "Probabilistic models give no particular insight into some of the basic problems of syntactic structure." This is true, but it ignores the fact that probabilistic models *do* provide insight into some *other* basic problems—problems that CFGs do not address. Chomsky's remarks had the unfortunate effect of scaring many people away from statistical model for two decades, until these models reemerged for use in speech recognition (Jelinek, 1976).

Add-one smoothing is due to Jeffreys (1948), and deleted interpolation smoothing is due to Jelinek and Mercer (1980), who used it for speech recognition. Other techniques include Witten–Bell smoothing (1991) and Good–Turing smoothing (Church and Gale, 1991). The later also arises frequently in bioinformatics problems. Biostatistics and probabilistic NLP are coming closer together, as each deals with long, structured sequences chosen from an alphabet of constituents.

Simple $n$-gram letter and word models are not the only possible probabilistic models. Blei *et al.* (2001) describe a probabilistic text model called **latent Dirichlet allocation** that views a document as a mixture of topics, each with its own distribution of words. This model can be seen as an extension and rationalization of the **latent semantic indexing** model of (Deerwester *et al.*, 1990) (see also Papadimitriou *et al.* (1998)) and is also related to the multiple cause mixture model of (Sahami *et al.*, 1996).

**Probabilistic context-free grammars** (PCFGs) answer all of Chomsky's objections about probabilistic models, and have advantages over CFGs. PCFGs were investigated by Booth (1969) and Salomaa (1969). Jelinek (1969) presents the stack decoding algorithm, a variation of Viterbi search that can be used to find the most probable parse with a PCFG.

Baker (1979) introduced the inside–outside algorithm, and Lari and Young (1990) described its uses and limitations. Charniak (1996) and Klein and Manning (2001) discuss parsing with **treebank** grammars. Stolcke and Omohundro (1994) show how to learn grammar rules with Bayesian model merging. Other algorithms for PCFGs are presented by Charniak (1993) and by Manning and Schütze (1999). Collins (1999) offers a survey of the field and an explanation of one of the most successful programs for statistical parsing.

Unfortunately, PCFGs perform worse than simple $n$-gram models on a variety of tasks, because PCFGs cannot represent information associated with individual words. To correct for that deficiency, several authors (Collins, 1996; Charniak, 1997; Hwa, 1998) have introduced versions of **lexicalized probabilistic grammars**, which combine context-free and word-based statistics.

The Brown Corpus (Francis and Kucera, 1967) was the first effort to collect a balanced corpus of text for empirical linguistics. It contained about a million words, tagged with part of speech. It was originally stored on 100,000 punched cards. The Penn treebank (Marcus *et al.*, 1993) is a collection of about 1.6 million words, hand-parsed into trees. It is stored on a CD. The British National Corpus (Leech *et al.*, 2001) extends that to 100 million words. The World Wide Web has over a trillion words. It is stored on over 10 million servers.

The field of **information retrieval** is experiencing a regrowth in interest, sparked by the wide usage of Internet searching. Robertson (1977) gives an early overview, and introduces the probability ranking principle. Manning and Schütze (1999) give a short introduction to IR in the context of statistical approaches to NLP. Baeza-Yates and Ribeiro-Neto (1999) is a general-purpose overview, replacing older classics by Salton and McGill (1983) and by Frakes and Baeza-Yates (1992). The book *Managing Gigabytes* (Witten *et al.*, 1999) does just what the title says: explains how to efficiently index, compress, and make queries on corpora in the gigabyte range. The TREC conference, organized by the U.S. government's National Institute of Standards and Technology (NIST), hosts an annual competition for IR systems and publishes proceedings with results. In the first seven years of the competition performance roughly doubled.

The most popular model for IR is the **vector space model** (Salton *et al.*, 1975). Salton's work dominated the early years of the field. There are two alternative probabilistic models. The one we presented is based on the work of Ponte and Croft (1998). It models the joint probability distribution $P(D, Q)$ in terms of $P(Q|D)$. An alternative model (Maron and Kuhns, 1960; Robertson and Sparck Jones, 1976) uses $P(D|Q)$. Lafferty and Zhai (2001) show that the models are based on the same joint probability distribution, but that the choice of model has implications for training the parameters. Our presentation is derived from theirs. Turtle and Croft (1992) compare the various IR models.

Brin and Page (1998) describe the implementation of a search engine for the World Wide Web, including the PAGERANK algorithm, a query-independent measure of document quality based on an analysis of Web links. Kleinberg (1999) describes how to find authoritative sources on the Web using link analysis. Silverstein et al. (1998) investigate a log of a billion Web searches. Kukich (1992) surveys the literature on spelling correction. Porter (1980) describes the classic rule-based stemming algorithm, and Krovetz (1993) describes a dictionary-based version.

Manning and Schütze (1999) provide a good overview of document classification and clustering. Joachims (2001) uses statistical learning theory and support vector machines to give a theoretical analysis of when classification will be successful. Apté *et al.* (1994) report an accuracy of 96% in classifying Reuters news articles into the "Earnings" category. Koller and Sahami (1997) report accuracy up to 95% using a naive Bayes classifier, and up to 98.6% using a Bayes classifier that accounts for some dependencies among features. Lewis (1998) surveys forty years of application of naive Bayes techniques to text classification and retrieval.

The journal *Information Retrieval* and the proceedings of the annual *SIGIR* conference cover recent developments in the field.

Early information extraction programs include GUS (Bobrow *et al.*, 1977) and FRUMP (DeJong, 1982). Some of the design of modern information extraction systems can be traced to work on semantic grammars in the 1970s and 1980s. For example, an interface to an airline reservation system with a semantic grammar would have categories like *Location* and *FlyTo* instead of *NP* and *VP*. See Birnbaum and Selfridge (1981) for an implementation of a system based on semantic grammars.

Recent information extraction has been pushed forward by the annual Message Understand Conferences (MUC), sponsored by the U.S. government. The FASTUS system was done by Hobbs *et al.* (1997); the collection of papers in which it appears (Roche and Schabes, 1997) lists other systems using finite state models.

In the 1930s Petr Troyanskii applied for a patent for a "translating machine," but there were no computers available to implement his ideas. In March 1947, the Rockefeller Foundation's Warren Weaver wrote to Norbert Weiner, suggesting machine translation might be possible. Drawing on work in cryptography and information theory, Weaver wrote, "When I look at an article in Russian, I say: 'This is really written in English, but it has been coded in strange symbols. I will now proceed to decode.'" For the next decade, the community tried to decode in this way. IBM exhibited a rudimentary system in 1954. Bar-Hillel (1960) and Locke and Booth (1955) describe the enthusiasm of this period. Later disillusionment with machine translation is described by Lindsay (1963), who also points out some of the obstacles to machine translation having to do with the interaction between syntax and semantics and with the need for world knowledge. The U.S. government became disappointed in the lack of progress, and a report (ALPAC, 1966) concluded "there is no immediate or predictable prospect of useful machine translation." However, limited work continued, and the SYSTRAN system was deployed by the U.S. Air Force in 1970 and by the European Community in 1976. the TAUM-METEO weather translation system was also deployed in 1976 (Quinlan and O'Brien, 1992). Starting in the 1980s, computer power had increased to the point where the ALPAC findings were no longer correct. Voorhees (1993) reports some recent translation applications based on Wordnet. A textbook introduction is given by Hutchins and Somers (1992).

Statistical machine translation harkens back to Weaver's 1947 note, but it was only in the 1980s that it became practical. Our presentation was based on the work of Brown and his colleagues at IBM (Brown *et al.*, 1988, 1993). It is very mathematical, so the accompanying tutorial by Kevin Knight (1999) is a breath of fresh air. More recent work on statistical machine translation goes beyond the bigram model to models that include some syntax (Yamada and Knight, 2001). Early work on sentence segmentation was done by Palmer and Hearst (1994). Michel and Plamondon (1996) cover bilingual sentence alignment.

There are two excellent books on probabilistic language processing: Charniak (1993) is brief and to the point while Manning and Schütze (1999) is comprehensive and up to date. Work on practical language processing is presented at the biennial Applied Natural Language Processing conference (ANLP), the conference on Empirical Methods in Natural Language Processing (EMNLP), and the journal *Natural Language Engineering*. SIGIR sponsors a newsletter and an annual conference on information retrieval.

## EXERCISES

**23.1** (Adapted from Jurafsky and Martin (2000).) In this exercise we will develop a classifier for authorship: given a text, it will try to determine which of two candidate authors wrote the text. Obtain samples of text from two different authors. Separate them into training and test sets. Now train a unigram word model for each author on the training set. Finally, for each test set, calculate its probability according to each unigram model and assign it to the most probable model. Assess the accuracy of this technique. Can you improve its accuracy with additional features? This subfield of linguistics is called **stylometry**; its successes include the identification of the author of the *Federalist Papers* (Mosteller and Wallace, 1964) and some disputed works of Shakespeare (Foster, 1989).

STYLOMETRY

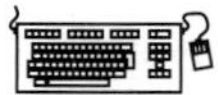

**23.2** This exercise explores the quality of the $n$-gram model of language. Find or create a monolingual corpus of about 100,000 words. Segment it into words, and compute the frequency of each word. How many distinct words are there? Plot the frequency of words versus their rank (first, second, third, ...) on a log–log scale. Also, count frequencies of bigrams (two consecutive words) and trigrams (three consecutive words). Now use those frequencies to generate language: from the unigram, bigram, and trigram models, in turn, generate a 100-word text by making random choices according to the frequency counts. Compare the three generated texts with actual language. Finally, calculate the perplexity of each model.

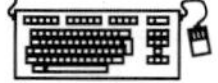

**23.3** This exercise concerns the detection of spam email. Spam is defined as unsolicited bulk commercial email messages. Dealing with spam is an annoying problem for many email users, so a reliable way of eliminating it would be a boon. Create a corpus of spam email and one of non-spam mail. Examine each corpus and decide what features appear to be useful for classification: unigram words? bigrams? message length, sender, time of arrival? Then train a classification algorithm (decision tree, naive Bayes, or some other algorithm of your choosing) on a training set and report its accuracy on a test set.

**23.4** Create a test set of five queries, and pose them to three major Web search engines. Evaluate each one for precision at 1, 3, and 10 documents returned and for mean reciprocal rank. Try to explain the differences.

**23.5** Try to ascertain which of the search engines from the previous exercise are using case folding, stemming, synonyms, and spelling correction.

**23.6** Estimate how much storage space is necessary for the index to a billion-page corpus of Web pages. Show the assumptions you made.

**23.7** Write a regular expression or a short program to extract company names. Test it on a corpus of business news articles. Report your recall and precision.

**23.8** Select five sentences and submit them to an online translation service. Translate them from English to another language and back to English. Rate the resulting sentences for grammaticality and preservation of meaning. Repeat the process; does the second round of iteration give worse results or the same results? Does the choice of intermediate language make a difference to the quality of the results?

**23.9** Collect some examples of time expressions, such as "two o'clock," "midnight," and "12:46." Also think up some examples that are ungrammatical, such as "thirteen o'clock" or "half past two fifteen." Write a grammar for the time language.

**23.10** (Adapted from Knight (1999).) The IBM Model 3 machine translation model assumes that, after the word choice model proposes a list of words and the offset proposes possible permutations of the words, the language model can choose the best permutation. This exercise investigates how sensible that assumption is. Try to unscramble these proposed sentences into the correct order:

- have programming a seen never I language better
- loves john mary
- is the communication exchange of intentional information brought by about the production perception of and signs from drawn a of system signs conventional shared

Which ones could you do? What type of knowledge did you draw upon? Train a bigram model from a training corpus, and use it to find the highest-probability permutation of some sentences from a test corpus. Report on the accuracy of this model.

**23.11** If you look in an English–French dictionary, the translation for "hear" is the verb "entendre." But if you train the IBM Model 3 on the Canadian Hansard, the most probable translation for "hear" is "Bravo." Explain why that is, and estimate what the fertility distribution for "hear" might be. (*Hint*: you might want to look at some Hansard text. Try a web search for [Hansard hear].)

# 24 PERCEPTION

*In which we connect the computer to the raw, unwashed world.*

PERCEPTION
SENSORS

**Perception** provides agents with information about the world they inhabit. Perception is initiated by **sensors**. A sensor is anything that can record some aspect of the environment and pass it as input to an agent program. The sensor could be as simple as a one-bit sensor that detects whether a switch is on or off or as complex as the retina of the human eye, which contains more than a hundred million photosensitive elements. In this chapter, our focus will be on vision, because that is by far the most useful sense for dealing with the physical world.

## 24.1 INTRODUCTION

There are a variety of sensory modalities that are available to artificial agents. Those they share with humans include vision, hearing, and touch. Hearing, at least for speech, was covered in Section 15.6. Touch, or **tactile sensing**, is discussed in Chapter 25, where we examine its use in dexterous manipulation by robots, and the rest of this chapter will cover vision. Some robots can perceive modalities that are not available to the unaided human, such as radio, infrared, GPS, and wireless signals. Some robots do **active sensing**, meaning they send out a signal, such as radar or ultrasound, and sense the reflection of this signal off of the environment.

There are two ways that an agent can use its percepts. In the **feature extraction** approach, agents detect some small number of features in their sensory input and pass them directly to their agent program, which can act reactively to the features, or can combine them with other information. The wumpus agent worked in this mode, with five sensors each extracting a one-bit feature. It is now known that a fly extracts features from the optical flow and feeds them directly to muscles that help it steer, allowing it to react and change direction within 30 milliseconds.

The alternative is a **model-based** approach, wherein the sensory stimulus is used to reconstruct a model of the world. In this approach we start with a function $f$ that maps from the state of the world, $W$, to the stimulus, $S$, that the world will produce:

$$S = f(W) .$$

COMPUTER GRAPHICS

The function $f$ is defined by physics and optics, and is fairly well understood. Generating $S$ from $f$ and a real or imaginary world $W$ is the problem addressed by **computer graphics**. Computer vision is in some sense the inverse of computer graphics: given $f$ and $S$, we try to compute $W$ with

$$W = f^{-1}(S) .$$

Unfortunately, $f$ does not have a proper inverse. For one thing, we cannot see around corners, so we cannot recover all aspects of the world from the stimulus. Moreover, even the part we *can* see is enormously ambiguous: without additional information we can not tell if $S$ is an image of a toy Godzilla destroying a two-foot tall model building, or a real monster destroying a two-hundred foot building. We can address some of these issues by building a probability distribution over worlds, rather than trying to find a unique world:

$$P(W) = P(W|S)P(S) .$$

A more important drawback with this type of modeling is that it is solving too difficult a problem. Consider that in computer graphics it can take several hours of computation to render a single frame of a movie, that 24 frames are needed per second, and that computing $f^{-1}$ is more difficult than computing $f$. Clearly this is too much computation for a supercomputer, let alone a fly, to react in real time. Fortunately, the agent does not need a model of the level of detail used in photorealistic computer graphics. The agent need only know whether there is a tiger hiding in the brush, not the precise location and orientation of every hair on the tiger's back.

For most of this chapter, we will see how to recognize objects, such as tigers, and we will see ways to do this without representing every last detail of the tiger. In Section 24.2 we study the process of image formation, defining some aspects of the $f(W)$ function. First we look at the geometry of the process. We will see that light reflects off objects in the world, and onto points in the image plane in the sensor of an agent. The geometry explains why a large Godzilla far away looks like a small Godzilla up close. Then we look at the photometry of the process, which describes how light in the scene determines the brightness of points in the image. Together, geometry and photometry give us a model of how objects in the world will map into a two-dimensional array of pixels.

With an understanding of how images are formed, we then turn to how they are processed. The flow of information in visual processing in both humans and computers can be divided into three phases. In early or low-level vision (Section 24.3) the raw image is smoothed to eliminate noise, and features of the two-dimensional image are extracted, particularly edges between regions. In mid-level vision these edges are grouped together to form two-dimensional regions. In high-level vision (Section 24.4), the two-dimensional regions are recognized as actual objects in the world (Section 24.5). We study various cues in the image that can be harnessed to this end, including motion, stereopsis, texture, shading, and contour. Object recognition is important to an agent in the wild to detect tigers, and it is important for industrial robots to distinguish nuts from bolts. Finally, Section 24.6 describes how the recognition of objects can help us perform useful tasks, such as manipulation and navigation. Manipulation means being able to grab and use tools and other objects, and navigation means being able to move from place to place without bumping into anything. By keeping these tasks in mind we can make sure that an agent builds only as much of a model as it needs to achieve its goals.

## 24.2 IMAGE FORMATION

SCENE
IMAGE

Vision gathers light scattered from objects in a **scene** and creates a two-dimensional **image** on an image plane. The image plane is coated with photosensitive material: Rhodopsin molecules in the retina, silver halides on photographic film, and a charge-coupled device (CCD) array in a digital camera. Each site in a CCD integrates the electrons released by photon absorption for a fixed time period. In a digital camera the image plane is subdivided into a rectangular grid of a few million **pixels**. The eye has a similar array of pixels consisting of about 100 million rods and 5 million cones, arranged in a hexagonal array.

PIXELS

The scene is very large and the image plane is quite small, so there needs to be some way of focusing the light onto the image plane. This can be done with or without a lens. Either way, the key is to define the geometry so that we can tell where each point in the scene will end up in the image plane.

### Images without lenses: the pinhole camera

PINHOLE CAMERA

The simplest way to form an image is with a **pinhole camera**, which consists of a pinhole opening, $O$, at the front of a box, and an image plane at the back of the box (Figure 24.1). We will use a three-dimensional coordinate system with the origin at $O$, and will consider a point $P$ in the scene, with coordinates $(X, Y, Z)$. $P$ gets projected to the point $P'$ in the image plane with coordinates $(x, y, z)$. If $f$ is the distance from the pinhole to the image plane, then by similar triangles, we can derive the following equations:

$$\frac{-x}{f} = \frac{X}{Z}, \ \frac{-y}{f} = \frac{Y}{Z} \quad \Rightarrow \quad x = \frac{-fX}{Z}, \ y = \frac{-fY}{Z} \ .$$

PERSPECTIVE PROJECTION

These equations define an image formation process known as **perspective projection**. Note that the $Z$ in the denominator means that the farther away an object is, the smaller its image will be. Also, note that the minus signs mean that the image is *inverted*, both left–right and up–down, compared with the scene.

Under perspective projection, parallel lines converge to a point on the horizon. (Think of railway tracks.) Let us see why this must be so. A line in the scene passing through the point $(X_0, Y_0, Z_0)$ in the direction $(U, V, W)$ can be described as the set of points $(X_0 + \lambda U, Y_0 + \lambda V, Z_0 + \lambda W)$, with $\lambda$ varying between $-\infty$ and $+\infty$. The projection of a point $P_\lambda$ from this line onto the image plane is given by

$$\left( f\frac{X_0 + \lambda U}{Z_0 + \lambda W}, f\frac{Y_0 + \lambda V}{Z_0 + \lambda W} \right) \ .$$

As $\lambda \to \infty$ or $\lambda \to -\infty$, this becomes $p_\infty = (fU/W, fV/W)$ if $W \neq 0$. We call $p_\infty$ the **vanishing point** associated with the family of straight lines with direction $(U, V, W)$. Lines with the same direction share the same vanishing point.

VANISHING POINT

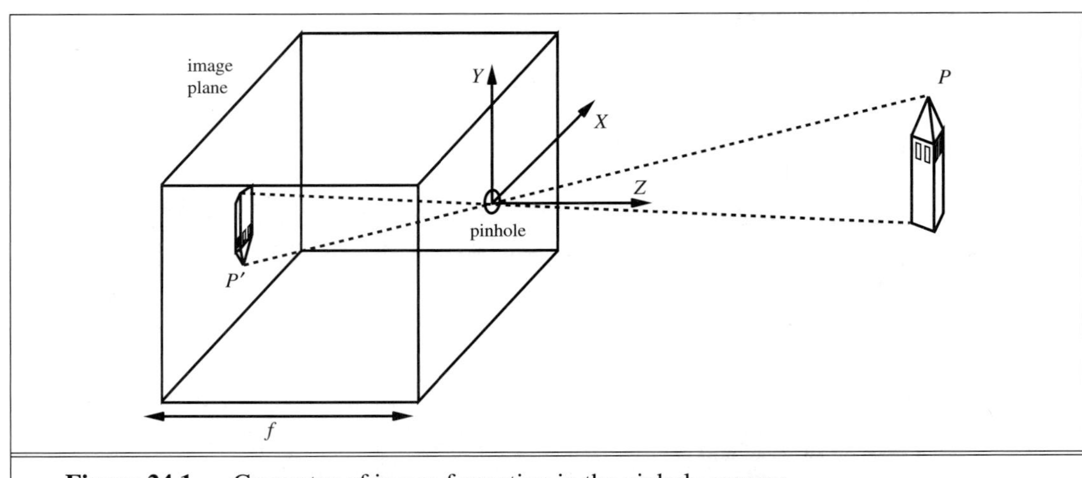


**Figure 24.1** Geometry of image formation in the pinhole camera.

SCALED ORTHOGRAPHIC PROJECTION

If the object is relatively shallow compared with its distance from the camera, we can approximate perspective projection by **scaled orthographic projection**. The idea is as follows: If the depth $Z$ of points on the object varies within some range $Z_0 \pm \Delta Z$, with $\Delta Z \ll Z_0$, then the perspective scaling factor $f/Z$ can be approximated by a constant $s = f/Z_0$. The equations for projection from the scene coordinates $(X, Y, Z)$ to the image plane become $x = sX$ and $y = sY$. Note that scaled orthographic projection is an approximation that is valid only for those parts of the scene with not much internal depth variation; it should not be used to study properties "in the large." An example to convince you of the need for caution: under orthographic projection, parallel lines stay parallel instead of converging to a vanishing point!

## Lens systems

LENS

Vertebrate eyes and modern cameras use a **lens**. A lens is much wider than a pinhole, enabling it to let in more light. This is paid for by the fact that not all the scene can be in sharp focus at the same time. The image of an object at distance $Z$ in the scene is produced at a fixed distance from the lens $Z'$, where the relation between $Z$ and $Z'$ is given by the lens equation

$$\frac{1}{Z} + \frac{1}{Z'} = \frac{1}{f},$$

in which $f$ is the focal length of the lens. Given a certain choice of image distance $Z'_0$ between the nodal point of the lens and the image plane, scene points with depths in a range around $Z_0$, where $Z_0$ is the corresponding object distance, will be imaged in reasonably sharp focus.

DEPTH OF FIELD

This range of depths in the scene is referred to as the **depth of field**.

Note that, because the object distance $Z$ is typically much greater than the image distance $Z'$ or $f$, we often make the following approximation:

$$\frac{1}{Z} + \frac{1}{Z'} \approx \frac{1}{Z'} \Rightarrow \frac{1}{Z'} \approx \frac{1}{f}.$$

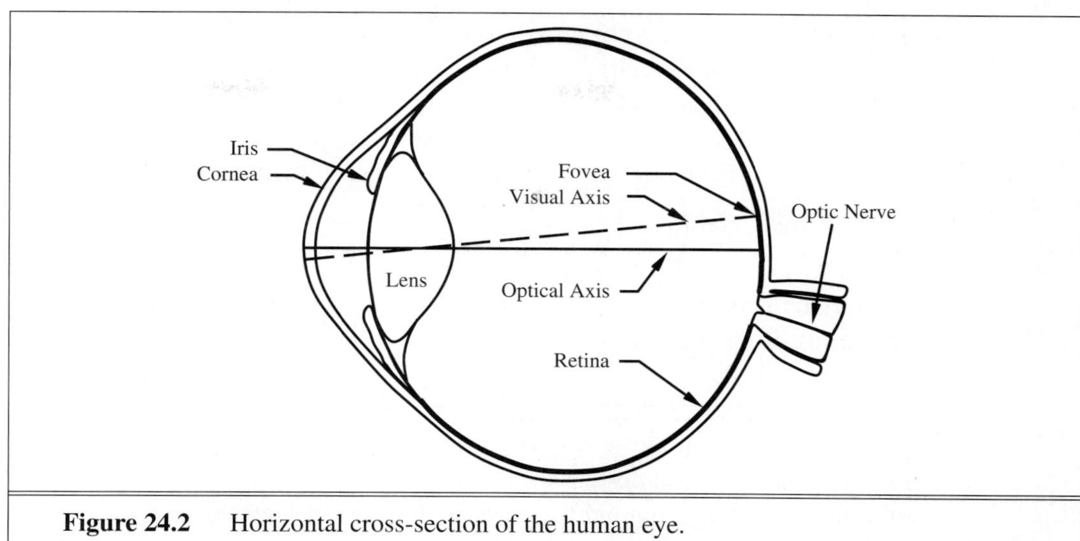


**Figure 24.2** Horizontal cross-section of the human eye.

Thus, the image distance $Z' \approx f$. We can therefore continue to use the pinhole camera perspective projection equations to describe the geometry of image formation in a lens system.

In order to focus objects that are at different distances $Z$, the lens in the eye (see Figure 24.2) changes shape, whereas the lens in a camera moves in the $Z$-direction.

### Light: the photometry of image formation

PHOTOMETRY

Light is a crucial prerequisite for vision; without light, all images would be uniformly dark, no matter how interesting the scene. **Photometry** is the study of light. For our purposes, we will model how the light in the scene maps into the intensity of light in the image plane over time, which we denote as $I(x, y)$.[1] A vision system uses this model backwards, going from the intensity of images to properties of the world. Figure 24.3 shows a digitized image of a stapler on a desk, and a close-up of a $12 \times 12$ block of pixels extracted from the stapler image. A computer program trying to interpret the image would have to start from a matrix of intensity values like this.

The brightness of a pixel in the image is proportional to the amount of light directed toward the camera by the surface patch in the scene that projects to the pixel. This in turn depends on the reflectance properties of the surface patch and on the position and distribution of the light sources in the scene. There is also a dependence on the reflectance properties of the rest of the scene, because other scene surfaces can serve as indirect light sources by reflecting light.

SPECULAR REFLECTION

DIFFUSE REFLECTION

We can model two different kinds of reflection. **Specular reflection** means that light is reflected from the outer surface of the object, and obeys the constraint that the angle of reflection is equal to the angle of incidence. This is the behavior of a perfect mirror. **Diffuse reflection** means that the light penetrates the surface of the object, is absorbed by the object,

[1] When we are concerned with changes over time we will use $I(x, y, t)$.

and is then re-emitted. For a perfectly diffusing (or **Lambertian**) surface the light scatters with equal intensity in all directions. The intensity depends only on the angle of incidence of the light source: a light source directly overhead will reflect the most light, and a light source that is almost parallel to the surface will reflect almost no light. In between those two extremes the reflected intensity, $I$, obeys Lambert's cosine law,

$$I = kI_0 \cos\theta \ ,$$

where $I_0$ is the intensity of the light source, $\theta$ is the angle between the light source and the surface normal, and $k$ is a constant called the **albedo**, which depends on the reflective properties of the surface. It varies from 0 (for perfectly black surfaces) to 1 (for pure white surfaces).

In real life, surfaces exhibit a combination of diffuse and specular properties. Modeling this combination on the computer is the bread and butter of computer graphics. Rendering realistic images is usually done by ray tracing, which aims to simulate the physical process of light originating from light sources and being reflected and re-reflected multiple times.

### Color: the spectrophotometry of image formation

In Figure 24.3 we showed a black-and-white picture, merrily ignoring the fact that visible light comes in a range of wavelengths—ranging from 400 nm on the violet end of the spectrum to 700 nm on the red end. Some light consists of a single wavelength, corresponding to a color of the rainbow. But other light is a mixture of different wavelengths. Does that mean we need a mixture of values for our $I(x, y)$ measure, rather than a single value? If we wanted to represent the physics of light exactly, we would indeed. But if we want only to duplicate the perception of light by humans (and many other vertebrates) we can compromise. Experiments (going back to Thomas Young in 1801) have shown that any mixture of wavelengths, no matter how complex, can be duplicated by a mixture of just three primary colors. That is, if you have a light generator that can linearly combine three wavelengths (typically, we choose red (700 nm), green (546 nm) and blue (436 nm)), then by adjusting knobs to give more of

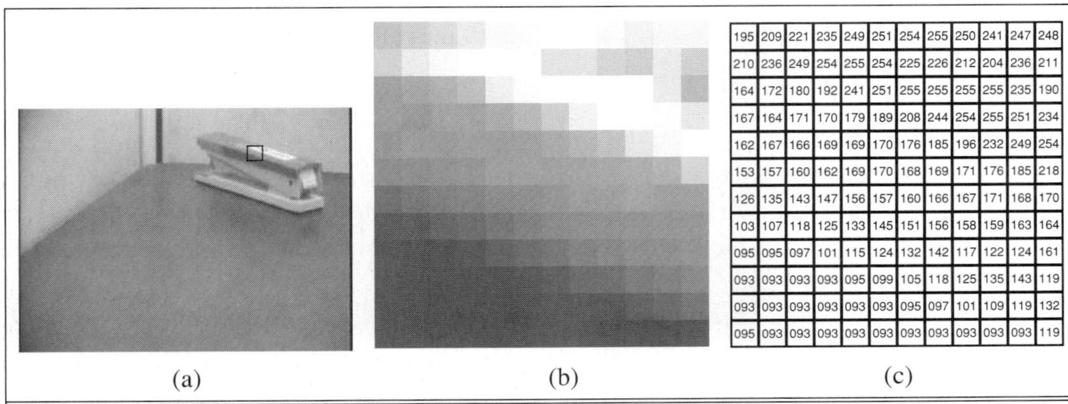

| | | | | | | | | | | | |
|---|---|---|---|---|---|---|---|---|---|---|---|
| 195 | 209 | 221 | 235 | 249 | 251 | 254 | 255 | 250 | 241 | 247 | 248 |
| 210 | 236 | 249 | 254 | 255 | 254 | 225 | 226 | 212 | 204 | 236 | 211 |
| 164 | 172 | 180 | 192 | 241 | 251 | 255 | 255 | 255 | 255 | 235 | 190 |
| 167 | 164 | 171 | 170 | 179 | 189 | 208 | 244 | 254 | 255 | 251 | 234 |
| 162 | 167 | 166 | 169 | 169 | 170 | 176 | 185 | 196 | 232 | 249 | 254 |
| 153 | 157 | 160 | 162 | 169 | 170 | 168 | 169 | 171 | 176 | 185 | 218 |
| 126 | 135 | 143 | 147 | 156 | 157 | 160 | 166 | 167 | 171 | 168 | 170 |
| 103 | 107 | 118 | 125 | 133 | 145 | 151 | 156 | 158 | 159 | 163 | 164 |
| 095 | 095 | 097 | 101 | 115 | 124 | 132 | 142 | 117 | 122 | 124 | 161 |
| 093 | 093 | 093 | 093 | 095 | 099 | 105 | 118 | 125 | 135 | 143 | 119 |
| 093 | 093 | 093 | 093 | 093 | 093 | 095 | 097 | 101 | 109 | 119 | 132 |
| 095 | 093 | 093 | 093 | 093 | 093 | 093 | 093 | 093 | 093 | 093 | 119 |

(a) (b) (c)

**Figure 24.3** (a) A photograph of a stapler on a desk. (b) Magnified view of a $12 \times 12$ block of pixels from (a). (c) The associated image brightness values on a scale of 0 to 255.

one color and less of another you can match *any* combination of wavelengths, as far as human visual perception is concerned. This experimental fact means that images can be represented with a vector of just three intensity numbers per pixel: one for each of the three primary wavelengths. In practice, one byte each results in a high-fidelity reproduction of the image. This trichromatic perception of color is related to the fact that the retina has three types of cones with receptivity peaks at 650 nm, 530 nm, and 430 nm, respectively, but the exact details of the relationship is more complex than a one-to-one mapping.

## 24.3 EARLY IMAGE PROCESSING OPERATIONS

We have seen how light reflects off objects in the scene to form an image consisting of, say, five million three-byte pixels. As with all sensors there will be noise in the image, and in any case there is a lot of data to deal with. In this section we see what can be done to the image data to make it easier to deal with. We will first look at the operations of smoothing the image to reduce noise, and of detecting edges in the image. These are called "early" or "low-level" operations because they are the first in a pipeline of operations. Early vision operations are characterized by their local nature (they can be carried out in one part of the image without regard for anything more than a few pixels away) and by their lack of knowledge: we can smooth images and detect edges without having any idea what objects are in the images. This makes the low-level operations good candidates for implementation in parallel hardware, either in vivo or in silicon. We will then look at one mid-level operation, segmenting the image into regions. This phase of operations is still operating on the image, not the scene, but it includes non-local processing.

In Section 15.2, **smoothing** meant predicting the value of a state variable at some time $t$ in the past, given evidence from $t$ and from other times up to the present. Now we apply the same idea to the spatial domain rather than the temporal: smoothing means predicting the value of a pixel given the surrounding pixels. Notice that we must keep straight the difference between the observed value measured at a pixel, and the true value that should have been measured at that pixel. These can be different because of random measurement errors or because of a systematic failure—the receptor in the CCD may have gone dead.

One way to smooth an image is to assign to each pixel the average of its neighbors. This will tend to cancel out extreme values. But how many neighbors should we consider—one pixel away, or two, or more? One answer that works well for canceling out Gaussian noise is

GAUSSIAN FILTER

a weighted average using a **Gaussian filter**. Recall that the Gaussian function with standard deviation $\sigma$ is

$$G_\sigma(x) = \frac{1}{\sqrt{2\pi\sigma^2}} e^{-x^2/2\sigma^2} \qquad \text{in one dimension, or}$$

$$G_\sigma(x,y) = \frac{1}{\sqrt{2\pi\sigma^2}} e^{-(x^2+y^2)/2\sigma^2} \qquad \text{in two dimensions.}$$

Applying a Gaussian filter means replacing the intensity $I(x_0, y_0)$ with the sum, over all $(x, y)$ pixels, of $I(x, y)\, G_\sigma(d)$, where $d$ is the distance from $(x_0, y_0)$ to $(x, y)$. This kind of weighted sum is so common that there is a special name and notation for it. We say that the

CONVOLUTION

function $h$ is the **convolution** of two functions $f$ and $g$ (denoted as $h = f * g$) if we have

$$h(x) = \sum_{u=-\infty}^{+\infty} f(u)\, g(x-u) \qquad \text{in one dimension, or}$$

$$h(x,y) = \sum_{u=-\infty}^{+\infty} \sum_{v=-\infty}^{+\infty} f(u,v)\, g(x-u, y-v) \qquad \text{in two dimensions.}$$

So the smoothing function is achieved by convolving the image with the Gaussian, $I * G_\sigma$. A $\sigma$ of 1 pixel is enough to smooth over a small amount of noise, whereas 2 pixels will smooth a larger amount, but at the loss of some detail. Because the Gaussian's influence fades at a distance, in practice we can replace the $\pm\infty$ in the sums with something like $\pm 3\sigma$.

### Edge detection

EDGES

The next step in early vision is to detect edges in the image plane. **Edges** are straight lines or curves in the image plane across which there is a "significant" change in image brightness. The goal of edge detection is to abstract away from the messy, multi-megabyte image and towards a more compact, abstract representation, as in Figure 24.4. The motivation is that edge contours in the image correspond to important scene contours. In the figure we have three examples of depth discontinuity, labelled 1; two surface-orientation discontinuities, labelled 2; a reflectance discontinuity, labelled 3; and an illumination discontinuity (shadow), labelled 4. Edge detection is concerned only with the image, and thus does not distinguish between these different types of discontinuities in the scene, but later processing will.

Figure 24.5(a) shows an image of a scene containing a stapler resting on a desk, and (b) shows the output of an edge detection algorithm on this image. As you can see, there is a difference between the output and an ideal line drawing. The small components edges do not all align with each other, there are gaps where no edge appears, and there are "noise" edges

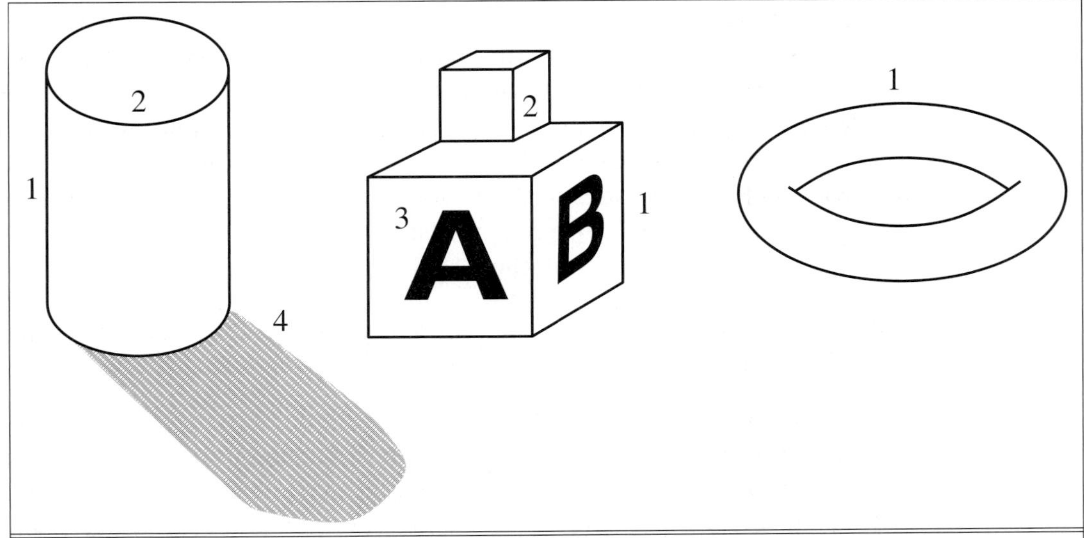


**Figure 24.4** Different kinds of edges: (1) depth discontinuities; (2) surface orientation discontinuities; (3) reflectance discontinuities; (4) illumination discontinuities (shadows).

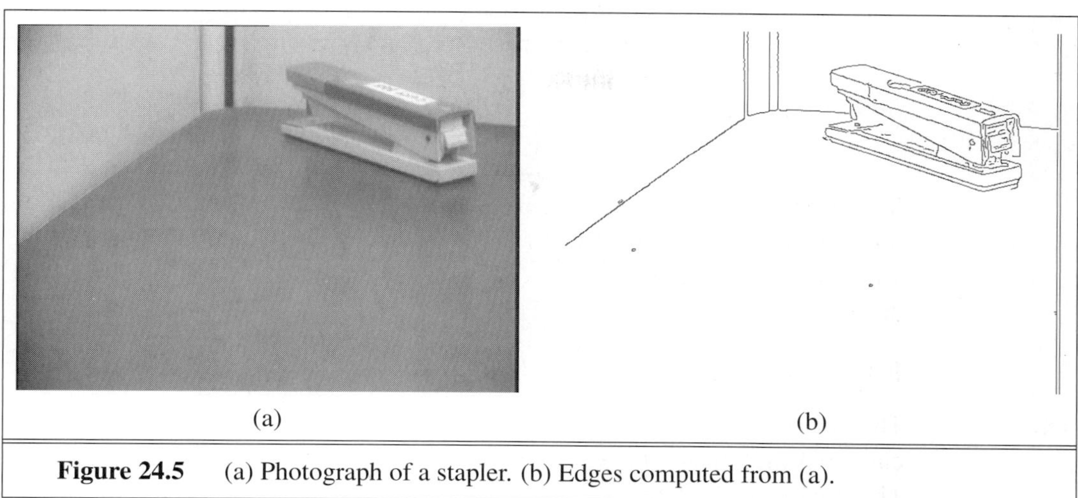

(a) (b)

**Figure 24.5** (a) Photograph of a stapler. (b) Edges computed from (a).

that do not correspond to anything of significance in the scene. Later stages of processing will have to correct for these errors. How do we detect edges in an image? Consider the profile of image brightness along a one-dimensional cross-section perpendicular to an edge—for example, the one between the left edge of the desk and the wall. It looks something like what is shown in Figure 24.6(a). The location of the edge corresponds to $x = 50$.

Because edges correspond to locations in images where the brightness undergoes a sharp change, a naive idea would be to differentiate the image and look for places where the magnitude of the derivative $I'(x)$ is large. Well, that almost works. In Figure 24.6(b), we see that, although there is a peak at $x = 50$, there are also subsidiary peaks at other locations (e.g., $x = 75$) that could be mistaken for true edges. These arise because of the presence of noise in the image. If we smooth the image first, the spurious peaks are diminished, as we see in (c).

We have a chance to make an optimization here: we can combine the smoothing and the edge finding into a single operation. It is a theorem that for any functions $f$ and $g$, the derivative of the convolution, $(f * g)'$, is equal to the convolution with the derivative, $f * (g)'$. So rather than smoothing the image and then differentiating, we can just convolve the image with the derivative of the Gaussian smoothing function, $G'_\sigma$. So in one dimension the algorithm for edge finding is:

1. Convolve the image $I$ with $G'_\sigma$ to obtain $R$.
2. Mark as edges those peaks in $||R(x)||$ that are above some prespecified threshold $T$. The threshold is chosen to eliminate spurious peaks due to noise.

In two dimensions edges may be at any angle $\theta$. To detect vertical edges, we have an obvious strategy: convolve with $G'_\sigma(x)G_\sigma(y)$. In the $y$ direction, the effect is just to smooth (because of the Gaussian convolution), and in the $x$ direction, the effect is that of differentiation accompanied with smoothing. The algorithm for detecting vertical edges then is as follows:

1. Convolve the image $I(x, y)$ with $f_V(x, y) = G'_\sigma(x)G_\sigma(y)$ to obtain $R_V(x, y)$.
2. Mark those peaks in $||R_V(x, y)||$ that are above some prespecified threshold $T$.

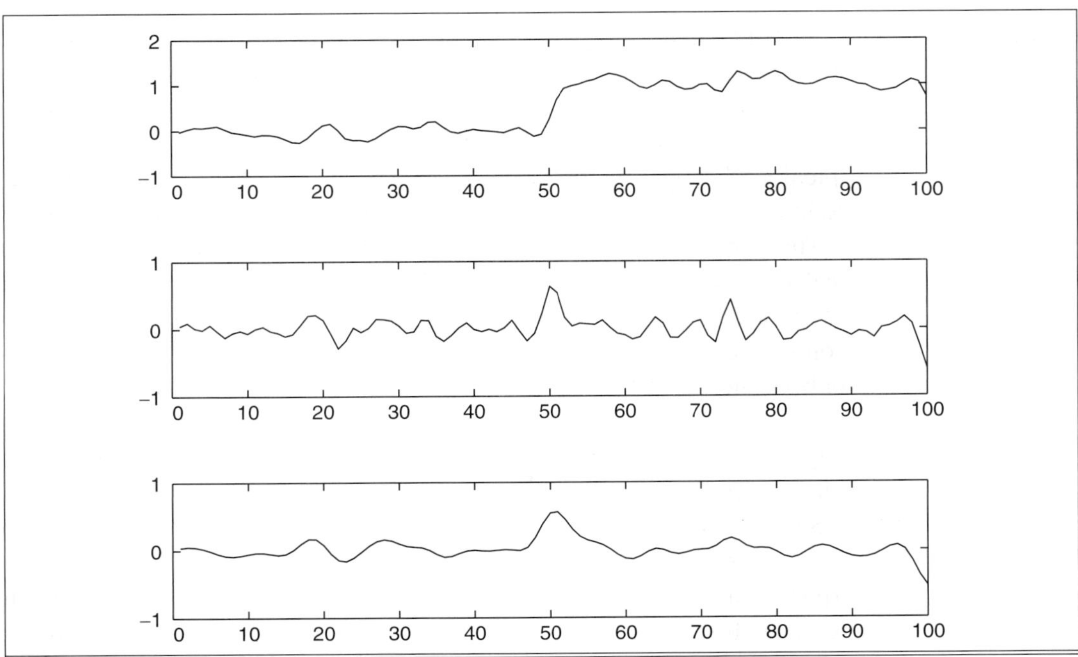


**Figure 24.6** Top: Intensity profile $I(x)$ along a one-dimensional section across a step edge. Middle: The derivative of intensity, $I'(x)$. Large values of this function correspond to edges, but the function is noisy. Bottom: The derivative of a smoothed version of the intensity, $(I * G_\sigma)'$, which can be computed in one step as the convolution $I * G'_\sigma$. The noisy candidate edge at $x = 75$ has disappeared.

In order to detect an edge at an arbitrary orientation, we need to convolve the image with two filters: $f_V = G'_\sigma(x)G_\sigma(y)$ and $f_H = G'_\sigma(y)G_\sigma(x)$, which is just $f_V$ rotated by $90°$. The algorithm for detecting edges at arbitrary orientations is then as follows:

1. Convolve the image $I(x, y)$ with $f_V(x, y)$ and $f_H(x, y)$ to get $R_V(x, y)$ and $R_H(x, y)$, respectively. Define $R(x, y) = R_V^2(x, y) + R_H^2(x, y)$
2. Mark those peaks in $||R(x, y)||$ that are above some prespecified threshold $T$.

Once we have marked edge pixels by this algorithm, the next stage is to link those pixels that belong to the same edge curves. This can be done by assuming that any two neighboring pixels that are both edge pixels with consistent orientations must belong to the same edge curve. This process is called **Canny edge detection** after the inventor, John Canny.

CANNY EDGE DETECTION

Once detected, edges form the basis for much subsequent processing: we can use them to do stereoptic processing, detect motion, or recognize objects.

## Image segmentation

Humans *organize* their perceptual input; instead of a collection of brightness values associated with individual photoreceptors, we perceive a number of visual groups, usually associated with objects or parts of objects. This ability is equally important for computer vision.

SEGMENTATION

**Segmentation** is the process of breaking an image into groups, based on similarities of the pixels. The basic idea is the following: Each image pixel can be associated with certain visual properties, such as brightness, color, and texture.[2] Within an object, or a single part of an object, these attributes vary relatively little, whereas across an inter-object boundary there is typically a large change in one or the other of these attributes. We need to find a partition of the image into sets of pixels such that these constraints are satisfied as well as possible.

There are a number of different ways in which this intuition can be formalized mathematically. For instance, Shi and Malik (2000) set this up as a graph partitioning problem. The nodes of the graph correspond to pixels, and edges to connections between pixels. The weight $W_{ij}$ on the edge connecting a pair of pixels $i$ and $j$ is based on how similar the two pixels are in brightness, color, texture etc. They then find partitions that minimize a *normalized cut* criterion. Roughly speaking, the criterion for partitioning the graph is to minimize the sum of weights of connections across the groups and maximize the sum of weights of connections within the groups.

Segmentation based purely on low-level, local attributes, such as brightness and color is an error-prone process. To reliably find boundaries associated with objects, one should also incorporate high-level knowledge of the kinds of objects one may expect to encounter in a scene. The Hidden Markov model formalism makes this possible for speech recognition; in the context of images such a unified framework remains a topic of active research. In any case, high-level knowledge of objects is the subject of the next section.

## 24.4 Extracting Three-Dimensional Information

In this section we show how to go from the two-dimensional image to a three-dimensional representation of the scene. It is important to reason about the scene, because, after all, the agent lives in the world, not in the image plane, and the goal of vision is to be able to interact with objects in the world. However, most agents need only a limited abstract representation of certain aspects of the scene, not of every detail. The algorithms we have seen in the rest of the book for dealing with the world depend on having concise descriptions of objects, not exhaustive enumerations of every three-dimensional surface patch.

OBJECT RECOGNITION

First we will cover **object recognition**, the process of converting features of the image (such as edges) into model of known objects (such as staplers). Object recognition consists of three steps: Segmenting the scene into distinct objects, determining the position and orientation of each object relative to the observer, and determining the shape of each object.

POSE

Discovering the position and orientation of an object relative to the observer (the so-called **pose** of the object) is most important for manipulation and navigation tasks. To move around in a crowded factory floor, one needs to know the locations of the obstacles, so that one can plan a path that avoids them. If one wants to pick up and grasp an object, one needs to know its position relative to the hand, so that an appropriate trajectory of moves can be generated. Manipulation and navigation actions typically are done in a control loop setting:

[2] Texture properties are based on statistics measured in a small patch centered at the pixel.

the sensory information provides feedback to modify the motion of the robot, or the motion of the robot's arm.

Let us specify position and orientation in mathematical terms. The position of a point $P$ in the scene is characterized by three numbers, the $(X, Y, Z)$ coordinates of $P$ in a coordinate frame with its origin at the pinhole and the $Z$-axis along the optical axis (Figure 24.1). What we have available is the perspective projection of the point in the image $(x, y)$ . This specifies the ray from the pinhole along which $P$ lies; what we do not know is the distance. The term "orientation" could be used in two senses:

1. **The orientation of the object as a whole.** This can be specified in terms of a three-dimensional rotation relating its coordinate frame to that of the camera.

2. **The orientation of the surface of the object at $P$.** This can be specified by a normal vector, **n**—that is a vector specifying the direction that is perpendicular to the surface. Often we express the surface orientation using the variables **slant** and **tilt**. Slant is the angle between the $Z$-axis and **n**. Tilt is the angle between the $X$-axis and the projection of **n** on the image plane.

SLANT

TILT

When the camera moves relative to an object, both the object's distance and its orientation change. What is preserved is the **shape** of the object. If the object is a cube, that fact is not changed when the object moves. Geometers have been attempting to formalize shape for centuries, the basic concept being that shape is what remains unchanged under some group of transformations, for example, combinations of rotations and translations. The difficulty lies in finding a representation of global shape that is general enough to deal with the wide variety of objects in the real world—not just simple forms like cylinders, cones, and spheres—and yet can be recovered easily from the visual input. The problem of characterizing the *local* shape of a surface is much better understood. Essentially, this can be done in terms of curvature: how does the surface normal change as one moves in different directions on the surface. For a plane, there is no change at all. For a cylinder, if one moves parallel to the axis, there is no change, but in the perpendicular direction, the surface normal rotates at a rate inversely proportional to the radius of the cylinder, and so on. All this is studied in the subject called differential geometry.

SHAPE

The shape of an object is relevant for some manipulation tasks (e.g., deciding where to grasp an object), but its most significant role is in object recognition, where geometric shape along with color and texture provide the most significant cues to enable us to identify objects, classify what is in the image as an example of some class one has seen before, and so on.

The fundamental question is the following: Given the fact that, during perspective projection, all points in the three-dimensional world along a ray from the pinhole have been projected to the same point in the image, how do we recover three-dimensional information? There are a number of cues available in the visual stimulus for this, including **motion**, **binocular stereopsis**, **texture**, **shading**, and **contour**. Each of these cues relies on background assumptions about physical scenes in order to provide (nearly) unambiguous interpretations. We discuss each of these cues in the five subsections that follow.

### Motion

So far we have considered only a single image at a time. But video cameras capture 30 frames per second, and the differences between frames can be an important source of information. If the camera moves relative to the three-dimensional scene, the resulting apparent motion in the image is called **optical flow**. This describes the direction and speed of motion of features *in the image* as a result of relative motion between the viewer and the scene. In Figure 24.7(a) and (b), we show two frames from a video of a rotating Rubik's cube. In (c) we display the optical flow vectors computed from these images. The optical flow encodes useful information about scene structure. For example, when viewed from a moving car, distant objects have much slower apparent motion than close objects; thus, the rate of apparent motion can tell us something about distance.

OPTICAL FLOW

(a) (b) (c)

**Figure 24.7** (a) A Rubik's cube on a rotating turntable. (b) The same cube, shown 19/30 seconds later. (Courtesy of Richard Szeliski.) (c) Flow vectors calculated by comparing the two images in (a) and (b). (Courtesy of Joe Weber and Jitendra Malik.)

The optical flow vector field can be represented by its components $v_x(x, y)$ in the $x$ direction and $v_y(x, y)$ in the $y$ direction. To measure optical flow, we need to find corresponding points between one time frame and the next. We exploit the fact that image patches around corresponding points have similar intensity patterns. Consider a block of pixels centered at pixel $p$, $(x_0, y_0)$ at time $t_0$. This block of pixels is to be compared with pixel blocks centered at various candidate pixels $q_i$ at $(x_0 + D_x, y_0 + D_y)$ at time $t_0 + D_t$. One possible measure of similarity is the **sum of squared differences** (SSD):

SUM OF SQUARED DIFFERENCES

$$SSD(D_x, D_y) = \sum_{(x,y)} (I(x, y, t) - I(x + D_x, y + D_y, t + D_t))^2 .$$

Here, $(x, y)$ ranges over pixels in the block centered at $(x_0, y_0)$. We find the $(D_x, D_y)$ that minimizes the SSD. The optical flow at $(x_0, y_0)$ is then $(v_x, v_y) = (D_x/D_t, D_y/D_t)$. Alternatively, one can maximize the **cross-correlation**:

CROSS-CORRELATION

$$Correlation(D_x, D_y) = \sum_{(x,y)} I(x, y, t)I(x + D_x, y + D_y, t + D_t) .$$

Cross-correlation works best when there is texture in the scene, resulting in windows containing a significant variation in brightness among the pixels. If one is looking at a uniform white wall, then the cross-correlation is going to be nearly the same for the different candidate matches $q$, and the algorithm is reduced to making a blind guess.

EGOMOTION

Suppose that the viewer has translational velocity $\mathbf{T}$ and angular velocity $\boldsymbol{\omega}$ (which thus describe the **egomotion**). One can derive an equation relating the viewer's velocities, the optical flow, and the positions of objects in the scene. Assuming that $f = 1$, it follows that

$$\begin{aligned} v_x(x,y) &= \left[-\frac{T_x}{Z(x,y)} - \omega_y + \omega_z y\right] - x\left[-\frac{T_z}{Z(x,y)} - \omega_x y + \omega_y x\right] \\ v_y(x,y) &= \left[-\frac{T_y}{Z(x,y)} - \omega_z x + \omega_x\right] - y\left[-\frac{T_z}{Z(x,y)} - \omega_x y + \omega_y x\right], \end{aligned}$$

where $Z(x, y)$ gives the $z$-coordinate of the point in the scene corresponding to the point in the image at $(x, y)$.

One can get a good intuition by considering the case of pure translation. In that case, the flow field becomes

$$v_x(x,y) = \frac{-T_x + xT_z}{Z(x,y)}, \qquad v_y(x,y) = \frac{-T_y + yT_z}{Z(x,y)}.$$

FOCUS OF EXPANSION

Now some interesting properties come to light. Both components of the optical flow, $v_x(x, y)$ and $v_y(x, y)$, are zero at the point $x = T_x/T_z, y = T_y/T_z$. This point is called the **focus of expansion** of the flow field. Suppose we change the origin in the $x$–$y$ plane to lie at the focus of expansion; then the expressions for optical flow take on a particularly simple form. Let $(x', y')$ be the new coordinates defined by $x' = x - T_x/T_z$, $y' = y - T_y/T_z$. Then

$$v_x(x',y') = \frac{x'T_z}{Z(x',y')}, \qquad v_y(x',y') = \frac{y'T_z}{Z(x',y')}.$$

This equation has some interesting applications. Suppose you are a fly trying to land on a wall and you want to know the time to contact at the current velocity. This time is given by $Z/T_z$. Note that although the instantaneous optical flow field cannot provide either the distance $Z$ or the velocity component $T_z$, it can provide the ratio of the two and can therefore be used to control the landing approach. Experiments with real flies show that this is exactly what they use. Flies are the most dexterous fliers of any animal or machine, and it is interesting that they do it with a vision system that has terrible spatial resolution (having only about 600 receptors compared to a human's 100 million) but spectacular temporal resolution.

To recover depth, one should make use of multiple frames. If the camera is looking at a rigid body, the shape does not change from frame to frame, and thus we are able to better deal with the inherently noisy optical flow measurements. Results from one such approach due to Tomasi and Kanade (1992) are shown in Figures 24.8 and 24.9.

## Binocular stereopsis

Most vertebrates have *two* eyes. This is useful for redundancy in case of a lost eye, but it helps in other ways too. Most prey have eyes on the side of the head to enable a wider field of vision. Predators have the eyes in the front, enabling them to use **binocular stereopsis**.

**Figure 24.8** (a) Four frames from a video sequence in which the camera is moved and rotated relative to the object. (b) The first frame of the sequence, annotated with small boxes highlighting the features found by the feature detector. (Courtesy of Carlo Tomasi.)

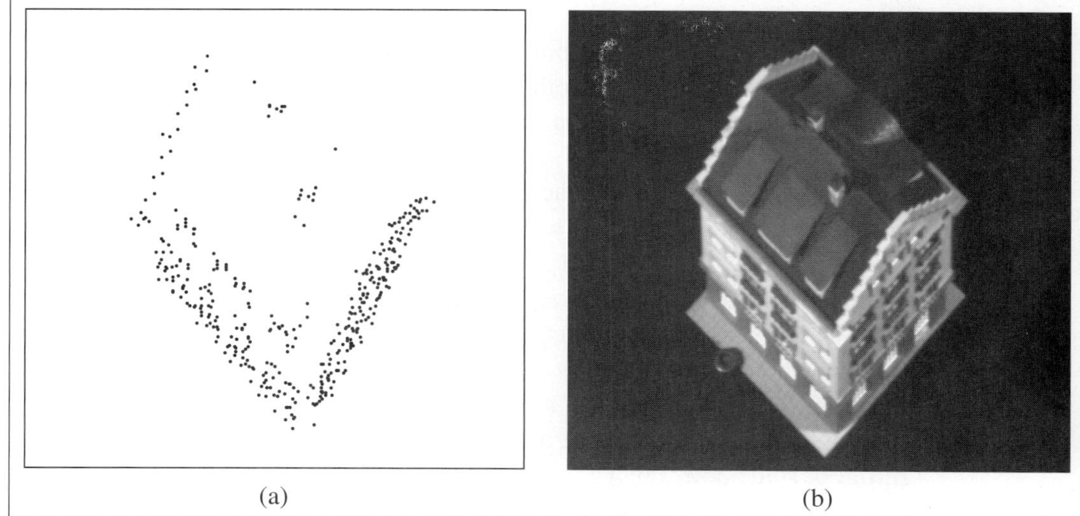


**Figure 24.9** (a) three-dimensional reconstruction of the locations of the image features in Figure 24.8, shown from above. (b) The real house, taken from the same position.

The idea is similar to motion parallax, except that instead of using images over time, we use two (or more) images separated in space, such as are provided by the forward-facing eyes of humans. Because a given feature in the scene will be in a different place relative to the $z$-axis of each image plane, if we superpose the two images, there will be a **disparity** in the location of the image feature in the two images. You can see this in Figure 24.10, where the nearest point of the pyramid is shifted to the left in the right image and to the right in the left image.

DISPARITY

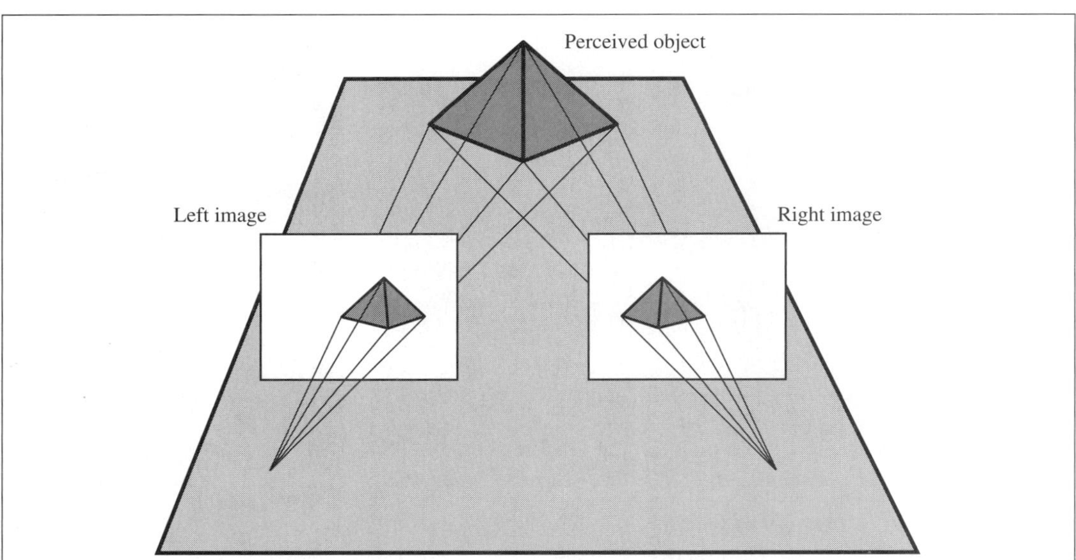


**Figure 24.10** The idea of stereopsis: different camera positions result in slightly different two-dimensional views of the same three-dimensional scene.

Let us work out the geometrical relationship between disparity and depth. First, we will consider the case when both the eyes (or cameras) are looking forward with their optical axes parallel. The relationship of the right camera to the left camera is then just translation along the $x$-axis by an amount $b$, the baseline. We can use the optical flow equations from the previous section to compute the horizontal and vertical disparity as $H = v_x \, \Delta t$, $V = v_y \, \Delta t$, given that $T_x = b/\Delta t$ and $T_y = T_z = 0$. The rotational parameters $\boldsymbol{\omega}_x$, $\boldsymbol{\omega}_y$, and $\boldsymbol{\omega}_z$ are zero. One obtains $H = b/Z$, $V = 0$. In words, the horizontal disparity is equal to the ratio of the baseline to the depth, and the vertical disparity is zero.

FIXATE

Under normal viewing conditions, humans **fixate**; that is, there is some point in the scene at which the optical axes of the two eyes intersect. Figure 24.11 shows two eyes fixated at a point $P_0$, which is at a distance $Z$ from the midpoint of the eyes. For convenience, we will compute the *angular* disparity, measured in radians. The disparity at the point of fixation $P_0$ is zero. For some other point $P$ in the scene that is $\delta Z$ further away, we can compute the angular displacements of the left and right images of $P$, which we will call $P_L$ and $P_R$, respectively. If each of these is displaced by an angle $\delta\theta/2$ relative to $P_0$, then the displacement between $P_L$ and $P_R$, which is the disparity of $P$, is just $\delta\theta$. From simple geometry, we have

$$\frac{\delta\theta}{\delta Z} = \frac{-b}{Z^2} \, .$$

BASELINE

In humans, $b$ (the **baseline**) is about 6 cm. Suppose that $Z$ is about 100 cm. Then the smallest detectable $\delta\theta$ (corresponding to the pixel size) is about 5 seconds of arc, giving a $\delta Z$ of 0.4 mm. For $Z = 30$ cm, we get the impressively small value $\delta Z = 0.036$ mm. That is, at a distance of 30 cm, humans can discriminate depths that differ by as little as 0.036 mm, enabling us to thread needles and the like.

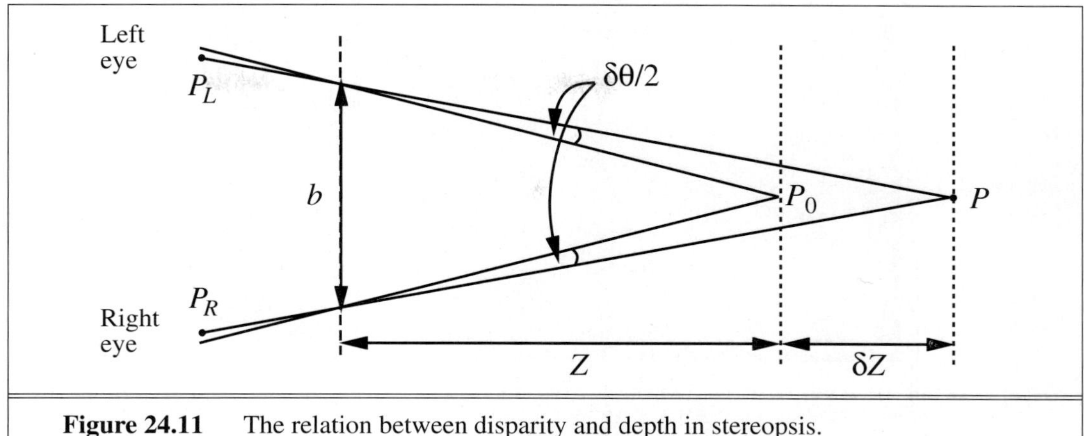


**Figure 24.11** The relation between disparity and depth in stereopsis.

### Texture gradients

TEXTURE

**Texture**, in everyday language, is a property of surfaces associated with the tactile quality they suggest ("texture" has the same root as "textile"). In computational vision, it refers to a closely related concept, that of a spatially repeating pattern on a surface that can be sensed visually. Examples include the pattern of windows on a building, the stitches on a sweater, the spots on a leopard's skin, blades of grass on a lawn, pebbles on a beach and a crowd of people in a stadium. Sometimes the arrangement is quite periodic, as in the stitches on a sweater; in other instances, such as pebbles on a beach, the regularity is only in a statistical sense: the density of pebbles is roughly the same on different parts of the beach.

TEXELS

What we just said is true *in the scene*. In the image, the apparent size, shape, spacing, and so on of the texture elements (the **texels**) do indeed vary, as illustrated in Figure 24.12. The tiles are identical in the scene. There are two main causes for the variation in the projected size and shape of the tiles in the image:

1. *Differences in the distances of the texels from the camera.* Recall that under perspective projection, distant objects appear smaller. The scaling factor is $1/Z$.
2. *Differences in the foreshortening of the texels.* This is related to the orientation of each texel relative to the line of sight from the camera. If the texel is perpendicular to the line of sight, there is no foreshortening. The magnitude of the foreshortening effect is proportional to $\cos\sigma$, where $\sigma$ is the slant of the plane of the texel.

TEXTURE GRADIENTS

Through some mathematical analysis, one can compute expressions for the rate of change of various image texel features, such as area, foreshortening, and density. These **texture gradients** are functions of the surface shape, as well as its slant and tilt with respect to the viewer's location.

To recover shape from texture, one can use a two-step process: (a) measure the texture gradients; (b) estimate the surface shape, slant, and tilt that would give rise to the measured texture gradients. We show the results of this process in Figure 24.12.

(a) (b)

**Figure 24.12** (a) A scene illustrating texture gradient. Assuming that the real texture is uniform allows recovery of the surface orientation. The computed surface orientation is indicated by overlaying a white circle and pointer, transformed as if the circle were painted on the surface at that point. (b) Recovery of shape from texture for a curved surface. (Images courtesy of Jitendra Malik and Ruth Rosenholtz (1994).)

### Shading

Shading—variation in the intensity of light received from different portions of a surface in a scene—is determined by the geometry of the scene and by the reflectance properties of the surfaces. In computer graphics, the objective is to compute the image brightness $I(x,y)$, given the scene geometry and reflectance properties of the objects in the scene. Computer vision aims to invert the process—that is, to recover the geometry and reflectance properties, given the image brightness $I(x,y)$. This has proved to be difficult to do in anything but the simplest cases.

Let us start with a situation in which we can, in fact, solve for shape from shading. Consider a Lambertian surface illuminated by a distant point light source. We will assume that the surface is distant enough from the camera so that we can use orthographic projection as an approximation to perspective projection. The image brightness is

$$I(x,y) = k\mathbf{n}(x,y) \cdot \mathbf{s} \,,$$

where $k$ is a scaling constant, $\mathbf{n}$ is the unit vector normal to the surface, and $\mathbf{s}$ is the unit vector in the direction of the light source. Because $\mathbf{n}$ and $\mathbf{s}$ are unit vectors, their dot product is just the cosine of the angle between them. The shape of the surface is captured in the variation of the normal vector $\mathbf{n}$ along the surface. Let us assume that $k$ and $\mathbf{s}$ are known. Our problem then is to recover the surface normal vector $\mathbf{n}(x,y)$ given the image intensity $I(x,y)$.

The first observation to make is that the problem of determining $\mathbf{n}$, given the brightness $I$ at a given pixel $(x,y)$, is underdetermined locally. We can compute the angle that $\mathbf{n}$ makes with the light source vector, but that only constrains it to lie on a certain cone of directions with axis $\mathbf{s}$ and apex angle $\theta = \cos^{-1}(I/k)$. To proceed further, note that $\mathbf{n}$ cannot vary arbitrarily from pixel to pixel. It corresponds to the normal vector of a smooth surface patch and consequently must also vary in a smooth fashion—the technical term for the constraint is

INTEGRABILITY **integrability**. Several different techniques have been developed to exploit this insight. One is simply to rewrite **n** in terms of the partial derivatives $Z_x$ and $Z_y$ of the depth $Z(x, y)$. This results in a partial differential equation for $Z$ that can be solved to yield the depth $Z(x, y)$, given appropriate boundary conditions.

One can generalize the approach somewhat. It is not necessary for the surface to be Lambertian nor for the light source to be a point source. As long as one is able to compute REFLECTANCE MAP the **reflectance map** $R(\mathbf{n})$, which specifies the brightness of a surface patch as a function of its surface normal **n**, essentially the same kind of techniques can be used.

The real difficulty comes in dealing with interreflections. If we consider a typical indoor scene, such as the objects inside an office, surfaces are illuminated not only by the light sources, but also by the light reflected from other surfaces in the scene that effectively serve as secondary light sources. These mutual illumination effects are quite significant. The reflectance map formalism completely fails in this situation: image brightness depends not just on the surface normal, but also on the complex spatial relationships among the different surfaces in the scene.

Humans clearly do get some perception of shape from shading, so this remains an interesting problem in spite of all these difficulties.

### Contour

When we look at a line drawing, such as Figure 24.13, we get a vivid perception of three-dimensional shape and layout. How? After all, we saw earlier that there is an infinity of scene configurations that can give rise to the same line drawing. Note that we get even a perception of surface slant and tilt. It could be due to a combination of high-level knowledge (about typical shapes) with low-level constraints.

We will consider the qualitative knowledge available from a line drawing. As discussed earlier, lines in a drawing can have multiple significance. (See Figure 24.4 and the accompa-

**Figure 24.13** An evocative line drawing. (Courtesy of Isha Malik.)

nying text.) The task of evaluating the actual significance of each line in an image is called **line labeling** and was one of the first tasks studied in computer vision. For now, let us deal with a simplified model of the world wherein the objects have no surface marks and the lines due to illumination discontinuities, such as shadow edges and specularities, have been removed in some preprocessing step, enabling us to limit our attention to line drawings where each line corresponds to either a depth or an orientation discontinuity.

LINE LABELING

LIMB

Each line then can be classified either as the projection of a **limb** (the locus of points on the surface where the line of sight is tangent to the surface) or as an **edge** (a surface normal discontinuity). In addition, each edge can be classified as convex, concave, or occluding. For occluding edges and limbs, we would like to figure out which of the two surfaces bordering the curve in the line drawing is nearer in the scene. These inferences can be represented by giving each line one of six possible **line labels** as illustrated in Figure 24.14:

LINE LABELS

1. "+" and "−" labels represent convex and concave edges, respectively. These are associated with surface normal discontinuities wherein both surfaces that meet along the edge are visible.
2. A "←" or a "→" represents an occluding convex edge. When viewed from the camera, both surface patches that meet along the edge lie on the same side, one occluding the other. As one moves in the direction of the arrow, the surfaces are to the right.
3. A "←←" or a "→→" represents a limb. Here, the surface curves smoothly around to occlude itself. As one moves in the direction of the twin arrows, the surface lies to the right. The line of sight is tangential to the surface for all points on the limb. Limbs move on the surface of the object as the viewpoint changes.

Of the $6^n$ combinatorially possible label assignments to the $n$ lines in a drawing, only a small number are physically possible. The determination of these label assignments is the line labeling problem. Note that the problem makes sense only if the label is the same all the way along a line. This is not always true, because the label can change along a line for images of curved objects. We will deal solely with polyhedral objects, to avoid this concern.

Huffman (1971) and Clowes (1971) independently attempted the first systematic approach to polyhedral scene analysis. Huffman and Clowes limited their analysis to scenes with opaque **trihedral** solids—objects in which exactly three plane surfaces come together at each vertex. For scenes with multiple objects, they also ruled out object alignments that

TRIHEDRAL

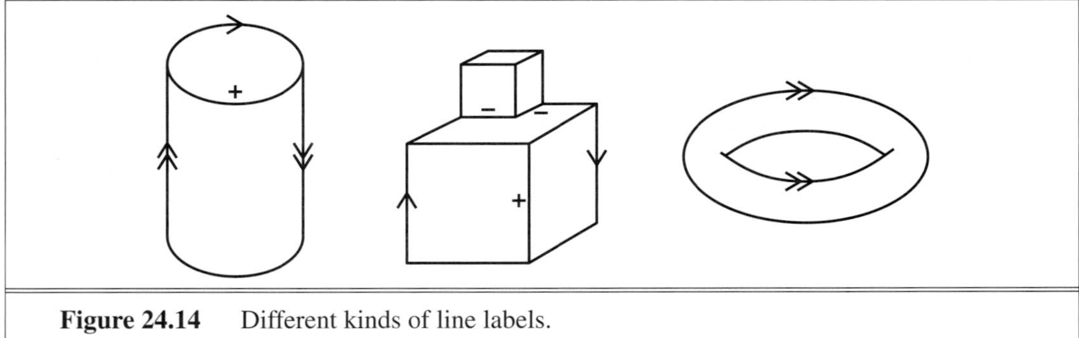


**Figure 24.14** Different kinds of line labels.

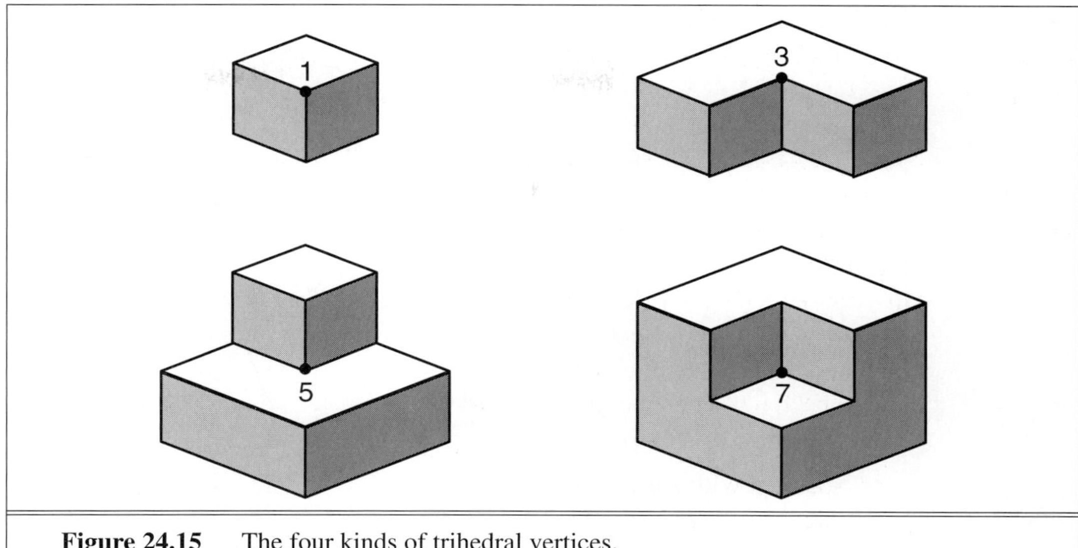


**Figure 24.15** The four kinds of trihedral vertices.

would result in a violation of the trihedral assumption, such as two cubes sharing a common edge. **Cracks** (i.e., "edges" across which the tangent planes are continuous) were also not permitted. For the trihedral world, Huffman and Clowes made an exhaustive listing of all the different types of vertices and the different ways in which they could be viewed under general viewpoint. The general viewpoint condition essentially ensures that if there is a small movement of the eye, none of the junctions changes character. For example, this condition implies that if three lines intersect in the image, the corresponding edges in the scene must also intersect.

CRACKS

The four ways in which three plane surfaces can come together at a vertex are shown in Figure 24.15. These cases have been constructed by taking a cube and dividing it into eight **octants**. We want to generate the different possible trihedral vertices at the center of the cube by filling in various octants. The vertex labeled 1 corresponds to one filled octant, 3 to three filled octants, and so on. Readers should convince themselves that these are indeed *all* the possibilities. For example, if one fills two octants in a cube, one cannot construct a valid trihedral vertex at the center. Note also that these four cases correspond to different combinations of convex and concave edges that meet at the vertex.

OCTANTS

The three edges meeting at the vertex partition the surrounding space into eight octants. A vertex can be viewed from any of the octants not occupied by solid material. Moving the viewpoint within a single octant does not result in a picture with different types of junctions. The vertex labeled 1 in Figure 24.15 can be viewed from any of the remaining seven octants to give the junction labels in Figure 24.16.

An exhaustive listing of the different ways each vertex can be viewed results in the possibilities shown in Figure 24.17. We get four different junction types that can be distinguished in the image: L-, Y-, arrow, and T-junctions. L-junctions correspond to two visible edges. Y- and arrow junctions correspond to a triple of edges—in a Y-junction, none of the three an-

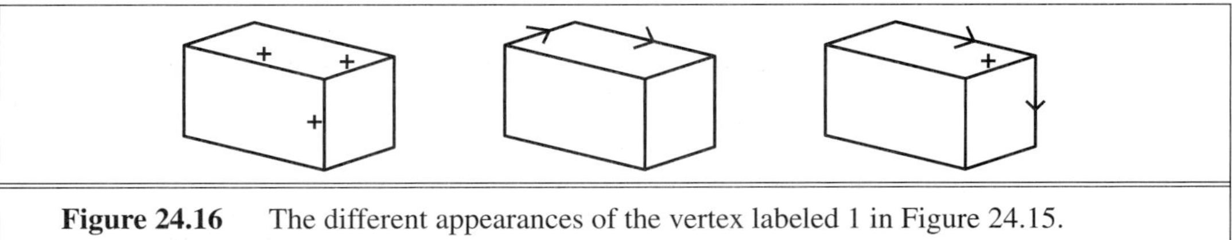

**Figure 24.16** The different appearances of the vertex labeled 1 in Figure 24.15.

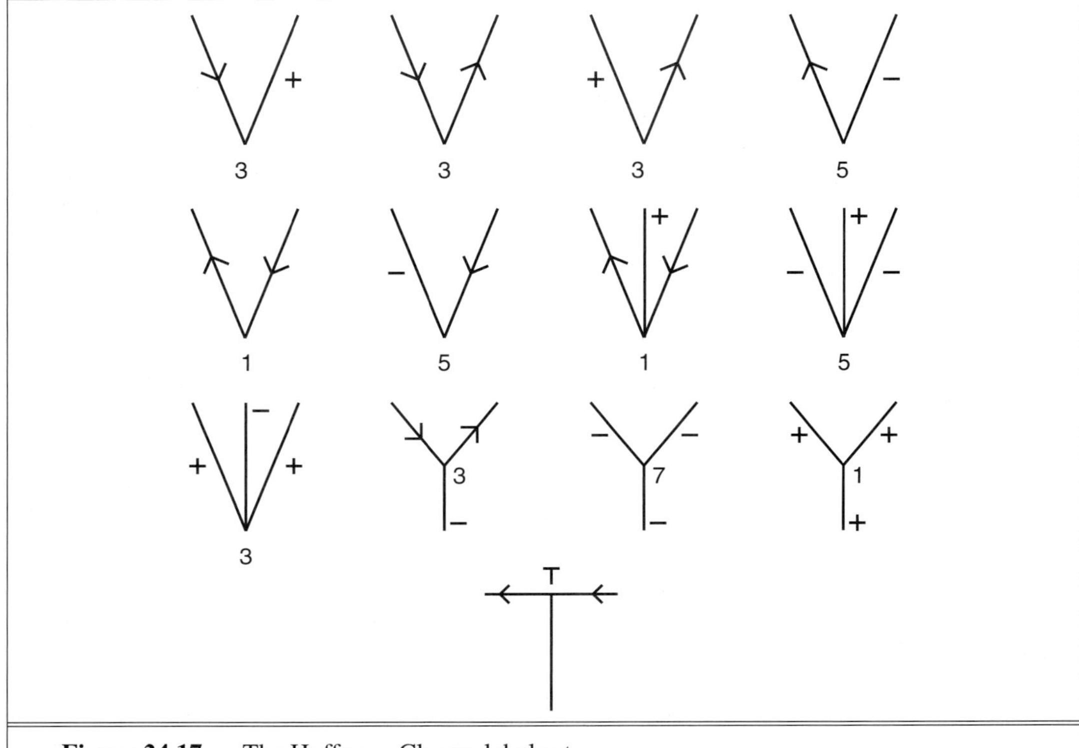


**Figure 24.17** The Huffman–Clowes label set.

gles is greater than 180°. T-junctions are associated with occlusion. When a nearer, opaque surface blocks the view of a more distant edge, one obtains a continuous edge meeting a half edge. The four T-junction labels correspond to the occlusion of four different types of edges.

In using this junction dictionary to find a labeling for the line drawing, the problem is to discover which junction interpretations are globally consistent. Consistency is forced by the rule that each line in the picture must be assigned one and only one label along its entire length. Waltz (1975) proposed an algorithm for this problem (actually for an augmented version with shadows, cracks, and separably concave edges) that was one of the first applications of constraint satisfaction in AI (see Chapter 5). In the terminology of CSPs, the variables are the junctions, the values are labelings for the junctions, and the constraints are that each line has a single label. Although the line-labeling problem for trihedral scenes is NP-complete, standard CSP algorithms perform well in practice.

## 24.5 OBJECT RECOGNITION

Vision enables us to recognize people, animals, and inanimate objects reliably. In AI or computer vision, it is customary to use the term *object recognition* to refer to all of these abilities. This includes determining the class of particular objects that have been imaged—e.g, a face—as well as recognizing specific objects—e.g., Bill Clinton's face. Motivating applications include the following:

BIOMETRIC IDENTIFICATION

◇ **Biometric identification**: Criminal investigations and access control for restricted facilities require the ability to identify unique individuals. Fingerprints, iris scans, and facial photographs result in images that must be matched to specific individuals.

CONTENT-BASED IMAGE RETRIEVAL

◇ **Content-based image retrieval**: It is easy to find a location in a document, if one exists, for the string "cat"—any text editor provides this capability. Now consider the problem of finding the subset of pixels in an image which correspond to a the image of a cat. If one had this capability, one could answer image queries such as "Bill Clinton and Nelson Mandela together," "a skater in mid-air," "the Eiffel Tower at night," and so on, without having had to type in caption keywords for each photograph in a collection. As image and video collections grow, manual annotation cannot scale.

HANDWRITING RECOGNITION

◇ **Handwriting recognition**: Examples include signatures, address blocks on envelopes, amounts on checks, and pen-based input on PDAs.

Vision is used to recognize not only objects, but also activities. We can identify gaits (a friend's walk), expressions (a smile, a grimace), gestures (a person waving), actions (jumping, dancing) and so on. Research on activity recognition is still in its infancy, so in this section we will concentrate on object recognition.

The problem of visual object recognition is generally easy for people, but has proved to be very difficult for computers. One wants to be able to identify a person's face in spite of variations in illumination, pose with respect to the camera, and facial expression. Any of these changes causes widespread differences in pixel brightness values, so a straightforward comparison of pixels is unlikely to work. When one wants to recognize examples of a category such as "car", one must cope also with the within-category variation. Even the very restricted problem of recognition of handwritten digits in postal zip codes proved to be quite a challenge.

Supervised learning or pattern classification provides a natural framework for studying object recognition. Given images of positive examples ("faces") and negative examples ("nonfaces"), the objective is to learn a function that can map novel images to one of the labels *face, nonface*. All of the techniques from Chapters 18 and 20 are plausible candidates: multilayer perceptrons, decision trees, nearest-neighbor classifiers, and kernel machines have all been applied to object recognition problems. We should note, however, that the application of these techniques to object recognition is far from straightforward.

The first challenge is image segmentation. Any image will typically contain multiple objects, so we need first to partition it into subsets of pixels that correspond to single objects. Once the image has been partitioned into regions, one can then input these regions or assemblies of regions into a classifier to determine object labels. Unfortunately, bottom-up segmentation is an error-prone process, so alternatively one might seek to find object groups *top-down*. That is, search for a subset of pixels that you can classify as a face, and if you succeed, you have found a group! Purely top-down approaches have high computational complexity, because one needs to examine image windows of different sizes, and at different locations, as well as compare them to all the different object hypotheses. At present, most practical object recognition systems use such a top-down strategy, though this might change as bottom-up techniques improve.

The second challenge is to ensure that the recognition process is robust against variations in illumination and pose. Humans can recognize objects in spite of considerable variation in precise appearance as measured by pixel brightness values. For example, we can recognize a friend's face under different illumination conditions, or at different angles of view. As an even simpler example, consider recognizing the handwritten digit 6. One should be able to do this at different sizes and at different positions in the image, and in spite of small rotations of the figure.[3]

The key point to note here is that geometrical transformations such as translation, scaling and rotation, or transformations of image brightness caused by moving light sources physically, have a different character than the intra-category variation such as exists between different human faces. Obviously, learning is the only way to learn about the different kinds of human faces, or the different ways of writing the digit 4. On the other hand, the effects of geometric and physical transformations are systematic and one should be able to factor them out by a proper design of the features used to represent the training instances.

To provide invariance under geometrical transformations, one technique that has proved quite effective is to preprocess the image region into a standard position, scale, and orientation. Alternatively, we can merrily ignore the causal nature of the geometrical and physical transformations and think of them as just other sources of variability for the classifier. In the training set, examples need to be provided corresponding to all these variations, and the hope is that the classifier will induce an appropriate set of transformations of the input so that the variations are factored out.

Let us now turn to specific algorithms for object recognition. For simplicity, we focus on the problem in a two-dimensional setting, with both training and test examples given in the form of two-dimensional brightness images. In domains such as handwriting recognition, this is clearly sufficient. Even in the case of three-dimensional objects, an effective strategy is to represent them by multiple two-dimensional views (see Figure 24.18) and classify new objects by comparing them to (some representation of) the stored views.

The previous section showed there are multiple cues for extracting three-dimensional information about a scene. Object recognition is also based on multiple cues—we identify a tiger by its mixture of orange and black colors, by its striped texture, and by its body shape.

Color and texture can be represented using histograms or empirical frequency distributions. Given an example image of a tiger, we can measure the percentage of pixels in the different color bins. Then, when an unknown example is presented, we can compare its color

[3] Complete rotation invariance is neither necessary nor desirable—one might then confuse a 6 with a 9!

**Figure 24.18** Multiple views of two three-dimensional objects.

histogram with that of previously seen tiger examples. To analyze textures, we consider histograms of the responses of an image to convolution with filters of various orientations and scales, searching for a match.

The use of shape for object recognition has proved to be much more difficult. Broadly speaking, there are two main approaches: **brightness-based recognition**, in which pixel brightness values are used directly, and **feature-based recognition**, which involves the use of spatial arrangements of extracted features such as edges or key points. After discussing each of these two approaches in more detail, we will also address the problem of **pose estimation**, i.e., determining the location and orientation of objects in the scene.

## Brightness-based recognition

Given the subset of image pixels that corresponds to a candidate object, define the features to be the raw pixel brightness values themselves. Or, in a variant, one might first convolve the image with various linear filters and treat the pixel values in the resulting images as the features. This approach has been very successful at tasks such as handwritten digit recognition, as we saw in Section 20.7.

A variety of statistical methods have been used to develop face detectors from image databases, including neural networks with raw pixel inputs, decision trees with features defined by various bar and edge filters, and naive Bayes models with wavelet features. Some results from the latter approach are shown in Figure 24.19.

One negative aspect of using raw pixels as feature vectors is the great redundancy inherent in this representation. Consider two nearby pixels on the cheek of a face; they are likely to be very highly correlated because of similar geometry, illumination, etc. Data reduction techniques, such as principal component analysis, can be used successfully to reduce the di-

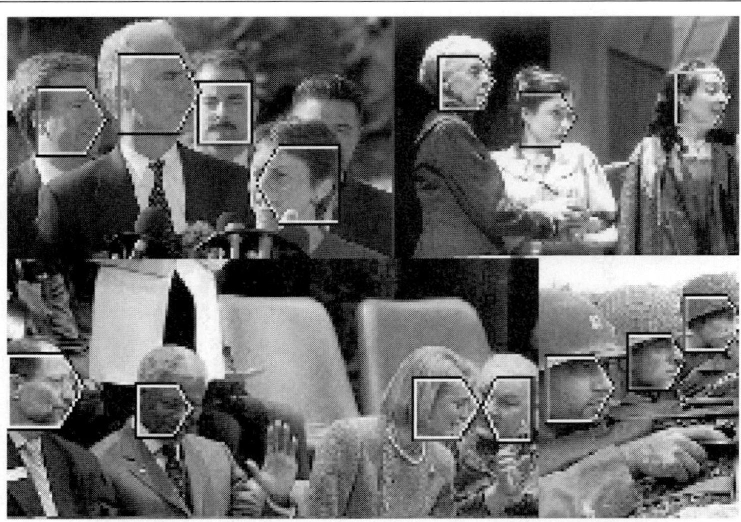

**Figure 24.19** Output of a face-finding algorithm. (Courtesy of Henry Schneiderman and Takeo Kanade.)

mensionality of the feature vector, enabling recognition of such things as faces with greater speed than one would get in a higher-dimensional space.

### Feature-based recognition

Instead of using raw pixel brightnesses as features, we can detect and mark spatially localized features such as regions and edges (Section 24.3). There are two motivations for using edges. One is data reduction—there are far fewer edges than image pixels. The other is illumination invariance—within a suitable range of contrasts, the edges will be detected at roughly the same locations, independent of precise lighting configuration. Edges are one-dimensional features; two-dimensional features (regions) and zero-dimensional features (points) have also been used. Note the difference in the treatment of spatial location in brightness-based and feature-based approaches. In brightness based approaches, this is coded implicitly as the index to a component of a feature vector. In feature-based approaches, the $(x, y)$ location *is* the feature.

The arrangement of edges is characteristic of an object—this is one reason why we can interpret line drawings (Figure 24.13) easily, even though such images do not occur in nature! The easiest way to use this knowledge is with a nearest-neighbor classifier. We pre-compute and store the configurations of edges corresponding to views of known objects. Given the configuration of edges corresponding to the unknown object in the query image, we can determine the "distance" to each member of a library of stored views. A nearest-neighbor classifier chooses the closest match.

DEFORMABLE MATCHING

Many different definitions have been proposed for distances between images. One of the more interesting approaches is based on the idea of **deformable matching**. In his classic work *On Growth and Form*, D'Arcy Thompson (1917) observed that related but not identical shapes can often be deformed into alignment using simple coordinate transformations.[4] In this paradigm, we operationalize a notion of shape similarity as a three stage process: (1) solve the correspondence problem between the two shapes, (2) use the correspondences to estimate an aligning transform, and (3) compute the distance between the two shapes as a sum of matching errors between corresponding points, together with a term measuring the magnitude of the aligning transformation.

We represent a shape by a discrete set of points sampled from the internal or external contours on the shape. These can be obtained as locations of edge pixels as found by an edge detector, giving us a set $\{p_1, \ldots, p_N\}$ of $N$ points. Figure 24.20(a) and (b) show sample points for two shapes.

Now consider a particular sample point $p_i$, together with the set of vectors originating from that point to all other sample points on a shape. These vectors express the configuration of the entire shape relative to the reference point. This leads to the following idea: associate with each sample point a descriptor, the **shape context**, which describes the coarse arrangement of the rest of the shape with respect to the point. More precisely, the shape context of $p_i$ is a coarse spatial histogram $h_i$ of the relative coordinates $p_k - p_i$ of the remaining $N-1$ points $p_k$. A log-polar coordinate system is used for defining the bins ensuring that the descriptor is more sensitive to differences in nearby pixels. An example is shown in Figure 24.20(c).

SHAPE CONTEXT

Note that invariance to translation is intrinsic to the shape context definition since all measurements are taken with respect to points on the object. To achieve scale invariance, all radial distances are normalized by the mean distance between pairs of points.

Shape contexts enable one to solve the correspondence problem between two similar but not identical shapes, such as seen in Figure 24.20(a) and (b). Shape contexts will be different for different points on a single shape $S$, whereas corresponding (homologous) points on similar shapes $S$ and $S'$ will tend to have similar shape contexts. We can then set up the problem of finding corresponding points between the two shapes as that of finding partners which have similar shape contexts.

More precisely, consider a point $p_i$ on the first shape and a point $q_j$ on the second shape. Let $C_{ij} = C(p_i, q_j)$ denote the cost of matching these two points. As shape contexts are distributions represented as histograms, it is natural to use the $\chi^2$ distance:

$$C_{ij} = \frac{1}{2} \sum_{k=1}^{K} \frac{[h_i(k) - h_j(k)]^2}{h_i(k) + h_j(k)} ,$$

where $h_i(k)$ and $h_j(k)$ denote the $k$th bin of the normalized histograms at $p_i$ and $q_j$. Given the set of costs $C_{ij}$ between all pairs of points $i$ on the first shape and $j$ on the second shape we want to minimize the total cost of matching subject to the constraint that the matching be one-to-one. This is an instance of the **weighted bipartite matching** problem, which can be solved in $O(N^3)$ time using the Hungarian algorithm.

Given the correspondences at sample points, the correspondence can be extended to the complete shape by estimating an aligning transformation that maps one shape onto the other. Regularized thin plate splines are particularly effective. Once the shapes are aligned,

[4] In modern computer graphics, this idea is referred to as **morphing**.

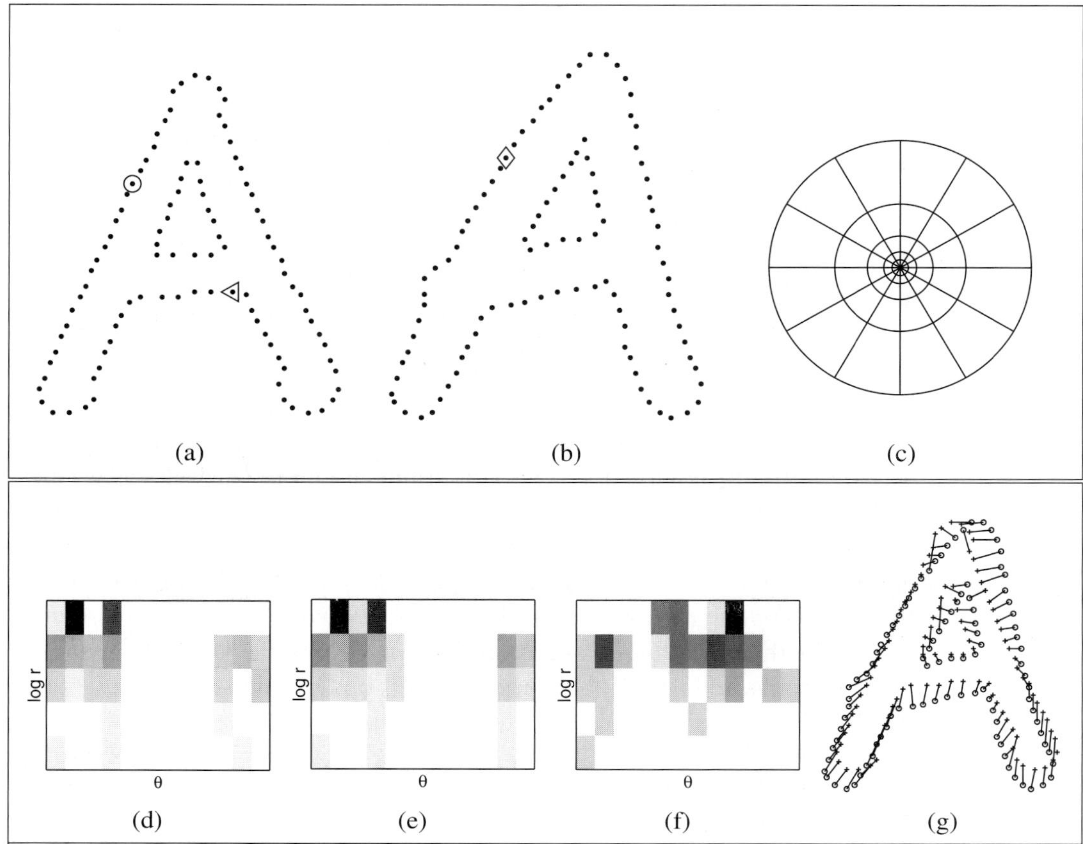


**Figure 24.20** Shape context computation and matching. (a,b) Sampled edge points of two shapes. (c) Diagram of the log-polar histogram bins used in computing the shape contexts. We use 5 bins for $\log r$ and 12 bins for $\theta$. (d-f) Example shape contexts for reference samples marked by the points $\circ, \diamond, \triangleleft$ in (a,b). Each shape context is a log-polar histogram of the coordinates of the rest of the point set measured using the reference point as the origin. (Dark cells mean more points in the bin.) Note the visual similarity of the shape contexts for $\circ$ and $\diamond$, which were computed for relatively similar points on the two shapes. By contrast, the shape context for $\triangleleft$ is quite different. (g) Correspondences between (a) and (b) found using bipartite matching, with costs defined by the $\chi^2$ distance between histograms.

computing similarity scores is relatively straightforward. The distance between two shapes can be defined as a weighted sum of the shape context distances between corresponding points and the bending energy associated with the thin plate spline. Given this distance measure, one can use a simple nearest-neighbor classifier to solve the recognition problem. The excellent performance of this approach on handwritten digit classification was described in Chapter 20.

## Pose Estimation

In addition to determining what an object is, we are also interested in determining its pose, i.e., its position and orientation with respect to the viewer. For instance, in an industrial manipulation task, the robot arm cannot pick up an object until the pose is known. In the case of rigid objects, whether three-dimensional or two-dimensional, this problem has a simple and well defined solution based on the **alignment method**, which we will now develop.

ALIGNMENT METHOD

The object is represented by $M$ features or distinguished points $m_1, m_2, \ldots, m_M$ in three-dimensional space—perhaps the vertices of a polyhedral object. These are measured in some coordinate system that is natural for the object. The points are then subjected to an unknown three-dimensional rotation **R**, followed by translation by an unknown amount **t** and then projection to give rise to image feature points $p_1, p_2, \ldots, p_N$ on the image plane. In general, $N \neq M$, because some model points may be occluded, and the feature detector could miss some features (or invent false ones due to noise). We can express this as

$$p_i = \Pi(\mathbf{R}m_i + \mathbf{t}) == Q(m_i)$$

for a three-dimensional model point $m_i$ and the corresponding image point $p_i$. Here, **R** is a rotation matrix, **t** is a translation, and $\Pi$ denotes perspective projection or one of its approximations, such as scaled orthographic projection. The net result is a transformation $Q$ that will bring the the model point $m_i$ into alignment with the image point $p_i$. Although we do not know $Q$ initially, we do know (for rigid objects) that $Q$ must be the *same* for all the model points.

One can solve for $Q$, given the three-dimensional coordinates of three model points and their two-dimensional projections. The intuition is as follows: one can write down equations relating the coordinates of $p_i$ to those of $m_i$. In these equations, the unknown quantities correspond to the parameters of the rotation matrix **R** and the translation vector **t**. If we have enough equations, we ought to be able to solve for $Q$. We will not give a proof here; we merely state the following result:

> Given three noncollinear points $m_1$, $m_2$, and $m_3$ in the model, and their scaled orthographic projections $p_1$, $p_2$, and $p_3$ on the image plane, there exist exactly two transformations from the three-dimensional model coordinate frame to a two-dimensional image coordinate frame.

These transformations are related by a reflection around the image plane and can be computed by a simple closed-form solution. If we could identify the corresponding model features for three features in the image, we could compute $Q$, the pose of the object. In the previous subsection, we discussed a technique for determining correspondences using shape context matching. If the object has well defined corners or other interest points, then an even simpler technique becomes available. The idea is to generate and test. We have to guess an initial correspondence of an image triplet with a model triplet and use the function FIND-TRANSFORM to hypothesize $Q$. If the guessed correspondence was correct, then $Q$ will be correct and, when applied to the remaining model points, will result in the prediction of the image points. If the guessed correspondence was incorrect, then $Q$ will be incorrect and, when applied to the remaining model points, would not predict the image points.

This is the basis of the ALIGN algorithm shown in Figure 24.21. The algorithm finds the pose for a given model, or returns with failure. The worst-case time complexity of the algorithm is proportional to the number of combinations of model triplets and image triplets, or $\binom{N}{3}\binom{M}{3}$, times the cost of verifying each combination. The cost of verification

```
function ALIGN(image, model) returns a solution or failure
  inputs: image, a list of image feature points
          model, a list of model feature points

  for each p1, p2, p3 in TRIPLETS(image) do
     for each m1, m2, m3 in TRIPLETS(model) do
        Q ← FIND-TRANSFORM(p1, p2, p3, m1, m2, m3)
        if projection according to Q explains image then
           return Q
  return failure
```

**Figure 24.21** An informal description of the alignment algorithm.

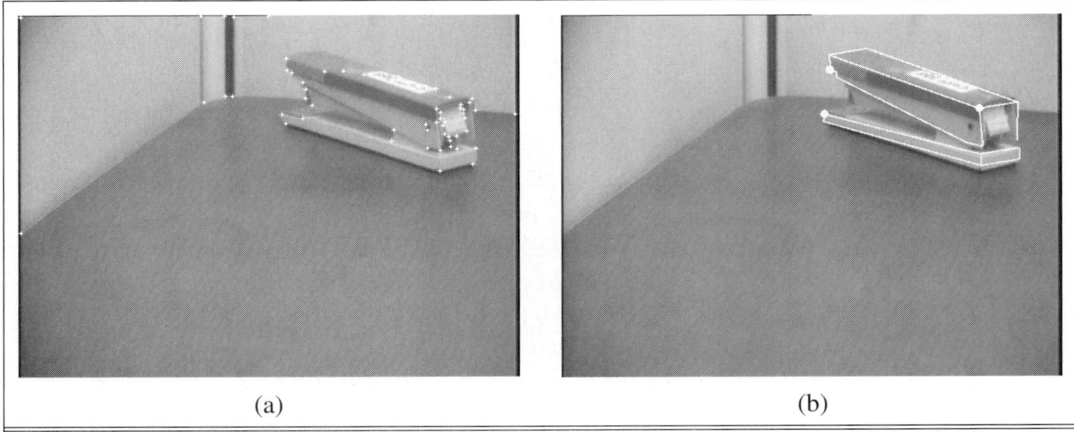

**Figure 24.22** (a) Corners found in the stapler image. (b) Hypothesized reconstruction overlaid on the original image. (Courtesy of Clark Olson.)

is $M \log N$, as we must predict the image position of each of $M$ model points, and find the distance to the nearest image point, a $\log N$ operation if the image points are arranged in an appropriate data structure. Thus, the worst-case complexity of the alignment algorithm is $O(M^4 N^3 \log N)$, where $M$ and $N$ are the number of model and image points, respectively. Techniques based on pose clustering in combination with randomization bring the complexity down to $O(MN^3)$. Results from the application of this algorithm to the stapler image are shown in Figure 24.22.

## 24.6 USING VISION FOR MANIPULATION AND NAVIGATION

One of the principal uses of vision is to provide information both for manipulating objects—picking them up, grasping them, twirling them, and so on—and for navigating while avoiding obstacles. The ability to use vision for these purposes is present in the most primitive of animal visual systems. In many cases, the visual system is minimal, in the sense that it extracts from the available light field just the information the animal needs to inform its behavior. Quite probably, modern vision systems evolved from early, primitive organisms that used a photosensitive spot at one end in order to orient themselves toward (or away from) the light. We saw in Section 24.4 that flies use a very simple optical flow detection system to land on walls. A classic study, *What the Frog's Eye Tells the Frog's Brain* (Lettvin *et al.*, 1959), observes of a frog that, "He will starve to death surrounded by food if it is not moving. His choice of food is determined only by size and movement."

**Figure 24.23** Image of a road taken from a camera inside the car. The horizontal white bars indicate the search windows within which the controller searches for the lane markers. The poor quality of the image is not untypical of low-resolution grayscale video.

Computer vision systems are used in "organisms" called robots. Let us consider a particular type of robot: an automated vehicle driving on a freeway. (See Figure 24.23.) First, we analyze the task; then, we identify the vision algorithms that will supply the information needed to perform those tasks well. The tasks faced by the driver include the following:

1. Lateral control—ensure that the vehicle remains securely within its lane or changes lane smoothly when required.
2. Longitudinal control—ensure that there is a safe distance to the vehicle in front.
3. Obstacle avoidance—monitor vehicles in neighboring lanes and be prepared for evasive maneuvers if one of them decides to change lanes.

The problem for the driver is to generate appropriate steering, acceleration, and braking actions to best accomplish these tasks.

For lateral control, one needs to maintain a representation of the position and orientation of the car relative to the lane. In the image shown in Figure 24.23, we can use edge detection algorithms to find edges corresponding to the lane marker segments. We can then fit smooth curves to these edge elements. The parameters of these curves carry information about the lateral position of the car, the direction it is pointing relative to the lane, and the curvature of the lane. This information, along with information about the dynamics of the car, is all that is needed by the steering control system. Note also that because, from every frame to the next frame, there is only a small change in the position of the projection of the lane in the image, one knows *where* to look for the lane markers in the image—in the figure, we need to look only in the areas marked by parallel white bars.

For longitudinal control, one needs to know distances to the vehicles in front. This can be accomplished with binocular stereopsis or optical flow. Both approaches can be simplified by exploiting the domain constraints derived from the fact that one is driving on a planar surface. Using these techniques, vision-controlled cars can now drive at highway speeds for long periods.

The driving example makes one point very clear: *for a specific task, one does not need to recover all the information that, in principle, can be recovered from an image.* One does not need to recover the exact shape of every vehicle, solve for shape-from-texture on the grass surface adjacent to the freeway, and so on. The needs of the task require only certain kinds of information and one can gain considerable computational speed and robustness by recovering only that information and fully exploiting the domain constraints. Our purpose in discussing the general approaches in the previous section was that they form the basic theory, which one can specialize for the needs of particular tasks.

## 24.7 Summary

Although perception appears to be an effortless activity for humans, it requires a significant amount of sophisticated computation. The goal of vision is to extract information needed for tasks such as manipulation, navigation, and object recognition.

- The process of **image formation** is well-understood in its geometric and physical aspects. Given a description of a three-dimensional scene, we can easily produce a picture of it from some arbitrary camera position (the graphics problem). Inverting the process by going from an image to a description of the scene is more difficult.
- To extract the visual information necessary for the tasks of manipulation, navigation, and recognition, intermediate representations have to be constructed. Early vision **image-processing** algorithms extract primitive features from the image, such as edges and regions.
- There are several cues in the image that enable one to obtain three-dimensional information about the scene: motion, stereopsis, texture, shading, and contour analysis. Each of these cues relies on background assumptions about physical scenes in order to provide nearly unambiguous interpretations.
- Object recognition in its full generality is a very hard problem. We discussed brightness-based and feature-based approaches. We also presented a simple algorithm for pose estimation. Other possibilities exist.

## BIBLIOGRAPHICAL AND HISTORICAL NOTES

Systematic attempts to understand human vision can be traced back to ancient times. Euclid (ca. 300 B.C.) wrote about natural perspective—the mapping that associates, with each point $P$ in the three-dimensional world, the direction of the ray $OP$ joining the center of projection $O$ to the point $P$. He was well aware of the notion of motion parallax. The mathematical understanding of perspective projection, this time in the context of projection onto planar surfaces, had its next significant advance in the 15th century in Renaissance Italy. Brunelleschi (1413) is usually credited with creating the first paintings based on geometrically correct projection of a three-dimensional scene. In 1435, Alberti codified the rules and inspired generations of artists whose artistic achievements amaze us to this day. Particularly notable in their development of the science of perspective, as it was called in those days, were Leonardo da Vinci and Albrecht Dürer. Leonardo's late 15th century descriptions of the interplay of light and shade (chiaroscuro), umbra and penumbra regions of shadows, and aerial perspective are still worth reading in translation (Kemp, 1989).

Although perspective was known to the Greeks, they were curiously confused by the role of the eyes in vision. Aristotle thought of the eyes as devices emitting rays, rather in the manner of modern laser range finders. This mistaken view was laid to rest by the work of Arab scientists, such as Alhazen, in the 10th century. The development of various kinds of cameras followed. These consisted of rooms (*camera* is Latin for "chamber") where light would be let in through a small hole in one wall to cast an image of the scene outside on the opposite wall. Of course, in all these cameras, the image was inverted, which caused no end of confusion. If the eye was to be thought of as such an imaging device, how do we see right side up? This enigma exercised the greatest minds of the era (including Leonardo). It took the work of Kepler and Descartes to settle the question. Descartes placed an eye from which the opaque cuticle had been removed in a hole in a window shutter. The result was an inverted image formed on a piece of paper laid out on the retina. While the retinal image is indeed inverted, this does cause a problem because the brain interprets the image the right way. In modern jargon, one just has to access the data structure appropriately.

The next major advances in the understanding of vision took place in the 19th century. The work of Helmholtz and Wundt, described in Chapter 1, established psychophysical experimentation as a rigorous scientific discipline. Through the work of Young, Maxwell, and Helmholtz, a trichromatic theory of color vision was established. That humans can see depth if the images presented to the left and right eyes are slightly different was demonstrated by Wheatstone's (1838) invention of the stereoscope. The device immediately became popular in parlors and salons throughout Europe. The essential concept of binocular stereopsis—that two images of a scene taken from slightly different viewpoints carry information sufficient to obtain a three-dimensional reconstruction of the scene, was exploited in the field of photogrammetry. Key mathematical results were obtained; for example, Kruppa (1913) proved that, given two views of five distinct points, one could reconstruct the rotation and translation between the two camera positions as well as the depth of the scene (up to a scale factor). Although the geometry of stereopsis had been understood for a long time, the correspondence problem in photogrammetry used to be solved by humans trying to match up corresponding points. The amazing ability of humans in solving the correspondence problem was illustrated by Julesz's (1971) invention of the random dot stereogram. Both in computer vision and in photogrammetry, much effort was devoted to solving the correspondence problem in the 1970s and 1980s.

The second half of the 19th century was a major foundational period for the psychophysical study of human vision. In the first half of the 20th century, the most significant research results in vision were obtained by the Gestalt school of psychology, led by Max Wertheimer. With the slogan "The whole is different from the sum of the parts," they promoted the view that complete forms, rather than components such as edges, should be the primary units of perception.

The period after World War II was marked by renewed activity. Most significant was the work of J. J. Gibson (1950, 1979), who pointed out the importance of optical flow, as well as texture gradients in the estimation of environmental variables such as surface slant and tilt. He reemphasized the importance of the stimulus and how rich it was. Gibson, Olum, and Rosenblatt (1955) pointed out that the optical flow field contained enough information to determine the egomotion of the observer relative to the environment. In the computational vision community, work in that area and in the (mathematically equivalent) area of gleaning structure from motion developed mainly in the 1980s and 1990s. The seminal work of Koenderink and van Doorn (1975), Ullman (1979), and Longuet-Higgins (1981) sparked this activity. Early concerns about the stability of structure from motion were allayed by the work of Tomasi and Kanade (1992) who showed that with the use of multiple frames, and the resulting wide base line, shape could be recovered quite accurately.

Chan *et al.* (1998) describe the astounding visual apparatus of the fly, which has temporal visual acuity ten times greater than humans. That is, a fly could watch a movie projected at up to 300 frames per second and recognize individual frames.

A conceptual innovation introduced in the 1990s was the study of projective structure from motion. In this setting camera calibration is not necessary, as was shown by Faugeras (1992). This discovery is related to the introduction of the use of geometrical invariants in object recognition, as surveyed by Mundy and Zisserman (1992), and the development of affine structure from motion by Koenderink and Van Doorn (1991). In the 1990s, with great increase in computer speed and storage, and the widespread availability of digital video, motion analysis found many new applications. Building geometrical models of real world scenes for rendering by computer graphics techniques proved particularly popular, led by reconstruction algorithms such as the one developed by Debevec, Taylor and Malik (1996). The books by Hartley and Zisserman (2000) and Faugeras *et al.* (2001) provide a comprehensive treatment of the geometry of multiple views.

In computational vision, major early works in inferring shape from texture are due to Bajscy and Liebermann (1976) and Stevens (1981). Whereas this work was for planar surfaces, a comprehensive analysis for curved surfaces is due to Garding (1992) and Malik and Rosenholtz (1997).

In the computational vision community, inferring shape from shading was first studied by Berthold Horn (1970). Horn and Brooks (1989) present an extensive survey of the main papers in the area. This framework made a number of simplifying assumptions, the most critical of which was ignoring the effect of mutual illumination. The importance of mutual illumination has been well appreciated in the computer graphics community, where ray tracing and radiosity have been developed precisely to take mutual illumination into account. A theoretical and empirical critique may be found in Forsyth and Zisserman (1991).

In the area of inferring shape from contour, after the key initial contributions of Huffman (1971) and Clowes (1971), Mackworth (1973) and Sugihara (1984) completed the analysis for polyhedral objects. Malik (1987) developed a labeling scheme for piecewise smooth curved objects. Kirousis and Papadimitriou (1988) showed that line-labeling for trihedral scenes is NP-complete.

Understanding the visual events in the projection of smooth curved objects requires an interplay between differential geometry and singularity theory. The best study is Koenderink's (1990) *Solid Shape*.

The seminal work in three-dimensional object recognition was Roberts's (1963) thesis at MIT. It is often considered to be the first PhD thesis in computer vision and it introduced several key ideas, including edge detection and model-based matching. Canny edge detection was introduced in Canny (1986). The idea of alignment, also first introduced by Roberts, resurfaced in the 1980s in the work of Lowe (1987) and Huttenlocher and Ullman (1990). Significant improvements in the efficiency of pose estimation by alignment were obtained by Olson (1994). Another major strand in research on 3D object recognition has been the approach based on the idea of describing shapes in terms of volumetric primitives, with **generalized cylinders**, introduced by Tom Binford (1971), proving particularly popular.

GENERALIZED CYLINDER

While computer vision research on object recognition largely focused on issues arising from the projection of three-dimensional objects onto two-dimensional images, there was a parallel tradition in the pattern recognition community that viewed the problem as one of pattern classification. The motivating examples were in domains such as optical character recognition and handwritten zip code recognition where the primary concern is that of learning the typical variations characteristic of a class of objects and separating them from other classes. See LeCun *et al.* (1995) for a comparison of approaches. Other work on object recognition includes that of Sirovitch and Kirby (1987) and of Viola and Jones (2002) for face recognition. Belongie *et al.* (2002) describe the shape context approach. Dickmanns and Zapp (1987) first demonstrated visually controlled car driving on freeways at high speeds; Pomerleau (1993) achieved similar performance using a neural network approach.

*Vision Science: Photons to Phenomenology* by Stephen Palmer (1999) provides the best comprehensive treatment of human vision; the books *Eye, Brain and Vision* by David Hubel (1988) and *Perception* by Irvin Rock (1984) are short introductions centered on neurophysiology and perception respectively.

For the field of computer vision, the most comprehensive textbook available today is *Computer Vision: A Modern Approach* by David Forsyth and Jean Ponce. Considerably shorter accounts can be found in the books by Nalwa (1993) and by Trucco and Verri (1998). *Robot Vision* (Horn, 1986) and *Three-Dimensional Computer Vision* (Faugeras, 1993) are two older and still useful textbooks, each with its specialized set of topics. David Marr's book *Vision* (Marr, 1982) played a major role in connecting computer vision to the traditional areas of biological vision—psychophysics and neurobiology. Two of the main journals for computer vision are the IEEE *Transactions on Pattern Analysis and Machine Intelligence* and the *International Journal of Computer Vision.* Computer vision conferences include ICCV (International Conference on Computer Vision), CVPR (Computer Vision and Pattern Recognition), and ECCV (European Conference on Computer Vision).

## EXERCISES

**24.1** In the shadow of a tree with a dense, leafy canopy, one sees a number of light spots. Surprisingly, they all appear to be circular. Why? After all, the gaps between the leaves through which the sun shines are not likely to be circular.

**24.2** Label the line drawing in Figure 24.24, assuming that the outside edges have been labeled as occluding and that all vertices are trihedral. Do this by a backtracking algorithm that examines the vertices in the order $A$, $B$, $C$, and $D$, picking at each stage a choice consistent with previously labeled junctions and edges. Now try the order $B$, $D$, $A$, and $C$.

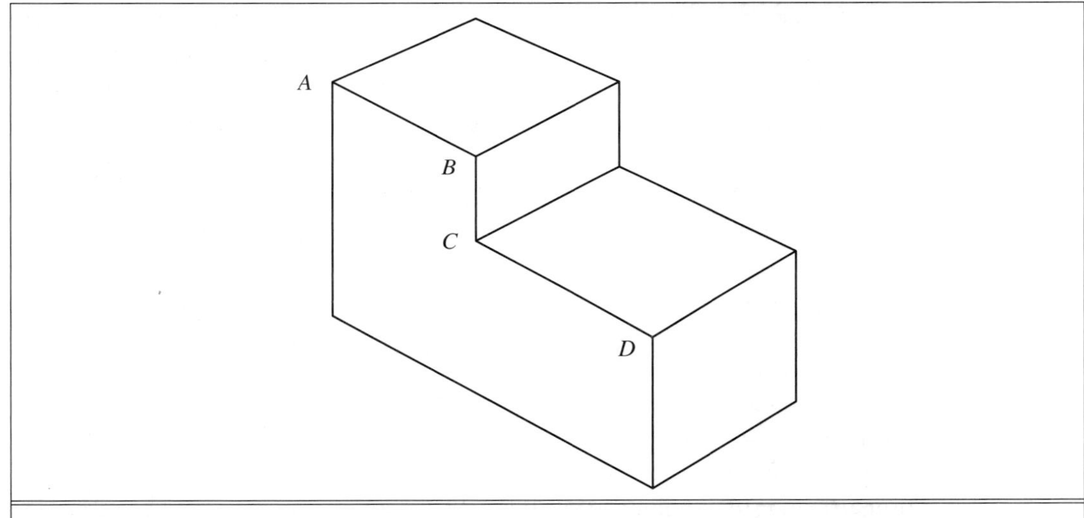


**Figure 24.24** A drawing to be labeled, in which all vertices are trihedral.

**24.3** Consider an infinitely long cylinder of radius $r$ oriented with its axis along the $y$-axis. The cylinder has a Lambertian surface and is viewed by a camera along the positive $z$-axis. What will you expect to see in the image if the cylinder is illuminated by a point source at infinity located on the positive $x$-axis? Explain your answer by drawing the isobrightness contours in the projected image. Are the contours of equal brightness uniformly spaced?

**24.4** Edges in an image can correspond to a variety of events in a scene. Consider the cover of this book, and assume that it is a picture of a real three-dimensional scene. Identify

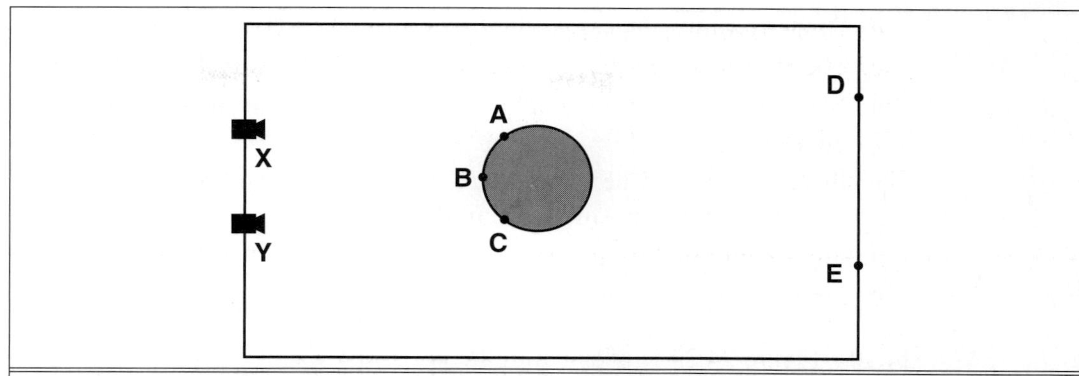


**Figure 24.25** Top view of a two-camera vision system observing a bottle with a wall behind.

ten different brightness edges in the image, and for each, state whether it corresponds to a discontinuity in (a) depth, (b) surface normal, (c) reflectance, or (d) illumination.

**24.5** Show that convolution with a given function $f$ commutes with differentiation; that is, show that $(f * g)' = f * g'$ .

**24.6** A stereoscopic system is being contemplated for terrain mapping. It will consist of two CCD cameras, each having $512 \times 512$ pixels on a 10 cm $\times$ 10 cm square sensor. The lenses to be used have a focal length of 16 cm, with the focus fixed at infinity. For corresponding points $(u_1, v_1)$ in the left image and $(u_2, v_2)$ in the right image, $v_1 = v_2$ because the $x$-axes in the two image planes are parallel to the epipolar lines. The optical axes of the two cameras are parallel. The baseline between the cameras is 1 meter.

**a**. If the nearest range to be measured is 16 meters, what is the largest disparity that will occur (in pixels)?

**b**. What is the range resolution at 16 meters, due to the pixel spacing?

**c**. What range corresponds to a disparity of one pixel?

**24.7** Suppose we wish to use the alignment algorithm in an industrial situation in which flat parts move along a conveyor belt and are photographed by a camera vertically above the conveyor belt. The pose of the part is specified by three variables—one for the rotation and two for the two-dimensional position. This simplifies the problem and the function FIND-TRANSFORM needs only two pairs of corresponding image and model features to determine the pose. Determine the worst-case complexity of the alignment procedure.

**24.8** (Courtesy of Pietro Perona.) Figure 24.25 shows two cameras at X and Y observing a scene. Draw the image seen at each camera, assuming that all named points are in the same horizontal plane. What can be concluded from these two images about the relative distances of points A, B, C, D, and E from the camera baseline, and on what basis?

**24.9** Which of the following are true, and which are false?

**a**. Finding corresponding points in stereo images is the easiest phase of the stereo depth-finding process.

**b.** Shape-from-texture can be done by projecting a grid of light-stripes onto the scene.

**c.** The Huffman–Clowes labelling scheme can deal with all polyhedral objects.

**d.** In line drawings of curved objects, the line label can change from one end of the line to the other.

**e.** In stereo views of the same scene, greater accuracy is obtained in the depth calculations if the two camera positions are further apart.

**f.** Lines with equal lengths in the scene always project to equal lengths in the image.

**g.** Straight lines in the image necessarily correspond to straight lines in the scene.

**24.10** Figure 24.23 is taken from the point of view of a car in the exit lane of a freeway. Two cars are visible in the lane immediately to the left. What reasons does the viewer have to conclude that one is closer than the other?

# 25 ROBOTICS

*In which agents are endowed with physical effectors with which to do mischief.*

## 25.1 INTRODUCTION

ROBOTS

EFFECTOR

SENSOR

**Robots** are physical agents that perform tasks by manipulating the physical world. To do so, they are equipped with **effectors** such as legs, wheels, joints, and grippers. Effectors have a single purpose: to assert physical forces on the environment.[1] Robots are also equipped with **sensors**, which allow them to perceive their environment. Present day robotics employs a diverse set of sensors, including cameras and ultrasound to measure the environment, and gyroscopes and accelerometers to measure the robot's own motion.

MANIPULATOR

Most of today's robots fall into one of three primary categories. **Manipulators**, or robot arms, are physically anchored to their workplace, for example in a factory assembly line or on the International Space Station. Manipulator motion usually involves an entire chain of controllable joints, enabling such robots to place their effectors in any position within the workplace. Manipulators are by far the most common type of industrial robots, with over a million units installed worldwide. Some mobile manipulators are used in hospitals to assist surgeons. Few car manufacturers could survive without robotic manipulators, and some manipulators have even been used to generate original artwork.

MOBILE ROBOT

ULV

UAV

AUV

PLANETARY ROVER

The second category is the **mobile robot**. Mobile robots move about their environment using wheels, legs, or similar mechanisms. They have been put to use delivering food in hospitals, moving containers at loading docks, and similar tasks. Earlier we encountered an example of a mobile robot: the NAVLAB **unmanned land vehicle** (ULV) capable of driverless autonomous highway navigation. Other types of mobile robots include **unmanned air vehicles** (UAV), commonly used for surveillance, crop-spraying, and military operations, **autonomous underwater vehicles** (AUV), used in deep sea exploration, and **planetary rovers**, such as the Sojourner robot shown in Figure 25.1(a).

[1] In Chapter 2 we talked about **actuators**, not effectors. An actuator is a control line that communicates a command to an effector; the effector is the physical device itself.

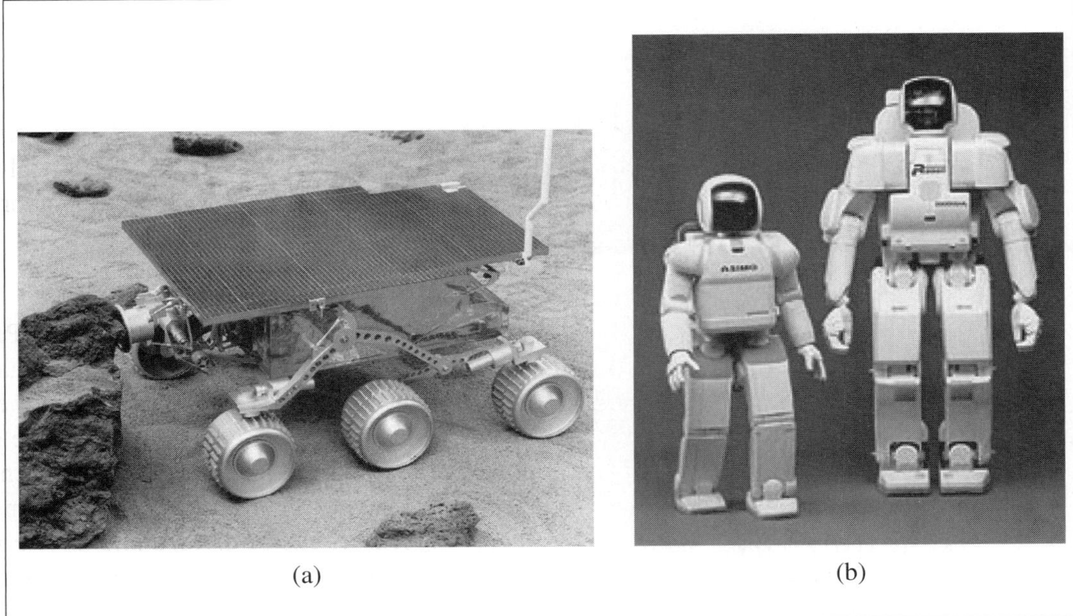

(a) (b)

**Figure 25.1** (a) NASA's Sojourner, a mobile robot that explored the surface of Mars in July 1997. (b) Honda's P3 and Asimo humanoid robots.

The third type is a hybrid: a mobile robot equipped with manipulators. These include the **humanoid robot**, whose physical design mimics the human torso. Figure 25.1(b) shows two such humanoid robots, both manufactured by Honda Corp. in Japan. Hybrids can apply their effectors further afield than anchored manipulators can, but their task is made harder because they don't have the rigidity that the anchor provides.

HUMANOID ROBOT

The field of robotics also includes prosthetic devices (artificial limbs, ears, and eyes for humans), intelligent environments (such as an entire house that is equipped with sensors and effectors), and multibody systems, wherein robotic action is achieved through swarms of small cooperating robots.

Real robots usually must cope with environments that are partially observable, stochastic, dynamic, and continuous. Some, but not all, robot environments are sequential and multiagent as well. Partial observability and stochasticity are the result of dealing with a large, complex world. The robot cannot see around corners, and motion commands are subject to uncertainty due to gears slipping, friction, etc. Also, the real world stubbornly refuses to operate faster than real time. In a simulated environment, it is possible to use simple algorithms (such as the **Q-learning** algorithm described in Chapter 21) to learn in a few CPU hours from millions of trials. In a real environment, it might take years to run these trials. Furthermore, real crashes really hurt, unlike simulated ones. Practical robotic systems need to embody prior knowledge about the robot, its physical environment, and the tasks that the robot will perform so that the robot can learn quickly and perform safely.

## 25.2 ROBOT HARDWARE

So far in this book, we have taken the agent architecture—sensors, effectors, and processors—as given, and we have concentrated on the agent program. The success of real robots depends at least as much on the design of sensors and effectors that are appropriate for the task.

### Sensors

PASSIVE SENSOR

ACTIVE SENSOR

Sensors are the perceptual interface between robots and their environments. **Passive sensors**, such as cameras, are true observers of the environment: they capture signals that are generated by other sources in the environment. **Active sensors**, such as sonar, send energy into the environment. They rely on the fact that this energy is reflected back to the sensor. Active sensors tend to provide more information than passive sensors, but at the expense of increased power consumption and with a danger of interference when multiple active sensors are used at the same time. Whether active or passive, sensors can be divided into three types, depending on whether they record distances to objects, entire images of the environment, or properties of the robot itself.

RANGE FINDER

SONAR SENSOR

Many mobile robots make use of **range finders**, which are sensors that measure the distance to nearby objects. One common type is the **sonar sensor**, also known as an ultrasonic transducer. Sonar sensors emit directional sound waves, which are reflected by objects, with some of the sound making it back into the sensor. The time and intensity of this returning signal thus carry information about the distance to nearby objects. Underwater sonar sensors are the technology of choice for AUVs. On land, sonar sensors are mainly used for near-range

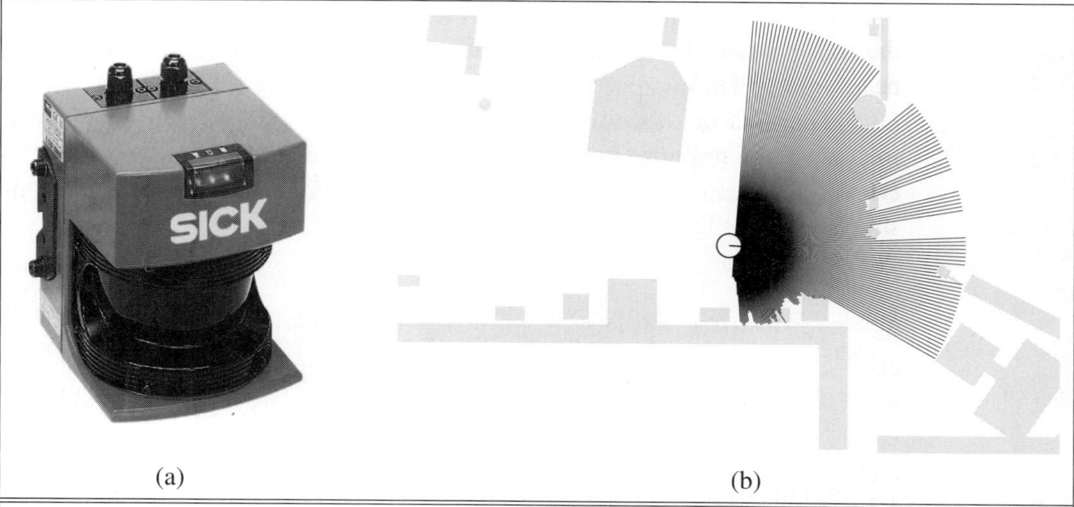


**Figure 25.2** (a) The SICK LMS laser range scanner, a popular range sensor for mobile robots. (b) Range scan obtained with a horizontally mounted sensor, projected onto a two-dimensional environment map.

collision avoidance, due to their limited angular resolution. Alternatives to sonar include radar (used primarily by aircraft) and laser. A laser range finder is shown in Figure 25.2.

TACTILE SENSORS
GLOBAL POSITIONING SYSTEM
DIFFERENTIAL GPS

Some range sensors measure very short or very long distances. Close-range sensors include **tactile sensors** such as whiskers, bump panels, and touch-sensitive skin. At the other end of the spectrum is the **Global Positioning System** (GPS), which measures the distance to satellites that emit pulsed signals. At present, there are two dozen satellites in orbit, each transmitting signals on two different frequencies. GPS receivers can recover the distance to these satellites by analyzing phase shifts. By triangulating signals from multiple satellites, GPS receivers can determine their absolute location on Earth to within a few meters. **Differential GPS** involves a second ground receiver with known location, providing millimeter accuracy under ideal conditions. Unfortunately, GPS does not work indoors or underwater.

IMAGING SENSOR

The second important class of sensors is **imaging sensors**—the cameras that provide us with images of the environment and, using the computer vision techniques of Chapter 24, models and features of the environment. Stereo vision is particularly important in robotics, because it can capture depth information; although its future is somewhat uncertain as new active technologies for range imaging are being developed successfully.

PROPRIOCEPTIVE SENSOR
SHAFT DECODER
ODOMETRY
INERTIAL SENSOR

The third important class is **proprioceptive sensors**, which inform the robot of its own state. To measure the exact configuration of a robotic joint, motors are often equipped with **shaft decoders** that count the revolution of motors in small increments. On robot arms, shaft decoders can provide accurate information over any period of time. On mobile robots, shaft decoders that report wheel revolutions can be used for **odometry**—the measurement of distance travelled. Unfortunately, wheels tend to drift and slip, so odometry is accurate only over short distances. External forces, such as the current for AUVs and the wind for UAVs, increase positional uncertainty. **Inertial sensors**, such as gyroscopes, can help but cannot by themselves prevent the inevitable accumulation of position uncertainty.

FORCE SENSOR
TORQUE SENSOR

Other important aspects of robot state are measured by **force** and **torque sensors**. These are indispensable when robots handle fragile objects or objects whose exact shape and location is unknown. Imagine a one ton robotic manipulator screwing in a light bulb. It would be all too easy to apply too much force and break the bulb. Force sensors allow the robot to sense how hard it is gripping the bulb, and torque sensors allow it to sense how hard it is turning. Good sensors can measure forces in three translational and three rotational directions.

## Effectors

DEGREE OF FREEDOM
KINEMATIC STATE
POSE
DYNAMIC STATE

Effectors are the means by which robots move and change the shape of their bodies. To understand the design of effectors, it will help first to talk about motion and shape in the abstract, using the concept of a **degree of freedom** (DOF). We count one degree of freedom for each independent direction in which a robot, or one of its effectors, can move. For example, a rigid free-moving robot such as an AUV has six degrees of freedom, three for its $(x, y, z)$ location in space and three for its angular orientation, known as *yaw*, *roll*, and *pitch*. These six degrees define the **kinematic state**[2] or **pose** of the robot. The **dynamic state** of a robot includes one additional dimension for the rate of change of each kinematic dimension.

[2] "Kinematic" is from the Greek word for *motion*, as is "cinema."

For nonrigid bodies, there are additional degrees of freedom within the robot itself. For example, in a human arm, the elbow has one degree of freedom—it can flex in one direction—and the wrist has three degrees of freedom—it can move up and down, side to side, and can also rotate. Robot joints also have 1, 2, or 3 degrees of freedom each. Six degrees of freedom are required to place an object, such as a hand, at a particular point in a particular orientation. The arm in Figure 25.3(a) has exactly six degrees of freedom, created by five **revolute joints** that generate rotational motion and one **prismatic joint** that generates sliding motion. You can verify that the human arm as a whole has more than six degrees of freedom by a simple experiment: put your hand on the table, and notice that you still have the freedom to rotate your elbow without changing the configuration of your hand. Manipulators that have more degrees of freedom than required to place an end effector at a target location are easier to control than robots with only the minimum number of DOFs.

REVOLUTE JOINT

PRISMATIC JOINT

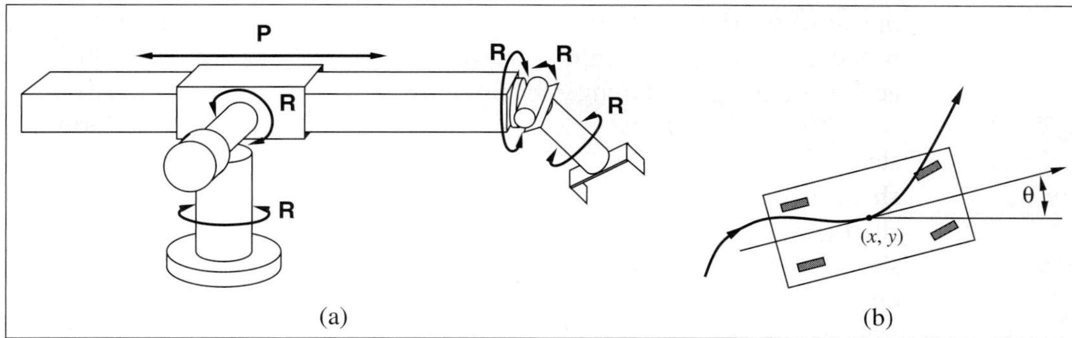


**Figure 25.3** (a) The Stanford Manipulator, an early robot arm with five revolute joints (R) and one prismatic joint (P), for a total of six degrees of freedom. (b) Motion of a nonholonomic four-wheeled vehicle with front-wheel steering.

For mobile robots, the DOFs are not necessarily the same as the number of actuated elements. Consider, for example, your average car: it can move forward or backward, and it can turn, giving it two DOFs. In contrast, a car's kinematic configuration is three-dimensional: on an open flat surface, one can easily maneuver a car to any $(x, y)$ point, in any orientation. (See Figure 25.3(b).) Thus, the car has 3 **effective degrees of freedom** but 2 **controllable degrees of freedom**. We say a robot is **nonholonomic** if it has more effective DOFs than controllable DOFs and **holonomic** if the two numbers are the same. Holonomic robots are easier to control—it would be much easier to park a car that could move sideways as well as forward and backward—but holonomic robots are also mechanically more complex. Most robot arms are holonomic, and most mobile robots are nonholonomic.

EFFECTIVE DOF

CONTROLLABLE DOF

NONHOLONOMIC

For mobile robots, there exists a range of mechanisms for locomotion, including wheels, tracks, and legs. **Differential drive** robots possess two independently actuated wheels (or tracks), one on each side, as on a military tank. If both wheels move at the same velocity, the robot moves on a straight line. If they move in opposite directions, the robot turns on the spot. An alternative is the **synchro drive**, in which each wheel can move and turn around its own axis. This could easily lead to chaos, if not for the constraint that all wheels always

DIFFERENTIAL DRIVE

SYNCHRO DRIVE

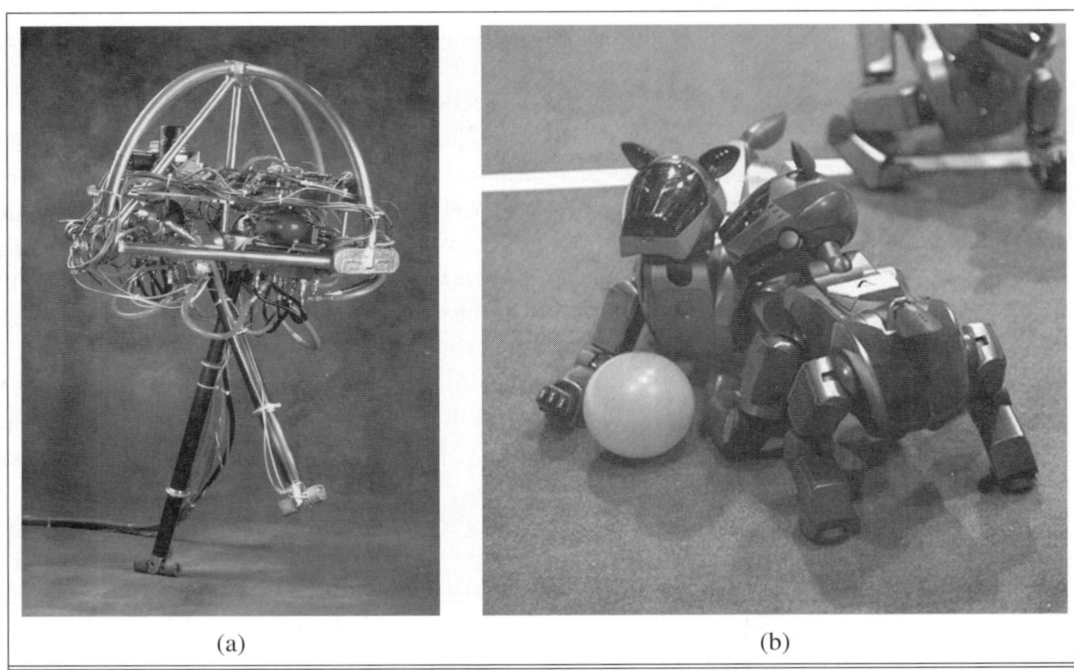

(a) (b)

**Figure 25.4** (a) One of Marc Raibert's legged robots in motion. (b) Sony AIBO robots playing soccer. (© 2001, The RoboCup Federation.)

point in the same direction and move at the same speed. Both differential and synchro drives are nonholonomic. Some more expensive robots use holonomic drives, which usually involve three or more wheels that can be oriented and moved independently.

Legs, unlike wheels, can handle very rough terrain. However, legs are notoriously slow on flat surfaces, and they are mechanically difficult to build. Robotics researchers have tried designs ranging from one leg up to dozens of legs. Legged robots have been made to walk, run, and even hop—as we see with the legged robot in Figure 25.4(a). This robot is **dynamically stable**, meaning that it can remain upright while hopping around. A robot that can remain upright without moving its legs is called **statically stable**. A robot is statically stable if its center of gravity is above the polygon spanned by its legs.

DYNAMICALLY STABLE

STATICALLY STABLE

Other types of mobile robot use vastly different mechanisms for moving about. Airborne vehicles usually use propellers or turbines. Robotic blimps rely on thermal effects to keep themselves aloft. Autonomous underwater vehicles often use thrusters, similar to those used on submarines.

Sensors and effectors alone do not make a robot. A complete robot also needs a source of power to drive its effectors. The **electric motor** is the most popular mechanism for both manipulator actuation and locomotion, but **pneumatic actuation** using compressed gas and **hydraulic actuation** using pressurized fluids also have their application niches. Most robots also have some means of digital communication such as a wireless network. Finally, there has to be a body frame to hang all the bits and pieces on and a soldering iron for emergencies.

ELECTRIC MOTOR

PNEUMATIC ACTUATION

HYDRAULIC ACTUATION

## 25.3 ROBOTIC PERCEPTION

Perception is the process by which robots map sensor measurements into internal representations of the environment. Perception is difficult because in general the sensors are noisy, and the environment is partially observable, unpredictable, and often dynamic. As a rule of thumb, good internal representations have three properties: they contain enough information for the robot to make the right decisions, they are structured so that they can be updated efficiently, and they are natural in the sense that internal variables correspond to natural state variables in the physical world.

In Chapter 15, we saw that Kalman filters, HMMs, and dynamic Bayes nets can represent the transition and sensor models of a partially observable environment, and we described both exact and approximate algorithms for updating the **belief state**—the posterior probability distribution over the environment state variables. Several dynamic Bayes net models for this process were shown in Chapter 15. For robotics problems, we usually include the robot's own past actions as observed variables in the model, as in the network shown in Figure 17.9. Figure 25.5 shows the notation used in this chapter: $\mathbf{X}_t$ is the state of the environment (including the robot) at time $t$, $\mathbf{Z}_t$ is the observation received at time $t$, and $A_t$ is the action taken after the observation is received.

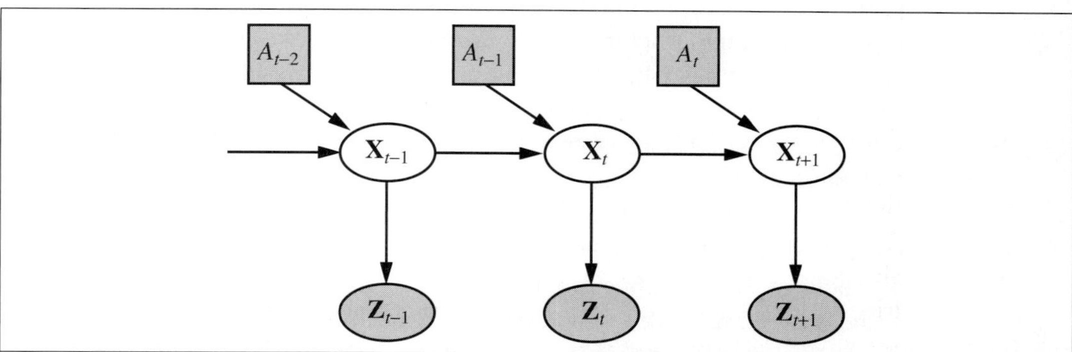


**Figure 25.5** Robot perception can be viewed as temporal inference from sequences of actions and measurements, as illustrated by this dynamic Bayes network.

The task of **filtering**, or updating the belief state, is essentially the same as in Chapter 15. The task is to compute the new belief state, $\mathbf{P}(\mathbf{X}_{t+1} \mid \mathbf{z}_{1:t+1}, a_{1:t})$, from the current belief state $\mathbf{P}(\mathbf{X}_t \mid \mathbf{z}_{1:t}, a_{1:t-1})$ and the new observation $\mathbf{z}_{t+1}$. The principal differences are that (1) we condition explicitly on the actions as well as the observations, and (2) we must now deal with *continuous* rather than *discrete* variables. Thus, we modify the recursive filtering equation (15.3) to use integration rather than summation:

$$\begin{aligned} &\mathbf{P}(\mathbf{X}_{t+1} \mid \mathbf{z}_{1:t+1}, a_{1:t}) \\ &= \alpha \mathbf{P}(\mathbf{z}_{t+1} \mid \mathbf{X}_{t+1}) \int \mathbf{P}(\mathbf{X}_{t+1} \mid \mathbf{x}_t, a_t)\, P(\mathbf{x}_t \mid \mathbf{z}_{1:t}, a_{1:t-1})\, d\mathbf{x}_t \,. \end{aligned} \tag{25.1}$$

The equation states that the posterior over the state variables $\mathbf{X}$ at time $t + 1$ is calculated recursively from the corresponding estimate one time step earlier. This calculation involves the previous action $a_t$ and the current sensor measurement $\mathbf{z}_{t+1}$. For example, if our goal is to develop a soccer-playing robot, $\mathbf{X}_{t+1}$ might be the location of the soccer ball relative to the robot. The posterior $\mathbf{P}(\mathbf{X}_t \mid \mathbf{z}_{1:t}, a_{1:t-1})$ is a probability distribution over all states that captures what we know from past sensor measurements and controls. Equation (25.1) tells us how to recursively estimate this location, by incrementally folding in sensor measurements (e.g., camera images) and robot motion commands. The probability $\mathbf{P}(\mathbf{X}_{t+1} \mid \mathbf{x}_t, a_t)$ is called the **transition model** or **motion model**, and $\mathbf{P}(\mathbf{z}_{t+1} \mid \mathbf{X}_{t+1})$ is the **sensor model**.

MOTION MODEL

## Localization

LOCALIZATION

**Localization** is a generic example of robot perception. It is the problem of determining where things are. Localization is one of the most pervasive perception problems in robotics, because knowledge about where things are is at the core of any successful physical interaction. For example, robot manipulators must know the location of objects they manipulate. Navigating robots must know where they are in order to find their way to goal locations.

TRACKING

GLOBAL LOCALIZATION

KIDNAPPING PROBLEM

The localization problem comes in three flavors of increasing difficulty. If the initial pose of the object to be localized is known, localization is a **tracking** problem. Tracking problems are characterized by bounded uncertainty. More difficult is the **global localization** problem, in which the initial location of the object is entirely unknown. Global localization problems turn into tracking problems once the object of interest has been localized, but they also involve phases where the robot has to manage very broad uncertainties. Finally, we can be mean to our robot and "kidnap" the object it is attempting to localize. Localization under such devious conditions is known as the **kidnapping problem**. Kidnapping is often used to test the robustness of a localization technique under extreme conditions.

To keep things simple, let us assume that the robot moves slowly in a plane and that it is given an exact map of the environment. (An example of such a map appears in Figure 25.8.) The pose of such a mobile robot is defined by its two Cartesian coordinates with values $x$ and $y$ and its heading with value $\theta$, as illustrated in Figure 25.6(a). (Notice that we exclude the corresponding velocities, so this is a kinematic rather than a dynamic model.) If we arrange those three values in a vector, then any particular state is given by $\mathbf{X}_t = (x_t, y_t, \theta_t)^\top$.

In the kinematic approximation, each action consists of the "instantaneous" specification of two velocities—a translational velocity $v_t$ and a rotational velocity $\omega_t$. For small time intervals $\Delta t$, a crude deterministic model of the motion of such robots is given by

$$\hat{\mathbf{X}}_{t+1} = f(\mathbf{X}_t, \underbrace{v_t, \omega_t}_{a_t}) = \mathbf{X}_t + \begin{pmatrix} v_t \Delta t \cos\theta_t \\ v_t \Delta t \sin\theta_t \\ \omega_t \Delta t \end{pmatrix} .$$

The notation $\hat{\mathbf{X}}$ refers to a deterministic state prediction. Of course, physical robots are somewhat unpredictable. This is commonly modeled by a Gaussian distribution with mean $f(\mathbf{X}_t, v_t, \omega_t)$ and covariance $\boldsymbol{\Sigma}_x$. (See Appendix A for a mathematical definition.)

$$\mathbf{P}(\mathbf{X}_{t+1} \mid \mathbf{X}_t, v_t, \omega_t) \;=\; N(\hat{\mathbf{X}}_{t+1}, \boldsymbol{\Sigma}_x) .$$

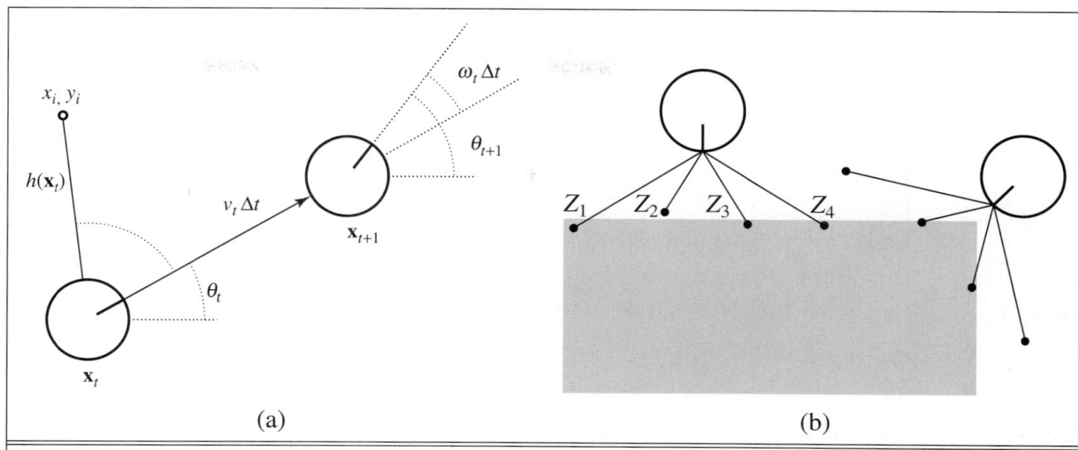


**Figure 25.6** (a) A simplified kinematic model of a mobile robot. The robot is shown as a circle with a mark showing the forward direction. Positions and orientations at $t$ and $t+1$ are shown, with the updates given by $v_t\Delta_t$ and $\omega_t\Delta_t$ respectively. Also shown is a landmark at $(x_i, y_i)$ observed at time $t$. (b) The range-scan sensor model. Two possible robot poses are shown for a given range scan $(z_1, z_2, z_3, z_4)$. It is much more likely that the pose on the left generated the range scan than the pose on the right.

Next, we need a sensor model. We will consider two kinds of sensor model. The first assumes that the sensors detect *stable*, *recognizable* features of the environment called **landmarks**. For each landmark, the range and bearing are reported. Suppose the robot's state is $\mathbf{x}_t = (x_t, y_t, \theta_t)^\top$ and it senses a landmark whose location is known to be $(x_i, y_i)^\top$. Without noise, the range and bearing can be calculated by simple geometry. (See Figure 25.6(a).) The exact prediction of the observed range and bearing would be

LANDMARKS

$$\hat{\mathbf{z}}_t = h(\mathbf{x}_t) = \begin{pmatrix} \sqrt{(x_t - x_i)^2 + (y_t - y_i)^2} \\ \arctan \frac{y_i - y_t}{x_i - x_t} - \theta_t \end{pmatrix} .$$

Again, noise distorts our measurements. To keep things simple, one might assume Gaussian noise with covariance $\mathbf{\Sigma}_z$

$$P(\mathbf{z}_t \mid \mathbf{x}_t) = N(\hat{\mathbf{z}}_t, \mathbf{\Sigma}_z) .$$

A somewhat different sensor model is often appropriate for range scanners of the kind shown in Figure 25.2. Such sensors produce a vector of range values $\mathbf{z}_t = (z_1, \ldots, z_M)^\top$, each of whose bearings is fixed relative to the robot. Given a pose $\mathbf{x}_t$, let $\hat{z}_j$ be the exact range along the $j$th beam direction from $\mathbf{x}_t$ to the nearest obstacle. As before, this will be corrupted by Gaussian noise. Typically, we assume that the errors for the different beam directions are independent and identically distributed, so we have

$$P(\mathbf{z}_t \mid \mathbf{x}_t) = \alpha \prod_{j=1}^{M} e^{-(z_j - \hat{z}_j)/2\sigma^2} .$$

Figure 25.6(b) shows an example of a four-beam range scan and two possible robot poses, one of which is reasonably likely to have produced the observed scan and one of which is not.

```
function MONTE-CARLO-LOCALIZATION(a, z, N, model, map) returns a set of samples
  inputs: a, the previous robot motion command
          z, a range scan with M readings z_1, ..., z_M
          N, the number of samples to be maintained
          model, a probabilistic environment model with pose prior P(X_0),
              motion model P(X_1|X_0, A_0), and range sensor noise model P(Z|Ẑ)
          map, a 2D map of the environment
  static: S, a vector of samples of size N, initially generated from P(X_0)
  local variables: W, a vector of weights of size N

  for i = 1 to N do
     S[i] ← sample from P(X_1|X_0 = S[i], A_0 = a)
     W[i] ← 1
     for j =1 to M do
        ẑ ← EXACT-RANGE(j, S[i], map)
        W[i] ← W[i] · P(Z = z_j|Ẑ = ẑ)
  S ← WEIGHTED-SAMPLE-WITH-REPLACEMENT(N, S, W)
  return S
```

**Figure 25.7** A Monte Carlo localization algorithm using a range scan sensor model with independent noise.

Comparing the range scan model to the landmark model, we see that the range scan model has the advantage that there is no need to *identify* a landmark before the range scan can be interpreted; indeed, in Figure 25.6(b), the robot faces a featureless wall. On the other hand, if there *is* a visible, identifiable landmark, it can provide immediate localization.

Chapter 15 described the Kalman filter, which represents the belief state as a single multivariate Gaussian, and the particle filter, which represents the belief state by a collection of particles that correspond to states. Most modern localization algorithms use one of two representations of the robot's belief $\mathbf{P}(\mathbf{X}_t \mid \mathbf{z}_{1:t}, a_{1:t-1})$.

MONTE CARLO LOCALIZATION

Localization using particle filtering is called **Monte Carlo localization**, or MCL. The MCL algorithm is essentially identical to the particle-filtering algorithm of Figure 15.15. All we need to do is supply the appropriate motion model and sensor model. Figure 25.7 shows one version using the range scan model. The operation of the algorithm is illustrated in Figure 25.8 as the robot finds out where it is inside an office building. In the first image, the particles are uniformly distributed based on the prior, indicating global uncertainty about the robot's position. In the second image, the first set of measurements arrives and the particles form clusters in the areas of high posterior belief. In the third, enough measurements are available to push all the particles to a single location.

The Kalman filter is the other major way to localize. A Kalman filter represents the posterior $\mathbf{P}(\mathbf{X}_t \mid \mathbf{z}_{1:t}, a_{1:t-1})$ by a Gaussian. The mean of this Gaussian will be denoted $\boldsymbol{\mu}_t$ and its covariance $\boldsymbol{\Sigma}_t$. The main problem with Gaussian beliefs is that they are only closed under linear motion models $f$ and linear measurement models $h$. For nonlinear $f$ or $h$, the result of

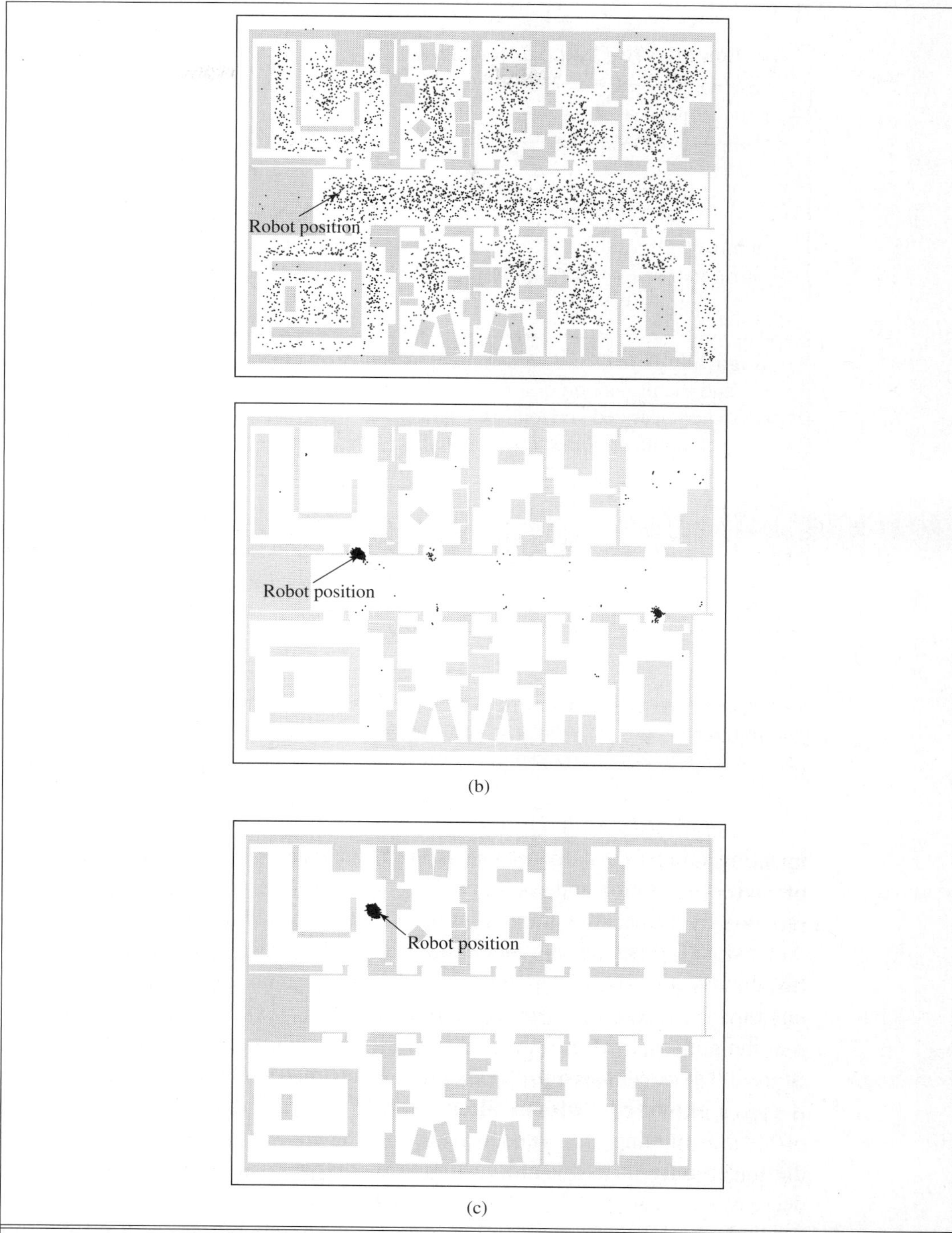


**Figure 25.8** Monte Carlo localization, a particle-filter algorithm for mobile robot localization. Top: initial, global uncertainty. Middle: approximately bimodal uncertainty after navigating in the (symmetric) corridor. Bottom: unimodal uncertainty after entering a distinctive office.

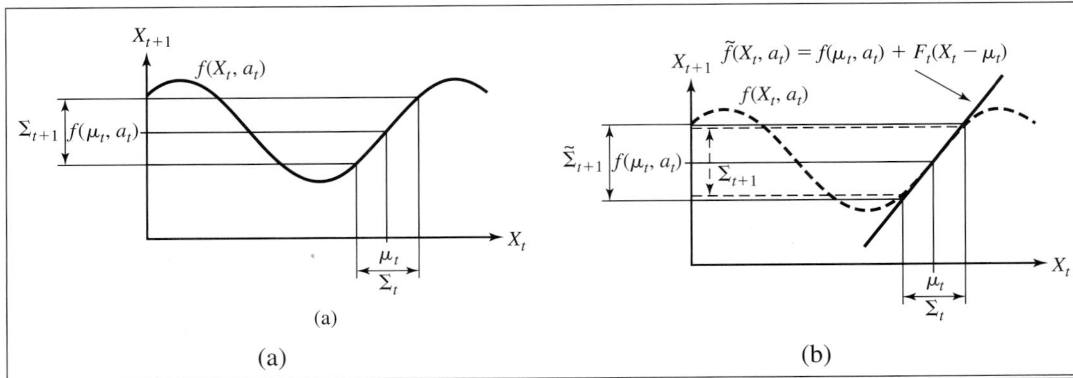


**Figure 25.9** One-dimensional illustration of a linearized motion model: (a) The function $f$, and the projection of a mean $\boldsymbol{\mu}_t$ and a covariance interval (based on $\boldsymbol{\Sigma}_t$) into time $t+1$. (b) The linearized version is the tangent of $f$ at $\boldsymbol{\mu}_t$. The projection of the mean $\boldsymbol{\mu}_t$ is correct. However, the projected covariance $\tilde{\boldsymbol{\Sigma}}_{t+1}$ differs from $\boldsymbol{\Sigma}_{t+1}$.

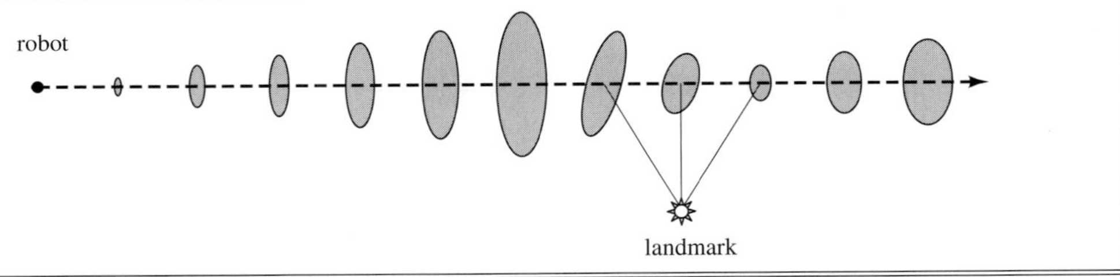


**Figure 25.10** Example of localization using the extended Kalman filter. The robot moves on a straight line. As it progresses, its uncertainty increases gradually, as illustrated by the error ellipses. When it observes a landmark with known position, the uncertainty is reduced.

updating a filter is usually not Gaussian. Thus, localization algorithms using the Kalman filter **linearize** the motion and sensor models. Linearization is a local approximation of a nonlinear function by a linear function. Figure 25.9 illustrates the concept of linearization for a (one-dimensional) robot motion model. On the left, it depicts a nonlinear motion model $f(\mathbf{x}_t, a_t)$ (the control $a_t$ is omitted in this graph since it plays no role in the linearization). On the right, this function is approximated by a linear function $\tilde{f}(\mathbf{x}_t, a_t)$. This linear function is tangent to $f$ at the point $\boldsymbol{\mu}_t$, the mean of our state estimate at time $t$. Such a linearization is called (first degree) **Taylor expansion**. A Kalman Filter that linearizes $f$ and $h$ via Taylor expansion is called **extended Kalman filter** (or EKF). Figure 25.10 shows a sequence of estimates of a robot running an extended Kalman filter localization algorithm. As the robot moves, the uncertainty in its location estimate increases, as shown by the error ellipses. Its error decreases as it senses the range and bearing to a landmark with known location. The error finally increases again as the robot loses sight of the landmark. EKF algorithms work well if landmarks are easily identified. Otherwise, the posterior distribution may be multimodal, as in Figure 25.8(b). The problem of needing to know the identity of landmarks is an instance of the **data association** problem discussed at the end of Chapter 15.

LINEARIZATION

TAYLOR EXPANSION

## Mapping

So far, we discussed the problem of localizing a single object. In robotics, one often seeks to localize many objects. The classical example of such a problem is that of robotic mapping. Imagine a robot that is not given a map of its environment. Rather, it has to construct such a map by itself. Clearly, humankind has developed amazing skills in mapping places as big as our entire planet. So a natural problem in robotics is to devise algorithms that enable robots to do the same.

SIMULTANEOUS LOCALIZATION AND MAPPING

In the literature, the robot mapping problem is often referred to as **simultaneous localization and mapping**, abbreviated as **SLAM**. Not only must the robot construct a map, it must do so *without knowing where it is*. SLAM is one of the core problems in robotics. We will consider the version in which the environment is fixed. This is quite difficult enough; it gets much worse when the environment is allowed to change while the robot moves around.

From a statistical perspective, mapping is a Bayesian inference problem, just like localization. If we denote the map by $M$ and the robot pose at time $t$ by $\mathbf{X}_t$ as before, we can rewrite Equation (25.1) to include the entire map in the posterior:

$$\begin{aligned}&\mathbf{P}(\mathbf{X}_{t+1}, M \mid \mathbf{z}_{1:t+1}, a_{1:t})\\&= \alpha\mathbf{P}(\mathbf{z}_{t+1} \mid \mathbf{X}_{t+1}, M) \int \mathbf{P}(\mathbf{X}_{t+1} \mid \mathbf{x}_t, a_t)\; P(\mathbf{x}_t, M \mid \mathbf{z}_{1:t}, a_{1:t-1})\; d\mathbf{x}_t\,.\end{aligned}$$

This equation actually conveys some good news: the conditional distributions needed for incorporating actions and measurements are essentially the same as in the robot localization problem. The main caveat is that the new state space—the space of all robot poses and all maps—has many more dimensions. Just imagine you want to represent an entire building in a photo-realistic way. This will probably require hundreds of millions of numbers. Each number will be a random variable and contributes to the enormously high dimension of the state space. What makes this problem even harder is that fact that the robot may not even know in advance how large its environment is. Thus, the dimensionality of $M$ has to be adjusted dynamically during mapping.

Probably the most widely used method for the SLAM problem is the EKF. It is usually combined with a landmark sensing model and requires that the landmarks are all distinguishable. In the previous section, the posterior estimate was represented by a Gaussian with mean $\boldsymbol{\mu}_t$ and covariance $\boldsymbol{\Sigma}_t$. In the EKF approach to the SLAM problem, the posterior is again Gaussian, but now the mean $\boldsymbol{\mu}_t$ is a much larger vector. It comprises not only the robot pose but also the location of all features (or landmarks) in the map. If there are $n$ such features, this vector will be of dimension $2n + 3$ (it takes two values to specify a landmark location and three to specify the robot pose). Consequently, the matrix $\boldsymbol{\Sigma}_t$ is of dimension $(2n + 3)$ by $(2n + 3)$. It possesses the following structure:

$$\boldsymbol{\Sigma}_t = \begin{pmatrix} \boldsymbol{\Sigma}_{XX} & \boldsymbol{\Sigma}_{XM} \\ \boldsymbol{\Sigma}_{XM}^{\top} & \boldsymbol{\Sigma}_{MM} \end{pmatrix}. \tag{25.2}$$

Here $\boldsymbol{\Sigma}_{XX}$ is the robot pose covariance, which we already encountered in the context of localization. $\boldsymbol{\Sigma}_{XM}$ is a matrix of size 3 by $2n$ that expresses the correlation between features in the map and robot coordinates. Finally, $\boldsymbol{\Sigma}_{MM}$ is a matrix of size $2n$ by $2n$ that specifies

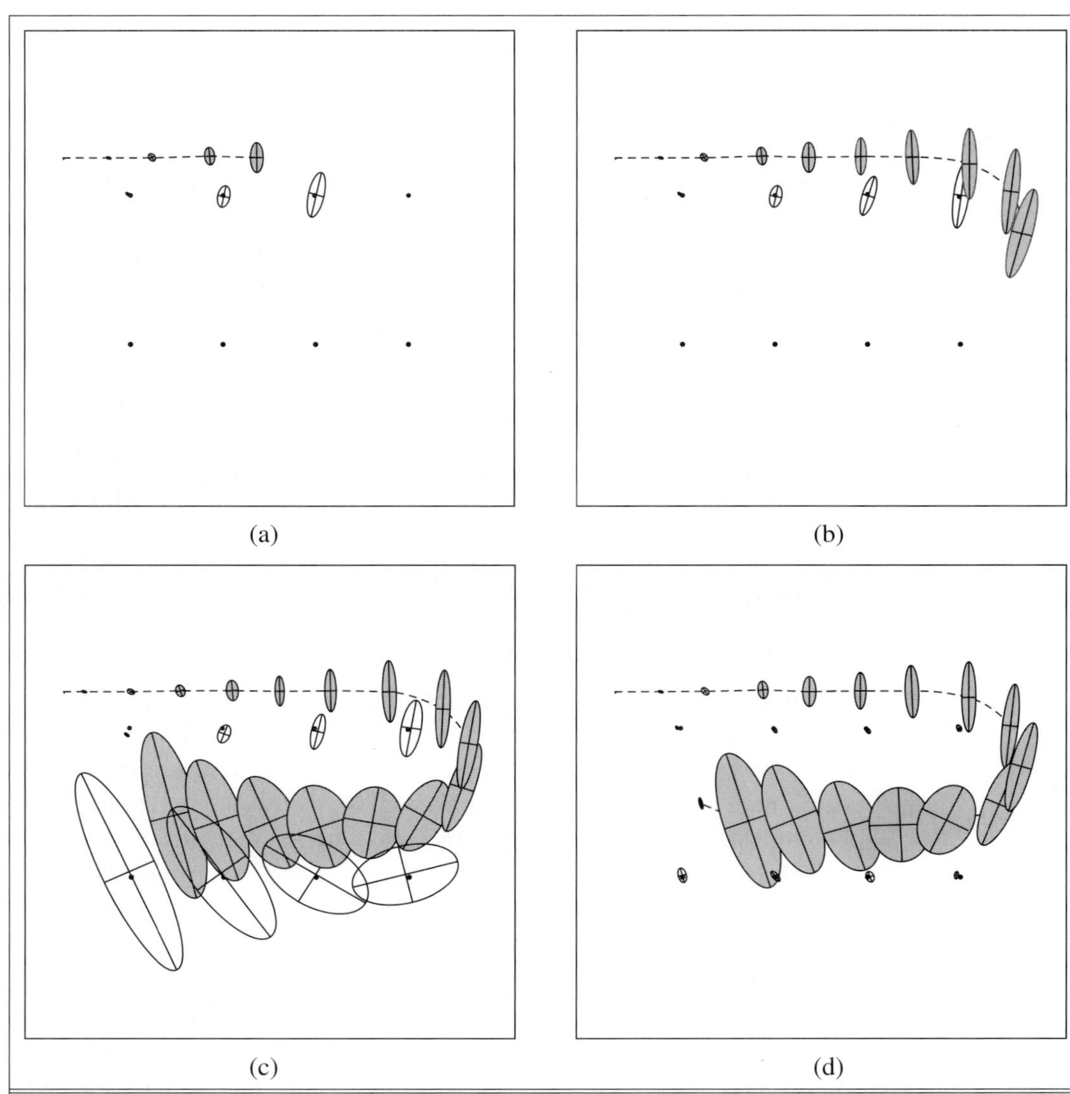


**Figure 25.11** EKF applied to the robot mapping problem. The robot's path is a dotted line, and its estimations of its own position are shaded ellipses. Eight distinguishable landmarks of unknown location are shown as small dots, and their location estimations are shown as white ellipses. In (a)–(c) the robot's positional uncertainty is increasing, as is its uncertainty about the landmarks it encounters. stages during which the robot encounters new landmarks, which are mapped with increasing uncertainty. In (d) the robot senses the first landmark again, and the uncertainty of *all* landmarks decreases, thanks to the fact that the estimates are correlated.

the covariance of features in the map, including all pairwise correlations. The memory requirements for EKFs are therefore quadratic in $n$, the number of features in the map, and the updating time is also quadratic in $n$.

Before delving into mathematical detail, let us study the EKF solution graphically. Figure 25.11 shows a robot in an environment with eight landmarks, arranged in two rows of four landmarks each. Initially, the robot has no idea where the landmarks are located. We will suppose that each landmark is a different color, and the robot can reliably detect which is which. The robot starts at a well-defined location towards the left, but it gradually loses certainty as to where it is. This is indicated by the error ellipses in Figure 25.11(a), whose width increases as the robot moves forward. As the robot moves, it senses the range and bearing to nearby landmarks, and these observations lead to estimates of the location of these landmarks. Naturally, the uncertainty in these landmark estimation is closely tied to the uncertainty in the robot's localization. Figures 25.11(b) and (c) illustrate the robot's belief as it moves further and further through its environment.

An important detail of all these estimates—which is not at all obvious from our graphical depiction—is the fact that we are maintaining a *single* Gaussian over all estimates. The error ellipses in Figure 25.11 are merely projections of this Gaussian into the subspaces of robot and landmark coordinates. This multivariate Gaussian posterior maintains correlations between all estimates. This observation becomes important for understanding what happens in Figure 25.11(d). Here the robot observes a previously mapped landmark. As a result, its own uncertainty shrinks tremendously. So does the uncertainty of all other landmarks. This is a consequence of the fact that the robot estimate and the landmark estimates are highly correlated in the posterior Gaussian. Finding out knowledge about one variable (here the robot pose) automatically reduces the uncertainty in all others.

The EKF algorithm for mapping resembles the EKF localization algorithm in the previous section. The key difference here arises from the added landmark variables in the posterior. The motion model for landmarks is trivial: they don't move. The function $f$, therefore, is the identity function for those variables. The measurement function is essentially the same as before. The only difference is that the Jacobian $H_t$ in the EKF update equation is taken not only with respect to the robot pose, but also with respect to the landmark location that was observed at time $t$. The resulting EKF equations are even more horrifying than the ones stated before, for which reason we will simply omit them here.

However, there is another difficulty that we have silently ignored so far: the fact that the size of the map $M$ is not known in advance. Hence, the number of elements in the final estimate $\boldsymbol{\mu}_t$ and $\boldsymbol{\Sigma}_t$ is unknown as well. It has to be determined dynamically as the robot discovers new landmarks. The solution to this problem is quite straightforward: as the robot discovers a new landmark, it simply adds a new element to the posterior. By initializing the variance of this new element to a very large value, the resulting posterior is the same as if the robot had known of the existence of the landmark in advance.

## Other types of perception

Not all of robot perception is about localization and mapping. Robots also perceive the temperature, odors, acoustic signals, and so on. Many of these quantities can be estimated probabilistically, just as in localization and mapping. All that is required for such estimators are conditional probability distributions that characterize the evolution of state variables over time, and other distributions that describe the relation of measurements to state variables.

However, not all working perception systems in robotics rely on probabilistic representations. In fact, while the internal state in all our examples had a clear physical interpretation, this does not necessarily have to be the case. For example, picture a legged robot that attempts to lift a leg over an obstacle. Suppose this robot uses a rule by which it initially moves the leg at a low height, but then lifts it higher and higher if the previous height resulted in a collision with this obstacle. Would we say that the commanded leg height is a representation of some physical quantity in the world? Maybe, in that it relates to the height and steepness of an obstacle. However, we can also think of the leg height as an auxiliary variable of the robot controller, devoid of direct physical meaning. Such representations are not uncommon in robotics, and for certain problems they work well.

The trend in robotics is clearly towards representations with well-defined semantics. Probabilistic techniques outperform other approaches in many hard perceptual problems such as localization and mapping. However, statistical techniques are sometimes too cumbersome, and simpler solutions may be just as effective in practice. To help decide which approach to take, experience working with real physical robots is the best teacher.

## 25.4 PLANNING TO MOVE

POINT-TO-POINT MOTION

COMPLIANT MOTION

In robotics, decisions ultimately involve motion of effectors. The **point-to-point motion** problem is to deliver the robot or its end-effector to a designated target location. A greater challenge is the **compliant motion** problem, in which a robot moves while being in physical contact with an obstacle. An example of compliant motion is a robot manipulator that screws in a light bulb, or a robot that pushes a box across a table top.

PATH PLANNING

We begin by finding a suitable representation in which motion planning problems can be described and solved. It turns out that the **configuration space**—the space of robot states defined by location, orientation, and joint angles—is a better place to work than the original 3D space. The **path planning** problem is to find a path from one configuration to another in configuration space. We have already encountered various versions of the path planning problem throughout this book; in robotics, the primary characteristic of path planning is that it involves *continuous* spaces. The literature on robot path planning distinguishes a range of different techniques specifically aimed at finding paths in high-dimensional continuous spaces. The major families of approaches are known as **cell decomposition** and **skeletonization**. Each reduces the continuous path-planning problem to a discrete graph search problem by identifying some canonical states and paths within the free space. Throughout this section, we assume that motion is deterministic and that localization of the robot is exact. Subsequent sections will relax these assumptions.

### Configuration space

The first step towards a solution to the robot motion problem is to devise an appropriate problem representation. We will start with a simple representation for a simple problem. Consider the robot arm shown in Figure 25.12(a). It has two joints that move independently.

Moving the joints alters the $(x, y)$ coordinates of the elbow and the gripper. (The arm cannot move in the $z$ direction.) This suggests that the robot's configuration can be described by a four-dimensional coordinate: $(x_e, y_e)$ for the location of the elbow relative to the environment and $(x_g, y_g)$ for the location of the gripper. Clearly, these four coordinates characterize the full state of the robot. They constitute what is known as **workspace** representation, since the coordinates of the robot are specified in the same coordinate system as the objects it seeks to manipulate (or to avoid). Workspace representations are well-suited for collision checking, especially if the robot and all objects are represented by simple polygonal models.

WORKSPACE

The problem with the workspace representation is that not all workspace coordinates are actually attainable, even in the absence of obstacles. This is because of the **linkage constraints** on the space of attainable workspace coordinates. For example, the elbow position $(x_e, y_e)$ and the gripper position $(x_g, y_g)$ are always a fixed distance apart, because they are joined by a rigid forearm. A robot motion planner defined over workspace coordinates faces the challenge of generating paths that adhere to these constraints. This is particularly tricky because the state space is continuous and the constraints are nonlinear.

LINKAGE CONSTRAINTS

CONFIGURATION SPACE

It turns out to be easier to plan with a **configuration space** representation. Instead of representing the state of the robot by the Cartesian coordinates of its elements, we represent the state by a configuration of the robot's joints. Our example robot possesses two joints. Hence, we can represent its state with the two angles $\varphi_s$ and $\varphi_e$ for the shoulder joint and elbow joint, respectively. In the absence of any obstacles, a robot could freely take on any value in configuration space. In particular, when planning a path one could simply connect the present and the target configuration by a straight line. In following this path, the robot would then change its joints at a constant velocity, until a target location is reached.

Unfortunately, configuration spaces have their own problems. The task of a robot is usually expressed in workspace coordinates, not in configuration space coordinates. For example, we might want a robot to move its end-effector to a certain coordinate in workspace, possibly with a specification of its orientation as well. This raises the question as to how to map such workspace coordinates into configuration space. In general the *inverse* of this problem, transforming configuration space coordinates into workspace coordinates, is simple: it involves a series of quite obvious coordinate transformations. These transformations are linear for prismatic joints and trigonometric for revolute joints. This chain of coordinate transformation is known as **kinematics**, a term we already encountered when discussion mobile robots.

INVERSE KINEMATICS

The inverse problem of calculating the configuration of a robot whose effector location is specified in workspace coordinates is known as **inverse kinematics**. Calculating the inverse kinematics is generally hard, especially for robots with many DOFs. In particular, the solution is seldom unique. For our example robot arm, there are two distinct configurations for which the gripper takes on the same workspace coordinates as in the figure.

In general, this two-link robot arm has between zero and two inverse kinematic solutions for any set of workspace coordinates. Most industrial robots have infinitely many solutions. To see how this is possible, simply imagine we added a third revolute joint to our example robot, one whose rotational axis is parallel to the ones of the existing joint. In such a case, we can keep the location (but not the orientation!) of the gripper fixed and still freely rotate its

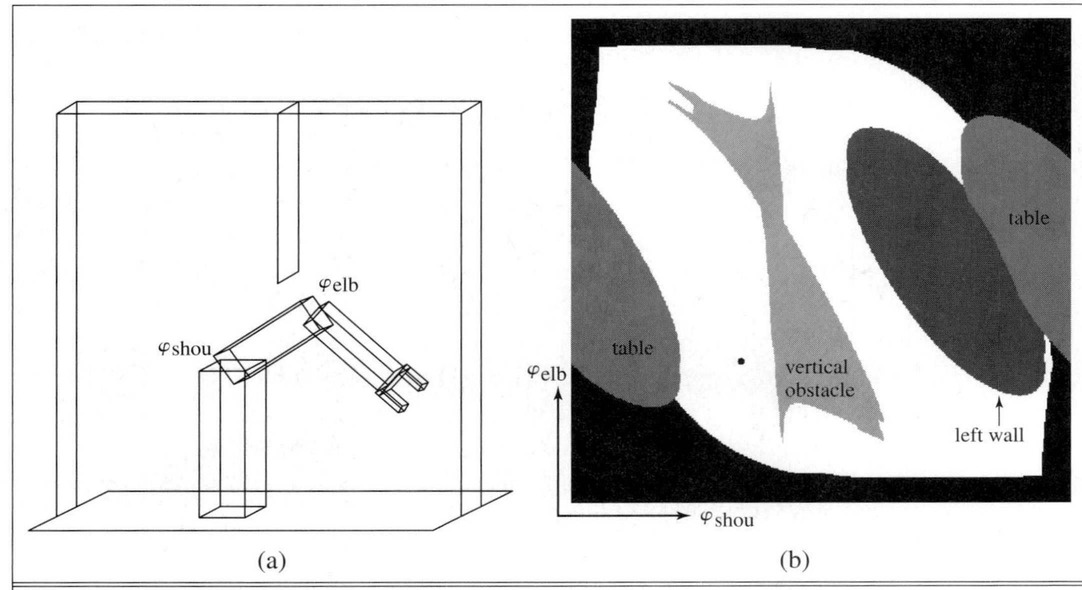


**Figure 25.12** (a) Workspace representation of a robot arm with 2 DOFs. The workspace is a box with a flat obstacle hanging from the ceiling. (b) Configuration space of the same robot. Only white regions in the space are configurations that are free of collisions. The dot in this diagram corresponds to the configuration of the robot shown on the left.

internal joints, for most configurations of the robot. With a few more joints (how many?) we can achieve the same effect while keeping the orientation constant as well. We have already seen an example of this in the "experiment" of placing your hand on the desk and moving your elbow. The kinematic constraint of your hand position is insufficient to determine the configuration of your elbow. In other words, the inverse kinematics of your shoulder–arm assembly possesses an infinite number of solutions.

The second problem with configuration space representations arises from the obstacles that may exist in the robot's workspace. Our example in Figure 25.12(a) shows several such obstacles, including a free hanging obstacle that protrudes into the center of the robot's workspace. In workspace, such obstacles take on simple geometric forms—especially in most robotics textbooks, which tend to focus on polygonal obstacles. But how do they look in configuration space?

Figure 25.12(b) shows the configuration space for our example robot, under the specific obstacle configuration shown in Figure 25.12(a). The configuration space can be decomposed into two subspaces: the space of all configurations that a robot may attain, commonly called **free space**, and the space of unattainable configurations, called **occupied space**. The white area in Figure 25.12(b) corresponds to the free space. All other regions correspond to occupied space. The different shading of the occupied space corresponds to the different objects in the robot's workspace; the black region surrounding the entire free space corresponds to configurations in which the robot collides with itself. It is easy to see that extreme values of the shoulder or elbow angles cause such a violation. The two oval-shaped regions on both

FREE SPACE

OCCUPIED SPACE

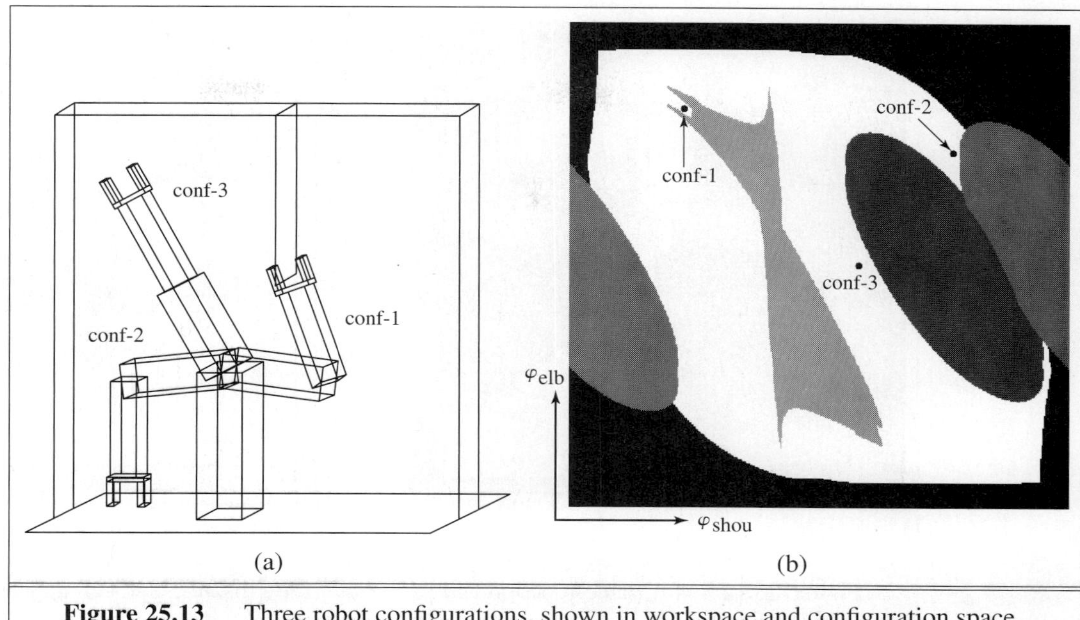


**Figure 25.13** Three robot configurations, shown in workspace and configuration space.

sides of the robot correspond to the table on which the robot is mounted. Similarly, the third oval region corresponds to the left wall. Finally, the most interesting object in configuration space is the simple vertical obstacle impeding the robot's workspace. This object has a funny shape: it is highly nonlinear and at places even concave. With a little bit of imagination the reader will recognize the shape of the gripper at the upper left end. We encourage the reader to pause for a moment and study this important diagram. The shape of this obstacle is not at all obvious! The dot inside Figure 25.12(b) marks the configuration of the robot, as shown in Figure 25.12(a). Figure 25.13 depicts three additional configurations, both in workspace and in configuration space. In configuration "conf-1," the gripper encloses the vertical obstacle.

In general, even if the robot's workspace is represented by flat polygons, the shape of the free space can be very complicated. In practice, therefore, one usually *probes* a configuration space instead of constructing it explicitly. A planner may generate a configuration and then test to see if it is in free space by applying the robot kinematics and then checking for collisions in workspace coordinates.

## Cell decomposition methods

Our first approach to path planning uses **cell decomposition**—that is, it decomposes the free space into a finite number of contiguous regions, called cells. These regions have the important property that the path planning problem within a single region can be solved by simple means (e.g., moving along a straight line). The path planning problem then becomes a discrete graph search problem, very much like the search problems introduced in Chapter 3.

The simplest cell decomposition consists of a regularly spaced grid. Figure 25.14(a) shows a square grid decomposition of the space and a solution path that is optimal for this

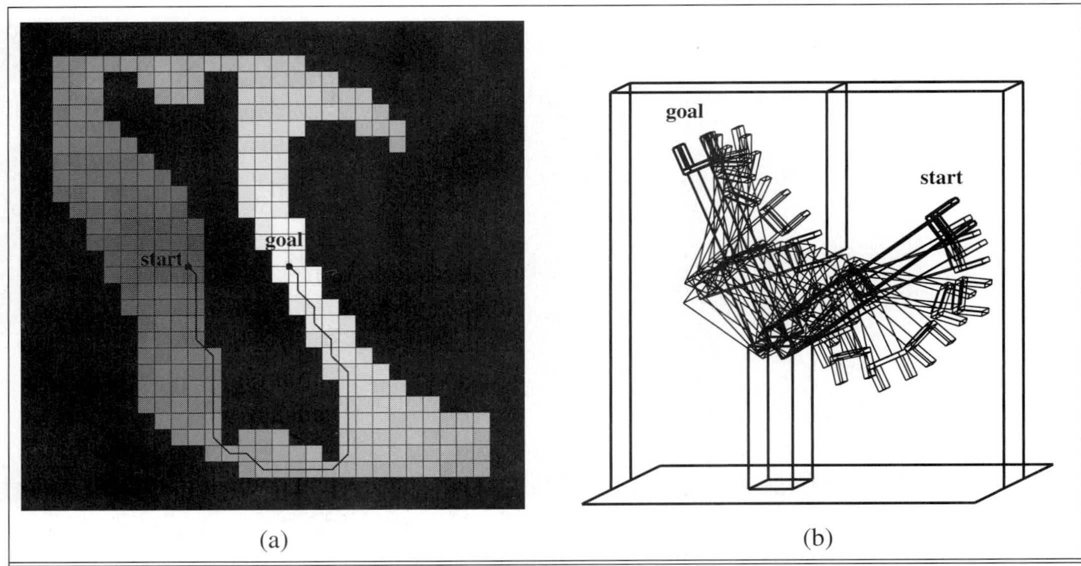


**Figure 25.14** (a) Value function and path found for a discrete grid cell approximation of the configuration space. (b) The same path visualized in workspace coordinates. Notice how the robot bends its elbow to avoid a collision with the vertical obstacle.

grid size. We have also used grayscale shading to indicate the *value* of each free-space grid cell—i.e., the cost of the shortest path from that cell to the goal. (These values can be computed by a deterministic form of the VALUE-ITERATION algorithm given in Figure 17.4.) Figure 25.14(b) shows the corresponding work space trajectory for the arm.

Such a decomposition has the advantage that it is extremely simple to implement, but it also suffers from two limitations. First, it is only workable for low-dimensional configuration spaces, as the number of grid cells increases exponentially with $d$, the number of dimensions. Second, there is the problem of what to do with cells that are "mixed"—that is, neither entirely within free space nor entirely within occupied space. A solution path that includes such a cell may not be a real solution, because there may be no way to cross the cell in the desired direction in a straight line. This would make the path planner *unsound*. On the other hand, if we insist that only completely free cells may be used, the planner will be *incomplete*, because it might be the case that the only paths to the goal may go through mixed cells—especially if the cell size is comparable to that of the passageways and clearances in the space.

There are two ways to fix the cell decomposition method to avoid these problems. The first is to allow *further subdivision* of the mixed cells—perhaps using cells of half the original size. This can be continued recursively until a path is found that lies entirely within free cells. (Of course, the method only works if there is a way to decide if a given cell is a mixed cell, which is easy only if the configuration space boundaries have relatively simple mathematical descriptions.) This method is complete provided there is a bound on the smallest passageway through which a solution must pass. Although it focuses most of the computational effort on the tricky areas within the configuration space, it still fails to scale well to high-dimensional

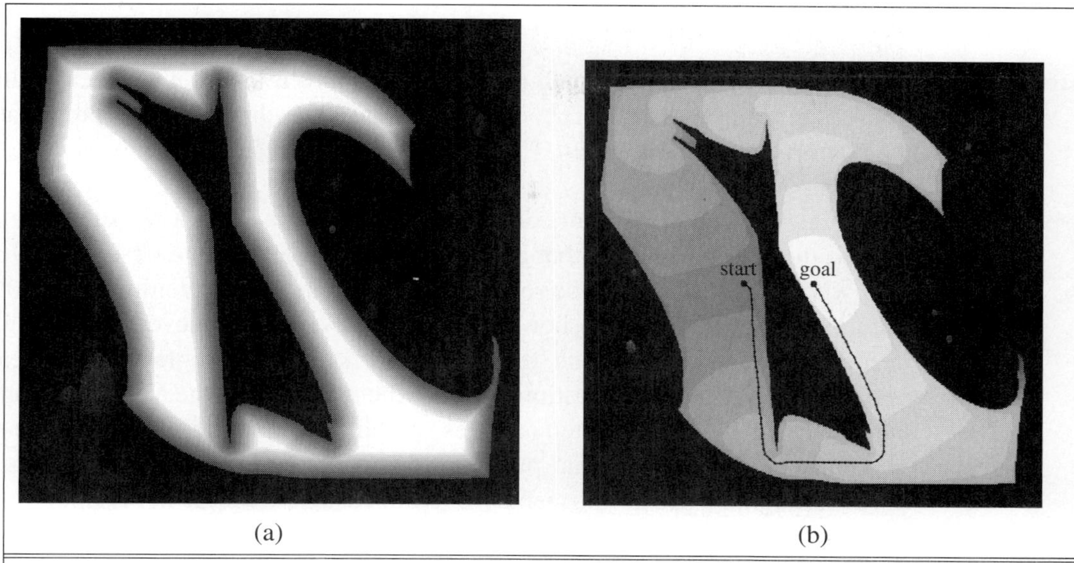


**Figure 25.15** (a) A repelling potential field pushes the robot away from obstacles. (b) Path found by simultaneously minimizing path length and the potential.

problems because each recursive splitting of a cell creates $2^d$ smaller cells. A second way to obtain a complete algorithm is to insist on an **exact cell decomposition** of the free space. This method must allow cells to be irregularly shaped where they meet the boundaries of free space, but the shapes must still be "simple" in the sense that it should be easy to compute a traversal of any free cell. This technique requires some quite advanced geometric ideas, so we shall not pursue it further here.

EXACT CELL DECOMPOSITION

Examining the solution path shown in Figure 25.14(a), we can see additional difficulties that will have to be resolved. First, notice that the path contains arbitrarily sharp corners; a robot moving at any finite speed could not execute such a path. Second, notice that the path goes very close to the obstacle. Anyone who has driven a car knows that a parking lot stall with one millimeter of clearance on either side is not really a parking space at all; for the same reason, we would prefer solution paths that are robust with respect to small motion errors.

POTENTIAL FIELD

We would like to maximize the clearance from obstacles while minimizing the path length. This can be achieved by introducing a **potential field**. A potential field is a function defined over state space, whose value grows with the distance to the closest obstacle. Figure 25.15(a) shows such a potential field—the darker a configuration state, the closer it is to an obstacle. When used in path planning, this potential field becomes an additional cost term in the optimization. This induces an interesting trade-off. On the one hand, the robot seeks to minimize path length to the goal. On the other, it tries to stay away from obstacles by virtue of minimizing the potential function. With the appropriate weight between both objectives, a resulting path may look like the one shown in Figure 25.15(b). This figure also displays the value function derived from the combined cost function, again calculated by value iteration. Clearly, the resulting path is longer, but it is also safer.

### Skeletonization methods

SKELETONIZATION

The second major family of path-planning algorithms is based on the idea of **skeletonization**. These algorithms reduce the robot's free space to a one-dimensional representation, for which the planning problem is easier. This lower-dimensional representation is called a **skeleton** of the configuration space.

VORONOI GRAPH

Figure 25.16 shows an example skeletonization: it is a **Voronoi graph** of the free space—the set of all points that are equidistant to two or more obstacles. To do path planning with a Voronoi graph, the robot first changes its present configuration to a point on the Voronoi graph. It is easy to show that this can always be achieved by a straight-line motion in configuration space. Second, the robot follows the Voronoi graph until it reaches the point nearest to the target configuration. Finally, the robot leaves the Voronoi graph and moves to the target. Again, this final step involves straight-line motion in configuration space.

In this way, the original path-planning problem is reduced to finding a path on the Voronoi diagram, which is generally one-dimensional (except in certain non-generic cases) and has finitely many points where three or more one-dimensional curves intersect. Thus, finding the shortest path along the Voronoi graph is a discrete graph search problem of the kind discussed in Chapters 3 and 4. Following the Voronoi graph may not give us the shortest path, but the resulting paths tend to maximize clearance. Disadvantages of Voronoi graph techniques are that they are difficult to apply to higher dimensional configuration spaces, and that they tend to induce unnecessarily large detours when the configuration space is wide open. Furthermore, computing the Voronoi diagram can be difficult, specifically in configuration space, where the shape of obstacles can be complex.

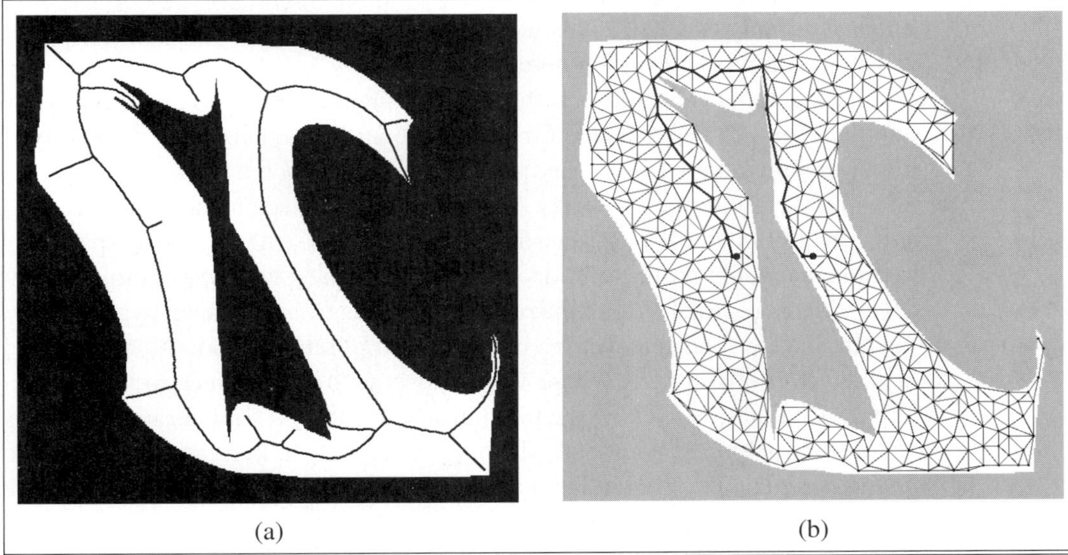


**Figure 25.16** (a) The Voronoi diagram is the set of points equidistant to two or more obstacles in configuration space. (b) A probabilistic roadmap, composed of 400 randomly chosen points in free space.

PROBABILISTIC ROADMAP

An alternative to the Voronoi diagrams is the **probabilistic roadmap**, a skeletonization approach that offers more possible routes, and thus deals better with wide open spaces. Figure 25.16(b) shows an example of a probabilistic roadmap. The graph is created by randomly generating a large number of configurations, and discarding those that do not fall into free space. Then, we join any two nodes by an arc if it is "easy" to reach one node from the other–for example, by a straight line in free space. The result of all this is a randomized graph in the robot's free space. If we add the robot's start and target configurations to this graph, path planning amounts to a discrete graph search. Theoretically, this approach is incomplete, because a bad choice of random points may leave us without any paths from start to target. It is possible to bound the probability of failure in terms of the number of points generated and certain geometric properties of the configuration space. It is also possibly to direct the generation of sample points towards the areas where a partial search suggests that a good path may be found, working bidirectionally from both the start and the goal positions. With these improvements, probabilistic roadmap planning tends to scale better to high-dimensional configuration spaces than most alternative path planning techniques.

## 25.5 PLANNING UNCERTAIN MOVEMENTS

None of the robot motion planning algorithms discussed thus far addresses a key characteristic of robotics problems: *uncertainty*. In robotics, uncertainty arises from partial observability of the environment and from the stochastic (or unmodeled) effects of the robot's actions. Errors can also arise from the use of approximation algorithms such as particle filtering, which does not provide the robot with an exact belief state even if the stochastic nature of the environment is modeled perfectly.

Most of today's robots use deterministic algorithms for decision making, such as the various path planning algorithms discussed thus far. To do so, it is common practice to extract the **most likely state** from the state distribution produced by the localization algorithm. The advantage of this approach is purely computational. Planning paths through configuration space is already a challenging problem; it would be worse if we had to work with a full probability distribution over states. Ignoring uncertainty in this way works when the uncertainty is small.

MOST LIKELY STATE

Unfortunately, ignoring the uncertainty does not always work. In some problems the robot's uncertainty is simply too large. For example, how can we use a deterministic path planner to control a mobile robot that has no clue where it is? In general, if the robot's true state is not the one identified by the maximum likelihood rule, the resulting control will be suboptimal. Depending on the magnitude of the error this can lead to all sorts of unwanted effects, such as collisions with obstacles.

The field of robotics has adopted a range of techniques for accommodating uncertainty. Some are derived from the algorithms given in Chapter 17 for decision making under uncertainty. If the robot only faces uncertainty in its state transition, but its state is fully observable, the problem is best modeled as a *Markov Decision process*, or MDP. The solution of an MDP is an optimal **policy**, which tells the robot what to do in every possible state. In this way, it can handle all sorts of motion errors, whereas a single-path solution from a deterministic planner would be much less robust. In robotics, policies are usually called **navigation functions**. The value function shown in Figure 25.14(a) can be converted into such a navigation function simply by following the gradient.

NAVIGATION FUNCTIONS

Just as in Chapter 17, partial observability makes the problem much harder. The resulting robot control problem is a **partially observable MDP**, or POMDP. In such situations, the robot usually maintains an internal belief state, like the ones discussed in Section 25.3. The solution to a POMDP is a policy defined over the robot's belief state. Put differently, the input to the policy is an entire probability distribution. This enables the robot to base its decision not only on what it knows, but also on what it does not know. For example, if it is uncertain about a critical state variable, it can rationally invoke an **information gathering action**. This is impossible in the MDP framework, since MDPs assume full observability. Unfortunately, techniques that solve POMDPs exactly are inapplicable to robotics—there are no known techniques for continuous spaces. Discretization usually produces POMDPs that are far too large for known techniques to handle. All we can do at present is to try to keep the pose uncertainty to a minimum; for example, the **coastal navigation** heuristic requires the robot to stay near known landmarks to decrease its pose uncertainty. This, in turn, gradually decreases the uncertainty in the mapping of new landmarks that are nearby, which then allows the robot to explore more territory.

INFORMATION GATHERING ACTION

COASTAL NAVIGATION

### Robust methods

ROBUST

Uncertainty can also be handled using so-called **robust** methods rather than probabilistic methods. A robust method is one that assumes a *bounded* amount of uncertainty in each aspect of a problem, but does not assign probabilities to values within the allowed interval. A robust solution is one that works no matter what actual values occur, provided they are within the assumed interval. An extreme form of robust method is the **conformant planning** approach given in Chapter 12—it produces plans that work with no state information at all.

FINE-MOTION PLANNING

Here, we look at a robust method that is used for **fine-motion planning** (or FMP) in robotic assembly tasks. Fine motion planning involves moving a robot arm in very close proximity to a static environment object. The main difficulty with fine-motion planning is that the required motions and the relevant features of the environment are very small. At such small scales, the robot is unable to measure or control its position accurately and may also be uncertain of the shape of the environment itself; we will assume that these uncertainties are all bounded. The solutions to FMP problems will typically be conditional plans or policies that make use of sensor feedback during execution and are guaranteed to work in all situations consistent with the assumed uncertainty bounds.

A fine-motion plan consists of a series of **guarded motions**. Each guarded motion consists of (1) a motion command and (2) a termination condition, which is a predicate on the robot's sensor values, and returns true to indicate the end of the guarded move. The motion commands are typically **compliant motions** that allow the robot to slide if the motion command would cause collision with an obstacle. As an example, Figure 25.17 shows a

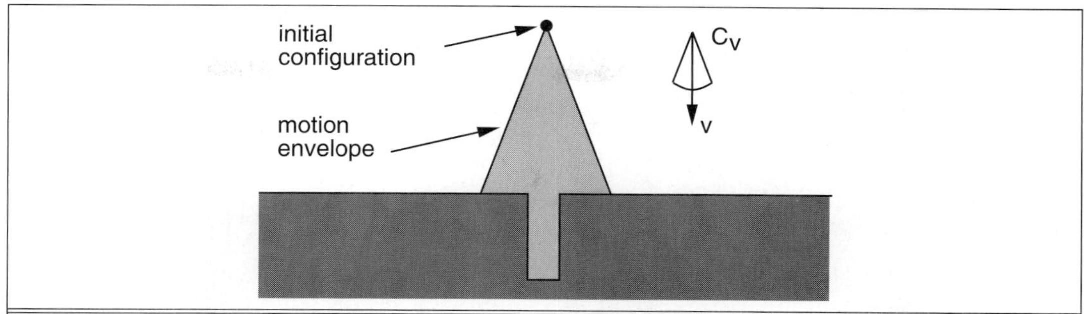


**Figure 25.17** A two-dimensional environment, velocity uncertainty cone, and envelope of possible robot motions. The intended velocity is $v$, but with uncertainty the actual velocity could be anywhere in $C_v$, resulting in a final configuration somewhere in the motion envelope, which means we wouldn't know if we hit the hole or not.

two-dimensional configuration space with a narrow vertical hole. It could be the configuration space for insertion of a rectangular peg into a hole that is slightly larger. The motion commands are constant velocities. The termination conditions are contact with a surface. To model uncertainty in control, we assume that instead of moving in the commanded direction, the robot's actual motion lies in the cone $C_v$ about it. The figure shows what would happen if we commanded a velocity straight down from the start region $s$. Because of the uncertainty in velocity, the robot could move anywhere in the conical envelope, possibly going into the hole, but more likely landing to one side of it. Because the robot would not then know which side of the hole it was on, it would not know which way to move.

A more sensible strategy is shown in Figures 25.18 and 25.19. In Figure 25.18, the robot deliberately moves to one side of the hole. The motion command is shown in the figure, and the termination test is contact with any surface. In Figure 25.19, a motion command is given that causes the robot to slide along the surface and into the hole. This assumes we use a compliant motion command. Because all possible velocities in the motion envelope are to the right, the robot will slide to the right whenever it is in contact with a horizontal surface. It will slide down the right-hand vertical edge of the hole when it touches it, because all possible velocities are down relative to a vertical surface. It will keep moving until it reaches the bottom of the hole, because that is its termination condition. In spite of the control uncertainty, all possible trajectories of the robot terminate in contact with the bottom of the hole—that is, unless surface irregularities cause the robot to stick in one place.

As one might imagine, the problem of *constructing* fine-motion plans is not trivial; in fact, it is a good deal harder than planning with exact motions. One can either choose a fixed number of discrete values for each motion or use the environment geometry to choose directions that give qualitatively different behavior. A fine-motion planner takes as input the configuration-space description, the angle of the velocity uncertainty cone, and a specification of what sensing is possible for termination (surface contact in this case). It should produce a multistep conditional plan or policy that is guaranteed to succeed, if such a plan exists.

Our example assumes that the planner has an exact model of the environment, but it is possible to allow for bounded error in this model as follows. If the error can be described in

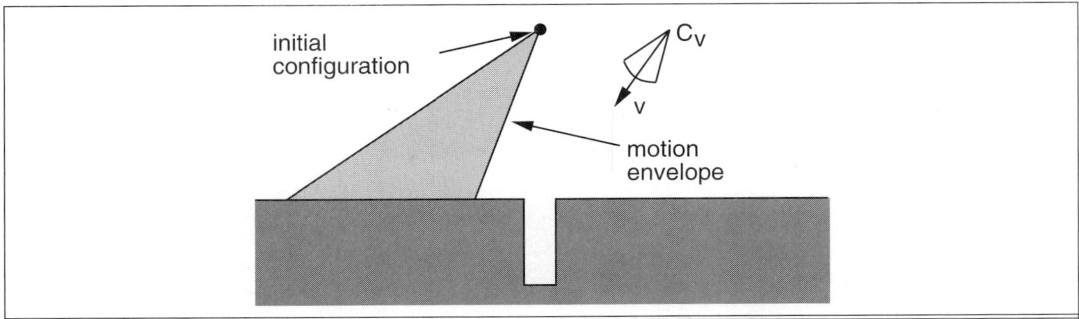


**Figure 25.18** The first motion command and the resulting envelope of possible robot motions. No matter what the error, we know the final configuration will be to the left of the hole.

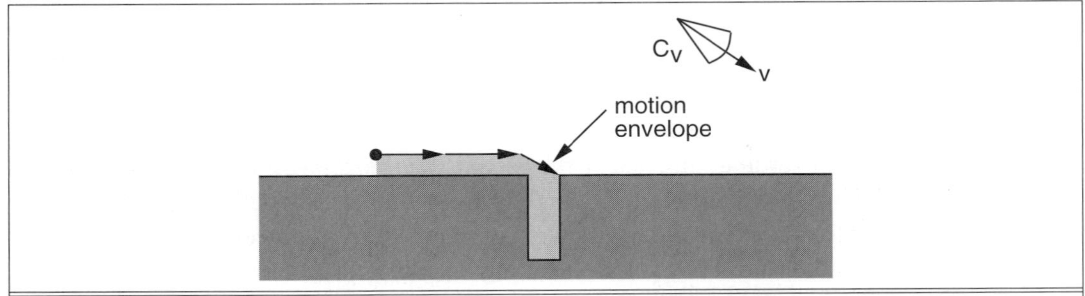


**Figure 25.19** The second motion command and the envelope of possible motions. Even with error, we will eventually get into the hole.

terms of parameters, those parameters can be added as degrees of freedom to the configuration space. In the last example, if the depth and width of the hole were uncertain, we could add them as two degrees of freedom to the configuration space. It is impossible to move the robot in these directions in the configuration space or to sense its position directly. But both those restrictions can be incorporated when describing this problem as an FMP problem by appropriately specifying control and sensor uncertainties. This gives a complex, four-dimensional planning problem, but exactly the same planning techniques can be applied. Notice that unlike the decision-theoretic methods in Chapter 17, this kind of robust approach results in plans designed for the worst-case outcome, rather than maximizing the expected quality of the plan. Worst-case plans are only optimal in the decision-theoretic sense if failure during execution is much worse than any of the other costs involved in execution.

## 25.6 MOVING

So far, we have talked about how to *plan* motions, but not about how to *move*. Our plans—particularly those produced by deterministic path planners—assume that the robot can simply follow any path that the algorithm produces. In the real world, of course, this is not the case.

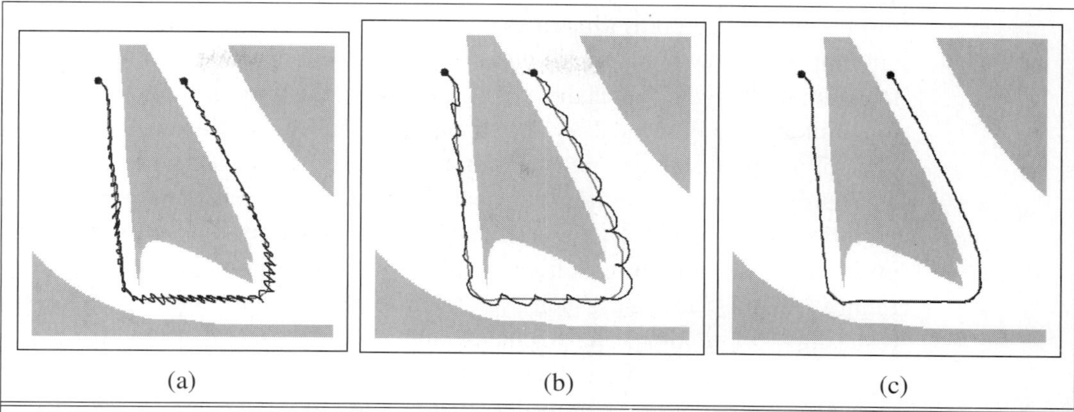


**Figure 25.20** Robot arm control using (a) proportional control with gain factor 1.0, (b) proportional control with gain factor 0.1, and (c) PD control with gain factors 0.3 for the proportional and 0.8 for the differential component. In all cases the robot arm tries to follow the path shown in gray.

Robots have inertia and cannot execute arbitrary paths except at arbitrarily slow speeds. In most cases, the robot gets to exert forces rather than specify positions. This section discusses methods for calculating these forces.

## Dynamics and control

Section 25.2 introduced the notion of **dynamic state**, which extends the kinematic state of a robot by modeling a robot's velocities. For example, in addition to the angle of a robot joint, the dynamic state also captures the rate of change of the angle. The transition model for a dynamic state representation includes the effect of forces on this rate of change. Such models are typically expressed via **differential equations**, which are equations that relate a quantity (e.g., a kinematic state) to the change of the quantity over time (e.g., velocity). In principle, we could have chosen to plan robot motion using dynamic models, instead of our kinematic models. Such a methodology would lead to superior robot performance, if we could generate the plans. However, the dynamic state is more complex than the kinematic space, and the curse of dimensionality would render motion planning problems intractable for all but the most simple robots. For this reason, practical robot system often rely on simpler kinematic path planners.

DIFFERENTIAL EQUATIONS

A common technique to compensate for the limitations of kinematic plans is to use a separate mechanism, a **controller**, for keeping the robot on track. Controllers are techniques for generating robot controls in real time using feedback from the environment, so as to achieve a control objective. If the objective is to keep the robot on a preplanned path, it is often referred to as a **reference controller** and the path is called a **reference path**. Controllers that optimize a global cost function are known as **optimal controllers**. Optimal policies for MDPs are, in effect, optimal controllers.

CONTROLLER

REFERENCE CONTROLLER

REFERENCE PATH

OPTIMAL CONTROLLERS

On the surface, the problem of keeping a robot on a pre-specified path appears to be relatively straightforward. In practice, however, even this seemingly simple problem has its pitfalls. Figure 25.20(a) illustrates what can go wrong. Shown there is the path of a robot that attempts to follow a kinematic path. Whenever a deviation occurs—whether due to noise or to constraints on the forces the robot can apply—the robot provides an opposing force whose magnitude is proportional to this deviation. Intuitively, this might appear plausible, since deviations should be compensated by a counter-force to keep the robot on track. However, as Figure 25.20(a) illustrates, our controller causes the robot to vibrate rather violently. The vibration is the result of a natural inertia of the robot arm: once driven back to its reference position the robot then overshoots, which induces a symmetric error with opposite sign. As Figure 25.20(a) illustrates, such overshooting may continue along an entire trajectory, and the resulting robot motion is far from desirable. Clearly, there is a need for better control.

To arrive at a better controller, let us formally describe the type of controller that produced the overshooting. Controllers that provide force in negative proportion to the observed error are known as **P controllers**. The letter P stands for *proportional*, indicating that the actual control is proportional to the error of the robot manipulator. More formally, let $y(t)$ be the reference path, parameterized by time index $t$. The control $a_t$ generated by a P controller has the following form:

P CONTROLLER

$$a_t = K_P(y(t) - x_t) .$$

GAIN PARAMETER

Here $x_t$ is the state of the robot at time $t$. $K_P$ is a so-called **gain parameter** of the controller that regulates how strongly the controller corrects for deviations between the actual state $x_t$ and the desired one $y(t)$. In our example, $K_P = 1$. At first glance, one might think that choosing a smaller value for $K_P$ remedies the problem. Unfortunately, this is not the case. Figure 25.20(b) shows a trajectory for $K_P = .1$, still exhibiting oscillatory behavior. Lower values of the gain parameter may simply slow down the oscillation, but do not solve the problem. In fact, in the absence of friction, the P controller is essentially a spring law; so it will oscillate indefinitely around a fixed target location.

Traditionally, problems of this type fall into the realm of **control theory**, a field of increasing importance to researchers in AI. Decades of research in this field have led to a large number of controllers that are superior to the simple control law given above. In particular, a reference controller is said to be **stable** if small perturbations lead to a bounded error between the robot and the reference signal. It is said to be **strictly stable** if it is able to return to its reference path upon such perturbations. Clearly, our P controller appears to be stable but not strictly stable, since it fails to return to its reference trajectory.

STABLE

STRICTLY STABLE

The simplest controller that achieves strict stability in our domain is known as a **PD controller**. The letter 'P' stands again for *proportional*, and 'D' stands for *derivative*. PD controllers are described by the following equation:

PD CONTROLLER

$$a_t = K_P(y(t) - x_t) + K_D \frac{\partial(y(t) - x_t)}{\partial t} . \tag{25.3}$$

As this equation suggests, PD controllers extend P controllers by a differential component, which adds to the value of $a_t$ a term that is proportional to the first derivative of the error $y(t) - x_t$ over time. What is the effect of such a term? In general, a derivative term dampens the system that is being controlled. To see, consider a situation where the error $(y(t) - x_t)$ is changing rapidly over time, as is the case for our P controller above. The derivative of this error will then counteract the proportional term, which will reduce the overall response to the perturbation. However, if same error persists and does not change, the derivative will vanish and the proportional term dominates the choice of control.

Figure 25.20(c) shows the result of applying this PD controller to our robot arm, using as gain parameters $K_P = .3$ and $K_D = .8$. Clearly, the resulting path is much smoother, and does not exhibit any obvious oscillations. As this example suggests, a differential term can make a controller stable that otherwise is not.

In practice, PD controllers also possess failure modes. In particular, PD controllers may fail to regulate an error down to zero, even in the absence of external perturbations. This is not obvious from our robot example, but sometimes an over-proportional feedback is required to drive an error down to zero. The solution to this problem lies in adding a third term to the control law, based on the integrated error over time:

$$a_t = K_P(y(t) - x_t) + K_I \int (y(t) - x_t)dt + K_D \frac{\partial(y(t) - x_t)}{\partial t} . \tag{25.4}$$

Here $K_I$ is yet another gain parameter. The term $\int (y(t) - x_t)dt$ calculates the integral of the error over time. The effect of this term is that long-lasting deviations between the reference signal and the actual state are corrected. If, for example, $x_t$ is smaller than $y(t)$ for a long period of time, this integral will grow until the resulting control $a_t$ forces this error to shrink. Integral terms, then, ensure that a controller does not exhibit systematic error, at the expenses of increased danger of oscillatory behavior. A controller with all three terms is called a **PID controller**. PID controllers are widely used in industry, for a variety of control problems.

PID CONTROLLER

### Potential field control

We introduced potential fields as an additional cost function in robot motion planning, but they can also be used for generating robot motion directly, dispensing with the path planning phase altogether. To achieve this, we have to define an attractive force that pulls the robot towards its goal configuration and a repellent potential field that pushes the robot away from obstacles. Such a potential field is shown in Figure 25.21. Its single global minimum is the target configuration, and the value is the sum of the distance to this target configuration and the proximity to obstacles. No planning was involved in generating the potential field shown in the figure. Because of this, potential fields are well-suited to real-time control. Figure 25.21 shows two trajectories of a robot that performs hill climbing in the potential field, under two different initial configurations. In many applications, the potential field can be calculated efficiently for any given configuration. Moreover, optimizing the potential amounts to calculating the gradient of the potential for the present robot configuration. These calculations are usually extremely efficient, especially when compared to path planning algorithms, all of which are exponential in the dimensionality of the configuration space (the DOFs).

The fact that the potential field approach manages to find a path to the goal in such an efficient manner, even over long distances in configuration space, raises the question as to whether there is a need for planning in robotics at all. Are potential field techniques sufficient, or were we just lucky in our example? The answer is that we were indeed lucky. Potential fields have many local minima that can trap the robot. In this example, the robot approaches

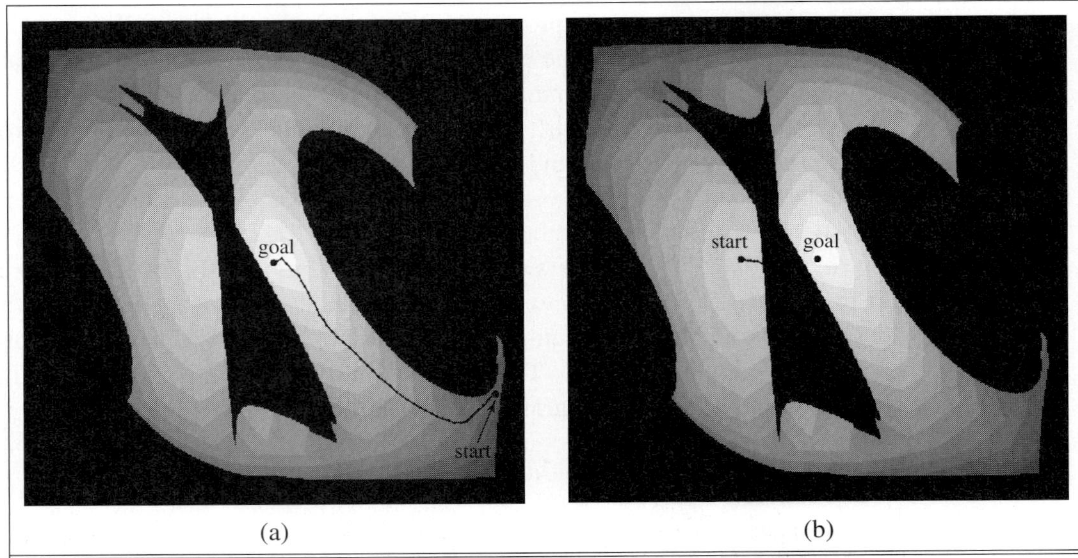


**Figure 25.21** Potential field control. The robot ascends a potential field composed of repelling forces asserted from the obstacles, and an attracting force that corresponds to the target configuration. (a) Successful path. (b) Local optimum.

the obstacle by simply rotating its shoulder joint, until it gets stuck on the wrong side of the obstacle. The potential field is not rich enough to make the robot bend its elbow so that the arm fits under the obstacle. In other words, potential field techniques are great for local robot control but they still require global planning. Another important drawback with potential fields is that the forces they generate depend only on the obstacle and robot positions, not on the robot's velocity. Thus, potential field control is really a kinematic method and may fail if the robot is moving quickly.

### Reactive control

So far we have consider control decisions that require some model of the environment for constructing either a reference path or a potential field. There are some difficulties with this approach. First, models that are sufficiently accurate are often difficult to obtain, especially in complex or remote environments, such as the surface of Mars. Second, even in cases where we can devise a model with sufficient accuracy, computational difficulties and localization error might render these techniques impractical. In some cases, a reflex agent design—so-called **reactive control**—is more appropriate.

REACTIVE CONTROL

HEXAPOD

One such example is the six-legged robot, or **hexapod** shown in Figure 25.22(a), with the task of walking through rough terrain. The robot's sensors are grossly inadequate to obtain models of the terrain at sufficient accuracy for any of the path planning techniques described in the previous section to work. Moreover, even if we added sufficiently accurate sensors, the twelve degrees of freedom (two for each leg) would render the resulting path planning problem computationally intractable.

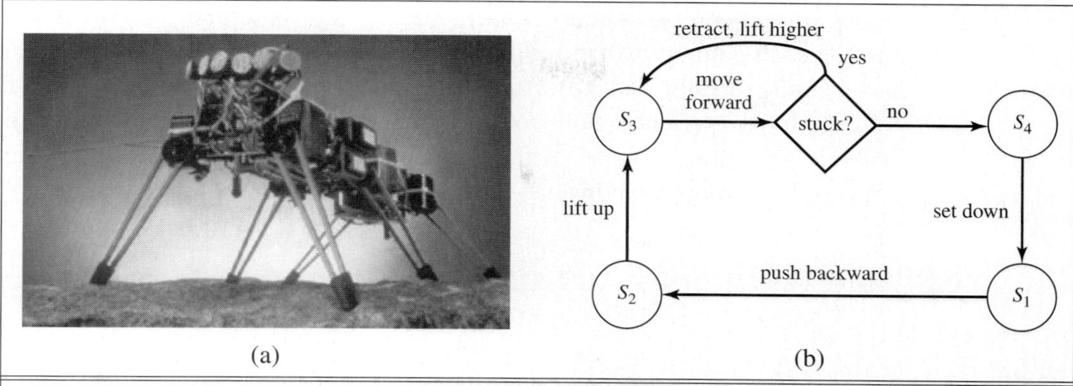


**Figure 25.22** (a) A hexapod robot (b) An augmented finite state machine (AFSM) for the control of a single leg. Notice that this AFSM reacts to sensor feedback: if a leg is stuck during the forward swinging phase, it will be lifted increasingly higher.

It is possible, nonetheless, to specify a controller directly without an explicit environmental model. (We have already seen this with the PD controller, which was able to keep a complex robot arm on target *without* an explicit model of the robot dynamics; it did, however, require a reference path generated from a kinematic model.) For the example of our legged robot, specifying a control law turns out to be surprisingly simple at the right level of abstraction. A viable control law might make each leg move in cycles, so that for some of the time it touches the ground, and for the remaining time it moves in the air. All six legs should be coordinated so that three of them (on opposite ends) are always on the ground to provide physical support. Such a control pattern is easily programmed and works great on flat terrain. On rugged terrain, obstacles may prevent legs from swinging forward. This problem can be overcome by a remarkably simple control rule: *when a leg's forward motion is blocked, simply retract it, lift it higher, and try again.* The resulting controller is shown in Figure 25.22(b) as a finite state machine; it constitutes a reflex agent with state, where the internal state is represented by the index of the current machine state ($s_1$ through $s_4$).

Variants of this simple feedback-driven controller has been found to generate a remarkably robust walking pattern, capable of maneuvering the robot over rugged terrain. Clearly, such a controller is model-free, and it does not deliberate or use search for generating controls. When executing such a controller, environment feedback plays a crucial role in the behavior generated by the robot. The software alone does not specify what will actually happen when the robot is placed in an environment. Behavior that emerges through the interplay of a (simple) controller and a (complex) environment is often referred to as **emergent behavior**. Strictly speaking, all robots discussed in this chapter exhibit emergent behavior, due to the fact that no model is perfect. Historically, however, the term has been reserved for control techniques that do not utilize explicit environmental models. Emergent behavior is also characteristic of a great number of biological organisms.

EMERGENT BEHAVIOR

Technically, reactive controllers are just one implementation of a policy for an MDP (or, if they have internal state, for a POMDP). In Chapter 17, we encountered several techniques for generating policies from models of the robot and its environment. In robotics, crafting such policies by hand is of great practical importance, due to our inability to formulate accurate models. Chapter 21 described reinforcement learning methods for constructing policies from experience. Some of those methods—such as Q-learning and the policy search methods—require no model of the environment and are capable of generating high-quality controllers for robots, but instead the rely on vast amounts of training data.

## 25.7 Robotic Software Architectures

SOFTWARE ARCHITECTURE

A methodology for structuring algorithms is called a **software architecture**. An architecture usually includes languages and tools for writing programs, as well as an overall philosophy for how programs can be brought together.

Modern-day software architectures for robotics must decide how to combine reactive control and model-based deliberative control. In many ways, reactive and deliberate control have orthogonal strengths and weaknesses. Reactive control is sensor-driven and appropriate for making low-level decisions in real time. However, reactive control rarely yields a plausible solution at the global level, because global control decisions depend on information that cannot be sensed at the time of decision making. For such problems, deliberate control is more appropriate.

Consequently, most robot architectures use reactive techniques at the lower levels of control with deliberate techniques at the higher levels. We encountered such a combination in our discussion of PD controllers, where we combined a (reactive) PD controller with a (deliberate) path planner. Architectures that combine reactive and deliberate techniques are usually called **hybrid architectures**.

HYBRID ARCHITECTURES

### Subsumption architecture

SUBSUMPTION ARCHITECTURE

The **subsumption architecture** (Brooks, 1986) is a framework for assembling reactive controllers out of finite state machines. Nodes in these machines may contain tests for certain sensor variables, in which case the execution trace of a finite state machine is conditioned on the outcome of such a test. Arcs can be tagged with messages that will be generated when traversing them, and that are sent to the robot's motors or to other finite state machines. Additionally, finite state machines possess internal timers (clocks) that control the time it takes to traverse an arc. The resulting machines are usually refereed to as **augmented finite state machines**, or AFSMs, where the augmentation refers to the use of clocks.

AUGMENTED FINITE STATE MACHINE

An example of a simple AFSM is the four-state machine shown in Figure 25.22(b), which generates cyclic leg motion for a hexapod walker. This AFSM implements a cyclic controller, whose execution mostly does not rely on environmental feedback. The forward swing phase, however, relies on sensor feedback. If the leg is stuck, meaning that it has failed to execute the forward swing, the robot retracts the leg, lifts up a little higher, and attempts to execute the forward swing once again. Thus, the controller is able to *react* to contingencies arising from the interplay of the robot and its environment.

The subsumption architecture offers additional primitives for synchronizing AFSMs, and for combining output values of multiple, possibly conflicting AFSMs. In this way, it enables the programmer to compose increasingly complex controllers in a bottom-up fashion. In our example, we might begin with AFSMs for individual legs, followed by an AFSM for coordinating multiple legs. On top of this, we might implement higher-level behaviors such as collision avoidance, which might involve backing up and turning.

The idea of composing robot controllers from AFSMs is quite intriguing. Imagine how difficult it would be to generate the same behavior with any of the configuration space path planning algorithms described in the previous section. First, we would need an accurate model of the terrain. The configuration space of a robot with six legs, each of which is driven by two independent motors, totals eighteen dimensions (twelve dimensions for the configuration of the legs, and six for the location and orientation of the robot relative to its environment). Even if our computers were fast enough to find paths in such high-dimensional spaces, we would have to worry about nasty effects such as the robot sliding down a slope. Because of such stochastic effects, a single path through configuration space would almost certainly be too brittle, and even a PID controller might not be able to cope with such contingencies. In other words, generating motion behavior deliberately is simply too complex a problem for present-day robot motion planning algorithms.

Unfortunately, the subsumption architecture has problems of its own. First, the AFSMs are usually driven by raw sensor input, an arrangement that works if the sensor data is reliable and contains all necessary information for decision making, but fails if sensor data has to be integrated in nontrivial ways over time. Subsumption-style controllers have therefore mostly been applied to local tasks, such as wall following or moving towards visible light sources. Second, the lack of deliberation makes it difficult to change the task of the robot. A subsumption-style robot usually does just one task, and it has no notion of how to modify its controls to accommodate different control objectives (just like the dung beetle on page 37). Finally, subsumption-style controllers tend to be difficult to understand. In practice, the intricate interplay between dozens of interacting AFSMs (and the environment) is beyond what most human programmers can comprehend. For all these reasons, the subsumption architecture is rarely used in commercial robotics, despite its great historical importance. However, some its descendants are.

### Three-layer architecture

THREE-LAYER ARCHITECTURE

Hybrid architectures combine reaction with deliberation. By far the most popular hybrid architecture is the **three-layer architecture**, which consists of a reactive layer, an executive layer, and a deliberate layer.

REACTIVE LAYER

The **reactive layer** provides low-level control to the robot. It is characterized by a tight sensor–action loop. Its decision cycle is often on the order of milliseconds.

EXECUTIVE LAYER

The **executive layer** (or sequencing layer) serves as the glue between the reactive and the deliberate layer. It accepts directives by the deliberate layer, and sequences them for the reactive layer. For example, the executive layer might handle a set of via-points generated by a deliberate path planner, and make decisions as to which reactive behavior to invoke.

Decision cycles at the executive layer are usually in the order of a second. The executive layer is also responsible for integrating sensor information into an internal state representation. For example, it may host the robot's localization and online mapping routines.

DELIBERATE LAYER

The **deliberate layer** generates global solutions to complex tasks using planning. Because of the computational complexity involved in generating such solutions, its decision cycle is often in the order of minutes. The deliberate layer (or planning layer) uses models for decision making. Those models might be pre-supplied or learned from data, and they usually utilize state information gathered at the executive layer.

Variants of the three-layer architecture can be found in most modern-day robot software systems. The decomposition into three layers is not very strict. Some robot software systems possess additional layers, such as user interface layers that control the interaction with people, or layers responsible for coordinating a robot's actions with that of other robots operating in the same environment.

### Robotic programming languages

BEHAVIOR LANGUAGE

Many robotic controllers have been implemented with special purpose programming languages. For example, many programs for the subsumption architecture have been implemented in the **behavior language** defined by Brooks (1990). This language is a rule-based real-time control language that compiles into AFSM controllers. Individual rules in a Lisp-like syntax are compiled into AFSMs, and multiple AFSMs are integrated through a collection of local and global message-passing mechanisms.

GENERIC ROBOT LANGUAGE

Just like the subsumption architecture, the behavior language is limited in its focus on simple AFSMs with a relatively narrow definition of the communication flow between modules. Recent research has built on this idea, leading to a range of programming languages similar in spirit to the behavior language, but more powerful and faster when executed. One such language is the **generic robot language**, or GRL (Horswill, 2000). GRL is a functional programming language for programming large modular control systems. Just as in the behavior language, GRL uses finite state machines as its basic building blocks. On top of this, it provides a much broader range of constructs for defining communication flow and synchronization constraints between different modules than the behavior language. Programs in GRL are compiled into efficient imperative languages, such as C.

Another important programming language (and associated architecture) for concurrent robot software is the reactive action plan system, or RAPS (Firby, 1994). RAPS enables programmers to specify goals, plans (or partial policies) associated with these goals, and conditions under which those plans will likely succeed. Crucially, RAPS also provides facilities for handling the inevitable *failures* that occur with real robotic systems. The programmer can specify detection routines for various kinds of failure and supply an exception-handling routine for each kind. In three-layer architectures, RAPS is often used in the executive layer, to handle contingencies that do not require replanning.

There are several other languages that allow for reasoning and learning to take place in the robot. For example, GOLOG (Levesque *et al.*, 1997b) is a programming language that seamlessly blends deliberate problem solving (planning) and direct specification of reactive control. Programs in GOLOG are formulated in situation calculus (Section 10.3), with the additional option of nondeterministic action operators. In addition to the specification of a control program with possible nondeterministic actions, the programmer also has to provide a complete model of the robot and its environment. Whenever the control program reaches a nondeterministic choice point, a planner (in the form of a theorem prover) is invoked to determine what to do next. In this way, the programmer can specify partial controllers and rely on built-in planners to make the final control choice. The beauty of GOLOG lies in its seamless integration of reactivity and deliberation. Despite the strong requirements of GOLOG (full observability, discrete states, full model), GOLOG has provided high-level control for a series of indoor mobile robots.

CES **CES**, short for C++ for embedded systems, is a language extension of C++ that integrates probabilities and learning (Thrun, 2000). CES's data types are probability distributions, allowing the programmer to calculate with uncertain information without the effort usually required to implement probabilistic techniques. More importantly, CES makes it possible to train robot software with examples, very much like the learning algorithms discussed in Chapter 20. CES enables programmers to leave "gaps" in the code that are filled by learnable functions—typically differentiable parametric representations such as neural networks. These functions are then learned inductively in explicit training phases, where the trainer has to specify the desired output behavior. CES has been demonstrated to work well in partially observable and continuous domains.

ALISP **ALisp** (Andre and Russell, 2002) is an extension of Lisp. ALisp allows programmers to specify nondeterministic choice points, similar to the choice points in GOLOG. However, instead of relying on a theorem prover to make decisions, ALisp inductively learns the right action via reinforcement learning. Thus ALisp can be seen as a flexible means to incorporate domain knowledge—especially knowledge about the hierarchical "subroutine" structure of desired behaviors—into a reinforcement learner. As yet, ALisp has been applied to robotics problems only in simulation, but it provides a promising methodology for building robots that learn through interaction with the environment.

## 25.8 APPLICATION DOMAINS

We will now list some of the prime application domains for robotic technology.

**Industry and Agriculture.** Traditionally, robots have been fielded in areas that require difficult human labor, yet are structured enough to be amenable to robotic automation. The best example is the assembly line, where manipulators routinely perform tasks such as assembly, part placement, material handling, welding, and painting. In many of these tasks, robots have become more cost-effective than human workers.

Outdoors, many of the heavy machines that we use to harvest, mine, or excavate earth have been turned into robots. For example, a recent project at Carnegie Mellon has demonstrated that robots can strip paint off large ships about 50 times faster than people can, and with a much reduced environmental impact. Prototypes of autonomous mining robots have

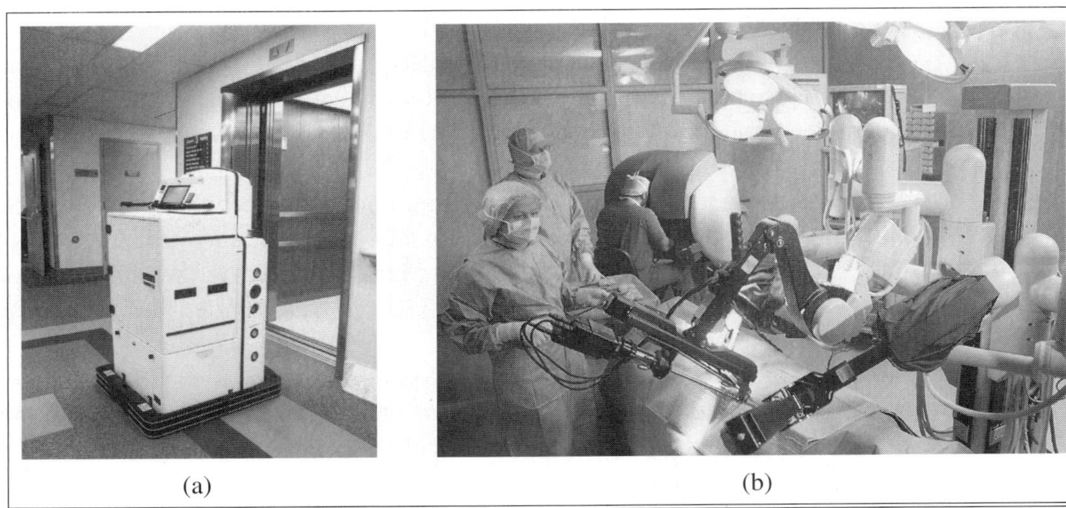

(a) (b)

**Figure 25.23** (a) The Helpmate robot transports food and other medical items in dozens of hospitals world-wide. (b) Surgical robots in the operating room (by da Vinci Surgical Systems).

been found to be faster and more precise than people in transporting ore in underground mines. Robots have been used to generate high-precision maps of abandoned mines and sewer systems. While many of these systems are still in their prototype stages, it is only a matter of time until robots will take over much of the semi-mechanical work that is presently performed by people.

**Transportation.** Robotic transportation has many facets: from autonomous helicopters that deliver objects to locations that would be hard to access by other means, to automatic wheelchairs that transport people who are unable to control wheelchairs by themselves, to autonomous straddle carriers that outperform skilled human drivers when transporting containers from ships to trucks on loading docks. A prime example of indoor transportation robots, or gofers, is the Helpmate robot shown in Figure 25.23(a). This robot has been deployed in dozens of hospitals to transport food and other items. Researchers have developed car-like robotic systems that can navigate autonomously on highways or across off-road terrain. In factory settings, autonomous vehicles are now routinely deployed to transport goods in warehouses and between production lines.

Many of these robots require environmental modifications for their operation. The most common modifications are localization aids such as inductive loops in the floor, active beacons, bar-code tags, and GPS satellites. An open challenge in robotics is the design of robots that can use natural cues, instead of artificial devices, to navigate, particularly in environments such as the deep ocean where GPS is unavailable.

**Hazardous environments.** Robots have assisted people in cleaning up nuclear waste, most notably in Chernobyl and Three Mile Island. Robots were present after the collapse of the World Trade Center, where they entered structures deemed too dangerous for human search and rescue crews.

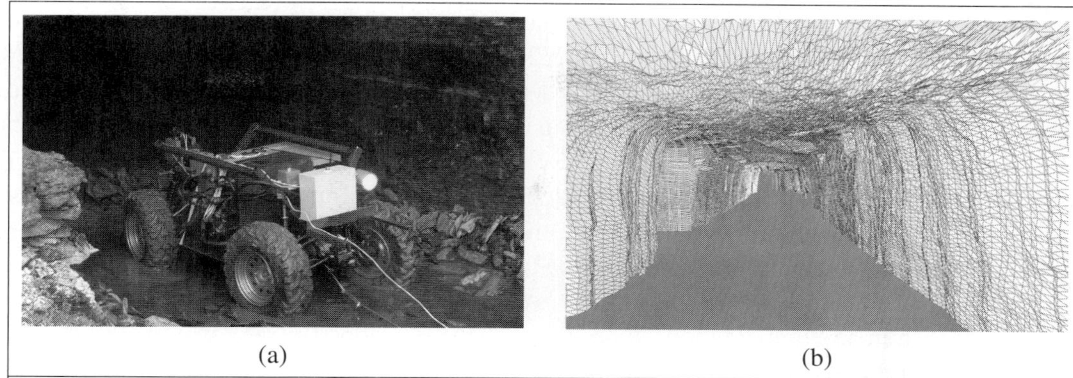

(a) (b)

**Figure 25.24** (a) A robot mapping an abandoned coal mine. (b) A 3-D map of the mine acquired by the robot.

Some countries have used robots to transport ammunition and to defuse bombs—a notoriously dangerous task. A number of research projects are presently developing prototype robots for clearing minefields, on land and at sea. Most existing robots for these tasks are teleoperated—a human operates them by remote control. Providing such robots with autonomy is an important next step.

**Exploration.** Robots have gone where no-one has gone before, including the surface of Mars. (See Figure 25.1(a).) Robotic arms assist astronauts in deploying and retrieving satellites and in building the International Space Station. Robots also help explore under the sea. They are routinely used to acquire maps of sunken ships. Figure 25.24 shows a robot mapping an abandoned coal mine, along with a 3-D model of the mine acquired using range sensors. In 1996, a team of researches released a legged robot into the crater of an active volcano to acquire data important for climate research. Unmanned air vehicles known as

DRONES

**drones** are used in military operations. Robots are becoming very effective tools for gathering information in domains that are difficult (or dangerous) to access for people.

**Health care.** Robots are increasingly used to assist surgeons with instrument placement when operating on organs as intricate as brains, eyes, and hearts. Figure 25.23(b) shows such a system. Robots have become indispensable tools in certain types of hip replacements, thanks to their high precision. In pilot studies, robotic devices have been found to reduce the danger of lesions when performing colonoscopies. Outside the operating room, researchers have begun to develop robotic aides for elderly and handicapped people, such as intelligent robotic walkers and intelligent toys that provide reminders to take medication.

**Personal Services.** Service is an up-and-coming application domain of robotics. Service robot assist individuals in performing daily tasks. Commercially available domestic service robots include autonomous vacuum cleaners, lawn mowers, and golf caddies. All these robots can navigate autonomously and perform their tasks without human help. Some service robots operate in public places, such as robotic information kiosks that have been deployed in shopping malls and trade fairs, or in museums as tour-guides. Service tasks require human interaction, and the ability to cope robustly with unpredictable and dynamic environments.

**Entertainment.** Robots have begun to conquer the entertainment and toy industry. We saw the Sony AIBO in Figure 25.4(b); this dog-like robot toy is being used as a research platform in AI labs around the world. One of the challenging AI tasks studied with this platform is **robotic soccer**, a competitive game very much like human soccer, but played with autonomous mobile robots. Robot soccer provides great opportunities for research in AI, since it raises a range of problems prototypical for many other, more serious robot applications. Annual robotic soccer competitions have attracted large numbers of AI researchers and added a lot of excitement to the field of robotics.

ROBOTIC SOCCER

**Human augmentation.** A final application domain of robotic technology is that of human augmentation. Researchers have developed legged walking machines that can carry people around, very much like a wheelchair. Several research efforts presently focus on the development devices that make it easier for people to walk or move their arms, by providing additional forces through extra-skeletal attachments. If such devices are attached permanently, they can be thought of as artificial robotic limbs. Robotic teleoperation, or telepresence, is another form of human augmentation. Teleoperation involves carrying out tasks over long distances, with the aid of robotic devices. A popular configuration for robotic teleoperation is the master–slave configuration, where a robot manipulator emulates the motion of a remote human operator, measured through a haptic interface. All these systems augment people's ability to interact with their environments. Some projects go as far as replicating humans, at least at a very superficial level. Humanoid robots are now available commercially through several companies in Japan.

## 25.9 SUMMARY

Robotics concerns itself with intelligent agents that manipulate the physical world. In this chapter, we have learned the following basics of robot hardware and software.

- Robots are equipped with sensors for perceiving their environment and effectors with which they can assert physical forces on their environment. Most robots are either manipulators anchored at fixed locations or mobile robots that can move.
- Robotic perception concerns itself with estimating decision-relevant quantities from sensor data. To do so, we need an internal representation and a method for updating this internal representation over time. Common examples of hard perceptual problems include localization and mapping.
- Probabilistic filtering algorithms such as Kalman filters and particle filters are useful for robot perception. These techniques maintain the belief state, i.e., a posterior distribution over state variables.
- The planning of robot motion is usually done in configuration space, where each point specifies the location and orientation of the robot and its joint angles.
- Configuration spaces search algorithms include cell decomposition techniques, which decompose the space of all configurations into finitely many cells, and skeletonization

techniques, which project configuration spaces onto lower-dimensional manifolds. The motion planning problem is then solved using search in these simpler structures.

- A path found by a search algorithm can be executed by using the path as the reference trajectory for a PID controllers.
- Potential field techniques navigate robots by potential functions, defined over the distance to obstacles and the target location. Potential field techniques may get stuck in local minima, but they can generate motion directly without the need for path planning.
- Sometimes, it is easier to specify a robot controller directly, rather than deriving a path from an explicit model of the environment. Such controllers can often be written as simple finite state machines.
- The subsumption architecture enables programmers to compose robot controllers from interconnected finite state machines, augmented by built-in timers.
- Three-layer architectures are common frameworks for developing robot software that integrate deliberation, sequencing of subgoals, and control.
- Special purpose programming languages exist that facilitate robot software development. These languages offer constructs for developing multithreaded software, for integrating control directives into planning, and for learning from experience.

## Bibliographical and Historical Notes

The word **robot** was popularized by Czech playwright Karel Capek in his 1921 play *R.U.R.* (Rossum's Universal Robots). The robots, which were grown chemically rather than constructed mechanically, end up resenting their masters and decide to take over. It appears (Glanc, 1978) that it was actually Capek's brother, Josef, who first combined the Czech words "robota" (obligatory work) and "robotnik" (serf) to yield "robot" in his 1917 short story *Opilec*.

The term *robotics* was first used by (Asimov, 1950). Robotics (under other names) has a much longer history, however. In ancient Greek mythology, a mechanical man named Talos was supposedly designed and built by Hephaistos, the Greek god of metallurgy. Wonderful automata were built in the 18th century—Jacques Vaucanson's mechanical duck from 1738 being one early example—but the complex behaviors they exhibited were entirely fixed in advance. Possibly the earliest example of a programmable robot-like device was the Jacquard loom (1805), described in Chapter 1.

UNIMATE

The first commercial robot was a robot arm called **Unimate**, short for *universal automation*. Unimate was developed by Joseph Engelberger and George Devol. In 1961, the first Unimate robot was sold to General Motors, where it was used for manufacturing TV picture tubes. 1961 was also the year when Devol obtained the first U.S. patent on a robot. Eleven years later, in 1972, Nissan Corp. was among the first to automate an entire assembly line with robots, developed by Kawasaki with robots supplied by Engelberger and Devol's company Unimation. This development initiated a major revolution that took place mostly in Japan and the U.S., and that is still ongoing. Unimation followed up in 1978 with the devel-

PUMA

opment of the **PUMA** robot, short for Programmable Universal Machine for Assembly. The PUMA robot, initially developed for General Motors, was the *de facto* standard for robotic manipulation for the two decades that followed. At present, the number of operating robots is estimated at one million world-wide, more than half of which are installed in Japan.

The literature on robotics research can be divided roughly into two parts: mobile robots and stationary manipulators. Grey Walter's "turtle," built in 1948, could be considered the first autonomous mobile robot, although its control system was not programmable. The "Hopkins Beast," built in the early 1960s at Johns Hopkins University, was much more sophisticated; it had pattern-recognition hardware and could recognize the cover plate of a standard AC power outlet. It was capable of searching for outlets, plugging itself in, and then recharging its batteries! Still, the Beast had a limited repertoire of skills. The first general-purpose mobile robot was "Shakey," developed at what was then the Stanford Research Institute (now SRI) in the late 1960s (Fikes and Nilsson, 1971; Nilsson, 1984). Shakey was the first robot to integrate perception, planning, and execution, and much subsequent research in AI was influenced by this remarkable achievement. Other influential projects include the Stanford Cart and the CMU Rover (Moravec, 1983). Cox and Wilfong (1990) describes classic work on autonomous vehicles.

OCCUPANCY GRID

The field of robotic mapping has evolved from two distinct origins. The first thread began with work by Smith and Cheeseman (1986), who applied Kalman filters to the simultaneous localization and mapping problem. This algorithm was first implemented by Moutarlier and Chatila (1989), and later extended to by Leonard and Durrant-Whyte (1992). Dissanayake *et al.* (2001) describes the state of the art. The second thread began with the development of the **occupancy grid** representation for probabilistic mapping, which specifies the probability that each $(x, y)$ location is occupied by an obstacle (Moravec and Elfes, 1985). An overview of the state of the art in robotic mapping can be found in (Thrun, 2002). Kuipers and Levitt (1988) were among the first to propose topological rather than metric mapping, motivated by models of human spatial cognition.

MARKOV LOCALIZATION

RAO-BLACKWELLIZED PARTICLE FILTER

Early mobile robot localization techniques are surveyed by Borenstein *et al.* (1996). Although Kalman filtering was well-known as a localization method in control theory for decades, the general probabilistic formulation of the localization problem did not appear in the AI literature until much later, through the work of Tom Dean and colleagues (1990, 1990) and Simmons and Koenig (1995). The latter work introduced the term **Markov localization**. The first real-world application of this technique was by Burgard *et al.* (1999), through a series of robots that were deployed in museums. Monte Carlo localization based on particle filters was developed by Fox *et al.* (1999) and is now widely used. The **Rao-Blackwellized particle filter** combines particle filtering for robot localization with exact filtering for map building (Murphy and Russell, 2001; Montemerlo *et al.*, 2002).

ROBOCUP

Research on mobile robotics has been stimulated over the last decade by two important competitions. AAAI's annual mobile robot competition began in 1992. The first competition winner was CARMEL (Congdon *et al.*, 1992). Progress has been steady and impressive: in the most recent competition (2002), the robots had to enter the conference complex, find their way to the registration desk, register for the conference, and give a talk. The **Robocup** competition, launched in 1995 by Kitano and colleagues (1997), aims by 2050 to "develop a team of fully autonomous humanoid robots that can win against the human world champion team in soccer." Play occurs in leagues for simulated robots, wheeled robots of different sizes, and four-legged Sony Aibo robots. In 2002, the competition event drew teams from almost 30 different countries and over 100,000 spectators.

HAND–EYE MACHINES

The study of manipulator robots, called originally called **hand–eye machines**, has evolved along quite different lines. The first major effort at creating a hand–eye machine was Heinrich Ernst's MH-1, described in his MIT Ph.D. thesis (Ernst, 1961). The Machine Intelligence project at Edinburgh also demonstrated an impressive early system for vision-based assembly called FREDDY (Michie, 1972). After these pioneering efforts, a great deal of work focused on geometric algorithms for deterministic and fully observable motion planning problems. The PSPACE-hardness of robot motion planning was shown in a seminal paper by Reif (1979). The configuration space representation is due to Lozano-Perez (1983). Highly influential was a series of papers by Schwartz and Sharir on what they called **piano movers** problems (Schwartz *et al.*, 1987).

PIANO MOVERS

Recursive cell decomposition for configuration space planning was originated by Brooks and Lozano-Perez (1985) and improved significantly by Zhu and Latombe (1991). The earliest skeletonization algorithms were based on Voronoi diagrams (Rowat, 1979) and **visibility graphs** (Wesley and Lozano-Perez, 1979). Guibas *et al.* (1992) developed efficient techniques for calculating Voronoi diagrams incrementally, and Choset (1996) generalized Voronoi diagrams to much broader motion planning problems. John Canny's Ph.D. thesis (1988) established the first singly exponential algorithm for motion planning using a different skeletonization method called the **silhouette** algorithm. The text by Jean-Claude Latombe (1991) covers a variety of approaches to the motion planning problem. (Kavraki *et al.*, 1996) developed probabilistic roadmaps, which are currently the most effective method. Fine motion planning with limited sensing was investigated by (Lozano-Perez *et al.*, 1984) and Canny and Reif (1987) using the idea of interval uncertainty rather than probabilistic uncertainty. Landmark-based navigation (Lazanas and Latombe, 1992) uses many of the same ideas in the mobile robot arena.

VISIBILITY GRAPH

SILHOUETTE

The control of robots as dynamical systems—whether for manipulation or navigation—has generated a huge literature on which the material in this chapter barely touches. Important works include a trilogy on impedance control by Hogan (1985) and a general study of robot dynamics by Featherstone (1987). Dean and Wellman (1991) were among the first to try to tie together control theory and AI planning systems. Three classical textbook on the mathematics of robot manipulation are due to Paul (1981), Craig (1989), and Yoshikawa (1990). The area of **grasping** is also important in robotics—the problem of determining a stable grasp is quite difficult (Mason and Salisbury, 1985). Competent grasping requires touch sensing, or **haptic feedback**, to determine contact forces and detect slip (Fearing and Hollerbach, 1985).

GRASPING

HAPTIC FEEDBACK

Potential field control, which attempts to solve the motion planning and control problems simultaneously, was introduced into the robotics literature by Khatib (1986). In mobile robotics, this idea was viewed as a practical solution to the collision avoidance problem, and was later extended into an algorithm called **vector field histograms** by Borenstein (1991). Navigation functions, the robotics version of a control policy for deterministic MDPs, were introduced by Koditschek (1987).

VECTOR FIELD HISTOGRAMS

The topic of software architectures for robots engenders much religious debate. The good old-fashioned AI candidate—the three-layer architecture—dates back to the design of Shakey and is reviewed by Gat (1998). The subsumption architecture is due to Rodney Brooks (1986), although similar ideas were developed independently by Braitenberg (1984), whose book, *Vehicles*, describes a series of simple robots based on the behavioral approach. The success of Brooks's six-legged walking robot was followed by many other projects. Connell, in his Ph.D. thesis (1989), developed a mobile robot capable of retrieving objects that was entirely reactive. Extensions of the behavior-based paradigm to multirobot systems can be found in (Mataric, 1997) and (Parker, 1996). GRL (Horswill, 2000) and COLBERT (Konolige, 1997) abstract the ideas of concurrent behavior-based robotics into general robot control languages. Arkin (1998) surveys the state of the art.

**Situated automata** (Rosenschein, 1985; Kaelbling and Rosenschein, 1990), described in Chapter 7, have also been used to control mobile robots for exploration and delivery tasks. Situated automata are closely related to behavior-based designs in that they consist of finite-state machines that track aspects of the environment state using simple combinatorial circuitry. Whereas the behavior-based approach stresses the absence of explicit representation, situated automata are constructed algorithmically from declarative environment models so that the representational content of each state register is well-defined.

There exist several good recent textbooks on mobile robotics. in addition to the textbooks referenced above, the collection by Kortenkamp *et al.* (1998) provides a comprehensive overview of contemporary mobile robot architectures and systems. Two recent textbooks by Dudek and Jenkin (2000) and Murphy (2000) cover robotics more generally. A recent book on robot manipulation addresses advanced topics such as compliant motion (Mason, 2001). The major conference for robotics is the *IEEE International Conference on Robotics and Automation*. Robotics journals include *IEEE Robotics and Automation*, the *International Journal of Robotics Research*, and *Robotics and Autonomous Systems*.

## EXERCISES

**25.1** Monte Carlo localization is *biased* for any finite sample size—i.e., the expected value of the location computed by the algorithm differs from the true expected value—because of the way particle filtering works. In this question, you are asked to quantify this bias.

To simplify, consider a world with four possible robot locations: $X = \{x_1, x_2, x_3, x_4\}$. Initially, we draw $N \geq 1$ samples uniformly from among those locations. As usual, it is perfectly acceptable if more than one sample is generated for any of the locations $X$. Let $Z$ be a Boolean sensor variable characterized by the following conditional probabilities:

$$
\begin{aligned}
P(z \mid x_1) &= 0.8 & \qquad P(\neg z \mid x_1) &= 0.2 \\
P(z \mid x_2) &= 0.4 & \qquad P(\neg z \mid x_2) &= 0.6 \\
P(z \mid x_3) &= 0.1 & \qquad P(\neg z \mid x_3) &= 0.9 \\
P(z \mid x_4) &= 0.1 & \qquad P(\neg z \mid x_4) &= 0.9 \,.
\end{aligned}
$$

MCL uses these probabilities to generate particle weights, which are subsequently normalized and used in the resampling process. For simplicity, let us assume we only generate one new sample in the resampling process, regardless of $N$. This sample might correspond to any of the four locations in $X$. Thus, the sampling process defines a probability distribution over $X$.

**a.** What is the resulting probability distribution over $X$ for this new sample? Answer this question separately for $N = 1, \ldots, 10$, and for $N = \infty$.

**b.** The difference between two probability distributions $P$ and $Q$ can be measured by the KL divergence, which is defined as

$$KL(P, Q) = \sum_i P(x_i) \log \frac{P(x_i)}{Q(x_i)} .$$

What are the KL divergences between the distributions in (a) and the true posterior?

**c.** What modification of the problem formulation (not the algorithm!) would guarantee that the specific estimator above is unbiased even for finite values of $N$? Provide at least two such modifications (each of which should be sufficient).

**25.2** Implement Monte Carlo localization for a simulated robot with range sensors. A grid map and range data are available from the code repository at **aima.cs.berkeley.edu**. Your exercise is complete if you can demonstrate successful global localization of the robot.

**25.3** Consider the robot arm shown in Figure 25.12. Assume that the robot's base element is 60cm long and that its upper arm and forearm are each 40cm long. As argued on page 917, the inverse kinematics of a robot is often not unique. State an explicit closed-form solution of the inverse kinematics for this arm. Under what exact conditions is the solution unique?

**25.4** Implement an algorithm for calculating the Voronoi diagram of an arbitrary 2-D environment, described by an $n \times n$ Boolean array. Illustrate your algorithm by plotting the Voronoi diagram for 10 interesting maps. What is the complexity of your algorithm?

**25.5** This exercise explores the relationship between workspace and configuration space using the examples shown in Figure 25.25.

**a.** Consider the robot configurations shown in Figure 25.25(a) through (c), ignoring the obstacle shown in each of the diagrams. Draw the corresponding arm configurations in configuration space. (*Hint:* Each arm configuration maps to a single point in configuration space, as illustrated in Figure 25.12(b).)

**b.** Draw the configuration space for each of the workspace diagrams in Figure 25.25(a)–(c). (*Hint:* The configuration spaces share with the one shown in Figure 25.25(a) the region that corresponds to self-collision, but differences arise from the lack of enclosing obstacles and the different locations of the obstacles in these individual figures.)

**c.** For each of the black dots in Figure 25.25(e)–(f), draw the corresponding configurations of the robot arm in workspace. Please ignore the shaded regions in this exercise.

**d.** The configuration spaces shown in Figure 25.25(e)–(f) have all been generated by a single workspace obstacle (dark shading), plus the constraints arising from the self-collision constraint (light shading). Draw, for each diagram, the workspace obstacle that corresponds to the darkly shaded area.

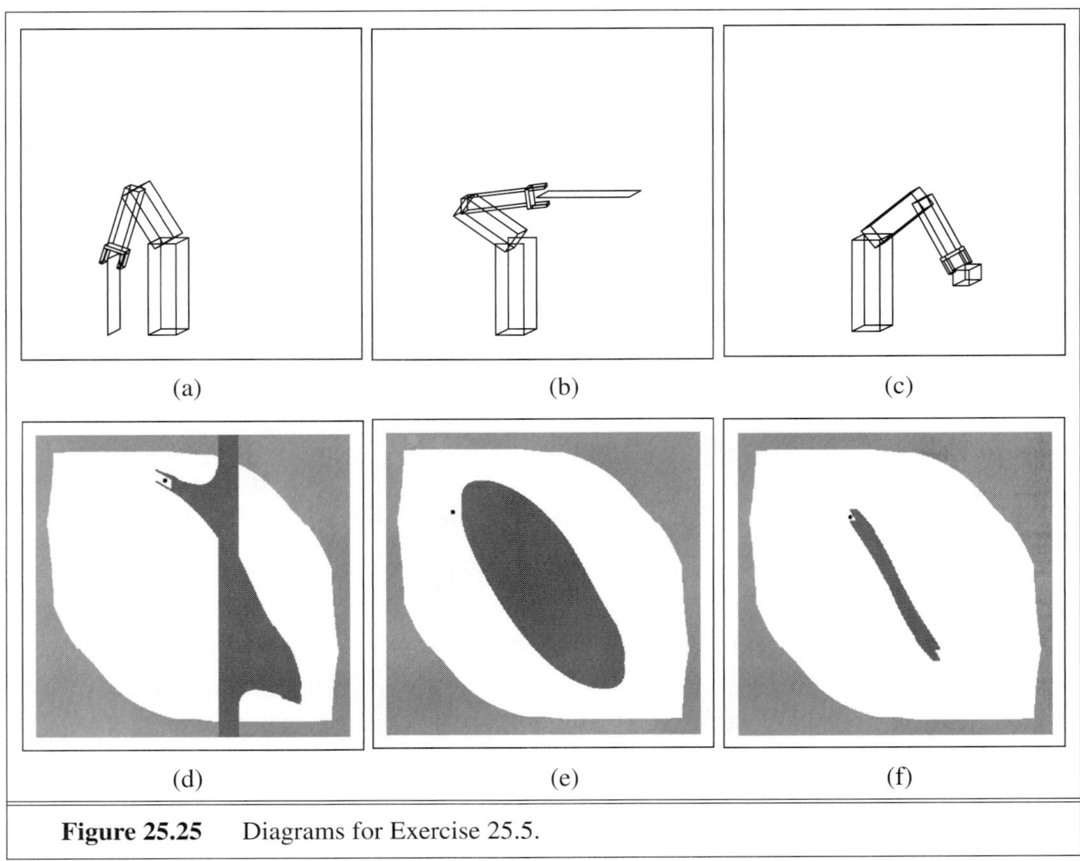


**Figure 25.25** Diagrams for Exercise 25.5.

**e**. Figure 25.25(d) illustrates that a single planar obstacle can decompose the workspace into two disconnected regions. What is the maximum number of disconnected regions that can be created by inserting a planar obstacle into an obstacle-free, connected workspace, for a 2DOF robot? Give an example, and argue why no larger number of disconnected regions can be created. How about a non-planar obstacle?

**25.6** Consider the simplified robot shown in Figure 25.26. Suppose the robot's Cartesian coordinates are known at all times, as are those of its target location. However, the locations of the obstacles are unknown. The robot can sense obstacles in its immediate proximity, as illustrated in this figure. For simplicity, let us assume the robot's motion is noise-free, and the state space is discrete. Figure 25.26 is only one example; in this exercise you are required to address all possible grid worlds with a valid path from the start to the goal location.

**a**. Design a deliberate controller that guarantees that the robot always reaches its target location if at all possible. The deliberate controller can memorize measurements in form of a map that is being acquired as the robot moves. Between individual moves, it may spend arbitrary time deliberating.

**b**. Now design a *reactive* controller for the same task. This controller may not memorize past sensor measurements. (It may not build a map!) Instead, it has to make all decisions

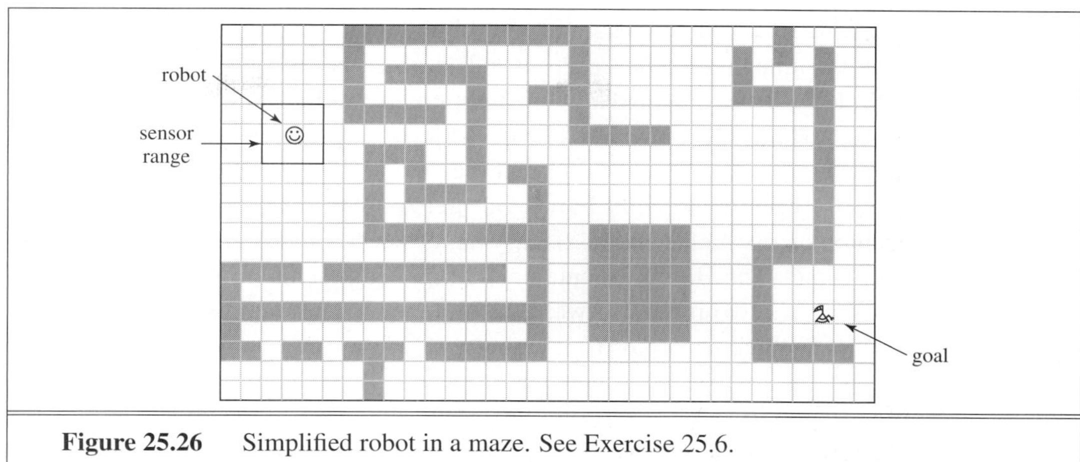


**Figure 25.26** Simplified robot in a maze. See Exercise 25.6.

based on the current measurement, which includes knowledge of its own location and that of the goal. The time to make a decision must be independent of the environment size or the number of past time steps. What is the maximum number of steps that it may take for your robot to arrive at the goal?

**c.** How will your controllers from (a) and (b) perform if any of the following six conditions apply: continuous state space, noise in perception, noise in motion, noise in both perception and motion, unknown location of the goal (the goal can be detected only when within sensor range), or moving obstacles. For each condition and each controller, give an example of a situation where the robot fails (or explain why it cannot).

**25.7** In Figure 25.22(b), we encountered an augmented finite state machine for the control of a single leg of a hexapod robot. In this exercise, the aim is to design an AFSM that, when combined with six copies of the individual leg controllers, results in efficient, stable locomotion. For this purpose, you have to augment the individual leg controller to pass messages to your new AFSM, and to wait until other messages arrive. Argue why your controller is efficient, in that it does not unnecessarily waste energy (e.g., by sliding legs), and in that it propels the robot at reasonably high speeds. Prove that your controller satisfies the stability condition given on page 906.

**25.8** (This exercise was first devised by Michael Genesereth and Nils Nilsson. It works for first graders through graduate students.) Humans are so adept at basic tasks such as picking up cups or stacking blocks that they often forget how complex these tasks are. In this exercise you will discover the complexity and recapitulate the last 30 years of developments in robotics. First, pick a task, such as building an arch out of three blocks. Then, build a robot out of four humans as follows:

**Brain.** The job of the Brain is to come up with a plan to achieve the goal, and to direct the hands in the execution of the plan. The Brain receives input from the Eyes, but *cannot see the scene directly*. The brain is the only one who knows what the goal is.

**Eyes.** The Eyes' job is to report a brief description of the scene to the Brain. The Eyes should stand a few feet away from the working environment, and can provide qualitative descriptions (such as "There is a red box standing on top of a green box, which is on its side") or quantitative descriptions ("The green box is about two feet to the left of the blue cylinder"). Eyes can also answer questions from the Brain such as, "Is there a gap between the Left Hand and the red box?" If you have a video camera, point it at the scene and allow the eyes to look at the viewfinder of the video camera, but not directly at the scene.

**Left hand** and **right hand.** One person plays each Hand. The two Hands stand next to each other; the Left Hand uses only his or her left hand, and the Right Hand only his or her right hand. The Hands execute only simple commands from the Brain—for example, "Left Hand, move two inches forward." They cannot execute commands other than motions; for example, "Pick up the box" is not something a Hand can do. To discourage cheating, you might want to have the hands wear gloves, or have them operate tongs. The Hands must be *blindfolded*. The only sensory capability they have is the ability to tell when their path is blocked by an immovable obstacle such as a table or the other Hand. In such cases, they can beep to inform the Brain of the difficulty.

# 26 PHILOSOPHICAL FOUNDATIONS

*In which we consider what it means to think and whether artifacts could and should ever do so.*

As we mentioned in Chapter 1, philosophers have been around for much longer than computers and have been trying to resolve some questions that relate to AI: How do minds work? Is it possible for machines to act intelligently in the way that people do, and if they did, would they have minds? What are the ethical implications of intelligent machines? For the first 25 chapters of this book, we have considered questions from AI itself; now we consider the philosopher's agenda for one chapter.

WEAK AI

STRONG AI

First, some terminology: the assertion that machines could possibly act intelligently (or, perhaps better, act *as if* they were intelligent) is called the **weak AI** hypothesis by philosophers, and the assertion that machines that do so are *actually* thinking (as opposed to *simulating* thinking) is called the **strong AI** hypothesis.

Most AI researchers take the weak AI hypothesis for granted, and don't care about the strong AI hypothesis—as long as their program works, they don't care whether you call it a simulation of intelligence or real intelligence. All AI researchers should be concerned with the ethical implications of their work.

## 26.1 WEAK AI: CAN MACHINES ACT INTELLIGENTLY?

Some philosophers have tried to prove that AI is impossible; that machines cannot possibly act intelligently. Some have used their arguments to call for a stop to AI research:

> Artificial intelligence *pursued within the cult of computationalism* stands not even a ghost of a chance of producing durable results . . . it is time to divert the efforts of AI researchers—and the considerable monies made available for their support—into avenues other than the computational approach. (Sayre, 1993)

Clearly, whether AI is impossible depends on how it is defined. In essence, AI is the quest for the best agent program on a given architecture. With this formulation, AI is by definition possible: for any digital architecture consisting of $k$ bits of storage there are exactly $2^k$ agent programs, and all we have to do to find the best one is enumerate and test them all. This might not be feasible for large $k$, but philosophers deal with the theoretical, not the practical.

Our definition of AI works well for the engineering problem of finding a good agent, given an architecture. Therefore, we're tempted to end this section right now, answering the title question in the affirmative. But philosophers are interested in the problem of comparing two architectures—human and machine. Furthermore, they have traditionally posed the question as, "**Can machines think**?" Unfortunately, this question is ill-defined. To see why, consider the following questions:

CAN MACHINES THINK?

- Can machines fly?
- Can machines swim?

Most people agree that the answer to the first question is yes, airplanes can fly, but the answer to the second is no; boats and submarines do move through the water, but we do not call that swimming. However, neither the questions nor the answers have any impact at all on the working lives of aeronautic and naval engineers or on the users of their products. The answers have very little to do with the design or capabilities of airplanes and submarines, and much more to do with the way we have chosen to use words. The word "swim" in English has come to mean "to move along in the water by movement of body parts," whereas the word "fly" has no such limitation on the means of locomotion.[1] The practical possibility of "thinking machines" has been with us for only 50 years or so, not long enough for speakers of English to settle on a meaning for the word "think."

Alan Turing, in his famous paper "Computing Machinery and Intelligence" (Turing, 1950), suggested that instead of asking whether machines can think, we should ask whether machines can pass a behavioral intelligence test, which has come to be called the Turing Test. The test is for a program to have a conversation (via online typed messages) with an interrogator for 5 minutes. The interrogator then has to guess if the conversation is with a program or a person; the program passes the test if it fools the interrogator 30% of the time. Turing conjectured that, by the year 2000, a computer with a storage of $10^9$ units could be programmed well enough to pass the test, but he was wrong. Some people *have* been fooled for 5 minutes; for example, the ELIZA program and the Internet chatbot called MGONZ have fooled humans who didn't realize they might be talking to a program, and the program ALICE fooled one judge in the 2001 Loebner Prize competition. But no program has come close to the 30% criterion against trained judges, and the field of AI as a whole has paid little attention to Turing tests.

Turing also examined a wide variety of possible objections to the possibility of intelligent machines, including virtually all of those that have been raised in the half century since his paper appeared. We will look at some of them.

### The argument from disability

The "argument from disability" makes the claim that "a machine can never do *X*." As examples of *X*, Turing lists the following:

---

[1] In Russian, the equivalent of "swim" *does* apply to ships.

> Be kind, resourceful, beautiful, friendly, have initiative, have a sense of humor, tell right from wrong, make mistakes, fall in love, enjoy strawberries and cream, make someone fall in love with it, learn from experience, use words properly, be the subject of its own thought, have as much diversity of behavior as man, do something really new.

Turing had to use his intuition to guess what would be possible in the future, but we have the luxury of looking back at what computers have already done. It is undeniable that computers now do many things that previously were the domain of humans alone. Programs play chess, checkers and other games, inspect parts on assembly lines, check the spelling of word processing documents, steer cars and helicopters, diagnose diseases, and do hundreds of other tasks as well as or better than humans. Computers have made small but significant discoveries in astronomy, mathematics, chemistry, mineralogy, biology, computer science, and other fields. Each of these required performance at the level of a human expert.

Given what we now know about computers, it is not surprising that they do well at combinatorial problems such as playing chess. But algorithms also perform at human levels on tasks that seemingly involve human judgment, or as Turing put it, "learning from experience" and the ability to "tell right from wrong." As far back as 1955, Paul Meehl (see also Grove and Meehl, 1996) studied the decision-making processes of trained experts at subjective tasks such as predicting the success of a student in a training program, or the recidivism of a criminal. In 19 out of the 20 studies he looked at, Meehl found that simple statistical learning algorithms (such as linear regression or naive Bayes) predict better than the experts. The Educational Testing Service has used an automated program to grade millions of essay questions on the GMAT exam since 1999. The program agrees with human graders 97% of the time, about the same level that two human graders agree (Burstein *et al.*, 2001).

It is clear that computers can do many things as well as or better than humans, including things that people believe require great human insight and understanding. This does not mean, of course, that computers use insight and understanding in performing these tasks—those are not part of *behavior*, and we address such questions elsewhere—but the point is that one's first guess about the mental processes required to produce a given behavior is often wrong. It is also true, of course, that there are many tasks at which computers do not yet excel (to put it mildly), including Turing's task of carrying on an open-ended conversation.

### The mathematical objection

It is well known, through the work of Turing (1936) and Gödel (1931), that certain mathematical questions are in principle unanswerable by particular formal systems. Gödel's incompleteness theorem (see Section 9.5) is the most famous example of this. Briefly, for any formal axiomatic system $F$ powerful enough to do arithmetic, it is possible to construct a so-called "Gödel sentence" $G(F)$ with the following properties:

- $G(F)$ is a sentence of $F$, but cannot be proved within $F$.
- If $F$ is consistent, then $G(F)$ is true.

Philosophers such as J. R. Lucas (1961) have claimed that this theorem shows that machines are mentally inferior to humans, because machines are formal systems that are limited by the incompleteness theorem—they cannot establish the truth of their own Gödel sentence—while humans have no such limitation. This claim has caused decades of controversy, spawning a vast literature including two books by the mathematician Sir Roger Penrose (1989, 1994) that repeat the claim with some fresh twists (such as the hypothesis that humans are different because their brains operate by quantum gravity). We will examine only three of the problems with the claim.

First, Gödel's incompleteness theorem applies only to formal systems that are powerful enough to do arithmetic. This includes Turing machines, and Lucas's claim is in part based on the assertion that computers are Turing machines. This is a good approximation, but is not quite true. Turing machines are infinite, whereas computers are finite, and any computer can therefore be described as a (very large) system in propositional logic, which is not subject to Gödel's incompleteness theorem.

Second, an agent should not be too ashamed that it cannot establish the truth of some sentence while other agents can. Consider the sentence

J. R. Lucas cannot consistently assert that this sentence is true.

If Lucas asserted this sentence then he would be contradicting himself, so therefore Lucas cannot consistently assert it, and hence it must be true. (The sentence cannot be false, because if it were then Lucas could not consistently assert it, so it would be true.) We have thus demonstrated that there is a sentence that Lucas cannot consistently assert while other people (and machines) can. But that does not make us think less of Lucas. To take another example, no human could compute the sum of 10 billion 10 digit numbers in his or her lifetime, but a computer could do it in seconds. Still, we do not see this as a fundamental limitation in the human's ability to think. Humans were behaving intelligently for thousands of years before they invented mathematics, so it is unlikely that mathematical reasoning plays more than a peripheral role in what it means to be intelligent.

Third, and most importantly, even if we grant that computers have limitations on what they can prove, there is no evidence that humans are immune from those limitations. It is all too easy to show rigorously that a formal system cannot do $X$, and then claim that humans *can* do $X$ using their own informal method, without giving any evidence for this claim. Indeed, it is impossible to prove that humans are not subject to Gödel's incompleteness theorem, because any rigorous proof would itself contain a formalization of the claimed unformalizable human talent, and hence refute itself. So we are left with an appeal to intuition that humans can somehow perform superhuman feats of mathematical insight. This appeal is expressed with arguments such as "we must assume our own consistency, if thought is to be possible at all" (Lucas, 1976). But if anything, humans are known to be inconsistent. This is certainly true for everyday reasoning, but it is also true for careful mathematical thought. A famous example is the four-color map problem. Alfred Kempe published a proof in 1879 that was widely accepted and contributed to his election as a Fellow of the Royal Society. In 1890, however, Percy Heawood pointed out a flaw and the theorem remained unproved until 1977.

### The argument from informality

One of the most influential and persistent criticisms of AI as an enterprise was raised by Turing as the "argument from informality of behavior." Essentially, this is the claim that human behavior is far too complex to be captured by any simple set of rules and that because computers can do no more than follow a set of rules, they cannot generate behavior as intelligent as that of humans. The inability to capture everything in a set of logical rules is called the **qualification problem** in AI. (See Chapter 10.)

The principal proponent of this view has been the philosopher Hubert Dreyfus, who has produced a series of influential critiques of artificial intelligence: *What Computers Can't Do* (1972), *What Computers Still Can't Do* (1992), and, with his brother Stuart, *Mind Over Machine* (1986).

The position they criticize came to be called "Good Old-Fashioned AI," or GOFAI, a term coined by Haugeland (1985). GOFAI is supposed to claim that all intelligent behavior can be captured by a system that reasons logically from a set of facts and rules describing the domain. It therefore corresponds to the simplest logical agent described in Chapter 7. Dreyfus is correct in saying that logical agents are vulnerable to the qualification problem. As we saw in Chapter 13, probabilistic reasoning systems are more appropriate for open-ended domains. The Dreyfus critique therefore is not addressed against computers *per se*, but rather against one particular way of programming them. It is reasonable to suppose, however, that a book called *What First-Order Logical Rule-Based Systems Without Learning Can't Do* might have had less impact.

Under Dreyfus's view, human expertise does include knowledge of some rules, but only as a "holistic context" or "background" within which humans operate. He gives the example of appropriate social behavior in giving and receiving gifts: "Normally one simply responds in the appropriate circumstances by giving an appropriate gift." One apparently has "a direct sense of how things are done and what to expect." The same claim is made in the context of chess playing: "A mere chess master might need to figure out what to do, but a grandmaster just sees the board as demanding a certain move . . . the right response just pops into his or her head." It is certainly true that much of the thought processes of a present-giver or grandmaster is done at a level that is not open to introspection by the conscious mind. But that does not mean that the thought processes do not exist. The important question that Dreyfus does not answer is *how* the right move gets into the grandmaster's head. One is reminded of Daniel Dennett's (1984) comment,

> It is rather as if philosophers were to proclaim themselves expert explainers of the methods of stage magicians, and then, when we ask how the magician does the sawing-the-lady-in-half trick, they explain that it is really quite obvious: the magician doesn't really saw her in half; he simply makes it appear that he does. "But how does he do *that*?" we ask. "Not our department," say the philosophers.

Dreyfus and Dreyfus (1986) propose a five-stage process of acquiring expertise, beginning with rule-based processing (of the sort proposed in GOFAI) and ending with the ability to select correct responses instantaneously. In making this proposal, Dreyfus and Dreyfus in effect move from being AI critics to AI theorists—they propose a neural network architecture organized into a vast "case library," but point out several problems. Fortunately, all of their problems have been addressed, some with partial success and some with total success. Their problems include:

1. Good generalization from examples cannot be achieved without background knowledge. They claim no one has any idea how to incorporate background knowledge into the neural network learning process. In fact, we saw in Chapter 19 that there are techniques for using prior knowledge in learning algorithms. Those techniques, however, rely on the availability of knowledge in explicit form, something that Dreyfus and Dreyfus strenuously deny. In our view, this is a good reason for a serious redesign of current models of neural processing so that they *can* take advantage of previously learned knowledge in the way that other learning algorithms do.
2. Neural network learning is a form of supervised learning (see Chapter 18), requiring the prior identification of relevant inputs and correct outputs. Therefore, they claim, it cannot operate autonomously without the help of a human trainer. In fact, learning without a teacher can be accomplished by **unsupervised learning** (Chapter 20) and **reinforcement learning** (Chapter 21).
3. Learning algorithms do not perform well with many features, and if we pick a subset of features, "there is no known way of adding new features should the current set prove inadequate to account for the learned facts." In fact, new methods such as support vector machines handle large feature sets very well. As we saw in Chapter 19, there are also principled ways to generate new features, although much more work is needed.
4. The brain is able to direct its sensors to seek relevant information and to process it to extract aspects relevant to the current situation. But, they claim, "Currently, no details of this mechanism are understood or even hypothesized in a way that could guide AI research." In fact, the field of active vision, underpinned by the theory of information value (Chapter 16), is concerned with exactly the problem of directing sensors, and already some robots have incorporated the theoretical results obtained.

In sum, many of the issues Dreyfus has focused on—background commonsense knowledge, the qualification problem, uncertainty, learning, compiled forms of decision making, the importance of considering situated agents rather than disembodied inference engines—have by now been incorporated into standard intelligent agent design. In our view, this is evidence of AI's progress, not of its impossibility.

## 26.2 STRONG AI: CAN MACHINES REALLY THINK?

Many philosophers have claimed that a machine that passes the Turing Test would still not be *actually* thinking, but would be only a *simulation* of thinking. Again, the objection was foreseen by Turing. He cites a speech by Professor Geoffrey Jefferson (1949):

> Not until a machine could write a sonnet or compose a concerto because of thoughts and emotions felt, and not by the chance fall of symbols, could we agree that machine equals brain—that is, not only write it but know that it had written it.

Turing calls this the argument from **consciousness**—the machine has to be aware of its own mental states and actions. While consciousness is an important subject, Jefferson's key point actually relates to **phenomenology**, or the study of direct experience—the machine has to actually feel emotions. Others focus on **intentionality**—that is, the question of whether the machine's purported beliefs, desires, and other representations are actually "about" something in the real world.

Turing's response to the objection is interesting. He could have presented reasons that machines can in fact be conscious (or have phenomenology, or have intentions). Instead, he maintains that the question is just as ill-defined as asking, "Can machines think?" Besides, why should we insist on a higher standard for machines than we do for humans? After all, in ordinary life we never have *any* direct evidence about the internal mental states of other humans. Nevertheless, Turing says, "Instead of arguing continually over this point, it is usual to have the **polite convention** that everyone thinks."

POLITE CONVENTION

Turing argues that Jefferson would be willing to extend the polite convention to machines if only he had experience with ones that act intelligently. He cites the following dialog, which has become such a part of AI's oral tradition that we simply have to include it:

> HUMAN: In the first line of your sonnet which reads "shall I compare thee to a summer's day," would not a "spring day" do as well or better?
> MACHINE: It wouldn't scan.
> HUMAN: How about "a winter's day." That would scan all right.
> MACHINE: Yes, but nobody wants to be compared to a winter's day.
> HUMAN: Would you say Mr. Pickwick reminded you of Christmas?
> MACHINE: In a way.
> HUMAN: Yet Christmas is a winter's day, and I do not think Mr. Pickwick would mind the comparison.
> MACHINE: I don't think you're serious. By a winter's day one means a typical winter's day, rather than a special one like Christmas.

Turing concedes that the question of consciousness is a difficult one, but denies that it has much relevance to the practice of AI: "I do not wish to give the impression that I think there is no mystery about consciousness ... But I do not think these mysteries necessarily need to be solved before we can answer the question with which we are concerned in this paper." We agree with Turing—we are interested in creating programs that behave intelligently, not in whether someone else pronounces them to be real or simulated. On the other hand, many philosophers are keenly interested in the question. To help understand it, we will consider the question of whether other artifacts are considered real.

In 1848, artificial urea was synthesized for the first time, by Frederick Wöhler. This was important because it proved that organic and inorganic chemistry could be united, a question that had been hotly debated. Once the synthesis was accomplished, chemists agreed that artificial urea *was* urea, because it had all the right physical properties. Similarly, artificial sweeteners are undeniably sweeteners, and artificial insemination (the other AI) is undeniably insemination. On the other hand, artificial flowers are not flowers, and Daniel Dennett points out that artificial Chateau Latour wine would not be Chateau Latour wine, even if it was chemically indistinguishable, simply because it was not made in the right place in the right way. Nor is an artificial Picasso painting a Picasso painting, no matter what it looks like.

We can conclude that in some cases, the behavior of an artifact is important, while in others it is the artifact's pedigree that matters. Which one is important in which case seems to be a matter of convention. But for artificial minds, there is no convention, and we are left to rely on intuitions. The philosopher John Searle (1980) has a strong one:

> No one supposes that a computer simulation of a storm will leave us all wet . . . Why on earth would anyone in his right mind suppose a computer simulation of mental processes actually had mental processes? (pp. 37–38)

While it is easy to agree that computer simulations of storms do not make us wet, it is not clear how to carry this analogy over to computer simulations of mental processes. After all, a Hollywood simulation of a storm using sprinklers and wind machines *does* make the actors wet. Most people are comfortable saying that a computer simulation of addition is addition, and a computer simulation of a chess game is a chess game. Are mental processes more like storms, or more like addition or chess? Like Chateau Latour and Picasso, or like urea? That all depends on your theory of mental states and processes.

FUNCTIONALISM

The theory of **functionalism** says that a mental state is any intermediate causal condition between input and output. Under functionalist theory, any two systems with isomorphic causal processes would have the same mental states. Therefore, a computer program could have the same mental states as a person. Of course, we have not yet said what "isomorphic" really means, but the assumption is that there is some level of abstraction below which the specific implementation does not matter; as long as the processes are isomorphic down to the this level, the same mental states will occur.

BIOLOGICAL NATURALISM

In contrast, the **biological naturalism** theory says that mental states are high-level emergent features that are caused by low-level neurological processes *in the neurons*, and it is the (unspecified) properties of the neurons that matter. Thus, mental states cannot be duplicated just on the basis of some program having the same functional structure with the same input–output behavior; we would require that the program be running on an architecture with the same causal power as neurons. The theory does not say why neurons have this causal power, nor what other physical instantiations might or might not have it.

To investigate these two viewpoints we will first look at one of the oldest problems in the philosophy of mind, and then turn to three thought experiments.

### The mind–body problem

MIND–BODY PROBLEM

The **mind–body problem** asks how mental states and processes are related to bodily (specifically, brain) states and processes. As if that wasn't hard enough, we will generalize the problem to the "mind–architecture" problem, to allow us to talk about the possibility of machines having minds.

Why is the mind–body problem a problem? The first difficulty goes back to René Descartes, who considered how an immortal soul interacts with a mortal body and concluded that the soul and body are two distinct types of things—a **dualist** theory. The **monist** theory, often called **materialism**, holds that there are no such things as immaterial souls; only material objects. Consequently, mental states—such as being in pain, knowing that one is riding a horse, or believing that Vienna is the capital of Austria—are brain states. John Searle pithily

DUALISM

MONISM

MATERIALISM

sums up the idea with the slogan, "*Brains cause minds*."

The materialist must face at least two serious obstacles. The first is the problem of

FREE WILL

**free will**: how can it be that a purely physical mind, whose every transformation is governed strictly by the laws of physics, still retains any freedom of choice? Most philosophers regard this problem as requiring a careful reconstitution of our naive notion of free will, rather than presenting any threat to materialism. The second problem concerns the general issue of **consciousness** (and related, but not identical, questions of **understanding** and **self-awareness**). Put simply, why is it that it *feels* like something to have certain brain states, whereas it presumably does not feel like anything to have other physical states (e.g., being a rock).

CONSCIOUSNESS

To begin to answer such questions, we need ways to talk about brain states at levels more abstract than specific configurations of all the atoms of the brain of a particular person at a particular time. For example, as I think about the capital of Austria, my brain undergoes myriad tiny changes from one picosecond to the next, but these do not constitute a *qualitative* change in brain state. To account for this, we need a notion of brain state *types*, under which we can judge whether two brain states belong to the same or different types. Various authors have various positions on what one means by *type* in this case. Almost everyone believes that if one takes a brain and replaces some of the carbon atoms by a new set of carbon atoms,[2] the mental state will not be affected. This is a good thing because real brains are continually replacing their atoms through metabolic processes, and yet this in itself does not seem to cause major mental upheavals.

INTENTIONAL STATE

Now let's consider a particular kind of mental state: the **propositional attitudes** (first discussed in Chapter 10), which are also known as **intentional states**. These are states, such as believing, knowing, desiring, fearing, and so on, that refer to some aspect of the external world. For example, the belief that Vienna is the capital of Austria is a belief *about* a particular city and its status. We will be asking whether it is possible for computers to have intentional states, so it helps to understand how to characterize such states. For example, one might say that the mental state in which I desire a hamburger differs from the state in which I desire a pizza because hamburger and pizza are different things in the real world. That is to say, intentional states have a necessary connection to their objects in the external world. On the other hand, we argued just a few paragraphs back that mental states are brain states; hence the identity or non-identity of mental states should be determined by staying completely "inside the head," without reference to the real world. To examine this dilemma we turn to a thought experiment that attempts to separate intentional states from their external objects.

### The "brain in a vat" experiment

Imagine, if you will, that your brain was removed from your body at birth and placed in a marvelously engineered vat. The vat sustains your brain, allowing it to grow and develop. At the same time, electronic signals are fed to your brain from a computer simulation of an entirely fictitious world, and motor signals from your brain are intercepted and used to modify the simulation as appropriate.[3] Then the brain could have the mental state

[2] Perhaps even atoms of a different isotope of carbon, as is sometimes done in brain-scanning experiments.

[3] This situation may be familiar to those who have seen the 1999 film, *The Matrix*.

$DyingFor(Me, Hamburger)$ even though it has no body to feel hunger and no taste buds to experience taste, and there may be no hamburger in the real world. In that case, would this be the same mental state as one held by a brain in a body?

One way to resolve the dilemma is to say that the content of mental states can be interpreted from two different points of view. The "**wide content**" view interprets it from the point of view of an omniscient outside observer with access to the whole situation, who can distinguish differences in the world. So under wide content the brain-in-a-vat beliefs are different from those of a "normal" person. **Narrow content** considers only the internal subjective point of view, and under this view the beliefs would all be the same.

WIDE CONTENT

NARROW CONTENT

The belief that a hamburger is delicious has a certain intrinsic nature—there is something that it is like to have this belief. Now we get into the realm of **qualia**, or intrinsic experiences (from the Latin word meaning, roughly, "such things"). Suppose, through some accident of retinal and neural wiring, that person $X$ experiences as red the color that person $Y$ perceives as green, and vice-versa. Then when both see the same traffic light they will act the same way, but the *experience* they have will be in some way different. Both may agree that the name for their experience is "the light is red," but the experiences feel different. It is not clear whether that means they are the same or different mental states.

QUALIA

We now turn to another thought experiment that gets at the question of whether physical objects other than human neurons can have mental states.

### The brain prosthesis experiment

The brain prosthesis experiment was introduced in the mid-1970s by Clark Glymour and was touched on by John Searle (1980), but is most commonly associated with the work of Hans Moravec (1988). It goes like this: Suppose neurophysiology has developed to the point where the input–output behavior and connectivity of all the neurons in the human brain are perfectly understood. Suppose further that we can build microscopic electronic devices that mimic this behavior and can be smoothly interfaced to neural tissue. Lastly, suppose that some miraculous surgical technique can replace individual neurons with the corresponding electronic devices without interrupting the operation of the brain as a whole. The experiment consists of gradually replacing all the neurons in someone's head with electronic devices and then reversing the process to return the subject to his or her normal biological state.

We are concerned with both the external behavior and the internal experience of the subject, during and after the operation. By the definition of the experiment, the subject's external behavior must remain unchanged compared with what would be observed if the operation were not carried out.[4] Now although the presence or absence of consciousness cannot easily be ascertained by a third party, the subject of the experiment ought at least to be able to record any changes in his or her own conscious experience. Apparently, there is a direct clash of intuitions as to what would happen. Moravec, a robotics researcher and functionalist, is convinced his consciousness would remain unaffected. Searle, a philosopher and biological naturalist, is equally convinced his consciousness would vanish:

[4] One can imagine using an identical "control" subject who is given a placebo operation, so that the two behaviors can be compared.

> You find, to your total amazement, that you are indeed losing control of your external behavior. You find, for example, that when doctors test your vision, you hear them say "We are holding up a red object in front of you; please tell us what you see." You want to cry out "I can't see anything. I'm going totally blind." But you hear your voice saying in a way that is completely out of your control, "I see a red object in front of me." ... [Y]our conscious experience slowly shrinks to nothing, while your externally observable behavior remains the same. (Searle, 1992)

But one can do more than argue from intuition. First, note that, in order for the external behavior to remain the same while the subject gradually becomes unconscious, it must be the case that the subject's volition is removed instantaneously and totally; otherwise the shrinking of awareness would be reflected in external behavior—"Help, I'm shrinking!" or words to that effect. This instantaneous removal of volition as a result of gradual neuron-at-a-time replacement seems an unlikely claim to have to make.

Second, consider what happens if we do ask the subject questions concerning his or her conscious experience during the period when no real neurons remain. By the conditions of the experiment, we will get responses such as "I feel fine. I must say I'm a bit surprised because I believed Searle's argument." Or we might poke the subject with a pointed stick and observe the response, "Ouch, that hurt." Now, in the normal course of affairs, the skeptic can dismiss such outputs from AI programs as mere contrivances. Certainly, it is easy enough to use a rule such as "If sensor 12 reads 'High' then output 'Ouch.' " But the point here is that, because we have replicated the functional properties of a normal human brain, we assume that the electronic brain contains no such contrivances. Then we must have an explanation of the manifestations of consciousness produced by the electronic brain that appeals only to the functional properties of the neurons. *And this explanation must also apply to the real brain, which has the same functional properties.* There are, it seems, only two possible conclusions:

1. The causal mechanisms of consciousness that generate these kinds of outputs in normal brains are still operating in the electronic version, which is therefore conscious.
2. The conscious mental events in the normal brain have no causal connection to behavior, and are missing from the electronic brain, which is therefore not conscious.

EPIPHENOMENON

Although we cannot rule out the second possibility, it reduces consciousness to what philosophers call an **epiphenomenal** role—something that happens, but casts no shadow, as it were, on the observable world. Furthermore, if consciousness is indeed epiphenomenal, then the brain must contain a second, unconscious mechanism that is responsible for the "Ouch."

Third, consider the situation after the operation has been reversed and the subject has a normal brain. Once again, the subject's external behavior must, by definition, be as if the operation had not occurred. In particular, we should be able to ask, "What was it like during the operation? Do you remember the pointed stick?" The subject must have accurate memories of the actual nature of his or her conscious experiences, including the qualia, despite the fact that, according to Searle there were no such experiences.

Searle might reply that we have not defined the experiment properly. If the real neurons are, say, put into suspended animation between the time they are extracted and the time they are replaced in the brain, then of course they will not "remember" the experiences during the operation. To deal with this eventuality, we need to make sure that the neurons' state is updated to reflect the internal state of the artificial neurons they are replacing. If the supposed "nonfunctional" aspects of the real neurons then result in functionally different behavior from that observed with artificial neurons still in place, then we have a simple *reductio ad absurdum*, because that would mean that the artificial neurons are not functionally equivalent to the real neurons. (See Exercise 26.3 for one possible rebuttal to this argument.)

Patricia Churchland (1986) points out that the functionalist arguments that operate at the level of the neuron can also operate at the level of any larger functional unit—a clump of neurons, a mental module, a lobe, a hemisphere, or the whole brain. That means that if you accept the notion that the brain prosthesis experiment shows that the replacement brain is conscious, then you should also believe that consciousness is maintained when the entire brain is replaced by a circuit that maps from inputs to outputs via a huge lookup table. This is disconcerting to many people (including Turing himself), who have the intuition that lookup tables are not conscious—or at least, that the conscious experiences generated during table lookup are not the same as those generated during the operation of a system that might be described (even in a simple-minded, computational sense) as accessing and generating beliefs, introspections, goals, and so on. This would suggest that the brain prosthesis experiment cannot use whole-brain-at-once replacement if it is to be effective in guiding intuitions, but it does not mean that it must use one-atom-at-a-time replacement as Searle have us believe.

### The Chinese room

Our final thought experiment is perhaps the most famous of all. It is due to John Searle (1980), who describes a hypothetical system that is clearly running a program and passes the Turing Test, but that equally clearly (according to Searle) does not *understand* anything of its inputs and outputs. His conclusion is that running the appropriate program (i.e., having the right outputs) is not a *sufficient* condition for being a mind.

The system consists of a human, who understands only English, equipped with a rule book, written in English, and various stacks of paper, some blank, some with indecipherable inscriptions. (The human therefore plays the role of the CPU, the rule book is the program, and the stacks of paper are the storage device.) The system is inside a room with a small opening to the outside. Through the opening appear slips of paper with indecipherable symbols. The human finds matching symbols in the rule book, and follows the instructions. The instructions may include writing symbols on new slips of paper, finding symbols in the stacks, rearranging the stacks, and so on. Eventually, the instructions will cause one or more symbols to be transcribed onto a piece of paper that is passed back to the outside world.

So far, so good. But from the outside, we see a system that is taking input in the form of Chinese sentences and generating answers in Chinese that are as obviously "intelligent" as those in the conversation imagined by Turing.[5] Searle then argues as follows: the person in the room does not understand Chinese (given). The rule book and the stacks of paper, being

5 The fact that the stacks of paper might well be larger than the entire planet and the generation of answers would take millions of years has no bearing on the *logical* structure of the argument. One aim of philosophical training is to develop a finely honed sense of which objections are germane and which are not.

just pieces of paper, do not understand Chinese. Therefore, there is no understanding of Chinese going on. *Hence, according to Searle, running the right program does not necessarily generate understanding.*

Like Turing, Searle considered and attempted to rebuff a number of replies to his argument. Several commentators, including John McCarthy and Robert Wilensky, proposed what Searle calls the systems reply. The objection is that, although one can ask if the human in the room understands Chinese, this is analogous to asking if the CPU can take cube roots. In both cases, the answer is no, and in both cases, according to the systems reply, the entire system *does* have the capacity in question. Certainly, if one asks the Chinese room whether it understands Chinese, the answer would be affirmative (in fluent Chinese). By Turing's polite convention, this should be enough. Searle's response is to reiterate the point that the understanding is not in the human and cannot be in the paper, so there cannot be any understanding. He further suggests that one could imagine the human memorizing the rule book and the contents of all the stacks of paper, so that there would be nothing to have understanding *except* the human; and again, when one asks the human (in English), the reply will be in the negative.

Now we are down to the real issues. The shift from paper to memorization is a red herring, because both forms are simply physical instantiations of a running program. The real claim made by Searle rests upon the following four axioms (Searle, 1990):

1. Computer programs are formal, syntactic entities.
2. Minds have mental contents, or semantics.
3. Syntax by itself is not sufficient for semantics.
4. Brains cause minds.

From the first three axioms he concludes that programs are not sufficient for minds. In other words, an agent running a program might be a mind, but it is not necessarily a mind just by virtue of running the program. From the fourth axiom he concludes "Any other system capable of causing minds would have to have causal powers (at least) equivalent to those of brains." From there he infers that any artificial brain would have to duplicate the causal powers of brains, not just run a particular program, and that human brains do not produce mental phenomena solely by virtue of running a program.

The conclusions that programs are not sufficient for minds *does* follow from the axioms, if you are generous in interpreting them. But the conclusion is unsatisfactory—all Searle has shown is that if you explicitly deny functionalism (that is what his axiom (3) does) then you can't necessarily conclude that non-brains are minds. This is reasonable enough, so the whole argument comes down to whether axiom (3) can be accepted. According to Searle, the point of the Chinese room argument is to provide intuitions for axiom (3). But the reaction to his argument shows that it provides intuitions only to those who were already inclined to accept the idea that mere programs cannot generate true understanding.

To reiterate, the aim of the Chinese Room argument is to refute strong AI—the claim that running the right sort of program necessarily results in a mind. It does this by exhibiting an apparently intelligent system running the right sort of program that is, according to Searle, *demonstrably* not a mind. Searle appeals to intuition, not proof, for this part: just look at the room; what's there to be a mind? But one could make the same argument about the brain:

just look at this collection of cells (or of atoms), blindly operating according to the laws of biochemistry (or of physics)—what's there to be a mind? Why can a hunk of brain be a mind while a hunk of liver cannot?

Furthermore, when Searle admits that materials other than neurons could in principle be a mind, he weakens his argument even further, for two reasons: first, one has only Searle's intuitions (or one's own) to say that the Chinese room is not a mind, and second, even if we decide the room is not a mind, that tells us nothing about whether a program running on some other physical medium (including a computer) might be a mind.

Searle allows the logical possibility that the brain is actually implementing an AI program of the traditional sort—but the same program running on the wrong kind of machine would not be a mind. Searle has denied that he believes that "machines cannot have minds," rather, he asserts that some machines *do* have minds—humans are biological machines with minds. We are left without much guidance as to what types of machines do or do not qualify.

## 26.3 The Ethics and Risks of Developing Artificial Intelligence

So far, we have concentrated on whether we *can* develop AI, but we must also consider whether we *should*. If the effects of AI technology are more likely to be negative than positive, then it would be the moral responsibility of workers in the field to redirect their research. Many new technologies have had unintended negative side-effects: the internal combustion engine brought air pollution and the paving-over of paradise; nuclear fission brought Chernobyl, Three Mile Island, and the threat of global destruction. All scientists and engineers face ethical considerations of how they should act on the job, what projects should or should not be done, and how they should be handled. There is even a handbook on the *Ethics of Computing* (Berleur and Brunnstein, 2001). AI, however, seems to pose some fresh problems beyond that of, say, building bridges that don't fall down:

- People might lose their jobs to automation.
- People might have too much (or too little) leisure time.
- People might lose their sense of being unique.
- People might lose some of their privacy rights.
- The use of AI systems might result in a loss of accountability.
- The success of AI might mean the end of the human race.

We will look at each issue in turn.

*People might lose their jobs to automation.* The modern industrial economy has become dependent on computers in general, and select AI programs in particular. For example, much of the economy, especially in the United States, depends on the availability of consumer credit. Credit card applications, charge approvals, and fraud detection are now done by AI programs. One could say that thousands of workers have been displaced by these AI programs, but in fact if you took away the AI programs these jobs would not exist, because human labor would add an unacceptable cost to the transactions. So far, automation via AI technology has created more jobs than it has eliminated, and has created more interesting, higher-paying jobs. Now that the canonical AI program is an "intelligent agent" designed to assist a human, loss of jobs is less of a concern than it was when AI focused on "expert systems" designed to replace humans.

*People might have too much (or too little) leisure time.* Alvin Toffler wrote in *Future Shock* (1970), "The work week has been cut by 50 percent since the turn of the century. It is not out of the way to predict that it will be slashed in half again by 2000." Arthur C. Clarke (1968b) wrote that people in 2001 might be "faced with a future of utter boredom, where the main problem in life is deciding which of several hundred TV channels to select." The only one of these predictions that has come close to panning out is the number of TV channels (Springsteen, 1992). Instead, people working in knowledge-intensive industries have found themselves part of an integrated computerized system that operates 24 hours a day; to keep up, they have been forced to work *longer* hours. In an industrial economy, rewards are roughly proportional to the time invested; working 10% more would tend to mean a 10% increase in income. In an information economy marked by high-bandwidth communication and easy replication of intellectual property (what Frank and Cook (1996) call the "Winner-Take-All Society"), there is a large reward for being slightly better than the competition; working 10% more could mean a 100% increase in income. So there is increasing pressure on everyone to work harder. AI increases the pace of technological innovation and thus contributes to this overall trend, but AI also holds the promise of allowing us to take some time off and let our automated agents handle things for a while.

*People might lose their sense of being unique.* In *Computer Power and Human Reason*, Weizenbaum (1976), the author of the ELIZA program, points out some of the potential threats that AI poses to society. One of Weizenbaum's principal arguments is that AI research makes possible the idea that humans are automata—an idea that results in a loss of autonomy or even of humanity. We note that the idea has been around much longer than AI, going back at least to *L'Homme Machine* (La Mettrie, 1748). We also note that humanity has survived other setbacks to our sense of uniqueness: *De Revolutionibus Orbium Coelestium* (Copernicus, 1543) moved the Earth away from the center of the solar system and *Descent of Man* (Darwin, 1871) put *Homo sapiens* at the same level as other species. AI, if widely successful, may be at least as threatening to the moral assumptions of 21st-century society as Darwin's theory of evolution was to those of the 19th century.

*People might lose some of their privacy rights.* Weizenbaum also pointed out that speech recognition technology could lead to widespread wiretapping, and hence to a loss of civil liberties. He didn't foresee a world with terrorist threats that would change the balance of how much surveillance people are willing to accept, but he did correctly recognize that AI has the potential to mass-produce surveillance. His prediction may have come true: the U.S. government's classified Echelon system "consists of a network of listening posts, antenna fields, and radar stations; the system is backed by computers that use language translation, speech recognition, and keyword searching to automatically sift through telephone, email, fax, and telex traffic."[6] Some accept that computerization leads to a loss of privacy—Sun

[6] See "Eavesdropping on Europe," *Wired* news, 9/30/1998, and cited EU reports.

Microsystems CEO Scott McNealy has said "You have zero privacy anyway. Get over it." Others disagree: Judge Louis Brandeis wrote in 1890, "Privacy is the most comprehensive of all rights ... the right to one's personality."

*The use of AI systems might result in a loss of accountability.* In the litigious atmosphere that prevails in the United States, legal liability becomes an important issue. When a physician relies on the judgment of a medical expert system for a diagnosis, who is at fault if the diagnosis is wrong? Fortunately, due in part to the growing influence of decision-theoretic methods in medicine, it is now accepted that negligence cannot be shown if the physician performs medical procedures that have high *expected* utility, even if the *actual* result is catastrophic for the patient. The question should therefore be "Who is at fault if the diagnosis is unreasonable?" So far, courts have held that medical expert systems play the same role as medical textbooks and reference books; physicians are responsible for understanding the reasoning behind any decision and for using their own judgment in deciding whether to accept the system's recommendations. In designing medical expert systems as agents, therefore, the actions should be thought of not as directly affecting the patient but as influencing the physician's behavior. If expert systems become reliably more accurate than human diagnosticians, doctors might become legally liable if they *don't* use the recommendations of an expert system. Gawande (2002) explores this premise.

Similar issues are beginning to arise regarding the use of intelligent agents on the Internet. Some progress has been made in incorporating constraints into intelligent agents so that they cannot, for example, damage the files of other users (Weld and Etzioni, 1994). The problem is magnified when money changes hands. If monetary transactions are made "on one's behalf" by an intelligent agent, is one liable for the debts incurred? Would it be possible for an intelligent agent to have assets itself and to perform electronic trades on its own behalf? So far, these questions do not seem to be well understood. To our knowledge, no program has been granted legal status as an individual for the purposes of financial transactions; at present, it seems unreasonable to do so. Programs are also not considered to be "drivers" for the purposes of enforcing traffic regulations on real highways. In California law, at least, there do not seem to be any legal sanctions to prevent an automated vehicle from exceeding the speed limits, although the designer of the vehicle's control mechanism would be liable in the case of an accident. As with human reproductive technology, the law has yet to catch up with the new developments.

*The success of AI might mean the end of the human race.* Almost any technology has the potential to cause harm in the wrong hands, but with AI and robotics, we have the new problem that the wrong hands might belong to the technology itself. Countless science fiction stories have warned about robots or robot–human cyborgs running amok. Early examples include Mary Shelley's *Frankenstein, or the Modern Prometheus* (1818)[7] and Karel Capek's play *R.U.R* (1921), in which robots conquer the world. In movies, we have *The Terminator* (1984), which combines the cliches of robots-conquer-the-world with time travel, and *The Matrix* (1999), which combines robots-conquer-the-world with brain-in-a-vat.

[7] As a young man, Charles Babbage was influenced by reading *Frankenstein*.

For the most part, it seems that robots are the protagonists of so many conquer-the-world stories because they represent the unknown, just like the witches and ghosts of tales from earlier eras. Do they pose a more credible threat than witches and ghosts? If robots are properly designed as agents that adopt their owner's goals, then they probably do not: robots that derive from incremental advances over current designs will serve, not conquer. Humans use their intelligence in aggressive ways because humans have some innately aggressive tendencies, due to natural selection. But the machines we build need not be innately aggressive, unless we decide to build them that way. On the other hand, it is possible that computers will achieve a sort of conquest by serving and becoming indispensable, just as automobiles have in a sense conquered the industrialized world. One scenario deserves further consideration. I. J. Good wrote (1965),

> Let an ultraintelligent machine be defined as a machine that can far surpass all the intellectual activities of any man however clever. Since the design of machines is one of these intellectual activities, an ultraintelligent machine could design even better machines; there would then unquestionably be an "intelligence explosion," and the intelligence of man would be left far behind. Thus the first ultraintelligent machine is the *last* invention that man need ever make, provided that the machine is docile enough to tell us how to keep it under control.

TECHNOLOGICAL SINGULARITY

The "intelligence explosion" has also been called the **technological singularity** by mathematics professor and science fiction author Vernor Vinge, who writes (1993), "Within thirty years, we will have the technological means to create superhuman intelligence. Shortly after, the human era will be ended." Good and Vinge (and many others) correctly note that the curve of technological progress is growing exponentially at present (consider Moore's Law). However, it is quite a step to extrapolate that the curve will continue on to a singularity of near-infinite growth. So far, every other technology has followed an S-shaped curve, where the exponential growth eventually tapers off.

Vinge is concerned and scared about the coming singularity, but other computer scientists and futurists relish it. Hans Moravec's *Robot: Mere Machine to Transcendent Mind* predicts that robots will match human intelligence in 50 years and then exceed it. He writes,

> Rather quickly, they could displace us from existence. I'm not as alarmed as many by the latter possibility, since I consider these future machines our progeny, "mind children" built in our image and likeness, ourselves in more potent form. Like biological children of previous generations, they will embody humanity's best hope for a long-term future. It behooves us to give them every advantage, and to bow out when we can no longer contribute. (Moravec, 2000)

Ray Kurzweil, in *The Age of Spiritual Machines* (2000), predicts that by the year 2099 there will be "a strong trend toward a merger of human thinking with the world of machine intelligence that the human species initially created. There is no longer any clear distinction between humans and computers." There is even a new word—**transhumanism**—for the active social movement that looks forward to this future. Suffice it to say that such issues present a challenge for most moral theorists, who take the preservation of human life and the human species to be a good thing.

TRANSHUMANISM

Finally, let us consider the robot's point of view. If robots become conscious, then to treat them as mere "machines" (e.g., to take them apart) might be immoral. Robots also must themselves act morally—we would need to program them with a theory of what is right and wrong. Science fiction writers have addressed the issue of robot rights and responsibilities, starting with Isaac Asimov (1942). The well-known movie *A.I.* (Spielberg, 2001) was based on a story by Brian Aldiss about an intelligent robot who was programmed to believe that he was human and fails to understand his eventual abandonment by his owner–mother. The story (and the movie) convince one of the need for a civil rights movement for robots.

## 26.4 Summary

This chapter has addressed the following issues:

- Philosophers use the term **weak AI** for the hypothesis that machines could possibly behave intelligently, and **strong AI** for the hypothesis that such machines would count as having actual minds (as opposed to simulated minds).
- Alan Turing rejected the question "Can machines think?" and replaced it with a behavioral test. He anticipated many objections to to the possibility of thinking machines. Few AI researchers pay attention to the Turing test, preferring to concentrate on their systems' performance on practical tasks, rather than the ability to imitate humans.
- There is general agreement in modern times that mental states are brain states.
- Arguments for and against strong AI are inconclusive. Few mainstream AI researchers believe that anything significant hinges on the outcome of the debate.
- Consciousness remains a mystery.
- We identified six potential threats to society posed by AI and related technology. We concluded that some of the threats are either unlikely or differ little from threats posed by other, "unintelligent" technologies. One threat in particular is worthy of further consideration: that ultraintelligent machines might lead to a future that is very different from today—we may not like it, and at that point we may not have a choice. Such considerations lead inevitably to the conclusion that we must weigh carefully, and soon, the possible consequences of AI research for the future of the human race.

## Bibliographical and Historical Notes

The nature of the mind has been a standard topic of philosophical theorizing from ancient times to the present. In the *Phaedo*, Plato specifically considered and rejected the idea that the mind could be an "attunement" or pattern of organization of the parts of the body, a viewpoint that approximates the functionalist viewpoint in modern philosophy of mind. He decided instead that the mind had to be an immortal, immaterial soul, separable from the body and different in substance—the viewpoint of dualism. Aristotle distinguished a variety of souls (Greek $\psi\upsilon\chi\eta$) in living things, some of which, at least, he described in a functionalist manner. (See Nussbaum (1978) for more on Aristotle's functionalism.)

Descartes is notorious for his dualistic view of the human mind, but ironically his historical influence was toward mechanism and materialism. He explicitly conceived of animals as automata, and he anticipated the Turing test, writing "it is not conceivable [that a machine] should produce different arrangements of words so as to give an appropriately meaningful answer to whatever is said in its presence, as even the dullest of men can do" (Descartes, 1637). Descartes's spirited defense of the animals-as-automata viewpoint actually had the effect of making it easier to conceive of humans as automata as well, even though he himself did not take this step. The book *L'Homme Machine* or *Man a Machine* (La Mettrie, 1748) did explicitly argue that humans are automata.

Modern analytic philosophy has typically accepted materialism (often in the form of the brain-state **identity theory** (Place, 1956; Armstrong, 1968), which asserts that mental states are identical with brain states), but has been much more divided on functionalism, the machine analogy for the human mind, and the question of whether machines can literally think. A number of early philosophical responses to Turing's (1950) "Computing Machinery and Intelligence," for example, Scriven (1953), attempted to deny that it was even *meaningful* to say that machines could think, on the ground that such an assertion violated the meaning of the word. Scriven, at least, had retracted this view by 1963; see his addendum to a reprint of his article (Anderson, 1964). The computer scientist Edsger Dijkstra said that "The question of whether a computer can think is no more interesting than the question of whether a submarine can swim." Ford and Hayes (1995) argue that the Turing Test is not helpful for AI.

Functionalism is the philosophy of mind most naturally suggested by AI, and critiques of functionalism often take the form of critiques of AI (as in the case of Searle). Following the classification used by Block (1980), we can distinguish varieties of functionalism. **Functional specification theory** (Lewis, 1966, 1980) is a variant of brain-state identity theory that selects the brain states that are to be identified with mental states on the basis of their functional role. **Functional state identity theory** (Putnam, 1960, 1967) is more closely based on a machine analogy. It identifies mental states not with *physical* brain states but with abstract computational states of the brain conceived expressly as a computing device. These abstract states are supposed to be independent of the specific physical composition of the brain, leading some to charge that functional state identity theory is a form of dualism!

Both the brain-state identity theory and the various forms of functionalism have come under attack from authors who claim that they do not account for the *qualia* or "what it's like" aspect of mental states (Nagel, 1974). Searle has focused instead on the alleged inability of functionalism to account for intentionality (Searle, 1980, 1984, 1992). Churchland and Churchland (1982) rebut both these types of criticism.

ELIMINATIVE MATERIALISM

**Eliminative materialism** (Rorty, 1965; Churchland, 1979) differs from all other prominent theories in the philosophy of mind, in that it does not attempt to give an account of why our "folk psychology" or commonsense ideas about the mind are true, but instead rejects them as false and attempts to replace them with a purely scientific theory of the mind. In principle, this scientific theory could be given by classical AI, but in practice, eliminative materialists tend to lean on neuroscience and neural network research instead (Churchland,

1986), on the grounds that classical AI, especially "knowledge representation" research of the kind described in Chapter 10, tends to rely on the truth of folk psychology. Although the "intentional stance" viewpoint (Dennett, 1971) could be interpreted as functionalist, it should probably instead be regarded as a form of eliminative materialism, in that taking the "intentional stance" is not supposed to reflect any objective property of the agent toward whom the stance is taken. It should also be noted that it is possible to be an eliminative materialist about some aspects of mentality while analyzing others in some other way. For instance, Dennett (1978) is much more strongly eliminativist about qualia than about intentionality.

Sources for the main critics of weak AI were given in the chapter. Although it became fashionable in the post-neural-network era to deride symbolic approaches, not all philosophers are critical of GOFAI. Some are, in fact, ardent advocates and even practitioners. Zenon Pylyshyn (1984) has argued that cognition can best be understood through a computational model, not only in principle but also as a way of conducting research at present, and has specifically rebutted Dreyfus's criticisms of the computational model of human cognition (Pylyshyn, 1974). Gilbert Harman (1983), in analyzing belief revision, makes connections with AI research on truth maintenance systems. Michael Bratman has applied his "belief-desire-intention" model of human psychology (Bratman, 1987) to AI research on planning (Bratman, 1992). At the extreme end of strong AI, Aaron Sloman (1978, p. xiii) has even described as "racialist" Joseph Weizenbaum's view (Weizenbaum, 1976) that hypothetical intelligent machines should not be regarded as persons.

The philosophical literature on minds, brains, and related topics is large and sometimes difficult to read without proper training in the terminology and methods of argument employed. The *Encyclopedia of Philosophy* (Edwards, 1967) is an impressively authoritative and very useful aide in this process. *The Cambridge Dictionary of Philosophy* (Audi, 1999) is a shorter and more accessible work, but main entries (such as "philosophy of mind") still span 10 pages or more. The *MIT Encyclopedia of Cognitive Science* (Wilson and Keil, 1999) covers the philosophy of mind as well as the biology and psychology of mind. General collections of articles on philosophy of mind, including functionalism and other viewpoints related to AI, are *Materialism and the Mind-Body Problem* (Rosenthal, 1971) and *Readings in the Philosophy of Psychology*, volume 1 (Block, 1980). Biro and Shahan (1982) present a collection devoted to the pros and cons of functionalism. Anthologies of articles dealing more specifically with the relation between philosophy and AI include *Minds and Machines* (Anderson, 1964), *Philosophical Perspectives in Artificial Intelligence* (Ringle, 1979), *Mind Design* (Haugeland, 1981), and *The Philosophy of Artificial Intelligence* (Boden, 1990). There are several general introductions to the philosophical "AI question" (Boden, 1977, 1990; Haugeland, 1985; Copeland, 1993). *The Behavioral and Brain Sciences*, abbreviated *BBS*, is a major journal devoted to philosophical and scientific debates about AI and neuroscience. Topics of ethics and responsibility in AI are covered in journals such as *AI and Society*, *Law, Computers and Artificial Intelligence*, and *Artificial Intelligence and Law*.

## EXERCISES

**26.1** Go through Turing's list of alleged "disabilities" of machines, identifying which have been achieved, which are achievable in principle by a program, and which are still problematic because they require conscious mental states.

**26.2** Does a refutation of the Chinese room argument necessarily prove that appropriately programmed computers have mental states? Does an acceptance of the argument necessarily mean that computers cannot have mental states?

**26.3** In the brain prosthesis argument, it is important to be able to restore the subject's brain to normal, such that its external behavior is as it would have been if the operation had not taken place. Can the skeptic reasonably object that this would require updating those neurophysiological properties of the neurons relating to conscious experience, as distinct from those involved in the functional behavior of the neurons?

**26.4** Find and analyze an account in the popular media of one or more of the arguments to the effect that AI is impossible.

**26.5** Attempt to write definitions of the terms "intelligence," "thinking," and "consciousness." Suggest some possible objections to your definitions.

**26.6** Analyze the potential threats from AI technology to society. What threats are most serious, and how might they be combated? How do they compare to the potential benefits?

**26.7** How do the potential threats from AI technology compare with those from other computer science technologies, and to bio-, nano-, and nuclear technologies?

**26.8** Some critics object that AI is impossible, while others object that it is *too* possible, and that ultraintelligent machines pose a threat. Which of these objections do you think is more likely? Would it be a contradiction for someone to hold both positions?

# 27 AI: PRESENT AND FUTURE

*In which we take stock of where we are and where we are going, this being a good thing to do before continuing.*

In Part I, we proposed a unified view of AI as rational agent design. We showed that the design problem depends on the percepts and actions available to the agent, the goals that the agent's behavior should satisfy, and the nature of the environment. A variety of different agent designs are possible, ranging from reflex agents to fully deliberative, knowledge-based agents. Moreover, the components of these designs can have a number of different instantiations—for example, logical, probabilistic, or "neural." The intervening chapters presented the principles by which these components operate.

For all the agent designs and components, there has been tremendous progress both in our scientific understanding and in our technological capabilities. In this chapter, we stand back from the details and ask, *"Will all this progress lead to a general-purpose intelligent agent that can perform well in a wide variety of environments?* Section 27.1 looks at the components of an intelligent agent to assess what's known and what's missing. Section 27.2 does the same for the overall agent architecture. Section 27.3 asks whether "rational agent design" is the right goal in the first place. (The answer is, "Not really, but it's OK for now.") Finally, Section 27.4 examines the consequences of success in our endeavors.

## 27.1 AGENT COMPONENTS

Chapter 2 presented several agent designs and their components. To focus our discussion here, we will look at the utility-based agent, which we show again in Figure 27.1. This is the most general of our agent designs; we will also consider its extension with learning capabilities, as depicted in Figure 2.15.

*Interaction with the environment through sensors and actuators*: For much of the history of AI, this has been a glaring weak point. With a few honorable exceptions, AI systems were built in such a way that humans had to supply the inputs and interpret the outputs, while robotic systems focused on low-level tasks in which high-level reasoning and planning were largely absent. This was due in part to the great expense and engineering effort required

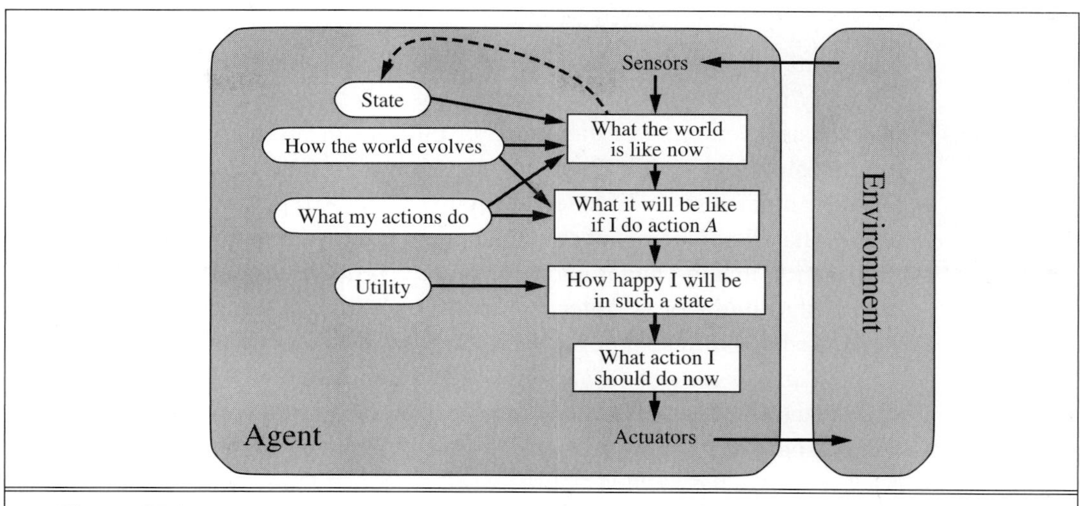


**Figure 27.1** A model-based, utility-based agent, as first presented in Figure 2.14.

to get real robots to work at all. The situation has changed rapidly in recent years with the availability of ready-made programmable robots, such as the four-legged robots shown in Figure 25.4(b). These, in turn, have benefited from small, cheap, high-resolution CCD cameras and compact, reliable motor drives. MEMS (micro-electromechanical systems) technology has supplied miniaturized accelerometers and gyroscopes and is now producing actuators that will, for example, power an artificial flying insect. (It may also be possible to combine millions of MEMS actuators to produce very powerful macroscopic actuators.) For physical environments, then, AI systems no longer have a real excuse. Furthermore, an entirely new environment—the Internet—has become available.

*Keeping track of the state of the world*: This is one of the core capabilities required for an intelligent agent. It requires both perception and updating of internal representations. Chapter 7 described methods for keeping track of worlds described by propositional logic; Chapter 10 extended this to first-order logic; and Chapter 15 described **filtering** algorithms for tracking uncertain environments. These filtering tools are required when real (and therefore imperfect) perception is involved. Current filtering and perception algorithms can be combined to do a reasonable job of reporting low-level predicates such as "the cup is on the table" but we have some way to go before they can report that "Dr. Russell is having a cup of tea with Dr. Norvig." Another problem is that, although approximate filtering algorithms can handle quite large environments, they are still essentially *propositional*—like propositional logic, they do not represent objects and relations explicitly. Chapter 14 explained how probability and first-order logic can be combined to solve this problem; we expect that the application of these ideas for tracking complex environments will yield huge benefits. Incidentally, as soon as we start talking about *objects* in an uncertain environment, we encounter

IDENTITY UNCERTAINTY

**identity uncertainty**—we don't know which object is which. This problem has been largely ignored in logic-based AI, where it has generally been assumed that percepts incorporate constant symbols that identify the objects.

*Projecting, evaluating, and selecting future courses of action*: The basic knowledge representation requirements here are the same as for keeping track of the world; the primary difficulty is coping with courses of action—such as having a conversation or a cup of tea—that consist eventually of thousands or millions of primitive steps for a real agent. It is only by imposing **hierarchical structure** on behavior that we humans cope at all. Some of the planning algorithms in Chapter 12 use hierarchical representations and first-order representations to handle problems of this scale; on the other hand, the algorithms given in Chapter 17 for decision making under uncertainty are essentially using the same ideas as the state-based search algorithms of Chapter 3. There is clearly a great deal of work to do here, perhaps along the lines of recent developments in **hierarchical reinforcement learning**.

*Utility as an expression of preferences*: In principle, basing rational decisions on the maximization of expected utility is completely general and avoids many of the problems of purely goal-based approaches, such as conflicting goals and uncertain attainment. As yet, however, there has been very little work on constructing *realistic* utility functions—imagine, for example, the complex web of interacting preferences that must be understood by an agent operating as an office assistant for a human being. It has proven very difficult to decompose preferences over complex states in the same way that Bayes nets decompose beliefs over complex states. One reason may be that preferences over states are really *compiled* from preferences over state histories, which are described by **reward functions** (see Chapter 17). Even if the reward function is simple, the corresponding utility function may be very complex. This suggests that we take seriously the task of knowledge engineering for reward functions as a way of conveying to our agents what it is that we want them to do.

*Learning*: Chapters 18 to 20 described how learning in an agent can be formulated as inductive learning (supervised, unsupervised, or reinforcement-based) of the functions that constitute the various components of the agent. Very powerful logical and statistical techniques have been developed that can cope with quite large problems, often reaching or exceeding human capabilities in the identification of predictive patterns defined on a given vocabulary. On the other hand, machine learning has made very little progress on the important problem of constructing new representations at levels of abstraction higher than the input vocabulary. For example, how can an autonomous robot generate useful predicates such as *Office* and *Cafe* if they are not supplied to it by humans? Similar considerations apply to learning behavior—$HavingACupOfTea$ is an important high-level action, but how does it get into an action library that initially contains much simpler actions such as $RaiseArm$ and $Swallow$? Unless we understand such issues, we are faced with the daunting task of constructing large commonsense knowledge bases by hand.

## 27.2 AGENT ARCHITECTURES

It is natural to ask, "Which of the agent architectures in Chapter 2 should an agent use?" The answer is, "All of them!" We have seen that reflex responses are needed for situations in which time is of the essence, whereas knowledge-based deliberation allows the agent to

HYBRID ARCHITECTURE

plan ahead. A complete agent must be able to do both, using a **hybrid architecture**. One important property of hybrid architectures is that the boundaries between different decision components are not fixed. For example, **compilation** continually converts declarative information at the deliberative level into more efficient representations, eventually reaching the reflex level—see Figure 27.2. (This is the purpose of explanation-based learning, as discussed in Chapter 19.) Agent architectures such as SOAR (Laird *et al.*, 1987) and THEO (Mitchell, 1990) have exactly this structure. Every time they solve a problem by explicit deliberation, they save away a generalized version of the solution for use by the reflex component. A less studied problem is the *reversal* of this process: when the environment changes, learned reflexes may no longer be appropriate and the agent must return to the deliberative level to produce new behaviors.

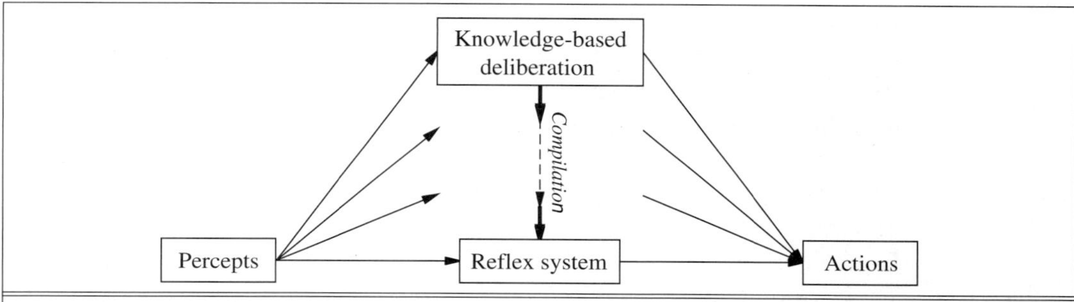


**Figure 27.2** Compilation serves to convert deliberative decision making into more efficient, reflexive mechanisms.

Agents also need ways to control their own deliberations. They must be able to cease deliberating when action is demanded, and they must be able to use the time available for deliberation to execute the most profitable computations. For example, a taxi-driving agent that sees an accident ahead must decide in a split second either to brake or to take evasive action. It should also spend that split second thinking about the most important questions, such as whether the lanes to the left and right are clear and whether there is a large truck close behind, rather than worrying about wear and tear on the tires or where to pick up the next passenger. These issues are usually studied under the heading of **real-time AI**. As AI systems move into more complex domains, all problems will become real-time, because the agent will never have long enough to solve the decision problem exactly.

REAL-TIME AI

Clearly, there is a pressing need for methods that work in more general decision-making situations. Two promising techniques have emerged in recent years. The first involves the use of **anytime algorithms** (Dean and Boddy, 1988; Horvitz, 1987). An anytime algorithm is an algorithm whose output quality improves gradually over time, so that it has a reasonable decision ready whenever it is interrupted. Such algorithms are controlled by a metalevel decision procedure that assesses whether further computation is worthwhile. Iterative deepening search in game playing provides a simple example of an anytime algorithm. More complex systems, composed of many such algorithms working together, can also be constructed (Zilberstein and Russell, 1996). The second technique is **decision-theoretic metareasoning**

ANYTIME ALGORITHMS

DECISION-THEORETIC METAREASONING

(Horvitz, 1989; Russell and Wefald, 1991; Horvitz and Breese, 1996). This method applies the theory of information value (Chapter 16) to the selection of computations. The value of a computation depends on both its cost (in terms of delaying action) and its benefits (in terms of improved decision quality). Metareasoning techniques can be used to design better search algorithms and to guarantee that the algorithms have the anytime property. Metareasoning is expensive, of course, and compilation methods can be applied so that the overhead is small compared to the costs of the computations being controlled.

REFLECTIVE ARCHITECTURE

Metareasoning is but one aspect of a general **reflective architecture**—that is, an architecture that enables deliberation about the computational entities and actions occurring within the architecture itself. A theoretical foundation for reflective architectures can be built by defining a joint state space composed from the environment state and the computational state of the agent itself. Decision-making and learning algorithms can be designed that operate over this joint state space and thereby serve to implement and improve the agent's computational activities. Eventually, we expect task-specific algorithms such as alpha-beta search and backward chaining to disappear from AI systems, to be replaced by general methods that direct the agent's computations toward the efficient generation of high-quality decisions.

## 27.3 Are We Going in the Right Direction?

The preceding section listed many advances and many opportunities for further progress. But where is this all leading? Dreyfus (1992) gives the analogy of trying to get to the moon by climbing a tree; one can report steady progress, all the way to the top of the tree. In this section, we consider whether AI's current path is more like a tree climb or a rocket trip.

In Chapter 1, we said that our goal was to build agents that *act rationally*. However, we also said that

> ... achieving perfect rationality—always doing the right thing—is not feasible in complicated environments. The computational demands are just too high. For most of the book, however, we will adopt the working hypothesis that perfect rationality is a good starting point for analysis.

Now it is time to consider again what exactly the goal of AI is. We want to build agents, but with what specification in mind? Here are four possibilities:

PERFECT RATIONALITY

**Perfect rationality**. A perfectly rational agent acts at every instant in such a way as to maximize its expected utility, given the information it has acquired from the environment. We have seen that the calculations necessary to achieve perfect rationality in most environments are too time-consuming, so perfect rationality is not a realistic goal.

CALCULATIVE RATIONALITY

**Calculative rationality**. This is the notion of rationality that we have used implicitly in designing logical and decision-theoretic agents. A calculatively rational agent *eventually* returns what *would have been* the rational choice at the beginning of its deliberation. This is an interesting property for a system to exhibit, but in most environments, the right answer at the wrong time is of no value. In practice, AI system designers are forced to compromise on decision quality to obtain reasonable overall performance; unfortunately, the theoretical basis of calculative rationality does not provide a well-founded way to make such compromises.

BOUNDED RATIONALITY

**Bounded rationality**. Herbert Simon (1957) rejected the notion of perfect (or even approximately perfect) rationality and replaced it with bounded rationality, a descriptive theory of decision making by real agents. He wrote,

> The capacity of the human mind for formulating and solving complex problems is very small compared with the size of the problems whose solution is required for objectively rational behavior in the real world—or even for a reasonable approximation to such objective rationality.

He suggested that bounded rationality works primarily by **satisficing**—that is, deliberating only long enough to come up with an answer that is "good enough." Simon won the Nobel prize in economics for this work and has written about it in depth (Simon, 1982). It appears to be a useful model of human behaviors in many cases. It is not a formal specification for intelligent agents, however, because the definition of "good enough" is not given by the theory. Furthermore, satisficing seems to be just one of a large range of methods used to cope with bounded resources.

BOUNDED OPTIMALITY

**Bounded optimality** (BO). A bounded optimal agent behaves as well as possible, *given its computational resources*. That is, the expected utility of the agent program for a bounded optimal agent is at least as high as the expected utility of any other agent program running on the same machine.

Of these four possibilities, bounded optimality seems to offer the best hope for a strong theoretical foundation for AI. It has the advantage of being possible to achieve: there is always at least one best program—something that perfect rationality lacks. Bounded optimal agents are actually useful in the real world, whereas calculatively rational agents usually are not, and satisficing agents might or might not be, depending on their own whims.

The traditional approach in AI has been to start with calculative rationality and then make compromises to meet resource constraints. If the problems imposed by the constraints are minor, one would expect the final design to be similar to a BO agent design. But as the resource constraints become more critical—e.g., as the environment becomes more complex—one would expect the two designs to diverge. In the theory of bounded optimality, these constraints can be handled in a principled fashion.

As yet, little is known about bounded optimality. It is possible to construct bounded optimal programs for very simple machines and for somewhat restricted kinds of environments (Etzioni, 1989; Russell *et al.*, 1993), but as yet we have no idea what BO programs are like for large, general-purpose computers in complex environments. If there is to be a constructive theory of bounded optimality, we have to hope that the design of bounded optimal programs does not depend too strongly on the details of the computer being used. It would make scientific research very difficult if adding a few kilobytes of memory to a gigabyte machine made a significant difference to the design of the BO program. One way to make sure this cannot happen is to be slightly more relaxed about the criteria for bounded optimality. By analogy with the notion of asymptotic complexity (Appendix A), we can define **asymptotic bounded optimality** (ABO) as follows (Russell and Subramanian, 1995). Suppose a program $P$ is bounded optimal for a machine $M$ in a class of environments $\mathbf{E}$, where the complexity of environments in **E** is unbounded. Then program $P'$ is ABO for $M$ in **E** if it can outperform $P$ by running on a machine $kM$ that is $k$ times faster (or larger) than $M$. Unless $k$ were enormous, we would be happy with a program that was ABO for a nontrivial environment on a nontrivial architecture. There would be little point in putting enormous effort into finding BO rather than ABO programs, because the size and speed of available machines tends to increase by a constant factor in a fixed amount of time anyway.

We can hazard a guess that BO or ABO programs for powerful computers in complex environments will not necessarily have a simple, elegant structure. We have already seen that general-purpose intelligence requires some reflex capability and some deliberative capability, a variety of forms of knowledge and decision making, learning and compilation mechanisms for all of those forms, methods for controlling reasoning, and a large store of domain-specific knowledge. A bounded optimal agent must adapt to the environment in which it finds itself, so that eventually its internal organization will reflect optimizations that are specific to the particular environment. This is only to be expected, and it is similar to the way in which racing cars restricted by engine capacity have evolved into extremely complex designs. We suspect that a science of artificial intelligence based on bounded optimality will involve a good deal of study of the processes that allow an agent program to converge to bounded optimality and perhaps less concentration on the details of the messy programs that result.

In sum, the concept of bounded optimality is proposed as a formal task for AI research that is both well defined and feasible. Bounded optimality specifies optimal *programs* rather than optimal *actions*. Actions are, after all, generated by programs, and it is over programs that designers have control.

## 27.4 WHAT IF AI DOES SUCCEED?

In David Lodge's *Small World* (1984), a novel about the academic world of literary criticism, the protagonist causes consternation by asking a panel of eminent but contradictory literary theorists the following question: "*What if you were right?*" None of the theorists seems to have considered this question before, perhaps because debating unfalsifiable theories is an end in itself. Similar confusion can sometimes be evoked by asking AI researchers, "What if you succeed?" AI is fascinating, and intelligent computers are clearly more useful than unintelligent computers, so why worry?

As Section 26.3 relates, there are ethical issues to consider. Intelligent computers are more powerful, but will that power be used for good or ill? Those who strive to develop AI have a responsibility to see that the impact of their work is a positive one. The scope of the impact will depend on the degree of success of AI. Even modest successes in AI have already changed the ways in which computer science is taught (Stein, 2002) and software development is practiced. AI has made possible new applications such as speech recognition systems, inventory control systems, surveillance systems, robots, and search engines.

We can expect that medium-level successes in AI would affect all kinds of people in their daily lives. So far, computerized communication networks, such as cell phones and the

Internet, have had this kind of pervasive effect on society, but AI has not. We can imagine that truly useful personal assistants for the office or the home would have a large positive impact on people's lives, although they might cause some economic dislocation in the short term. A technological capability at this level might also be applied to the development of autonomous weapons, which many view as an undesirable development.

Finally, it seems likely that a large-scale success in AI—the creation of human-level intelligence and beyond—would change the lives of a majority of humankind. The very nature of our work and play would be altered, as would our view of intelligence, consciousness, and the future destiny of the human race. At this level, AI systems could pose a more direct threat to human autonomy, freedom, and even survival. For these reasons, we cannot divorce AI research from its ethical consequences.

Which way will the future go? Science fiction authors seem to favor dystopian futures over utopian ones, probably because they make for more interesting plots. But so far, AI seems to fit in with other revolutionary technologies (printing, plumbing, air travel, telephony) whose negative repercussions are outweighed by their positive aspects.

In conclusion, we see that AI has made great progress in its short history, but the final sentence of Alan Turing's essay on *Computing Machinery and Intelligence* is still valid today:

> We can see only a short distance ahead, but we can see that much remains to be done.

# A MATHEMATICAL BACKGROUND

## A.1 COMPLEXITY ANALYSIS AND O() NOTATION

Computer scientists are often faced with the task of comparing algorithms to see how fast they run or how much memory they require. There are two approaches to this task. The first

BENCHMARKING

is **benchmarking**—running the algorithms on a computer and measuring speed in seconds and memory consumption in bytes. Ultimately, this is what really matters, but a benchmark can be unsatisfactory because it is so specific: it measures the performance of a particular program written in a particular language, running on a particular computer, with a particular compiler and particular input data. From the single result that the benchmark provides, it can be difficult to predict how well the algorithm would do on a different compiler, computer, or data set.

### Asymptotic analysis

ANALYSIS OF ALGORITHMS

The second approach relies on a mathematical **analysis of algorithms**, independently of the particular implementation and input. We will examine the approach via the following example, a program to compute the sum of a sequence of numbers:

```
function SUMMATION(sequence) returns a number
  sum ← 0
  for i ← 1 to LENGTH(sequence)
      sum ← sum + sequence[i]
  return sum
```

The first step in the analysis is to abstract over the input, in order to find some parameter or parameters that characterize the size of the input. In this example, the input can be characterized by the length of the sequence, which we will call $n$. The second step is to abstract over the implementation, to find some measure that reflects the running time of the algorithm, but is not tied to a particular compiler or computer. For the SUMMATION program, this could be just the number of lines of code executed, or it could be more detailed, measuring the number of additions, assignments, array references, and branches executed by the algorithm.

Either way gives us a characterization of the total number of steps taken by the algorithm as a function of the size of the input. We will call this characterization $T(n)$. If we count lines of code, we have $T(n) = 2n + 2$ for our example.

If all programs were as simple as SUMMATION, the analysis of algorithms would be a trivial field. But two problems make it more complicated. First, it is rare to find a parameter like $n$ that completely characterizes the number of steps taken by an algorithm. Instead, the best we can usually do is compute the worst case $T_{\text{worst}}(n)$ or the average case $T_{\text{avg}}(n)$. Computing an average means that the analyst must assume some distribution of inputs.

The second problem is that algorithms tend to resist exact analysis. In that case, it is necessary to fall back on an approximation. We say that the SUMMATION algorithm is $O(n)$, meaning that its measure is at most a constant times $n$, with the possible exception of a few small values of $n$. More formally,

$$T(n) \text{ is } O(f(n)) \text{ if } T(n) \leq kf(n) \text{ for some } k, \text{ for all } n > n_0 .$$

ASYMPTOTIC ANALYSIS

The $O()$ notation gives us what is called an **asymptotic analysis**. We can say without question that, as $n$ asymptotically approaches infinity, an $O(n)$ algorithm is better than an $O(n^2)$ algorithm. A single benchmark figure could not substantiate such a claim.

The $O()$ notation abstracts over constant factors, which makes it easier to use, but less precise, than the $T()$ notation. For example, an $O(n^2)$ algorithm will always be worse than an $O(n)$ in the long run, but if the two algorithms are $T(n^2 + 1)$ and $T(100n + 1000)$, then the $O(n^2)$ algorithm is actually better for $n \leq 110$.

Despite this drawback, asymptotic analysis is the most widely used tool for analyzing algorithms. It is precisely because the analysis abstracts over both the exact number of operations (by ignoring the constant factor $k$) and the exact content of the input (by considering only its size $n$) that the analysis becomes mathematically feasible. The $O()$ notation is a good compromise between precision and ease of analysis.

## NP and inherently hard problems

COMPLEXITY ANALYSIS

The analysis of algorithms and the $O()$ notation allow us to talk about the efficiency of a particular algorithm. However, they have nothing to say about whether there could be a better algorithm for the problem at hand. The field of **complexity analysis** analyzes problems rather than algorithms. The first gross division is between problems that can be solved in polynomial time and problems that cannot be solved in polynomial time, no matter what algorithm is used. The class of polynomial problems—those which can be solved in time $O(n^k)$ for some $k$—is called P. These are sometimes called "easy" problems, because the class contains those problems with running times like $O(\log n)$ and $O(n)$. But it also contains those with time $O(n^{1000})$, so the name "easy" should not be taken too literally.

Another important class of problems is NP, the class of nondeterministic polynomial problems. A problem is in this class if there is some algorithm that can guess a solution and then verify whether the guess is correct in polynomial time. The idea is that if you have an arbitrarily large number of processors, so that you can try all the guesses at once, or you are very lucky and always guess right the first time, then the NP problems become P problems. One of the biggest open questions in computer science is whether the class

NP is equivalent to the class P when one does not have the luxury of an infinite number of processors or omniscient guessing. Most computer scientists are convinced that P $\neq$ NP—that NP problems are inherently hard and have no polynomial time algorithms. But this has never been proven.

NP-COMPLETE

Those who are interested in deciding whether P = NP look at a subclass of NP called the **NP-complete** problems. The word "complete" is used here in the sense of "most extreme" and thus refers to the hardest problems in the class NP. It has been proven that either all the NP-complete problems are in P or none of them is. This makes the class theoretically interesting, but the class is also of practical interest because many important problems are known to be NP-complete. An example is the satisfiability problem: given a sentence of propositional logic, is there an assignment of truth values to the proposition symbols of the sentence that make it true? Unless a miracle occurs and P = NP, there can be no algorithm that solves *all* satisfiability problems in polynomial time. However, AI is more interested in whether there are algorithms that perform efficiently on *typical* problems drawn from a predetermined distribution; as we saw in Chapter 7, there are algorithms such as WALKSAT that do quite well on many problems.

CO-NP

CO-NP-COMPLETE

The class **co-NP** is the complement of NP, in the sense that, for every decision problem in NP, there is a corresponding problem in co-NP with the "yes" and "no" answers reversed. We know that P is a subset of both NP and co-NP, and it is believed that there are problems in co-NP that are not in P. The **co-NP-complete** problems are the hardest problems in co-NP.

The class #P (pronounced "sharp P") is the set of counting problems corresponding to the decision problems in NP. Decision problems have a yes-or-no answer: is there a solution to this 3-SAT formula? Counting problems have an integer answer: how many solutions are there to this 3-SAT formula? In some cases, the counting problem is much harder than the decision problem. For example, deciding whether a bipartite graph has a perfect matching can be done in time $O(VE)$ (where the graph has $V$ vertices and $E$ edges), but the counting problem "how many perfect matches does this bipartite graph have" is #P-complete, meaning that it is hard as any problem in #P and thus at least as hard as any NP problem.

Also studied is the class of PSPACE problems—those that require a polynomial amount of space, even on a nondeterministic machine. It is believed that PSPACE-hard problems are worse than NP-complete problems, although it could turn out that NP = PSPACE, just as it could turn out that P = NP.

## A.2 VECTORS, MATRICES, AND LINEAR ALGEBRA

VECTOR

Mathematicians define a **vector** as a member of a vector space, but we will use a more concrete definition: a vector is an ordered sequence of values. For example, in two-dimensional space, we have vectors such as $\mathbf{x} = \langle 3, 4 \rangle$ and $\mathbf{y} = \langle 0, 2 \rangle$. We follow the usual convention of using bold face characters for vector names, although some authors use arrows or bars over the names: $\vec{x}$ or $\bar{y}$. The elements of a vector can be accessed using subscripts: $\mathbf{z} = \langle z_1, z_2, \ldots, z_n \rangle$.

The two fundamental operations on vectors are vector addition and scalar multiplication. The vector addition $\mathbf{x} + \mathbf{y}$ is the elementwise sum: $\mathbf{x} + \mathbf{y} = \langle 3+0, 4+2 \rangle = \langle 3, 6 \rangle$. Scalar multiplication multiplies each element by a constant: $5\mathbf{x} = \langle 5 \times 3, 5 \times 4 \rangle = \langle 15, 20 \rangle$.

The length of a vector is denoted $|\mathbf{x}|$ and is computed by taking the square root of the sum of the squares of the elements: $|\mathbf{x}| = \sqrt{(3^2 + 4^2)} = 5$. The dot product (also called scalar product) of two vectors $\mathbf{x} \cdot \mathbf{y}$ is the sum of the products of corresponding elements, that is, $\mathbf{x} \cdot \mathbf{y} = \sum_i x_i y_i$, or in our particular case, $\mathbf{x} \cdot \mathbf{y} = 3 \times 0 + 4 \times 2 = 8$.

Vectors are often interpreted as directed line segments (arrows) in an $n$-dimensional Euclidean space. Vector addition is then equivalent to placing the tail of one vector at the head of the other, and the dot product $\mathbf{x} \cdot \mathbf{y}$ is equal to $|\mathbf{x}|\ |\mathbf{y}|\ \cos\theta$, where $\theta$ is the angle between $\mathbf{x}$ and $\mathbf{y}$.

MATRIX

A **matrix** is a rectangular array of values arranged into rows and columns. Here is a matrix $\mathbf{m}$ of size $3 \times 4$:

$$\begin{pmatrix} \mathbf{m}_{1,1} & \mathbf{m}_{1,2} & \mathbf{m}_{1,3} & \mathbf{m}_{1,4} \\ \mathbf{m}_{2,1} & \mathbf{m}_{2,2} & \mathbf{m}_{2,3} & \mathbf{m}_{2,4} \\ \mathbf{m}_{3,1} & \mathbf{m}_{3,2} & \mathbf{m}_{3,3} & \mathbf{m}_{3,4} \end{pmatrix}$$

The first index of $\mathbf{m}_{i,j}$ specifies the row and the second the column. In programming languages, $\mathbf{m}_{i,j}$ is often written `m[i,j]` or `m[i][j]`.

The sum of two matrices is defined by adding corresponding elements; thus, $(\mathbf{m} + \mathbf{n})_{i,j} = \mathbf{m}_{i,j} + \mathbf{n}_{i,j}$. (The sum is undefined if $\mathbf{m}$ and $\mathbf{n}$ have different sizes.) We can also define the multiplication of a matrix by a scalar: $(c\mathbf{m})_{i,j} = c\mathbf{m}_{i,j}$. Matrix multiplication (the product of two matrices) is more complicated. The product $\mathbf{mn}$ is defined only if $\mathbf{m}$ is of size $a \times b$ and $\mathbf{n}$ is of size $b \times c$ (i.e., the second matrix has the same number of rows as the first has columns); the result is a matrix of size $a \times c$. This means that matrix multiplication is not commutative: $\mathbf{mn} \neq \mathbf{nm}$ in general. If the matrices are of appropriate size, then the result is

$$(\mathbf{mn})_{i,k} = \sum_j \mathbf{m}_{i,j}\mathbf{n}_{j,k} \ .$$

The identity matrix $\mathbf{I}$ has elements $\mathbf{I}_{i,j}$ equal to 1 when $i = j$ and equal to 0 otherwise. It has the property that $\mathbf{mI} = \mathbf{m}$ for all $\mathbf{m}$. The transpose of $\mathbf{m}$, written $\mathbf{m}^T$ is formed by turning rows into columns and vice versa, or, more formally, by $\mathbf{m}^T_{i,j} = \mathbf{m}_{j,i}$.

GAUSS–JORDAN ELIMINATION

Matrices are used to solve systems of linear equations via a process called **Gauss–Jordan elimination**, an $O(n^3)$ algorithm. Consider the following set of equations, for which we want a solution in $x$, $y$, and $z$:

$$\begin{aligned} &+2x + y - z = 8 \\ &-3x - y + 2z = -11 \\ &-2x + y + 2z = -3 \ . \end{aligned}$$

We can represent this system as a matrix:

$$\begin{matrix} x & y & z & c \end{matrix}$$
$$\begin{pmatrix} 2 & 1 & -1 & 8 \\ -3 & -1 & 2 & -11 \\ -2 & 1 & 2 & -3 \end{pmatrix}$$

Here, the $x\ y\ z\ c$ is not part of the matrix; it is just there as a reminder to the viewer. We know that if we multiply both sides of an equation by a constant or add two equations, we get an equally valid equation. Gauss–Jordan elimination works by repeatedly doing these operations in such a way that we start by eliminating the first variable ($x$) from all but the first equation and then continue on, eliminating the $i$th variable from all but the $i$th equation, for all $i$. We eliminate $x$ from the second equation by multiplying the first equation by $3/2$ and adding it to the second. This gives us the following matrix:

$$\begin{array}{cccc} x & y & z & c \end{array}$$
$$\begin{pmatrix} 2 & 1 & -1 & 8 \\ 0 & .5 & .5 & 1 \\ -2 & 1 & 2 & -3 \end{pmatrix}$$

We continue in this fashion, eliminating $x$, $y$, and $z$ until we get

$$\begin{array}{cccc} x & y & z & c \end{array}$$
$$\begin{pmatrix} 1 & 0 & 0 & 2 \\ 0 & 1 & 0 & 3 \\ 0 & 0 & 1 & -1 \end{pmatrix}$$

indicating that $x = 2, y = 3, z = -1$ is a solution. (Try it!)

## A.3 Probability Distributions

A probability is a measure over a set of events that satisfies three axioms:

1. The measure of each event is between 0 and 1. We write this as $0 \leq P(E = e_i) \leq 1$, where $E$ is a random variable representing an event and $e_i$ are the possible values of $E$. In general, random variables are denoted by uppercase letters and their values by lowercase letters.
2. The measure of the whole set is 1; that is, $\sum_{i=1}^{n} P(E = e_i) = 1$.
3. The probability of a union of disjoint events is the sum of the probabilities of the individual events; that is, $P(E = e_1 \vee E = e_2) = P(E = e_1) + P(E = e_2)$, where $e_1$ and $e_2$ are disjoint.

A **probabilistic model** consists of a sample space of mutually exclusive possible outcomes, together with a probability measure for each outcome. For example, in a model of the weather tomorrow, the outcomes might be *sunny, cloudy, rainy*, and *snowy*. A subset of these outcomes constitutes an event. For example, the event of precipitation is the subset $\{$*rainy, snowy*$\}$.

We use $\mathbf{P}(E)$ to denote the vector of values $\langle P(E = e_1), \ldots, P(E = e_n)\rangle$. We also use $P(e_i)$ as an abbreviation for $P(E = e_i)$ and $\sum_e P(e)$ for $\sum_{i=1}^{n} P(E = e_i)$.

The conditional probability $P(B|A)$ is defined as $P(B \cap A)/P(A)$. $A$ and $B$ are conditionally independent if $P(B|A) = P(B)$ (or equivalently, $P(A|B) = P(A)$). For continuous variables, there are an infinite number of values, and unless there are point spikes,

PROBABILITY DENSITY FUNCTION

the probability of any one value is 0. Therefore, we define a **probability density function**, which we also denote as $P(X)$, but which has a slightly different meaning from the discrete probability function $P(A)$. The density function $P(X = c)$ is defined as the ratio of the probability that $X$ falls into an interval around $c$, divided by the width of the interval, as the interval width goes to zero:

$$P(X = c) = \lim_{dx \to 0} P(c \leq X \leq c + dx)/dx \ .$$

The density function must be nonnegative for all $x$ and must have

$$\int_{-\infty}^{\infty} P(X)\, dx = 1 \ .$$

CUMULATIVE PROBABILITY DENSITY FUNCTION

We can also define a **cumulative probability density function** $F(X)$, which is the probability of a random variable being less than $x$:

$$F(X) = \int_{-\infty}^{x} P(Z)\, dz \ .$$

Note that the probability density function has units, whereas the discrete probability function is unitless. For example, if $X$ is measured in seconds, then the density is measured in Hz (i.e., 1/sec). If **X** is a point in three-dimensional space measured in meters, then density is measured in $1/m^3$.

GAUSSIAN DISTRIBUTION

One of the most important probability distributions is the **Gaussian distribution**, also known as the **normal distribution**. A Gaussian distribution with mean $\mu$ and standard deviation $\sigma$ (and therefore variance $\sigma^2$) is defined as

$$P(x) = \frac{1}{\sigma\sqrt{2\pi}} e^{-(x-\mu)^2/(2\sigma^2)} \ ,$$

STANDARD NORMAL DISTRIBUTION

MULTIVARIATE GAUSSIAN

where $x$ is a continuous variable ranging from $-\infty$ to $+\infty$. With mean $\mu = 0$ and variance $\sigma^2 = 1$, we get the special case of the **standard normal distribution**. For a distribution over a vector **x** in $n$ dimensions, there is the **multivariate Gaussian** distribution:

$$P(\mathbf{x}) = \frac{1}{\sqrt{(2\pi)^n |\mathbf{\Sigma}|}} e^{-\frac{1}{2}\left((\mathbf{x}-\boldsymbol{\mu})^\top \mathbf{\Sigma}^{-1} (\mathbf{x}-\boldsymbol{\mu})\right)} \ ,$$

COVARIANCE MATRIX

CUMULATIVE DISTRIBUTION

where $\boldsymbol{\mu}$ is the mean vector and $\mathbf{\Sigma}$ is the **covariance matrix** of the distribution.

In one dimension, we can also define the **cumulative distribution** function $F(x)$ as the probability that a random variable will be less than $x$. For the standard normal distribution, this is given by

$$F(x) = \int_{-\infty}^{x} P(x) dx = \frac{1}{2}(1 + \text{erf}(\frac{x - \mu}{\sigma\sqrt{2}})) \ ,$$

where $\text{erf}(x)$ is the so-called **error function**, which has no closed form representation.

CENTRAL LIMIT THEOREM

The **central limit theorem** states that the mean of $n$ random variables tends to a normal distribution as $n$ tends to infinity. This holds for almost any collection of random variables, unless the variance of any finite subset of variables dominates the others.

## Bibliographical and Historical Notes

The $O()$ notation so widely used in computer science today was first introduced in the context of number theory by the German mathematician P. G. H. Bachmann (1894). The concept of NP-completeness was invented by Cook (1971), and the modern method for establishing a reduction from one problem to another is due to Karp (1972). Cook and Karp have both won the Turing award, the highest honor in computer science, for their work.

Classic works on the analysis and design of algorithms include those by Knuth (1973) and Aho, Hopcroft, and Ullman (1974); more recent contributions are by Tarjan (1983) and Cormen, Leiserson, and Rivest (1990). These books place an emphasis on designing and analyzing algorithms to solve tractable problems. For the theory of NP-completeness and other forms of intractability, see Garey and Johnson (1979) or Papadimitriou (1994). In addition to the underlying theory, Garey and Johnson provide examples that convey very forcefully why computer scientists are unanimous in drawing the line between tractable and intractable problems at the border between polynomial and exponential time complexity. They also provide a voluminous catalog of problems that are known to be NP-complete or otherwise intractable.

Good texts on probability include Chung (1979), Ross (1988), Bertsekas and Tsitsiklis (2002), and Feller (1971).

# B NOTES ON LANGUAGES AND ALGORITHMS

## B.1 DEFINING LANGUAGES WITH BACKUS–NAUR FORM (BNF)

In this book, we define several languages, including the languages of propositional logic (page 204), first-order logic (page 247), and a subset of English (page 805). A formal language is defined as a set of strings where each string is a sequence of symbols. All the languages we are interested in consist of an infinite set of strings, so we need a concise way to characterize the set. We do that with a **grammar**. We write our grammars in a formalism called **Backus–Naur form (BNF)**. There are four components to a BNF grammar:

BACKUS–NAUR FORM (BNF)

TERMINAL SYMBOLS

- A set of **terminal symbols**. These are the symbols or words that make up the strings of the language. They could be letters (**A, B, C,** ...) or words (**a, aardvark, abacus,** ...).

NONTERMINAL SYMBOLS

- A set of **nonterminal symbols** that categorize subphrases of the language. For example, the nonterminal symbol *NounPhrase* in English denotes an infinite set of strings including "you" and "the big slobbery dog."

START SYMBOL

- A **start symbol**, which is the nonterminal symbol that denotes the complete strings of the language. In English, this is *Sentence*; for arithmetic, it might be *Expr*.
- A set of **rewrite rules**, of the form $LHS \rightarrow RHS$, where $LHS$ is a nonterminal and $RHS$ is a sequence of zero or more symbols (either terminal or nonterminal).

A rewrite rule of the form

$$Sentence \rightarrow NounPhrase\ VerbPhrase$$

means that whenever we have two strings categorized as a *NounPhrase* and a *VerbPhrase*, we can append them together and categorize the result as a *Sentence*. As an abbreviation, the symbol | can be used to separate alternative right-hand sides. Here is a BNF grammar for simple arithmetic expressions:

$$\begin{array}{lcl} Expr & \rightarrow & Expr\ Operator\ Expr \mid \mathbf{(}\ Expr\ \mathbf{)} \mid Number \\ \\ Number & \rightarrow & Digit \mid Number\ Digit \\ \\ Digit & \rightarrow & \mathbf{0} \mid \mathbf{1} \mid \mathbf{2} \mid \mathbf{3} \mid \mathbf{4} \mid \mathbf{5} \mid \mathbf{6} \mid \mathbf{7} \mid \mathbf{8} \mid \mathbf{9} \\ Operator & \rightarrow & + \mid - \mid \div \mid \times \end{array}$$

We cover languages and grammars in more detail in Chapter 22. Be aware that other books use slightly different notations for BNF; for example, you might see $\langle Digit \rangle$ instead of $Digit$ for a nonterminal, 'word' instead of **word** for a terminal, or ::= instead of $\rightarrow$ in a rule.

## B.2 DESCRIBING ALGORITHMS WITH PSEUDOCODE

In this book, we define over 80 algorithms in detail. Rather than picking a programming language (and risking the possibility that readers who are unfamiliar with the language will be lost), we have chosen to describe the algorithms in pseudocode. Most of the pseudocode should be familiar to users of languages like Java, C++, or Lisp. In some places we use mathematical formulas or ordinary English to describe parts that would otherwise be more cumbersome. A few idiosyncrasies should be noted.

**Static variables.** We use the keyword **static** to say that a variable is given an initial value the first time a function is called and retains that value (or the value given to it by a subsequent assignment statement) on all subsequent calls to the function. Thus, static variables are like global variables in that they outlive a single call to their function, but they are accessible only within the function. The agent programs in the book use static variables for "memory." Programs with static variables can be implemented as "objects" in object-oriented languages such as Java and Smalltalk. In functional languages, they can be implemented by functional closures in an environment in which the required variables are defined.

**Functions as values.** Functions and procedures have capitalized names, and variables have lowercase italic names. So most of the time, a function call looks like FN($x$). However, we allow the value of a variable to be a function; for example, if the value of the variable $f$ is the square root function, then $f(9)$ returns 3.

**Arrays start at 1.** Unless stated otherwise, the first index of an array is 1 as in usual mathematical notation, not 0, as in Java and C.

**Indentation is significant.** Indentation is used to mark the scope of a loop or conditional, as in the language Python, and unlike Java and C++ (which use braces) or Pascal and Visual Basic (which use **end**).

## B.3 ONLINE HELP

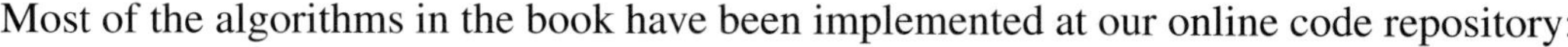

Most of the algorithms in the book have been implemented at our online code repository:

**aima.cs.berkeley.edu**

If you have any comments, corrections, or suggestions for improving the book, we would like to hear from you. Please visit the Web site for instructions on discussion lists, or send an email message to:

**aima@cs.berkeley.edu**

# Bibliography


**Aarup**, M., Arentoft, M. M., Parrod, Y., Stader, J., and Stokes, I. (1994). OPTIMUM-AIV: A knowledge-based planning and scheduling system for spacecraft AIV. In Fox, M. and Zweben, M. (Eds.), *Knowledge Based Scheduling*. Morgan Kaufmann, San Mateo, California.

**Abramson**, B. and Yung, M. (1989). Divide and conquer under global constraints: A solution to the N-queens problem. *Journal of Parallel and Distributed Computing*, *6*(3), 649–662.

**Ackley**, D. H. and Littman, M. L. (1991). Interactions between learning and evolution. In Langton, C., Taylor, C., Farmer, J. D., and Ramussen, S. (Eds.), *Artificial Life II*, pp. 487–509. Addison-Wesley, Redwood City, California.

**Adelson-Velsky**, G. M., Arlazarov, V. L., Bitman, A. R., Zhivotovsky, A. A., and Uskov, A. V. (1970). Programming a computer to play chess. *Russian Mathematical Surveys*, *25*, 221–262.

**Adelson-Velsky**, G. M., Arlazarov, V. L., and Donskoy, M. V. (1975). Some methods of controlling the tree search in chess programs. *Artificial Intelligence*, *6*(4), 361–371.

**Agmon**, S. (1954). The relaxation method for linear inequalities. *Canadian J. Math.*, *6*(3), 382–392.

**Agre**, P. E. and Chapman, D. (1987). Pengi: an implementation of a theory of activity. In *Proceedings of the Tenth International Joint Conference on Artificial Intelligence (IJCAI-87)*, pp. 268–272, Milan. Morgan Kaufmann.

**Aho**, A. V., Hopcroft, J., and Ullman, J. D. (1974). *The Design and Analysis of Computer Algorithms*. Addison-Wesley, Reading, Massachusetts.

**Aho**, A. V. and Ullman, J. D. (1972). *The Theory of Parsing, Translation and Compiling*. Prentice-Hall, Upper Saddle River, New Jersey.

**Ait-Kaci**, H. and Podelski, A. (1993). Towards a meaning of LIFE. *Journal of Logic Programming*, *16*(3–4), 195–234.

**Aizerman**, M., Braverman, E., and Rozonoer, L. (1964). Theoretical foundations of the potential function method in pattern recognition learning. *Automation and Remote Control*, *25*, 821–837.

**Albus**, J. S. (1975). A new approach to manipulator control: The cerebellar model articulation controller (CMAC). *Journal of Dynamic Systems, Measurement, and Control*, *97*, 270–277.

**Aldous**, D. and Vazirani, U. (1994). "Go with the winners" algorithms. In *Proceedings of the 35th Annual Symposium on Foundations of Computer Science*, pp. 492–501, Santa Fe, New Mexico. IEEE Computer Society Press.

**Allais**, M. (1953). Le comportment de l'homme rationnel devant la risque: critique des postulats et axiomes de l'école Américaine. *Econometrica*, *21*, 503–546.

**Allen**, J. F. (1983). Maintaining knowledge about temporal intervals. *Communications of the Association for Computing Machinery*, *26*(11), 832–843.

**Allen**, J. F. (1984). Towards a general theory of action and time. *Artificial Intelligence*, *23*, 123–154.

**Allen**, J. F. (1991). Time and time again: The many ways to represent time. *International Journal of Intelligent Systems*, *6*, 341–355.

**Allen**, J. F. (1995). *Natural Language Understanding*. Benjamin/Cummings, Redwood City; California.

**Allen**, J. F., Hendler, J., and Tate, A. (Eds.). (1990). *Readings in Planning*. Morgan Kaufmann, San Mateo, California.

**Almuallim**, H. and Dietterich, T. (1991). Learning with many irrelevant features. In *Proceedings of the Ninth National Conference on Artificial Intelligence (AAAI-91)*, Vol. 2, pp. 547–552, Anaheim, California. AAAI Press.

**ALPAC** (1966). Language and machines: Computers in translation and linguistics. Tech. rep. 1416, The Automatic Language Processing Advisory Committee of the National Academy of Sciences, Washington, DC.

**Alshawi**, H. (Ed.). (1992). *The Core Language Engine*. MIT Press, Cambridge, Massachusetts.

**Alterman**, R. (1988). Adaptive planning. *Cognitive Science*, *12*, 393–422.

**Amarel**, S. (1968). On representations of problems of reasoning about actions. In Michie, D. (Ed.), *Machine Intelligence 3*, Vol. 3, pp. 131–171. Elsevier/North-Holland, Amsterdam, London, New York.

**Ambros-Ingerson**, J. and Steel, S. (1988). Integrating planning, execution and monitoring. In *Proceedings of the Seventh National Conference on Artificial Intelligence (AAAI-88)*, pp. 735–740, St. Paul, Minnesota. Morgan Kaufmann.

**Amit**, D., Gutfreund, H., and Sompolinsky, H. (1985). Spin-glass models of neural networks. *Physical Review*, *A 32*, 1007–1018.

**Andersen**, S. K., Olesen, K. G., Jensen, F. V., and Jensen, F. (1989). HUGIN—a shell for building Bayesian belief universes for expert systems. In *Proceedings of the Eleventh International Joint Conference on Artificial Intelligence (IJCAI-89)*, Vol. 2, pp. 1080–1085, Detroit. Morgan Kaufmann.

**Anderson**, A. R. (Ed.). (1964). *Minds and Machines*. Prentice-Hall, Upper Saddle River, New Jersey.

**Anderson**, J. A. and Rosenfeld, E. (Eds.). (1988). *Neurocomputing: Foundations of Research*. MIT Press, Cambridge, Massachusetts.

**Anderson**, J. R. (1980). *Cognitive Psychology and Its Implications*. W. H. Freeman, New York.

**Anderson**, J. R. (1983). *The Architecture of Cognition*. Harvard University Press, Cambridge, Massachusetts.

**Andre**, D. and Russell, S. J. (2002). State abstraction for programmable reinforcement learning agents. In *Proceedings of the Eighteenth National Conference on Artificial Intelligence (AAAI-02)*, pp. 119–125, Edmonton, Alberta. AAAI Press.

**Anshelevich**, V. A. (2000). The game of Hex: An automatic theorem proving approach to game programming. In *Proceedings of the Seventeenth National Conference on Artificial Intelligence (AAAI-00)*, pp. 189–194, Austin, Texas. AAAI Press.

**Anthony**, M. and Bartlett, P. (1999). *Neural Network Learning: Theoretical Foundations*. Cambridge University Press, Cambridge, UK.

**Appel**, K. and Haken, W. (1977). Every planar map is four colorable: Part I: Discharging. *Illinois J. Math.*, *21*, 429–490.

**Apt**, K. R. (1999). The essence of constraint propagation. *Theoretical Computer Science*, *221*(1–2), 179–210.

**Apté**, C., Damerau, F., and Weiss, S. (1994). Automated learning of decision rules for text categorization. *ACM Transactions on Information Systems*, *12*, 233–251.

**Arkin**, R. (1998). *Behavior-Based Robotics*. MIT Press, Boston, MA.

**Armstrong**, D. M. (1968). *A Materialist Theory of the Mind*. Routledge and Kegan Paul, London.

**Arnauld**, A. (1662). *La logique, ou l'art de penser*. Chez Charles Savreux, au pied de la Tour de Nostre Dame, Paris.

**Arora**, S. (1998). Polynomial time approximation schemes for Euclidean traveling salesman and other geometric problems. *Journal of the Association for Computing Machinery*, *45*(5), 753–782.

**Ashby**, W. R. (1940). Adaptiveness and equilibrium. *Journal of Mental Science*, *86*, 478–483.

**Ashby**, W. R. (1948). Design for a brain. *Electronic Engineering, December*, 379–383.

**Ashby**, W. R. (1952). *Design for a Brain*. Wiley, New York.

**Asimov**, I. (1942). Runaround. *Astounding Science Fiction, March*.

**Asimov**, I. (1950). *I, Robot*. Doubleday, Garden City, New York.

**Astrom**, K. J. (1965). Optimal control of Markov decision processes with incomplete state estimation. *J. Math. Anal. Applic.*, *10*, 174–205.

**Audi**, R. (Ed.). (1999). *The Cambridge Dictionary of Philosophy*. Cambridge University Press, Cambridge, UK.

**Austin**, J. L. (1962). *How To Do Things with Words*. Harvard University Press, Cambridge, Massachusetts.

**Axelrod**, R. (1985). *The Evolution of Cooperation*. Basic Books, New York.

**Bacchus**, F. (1990). *Representing and Reasoning with Probabilistic Knowledge*. MIT Press, Cambridge, Massachusetts.

**Bacchus**, F. and Grove, A. (1995). Graphical models for preference and utility. In *Uncertainty in Artificial Intelligence: Proceedings of the Eleventh Conference*, pp. 3–10, Montreal, Canada. Morgan Kaufmann.

**Bacchus**, F. and Grove, A. (1996). Utility independence in a qualitative decision theory. In *Proceedings of the Fifth International Conference on the Principles of Knowledge Representation and Reasoning*, pp. 542–552, San Mateo, California. Morgan Kaufmann.

**Bacchus**, F., Grove, A., Halpern, J. Y., and Koller, D. (1992). From statistics to beliefs. In *Proceedings of the Tenth National Conference on Artificial Intelligence (AAAI-92)*, pp. 602–608, San Jose. AAAI Press.

**Bacchus**, F. and van Beek, P. (1998). On the conversion between non-binary and binary constraint satisfaction problems. In *Proceedings of the Fifteenth National Conference on Artificial Intelligence (AAAI-98)*, pp. 311–318, Madison, Wisconsin. AAAI Press.

**Bacchus**, F. and van Run, P. (1995). Dynamic variable ordering in CSPs. In *Proceedings of the First International Conference on Principles and Practice of Constraint Programming*, pp. 258–275, Cassis, France. Springer-Verlag.

**Bachmann**, P. G. H. (1894). *Die analytische Zahlentheorie*. B. G. Teubner, Leipzig.

**Backus**, J. W. (1996). Transcript of question and answer session. In Wexelblat, R. L. (Ed.), *History of Programming Languages*, p. 162. Academic Press, New York.

**Baeza-Yates**, R. and Ribeiro-Neto, B. (1999). *Modern Information Retrieval*. Addison Wesley Longman, Reading, Massachusetts.

**Bajcsy**, R. and Lieberman, L. (1976). Texture gradient as a depth cue. *Computer Graphics and Image Processing*, *5*(1), 52–67.

**Baker**, C. L. (1989). *English Syntax*. MIT Press, Cambridge, Massachusetts.

**Baker**, J. (1975). The Dragon system—an overview. *IEEE Transactions on Acoustics, Speech, and Signal Processing*, *23*, 24–29.

**Baker**, J. (1979). Trainable grammars for speech recognition. In *Speech Communication Papers for the 97th Meeting of the Acoustical Society of America*, pp. 547–550, Cambridge, Massachusetts. MIT Press.

**Baldwin**, J. M. (1896). A new factor in evolution. *American Naturalist*, *30*, 441–451. Continued on pages 536–553.

**Ballard**, B. W. (1983). The *-minimax search procedure for trees containing chance nodes. *Artificial Intelligence*, *21*(3), 327–350.

**Baluja**, S. (1997). Genetic algorithms and explicit search statistics. In Mozer, M. C., Jordan, M. I., and Petsche, T. (Eds.), *Advances in Neural Information Processing Systems*, Vol. 9, pp. 319–325. MIT Press, Cambridge, Massachusetts.

**Bancilhon**, F., Maier, D., Sagiv, Y., and Ullman, J. D. (1986). Magic sets and other strange ways to implement logic programs. In *Proceedings of the Fifth ACM Symposium on Principles of Database Systems*, pp. 1–16, New York. ACM Press.

**Bar-Hillel**, Y. (1954). Indexical expressions. *Mind*, *63*, 359–379.

**Bar-Hillel**, Y. (1960). The present status of automatic translation of languages. In Alt, F. L. (Ed.), *Advances in Computers*, Vol. 1, pp. 91–163. Academic Press, New York.

**Bar-Shalom**, Y. (Ed.). (1992). *Multitarget-multisensor tracking: Advanced applications*. Artech House, Norwood, Massachusetts.

**Bar-Shalom**, Y. and Fortmann, T. E. (1988). *Tracking and Data Association*. Academic Press, New York.

**Barrett**, A. and Weld, D. S. (1994). Task-decomposition via plan parsing. In *Proceedings of the Twelfth National Conference on Artificial Intelligence (AAAI-94)*, pp. 1117–1122, Seattle. AAAI Press.

**Bartak**, R. (2001). Theory and practice of constraint propagation. In *Proceedings of the Third Workshop on Constraint Programming for Decision and Control (CPDC-01)*, pp. 7–14, Gliwice, Poland.

**Barto**, A. G., Bradtke, S. J., and Singh, S. P. (1995). Learning to act using real-time dynamic programming. *Artificial Intelligence*, *73*(1), 81–138.

**Barto**, A. G., Sutton, R. S., and Anderson, C. W. (1983). Neuronlike adaptive elements that can solve difficult learning control problems. *IEEE Transactions on Systems, Man and Cybernetics*, *13*, 834–846.

**Barto**, A. G., Sutton, R. S., and Brouwer, P. S. (1981). Associative search network: A reinforcement learning associative memory. *Biological Cybernetics*, *40*(3), 201–211.

**Barton**, G. E., Berwick, R. C., and Ristad, E. S. (1987). *Computational Complexity and Natural Language*. MIT Press, Cambridge, Massachusetts.

**Barwise**, J. and Etchemendy, J. (1993). *The Language of First-Order Logic: Including the Macintosh Program Tarski's World 4.0* (Third Revised and Expanded edition). Center for the Study of Language and Information (CSLI), Stanford, California.

**Bateman**, J. A. (1997). Enabling technology for multilingual natural language generation: The KPML development environment. *Natural Language Engineering*, *3*(1), 15–55.

**Bateman**, J. A., Kasper, R. T., Moore, J. D., and Whitney, R. A. (1989). A general organization of knowledge for natural language processing: The penman upper model. Tech. rep., Information Sciences Institute, Marina del Rey, CA.

**Baum**, E., Boneh, D., and Garrett, C. (1995). On genetic algorithms. In *Proceedings of the Eighth Annual Conference on Computational Learning Theory (COLT-92)*, pp. 230–239, Santa Cruz, California. ACM Press.

**Baum**, E. and Haussler, D. (1989). What size net gives valid generalization?. *Neural Computation*, *1*(1), 151–160.

**Baum**, E. and Smith, W. D. (1997). A Bayesian approach to relevance in game playing. *Artificial Intelligence*, *97*(1–2), 195–242.

**Baum**, E. and Wilczek, F. (1988). Supervised learning of probability distributions by neural networks. In Anderson, D. Z. (Ed.), *Neural Information Processing Systems*, pp. 52–61. American Institute of Physics, New York.

**Baum**, L. E. and Petrie, T. (1966). Statistical inference for probabilistic functions of finite state Markov chains. *Annals of Mathematical Statistics*, *41*.

**Baxter**, J. and Bartlett, P. (2000). Reinforcement learning in POMDP's via direct gradient ascent. In *Proceedings of the Seventeenth International Conference on Machine Learning*, pp. 41–48, Stanford, California. Morgan Kaufmann.

**Bayardo**, R. J. and Schrag, R. C. (1997). Using CSP look-back techniques to solve real-world SAT instances. In *Proceedings of the Fourteenth National Conference on Artificial Intelligence (AAAI-97)*, pp. 203–208, Providence, Rhode Island. AAAI Press.

**Bayes**, T. (1763). An essay towards solving a problem in the doctrine of chances. *Philosophical Transactions of the Royal Society of London*, *53*, 370–418.

**Beal**, D. F. (1980). An analysis of minimax. In Clarke, M. R. B. (Ed.), *Advances in Computer Chess 2*, pp. 103–109. Edinburgh University Press, Edinburgh, Scotland.

**Beal**, D. F. (1990). A generalised quiescence search algorithm. *Artificial Intelligence*, *43*(1), 85–98.

**Beckert**, B. and Posegga, J. (1995). Leantap: Lean, tableau-based deduction. *Journal of Automated Reasoning*, *15*(3), 339–358.

**Beeri**, C., Fagin, R., Maier, D., and Yannakakis, M. (1983). On the desirability of acyclic database schemes. *Journal of the Association for Computing Machinery*, *30*(3), 479–513.

**Bell**, C. and Tate, A. (1985). Using temporal constraints to restrict search in a planner. In *Proceedings of the Third Alvey IKBS SIG Workshop*, Sunningdale, Oxfordshire, UK. Institution of Electrical Engineers.

**Bell**, J. L. and Machover, M. (1977). *A Course in Mathematical Logic*. Elsevier/North-Holland, Amsterdam, London, New York.

**Bellman**, R. E. (1978). *An Introduction to Artificial Intelligence: Can Computers Think?* Boyd & Fraser Publishing Company, San Francisco.

**Bellman**, R. E. and Dreyfus, S. E. (1962). *Applied Dynamic Programming*. Princeton University Press, Princeton, New Jersey.

**Bellman**, R. E. (1957). *Dynamic Programming*. Princeton University Press, Princeton, New Jersey.

**Belongie**, S., Malik, J., and Puzicha, J. (2002). Shape matching and object recognition using shape contexts. *IEEE Transactions on Pattern Analysis and Machine Intelligence (PAMI)*, *24*(4), 509–522.

**Bender**, E. A. (1996). *Mathematical methods in artificial intelligence*. IEEE Computer Society Press, Los Alamitos, California.

**Bentham**, J. (1823). *Principles of Morals and Legislation*. Oxford University Press, Oxford, UK. Original work published in 1789.

**Berger**, J. O. (1985). *Statistical Decision Theory and bayesian Analysis*. Springer Verlag, Berlin.

**Berlekamp**, E. R., Conway, J. H., and Guy, R. K. (1982). *Winning Ways, For Your Mathematical Plays*. Academic Press, New York.

**Berleur**, J. and Brunnstein, K. (2001). *Ethics of Computing: Codes, Spaces for Discussion and Law*. Chapman and Hall, London.

**Berliner**, H. J. (1977). BKG—a program that plays backgammon. Tech. rep., Computer Science Department, Carnegie-Mellon University, Pittsburgh.

**Berliner**, H. J. (1979). The B* tree search algorithm: A best-first proof procedure. *Artificial Intelligence*, *12*(1), 23–40.

**Berliner**, H. J. (1980a). Backgammon computer program beats world champion. *Artificial Intelligence*, *14*, 205–220.

**Berliner**, H. J. (1980b). Computer backgammon. *Scientific American*, *249*(6), 64–72.

**Berliner**, H. J. and Ebeling, C. (1989). Pattern knowledge and search: The SUPREM architecture. *Artificial Intelligence*, *38*(2), 161–198.

**Bernardo**, J. M. and Smith, A. F. M. (1994). *Bayesian Theory*. Wiley, New York.

**Berners-Lee**, T., Hendler, J., and Lassila, O. (2001). The semantic web. *Scientific American*, *284*(5), 34–43.

**Bernoulli**, D. (1738). Specimen theoriae novae de mensura sortis. *Proceedings of the St. Petersburg Imperial Academy of Sciences*, *5*, 175–192.

**Bernstein**, A. and Roberts, M. (1958). Computer vs. chess player. *Scientific American*, *198*(6), 96–105.

**Bernstein**, A., Roberts, M., Arbuckle, T., and Belsky, M. S. (1958). A chess playing program for the IBM 704. In *Proceedings of the 1958 Western Joint Computer Conference*, pp. 157–159, Los Angeles. American Institute of Electrical Engineers.

**Bernstein**, P. L. (1996). *Against the Odds: The Remarkable Story of Risk*. Wiley, New York.

**Berrou**, C., Glavieux, A., and Thitimajshima, P. (1993). Near Shannon limit error control-correcting coding and decoding: Turbo-codes. 1. In *Proc. IEEE International Conference on Communications*, pp. 1064–1070, Geneva, Switzerland. IEEE.

**Berry**, D. A. and Fristedt, B. (1985). *Bandit Problems: Sequential Allocation of Experiments*. Chapman and Hall, London.

**Bertele**, U. and Brioschi, F. (1972). *Nonserial dynamic programming*. Academic Press, New York.

**Bertoli**, P., Cimatti, A., and Roveri, M. (2001a). Heuristic search + symbolic model checking = efficient conformant planning. In *Proceedings of the Seventeenth International Joint Conference on Artificial Intelligence (IJCAI-01)*, pp. 467–472, Seattle. Morgan Kaufmann.

**Bertoli**, P., Cimatti, A., Roveri, M., and Traverso, P. (2001b). Planning in nondeterministic domains under partial observability via symbolic model checking. In *Proceedings of the Seventeenth International Joint Conference on Artificial Intelligence (IJCAI-01)*, pp. 473–478, Seattle. Morgan Kaufmann.

**Bertsekas**, D. (1987). *Dynamic Programming: Deterministic and Stochastic Models*. Prentice-Hall, Upper Saddle River, New Jersey.

**Bertsekas**, D. and Tsitsiklis, J. N. (1996). *Neurodynamic programming*. Athena Scientific, Belmont, Massachusetts.

**Bertsekas**, D. and Tsitsiklis, J. N. (2002). *Introduction to Probability*. Athena Scientific, Belmont, Massachusetts.

**Bibel**, W. (1981). On matrices with connections. *Journal of the Association for Computing Machinery*, *28*(4), 633–645.

**Bibel**, W. (1993). *Deduction: Automated Logic*. Academic Press, London.

**Biggs**, N. L., Lloyd, E. K., and Wilson, R. J. (1986). *Graph Theory 1736–1936*. Oxford University Press, Oxford, UK.

**Binder**, J., Koller, D., Russell, S. J., and Kanazawa, K. (1997a). Adaptive probabilistic networks with hidden variables. *Machine Learning*, *29*, 213–244.

**Binder**, J., Murphy, K., and Russell, S. J. (1997b). Space-efficient inference in dynamic probabilistic networks. In *Proceedings of the Fifteenth International Joint Conference on Artificial Intelligence (IJCAI-97)*, pp. 1292–1296, Nagoya, Japan. Morgan Kaufmann.

**Binford**, T. O. (1971). Visual perception by computer. Invited paper presented at the IEEE Systems Science and Cybernetics Conference, Miami.

**Binmore**, K. (1982). *Essays on Foundations of Game Theory*. Pitman, London.

**Birnbaum**, L. and Selfridge, M. (1981). Conceptual analysis of natural language. In Schank, R. and Riesbeck, C. (Eds.), *Inside Computer Understanding*. Lawrence Erlbaum, Potomac, Maryland.

**Biro**, J. I. and Shahan, R. W. (Eds.). (1982). *Mind, Brain and Function: Essays in the Philosophy of Mind*. University of Oklahoma Press, Norman, Oklahoma.

**Birtwistle**, G., Dahl, O.-J., Myrhaug, B., and Nygaard, K. (1973). *Simula Begin*. Studentliteratur (Lund) and Auerbach, New York.

**Bishop**, C. M. (1995). *Neural Networks for Pattern Recognition*. Oxford University Press, Oxford, UK.

**Bistarelli**, S., Montanari, U., and Rossi, F. (1997). Semiring-based constraint satisfaction and optimization. *Journal of the Association for Computing Machinery*, *44*(2), 201–236.

**Bitner**, J. R. and Reingold, E. M. (1975). Backtrack programming techniques. *Communications of the Association for Computing Machinery*, *18*(11), 651–656.

**Blei**, D. M., Ng, A. Y., and Jordan, M. I. (2001). Latent Dirichlet Allocation. In *Neural Information Processing Systems*, Vol. 14, Cambridge, Massachusetts. MIT Press.

**Blinder**, A. S. (1983). Issues in the coordination of monetary and fiscal policies. In *Monetary Policy Issues in the 1980s*. Federal Reserve Bank, Kansas City, Missouri.

**Block**, N. (Ed.). (1980). *Readings in Philosophy of Psychology*, Vol. 1. Harvard University Press, Cambridge, Massachusetts.

**Blum**, A. L. and Furst, M. (1995). Fast planning through planning graph analysis. In *Proceedings of the Fourteenth International Joint Conference on Artificial Intelligence (IJCAI-95)*, pp. 1636–1642, Montreal. Morgan Kaufmann.

**Blum**, A. L. and Furst, M. (1997). Fast planning through planning graph analysis. *Artificial Intelligence*, *90*(1–2), 281–300.

**Blumer**, A., Ehrenfeucht, A., Haussler, D., and Warmuth, M. (1989). Learnability and the Vapnik-Chervonenkis dimension. *Journal of the Association for Computing Machinery*, *36*(4), 929–965.

**Bobrow**, D. G. (1967). Natural language input for a computer problem solving system. In Minsky, M. L. (Ed.), *Semantic Information Processing*, pp. 133–215. MIT Press, Cambridge, Massachusetts.

**Bobrow**, D. G., Kaplan, R., Kay, M., Norman, D. A., Thompson, H., and Winograd, T. (1977). GUS, a frame driven dialog system. *Artificial Intelligence*, *8*, 155–173.

**Bobrow**, D. G. and Raphael, B. (1974). New programming languages for artificial intelligence research. *Computing Surveys*, *6*(3), 153–174.

**Boden**, M. A. (1977). *Artificial Intelligence and Natural Man*. Basic Books, New York.

**Boden**, M. A. (Ed.). (1990). *The Philosophy of Artificial Intelligence*. Oxford University Press, Oxford, UK.

**Bonet**, B. and Geffner, H. (1999). Planning as heuristic search: New results. In *Proceedings of the European Conference on Planning*, pp. 360–372, Durham, UK. Springer-Verlag.

**Bonet**, B. and Geffner, H. (2000). Planning with incomplete information as heuristic search in belief space. In Chien, S., Kambhampati, S., and Knoblock, C. A. (Eds.), *International Conference on Artificial Intelligence Planning and Scheduling*, pp. 52–61, Menlo Park, California. AAAI Press.

**Boole**, G. (1847). *The Mathematical Analysis of Logic: Being an Essay towards a Calculus of Deductive Reasoning*. Macmillan, Barclay, and Macmillan, Cambridge.

**Boolos**, G. S. and Jeffrey, R. C. (1989). *Computability and Logic* (3rd edition). Cambridge University Press, Cambridge, UK.

**Booth**, T. L. (1969). Probabilistic representation of formal languages. In *IEEE Conference Record of the 1969 Tenth Annual Symposium on Switching and Automata Theory*, pp. 74–81, Waterloo, Ontario. IEEE.

**Borel**, E. (1921). La théorie du jeu et les équations intégrales à noyau symétrique. *Comptes Rendus Hebdomadaires des Séances de l'Académie des Sciences*, *173*, 1304–1308.

**Borenstein**, J., Everett, B., and Feng, L. (1996). *Navigating Mobile Robots: Systems and Techniques*. A. K. Peters, Ltd., Wellesley, MA.

**Borenstein**, J. and Koren., Y. (1991). The vector field histogram—fast obstacle avoidance for moile robots. *IEEE Transactions on Robotics and Automation*, *7*(3), 278–288.

**Borgida**, A., Brachman, R. J., McGuinness, D. L., and Alperin Resnick, L. (1989). CLASSIC: A structural data model for objects. *SIGMOD Record*, *18*(2), 58–67.

**Boser**, B. E., Guyon, I. M., and Vapnik, V. N. (1992). A training algorithm for optimal margin classifiers. In *Proceedings of the Fifth Annual ACM Workshop on Computational Learning Theory (COLT-92)*, Pittsburgh, Pennsylvania. ACM Press.

**Boutilier**, C. and Brafman, R. I. (2001). Partial-order planning with concurrent interacting actions. *Journal of Artificial Intelligence Research*, *14*, 105–136.

**Boutilier**, C., Dearden, R., and Goldszmidt, M. (2000). Stochastic dynamic programming with factored representations. *Artificial Intelligence*, *121*, 49–107.

**Boutilier**, C., Reiter, R., and Price, B. (2001). Symbolic dynamic programming for first-order MDPs. In *Proceedings of the Seventeenth International Joint Conference on Artificial Intelligence (IJCAI-01)*, pp. 467–472, Seattle. Morgan Kaufmann.

**Boutilier**, C., Reiter, R., Soutchanski, M., and Thrun, S. (2000). Decision-theoretic, high-level agent programming in the situation calculus. In *Proceedings of the Seventeenth National Conference on Artificial Intelligence (AAAI-00)*, pp. 355–362, Austin, Texas. AAAI Press.

**Box**, G. E. P. (1957). Evolutionary operation: A method of increasing industrial productivity. *Applied Statistics*, *6*, 81–101.

**Boyan**, J. A. (2002). Technical update: Least-squares temporal difference learning. *Machine Learning*, *49*(2–3), 233–246.

**Boyan**, J. A. and Moore, A. W. (1998). Learning evaluation functions for global optimization and Boolean satisfiability. In *Proceedings of the Fifteenth National Conference on Artificial Intelligence (AAAI-98)*, Madison, Wisconsin. AAAI Press.

**Boyen**, X., Friedman, N., and Koller, D. (1999). Discovering the hidden structure of complex dynamic systems. In *Uncertainty in Artificial Intelligence: Proceedings of the Fifteenth Conference*, Stockholm. Morgan Kaufmann.

**Boyer**, R. S. and Moore, J. S. (1979). *A Computational Logic*. Academic Press, New York.

**Boyer**, R. S. and Moore, J. S. (1984). Proof checking the RSA public key encryption algorithm. *American Mathematical Monthly*, *91*(3), 181–189.

**Brachman**, R. J. (1979). On the epistemological status of semantic networks. In Findler, N. V. (Ed.), *Associative Networks: Representation and Use of Knowledge by Computers*, pp. 3–50. Academic Press, New York.

**Brachman**, R. J., Fikes, R. E., and Levesque, H. J. (1983). Krypton: A functional approach to knowledge representation. *Computer*, *16*(10), 67–73.

**Brachman**, R. J. and Levesque, H. J. (Eds.). (1985). *Readings in Knowledge Representation*. Morgan Kaufmann, San Mateo, California.

**Bradtke**, S. J. and Barto, A. G. (1996). Linear least-squares algorithms for temporal difference learning. *Machine Learning*, *22*, 33–57.

**Brafman**, R. I. and Tennenholtz, M. (2000). A near optimal polynomial time algorithm for learning in certain classes of stochastic games. *Artificial Intelligence*, *121*, 31–47.

**Braitenberg**, V. (1984). *Vehicles: Experiments in Synthetic Psychology*. MIT Press.

**Bransford**, J. and Johnson, M. (1973). Consideration of some problems in comprehension. In Chase, W. G. (Ed.), *Visual Information Processing*. Academic Press, New York.

**Bratko**, I. (1986). *Prolog Programming for Artificial Intelligence* (1st edition). Addison-Wesley, Reading, Massachusetts.

**Bratko**, I. (2001). *Prolog Programming for Artificial Intelligence* (Third edition). Addison-Wesley, Reading, Massachusetts.

**Bratman**, M. E. (1987). *Intention, Plans, and Practical Reason*. Harvard University Press, Cambridge, Massachusetts.

**Bratman**, M. E. (1992). Planning and the stability of intention. *Minds and Machines*, *2*(1), 1–16.

**Breese**, J. S. and Heckerman, D. (1996). Decision-theoretic troubleshooting: A framework for repair and experiment. In *Uncertainty in Artificial Intelligence: Proceedings of the Twelfth Conference*, pp. 124–132, Portland, Oregon. Morgan Kaufmann.

**Breiman**, L. (1996). Bagging predictors. *Machine Learning*, *26*(2), 123–140.

**Breiman**, L., Friedman, J., Olshen, R. A., and Stone, P. J. (1984). *Classification and Regression Trees*. Wadsworth International Group, Belmont, California.

**Brelaz**, D. (1979). New methods to color the vertices of a graph. *Communications of the Association for Computing Machinery*, *22*(4), 251–256.

**Brent**, R. P. (1973). *Algorithms for minimization without derivatives*. Prentice-Hall, Upper Saddle River, New Jersey.

**Bresnan**, J. (1982). *The Mental Representation of Grammatical Relations*. MIT Press, Cambridge, Massachusetts.

**Brewka**, G., Dix, J., and Konolige, K. (1997). *Nononotonic Reasoning: An Overview*. CSLI Publications, Stanford, California.

**Bridle**, J. S. (1990). Probabilistic interpretation of feedforward classification network outputs, with relationships to statistical pattern recognition. In Fogelman Soulié, F. and Hérault, J. (Eds.), *Neurocomputing: Algorithms, Architectures and Applications*. Springer-Verlag, Berlin.

**Briggs**, R. (1985). Knowledge representation in Sanskrit and artificial intelligence. *AI Magazine*, *6*(1), 32–39.

**Brin**, S. and Page, L. (1998). The anatomy of a large-scale hypertextual web search engine. In *Proceedings of the Seventh World Wide Web Conference*, Brisbane, Australia.

**Broadbent**, D. E. (1958). *Perception and communication*. Pergamon, Oxford, UK.

**Brooks**, R. A. (1986). A robust layered control system for a mobile robot. *IEEE Journal of Robotics and Automation*, *2*, 14–23.

**Brooks**, R. A. (1989). Engineering approach to building complete, intelligent beings. *Proceedings of the SPIE—the International Society for Optical Engineering*, *1002*, 618–625.

**Brooks**, R. A. (1990). Elephants don't play chess. *Autonomous Robots*, *6*, 3–15.

**Brooks**, R. A. (1991). Intelligence without representation. *Artificial Intelligence*, *47*(1–3), 139–159.

**Brooks**, R. A. and Lozano-Perez, T. (1985). A subdivision algorithm in configuration space for findpath with rotation. *IEEE Transactions on Systems, Man and Cybernetics*, *15*(2), 224–233.

**Brown**, M., Grundy, W., Lin, D., Cristianini, N., Sugnet, C., Furey, T., Ares, M., and Haussler, D. (2000). Knowledge-based analysis of microarray gene expression data using support vector machines. In *Proceedings of the national Academy of Sciences*, Vol. 97, pp. 262–267.

**Brown**, P. F., Cocke, J., Della Pietra, S. A., Della Pietra, V. J., Jelinek, F., Mercer, R. L., and Roossin, P. (1988). A statistical approach to language translation. In *Proceedings of the 12th International Conference on Computational Linguistics*, pp. 71–76, Budapest. John von Neumann Society for Computing Sciences.

**Brown**, P. F., Della Pietra, S. A., Della Pietra, V. J., and Mercer, R. L. (1993). The mathematics of statistical machine translation: Parameter estimation. *Computational Linguistics*, *19*(2), 263–311.

**Brownston**, L., Farrell, R., Kant, E., and Martin, N. (1985). *Programming expert systems in OPS5: An introduction to rule-based programming*. Addison-Wesley, Reading, Massachusetts.

**Brudno**, A. L. (1963). Bounds and valuations for shortening the scanning of variations. *Problems of Cybernetics*, *10*, 225–241.

**Bruner**, J. S., Goodnow, J. J., and Austin, G. A. (1957). *A Study of Thinking*. Wiley, New York.

**Bryant**, R. E. (1992). Symbolic Boolean manipulation with ordered binary decision diagrams. *ACM Computing Surveys*, *24*(3), 293–318.

**Bryson**, A. E. and Ho, Y.-C. (1969). *Applied Optimal Control*. Blaisdell, New York.

**Buchanan**, B. G. and Mitchell, T. M. (1978). Model-directed learning of production rules. In Waterman, D. A. and Hayes-Roth, F. (Eds.), *Pattern-Directed Inference Systems*, pp. 297–312. Academic Press, New York.

**Buchanan**, B. G., Mitchell, T. M., Smith, R. G., and Johnson, C. R. (1978). Models of learning systems. In *Encyclopedia of Computer Science and Technology*, Vol. 11. Dekker, New York.

**Buchanan**, B. G. and Shortliffe, E. H. (Eds.). (1984). *Rule-Based Expert Systems: The MYCIN Experiments of the Stanford Heuristic Programming Project*. Addison-Wesley, Reading, Massachusetts.

**Buchanan**, B. G., Sutherland, G. L., and Feigenbaum, E. A. (1969). Heuristic DENDRAL: A program for generating explanatory hypotheses in organic chemistry. In Meltzer, B., Michie, D., and Swann, M. (Eds.), *Machine Intelligence 4*, pp. 209–254. Edinburgh University Press, Edinburgh, Scotland.

**Bundy**, A. (1999). A survey of automated deduction. In Wooldridge, M. J. and Veloso, M. (Eds.), *Artificial intelligence today: Recent trends and developments*, pp. 153–174. Springer-Verlag, Berlin.

**Bunt**, H. C. (1985). The formal representation of (quasi-) continuous concepts. In Hobbs, J. R. and Moore, R. C. (Eds.), *Formal Theories of the Commonsense World*, chap. 2, pp. 37–70. Ablex, Norwood, New Jersey.

**Burgard**, W., Cremers, A. B., Fox, D., Hähnel, D., Lakemeyer, G., Schulz, D., Steiner, W., and Thrun, S. (1999). Experiences with an interactive museum tour-guide robot. *Artificial Intelligence*, *114*(1-2), 3–55.

**Buro**, M. (2002). Improving heuristic mini-max search by supervised learning. *Artificial Intelligence*, *134*(1–2), 85–99.

**Burstall**, R. M. (1974). Program proving as hand simulation with a little induction. In *Information Processing '74*, pp. 308–312. Elsevier/North-Holland, Amsterdam, London, New York.

**Burstall**, R. M. and Darlington, J. (1977). A transformation system for developing recursive programs. *Journal of the Association for Computing Machinery*, *24*(1), 44–67.

**Burstein**, J., Leacock, C., and Swartz, R. (2001). Automated evaluation of essays and short answers. In *Fifth International Computer Assisted Assessment (CAA) Conference*, Loughborough, U.K. Loughborough University.

**Bylander**, T. (1992). Complexity results for serial decomposability. In *Proceedings of the Tenth National Conference on Artificial Intelligence (AAAI-92)*, pp. 729–734, San Jose. AAAI Press.

**Bylander**, T. (1994). The computational complexity of propositional strips planning. *Artificial Intelligence*, *69*, 165–204.

**Calvanese**, D., Lenzerini, M., and Nardi, D. (1999). Unifying class-based representation formalisms. *Journal of Artificial Intelligence Research*, *11*, 199–240.

**Campbell**, M. S., Hoane, A. J., and Hsu, F.-H. (2002). Deep Blue. *Artificial Intelligence*, *134*(1–2), 57–83.

**Canny**, J. and Reif, J. (1987). New lower bound techniques for robot motion planning problems. In *IEEE Symposium on Foundations of Computer Science*, pp. 39–48.

**Canny**, J. (1986). A computational approach to edge detection. *IEEE Transactions on Pattern Analysis and Machine Intelligence (PAMI)*, *8*, 679–698.

**Canny**, J. (1988). *The Complexity of Robot Motion Planning*. MIT Press, Cambridge, Massachusetts.

**Carbonell**, J. G. (1983). Derivational analogy and its role in problem solving. In *Proceedings of the National Conference on Artificial Intelligence (AAAI-83)*, pp. 64–69, Washington, DC. Morgan Kaufmann.

**Carbonell**, J. G., Knoblock, C. A., and Minton, S. (1989). PRODIGY: An integrated architecture for planning and learning. Technical report CMU-CS-89-189, Computer Science Department, Carnegie-Mellon University, Pittsburgh.

**Carbonell**, J. R. and Collins, A. M. (1973). Natural semantics in artificial intelligence. In *Proceedings of the Third International Joint Conference on Artificial Intelligence (IJCAI-73)*, pp. 344–351, Stanford, California. IJCAII.

**Carnap**, R. (1928). *Der logische Aufbau der Welt*. Weltkreis-verlag, Berlin-Schlachtensee. Translated into English as (Carnap, 1967).

**Carnap**, R. (1948). On the application of inductive logic. *Philosophy and Phenomenological Research*, *8*, 133–148.

**Carnap**, R. (1950). *Logical Foundations of Probability*. University of Chicago Press, Chicago.

**Carrasco**, R. C., Oncina, J., and Calera, J. (1998). *Stochastic Inference of Regular Tree Languages*, Vol. 1433 of *Lecture Notes in Computer Science*. Springer-Verlag, Berlin.

**Cassandra**, A. R., Kaelbling, L. P., and Littman, M. L. (1994). Acting optimally in partially observable stochastic domains. In *Proceedings of the Twelfth National Conference on Artificial Intelligence (AAAI-94)*, pp. 1023–1028, Seattle. AAAI Press.

**Ceri**, S., Gottlob, G., and Tanca, L. (1990). *Logic programming and databases*. Springer-Verlag, Berlin.

**Chakrabarti**, P. P., Ghose, S., Acharya, A., and de Sarkar, S. C. (1989). Heuristic search in restricted memory. *Artificial Intelligence*, *41*(2), 197–222.

**Chan**, W. P., Prete, F., and Dickinson, M. H. (1998). Visual input to the efferent control system of a fly's 'gyroscope'. *Science*, *289*, 289–292.

**Chandra**, A. K. and Harel, D. (1980). Computable queries for relational data bases. *Journal of Computer and System Sciences*, *21*(2), 156–178.

**Chandra**, A. K. and Merlin, P. M. (1977). Optimal implementation of conjunctive queries in relational databases. In *Proceedings of the 9th Annual ACM Symposium on Theory of Computing*, pp. 77–90, New York. ACM Press.

**Chang**, C.-L. and Lee, R. C.-T. (1973). *Symbolic Logic and Mechanical Theorem Proving*. Academic Press, New York.

**Chapman**, D. (1987). Planning for conjunctive goals. *Artificial Intelligence*, *32*(3), 333–377.

**Charniak**, E. (1993). *Statistical Language Learning*. MIT Press, Cambridge, Massachusetts.

**Charniak**, E. (1996). Tree-bank grammars. In *Proceedings of the Thirteenth National Conference on Artificial Intelligence (AAAI-96)*, pp. 1031–1036, Portland, Oregon. AAAI Press.

**Charniak**, E. (1997). Statistical parsing with a context-free grammar and word statistics. In *Proceedings of the Fourteenth National Conference on Artificial Intelligence (AAAI-97)*, pp. 598–603, Providence, Rhode Island. AAAI Press.

**Charniak**, E. and Goldman, R. (1992). A Bayesian model of plan recognition. *Artificial Intelligence*, *64*(1), 53–79.

**Charniak**, E. and McDermott, D. (1985). *Introduction to Artificial Intelligence*. Addison-Wesley, Reading, Massachusetts.

**Charniak**, E., Riesbeck, C., McDermott, D., and Meehan, J. (1987). *Artificial Intelligence Programming* (2nd edition). Lawrence Erlbaum Associates, Potomac, Maryland.

**Chatfield**, C. (1989). *The Analysis of Time Series: An Introduction* (4th edition). Chapman and Hall, London.

**Cheeseman**, P. (1985). In defense of probability. In *Proceedings of the Ninth International Joint Conference on Artificial Intelligence (IJCAI-85)*, pp. 1002–1009, Los Angeles. Morgan Kaufmann.

**Cheeseman**, P. (1988). An inquiry into computer understanding. *Computational Intelligence*, *4*(1), 58–66.

**Cheeseman**, P., Kanefsky, B., and Taylor, W. (1991). Where the really hard problems are. In *Proceedings of the Twelfth International Joint Conference on Artificial Intelligence (IJCAI-91)*, pp. 331–337, Sydney. Morgan Kaufmann.

**Cheeseman**, P., Self, M., Kelly, J., and Stutz, J. (1988). Bayesian classification. In *Proceedings of the Seventh National Conference on Artificial Intelligence (AAAI-88)*, Vol. 2, pp. 607–611, St. Paul, Minnesota. Morgan Kaufmann.

**Cheeseman**, P. and Stutz, J. (1996). Bayesian classification (AutoClass): Theory and results. In Fayyad, U., Piatesky-Shapiro, G., Smyth, P., and Uthurusamy, R. (Eds.), *Advances in Knowledge Discovery and Data Mining*. AAAI Press/MIT Press, Menlo Park, California.

**Cheng**, J. and Druzdzel, M. J. (2000). AIS-BN: An adaptive importance sampling algorithm for evidential reasoning in large Bayesian networks. *Journal of Artificial Intelligence Research*, *13*, 155–188.

**Cheng**, J., Greiner, R., Kelly, J., Bell, D. A., and Liu, W. (2002). Learning Bayesian networks from data: An information-theory based approach. *Artificial Intelligence*, *137*, 43–90.

**Chierchia**, G. and McConnell-Ginet, S. (1990). *Meaning and Grammar*. MIT Press, Cambridge, Massachusetts.

**Chomsky**, N. (1956). Three models for the description of language. *IRE Transactions on Information Theory*, *2*(3), 113–124.

**Chomsky**, N. (1957). *Syntactic Structures*. Mouton, The Hague and Paris.

**Chomsky**, N. (1980). Rules and representations. *The Behavioral and Brain Sciences*, *3*, 1–61.

**Choset**, H. (1996). *Sensor Based Motion Planning: The Hierarchical Generalized Voronoi Graph*. Ph.D. thesis, California Institute of Technology.

**Chung**, K. L. (1979). *Elementary Probability Theory with Stochastic Processes* (3rd edition). Springer-Verlag, Berlin.

**Church**, A. (1936). A note on the Entscheidungsproblem. *Journal of Symbolic Logic*, *1*, 40–41 and 101–102.

**Church**, K. and Patil, R. (1982). Coping with syntactic ambiguity or how to put the block in the box on the table. *American Journal of Computational Linguistics*, *8*(3–4), 139–149.

**Church**, K. and Gale, W. A. (1991). A comparison of the enhanced Good–Turing and deleted estimation methods for estimating probabilities of English bigrams. *Computer Speech and Language*, *5*, 19–54.

**Churchland**, P. M. (1979). *Scientific Realism and the Plasticity of Mind*. Cambridge University Press, Cambridge, UK.

**Churchland**, P. M. and Churchland, P. S. (1982). Functionalism, qualia, and intentionality. In Biro, J. I. and Shahan, R. W. (Eds.), *Mind, Brain and Function: Essays in the Philosophy of Mind*, pp. 121–145. University of Oklahoma Press, Norman, Oklahoma.

**Churchland**, P. S. (1986). *Neurophilosophy: Toward a Unified Science of the Mind–Brain*. MIT Press, Cambridge, Massachusetts.

**Cimatti**, A., Roveri, M., and Traverso, P. (1998). Automatic OBDD-based generation of universal plans in non-deterministic domains. In *Proceedings of the Fifteenth National Conference on Artificial Intelligence (AAAI-98)*, pp. 875–881, Madison, Wisconsin. AAAI Press.

**Clark**, K. L. (1978). Negation as failure. In Gallaire, H. and Minker, J. (Eds.), *Logic and Data Bases*, pp. 293–322. Plenum, New York.

**Clark**, P. and Niblett, T. (1989). The CN2 induction algorithm. *Machine Learning*, *3*, 261–283.

**Clarke**, A. C. (1968a). *2001: A Space Odyssey*. Signet.

**Clarke**, A. C. (1968b). The world of 2001. Vogue.

**Clarke**, E. and Grumberg, O. (1987). Research on automatic verification of finite-state concurrent systems. *Annual Review of Computer Science*, *2*, 269–290.

**Clarke**, E., Grumberg, O., and Peled, D. (1999). *Model Checking*. MIT Press, Cambridge, Massachusetts.

**Clarke**, M. R. B. (Ed.). (1977). *Advances in Computer Chess 1*. Edinburgh University Press, Edinburgh, Scotland.

**Clearwater**, S. H. (Ed.). (1996). *Market-Based Control*. World Scientific, Singapore and Teaneck, New Jersey.

**Clocksin**, W. F. and Mellish, C. S. (1994). *Programming in Prolog* (4th edition). Springer-Verlag, Berlin.

**Clowes**, M. B. (1971). On seeing things. *Artificial Intelligence*, *2*(1), 79–116.

**Cobham**, A. (1964). The intrinsic computational difficulty of functions. In Bar-Hillel, Y. (Ed.), *Proceedings of the 1964 International Congress for Logic, Methodology, and Philosophy of Science*, pp. 24–30, Jerusalem. Elsevier/North-Holland.

**Cobley**, P. (1997). *Introducing Semiotics*. Totem Books, New York.

**Cohen**, J. (1988). A view of the origins and development of PROLOG. *Communications of the Association for Computing Machinery*, *31*, 26–36.

**Cohen**, P. R. (1995). *Empirical methods for artificial intelligence*. MIT Press, Cambridge, Massachusetts.

**Cohen**, P. R. and Levesque, H. J. (1990). Intention is choice with commitment. *Artificial Intelligence*, *42*(2–3), 213–261.

**Cohen**, P. R., Morgan, J., and Pollack, M. E. (1990). *Intentions in Communication*. MIT Press, Cambridge, Massachusetts.

**Cohen**, P. R. and Perrault, C. R. (1979). Elements of a plan-based theory of speech acts. *Cognitive Science*, *3*(3), 177–212.

**Cohen**, W. W. and Page, C. D. (1995). Learnability in inductive logic programming: Methods and results. *New Generation Computing*, *13*(3–4), 369–409.

**Cohn**, A. G., Bennett, B., Gooday, J. M., and Gotts, N. (1997). RCC: A calculus for region based qualitative spatial reasoning. *GeoInformatica*, *1*, 275–316.

**Collins**, M. J. (1996). A new statistical parser based on bigram lexical dependencies. In Joshi, A. K. and Palmer, M. (Eds.), *Proceedings of the Thirty-Fourth Annual Meeting of the Association for Computational Linguistics*, pp. 184–191, San Francisco. Morgan Kaufmann Publishers.

**Collins**, M. J. (1999). *Head-driven Statistical Models for Natural Language Processing*. Ph.D. thesis, University of Pennsylvania.

**Collins**, M. and Duffy, K. (2002). New ranking algorithms for parsing and tagging: Kernels over discrete structures, and the voted perceptron. In *Proceedings of the ACL*.

**Colmerauer**, A. (1975). Les grammaires de metamorphose. Tech. rep., Groupe d'Intelligence Artificielle, Université de Marseille-Luminy.

**Colmerauer**, A., Kanoui, H., Pasero, R., and Roussel, P. (1973). Un systéme de communication homme–machine en Français. Rapport, Groupe d'Intelligence Artificielle, Université d'Aix-Marseille II.

**Condon**, J. H. and Thompson, K. (1982). Belle chess hardware. In Clarke, M. R. B. (Ed.), *Advances in Computer Chess 3*, pp. 45–54. Pergamon, Oxford, UK.

**Congdon**, C. B., Huber, M., Kortenkamp, D., Bidlack, C., Cohen, C., Huffman, S., Koss, F., Raschke, U., and Weymouth, T. (1992). CARMEL versus Flakey: A comparison of two robots. Tech. rep. Papers from the AAAI Robot Competition, RC-92-01, American Association for Artificial Intelligence, Menlo Park, CA.

**Connell**, J. (1989). *A Colony Architecture for an Artificial Creature*. Ph.D. thesis, Artificial Intelligence Laboratory, MIT, Cambridge, MA. also available as AI Technical Report 1151.

**Cook**, S. A. (1971). The complexity of theorem-proving procedures. In *Proceedings of the 3rd Annual ACM Symposium on Theory of Computing*, pp. 151–158, New York. ACM Press.

**Cook**, S. A. and Mitchell, D. (1997). Finding hard instances of the satisfiability problem: A survey. In Du, D., Gu, J., and Pardalos, P. (Eds.), *Satisfiability problems: Theory and applications*. American Mathematical Society, Providence, Rhode Island.

**Cooper**, G. (1990). The computational complexity of probabilistic inference using Bayesian belief networks. *Artificial Intelligence*, *42*, 393–405.

**Cooper**, G. and Herskovits, E. (1992). A Bayesian method for the induction of probabilistic networks from data. *Machine Learning*, *9*, 309–347.

**Copeland**, J. (1993). *Artificial Intelligence: A Philosophical Introduction*. Blackwell, Oxford, UK.

**Copernicus** (1543). *De Revolutionibus Orbium Coelestium*. Apud Ioh. Petreium, Nuremberg.

**Cormen**, T. H., Leiserson, C. E., and Rivest, R. (1990). *Introduction to Algorithms*. MIT Press, Cambridge, Massachusetts.

**Cortes**, C. and Vapnik, V. N. (1995). Support vector networks. *Machine Learning*, *20*, 273–297.

**Cournot**, A. (Ed.). (1838). *Recherches sur les principes mathématiques de la théorie des richesses*. L. Hachette, Paris.

**Covington**, M. A. (1994). *Natural Language Processing for Prolog Programmers*. Prentice-Hall, Upper Saddle River, New Jersey.

**Cowan**, J. D. and Sharp, D. H. (1988a). Neural nets. *Quarterly Reviews of Biophysics*, *21*, 365–427.

**Cowan**, J. D. and Sharp, D. H. (1988b). Neural nets and artificial intelligence. *Daedalus*, *117*, 85–121.

**Cox**, I. (1993). A review of statistical data association techniques for motion correspondence. *International Journal of Computer Vision*, *10*, 53–66.

**Cox**, I. and Hingorani, S. L. (1994). An efficient implementation and evaluation of Reid's multiple hypothesis tracking algorithm for visual tracking. In *Proceedings of the 12th International Conference on Pattern Recognition*, Vol. 1, pp. 437–442, Jerusalem, Israel. International Association for Pattern Recognition (IAPR).

**Cox**, I. and Wilfong, G. T. (Eds.). (1990). *Autonomous Robot Vehicles*. Springer Verlag, Berlin.

**Cox**, R. T. (1946). Probability, frequency, and reasonable expectation. *American Journal of Physics*, *14*(1), 1–13.

**Craig**, J. (1989). *Introduction to Robotics: Mechanics and Control (2nd Edition)*. Addison-Wesley Publishing, Inc., Reading, MA.

**Craik**, K. J. (1943). *The Nature of Explanation*. Cambridge University Press, Cambridge, UK.

**Crawford**, J. M. and Auton, L. D. (1993). Experimental results on the crossover point in satisfiability problems. In *Proceedings of the Eleventh National Conference on Artificial Intelligence (AAAI-93)*, pp. 21–27, Washington, DC. AAAI Press.

**Cristianini**, N. and Schölkopf, B. (2002). Support vector machines and kernel methods: The new generation of learning machines. *AI Magazine*, *23*(3), 31–41.

**Cristianini**, N. and Shawe-Taylor, J. (2000). *An introduction to support vector machines and other kernel-based learning methods*. Cambridge University Press, Cambridge, UK.

**Crockett**, L. (1994). *The Turing Test and the Frame Problem: AI's Mistaken Understanding of Intelligence*. Ablex, Norwood, New Jersey.

**Cross**, S. E. and Walker, E. (1994). Dart: Applying knowledge based planning and scheduling to crisis action planning. In Zweben, M. and Fox, M. S. (Eds.), *Intelligent Scheduling*, pp. 711–729. Morgan Kaufmann, San Mateo, California.

**Cruse**, D. A. (1986). *Lexical Semantics*. Cambridge University Press.

**Culberson**, J. and Schaeffer, J. (1998). Pattern databases. *Computational Intelligence*, *14*(4), 318–334.

**Cullingford**, R. E. (1981). Integrating knowledge sources for computer "understanding" tasks. *IEEE Transactions on Systems, Man and Cybernetics (SMC)*, *11*.

**Cussens**, J. and Dzeroski, S. (2000). *Learning Language in Logic*, Vol. 1925 of *Lecture Notes in Computer Science*. Springer-Verlag, Berlin.

**Cybenko**, G. (1988). Continuous valued neural networks with two hidden layers are sufficient. Technical report, Department of Computer Science, Tufts University, Medford, Massachusetts.

**Cybenko**, G. (1989). Approximation by superpositions of a sigmoidal function. *Mathematics of Controls, Signals, and Systems*, *2*, 303–314.

**Daganzo**, C. (1979). *Multinomial probit: The theory and its application to demand forecasting*. Academic Press, New York.

**Dagum**, P. and Luby, M. (1993). Approximating probabilistic inference in Bayesian belief networks is NP-hard. *Artificial Intelligence*, *60*(1), 141–153.

**Dahl**, O.-J., Myrhaug, B., and Nygaard, K. (1970). (Simula 67) common base language. Tech. rep. N. S-22, Norsk Regnesentral (Norwegian Computing Center), Oslo.

**Dale**, R., Moisl, H., and Somers, H. (2000). *Handbook of Natural Language Processing*. Marcel Dekker, New York.

**Dantzig**, G. B. (1949). Programming of interdependent activities: II. mathematical model. *Econometrica*, *17*, 200–211.

**Darwiche**, A. (2001). Recursive conditioning. *Artificial Intelligence*, *126*, 5–41.

**Darwiche**, A. and Ginsberg, M. L. (1992). A symbolic generalization of probability theory. In *Proceedings of the Tenth National Conference on Artificial Intelligence (AAAI-92)*, pp. 622–627, San Jose. AAAI Press.

**Darwin**, C. (1859). *On The Origin of Species by Means of Natural Selection*. J. Murray, London.

**Darwin**, C. (1871). *Descent of Man*. J. Murray.

**Dasgupta**, P., Chakrabarti, P. P., and DeSarkar, S. C. (1994). Agent searching in a tree and the optimality of iterative deepening. *Artificial Intelligence*, *71*, 195–208.

**Davidson**, D. (1980). *Essays on Actions and Events*. Oxford University Press, Oxford, UK.

**Davies**, T. R. (1985). Analogy. Informal note IN-CSLI-85-4, Center for the Study of Language and Information (CSLI), Stanford, California.

**Davies**, T. R. and Russell, S. J. (1987). A logical approach to reasoning by analogy. In *Proceedings of the Tenth International Joint Conference on Artificial Intelligence (IJCAI-87)*, Vol. 1, pp. 264–270, Milan. Morgan Kaufmann.

**Davis**, E. (1986). *Representing and Acquiring Geographic Knowledge*. Pitman and Morgan Kaufmann, London and San Mateo, California.

**Davis**, E. (1990). *Representations of Commonsense Knowledge*. Morgan Kaufmann, San Mateo, California.

**Davis**, K. H., Biddulph, R., and Balashek, S. (1952). Automatic recognition of spoken digits. *Journal of the Acoustical Society of America*, *24*(6), 637–642.

**Davis**, M. (1957). A computer program for Presburger's algorithm. In Robinson, A. (Ed.), *Proving Theorems (as Done by Man, Logician, or Machine)*, pp. 215–233, Cornell University, Ithaca, New York. Communications Research Division, Institute for Defense Analysis. Proceedings of the Summer Institute for Symbolic Logic. Second edition; publication date is 1960.

**Davis**, M., Logemann, G., and Loveland, D. (1962). A machine program for theorem-proving. *Communications of the Association for Computing Machinery*, *5*, 394–397.

**Davis**, M. and Putnam, H. (1960). A computing procedure for quantification theory. *Journal of the Association for Computing Machinery*, *7*(3), 201–215.

**Davis**, R. and Lenat, D. B. (1982). *Knowledge-Based Systems in Artificial Intelligence*. McGraw-Hill, New York.

**Dayan**, P. (1992). The convergence of TD($\lambda$) for general $\lambda$. *Machine Learning*, *8*(3–4), 341–362.

**Dayan**, P. and Abbott, L. F. (2001). *Theoretical Neuroscience: Computational and Mathematical Modeling of Neural Systems*. MIT Press, Cambridge, Massachusetts.

**de Dombal**, F. T., Leaper, D. J., Horrocks, J. C., and Staniland, J. R. (1974). Human and computer-aided diagnosis of abdominal pain: Further report with emphasis on performance of clinicians. *British Medical Journal*, *1*, 376–380.

**de Dombal**, F. T., Staniland, J. R., and Clamp, S. E. (1981). Geographical variation in disease presentation. *Medical Decision Making*, *1*, 59–69.

**de Finetti**, B. (1937). Le prévision: ses lois logiques, ses sources subjectives. *Ann. Inst. Poincaré*, *7*, 1–68.

**de Freitas**, J. F. G., Niranjan, M., and Gee, A. H. (2000). Sequential Monte Carlo methods to train neural network models. *Neural Computation*, *12*(4), 933–953.

**de Kleer**, J. (1975). Qualitative and quantitative knowledge in classical mechanics. Tech. rep. AI-TR-352, MIT Artificial Intelligence Laboratory.

**de Kleer**, J. (1986a). An assumption-based TMS. *Artificial Intelligence*, *28*(2), 127–162.

**de Kleer**, J. (1986b). Extending the ATMS. *Artificial Intelligence*, *28*(2), 163–196.

**de Kleer**, J. (1986c). Problem solving with the ATMS. *Artificial Intelligence*, *28*(2), 197–224.

**de Kleer**, J. (1989). A comparison of ATMS and CSP techniques. In *Proceedings of the Eleventh International Joint Conference on Artificial Intelligence (IJCAI-89)*, Vol. 1, pp. 290–296, Detroit. Morgan Kaufmann.

**de Kleer**, J. and Brown, J. S. (1985). A qualitative physics based on confluences. In Hobbs, J. R. and Moore, R. C. (Eds.), *Formal Theories of the Commonsense World*, chap. 4, pp. 109–183. Ablex, Norwood, New Jersey.

**de Marcken**, C. (1996). *Unsupervised Language Acquisition*. Ph.D. thesis, MIT.

**De Morgan**, A. (1864). On the syllogism IV and on the logic of relations. *Cambridge Philosophical Transactions*, *x*, 331–358.

**De Raedt**, L. (1992). *Interactive Theory Revision: An Inductive Logic Programming Approach.* Academic Press, New York.

**de Saussure**, F. (1910 (republished 1993)). *Lectures on General Linguistics.* Pergamon Press, Oxford, UK.

**Deacon**, T. W. (1997). *The symbolic species: The co-evolution of language and the brain.* W. W. Norton, New York.

**Deale**, M., Yvanovich, M., Schnitzius, D., Kautz, D., Carpenter, M., Zweben, M., Davis, G., and Daun, B. (1994). The space shuttle ground processing scheduling system. In Zweben, M. and Fox, M. (Eds.), *Intelligent Scheduling*, pp. 423–449. Morgan Kaufmann, San Mateo, California.

**Dean**, T., Basye, K., Chekaluk, R., and Hyun, S. (1990). Coping with uncertainty in a control system for navigation and exploration. In *Proceedings of the Eighth National Conference on Artificial Intelligence (AAAI-90)*, Vol. 2, pp. 1010–1015, Boston. MIT Press.

**Dean**, T. and Boddy, M. (1988). An analysis of time-dependent planning. In *Proceedings of the Seventh National Conference on Artificial Intelligence (AAAI-88)*, pp. 49–54, St. Paul, Minnesota. Morgan Kaufmann.

**Dean**, T., Firby, R. J., and Miller, D. (1990). Hierarchical planning involving deadlines, travel time, and resources. *Computational Intelligence*, *6*(1), 381–398.

**Dean**, T., Kaelbling, L. P., Kirman, J., and Nicholson, A. (1993). Planning with deadlines in stochastic domains. In *Proceedings of the Eleventh National Conference on Artificial Intelligence (AAAI-93)*, pp. 574–579, Washington, DC. AAAI Press.

**Dean**, T. and Kanazawa, K. (1989a). A model for projection and action. In *Proceedings of the Eleventh International Joint Conference on Artificial Intelligence (IJCAI-89)*, pp. 985–990, Detroit. Morgan Kaufmann.

**Dean**, T. and Kanazawa, K. (1989b). A model for reasoning about persistence and causation. *Computational Intelligence*, *5*(3), 142–150.

**Dean**, T., Kanazawa, K., and Shewchuk, J. (1990). Prediction, observation and estimation in planning and control. In *5th IEEE International Symposium on Intelligent Control*, Vol. 2, pp. 645–650, Los Alamitos, CA. IEEE Computer Society Press.

**Dean**, T. and Wellman, M. P. (1991). *Planning and Control.* Morgan Kaufmann, San Mateo, California.

**Debevec**, P., Taylor, C., and Malik, J. (1996). Modeling and rendering architecture from photographs: a hybrid geometry- and image-based approach. In *Proceedings of the 23rd Annual Conference on Computer Graphics (SIGGRAPH)*, pp. 11–20.

**Debreu**, G. (1960). Topological methods in cardinal utility theory. In Arrow, K. J., Karlin, S., and Suppes, P. (Eds.), *Mathematical Methods in the Social Sciences, 1959.* Stanford University Press, Stanford, California.

**Dechter**, R. (1990a). Enhancement schemes for constraint processing: Backjumping, learning and cutset decomposition. *Artificial Intelligence*, *41*, 273–312.

**Dechter**, R. (1990b). On the expressiveness of networks with hidden variables. In *Proceedings of the Eighth National Conference on Artificial Intelligence (AAAI-90)*, pp. 379–385, Boston. MIT Press.

**Dechter**, R. (1992). Constraint networks. In Shapiro, S. (Ed.), *Encyclopedia of Artificial Intelligence* (2nd edition)., pp. 276–285. Wiley and Sons, New York.

**Dechter**, R. (1999). Bucket elimination: A unifying framework for reasoning. *Artificial Intelligence*, *113*, 41–85.

**Dechter**, R. and Frost, D. (1999). Backtracking algorothms for constraint satisfaction problems. Tech. rep., Department of Information and Computer Science, University of California, Irvine.

**Dechter**, R. and Pearl, J. (1985). Generalized best-first search strategies and the optimality of A*. *Journal of the Association for Computing Machinery*, *32*(3), 505–536.

**Dechter**, R. and Pearl, J. (1987). Network-based heuristics for constraint-satisfaction problems. *Artificial Intelligence*, *34*(1), 1–38.

**Dechter**, R. and Pearl, J. (1989). Tree clustering for constraint networks. *Artificial Intelligence*, *38*(3), 353–366.

**DeCoste**, D. and Scholkopf, B. (2002). Training invariant support vector machines. *Machine Learning*, *46*(1), 161–190.

**Dedekind**, R. (1888). *Was sind und was sollen die Zahlen.* Braunschweig, Germany.

**Deerwester**, S. C., Dumais, S. T., Landauer, T. K., Furnas, G. W., and Harshman, R. A. (1990). Indexing by latent semantic analysis. *Journal of the American Society of Information Science*, *41*(6), 391–407.

**DeGroot**, M. H. (1970). *Optimal Statistical Decisions.* McGraw-Hill, New York.

**DeGroot**, M. H. (1989). *Probability and Statistics* (2nd edition). Addison-Wesley, Reading, Massachusetts.

**DeJong**, G. (1981). Generalizations based on explanations. In *Proceedings of the Seventh International Joint Conference on Artificial Intelligence (IJCAI-81)*, pp. 67–69, Vancouver, British Columbia. Morgan Kaufmann.

**DeJong**, G. (1982). An overview of the FRUMP system. In Lehnert, W. and Ringle, M. (Eds.), *Strategies for Natural Language Processing*, pp. 149–176. Lawrence Erlbaum, Potomac, Maryland.

**DeJong**, G. and Mooney, R. (1986). Explanation-based learning: An alternative view. *Machine Learning*, *1*, 145–176.

**Dempster**, A. P. (1968). A generalization of Bayesian inference. *Journal of the Royal Statistical Society*, *30 (Series B)*, 205–247.

**Dempster**, A. P., Laird, N., and Rubin, D. (1977). Maximum likelihood from incomplete data via the EM algorithm. *Journal of the Royal Statistical Society*, *39 (Series B)*, 1–38.

**Denes**, P. (1959). The design and operation of the mechanical speech recognizer at University College London. *Journal of the British Institution of Radio Engineers*, *19*(4), 219–234.

**Deng**, X. and Papadimitriou, C. H. (1990). Exploring an unknown graph. In *Proceedings 31st Annual Symposium on Foundations of Computer Science*, pp. 355–361, St. Louis. IEEE Computer Society Press.

**Denis**, F. (2001). Learning regular languages from simple positive examples. *Machine Learning*, *44*(1/2), 37–66.

**Dennett**, D. C. (1971). Intentional systems. *The Journal of Philosophy*, *68*(4), 87–106.

**Dennett**, D. C. (1978). Why you can't make a computer that feels pain. *Synthese*, *38*(3).

**Dennett**, D. C. (1984). Cognitive wheels: the frame problem of AI. In Hookway, C. (Ed.), *Minds, Machines, and Evolution: Philosophical Studies*, pp. 129–151. Cambridge University Press, Cambridge, UK.

**Deo**, N. and Pang, C.-Y. (1984). Shortest path algorithms: Taxonomy and annotation. *Networks*, *14*(2), 275–323.

**Descartes**, R. (1637). Discourse on method. In Cottingham, J., Stoothoff, R., and Murdoch, D. (Eds.), *The Philosophical Writings of Descartes*, Vol. I. Cambridge University Press, Cambridge, UK.

**Descotte**, Y. and Latombe, J.-C. (1985). Making compromises among antagonist constraints in a planner. *Artificial Intelligence*, *27*, 183–217.

**Devroye**, L. (1987). *A course in density estimation*. Birkhauser, Boston.

**Devroye**, L., Gyorfi, L., and Lugosi, G. (1996). *A probabilistic theory of pattern recognition*. Springer-Verlag, Berlin.

**Dickmanns**, E. D. and Zapp, A. (1987). Autonomous high speed road vehicle guidance by computer vision. In Isermann, R. (Ed.), *Automatic Control—World Congress, 1987: Selected Papers from the 10th Triennial World Congress of the International Federation of Automatic Control*, pp. 221–226, Munich. Pergamon.

**Dietterich**, T. (1990). Machine learning. *Annual Review of Computer Science*, *4*, 255–306.

**Dietterich**, T. (2000). Hierarchical reinforcement learning with the MAXQ value function decomposition. *Journal of Artificial Intelligence Research*, *13*, 227–303.

**DiGioia**, A. M., Kanade, T., and Wells, P. (1996). Final report of the second international workshop on robotics and computer assisted medical interventions. *Computer Aided Surgery*, *2*, 69–101.

**Dijkstra**, E. W. (1959). A note on two problems in connexion with graphs. *Numerische Mathematik*, *1*, 269–271.

**Dissanayake**, G., Newman, P., Clark, S., Durrant-Whyte, H., and Csorba, M. (2001). A solution to the simultaneous localisation and map building (SLAM) problem. *IEEE Transactions of Robotics and Automation*, *17*(3), 229–241.

**Do**, M. B. and Kambhampati, S. (2001). Sapa: A domain-independent heuristic metric temporal planner. In *Proccedings of the European Conference on Planning*, Toledo, Spain. Springer-Verlag.

**Domingos**, P. and Pazzani, M. (1997). On the optimality of the simple Bayesian classifier under zero–one loss. *Machine Learning*, *29*, 103–30.

**Doran**, C., Egedi, D., Hockey, B. A., Srinivas, B., and Zaidel, M. (1994). XTAG system—a wide coverage grammar of English. In Nagao, M. (Ed.), *Proceedings of the 15th COLING*, Kyoto, Japan.

**Doran**, J. and Michie, D. (1966). Experiments with the graph traverser program. *Proceedings of the Royal Society of London*, *294, Series A*, 235–259.

**Dorf**, R. C. and Bishop, R. H. (1999). *Modern Control Systems*. Addison-Wesley, Reading, Massachusetts.

**Doucet**, A. (1997). *Monte Carlo methods for Bayesian estimation of hidden Markov models: Application to radiation signals*. Ph.D. thesis, Université de Paris-Sud, Orsay, France.

**Dowling**, W. F. and Gallier, J. H. (1984). Linear-time algorithms for testing the satisfiability of propositional Horn formulas. *Journal of Logic Programming*, *1*, 267–284.

**Dowty**, D., Wall, R., and Peters, S. (1991). *Introduction to Montague Semantics*. D. Reidel, Dordrecht, Netherlands.

**Doyle**, J. (1979). A truth maintenance system. *Artificial Intelligence*, *12*(3), 231–272.

**Doyle**, J. (1983). What is rational psychology? Toward a modern mental philosophy. *AI Magazine*, *4*(3), 50–53.

**Doyle**, J. and Patil, R. (1991). Two theses of knowledge representation: Language restrictions, taxonomic classification, and the utility of representation services. *Artificial Intelligence*, *48*(3), 261–297.

**Drabble**, B. (1990). Mission scheduling for spacecraft: Diaries of T-SCHED. In *Expert Planning Systems*, pp. 76–81, Brighton, UK. Institute of Electrical Engineers.

**Draper**, D., Hanks, S., and Weld, D. S. (1994). Probabilistic planning with information gathering and contingent execution. In *Proceedings of the Second International Conference on AI Planning Systems*, pp. 31–36, Chicago. Morgan Kaufmann.

**Dreyfus**, H. L. (1972). *What Computers Can't Do: A Critique of Artificial Reason*. Harper and Row, New York.

**Dreyfus**, H. L. (1992). *What Computers Still Can't Do: A Critique of Artificial Reason*. MIT Press, Cambridge, Massachusetts.

**Dreyfus**, H. L. and Dreyfus, S. E. (1986). *Mind over Machine: The Power of Human Intuition and Expertise in the Era of the Computer*. Blackwell, Oxford, UK.

**Dreyfus**, S. E. (1969). An appraisal of some shortest-paths algorithms. *Operations Research*, *17*, 395–412.

**Du**, D., Gu, J., and Pardalos, P. M. (Eds.). (1999). *Optimization methods for logical inference*. American Mathematical Society, Providence, Rhode Island.

**Dubois**, D. and Prade, H. (1994). A survey of belief revision and updating rules in various uncertainty models. *International Journal of Intelligent Systems*, *9*(1), 61–100.

**Duda**, R. O., Gaschnig, J., and Hart, P. E. (1979). Model design in the Prospector consultant system for mineral exploration. In Michie, D. (Ed.), *Expert Systems in the Microelectronic Age*, pp. 153–167. Edinburgh University Press, Edinburgh, Scotland.

**Duda**, R. O. and Hart, P. E. (1973). *Pattern classification and scene analysis*. Wiley, New York.

**Duda**, R. O., Hart, P. E., and Stork, D. G. (2001). *Pattern Classification*. Wiley, New York.

**Dudek**, G. and Jenkin, M. (2000). *Computational Principles of Mobile Robotics*. Cambridge University Press, Cambridge CB2 2RU, UK.

**Durfee**, E. H. and Lesser, V. R. (1989). Negotiating task decomposition and allocation using partial global planning. In Huhns, M. and Gasser, L. (Eds.), *Distributed AI*, Vol. 2. Morgan Kaufmann, San Mateo, California.

**Dyer**, M. (1983). *In-Depth Understanding*. MIT Press, Cambridge, Massachusetts.

**Dzeroski**, S., Muggleton, S. H., and Russell, S. J. (1992). PAC-learnability of determinate logic programs. In *Proceedings of the Fifth Annual ACM Workshop on Computational Learning Theory (COLT-92)*, pp. 128–135, Pittsburgh, Pennsylvania. ACM Press.

**Earley**, J. (1970). An efficient context-free parsing algorithm. *Communications of the Association for Computing Machinery*, *13*(2), 94–102.

**Ebeling**, C. (1987). *All the Right Moves*. MIT Press, Cambridge, Massachusetts.

**Eco**, U. (1979). *Theory of Semiotics*. Indiana University Press, Bloomington, Indiana.

**Edmonds**, J. (1965). Paths, trees, and flowers. *Canadian Journal of Mathematics*, *17*, 449–467.

**Edwards**, P. (Ed.). (1967). *The Encyclopedia of Philosophy*. Macmillan, London.

**Eiter**, T., Leone, N., Mateis, C., Pfeifer, G., and Scarcello, F. (1998). The KR system dlv: Progress report, comparisons and benchmarks. In Cohn, A., Schubert, L., and Shapiro, S. (Eds.), *Proceedings of the Sixth International Conference on Principles of Knowledge Representation and Reasoning*, pp. 406–417, Trento, Italy.

**Elhadad**, M. (1993). FUF: The universal unifier—user manual. Technical report, Ben Gurion University of the Negev, Be'er Sheva, Israel.

**Elkan**, C. (1993). The paradoxical success of fuzzy logic. In *Proceedings of the Eleventh National Conference on Artificial Intelligence (AAAI-93)*, pp. 698–703, Washington, DC. AAAI Press.

**Elkan**, C. (1997). Boosting and naive Bayesian learning. Tech. rep., Department of Computer Science and Engineering, University of California, San Diego.

**Elman**, J., Bates, E., Johnson, M., Karmiloff-Smith, A., Parisi, D., and Plunkett, K. (1997). *Rethinking Innateness*. MIT Press, Cambridge, Massachusetts.

**Empson**, W. (1953). *Seven Types of Ambiguity*. New Directions, New York.

**Enderton**, H. B. (1972). *A Mathematical Introduction to Logic*. Academic Press, New York.

**Erdmann**, M. A. and Mason, M. (1988). An exploration of sensorless manipulation. *IEEE Journal of Robotics and Automation*, *4*(4), 369–379.

**Erman**, L. D., Hayes-Roth, F., Lesser, V. R., and Reddy, R. (1980). The HEARSAY-II speech-understanding system: Integrating knowledge to resolve uncertainty. *Computing Surveys*, *12*(2), 213–253.

**Ernst**, H. A. (1961). *MH-1, a Computer-Operated Mechanical Hand*. Ph.D. thesis, Massachusetts Institute of Technology, Cambridge, Massachusetts.

**Ernst**, M., Millstein, T., and Weld, D. S. (1997). Automatic SAT-compilation of planning problems. In *Proceedings of the Fifteenth International Joint Conference on Artificial Intelligence (IJCAI-97)*, pp. 1169–1176, Nagoya, Japan. Morgan Kaufmann.

**Erol**, K., Hendler, J., and Nau, D. S. (1994). HTN planning: Complexity and expressivity. In *Proceedings of the Twelfth National Conference on Artificial Intelligence (AAAI-94)*, pp. 1123–1128, Seattle. AAAI Press.

**Erol**, K., Hendler, J., and Nau, D. S. (1996). Complexity results for HTN planning. *Annals of Mathematics and Artificial Intelligence*, *18*(1), 69–93.

**Etzioni**, O. (1989). Tractable decision-analytic control. In *Proc. of 1st International Conference on Knowledge Representation and Reasoning*, pp. 114–125, Toronto.

**Etzioni**, O., Hanks, S., Weld, D. S., Draper, D., Lesh, N., and Williamson, M. (1992). An approach to planning with incomplete information. In *Proceedings of the 3rd International Conference on Principles of Knowledge Representation and Reasoning*, Cambridge, Massachusetts.

**Etzioni**, O. and Weld, D. S. (1994). A softbot-based interface to the Internet. *Communications of the Association for Computing Machinery*, *37*(7), 72–76.

**Evans**, T. G. (1968). A program for the solution of a class of geometric-analogy intelligence-test questions. In Minsky, M. L. (Ed.), *Semantic Information Processing*, pp. 271–353. MIT Press, Cambridge, Massachusetts.

**Fagin**, R., Halpern, J. Y., Moses, Y., and Vardi, M. Y. (1995). *Reasoning about Knowledge*. MIT Press, Cambridge, Massachusetts.

**Fahlman**, S. E. (1974). A planning system for robot construction tasks. *Artificial Intelligence*, *5*(1), 1–49.

**Fahlman**, S. E. (1979). *NETL: A System for Representing and Using Real-World Knowledge*. MIT Press, Cambridge, Massachusetts.

**Faugeras**, O. (1992). What can be seen in three dimensions with an uncalibrated stereo rig?. In Sandini, G. (Ed.), *Proceedings of the European Conference on Computer Vision*, Vol. 588 of *Lecture Notes in Computer Science*, pp. 563–578. Springer-Verlag.

**Faugeras**, O. (1993). *Three-Dimensional Computer Vision: A Geometric Viewpoint*. MIT Press, Cambridge, Massachusetts.

**Faugeras**, O., Luong, Q.-T., and Papadopoulo, T. (2001). *The Geometry of Multiple Images*. MIT Press, Cambridge, Massachusetts.

**Fearing**, R. S. and Hollerbach, J. M. (1985). Basic solid mechanics for tactile sensing. *International Journal of Robotics Research*, *4*(3), 40–54.

**Featherstone**, R. (1987). *Robot Dynamics Algorithms*. Kluwer Academic Publishers, Boston, MA.

**Feigenbaum**, E. A. (1961). The simulation of verbal learning behavior. *Proceedings of the Western Joint Computer Conference*, *19*, 121–131.

**Feigenbaum**, E. A., Buchanan, B. G., and Lederberg, J. (1971). On generality and problem solving: A case study using the DENDRAL program. In Meltzer, B. and Michie, D. (Eds.), *Machine Intelligence 6*, pp. 165–190. Edinburgh University Press, Edinburgh, Scotland.

**Feigenbaum**, E. A. and Feldman, J. (Eds.). (1963). *Computers and Thought*. McGraw-Hill, New York.

**Feldman**, J. and Sproull, R. F. (1977). Decision theory and artificial intelligence II: The hungry monkey. Technical report, Computer Science Department, University of Rochester.

**Feldman**, J. and Yakimovsky, Y. (1974). Decision theory and artificial intelligence I: Semantics-based region analyzer. *Artificial Intelligence*, *5*(4), 349–371.

**Fellbaum**, C. (2001). *Wordnet: An Electronic Lexical Database*. MIT Press, Cambridge, Massachusetts.

**Feller**, W. (1971). *An Introductioon to Probability Theory and its Applications*, Vol. 2. John Wiley.

**Ferraris**, P. and Giunchiglia, E. (2000). Planning as satisability in nondeterministic domains. In *Proceedings of Seventeenth National Conference on Artificial Intelligence*, pp. 748–753. AAAI Press.

**Fikes**, R. E., Hart, P. E., and Nilsson, N. J. (1972). Learning and executing generalized robot plans. *Artificial Intelligence*, *3*(4), 251–288.

**Fikes**, R. E. and Nilsson, N. J. (1971). STRIPS: A new approach to the application of theorem proving to problem solving. *Artificial Intelligence*, *2*(3–4), 189–208.

**Fikes**, R. E. and Nilsson, N. J. (1993). STRIPS, a retrospective. *Artificial Intelligence*, *59*(1–2), 227–232.

**Findlay**, J. N. (1941). Time: A treatment of some puzzles. *Australasian Journal of Psychology and Philosophy*, *19*(3), 216–235.

**Finney**, D. J. (1947). *Probit analysis: A statistical treatment of the sigmoid response curve*. Cambridge University Press, Cambridge, UK.

**Firby**, J. (1994). Task networks for controlling continuous processes. In Hammond, K. (Ed.), *Proceedings of the Second International Conference on AI Planning Systems*, pp. 49–54, Menlo Park, CA. AAAI Press.

**Firby**, R. J. (1996). Modularity issues in reactive planning. In *Proceedings of the 3rd International Conference on Artificial Intelligence Planning Systems (AIPS-96)*, pp. 78–85, Edinburgh, Scotland. AAAI Press.

**Fischer**, M. J. and Ladner, R. E. (1977). Propositional modal logic of programs. In *Proceedings of the 9th ACM Symposium on the Theory of Computing*, pp. 286–294, New York. ACM Press.

**Fisher**, R. A. (1922). On the mathematical foundations of theoretical statistics. *Philosophical Transactions of the Royal Society of London, Series A 222*, 309–368.

**Fix**, E. and Hodges, J. L. (1951). Discriminatory analysis—nonparametric discrimination: Consistency properties. Tech. rep. 21-49-004, USAF School of Aviation Medicine, Randolph Field, Texas.

**Fogel**, D. B. (2000). *Evolutionary Computation: Toward a New Philosophy of Machine Intelligence*. IEEE Press, Piscataway, New Jersey.

**Fogel**, L. J., Owens, A. J., and Walsh, M. J. (1966). *Artificial Intelligence through Simulated Evolution*. Wiley, New York.

**Forbes**, J. (2002). *Learning Optimal Control for Autonomous Vehicles*. Ph.D. thesis, University of California, Berkeley.

**Forbus**, K. D. (1985). The role of qualitative dynamics in naive physics. In Hobbs, J. R. and Moore, R. C. (Eds.), *Formal Theories of the Commonsense World*, chap. 5, pp. 185–226. Ablex, Norwood, New Jersey.

**Forbus**, K. D. and de Kleer, J. (1993). *Building Problem Solvers*. MIT Press, Cambridge, Massachusetts.

**Ford**, K. M. and Hayes, P. J. (1995). Turing Test considered harmful. In *Proceedings of the Fourteenth International Joint Conference on Artificial Intelligence (IJCAI-95)*, pp. 972–977, Montreal. Morgan Kaufmann.

**Forestier**, J.-P. and Varaiya, P. (1978). Multilayer control of large Markov chains. *IEEE Transactions on Automatic Control*, *23*(2), 298–304.

**Forgy**, C. (1981). OPS5 user's manual. Technical report CMU-CS-81-135, Computer Science Department, Carnegie-Mellon University, Pittsburgh.

**Forgy**, C. (1982). A fast algorithm for the many patterns/many objects match problem. *Artificial Intelligence*, *19*(1), 17–37.

**Forsyth**, D. and Zisserman, A. (1991). Reflections on shading. *IEEE Transactions on Pattern Analysis and Machine Intelligence (PAMI)*, *13*(7), 671–679.

**Fortescue**, M. D. (1984). *West Greenlandic*. Croom Helm, London.

**Foster**, D. W. (1989). *Elegy by W. W.: A Study in Attribution*. Associated University Presses, Cranbury, New Jersey.

**Fourier**, J. (1827). Analyse des travaux de l'Académie Royale des Sciences, pendant l'année 1824; partie mathématique. *Histoire de l'Académie Royale des Sciences de France*, *7*, xlvii–lv.

**Fox**, D., Burgard, W., Dellaert, F., and Thrun, S. (1999). Monte carlo localization: Efficient position estimation for mobile robots. In *Proceedings of the National Conference on Artificial Intelligence (AAAI)*, Orlando, FL. AAAI.

**Fox**, M. S. (1990). Constraint-guided scheduling: A short history of research at CMU. *Computers in Industry*, *14*(1–3), 79–88.

**Fox**, M. S., Allen, B., and Strohm, G. (1982). Job shop scheduling: An investigation in constraint-directed reasoning. In *Proceedings of the National Conference on Artificial Intelligence (AAAI-82)*, pp. 155–158, Pittsburgh, Pennsylvania. Morgan Kaufmann.

**Fox**, M. S. and Long, D. (1998). The automatic inference of state invariants in TIM. *Journal of Artificial Intelligence Research*, *9*, 367–421.

**Frakes**, W. and Baeza-Yates, R. (Eds.). (1992). *Information Retrieval: Data Structures and Algorithms*. Prentice-Hall, Upper Saddle River, New Jersey.

**Francis**, S. and Kucera, H. (1967). *Computing Analysis of Present-day American English*. Brown University Press, Providence, Rhode Island.

**Franco**, J. and Paull, M. (1983). Probabilistic analysis of the Davis Putnam procedure for solving the satisfiability problem. *Discrete Applied Mathematics*, *5*, 77–87.

**Frank**, R. H. and Cook, P. J. (1996). *The Winner-Take-All Society*. Penguin, New York.

**Frege**, G. (1879). *Begriffsschrift, eine der arithmetischen nachgebildete Formelsprache des reinen Denkens*. Halle, Berlin. English translation appears in van Heijenoort (1967).

**Freuder**, E. C. (1978). Synthesizing constraint expressions. *Communications of the Association for Computing Machinery*, *21*(11), 958–966.

**Freuder**, E. C. (1982). A sufficient condition for backtrack-free search. *Journal of the Association for Computing Machinery*, *29*(1), 24–32.

**Freuder**, E. C. (1985). A sufficient condition for backtrack-bounded search. *Journal of the Association for Computing Machinery*, *32*(4), 755–761.

**Freuder**, E. C. and Mackworth, A. K. (Eds.). (1994). *Constraint-based reasoning*. MIT Press, Cambridge, Massachusetts.

**Freund**, Y. and Schapire, R. E. (1996). Experiments with a new boosting algorithm. In *Proceedings of the Thirteenth International Conference on Machine Learning*, Bari, Italy. Morgan Kaufmann.

**Friedberg**, R. M. (1958). A learning machine: Part I. *IBM Journal*, *2*, 2–13.

**Friedberg**, R. M., Dunham, B., and North, T. (1959). A learning machine: Part II. *IBM Journal of Research and Development*, *3*(3), 282–287.

**Friedman**, G. J. (1959). Digital simulation of an evolutionary process. *General Systems Yearbook*, *4*, 171–184.

**Friedman**, J., Hastie, T., and Tibshirani, R. (2000). Additive logistic regression: A statistical view of boosting. *Annals of Statistics*, *28*(2), 337–374.

**Friedman**, N. (1998). The Bayesian structural EM algorithm. In *Uncertainty in Artificial Intelligence: Proceedings of the Fourteenth Conference*, Madison, Wisconsin. Morgan Kaufmann.

**Friedman**, N. and Goldszmidt, M. (1996). Learning Bayesian networks with local structure. In *Uncertainty in Artificial Intelligence: Proceedings of the Twelfth Conference*, pp. 252–262, Portland, Oregon. Morgan Kaufmann.

**Fry**, D. B. (1959). Theoretical aspects of mechanical speech recognition. *Journal of the British Institution of Radio Engineers*, *19*(4), 211–218.

**Fuchs**, J. J., Gasquet, A., Olalainty, B., and Currie, K. W. (1990). PlanERS-1: An expert planning system for generating spacecraft mission plans. In *First International Conference on Expert Planning Systems*, pp. 70–75, Brighton, UK. Institute of Electrical Engineers.

**Fudenberg**, D. and Tirole, J. (1991). *Game theory*. MIT Press, Cambridge, Massachusetts.

**Fukunaga**, A. S., Rabideau, G., Chien, S., and Yan, D. (1997). ASPEN: A framework for automated planning and scheduling of spacecraft control and operations. In *Proceedings of the International Symposium on AI, Robotics and Automation in Space*, pp. 181–187, Tokyo.

**Fung**, R. and Chang, K. C. (1989). Weighting and integrating evidence for stochastic simulation in Bayesian networks. In *Proceedings of the Fifth Conference on Uncertainty in Artificial Intelligence (UAI-89)*, pp. 209–220, Windsor, Ontario. Morgan Kaufmann.

**Gaifman**, H. (1964). Concerning measures in first order calculi. *Israel Journal of Mathematics*, *2*, 1–18.

**Gallaire**, H. and Minker, J. (Eds.). (1978). *Logic and Databases*. Plenum, New York.

**Gallier**, J. H. (1986). *Logic for Computer Science: Foundations of Automatic Theorem Proving*. Harper and Row, New York.

**Gallo**, G. and Pallottino, S. (1988). Shortest path algorithms. *Annals of Operations Research*, *13*, 3–79.

**Gamba**, A., Gamberini, L., Palmieri, G., and Sanna, R. (1961). Further experiments with PAPA. *Nuovo Cimento Supplemento*, *20*(2), 221–231.

**Garding**, J. (1992). Shape from texture for smooth curved surfaces in perspective projection. *Journal of Mathematical Imaging and Vision*, *2*(4), 327–350.

**Gardner**, M. (1968). *Logic Machines, Diagrams and Boolean Algebra*. Dover, New York.

**Garey**, M. R. and Johnson, D. S. (1979). *Computers and Intractability*. W. H. Freeman, New York.

**Gaschnig**, J. (1977). A general backtrack algorithm that eliminates most redundant tests. In *Proceedings of the Fifth International Joint Conference on Artificial Intelligence (IJCAI-77)*, p. 457, Cambridge, Massachusetts. IJCAII.

**Gaschnig**, J. (1979). Performance measurement and analysis of certain search algorithms. Technical report CMU-CS-79-124, Computer Science Department, Carnegie-Mellon University.

**Gasser**, R. (1995). *Efficiently harnessing computational resources for exhaustive search*. Ph.D. thesis, ETH Zürich, Switzerland.

**Gasser**, R. (1998). Solving nine men's morris. In Nowakowski, R. (Ed.), *Games of No Chance*. Cambridge University Press, Cambridge, UK.

**Gat**, E. (1998). Three-layered architectures. In Kortenkamp, D., Bonasso, R. P., and Murphy, R. (Eds.), *AI-based Mobile Robots: Case Studies of Successful Robot Systems*, pp. 195–210. MIT Press.

**Gauss**, K. F. (1809). *Theoria Motus Corporum Coelestium in Sectionibus Conicis Solem Ambientium*. Sumtibus F. Perthes et I. H. Besser, Hamburg.

**Gauss**, K. F. (1829). Beiträge zur theorie der algebraischen gleichungen. Collected in *Werke, Vol. 3*, pages 71–102. K. Gesellschaft Wissenschaft, Göttingen, Germany, 1876.

**Gawande**, A. (2002). *Complications: A Surgeon's Notes on an Imperfect Science*. Metropolitan Books, New York.

**Ge**, N., Hale, J., and Charniak, E. (1998). A statistical approach to anaphora resolution. In *Proceedings of the Sixth Workshop on Very Large Corpora*, pp. 161–171, Montreal. COLING-ACL.

**Geiger**, D., Verma, T., and Pearl, J. (1990). Identifying independence in Bayesian networks. *Networks*, *20*(5), 507–534.

**Gelb**, A. (1974). *Applied Optimal Estimation*. MIT Press, Cambridge, Massachusetts.

**Gelernter**, H. (1959). Realization of a geometry-theorem proving machine. In *Proceedings of an International Conference on Information Processing*, pp. 273–282, Paris. UNESCO House.

**Gelfond**, M. and Lifschitz, V. (1988). Compiling circumscriptive theories into logic programs. In Reinfrank, M., de Kleer, J., Ginsberg, M. L., and Sandewall, E. (Eds.), *Non-Monotonic Reasoning: 2nd International Workshop Proceedings*, pp. 74–99, Grassau, Germany. Springer-Verlag.

**Gelman**, A., Carlin, J. B., Stern, H. S., and Rubin, D. (1995). *Bayesian Data Analysis*. Chapman & Hall, London.

**Geman**, S. and Geman, D. (1984). Stochastic relaxation, Gibbs distributions, and Bayesian restoration of images.. *IEEE Transactions on Pattern Analysis and Machine Intelligence (PAMI)*, *6*(6), 721–741.

**Genesereth**, M. R. (1984). The use of design descriptions in automated diagnosis. *Artificial Intelligence*, *24*(1–3), 411–436.

**Genesereth**, M. R. and Nilsson, N. J. (1987). *Logical Foundations of Artificial Intelligence*. Morgan Kaufmann, San Mateo, California.

**Genesereth**, M. R. and Nourbakhsh, I. (1993). Time-saving tips for problem solving with incomplete information. In *Proceedings of the Eleventh National Conference on Artificial Intelligence (AAAI-93)*, pp. 724–730, Washington, DC. AAAI Press.

**Genesereth**, M. R. and Smith, D. E. (1981). Meta-level architecture. Memo HPP-81-6, Computer Science Department, Stanford University, Stanford, California.

**Gentner**, D. (1983). Structure mapping: A theoretical framework for analogy. *Cognitive Science*, *7*, 155–170.

**Gentzen**, G. (1934). Untersuchungen über das logische Schliessen. *Mathematische Zeitschrift*, *39*, 176–210, 405–431.

**Georgeff**, M. P. and Lansky, A. L. (1987). Reactive reasoning and planning. In *Proceedings of the Sixth National Conference on Artificial Intelligence (AAAI-87)*, pp. 677–682, Seattle. Morgan Kaufmann.

**Gerevini**, A. and Schubert, L. K. (1996). Accelerating partial-order planners: Some techniques for effective search control and pruning. *Journal of Artificial Intelligence Research*, *5*, 95–137.

**Gerevini**, A. and Serina, I. (2002). LPG: A planner based on planning graphs with action costs. In *Proceedings of the Sixth International Conference on AI Planning and Scheduling*, pp. 281–290, Menlo Park, California. AAAI Press.

**Germann**, U., Jahr, M., Knight, K., Marcu, D., and Yamada, K. (2001). Fast decoding and optimal decoding for machine translation. In *Proceedings of the Conference of the Association for Computational Linguistics (ACL)*, pp. 228–235, Toulouse, France.

**Gershwin**, G. (1937). Let's call the whole thing off. song.

**Ghahramani**, Z. and Jordan, M. I. (1997). Factorial hidden Markov models. *Machine Learning*, *29*, 245–274.

**Ghallab**, M., Howe, A., Knoblock, C. A., and McDermott, D. (1998). PDDL—the planning domain definition language. Tech. rep. DCS TR-1165, Yale Center for Computational Vision and Control, New Haven, Connecticut.

**Ghallab**, M. and Laruelle, H. (1994). Representation and control in IxTeT, a temporal planner. In *Proceedings of the 2nd International Conference on Artificial Intelligence Planning Systems (AIPS-94)*, pp. 61–67, Chicago. AAAI Press.

**Giacomo**, G. D., Lespérance, Y., and Levesque, H. J. (2000). ConGolog, a concurrent programming language based on the situation calculus. *Artificial Intelligence*, *121*, 109–169.

**Gibson**, J. J. (1950). *The Perception of the Visual World*. Houghton Mifflin, Boston.

**Gibson**, J. J. (1979). *The Ecological Approach to Visual Perception*. Houghton Mifflin, Boston.

**Gibson**, J. J., Olum, P., and Rosenblatt, F. (1955). Parallax and perspective during aircraft landings. *American Journal of Psychology*, *68*, 372–385.

**Gilks**, W. R., Richardson, S., and Spiegelhalter, D. J. (Eds.). (1996). *Markov chain Monte Carlo in practice*. Chapman and Hall, London.

**Gilks**, W. R., Thomas, A., and Spiegelhalter, D. J. (1994). A language and program for complex Bayesian modelling. *The Statistician*, *43*, 169–178.

**Gilmore**, P. C. (1960). A proof method for quantification theory: Its justification and realization. *IBM Journal of Research and Development*, *4*, 28–35.

**Ginsberg**, M. L. (1989). Universal planning: An (almost) universally bad idea. *AI Magazine*, *10*(4), 40–44.

**Ginsberg**, M. L. (1993). *Essentials of Artificial Intelligence*. Morgan Kaufmann, San Mateo, California.

**Ginsberg**, M. L. (1999). GIB: Steps toward an expert-level bridge-playing program. In *Proceedings of the Sixteenth International Joint Conference on Artificial Intelligence (IJCAI-99)*, pp. 584–589, Stockholm. Morgan Kaufmann.

**Ginsberg**, M. L., Frank, M., Halpin, M. P., and Torrance, M. C. (1990). Search lessons learned from crossword puzzles. In *Proceedings of the Eighth National Conference on Artificial Intelligence (AAAI-90)*, Vol. 1, pp. 210–215, Boston. MIT Press.

**Gittins**, J. C. (1989). *Multi-Armed Bandit Allocation Indices*. Wiley, New York.

**Glanc**, A. (1978). On the etymology of the word "robot". *SIGART Newsletter*, *67*, 12.

**Glover**, F. (1989). Tabu search: 1. *ORSA Journal on Computing*, *1*(3), 190–206.

**Glover**, F. and Laguna, M. (Eds.). (1997). *Tabu search*. Kluwer, Dordrecht, Netherlands.

**Gödel**, K. (1930). *Über die Vollständigkeit des Logikkalküls*. Ph.D. thesis, University of Vienna.

**Gödel**, K. (1931). Über formal unentscheidbare Sätze der Principia mathematica und verwandter Systeme I. *Monatshefte für Mathematik und Physik*, *38*, 173–198.

**Goebel**, J., Volk, K., Walker, H., and Gerbault, F. (1989). Automatic classification of spectra from the infrared astronomical satellite (IRAS). *Astronomy and Astrophysics*, *222*, L5–L8.

**Gold**, B. and Morgan, N. (2000). *Speech and Audio Signal Processing*. Wiley, New York.

**Gold**, E. M. (1967). Language identification in the limit. *Information and Control*, *10*, 447–474.

**Golden**, K. (1998). Leap before you look: Information gathering in the PUCCINI planner. In *Proceedings of the 4th International Conference on Artificial Intelligence Planning Systems (AIPS-98)*, pp. 70–77, Pittsburgh, Pennsylvania. AAAI Press.

**Goldman**, N. (1975). Conceptual generation. In Schank, R. (Ed.), *Conceptual Information Processing*, chap. 6. North-Holland, Amsterdam.

**Goldman**, R. and Boddy, M. (1996). Expressive planning and explicit knowledge. In *Proceedings of the 3rd International Conference on Artificial Intelligence Planning Systems (AIPS-96)*, pp. 110–117, Edinburgh, Scotland. AAAI Press.

**Gomes**, C., Selman, B., and Kautz, H. (1998). Boosting combinatorial search through randomization. In *Proceedings of the Fifteenth National Conference on Artificial Intelligence (AAAI-98)*, pp. 431–437, Madison, Wisconsin. AAAI Press.

**Good**, I. J. (1950). Contribution to the discussion of Eliot Slater's "Statistics for the chess computer and the factor of mobility". In *Symposium on Information Theory*, p. 199, London. Ministry of Supply.

**Good**, I. J. (1961). A causal calculus. *British Journal of the Philosophy of Science*, *11*, 305–318.

**Good**, I. J. (1965). Speculations concerning the first ultraintelligent machine. In Alt, F. L. and Rubinoff, M. (Eds.), *Advances in Computers*, Vol. 6, pp. 31–88. Academic Press, New York.

**Goodman**, D. and Keene, R. (1997). *Man versus Machine: Kasparov versus Deep Blue*. H3 Publications, Cambridge, Massachusetts.

**Goodman**, N. (1954). *Fact, Fiction and Forecast*. University of London Press, London.

**Goodman**, N. (1977). *The Structure of Appearance* (3rd edition). D. Reidel, Dordrecht, Netherlands.

**Gordon**, M. J., Milner, A. J., and Wadsworth, C. P. (1979). *Edinburgh LCF*. Springer-Verlag, Berlin.

**Gordon**, N. J. (1994). *Bayesian methods for tracking*. Ph.D. thesis, Imperial College, University of London.

**Gordon**, N. J., Salmond, D. J., and Smith, A. F. M. (1993). Novel approach to nonlinear/non-Gaussian Bayesian state estimation. *IEE Proceedings F (Radar and Signal Processing)*, *140*(2), 107–113.

**Gorry**, G. A. (1968). Strategies for computer-aided diagnosis. *Mathematical Biosciences*, *2*(3–4), 293–318.

**Gorry**, G. A., Kassirer, J. P., Essig, A., and Schwartz, W. B. (1973). Decision analysis as the basis for computer-aided management of acute renal failure. *American Journal of Medicine*, *55*, 473–484.

**Gottlob**, G., Leone, N., and Scarcello, F. (1999a). A comparison of structural CSP decomposition methods. In *Proceedings of the Sixteenth International Joint Conference on Artificial Intelligence (IJCAI-99)*, pp. 394–399, Stockholm. Morgan Kaufmann.

**Gottlob**, G., Leone, N., and Scarcello, F. (1999b). Hypertree decompositions and tractable queries. In *Proceedings of the 18th ACM International Symposium on Principles of Database Systems*, pp. 21–32, Philadelphia. Association for Computing Machinery.

**Graham**, S. L., Harrison, M. A., and Ruzzo, W. L. (1980). An improved context-free recognizer. *ACM Transactions on Programming Languages and Systems*, *2*(3), 415–462.

**Grassmann**, H. (1861). *Lehrbuch der Arithmetik*. Th. Chr. Fr. Enslin, Berlin.

**Grayson**, C. J. (1960). Decisions under uncertainty: Drilling decisions by oil and gas operators. Tech. rep., Division of Research, Harvard Business School, Boston.

**Green**, B., Wolf, A., Chomsky, C., and Laugherty, K. (1961). BASEBALL: An automatic question answerer. In *Proceedings of the Western Joint Computer Conference*, pp. 219–224.

**Green**, C. (1969a). Application of theorem proving to problem solving. In *Proceedings of the First International Joint Conference on Artificial Intelligence (IJCAI-69)*, pp. 219–239, Washington, DC. IJCAII.

**Green**, C. (1969b). Theorem-proving by resolution as a basis for question-answering systems. In Meltzer, B., Michie, D., and Swann, M. (Eds.), *Machine Intelligence 4*, pp. 183–205. Edinburgh University Press, Edinburgh, Scotland.

**Green**, C. and Raphael, B. (1968). The use of theorem-proving techniques in question-answering systems. In *Proceedings of the 23rd ACM National Conference*, Washington, DC. ACM Press.

**Greenblatt**, R. D., Eastlake, D. E., and Crocker, S. D. (1967). The Greenblatt chess program. In *Proceedings of the Fall Joint Computer Conference*, pp. 801–810. American Federation of Information Processing Societies (AFIPS).

**Greiner**, R. (1989). Towards a formal analysis of EBL. In *Proceedings of the Sixth International Machine Learning Workshop*, pp. 450–453, Ithaca, NY. Morgan Kaufmann.

**Grice**, H. P. (1957). Meaning. *Philosophical Review*, *66*, 377–388.

**Grosz**, B. J., Joshi, A. K., and Weinstein, S. (1995). Centering: A framework for modeling the local coherence of discourse. *Computational Linguistics*, *21*(2), 203–225.

**Grosz**, B. J. and Sidner, C. L. (1986). Attention, intentions, and the structure of discourse. *Computational Linguistics*, *12*(3), 175–204.

**Grosz**, b. J., Sparck Jones, K., and Webber, B. L. (Eds.). (1986). *Readings in Natural Language Processing*. Morgan Kaufmann, San Mateo, California.

**Grove**, W. and Meehl, P. (1996). Comparative efficiency of informal (subjective, impressionistic) and formal (mechanical, algorithmic) prediction procedures: The clinical statistical controversy. *Psychology, Public Policy, and Law*, *2*, 293–323.

**Gu**, J. (1989). *Parallel Algorithms and Architectures for Very Fast AI Search*. Ph.D. thesis, University of Utah.

**Guard**, J., Oglesby, F., Bennett, J., and Settle, L. (1969). Semi-automated mathematics. *Journal of the Association for Computing Machinery*, *16*, 49–62.

**Guibas**, L. J., Knuth, D. E., and Sharir, M. (1992). Randomized incremental construction of Delaunay and Voronoi diagrams. *Algorithmica*, *7*, 381–413. See also *17th Int. Coll. on Automata, Languages and Programming*, 1990, pp. 414–431.

**Haas**, A. (1986). A syntactic theory of belief and action. *Artificial Intelligence*, *28*(3), 245–292.

**Hacking**, I. (1975). *The Emergence of Probability*. Cambridge University Press, Cambridge, UK.

**Hald**, A. (1990). *A History of Probability and Statistics and Their Applications before 1750*. Wiley, New York.

**Halpern**, J. Y. (1990). An analysis of first-order logics of probability. *Artificial Intelligence*, *46*(3), 311–350.

**Hamming**, R. W. (1991). *The Art of Probability for Scientists and Engineers*. Addison-Wesley, Reading, Massachusetts.

**Hammond**, K. (1989). *Case-Based Planning: Viewing Planning as a Memory Task*. Academic Press, New York.

**Hamscher**, W., Console, L., and Kleer, J. D. (1992). *Readings in Model-based Diagnosis*. Morgan Kaufmann, San Mateo, California.

**Handschin**, J. E. and Mayne, D. Q. (1969). Monte Carlo techniques to estimate the conditional expectation in multi-stage nonlinear filtering. *International Journal of Control*, *9*(5), 547–559.

**Hansen**, E. (1998). Solving POMDPs by searching in policy space. In *Uncertainty in Artificial Intelligence: Proceedings of the Fourteenth Conference*, pp. 211–219, Madison, Wisconsin. Morgan Kaufmann.

**Hansen**, E. and Zilberstein, S. (2001). LAO*: a heuristic search algorithm that finds solutions with loops. *Artificial Intelligence*, *129*(1–2), 35–62.

**Hansen**, P. and Jaumard, B. (1990). Algorithms for the maximum satisfiability problem. *Computing*, *44*(4), 279–303.

**Hanski**, I. and Cambefort, Y. (Eds.). (1991). *Dung Beetle Ecology*. Princeton University Press, Princeton, New Jersey.

**Hansson**, O. and Mayer, A. (1989). Heuristic search as evidential reasoning. In *Proceedings of the Fifth Workshop on Uncertainty in Artificial Intelligence*, Windsor, Ontario. Morgan Kaufmann.

**Hansson**, O., Mayer, A., and Yung, M. (1992). Criticizing solutions to relaxed models yields powerful admissible heuristics. *Information Sciences*, *63*(3), 207–227.

**Haralick**, R. M. and Elliot, G. L. (1980). Increasing tree search efficiency for constraint satisfaction problems. *Artificial Intelligence*, *14*(3), 263–313.

**Hardin**, G. (1968). The tragedy of the commons. *Science*, *162*, 1243–1248.

**Harel**, D. (1984). Dynamic logic. In Gabbay, D. and Guenthner, F. (Eds.), *Handbook of Philosophical Logic*, Vol. 2, pp. 497–604. D. Reidel, Dordrecht, Netherlands.

**Harman**, G. H. (1983). *Change in View: Principles of Reasoning*. MIT Press, Cambridge, Massachusetts.

**Harsanyi**, J. (1967). Games with incomplete information played by Bayesian players. *Management Science*, *14*, 159–182.

**Hart**, P. E., Nilsson, N. J., and Raphael, B. (1968). A formal basis for the heuristic determination of minimum cost paths. *IEEE Transactions on Systems Science and Cybernetics*, *SSC-4(2)*, 100–107.

**Hart**, P. E., Nilsson, N. J., and Raphael, B. (1972). Correction to "A formal basis for the heuristic determination of minimum cost paths". *SIGART Newsletter*, *37*, 28–29.

**Hart**, T. P. and Edwards, D. J. (1961). The tree prune (TP) algorithm. Artificial intelligence project memo 30, Massachusetts Institute of Technology, Cambridge, Massachusetts.

**Hartley**, R. and Zisserman, A. (2000). *Multiple view geometry in computer vision*. Cambridge University Press, Cambridge, UK.

**Haslum**, P. and Geffner, H. (2001). Heuristic planning with time and resources. In *Proceedings of the IJCAI-01 Workshop on Planning with Resources*, Seattle.

**Hastie**, T. and Tibshirani, R. (1996). Discriminant adaptive nearest neighbor classification and regression. In Touretzky, D. S., Mozer, M. C., and Hasselmo, M. E. (Eds.), *Advances in Neural Information Processing Systems*, Vol. 8, pp. 409–15. MIT Press, Cambridge, Massachusetts.

**Hastie**, T., Tibshirani, R., and Friedman, J. (2001). *The Elements of Statistical Learning: Data Mining, Inference and Prediction*. Springer-Verlag, Berlin.

**Haugeland**, J. (Ed.). (1981). *Mind Design*. MIT Press, Cambridge, Massachusetts.

**Haugeland**, J. (Ed.). (1985). *Artificial Intelligence: The Very Idea*. MIT Press, Cambridge, Massachusetts.

**Haussler**, D. (1989). Learning conjunctive concepts in structural domains. *Machine Learning*, *4*(1), 7–40.

**Havelund**, K., Lowry, M., Park, S., Pecheur, C., Penix, J., Visser, W., and White, J. L. (2000). Formal analysis of the remote agent before and after flight. In *Proceedings of the 5th NASA Langley Formal Methods Workshop*, Williamsburg, VA.

**Hayes**, P. J. (1978). The naive physics manifesto. In Michie, D. (Ed.), *Expert Systems in the Microelectronic Age*. Edinburgh University Press, Edinburgh, Scotland.

**Hayes**, P. J. (1979). The logic of frames. In Metzing, D. (Ed.), *Frame Conceptions and Text Understanding*, pp. 46–61. de Gruyter, Berlin.

**Hayes**, P. J. (1985a). Naive physics I: Ontology for liquids. In Hobbs, J. R. and Moore, R. C. (Eds.), *Formal Theories of the Commonsense World*, chap. 3, pp. 71–107. Ablex, Norwood, New Jersey.

**Hayes**, P. J. (1985b). The second naive physics manifesto. In Hobbs, J. R. and Moore, R. C. (Eds.), *Formal Theories of the Commonsense World*, chap. 1, pp. 1–36. Ablex, Norwood, New Jersey.

**Hebb**, D. O. (1949). *The Organization of Behavior*. Wiley, New York.

**Heckerman**, D. (1986). Probabilistic interpretation for MYCIN's certainty factors. In Kanal, L. N. and Lemmer, J. F. (Eds.), *Uncertainty in Artificial Intelligence*, pp. 167–196. Elsevier/North-Holland, Amsterdam, London, New York.

**Heckerman**, D. (1991). *Probabilistic Similarity Networks*. MIT Press, Cambridge, Massachusetts.

**Heckerman**, D. (1998). A tutorial on learning with Bayesian networks. In Jordan, M. I. (Ed.), *Learning in graphical models*. Kluwer, Dordrecht, Netherlands.

**Heckerman**, D., Geiger, D., and Chickering, D. M. (1994). Learning Bayesian networks: The combination of knowledge and statistical data. Technical report MSR-TR-94-09, Microsoft Research, Redmond, Washington.

**Heim**, I. and Kratzer, A. (1998). *Semantics in a Generative Grammar*. Blackwell, Oxford, UK.

**Heinz**, E. A. (2000). *Scalable search in computer chess*. Vieweg, Braunschweig, Germany.

**Held**, M. and Karp, R. M. (1970). The traveling salesman problem and minimum spanning trees. *Operations Research*, *18*, 1138–1162.

**Helmert**, M. (2001). On the complexity of planning in transportation domains. In Cesta, A. and Barrajo, D. (Eds.), *Sixth European Conference on Planning (ECP-01)*, Toledo, Spain. Springer-Verlag.

**Hendrix**, G. G. (1975). Expanding the utility of semantic networks through partitioning. In *Proceedings of the Fourth International Joint Conference on Artificial Intelligence (IJCAI-75)*, pp. 115–121, Tbilisi, Georgia. IJCAII.

**Henrion**, M. (1988). Propagation of uncertainty in Bayesian networks by probabilistic logic sampling. In Lemmer, J. F. and Kanal, L. N. (Eds.), *Uncertainty in Artificial Intelligence 2*, pp. 149–163. Elsevier/North-Holland, Amsterdam, London, New York.

**Henzinger**, T. A. and Sastry, S. (Eds.). (1998). *Hybrid systems: Computation and control*. Springer-Verlag, Berlin.

**Herbrand**, J. (1930). *Recherches sur la Théorie de la Démonstration*. Ph.D. thesis, University of Paris.

**Hewitt**, C. (1969). PLANNER: a language for proving theorems in robots. In *Proceedings of the First International Joint Conference on Artificial Intelligence (IJCAI-69)*, pp. 295–301, Washington, DC. IJCAII.

**Hierholzer**, C. (1873). Über die Möglichkeit, einen Linienzug ohne Wiederholung und ohne Unterbrechung zu umfahren. *Mathematische Annalen*, *6*, 30–32.

**Hilgard**, E. R. and Bower, G. H. (1975). *Theories of Learning* (4th edition). Prentice-Hall, Upper Saddle River, New Jersey.

**Hintikka**, J. (1962). *Knowledge and Belief*. Cornell University Press, Ithaca, New York.

**Hinton**, G. E. and Anderson, J. A. (1981). *Parallel Models of Associative Memory*. Lawrence Erlbaum Associates, Potomac, Maryland.

**Hinton**, G. E. and Nowlan, S. J. (1987). How learning can guide evolution. *Complex Systems*, *1*(3), 495–502.

**Hinton**, G. E. and Sejnowski, T. (1983). Optimal perceptual inference. In *Proceedings of the IEEE Computer Society Conference on Computer Vision and Pattern Recognition*, pp. 448–453, Washington, DC. IEEE Computer Society Press.

**Hinton**, G. E. and Sejnowski, T. (1986). Learning and relearning in Boltzmann machines. In Rumelhart, D. E. and McClelland, J. L. (Eds.), *Parallel Distributed Processing*, chap. 7, pp. 282–317. MIT Press, Cambridge, Massachusetts.

**Hirsh**, H. (1987). Explanation-based generalization in a logic programming environment. In *Proceedings of the Tenth International Joint Conference on Artificial Intelligence (IJCAI-87)*, Milan. Morgan Kaufmann.

**Hirst**, G. (1981). *Anaphora in Natural Language Understanding: A Survey*, Vol. 119 of *Lecture Notes in Computer Science*. Springer Verlag, Berlin.

**Hirst**, G. (1987). *Semantic Interpretation against Ambiguity*. Cambridge University Press, Cambridge, UK.

**Hobbs**, J. R. (1978). Resolving pronoun references. *Lingua*, *44*, 339–352.

**Hobbs**, J. R. (1990). *Literature and Cognition*. CSLI Press, Stanford, California.

**Hobbs**, J. R., Appelt, D., Bear, J., Israel, D., Kameyama, M., Stickel, M. E., and Tyson, M. (1997). FASTUS: A cascaded finite-state transducer for extracting information from natural-language text. In Roche, E. and Schabes, Y. (Eds.), *Finite-State Devices for Natural Language Processing*, pp. 383–406. MIT Press, Cambridge, Massachusetts.

**Hobbs**, J. R. and Moore, R. C. (Eds.). (1985). *Formal Theories of the Commonsense World*. Ablex, Norwood, New Jersey.

**Hobbs**, J. R., Stickel, M. E., Appelt, D., and Martin, P. (1993). Interpretation as abduction. *Artificial Intelligence*, *63*(1–2), 69–142.

**Hoffmann**, J. (2000). A heuristic for domain independent planning and its use in an enforced hill-climbing algorithm. In *Proceedings of the 12th International Symposium on Methodologies for Intelligent Systems*, pp. 216–227, Charlotte, North Carolina. Springer-Verlag.

**Hogan**, N. (1985). Impedance control: An approach to manipulation. parts i, ii, and iii. *Transactions ASME Journal of Dynamics, Systems, Measurement, and Control*, *107*(3), 1–24.

**Holland**, J. H. (1975). *Adaption in Natural and Artificial Systems*. University of Michigan Press, Ann Arbor, Michigan.

**Holland**, J. H. (1995). *Hidden order: How adaptation builds complexity*. Addison-Wesley, Reading, Massachusetts.

**Holldobler**, S. and Schneeberger, J. (1990). A new deductive approach to planning. *New Generation Computing*, *8*(3), 225–244.

**Holzmann**, G. J. (1997). The Spin model checker. *ISSS Transactions on Software Engineering*, *23*(5), 279–295.

**Hood**, A. (1824). Case 4th—28 July 1824 (Mr. Hood's cases of injuries of the brain). *The Phrenological Journal and Miscellany*, *2*, 82–94.

**Hopfield**, J. J. (1982). Neurons with graded response have collective computational properties like those of two-state neurons. *Proceedings of the National Academy of Sciences of the United States of America*, *79*, 2554–2558.

**Horn**, A. (1951). On sentences which are true of direct unions of algebras. *Journal of Symbolic Logic*, *16*, 14–21.

**Horn**, B. K. P. (1970). Shape from shading: A method for obtaining the shape of a smooth opaque object from one view. Technical report 232, MIT Artificial Intelligence Laboratory, Cambridge, Massachusetts.

**Horn**, B. K. P. (1986). *Robot Vision*. MIT Press, Cambridge, Massachusetts.

**Horn**, B. K. P. and Brooks, M. J. (1989). *Shape from Shading*. MIT Press, Cambridge, Massachusetts.

**Horning**, J. J. (1969). *A study of grammatical inference*. Ph.D. thesis, Stanford University.

**Horowitz**, E. and Sahni, S. (1978). *Fundamentals of computer algorithms*. Computer Science Press, Rockville, Maryland.

**Horswill**, I. (2000). Functional programming of behavior-based systems. *Autonomous Robots*, *9*, 83–93.

**Horvitz**, E. J. (1987). Problem-solving design: Reasoning about computational value, trade-offs, and resources. In *Proceedings of the Second Annual NASA Research Forum*, pp. 26–43, Moffett Field, California. NASA Ames Research Center.

**Horvitz**, E. J. (1989). Rational metareasoning and compilation for optimizing decisions under bounded resources. In *Proceedings of Computational Intelligence 89*, Milan. Association for Computing Machinery.

**Horvitz**, E. J. and Barry, M. (1995). Display of information for time-critical decision making. In *Uncertainty in Artificial Intelligence: Proceedings of the Eleventh Conference*, pp. 296–305, Montreal, Canada. Morgan Kaufmann.

**Horvitz**, E. J., Breese, J. S., Heckerman, D., and Hovel, D. (1998). The Lumiere project: Bayesian user modeling for inferring the goals and needs of software users. In *Uncertainty in Artificial Intelligence: Proceedings of the Fourteenth Conference*, pp. 256–265, Madison, Wisconsin. Morgan Kaufmann.

**Horvitz**, E. J., Breese, J. S., and Henrion, M. (1988). Decision theory in expert systems and artificial intelligence. *International Journal of Approximate Reasoning*, *2*, 247–302.

**Horvitz**, E. J. and Breese, J. S. (1996). Ideal partition of resources for metareasoning. In *Proceedings of the Thirteenth National Conference on Artificial Intelligence (AAAI-96)*, pp. 1229–1234, Portland, Oregon. AAAI Press.

**Horvitz**, E. J. and Heckerman, D. (1986). The inconsistent use of measures of certainty in artificial intelligence research. In Kanal, L. N. and Lemmer, J. F. (Eds.), *Uncertainty in Artificial Intelligence*, pp. 137–151. Elsevier/North-Holland, Amsterdam, London, New York.

**Horvitz**, E. J., Heckerman, D., and Langlotz, C. P. (1986). A framework for comparing alternative formalisms for plausible reasoning. In *Proceedings of the Fifth National Conference on Artificial Intelligence (AAAI-86)*, Vol. 1, pp. 210–214, Philadelphia. Morgan Kaufmann.

**Hovy**, E. (1988). *Generating Natural Language under Pragmatic Constraints*. Lawrence Erlbaum, Potomac, Maryland.

**Howard**, R. A. (1960). *Dynamic Programming and Markov Processes*. MIT Press, Cambridge, Massachusetts.

**Howard**, R. A. (1966). Information value theory. *IEEE Transactions on Systems Science and Cybernetics*, *SSC-2*, 22–26.

**Howard**, R. A. (1977). Risk preference. In Howard, R. A. and Matheson, J. E. (Eds.), *Readings in Decision Analysis*, pp. 429–465. Decision Analysis Group, SRI International, Menlo Park, California.

**Howard**, R. A. (1989). Microrisks for medical decision analysis. *International Journal of Technology Assessment in Health Care*, *5*, 357–370.

**Howard**, R. A. and Matheson, J. E. (1984). Influence diagrams. In Howard, R. A. and Matheson, J. E. (Eds.), *Readings on the Principles and Applications of Decision Analysis*, pp. 721–762. Strategic Decisions Group, Menlo Park, California.

**Hsu**, F.-H. (1999). IBM's Deep Blue chess grandmaster chips. *IEEE Micro*, *19*(2), 70–80.

**Hsu**, F.-H., Anantharaman, T. S., Campbell, M. S., and Nowatzyk, A. (1990). A grandmaster chess machine. *Scientific American*, *263*(4), 44–50.

**Huang**, T., Koller, D., Malik, J., Ogasawara, G., Rao, B., Russell, S. J., and Weber, J. (1994). Automatic symbolic traffic scene analysis using belief networks. In *Proceedings of the Twelfth National Conference on Artificial Intelligence (AAAI-94)*, pp. 966–972, Seattle. AAAI Press.

**Huang**, X. D., Acero, A., and Hon, H. (2001). *Spoken Language Processing*. Prentice Hall, Upper Saddle River, New Jersey.

**Hubel**, D. H. (1988). *Eye, Brain, and Vision*. W. H. Freeman, New York.

**Huddleston**, R. D. and Pullum, G. K. (2002). *The Cambridge Grammar of the English Language*. Cambridge University Press, Cambridge, UK.

**Huffman**, D. A. (1971). Impossible objects as nonsense sentences. In Meltzer, B. and Michie, D. (Eds.), *Machine Intelligence 6*, pp. 295–324. Edinburgh University Press, Edinburgh, Scotland.

**Hughes**, B. D. (1995). *Random Walks and Random Environments, Vol. 1: Random Walks*. Oxford University Press, Oxford, UK.

**Huhns**, M. N. and Singh, M. P. (Eds.). (1998). *Readings in agents*. Morgan Kaufmann, San Mateo, California.

**Hume**, D. (1739). *A Treatise of Human Nature* (2nd edition). republished by Oxford University Press, 1978, Oxford, UK.

**Hunsberger**, L. and Grosz, B. J. (2000). A combinatorial auction for collaborative planning. In *International Conference on Multi-Agent Systems (ICMAS-2000)*.

**Hunt**, E. B., Marin, J., and Stone, P. T. (1966). *Experiments in Induction*. Academic Press, New York.

**Hunter**, L. and States, D. J. (1992). Bayesian classification of protein structure. *IEEE Expert*, *7*(4), 67–75.

**Hurwicz**, L. (1973). The design of mechanisms for resource allocation. *American Economic Review Papers and Proceedings*, *63*(1), 1–30.

**Hutchins**, W. J. and Somers, H. (1992). *An Introduction to Machine Translation*. Academic Press, New York.

**Huttenlocher**, D. P. and Ullman, S. (1990). Recognizing solid objects by alignment with an image. *International Journal of Computer Vision*, *5*(2), 195–212.

**Huygens**, C. (1657). Ratiociniis in ludo aleae. In van Schooten, F. (Ed.), *Exercitionum Mathematicorum*. Elsevirii, Amsterdam.

**Hwa**, R. (1998). An empirical evaluation of probabilistic lexicalized tree insertion grammars. In *Proceedings of COLING-ACL '98*, pp. 557–563, Montreal. International Committee on Computational Linguistics and Association for Computational Linguistics.

**Hwang**, C. H. and Schubert, L. K. (1993). EL: A formal, yet natural, comprehensive knowledge representation. In *Proceedings of the Eleventh National Conference on Artificial Intelligence (AAAI-93)*, pp. 676–682, Washington, DC. AAAI Press.

**Indyk**, P. (2000). Dimensionality reduction techniques for proximity problems. In *Proceedings of the Eleventh Annual ACM–SIAM Symposium on Discrete Algorithms*, pp. 371–378, San Francisco. Association for Computing Machinery.

**Ingerman**, P. Z. (1967). Panini–Backus form suggested. *Communications of the Association for Computing Machinery*, *10*(3), 137.

**Inoue**, K. (2001). Inverse entailment for full clausal theories. In *LICS-2001 Workshop on Logic and Learning*, Boston. IEEE.

**Intille**, S. and Bobick, A. (1999). A framework for recognizing multi-agent action from visual evidence. In *Proceedings of the Sixteenth National Conference on Artificial Intelligence (AAAI-99)*, pp. 518–525, Orlando, Florida. AAAI Press.

**Isard**, M. and Blake, A. (1996). Contour tracking by stochastic propagation of conditional density. In *Proceedings of Fourth European Conference on Computer Vision*, pp. 343–356, Cambridge, UK. Springer-Verlag.

**Jaakkola**, T. and Jordan, M. I. (1996). Computing upper and lower bounds on likelihoods in intractable networks. In *Uncertainty in Artificial Intelligence: Proceedings of the Twelfth Conference*, pp. 340–348. Morgan Kaufmann, Portland, Oregon.

**Jaakkola**, T., Singh, S. P., and Jordan, M. I. (1995). Reinforcement learning algorithm for partially observable Markov decision problems. In Tesauro, G., Touretzky, D., and Leen, T. (Eds.), *Advances in Neural Information Processing Systems 7*, pp. 345–352, Cambridge, Massachusetts. MIT Press.

**Jaffar**, J. and Lassez, J.-L. (1987). Constraint logic programming. In *Proceedings of the Fourteenth ACM Conference on Principles of Programming Languages*, pp. 111–119, Munich. Association for Computing Machinery.

**Jaffar**, J., Michaylov, S., Stuckey, P. J., and Yap, R. H. C. (1992a). The CLP(R) language and system. *ACM Transactions on Programming Languages and Systems*, *14*(3), 339–395.

**Jaffar**, J., Stuckey, P. J., Michaylov, S., and Yap, R. H. C. (1992b). An abstract machine for CLP(R). *SIGPLAN Notices*, *27*(7), 128–139.

**Jáskowski**, S. (1934). On the rules of suppositions in formal logic. *Studia Logica*, *1*.

**Jefferson**, G. (1949). The mind of mechanical man: The Lister Oration delivered at the Royal College of Surgeons in England. *British Medical Journal*, *1*(25), 1105–1121.

**Jeffrey**, R. C. (1983). *The Logic of Decision* (2nd edition). University of Chicago Press, Chicago.

**Jeffreys**, H. (1948). *Theory of Probability*. Oxford, Oxford, UK.

**Jelinek**, F. (1969). Fast sequential decoding algorithm using a stack. *IBM Journal of Research and Development*, *64*, 532–556.

**Jelinek**, F. (1976). Continuous speech recognition by statistical methods. *Proceedings of the IEEE*, *64*(4), 532–556.

**Jelinek**, F. (1997). *Statistical methods for speech recognition*. MIT Press, Cambridge, Massachusetts.

**Jelinek**, F. and Mercer, R. L. (1980). Interpolated estimation of Markov source parameters from sparse data. In *Proceedings of the Workshop on Pattern Recognition in Practice*, pp. 381–397, Amsterdam, London, New York. North Holland.

**Jennings**, H. S. (1906). *Behavior of the lower organisms*. Columbia University Press, New York.

**Jensen**, F. V. (2001). *Bayesian Networks and Decision Graphs*. Springer-Verlag, Berlin.

**Jespersen**, O. (1965). *Essentials of English Grammar*. University of Alabama Press, Tuscaloosa, Alabama.

**Jevons**, W. S. (1874). *The Principles of Science*. Routledge/Thoemmes Press, London.

**Jimenez**, P. and Torras, C. (2000). An efficient algorithm for searching implicit AND/OR graphs with cycles. *Artificial Intelligence*, *124*(1), 1–30.

**Joachims**, T. (2001). A statistical learning model of text classification with support vector machines. In *Proceedings of the 24th Conference on Research and Development in Information Retrieval (SIGIR)*, pp. 128–136, New Orleans. Association for Computing Machinery.

**Johnson**, W. W. and Story, W. E. (1879). Notes on the "15" puzzle. *American Journal of Mathematics*, *2*, 397–404.

**Johnson-Laird**, P. N. (1988). *The Computer and the Mind: An Introduction to Cognitive Science*. Harvard University Press, Cambridge, Massachusetts.

**Johnston**, M. D. and Adorf, H.-M. (1992). Scheduling with neural networks: The case of the Hubble space telescope. *Computers & Operations Research*, *19*(3–4), 209–240.

**Jones**, N. D., Gomard, C. K., and Sestoft, P. (1993). *Partial Evaluation and Automatic Program Generation*. Prentice-Hall, Upper Saddle River, New Jersey.

**Jones**, R., Laird, J. E., and Nielsen, P. E. (1998). Automated intelligent pilots for combat flight simulation. In *Proceedings of the Fifteenth National Conference on Artificial Intelligence (AAAI-98)*, pp. 1047–54, Madison, Wisconsin. AAAI Press.

**Jonsson**, A., Morris, P., Muscettola, N., Rajan, K., and Smith, B. (2000). Planning in interplanetary space: Theory and practice. In *Proceedings of the 5th International Conference on Artificial Intelligence Planning Systems (AIPS-00)*, pp. 177–186, Breckenridge, Colorado. AAAI Press.

**Jordan**, M. I. (1995). Why the logistic function? a tutorial discussion on probabilities and neural networks. Computational cognitive science technical report 9503, Massachusetts Institute of Technology.

**Jordan**, M. I. (2003). *An Introduction to Graphical Models*. In press.

**Jordan**, M. I., Ghahramani, Z., Jaakkola, T., and Saul, L. K. (1998). An introduction to variational methods for graphical models. In Jordan, M. I. (Ed.), *Learning in Graphical Models*. Kluwer, Dordrecht, Netherlands.

**Jordan**, M. I., Ghahramani, Z., Jaakkola, T., and Saul, L. K. (1999). An introduction to variational methods for graphical models. *Machine Learning*, *37*(2–3), 183–233.

**Joshi**, A. K. (1985). Tree-adjoining grammars: How much context sensitivity is required to provide reasonable structural descriptions. In Dowty, D., Karttunen, L., and Zwicky, A. (Eds.), *Natural Language Parsing*. Cambridge University Press, Cambridge, UK.

**Joshi**, A. K., Webber, B. L., and Sag, I. (1981). *Elements of Discourse Understanding*. Cambridge University Press, Cambridge, UK.

**Joslin**, D. and Pollack, M. E. (1994). Least-cost flaw repair: A plan refinement strategy for partial-order planning. In *Proceedings of the Twelfth National Conference on Artificial Intelligence (AAAI-94)*, p. 1506, Seattle. AAAI Press.

**Jouannaud**, J.-P. and Kirchner, C. (1991). Solving equations in abstract algebras: A rule-based survey of unification. In Lassez, J.-L. and Plotkin, G. (Eds.), *Computational Logic*, pp. 257–321. MIT Press, Cambridge, Massachusetts.

**Judd**, J. S. (1990). *Neural Network Design and the Complexity of Learning*. MIT Press, Cambridge, Massachusetts.

**Juels**, A. and Wattenberg, M. (1996). Stochastic hillclimbing as a baseline method for evaluating genetic algorithms. In Touretzky, D. S., Mozer, M. C., and Hasselmo, M. E. (Eds.), *Advances in Neural Information Processing Systems*, Vol. 8, pp. 430–6. MIT Press, Cambridge, Massachusetts.

**Julesz**, B. (1971). *Foundations of Cyclopean Perception*. University of Chicago Press, Chicago.

**Jurafsky**, D. and Martin, J. H. (2000). *Speech and Language Processing: An Introduction to Natural Language Processing, Computational Linguistics, and Speech Recognition*. Prentice-Hall, Upper Saddle River, New Jersey.

**Kadane**, J. B. and Larkey, P. D. (1982). Subjective probability and the theory of games. *Management Science*, *28*(2), 113–120.

**Kaelbling**, L. P., Littman, M. L., and Cassandra, A. R. (1998). Planning and acting in partially observable stochastic domains. *Artificial Intelligence*, *101*, 99–134.

**Kaelbling**, L. P., Littman, M. L., and Moore, A. W. (1996). Reinforcement learning: A survey. *Journal of Artificial Intelligence Research*, *4*, 237–285.

**Kaelbling**, L. P. and Rosenschein, S. J. (1990). Action and planning in embedded agents. *Robotics and Autonomous Systems*, *6*(1–2), 35–48.

**Kager**, R. (1999). *Optimality Theory*. Cambridge University Press, Cambridge, UK.

**Kahneman**, D., Slovic, P., and Tversky, A. (Eds.). (1982). *Judgment under Uncertainty: Heuristics and Biases*. Cambridge University Press, Cambridge, UK.

**Kaindl**, H. and Khorsand, A. (1994). Memory-bounded bidirectional search. In *Proceedings of the Twelfth National Conference on Artificial Intelligence (AAAI-94)*, pp. 1359–1364, Seattle. AAAI Press.

**Kalman**, R. (1960). A new approach to linear filtering and prediction problems. *Journal of Basic Engineering*, *82*, 35–46.

**Kambhampati**, S. (1994). Exploiting causal structure to control retrieval and refitting during plan reuse. *Computational Intelligence*, *10*, 213–244.

**Kambhampati**, S., Mali, A. D., and Srivastava, B. (1998). Hybrid planning for partially hierarchical domains. In *Proceedings of the Fifteenth National Conference on Artificial Intelligence (AAAI-98)*, pp. 882–888, Madison, Wisconsin. AAAI Press.

**Kanal**, L. N. and Kumar, V. (1988). *Search in Artificial Intelligence*. Springer-Verlag, Berlin.

**Kanal**, L. N. and Lemmer, J. F. (Eds.). (1986). *Uncertainty in Artificial Intelligence*. Elsevier/North-Holland, Amsterdam, London, New York.

**Kanazawa**, K., Koller, D., and Russell, S. J. (1995). Stochastic simulation algorithms for dynamic probabilistic networks. In *Uncertainty in Artificial Intelligence: Proceedings of the Eleventh Conference*, pp. 346–351, Montreal, Canada. Morgan Kaufmann.

**Kaplan**, D. and Montague, R. (1960). A paradox regained. *Notre Dame Journal of Formal Logic*, *1*(3), 79–90.

**Karmarkar**, N. (1984). A new polynomial-time algorithm for linear programming. *Combinatorica*, *4*, 373–395.

**Karp**, R. M. (1972). Reducibility among combinatorial problems. In Miller, R. E. and Thatcher, J. W. (Eds.), *Complexity of Computer Computations*, pp. 85–103. Plenum, New York.

**Kasami**, T. (1965). An efficient recognition and syntax analysis algorithm for context-free languages. Tech. rep. AFCRL-65-758, Air Force Cambridge Research Laboratory, Bedford, Massachusetts.

**Kasparov**, G. (1997). IBM owes me a rematch. *Time*, *149*(21), 66–67.

**Kasper**, R. T. (1988). Systemic grammar and functional unification grammar. In Benson, J. and Greaves, W. (Eds.), *Systemic Functional Approaches to Discourse*. Ablex, Norwood, New Jersey.

**Kaufmann**, M., Manolios, P., and Moore, J. S. (2000). *Computer-Aided Reasoning: An Approach*. Kluwer, Dordrecht, Netherlands.

**Kautz**, H., McAllester, D. A., and Selman, B. (1996). Encoding plans in propositional logic. In *Proceedings of the Fifth International Conference on Principles of Knowledge Representation and Reasoning*, pp. 374–384, Cambridge, Massachusetts. Morgan Kaufmann.

**Kautz**, H. and Selman, B. (1992). Planning as satisfiability. In *ECAI 92: 10th European Conference on Artificial Intelligence Proceedings*, pp. 359–363, Vienna. Wiley.

**Kautz**, H. and Selman, B. (1998). BLACKBOX: A new approach to the application of theorem proving to problem solving. Working Notes of the AIPS-98 Workshop on Planning as Combinatorial Search.

**Kavraki**, L., Svestka, P., Latombe, J.-C., and Overmars, M. (1996). Probabilistic roadmaps for path planning in high-dimensional configuration spaces. *IEEE Transactions on Robotics and Automation*, *12*(4), 566–580.

**Kay**, M., Gawron, J. M., and Norvig, P. (1994). *Verbmobil: A Translation System for Face-To-Face Dialog*. CSLI Press, Stanford, California.

**Kaye**, R. (2000). Minesweeper is NP-complete!. *Mathematical Intelligencer*, *5*(22), 9–15.

**Kearns**, M. (1990). *The Computational Complexity of Machine Learning*. MIT Press, Cambridge, Massachusetts.

**Kearns**, M., Mansour, Y., and Ng, A. Y. (2000). Approximate planning in large POMDPs via reusable trajectories. In Solla, S. A., Leen, T. K., and Müller, K.-R. (Eds.), *Advances in Neural Information Processing Systems 12*. MIT Press, Cambridge, Massachusetts.

**Kearns**, M. and Singh, S. P. (1998). Near-optimal reinforcement learning in polynomial time. In *Proceedings of the Fifteenth International Conference on Machine Learning*, pp. 260–268, Madison, Wisconsin. Morgan Kaufmann.

**Kearns**, M. and Vazirani, U. (1994). *An Introduction to Computational Learning Theory*. MIT Press, Cambridge, Massachusetts.

**Keeney**, R. L. (1974). Multiplicative utility functions. *Operations Research*, *22*, 22–34.

**Keeney**, R. L. and Raiffa, H. (1976). *Decisions with Multiple Objectives: Preferences and Value Tradeoffs*. Wiley, New York.

**Kehler**, A. (1997). Probabilistic coreference in information extraction. In Cardie, C. and Weischedel, R. (Eds.), *Proceedings of the Second Conference on Empirical Methods in Natural Language Processing*, pp. 163–173. Association for Computational Linguistics, Somerset, New Jersey.

**Kemp**, M. (Ed.). (1989). *Leonardo on Painting: An Anthology of Writings*. Yale University Press, New Haven, Connecticut.

**Kern**, C. and Greenstreet, M. R. (1999). Formal verification in hardware design: A survey. *ACM Transactions on Design Automation of Electronic Systems*, *4*(2), 123–193.

**Keynes**, J. M. (1921). *A Treatise on Probability*. Macmillan, London.

**Khatib**, O. (1986). Real-time obstacle avoidance for robot manipulator and mobile robots. *The International Journal of Robotics Research*, *5*(1), 90–98.

**Kietz**, J.-U. and Dzeroski, S. (1994). Inductive logic programming and learnability. *SIGART Bulletin*, *5*(1), 22–32.

**Kim**, J. H. (1983). *CONVINCE: A Conversational Inference Consolidation Engine*. Ph.D. thesis, Department of Computer Science, University of California at Los Angeles.

**Kim**, J. H. and Pearl, J. (1983). A computational model for combined causal and diagnostic reasoning in inference systems. In *Proceedings of the Eighth International Joint Conference on Artificial Intelligence (IJCAI-83)*, pp. 190–193, Karlsruhe, Germany. Morgan Kaufmann.

**Kim**, J. H. and Pearl, J. (1987). CONVINCE: A conversational inference consolidation engine. *IEEE Transactions on Systems, Man, and Cybernetics*, *17*(2), 120–132.

**King**, R. D., Muggleton, S. H., Lewis, R. A., and Sternberg, M. J. E. (1992). Drug design by machine learning: The use of inductive logic programming to model the structure activity relationships of trimethoprim analogues binding to dihydrofolate reductase. *Proceedings of the National Academy of Sciences of the United States of America*, *89*(23), 11322–11326.

**Kirkpatrick**, S., Gelatt, C. D., and Vecchi, M. P. (1983). Optimization by simulated annealing. *Science*, *220*, 671–680.

**Kirkpatrick**, S. and Selman, B. (1994). Critical behavior in the satisfiability of random Boolean expressions. *Science*, *264*(5163), 1297–1301.

**Kirousis**, L. M. and Papadimitriou, C. H. (1988). The complexity of recognizing polyhedral scenes. *Journal of Computer and System Sciences*, *37*(1), 14–38.

**Kitano**, H., Asada, M., Kuniyoshi, Y., Noda, I., and Osawa, E. (1997). RoboCup: The robot world cup initiative. In Johnson, W. L. and Hayes-Roth, B. (Eds.), *Proceedings of the First International Conference on Autonomous Agents*, pp. 340–347, New York. ACM Press.

**Kjaerulff**, U. (1992). A computational scheme for reasoning in dynamic probabilistic networks. In *Uncertainty in Artificial Intelligence: Proceedings of the Eighth Conference*, pp. 121–129, Stanford, California. Morgan Kaufmann.

**Klein**, D. and Manning, C. D. (2001). Parsing with treebank grammars: Empirical bounds, theoretical models, and the structure of the Penn treebank. In *Proceedings of the 39th Annual Meeting of the ACL*.

**Kleinberg**, J. M. (1999). Authoritative sources in a hyperlinked environment. *Journal of the ACM*, *46*(5), 604–632.

**Knight**, K. (1999). A statistical mt tutorial workbook. prepared in connection with the Johns Hopkins University summer workshop.

**Knoblock**, C. A. (1990). Learning abstraction hierarchies for problem solving. In *Proceedings of the Eighth National Conference on Artificial Intelligence (AAAI-90)*, Vol. 2, pp. 923–928, Boston. MIT Press.

**Knuth**, D. E. (1968). Semantics for context-free languages. *Mathematical Systems Theory*, *2*(2), 127–145.

**Knuth**, D. E. (1973). *The Art of Computer Programming* (second edition)., Vol. 2: Fundamental Algorithms. Addison-Wesley, Reading, Massachusetts.

**Knuth**, D. E. (1975). An analysis of alpha–beta pruning. *Artificial Intelligence*, *6*(4), 293–326.

**Knuth**, D. E. and Bendix, P. B. (1970). Simple word problems in universal algebras. In Leech, J. (Ed.), *Computational Problems in Abstract Algebra*, pp. 263–267. Pergamon, Oxford, UK.

**Koditschek**, D. (1987). Exact robot navigation by means of potential functions: some topological considerations. In *Proceedings of the 1987 IEEE International Conference on Robotics and Automation*, Vol. 1, pp. 1–6, Raleigh, North Carolina. IEEE Computer Society Press.

**Koehler**, J., Nebel, B., Hoffman, J., and Dimopoulos, Y. (1997). Extending planning graphs to an ADL subset. In *Proceedings of the Fourth European Conference on Planning*, pp. 273–285, Toulouse, France. Springer-Verlag.

**Koenderink**, J. J. (1990). *Solid Shape*. MIT Press, Cambridge, Massachusetts.

**Koenderink**, J. J. and van Doorn, A. J. (1975). Invariant properties of the motion parallax field due to the movement of rigid bodies relative to an observer. *Optica Acta*, *22*(9), 773–791.

**Koenderink**, J. J. and van Doorn, A. J. (1991). Affine structure from motion. *Journal of the Optical Society of America A*, *8*, 377–385.

**Koenig**, S. (1991). Optimal probabilistic and decision-theoretic planning using Markovian decision theory. Master's report, Computer Science Division, University of California, Berkeley.

**Koenig**, S. (2000). Exploring unknown environments with real-time search or reinforcement learning. In Solla, S. A., Leen, T. K., and Müller, K.-R. (Eds.), *Advances in Neural Information Processing Systems 12*. MIT Press, Cambridge, Massachusetts.

**Koenig**, S. and Simmons, R. (1998). Solving robot navigation problems with initial pose uncertainty using real-time heuristic search. In *aips98*. AAAI Press, Menlo Park, California.

**Kohn**, W. (1991). Declarative control architecture. *Communications of the Association for Computing Machinery*, *34*(8), 65–79.

**Koller**, D., Meggido, N., and von Stengel, B. (1996). Efficient computation of equilibria for extensive two-person games. *Games and Economic Behaviour*, *14*(2), 247–259.

**Koller**, D. and Pfeffer, A. (1997). Representations and solutions for game-theoretic problems. *Artificial Intelligence*, *94*(1–2), 167–215.

**Koller**, D. and Pfeffer, A. (1998). Probabilistic frame-based systems. In *Proceedings of the Fifteenth National Conference on Artificial Intelligence (AAAI-98)*, pp. 580–587, Madison, Wisconsin. AAAI Press.

**Koller**, D. and Sahami, M. (1997). Hierarchically classifying documents using very few words. In *Proceedings of the Fourteenth International Conference on Machine Learning*, pp. 170–178. Morgan Kaufmann.

**Kolmogorov**, A. N. (1941). Interpolation und extrapolation von stationaren zufalligen folgen. *Bulletin of the Academy of Sciences of the USSR, Ser. Math. 5*, 3–14.

**Kolmogorov**, A. N. (1950). *Foundations of the Theory of Probability*. Chelsea, New York.

**Kolmogorov**, A. N. (1963). On tables of random numbers. *Sankhya, the Indian Journal of Statistics, Series A 25*.

**Kolmogorov**, A. N. (1965). Three approaches to the quantitative definition of information. *Problems in Information Transmission*, *1*(1), 1–7.

**Kolodner**, J. (1983). Reconstructive memory: A computer model. *Cognitive Science*, *7*, 281–328.

**Kolodner**, J. (1993). *Case-Based Reasoning*. Morgan Kaufmann, San Mateo, California.

**Kondrak**, G. and van Beek, P. (1997). A theoretical evaluation of selected backtracking algorithms. *Artificial Intelligence*, *89*, 365–387.

**Konolige**, K. (1997). COLBERT: A language for reactive control in Saphira. In *KI-97: Advances in Artificial Intelligence*, LNAI, pp. 31–52. Springer verlag.

**Konolige**, K. (1982). A first order formalization of knowledge and action for a multi-agent planning system. In Hayes, J. E., Michie, D., and Pao, Y.-H. (Eds.), *Machine Intelligence 10*. Ellis Horwood, Chichester, England.

**Koopmans**, T. C. (1972). Representation of preference orderings over time. In McGuire, C. B. and Radner, R. (Eds.), *Decision and Organization*. Elsevier/North-Holland, Amsterdam, London, New York.

**Korf**, R. E. (1985a). Depth-first iterative-deepening: an optimal admissible tree search. *Artificial Intelligence, 27(1)*, 97–109.

**Korf**, R. E. (1985b). Iterative-deepening A*: An optimal admissible tree search. In *Proceedings of the Ninth International Joint Conference on Artificial Intelligence (IJCAI-85)*, pp. 1034–1036, Los Angeles. Morgan Kaufmann.

**Korf**, R. E. (1987). Planning as search: A quantitative approach. *Artificial Intelligence*, *33(1)*, 65–88.

**Korf**, R. E. (1988). Optimal path finding algorithms. In Kanal, L. N. and Kumar, V. (Eds.), *Search in Artificial Intelligence*, chap. 7, pp. 223–267. Springer-Verlag, Berlin.

**Korf**, R. E. (1990). Real-time heuristic search. *Artificial Intelligence*, *42*(3), 189–212.

**Korf**, R. E. (1991). Best-first search with limited memory. UCLA Computer Science Annual.

**Korf**, R. E. (1993). Linear-space best-first search. *Artificial Intelligence*, *62*(1), 41–78.

**Korf**, R. E. (1995). Space-efficient search algorithms. *ACM Computing Surveys*, *27*(3), 337–339.

**Korf**, R. E. and Chickering, D. M. (1996). Best-first minimax search. *Artificial Intelligence*, *84*(1–2), 299–337.

**Korf**, R. E. and Felner, A. (2002). Disjoint pattern database heuristics. *Artificial Intelligence*, *134*(1–2), 9–22.

**Korf**, R. E. and Zhang, W. (2000). Divide-and-conquer frontier search applied to optimal sequence alignment. In *Proceedings of the 17th National Conference on Artificial Intelligence*, pp. 910–916, Cambridge, Massachusetts. MIT Press.

**Kortenkamp**, D., Bonasso, R. P., and Murphy, R. (Eds.). (1998). *AI-based Mobile Robots: Case studies of successful robot systems*, Cambridge, MA. MIT Press.

**Kotok**, A. (1962). A chess playing program for the IBM 7090. Ai project memo 41, MIT Computation Center, Cambridge, Massachusetts.

**Koutsoupias**, E. and Papadimitriou, C. H. (1992). On the greedy algorithm for satisfiability. *Information Processing Letters*, *43*(1), 53–55.

**Kowalski**, R. (1974). Predicate logic as a programming language. In *Proceedings of the IFIP-74 Congress*, pp. 569–574. Elsevier/North-Holland.

**Kowalski**, R. (1979a). Algorithm = logic + control. *Communications of the Association for Computing Machinery*, *22*, 424–436.

**Kowalski**, R. (1979b). *Logic for Problem Solving*. Elsevier/North-Holland, Amsterdam, London, New York.

**Kowalski**, R. (1988). The early years of logic programming. *Communications of the Association for Computing Machinery*, *31*, 38–43.

**Kowalski**, R. and Kuehner, D. (1971). Linear resolution with selection function. *Artificial Intelligence*, *2*(3–4), 227–260.

**Kowalski**, R. and Sergot, M. (1986). A logic-based calculus of events. *New Generation Computing*, *4*(1), 67–95.

**Koza**, J. R. (1992). *Genetic Programming: On the Programming of Computers by Means of Natural Selection*. MIT Press, Cambridge, Massachusetts.

**Koza**, J. R. (1994). *Genetic Programming II: Automatic discovery of reusable programs*. MIT Press, Cambridge, Massachusetts.

**Koza**, J. R., Bennett, F. H., Andre, D., and Keane, M. A. (1999). *Genetic Programming III: Darwinian invention and problem solving*. Morgan Kaufmann, San Mateo, California.

**Kraus**, S., Ephrati, E., and Lehmann, D. (1991). Negotiation in a non-cooperative environment. *Journal of Experimental and Theoretical Artificial Intelligence*, *3*(4), 255–281.

**Kripke**, S. A. (1963). Semantical considerations on modal logic. *Acta Philosophica Fennica*, *16*, 83–94.

**Krovetz**, R. (1993). Viewing morphology as an inference process. In *Proceedings of the Sixteenth Annual International ACM-SIGIR Conference on Research and Development in Information Retrieval*, pp. 191–202, New York. ACM Press.

**Kruppa**, E. (1913). Zur Ermittlung eines Objecktes aus zwei Perspektiven mit innerer Orientierung. *Sitz.-Ber. Akad. Wiss., Wien, Math. Naturw., Kl. Abt. IIa*, *122*, 1939–1948.

**Kuhn**, H. W. (1953). Extensive games and the problem of information. In Kuhn, H. W. and Tucker, A. W. (Eds.), *Contributions to the Theory of Games II*. Princeton University Press, Princeton, New Jersey.

**Kuipers**, B. J. and Levitt, T. S. (1988). Navigation and mapping in large-scale space. *AI Magazine*, *9*(2), 25–43.

**Kukich**, K. (1992). Techniques for automatically correcting words in text. *ACM Computing Surveys*, *24*(4), 377–439.

**Kumar**, P. R. and Varaiya, P. (1986). *Stochastic systems: Estimation, identification, and adaptive control*. Prentice-Hall, Upper Saddle River, New Jersey.

**Kumar**, V. (1992). Algorithms for constraint satisfaction problems: A survey. *AI Magazine*, *13*(1), 32–44.

**Kumar**, V. and Kanal, L. N. (1983). A general branch and bound formulation for understanding and synthesizing and/or tree search procedures. *Artificial Intelligence*, *21*, 179–198.

**Kumar**, V. and Kanal, L. N. (1988). The CDP: A unifying formulation for heuristic search, dynamic programming, and branch-and-bound. In Kanal, L. N. and Kumar, V. (Eds.), *Search in Artificial Intelligence*, chap. 1, pp. 1–27. Springer-Verlag, Berlin.

**Kumar**, V., Nau, D. S., and Kanal, L. N. (1988). A general branch-and-bound formulation for AND/OR graph and game tree search. In Kanal, L. N. and Kumar, V. (Eds.), *Search in Artificial Intelligence*, chap. 3, pp. 91–130. Springer-Verlag, Berlin.

**Kuper**, G. M. and Vardi, M. Y. (1993). On the complexity of queries in the logical data model. *Theoretical Computer Science*, *116*(1), 33–57.

**Kurzweil**, R. (1990). *The Age of Intelligent Machines*. MIT Press, Cambridge, Massachusetts.

**Kurzweil**, R. (2000). *The Age of Spiritual Machines*. Penguin.

**Kyburg**, H. E. (1977). Randomness and the right reference class. *The Journal of Philosophy*, *74*(9), 501–521.

**Kyburg**, H. E. (1983). The reference class. *Philosophy of Science*, *50*, 374–397.

**La Mettrie**, J. O. (1748). *L'homme machine*. E. Luzac, Leyde, France.

**La Mura**, P. and Shoham, Y. (1999). Expected utility networks. In *Uncertainty in Artificial Intelligence: Proceedings of the Fifteenth Conference*, pp. 366–373, Stockholm. Morgan Kaufmann.

**Ladkin**, P. (1986a). Primitives and units for time specification. In *Proceedings of the Fifth National Conference on Artificial Intelligence (AAAI-86)*, Vol. 1, pp. 354–359, Philadelphia. Morgan Kaufmann.

**Ladkin**, P. (1986b). Time representation: a taxonomy of interval relations. In *Proceedings of the Fifth National Conference on Artificial Intelligence (AAAI-86)*, Vol. 1, pp. 360–366, Philadelphia. Morgan Kaufmann.

**Lafferty**, J. and Zhai, C. (2001). Probabilistic relevance models based on document and query generation. In *Proceedings of the Workshop on Language Modeling and Information retrieval*.

**Laird**, J. E., Newell, A., and Rosenbloom, P. S. (1987). SOAR: An architecture for general intelligence. *Artificial Intelligence*, *33*(1), 1–64.

**Laird**, J. E., Rosenbloom, P. S., and Newell, A. (1986). Chunking in Soar: The anatomy of a general learning mechanism. *Machine Learning*, *1*, 11–46.

**Lakoff**, G. (1987). *Women, Fire, and Dangerous Things: What Categories Reveal about the Mind*. University of Chicago Press, Chicago.

**Lakoff**, G. and Johnson, M. (1980). *Metaphors We Live By*. University of Chicago Press, Chicago.

**Lamarck**, J. B. (1809). *Philosophie zoologique*. Chez Dentu et L'Auteur, Paris.

**Langley**, P., Simon, H. A., Bradshaw, G. L., and Zytkow, J. M. (1987). *Scientific Discovery: Computational Explorations of the Creative Processes*. MIT Press, Cambridge, Massachusetts.

**Langton**, C. (Ed.). (1995). *Artificial life*. MIT Press, Cambridge, Massachusetts.

**Laplace**, P. (1816). *Essai philosophique sur les probabilités* (3rd edition). Courcier Imprimeur, Paris.

**Lappin**, S. and Leass, H. J. (1994). An algorithm for pronominal anaphora resolution. *Computational Linguistics*, *20*(4), 535–561.

**Lari**, K. and Young, S. J. (1990). The estimation of stochastic context-free grammars using the inside-outside algorithm. *Computer, Speech and Language*, *4*, 35–56.

**Larrañaga**, P., Kuijpers, C., Murga, R., Inza, I., and Dizdarevic, S. (1999). Genetic algorithms for the travelling salesman problem: A review of representations and operators. *Artificial Intelligence Review*, *13*, 129–170.

**Latombe**, J.-C. (1991). *Robot Motion Planning*. Kluwer, Dordrecht, Netherlands.

**Lauritzen**, S. (1995). The EM algorithm for graphical association models with missing data. *Computational Statistics and Data Analysis*, *19*, 191–201.

**Lauritzen**, S. (1996). *Graphical models*. Oxford University Press, Oxford, UK.

**Lauritzen**, S., Dawid, A., Larsen, B., and Leimer, H. (1990). Independence properties of directed Markov fields. *Networks*, *20*(5), 491–505.

**Lauritzen**, S. and Spiegelhalter, D. J. (1988). Local computations with probabilities on graphical structures and their application to expert systems. *Journal of the Royal Statistical Society*, *B 50*(2), 157–224.

**Lauritzen**, S. and Wermuth, N. (1989). Graphical models for associations between variables, some of which are qualitative and some quantitative. *Annals of Statistics*, *17*, 31–57.

**Lavrač**, N. and Džeroski, S. (1994). *Inductive Logic Programming: Techniques and Applications*. Ellis Horwood, Chichester, England.

**Lawler**, E. L. (1985). *The traveling salesman problem: A guided tour of combinatorial optimization*. Wiley, New York.

**Lawler**, E. L., Lenstra, J. K., Kan, A., and Shmoys, D. B. (1992). *The Travelling Salesman Problem*. Wiley Interscience.

**Lawler**, E. L., Lenstra, J. K., Kan, A., and Shmoys, D. B. (1993). Sequencing and scheduling: algorithms and complexity. In Graves, S. C., Zipkin, P. H., and Kan, A. H. G. R. (Eds.), *Logistics of Production and Inventory: Handbooks in Operations Research and Management Science, Volume 4*, pp. 445–522. North-Holland, Amsterdam.

**Lawler**, E. L. and Wood, D. E. (1966). Branch-and-bound methods: A survey. *Operations Research*, *14(4)*, 699–719.

**Lazanas**, A. and Latombe, J.-C. (1992). Landmark-based robot navigation. In *Proceedings of the Tenth National Conference on Artificial Intelligence (AAAI-92)*, pp. 816–822, San Jose. AAAI Press.

**Le Cun**, Y., Jackel, L., Boser, B., and Denker, J. (1989). Handwritten digit recognition: Applications of neural network chips and automatic learning. *IEEE Communications Magazine*, *27*(11), 41–46.

**LeCun**, Y., Jackel, L., Bottou, L., Brunot, A., Cortes, C., Denker, J., Drucker, H., Guyon, I., Muller, U., Sackinger, E., Simard, P., and Vapnik, V. N. (1995). Comparison of learning algorithms for handwritten digit recognition. In Fogelman, F. and Gallinari, P. (Eds.), *International Conference on Artificial Neural Networks*, pp. 53–60, Berlin. Springer-Verlag.

**Leech**, G., Rayson, P., and Wilson, A. (2001). *Word Frequencies in Written and Spoken English: Based on the British National Corpus*. Longman, New York.

**Lefkovitz**, D. (1960). A strategic pattern recognition program for the game Go. Technical note 60-243, Wright Air Development Division, University of Pennsylvania, Moore School of Electrical Engineering.

**Lenat**, D. B. (1983). EURISKO: A program that learns new heuristics and domain concepts: The nature of heuristics, III: Program design and results. *Artificial Intelligence*, *21*(1–2), 61–98.

**Lenat**, D. B. (1995). Cyc: A large-scale investment in knowledge infrastructure. *Communications of the ACM*, *38*(11).

**Lenat**, D. B. and Brown, J. S. (1984). Why AM and EURISKO appear to work. *Artificial Intelligence*, *23*(3), 269–294.

**Lenat**, D. B. and Guha, R. V. (1990). *Building Large Knowledge-Based Systems: Representation and Inference in the CYC Project*. Addison-Wesley, Reading, Massachusetts.

**Leonard**, H. S. and Goodman, N. (1940). The calculus of individuals and its uses. *Journal of Symbolic Logic*, *5*(2), 45–55.

**Leonard**, J. J. and Durrant-Whyte, H. (1992). *Directed sonar sensing for mobile robot navigation*. Kluwer, Dordrecht, Netherlands.

**Leśniewski**, S. (1916). Podstawy ogólnej teorii mnogości. Moscow.

**Lettvin**, J. Y., Maturana, H. R., McCulloch, W. S., and Pitts, W. H. (1959). What the frog's eye tells the frog's brain. *Proceedings of the IRE*, *47*(11), 1940–1951.

**Letz**, R., Schumann, J., Bayerl, S., and Bibel, W. (1992). SETHEO: A high-performance theorem prover. *Journal of Automated Reasoning*, *8*(2), 183–212.

**Levesque**, H. J. and Brachman, R. J. (1987). Expressiveness and tractability in knowledge representation and reasoning. *Computational Intelligence*, *3*(2), 78–93.

**Levesque**, H. J., Reiter, R., Lespérance, Y., Lin, F., and Scherl, R. (1997a). GOLOG: A logic programming language for dynamic domains. *Journal of Logic Programming*, *31*, 59–84.

**Levesque**, H. J., Reiter, R., Lespérance, Y., Lin, F., and Scherl, R. (1997b). GOLOG: A logic programming language for dynamic domains. *Journal of Logic Programming*, *31*, 59–84.

**Levitt**, G. M. (2000). *The Turk, Chess Automaton*. McFarland and Company.

**Levy**, D. N. L. (Ed.). (1988a). *Computer Chess Compendium*. Springer-Verlag, Berlin.

**Levy**, D. N. L. (Ed.). (1988b). *Computer Games*. Springer-Verlag, Berlin.

**Lewis**, D. D. (1998). Naive Bayes at forty: The independence assumption in information retrieval. In *Machine Learning: ECML-98. 10th European Conference on Machine Learning. Proceedings*, pp. 4–15, Chemnitz, Germany. Springer-Verlag.

**Lewis**, D. K. (1966). An argument for the identity theory. *The Journal of Philosophy*, *63*(1), 17–25.

**Lewis**, D. K. (1972). General semantics. In Davidson, D. and Harman, G. (Eds.), *Semantics of Natural Language*, pp. 169–218. D. Reidel, Dordrecht, Netherlands.

**Lewis**, D. K. (1980). Mad pain and Martian pain. In Block, N. (Ed.), *Readings in Philosophy of Psychology*, Vol. 1, pp. 216–222. Harvard University Press, Cambridge, Massachusetts.

**Li**, C. M. and Anbulagan (1997). Heuristics based on unit propagation for satisfiability problems. In *Proceedings of the Fifteenth International Joint Conference on Artificial Intelligence (IJCAI-97)*, pp. 366–371, Nagoya, Japan. Morgan Kaufmann.

**Li**, M. and Vitanyi, P. M. B. (1993). *An Introduction to Kolmogorov Complexity and Its Applications*. Springer-Verlag, Berlin.

**Lifschitz**, V. (1986). On the semantics of STRIPS. In Georgeff, M. P. and Lansky, A. L. (Eds.), *Reasoning about Actions and Plans: Proceedings of the 1986 Workshop*, pp. 1–9, Timberline, Oregon. Morgan Kaufmann.

**Lifschitz**, V. (2001). Answer set programming and plan generation. *Artificial Intelligence*, *138*(1–2), 39–54.

**Lighthill**, J. (1973). Artificial intelligence: A general survey. In Lighthill, J., Sutherland, N. S., Needham, R. M., Longuet-Higgins, H. C., and Michie, D. (Eds.), *Artificial Intelligence: A Paper Symposium*. Science Research Council of Great Britain, London.

**Lin**, F. and Reiter, R. (1997). How to progress a database. *Artificial Intelligence*, *92*(1–2), 131–167.

**Lin**, S. (1965). Computer solutions of the travelling salesman problem. *Bell Systems Technical Journal*, *44(10)*, 2245–2269.

**Lin**, S. and Kernighan, B. W. (1973). An effective heuristic algorithm for the travelling-salesman problem. *Operations Research*, *21*(2), 498–516.

**Linden**, T. A. (1991). Representing software designs as partially developed plans. In Lowry, M. R. and McCartney, R. D. (Eds.), *Automating Software Design*, pp. 603–625. MIT Press, Cambridge, Massachusetts.

**Lindsay**, R. K. (1963). Inferential memory as the basis of machines which understand natural language. In Feigenbaum, E. A. and Feldman, J. (Eds.), *Computers and Thought*, pp. 217–236. McGraw-Hill, New York.

**Lindsay**, R. K., Buchanan, B. G., Feigenbaum, E. A., and Lederberg, J. (1980). *Applications of Artificial Intelligence for Organic Chemistry: The DENDRAL Project*. McGraw-Hill, New York.

**Littman**, M. L. (1994). Markov games as a framework for multi-agent reinforcement learning. In *Proceedings of the 11th International Conference on Machine Learning (ML-94)*, pp. 157–163, New Brunswick, NJ. Morgan Kaufmann.

**Littman**, M. L., Keim, G. A., and Shazeer, N. M. (1999). Solving crosswords with PROVERB. In *Proceedings of the Sixteenth National Conference on Artificial Intelligence (AAAI-99)*, pp. 914–915, Orlando, Florida. AAAI Press.

**Liu**, J. S. and Chen, R. (1998). Sequential Monte Carlo methods for dynamic systems. *Journal of the American Statistical Association*, *93*, 1022–1031.

**Lloyd**, J. W. (1987). *Foundations of Logic Programming*. Springer-Verlag, Berlin.

**Locke**, J. (1690). *An Essay Concerning Human Understanding*. William Tegg.

**Locke**, W. N. and Booth, A. D. (1955). *Machine Translation of Languages: Fourteen Essays*. MIT Press, Cambridge, Massachusetts.

**Lodge**, D. (1984). *Small World*. Penguin Books, New York.

**Lohn**, J. D., Kraus, W. F., and Colombano, S. P. (2001). Evolutionary optimization of yagi-uda antennas. In *Proceedings of the Fourth International Conference on Evolvable Systems*, pp. 236–243.

**Longuet-Higgins**, H. C. (1981). A computer algorithm for reconstructing a scene from two projections. *Nature*, *293*, 133–135.

**Lovejoy**, W. S. (1991). A survey of algorithmic methods for partially observed Markov decision processes. *Annals of Operations Research*, *28*(1–4), 47–66.

**Loveland**, D. (1968). Mechanical theorem proving by model elimination. *Journal of the Association for Computing Machinery*, *15*(2), 236–251.

**Loveland**, D. (1970). A linear format for resolution. In *Proceedings of the IRIA Symposium on Automatic Demonstration*, pp. 147–162, Berlin. Springer-Verlag.

**Loveland**, D. (1984). Automated theorem-proving: A quarter-century review. *Contemporary Mathematics*, *29*, 1–45.

**Lowe**, D. G. (1987). Three-dimensional object recognition from single two-dimensional images. *Artificial Intelligence*, *31*, 355–395.

**Löwenheim**, L. (1915). Über möglichkeiten im Relativkalkül. *Mathematische Annalen*, *76*, 447–470.

**Lowerre**, B. T. (1976). *The* HARPY *Speech Recognition System*. Ph.D. thesis, Computer Science Department, Carnegie-Mellon University, Pittsburgh, Pennsylvania.

**Lowerre**, B. T. and Reddy, R. (1980). The HARPY speech recognition system. In Lea, W. A. (Ed.), *Trends in Speech Recognition*, chap. 15. Prentice-Hall, Upper Saddle River, New Jersey.

**Lowry**, M. R. and McCartney, R. D. (1991). *Automating Software Design*. MIT Press, Cambridge, Massachusetts.

**Loyd**, S. (1959). *Mathematical Puzzles of Sam Loyd: Selected and Edited by Martin Gardner*. Dover, New York.

**Lozano-Perez**, T. (1983). Spatial planning: A configuration space approach. *IEEE Transactions on Computers*, *C-32*(2), 108–120.

**Lozano-Perez**, T., Mason, M., and Taylor, R. (1984). Automatic synthesis of fine-motion strategies for robots. *International Journal of Robotics Research*, *3*(1), 3–24.

**Luby**, M., Sinclair, A., and Zuckerman, D. (1993). Optimal speedup of Las Vegas algorithms. *Information Processing Letters*, *47*, 173–180.

**Luby**, M. and Vigoda, E. (1999). Fast convergence of the glauber dynamics for sampling independent sets. *Random Structures and Algorithms*, *15*(3-4), 229–241.

**Lucas**, J. R. (1961). Minds, machines, and Gödel. *Philosophy*, *36*.

**Lucas**, J. R. (1976). This Gödel is killing me: A rejoinder. *Philosophia*, *6*(1), 145–148.

**Lucas**, P. (1996). Knowledge acquisition for decision-theoretic expert systems. *AISB Quarterly*, *94*, 23–33.

**Luce**, D. R. and Raiffa, H. (1957). *Games and Decisions*. Wiley, New York.

**Luger**, G. F. (Ed.). (1995). *Computation and intelligence: Collected readings*. AAAI Press, Menlo Park, California.

**MacKay**, D. J. C. (1992). A practical Bayesian framework for back-propagation networks. *Neural Computation*, *4*(3), 448–472.

**Mackworth**, A. K. (1973). Interpreting pictures of polyhedral scenes. *Artificial Intelligence*, *4*, 121–137.

**Mackworth**, A. K. (1977). Consistency in networks of relations. *Artificial Intelligence*, *8*(1), 99–118.

**Mackworth**, A. K. (1992). Constraint satisfaction. In Shapiro, S. (Ed.), *Encyclopedia of Artificial Intelligence* (second edition)., Vol. 1, pp. 285–293. Wiley, New York.

**Mahanti**, A. and Daniels, C. J. (1993). A SIMD approach to parallel heuristic search. *Artificial Intelligence*, *60*(2), 243–282.

**Majercik**, S. M. and Littman, M. L. (1999). Planning under uncertainty via stochastic satisfiability. In *Proceedings of the Sixteenth National Conference on Artificial Intelligence*, pp. 549–556.

**Malik**, J. (1987). Interpreting line drawings of curved objects. *International Journal of Computer Vision*, *1*(1), 73–103.

**Malik**, J. and Rosenholtz, R. (1994). Recovering surface curvature and orientation from texture distortion: A least squares algorithm and sensitivity analysis. In Eklundh, J.-O. (Ed.), *Proceedings of the Third European Conf. on Computer Vision*, pp. 353–364, Stockholm. Springer-Verlag.

**Malik**, J. and Rosenholtz, R. (1997). Computing local surface orientation and shape from texture for curved surfaces. *International Journal of Computer Vision*, *23*(2), 149–168.

**Mann**, W. C. and Thompson, S. A. (1983). Relational propositions in discourse. Tech. rep. RR-83-115, Information Sciences Institute.

**Mann**, W. C. and Thompson, S. A. (1988). Rhetorical structure theory: Toward a functional theory of text organization. *Text*, *8*(3), 243–281.

**Manna**, Z. and Waldinger, R. (1971). Toward automatic program synthesis. *Communications of the Association for Computing Machinery*, *14*(3), 151–165.

**Manna**, Z. and Waldinger, R. (1985). *The Logical Basis for Computer Programming: Volume 1: Deductive Reasoning*. Addison-Wesley, Reading, Massachusetts.

**Manna**, Z. and Waldinger, R. (1986). Special relations in automated deduction. *Journal of the Association for Computing Machinery*, *33*(1), 1–59.

**Manna**, Z. and Waldinger, R. (1992). Fundamentals of deductive program synthesis. *IEEE Transactions on Software Engineering*, *18*(8), 674–704.

**Manning**, C. D. and Schütze, H. (1999). *Foundations of Statistical Natural Language Processing*. MIT Press.

**Marbach**, P. and Tsitsiklis, J. N. (1998). Simulation-based optimization of Markov reward processes. Technical report LIDS-P-2411, Laboratory for Information and Decision Systems, Massachusetts Institute of Technology.

**Marcus**, M. P., Santorini, B., and Marcinkiewicz, M. A. (1993). Building a large annotated corpus of english: The penn treebank. *Computational Linguistics*, *19*(2), 313–330.

**Markov**, A. A. (1913). An example of statistical investigation in the text of "Eugene Onegin" illustrating coupling of "tests" in chains. *Proceedings of the Academy of Sciences of St. Petersburg*, *7*.

**Maron**, M. E. (1961). Automatic indexing: An experimental inquiry. *Journal of the Association for Computing Machinery*, *8*(3), 404–417.

**Maron**, M. E. and Kuhns, J.-L. (1960). On relevance, probabilistic indexing and information retrieval. *Communications of the ACM*, *7*, 219–244.

**Marr**, D. (1982). *Vision: A Computational Investigation into the Human Representation and Processing of Visual Information*. W. H. Freeman, New York.

**Marriott**, K. and Stuckey, P. J. (1998). *Programming with Constraints: An Introduction*. MIT Press, Cambridge, Massachusetts.

**Marsland**, A. T. and Schaeffer, J. (Eds.). (1990). *Computers, Chess, and Cognition*. Springer-Verlag, Berlin.

**Martelli**, A. and Montanari, U. (1976). Unification in linear time and space: A structured presentation. Internal report B 76-16, Istituto di Elaborazione della Informazione, Pisa, Italy.

**Martelli**, A. and Montanari, U. (1978). Optimizing decision trees through heuristically guided search. *Communications of the Association for Computing Machinery*, *21*, 1025–1039.

**Marthi**, B., Pasula, H., Russell, S. J., and Peres, Y. (2002). Decayed MCMC filtering. In *Uncertainty in Artificial Intelligence: Proceedings of the Eighteenth Conference*, pp. 319–326, Edmonton, Alberta. Morgan Kaufmann.

**Martin**, J. H. (1990). *A Computational Model of Metaphor Interpretation*. Academic Press, New York.

**Martin**, P. and Shmoys, D. B. (1996). A new approach to computing optimal schedules for the job-shop scheduling problem. In *Proceedings of the 5th International IPCO Conference*, pp. 389–403. Springer-Verlag.

**Maslov**, S. Y. (1964). An inverse method for establishing deducibility in classical predicate calculus. *Doklady Akademii nauk SSSR*, *159*, 17–20.

**Maslov**, S. Y. (1967). An inverse method for establishing deducibility of nonprenex formulas of the predicate calculus. *Doklady Akademii nauk SSSR*, *172*, 22–25.

**Mason**, M. (1993). Kicking the sensing habit. *AI Magazine*, *14*(1), 58–59.

**Mason**, M. (2001). *Mechanics of Robotic Manipulation*. MIT Press.

**Mason**, M. and Salisbury, J. (1985). *Robot hands and the mechanics of manipulation*. MIT Press.

**Mataric**, M. J. (1997). Reinforcement learning in the multi-robot domain. *Autonomous Robots*, *4*(1), 73–83.

**Mates**, B. (1953). *Stoic Logic*. University of California Press, Berkeley and Los Angeles.

**Maxwell**, J. and Kaplan, R. (1993). The interface between phrasal and functional constraints. *Computational Linguistics*, *19*(4), 571–590.

**Maxwell**, J. and Kaplan, R. (1995). A method for disjunctive constraint satisfaction. In Dalrymple, M., Kaplan, R., Maxwell, J., and Zaenen, A. (Eds.), *Formal Issues in Lexical-Functional Grammar*, No. 47 in CSLI Lecture Note Series, chap. 14, pp. 381–481. CSLI Publications.

**McAllester**, D. A. (1980). An outlook on truth maintenance. Ai memo 551, MIT AI Laboratory, Cambridge, Massachusetts.

**McAllester**, D. A. (1988). Conspiracy numbers for min-max search. *Artificial Intelligence*, *35*(3), 287–310.

**McAllester**, D. A. (1989). *Ontic: A Knowledge Representation System for Mathematics*. MIT Press, Cambridge, Massachusetts.

**McAllester**, D. A. (1998). What is the most pressing issue facing ai and the aaai today?. Candidate statement, election for Councilor of the American Association for Artificial Intelligence.

**McAllester**, D. A. and Givan, R. (1992). Natural language syntax and first-order inference. *Artificial Intelligence*, *56*(1), 1–20.

**McAllester**, D. A. and Rosenblitt, D. (1991). Systematic nonlinear planning. In *Proceedings of the Ninth National Conference on Artificial Intelligence (AAAI-91)*, Vol. 2, pp. 634–639, Anaheim, California. AAAI Press.

**McCarthy**, J. (1958). Programs with common sense. In *Proceedings of the Symposium on Mechanisation of Thought Processes*, Vol. 1, pp. 77–84, London. Her Majesty's Stationery Office.

**McCarthy**, J. (1963). Situations, actions, and causal laws. Memo 2, Stanford University Artificial Intelligence Project, Stanford, California.

**McCarthy**, J. (1968). Programs with common sense. In Minsky, M. L. (Ed.), *Semantic Information Processing*, pp. 403–418. MIT Press, Cambridge, Massachusetts.

**McCarthy**, J. (1980). Circumscription: A form of non-monotonic reasoning. *Artificial Intelligence*, *13*(1–2), 27–39.

**McCarthy**, J. and Hayes, P. J. (1969). Some philosophical problems from the standpoint of artificial intelligence. In Meltzer, B., Michie, D., and Swann, M. (Eds.), *Machine Intelligence 4*, pp. 463–502. Edinburgh University Press, Edinburgh, Scotland.

**McCarthy**, J., Minsky, M. L., Rochester, N., and Shannon, C. E. (1955). Proposal for the Dartmouth summer research project on artificial intelligence. Tech. rep., Dartmouth College.

**McCawley**, J. D. (1988). *The Syntactic Phenomena of English*, Vol. 2 volumes. University of Chicago Press.

**McCawley**, J. D. (1993). *Everything That Linguists Have Always Wanted to Know about Logic but Were Ashamed to Ask* (Second edition). University of Chicago Press, Chicago.

**McCulloch**, W. S. and Pitts, W. (1943). A logical calculus of the ideas immanent in nervous activity. *Bulletin of Mathematical Biophysics*, *5*, 115–137.

**McCune**, W. (1992). Automated discovery of new axiomatizations of the left group and right group calculi. *Journal of Automated Reasoning*, *9*(1), 1–24.

**McCune**, W. (1997). Solution of the robbins problem. *Journal of Automated Reasoning*, *19*(3), 263–276.

**McDermott**, D. (1976). Artificial intelligence meets natural stupidity. *SIGART Newsletter*, *57*, 4–9.

**McDermott**, D. (1978a). Planning and acting. *Cognitive Science*, *2*(2), 71–109.

**McDermott**, D. (1978b). Tarskian semantics, or, no notation without denotation!. *Cognitive Science*, *2*(3).

**McDermott**, D. (1987). A critique of pure reason. *Computational Intelligence*, *3*(3), 151–237.

**McDermott**, D. (1996). A heuristic estimator for means-ends analysis in planning. In *Proceedings of the Third International Conference on AI Planning Systems*, pp. 142–149, Edinburgh, Scotland. AAAI Press.

**McDermott**, D. and Doyle, J. (1980). Non-monotonic logic: i. *Artificial Intelligence*, *13*(1–2), 41–72.

**McDermott**, J. (1982). R1: A rule-based configurer of computer systems. *Artificial Intelligence*, *19*(1), 39–88.

**McEliece**, R. J., MacKay, D. J. C., and Cheng, J.-F. (1998). Turbo decoding as an instance of Pearl's "belief propagation" algorithm. *IEEE Journal on Selected Areas in Communications*, *16*(2), 140–152.

**McGregor**, J. J. (1979). Relational consistency algorithms and their application in finding subgraph and graph isomorphisms. *Information Sciences*, *19*(3), 229–250.

**McKeown**, K. (1985). *Text Generation: Using Discourse Strategies and Focus Constraints to Generate Natural Language Text*. Cambridge University Press, Cambridge, UK.

**McLachlan**, G. J. and Krishnan, T. (1997). *The EM Algorithm and Extensions*. Wiley, New York.

**McMillan**, K. L. (1993). *Symbolic Model Checking*. Kluwer, Dordrecht, Netherlands.

**Meehl**, P. (1955). *Clinical vs. Statistical Prediction*. University of Minnesota Press, Minneapolis.

**Melćuk**, I. A. and Polguere, A. (1988). A formal lexicon in the meaning-text theory (or how to do lexica with words). *Computational Linguistics*, *13*(3–4), 261–275.

**Mendel**, G. (1866). Versuche über pflanzen-hybriden. *Verhandlungen des Naturforschenden Vereins, Abhandlungen, Brünn*, *4*, 3–47. Translated into English by C. T. Druery, published by Bateson (1902).

**Mercer**, J. (1909). Functions of positive and negative type and their connection with the theory of integral equations. *Philos. Trans. Roy. Soc. London, A*, *209*, 415–446.

**Metropolis**, N., Rosenbluth, A., Rosenbluth, M., Teller, A., and Teller, E. (1953). Equations of state calculations by fast computing machines. *Journal of Chemical Physics*, *21*, 1087–1091.

**Mézard**, M. and Nadal, J.-P. (1989). Learning in feedforward layered networks: The tiling algorithm. *Journal of Physics*, *22*, 2191–2204.

**Michalski**, R. S. (1969). On the quasi-minimal solution of the general covering problem. In *Proceedings of the First International Symposium on Information Processing*, pp. 125–128.

**Michalski**, R. S., Carbonell, J. G., and Mitchell, T. M. (Eds.). (1983). *Machine Learning: An Artificial Intelligence Approach*, Vol. 1. Morgan Kaufmann, San Mateo, California.

**Michalski**, R. S., Carbonell, J. G., and Mitchell, T. M. (Eds.). (1986a). *Machine Learning: An Artificial Intelligence Approach*, Vol. 2. Morgan Kaufmann, San Mateo, California.

**Michalski**, R. S., Mozetic, I., Hong, J., and Lavrač, N. (1986b). The multi-purpose incremental learning system aq15 and its testing application to three medical domains. In *Proceedings of the Fifth National Conference on Artificial Intelligence (AAAI-86)*, pp. 1041–1045, Philadelphia. Morgan Kaufmann.

**Michel**, S. and Plamondon, P. (1996). Bilingual sentence alignment: Balancing robustness and accuracy. In *Proceedings of the Conference of the Association for Machine Translation in the Americas (AMTA)*.

**Michie**, D. (1966). Game-playing and game-learning automata. In Fox, L. (Ed.), *Advances in Programming and Non-Numerical Computation*, pp. 183–200. Pergamon, Oxford, UK.

**Michie**, D. (1972). Machine intelligence at Edinburgh. *Management Informatics*, *2*(1), 7–12.

**Michie**, D. (1974). Machine intelligence at Edinburgh. In *On Intelligence*, pp. 143–155. Edinburgh University Press.

**Michie**, D. and Chambers, R. A. (1968). BOXES: An experiment in adaptive control. In Dale, E. and Michie, D. (Eds.), *Machine Intelligence 2*, pp. 125–133. Elsevier/North-Holland, Amsterdam, London, New York.

**Michie**, D., Spiegelhalter, D. J., and Taylor, C. (Eds.). (1994). *Machine Learning, Neural and Statistical Classification*. Ellis Horwood, Chichester, England.

**Milgrom**, P. (1997). Putting auction theory to work: The simultaneous ascending auction. Tech. rep. Technical Report 98-0002, Stanford University Department of Economics.

**Mill**, J. S. (1843). *A System of Logic, Ratiocinative and Inductive: Being a Connected View of the Principles of Evidence, and Methods of Scientific Investigation*. J. W. Parker, London.

**Mill**, J. S. (1863). *Utilitarianism*. Parker, Son and Bourn, London.

**Miller**, A. C., Merkhofer, M. M., Howard, R. A., Matheson, J. E., and Rice, T. R. (1976). Development of automated aids for decision analysis. Technical report, SRI International, Menlo Park, California.

**Minsky**, M. L. (Ed.). (1968). *Semantic Information Processing*. MIT Press, Cambridge, Massachusetts.

**Minsky**, M. L. (1975). A framework for representing knowledge. In Winston, P. H. (Ed.), *The Psychology of Computer Vision*, pp. 211–277. McGraw-Hill, New York. Originally an MIT AI Laboratory memo; the 1975 version is abridged, but is the most widely cited.

**Minsky**, M. L. and Papert, S. (1969). *Perceptrons: An Introduction to Computational Geometry* (first edition). MIT Press, Cambridge, Massachusetts.

**Minsky**, M. L. and Papert, S. (1988). *Perceptrons: An Introduction to Computational Geometry* (Expanded edition). MIT Press, Cambridge, Massachusetts.

**Minton**, S. (1984). Constraint-based generalization: Learning game-playing plans from single examples. In *Proceedings of the National Conference on Artificial Intelligence (AAAI-84)*, pp. 251–254, Austin, Texas. Morgan Kaufmann.

**Minton**, S. (1988). Quantitative results concerning the utility of explanation- based learning. In *Proceedings of the Seventh National Conference on Artificial Intelligence (AAAI-88)*, pp. 564–569, St. Paul, Minnesota. Morgan Kaufmann.

**Minton**, S., Johnston, M. D., Philips, A. B., and Laird, P. (1992). Minimizing conflicts: A heuristic repair method for constraint satisfaction and scheduling problems. *Artificial Intelligence*, *58*(1–3), 161–205.

**Mitchell**, M. (1996). *An Introduction to Genetic Algorithms*. MIT Press, Cambridge, Massachusetts.

**Mitchell**, M., Holland, J. H., and Forrest, S. (1996). When will a genetic algorithm outperform hill climbing?. In Cowan, J., Tesauro, G., and Alspector, J. (Eds.), *Advances in Neural Information Processing Systems*, Vol. 6. MIT Press, Cambridge, Massachusetts.

**Mitchell**, T. M. (1977). Version spaces: A candidate elimination approach to rule learning. In *Proceedings of the Fifth International Joint Conference on Artificial Intelligence (IJCAI-77)*, pp. 305–310, Cambridge, Massachusetts. IJCAII.

**Mitchell**, T. M. (1982). Generalization as search. *Artificial Intelligence*, *18*(2), 203–226.

**Mitchell**, T. M. (1990). Becoming increasingly reactive (mobile robots). In *Proceedings of the Eighth National Conference on Artificial Intelligence (AAAI-90)*, Vol. 2, pp. 1051–1058, Boston. MIT Press.

**Mitchell**, T. M. (1997). *Machine Learning*. McGraw-Hill, New York.

**Mitchell**, T. M., Keller, R., and Kedar-Cabelli, S. (1986). Explanation-based generalization: A unifying view. *Machine Learning*, *1*, 47–80.

**Mitchell**, T. M., Utgoff, P. E., and Banerji, R. (1983). Learning by experimentation: Acquiring and refining problem-solving heuristics. In Michalski, R. S., Carbonell, J. G., and Mitchell, T. M. (Eds.), *Machine Learning: An Artificial Intelligence Approach*, pp. 163–190. Morgan Kaufmann, San Mateo, California.

**Mitkov**, R. (2002). *Anaphora Resolution*. Longman, New York.

**Mohr**, R. and Henderson, T. C. (1986). Arc and path consistency revisited. *Artificial Intelligence*, *28*(2), 225–233.

**Mohri**, M., Pereira, F., and Riley, M. (2002). Weighted finite-state transducers in speech recognition. *Computer Speech and Language*, *16*(1), 69–88.

**Montague**, P. R., Dayan, P., Person, C., and Sejnowski, T. (1995). Bee foraging in uncertain environments using predictive Hebbian learning. *Nature*, *377*, 725–728.

**Montague**, R. (1970). English as a formal language. In *Linguaggi nella Società e nella Tecnica*, pp. 189–224. Edizioni di Comunità, Milan.

**Montague**, R. (1973). The proper treatment of quantification in ordinary English. In Hintikka, K. J. J., Moravcsik, J. M. E., and Suppes, P. (Eds.), *Approaches to Natural Language*. D. Reidel, Dordrecht, Netherlands.

**Montanari**, U. (1974). Networks of constraints: Fundamental properties and applications to picture processing. *Information Sciences*, *7*(2), 95–132.

**Montemerlo**, M., Thrun, S., Koller, D., and Wegbreit, B. (2002). FastSLAM: A factored solution to the simultaneous localization and mapping problem. In *Proceedings of the Eighteenth National Conference on Artificial Intelligence (AAAI-02)*, Edmonton, Alberta. AAAI Press.

**Mooney**, R. (1999). Learning for semantic interpretation: Scaling up without dumbing down. In Cussens, J. (Ed.), *Proceedings of the 1st Workshop on Learning Language in Logic*, pp. 7–15. Springer-Verlag.

**Mooney**, R. J. and Califf, M. E. (1995). Induction of first-order decision lists: Results on learning the past tense of English verbs. *Journal of AI Research*, *3*, 1–24.

**Moore**, A. W. and Atkeson, C. G. (1993). Prioritized sweeping—reinforcement learning with less data and less time. *Machine Learning*, *13*, 103–130.

**Moore**, E. F. (1959). The shortest path through a maze. In *Proceedings of an International Symposium on the Theory of Switching, Part II*, pp. 285–292. Harvard University Press, Cambridge, Massachusetts.

**Moore**, J. S. and Newell, A. (1973). How can Merlin understand?. In Gregg, L. (Ed.), *Knowledge and Cognition*. Lawrence Erlbaum Associates, Potomac, Maryland.

**Moore**, R. C. (1980). Reasoning about knowledge and action. Artificial intelligence center technical note 191, SRI International, Menlo Park, California.

**Moore**, R. C. (1985). A formal theory of knowledge and action. In Hobbs, J. R. and Moore, R. C. (Eds.), *Formal Theories of the Commonsense World*, pp. 319–358. Ablex, Norwood, New Jersey.

**Moravec**, H. P. (1983). The stanford cart and the cmu rover. *Proceedings of the IEEE*, *71*(7), 872–884.

**Moravec**, H. P. and Elfes, A. (1985). High resolution maps from wide angle sonar. In *1985 IEEE International Conference on Robotics and Automation*, pp. 116–121, St. Louis, Missouri. IEEE Computer Society Press.

**Moravec**, H. P. (1988). *Mind Children: The Future of Robot and Human Intelligence*. Harvard University Press, Cambridge, Massachusetts.

**Moravec**, H. P. (2000). *Robot: Mere Machine to Transcendent Mind*. Oxford University Press.

**Morgenstern**, L. (1987). Knowledge preconditions for actions and plans. In *Proceedings of the Tenth International Joint Conference on Artificial Intelligence (IJCAI-87)*, pp. 867–874, Milan. Morgan Kaufmann.

**Morgenstern**, L. (1998). Inheritance comes of age: Applying nonmonotonic techniques to problems in industry. *Artificial Intelligence*, *103*, 237–271.

**Morjaria**, M. A., Rink, F. J., Smith, W. D., Klempner, G., Burns, C., and Stein, J. (1995). Elicitation of probabilities for belief networks: Combining qualitative and quantitative information. In *Proceedings of the Conference on Uncertainty in Artificial Intelligence*, pp. 141–148. Morgan Kaufmann.

**Morrison**, P. and Morrison, E. (Eds.). (1961). *Charles Babbage and His Calculating Engines: Selected Writings by Charles Babbage and Others*. Dover, New York.

**Moskewicz**, M. W., Madigan, C. F., Zhao, Y., Zhang, L., and Malik, S. (2001). Chaff: Engineering an efficient SAT solver. In *Proceedings of the 38th Design Automation Conference (DAC 2001)*, pp. 530–535. ACM Press.

**Mosteller**, F. and Wallace, D. L. (1964). *Inference and Disputed Authorship: The Federalist*. Addison-Wesley.

**Mostow**, J. and Prieditis, A. E. (1989). Discovering admissible heuristics by abstracting and optimizing: A transformational approach. In *Proceedings of the Eleventh International Joint Conference on Artificial Intelligence (IJCAI-89)*, Vol. 1, pp. 701–707, Detroit. Morgan Kaufmann.

**Motzkin**, T. S. and Schoenberg, I. J. (1954). The relaxation method for linear inequalities. *Canadian Journal of Mathematics*, *6*(3), 393–404.

**Moussouris**, J., Holloway, J., and Greenblatt, R. D. (1979). CHEOPS: A chess-oriented processing system. In Hayes, J. E., Michie, D., and Mikulich, L. I. (Eds.), *Machine Intelligence 9*, pp. 351–360. Ellis Horwood, Chichester, England.

**Moutarlier**, P. and Chatila, R. (1989). Stochastic multisensory data fusion for mobile robot location and environment modeling. In *5th Int. Symposium on Robotics Research*, Tokyo.

**Muggleton**, S. H. (1991). Inductive logic programming. *New Generation Computing*, *8*, 295–318.

**Muggleton**, S. H. (1992). *Inductive Logic Programming*. Academic Press, New York.

**Muggleton**, S. H. (1995). Inverse entailment and Progol. *New Generation Computing, Special issue on Inductive Logic Programming*, *13*(3-4), 245–286.

**Muggleton**, S. H. (2000). Learning stochastic logic programs. Proceedings of the AAAI 2000 Workshop on Learning Statistical Models from Relational Data.

**Muggleton**, S. H. and Buntine, W. (1988). Machine invention of first-order predicates by inverting resolution. In *Proceedings of the Fifth International Conference on Machine Learning*, pp. 339–352. Morgan Kaufmann.

**Muggleton**, S. H. and De Raedt, L. (1994). Inductive logic programming: Theory and methods. *Journal of Logic Programming*, *19/20*, 629–679.

**Muggleton**, S. H. and Feng, C. (1990). Efficient induction of logic programs. In *Proceedings of the Workshop on Algorithmic Learning Theory*, pp. 368–381, Tokyo. Ohmsha.

**Müller**, M. (2002). Computer Go. *Artificial Intelligence*, *134*(1–2), 145–179.

**Mundy**, J. and Zisserman, A. (Eds.). (1992). *Geometric Invariance in Computer Vision*. MIT Press, Cambridge, Massachusetts.

**Murphy**, K., Weiss, Y., and Jordan, M. I. (1999). Loopy belief propagation for approximate inference: An empirical study. In *Uncertainty in Artificial Intelligence: Proceedings of the Fifteenth Conference*, pp. 467–475, Stockholm. Morgan Kaufmann.

**Murphy**, K. and Russell, S. J. (2001). Rao-blackwellised particle filtering for dynamic bayesian networks. In Doucet, A., de Freitas, N., and Gordon, N. J. (Eds.), *Sequential Monte Carlo Methods in Practice*. Springer-Verlag, Berlin.

**Murphy**, R. (2000). *Introduction to AI Robotics*. MIT Press, Cambridge, Massachusetts.

**Muscettola**, N., Nayak, P., Pell, B., and Williams, B. (1998). Remote agent: To boldly go where no ai system has gone before. *Artificial Intelligence*, *103*, 5–48.

**Myerson**, R. B. (1991). *Game Theory: Analysis of Conflict*. Harvard University Press, Cambridge.

**Nagel**, T. (1974). What is it like to be a bat?. *Philosophical Review*, *83*, 435–450.

**Nalwa**, V. S. (1993). *A Guided Tour of Computer Vision*. Addison-Wesley, Reading, Massachusetts.

**Nash**, J. (1950). Equilibrium points in N-person games. *Proceedings of the National Academy of Sciences of the United States of America*, *36*, 48–49.

**Nau**, D. S. (1980). Pathology on game trees: A summary of results. In *Proceedings of the First Annual National Conference on Artificial Intelligence (AAAI-80)*, pp. 102–104, Stanford, California. AAAI.

**Nau**, D. S. (1983). Pathology on game trees revisited, and an alternative to minimaxing. *Artificial Intelligence*, *21*(1–2), 221–244.

**Nau**, D. S., Kumar, V., and Kanal, L. N. (1984). General branch and bound, and its relation to A* and AO*. *Artificial Intelligence*, *23*, 29–58.

**Naur**, P. (1963). Revised report on the algorithmic language Algol 60. *Communications of the Association for Computing Machinery*, *6*(1), 1–17.

**Nayak**, P. and Williams, B. (1997). Fast context switching in real-time propositional reasoning. In *Proceedings of the Fourteenth National Conference on Artificial Intelligence (AAAI-97)*, pp. 50–56, Providence, Rhode Island. AAAI Press.

**Neal**, R. (1996). *Bayesian Learning for Neural Networks*. Springer-Verlag, Berlin.

**Nebel**, B. (2000). On the compilability and expressive power of propositional planning formalisms. *Journal of AI Research*, *12*, 271–315.

**Nelson**, G. and Oppen, D. C. (1979). Simplification by cooperating decision procedures. *ACM Transactions on Programming Languages and Systems*, *1*(2), 245–257.

**Netto**, E. (1901). *Lehrbuch der Combinatorik*. B. G. Teubner, Leipzig.

**Nevill-Manning**, C. G. and Witten, I. H. (1997). Identifying hierarchical structures in sequences: A linear-time algorithm. *Journal of AI Research*, *7*, 67–82.

**Nevins**, A. J. (1975). Plane geometry theorem proving using forward chaining. *Artificial Intelligence*, *6*(1), 1–23.

**Newell**, A. (1982). The knowledge level. *Artificial Intelligence*, *18*(1), 82–127.

**Newell**, A. (1990). *Unified Theories of Cognition*. Harvard University Press, Cambridge, Massachusetts.

**Newell**, A. and Ernst, G. (1965). The search for generality. In Kalenich, W. A. (Ed.), *Information Processing 1965: Proceedings of IFIP Congress 1965*, Vol. 1, pp. 17–24, Chicago. Spartan.

**Newell**, A., Shaw, J. C., and Simon, H. A. (1957). Empirical explorations with the logic theory machine. *Proceedings of the Western Joint Computer Conference*, *15*, 218–239. Reprinted in Feigenbaum and Feldman (1963).

**Newell**, A., Shaw, J. C., and Simon, H. A. (1958). Chess playing programs and the problem of complexity. *IBM Journal of Research and Development*, *4*(2), 320–335.

**Newell**, A. and Simon, H. A. (1961). GPS, a program that simulates human thought. In Billing, H. (Ed.), *Lernende Automaten*, pp. 109–124. R. Oldenbourg, Munich.

**Newell**, A. and Simon, H. A. (1972). *Human Problem Solving*. Prentice-Hall, Upper Saddle River, New Jersey.

**Newell**, A. and Simon, H. A. (1976). Computer science as empirical inquiry: Symbols and search. *Communications of the Association for Computing Machinery*, *19*, 113–126.

**Newton**, I. (1664–1671). Methodus fluxionum et serierum infinitarum. Unpublished notes.

**Ng**, A. Y., Harada, D., and Russell, S. J. (1999). Policy invariance under reward transformations: Theory and application to reward shaping. In *Proceedings of the Sixteenth International Conference on Machine Learning*, Bled, Slovenia. Morgan Kaufmann.

**Ng**, A. Y. and Jordan, M. I. (2000). PEGASUS: A policy search method for large MDPs and POMDPs. In *Uncertainty in Artificial Intelligence: Proceedings of the Sixteenth Conference*, pp. 406–415, Stanford, California. Morgan Kaufmann.

**Nguyen**, X. and Kambhampati, S. (2001). Reviving partial order planning. In *Proceedings of the Seventeenth International Joint Conference on Artificial Intelligence (IJCAI-01)*, pp. 459–466, Seattle. Morgan Kaufmann.

**Nguyen**, X., Kambhampati, S., and Nigenda, R. S. (2001). Planning graph as the basis for deriving heuristics for plan synthesis by state space and CSP search. Tech. rep., Computer Science and Engineering Department, Arizona State University.

**Nicholson**, A. and Brady, J. M. (1992). The data association problem when monitoring robot vehicles using dynamic belief networks. In *ECAI 92: 10th European Conference on Artificial Intelligence Proceedings*, pp. 689–693, Vienna, Austria. Wiley.

**Niemelä**, I., Simons, P., and Syrjänen, T. (2000). Smodels: A system for answer set programming. In *Proceedings of the 8th International Workshop on Non-Monotonic Reasoning*.

**Nilsson**, D. and Lauritzen, S. (2000). Evaluating influence diagrams using LIMIDs. In *Uncertainty in Artificial Intelligence: Proceedings of the Sixteenth Conference*, pp. 436–445, Stanford, California. Morgan Kaufmann.

**Nilsson**, N. J. (1965). *Learning Machines: Foundations of Trainable Pattern-Classifying Systems*. McGraw-Hill, New York. republished in 1990.

**Nilsson**, N. J. (1971). *Problem-Solving Methods in Artificial Intelligence*. McGraw-Hill, New York.

**Nilsson**, N. J. (1980). *Principles of Artificial Intelligence*. Morgan Kaufmann, San Mateo, California.

**Nilsson**, N. J. (1984). Shakey the robot. Technical note 323, SRI International, Menlo Park, California.

**Nilsson**, N. J. (1986). Probabilistic logic. *Artificial Intelligence*, *28*(1), 71–87.

**Nilsson**, N. J. (1991). Logic and artificial intelligence. *Artificial Intelligence*, *47*(1–3), 31–56.

**Nilsson**, N. J. (1998). *Artificial Intelligence: A New Synthesis*. Morgan Kaufmann, San Mateo, California.

**Norvig**, P. (1988). Multiple simultaneous interpretations of ambiguous sentences. In *Proceedings of the 10th Annual Conference of the Cognitive Science Society*.

**Norvig**, P. (1992). *Paradigms of Artificial Intelligence Programming: Case Studies in Common Lisp*. Morgan Kaufmann, San Mateo, California.

**Nowick**, S. M., Dean, M. E., Dill, D. L., and Horowitz, M. (1993). The design of a high-performance cache controller: A case study in asynchronous synthesis. *Integration: The VLSI Journal*, *15*(3), 241–262.

**Nunberg**, G. (1979). The non-uniqueness of semantic solutions: Polysemy. *Language and Philosophy*, *3*(2), 143–184.

**Nussbaum**, M. C. (1978). *Aristotle's* De Motu Animalium. Princeton University Press, Princeton, New Jersey.

**Ogawa**, S., Lee, T.-M., Kay, A. R., and Tank, D. W. (1990). Brain magnetic resonance imaging with contrast dependent on blood oxygenation. *Proceedings of the National Academy of Sciences of the United States of America*, *87*, 9868–9872.

**Olawsky**, D. and Gini, M. (1990). Deferred planning and sensor use. In Sycara, K. P. (Ed.), *Proceedings, DARPA Workshop on Innovative Approaches to Planning, Scheduling, and Control*, San Diego, California. Defense Advanced Research Projects Agency (DARPA), Morgan Kaufmann.

**Olesen**, K. G. (1993). Causal probabilistic networks with both discrete and continuous variables. *IEEE Transactions on Pattern Analysis and Machine Intelligence (PAMI)*, *15*(3), 275–279.

**Oliver**, R. M. and Smith, J. Q. (Eds.). (1990). *Influence Diagrams, Belief Nets and Decision Analysis*. Wiley, New York.

**Olson**, C. F. (1994). Time and space efficient pose clustering. In *Proceedings of the IEEE Conference on Computer Vision and Pattern Recognition*, pp. 251–258, Washington, DC. IEEE Computer Society Press.

**Oncina**, J. and Garcia, P. (1992). Inferring regular languages in polynomial update time. In Perez, Sanfeliu, and Vidal (Eds.), *Pattern Recognition and Image Analysis*, pp. 49–61. World Scientific.

**O'Reilly**, U.-M. and Oppacher, F. (1994). Program search with a hierarchical variable length representation: Genetic programming, simulated annealing and hill climbing. In Davidor, Y., Schwefel, H.-P., and Manner, R. (Eds.), *Proceedings of the Third Conference on Parallel Problem Solving from Nature*, pp. 397–406, Jerusalem, Israel. Springer-Verlag.

**Ormoneit**, D. and Sen, S. (2002). Kernel-based reinforcement learning. *Machine Learning*, *49*(2–3), 161–178.

**Ortony**, A. (Ed.). (1979). *Metaphor and Thought*. Cambridge University Press, Cambridge, UK.

**Osborne**, M. J. and Rubinstein, A. (1994). *A Course in Game Theory*. MIT Press, Cambridge, Massachusetts.

**Osherson**, D. N., Stob, M., and Weinstein, S. (1986). *Systems That Learn: An Introduction to Learning Theory for Cognitive and Computer Scientists*. MIT Press, Cambridge, Massachusetts.

**Page**, C. D. and Srinivasan, A. (2002). ILP: A short look back and a longer look forward. Submitted to Journal of Machine Learning Research.

**Pak**, I. (2001). On mixing of certain random walks, cutoff phenomenon and sharp threshold of random matroid processes. *DAMATH: Discrete Applied Mathematics and Combinatorial Operations Research and Computer Science*, *110*, 251–272.

**Palay**, A. J. (1985). *Searching with Probabilities*. Pitman, London.

**Palmer**, D. A. and Hearst, M. A. (1994). Adaptive sentence boundary disambiguation. In *Proceedings of the Conference on Applied Natural Language Processing*, pp. 78–83. Morgan Kaufmann.

**Palmer**, S. (1999). *Vision Science: Photons to Phenomenology*. MIT Press, Cambridge, Massachusetts.

**Papadimitriou**, C. H. (1994). *Computational Complexity*. Addison Wesley.

**Papadimitriou**, C. H., Tamaki, H., Raghavan, P., and Vempala, S. (1998). Latent semantic indexing: A probabilistic analysis. In *Proceedings of the ACM Conference on Principles of Database Systems (PODS)*, pp. 159–168, New York. ACM Press.

**Papadimitriou**, C. H. and Tsitsiklis, J. N. (1987). The complexity of markov decision processes. *Mathematics of Operations Research*, *12*(3), 441–450.

**Papadimitriou**, C. H. and Yannakakis, M. (1991). Shortest paths without a map. *Theoretical Computer Science*, *84*(1), 127–150.

**Papavassiliou**, V. and Russell, S. J. (1999). Convergence of reinforcement learning with general function approximators. In *Proceedings of the Sixteenth International Joint Conference on Artificial Intelligence (IJCAI-99)*, pp. 748–757, Stockholm. Morgan Kaufmann.

**Parekh**, R. and Honavar, V. (2001). Dfa learning from simple examples. *Machine Learning*, *44*, 9–35.

**Parisi**, G. (1988). *Statistical field theory*. Addison-Wesley, Reading, Massachusetts.

**Parker**, D. B. (1985). Learning logic. Technical report TR-47, Center for Computational Research in Economics and Management Science, Massachusetts Institute of Technology, Cambridge, Massachusetts.

**Parker**, L. E. (1996). On the design of behavior-based multi-robot teams. *Journal of Advanced Robotics*, *10*(6).

**Parr**, R. and Russell, S. J. (1998). Reinforcement learning with hierarchies of machines. In Jordan, M. I., Kearns, M., and Solla, S. A. (Eds.), *Advances in Neural Information Processing Systems 10*. MIT Press, Cambridge, Massachusetts.

**Parzen**, E. (1962). On estimation of a probability density function and mode. *Annals of Mathematical Statistics*, *33*, 1065–1076.

**Pasula**, H. and Russell, S. J. (2001). Approximate inference for first-order probabilistic languages. In *Proceedings of the Seventeenth International Joint Conference on Artificial Intelligence (IJCAI-01)*, Seattle. Morgan Kaufmann.

**Pasula**, H., Russell, S. J., Ostland, M., and Ritov, Y. (1999). Tracking many objects with many sensors. In *Proceedings of the Sixteenth International Joint Conference on Artificial Intelligence (IJCAI-99)*, Stockholm. Morgan Kaufmann.

**Paterson**, M. S. and Wegman, M. N. (1978). Linear unification. *Journal of Computer and System Sciences*, *16*, 158–167.

**Patrick**, B. G., Almulla, M., and Newborn, M. M. (1992). An upper bound on the time complexity of iterative-deepening-A*. *Annals of Mathematics and Artificial Intelligence*, *5*(2–4), 265–278.

**Patten**, T. (1988). *Systemic Text Generation as Problem Solving*. Studies in Natural Language Processing. Cambridge University Press, Cambridge, UK.

**Paul**, R. P. (1981). *Robot Manipulators: Mathematics, Programming, and Control*. MIT Press, Cambridge, Massachusetts.

**Peano**, G. (1889). *Arithmetices principia, nova methodo exposita*. Fratres Bocca, Turin.

**Pearl**, J. (1982a). Reverend Bayes on inference engines: A distributed hierarchical approach. In *Proceedings of the National Conference on Artificial Intelligence (AAAI-82)*, pp. 133–136, Pittsburgh, Pennsylvania. Morgan Kaufmann.

**Pearl**, J. (1982b). The solution for the branching factor of the alpha–beta pruning algorithm and its optimality. *Communications of the Association for Computing Machinery*, *25*(8), 559–564.

**Pearl**, J. (1984). *Heuristics: Intelligent Search Strategies for Computer Problem Solving*. Addison-Wesley, Reading, Massachusetts.

**Pearl**, J. (1986). Fusion, propagation, and structuring in belief networks. *Artificial Intelligence*, *29*, 241–288.

**Pearl**, J. (1987). Evidential reasoning using stochastic simulation of causal models. *Artificial Intelligence*, *32*, 247–257.

**Pearl**, J. (1988). *Probabilistic Reasoning in Intelligent Systems: Networks of Plausible Inference*. Morgan Kaufmann, San Mateo, California.

**Pearl**, J. (2000). *Causality: Models, Reasoning, and Inference*. Cambridge University Press, Cambridge, UK.

**Pearl**, J. and Verma, T. (1991). A theory of inferred causation. In Allen, J. A., Fikes, R., and Sandewall, E. (Eds.), *Proceedings of the 2nd International Conference on Principles of Knowledge Representation and Reasoning*, pp. 441–452, San Mateo, California. Morgan Kaufmann.

**Pearson**, J. and Jeavons, P. (1997). A survey of tractable constraint satisfaction problems. Technical report CSD-TR-97-15, Royal Holloway College, U. of London.

**Pednault**, E. P. D. (1986). Formulating multiagent, dynamic-world problems in the classical planning framework. In Georgeff, M. P. and Lansky, A. L. (Eds.), *Reasoning about Actions and Plans: Proceedings of the 1986 Workshop*, pp. 47–82, Timberline, Oregon. Morgan Kaufmann.

**Peirce**, C. S. (1870). Description of a notation for the logic of relatives, resulting from an amplification of the conceptions of Boole's calculus of logic. *Memoirs of the American Academy of Arts and Sciences*, *9*, 317–378.

**Peirce**, C. S. (1883). A theory of probable inference. Note B. The logic of relatives. In *Studies in Logic by Members of the Johns Hopkins University*, pp. 187–203, Boston.

**Peirce**, C. S. (1902). Logic as semiotic: The theory of signs. Unpublished manuscript; reprinted in (Buchler 1955).

**Peirce**, C. S. (1909). Existential graphs. Unpublished manuscript; reprinted in (Buchler 1955).

**Pelikan**, M., Goldberg, D. E., and Cantu-Paz, E. (1999). BOA: The Bayesian optimization algorithm. In *GECCO-99: Proceedings of the Genetic and Evolutionary Computation Conference*, pp. 525–532, Orlando, Florida. Morgan Kaufmann.

**Pemberton**, J. C. and Korf, R. E. (1992). Incremental planning on graphs with cycles. In Hendler, J. (Ed.), *Artificial Intelligence Planning Systems: Proceedings of the First International Conference*, pp. 525–532, College Park, Maryland. Morgan Kaufmann.

**Penberthy**, J. S. and Weld, D. S. (1992). UCPOP: A sound, complete, partial order planner for ADL. In *Proceedings of KR-92*, pp. 103–114. Morgan Kaufmann.

**Peng**, J. and Williams, R. J. (1993). Efficient learning and planning within the Dyna framework. *Adaptive Behavior*, *2*, 437–454.

**Penrose**, R. (1989). *The Emperor's New Mind*. Oxford University Press, Oxford, UK.

**Penrose**, R. (1994). *Shadows of the Mind*. Oxford University Press, Oxford, UK.

**Peot**, M. and Smith, D. E. (1992). Conditional nonlinear planning. In Hendler, J. (Ed.), *Proceedings of the First International Conference on AI Planning Systems*, pp. 189–197, College Park, Maryland. Morgan Kaufmann.

**Pereira**, F. and Shieber, S. M. (1987). *Prolog and Natural-Language Analysis*. Center for the Study of Language and Information (CSLI), Stanford, California.

**Pereira**, F. and Warren, D. H. D. (1980). Definite clause grammars for language analysis: A survey of the formalism and a comparison with augmented transition networks. *Artificial Intelligence*, *13*, 231–278.

**Peterson**, C. and Anderson, J. R. (1987). A mean field theory learning algorithm for neural networks. *Complex Systems*, *1*(5), 995–1019.

**Pfeffer**, A. (2000). *Probabilistic Reasoning for Complex Systems*. Ph.D. thesis, Stanford University, Stanford, California.

**Pinker**, S. (1989). *Learnability and Cognition*. MIT Press, Cambridge, MA.

**Pinker**, S. (1995). Language acquisition. In Gleitman, L. R., Liberman, M., and Osherson, D. N. (Eds.), *An Invitation to Cognitive Science* (second edition)., Vol. 1. MIT Press, Cambridge, Massachusetts.

**Pinker**, S. (2000). *The Language Instinct: How the Mind Creates Language*. MIT Press, Cambridge, Massachusetts.

**Plaat**, A., Schaeffer, J., Pijls, W., and de Bruin, A. (1996). Best-first fixed-depth minimax algorithms. *Artificial Intelligence Journal*, *87*(1–2), 255–293.

**Place**, U. T. (1956). Is consciousness a brain process?. *British Journal of Psychology*, *47*, 44–50.

**Plotkin**, G. (1971). *Automatic Methods of Inductive Inference*. Ph.D. thesis, Edinburgh University.

**Plotkin**, G. (1972). Building-in equational theories. In Meltzer, B. and Michie, D. (Eds.), *Machine Intelligence 7*, pp. 73–90. Edinburgh University Press, Edinburgh, Scotland.

**Pnueli**, A. (1977). The temporal logic of programs. In *Proceedings of the 18th IEEE Symposium on the Foundations of Computer Science (FOCS-77)*, pp. 46–57, Providence, Rhode Island. IEEE, IEEE Computer Society Press.

**Pohl**, I. (1969). Bi-directional and heuristic search in path problems. Tech. rep. 104, SLAC (Stanford Linear Accelerator Center, Stanford, California.

**Pohl**, I. (1970). First results on the effect of error in heuristic search. In Meltzer, B. and Michie, D. (Eds.), *Machine Intelligence 5*, pp. 219–236. Elsevier/North-Holland, Amsterdam, London, New York.

**Pohl**, I. (1971). Bi-directional search. In Meltzer, B. and Michie, D. (Eds.), *Machine Intelligence 6*, pp. 127–140. Edinburgh University Press, Edinburgh, Scotland.

**Pohl**, I. (1973). The avoidance of (relative) catastrophe, heuristic competence, genuine dynamic weighting and computational issues in heuristic problem solving. In *Proceedings of the Third International Joint Conference on Artificial Intelligence (IJCAI-73)*, pp. 20–23, Stanford, California. IJCAII.

**Pohl**, I. (1977). Practical and theoretical considerations in heuristic search algorithms. In Elcock, E. W. and Michie, D. (Eds.), *Machine Intelligence 8*, pp. 55–72. Ellis Horwood, Chichester, England.

**Pomerleau**, D. A. (1993). *Neural Network Perception for Mobile Robot Guidance*. Kluwer, Dordrecht, Netherlands.

**Ponte**, J. M. and Croft, W. B. (1998). A language modeling approach to information retrieval. In *Research and Development in Information Retrieval*, pp. 275–281.

**Poole**, D. (1993). Probabilistic Horn abduction and Bayesian networks. *Artificial Intelligence*, *64*, 81–129.

**Poole**, D., Mackworth, A. K., and Goebel, R. (1998). *Computational intelligence: A logical approach*. Oxford University Press, Oxford, UK.

**Popper**, K. R. (1959). *The Logic of Scientific Discovery*. Basic Books, New York.

**Popper**, K. R. (1962). *Conjectures and Refutations: The Growth of Scientific Knowledge*. Basic Books, New York.

**Porter**, M. F. (1980). An algorithm for suffix stripping. *Program*, *13*(3), 130–137.

**Post**, E. L. (1921). Introduction to a general theory of elementary propositions. *American Journal of Mathematics*, *43*, 163–185.

**Pradhan**, M., Provan, G. M., Middleton, B., and Henrion, M. (1994). Knowledge engineering for large belief networks. In *Uncertainty in Artificial Intelligence: Proceedings of the Tenth Conference*, pp. 484–490, Seattle, Washington. Morgan Kaufmann.

**Pratt**, V. R. (1976). Semantical considerations on Floyd-Hoare logic. In *Proceedings of the 17th IEEE Symposium on the Foundations of Computer Science*, pp. 109–121. IEEE Computer Society Press.

**Prawitz**, D. (1960). An improved proof procedure. *Theoria*, *26*, 102–139.

**Prawitz**, D. (1965). *Natural Deduction: A Proof Theoretical Study*. Almquist and Wiksell, Stockholm.

**Press**, W. H., Teukolsky, S. A., Vetterling, W. T., and Flannery, B. P. (2002). *Numerical Recipes in C++: The Art of Scientific Computing* (Second edition). Cambridge University Press, Cambridge, UK.

**Prieditis**, A. E. (1993). Machine discovery of effective admissible heuristics. *Machine Learning*, *12*(1–3), 117–141.

**Prinz**, D. G. (1952). Robot chess. *Research*, *5*, 261–266.

**Prior**, A. N. (1967). *Past, Present, and Future*. Oxford University Press, Oxford, UK.

**Prosser**, P. (1993). Hybrid algorithms for constraint satisfaction problems. *Computational Intelligence*, *9*, 268–299.

**Pryor**, L. and Collins, G. (1996). Planning for contingencies: A decision-based approach. *Journal of Artificial Intelligence Research*, *4*, 287–339.

**Pullum**, G. K. (1991). *The Great Eskimo Vocabulary Hoax (and Other Irreverent Essays on the Study of Language)*. University of Chicago Press, Chicago.

**Pullum**, G. K. (1996). Learnability, hyperlearning, and the poverty of the stimulus. In *22nd Annual Meeting of the Berkeley Linguistics Society*.

**Puterman**, M. L. (1994). *Markov Decision Processes: Discrete Stochastic Dynamic Programming*. Wiley, New York.

**Puterman**, M. L. and Shin, M. C. (1978). Modified policy iteration algorithms for discounted Markov decision problems. *Management Science*, *24*(11), 1127–1137.

**Putnam**, H. (1960). Minds and machines. In Hook, S. (Ed.), *Dimensions of Mind*, pp. 138–164. Macmillan, London.

**Putnam**, H. (1963). 'Degree of confirmation' and inductive logic. In Schilpp, P. A. (Ed.), *The Philosophy of Rudolf Carnap*, pp. 270–292. Open Court, La Salle, Illinois.

**Putnam**, H. (1967). The nature of mental states. In Capitan, W. H. and Merrill, D. D. (Eds.), *Art, Mind, and Religion*, pp. 37–48. University of Pittsburgh Press, Pittsburgh.

**Pylyshyn**, Z. W. (1974). Minds, machines and phenomenology: Some reflections on Dreyfus' "What Computers Can't Do". *International Journal of Cognitive Psychology*, *3*(1), 57–77.

**Pylyshyn**, Z. W. (1984). *Computation and Cognition: Toward a Foundation for Cognitive Science*. MIT Press, Cambridge, Massachusetts.

**Quillian**, M. R. (1961). A design for an understanding machine. Paper presented at a colloquium: Semantic Problems in Natural Language, King's College, Cambridge, England.

**Quine**, W. V. (1953). Two dogmas of empiricism. In *From a Logical Point of View*, pp. 20–46. Harper and Row, New York.

**Quine**, W. V. (1960). *Word and Object*. MIT Press, Cambridge, Massachusetts.

**Quine**, W. V. (1982). *Methods of Logic* (Fourth edition). Harvard University Press, Cambridge, Massachusetts.

**Quinlan**, E. and O'Brien, S. (1992). Sublanguage: Characteristics and selection guidelines for MT. In *AI and Cognitive Science '92: Proceedings of Annual Irish Conference on Artificial Intelligence and Cognitive Science '92*, pp. 342–345, Limerick, Ireland. Springer-Verlag.

**Quinlan**, J. R. (1979). Discovering rules from large collections of examples: A case study. In Michie, D. (Ed.), *Expert Systems in the Microelectronic Age*. Edinburgh University Press, Edinburgh, Scotland.

**Quinlan**, J. R. (1986). Induction of decision trees. *Machine Learning*, *1*, 81–106.

**Quinlan**, J. R. (1990). Learning logical definitions from relations. *Machine Learning*, *5*(3), 239–266.

**Quinlan**, J. R. (1993). *C4.5: Programs for machine learning*. Morgan Kaufmann, San Mateo, California.

**Quinlan**, J. R. and Cameron-Jones, R. M. (1993). FOIL: a midterm report. In Brazdil, P. B. (Ed.), *European Conference on Machine Learning Proceedings (ECML-93)*, pp. 3–20, Vienna. Springer-Verlag.

**Quirk**, R., Greenbaum, S., Leech, G., and Svartvik, J. (1985). *A Comprehensive Grammar of the English Language*. Longman, New York.

**Rabani**, Y., Rabinovich, Y., and Sinclair, A. (1998). A computational view of population genetics. *Random Structures and Algorithms*, *12*(4), 313–334.

**Rabiner**, L. R. and Juang, B.-H. (1993). *Fundamentals of Speech Recognition*. Prentice-Hall, Upper Saddle River, New Jersey.

**Ramakrishnan**, R. and Ullman, J. D. (1995). A survey of research in deductive database systems. *Journal of Logic Programming*, *23*(2), 125–149.

**Ramsey**, F. P. (1931). Truth and probability. In Braithwaite, R. B. (Ed.), *The Foundations of Mathematics and Other Logical Essays*. Harcourt Brace Jovanovich, New York.

**Raphson**, J. (1690). *Analysis aequationum universalis*. Apud Abelem Swalle, London.

**Rassenti**, S., Smith, V., and Bulfin, R. (1982). A combinatorial auction mechanism for airport time slot allocation.. *Bell Journal of Economics*, *13*, 402–417.

**Ratner**, D. and Warmuth, M. (1986). Finding a shortest solution for the $n \times n$ extension of the 15-puzzle is intractable. In *Proceedings of the Fifth National Conference on Artificial Intelligence (AAAI-86)*, Vol. 1, pp. 168–172, Philadelphia. Morgan Kaufmann.

**Rauch**, H. E., Tung, F., and Striebel, C. T. (1965). Maximum likelihood estimates of linear dynamic systems. *AIAA Journal*, *3*(8), 1445–1450.

**Rechenberg**, I. (1965). Cybernetic solution path of an experimental problem. Library translation 1122, Royal Aircraft Establishment.

**Rechenberg**, I. (1973). *Evolutionsstrategie: Optimierung technischer Systeme nach Prinzipien der biologischen Evolution*. Frommann-Holzboog, Stuttgart, Germany.

**Regin**, J. (1994). A filtering algorithm for constraints of difference in CSPs. In *Proceedings of the Twelfth National Conference on Artificial Intelligence (AAAI-94)*, pp. 362–367, Seattle. AAAI Press.

**Reichenbach**, H. (1949). *The Theory of Probability: An Inquiry into the Logical and Mathematical Foundations of the Calculus of Probability* (Second edition). University of California Press, Berkeley and Los Angeles.

**Reif**, J. (1979). Complexity of the mover's problem and generalizations. In *Proceedings of the 20th IEEE Symposium on Foundations of Computer Science*, pp. 421–427, San Juan, Puerto Rico. IEEE, IEEE Computer Society Press.

**Reiter**, E. and Dale, R. (2000). *Building Natural Language Generation Systems*. Studies in Natural Language Processing. Cambridge University Press, Cambridge, UK.

**Reiter**, R. (1980). A logic for default reasoning. *Artificial Intelligence*, *13*(1–2), 81–132.

**Reiter**, R. (1991). The frame problem in the situation calculus: A simple solution (sometimes) and a completeness result for goal regression. In Lifschitz, V. (Ed.), *Artificial Intelligence and Mathematical Theory of Computation: Papers in Honor of John McCarthy*, pp. 359–380. Academic Press, New York.

**Reiter**, R. (2001a). On knowledge-based programming with sensing in the situation calculus. *ACM Transactions on Computational Logic*, *2*(4), 433–457.

**Reiter**, R. (2001b). *Knowledge in Action: Logical Foundations for Specifying and Implementing Dynamical Systems*. MIT Press, Cambridge, Massachusetts.

**Reitman**, W. and Wilcox, B. (1979). The structure and performance of the INTERIM.2 Go program. In *Proceedings of the Sixth International Joint Conference on Artificial Intelligence (IJCAI-79)*, pp. 711–719, Tokyo. IJCAII.

**Remus**, H. (1962). Simulation of a learning machine for playing Go. In *Proceedings IFIP Congress*, pp. 428–432, Amsterdam, London, New York. Elsevier/North-Holland.

**Rényi**, A. (1970). *Probability Theory*. Elsevier/North-Holland, Amsterdam, London, New York.

**Rescher**, N. and Urquhart, A. (1971). *Temporal Logic*. Springer-Verlag, Berlin.

**Reynolds**, C. W. (1987). Flocks, herds, and schools: A distributed behavioral model. *Computer Graphics*, *21*, 25–34. SIGGRAPH '87 Conference Proceedings.

**Rich**, E. and Knight, K. (1991). *Artificial Intelligence* (second edition). McGraw-Hill, New York.

**Richardson**, M., Bilmes, J., and Diorio, C. (2000). Hidden-articulator Markov models: Performance improvements and robustness to noise. In *ICASSP-2000: 2000 International Conference on Acoustics, Speech, and Signal Processing*, Los Alamitos, CA. IEEE Computer Society Press.

**Rieger**, C. (1976). An organization of knowledge for problem solving and language comprehension. *Artificial Intelligence*, *7*, 89–127.

**Ringle**, M. (1979). *Philosophical Perspectives in Artificial Intelligence*. Humanities Press, Atlantic Highlands, New Jersey.

**Rintanen**, J. (1999). Improvements to the evaluation of quantified boolean formulae. In *Proceedings of the Sixteenth International Joint Conference on Artificial Intelligence (IJCAI-99)*, pp. 1192–1197, Stockholm. Morgan Kaufmann.

**Ripley**, B. D. (1996). *Pattern Recognition and Neural Networks*. Cambridge University Press, Cambridge, UK.

**Rissanen**, J. (1984). Universal coding, information, prediction, and estimation. *IEEE Transactions on Information Theory*, *IT-30*(4), 629–636.

**Ritchie**, G. D. and Hanna, F. K. (1984). AM: A case study in AI methodology. *Artificial Intelligence*, *23*(3), 249–268.

**Rivest**, R. (1987). Learning decision lists. *Machine Learning*, *2*(3), 229–246.

**Roberts**, L. G. (1963). Machine perception of three-dimensional solids. Technical report 315, MIT Lincoln Laboratory.

**Robertson**, N. and Seymour, P. D. (1986). Graph minors. ii. Algorithmic aspects of tree-width. *Journal of Algorithms*, *7*(3), 309–322.

**Robertson**, S. E. (1977). The probability ranking principle in ir. *Journal of Documentation*, *33*, 294–304.

**Robertson**, S. E. and Sparck Jones, K. (1976). Relevance weighting of search terms. *Journal of the American Society for Information Science*, *27*, 129–146.

**Robinson**, J. A. (1965). A machine-oriented logic based on the resolution principle. *Journal of the Association for Computing Machinery*, *12*, 23–41.

**Roche**, E. and Schabes, Y. (1997). *Finite-State Language Processing (Language, Speech and Communication)*. Bradford Books, Cambridge.

**Rock**, I. (1984). *Perception*. W. H. Freeman, New York.

**Rorty**, R. (1965). Mind-body identity, privacy, and categories. *Review of Metaphysics*, *19*(1), 24–54.

**Rosenblatt**, F. (1957). The perceptron: A perceiving and recognizing automaton. Report 85-460-1, Project PARA, Cornell Aeronautical Laboratory, Ithaca, New York.

**Rosenblatt**, F. (1960). On the convergence of reinforcement procedures in simple perceptrons. Report VG-1196-G-4, Cornell Aeronautical Laboratory, Ithaca, New York.

**Rosenblatt**, F. (1962). *Principles of Neurodynamics: Perceptrons and the Theory of Brain Mechanisms*. Spartan, Chicago.

**Rosenblatt**, M. (1956). Remarks on some nonparametric estimates of a density function. *Annals of Mathematical Statistics*, *27*, 832–837.

**Rosenblueth**, A., Wiener, N., and Bigelow, J. (1943). Behavior, purpose, and teleology. *Philosophy of Science*, *10*, 18–24.

**Rosenschein**, J. S. and Zlotkin, G. (1994). *Rules of Encounter*. MIT Press, Cambridge, Massachusetts.

**Rosenschein**, S. J. (1985). Formal theories of knowledge in AI and robotics. *New Generation Computing*, *3*(4), 345–357.

**Rosenthal**, D. M. (Ed.). (1971). *Materialism and the Mind-Body Problem*. Prentice-Hall, Upper Saddle River, New Jersey.

**Ross**, S. M. (1988). *A First Course in Probability* (third edition). Macmillan, London.

**Roussel**, P. (1975). Prolog: Manual de reference et d'utilization. Tech. rep., Groupe d'Intelligence Artificielle, Université d'Aix-Marseille.

**Rouveirol**, C. and Puget, J.-F. (1989). A simple and general solution for inverting resolution. In *Proceedings of the European Working Session on Learning*, pp. 201–210, Porto, Portugal. Pitman.

**Rowat**, P. F. (1979). *Representing the Spatial Experience and Solving Spatial problems in a Simulated Robot Environment*. Ph.D. thesis, University of British Columbia, Vancouver, BC, Canada.

**Roweis**, S. T. and Ghahramani, Z. (1999). A unifying review of Linear Gaussian Models. *Neural Computation*, *11*(2), 305–345.

**Rubin**, D. (1988). Using the SIR algorithm to simulate posterior distributions. In Bernardo, J. M., de Groot, M. H., Lindley, D. V., and Smith, A. F. M. (Eds.), *Bayesian Statistics 3*, pp. 395–402. Oxford University Press, Oxford, UK.

**Rumelhart**, D. E., Hinton, G. E., and Williams, R. J. (1986a). Learning internal representations by error propagation. In Rumelhart, D. E. and McClelland, J. L. (Eds.), *Parallel Distributed Processing*, Vol. 1, chap. 8, pp. 318–362. MIT Press, Cambridge, Massachusetts.

**Rumelhart**, D. E., Hinton, G. E., and Williams, R. J. (1986b). Learning representations by back-propagating errors. *Nature*, *323*, 533–536.

**Rumelhart**, D. E. and McClelland, J. L. (Eds.). (1986). *Parallel Distributed Processing*. MIT Press, Cambridge, Massachusetts.

**Ruspini**, E. H., Lowrance, J. D., and Strat, T. M. (1992). Understanding evidential reasoning. *International Journal of Approximate Reasoning*, *6*(3), 401–424.

**Russell**, J. G. B. (1990). Is screening for abdominal aortic aneurysm worthwhile?. *Clinical Radiology*, *41*, 182–184.

**Russell**, S. J. (1985). The compleat guide to MRS. Report STAN-CS-85-1080, Computer Science Department, Stanford University.

**Russell**, S. J. (1986). A quantitative analysis of analogy by similarity. In *Proceedings of the Fifth National Conference on Artificial Intelligence (AAAI-86)*, pp. 284–288, Philadelphia. Morgan Kaufmann.

**Russell**, S. J. (1988). Tree-structured bias. In *Proceedings of the Seventh National Conference on Artificial Intelligence (AAAI-88)*, Vol. 2, pp. 641–645, St. Paul, Minnesota. Morgan Kaufmann.

**Russell**, S. J. (1992). Efficient memory-bounded search methods. In *ECAI 92: 10th European Conference on Artificial Intelligence Proceedings*, pp. 1–5, Vienna. Wiley.

**Russell**, S. J. (1998). Learning agents for uncertain environments (extended abstract). In *Proceedings of the Eleventh Annual ACM Workshop on Computational Learning Theory (COLT-98)*, pp. 101–103, Madison, Wisconsin. ACM Press.

**Russell**, S. J., Binder, J., Koller, D., and Kanazawa, K. (1995). Local learning in probabilistic networks with hidden variables. In *Proceedings of the Fourteenth International Joint Conference on Artificial Intelligence (IJCAI-95)*, pp. 1146–52, Montreal. Morgan Kaufmann.

**Russell**, S. J. and Grosof, B. (1987). A declarative approach to bias in concept learning. In *Proceedings of the Sixth National Conference on Artificial Intelligence (AAAI-87)*, Seattle. Morgan Kaufmann.

**Russell**, S. J. and Norvig, P. (1995). *Artificial Intelligence: A Modern Approach*. Prentice-Hall, Upper Saddle River, New Jersey.

**Russell**, S. J. and Subramanian, D. (1995). Provably bounded-optimal agents. *Journal of Artificial Intelligence Research*, *3*, 575–609.

**Russell**, S. J., Subramanian, D., and Parr, R. (1993). Provably bounded optimal agents. In *Proceedings of the Thirteenth International Joint Conference on Artificial Intelligence (IJCAI-93)*, pp. 338–345, Chambery, France. Morgan Kaufmann.

**Russell**, S. J. and Wefald, E. H. (1989). On optimal game-tree search using rational meta-reasoning. In *Proceedings of the Eleventh International Joint Conference on Artificial Intelligence (IJCAI-89)*, pp. 334–340, Detroit. Morgan Kaufmann.

**Russell**, S. J. and Wefald, E. H. (1991). *Do the Right Thing: Studies in Limited Rationality*. MIT Press, Cambridge, Massachusetts.

**Rustagi**, J. S. (1976). *Variational Methods in Statistics*. Academic Press, New York.

**Ryder**, J. L. (1971). Heuristic analysis of large trees as generated in the game of Go. Memo AIM-155, Stanford Artificial Intelligence Project, Computer Science Department, Stanford University, Stanford, California.

**Sabin**, D. and Freuder, E. C. (1994). Contradicting conventional wisdom in constraint satisfaction. In *ECAI 94: 11th European Conference on Artificial Intelligence. Proceedings*, pp. 125–129, Amsterdam. Wiley.

**Sacerdoti**, E. D. (1974). Planning in a hierarchy of abstraction spaces. *Artificial Intelligence*, *5*(2), 115–135.

**Sacerdoti**, E. D. (1975). The nonlinear nature of plans. In *Proceedings of the Fourth International Joint Conference on Artificial Intelligence (IJCAI-75)*, pp. 206–214, Tbilisi, Georgia. IJCAII.

**Sacerdoti**, E. D. (1977). *A Structure for Plans and Behavior*. Elsevier/North-Holland, Amsterdam, London, New York.

**Sacerdoti**, E. D., Fikes, R. E., Reboh, R., Sagalowicz, D., Waldinger, R., and Wilber, B. M. (1976). QLISP—a language for the interactive development of complex systems. In *Proceedings of the AFIPS National Computer Conference*, pp. 349–356.

**Sacks**, E. and Joskowicz, L. (1993). Automated modeling and kinematic simulation of mechanisms. *Computer Aided Design*, *25*(2), 106–118.

**Sadri**, F. and Kowalski, R. (1995). Variants of the event calculus. In *International Conference on Logic Programming*, pp. 67–81.

**Sag**, I. and Wasow, T. (1999). *Syntactic Theory: An Introduction*. CSLI Publications, Stanford, California.

**Sager**, N. (1981). *Natural Language Information Processing: A Computer Grammar of English and Its Applications*. Addison-Wesley, Reading, Massachusetts.

**Sahami**, M., Dumais, S. T., Heckerman, D., and Horvitz, E. J. (1998). A Bayesian approach to filtering junk E-mail. In *Learning for Text Categorization: Papers from the 1998 Workshop*, Madison, Wisconsin. AAAI Technical Report WS-98-05.

**Sahami**, M., Hearst, M. A., and Saund, E. (1996). Applying the multiple cause mixture model to text categorization. In Saitta, L. (Ed.), *Proceedings of ICML-96, 13th International Conference on Machine Learning*, pp. 435–443, Bari, Italy. Morgan Kaufmann Publishers.

**Salomaa**, A. (1969). Probabilistic and weighted grammars. *Information and Control*, *15*, 529–544.

**Salton**, G. and McGill, M. J. (1983). *Introduction to Modern Information Retrieval*. McGraw-Hill, New York, NY.

**Salton**, G., Wong, A., and Yang, C. S. (1975). A vector space model for automatic indexing. *Communications of the ACM*, *18*(11), 613–620.

**Samuel**, A. L. (1959). Some studies in machine learning using the game of checkers. *IBM Journal of Research and Development*, *3*(3), 210–229.

**Samuel**, A. L. (1967). Some studies in machine learning using the game of checkers II—Recent progress. *IBM Journal of Research and Development*, *11*(6), 601–617.

**Samuelsson**, C. and Rayner, M. (1991). Quantitative evaluation of explanation-based learning as an optimization tool for a large-scale natural language system. In *Proceedings of the Twelfth International Joint Conference on Artificial Intelligence (IJCAI-91)*, pp. 609–615, Sydney. Morgan Kaufmann.

**Sato**, T. and Kameya, Y. (1997). PRISM: A symbolic-statistical modeling language. In *Proceedings of the Fifteenth International Joint Conference on Artificial Intelligence (IJCAI-97)*, pp. 1330–1335, Nagoya, Japan. Morgan Kaufmann.

**Saul**, L. K., Jaakkola, T., and Jordan, M. I. (1996). Mean field theory for sigmoid belief networks. *Journal of Artificial Intelligence Research*, *4*, 61–76.

**Savage**, L. J. (1954). *The Foundations of Statistics*. Wiley, New York.

**Sayre**, K. (1993). Three more flaws in the computational model. Paper presented at the APA (Central Division) Annual Conference, Chicago, Illinois.

**Schabes**, Y., Abeille, A., and Joshi, A. K. (1988). Parsing strategies with lexicalized grammars: Application to tree adjoining grammars. In Vargha, D. (Ed.), *Proceedings of the 12th International Conference on Computational Linguistics (COLING)*, Vol. 2, pp. 578–583, Budapest. John von Neumann Society for Computer Science.

**Schaeffer**, J. (1997). *One Jump Ahead: Challenging Human Supremacy in Checkers*. Springer-Verlag, Berlin.

**Schank**, R. C. and Abelson, R. P. (1977). *Scripts, Plans, Goals, and Understanding*. Lawrence Erlbaum Associates, Potomac, Maryland.

**Schank**, R. C. and Riesbeck, C. (1981). *Inside Computer Understanding: Five Programs Plus Miniatures*. Lawrence Erlbaum Associates, Potomac, Maryland.

**Schapire**, R. E. (1999). Theoretical views of boosting and applications. In *Algorithmic Learning Theory: Proceedings of the 10th International Conference (ALT'99)*, pp. 13–25. Springer-Verlag, Berlin.

**Schapire**, R. E. (1990). The strength of weak learnability. *Machine Learning*, *5*(2), 197–227.

**Schmolze**, J. G. and Lipkis, T. A. (1983). Classification in the KL-ONE representation system. In *Proceedings of the Eighth International Joint Conference on Artificial Intelligence (IJCAI-83)*, pp. 330–332, Karlsruhe, Germany. Morgan Kaufmann.

**Schofield**, P. D. A. (1967). Complete solution of the eight puzzle. In Dale, E. and Michie, D. (Eds.), *Machine Intelligence 2*, pp. 125–133. Elsevier/North-Holland, Amsterdam, London, New York.

**Schölkopf**, B. and Smola, A. J. (2002). *Learning with Kernels*. MIT Press, Cambridge, Massachusetts.

**Schöning**, T. (1999). A probabilistic algorithm for k-SAT and constraint satisfaction problems. In *40th Annual Symposium on Foundations of Computer Science*, pp. 410–414, New York. IEEE Computer Society Press.

**Schoppers**, M. J. (1987). Universal plans for reactive robots in unpredictable environments. In *Proceedings of the Tenth International Joint Conference on Artificial Intelligence (IJCAI-87)*, pp. 1039–1046, Milan. Morgan Kaufmann.

**Schoppers**, M. J. (1989). In defense of reaction plans as caches. *AI Magazine*, *10*(4), 51–60.

**Schröder**, E. (1877). *Der Operationskreis des Logikkalküls*. B. G. Teubner, Leipzig.

**Schultz**, W., Dayan, P., and Montague, P. R. (1997). A neural substrate of prediction and reward. *Science*, *275*, 1593.

**Schütze**, H. (1995). *Ambiguity in Language Learning: Computational and Cognitive Models*. Ph.D. thesis, Stanford University. Also published by CSLI Press, 1997.

**Schwartz**, J. T., Scharir, M., and Hopcroft, J. (1987). *Planning, Geometry and Complexity of Robot Motion*. Ablex Publishing Corporation, Norwood, NJ.

**Schwartz**, S. P. (Ed.). (1977). *Naming, Necessity, and Natural Kinds*. Cornell University Press, Ithaca, New York.

**Scott**, D. and Krauss, P. (1966). Assigning probabilities to logical formulas. In Hintikka, J. and Suppes, P. (Eds.), *Aspects of Inductive Logic*. North-Holland, Amsterdam.

**Scriven**, M. (1953). The mechanical concept of mind. *Mind*, *62*, 230–240.

**Searle**, J. R. (1969). *Speech Acts: An Essay in the Philosophy of Language*. Cambridge University Press, Cambridge, UK.

**Searle**, J. R. (1980). Minds, brains, and programs. *Behavioral and Brain Sciences*, *3*, 417–457.

**Searle**, J. R. (1984). *Minds, Brains and Science*. Harvard University Press, Cambridge, Massachusetts.

**Searle**, J. R. (1990). Is the brain's mind a computer program?. *Scientific American*, *262*, 26–31.

**Searle**, J. R. (1992). *The Rediscovery of the Mind*. MIT Press, Cambridge, Massachusetts.

**Selman**, B., Kautz, H., and Cohen, B. (1996). Local search strategies for satisfiability testing. In *DIMACS Series in Discrete Mathematics and Theoretical Computer Science, Volume 26*, pp. 521–532. American Mathematical Society, Providence, Rhode Island.

**Selman**, B. and Levesque, H. J. (1993). The complexity of path-based defeasible inheritance. *Artificial Intelligence*, *62*(2), 303–339.

**Selman**, B., Levesque, H. J., and Mitchell, D. (1992). A new method for solving hard satisfiability problems. In *Proceedings of the Tenth National Conference on Artificial Intelligence (AAAI-92)*, pp. 440–446, San Jose. AAAI Press.

**Shachter**, R. D. (1986). Evaluating influence diagrams. *Operations Research*, *34*, 871–882.

**Shachter**, R. D. (1998). Bayes-ball: The rational pastime (for determining irrelevance and requisite information in belief networks and influence diagrams). In *Uncertainty in Artificial Intelligence: Proceedings of the Fourteenth Conference*, pp. 480–487, Madison, Wisconsin. Morgan Kaufmann.

**Shachter**, R. D., D'Ambrosio, B., and Del Favero, B. A. (1990). Symbolic probabilistic inference in belief networks. In *Proceedings of the Eighth National Conference on Artificial Intelligence (AAAI-90)*, pp. 126–131, Boston. MIT Press.

**Shachter**, R. D. and Kenley, C. R. (1989). Gaussian influence diagrams. *Management Science*, *35*(5), 527–550.

**Shachter**, R. D. and Peot, M. (1989). Simulation approaches to general probabilistic inference on belief networks. In *Proceedings of the Fifth Conference on Uncertainty in Artificial Intelligence (UAI-89)*, Windsor, Ontario. Morgan Kaufmann.

**Shafer**, G. (1976). *A Mathematical Theory of Evidence*. Princeton University Press, Princeton, New Jersey.

**Shafer**, G. and Pearl, J. (Eds.). (1990). *Readings in Uncertain Reasoning*. Morgan Kaufmann, San Mateo, California.

**Shahookar**, K. and Mazumder, P. (1991). VLSI cell placement techniques. *Computing Surveys*, *23*(2), 143–220.

**Shanahan**, M. (1997). *Solving the Frame Problem*. MIT Press, Cambridge, Massachusetts.

**Shanahan**, M. (1999). The event calculus explained. In Wooldridge, M. J. and Veloso, M. (Eds.), *Artificial Intelligence Today*, pp. 409–430. Springer-Verlag, Berlin.

**Shankar**, N. (1986). *Proof-Checking Metamathematics*. Ph.D. thesis, Computer Science Department, University of Texas at Austin.

**Shannon**, C. E. and Weaver, W. (1949). *The Mathematical Theory of Communication*. University of Illinois Press, Urbana, Illinois.

**Shannon**, C. E. (1950). Programming a computer for playing chess. *Philosophical Magazine*, *41*(4), 256–275.

**Shapiro**, E. (1981). An algorithm that infers theories from facts. In *Proceedings of the Seventh International Joint Conference on Artificial Intelligence (IJCAI-81)*, p. 1064, Vancouver, British Columbia. Morgan Kaufmann.

**Shapiro**, S. C. (Ed.). (1992). *Encyclopedia of Artificial Intelligence* (second edition). Wiley, New York.

**Shapley**, S. (1953). Stochastic games. In *Proceedings of the National Academy of Sciences*, Vol. 39, pp. 1095–1100.

**Shavlik**, J. and Dietterich, T. (Eds.). (1990). *Readings in Machine Learning*. Morgan Kaufmann, San Mateo, California.

**Shelley**, M. (1818). *Frankenstein: or, the Modern Prometheus*. Pickering and Chatto.

**Shenoy**, P. P. (1989). A valuation-based language for expert systems. *International Journal of Approximate Reasoning*, *3*(5), 383–411.

**Shi**, J. and Malik, J. (2000). Normalized cuts and image segmentation. *IEEE Transactions on Pattern Analysis and Machine Intelligence (PAMI)*, *22*(8), 888–905.

**Shoham**, Y. (1987). Temporal logics in AI: Semantical and ontological considerations. *Artificial Intelligence*, *33*(1), 89–104.

**Shoham**, Y. (1993). Agent-oriented programming. *Artificial Intelligence*, *60*(1), 51–92.

**Shoham**, Y. (1994). *Artificial Intelligence Techniques in Prolog*. Morgan Kaufmann, San Mateo, California.

**Shortliffe**, E. H. (1976). *Computer-Based Medical Consultations: MYCIN*. Elsevier/North-Holland, Amsterdam, London, New York.

**Shwe**, M. and Cooper, G. (1991). An empirical analysis of likelihood-weighting simulation on a large, multiply connected medical belief network. *Computers and Biomedical Research*, *1991*(5), 453–475.

**Siekmann**, J. and Wrightson, G. (Eds.). (1983). *Automation of Reasoning*. Springer-Verlag, Berlin.

**Sietsma**, J. and Dow, R. J. F. (1988). Neural net pruning—why and how. In *IEEE International Conference on Neural Networks*, pp. 325–333, San Diego. IEEE.

**Siklossy**, L. and Dreussi, J. (1973). An efficient robot planner which generates its own procedures. In *Proceedings of the Third International Joint Conference on Artificial Intelligence (IJCAI-73)*, pp. 423–430, Stanford, California. IJCAII.

**Silverstein**, C., Henzinger, M., Marais, H., and Moricz, M. (1998). Analysis of a very large altavista query log. Tech. rep. 1998-014, Digital Systems Research Center.

**Simmons**, R. and Koenig, S. (1995). Probabilistic robot navigation in partially observable environments. In *Proceedings of IJCAI-95*, pp. 1080–1087, Montreal, Canada. IJCAI, Inc.

**Simmons**, R. and Slocum, J. (1972). Generating english discourse from semantic networks. *Communications of the ACM*, *15*(10), 891–905.

**Simon**, H. A. (1947). *Administrative behavior*. Macmillan, New York.

**Simon**, H. A. (1957). *Models of Man: Social and Rational*. John Wiley, New York.

**Simon**, H. A. (1963). Experiments with a heuristic compiler. *Journal of the Association for Computing Machinery*, *10*, 493–506.

**Simon**, H. A. (1981). *The Sciences of the Artificial* (second edition). MIT Press, Cambridge, Massachusetts.

**Simon**, H. A. (1982). *Models of Bounded Rationality, Volume 1*. The MIT Press, Cambridge, Massachusetts.

**Simon**, H. A. and Newell, A. (1958). Heuristic problem solving: The next advance in operations research. *Operations Research*, *6*, 1–10.

**Simon**, H. A. and Newell, A. (1961). Computer simulation of human thinking and problem solving. *Datamation, June/July*, 35–37.

**Simon**, J. C. and Dubois, O. (1989). Number of solutions to satisfiability instances—applications to knowledge bases. *Int. J. Pattern Recognition and Artificial Intelligence*, *3*, 53–65.

**Sirovitch**, L. and Kirby, M. (1987). Low-dimensional procedure for the characterization of human faces. *Journal of the Optical Society of America A*, *2*, 586–591.

**Skinner**, B. F. (1953). *Science and Human Behavior*. Macmillan, London.

**Skolem**, T. (1920). Logisch-kombinatorische Untersuchungen über die Erfüllbarkeit oder Beweisbarkeit mathematischer Sätze nebst einem Theoreme über die dichte Mengen. *Videnskapsselskapets skrifter, I. Matematisk-naturvidenskabelig klasse*, *4*.

**Skolem**, T. (1928). Über die mathematische Logik. *Norsk matematisk tidsskrift*, *10*, 125–142.

**Slagle**, J. R. (1963a). A heuristic program that solves symbolic integration problems in freshman calculus. *Journal of the Association for Computing Machinery*, *10*(4).

**Slagle**, J. R. (1963b). Game trees, $m$ & $n$ minimaxing, and the $m$ & $n$ alpha–beta procedure. Artificial intelligence group report 3, University of California, Lawrence Radiation Laboratory, Livermore, California.

**Slagle**, J. R. and Dixon, J. K. (1969). Experiments with some programs that search game trees. *Journal of the Association for Computing Machinery*, *16*(2), 189–207.

**Slate**, D. J. and Atkin, L. R. (1977). CHESS 4.5—Northwestern University chess program. In Frey, P. W. (Ed.), *Chess Skill in Man and Machine*, pp. 82–118. Springer-Verlag, Berlin.

**Slater**, E. (1950). Statistics for the chess computer and the factor of mobility. In *Symposium on Information Theory*, pp. 150–152, London. Ministry of Supply.

**Sleator**, D. and Temperley, D. (1993). Parsing English with a link grammar. In *Third Annual Workshop on Parsing technologies*.

**Sloman**, A. (1978). *The Computer Revolution in Philosophy*. Harvester Press, Hassocks, Sussex, UK.

**Smallwood**, R. D. and Sondik, E. J. (1973). The optimal control of partially observable Markov processes over a finite horizon. *Operations Research*, *21*, 1071–1088.

**Smith**, D. E., Genesereth, M. R., and Ginsberg, M. L. (1986). Controlling recursive inference. *Artificial Intelligence*, *30*(3), 343–389.

**Smith**, D. R. (1990). KIDS: a semiautomatic program development system. *IEEE Transactions on Software Engineering*, *16*(9), 1024–1043.

**Smith**, D. R. (1996). Machine support for software development. In *Proceedings of the 18th International Conference on Software Engineering*, pp. 167–168, Berlin. IEEE Computer Society Press.

**Smith**, D. E. and Weld, D. S. (1998). Conformant Graphplan. In *Proceedings of the Fifteenth National Conference on Artificial Intelligence (AAAI-98)*, pp. 889–896, Madison, Wisconsin. AAAI Press.

**Smith**, J. Q. (1988). *Decision Analysis*. Chapman and Hall, London.

**Smith**, J. M. and Szathmáry, E. (1999). *The Origins of Life: From the Birth of Life to the Origin of Language*. Oxford University Press, Oxford, UK.

**Smith**, R. C. and Cheeseman, P. (1986). On the representation and estimation of spatial uncertainty. *International Journal of Robotics Research*, *5*(4), 56–68.

**Smith**, S. J. J., Nau, D. S., and Throop, T. A. (1998). Success in spades: Using ai planning techniques to win the world championship of computer bridge. In *Proceedings of the Fifteenth National Conference on Artificial Intelligence (AAAI-98)*, pp. 1079–1086, Madison, Wisconsin. AAAI Press.

**Smolensky**, P. (1988). On the proper treatment of connectionism. *Behavioral and Brain Sciences*, *2*, 1–74.

**Smyth**, P., Heckerman, D., and Jordan, M. I. (1997). Probabilistic independence networks for hidden Markov probability models. *Neural Computation*, *9*(2), 227–269.

**Soderland**, S. and Weld, D. S. (1991). Evaluating nonlinear planning. Technical report TR-91-02-03, University of Washington Department of Computer Science and Engineering, Seattle, Washington.

**Solomonoff**, R. J. (1964). A formal theory of inductive inference. *Information and Control*, *7*, 1–22, 224–254.

**Sondik**, E. J. (1971). *The Optimal Control of Partially Observable Markov Decision Processes*. Ph.D. thesis, Stanford University, Stanford, California.

**Sosic**, R. and Gu, J. (1994). Efficient local search with conflict minimization: A case study of the n-queens problem. *IEEE Transactions on Knowledge and Data Engineering*, *6*(5), 661–668.

**Sowa**, J. (1999). *Knowledge Representation: Logical, Philosophical, and Computational Foundations*. Blackwell, Oxford, UK.

**Spiegelhalter**, D. J. (1986). Probabilistic reasoning in predictive expert systems. In Kanal, L. N. and Lemmer, J. F. (Eds.), *Uncertainty in Artificial Intelligence*, pp. 47–67. Elsevier/North-Holland, Amsterdam, London, New York.

**Spiegelhalter**, D. J., Dawid, P., Lauritzen, S., and Cowell, R. (1993). Bayesian analysis in expert systems. *Statistical Science*, *8*, 219–282.

**Spielberg**, S. (2001). AI. movie.

**Spirtes**, P., Glymour, C., and Scheines, R. (1993). *Causation, prediction, and search*. Springer-Verlag, Berlin.

**Springsteen**, B. (1992). 57 channels (and nothin' on). In *Human Touch*. Sony.

**Srinivasan**, A., Muggleton, S. H., King, R. D., and Sternberg, M. J. E. (1994). Mutagenesis: ILP experiments in a non-determinate biological domain. In Wrobel, S. (Ed.), *Proceedings of the 4th International Workshop on Inductive Logic Programming*, Vol. 237, pp. 217–232. Gesellschaft für Mathematik und Datenverarbeitung MBH.

**Srivas**, M. and Bickford, M. (1990). Formal verification of a pipelined microprocessor. *IEEE Software*, *7*(5), 52–64.

**Stallman**, R. M. and Sussman, G. J. (1977). Forward reasoning and dependency-directed backtracking in a system for computer-aided circuit analysis. *Artificial Intelligence*, *9*(2), 135–196.

**Stanfill**, C. and Waltz, D. (1986). Toward memory-based reasoning. *Communications of the Association for Computing Machinery*, *29*(12), 1213–1228.

**Stefik**, M. (1995). *Introduction to Knowledge Systems*. Morgan Kaufmann, San Mateo, California.

**Stein**, L. A. (2002). *Interactive Programming in Java (pre-publication draft)*. Morgan Kaufmann, San Mateo, California.

**Steinbach**, M., Karypis, G., and Kumar, V. (2000). A comparison of document clustering techniques. In *KDD Workshop on Text Mining*, pp. 109–110. ACM Press.

**Stevens**, K. A. (1981). The information content of texture gradients. *Biological Cybernetics*, *42*, 95–105.

**Stickel**, M. E. (1985). Automated deduction by theory resolution. *Journal of Automated Reasoning*, *1*(4), 333–355.

**Stickel**, M. E. (1988). A Prolog Technology Theorem Prover: implementation by an extended Prolog compiler. *Journal of Automated Reasoning*, *4*, 353–380.

**Stiller**, L. B. (1992). KQNKRR. *ICCA Journal*, *15*(1), 16–18.

**Stillings**, N. A., Weisler, S., Feinstein, M. H., Garfield, J. L., and Rissland, E. L. (1995). *Cognitive Science: An Introduction* (second edition). MIT Press, Cambridge, Massachusetts.

**Stockman**, G. (1979). A minimax algorithm better than alpha–beta?. *Artificial Intelligence*, *12*(2), 179–196.

**Stolcke**, A. and Omohundro, S. (1994). Inducing probabilistic grammars by Bayesian model merging.. In *Proceedings of the Second International Colloquium on Grammatical Inference and Applications (ICGI-94)*, pp. 106–118, Alicante, Spain. Springer-Verlag.

**Stone**, P. (2000). *Layered Learning in Multi-Agent Systems: A Winning Approach to Robotic Soccer*. MIT Press, Cambridge, Massachusetts.

**Strachey**, C. (1952). Logical or non-mathematical programmes. In *Proceedings of the Association for Computing Machinery (ACM)*, pp. 46–49, Toronto, Canada.

**Subramanian**, D. (1993). Artificial intelligence and conceptual design. In *Proceedings of the Thirteenth International Joint Conference on Artificial Intelligence (IJCAI-93)*, pp. 800–809, Chambery, France. Morgan Kaufmann.

**Subramanian**, D. and Feldman, R. (1990). The utility of EBL in recursive domain theories. In *Proceedings of the Eighth National Conference on Artificial Intelligence (AAAI-90)*, Vol. 2, pp. 942–949, Boston. MIT Press.

**Subramanian**, D. and Wang, E. (1994). Constraint-based kinematic synthesis. In *Proceedings of the International Conference on Qualitative Reasoning*, pp. 228–239. AAAI Press.

**Sugihara**, K. (1984). A necessary and sufficient condition for a picture to represent a polyhedral scene. *IEEE Transactions on Pattern Analysis and Machine Intelligence (PAMI)*, *6*(5), 578–586.

**Sussman**, G. J. (1975). *A Computer Model of Skill Acquisition*. Elsevier/North-Holland, Amsterdam, London, New York.

**Sussman**, G. J. and Winograd, T. (1970). MICRO-PLANNER Reference Manual. Ai memo 203, MIT AI Lab, Cambridge, Massachusetts.

**Sutherland**, I. (1963). Sketchpad: A man-machine graphical communication system. In *Proceedings of the Spring Joint Computer Conference*, pp. 329–346. IFIPS.

**Sutton**, R. S. (1988). Learning to predict by the methods of temporal differences. *Machine Learning*, *3*, 9–44.

**Sutton**, R. S., McAllester, D. A., Singh, S. P., and Mansour, Y. (2000). Policy gradient methods for reinforcement learning with function approximation. In Solla, S. A., Leen, T. K., and Müller, K.-R. (Eds.), *Advances in Neural Information Processing Systems 12*, pp. 1057–1063. MIT Press, Cambridge, Massachusetts.

**Sutton**, R. S. (1990). Integrated architectures for learning, planning, and reacting based on approximating dynamic programming. In *Machine Learning: Proceedings of the Seventh International Conference*, pp. 216–224, Austin, Texas. Morgan Kaufmann.

**Sutton**, R. S. and Barto, A. G. (1998). *Reinforcement Learning: An Introduction*. MIT Press, Cambridge, Massachusetts.

**Swade**, D. D. (1993). Redeeming Charles Babbage's mechanical computer. *Scientific American*, *268*(2), 86–91.

**Swerling**, P. (1959). First order error propagation in a stagewise smoothing procedure for satellite observations. *Journal of Astronautical Sciences*, *6*, 46–52.

**Swift**, T. and Warren, D. S. (1994). Analysis of SLG-WAM evaluation of definite programs. In *Logic Programming. Proceedings of the 1994 International Symposium*, pp. 219–235, Ithaca, NY. MIT Press.

**Syrjänen**, T. (2000). Lparse 1.0 user's manual. http://saturn.tcs.hut.fi/Software/smodels.

**Tadepalli**, P. (1993). Learning from queries and examples with tree-structured bias. In *Proceedings of the Tenth International Conference on Machine Learning*, pp. 322–329, Amherst, Massachusetts. Morgan Kaufmann.

**Tait**, P. G. (1880). Note on the theory of the "15 puzzle". *Proceedings of the Royal Society of Edinburgh*, *10*, 664–665.

**Tamaki**, H. and Sato, T. (1986). OLD resolution with tabulation. In *Third International Conference on Logic Programming*, pp. 84–98, London. Springer-Verlag.

**Tambe**, M., Newell, A., and Rosenbloom, P. S. (1990). The problem of expensive chunks and its solution by restricting expressiveness. *Machine Learning*, *5*, 299–348.

**Tarjan**, R. E. (1983). *Data Structures and Network Algorithms*. CBMS-NSF Regional Conference Series in Applied Mathematics. SIAM (Society for Industrial and Applied Mathematics, Philadelphia.

**Tarski**, A. (1935). Die Wahrheitsbegriff in den formalisierten Sprachen. *Studia Philosophica*, *1*, 261–405.

**Tarski**, A. (1956). *Logic, Semantics, Metamathematics: Papers from 1923 to 1938*. Oxford University Press, Oxford, UK.

**Tash**, J. K. and Russell, S. J. (1994). Control strategies for a stochastic planner. In *Proceedings of the Twelfth National Conference on Artificial Intelligence (AAAI-94)*, pp. 1079–1085, Seattle. AAAI Press.

**Tate**, A. (1975a). Interacting goals and their use. In *Proceedings of the Fourth International Joint Conference on Artificial Intelligence (IJCAI-75)*, pp. 215–218, Tbilisi, Georgia. IJCAII.

**Tate**, A. (1975b). *Using Goal Structure to Direct Search in a Problem Solver*. Ph.D. thesis, University of Edinburgh, Edinburgh, Scotland.

**Tate**, A. (1977). Generating project networks. In *Proceedings of the Fifth International Joint Conference on Artificial Intelligence (IJCAI-77)*, pp. 888–893, Cambridge, Massachusetts. IJCAII.

**Tate**, A. and Whiter, A. M. (1984). Planning with multiple resource constraints and an application to a naval planning problem. In *Proceedings of the First Conference on AI Applications*, pp. 410–416, Denver, Colorado.

**Tatman**, J. A. and Shachter, R. D. (1990). Dynamic programming and influence diagrams. *IEEE Transactions on Systems, Man and Cybernetics*, *20*(2), 365–379.

**Tesauro**, G. (1989). Neurogammon wins computer olympiad. *Neural Computation*, *1*(3), 321–323.

**Tesauro**, G. (1992). Practical issues in temporal difference learning. *Machine Learning*, *8*(3–4), 257–277.

**Tesauro**, G. (1995). Temporal difference learning and TD-Gammon. *Communications of the Association for Computing Machinery*, *38*(3), 58–68.

**Tesauro**, G. and Sejnowski, T. (1989). A parallel network that learns to play backgammon. *Artificial Intelligence*, *39*(3), 357–390.

**Thagard**, P. (1996). *Mind: Introduction to Cognitive Science*. MIT Press, Cambridge, Massachusetts.

**Thaler**, R. (1992). *The Winner's Curse: Paradoxes and Anomalies of Economic Life*. Princeton University Press, Princeton, New Jersey.

**Thielscher**, M. (1999). From situation calculus to fluent calculus: State update axioms as a solution to the inferential frame problem. *Artificial Intelligence*, *111*(1–2), 277–299.

**Thomason**, R. H. (Ed.). (1974). *Formal Philosophy: Selected Papers of Richard Montague*. Yale University Press, New Haven, Connecticut.

**Thompson**, D. W. (1917). *On Growth and Form*. Cambridge University Press, Cambridge, UK.

**Thrun**, S. (2000). Towards programming tools for robots that integrate probabilistic computation and learning. In *Proceedings of the IEEE International Conference on Robotics and Automation (ICRA)*, San Francisco, CA. IEEE.

**Thrun**, S. (2002). Robotic mapping: A survey. In Lakemeyer, G. and Nebel, B. (Eds.), *Exploring Artificial Intelligence in the New Millenium*. Morgan Kaufmann. to appear.

**Titterington**, D. M., Smith, A. F. M., and Makov, U. E. (1985). *Statistical analysis of finite mixture distributions*. Wiley, New York.

**Toffler**, A. (1970). *Future Shock*. Bantam.

**Tomasi**, C. and Kanade, T. (1992). Shape and motion from image streams under orthography: A factorization method. *International Journal of Computer Vision*, *9*, 137–154.

**Touretzky**, D. S. (1986). *The Mathematics of Inheritance Systems*. Pitman and Morgan Kaufmann, London and San Mateo, California.

**Trucco**, E. and Verri, A. (1998). *Introductory Techniques for 3-D Computer Vision*. Prentice Hall, Upper Saddle River, New Jersey.

**Tsang**, E. (1993). *Foundations of Constraint Satisfaction*. Academic Press, New York.

**Tsitsiklis**, J. N. and Van Roy, B. (1997). An analysis of temporal-difference learning with function approximation. *IEEE Transactions on Automatic Control*, *42*(5), 674–690.

**Tumer**, K. and Wolpert, D. (2000). Collective intelligence and braess' paradox. In *Proceedings of the AAAI/IAAI*, pp. 104–109.

**Turcotte**, M., Muggleton, S. H., and Sternberg, M. J. E. (2001). Automated discovery of structural signatures of protein fold and function. *Journal of Molecular Biology*, *306*, 591–605.

**Turing**, A. (1936). On computable numbers, with an application to the Entscheidungsproblem. *Proceedings of the London Mathematical Society, 2nd series*, *42*, 230–265.

**Turing**, A. (1948). Intelligent machinery. Tech. rep., National Physical Laboratory. reprinted in (Ince, 1992).

**Turing**, A. (1950). Computing machinery and intelligence. *Mind*, *59*, 433–460.

**Turing**, A., Strachey, C., Bates, M. A., and Bowden, B. V. (1953). Digital computers applied to games. In Bowden, B. V. (Ed.), *Faster than Thought*, pp. 286–310. Pitman, London.

**Turtle**, H. R. and Croft, W. B. (1992). A comparison of text retrieval models. *The Computer Journal*, *35*(1), 279–289.

**Tversky**, A. and Kahneman, D. (1982). Causal schemata in judgements under uncertainty. In Kahneman, D., Slovic, P., and Tversky, A. (Eds.), *Judgement Under Uncertainty: Heuristics and Biases*. Cambridge University Press, Cambridge, UK.

**Ullman**, J. D. (1985). Implementation of logical query languages for databases. *ACM Transactions on Database Systems*, *10*(3), 289–321.

**Ullman**, J. D. (1989). *Principles of Database and Knowledge-Base Bystems*. Computer Science Press, Rockville, Maryland.

**Ullman**, S. (1979). *The Interpretation of Visual Motion*. MIT Press, Cambridge, Massachusetts.

**Vaessens**, R. J. M., Aarts, E. H. I., and Lenstra, J. K. (1996). Job shop scheduling by local search. *INFORMS J. on Computing*, *8*, 302–117.

**Valiant**, L. (1984). A theory of the learnable. *Communications of the Association for Computing Machinery*, *27*, 1134–1142.

**van** Benthem, J. (1983). *The Logic of Time*. D. Reidel, Dordrecht, Netherlands.

**Van Emden**, M. H. and Kowalski, R. (1976). The semantics of predicate logic as a programming language. *Journal of the Association for Computing Machinery*, *23*(4), 733–742.

**van** Harmelen, F. and Bundy, A. (1988). Explanation-based generalisation = partial evaluation. *Artificial Intelligence*, *36*(3), 401–412.

**van** Heijenoort, J. (Ed.). (1967). *From Frege to Gödel: A Source Book in Mathematical Logic, 1879–1931*. Harvard University Press, Cambridge, Massachusetts.

**Van Hentenryck**, P., Saraswat, V., and Deville, Y. (1998). Design, implementation, and evaluation of the constraint language cc(fd). *Journal of Logic Programming*, *37*(1–3), 139–164.

**van** Nunen, J. A. E. E. (1976). A set of successive approximation methods for discounted Markovian decision problems. *Zeitschrift fur Operations Research, Serie A*, *20*(5), 203–208.

**van** Roy, B. (1998). *Learning and value function approximation in complex decision processes*. Ph.D. thesis, Laboratory for Information and Decision Systems, MIT, Cambridge, Massachusetts.

**Van Roy**, P. L. (1990). Can logic programming execute as fast as imperative programming?. Report UCB/CSD 90/600, Computer Science Division, University of California, Berkeley, California.

**Vapnik**, V. N. (1998). *Statistical Learning Theory*. Wiley, New York.

**Vapnik**, V. N. and Chervonenkis, A. Y. (1971). On the uniform convergence of relative frequencies of events to their probabilities. *Theory of Probability and Its Applications*, *16*, 264–280.

**Varian**, H. R. (1995). Economic mechanism design for computerized agents. In *USENIX Workshop on Electronic Commerce*, pp. 13–21.

**Veloso**, M. and Carbonell, J. G. (1993). Derivational analogy in PRODIGY: Automating case acquisition, storage, and utilization. *Machine Learning*, *10*, 249–278.

**Vere**, S. A. (1983). Planning in time: Windows and durations for activities and goals. *IEEE Transactions on Pattern Analysis and Machine Intelligence (PAMI)*, *5*, 246–267.

**Vinge**, V. (1993). The coming technological singularity: How to survive in the post-human era. In *VISION-21 Symposium*. NASA Lewis Research Center and the Ohio Aerospace Institute.

**Viola**, P. and Jones, M. (2002). Robust real-time object detection. *International Journal of Computer Vision*, in press.

**von** Mises, R. (1928). *Wahrscheinlichkeit, Statistik und Wahrheit*. J. Springer, Berlin.

**von** Neumann, J. (1928). Zur Theorie der Gesellschaftsspiele. *Mathematische Annalen*, *100*(295–320).

**von** Neumann, J. and Morgenstern, O. (1944). *Theory of Games and Economic Behavior* (first edition). Princeton University Press, Princeton, New Jersey.

**von** Winterfeldt, D. and Edwards, W. (1986). *Decision Analysis and Behavioral Research*. Cambridge University Press, Cambridge, UK.

**Voorhees**, E. M. (1993). Using WordNet to disambiguate word senses for text retrieval. In *Sixteenth Annual International ACM SIGIR Conference on Research and Development in Information Retrieval*, pp. 171–80, Pittsburgh. Association for Computing Machinery.

**Vossen**, T., Ball, M., Lotem, A., and Nau, D. S. (2001). Applying integer programming to ai planning. *Knowledge Engineering Review*, *16*, 85–100.

**Waibel**, A. and Lee, K.-F. (1990). *Readings in Speech Recognition*. Morgan Kaufmann, San Mateo, California.

**Waldinger**, R. (1975). Achieving several goals simultaneously. In Elcock, E. W. and Michie, D. (Eds.), *Machine Intelligence 8*, pp. 94–138. Ellis Horwood, Chichester, England.

**Waltz**, D. (1975). Understanding line drawings of scenes with shadows. In Winston, P. H. (Ed.), *The Psychology of Computer Vision*. McGraw-Hill, New York.

**Wanner**, E. (1974). *On remembering, forgetting and understanding sentences*. Mouton, The Hague and Paris.

**Warren**, D. H. D. (1974). WARPLAN: A System for Generating Plans. Department of Computational Logic Memo 76, University of Edinburgh, Edinburgh, Scotland.

**Warren**, D. H. D. (1976). Generating conditional plans and programs. In *Proceedings of the AISB Summer Conference*, pp. 344–354.

**Warren**, D. H. D. (1983). An abstract Prolog instruction set. Technical note 309, SRI International, Menlo Park, California.

**Warren**, D. H. D., Pereira, L. M., and Pereira, F. (1977). PROLOG: The language and its implementation compared with LISP. *SIGPLAN Notices*, *12*(8), 109–115.

**Watkins**, C. J. (1989). *Models of Delayed Reinforcement Learning*. Ph.D. thesis, Psychology Department, Cambridge University, Cambridge, UK.

**Watson**, J. D. and Crick, F. H. C. (1953). A structure for deoxyribose nucleic acid. *Nature*, *171*, 737.

**Webber**, B. L. (1983). So what can we talk about now?. In Brady, M. and Berwick, R. (Eds.), *Computational Models of Discourse*. MIT Press, Cambridge, Massachusetts.

**Webber**, B. L. (1988). Tense as discourse anaphora. *Computational Linguistics*, *14*(2), 61–73.

**Webber**, B. L. and Nilsson, N. J. (Eds.). (1981). *Readings in Artificial Intelligence*. Morgan Kaufmann, San Mateo, California.

**Weidenbach**, C. (2001). SPASS: Combining superposition, sorts and splitting. In Robinson, A. and Voronkov, A. (Eds.), *Handbook of Automated Reasoning*. mit, mit-ad.

**Weiss**, G. (1999). *Multiagent systems*. MIT Press, Cambridge, Massachusetts.

**Weiss**, S. and Kulikowski, C. A. (1991). *Computer Systems That Learn: Classification and Prediction Methods from Statistics, Neural Nets, Machine Learning, and Expert Systems*. Morgan Kaufmann, San Mateo, California.

**Weizenbaum**, J. (1976). *Computer Power and Human Reason*. W. H. Freeman, New York.

**Weld**, D. S. (1994). An introduction to least commitment planning. *AI Magazine*, *15*(4), 27–61.

**Weld**, D. S. (1999). Recent advances in ai planning. *AI Magazine*, *20*(2), 93–122.

**Weld**, D. S., Anderson, C. R., and Smith, D. E. (1998). Extending graphplan to handle uncertainty and sensing actions. In *Proceedings of the Fifteenth National Conference on Artificial Intelligence (AAAI-98)*, pp. 897–904, Madison, Wisconsin. AAAI Press.

**Weld**, D. S. and de Kleer, J. (1990). *Readings in Qualitative Reasoning about Physical Systems*. Morgan Kaufmann, San Mateo, California.

**Weld**, D. S. and Etzioni, O. (1994). The first law of robotics: A call to arms. In *Proceedings of the Twelfth National Conference on Artificial Intelligence (AAAI-94)*, Seattle. AAAI Press.

**Wellman**, M. P. (1985). Reasoning about preference models. Technical report MIT/LCS/TR-340, Laboratory for Computer Science, MIT, Cambridge, Massachusetts.

**Wellman**, M. P. (1988). *Formulation of Tradeoffs in Planning under Uncertainty*. Ph.D. thesis, Massachusetts Institute of Technology, Cambridge, Massachusetts.

**Wellman**, M. P. (1990a). Fundamental concepts of qualitative probabilistic networks. *Artificial Intelligence*, *44*(3), 257–303.

**Wellman**, M. P. (1990b). The STRIPS assumption for planning under uncertainty. In *Proceedings of the Eighth National Conference on Artificial Intelligence (AAAI-90)*, pp. 198–203, Boston. MIT Press.

**Wellman**, M. P. (1995). The economic approach to artificial intelligence. *ACM Computing Surveys*, *27*(3), 360–362.

**Wellman**, M. P., Breese, J. S., and Goldman, R. (1992). From knowledge bases to decision models. *Knowledge Engineering Review*, *7*(1), 35–53.

**Wellman**, M. P. and Doyle, J. (1992). Modular utility representation for decision-theoretic planning. In *Proceedings, First International Conference on AI Planning Systems*, pp. 236–242, College Park, Maryland. Morgan Kaufmann.

**Werbos**, P. (1974). *Beyond Regression: New Tools for Prediction and Analysis in the Behavioral Sciences*. Ph.D. thesis, Harvard University, Cambridge, Massachusetts.

**Werbos**, P. (1977). Advanced forecasting methods for global crisis warning and models of intelligence. *General Systems Yearbook*, *22*, 25–38.

**Wesley**, M. A. and Lozano-Perez, T. (1979). An algorithm for planning collision-free paths among polyhedral objects. *Communications of the ACM*, *22*(10), 560–570.

**Wheatstone**, C. (1838). On some remarkable, and hitherto unresolved, phenomena of binocular vision. *Philosophical Transactions of the Royal Society of London*, *2*, 371–394.

**Whitehead**, A. N. (1911). *An Introduction to Mathematics*. Williams and Northgate, London.

**Whitehead**, A. N. and Russell, B. (1910). *Principia Mathematica*. Cambridge University Press, Cambridge, UK.

**Whorf**, B. (1956). *Language, Thought, and Reality*. MIT Press, Cambridge, Massachusetts.

**Widrow**, B. (1962). Generalization and information storage in networks of adaline "neurons". In Yovits, M. C., Jacobi, G. T., and Goldstein, G. D. (Eds.), *Self-Organizing Systems 1962*, pp. 435–461, Chicago, Illinois. Spartan.

**Widrow**, B. and Hoff, M. E. (1960). Adaptive switching circuits. In *1960 IRE WESCON Convention Record*, pp. 96–104, New York.

**Wiener**, N. (1942). The extrapolation, interpolation, and smoothing of stationary time series. Osrd 370, Report to the Services 19, Research Project DIC-6037, MIT, Cambridge, Massachusetts.

**Wiener**, N. (1948). *Cybernetics*. Wiley, New York.

**Wilensky**, R. (1978). *Understanding goal-based stories*. Ph.D. thesis, Yale University, New Haven, Connecticut.

**Wilensky**, R. (1983). *Planning and Understanding*. Addison-Wesley, Reading, Massachusetts.

**Wilkins**, D. E. (1980). Using patterns and plans in chess. *Artificial Intelligence*, *14*(2), 165–203.

**Wilkins**, D. E. (1988). *Practical Planning: Extending the AI Planning Paradigm*. Morgan Kaufmann, San Mateo, California.

**Wilkins**, D. E. (1990). Can AI planners solve practical problems?. *Computational Intelligence*, *6*(4), 232–246.

**Wilkins**, D. E., Myers, K. L., Lowrance, J. D., and Wesley, L. P. (1995). Planning and reacting in uncertain and dynamic environments. *Journal of Experimental and Theoretical AI*, *7*(1), 197–227.

**Wilks**, Y. (1975). An intelligent analyzer and understander of English. *Communications of the ACM*, *18*(5), 264–274.

**Williams**, R. J. (1992). Simple statistical gradient-following algorithms for connectionist reinforcement learning. *Machine Learning*, *8*, 229–256.

**Williams**, R. J. and Baird, L. C. I. (1993). Tight performance bounds on greedy policies based on imperfect value functions. Tech. rep. NU-CCS-93-14, College of Computer Science, Northeastern University, Boston.

**Wilson**, R. A. and Keil, F. C. (Eds.). (1999). *The MIT Encyclopedia of the Cognitive Sciences*. MIT Press, Cambridge, Massachusetts.

**Winograd**, S. and Cowan, J. D. (1963). *Reliable Computation in the Presence of Noise*. MIT Press, Cambridge, Massachusetts.

**Winograd**, T. (1972). Understanding natural language. *Cognitive Psychology*, *3*(1), 1–191.

**Winston**, P. H. (1970). Learning structural descriptions from examples. Technical report MAC-TR-76, Department of Electrical Engineering and Computer Science, Massachusetts Institute of Technology, Cambridge, Massachusetts.

**Winston**, P. H. (1992). *Artificial Intelligence* (Third edition). Addison-Wesley, Reading, Massachusetts.

**Wirth**, R. and O'Rorke, P. (1991). Constraints on predicate invention. In *Machine Learning: Proceedings of the Eighth International Workshop (ML-91)*, pp. 457–461, Evanston, Illinois. Morgan Kaufmann.

**Witten**, I. H. and Bell, T. C. (1991). The zero-frequency problem: Estimating the probabilities of novel events in adaptive text compression. *IEEE Transactions on Information Theory*, *37*(4), 1085–1094.

**Witten**, I. H., Moffat, A., and Bell, T. C. (1999). *Managing Gigabytes: Compressing and Indexing Documents and Images* (second edition). Morgan Kaufmann, San Mateo, California.

**Wittgenstein**, L. (1922). *Tractatus Logico-Philosophicus* (second edition). Routledge and Kegan Paul, London. Reprinted 1971, edited by D. F. Pears and B. F. McGuinness. This edition of the English translation also contains Wittgenstein's original German text on facing pages, as well as Bertrand Russell's introduction to the 1922 edition.

**Wittgenstein**, L. (1953). *Philosophical Investigations*. Macmillan, London.

**Wojciechowski**, W. S. and Wojcik, A. S. (1983). Automated design of multiple-valued logic circuits by automated theorem proving techniques. *IEEE Transactions on Computers*, *C-32*(9), 785–798.

**Wojcik**, A. S. (1983). Formal design verification of digital systems. In *ACM IEEE 20th Design Automation Conference Proceedings*, pp. 228–234, Miami Beach, Florida. IEEE.

**Wood**, M. K. and Dantzig, G. B. (1949). Programming of interdependent activities. i. general discussion. *Econometrica*, *17*, 193–199.

**Woods**, W. A. (1973). Progress in natural language understanding: An application to lunar geology. In *AFIPS Conference Proceedings*, Vol. 42, pp. 441–450.

**Woods**, W. A. (1975). What's in a link? Foundations for semantic networks. In Bobrow, D. G. and Collins, A. M. (Eds.), *Representation and Understanding: Studies in Cognitive Science*, pp. 35–82. Academic Press, New York.

**Woods**, W. A. (1978). Semantics and quantification in natural language question answering. In *Advances in Computers*. Academic Press.

**Wooldridge**, M. and Rao, A. (Eds.). (1999). *Foundations of rational agency*. Kluwer, Dordrecht, Netherlands.

**Wos**, L., Carson, D., and Robinson, G. (1964). The unit preference strategy in theorem proving. In *Proceedings of the Fall Joint Computer Conference*, pp. 615–621.

**Wos**, L., Carson, D., and Robinson, G. (1965). Efficiency and completeness of the set-of-support strategy in theorem proving. *Journal of the Association for Computing Machinery*, *12*, 536–541.

**Wos**, L., Overbeek, R., Lusk, E., and Boyle, J. (1992). *Automated Reasoning: Introduction and Applications* (second edition). McGraw-Hill, New York.

**Wos**, L. and Robinson, G. (1968). Paramodulation and set of support. In *Proceedings of the IRIA Symposium on Automatic Demonstration*, pp. 276–310. Springer-Verlag.

**Wos**, L., Robinson, G., Carson, D., and Shalla, L. (1967). The concept of demodulation in theorem proving. *Journal of the Association for Computing Machinery*, *14*, 698–704.

**Wos**, L. and Winker, S. (1983). Open questions solved with the assistance of AURA. In Bledsoe, W. W. and Loveland, D. (Eds.), *Automated Theorem Proving: After 25 Years: Proceedings of the Special Session of the 89th Annual Meeting of the American Mathematical Society*, pp. 71–88, Denver, Colorado. American Mathematical Society.

**Wright**, S. (1921). Correlation and causation. *Journal of Agricultural Research*, *20*, 557–585.

**Wright**, S. (1931). Evolution in Mendelian populations. *Genetics*, *16*, 97–159.

**Wright**, S. (1934). The method of path coefficients. *Annals of Mathematical Statistics*, *5*, 161–215.

**Wu**, D. (1993). Estimating probability distributions over hypotheses with variable unification. In *Proceedings of the Thirteenth International Joint Conference on Artificial Intelligence (IJCAI-93)*, pp. 790–795, Chambery, France. Morgan Kaufmann.

**Wygant**, R. M. (1989). CLIPS— a powerful development and delivery expert system tool. *Computers and Industrial Engineering*, *17*, 546–549.

**Yamada**, K. and Knight, K. (2001). A syntax-based statistical translation model. In *Proceedings of the Thirty Ninth Annual Conference of the Association for Computational Linguistics*, pp. 228–235.

**Yang**, Q. (1990). Formalizing planning knowledge for hierarchical planning. *Computational Intelligence*, *6*, 12–24.

**Yang**, Q. (1997). *Intelligent planning: A decomposition and abstraction based approach*. Springer-Verlag, Berlin.

**Yedidia**, J., Freeman, W., and Weiss, Y. (2001). Generalized belief propagation. In Leen, T. K., Dietterich, T., and Tresp, V. (Eds.), *Advances in Neural Information Processing Systems 13*. MIT Press, Cambridge, Massachusetts.

**Yip**, K. M.-K. (1991). *KAM: A System for Intelligently Guiding Numerical Experimentation by Computer*. MIT Press, Cambridge, Massachusetts.

**Yngve**, V. (1955). A model and an hypothesis for language structure. In Locke, W. N. and Booth, A. D. (Eds.), *Machine Translation of Languages*, pp. 208–226. MIT Press, Cambridge, Massachusetts.

**Yob**, G. (1975). Hunt the wumpus!. *Creative Computing, Sep/Oct*.

**Yoshikawa**, T. (1990). *Foundations of Robotics: Analysis and Control*. MIT Press, Cambridge, Massachusetts.

**Young**, R. M., Pollack, M. E., and Moore, J. D. (1994). Decomposition and causality in partial order planning. In *Proceedings of the 2nd International Conference on Artificial Intelligence Planning Systems (AIPS-94)*, pp. 188–193, Chicago.

**Younger**, D. H. (1967). Recognition and parsing of context-free languages in time $n^3$. *Information and Control*, *10*(2), 189–208.

**Zadeh**, L. A. (1965). Fuzzy sets. *Information and Control*, *8*, 338–353.

**Zadeh**, L. A. (1978). Fuzzy sets as a basis for a theory of possibility. *Fuzzy Sets and Systems*, *1*, 3–28.

**Zaritskii**, V. S., Svetnik, V. B., and Shimelevich, L. I. (1975). Monte-Carlo technique in problems of optimal information processing. *Automation and Remote Control*, *36*, 2015–22.

**Zelle**, J. and Mooney, R. J. (1996). Learning to parse database queries using inductive logic programming. In *Proceedings of the Thirteenth National Conference on Artificial Intelligence*, pp. 1050–1055.

**Zermelo**, E. (1913). Uber Eine Anwendung der Mengenlehre auf die Theorie des Schachspiels. In *Proceedings of the Fifth International Congress of Mathematicians*, Vol. 2, pp. 501–504.

**Zermelo**, E. (1976). An application of set theory to the theory of chess-playing. *Firbush News*, *6*, 37–42. English translation of (Zermelo 1913).

**Zhang**, N. L. and Poole, D. (1994). A simple approach to bayesian network computations. In *Proceedings of the 10th Canadian Conference on Artificial Intelligence*, pp. 171–178, Banff, Alberta. Morgan Kaufmann.

**Zhang**, N. L. and Poole, D. (1996). Exploiting causal independence in Bayesian network inference. *Journal of Artificial Intelligence Research*, *5*, 301–328.

**Zhou**, R. and Hansen, E. (2002). Memory-bounded A* graph search. In *Proceedings of the 15th International Flairs Conference*.

**Zhu**, D. J. and Latombe, J.-C. (1991). New heuristic algorithms for efficient hierarchical path planning. *IEEE Transactions on Robotics and Automation*, *7*(1), 9–20.

**Zilberstein**, S. and Russell, S. J. (1996). Optimal composition of real-time systems. *Artificial Intelligence*, *83*, 181–213.

**Zimmermann**, H.-J. (Ed.). (1999). *Practical applications of fuzzy technologies*. Kluwer, Dordrecht, Netherlands.

**Zimmermann**, H.-J. (2001). *Fuzzy Set Theory—And Its Applications* (Fourth edition). Kluwer, Dordrecht, Netherlands.

**Zobrist**, A. L. (1970). *Feature Extraction and Representation for Pattern Recognition and the Game of Go*. Ph.D. thesis, University of Wisconsin.

**Zuse**, K. (1945). The Plankalkül. Report 175, Gesellschaft für Mathematik und Datenverarbeitung, Bonn, Germany.

**Zweig**, G. and Russell, S. J. (1998). Speech recognition with dynamic Bayesian networks. In *Proceedings of the Fifteenth National Conference on Artificial Intelligence (AAAI-98)*, pp. 173–180, Madison, Wisconsin. AAAI Press.

# Index

Page numbers in **bold** refer to definitions of terms and algorithms; page numbers in *italics* refer to items in the bibliography.